# Lecture Notes in Computer Science 13529

More information about this series at https://link.springer.com/bookseries/558

Elias Pimenidis · Plamen Angelov ·
Chrisina Jayne · Antonios Papaleonidas ·
Mehmet Aydin (Eds.)

# Artificial Neural Networks and Machine Learning – ICANN 2022

31st International Conference on Artificial Neural Networks
Bristol, UK, September 6–9, 2022
Proceedings, Part I

Springer

*Editors*
Elias Pimenidis (iD)
University of the West of England
Bristol, UK

Chrisina Jayne (iD)
Digital Innovation
Teesside University
Middlesbrough, UK

Mehmet Aydin (iD)
The University of the West of England
Bristol, UK

Plamen Angelov (iD)
Lancaster University
Lancaster, UK

Antonios Papaleonidas (iD)
Democritus University of Thrace
Xanthi, Greece

ISSN 0302-9743 ISSN 1611-3349 (electronic)
Lecture Notes in Computer Science
ISBN 978-3-031-15918-3 ISBN 978-3-031-15919-0 (eBook)
https://doi.org/10.1007/978-3-031-15919-0

# Organization

## General Chairs

Elias Pimenidis      University of the West of England, UK
Angelo Cangelosi      University of Manchester, UK

## Organizing Committee Chairs

Tim Brailsford      University of the West of England, UK
Larry Bull      University of the West of England, UK

## Honorary Chairs

Stefan Wermter (ENNS President)      University of Hamburg, Germany
Igor Farkaš      FMPI, Comenius University in Bratislava, Slovakia

## Program Committee Chairs

Plamen Angelov      Lancaster University, UK
Mehmet Aydin      University of the West of England, UK
Chrisina Jayne      Teesside University, UK
Elias Pimenidis      University of the West of England, UK

## Communication Chairs

Paolo Masulli      ENNS, Technical University of Denmark
Kristína Malinovská      FMPI, Comenius University in Bratislava, Slovakia
Antonios Papaleonidas      Democritus University of Thrace, Greece

## Steering Committee

Jérémie Cabessa      Université Versailles Saint-Quentin-en-Yvelines, France
Włodzisław Duch      Nicolaus Copernicus University, Torun, Poland
Igor Farkaš      Comenius University, Bratislava, Slovakia
Matthias Kerzel      Universität Hamburg, Germany
Věra Kůrková      Czech Academy of Sciences, Prague, Czechia

| | |
|---|---|
| Alessandra Lintas | Université de Lausanne, Switzerland |
| Paolo Masulli | iMotions A/S, Copenhagen, Denmark |
| Alessio Micheli | University of Pisa, Italy |
| Erkki Oja | Aalto University, Finland |
| Sebastian Otte | Universität Tübingen, Germany |
| Jaakko Peltonen | Tampere University, Finland |
| Antonio J. Pons | Universitat Politècnica de Catalunya, Barcelona, Spain |
| Igor V. Tetko | Helmholtz Zentrum München, Germany |
| Alessandro E. P. Villa | Université de Lausanne, Switzerland |
| Roseli Wedemann | Universidade do Estado do Rio de Janeiro, Brazil |
| Stefan Wermter | Universität Hamburg, Germany |

## Local Organizing Committee

| | |
|---|---|
| Nathan Duran | University of the West of England, UK |
| Haixia Liu | University of the West of England, UK |
| Zaheer Khan | University of the West of England, UK |
| Antonios Papaleonidas | Democritus University of Thrace, Greece |
| Nikolaos Polatidis | Brighton University, UK |
| Antisthenis Tsompanas | University of the West of England, UK |

## Hybrid Facilitation and Moderation Committee

| | |
|---|---|
| Anastasios Panagiotis Psathas | Democritus University of Thrace, Greece |
| Dimitris Boudas | Democritus University of Thrace, Greece |
| Ioanna-Maria Erentzi | Democritus University of Thrace, Greece |
| Ioannis Skopelitis | Democritus University of Thrace, Greece |
| Lambros Kazelis | Democritus University of Thrace, Greece |
| Leandros Tsatsaronis | Democritus University of Thrace, Greece |
| Nikiforos Mpotzoris | Democritus University of Thrace, Greece |
| Nikos Zervis | Democritus University of Thrace, Greece |
| Odysseas Tsonos | Hellenic Open University, Greece |
| Panagiotis Restos | Democritus University of Thrace, Greece |
| Tassos Giannakopoulos | Democritus University of Thrace, Greece |
| Vasilis Kokkinos | Democritus University of Thrace, Greece |

## Program Committee

| | |
|---|---|
| Abdelhamid Bouchachia | Bournemouth University, UK |
| Abdur Rakib | University of the West of England, UK |
| Abraham Yosipof | College of Law and Business, Israel |
| Akihiro Inokuchi | Kwansei Gakuin University, Japan |

| | |
|---|---|
| Alaa Zain | Hosei University, Japan |
| Albert Bifet | LTCI, Telecom ParisTech, France |
| Alejandro Cabana | Universidad Autónoma de Madrid, Spain |
| Alexander Claman | University of Miami, USA |
| Alexander Gepperth | ENSTA ParisTech, France |
| Alexander Ilin | Aalto University, Finland |
| Alexander Kovalenko | Czech Technical University in Prague, Czechia |
| Alexander Krawczyk | HAW Fulda, Germany |
| Ali Zoljodi | MDU, Sweden |
| Aluizio Araújo | Universidade Federal de Pernambuco, Brazil |
| Amit Kumar Kundu | University of Maryland, College Park, USA |
| An Xu | Donghua University, China |
| Anastasios Panagiotis Psathas | Democritus University of Thrace, Greece |
| André Artelt | Bielefeld University, Germany |
| Andre de Carvalho | University of São Paulo, Brazil |
| Andrea Castellani | Bielefeld University - CITEC, Germany |
| Andrea Galassi | University of Bologna, Italy |
| Angelo Cangelosi | University of Manchester, UK |
| Anmol Biswas | Indian Institute of Technology, Mumbai, India |
| Anna Jenul | Norwegian University of Life Sciences, Norway |
| Annie DeForge | Bentley University, USA |
| Anselm Haselhoff | Hochschule Ruhr West, Germany |
| Antisthenis Tsompanas | University of the West of England, UK |
| Antonio García-Díaz | Université libre de Bruxelles (ULB), Belgium |
| Antonio Pons | Universitat Politècnica de Catalunya, Spain |
| Antonios Papaleonidas | Democritus University of Thrace, Greece |
| Argyris Kalogeratos | CMLA, ENS Cachan, France |
| Asada | Osaka University, Japan |
| Asei Akanuma | Goldsmiths College, University of London, UK |
| Atsushi Koike | Tohoku University, Japan |
| Baris Serhan | University of Manchester, UK |
| Barkha Javed | University of the West of England, UK |
| Benedikt Bagus | Hochschule Fulda, Germany |
| Benyuan Liu | University of Massachusetts, Lowell, USA |
| Bernhard Pfahringer | University of Waikato, New Zealand |
| Bi Yan-Qing | National University of Defense Technology, China |
| Binyi Wu | TU Dresden, Germany |
| Binyu Zhao | Harbin Institute of Technology, China |
| Bo Mei | Texas Christian University, USA |
| Boyu Diao | ict, China |
| Cao Hongye | Northwestern Polytechnical University, China |

| | |
|---|---|
| Carsten Marr | German Research Center for Environmental Health, Germany |
| Chao Ma | Hong Kong Polytechnic University, Hong Kong, China |
| Cheng Feng | Fujitsu R&D Center, China |
| Ching-Chia Kao | Academia Sinica, Taiwan |
| Chrisina Jayne | Teesside University, UK |
| Christian Bauckhage | Fraunhofer IAIS, Sankt Augustin, Germany |
| Christian Oliva | Universidad Autónoma de Madrid, Spain |
| Christoph Linse | Universität zu Lübeck, Germany |
| Chuan Lu | Aberystwyth University, UK |
| Chuang Yu | University of Manchester, UK |
| Chunhong Cao | Xiangtan University, China |
| Chun-Shien Lu | Academia Sinica, Taiwan |
| Claudio Bellei | Elliptic, UK |
| Claudio Gallicchio | University of Pisa, Italy |
| Claudio Giorgio Giancaterino | Catholic University of Milan, Italy |
| Connor Gäde | University of Hamburg, Germany |
| Constantine Dovrolis | Georgia Institute of Technology, USA |
| Cornelius Weber | University of Hamburg, Germany |
| Coşku Can Horuz | University of Tübingen, Germany |
| Cui Wang | Macao Polytechnic University, China |
| Dan Fisher | University of North Carolina, Wilmington, USA |
| Daniel Kluvanec | Durham University, UK |
| David Dembinsky | German Research Center for Artificial Intelligence, Germany |
| David Martínez | DataSpartan Ltd., UK |
| Dayananda Herurkar | DFKI, Germany |
| Denise Gorse | University College London, UK |
| Dennis Becker | Lüneburg University, Germany |
| Dimitrios Bountas | Democritus University of Thrace, Greece |
| Dimitrios Michail | Harokopio University of Athens, Greece |
| Diyuan Lu | Frankfurt Institute for Advanced Studies, Germany |
| D. J. McMoran | University of North Carolina, Wilmington, USA |
| Domenico Tortorella | University of Pisa, Italy |
| Dominique Mercier | German Research Center for Artificial Intelligence, Germany |
| Doron Nevo | Bar-Ilan University, Israel |
| Douglas Nyabuga | Donghua University, China |
| Efe Bozkir | University of Tübingen, Germany |
| Eisuke Ito | Ritsumeikan University, Japan |

Elias Pimenidis                   University of the West of England, UK
Fabian Hinder                     Bielefeld University, Germany
Fanglin Chen                      Harbin Institute of Technology, Shenzhen, China
Fares Abawi                       University of Hamburg, Germany
Federico Tavella                  University of Manchester, UK
Feixiang Zhou                     University of Leicester, UK
Feng Wei                          York University, Canada
Florence Dupin de Saint-Cyr       IRIT, Université Paul Sabatier, France
Francesco Semeraro                University of Manchester, UK
Francois Blayo                    Neoinstinct, Switzerland
Frank Gyan Okyere                 Rothamsted Research, UK
Frederic Alexandre                Inria, France
Gang Yang                         Renmin University, China
Giannis Nikolentzos               Athens University of Economics and Business,
                                    Greece
Gonzalo Martínez-Muñoz            Universidad Autónoma de Madrid, Spain
Grégory Bourguin                  LISIC/ULCO, France
Guillermo Martín-Sánchez          Graduate Training Center of Neuroscience,
                                    Germany
Gulustan Dogan                    University of North Carolina, Wilmington, USA
Habib Khan                        Islamia College Peshawar, Pakistan
Hafez Farazi                      University of Bonn, Germany
Haixia Liu                        University of the West of England, UK
Haizhou Du                        Shanghai University of Electric Power, China
Hang Gao                          Institute of Software, Chinese Academy of
                                    Sciences, China
Haopeng Chen                      Shanghai Jiao Tong University, China
Hazrat Ali                        Hamad Bin Khalifa University, Qatar
Heitor Gomes                      University of Waikato, New Zealand
Hideaki Yamamoto                  Tohoku University, Japan
Hina Afridi                       NTNU, Norway
Hiroyoshi Ito                     University of Tsukuba, Japan
Hisham Ihshaish                   University of the West of England, UK
Hong Qing Yu                      University of Bedfordshire, UK
Hongchao Gao                      South China University of Technology, China
Honggang Zhang                    University of Massachusetts, Boston, USA
Hugo Eduardo Camacho Cruz         Universidad Autónoma de Tamaulipas, Mexico
Hugues Bersini                    Université libre de Bruxelles, Belgium
Huifang Ma                        Northwest Normal University, China
Huiyu Zhou                        University of Leicester, UK
Hy Dang                           Texas Christian University, USA
Igor Farkaš                       Comenius University in Bratislava, Slovakia

| | |
|---|---|
| Ioannis Pierros | Aristotle University of Thessaloniki, Greece |
| Iveta Bečková | Comenius University in Bratislava, Slovakia |
| Jae Hee Lee | University of Hamburg, Germany |
| James J. Q. Yu | Southern University of Science and Technology, Hong Kong, China |
| James Msonda | Aberystwyth University, UK |
| Jan Faigl | Czech Technical University in Prague, Czechia |
| Jan Feber | Czech Technical University in Prague, Czechia |
| Jan Kalina | Czech Academy of Sciences, Czechia |
| Jérémie Cabessa | University Paris 2, France |
| Jia Cai | Guangdong University of Finance & Economics, China |
| Jiajun Liu | CSIRO, Australia |
| Jianhua Xu | Nanjing Normal University, China |
| Jian-Wei Liu | China University of Petroleum, Beijing, China |
| Jianyong Chen | Shenzhen University, Shenzhen, China |
| Jichao Bi | Zhejiang University, China |
| Jie Shao | University of Science and Technology, Chengdu, China |
| Jim Smith | University of the West of England, UK |
| Jing Yang | Hefei University of Technology, China |
| Jingyi Yuan | Arizona State University, USA |
| Jingyun Jia | Florida Institute of Technology, USA |
| Johannes Brinkrolf | CITEC Centre of Excellence, Germany |
| Jonathan Jakob | Bielefeld University, Germany |
| Jonathan Lawry | University of Bristol, UK |
| Jonathan Mojoo | Hiroshima University, Japan |
| Jordi Cosp-Vilella | Universitat Politècnica de Catalunya, Spain |
| Jordi Madrenas | Universitat Politècnica de Catalunya, Spain |
| Joseph Jaja | University of Maryland, USA |
| Juan Liu | Wuhan University, China |
| K. L. Eddie Law | Macao Polytechnic University, Macao, China |
| Kamran Soomro | University of the West of England, UK |
| Katsiaryna Haitsiukevich | Aalto University, Finland |
| Kenneth Co | Imperial College London, UK |
| Koji Kyoda | RIKEN Center for Biosystems Dynamics Research, Japan |
| Koloud Alkhamaiseh | Western Michigan University, USA |
| Kostadin Cvejoski | Fraunhofer IAIS, Sankt Augustin, Germany |
| Kostantinos Demertzis | Democritus University of Thrace, Greece |
| Kristian Hovde Liland | Norwegian University of Life Sciences, Norway |
| Kuntal Ghosh | Indian Statistical Institute, India |

| | |
|---|---|
| Nermeen Abou Baker | Hochschule Ruhr West, Germany |
| Nikolaos Polatidis | University of Brighton, UK |
| Oleg Bakhteev | MIPT, Russia |
| Olga Grebenkova | Moscow Institute of Physics and Technology (MIPT), Russia |
| Or Elroy | CLB, Israel |
| Ozan Özdemir | University of Hamburg, Germany |
| Paulo Cortez | University of Minho, Portugal |
| Plamen Angelov | Lancaster University, UK |
| Rafet Durgut | Bandirma Onyedi Eylul University, Turkey |
| Roman Moucek | University of West Bohemia, Czechia |
| Roseli S. Wedemann | Universidade do Estado do Rio de Janeiro, Brazil |
| Ruijun Feng | Zhejiang University of Finance and Economics, China |
| Saikat Chakraborty | Kalinga Institute of Industrial Technology (KIIT), India |
| Sajjad Heydari | University of Manitoba, Winnipeg, Canada |
| Sander Bohte | CWI, Netherlands |
| Sandrine Mouysset | IRIT, France |
| Sebastián Basterrech | VSB-Technical University of Ostrava, Czechia |
| Sebastian Otte | University of Tübingen, Germany |
| Senwei Liang | Purdue University, USA |
| Shelan Jeawak | University of the West of England, UK |
| Shoubin Dong | South China University of Technology, China |
| Sidi Yang | RI-MUHC, Canada |
| Song Guo | Xi'an University of Architecture and Technology, China |
| Songlin Du | Southeast University, China |
| Stefan Wermter | University of Hamburg, Germany |
| Steve Battle | University of the West of England, UK |
| Sven Behnke | University of Bonn, Germany |
| Takaharu Yaguchi | Kobe University, Japan |
| Takeshi Ikenaga | Waseda University, Japan |
| Tang Kai | Toshiba, China |
| Tetsuya Hoya | Nihon University, Japan |
| Tianlin Zhang | University of the Chinese Academy of Sciences, China |
| Tieke He | Nanjing University, China |
| Tim Brailsford | University of the West of England, UK |
| Ting Bai | Hefei University of Technology, China |
| Toby Breckon | Durham University, UK |
| Varun Ojha | University of Reading, UK |

| | |
|---|---|
| Wenxin Yu | Southwest University of Science and Technology, China |
| Xi Cheng | Nanjing University of Science and Technology, China |
| Xia Feng | Civil Aviation University, China |
| Xian Zhong | Wuhan University of Technology, China |
| Xiang Zhang | National University of Defense Technology, China |
| Xiaoqing Liu | Kyushu University, Japan |
| Xiumei Li | Hangzhou Normal University, China |
| Xizhan Gao | University of Jinan, China |
| Xuan Yang | Shenzhen University, China |
| Yan Chen | Chinese Academy of Sciences, China |
| Yangguang Cui | East China Normal University, China |
| Yapeng Gao | University of Tübingen, Germany |
| Yaxi Chen | Wuhan University, China |
| Yiannis Aloimonos | University of Maryland, USA |
| Yihao Luo | Huazhong University of Science and Technology, China |
| Yipeng Yu | Tencent, China |
| Yuan Li | Academy of Military Science, China |
| Yuanyuan Chen | Sichuan University, China |
| Yuchen Zheng | Shihezi University, China |
| Yuchun Fang | Shanghai University, China |
| Yue Gao | Beijing University of Posts and Telecommunications, China |
| Yuji Kawai | Osaka University, Japan |
| Zhaoxiang Zang | China Three Gorges University, China |
| Zhaoyun Ding | National University of Defense Technology, China |
| Zhengfeng Yang | East China Normal University, Shanghai, China |
| Zhenjie Yao | CMCC, China |
| Zhiping Lai | Fudan University, China |
| Zhiqiang Zhang | Hosei University, Japan |
| Zhixin Li | Guangxi Normal University, China |
| Zhongnan Zhang | Xiamen University, China |

# Contents – Part I

# A Novel Deep Learning Based Method for Doppler Spectral Curve Detection

Keming Mao[1], Yitao Ren[1(✉)], Liancheng Yin[1], and Yan Jin[2]

[1] College of Software, Northeastern University, Shenyang, China
maokm@mail.neu.edu.cn, 2171341@stu.neu.edu.cn
[2] Department of Cardiovascular Surgery, General Hospital of Northern Theater Command, Shenyang, China

**Abstract.** This paper proposes a novel doppler spectral curve detection method. First, U-net model is used to obtain the coarse segmentation map from the spectral image. Then, in order to solve the problem of curve deviation and curve defect, two components, curve correction and curve filling, which adopt deep regression and Generative adversarial networks, are devised for spectrum curve refining operation. These two outputs are fused for final segmentation. The experiments are validated on a private collected Spectral Doppler Spectrum dataset. The results demonstrate the proposed method has achieved satisfactory performance.

**Keywords:** Deep learning · Spectrum curve detection · Medical image processing · Computer aided diagnosis

## 1 Introduction

Doppler Spectral Echo Echocardiography is important for clinical diagnosis by examining direction and velocity of blood flow represented by spectrum curve. An example of Doppler Spectral Echo Echocardiography is shown in Fig. 1. However, current spectrum curve methods mainly rely on manual observation, which is time-consuming and inconsistent. Therefore, it is worth exploring an accurate method to detect spectrum curves.

Deep learning based methods show good performance in medical image processing. Among these methods, U-net model has become the baseline since its lightweight, high efficiency and low data dependency [1]. It includes encoders and decoders with symmetrical structure, and skip connections are added in the same layer. So U-net model can integrate shallow and deep semantic features to prevent the loss of key features.

Many improved models based on U-net have shown excellent performance in various medical image processing tasks. [2] strengthened the information interaction between different layers on the basis of U-net. [3] added an attention gate to U-net to reduce redundant calculation and highlight the target region. [4] replaced the ordinary convolution in with recurrent residual convolution. [5] extended U-net from 2D to 3D to process 3D medical data. [6] proposed bridge

© The Author(s), under exclusive license to Springer Nature Switzerland AG 2022
E. Pimenidis et al. (Eds.): ICANN 2022, LNCS 13529, pp. 1–12, 2022.
https://doi.org/10.1007/978-3-031-15919-0_1

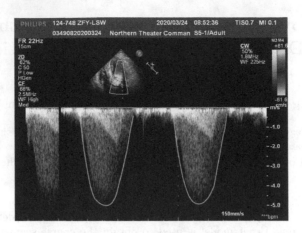

**Fig. 1.** A sample of Doppler Spectral Echo Cardio, the blood flow spectrum curve is marked with yellow solid line. (Color figure online)

U-net, namely, connecting two U-net models. [7] proposed to use two or three consecutive U-nets for image segmentation.

Although these models achieve better segmentation results, they are not available for spectral curve detection for the following two reasons. First, due to the large noise interference and heterogeneous texture, even the labels given by professional experts are usually not consistent. Second, different from the tasks such as lung nodule segmentation and skin lesion segmentation, which have an obvious target region, blood flow spectrum curve is obtained by measuring the blood flow velocity is always changing, and this may leads to the feature inconsistency of the target region and brings difficulties to curve detection. The above reasons may bring much deviations in detected curves and part of curves may be lost. Some researches proposed to refine the segmentation maps [8,9], however, they need to manually adjust the model parameters. This is not only time-consuming and laborious, but also inappropriate and inconvenient. What's more, deep learning based methods require large amount of data while there is relatively small size of doppler spectrum training data.

To handle these problems, a novel two-stage spectrum curve detection method is proposed in this paper. Firstly, typical U-net model is used for coarse segmentation. Secondly, two modules are designed to refine the initially segmentation result, which are curve correction module and curve filling module respectively. In curve correction module, an effective 1D U-net is trained for further deep curve regression. In curve filling module, GANs is adopted to fill the defect region automatically. Finally, these two modules are fused for final curve segmentation. This method is more effectively refine and accurate for final curve segmentation. To the best of our knowledge, this is the first deep learning based method for the task of doppler spectral curve detection. The main contributions of this paper are as follows:

- This paper proposes a novel framework for Doppler spectral curve detection, which combines the curve regression and defect region filling.
- GANs is adopted to solve the partial missing of detected curve. It transforms the incomplete segmentation filling to problem of automatic data generation.
- Extensive experiments from various aspects are evaluated to demonstrate the effectiveness of the proposed method.

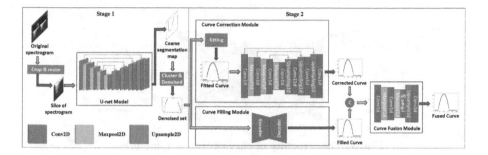

**Fig. 2.** The overall structure of the proposed method.

The remaining parts of this paper are organized as follows: Sect. 2 introduces the proposed method in detail; Sect. 3 presents the experimental evaluations; and Sect. 4 summarizes the whole paper.

## 2 Proposed Method

Figure 2 illustrates the mainframework. After pre-processing, the cropped and resized slices are coarsely segmented in Stage 1. In Stage 2, curve correction and curve filling are used for refinement, and the outputs of these two modules are fused to form the final segmentation. The detail are described as follows.

### 2.1 Preprocessing and Coarse Segmentation

Since the blood flow spectrum curve only exists in the spectral region, and the other regions do not need to be concerned. The whole image is first cropped into spectral region slices, and they are resized to size $W \times H \times C$, where $W$, $H$ and $C$ represent the width, height and channels respectively.

Denote the slice as $\mathbf{X} \in \mathbf{R}^{W \times H \times C}$, and it is used as the basic processing unit. The well-known U-net model is adopted for coarse segmentation in this research. The segmentation map obtained from U-net can be regarded as a two-dimensional representation $\mathbf{Y} \in \mathbf{R}^{W \times H}$.

The curve detected by U-net model often has deviation and defect, and curve correction and curve filling modules are used for further refinement. For convenience, segmentation map $\mathbf{Y}$ is converted to one dimension format. We first traverse $\mathbf{Y}$ to get edge pixel points with sample thresholding. Coordinate $p(x_{pixel}, y_{pixel})$ of selected edge pixel is added to curve set.

Moreover, DBSCAN is also used to eliminate the noise points that far away from curve edge. $P$ is used to represent the curve point set after noise removing, and it is the input for curve correction module and curve filling module.

## 2.2  Curve Correction

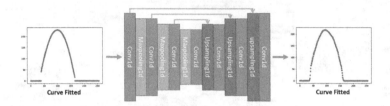

**Fig. 3.** The structure of curve correction module.

To deal with curve deviation, curve correction module is designed. It consists of two parts, an curve fitting transformation and a 1D-Unet for curve correction.

$P_{fitted}$ is first obtained with polynomial fitting of $P$. Then a correction operation $M_{correct}$ is constructed with a 1D-Unet structure. $P_{fitted}$ is further modified to curve point set $P_{corrected}$ with deep regression provided by $M_{correct}$, which is given in Eq. 1. Figure 3 demonstrates the curve correction module.

$$P_{corrected} = M_{correct}(P_{fitted}) \tag{1}$$

The difference between $P_{corrected}$ and ground truth label $P_{truth}$ is used as loss function to tune the parameter weight of model $M_{correct}$. As shown in Eq. 2, $L_{correction}$ is the $L_2$ distance among all curve point. $m$ is the number of curve point. $P_{corrected}^i$ and $P_{truth}^i$ represent position of $ith$ curve point in $P_{corrected}$ and $P_{truth}$. For simplicity, curve point $i$ is omitted in following equations.

$$L_{correction} = ||P_{corrected} - P_{truth}||_2$$
$$= \frac{1}{2m} \sum_{i=1}^{m} (P_{corrected}^i - P_{truth}^i)^2 \tag{2}$$

Using curve correction module, a continuous and smooth curve can be gained.

## 2.3  Curve Filling

Besides curve correction module, a curve filling module is also designed to deal with the curve defect problem.

In this subsection, the defect part of curve can be regarded as the masked area that is expected to be restored. The restoration of masked image has always been one of the key research directions by GANs. So far, many models with good performance have been proposed [10–12]. Inspired by pix2pix [13], we propose a curve filling module based on 1D-GANs to generate the missing curve. The structure of curve filling module is shown in Fig. 4. It includes an encoder decoder based generator and a PatchGAN based discriminator.

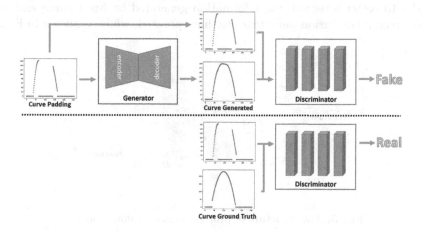

**Fig. 4.** The structure of curve filling.

$D$ and $G$ are used to represent the discriminator and the generator. The purpose of generator $G$ is to generate a new curve based on input $P$ that the missing parts are filled and the discriminator $D$ is to determine whether the given curve is the generated curve or not. These two parts are trained in an adversarial way. A well trained generator $G$ can produce a curve similar to the ground truth, which is denoted as $P_{filled}$.

The loss function of generator $G$ adopts $L_1$ distance, as shown in Eq. 3.

$$L_G(G) = \mathbb{E}_{P,P_{truth},z}(\|P_{truth} - G(P,z))\|_1) \tag{3}$$

Compared with other GANs models which adapt $L_2$ distance, $L_1$ distance can make the generated curve more close to the ground truth curve and further reduce the ambiguity so that the generated curve is more smooth. The loss function of discriminator $D$ is given in Eq. 4.

$$
\begin{aligned}
L_D(G,D) = & \mathbb{E}_{P,P_{truth}}[\log D(P_{truth},P] \\
& + \mathbb{E}_P[1 - \log(1 - D(P,G(P,z)]
\end{aligned} \tag{4}
$$

The goal of $G$ is to minimize the difference between the generated curve $P_{filled}$ and the truth label $P_{truth}$, while the goal of $D$ is to maximize it. Therefore, the whole objective function of curve filling module is given as Eq. 5.

$$L_{filling} = \arg\min_G \max_D L_D(G, D) + \lambda L_G(G) \qquad (5)$$

where $\lambda$ is a weight parameter. $G$ and $D$ can be trained simultaneously in an adversarial way.

## 2.4   Curve Fusion

In order to better integrate the information generated by filled curve and corrected curve, a late fusion module is also incorporated, which is shown in Fig. 5.

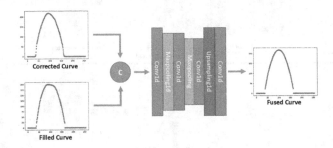

**Fig. 5.** The structure of proposed curve fusion model.

For fusion module, $P_{corrected}$ and $P_{filled}$ are used as inputs. They are first concatenated together, and then fully convolutions operations are used to form the final output curve $P_{fused}$. This process is shown in Eq. 6.

$$P_{fused} = M_{fuse}(P_{corrected}, P_{filled}) \qquad (6)$$

Similarly, to train the model $M_{fusion}$, $L_1$ distance between $P_{truth}$ and $P_{fused}$ is formed as the loss function, which is given in Eq. 7.

$$L_{fusion} = ||P_{truth} - P_{fused}||_1 \qquad (7)$$

## 2.5   Objective Function

We integrate the curve correction, curve filling and curve fusion modules together into stage 2, and the final objective function is shown in Eq. 8.

$$L_{total} = w_1 L_{correction} + w_2 L_{filling} + w_3 L_{fusion} \qquad (8)$$

The final loss function $L_{total}$ is represented as the weighted sum of the above 3 loss functions. $w_1$, $w_2$ and $w_3$ are their weight parameters respectively. Our proposed method is totally end-to-end framework and can be train automatically.

# 3 Experiment

## 3.1 Dataset

The data used in this paper is provided by the General Hospital of the North-eastern Theater Command, China. There are 44 spectral images in total, and they are cropped into 88 slices with size of 256 * 256 * 1. 71 samples are used for training and 17 samples are used for testing. Data augmentation is applied on 71 training slices and the augmented data are about 710.

## 3.2 Implementation Details

All models are trained for 50 epochs. Adam optimizer is adopted with learning rate 0.0004. All experiments are conducted on NVIDIA GeForce 1070Ti GPU, 32G RAM, and tensorflow 2.3 and keras 2.4 are selected for deep framework.

## 3.3 Quantitative Evaluation

Based on standard criteria provided by [14–16], optimal dataset scale (ODS) and the optimal image scale(OIS) are adopted to evaluate model performance. They are F-measure values with different threshold setting, which is shown in Eq. 9.

$$F - measure = \frac{2 \times precision \times recall}{precision + recall} \tag{9}$$

## 3.4 Performance Evaluation of Proposed Model Combined with U-net

To evaluate the performance of the proposed modules, 4 U-net models, Unet++ [2], Attention-Unet [3], R2-Unet [4] and BCD-Unet [17] are selected for coarse segmentation. Then they are combined with our proposed modules respectively. The comparison of results are shown in Table 1.

It can be seen from the result that our proposed modules can improve performance of base models with about 2% to 4% promotion. Moreover, Unet++ based improvement gets the optimal performance, with 82.92% and 82.97 % for ODS and OIS respectively.

Segmentation results of 4 different model settings are given in Fig. 6, Fig. 7, Fig. 8 and Fig. 9. They demonstrate the segmentation results obtain by the proposed method are more clear, smooth and less noisy compared with their counterparts, and they are more close to the ground truth labels.

**Table 1.** Comparison of OIS and ODS of U-net models with different modules.

| Model name | ODS | OIS |
|---|---|---|
| Unet++ | 78.88% | 78.90% |
| Unet++ with curve corr. | 80.76% | 80.81% |
| Unet++ with curve filling | 82.75% | 82.80% |
| **Unet++ with stage 2** | **82.92%** | **82.97%** |
| Attention-Unet | 78.88% | 78.89% |
| Attention-Unet with curve corr. | 80.93% | 80.97% |
| Attention-Unet with curve filling | 82.01% | 82.07% |
| **Attention-Unet with stage 2** | **82.23%** | **82.27%** |
| R2-Unet | 79.52% | 79.63% |
| R2-Unet with curve corr. | 81.84% | 81.88% |
| R2-Unet with curve filling | 81.36% | 81.41% |
| **R2-Unet with stage 2** | **81.89%** | **81.94%** |
| BCD-Unet | 78.88% | 78.89% |
| BCD-Unet with curve corr. | 81.93% | 81.95% |
| BCD-Unet with curve filling | 81.65% | 81.69% |
| **BCD-Unet with stage 2** | **81.96%** | **82.02%** |

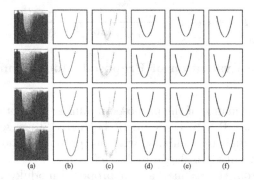

**Fig. 6.** Segmentation maps by Unet++ combined with different modules. (a) slices of spectrum, (b) ground truth label, (c) coarse segmentation maps, (d) segmentation maps with curve correction module, (e) segmentation maps with curve filling module, (f) segmentation maps combined with all modules.

We also compare our method with some state-of-the-art methods to further illustrate it's performance. These methods are all proposed in 2020 or 2021, which are latest and achieve satisfactory scores in their own domain. Same as the above U-net models, these models are also trained for 50 epochs with the cross entropy loss, Table 2 shows the comparison results.

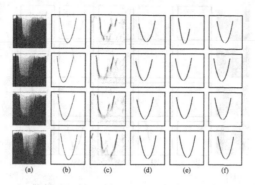

**Fig. 7.** Segmentation maps by Attention-Unet combined with different modules. (a) slices of spectrum, (b) ground truth label, (c) coarse segmentation maps, (d) segmentation maps with curve correction, (e) segmentation maps with curve filling, (f) segmentation maps combined with all modules.

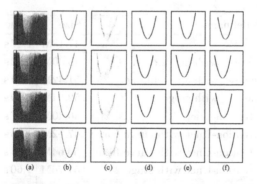

**Fig. 8.** Segmentation maps by R2-Unet combined with different modules. (a) slices of spectrum, (b) ground truth label, (c) coarse segmentation maps, (d) segmentation maps with curve correction, (e) segmentation maps with curve filling, (f) segmentation maps combined with all modules.

**Table 2.** Comparison of OIS and ODS of our method with state-of-the-art method.

| Model name | ODS | OIS |
|---|---|---|
| Lyu et al. [18] | 80.88% | 80.99% |
| Mirn et al. [19] | 79.27% | 79.32% |
| Sun et al. [20] | 81.59% | 81.66% |
| Gao et al. [21] | 80.50% | 80.63% |
| Li et al. [22] | 81.48% | 81.55% |
| Unet++ with stage 2 | 82.92% | 82.97% |
| Attention-Unet with stage 2 | 82.23% | 82.27% |
| R2-Unet with stage 2 | 81.89% | 81.94% |
| BCD-Unet with stage 2 | 81.96% | 82.02% |

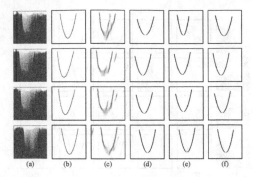

**Fig. 9.** Segmentation maps by BCD-Unet combined with different modules. (a) slices of spectrum, (b) ground truth label, (c) coarse segmentation maps, (d) segmentation maps with curve correction, (e) segmentation maps with curve filling, (f) segmentation maps combined with all modules.

**Table 3.** Comparison of model size and running time.

| Model name | Size | Time |
|---|---|---|
| Unet++ | 47.18M | 1.47 s |
| Unet++ with curve corr. | 48.30M | 1.62 s |
| Unet++ with curve filling | 51.42M | 1.64 s |
| Unet++ with stage 2 | 52.54M | 1.69 s |
| Attention-Unet | 46.40M | 1.37 s |
| Attention-Unet with curve corr. | 47.52M | 1.53 s |
| Attention-Unet with curve filling | 50.64M | 1.54 s |
| Attention-Unet with stage 2 | 51.76M | 1.60 s |
| R2U-net | 47.18M | 1.49 s |
| R2U-net with curve corr. | 47.92M | 1.64 s |
| R2U-net with curve filling | 51.04M | 1.66 s |
| R2U-net with stage 2 | 52.16M | 1.70 s |
| BCD-Unet | 48.20M | 2.91 s |
| BCD-Unet with curve corr. | 49.32M | 3.06 s |
| BCD-Unet with curve filling | 52.44M | 3.07 s |
| BCD-Unet with stage 2 | 53.56M | 3.13 s |

From Table 2 we know that compared with the state-of-the-art methods, our methods are more effective and have better performance. Besides, the proposed modules can be combined with other models easily to refine their segmentation maps, which means that our methods are adaptable.

According to our evaluation, performance of Unet++ combined with our proposed modules is the best choice. Meanwhile, other methods also show improvements than their basic models. These results illustrate the effectiveness of our proposed method.

### 3.5  Comparison of Model Efficiency

In order to further illustrate the model efficiency, we compare the size of the different models and their running time. The comparisons are shown in Table 3.

It can be seen from Table 3 that the proposed method consumes less expenses on extra model storage, with less 10%. For running efficiency, there needs about 15% extra time. It can be concluded that the efficiency of proposed method is acceptable and practical, and it can be deployed on mobile platform easily.

## 4  Conclusion

In this paper, we proposed a novel curve detection method for Doppler spectrum image. Due to the large noise interference and the heterogeneous texture, refinement stage of feature map based on two modules of curve correction and curve filling are designed. The coarse segmentation map obtained from U-net model are fitted, corrected, filled and fused. Finally a continuous and smooth spectrum curve is obtained. The experimental results show that the method proposed can effectively refine the coarse segmentation map. It improves the accuracy of segmentation result and outperforms some well known segmentation methods. Our future works will focus on more challenging medical scenarios.

## References

1. Ronneberger, O., Fischer, P., Brox, T.: U-net: convolutional networks for biomedical image segmentation. In: Navab, N., Hornegger, J., Wells, W.M., Frangi, A.F. (eds.) MICCAI 2015. LNCS, vol. 9351, pp. 234–241. Springer, Cham (2015). https://doi.org/10.1007/978-3-319-24574-4_28
2. Zhou, Z., Rahman Siddiquee, M.M., Tajbakhsh, N., Liang, J.: UNet++: a nested U-net architecture for medical image segmentation. In: Stoyanov, D., et al. (eds.) DLMIA/ML-CDS -2018. LNCS, vol. 11045, pp. 3–11. Springer, Cham (2018). https://doi.org/10.1007/978-3-030-00889-5_1
3. Okta, O., et al.: Attention U-net: learning where to look for the pancreas. arXiv:1804.03999 (2018)
4. Alom, M.Z., Hasan, M., Yakopcic, C., Taha, T.M., Asari, V.K.: Recurrent residual convolutional neural network based on U-net (R2U-net) for medical image segmentation. arXiv:1802.06955 (2018)
5. Çiçek, Ö., Abdulkadir, A., Lienkamp, S.S., Brox, T., Ronneberger, O.: 3D U-net: learning dense volumetric segmentation from sparse annotation. In: Ourselin, S., Joskowicz, L., Sabuncu, M.R., Unal, G., Wells, W. (eds.) MICCAI 2016. LNCS, vol. 9901, pp. 424–432. Springer, Cham (2016). https://doi.org/10.1007/978-3-319-46723-8_49
6. Chen, W., et al.: Prostate segmentation using 2D bridged U-net. In: 2019 International Joint Conference on Neural Networks, pp. 1–7 (2019)

7. Dalmı, M.U., et al.: Using deep learning to segment breast and fibroglandular tissue in MRI volumes. Med. Phys. **44**(2), 533–546 (2017)
8. Chen, L., Papandreou, G., Kokkinos, I., Murphy, K., Yuille, A.L.: DeepLab: semantic image segmentation with deep convolutional nets, atrous convolution, and fully connected CRFs. In: IEEE Transactions on Pattern Analysis and Machine Intelligence, vol. 40, no. 4, pp. 834–848 (2018)
9. Kamnitsas, K., et al.: Efficient multi-scale 3D CNN with fully connected CRF for accurate brain lesion segmentation. Med. Image Anal. **36**, 61–78 (2017)
10. Liu, H., Jiang, B., Xiao, Y., Yang, C.: Coherent semantic attention for image inpainting. In: 2019 IEEE/CVF International Conference on Computer Vision, pp. 4169–4178 (2019)
11. Zheng, C., Cham, T.J., Cai, J.: Pluralistic image completion. In: Proceedings of the IEEE/CVF Conference on Computer Vision and Pattern Recognition (2019)
12. Xiong, W., Lin, Z., Yang, J., Lu, X., Barnes, C., Luo, J.: Foreground-aware image inpainting. In: Proceedings of the IEEE/CVF Conference on Computer Vision and Pattern Recognition (2019)
13. Isola, P., Zhu, J., Zhou, T., Efros, A.A.: Image-to-image translation with conditional adversarial networks. In: 2017 IEEE Conference on Computer Vision and Pattern Recognition, pp. 5967–5976(2017)
14. Xie, S., Tu, Z.: Holistically-nested edge detection. In: 2015 IEEE International Conference on Computer Vision, pp. 1395–1403 (2015)
15. Liu, Y., Cheng, M., Hu, X., Wang, K., Bai, X.: Richer convolutional features for edge detection. In: 2017 IEEE Conference on Computer Vision and Pattern Recognition, pp. 5872–5881 (2017)
16. He, J., Zhang, S., Yang, M., Shan, Y., Huang, T.: Bi-directional cascade network for perceptual edge detection. In: Proceedings of the IEEE Conference on Computer Vision and Pat-tern Recognition, pp. 3828–3837 (2019)
17. Azad, R., Asadi-Aghbolaghi, M., Fathy, M., Escalera, S.: Bi-directional ConvLSTM U-net with densley connected convolutions. In: 2019 IEEE/CVF International Conference on Computer Vision Workshop, pp. 406–415 (2019)
18. Lyu, C., Shu, H.: A two-stage cascade model with variational autoencoders and attention gates for MRI brain tumor segmentation. In: Crimi, A., Bakas, S. (eds.) BrainLes 2020. LNCS, vol. 12658, pp. 435–447. Springer, Cham (2021). https://doi.org/10.1007/978-3-030-72084-1_39
19. Miron, R., Albert, R., Breaban, M.: A two-stage atrous convolution neural network for brain tumor segmentation and survival prediction. In: Crimi, A., Bakas, S. (eds.) BrainLes 2020. LNCS, vol. 12659, pp. 290–299. Springer, Cham (2021). https://doi.org/10.1007/978-3-030-72087-2_25
20. Sun, J., Darbehani, F., Zaidi, M., Wang, B.: SAUNet: shape attentive u-net for interpretable medical image segmentation. In: Martel, A.L., et al. (eds.) MICCAI 2020. LNCS, vol. 12264, pp. 797–806. Springer, Cham (2020). https://doi.org/10.1007/978-3-030-59719-1_77
21. Gao, Y., Zhou, M., Metaxas, D.N.: UTNet: a hybrid transformer architecture for medical image segmentation. In: de Bruijne, M., et al. (eds.) MICCAI 2021. LNCS, vol. 12903, pp. 61–71. Springer, Cham (2021). https://doi.org/10.1007/978-3-030-87199-4_6
22. Li, Y., et al.: GT U-net: a U-net like group transformer network for tooth root segmentation. In: Lian, C., Cao, X., Rekik, I., Xu, X., Yan, P. (eds.) MLMI 2021. LNCS, vol. 12966, pp. 386–395. Springer, Cham (2021). https://doi.org/10.1007/978-3-030-87589-3_40

# A Unified Multiple Inducible Co-attentions and Edge Guidance Network for Co-saliency Detection

Zhenshan Tan[ORCID] and Xiaodong Gu[✉][ORCID]

Department of Electronic Engineering, Fudan University, Shanghai 200433, China
{zstan19,xdgu}@fudan.edu.cn

**Abstract.** The learning-based methods have improved the performances of co-salient object detection (CoSOD). Mining the intra-image saliency individuals and exploring the inter-image co-attention are two challenges. In this paper, we propose a unified Multiple INducible co-attentions and Edge guidance network (MineNet) for CoSOD. Firstly, a classified inducible co-attention (CICA) is designed to model the classification interactions from a group of images. Secondly, a focal inducible co-attention (FICA) is employed to adaptively suppress and aggregate inter-image saliency features. CICA and FICA are jointly embedded into the network to predict the co-attention. The co-attentions of CICA and FICA are collaborative calibration and mutual optimization. Thirdly, we put forward an edge guidance module (EGM) to mine the intra-image saliency individuals, which aims to keep the consistency of co-attention during the feature transfer and refine the object edges. Finally, these three modules are merged into a unified and end-to-end network to predict the fine-grained boundary-preserving salient objects. Experimental results on three prevailing benchmarks show that our MineNet outperforms other competitors in terms of the evaluation metrics. In addition, the proposed method runs at the speed of more than 30 fps on a single GPU.

**Keywords:** Co-salient object detection · Co-attention · Edge guidance module

## 1 Introduction

Compared with single-image-based salient object detection (SOD) [17–19], co-saliency detection (CoSOD) aims to discover the most attractive and representative regions from a group of images. CoSOD has two basic rules: 1) extracting the co-attention from multiple images and 2) refining the individuals. Early CoSOD algorithms [1,8,12,14,23–25] mainly rely on hand-crafted features such as color, shape and texture of multiple foregrounds and backgrounds. However, due to the complexities of objects and surroundings in multiple diverse practical applications, these methods hardly explore high-level semantic information and detect co-salient objects. Recently, the learning-based methods especially the

E. Pimenidis et al. (Eds.): ICANN 2022, LNCS 13529, pp. 13–24, 2022.
https://doi.org/10.1007/978-3-031-15919-0_2

end-to-end networks have been introduced to CoSOD [6,13,20,28] and achieve competitive statistical results.

However, the learning-based methods still suffer from three issues: 1) Parts of previous researches [6,28] utilize the classification model to explore the inter-image interactions. Nevertheless, classification-based methods rely on the classified features extracted by backbone network, lacking the post-processing capability to correct the misled information caused by the complexities of multiple foregrounds and backgrounds. Similarly, the GCNs-based methods [13] have hit a same bottleneck; 2) Some methods [10,16,27] attempt to address CoSOD issue by feature concatenation. These methods concatenate the features extracted by the encoder and then explore the co-attention and calibrate the individuals after layer concatenation. However, they only rely on the feature fitting ability by neural networks while ignore the prior knowledge, causing the optimization difficulty and the feature redundancy; 3) For individual calibration, previous methods do not take the edge refinement into account. Recent learning-based methods mainly focus on the co-attention exploration. However, the important consistent convergence of co-attention and the edge preservation still need to be further considered.

With the above insights, we propose an end-to-end network named MineNet, including multiple inducible co-attentions to exploit the group-wise representations and an edge guidance module to predict the fine-grained boundary-preserving results. Concretely, to address the first and the second issues above, we combine feature classification and feature concatenation. We first propose a classified inducible co-attention (CICA) to mine the classification interactions of multiple images to induce the classified features. Then, to correct the potentially misled features of classification, we design a focal inducible co-attention (FICA) to aggregate multiple features. Besides, considering the optimization difficulty and the feature redundancy caused by concatenation-based model, we embed an adaptive focal attention redistribution (AFAR) into FICA to adaptively suppress and aggregate inter-image features. With the help of AFAR, the noises are filtered out and the important features are directly refined. Finally, to address the third issue above, we put forward an edge guidance module (EGM) to keep the consistency of co-attention and preserve the edges of object.

In a word, the main contributions can be highlighted as follows.

- We present a classified inducible co-attention to explore the co-attention of classification interactions among multiple images. The classified co-attention helps to induce the most distinctive classified features and reduce non-repetitive features.
- We design a focal inducible co-attention with an adaptive focal attention redistribution to adaptively suppress and aggregate inter-image features, which filters out the noises and highlights the important features.
- We put forward an edge guidance module in the intra-image feature extraction, aiming to constrain the co-attention and calibrate the boundary features.
- Visual and objective assessments on three prevailing datasets reveal that our MineNet outperforms other methods. And the ablation studies validate each proposed module.

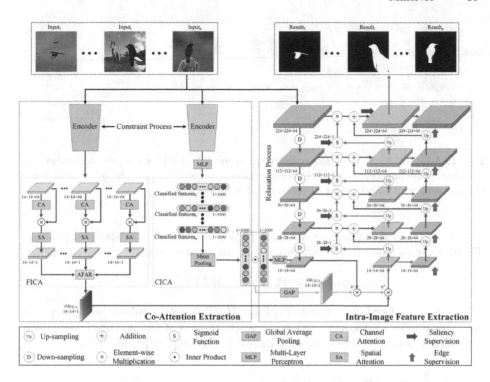

**Fig. 1.** Overall architecture of MineNet. AFAR denotes the adaptive focal attention redistribution and is shown in Fig. 2

## 2 Proposed Method

As illustrated in Fig. 1, we propose a unified multiple inducible co-attentions and edge guidance network for CoSOD. The multiple inducible co-attentions contain a classified co-attention to reduce non-repetitive features and a focal inducible co-attention to correct the misled features. The edge guidance module aims to keep the consistency of co-attention and calibrate the edges.

### 2.1 Classified Inducible Co-Attention

Inspired by previous methods [2,3,6,15,21,28], the proposed classified inducible co-attention (CICA) adopts a constrained pre-training model to explore the co-classified features. Structurally, as shown in Fig. 1, a constrained vgg16 is utilized to extract the classified features from $N$ relevant images $\mathcal{I} = \{I_n\}_{n=1}^N$. During the constraint process, the parameters will not be learned. After that, a mean-pooling is used to extract the classification interactions.

$$cls = P_{mean}(f_{vgg16}^{CICA}(\mathcal{I})), \tag{1}$$

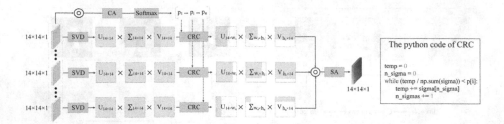

**Fig. 2.** Adaptive focal attention redistribution module. CRC is compression ratio calculation. ⊚ is concatenation. × is vector product. 'sigma' denotes the $\sum$. $w$ and $h$ are the reserved width and height of matrix and $w = h$.

where, $P_{mean}$ is the mean-pooling and $f_{vgg16}^{CICA}$ denotes the constrained process. Then, $cls$ is assigned to the individual feature maps to extract the co-attention.

$$ca_{CICA} = P_{gap}(cls \odot MLP(e_i^5)), \tag{2}$$

where, $P_{gap}$ is the global average pooling, $MLP$ denotes multi-layer perceptron and $e_i^5$ is the $5-th$ encoder feature maps. By the aid of CICA, the classification interactions are abstracted, which reduces the non-repetitive features.

## 2.2    Focal Inducible Co-attention

As CICA needs a post-processing model to recalibrate the possible misled classification features. Therefore, we propose a focal inducible co-attention module (FICA) to achieve this. Concretely, as shown in Fig. 1, we utilize another constrained vgg16 to extract the features $\mathcal{Z} = \{z_n\}_{n=1}^N$ of images.

$$z_i = f_{vgg16}^{FICA}(I_i), \tag{3}$$

where, $f_{vgg16}^{FICA}$ is the constrained process and the fully-connected layers of vgg16 are dropped. After that, a relaxed channel attention [11] is used to assign the feature map weights. During the relaxed process, the parameters are learned.

$$A_{ca_i}{}' = z_i \cdot \sigma(MLP'(P_{aap}{}'(z_i)) \oplus MLP'(P_{amp}{}'(z_i))), \tag{4}$$

where, $P_{aap}{}'$ and $P_{amp}{}'$ are average pooling and maximum pooling, and $\sigma$ denotes the sigmoid function. Then, a relaxed spatial attention [22] is utilized to predict the attention priors.

$$A_{sa_i}{}' = \sigma(f_{7\times7}{}'([P_{cap}{}'(A_{ca_i}{}'); P_{cmp}{}'(A_{ca_i}{}')])), \tag{5}$$

where, $P_{cap}{}'$ and $P_{cmp}{}'$ are channel-wise average pooling and channel-wise maximum pooling. The '[]' denote channel concatenation. $f_{7\times7}{}'$ is the convolutional layer with $7 \times 7$ kernel size. At the beginning of training, $A_{ca_i}{}'$ and $A_{sa_i}{}'$ assign more weights to the repetitive features. As the training progresses, $A_{ca_i}{}'$ and

$A_{sa_i}'$ can focus on the misled features. Accordingly, these two mechanisms make the network avoid falling into the sub-optimal results and this whole process can be called the focus shifting process. In addition, we also embed an adaptive focal attention redistribution (AFAR) into FICA to filter out the noises and fuse multiple attentions to predict the co-attention. As illustrated in Fig. 2, a relaxed channel attention distributes the weights of concatenated features, which calculates the probability and determines the importances.

$$A_{ca_i}'' = MLP''(P_{aap}''([A_{sa_n}']_{n=1}^N)) \oplus MLP''(P_{amp}''([A_{sa_n}']_{n=1}^N)) \quad (6)$$

Then, we use the singular value decomposition (SVD) to suppress the redundant features. The key point of SVD is how to select the number of singular values. To address this, we take the probabilities offered by the channel attention as the singular value selection, which is adaptive and interference free.

$$A_{svd_i} = SVD(A_{sa_i}', A_{ca_i}'') = U_{W \times w_i} \sum_{w_i \times h_i} V_{h_i \times H}^T, \quad (7)$$

where, $U$, $\sum$ and $V$ represent left singular vector, singular value and right singular vector, respectively. $W$ and $H$ are the size, $w$ and $h$ are the reserved size of selected singular values. The interference free probability makes the recovered features be better robustness. Finally, the more flexible and reliable co-attention is extracted by a relaxed spatial attention.

$$h_i'' = \sigma(f_{7 \times 7}''([P_{cap}''([A_{svd_i}]_{n=1}^N); P_{cap}''([A_{svd_i}]_{n=1}^N)])) \otimes h_i', \quad (8)$$

## 2.3   Individual Extraction

Individual extraction (intra-image feature extraction) directly determines the performance. It has two key points: 1) the co-attention consistency and 2) the edge refinement. The co-attention consistency means the individual should learn the co-attention and can not change the co-attention during feature transfer. The edge refinement requires the objects have the fine-grained contours. Therefore, we embed an edge guidance module (EGM) into individual extraction. Obviously, the object edges help to keep the consistency of co-attention because the complementarity between boundary features and saliency features. Besides, EGM can naturally optimize the edges.

The whole process of EGM can be found in Fig. 1. After the fusion with co-attention, the induced feature $h_i''$ is extracted and fed into the decoder layer. During the decoder, the co-attention is passed from down layers to top layers. Due to the stacks of convolutional layers, the noise features also appear. Limited by calculation speed and GPU memories, SVD is not suitable. Accordingly, to keep the consistency transfer of co-attention, we put forward an EGM.

$$g_i^q = f_{EGM}^q(d_i^q; \Theta_{EGM}^q), q = 1, 2, 3, 4, 5, \quad (9)$$

where, $\Theta_{EGM}^q$ denotes the parameters learned from the convolutional process $f_{EGM}^q$. Then, $g_i^q$ is used to predict the previous decoder. By the aid of the embedded EGM, the co-attention preserves consistent convergence in the process of feature transfer and the boundary features are refined.

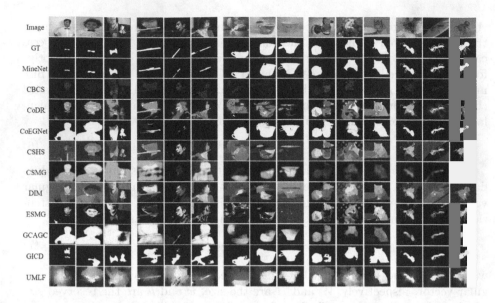

**Fig. 3.** Visual comparison with state-of-the-art methods.

## 2.4 Loss Function

In this paper, we use the Dice loss [7] to supervise the saliency features and the weighted BCE loss to supervise the boundary features. The Dice loss can be denoted as follows.

$$L_{Dice}^{(s)} = 1 - \frac{\sum_{(m,n)} GP}{\sum_{(m,n)} [G + P]} \qquad (10)$$

where, $G$ and $P$ represent the ground truth and predicted feature map, respectively. $m$ and $n$ are the pixel coordinate. And the weighted BCE loss is as follows.

$$L_{wBCE}^{(e)} = - \sum_{(m,n)} [\omega G log P + (1 - G)(1 - log P)], \qquad (11)$$

where, $L_{wBCE}^{(e)}$ is the loss of $e$-th layer. $\omega$ is the abbreviation $\omega(m,n)$ and we set $\omega(m,n) = \frac{\sharp 0\{m,n\}}{\sharp 1\{m,n\}}$, in which $\sharp 0\{m,n\}$ (or $\sharp 1\{m,n\}$) is the number of 0 (or 1). Compared with the background, the sparse edge foreground are assigned higher weights by $\omega$. The hybrid loss can be denoted as follows.

$$L = \sum_{s=1}^{S} L_{Dice}^{(s)} + \sum_{e=1}^{E} L_{wBCE}^{(e)}, \qquad (12)$$

where, $S$ and $E$ represent the layer number and are set as 5 and 5, respectively.

**Table 1.** Quantitative comparisons with state-of-the-art methods. Publish: Where and when the paper is published; '–' denotes no reports; '↑' denotes the larger the value, the better the results; '↓' denotes the lower the value, the better the results; Values with bold fonts indicate the best performance; Values with italics indicate suboptimal performance.

| Methods | Publish | CoSal2015 | | | | | CoSOD3k | | | | | CoCA | | | | |
|---|---|---|---|---|---|---|---|---|---|---|---|---|---|---|---|---|
| | | $F_\phi\uparrow$ | $\epsilon\downarrow$ | $F_\gamma\uparrow$ | $E_\phi\uparrow$ | $S_\alpha\uparrow$ | $F_\phi\uparrow$ | $\epsilon\downarrow$ | $F_\gamma\uparrow$ | $E_\phi\uparrow$ | $S_\alpha\uparrow$ | $F_\phi\uparrow$ | $\epsilon\downarrow$ | $F_\gamma\uparrow$ | $E_\phi\uparrow$ | $S_\alpha\uparrow$ |
| CBCS [8] | TIP 2013 | 0.591 | 0.234 | 0.514 | 0.657 | 0.545 | 0.526 | 0.225 | 0.455 | 0.653 | 0.450 | – | – | – | – | – |
| CSHS [14] | SPL 2013 | 0.633 | 0.312 | 0.437 | 0.686 | 0.594 | 0.555 | 0.307 | 0.393 | 0.663 | 0.568 | – | – | – | – | – |
| ESMG [12] | SPL 2014 | 0.531 | 0.248 | 0.471 | 0.640 | 0.552 | 0.463 | 0.239 | 0.418 | 0.638 | 0.534 | – | – | – | – | – |
| SACS [1] | TIP 2014 | 0.702 | 0.193 | 0.632 | 0.751 | 0.697 | – | – | – | – | – | – | – | – | – | – |
| CoDR [23] | SPL 2015 | 0.628 | 0.203 | 0.568 | 0.751 | 0.692 | 0.594 | 0.222 | 0.508 | 0.714 | 0.643 | – | – | – | – | – |
| DIM [24] | TNNLS 2015 | 0.638 | 0.311 | 0.429 | 0.696 | 0.595 | 0.560 | 0.327 | 0.384 | 0.668 | 0.561 | – | – | – | – | – |
| MIL [25] | ICCV 2015 | 0.677 | 0.209 | 0.611 | 0.722 | 0.676 | – | – | – | – | – | – | – | – | – | – |
| CoDW [26] | IJCV 2016 | 0.725 | 0.274 | 0.560 | 0.752 | 0.650 | – | – | – | – | – | – | – | – | – | – |
| UMLF [9] | TCSVT 2017 | 0.730 | 0.269 | 0.542 | 0.772 | 0.665 | 0.689 | 0.277 | 0.529 | 0.768 | 0.641 | – | – | – | – | – |
| GoNet [10] | ECCV 2018 | 0.781 | 0.159 | 0.692 | 0.806 | 0.754 | – | – | – | – | – | – | – | – | – | – |
| CSMG [27] | CVPR 2019 | 0.834 | 0.131 | 0.747 | 0.843 | 0.775 | 0.764 | 0.148 | 0.680 | 0.824 | 0.712 | 0.539 | 0.127 | 0.478 | **0.759** | 0.608 |
| IML [16] | NEUCOM 2020 | 0.712 | 0.155 | 0.620 | 0.788 | 0.736 | – | – | – | – | – | – | – | – | – | – |
| GICD [28] | ECCV 2020 | 0.867 | 0.071 | *0.834* | *0.886* | *0.843* | 0.799 | *0.079* | *0.763* | 0.848 | *0.797* | 0.547 | 0.126 | *0.503* | 0.714 | *0.657* |
| ERN [17] | ICANN 2020 | 0.805 | 0.098 | 0.771 | 0.845 | 0.812 | 0.730 | 0.112 | 0.699 | 0.801 | 0.762 | 0.440 | 0.175 | 0.402 | 0.653 | 0.602 |
| GCAGC [13] | TMM 2021 | 0.854 | 0.090 | 0.767 | 0.881 | 0.810 | *0.806* | 0.092 | 0.730 | *0.850* | 0.785 | **0.555** | *0.113* | 0.492 | 0.715 | 0.649 |
| CoEGNet [6] | TPAMI 2021 | *0.868* | 0.078 | 0.833 | 0.883 | 0.838 | 0.798 | 0.084 | 0.757 | 0.837 | 0.777 | 0.549 | **0.106** | 0.493 | 0.713 | 0.610 |
| MineNet | | **0.872** | **0.066** | **0.843** | **0.892** | **0.851** | **0.807** | **0.074** | **0.771** | **0.852** | **0.802** | *0.550* | 0.118 | **0.506** | *0.721* | **0.659** |

# 3 Experiments

## 3.1 Datasets and Evaluation Metrics

Following previous methods [6,28], we evaluate the proposed method on three prevailing datasets, including CoSal2015 [26], CoSOD3k [6] and CoCA [28]. We train our MineNet on the dataset of the method [28].Five widely used metrics, including F-measure ($F_\phi$), mean absolute error ($\epsilon$), average F-measure ($F_\gamma$), maximal enhanced-alignment measure ($E_\phi$) [5] and structural similarity measure ($S_\alpha$) [4], are applied to evaluate the performance of MineNet and other state-of-the-art methods.

## 3.2 Implementation Details

The overall framework is implemented on PyTorch platform with a GTX 2080 Ti GPU. All the 20 inputs are resized as 224 × 224. Following previous methods [6,28], the data augmentation algorithms such as normalization, random rotation and random horizontal flipping are adopted to reduce the over-fitting. Adam optimizer with default parameters is used. The initial learning rate is set to 1e−4 during 100 epochs. We do not apply any pre-processing or post-processing methods and fix the initialize random seed, which can obtain the same results of each process.

## 3.3 Comparison with the State-of-the-Art

**Quantitative Comparison.** We compare the proposed FRCNet against 15 CoSOD methods and 1 SOD method, including CBCS [8], CSHS [14], ESMG [12],

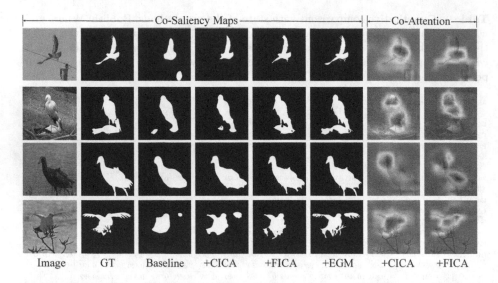

**Fig. 4.** Visualization the co-attention and the cooperation of each module.

SACS [1], CoDR [23], DIM [24], MIL [25], CoDW [26], UMLF [9], GoNet [10], CSMG [27], IML [16], GICD [28], ERN [17], GCAGC [13], CoEGNet [6]. ERN is a SOD method and others are CoSOD methods. As illustrated in Table 1, MineNet achieves consistent superiors against other methods across three datasets. Obviously, SOD cannot well address the CoSOD issue, which verifies that the co-attention is necessary. In addition, our method outperforms others on CoSal2015 and CoSOD3k datasets, and achieves two best results on CoCA dataset in terms of five indicators, which further demonstrates the effectiveness of our method.

**Visual Comparison.** As illustrated in Fig. 3, we visualize some results of MineNet and other state-of-the-art methods. The resulting saliency maps of MineNet achieve superior performances, which are closer to the ground truth in visual. Specifically, with the help of CICA and FICA, our model not only induces the salient regions (see Fig. 3 columns 1–6), but also suppress the background noises (see Fig. 3 columns 7–12). By the aid of the complementarity of saliency features and boundary features in EGM, MineNet is able to generate more complete and fine-grained boundary-preserving saliency maps even though in the complex background (see Fig. 3 columns 13–15). Furthermore, MineNet achieves these results without any pre-processing or post-processing.

### 3.4 Ablation Studies

To validate the effectiveness of each key component of MineNet, we train all the proposed modules on the same training dataset. Besides, the hyper-parameters keep consistent.

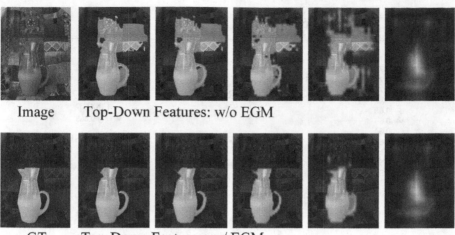

Fig. 5. Visualization of EGM. From the top row to the down row show the top-down features with or without EGM.

Table 2. Quantitative Comparisons of each proposed module. '↑' represents the larger the value, the better the results; '↓' represents the lower the value, the better the results; EGM is edge guidance module.

| | Modules | | | | CoSal2015 | | | | | CoSOD3k | | | | |
|---|---|---|---|---|---|---|---|---|---|---|---|---|---|---|
| | Baseline | CICA | FICA | EGM | $F_\phi\uparrow$ | $\epsilon\downarrow$ | $F_\gamma\uparrow$ | $E_\phi\uparrow$ | $S_\alpha\uparrow$ | $F_\phi\uparrow$ | $\epsilon\downarrow$ | $F_\gamma\uparrow$ | $E_\phi\uparrow$ | $S_\alpha\uparrow$ |
| (a) | ✓ | | | | 0.753 | 0.107 | 0.713 | 0.790 | 0.761 | 0.702 | 0.121 | 0.619 | 0.748 | 0.702 |
| (b) | ✓ | ✓ | | | 0.799 | 0.093 | 0.768 | 0.833 | 0.806 | 0.733 | 0.108 | 0.653 | 0.786 | 0.729 |
| (c) | ✓ | | ✓ | | 0.779 | 0.100 | 0.763 | 0.816 | 0.783 | 0.717 | 0.115 | 0.641 | 0.762 | 0.711 |
| (d) | ✓ | ✓ | ✓ | | 0.822 | 0.083 | 0.801 | 0.848 | 0.816 | 0.762 | 0.102 | 0.697 | 0.806 | 0.744 |
| (e) | ✓ | | | ✓ | 0.791 | 0.093 | 0.763 | 0.830 | 0.802 | 0.721 | 0.113 | 0.645 | 0.775 | 0.718 |
| (f) | ✓ | ✓ | ✓ | ✓ | 0.872 | 0.066 | 0.843 | 0.892 | 0.851 | 0.807 | 0.074 | 0.771 | 0.852 | 0.802 |

Figure 4 visualizes the cooperation of each proposed module. Obviously, the vanilla baseline without co-attention cannot filter out the noises (see row 1). The classification-based module CICA can roughly exploit the co-attention, and the concatenation-based module FICA can further purify the co-attention. As shown in the co-attention parts of Fig. 4, FICA is able to suppress the background noises. However, because of the lack of co-attention constraint and contour optimization in the decoder, CICA and FICA still suffer from incomplete resulting performances and noise interference. When EGM is embedded, the co-attention is constrained and the contours are calibrated, which is able to predict the fine-grained boundary-preserving co-salient objects.

Figure 5 visualizes the process of without or with EGM, it can be observed that in each decoder, the co-attention is consistent convergence, the noise features are filtered out and the contours are refined. In addition, Table 2 show

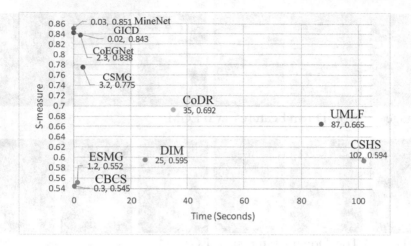

**Fig. 6.** Average running time and the statistical results of $S_\alpha$ on CoSal2015 dataset.

the statistical results of each module. Obviously, each module contributes to the predicted salient objects, which also verifies the effectiveness of each proposed component. In addition, our MineNet can run at the speed of 33 fps on a single GTX 2080Ti GPU. We also compare our MineNet against other methods on the CoSal2015 dataset in terms of the speed, which is shown in Fig. 6. Figure 6 shows that our method is not only faster than others, but also achieves the best performances. The time comparison also verifies the effectiveness of our method.

## 4   Conclusion

In this paper, we propose a unified multiple inducible co-attentions and edge guidance network for co-saliency detection. Firstly, to mine the classified co-attention from a group of images, a classified inducible co-attention module is designed to explore the co-classified prior guidance. Secondly, a focal inducible co-attention module is proposed to mutually recalibrate with the classified co-attention. Besides, to reduce the feature redundancy and the optimization difficult caused by the repeated convolution processes, an adaptive focal attention redistribution model is presented to adaptively suppress the noise features. Benefitting from the co-attention extraction mechanism, the classification and the concatenation are jointly optimized into a unified framework with better flexibility in terms of generating co-attention. Secondly, to keep the consistency of co-attention and refine the details, an edge guidance module is embedded into the individual extraction module. With the help of edge guidance module, the co-attention is convergent and the contour are calibrated. Finally, the co-attention is assigned to the individuals to predict the fine-grained boundary-preserving co-salient objects. Extensive experimental results on three prevailing datasets show that the proposed method achieves consistently superior results under the evaluation metrics. Besides, the ablation studies also verify the effectiveness of each module. In addition, our MineNet can run at the speed of more than 30 fps on a single GTX 2080Ti GPU.

**Acknowledgements.** This work was supported in part by National Natural Science Foundation of China under grant 62176062.

# References

1. Cao, X., Tao, Z., Zhang, B., et al.: Self-adaptively weighted co-saliency detection via rank constraint. IEEE Trans. Image Process. **23**(9), 4175–4186 (2014)
2. Chen, C., Tan, Z., Cheng, Q., et al.: UTC: a unified transformer with inter-task contrastive learning for visual dialog. In: Proceedings of the IEEE/CVF Conference on Computer Vision and Pattern Recognition, pp. 18103–18112. IEEE, New Orleans (2022)
3. Cheng, Q., Tan, Z., Wen, K., et al.: Semantic Pre-alignment and ranking learning with unified framework for cross-modal retrieval. IEEE Trans. Circ. Syst. Video Technol. (2022). https://doi.org/10.1109/TCSVT.2022.3182549
4. Fan, D., Cheng, M., Liu, Y., et al.: Structure-measure: a new way to evaluate foreground maps. In: Proceedings of the IEEE International Conference on Computer Vision, pp. 4548–4557. IEEE, Hawaii (2017)
5. Fan, D., Gong, C., Cao, Y., et al.: Enhanced-alignment measure for binary foreground map evaluation. In: Proceedings of the International Joint Conference on Artificial Intelligence (2018)
6. Fan, D., Li, T., Lin, Z., et al.: Re-thinking co-salient object detection. IEEE Trans. Pattern Anal. Mach. Intell. **44**, 4339–4354 (2021)
7. Fidon, L., et al.: Generalised Wasserstein dice score for imbalanced multi-class segmentation using holistic convolutional networks. In: Crimi, A., Bakas, S., Kuijf, H., Menze, B., Reyes, M. (eds.) BrainLes 2017. LNCS, vol. 10670, pp. 64–76. Springer, Cham (2018). https://doi.org/10.1007/978-3-319-75238-9_6
8. Fu, H., Cao, X., Tu, Z.: Cluster-based co-saliency detection. IEEE Trans. Image Process. **22**(10), 3766–3778 (2013)
9. Han, J., Cheng, G., Li, Z., et al.: A unified metric learning-based framework for co-saliency detection. IEEE Trans. Circ.Syst. Video Technol. **28**(10), 2473–2483 (2017)
10. Hsu, K.-J., Tsai, C.-C., Lin, Y.-Y., Qian, X., Chuang, Y.-Y.: Unsupervised CNN-based co-saliency detection with graphical optimization. In: Ferrari, V., Hebert, M., Sminchisescu, C., Weiss, Y. (eds.) ECCV 2018. LNCS, vol. 11209, pp. 485–501. Springer, Cham (2018). https://doi.org/10.1007/978-3-030-01228-1_30
11. Hu, J., Shen, L., Sun, G.: Squeeze-and-excitation networks. In: Proceedings of the IEEE conference on Computer Vision and Pattern Recognition, pp. 7132–7141. IEEE, Salt Lake (2018)
12. Li, Y., Fu, K., Liu, Z., et al.: Efficient saliency-model-guided visual co-saliency detection. IEEE Signal Process. Lett. **22**(5), 588–592 (2014)
13. Li, T., Zhang, K., Shen, S., et al.: Image co-saliency detection and instance co-segmentation using attention graph clustering based graph convolutional network. IEEE Trans. Multimed. **22**, 492–505 (2021)
14. Liu, Z., Zou, W., Li, L., et al.: Co-saliency detection based on hierarchical segmentation. IEEE Signal Process. Lett. **21**(1), 88–92 (2013)

15. Qin, Y., Gu, X., Tan, Z.: Visual context learning based on textual knowledge for image-text retrieval. Neural Netw. **152**, 434–449 (2022)
16. Ren, J., Liu, Z., Zhou, X., et al.: Co-saliency detection via integration of multi-layer convolutional features and inter-image propagation. Neurocomputing **371**, 137–146 (2020)
17. Tan, Z., Hua, Y., Gu, X.: Salient object detection with edge recalibration. In: Farkaš, I., Masulli, P., Wermter, S. (eds.) ICANN 2020. LNCS, vol. 12396, pp. 724–735. Springer, Cham (2020). https://doi.org/10.1007/978-3-030-61609-0_57
18. Tan, Z., Gu, X.: Scale balance network for accurate salient object detection. In: Proceedings of the International Joint Conference on Neural Networks, pp. 1–7. IEEE, Glasgow (2020)
19. Tan, Z., Gu, X.: Depth scale balance saliency detection with connective feature pyramid and edge guidance. Appl. Intell. **51**(8), 5775–5792 (2021). https://doi.org/10.1007/s10489-020-02150-z
20. Tan, Z., Gu, X.: Co-saliency detection with intra-group two-stage group semantics propagation and inter-group contrastive learning. Knowl.-Based Syst. **252**, 109356 (2022)
21. Wen, K., Tan, Z., Cheng, Q., et al.: Contrastive cross-modal knowledge sharing pre-training for vision-language representation learning and retrieval. arXiv preprint arXiv:2207.00733 (2022)
22. Woo, S., Park, J., Lee, J.-Y., Kweon, I.S.: CBAM: convolutional block attention module. In: Ferrari, V., Hebert, M., Sminchisescu, C., Weiss, Y. (eds.) ECCV 2018. LNCS, vol. 11211, pp. 3–19. Springer, Cham (2018). https://doi.org/10.1007/978-3-030-01234-2_1
23. Ye, L., Liu, Z., Li, J., et al.: Co-saliency detection via co-salient object discovery and recovery. IEEE Signal Process. Lett. **22**(11), 2073–2077 (2015)
24. Zhang, D., Han, J., et al.: Cosaliency detection based on intrasaliency prior transfer and deep intersaliency mining. IEEE Trans. Neural Netw. Learn. Syst. **27**(6), 1163–1176 (2015)
25. Zhang, D., Meng, D., Li, C., et al.: A self-paced multiple-instance learning framework for co-saliency detection. In: Proceedings of the IEEE International Conference on Computer Vision, pp. 594–602. IEEE, Santiago (2015)
26. Zhang, D., Han, J., Li, C., et al.: Detection of co-salient objects by looking deep and wide. Int. J. Comput. Vis. **120**(2), 215–232 (2016)
27. Zhang, K., Li, T., Liu, B., et al.: Co-saliency detection via mask-guided fully convolutional networks with multi-scale label smoothing. In: Proceedings of the IEEE/CVF Conference on Computer Vision and Pattern Recognition, pp. 3095–3104. IEEE, Long Beach (2019)
28. Zhang, Z., Jin, W., Xu, J., Cheng, M.-M.: Gradient-induced co-saliency detection. In: Vedaldi, A., Bischof, H., Brox, T., Frahm, J.-M. (eds.) ECCV 2020. LNCS, vol. 12357, pp. 455–472. Springer, Cham (2020). https://doi.org/10.1007/978-3-030-58610-2_27

# Attention Guided Network for Salient Object Detection in Optical Remote Sensing Images

Yuhan Lin[1], Han Sun[1(✉)], Ningzhong Liu[1], Yetong Bian[1], Jun Cen[1], and Huiyu Zhou[2]

[1] College of Computer Science and Technology,
Nanjing University of Aeronautics and Astronautics, Nanjing, China
`sunhan@nuaa.edu.cn`
[2] School of Computing and Mathematical Sciences, University of Leicester,
Leicester LE1 7RH, UK

**Abstract.** Due to the extreme complexity of scale and shape as well as the uncertainty of the predicted location, salient object detection in optical remote sensing images (RSI-SOD) is a very difficult task. The existing SOD methods can satisfy the detection performance for natural scene images, but they are not well adapted to RSI-SOD due to the above-mentioned image characteristics in remote sensing images. In this paper, we propose a novel Attention Guided Network (AGNet) for SOD in optical RSIs, including position enhancement stage and detail refinement stage. Specifically, the position enhancement stage consists of a semantic attention module and a contextual attention module to accurately describe the approximate location of salient objects. The detail refinement stage uses the proposed self-refinement module to progressively refine the predicted results under the guidance of attention and reverse attention. In addition, the hybrid loss is applied to supervise the training of the network, which can improve the performance of the model from three perspectives of pixel, region and statistics. Extensive experiments on two popular benchmarks demonstrate that AGNet achieves competitive performance compared to other state-of-the-art methods. The code will be available at https://github.com/NuaaYH/AGNet.

**Keywords:** Salient object detection · Optical remote sensing images · Position enhancement stage · Detail refinement stage

## 1 Introduction

Salient object detection (SOD) is used to simulate the human visual attention mechanism, which helps machine automatically search for the most attractive areas or objects in an image.

This work is supported in part by the Fundamental Research Funds for the Central Universities of China under Grant NZ2019009.

In the early days, the traditional methods for SOD are based on hand-crafted features. Such methods can meet the performance requirements of SOD tasks in specific scenarios, which also have the advantages of fast speed and convenient deployment. However, when application environment expands to a wide variety of scenarios, traditional methods do not have satisfactory generalization. In 2015, the SOD model was combined with deep learning technique and convolutional neural network (CNN) for the first time, which aroused the interest of researchers in the topic of CNN-based SOD methods.

At the present time, there has been a lot of excellent work on SOD tasks in natural scene images (NSIs) such as GateNet [20], F3Net [14], LDF [15], GCPANet [1]. However, as an emerging topic of sailency detection, the researches on SOD in optical remote sensing images (RSIs) is still relatively rare. Compared with NSIs, remote sensing images bring us more challenges. Specifically, RSIs are usually taken from a high altitude with a bird's-eye view through equipments such as aerial cameras or satellites, thus the location of salient objects may appear in various places in the frame. Meanwhile, various scales, complex shapes and indistinct boundaries are the unique features of objects in RSIs, which also hinder the accurate prediction of object details. Since the RSI-SOD datasets were constructed and opened, there have been some promising attempts to solve SOD tasks on remote sensing images, e.g., DAFNet [19], EMFINet [22], SARNet [5]. But none of them can solve the above-mentioned problems well, which includes the optimization of object positioning and object details.

As another huge vision task topic, attention mechanism and salient object detection have many similarities. Over the years, the attention mechanism has been widely used in SOD models and proved to be an extremely effective solution. In this paper, we aim at designing an attention guided network for accurate salient object detection in optical RSIs, called AGNet. To obtain accurate location prediction for salient objects, we propose a position enhancement stage including a semantic attention module and a contextual attention module, which provide the network with attention-guiding information from global semantic and local context perspectives, respectively. In order to obtain a more refined and complete saliency map, a self-refinement module is designed to build the detail refinement stage. The self-refinement module employs attention and reverse attention mechanisms to mine object details in high-confidence and low-confidence regions, thereby gradually improving the prediction results. At last, we evaluate the effectiveness of the proposed network.

## 2   Related Work

### 2.1   Attention Mechanism for SOD

In recent years, the attention mechanism is utilized to promote the performance of SOD models to a higher level. Zhao et al. [20] proposes a simple gate network to filter the noise in the encoder feature map and consider the difference in contributions from different encoder blocks. Wu et al. [16] designs a holistic attention module to expand the coverage of the initial saliency map, which helps to segment the entire salient object and optimize the boundaries. Yang et al. [18] designs a branch-wise attention module to adaptively aggregate multi-scale features so that salient objects can be efficiently localized and detected. Tang et al. [10] proposes a novel non-local cross-level attention, which can capture long-range feature dependencies to enhance the discriminative ability of complete salient objects. And Wang et al. [13] presents a pyramid attention structure to enable the network to pay more attention to saliency regions while exploiting multi-scale saliency information.

## 2.2 Salient Object Detection for RSIs

As we know, the RSI-SOD methods based on deep learning have become the main research idea since 2019. Zhang et al. [19] proposes a dense attention flow network, in which attention information flows from shallow layers to deep layers to guide the generation of high-level feature maps. Cong et al. [2] presents a graph structure-based reasoning module and a parallel multi-scale attention module, which greatly improve the accuracy and completeness of the saliency map. Zhou et al. [22] uses three encoders with different input scales to extract and fuse multi-scale features, and then introduces the guidance of edge information to obtain high-quality saliency maps. Huang et al. [5] integrates multiple high-level features to locate the object position and feed back the high-level features into the stage of shallow feature fusion. And in [11], a joint learning scheme based on bidirectional feature transformation is proposed to simultaneously optimize the boundaries and regions of salient objects.

In general, since the above deep learning-based RSI-SOD methods have made great progress, these solutions still show unsatisfactory performance when dealing with some difficult samples in Fig. 6. In our AGNet, we design an intuitively more natural method according to the image features of RSIs, which is implemented by position enhancement stage and detail refinement stage.

## 3 Approach

In this section, we will specify the details of the proposed network. The overall framework of AGNet is given in Fig. 1. From the figure, it is clear that the inference process of the proposed network consists of three main parts: feature encoding backbone, position enhancement stage and detail refinement stage. In the following, the above three components will be discussed in turn. Finally, we will also present the design of the used hybrid loss.

## 3.1 Feature Encoding Backbone

In this paper, we adopt the widely used Res2Net-50 [3] as the feature encoding backbone of AGNet. To reduce the computational complexity and the overall number of parameters in our network, a $1 \times 1$ convolutional layer is used to perform channel downscaling on the five convolutional block outputs of Res2Net.

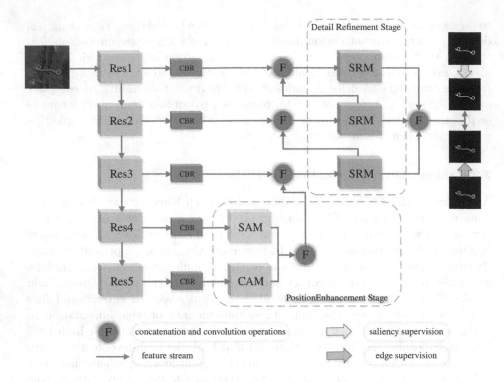

**Fig. 1.** The architecture of AGNet. CBR refers to the combination of convolutional layer, batch normalization operation, and activation function. SAM means semantic attention module, CAM denotes contextual attention module, and SRM refers to self-refinement module.

At last, all the five groups of feature maps are converted to 128 channels and ready for the next processing step. This process can be formulated as:

$$F_i = relu(bn(conv_{1 \times 1}(f_i))), i = 1...5 \tag{1}$$

in which $conv_{1 \times 1}$ denotes the $1 \times 1$ convolution operation, $bn$ refers to batch normalization operation, and $relu$ denotes the ReLU activation function. These series of operations will be represented by $CBR$ in this paper.

### 3.2    Position Enhancement Stage

Inspired by the coarse-to-fine strategy, we propose a position enhancement stage to locate potentially salient object position in the deep feature map. Specifically, the semantic attention module (SAM) is proposed to model semantic relations between different channels on the fourth layer feature map and the contextual attention module (CAM) is designed to estimate the accurate location information of salient objects on the last layer.

**Semantic Attention Module.** SENet [4] is the most widely used method for calculating channel attention. However, we think that the dimensionality reduction of channels in SENet will have the side effect of making some semantic information lost. Also, capturing the dependencies between all channels is inefficient and unnecessary [12]. Therefore, a novel semantic attention module without dimensionality reduction is designed in Fig. 2, which can be efficiently implemented via one-dimensional group convolution.

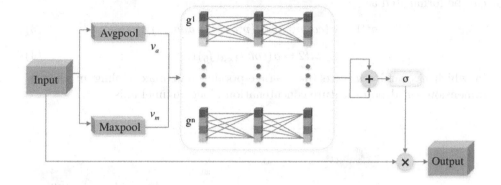

**Fig. 2.** The architecture of SAM.

Considering that the fourth layer feature map already has a large enough receptive field to describe the semantic information, we use this feature map as input to SAM. First, global average pooling and global maximum pooling are used on the feature map to obtain a global semantic representation of the features, denoted as $v_a$ and $v_m$. Then, we design a unique method for computing channel attention based on group convolution. Specifically, the above two channel vectors are used to compute local semantic correlations by two one-dimensional group convolutional layers. Each one-dimensional convolution kernel is computed with adjacent channel features, and thus the convolution results can reflect local cross-channel semantic interactions. In this paper, SAM is able to provide the maximum contribution to the network when we set the number of groups to 8. The semantic attention can be formulated as:

$$att = \sigma(gconv_{1\times1}(avgpool(f_4)) + gconv_{1\times1}(maxpool(f_4))) \qquad (2)$$

where $\sigma$ denotes the sigmoid activation function, $gconv_{1\times1}$ denotes the two $1 \times 1$ group convolutional layers, $avepool$ and $maxpool$ are the average-pooling and max-pooling in spatial dimension, respectively.

**Contextual Attention Module.** In RSIs, the location of the salient object is more randomly distributed than in NSIs, such as the center of the view or different corners of the image. Therefore, the contextual attention module is proposed to guide the network to provide the most accurate object position in the deepest layer.

As shown in Fig. 3, unlike previous spatial attention, our CAM calculates the saliency of the location from the channel dimension and the local spatial dimension, respectively. Specifically, one branch performs maximum pooling and average pooling on the input in the channel dimension, and then cascades the two single-channel feature maps to generate a spatial attention map by convolutional fusion. The other branch computes an attention map directly on the input using $3 \times 3$ convolution, which reflects the influence of neighboring pixels on the saliency of a location in the local spatial dimension. The contextual attention can be formulated as:

$$att1 = \sigma(conv_{3\times3}(cat(max(f_5), avg(f_5)))) \tag{3}$$

$$att2 = \sigma(conv_{3\times3}(f_5)) \tag{4}$$

in which $avg$ and $max$ are the average-pooling and max-pooling in channel dimension, $cat$ denotes feature concatenation along channel axis.

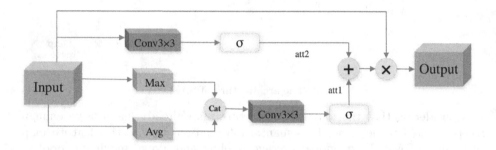

**Fig. 3.** The architecture of CAM.

### 3.3 Detail Refinement Stage

As shown in most researches, the shallow features of the network often tend to provide some additional information in terms of local details to the final prediction results. In this section, we will introduce the most critical component of the detail refinement stage, the self-refinement module (SRM), as shown in Fig. 4.

Specifically, the input to each SRM are the fused feature map, which are obtained from the deep feature of the previous layer and shallow feature of the corresponding layer. Subsequently, the convolution operation is used to compute the attention map reflecting the salient regions. At the same time, we invert this attention map to obtain the reverse attention map, which reflects some low-confidence regions ignored by the network. These two attention maps are multiplied with the fused feature map to guide the network to further mine the saliency information from the high-confidence salient regions and the low-confidence background regions. Finally, the two results are summed and fused by the convolutional layer to obtain the output of the SRM. This process can be formulated as:

$$att = \sigma(conv_{1\times1}(f)), att\_r = 1 - att \tag{5}$$

$$F = cbr(cbr(att * f) + cbr(att\_r * f)) \tag{6}$$

At last, to fully utilize the effect of SRM, the results of the three SRM modules are integrated to obtain the final prediction map of the network by concatenation and convolution operations, as shown in Fig. 1.

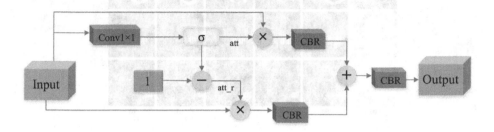

**Fig. 4.** The architecture of SRM.

### 3.4 Hybrid Loss of AGNet

In this paper, the widely used cross-entropy loss, IoU loss and recent F-value loss are introduced into hybrid loss to supervise the training of the network from the perspectives of pixels, regions, statistics. Furthermore, edge information is also added to the loss function. In the end, the total loss of the network can be described by the following equation:

$$loss = loss_{bce} + \lambda \cdot loss_{iou} + loss_f \tag{7}$$

$$Loss = loss(P, G_p) + \mu \cdot loss(E, G_e) \tag{8}$$

where $\lambda$ and $\mu$ are hyperparameters that balance the contributions of the three losses and the contributions of the two supervised objects. Empirically, we set $\lambda = 0.6$ and $\mu = 0.5$.

## 4 Experiment

### 4.1 Implementation Details

For the EORSSD [19] dataset and ORSSD [6] dataset, we expand their training sets to 11200 and 4800 samples by random flipping and random rotating. We train the proposed AGNet using the adam optimizer with initial learning rate of 1e−4, weight decay of 5e−4, and batch size of 8. Cosine annealing decay strategy is adopted to adjust the learning rate and the minimum learning rate is set to 1e−5. Our network is totally trained for 60 epochs and the input size is 224 × 224. For a fair comparison with other methods, four commonly used metrics including the mean absolute error (MAE), mean F-measure (mF), S-measure (Sm) and mean E-measure (mE) are adopted to evaluate the model performance as suggested in [5].

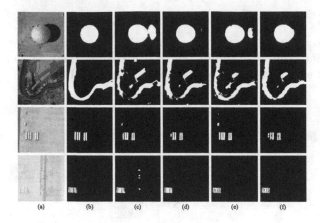

**Fig. 5.** Comparison of predictions among different networks. (a) Image; (b) Ground truth; (c) Baseline; (d) Baseline+PES; (e) Baseline+DRS; (f) Baseline+PES+DRS.

## 4.2  Ablation Studies

To demonstrate the effectiveness of the proposed method with convincing data, a series of ablation experiments are presented in this section. The same experimental parameter settings are used throughout the experiment. The qualitative comparison and quantitative comparison are shown in Fig. 5 and Table 1. Specifically, Baseline denotes the U-shaped model with Res2Net-50 as the backbone, PES means the position enhancement stage and DRS refers to the detail refinement stage.

**Effectiveness of PES.** From Table 1, it can be found that the addition of PES makes the performance of the network have obvious improvements in three main metrics, such as a gain of 0.83% in mF. The effectiveness of PES can be more thoroughly demonstrated in Fig. 5. The fourth column of each row is the saliency map predicted by the model combined with PES on the basis of the baseline. For example, the pictures in the first and second rows in Fig. 5 are representative of challenging scenes in the EORSSD dataset. The salient object in the image of the first row is accompanied by interference information such as shadows, while in the image of the second row, the color and texture features of the river are extremely similar to its surroundings, which can easily guide the network to output wrong results. Thanks to our proposed PES, the model has the ability to remove the background interference and accurately locate the object area, as shown in the third and fourth columns in Fig. 5.

**Effectiveness of DRS.** To prove the effectiveness of our DRS, we additionally train with a combination of baseline and DRS. The trained model shows the contribution of DRS to the network in Table 1, such as a 0.5% improvement on mF. The third and fourth rows of images in Fig. 5 are used to illustrate the effectiveness of DRS. As can be seen from the fifth column of Fig. 5, the gaps between closely spaced vehicles are more apparent compared to the baseline, while the shapes of the vehicles are more fully highlighted. This change is because DRS improves the prediction quality of the object details by the network. Our method can refine and supplement the details of salient objects, which is helpful for the application of RSI-SOD in earth observation, object counting, etc.

**Table 1.** Quantitative evaluation of ablation studies on the EORSSD dataset.

| Methods | EORSSD | | |
|---|---|---|---|
| | mF↑ | mE↑ | Sm↑ |
| Baseline | 0.8613 | 0.9554 | 0.9229 |
| Baseline+PES | 0.8696 | 0.9599 | 0.9248 |
| Baseline+DRS | 0.8663 | 0.9578 | 0.9247 |
| Baseline+PES+DRS | 0.8736 | 0.9614 | 0.9284 |

### 4.3 Comparison with State-of-the-arts

To demonstrate the validity of our proposed network, we compare the proposed method against other fourteen current state-of-the-art (SOTA) methods, including eight SOD methods for NSIs (i.e., ITSD [21], LDF [15], MINet [9], GCPANet [1], GateNet [20], F3Net [14], PA-KRN [17] and SUCA [8]), and six recent SOD methods for optical RSIs (i.e., CorrNet [7], DAFNet [19], EMFINet [22], LVNet [6], MJRBM [11] and SARNet [5]). All NSI-SOD methods are retrained using the original code projects published by their authors. For RSI-SOD methods, we use the saliency maps provided on the corresponding methods on github. Table 2 and Fig. 6 show the comparison of the different methods on the four metrics and visualization results, respectively.

**Quantitative Comparison.** In Table 2, we report the mF, mE, Sm, MAE of our method and fourteen other methods on two RSI-SOD datasets. Compared with other RSI-SOD methods, our method shows impressive performance. Specifically, on the EORSSD dataset, AGNet is much higher than the second-ranked method in mF, mE, e.g., mF: 0.8736 (AGNet) v.s. 0.8690 (CorrNet), and mE: 0.9614 (AGNet) v.s. 0.9512(CorrNet). Meanwhile, on MAE, our method is only slightly weaker than DAFNet by a gap of 0.0009. While on the ORSSD dataset, our method ranks first on mF, mE and MAE. Although our method fails to achieve the best score on both datasets on Sm, our method outperforms by achieving more impressive performance with smaller parameters, e.g., param: 26.60M (AGNet) vs 107.26M (EMFINet). And our AGNet also beats SARNet with the same scale of parameters, the former has about 26M and the latter has 40M. In competition with all NSI-SOD methods, our model and most RSI-SOD methods are a lot ahead of them, which further demonstrates the necessity of specially designing the model for the SOD of optical RSIs.

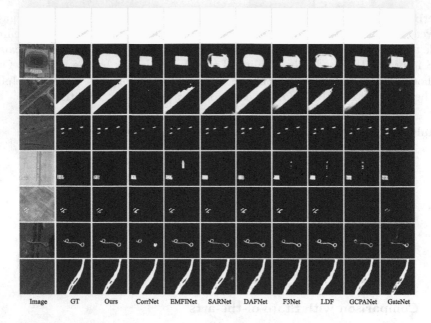

Image  GT  Ours  CorrNet  EMFINet  SARNet  DAFNet  F3Net  LDF  GCPANet  GateNet

**Fig. 6.** Visual comparisons of different methods

**Table 2.** Quantitative evaluation. The best three results are highlighted in red, blue, green.

| Methods | Type | EORSSD | | | | ORSSD | | | |
|---|---|---|---|---|---|---|---|---|---|
| | | mF↑ | MAE↓ | Sm↑ | mE↑ | mF↑ | MAE↓ | Sm↑ | mE↑ |
| ITSD | NSI | 0.8313 | 0.0109 | 0.9043 | 0.9265 | 0.8590 | 0.0172 | 0.9056 | 0.9410 |
| LDF | NSI | 0.8317 | 0.0087 | 0.9078 | 0.9464 | 0.8779 | 0.0137 | 0.9143 | 0.9518 |
| MINet | NSI | 0.8233 | 0.0097 | 0.9049 | 0.9190 | 0.8622 | 0.0153 | 0.9040 | 0.9355 |
| GCPANet | NSI | 0.7968 | 0.0104 | 0.8855 | 0.8993 | 0.8488 | 0.0177 | 0.9005 | 0.9253 |
| GateNet | NSI | 0.8314 | 0.0099 | 0.9090 | 0.9238 | 0.8769 | 0.0144 | 0.9192 | 0.9472 |
| PA-KRN | NSI | 0.8434 | 0.0109 | 0.9194 | 0.9416 | 0.8824 | 0.0145 | 0.9243 | 0.9566 |
| F3Net | NSI | 0.8164 | 0.0088 | 0.9030 | 0.9401 | 0.8677 | 0.0155 | 0.9160 | 0.9538 |
| SUCA | NSI | 0.8040 | 0.0102 | 0.8971 | 0.9131 | 0.8347 | 0.0150 | 0.8992 | 0.9349 |
| CorrNet | RSI | 0.8690 | 0.0087 | 0.9297 | 0.9512 | 0.9077 | 0.0107 | 0.9405 | 0.9687 |
| DAFNet | RSI | 0.8135 | 0.0060 | 0.9175 | 0.9295 | 0.8578 | 0.0111 | 0.9186 | 0.9496 |
| EMFINet | RSI | 0.8601 | 0.0079 | 0.9307 | 0.9445 | 0.9083 | 0.0104 | 0.9435 | 0.9662 |
| LVNet | RSI | 0.7488 | 0.0146 | 0.8639 | 0.8729 | 0.8107 | 0.0211 | 0.8807 | 0.9204 |
| MJRBM | RSI | 0.8162 | 0.0105 | 0.9068 | 0.9087 | 0.8679 | 0.0151 | 0.9190 | 0.9338 |
| SARNet | RSI | 0.8625 | 0.0091 | 0.9284 | 0.9482 | 0.8942 | 0.0105 | 0.9361 | 0.9596 |
| AGNet | RSI | 0.8736 | 0.0069 | 0.9284 | 0.9614 | 0.9109 | 0.0093 | 0.9392 | 0.9707 |

**Qualitative Comparison.** In Fig. 6, we show the saliency maps for the more difficult test samples. From the visual analysis of the saliency maps in the first to third rows, AGNet outperforms other methods when dealing with multi-scale objects, which is exactly the benefit of a powerful multi-scale feature extractor and multi-layer feature fusion strategy. The images in the fourth to sixth rows involve multiple small salient objects, which is a challenging problem in the RSI-SOD task. Our method can detect all salient objects and get refined segmentation results. For example, there are seven circular buildings in the image in the sixth row, all of which are clearly marked by our method with the help of PES. But other methods can only detect a part of the buildings, or make objects blend together, such as GateNet and DAFNet. In the last two rows in Fig. 6, we present the performance of all methods when encountering slender or complex-structured objects. For the ring-shaped buildings in the seventh row, our method provides the most complete and clear detection results due to the effect of DRS. For the two lands surrounded by the river in the eighth row, other methods either conflate them with the river or only show a hole in the saliency map, while our method successfully recognizes the two lands as the background, which further confirms the importance of self-refinement for the RSI-SOD task.

## 5   Conclusion

In this paper, a novel attention-guided network is proposed to solve the RSI-SOD task. To enhance the detection quality of salient object position, a semantic attention module and a contextual attention module are jointly used to guide the network to detect coarse but accurate object locations. In order to make the details of the object more refined and complete, a self-refinement module is designed to refine the feature map from high-confidence and low-confidence regions. Finally, an efficient hybrid loss is employed in the training of the network to boost performance. Experimental results demonstrate the robustness of our method in dealing with multi-scale objects, multiple small objects, and objects with complex structures. In the future, we will try to design a high-precision and lightweight network structure to further promote the application of the RSI-SOD model in real life.

## References

1. Chen, Z., Xu, Q., Cong, R., Huang, Q.: Global context-aware progressive aggregation network for salient object detection. In: Proceedings of the AAAI Conference on Artificial Intelligence, vol. 34, pp. 10599–10606 (2020)
2. Cong, R., et al.: RRNet: relational reasoning network with parallel multi-scale attention for salient object detection in optical remote sensing images. IEEE Trans. Geosci. Remote Sens. **60**, 1–11 (2021)
3. Gao, S.H., Cheng, M.M., Zhao, K., Zhang, X.Y., Yang, M.H., Torr, P.: Res2Net: a new multi-scale backbone architecture. IEEE Trans. Pattern Anal. Mach. Intell. **43**(2), 652–662 (2019)
4. Hu, J., Shen, L., Sun, G.: Squeeze-and-excitation networks. In: Proceedings of the IEEE Conference on Computer Vision and Pattern Recognition, pp. 7132–7141 (2018)

5. Huang, Z., Chen, H., Liu, B., Wang, Z.: Semantic-guided attention refinement network for salient object detection in optical remote sensing images. Remote Sens. **13**(11), 2163 (2021)
6. Li, C., Cong, R., Hou, J., Zhang, S., Qian, Y., Kwong, S.: Nested network with two-stream pyramid for salient object detection in optical remote sensing images. IEEE Trans. Geosci. Remote Sens. **57**(11), 9156–9166 (2019)
7. Li, G., Liu, Z., Bai, Z., Lin, W., Ling, H.: Lightweight salient object detection in optical remote sensing images via feature correlation. IEEE Trans. Geosci. Remote Sens. **60**, 1–12 (2022)
8. Li, J., Pan, Z., Liu, Q., Wang, Z.: Stacked u-shape network with channel-wise attention for salient object detection. IEEE Trans. Multimed. **23**, 1397–1409 (2020)
9. Pang, Y., Zhao, X., Zhang, L., Lu, H.: Multi-scale interactive network for salient object detection. In: Proceedings of the IEEE/CVF Conference on Computer Vision and Pattern Recognition, pp. 9413–9422 (2020)
10. Tang, L., Li, B.: CLASS: cross-level attention and supervision for salient objects detection. In: Proceedings of the Asian Conference on Computer Vision (2020)
11. Tu, Z., Wang, C., Li, C., Fan, M., Zhao, H., Luo, B.: ORSI salient object detection via multiscale joint region and boundary model. IEEE Trans. Geosci. Remote Sens. **60**, 1–13 (2021)
12. Wang, Q., Wu, B., Zhu, P., Li, P., Zuo, W., Hu, Q.: ECA-net: efficient channel attention for deep convolutional neural networks. In: 2020 IEEE/CVF Conference on Computer Vision and Pattern Recognition (CVPR), pp. 11531–11539 (2020)
13. Wang, W., Zhao, S., Shen, J., Hoi, S.C., Borji, A.: Salient object detection with pyramid attention and salient edges. In: Proceedings of the IEEE/CVF Conference on Computer Vision and Pattern Recognition, pp. 1448–1457 (2019)
14. Wei, J., Wang, S., Huang, Q.: F$^3$net: fusion, feedback and focus for salient object detection. In: Proceedings of the AAAI Conference on Artificial Intelligence, vol. 34, pp. 12321–12328 (2020)
15. Wei, J., Wang, S., Wu, Z., Su, C., Huang, Q., Tian, Q.: Label decoupling framework for salient object detection. In: Proceedings of the IEEE/CVF Conference on Computer Vision and Pattern Recognition, pp. 13025–13034 (2020)
16. Wu, Z., Su, L., Huang, Q.: Cascaded partial decoder for fast and accurate salient object detection. In: Proceedings of the IEEE/CVF Conference on Computer Vision and Pattern Recognition, pp. 3907–3916 (2019)
17. Xu, B., Liang, H., Liang, R., Chen, P.: Locate globally, segment locally: a progressive architecture with knowledge review network for salient object detection. In: Proceedings. of the AAAI Conference On Artificial Intelligence, pp. 1–9 (2021)
18. Yang, S., Lin, W., Lin, G., Jiang, Q., Liu, Z.: Progressive self-guided loss for salient object detection. IEEE Trans. Image Process. **30**, 8426–8438 (2021)
19. Zhang, Q., et al.: Dense attention fluid network for salient object detection in optical remote sensing images. IEEE Trans. Image Process. **30**, 1305–1317 (2020)
20. Zhao, X., Pang, Y., Zhang, L., Lu, H., Zhang, L.: Suppress and balance: a simple gated network for salient object detection. In: Vedaldi, A., Bischof, H., Brox, T., Frahm, J.-M. (eds.) ECCV 2020. LNCS, vol. 12347, pp. 35–51. Springer, Cham (2020). https://doi.org/10.1007/978-3-030-58536-5_3
21. Zhou, H., Xie, X., Lai, J.H., Chen, Z., Yang, L.: Interactive two-stream decoder for accurate and fast saliency detection. In: Proceedings of the IEEE/CVF Conference on Computer Vision and Pattern Recognition, pp. 9141–9150 (2020)
22. Zhou, X., Shen, K., Liu, Z., Gong, C., Zhang, J., Yan, C.: Edge-aware multiscale feature integration network for salient object detection in optical remote sensing images. IEEE Trans. Geosci. Remote Sens. **60**, 1–15 (2021)

# BiSMSM: A Hybrid MLP-Based Model of Global Self-Attention Processes for EEG-Based Emotion Recognition

Wei Li[1(✉)], Ye Tian[2], Bowen Hou[1], Jianzhang Dong[2], and Shitong Shao[1]

[1] School of Instrument Science and Engineering, Southeast University,
Nanjing 210096, Jiangsu, China
li-wei@seu.edu.cn
[2] College of Software Engineering, Southeast University,
Suzhou 215123, Jiangsu, China

**Abstract.** Due to the instability and complex distribution of electroencephalography (EEG) signals and the great cross-subject variations, extracting valuable and discriminative emotional information from EEG is still a significant challenge in EEG-based emotion recognition. In this paper, we proposed Bi-Stream MLP-SA Mixer (BiSMSM), a novel model for emotion recognition, which consists of two streams: the Spatial stream and the Temporal stream. The model captures signal information from four angles, from space to time, from local to global, aiming to encode more discriminative features describing emotions. The Spatial stream focuses on spatial information, while the Temporal stream concentrates on the correlation in the time domain. The structures of the two streams are similar, which both consist of an MLP-based module that extracts regional in-channel and cross-channel information. The module is followed by a global self-attention mechanism to focus on the global signal correlations. We conduct subject-independent experiments on the datasets DEAP and DREAMER to verify the performance of our model, whose results have excelled related methods. We obtained the average accuracy of 62.97% for valence classification and 61.87% for arousal classification on DEAP, and 60.87% for valence and 63.28% for arousal on DREAMER.

**Keywords:** Emotion recognition · Deep learning · Self-attention · EEG signals

## 1 Introduction

Emotion is a kind of human mental response to external stimuli, reflecting on the changes of facial expressions, body languages, physiological signals and other ways [18]. Currently, an increasing number of people are involved in the research of emotion recognition due to the development of Human-Computer Interaction

(HCI). Correct emotion recognition is important for the improvement of HCI which has a great application prospect in many fields, such as medical treatment, public security, artificial intelligent robot and so on. In the medical area, identifying a patient's emotion and psychological state can help doctors tailor treatment for the patients; In the field of public security, identifying the suspect's emotions accurately can help the police judge whether the suspect is lying during interrogation. And robots can interact with people better when they can correctly recognize people's emotions [12].

Research about emotion recognition is mainly based on two categories of signals: external signals and internal signals. External signals generally involve facial expressions [7], voices [1], and body languages [26]. And internal signals denote physiological signals, which refer to Electroencephalogram (EEG), Electrocardiogram (ECG), Electrooculography (EOG), and so forth [16]. However, external signals can be deceptive, such as expressions and actions. There is a certain probability that the results are unreliable and misleading when the testers dissembled their emotions. While the brain, as one of the critical parts of the central nervous system, acts unconsciously and has a pretty close relation to human perception. So the signals recorded on the cerebral cortex, the biggest region of the brain, can effectively and reliably reflect the changes in human emotions [3]. Furthermore, with the advancement of technology and Internet-of-Things devices, many wearable devices have been developed, making it easier and cheaper to pick up electrical signals from the brain. However, EEGs are highly random and non-stationary signals, which causes humans being difficult to straightly understand the meaning of the signals through direct observation. Specifically, the cross-subject scenario is one of the reasons which result in the drastic signal variation [16]. Although researchers have made substantial efforts to solve the above problems, these problems have not been completely overcome.

In this paper, we proposed a novel two-stream model called 'BiSMSM' for EEG-based emotion recognition. The novelty of this work is as follows:

- We designed two streams, Spatial stream and Temporal stream, which constituted the BiSMSM. The proposed BiSMSM could capture the correlation between signals from four perspectives, from space domain to time domain, from the local region to the global view. Therefore, BiSMSM succeeds in mining more effective and valuable information from EEG signals in which the distribution broadly differs among various individuals.
- We proposed an Multilayer Perceptron - Self-Attention Mixer (MLP-SA Mixer) shared by the two streams. It has an MLP-based module to simultaneously capture local in-channel and cross-channel information. A Self-Attention mechanism is utilized in the following part, which has an advantage in computing efficiency and capturing the intrinsic correlation and similarity between different segments of EEG from the global view. Finally, the model fuses the extracted information to construct more discriminative features.
- We designed a novel position-coding block in the Self-Attention part of the MLP-SA Mixer to describe the relative position of each electrode (or sample segment).

The rest of this paper is structured as follows. Section 2 is the related work. In Sect. 3, the proposed method is presented in detail. In Sect. 4, the experiments are described and discussed. Section 5 is the conclusion.

## 2    Related Work

It Generally, the whole procedures of EEG-based emotion recognition consist of: (1) Signal acquisition by specific devices; (2) Signal preprocessing; (3) Feature extraction; (4) Emotion Classification. Widely-used features include the time domain features (e.g., Higher order crossings), frequency domain features (e.g., Power spectra density), and time-frequency domain features (e.g., Differential entropy) [8]. In many researches, people extracted the statistical features of signals in time or spectral domain, and then used classifiers for emotion recognition. Al-shargie et al. [2] integrated the local cortical activations with dynamic functional connectivity networks patterns and then employed SVM to implement the emotion classification.

With the development of deep learning in recent years, people have explored diverse feature representation methods and recognize emotion through neural networks, which have shown promising performance. Jia et al. [9] designed a 3D dense network to obtain discriminative local patterns with the use of Spatial-Spectral/Temporal Attention mechanism. S.K. Khare et al. [11] proposed a novel time-order representation (TOR) based on S-transform which is derived from short-time fourier and wavelet transform. They employed the convolutional neural network (CNN) and took the TOR as input and then output the result. To Better capture the intrinsic correlation between multi-channel EEG signals and extract more discriminative features, Song et al. [20] proposed a novel dynamical graph convolutional neural network for emotion recognition which represented features by a dynamically learning adjacency matrix. It achieves satisfactory performance in both subject-dependent and independent experiments. And since Long Short-Term Memory (LSTM) was first proposed in 1998 [6], many researchers have used RNNs and LSTMs to extract information from EEG signals because the structures of RNN and LSTM contains loops, allowing persistence of information and being able to learn long-term dependency information. Xing et al. [25] presented a new framework that used Stack AutoEncoder to decompose the EEG source signals and build a linear EEG mixing model, and then employed LSTM-RNN to classify emotion based on the feature extracted. The framework improves classification accuracy by exploring the context correlation in EEG signals.

As to capture the spatio-temporal correlation in EEG signals, Zhang et al. [27] designed a novel deep learning framework called spatial-temporal recurrent neural network. He employed a SRNN and a TRNN to respectively extract information by taking advantage of RNN which can capture long term dependencies. This model can be applied in both emotion recognition and face recognition. Wang et al. [24] used phase-locking value (PLV) to model the graphic spatio-temporal representation of EEG signals, and then the graph data was input to graph convolution neural network for recognizing emotion which are termed as 'P-GCNN'. Peiyang *et al.* [15] also adopted PLV to measure the connection between brain regions to model the connection pattern for Emotional Analysis.

Recently, self-attention mechanism has achieved great interest of many researchers, which has shown promising results in the fields of Natural Language Processing (NLP) and Computer Vision (CV). Ashish Vaswani *et al.* [23] proposed the self-attention mechanism implementing the machine translation mission. Alexey Dosovitskiy *et al.* [4] applied the self-attention mechanism to the computer vision termed 'VIT', which has caught worldwide interest. In the area of EEG-based emotion recognition, Tao *et al.* [21] also proposed the attention-based convolutional recurrent neural network (ACRNN) to extract attentive spatial and temporal information to classify emotions. Priyasad *et al.* [17] proposed channel-specific encoders to learn the high-level features and model the spatial dependencies through graph attention networks.

LSTM and RNN have proved their excellent performance in capturing long-term association and dependence of signals in the reviewed research. However, each unit in them needs to wait for the state of the last node, which results in low efficiency. Furthermore, it is still affected by the difference of individual signal probability distribution and the large amount of noise. Therefore, for purpose of constructing more discriminative features, we propose a new method to mine correlations between signals from time to space, from local to global (Fig. 1).

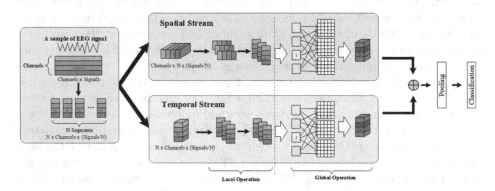

**Fig. 1.** The overview of the proposed method. The EEG signals converse in the time and space domain and respectively input to Spatial Stream and Temporal Stream. The two streams share similar architecture which termed 'MLP-SA Mixer' consisting of a regional MLP-based model and global self-attention processes. The output of two streams will be fused to discriminative features and finally classified into emotion labels.

# 3    Methods

## 3.1    Spatial/Temporal Stream

To extract more discriminative features, the proposed method employs a Spatial Stream and a Temporal Stream to extract the spatial and temporal features, respectively. Concretely, the structures of the two streams are similar. Each stream comprises a regional MLP-based module and a global self-attention mechanism, which are termed as MLP-SA Mixer. The former obtains cross-channel and in-channel correlation of regional signal segments through the MLP blocks. And the latter part parses the signal information from the global perspective. It can capture the intrinsic associations and abstract patterns between each pair of signal segments, even if the two segments are far apart in the time domain or space domain. So the whole module consisting of two streams can extract and fuse discriminative features from four angles, from spatial to temporal, from regional to global. Therefore, the data transmitted in the model should have the ability of being traversed in certain orders in time or space domain, such as multi-channel sequence signals (e.g., EEG). For the Temporal Stream, inspired by [22], we slice the data into N non-overlapping segments according to the temporal order, which is Sample $S = [s_1, s_2, ..., s_n]$, n is the number of segments. For example, if the original EEG signal has the size of $C \times S$, which C denotes the number of channels, and S is the dimension of each channel, then we can obtain the processed signal in size of $N \times C \times (S/N)$. And in the spatial stream, we converted the data from the time domain to the space domain, where the data was transformed into $C \times N \times (S/N)$. Such a form of data is beneficial for us to focus on the regional information, while the self-attention module would capture the information from the global perspective.

## 3.2    MLP-SA Mixer

Figure 2 demonstrates the overview structure of the Spatial/Temporal Stream. As the two streams share a similar architecture, we take Temporal Stream as an example. In the stream, we employ two MLP blocks to simultaneously learn the in-channel and cross-channel information between signals in the regional processing part. Each MLP block contains two fully-connected layers and an activation function to capture the correlation between and within channels through the transformation of input data. The MLP block can be written as follows:

$$\overline{S} = \mathcal{D}_2(\mathcal{FC}_2(\sigma(\mathcal{D}_1(\mathcal{FC}_1(S)))))  \tag{1}$$

where $D_1$ and $D_2$ are dropout functions to alleviate the over-fitting problem in emotion recognition due to the unstable nature of EEG signals. And $FC$ denotes the fully-connected layers. The first MLP block is applied to $s_i^T$ which is a transposition of segment $s_i$. It extracts cross-channel information of the sample segments. In contrast, the second block acts on each channel of segment $s_i$ to extract information within channels. A residual operator + is also employed to mix the cross-channel and in-channel information. Finally, the local features

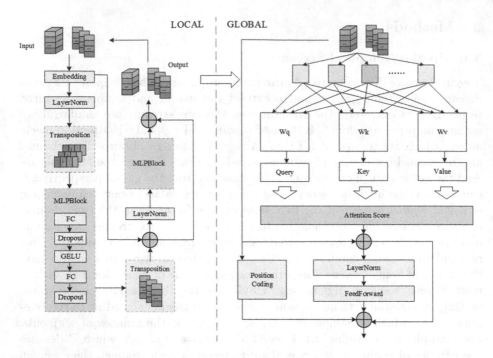

**Fig. 2.** The procedures of Spatial/Temporal Stream. The left part is about the local processes which is based on several MLP blocks. The right part is the correlation extraction from the global perspective based on the self-attention mechanism.

of the data are obtained. The whole process in the local MLP-based module components can be written as follows:

$$
\begin{aligned}
I_{cross-channel} &= S + (M_1(LN(S^T)))^T \\
I_{in-channel} &= M_2(LN(I_{cross-channel})) \\
I_{local} &= I_{cross-channel} + I_{in-channel}
\end{aligned}
\tag{2}
$$

where $M_1$ denotes the first MLP block, and $M_2$ is the second MLP aiming to capture in-channel correlation. $LN$ is LayerNorm.

In the previous study, many researchers intend to use RNN or LSTM to capture temporal information of EEG signals. However, no matter RNN or LSTM, when processing data at each time point, both networks need to wait until the state of the previous time stage is obtained, which unavoidably result in the low computing efficiency. In this paper, we use the self-attention mechanism to capture global connections between signals. The procedure of this part is illustrated in Fig. 2. $W_q, W_k, W_v$ are three learnable weight matrices. They operate on each segment of data so that each data segment will have a query vector, a key vector and a value vector. Each query will be matched with each key in the way of scaled dot-product in the Hilbert space to get the attention score. All the vectors compose Querys Matrix (Q), Keys Matrix (K), and Values Matrix (V).

So we only need to perform matrix operations to get the correlation between all the segments in the sample.

$$\begin{cases} q_i = W_q \cdot s_i \\ k_i = W_k \cdot s_i \quad i = 1, 2, ...N \\ v_i = W_v \cdot s_i \end{cases} \tag{3}$$

$$\begin{cases} Q = W_q \cdot S = [q_1\ q_2\ ...\ q_n] \\ K = W_k \cdot S = [k_1\ k_2\ ...\ k_n] \\ V = W_v \cdot S = [v_1\ v_2\ ...\ v_n] \end{cases} \tag{4}$$

Equation 3 and Eq. 4 are the calculating formula of query set Q, key set K, and value set V. $S = \{s_i | 1 \leq i \leq N\}$ is the set of sample segments. Each data segment is input into the three learnable matrices to achieve its corresponding query vector, key vector, and value vector. All the query vectors, key vectors and value vectors of data segments composed the matrices of Query, Key and Value. Then the correlation of each pair of segments is obtained by matching one node's query vector to the other's key vector. $\alpha_{i,j}$ means the correlation between segment $i$ and segment $j$.

$$\begin{aligned} A &= \begin{bmatrix} \alpha_{1,1} & \alpha_{1,2} & \cdots & \alpha_{1,n} \\ \alpha_{2,1} & \alpha_{2,2} & \cdots & \alpha_{2,n} \\ \vdots & \vdots & & \vdots \\ \alpha_{n,1} & \alpha_{n,2} & \cdots & \alpha_{n,n} \end{bmatrix} \\ &= \begin{bmatrix} k_1' \\ k_2' \\ \vdots \\ k_n' \end{bmatrix} \cdot [q_1\ q_2\ \cdots\ q_n] \\ &= K^T \cdot Q \end{aligned} \tag{5}$$

The formula for computing attention scores is written as follows:

$$SA(Q, K, V) = softmax(\frac{A \cdot V}{\sqrt{d_k}}) \tag{6}$$

where $\sqrt{d_k}$ denotes the length of Key. Moreover, we employ a learnable matrix to represent the relative position information of each segment to overcome the limitation of irregular distribution of effective information in EEG signal. Furthermore, a feedforward and residual operation are carried out after obtaining the attention score to obtain the global information $I_{global}$. Finally, the local and global information of time domain and space domain is integrated into more discriminative features. And then a pooling layer is also employed.

# 4  Experiments

## 4.1  Datasets

To verify the performance of our method, we conducted several experiments on two public acknowledged benchmark datasets, DEAP [13] and DREAMER [10]. DEAP is a multi-channel physiological signals dataset collected by Sander Koelstra *et al.* to study human emotional states for affection computing. In the data collection process, 32 subjects watched 40 one-minute-long music videos. The 40-channel (32-channel electroencephalogram and 8-channel peripheral physiological signals) signal for each subjects was recorded while testers watching the music videos with a sampling rate 512 Hz. Each video clip starts with a 3-second blank. Deap uses two indexes to describe emotional states in a continuous space, arousal (rating from 1 to 9) and valence (rating from 1 to 9). And we divided the trails into two classes according to value of valence (or arousal) and labeled 'High' if the value is higher or equal to 5 and as 'Low' if it is lower than 5.

In DREAMER, the EEG and ECG signals were recorded when the 23 subjects watched 18 film clips. They were asked to assess themselves from 3 dimensions of Arousal, Valence and Dominance rating from scale 1 to scale 5. Specifically, we only use the EEG signals with a downsampling rate 128 Hz in our experiments. Moreover, according to the author's recommendation, we only use the last-60-s signal. Similar to DEAP, we divided the trails into two classes based on the value of valence (or arousal) and labeled 'High' if the value is higher or equal to 3 and 'Low' if it is lower or equal to 3.

## 4.2  Experimental Setup

**Table 1.** Hyperparameters for model training

| Parameters | DEAP | DREAMER |
|---|---|---|
| Learning rate | 0.00003 | 0.00003 |
| Dropout rate | 0.25 | 0.1 |
| Hidden dimension | 128 | 128 |
| Local module loop number | 2 | 1 |
| Segment number | 10 | 10 |

We chose the data of the first 32 channels and the last 60 s that are more correlated with emotion according to the author's recommendation in DEAP. And in DREAMER, also to avoid extra emotional disturbance, only the last-60-s of data were used. We performed baseline removal on the signal and extracted the DE feature of the signal per second. At the same time, we cut a sample into N non-overlapping segments as so it can be reversed in the time domain and space domain. In conventional methods, researchers slice data for the purpose of data augmentation. In comparison, we transform data from two dimensions to three dimensions so that we could focus on the internal correlation of local data and better capture an identifying feature (Table 1).

In Table 2, we provide the model hyperparameters. We set the hidden dimension of the MLP Blocks as 128 for both datasets. For the training of the model, we initialize the learning rate as 0.00003 and the batchsize as 32. The dropout rate in the MLP Blocks are set as 0.25 on DEAP and 0.1 on DREAMER. The output of the layer will be the input of the next loop. We set the number of loop as 1 for DEAP and 2 for DREAMER. And in all experiments on the dataset DEAP and DREAMER, we all employ the Adam optimizer and use the cross-entropy as the loss function. Furthermore, the data are all segmented into 10 patches. We carry out the experiments in Python 3.7 on the PC with the CPU of Intel(R) Core(TM) i7-9700KF, the GPU of NVIDIA GeForce RTX 2060 SUPER, and the Memory of 16 GB.

**Table 2.** Comparison of performance with existing study on dataset deap (two classes: low/high)

| Researches | Accuracy (%) | | | |
|---|---|---|---|---|
| | DEAP | | DREAMER | |
| | Valence | Arousal | Valence | Arousal |
| Wang *et al.* [24] | 48.04 | 47.03 | 46.37 | 46.47 |
| Al-Shargie *et al.* [2] | 47.73 | 60.55 | 53.14 | **68.12** |
| Li *et al.* [15] | 53.63 | 55.55 | 60.63 | 62.46 |
| Li *et al.* [14] | 52.44 | 54.40 | 56.45 | 64.52 |
| Song *et al.* [19] | 51.25 | 52.97 | 53.70 | 61.11 |
| Tao *et al.* [21] | 53.84 | 59.45 | 56.33 | 62.08 |
| Jia *et al.* [9] | 55.44 | 60.10 | 56.45 | 64.52 |
| He *et al.* [5] | 51.53 | 52.11 | 54.47 | 52.78 |
| Ours | **62.97** | **61.87** | **60.86** | 63.28 |
| Ablation ex1 | 58.93 | 60.07 | 58.17 | 51.69 |
| Ablation ex2 | 55.78 | 58.51 | 58.69 | 59.17 |

### 4.3   Performance

We ran the proposed model with the above experimental parameters and compared the results with seven existing related advanced researches to verify the performance of our method. We conducted the subject-independent experiments in the manner of leave-one-subject-out. To be specific, we re-implemented the following seven researches recently proposed. Wang *et al.* [24] introduced the phase-locking value into graph convolutional neural networks to construct spatio-temporal features of EEG. Al-Shargie *et al.* [2] also designed a discriminative fusion feature to represent EEG signals, which mainly included the local cortical activations and the connection of dynamic functional networks. Li *et al.* [15] took spectrum analysis as the research focus and main feature, and their feature fused the activation pattern and connection pattern of the emotion. Li *et al.* [14] proposed an effective joint distribution adaptation (JDA) method and utilized the relation between adaptation strategies and functional layers for cross-subject classifying emotion. Song *et al.* [19] converted discrete EEG signals into continuous images, which are then fed into the graph-embedded convolutional neural network (GECNN). It explored the global functional features by dynamical graph filtering. In [21], channels were assigned weights through the attention mechanism, and then CNN was used to extract spatial information. An extended RNN with an extended self-attention mechanism was used to extract temporal information. And in [9], the author used 3D dense network to process the spatial-spectral representation and spatial-temporal representation and then combines the outputs to classify emotions. He *et al.* [5] utilized the feasibility of temporal convolutional networks and domain adaptation algorithms to overcome the domain shift across subjects with an unusual emotion labelling methods of K-means clustering. In their works, some of them carried out subject-dependent experiments. That is to say, the subjects in the training source domain are identical to the test target domain. Therefore, the source domain and target domain share similar distributions, which reduces the classification difficulty and improves the recognition accuracy to some extent. We tested these works under the conditions same as our experiment to compare the results. The results are presented in Table 2. Our method not only extracts information from the perspective of time and space, but also further combines local and global signal correlations. The results show that our approach yielded the best results on the dataset DEAP with the accuracy of 62.97% for valence classification and 61.87% for arousal classification. And in the experiments on dataset DREAMER, our methods got the accuracy of 63.28% for arousal and 60.86% for valence. Although our method is slightly lower than Al-Shargie's method by 5%, it still has good performance on valence which achieved the highest accuracy of 60.86%. Additionally, we also conducted ablation experiments by removing the local MLP-based module (ex1) and the global self-attention processes (ex2) respectively. According to Table 2, the performance of ex1 and ex2 verified the effectiveness of the two modules.

## 5   Conclusion

In this paper, a novel two-stream model termed as 'BiSMSM' is proposed. The model takes full advantage of the MLP blocks which can extract local information and simultaneously fuse the in-channel and cross-channel correlation. It also utilizes the spatial and temporal characteristics of EEG signals, which can be conversed in the time and space domain. So the self-attention mechanism can be applied to capture the connection between each pair of data segments from the global view. We also design a position encoding method to optimize the global information extracting. The model can extract more discriminative features from 4 angles: from spatial to temporal, from local to global. Finally, we compare our methods with several related work and our methods have shown a promising performance. Furthermore, the proposed method can not only be applied in EEG emotion recognition but also in other recognition or classification issues where input data can converse in time and space domain, such as speech-based emotion recognition.

**Acknowledgements.** This work was supported in part by the Aeronautical Science Foundation of China under Grant 20200058069001, in part by the Basic Research Project of Leading Technology of Jiangsu Province under Grant BK20192004, and in part by the Fundamental Research Funds for the Central Universities under Grant 2242021R41094.

# References

1. Abbaschian, B.J., Sierra-Sosa, D., Elmaghraby, A.: Deep learning techniques for speech emotion recognition, from databases to models. Sensors **21**(4), 1249 (2021)
2. Al-Shargie, F., Tariq, U., Alex, M., Mir, H., Al-Nashash, H.: Emotion recognition based on fusion of local cortical activations and dynamic functional networks connectivity: an EEG study. IEEE Access **7**, 143550–143562 (2019)
3. Alarcão, S.M., Fonseca, M.J.: Emotions recognition using EEG signals: a survey. IEEE Trans. Affect. Comput. **10**(3), 374–393 (2019)
4. Dosovitskiy, A., et al.: An image is worth 16×16 words: transformers for image recognition at scale. In: 9th International Conference on Learning Representations, ICLR 2021, Virtual Event, Austria, 3–7 May 2021. OpenReview.net (2021)
5. He, Z., Zhong, Y., Pan, J.: Joint temporal convolutional networks and adversarial discriminative domain adaptation for EEG-based cross-subject emotion recognition. In: ICASSP 2022–2022 IEEE International Conference on Acoustics, Speech and Signal Processing (ICASSP), pp. 3214–3218 (2022)
6. Hochreiter, S.: The vanishing gradient problem during learning recurrent neural nets and problem solutions. Internat. J. Uncertain. Fuzziness Knowl.-Based Syst. **6**(02), 107–116 (1998)
7. Jain, D.K., Shamsolmoali, P., Sehdev, P.: Extended deep neural network for facial emotion recognition. Pattern Recogn. Lett. **120**, 69–74 (2019)
8. Jenke, R., Peer, A., Buss, M.: Feature extraction and selection for emotion recognition from EEG. IEEE Trans. Affect. Comput. **5**(3), 327–339 (2014)
9. Jia, Z., Lin, Y., Cai, X., Chen, H., Gou, H., Wang, J.: SST-EmotionNet: spatial-spectral-temporal based attention 3D dense network for EEG emotion recognition. In: Proceedings of the 28th ACM International Conference on Multimedia, pp. 2909–2917 (2020)
10. Katsigiannis, S., Ramzan, N.: DREAMER: a database for emotion recognition through EEG and ECG signals from wireless low-cost off-the-shelf devices. IEEE J. Biomed. Health Inform. **22**(1), 98–107 (2018)
11. Khare, S., Nishad, A., Upadhyay, A., Bajaj, V.: Classification of emotions from EEG signals using time-order representation based on the S-transform and convolutional neural network. Electron. Lett. **56**(25), 1359–1361 (2020)

12. Kim, K.H., Bang, S.W., Kim, S.R.: Emotion recognition system using short-term monitoring of physiological signals. Med. Biol. Eng. Comput. **42**(3), 419–427 (2004)
13. Koelstra, S., et al.: DEAP: a database for emotion analysis using physiological signals. IEEE Trans. Affect. Comput. **3**(1), 18–31 (2012)
14. Li, J., Qiu, S., Du, C., Wang, Y., He, H.: Domain adaptation for EEG emotion recognition based on latent representation similarity. IEEE Trans. Cogn. Dev. Syst. **12**(2), 344–353 (2020)
15. Li, P., et al.: EEG based emotion recognition by combining functional connectivity network and local activations. IEEE Trans. Biomed. Eng. **66**(10), 2869–2881 (2019)
16. Li, W., Huan, W., Hou, B., Tian, Y., Zhang, Z., Song, A.: Can emotion be transferred?-a review on transfer learning for EEG-based emotion recognition. IEEE Trans. Cogn. Dev. Syst. (2021). https://doi.org/10.1109/TCDS.2021.3098842
17. Priyasad, D., Fernando, T., Denman, S., Sridharan, S., Fookes, C.: Affect recognition from scalp-EEG using channel-wise encoder networks coupled with geometric deep learning and multi-channel feature fusion. Knowl.-Based Syst. **250**, 109038 (2022)
18. Rached, T.S., Perkusich, A.: Emotion recognition based on brain-computer interface systems. In: Brain-Computer Interface Systems-recent Progress and Future Prospects, pp. 253–270 (2013)
19. Song, T., Zheng, W., Liu, S., Zong, Y., Cui, Z., Li, Y.: Graph-embedded convolutional neural network for image-based EEG emotion recognition. IEEE Trans. Emerg. Top. Comput. 1 (2021). https://doi.org/10.1109/TETC.2021.3087174
20. Song, T., Zheng, W., Song, P., Cui, Z.: EEG emotion recognition using dynamical graph convolutional neural networks. IEEE Trans. Affect. Comput. **11**(3), 532–541 (2020)
21. Tao, W., et al.: EEG-based emotion recognition via channel-wise attention and self attention. IEEE Trans. Affect. Comput. 1–12 (2020). https://doi.org/10.1109/TAFFC.2020.3025777
22. Tolstikhin, H., et al.: MLP-mixer: an all-MLP architecture for vision. Adv. Neural Inf. Process. Syst. **34**, 24261–24272 (2021)
23. Vaswani, A., et al.: Attention is all you need. Adv. Neural Inf. Process. Syst. **30**, 6000–6010 (2017)
24. Wang, Z., Tong, Y., Heng, X.: Phase-locking value based graph convolutional neural networks for emotion recognition. IEEE Access **7**, 93711–93722 (2019)
25. Xing, X., Li, Z., Xu, T., Shu, L., Hu, B., Xu, X.: SAE+LSTM: a new framework for emotion recognition from multi-channel EEG. Front. Neurorobot. **13**, 37(1)–37(14) (2019)
26. Yang, Z., Kay, A., Li, Y., Cross, W., Luo, J.: Pose-based body language recognition for emotion and psychiatric symptom interpretation. In: 2020 25th International Conference on Pattern Recognition (ICPR), pp. 294–301. IEEE, Milan (2021)
27. Zhang, T., Zheng, W., Cui, Z., Zong, Y., Li, Y.: Spatial-temporal recurrent neural network for emotion recognition. IEEE Trans. Cybern. **49**(3), 839–847 (2019)

# Boosting Both Robustness and Hardware Efficiency via Random Pruning Mask Selection

Ruixin Xue, Meiqi Wang$^{(\boxtimes)}$, and Zhongfeng Wang$^{(\boxtimes)}$

School of Electronic Science and Engineering, Nanjing University, Nanjing, China
{rxxue,mqwang}@smail.nju.edu.cn, zfwang@nju.edu.cn

**Abstract.** Deep neural networks (DNNs) are notorious for two key drawbacks: the vulnerability against adversarial attacks and the prohibitive cost of storage and computation, which greatly hinders DNNs' deployment on safety-critical yet resource-limited platforms. Although researchers have proposed adversary-aware pruning methods where adversarial training and network pruning are studied jointly to improve the robustness of pruned networks, they failed to attain a double-win, i.e., the achieved robustness is still limited and cannot surpass that of dense networks. In this work, pursuing a win-win in robustness and efficiency, we demonstrate that the robustness of pruned networks can be easily boosted by leveraging the stochastic policy. More specifically, we propose a Random Mask Selection (RMS) strategy where pruning masks are randomly sampled during inference to confuse attackers. Furthermore, a necessary hardware-aware algorithm optimization is introduced to eliminate the potential hardware overhead of RMS, and thus ensures a convenient implementation of RMS on existing hardware accelerators without sacrificing processing speed or power efficiency. Extensive experiments show that our approach achieves a double-win in robustness and compactness compared to dense models and outperforms the SOTA adversary-aware pruning method in terms of robustness.

**Keywords:** Model compression · Network pruning · Adversarial machine learning · Deep learning

## 1 Introduction

Due to the recent breakthroughs in deep learning, deep neural networks (DNNs) have been widely implemented on Internet of Things (IoT) devices to perform various real-world tasks, e.g., video tracking [16], natural language processing [2] and autonomous driving [1]. However, studies have shown that DNNs are vulnerable to adversarial attacks (i.e., a small perturbation added to the input will cause erroneous output) [7,11,15], which brings severe security issues to the application of DNNs. To improve the adversarial robustness of DNN-based models, prior works have proposed multiple defense methods including adversarial training [7,11], adversarial sample detection [3], etc.

© The Author(s), under exclusive license to Springer Nature Switzerland AG 2022
E. Pimenidis et al. (Eds.): ICANN 2022, LNCS 13529, pp. 49–60, 2022.
https://doi.org/10.1007/978-3-031-15919-0_5

Another barrier to deploying DNNs on IoT devices is their notoriously large storage and computation requirements. Although current model compression methods (e.g., quantization [10], weight/activation pruning [9], dynamic computing [4]) have shown promising results in reducing the size and computational complexity of DNNs, other works imply that directly compressed models may suffer from a worse robustness [8,13]. Such a contradiction between robustness and compactness greatly hinders the real-world application of deep learning. To tackle this challenge, recent works tried to develop adversary-aware model compression approaches to achieve robust yet efficient networks [13,14,18].

Inspired by the latest trend in the adversarial defense field where stochastic networks are introduced to confuse attackers, researchers explore the natural randomness that exists in model compression to aggressively improve the robustness without sacrificing the compression ratio. Particularly, Robust Scratch Tickets (RST) [5] points out that adversarial samples transfer poorly between sparse networks of different sparsity ratios. However, while RST leverages random sparsity ratios to achieve high robustness, their proposal will lead to unstable accuracy and low hardware efficiency due to the frequent on-chip/external memory accesses. Therefore, an accuracy-stable and hardware-efficient random network pruning solution is highly required.

In this work, we propose a hardware-aware Random Mask Selection (HW-RMS) method which boosts the robustness of pruned networks while achieving substantial speed-up. Our contributions are summarized as follows.

1) By leveraging the inborn randomness in network pruning, we generate sparse networks which dramatically surpass the dense ones in both robustness and compactness. A novel weight sharing scheme and iterative retraining method are introduced to maintain a stable accuracy among diverse pruned networks.
2) A hardware-aware algorithm optimization is proposed to eliminate the potential extra memory accesses, which ensures that RMS can be directly implemented on existing accelerators without sacrificing processing speed or power efficiency.
3) Extensive results show that our method achieves up to 10% robustness improvement under PGD-20 attacks than the state-of-the-art (SOTA) adversary-aware pruning method. Compared with RST, we achieve 2× lower latency and power consumption, making our method a more favorable solution for implementing random pruning strategies on DNNs.

## 2    Background and Related Works

### 2.1    Adversarial Attacks and Adversarial Training

DNNs' robustness against malicious attacks has attracted wide-ranging attention. Adversarial attacks, especially white-box adversarial attacks, can easily lead to a collapse of DNNs' accuracy by introducing small perturbation to input samples [7,11,15]. Assuming that the attacker knows our model $f_\theta$ and its parameters

$\theta$, white-box attacks generate the attack perturbation $\delta(||\delta|| \leq \epsilon)$ by maximizing the following objective:

$$\max_{||\delta|| \leq \epsilon} l(f_\theta(x + \delta), y), \tag{1}$$

where $x$ and $y$ denote the input sample and its label, $l$ is the loss function and $\epsilon$ is a scalar that limits the perturbation's magnitude. Specifically, the Fast Gradient Sign Method (FGSM) [7] generates $\delta$ by taking one step gradient update:

$$\delta = \epsilon \times \text{sign}(\nabla_x l(f_\theta(x + \delta), y)). \tag{2}$$

Projected Gradient Decent (PGD) [11] provides a stronger attack than FGSM by taking $t(t > 1)$ iterative steps of update with a smaller step size $\alpha$:

$$\delta_{t+1} = \text{clip}_\epsilon\{\delta_t + \alpha \times \text{sign}(\nabla_x l(f_\theta(x + \delta), y))\}. \tag{3}$$

Multiple approaches have been proposed to defend against adversarial attacks, among which adversarial training provides the most promising defense effect. Adversarial training introduces the above-mentioned attacks (i.e., FGSM and PGD) into the training process by optimizing the following min-max objective:

$$\min_\theta \sum_i \max_{||\delta|| \leq \epsilon} l(f_\theta(x_i + \delta), y_i). \tag{4}$$

Considering that white-box attacks are so far the strongest adversarial attack, we adopt it as our mainly targeted attack method and treat adversarially trained models as targeted models to be pruned.

## 2.2   Double-Win Network Pruning

As one of the most popular model compression methods, network pruning (i.e., or weight pruning) can significantly reduce the size and computational complexity of a pre-trained model by erasing unimportant weights. However, early experiments [8,13] showed that designing a robust pruned model is non-trivial since adversarial training always requires a larger model capacity. To achieve compressed yet robust networks, multiple adversary-aware pruning methods were proposed [13,14,18]. Instead of developing a novel pruning method, RST [5] finds that adversarial samples transfer poorly between sparse networks of different sparsity ratios (i.e., adversarial samples generated from one sparse network exhibit poor attacking effect on another one). Despite that RST gains appreciable robustness improvement via leveraging such a poor transferability, this proposal remains two severe issues: 1) Random sparsity ratios bring unstable accuracy and latency in multiple runs. 2) Non-consecutive weight reading leads to extra memory accesses which affects the on-chip processing speed and power efficiency, as it is illustrated in Sect. 3.3. Therefore, RST is not an ideal solution to implement the random network pruning strategy on IoT devices.

# 3  Method

In this section, we first provide the inspiration and a brief description of our Random Mask Selection (RMS) strategy in Sect. 3.1. Then in Sect. 3.2, we explain in detail how the pruned networks of different masks are properly retrained through an iterative retraining framework. Finally, a hardware-aware optimization technique is proposed in Sect. 3.3 to minimize the potential data reading overhead for deploying RMS on existing accelerators.

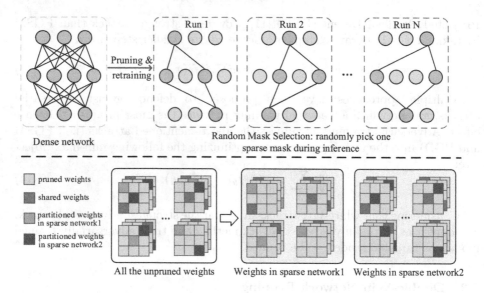

**Fig. 1.** Demonstration of the proposed Random Mask Selection strategy (top) and the sharing subnet scheme (bottom).

## 3.1  Random Mask Selection (RMS) Strategy

To achieve robust yet efficient pruned networks, we draw inspiration from the stochastic policy of game theory [12], where the two-person fight is modeled as a mouse-cat chasing game, just like defenders and attackers in adversarial attack scenarios. More specifically, we generate diverse sparse networks from a dense network to form a network pool, then randomly pick one during inference. Hence, even though attackers get access to all the sparse networks, they do not know which network defenders will choose and cannot generate the optimal attack, making it possible to achieve a double-win in robustness and efficiency.

There are two most straightforward ways to draw multiple pruned networks from a dense one: 1) by setting multiple pruning ratios; 2) by generating different masks (i.e., a pruning mask defines which weights are pruned). Although the former solution has proven to be effective in improving robustness, it is traded by the inevitable instability in accuracy and latency which is led by random sparsity ratios (e.g., in the final solution of RST [5], pruning ratios range from 40% to 97%). In contrast, generating different masks with the same pruning ratio can easily attain a stable accuracy and processing speed through multiple runs, making it a more favorable solution for real-world applications.

Following the above discussion, we propose the RMS strategy to boost the robustness of pruned networks, as depicted in Fig. 1. Specifically, RMS draws different pruning masks from the same dense network, and randomly samples masks during inference to confuse attackers. For simplicity, we call these pruned networks random-mask-networks (RMNs).

However, generating RMNs is non-trivial since in pruning, unpruned weights always play a critical role in keeping the model's accuracy. Therefore, directly scattering these most important weights across RMNs will lead to a collapse of accuracy. To tackle this issue, we adopt a subnet sharing scheme, where the most important weights serve as a **global sub-network** and are shared among RMNs to ensure an acceptable accuracy for each mask. To achieve subnet sharing, weights are first divided into shared weights $W_{shar}$, partitioned weights $W_{part}$ and pruned weights $W_{prun}$ depending on their importance. Following the widely used LWM-based pruning [9], we utilize magnitudes of weights to represent their importance:

$$\begin{cases} W_{shar}^l = \{w, |w| > w_{th,shar}\} \\ W_{part}^l = \{w, w_{th,shar} > |w| > w_{th,part}\} \\ W_{prun}^l = \{w, |w| < w_{th,part}\} \end{cases} \tag{5}$$

where $l$ denotes the index of the target layer, $w \subseteq W^l$ denotes every weight element in layer $l$, and $w_{th,shar}$ and $w_{th,part}$ are pruning thresholds that can be calculated by the pre-defined pruning ratio and the proportion of $W_{prun}$ in all unpruned weights. After weight division, shared weights, the most important weights, are shared between RMNs to maintain the accuracy of multiple sparse networks. Partitioned weights are scattered to different networks to further improve each RMN's accuracy while maintaining the structural diversity between RMNs. The least important weights are directly pruned off. In other words, RMNs share the same sub-network composed of $W_{shar}$ while still maintaining the adversarial gaps between them. We depict such a scheme in Fig. 1, and experiment results show that composed with the iterative retraining in Sect. 3.2, our method exhibits promising accuracy and robustness.

## 3.2   Iterative Retraining Framework

It is commonly known that retraining is necessary for improving pruned networks' accuracy. Nevertheless, naive retraining is not applicable for the above-mentioned subnet sharing scheme since training each RMN respectively will make values of $W_{shar}$ differ between RMNs, and storing them all will bring extra memory overhead. To eliminate this enormous redundancy, we design an iterative retraining framework to effectively retrain RMNs with a global sub-network. The detailed process of iterative retraining is shown in Algorithm 1.

**Algorithm 1.** The Iterative Retraining Framework

**Require:** Training dataset $D_{train}$, RMN group $\{f_\theta^n, n = 1, 2, ..., N\}$, retraining
  epochs $T$, the cross entropy loss $L$
1: **for** $epoch \in [1, T]$ **do**
2:     Fix partitioned weights
3:     **for** $(x, y) \in D_{train}$ **do**
4:         Randomly sample a RMN $f_\theta^i$ from $\{f_\theta^n, n = 1, 2, ..., N\}$
5:         Update shared weights with $L(f_\theta^i(x), y)$
6:     **for** $n \in [1, N]$ **do**
7:         Fix shared weights
8:         **for** $(x, y) \in D_{train}$ **do**
9:             Update partitioned weights of $f_\theta^n$ with $L(f_\theta^n(x), y)$
10: **return** retrained RMN group $\{f_\theta^{n'}, n = 1, 2, ..., N\}$

Briefly, the main idea of iterative retraining is to train $W_{shar}$ and $W_{part}$ in an
iterative manner, during which the global $W_{shar}$ is forced to adapt to the variation of $W_{part}$, and $W_{part}$ learns to cooperate with $W_{shar}$ to maximize each
RMN's accuracy while keeping decentralized.

### 3.3   Hardware-Aware RMS (HW-RMS)

**Hardware Overhead of Vanilla RMS.** So far our RMS has gained high
robustness while significantly reducing parameters and FLOPs (i.e., floating-point operations) during inference. However, as illustrated in [17], theoretical
FLOPs cannot represent on-chip latency or power, especially for RMS which
will implicitly change the on-chip processing. To find out the potential hardware
overhead caused by implementing RMS on existing accelerators, we provide a
thorough analysis of the dataflow of a typical sparse tensor accelerator, SparTen
[6]. Note that most other accelerators share a similar dataflow and only differ in
details that will not influence our analysis.

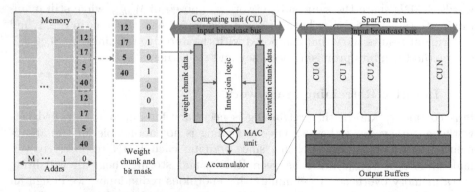

**Fig. 2.** The microarchitecture of SparTen. This figure is modified from [6].

The architecture of SparTen is shown in Fig. 2. In SparTen, data are stored in the memory waiting to be processed. Weights and activations are divided into chunks for parallel computing. Pairs of chunks are read out and fed into multiple computing units (CUs) to generate multiple outputs, and the corresponding bit-masks are utilized to skip computations of zero values. For simplicity, we focus on the processing of one CU. For a naive sparse network, SparTen reads one chunk of weights from memory per cycle, which guarantees that chunks are consecutively fed into this CU. Therefore, the CU can process these chunks constantly, leading to high utilization. Nevertheless, in RMS, because the global sub-network is shared between RMNs, $W_{shar}$ and $W_{part}$ have to be stored separately. Consequently, weights of one RMN are scattered in different addresses of the memory, forcing SparTen to read a chunk in more than one cycle, and thus will degrade the utilization of CUs and further lead to a longer processing time and higher power consumption. We depict such a characteristic in the left part of Fig. 3. It is also notable that the random pruning ratio strategy in RST [5] will face the same issue. The consequential inefficiency cannot be relieved without introducing algorithm optimization.

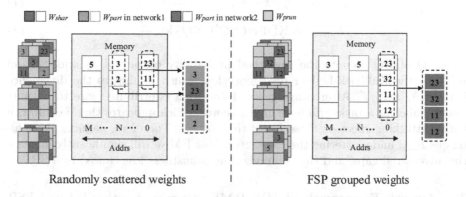

**Fig. 3.** Demonstration of data reading in vanilla RMS (left) and hardware-aware RMS with FSP technique (right). Assuming computing units require for the first weight chunk. In vanilla RMS, we have to read two different addresses in two clock cycles, yet in hardware-aware RMS, only one cycle is needed. Note that $W_{part}$ of different RMNs are not separated into different filters, since only $W_{part}$ of one RMN is read out in each run and it will not cause inefficiency.

**FSP: Towards the Practical Speed-Up of RMS.** To alleviate the above-mentioned hardware inefficiency, we draw inspiration from structured pruning, a pruning method that targets a similar challenge. In structured pruning, groups of weights (i.e., filters or channels) are completely pruned off to achieve a regular on-chip dataflow. Following this idea, we observe that when $W_{shar}$ and $W_{part}$ are grouped into separated filters rather than scattered among all filters, the on-chip data reading will be naturally consecutive, as shown in the right side of Fig. 3. Intuitively, we first determine important and unimportant filters as shared filters $F_{shar}$ and partitioned filters $F_{part}$ (i.e., as we have done in Sect. 3.1, importance is represented by magnitudes), then prune $F_{shar}$ to get $W_{shar}$ and prune $F_{part}$ to get $W_{part}$. By doing so, $W_{shar}$ and $W_{part}$ exist in completely different filters, which ensures a high data reading efficiency.

However, experiments show that this direct magnitude-based FSP will degrade the adversarial gaps between RMNs, which can be attributed to the less structural divergence caused by grouping $W_{part}$. To compensate for the robustness drop, we propose a knowledge distillation (KD) method to find adversary-sensitive filters to be $F_{part}$. More specifically, given a pre-trained dense model $f_\theta$ and its corresponding malicious perturbation $\delta$, we set scores (a score is a floating-point scaler) to all filters and pruned off the filters with lower scores in the forward path to get $f'_\theta$. Then we update all scores by optimizing the following distillation objective $L_{distill}$:

$$Q = f_\theta(x + \delta), \tag{6}$$

$$Q' = f'_\theta(x + \delta), \tag{7}$$

$$L_{distill} = \text{KLdiv}(Q, Q') = Q \cdot \log \frac{Q}{Q'}, \tag{8}$$

where $Q$ and $Q'$ denote the smoothed probability output of $f_\theta$ and $f'_\theta$, and $Kldiv$ is the Kullback-Leibler divergence loss which minimizes the divergence between $Q$ and $Q'$. After convergence, filters that contribute more to outputs under malicious attacks will have higher scores, which indicates that $\delta$ exhibits a better attacking effect on these filters than others. Therefore, defining these filters as $F_{part}$ and scattering their weights across RMNs will significantly increase the adversarial gaps, and thus minimize the robustness loss caused by FSP.

**The Overall Framework of HW-RMS.** Composed with KD-based FSP, RMS achieves robust yet efficient on-chip inference with neither extra computational cost nor extra hardware design effort. The overall framework of HW-RMS can be summarized as the following steps: 1) divide filters using the knowledge distillation in Eq. 8; 2) prune the dense network to get multiple sparse RMNs with the FSP technique; 3) retrain RMNs utilizing iterative retraining; 4) during inference, randomly pick an RMN to confuse attackers.

## 4    Experiments

### 4.1    Experiment Setup

**Networks and Datasets.** We evaluate the proposed HW-RMS on three networks and two datasets, i.e., ResNet18, WideResNet28-4 (WRN-28-4), and Pre-ActResNet 18 on CIFAR10/100. Note that if not otherwise specified, RMS denotes HW-RMS.

**Training Settings.** We adopt PGD-7 adversarial training method in both the pre-training stage and the retraining stage to get robust dense networks. Hyper-parameters for adversarial training are the same as the original paper [11] for fair comparisons. For pre-training, we train the model for 160 epochs with a batch size of 128 and an SGD optimizer with a momentum of 0.9. The initial learning rate is 0.1, and is decayed by 10 at both the 80-th and 120-th epochs. For iterative retraining in RMS, we retrain the pruned model for extra 20 epochs with the same batch size as pre-training and a learning rate of 0.01.

**Table 1.** Evaluating RMS and SOTA methods on CIFAR10/100.

| | Method | Pruning ratio (%) | ResNet18 | | WRN-28-4 | |
|---|---|---|---|---|---|---|
| | | | Natural acc (%) | PGD-20 acc (%) | Natural acc (%) | PGD-20 acc (%) |
| CIFAR10 | FGSM | 0 | 87.23 | 42.76 | 89.95 | 45.33 |
| | PGD-7 | 0 | 82.53 | 52.18 | 83.25 | 52.61 |
| | PGD-7 + Baseline | 90 | 81.94 | 50.30 | 80.92 | 50.39 |
| | PGD-7 + HYDRA† | 90 | 82.88 | 50.45 | 83.44 | 52.27 |
| | **PGD-7 + RMS** | **90** | **80.52** | **64.5** | **81.32** | **63.23** |
| CIFAR100 | FGSM | 0 | 57.60 | 26.14 | 59.40 | 27.14 |
| | PGD-7 | 0 | 56.31 | 28.23 | 57.31 | 29.12 |
| | PGD-7 + Baseline | 90 | 54.49 | 27.29 | 55.27 | 27.87 |
| | PGD-7 + HYDRA† | 90 | 56.62 | 27.82 | 57.96 | 28.56 |
| | **PGD-7 + RMS** | **90** | **55.04** | **40.81** | **55.23** | **39.93** |

† Our implementation

## 4.2 Benchmark with SOTA Methods

Here we compare our RMS with the latest adversarial defense methods, as summarized in Table 1. For the baseline, we choose the widely-adopted LWM-based pruning in [9] and retrain it with adversarial training. Other methods include the latest adversarial training methods (i.e., FGSM and PGD-7) and a SOTA adversary-aware pruning method, HYDRA [14]. We implement PGD-20 attack to evaluate the robustness against adversarial attacks.

**Comparison with Adversarial Training.** Compared with SOTA adversarially trained dense networks, our RMS achieves a double-win in robustness and compactness. Under 10× compression ratio, RMS achieves 12.32%/12.58% higher robustness on ResNet18 than PGD-7, which is one of the strongest adversarial training methods. On WRN-28-4, our RMS also achieves 12.62%/11.81% robustness improvement.

**Comparison with Adversary-Aware Pruning.** Our RMS show significantly higher robustness (i.e., more than 10%) than the baseline and the leading adversary-aware pruning method under the same pruning ratio. While other well-designed pruning methods can only compensate for the robustness drop compared to the dense network, RMS leverages random pruning to achieve a double-win in robustness and efficiency. This can be mainly attributed to the introduction of the stochastic policy which solves the robustness-efficiency conflict from a higher policy level.

### 4.3 Comparison with RST

As the counterpart of our RMS, RST also targets a double-win in robustness and compactness by leveraging random sparsity ratios. However, as discussed in Sect. 2.2, there are two main drawbacks of RST: 1) extra memory accesses; 2) unstable accuracy and processing

**Table 2.** Hardware metrics of RST, vanilla RMS and HW-RMS. For latency and energy, the lower the better.

| Method | Latency (ms) | Energy (mJ) |
|---|---|---|
| RST | 11.52 | 1.23 |
| Vanilla RMS | 8.30 | 1.14 |
| **HW-RMS** | **5.07** | **0.67** |

speed. We have theoretically analyzed the former one in Sect. 3.3, and for a better evaluation, we simulate the latency and energy consumption of RST, vanilla RMS and HW-RMS using the DNN-chip predictor in [19], as shown in Table 2. For a fair comparison, we implement both RST and RMS on PreActResNet18 following [5]. In RST, sparsity ratios range from 40% to 97% like the original paper [5]. Results show that thanks to the carefully designed hardware-aware FSP technique, our HW-RMS achieves nearly 2× lower latency and energy than RST.

To evaluate the accuracy and processing speed, we compare RMS and RST in terms of average accuracy, average parameters, and average FLOPs. Comparison results on CIFAR10 and CIFAR100 are shown in Table 3. We can see that although RST shows slightly higher robustness than RMS (less than 1%), it is traded by more than 2% accuracy drop and 2× more average parameters/FLOPs, not to mention that the extra memory accesses will bring much higher on-chip latency and power consumption. Therefore, our RMS is a more favorable solution for real-world scenarios.

**Table 3.** The comparisons between RST and RMS of PreActResNet18.

| Network | CIFAR10 | | CIFAR100 | | PARAMs (MB) | FLOPs (G) |
|---|---|---|---|---|---|---|
| | Natural acc (%) | PGD-20 acc (%) | Natural acc (%) | PGD-20 acc (%) | | |
| Dense | 82.53 | 52.18 | 56.88 | 26.94 | 11.20 | 1.81 |
| RST, 40%-97% | 77.49 | 63.93 | 52.12 | 41.01 | 2.24 | 0.36 |
| **RMS, 90%** | **80.35** | **63.80** | **54.11** | **40.20** | **1.12** | **0.18** |

### 4.4 Ablation Study of FSP and Adversarial Gaps

Adversarial gaps between different pruning masks play a critical role in determining the robustness gain of RMS. Higher gaps always come with higher robustness. To better show how KD-based FSP increases adversarial gaps, we present

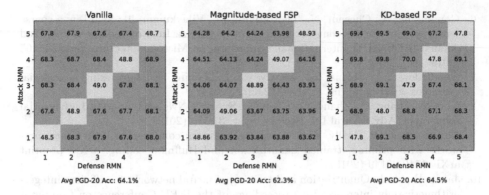

**Fig. 4.** Adversarial gaps in vanilla RMS (left), RMS with magnitude based FSP (middle) and RMS with knowledge distillation based FSP(right).

attack-defense heatmaps of different approaches in Fig. 4. It is observed that although the magnitude-based FSP degrades the gaps, the proposed knowledge distillation method can not only make up for this drop but also achieve even higher robustness than vanilla RMS.

# 5  Conclusion

Towards achieving a win-win in robustness and efficiency, we propose a strategy dubbed Random Mask Selection (RMS) which leverages random pruning masks to boost the robustness of pruned networks. Furthermore, a novel hardware-aware filter separation technique is introduced to eliminate the hardware overhead brought by RMS. Compared to its counterpart, RMS exhibits more stable accuracy and higher compression, making it a more favorable solution for real-world applications for IoT devices.

# References

1. Chen, C., Seff, A., Kornhauser, A., Xiao, J.: DeepDriving: learning affordance for direct perception in autonomous driving. In: Proceedings of the IEEE International Conference on Computer Vision, pp. 2722–2730 (2015)
2. Devlin, J., Chang, M.W., Lee, K., Toutanova, K.: BERT: pre-training of deep bidirectional transformers for language understanding. arXiv preprint arXiv:1810.04805 (2018)
3. Feinman, R., Curtin, R.R., Shintre, S., Gardner, A.B.: Detecting adversarial samples from artifacts. arXiv preprint arXiv:1703.00410 (2017)
4. Figurnov, M., et al.: Spatially adaptive computation time for residual networks. In: Proceedings of the IEEE Conference on Computer Vision and Pattern Recognition, pp. 1039–1048 (2017)
5. Fu, Y., et al.: Drawing robust scratch tickets: subnetworks with inborn robustness are found within randomly initialized networks. Adv. Neural Inf. Process. Syst. **34**, 20 (2021)

6. Gondimalla, A., Chesnut, N., Thottethodi, M., Vijaykumar, T.: SparTen: a sparse tensor accelerator for convolutional neural networks. In: Proceedings of the 52nd Annual IEEE/ACM International Symposium on Microarchitecture, pp. 151–165 (2019)
7. Goodfellow, I.J., Shlens, J., Szegedy, C.: Explaining and harnessing adversarial examples. arXiv preprint arXiv:1412.6572 (2014)
8. Guo, Y., Zhang, C., Zhang, C., Chen, Y.: Sparse DNNs with improved adversarial robustness. Adv. Neural Inf. Process. Syst. **31**, 10 (2018)
9. Han, S., Mao, H., Dally, W.J.: Deep compression: compressing deep neural networks with pruning, trained quantization and Huffman coding. arXiv preprint arXiv:1510.00149 (2015)
10. Jacob, B., et al.: Quantization and training of neural networks for efficient integer-arithmetic-only inference. In: Proceedings of the IEEE Conference on Computer Vision and Pattern Recognition, pp. 2704–2713 (2018)
11. Madry, A., Makelov, A., Schmidt, L., Tsipras, D., Vladu, A.: Towards deep learning models resistant to adversarial attacks. arXiv preprint arXiv:1706.06083 (2017)
12. Osborne, M.J., Rubinstein, A.: A Course in Game Theory. MIT Press, Cambridge (1994)
13. Rakin, A.S., He, Z., Yang, L., Wang, Y., Wang, L., Fan, D.: Robust sparse regularization: simultaneously optimizing neural network robustness and compactness. arXiv preprint arXiv:1905.13074 (2019)
14. Sehwag, V., Wang, S., Mittal, P., Jana, S.: HYDRA: pruning adversarially robust neural networks. Adv. Neural. Inf. Process. Syst. **33**, 19655–19666 (2020)
15. Szegedy, C., et al.: Intriguing properties of neural networks. arXiv preprint arXiv:1312.6199 (2013)
16. Wang, L., Liu, T., Wang, G., Chan, K.L., Yang, Q.: Video tracking using learned hierarchical features. IEEE Trans. Image Process. **24**(4), 1424–1435 (2015)
17. Wu, B., et al.: FBNet: hardware-aware efficient convnet design via differentiable neural architecture search. In: Proceedings of the IEEE/CVF Conference on Computer Vision and Pattern Recognition, pp. 10734–10742 (2019)
18. Ye, S., et al.: Adversarial robustness vs. model compression, or both? In: Proceedings of the IEEE/CVF International Conference on Computer Vision, pp. 111–120 (2019)
19. Zhao, Y., Li, C., Wang, Y., Xu, P., Zhang, Y., Lin, Y.: DNN-chip predictor: an analytical performance predictor for DNN accelerators with various dataflows and hardware architectures. In: ICASSP 2020–2020 IEEE International Conference on Acoustics, Speech and Signal Processing (ICASSP), pp. 1593–1597. IEEE (2020)

# Brain Tumor Segmentation Framework Based on Edge Cloud Cooperation and Deep Learning

Saifeng Feng[1], Jianhui Zhao[1]([✉]), Wenyuan Zhao[2], and Tingbao Zhang[2]

[1] School of Computer Science, Wuhan University, Wuhan, China
jianhuizhao@whu.edu.cn
[2] Zhongnan Hospital, Wuhan University, Wuhan, China

**Abstract.** Brain tumors have very high morbidity and mortality, and it is very time-consuming for clinicians to diagnose this disease. Computer-aided medical image analysis can improve the performance of tumor diagnosis and alleviate the pressure of clinicians. Most of the existing intelligent diagnosis platforms rely on the public cloud, which has high requirements for communication and network and can not provide offline operation. We propose a brain tumor segmentation framework based on deep learning and edge-cloud collaboration, which can realize computer-assisted medical diagnosis in both offline and online modes. We deploy segmentation network with different complexity in the edge and cloud, and the Dice coefficients in offline mode and online mode are 0.8098 and 0.8910 respectively. Compared with the offline mode, the average values of Dice, PPV, and Sensitivity increased by 8.12%, 2.65%, and 7.31% in the online mode. In addition, we also analyze the response time of the two modes. For the diagnosis of a patient, the offline mode and online mode take 27.610 s and 40.885 s respectively. Experimental data show that our method has an excellent performance in tumor diagnosis and response time, and the framework can be easily extended to other diseases diagnosis.

**Keywords:** Brain tumor segmentation · Edge cloud cooperation · Deep learning

## 1 Introduction

Brain tissue is one of the most important organs of the human body, which plays a vital role in human life. Early detection of lesion areas is a key step in the treatment of brain tumors, which not only needs the theoretical progress of clinical medicine but also needs the assistance of computer science and technology.

Magnetic resonance imaging (MRI) will not cause radiation damage to the human body and can present brain tissue structure and three-dimensional anatomical information. The segmentation of brain tumor MRI images can extract different tumor regions in the brain, which is the key to the treatment of brain tumors. However, experts segment images according to their own experience and knowledge. The segmentation results may not be the same if the experience of each expert is different. Manual reading is certainly time-consuming, laborious, and subjective. With the development of artificial intelligence and the Internet of Things, many studies have begun to involve the automatic segmentation of brain tumors. Developing an intelligent diagnosis system for brain tumors based on deep learning is of great significance to improve the efficiency of tumor diagnosis and reduce the workload of doctors.

According to different theories, the existing intelligent medical brain tumor diagnosis systems can be divided into the following categories: (1) Preprocessing images using mathematical morphology and extracting tumor regions using clustering techniques [4]. (2) Using machine learning algorithms to deal with brain tumors and improve segmentation accuracy, such as K-meas [8]. (3) Building brain tumor diagnostic tools based on deep learning methods, and then deploying them to cloud servers to work and improve diagnostic accuracy [11]. The medical device based on the cloud platform uploads the data from the terminal to the remote cloud, and the result is then returned to the terminal device. However, putting all the computing on the cloud platform can result in unbearable network load and latency. On the other hand, it is difficult to get a real-time response just by processing data in the cloud. Therefore, the intelligent medical platform should also focus on the development of computing resources at the edge [12].

In order to solve the challenges mentioned above and promote the innovation and progress of intelligent medical diagnosis framework. We propose the edge-cloud cooperation based brain tumor segmentation diagnosis (ECC-BTSD), which utilizes the efficiency of cloud computing to improve the efficiency and accuracy of diagnosis. In our framework, the edge end is the imaging equipment integrated with deep learning model in hospital, and the cloud uses the computing resources of the cloud platform. Our framework contains offline mode and online mode. In the offline mode, the edge equipment in the hospital collects brain tumor images and completes the preliminary segmentation diagnosis. In online mode, if the segmentation results of edge devices need to be improved, we upload the images to the cloud platform for secondary diagnosis to achieve better results. ECC-BTSD includes image acquisition and image segmentation, which is also an ideal form of brain tumor diagnostic equipment in an intelligent medical environment.

The proposed framework is shown in Fig. 1. It consists of three important components: brain tumor images acquisition equipment, edge computing platform, and cloud computing platform. The image acquisition equipment is used to obtain the multimodal brain tissue image in MRI format of patients. The edge computing platform is used to process MRI images obtained by imaging equipment in the offline mode, including data preprocessing and brain tumor segmentation based on deep learning. The platform is configured with a GeForce GTX 1080ti/11G GPU and the operating system is Ubuntu. The cloud platform is used to process MRI images in online mode, which also includes data preprocessing and brain tumor segmentation. The platform is configured with 8-core 64Gb CPU and NVIDIA-V100-32GB GPU. The specific workflow of our framework will be described in detail in the next section.

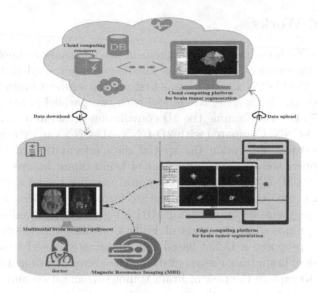

**Fig. 1.** The edge-cloud framework

The main contributions of this paper are as follows:

- In order to relieve the pressure of image reading for clinicians in the brain tumor department, we propose a brain tumor segmentation framework based on deep learning and edge-cloud collaboration, which can realize computer-aided brain tumor diagnosis in both offline and online modes.
- On the edge platform, we first make 2D slices of MRI images and then use Hybrid ResUnet algorithm to complete brain tumor segmentation. The segmentation task can be started immediately after imaging, which greatly improves the work efficiency of doctors and avoids missed diagnoses.
- In order to cooperate with the edge to complete the segmentation task, we make 3D blocks of MRI images and then use Vnet [13] algorithm with better accuracy to complete brain tumor segmentation on the cloud platform. On the one hand, it can make up for the defect of edge computing capabilities. On the other hand, it also improves the accuracy of brain tumor diagnosis, and further guarantees the safety of patients.
- We use the BraTS dataset provided by the Multimodal Brain Tumor Segmentation Challenge to validate and evaluate the segmentation performance on the edge and in the cloud. The experimental results show that our idea is suitable for intelligent brain tumor segmentation and diagnosis.

In the rest of this paper, the second part analyzes and discusses the current research status of brain tumor segmentation and intelligent medical system at home and abroad. The third part focuses on our proposed edge-cloud collaboration framework, including the device configuration and model selection at both ends. The fourth part is the experimental design and analysis.

## 2   Related Works

In recent years, with the rapid development of deep learning technology, convolutional neural network (CNN) [10] has also been widely used in brain tumor segmentation. The 2D-CNN network was first used to segment brain tumors, and the most classic one is the 2D-CNN model with two parallel paths proposed by havaei et al. [7]. By transforming the 2D convolution kernel into 3D, researchers put forward 3D-CNN. Compared with 2D-CNN, 3D-CNN can extract more data information features and retain the spatial data information of MRI images, which can improve the segmentation effect of brain tumor lesions. G. Urban et al. [17] trained a 3D-CNN convolutional neural network model with a depth of 22 layers, which used the SENet architecture formed by stacking SE blocks to automatically segment 3D brain tumor MRI images and achieved good results. U-Net [15] is proposed on the basis of Fully Convolutional Networks (FCN). Dong et al. [6] proposed a U-Net-based fully automatic model that performed well on the task of brain tumor segmentation. The above-mentioned methods use deep learning to explore the task of brain tumor segmentation and achieve better and better performance. In tumor segmentation, 2D networks are faster, but 3D networks are more accurate. Therefore, in practical applications, we need to combine the advantages of both. However, few people combine the advantages of 2D models and 3D models, and few people design an intelligent medical framework for brain tumor diagnosis based on this.

An intelligent medical imaging diagnosis system can identify lesions and cancerous tissues faster and more accurately by using artificial neural network and autonomous learning. It is widely used in the early screening of cancer, endoscopy, and pathological examination. Iuliana et al. [5] used the Verilog hardware language to develop a real-time image processing system for tumor screening, which facilitated the early diagnosis of tumors. M. Usman Akram et al. [2] developed a computer-aided system for brain tumor detection and segmentation, which completes the diagnosis through three stages: preprocessing, global threshold segmentation, and post-processing. H. Sulaiman et al. [16] proposed to use the Wavelet Transform Modulus Maxima method on a parallel computing system to construct a diagnostic platform, which can achieve high-performance visualization of tumor detection. T. Keerthana et al. [9] used data mining techniques to process medical datasets and adopted genetic algorithms to optimize features and SVM parameters, and then proposed an intelligent system for early assessment of brain tumors. The intracranial tumor MRI diagnostic software named BioMind uses centralized cloud computing to realize intelligent diagnosis of many types of intracranial tumors. However, the above diagnosis system either only uses local equipment or adopts centralized cloud processing, which does not make full use of the idea of edge cloud collaboration to develop a more efficient diagnosis system.

Medical data under centralized cloud service is uploaded from local to the cloud. The local device does not calculate and the cloud platform returns the result to the local end after calculation. The emergence of intelligent medical devices puts forward higher requirements for network load [1]. A large number of medical devices will produce huge data. If these data need to be uploaded to the cloud for processing, it will produce huge network load and network delay, and it is difficult to achieve a real-time response. The architecture based on edge collaboration can effectively reduce the burden of the cloud platform. It processes part of the computing tasks at the edge to meet the computing needs of medical data [14]. This edge-cloud collaboration method has been widely used in many real-time services and intelligent applications. This paper adopts the edge-cloud collaboration to design a brain tumor segmentation framework based on deep learning, including offline mode and online mode. Our framework can not only complete the task of brain tumor segmentation and improve the accuracy but also reduce the computational pressure on the edge.

## 3    Methods

This part is divided into 3 parts. Section 3.1 describes the workflow of the proposed edge-cloud collaborative brain tumor segmentation framework. Section 3.2 and Sect. 3.3 introduce the segmentation methods of edge and cloud respectively.

### 3.1    The Workflow of ECC-BTSD

To realize the accurate segmentation of brain tumors and give doctors suggestions on disease diagnosis, we designed a brain tumor segmentation framework based on deep learning under the cooperation of edge and cloud (Fig. 1). The workflow of our designed edge cloud collaboration framework is shown in Fig. 2, which includes five phases.

- Phase 1 (data preprocessing at the edge): MRI images acquired by brain tumor image acquisition equipment are multimodal 3D images. Firstly, the edge end standardizes each modal image, then cuts and slices each modal image and GT (ground truth) image to obtain 2D images. Finally, the slices of each modal are merged and saved.
- Phase 2 (brain tumor segmentation at the edge): The Hybrid ResUnet model is used at the edge end to analyze the preprocessed images obtained in the first phase and complete the segmentation of the brain tumor. This will result in a series of segmented 2D slices.
- Phase 3 (judgment of the results): If the segmentation performance indicators (the indicators used in this paper are Dice, Sensitivity, Positive Predictive Value, and Hausdorff Distance) in the second phase are reliable, the task is completed. If the segmentation result is not ideal, then start the online mode and enter the fourth phase.
- Phase 4 (data preprocessing in the cloud): For those samples whose segmentation results are judged to be unsatisfactory in the third phase, the edge sends the standardized and cropped images of these samples in the first phase to the cloud platform. Firstly, the cloud cuts different modal images and GT images to obtain 3D blocks. Finally, the blocks of each modal are merged and saved.

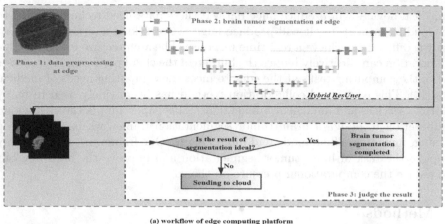

(a) workflow of edge computing platform

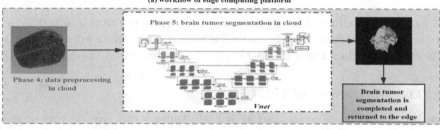

(b) workflow of cloud computing platform

**Fig. 2.** The workflow of our designed edge cloud collaboration framework.

- Phase 5 (brain tumor segmentation in the cloud): The cloud uses V-net model to analyze the preprocessed images obtained in the third phase and complete brain tumor segmentation, then returns the results to the edge for doctors to view.

## 3.2   The Edge End of ECC-BTSD

To relieve doctors' pressure of reading images and reduce the missed diagnosis rate of diseases, we need to develop an efficient tumor detection and segmentation algorithm that can run on the edge end for ECC-BTSD.

UNet consists of encoder and decoder is widely used in medical segmentation tasks. Many variant models based on Unet also perform well, such as RUNet, R2UNet [3] and Deep ReSUNet [18]. Among them, Deep ResUNet directly skips the outputs of previous layers and introduces them into the input of latter data layer. This design overcomes the problem that the learning efficiency becomes low and the accuracy cannot be improved due to the deepening of the network (also known as network degradation). But turning all double convolutions into ResNets would make the network overly complex and prone to overfitting the training data. Therefore, we adopt the hybrid ResUnet proposed later at the edge. It only uses ResBlocks in the down path of UNet, and still maintains double CNN layers in the up path. This not only simplifies the model but also increases the gradient flow on the downward path.

## 3.3  The Cloud End of ECC-BTSD

The Deep ReSUNet at the edge is a 2D network with low complexity, so it does not require much computing power. But at the same time, it can efficiently and quickly complete the task of brain tumor segmentation. If we use a network with higher precision, it may require the edge device to have more powerful computing resources, which will increase the cost of the edge device. So we choose to deploy the network with high complexity on the cloud platform, which can not only further improve the segmentation accuracy but also save the cost of the edge platform. ECC-BTSD deploys a 3D network with higher accuracy to the cloud platform, here is VNet. VNet requires the input to be 3D images, so the convolution kernel is also three-dimensional.

When the edge segmentation performance is not ideal, we can transmit MRI images to the cloud platform on the online mode. It uses VNet to complete segmentation, and then sends the results back to the edge. This edge-cloud cooperation method can not only improve the accuracy of tumor segmentation but also relieve the computational pressure at the edge. Compared with centralized cloud processing, it reduces network load and avoids abnormal jitter.

# 4  Experiments

To verify the performance of our proposed ECC-BSTD brain tumor segmentation framework, this section will design experiments to prove it. The experimental results are displayed, including the segmentation effect of edge and cloud and the synergistic effect of them.

## 4.1  The Dataset and Preprocessing

We use the dataset from the Multimodal Brain Tumor Image Segmentation Challenge (BraTS 2018) to train our algorithm, including 285 samples. These 285 samples are 3D images, which can be sliced into tens of thousands of 2D images. It is also one of the most commonly used datasets in the field of medical image segmentation. Compared with 2018, the challenge in 2019 gives 50 more samples, so we use the extra part as the test set. The experimental task is to accurately segment three tumor regions of patients, which are whole tumor (WT), tumor core (TC), and enhancing tumor (ET). For each patient sample, there are 4 modalities of MRI images and ground truth (GT) images. Figure 3 shows the MRI and GT of a patient.

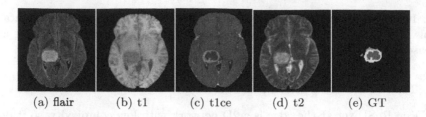

(a) flair      (b) t1      (c) t1ce      (d) t2      (e) GT

**Fig. 3.** (a), (b), (c) and (d) are 4 modalities. In GT (e), green represents peritumoral edema, yellow represents enhancing tumor, and red represents non-enhancing tumor. (Color figure online)

In our framework, the edge side uses a 2D model named Deep ReSUNet. So the original 3D MRI image needs to be processed before slicing. We use a 3D model named VNet in the cloud, so the block processing is used to alleviate the pressure of memory and graphics cards. Similar to 2D processing, the difference is that the slicing operation is replaced by cutting to blocks operation (the thickness of the block is 32 here).

### 4.2   Performance of ECC-BSTD in the Offline Mode

The ECC-BSTD framework adopts the Hybrid ResUnet algorithm to realize the task of brain tumor segmentation in offline mode. We verify the trained model on the test set and the performance of ECC-BSTD in the offline mode is as shown in Table 1. The mean Dice, mean PPV, mean Sensitivity, mean Hausdorff of WT, TC, and ET were 0.8098, 0.8476, 0.8578, and 0.2416 in the offline mode. These segmentation metrics reach or even exceed the effects of some clinicians, which shows that our method has achieved good results on brain tumor segmentation and can provide assistance for clinical diagnosis. On the other hand, it is not difficult to find that Dice, PPV, and Sensitivity are relatively low in the ET region. This may be because we slice the MRI images, which will lose some three-dimensional spatial connection. Other reasons may be that the parameters of Hybrid ResUnet are small, which will lead to low complexity of the model. Figure 4 shows the brain tumor segmentation result of a patient in the offline state. It takes 21.3723 s to segment the case, which is less than the judgment time of ordinary clinicians. This shows that ECC-BSTD framework can achieve high-precision result within 22 s in the offline mode, and has the ability to segment brain tumors in advance in clinical situations.

**Table 1.** Performance in the offline mode

| Part | Dice | PPV | Sensitivity | Hausdorff |
|------|------|-----|-------------|-----------|
| WT | 0.8402 | 0.8894 | 0.8538 | 0.2628 |
| TC | 0.8182 | 0.8351 | 0.9176 | 0.1804 |
| ET | 0.7709 | 0.8182 | 0.8019 | 0.2815 |

### 4.3    Performance of ECC-BSTD in the Online Mode

ECC-BSTD framework uses Vnet to realize tumor segmentation in online mode and unsatisfactory segmentation will be segmented again. We verify the trained model on the test set and the performance of ECC-BSTD in the online mode is as shown in Table 2. The mean Dice, mean PPV, mean Sensitivity, mean Hausdorff of WT, TC and ET were 0.8910, 0.8741, 0.9309, 0.3500 in the online mode. The performance of ECC-BSTD in the online mode has been greatly improved compared with the offline mode. The average values of Dice, PPV, and Sensitivity increased by 8.12%, 2.65%, and 7.31%, respectively. On the other hand, the edge-cloud collaboration method solves the problem of low performance of ET region in the offline mode. In the online mode, three regions have all achieved good segmentation results. This shows that we can achieve better performance by appropriately increasing the complexity of model. To relieve the computational pressure of edge devices, it is a feasible option to deploy a segmentation model with higher accuracy in the cloud. Figure 4 shows the segmentation result of a person in the online state. On the cloud platform, it was measured that it took 32.8272 s to segment the case. The time only increased by 11.4549 s while obtaining more effective results, which is still far less than the diagnosis time of ordinary clinicians. Our experiments show that ECC-BSTD significantly improves the performance of brain tumor segmentation. It can provide accurate predictions for brain tumor diagnosis, while also easing the computational pressure on edge devices.

**Table 2.** Performance in the Online Mode

| Part | Dice | PPV | Sensitivity | Hausdorff |
|------|------|-----|-------------|-----------|
| WT | 0.9138 | 0.8882 | 0.9492 | 0.2177 |
| TC | 0.8690 | 0.8376 | 0.9510 | 0.5619 |
| ET | 0.8901 | 0.8965 | 0.8924 | 0.2703 |

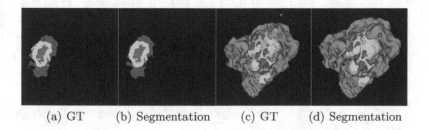

(a) GT        (b) Segmentation        (c) GT        (d) Segmentation

**Fig. 4.** (a) represents 2D GT of one patient and (b) represents the segmentation result in the offline mode. (c) represents 3D GT of a patient and (d) represents the segmentation result in the online mode.

## 4.4 ECC-BSTD Analysis Under Edge-Cloud Collaboration

To verify the performance of the ECC-BSTD framework under edge-cloud collaboration, we evaluate the performance and efficiency of the edge and the cloud. Figure 5 shows the performance metrics for 50 test cases in offline mode and online mode. The x-axis represents 50 patients and the y-axis represents the four performance metrics in three regions: WT, TC, and ET. The blue curve and red curve represent the evaluation values of 50 patients in online mode and offline mode, respectively. On average, the online mode performs better than the offline mode. We compared the response times in the two modes, as shown in Table 3. The average preprocessing time in online mode is 4.029 s, which also includes the network latency for uploading data to the cloud. The average response time is the sum of average preprocessing time and average segmentation time. It can be seen that the total time in online mode is only 13.275 s longer. In addition, we also deployed the Vnet in the online mode to the edge, and we have reduced the parameters. The measured average response time is 45.707 s. This takes longer than the cloud platform, which shows that the computing power of the cloud platform provides us with faster and more accurate results. It should be noted that the response time in both modes is far less than the diagnosis time of clinicians.

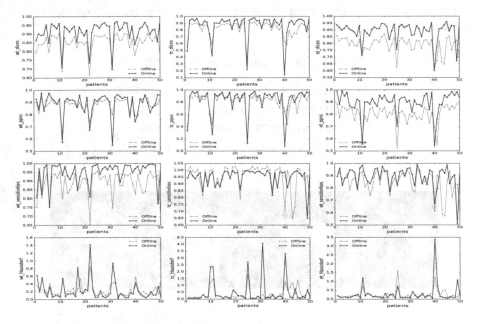

**Fig. 5.** The performance metrics for 50 test cases in the offline mode and the online mode

Table 3. Processing time in the offline and online mode

|  | Offline | Online |
| --- | --- | --- |
| Preprocessing time for 50 patient images | 155.949 s | 201.428 s |
| Average preprocessing time | 3.119 s | 4.029 s |
| Segmentation time for 50 patients | 1224.563 s | 1842.790 s |
| Average segmentation time | 24.491 s | 36.856 s |
| Average response time | 27.610 s | 40.885 s |

The above experiments show that under networking conditions, the online mode can provide offline mode with an opportunity of secondary segmentation with higher accuracy. Once the performance at the edge is not ideal, we can use the cloud to achieve a more ideal result. Usually, the offline mode can meet the needs of clinical prediction in a short time. We only need to pay a little extra time to get a more accurate result in online mode.

## 5 Conclusion

This paper proposes a brain tumor segmentation framework based on deep learning and edge-cloud collaboration, which can realize computer-assisted medical diagnosis in both offline and online modes. The framework utilizes the efficiency of cloud computing to improve the efficiency and accuracy of diagnosis. Our framework that integrates image acquisition and diagnosis is an ideal form for smart medical devices. Experiments show that our method improves diagnostic efficiency and reduces the risk of missed diagnosis. On the other hand, the framework solves the problem of insufficient computing power in edge devices and the safety of patients can also be further guaranteed. Last but not least, this intelligent medical framework can also be extended to other disease diagnoses.

**Acknowledgements.** The work was supported by Translational Medicine and Interdisciplinary Research Joint Fund of Zhongnan Hospital of Wuhan University (Grant No. ZNJC201926), in part by the National Natural Science Foundation of China (62073248).

## References

1. Adame, T., Bel, A., Carreras, A., Melia-Segui, J., Oliver, M., Pous, R.: Cuidats: an RFID-WSN hybrid monitoring system for smart health care environments. Futur. Gener. Comput. Syst. **78**, 602–615 (2018)
2. Akram, M.U., Usman, A.: Computer aided system for brain tumor detection and segmentation. In: International Conference on Computer Networks and Information Technology, pp. 299–302. IEEE (2011)
3. Alom, M.Z., Hasan, M., Yakopcic, C., Taha, T.M., Asari, V.K.: Recurrent residual convolutional neural network based on U-Net (R2U-Net) for medical image segmentation (2018)

4. Benson, C., Lajish, V., Rajamani, K.: Robust classification of mr brain images based on fractal dimension analysis. In: 2017 International Conference on Advances in Computing, Communications and Informatics (ICACCI), pp. 1135–1140. IEEE (2017)
5. Chiuchisan, I., Geman, O.: A review of hdl-based system for real-time image processing used in tumors screening. In: 2014 18th International Conference on System Theory, Control and Computing (ICSTCC), pp. 217–220. IEEE (2014)
6. Dong, H., Yang, G., Liu, F., Mo, Y., Guo, Y.: Automatic brain tumor detection and segmentation using U-Net based fully convolutional networks. In: Valdés Hernández, M., González-Castro, V. (eds.) MIUA 2017. CCIS, vol. 723, pp. 506–517. Springer, Cham (2017). https://doi.org/10.1007/978-3-319-60964-5_44
7. Havaei, M., et al.: Brain tumor segmentation with deep neural networks. Med. Image Anal. **35**, 18–31 (2017)
8. Hoyos, F.T., Martín-Landrove, M., Navarro, R.B., Villadiego, J.V., Cardenas, J.C.: Study of cervical cancer through fractals and a method of clustering based on quantum mechanics. Appl. Radiat. Isot. **150**, 182–191 (2019)
9. Keerthana, T., Xavier, S.: An intelligent system for early assessment and classification of brain tumor. In: 2018 Second International Conference on Inventive Communication and Computational Technologies (ICICCT), pp. 1265–1268. IEEE (2018)
10. Krizhevsky, A., Sutskever, I., Hinton, G.E.: Imagenet classification with deep convolutional neural networks. Adv. Neural. Inf. Process. Syst. **25**, 1097–1105 (2012)
11. Lenka, S., Kumar, S., Mishra, S., Jena, K.K.: An iot-cloud based fractal model for brain tumor image analysis. In: 2020 Fourth International Conference on I-SMAC (IoT in Social, Mobile, Analytics and Cloud)(I-SMAC), pp. 1–7. IEEE (2020)
12. Lin, P., Song, Q., Jamalipour, A.: Multidimensional cooperative caching in compintegrated ultra-dense cellular networks. IEEE Trans. Wireless Commun. **19**(3), 1977–1989 (2019)
13. Milletari, F., Navab, N., Ahmadi, S.A.: V-net: Fully convolutional neural networks for volumetric medical image segmentation. In: 2016 fourth international conference on 3D vision (3DV), pp. 565–571. IEEE (2016)
14. Ning, Z., Wang, X., Huang, J.: Mobile edge computing-enabled 5g vehicular networks: Toward the integration of communication and computing. IEEE Vehicular Technol. Mag. **14**(1), 54–61 (2018)
15. Ronneberger, O., Fischer, P., Brox, T.: U-Net: convolutional networks for biomedical image segmentation. In: Navab, N., Hornegger, J., Wells, W.M., Frangi, A.F. (eds.) MICCAI 2015. LNCS, vol. 9351, pp. 234–241. Springer, Cham (2015). https://doi.org/10.1007/978-3-319-24574-4_28
16. Sulaiman, H., Said, N.M., Ibrahim, A., Alias, N.: High performance visualization of human tumor detection using wtmm on parallel computing system. In: 2013 IEEE 9th International Colloquium on Signal Processing and its Applications, pp. 205–208. IEEE (2013)
17. Urban, G., Bendszus, M., Hamprecht, F., Kleesiek, J.: Multi-modal brain tumor segmentation using deep convolutional neural networks. MICCAI BraTS (brain tumor segmentation) challenge. Proceedings, winning contribution, pp. 31–35 (2014)
18. Zhang, Z., Liu, Q., Wang, Y.: Road extraction by deep residual U-Net. IEEE Geosci. Remote Sens. Lett. **15**(5), 749–753 (2018)

# CLTS+: A New Chinese Long Text Summarization Dataset with Abstractive Summaries

Xiaojun Liu[1,2], Shunan Zang[1,2], Chuang Zhang[1(✉)], Xiaojun Chen[1], and Yangyang Ding[1]

[1] Institute of Information Engineering, Chinese Academy of Sciences, Beijing, China
{liuxiaojun,zangshunan,zhangchuang,chenxiaojun,dingyangyang}@iie.ac.cn
[2] School of Cyber Security, University of Chinese Academy of Sciences, Beijing, China

**Abstract.** The abstractive methods lack of creative ability is particularly a problem in automatic text summarization. The summaries generated by models are mostly extracted from the source articles. One of the main causes for this problem is the lack of dataset with *abstractiveness*, especially for Chinese. In order to solve this problem, we paraphrase the reference summaries in CLTS, the **C**hinese **L**ong **T**ext **S**ummarization dataset, correct errors of factual inconsistencies, and propose the first Chinese Long Text Summarization dataset with a high level of *abstractiveness*, CLTS+, which contains more than 180K article-summary pairs and is available online. Additionally, we introduce an intrinsic metric based on co-occurrence words to evaluate the dataset we constructed. We analyze the extraction strategies used in CLTS+ summaries against other datasets to quantify the *abstractiveness* and difficulty of our new data and train several baselines on CLTS+ to verify the utility of it for improving the creative ability of models.

**Keywords:** Dataset resources · Automatic text summarization · Intrinsic evaluation

## 1 Introduction

In the process of human writing summaries, some words, phrases, and sentences that are not in the source article can be produced, which is one of the main differences between human-written and computer-generated summaries[1]. Therefore, in order to make summaries generated by computers as close as possible to the results of human-written, we hope that the model has creative ability, which means that it can generate some novel n-grams, rather than completely copy from the articles, especially for abstractive summarization.

In recent years, deep learning models have greatly improved the state-of-the-art for various supervised NLP problems [3,17,21], including automatic text

---

[1] https://github.com/lxj5957/CLTS-plus-Dataset.

© The Author(s), under exclusive license to Springer Nature Switzerland AG 2022
E. Pimenidis et al. (Eds.): ICANN 2022, LNCS 13529, pp. 73–84, 2022.
https://doi.org/10.1007/978-3-031-15919-0_7

summarization [2,13,19]. However, the sequence-to-sequence architecture based on deep neural networks is data-driven, which means that the quality and nature of the dataset have a great impact on training and testing the model. Therefore, a high-quality dataset can greatly improve the quality of the summaries generated.

However, there is no *abstractiveness* dataset in Chinese long text summarization: abstractive summaries describe the contents of articles primarily using new sentences. There is only one Chinese long text summarization dataset called CLTS [11]. It is an *extractiveness* dataset: extractive summaries frequently borrow words and phrases from their source text, which leads to the fact that models trained on CLTS will extract whole sentences from articles to form summaries when predicting. It makes a nonsense of abstractive and reduces the novelty of summaries generated.

In this work, we propose CLTS+ dataset, which is based on CLTS, the **C**hinese **L**ong **T**ext **S**ummarization dataset. We paraphrase the reference summaries in CLTS to reduce the number of samples that reference summaries are completely extracted from the source articles and make the dataset abstractive to improve the creative ability of models. Meanwhile, some inconsistencies will inevitably occur during the process of paraphrasing; for example, people and place names in summaries after paraphrasing can't be aligned with those in CLTS reference summaries. Therefore, we correct errors of factual inconsistencies to reduce the noise in the dataset and improve the prediction accuracy of models.

For data-driven learning-based methods (e.g., neural networks), the high quality of the training data ensures that models learn to perform a given task correctly. Therefore, we introduce an intrinsic metric based on co-occurrence words as a supplement to the existing indicators of the dataset quality. This metric focuses on the semantic dimension, and we apply it to CNN/DM, the most commonly used dataset in this field, to verify the reasonability of the metric.

We summarize our contributions as follows: (1)We propose a Chinese long text summarization dataset called CLTS+. To the best of our knowledge, it is the first Chinese long text summarization dataset with such a high level of *abstractiveness*. There are no article-summary pairs where the reference summary is completely extracted from the source article. (2)We provide an extensive analysis of the properties of this dataset to quantify the *abstractiveness* and difficulty of our new data. (3)We introduce an intrinsic metric based on co-occurrence words as a supplementary indicator to existing evaluation metrics on dataset. (4)We train and evaluate several baselines on CLTS+ dataset and test on the out-of-domain data to verify the dataset's utility for improving the creative ability of models.

## 2   Related Work

Recently, neural networks have shown great promise in text summarization, with both extractive [23,24] and abstractive [2,14,18,19] methods. End-to-end deep neural models are data-driven, and therefore, there is strong demand for high-quality and large-scale datasets.

However, Chinese datasets for automatic text summarization are only NLPCC, CLTS [11] and LCSTS [8]. The size of NLPCC is so small that it can't be used to train neural networks. Take NLPCC-2017 as an example; it only contains 50K article-summary pairs, which is mostly used for evaluation. LCSTS is a short text dataset collected from verified accounts on the Chinese microblogging website Sina Weibo, in which each article doesn't exceed 140 Chinese characters. It is only applicable to abstractive summarization and can only be used to generate a title from a short text. And CLTS, the only Chinese long text summarization dataset, is extracted from the source article, which leads to the fact that models trained on CLTS lose the ability to generate novel n-grams in prediction.

The current situation of English datasets for automatic text summarization is better than Chinese, not only in the number of datasets, but also in the types of them. Commonly used datasets in English include short text Gigaword [1, 18] and long text CNN/DM [7, 13, 19]. There are also multi-document datasets including DUC-2004 [15], TAC-2011 [16] and Multi-News [4]. In addition to news articles, researchers also introduce dialogue summarization corpus [5], patent documents [20] and scientific papers [22].

## 3 Dataset Construction

The process of constructing CLTS+ dataset is shown in Fig. 1. We leverage back translation to paraphrase reference summaries in CLTS dataset and correct factual inconsistencies such as people and place names. After the operations mentioned above, we obtain the reference summaries in CLTS+ dataset.

### 3.1 Back Translation

Back translation is a commonly used technique for text augmentation in Natural Language Process. It is equivalent to paraphrase the text, which means the semantic meaning remains the same while the expression of the text is completely different from the original. The key idea of back translation is very simple. We translate the original text from the source language into another language and then translate it back into the source language.

There are many machine translation services to translate to a different language and back to Chinese, such as Google Translate, Baidu Translate, etc. Google Translate is the most popular service among them. However, it is needed to get an API key to use it, and it is a paid service. Alternatively, we use a handy feature named GOOGLETRANSLATE() in Google Sheets[2] web app to leverage for our purpose. We translate the reference summaries in CLTS dataset from Chinese to English and then back again to Chinese. After the back translation

---

[2] https://www.google.cn/intl/zh_cn/sheets/about/.

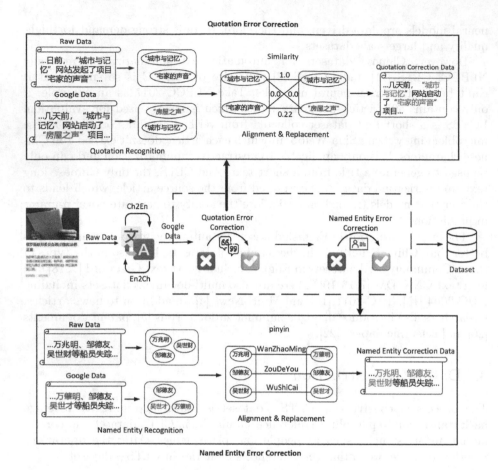

**Fig. 1.** Process of CLTS+ dataset construction. *Raw Data* refers to summaries in CLTS. *Google Data* refers to *Raw Data* after back translation. *Quotation Correction Data* and *Named Entity Correction Data* refers to *Google Data* after correcting quotation and named entity errors respectively.

process, we have achieved the purpose of paraphrasing the reference summaries in CLTS dataset, which formed by extractive fragments from the source articles have transformed into more abstractive ones.

## 3.2 Error Correction

Since most of the samples in the dataset are news articles, the reference summaries will contain the quotation of statements in the source articles, which includes but is not limited to important details of the speeches delivered by national leaders and the views of the interviewees on an event. These statements are also objective facts, and therefore, although the semantic meaning before and after back translation is the same, we still hope that the quotation of such statements should not be paraphrased.

We recognize quotations with regular expression in Raw Data $R$ and Google Data $G$, and then compute the similarity, which is defined by the normalized length of longest contiguous matching subsequence, between quotations in $R$ and $G$. Two quotations with a similarity higher than the threshold are regarded as aligned, and we replace the quotation in Google Data $G$ with the one in Raw Data $R$.

Additionally, during the process of back translation, errors of named entities will inevitably occur, among which the commonest are incorrect factual details such as people and place names. If these errors are not corrected, samples containing them are noise in the dataset, which will negatively affect model training and reduce the accuracy when inferring. Therefore, the errors of named entities need to be corrected so that models can predict accurately during testing.

We use jieba[3] to make word segmentation on Raw Data $R$ and Google Data $G$ respectively. We determine whether a word is a named entity based on surname and the length of it. After named entity recognition, we align named entities in $R$ and $G$ by pinyin, because as for people's name, the pinyin is always the same, although Chinese characters are different during the process of back-translation. Finally, we replace named entities in $G$ with those in $R$.

We correct 42,030 quotation errors and 263,822 named entity errors. After back translation and error correction, we offered CLTS+ dataset containing 181,401 samples.

### 3.3   Metric Based on Co-occurrence Words

High-quality data forms the bedrock for building meaningful statistical models in NLP. In order to ensure the quality of the dataset we constructed, we introduce an intrinsic metric based on co-occurrence words as a supplement to the existing indicators. The process is shown in Fig. 2, and the main steps are summarized as follows:

(1) Tokenize the article and remove stop words from it to get the Word set $\mathcal{W}$.
(2) Sort $\mathcal{W}$ in descending order according to the word and sentence frequency. Sentence frequency refers to a sentence that contains the word occurring how many times in the article. And then take the first N words to obtain the High-frequency Word set $\mathcal{HW}$.
(3) Perform sentence segmentation on the article to get the Sentence set $\mathcal{S}$. We define co-occurrence words as high-frequency words in $\mathcal{HW}$ appear in the same sentence. Sort the co-occurrence words in descending order according to the length and frequency of them to obtain the co-occurring word set and take the top-K co-occurrence words as Topic Word set $\mathcal{TW}$. We regard $\mathcal{TW}$ as a highly condensed expression of the article.

---

[3] https://github.com/fxsjy/jieba.

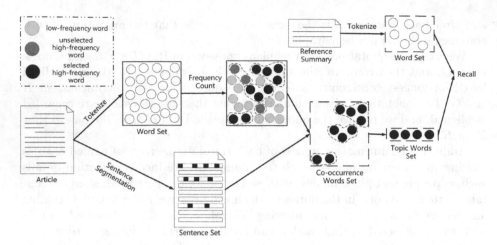

**Fig. 2.** Process of our metric based on co-occurrence words.

(4) Tokenize the reference summary and compute recall of the words in reference summary in $\mathcal{TW}$. This metric assigns a value $x \in [0, 1]$ to every document-summary pairs $(D_i, S_i)$ where 1 is the maximum score and example-level scores are averaged to yield a dataset-level score.

## 4    Analysis

### 4.1    Data Statistics

CLTS+ dataset contains 181,401 article-summary pairs, and is divided into training (145,120 samples, 80%), validation (19,954 samples, 11%) and testing (16,327 samples, 9%) sets. Table 1 shows the same article corresponding to different reference summaries in CLTS+ and CLTS respectively, which indicates that the reference summaries in CLTS+ are quite abstractive. Simple statistics on CLTS+ dataset compared to other datasets are shown in Table 2. To quantify *abstractiveness* in our dataset, we use one measure named novel n-grams, which refers to unique n-grams in the summary which are not in the article. The results are shown in Table 3.

### 4.2    Rouge of LEAD-3 and Oracle

LEAD-3, which selects the first three sentences of the article, is a strong baseline in automatic summarization. News articles adhere to a writing structure known in journalism as the "Inverted Pyramid." In this form, the initial paragraphs contain the most newsworthy information, which is followed by details and background. This structure makes LEAD-3 can be competitive with some state-of-art systems, although it is very simple.

**Table 1.** An example of CLTS+ and CLTS dataset. The red font means extractive fragments of an article-summary pair.

| Article(truncated) | ...工信部党组成员、总工程师张峰出席博览会并致辞。他在会上透露，接下来将着力完善三大体系，构筑工业互联网生态。...张峰提出，我国工业互联网应用场景丰富，模式创新活跃，但关键核心技术还不足。因此，要加强产业创新能力，夯实持续发展基础。...(... Zhang Feng, a member of the Party Leadership Group and Chief Engineer of the MIIT, attended the Expo and delivered a speech. He said at the meeting that three systems would be improved, and an industrial Internet ecosystem would be built in follow-up work. ... Zhang Feng pointed out that there are rich application scenarios and active innovation patterns in the industrial Internet in China. However, the key technologies are still insufficient. Therefore, it .si necessary to strengthen industrial innovation capabilities and consolidate the foundation for sustainable development. ... ) |
|---|---|
| **Summary in CLTS** | 工信部党组成员、总工程师张峰提出，我国工业互联网应用场景丰富，模式创新活跃，但关键核心技术还不足。因此，要加强产业创新能力，夯实持续发展基础。 |
| **Summary in CLTS+** | 工业和信息化部党组成员，总工程师张峰指出，我国的工业互联网具有丰富的应用场景和积极的模式创新，但关键的核心技术仍然不足。因此，有必要加强产业创新能力，夯实可持续发展基础。 |

**Table 2.** Dataset Statistics. For Chinese dataset, length is the number of Chinese characters, while for English, it is the number of words.

| Dataset | #docs(train/val/test) | avg.document length | | avg.summary length | | vocabulary size | |
|---|---|---|---|---|---|---|---|
| | | Words | Sentences | Words | Sentences | Documents | Summeries |
| CLTS+ | 145,118/19,954/16,327 | 1,584.76 | 32.53 | 68.79 | 1.95 | 215,553 | 23,773 |
| CLTS | 148,317/20,393/16,687 | 1,582.88 | 32.51 | 66.34 | 1.50 | 220,428 | 18,981 |
| CNN/DM | 287,227/13,368/11,490 | 791.36 | 42.65 | 62.75 | 4.85 | 722,715 | 197,771 |

Oracle represents the best possible performance of an ideal extractive system. Given an article $A$ and its summary $S$, Oracle summary refers to concatenating the fragments in $\mathcal{F}(A, S)$ [6] in the order they appear in the summary $S$.

We report ROUGE [10] scores, which measures the overlap of unigrams (ROUGE-1), bigrams (ROUGE-2), and longest common subsequence (ROUGE-L) between the candidate and reference summaries. If summaries generated by LEAD-3 and Oracle achieve a high ROUGE score, it means that the reference summaries are directly extracted from the source articles with no abstractiveness. In that case, the dataset can't be used to challenge the summarization task and verify the effectiveness of models because the nature of the dataset determines that the most sophisticated models can't surpass the simple, strong baseline LEAD-3 and Oracle.

Table 3 presents the ROUGE score of summaries predicted by LEAD-3 and Oracle on CLTS+, CLTS, and CNN/DM test sets. CLTS dataset has achieved the highest ROUGE score, whether on LEAD-3 or Oracle, which shows that the reference summaries in CLTS are all extracted from the source articles. The Oracle ROUGE score of CLTS+ is higher than CNN/DM. In comparison, the LEAD-3 score is lower than it and drops significantly compared with CLTS, which indicates that although the reference summaries in CLTS+ copy some words from the source articles, the reorganization of them also makes the summaries abstractive.

**Table 3.** ROUGE scores for LEAD-3 and Oracle on CLTS+, CLTS and a commonly used English dataset, CNN/DM.

| Dataset | % of novel n-grams in gold summary | | | | LEAD-3 | | | ORACLE | | |
|---------|----------|---------|----------|---------|------|------|------|------|------|------|
| | Unigrams | Bigrams | Trigrams | 4-grams | R-1 | R-2 | R-L | R-1 | R-2 | R-L |
| CLTS+ | 8.66% | 38.07% | 55.77% | 66.37% | 42.27 | 22.51 | 35.34 | 83.05 | 71.03 | 84.01 |
| CLTS | 0.57% | 3.23% | 5.38% | 7.10% | 49.87 | 37.78 | 45.73 | 99.50 | 99.08 | 99.50 |
| CNN/DM | 11.10% | 48.71% | 69.51% | 79.53% | 40.34 | 17.70 | 36.57 | 71.49 | 56.15 | 76.44 |

### 4.3 Human Evaluation

The metrics mentioned above are all automatic. In order to further verify the quality of CLTS+, we provide human evaluation of the different datasets on the reference summaries and articles. Human evaluation is centered around five dimensions, including fluency (individual sentences are well-written and grammatical), coherence (all sentences of the summary fit together and make sense collectively), consistency (factual details in the summary are aligned with the ones in the article), informativeness (summary captures the key points from the article) and novelty (words, phrases, and sentences of the summary are not in the article).

Evaluation is performed on 100 randomly sampled articles with the system-generated summaries of Pointer-Generator network. Each system-article pair is rated by five distinct judges, with the final score obtained by averaging the individual scores (out of 5).

**Table 4.** Human evaluation on the system-generated summaries of Pointer-Generator network trained on CLTS, CLTS+ and CNN/DM respectively.

| Dataset | Fluency | Coherence | Consistency | Informativeness | Novelty |
|---------|---------|-----------|-------------|-----------------|---------|
| CLTS | **3.92** | **3.87** | **3.90** | 2.09 | 0.03 |
| CLTS+ | 3.71 | 3.60 | 3.87 | 3.40 | **3.80** |
| CNN / DM | 3.56 | 3.39 | 3.62 | **3.55** | 3.73 |

Table 4 shows human evaluation results on CLTS, CLTS+ and CNN/DM. Reference summaries in CLTS get the highest fluency and coherence scores because they are completely extracted from the source articles. Although it ensures the correctness of syntactic, the novelty score is almost zero. CLTS+ exhibits similar to CNN/DM dataset on all scores, and it greatly improves the novelty score without sacrificing fluency and coherence.

### 4.4 Our Metric

When performing the metric we introduced on different datasets, We set $N = 8$ in Chinese, $N = 20$ in English, and $K = 1$. The average score on CLTS+, CLTS,

**Table 5.** ROUGE scores of different methods on CLTS, CLTS+ and non-anonymized version of CNN/DM dataset.

| Model | CLTS | | | CLTS+ | | | CNN/DM | | |
|---|---|---|---|---|---|---|---|---|---|
| | R-1 | R-2 | R-L | R-1 | R-2 | R-L | R-1 | R-2 | R-L |
| LEAD-3 | 43.18 | 35.79 | 40.54 | 37.01 | 20.89 | 34.76 | **40.34** | 17.70 | 36.57 |
| TextRank | 31.55 | 22.50 | 27.00 | 27.45 | 13.90 | 25.38 | 35.23 | 13.90 | 31.48 |
| Seq2seq-att | 48.05 | 37.00 | 43.34 | 41.35 | 24.03 | 36.47 | 31.33 | 11.81 | 28.83 |
| Pointer-gen | **51.68** | **41.17** | **47.18** | 42.06 | 24.90 | 37.11 | 36.44 | 15.66 | 33.42 |
| Pointer-gen+cov | 46.34 | 34.88 | 41.39 | 40.65 | 23.21 | 35.90 | 39.53 | 17.28 | 36.38 |
| Transformer | 48.92 | 37.91 | 44.27 | **43.27** | **26.17** | **37.97** | 40.05 | **17.72** | **36.77** |

and CNN/DM is 0.384, 0.522, and 0.496, respectively. The percentage of samples in the three datasets mentioned above get a score between (0.5, 1.0] is 27.27%, 46.21%, 44.48%. Compared with CNN/DM, the most commonly used dataset in automatic text summarization, CLTS+ achieves a similar distribution and high consistency with it, which demonstrates the high quality of the dataset we constructed and shows the reasonability of the metric.

# 5 Experiment

## 5.1 Baseline

We train and evaluate several summarization systems to understand the challenges of CLTS+ and its usefulness for training systems. We consider two unsupervised extractive systems including LEAD-3 and TextRank [12]. Additionally, we train four abstractive systems: Seq2seq with attention (Seq2seq-att) [1,14], Pointer-Generator (Pointer-gen) and a version with coverage mechanism (Pointer-gen+cov) [19] and Transformer [21].

## 5.2 Automatic Evaluation

For abstractive models mentioned above, we take the Chinese character as input and use OpenNMT-py [9] to re-implement them. The results are shown in Table 5.

All baselines perform better on CLTS+ compared to CNN/DM. Although ROUGE scores on CLTS+ are lower than CLTS, they are incomparable because their extractive strategies are different. The results on CLTS+ are consistent with CNN/DM, the most commonly used English dataset, which means that CLTS+ can be used as a benchmark dataset in automatic text summarization.

## 5.3 Results on Out-of-domain Data

In addition to generating summaries on the test set, we also evaluate Pointer-Generator network trained on CLTS and CLTS+ respectively on the out-of-domain data to verify the creative ability of the model. We randomly select 100

**Table 6.** An example on the out-of-domain data of Pointer-Generator model trained on CLTS and CLTS+ respectively. The underlined words are extractive fragments of an article-summary pair.

| | |
|---|---|
| **Article(truncated)** | 中新社北京10月20日电 (记者 于立霄)北京市政府新闻发言人徐和建在20日举行的疫情防控发布会上表示，要继续做好直航北京国际航班的管控，严格防疫措施和闭环管理；严防第三国人员中转入境进京。<br>徐和建指出，北京要密切关注重点地区疫情走势，对中高风险地区进京人员迅速排查、加强管控，落实核酸检测、医学观察等措施。同时，要加强进口冷链食品监管，严格口岸查控措施，督促承运企业落实主体责任，做好从业人员防护和运输装备、外包装消毒。... |
| **Model trained on CLTS** | 徐和建指出，北京要密切关注重点地区疫情走势，对中高风险地区进京人员迅速排查、加强管控，落实核酸检测、医学观察等措施。 |
| **Model trained on CLTS+** | 北京市政府新闻发言人 徐和建指出，北京必须密切关注重点地区的流行病，对中高风险地区进行迅速调查，加强管理控制，实施核酸检测、医学观察等措施。 |

news articles from Chinese news website such as ChinaNews[4], TencentNews[5] and SohuNews[6].

Table 6 is an example of computer-generated summaries of the models trained on CLTS and CLTS+ respectively, and the article is from ChinaNews[7]. The summary generated by the model trained on CLTS+ is not only abstractive but also informative, which includes the information "北京市政府新闻发言 " that is not in the system-generated summary of the model trained on CLTS.

## 6    Conclusion

We present CLTS+ dataset, the largest Chinese long text summarization dataset with a high level of *abstractiveness*, consisting of various articles and corresponding abstractive summaries. The results show that the dataset can improve the creative ability of models and be used as a benchmark. We hope that the new dataset will promote the development of automatic text summarization research as a new option for researchers to evaluate their systems.

## References

1. Chopra, S., Auli, M., Rush, A.M.: Abstractive sentence summarization with attentive recurrent neural networks. In: Proceedings of the 2016 Conference of the North American Chapter of the Association for Computational Linguistics: Human Language Technologies, pp. 93–98. Association for Computational Linguistics, San Diego, California (2016). https://doi.org/10.18653/v1/N16-1012

---

[4] https://www.chinanews.com/.
[5] https://news.qq.com/.
[6] http://news.sohu.com/.
[7] http://www.bj.chinanews.com/news/2020/1020/79344.html.

2. Cohan, A., et al.: A disicourse-aware attention model for abstractive summarization of long documents. In: Proceedings of the 2018 Conference of the North American Chapter of the Association for Computational Linguistics: Human Language Technologies, Volume 2 (Short Papers), pp. 615–621. Association for Computational Linguistics, New Orleans, Louisiana (2018). https://doi.org/10.18653/v1/N18-2097

3. Devlin, J., Chang, M.W., Lee, K., Toutanova, K.: BERT: pre-training of deep bidirectional transformers for language understanding. In: Proceedings of the 2019 Conference of the North American Chapter of the Association for Computational Linguistics: Human Language Technologies, Volume 1 (Long and Short Papers), pp. 4171–4186. Association for Computational Linguistics, Minneapolis, Minnesota (2019). https://doi.org/10.18653/v1/N19-1423

4. Fabbri, A., Li, I., She, T., Li, S., Radev, D.: Multi-news: a large-scale multi-document summarization dataset and abstractive hierarchical model. In: Proceedings of the 57th Annual Meeting of the Association for Computational Linguistics, pp. 1074–1084. Association for Computational Linguistics, Florence, Italy (2019). https://doi.org/10.18653/v1/P19-1102

5. Gliwa, B., Mochol, I., Biesek, M., Wawer, A.: SAMSum corpus: a human-annotated dialogue dataset for abstractive summarization. In: Proceedings of the 2nd Workshop on New Frontiers in Summarization, pp. 70–79. Association for Computational Linguistics, Hong Kong, China (2019). https://doi.org/10.18653/v1/D19-5409

6. Grusky, M., Naaman, M., Artzi, Y.: Newsroom: a dataset of 1.3 million summaries with diverse extractive strategies. In: Proceedings of the 2018 Conference of the North American Chapter of the Association for Computational Linguistics: Human Language Technologies, Volume 1 (Long Papers), pp. 708–719. Association for Computational Linguistics, New Orleans, Louisiana (2018). https://doi.org/10.18653/v1/N18-1065

7. Hermann, K.M., et al.: Teaching machines to read and comprehend. In: Advances in Neural Information Processing Systems, pp. 1693–1701 (2015)

8. Hu, B., Chen, Q., Zhu, F.: LCSTS: A large scale Chinese short text summarization dataset. In: Proceedings of the 2015 Conference on Empirical Methods in Natural Language Processing, pp. 1967–1972. Association for Computational Linguistics, Lisbon, Portugal (2015). https://doi.org/10.18653/v1/D15-1229

9. Klein, G., Kim, Y., Deng, Y., Senellart, J., Rush, A.: OpenNMT: open-source toolkit for neural machine translation. In: Proceedings of ACL 2017, System Demonstrations, pp. 67–72. Association for Computational Linguistics, Vancouver, Canada (2017)

10. Lin, C.Y.: ROUGE: a package for automatic evaluation of summaries. In: Text Summarization Branches Out, pp. 74–81. Association for Computational Linguistics, Barcelona, Spain (2004)

11. Liu, X., Zhang, C., Chen, X., Cao, Y., Li, J.: CLTS: a new Chinese long text summarization dataset. In: Zhu, X., Zhang, M., Hong, Yu., He, R. (eds.) NLPCC 2020. LNCS (LNAI), vol. 12430, pp. 531–542. Springer, Cham (2020). https://doi.org/10.1007/978-3-030-60450-9_42

12. Mihalcea, R., Tarau, P.: TextRank: bringing order into text. In: Proceedings of the 2004 Conference on Empirical Methods in Natural Language Processing, pp. 404–411. Association for Computational Linguistics, Barcelona, Spain (2004)

13. Nallapati, R., Zhai, F., Zhou, B.: SummaRuNNer: a recurrent neural network based sequence model for extractive summarization of documents. In: Proceedings of the AAAI Conference on Artificial Intelligence, vol. 31 (2017)

14. Nallapati, R., Zhou, B., dos Santos, C., Gulçehre, Ç., Xiang, B.: Abstractive text summarization using sequence-to-sequence RNNs and beyond. In: Proceedings of the 20th SIGNLL Conference on Computational Natural Language Learning, pp. 280–290. Association for Computational Linguistics, Berlin, Germany (2016). https://doi.org/10.18653/v1/K16-1028

15. Over, P., Yen, J.: An introduction to DUC-2004. Nat. Inst. Stan. Technol. (2004)

16. Owczarzak, K., Dang, H.T.: Overview of the TAC 2011 summarization track: Guided task and AESOP task. In: Proceedings of the Text Analysis Conference (TAC 2011), Gaithersburg, Maryland, USA, November (2011)

17. Paulus, R., Xiong, C., Socher, R.: A deep reinforced model for abstractive summarization. arXiv preprint arXiv:1705.04304 (2017)

18. Rush, A.M., Chopra, S., Weston, J.: A neural attention model for abstractive sentence summarization. In: Proceedings of the 2015 Conference on Empirical Methods in Natural Language Processing, pp. 379–389. Association for Computational Linguistics, Lisbon, Portugal (2015). https://doi.org/10.18653/v1/D15-1044

19. See, A., Liu, P.J., Manning, C.D.: Get to the point: summarization with pointer-generator networks. In: Proceedings of the 55th Annual Meeting of the Association for Computational Linguistics (Volume 1: Long Papers), pp. 1073–1083. Association for Computational Linguistics, Vancouver, Canada (2017). https://doi.org/10.18653/v1/P17-1099

20. Sharma, E., Li, C., Wang, L.: BIGPATENT: a large-scale dataset for abstractive and coherent summarization. In: Proceedings of the 57th Annual Meeting of the Association for Computational Linguistics, pp. 2204–2213. Association for Computational Linguistics, Florence, Italy (2019). https://doi.org/10.18653/v1/P19-1212

21. Vaswani, A., et al.: Attention is all you need. In: Advances in Neural Information Processing Systems, pp. 5998–6008 (2017)

22. Yasunaga, M., et al.: Scisummnet: a large annotated corpus and content-impact models for scientific paper summarization with citation networks. In: Proceedings of the AAAI Conference on Artificial Intelligence, vol. 33, pp. 7386–7393 (2019)

23. Zhong, M., Wang, D., Liu, P., Qiu, X., Huang, X.: A closer look at data bias in neural extractive summarization models. In: Proceedings of the 2nd Workshop on New Frontiers in Summarization, pp. 80–89. Association for Computational Linguistics, Hong Kong, China (2019). https://doi.org/10.18653/v1/D19-5410

24. Zhou, Q., Yang, N., Wei, F., Huang, S., Zhou, M., Zhao, T.: Neural document summarization by jointly learning to score and select sentences. In: Proceedings of the 56th Annual Meeting of the Association for Computational Linguistics (Volume 1: Long Papers), pp. 654–663. Association for Computational Linguistics, Melbourne, Australia (2018). https://doi.org/10.18653/v1/P18-1061

# Correlation-Based Transformer Tracking

Minghan Zhong[1,2], Fanglin Chen[1,2]([✉]), Jun Xu[1], and Guangming Lu[1,2]

[1] Harbin Institute of Technology, Shenzhen, China
zhongminghan@stu.hit.edu.cn,
{chenfanglin,xunjunqgy,luguangming}@hit.edu.cn
[2] Guangdong Provincial Key Laboratory of Novel Security Intelligence Technologies,
Shenzhen, China

**Abstract.** In recent studies on object tracking, Siamese tracking has achieved state-of-the-art performance due to its robustness and accuracy. Cross-correlation which is responsible for calculating similarity plays an important role in the development of Siamese tracking. However, the fact that general cross-correlation is a local operation leads to the lack of global contextual information. Although introducing transformer into tracking seems helpful to gain more semantic information, it will also bring more background interference, thus leads to the decline of the accuracy especially in long-term tracking. To address these problems, we propose a novel tracker, which adopts transformer architecture combined with cross-correlation, referred as correlation-based transformer tracking (CTT). When capturing global contextual information, the proposed CTT takes advantage of cross-correlation for more accurate feature fusion. This architecture is helpful to improve the tracking performance, especially long-term tracking. Extensive experimental results on large-scale benchmark datasets show that the proposed CTT achieves state-of-the-art performance, and particularly performs better than other trackers in long-term tracking.

**Keywords:** Object tracking · Transformer · Cross-correlation

## 1 Introduction

Visual object tracking is an attractive yet challenging topic in computer vision. Object tracking is widely applied in real-world scenarios such as self-driving, surveillance and autonomous robots. Despite the recent progress, it remains a challenging task as it is actually an ill-posed problem. In addition, object tracking becomes quite difficult in complex situations such as illumination variation, scale variation, background clutters and heavy occlusions.

In recent studies, Siamese tracking [1,4,8,13–15,26,31] becomes quite popular due to its robustness and accuracy. A general architecture of Siamese tracking is shown in Fig. 1(a). The most critical part in Siamese tracking is cross-correlation [1,13–15,26], which is specifically designed for feature fusion and realized simply by a local matching operation. However, general cross-correlation can

© The Author(s), under exclusive license to Springer Nature Switzerland AG 2022
E. Pimenidis et al. (Eds.): ICANN 2022, LNCS 13529, pp. 85–96, 2022.
https://doi.org/10.1007/978-3-031-15919-0_8

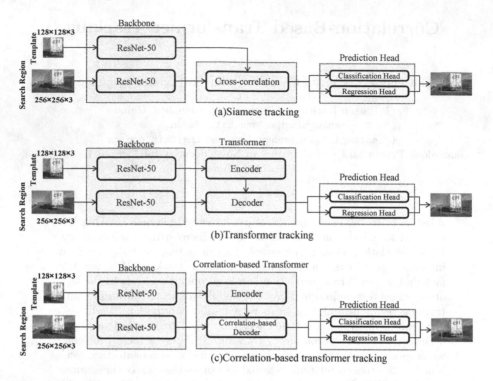

**Fig. 1.** The comparison of the proposed CTT with Siamese tracking and transformer tracking. (a) Siamese tracking. (b) Transformer tracking. (c) CTT. Each of them consists of three main parts.

only calculate similarity between local patches, thus global contextual information is ignored. This leads to the global semantic loss, so limits the performance of Siamese tracking.

Recently, following advances in object detection [2,6], transformer [20] and attention mechanism are introduced into object tracking [3,5,21,25,29]. Transformer contributes to the acquisition of global contextual information in tracking, thus reduces global semantic loss. Despite great success in detection with transformer, how to introduce and adapt the encoder-decoder architecture into tracking properly still remains a question. A general architecture of transformer tracking is shown in Fig. 1(b), in which transformer is responsible for feature fusion. Since feature fusion is a critical part in object tracking but not exists in object detection, traditional transformer from object detection is not proper in tracking. For example, when there are lots of similar objects in the search region, general semantic information is needed in detection to detect all these objects as possible. On the contrary in tracking, specific semantic information, which is generated by feature fusion from the template, is needed to distinguish the target from distractors. In other words, tracking is more vulnerable to the background interference, especially in long-term sequences. When transformer brings more semantic information, the background interference will also be stronger. In this case, more accurate feature fusion is needed in tracking, which becomes the bottleneck of designing high-accuracy tracking algorithms.

From the above analysis, the key to further improve tracking performance lies in two points. On the one hand, more global contextual information is crucial to reduce global semantic loss. On the other hand, more accurate feature fusion is needed to weaken the background interference. Based on this observation, a natural idea is to combine transformer with cross-correlation to take the advantages of both.

To overcome the restriction of Siamese tracking and the traditional transformer, we propose a novel tracker without complex structure, which adopts transformer combined with cross-correlation, referred as correlation-based transformer tracking (CTT) and the architecture is shown in Fig. 1(c). Specifically, the proposed tracker consists of three components, including backbone, correlation-based transformer and prediction head. Siamese network is used as backbone for feature extraction. Then correlation-based transformer is introduced for capturing global contextual information and realizing accurate feature fusion. Unlike traditional transformer, we design a novel transformer in which cross-correlation is responsible for feature fusion. This correlation operation consists of a two-stage pixel-wise correlation, including pixel-wise correlation in spatial and pixel-wise correlation in channel. By weakening the background interference, this architecture contributes to performance particularly in long-term tracking. After feature fusion, prediction head with classification branch and regression branch generates candidate bounding boxes with scores.

Comparing with recent Siamese trackers and transformer trackers, the proposed CTT shows outstanding results on prevalent large-scale tracking benchmarks. Especially on LaSOT [7], of which the average video length is more than 2,500 frames, CTT outperforms other trackers. It proves that CTT is effective in improving long-term tracking performance.

To summarize, the main contributions of this work are listed below in three-fold.

- We introduce a novel transformer tracker, referred as correlation-based transformer tracking (CTT). By introducing encoder-decoder architecture without complex design, the proposed CTT can capture global contextual information effectively.
- We propose a new transformer combined with two-stage pixel-wise correlation to realize more accurate and robust feature fusion. This architecture contributes to performance particularly in long-term tracking.
- Evaluated on large-scale datasets, in long-term tracking the proposed CTT significantly outperforms other trackers, and in short-term tracking it also achieves state-of-the-art performance.

## 2   Related Work

In this section, we will review the related work on Siamese tracking and cross-correlation which plays an important role in such methods. Then transformer tracking in recent years will be discussed.

**Siamese Tracking.** Siamese tracking [1] originally regards object tracking as a target matching problem and aims to learn a general similarity map between the template and the search region by cross-correlation. "Siamese" means that the two branches in backbone have the same architecture and shared weights. SiamFC [1] firstly adopts a fully convolutional network to build a Siamese tracking model. Based on SiamFC, SiamRPN [14] views tracking as a one-shot detection problem to take advantage of architectures in object detection. To address the problem that deep network does not work in tracking, SiamRPN++ [13] proposes a spatial aware sampling strategy. In recent progress, cross-correlation [13,15,26] becomes a research hot spot.

**Cross-Correlation in Tracking.** Cross-correlation [1] is one of the most important steps in Siamese tracking. SiamFC [1] adopts the convolutional layer to implement cross-correlation. Then SiamRPN++ [13] proposes a novel way to realize cross-correlation in which the kernel is decomposed in depth, referred as depth-wise correlation. Based on depth-wise correlation, the kernel of correlation is further decomposed into pixels in AlphaRefine [26] for extracting more precise spatial information. PGNet [15] extend cross-correlation from pixel to global for less background interference. Recently STMTracker [8] calculates similarity between pixels in the template and the search region by non-local neural network [22] to capture rich contextual information. Different from STMTracker, our tracker takes advantage of the encoder-decoder architecture to capture more contextual information.

**Transformer Tracking.** Transformer is firstly applied in machine translation [20] to learn the dependencies of sequences. In object detection, DETR [2] introduces transformer into detection task by viewing detection as a set prediction problem. Following DETR, STARK [25] introduces transformer into tracking the way almost same with DETR. To gain rich contextual dependencies, SiamAttn [28] proposes a tracker based on attention mechanism and TransT [3] presents an attention-based feature fusion network. Then to explore temporal context among frames, TrDimp [21] proposes a transformer architecture with two carefully designed branches. Although being effective, these methods ignore the background interference. In contrast, without adopting complex network structure, we combine transformer with cross-correlation, realizing more accurate feature fusion.

# 3  Correlation-Based Transformer Tracking

In this section, we will elaborate on the proposed correlation-based transformer tracking (CTT). In addition, we also present a tracker with traditional transformer with same other components in CTT, referred as TT-pos and the architecture is shown in Fig. 1(b).

To summarize, firstly we will introduce the whole architecture of CTT model. Secondly, the core part in the proposed tracker, correlation-based transformer, will be described in detail. At last, we briefly introduce the loss function adopted in CTT.

## 3.1  Architecture

As shown in Fig. 1(c), the input of our tracking model are patches of the search region and the template, of which the size is $256 \times 256$ and $128 \times 128$. Backbone for preliminary feature extraction is ResNet-50 [10] with a stride of 8, in which the last stage and the fully-connected layers are removed. After preliminary feature extraction, feature maps are transmitted to correlation-based transformer, which consists of 6 encoder layers and 6 decoder layers. This architecture is responsible for the enhancement of feature extraction and feature fusion. The prediction head, including classification head and regression head, takes output of correlation-based transformer as input for generating bounding boxes and classification scores. Final prediction of our tracking model is chosen from these bounding boxes with max classification score after post-processing.

## 3.2  Correlation-Based Transformer

We follow the encoder-decoder architecture [20] to build the core part of CTT, as shown in Fig. 2. By introducing transformer structure into tracking model, our tracker is capable of capturing global contextual information. In addition, different from directly adopting the traditional transformer in object detection [2] into tracking framework, we present a novel correlation-based transformer. Cross-correlation acts as an important role in decoder to realize more robust and accurate feature fusion.

**Encoder.** The input of the encoder is the feature map extracted from the template. We follow the encoder proposed in DETR [2]. Specifically, the encoder in CTT consists of 6 encoder layers. This architecture is responsible for establishing the connections between all elements in feature map to gain global contextual information.

**Correlation-Based Decoder.** Basically, we follow the architecture of the decoder proposed in DETR [2]. But different from DETR, in TT-pos, which adopts traditional transformer, queries is not generated by embedding layer but extracted from the search region. Specifically, the decoder in TT-pos takes

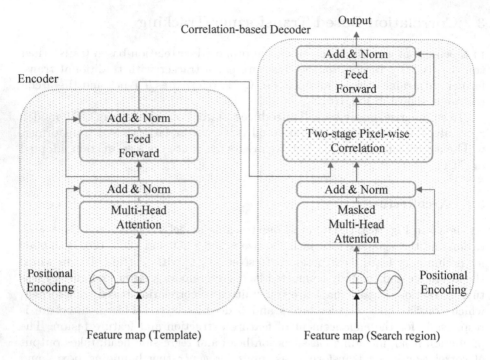

**Fig. 2.** Architecture of correlation-based transformer in the proposed CTT. Unlike traditional transformer, two-stage pixel-wise correlation is introduced into transformer for accurate feature fusion.

the feature map extracted from the search region as queries and the output of encoder as keys and values.

Unlike the decoder mentioned before, we propose a novel correlation-based decoder in CTT, which consists of three main parts (see Fig. 2), including self-attention, two-stage pixel-wise correlation and feed-forward network. Specifically, we introduce the two-stage pixel-wise correlation into the decoder to realize feature fusion, which is implemented by cross-attention in traditional transformer.

**Two-Stage Pixel-Wise Correlation.** As shown in Fig. 3, the proposed cross-correlation consists of two-stage pixel-wise correlation. Pixel-wise correlation is proposed in RANet [23] which can attend kernels of correlation to all positions in the template and the search region, thus it is good at retaining spatial information. Based on pixel-wise correlation, we propose a two-stage pixel-wise correlation to realize feature fusion for more spatial information and less background interference, which can be formulated as:

$$P = \{P_j \mid P_j = T_j * S\}_{j \in \{1,\ldots,H_0 \times W_0\}} \tag{1}$$

$$O = \{O_i \mid O_i = T_i * P\}_{i \in \{1,\ldots,C\}} \tag{2}$$

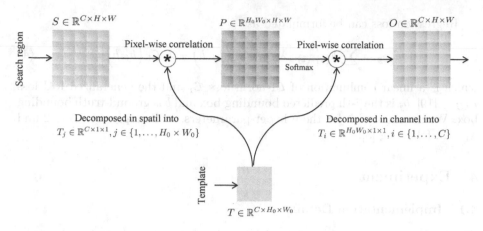

**Fig. 3.** Architecture of two-stage pixel-wise correlation, which consists of a two-stage operation, including pixel-wise correlation in spatial and pixel-wise correlation in channel.

Specifically, $*$ denotes cross-correlation in [1]. $S \in \mathbb{R}^{C \times H \times W}$ denotes feature map extracted from the search region, $T \in \mathbb{R}^{C \times H_0 \times W_0}$ denotes feature map extracted from the template. Firstly, $T$ is decomposed in spatial and channel into pixel-wise kernels $T_j \in \mathbb{R}^{C \times 1 \times 1}$ and channel-wise kernels $T_i \in \mathbb{R}^{H_0 W_0 \times 1 \times 1}$. $P \in \mathbb{R}^{H_0 W_0 \times H \times W}$ is calculated from $T_j$ and $S$ by cross-correlation. This operation is referred as pixel-wise correlation in spatial. After pixel-wise correlation in spatial, $O \in \mathbb{R}^{C \times H \times W}$ is calculated from $T_i$ and $P$ after softmax. Similarly, this operation can be referred as pixel-wise correlation in channel. Pixel-wise correlation in channel can weaken the background interference by taking advantage of information in channels [14]. In addition, comparing with pixel-wise correlation [23,26] or pixel-to-global matching process [15], stacking of cross-correlation in decoder layers further reinforces the feature fusion, thus allowing the model to learn more discriminative features for prediction.

### 3.3 Loss Function

The total loss function [3] are made up of two parts, including classification loss and regression loss.

We employ the standard binary cross-entropy loss for classification, which is formulated as

$$\mathcal{L}_{cls} = -\sum_j \left[ y_j \log \left( p_j \right) + \left( 1 - y_j \right) \log \left( 1 - p_j \right) \right], \tag{3}$$

where the ground-truth label of the $j$-th sample is defined as $y_j$, and the probability that the $j$-th sample belongs to the foreground is defined as $p_j$. When $y_j = 1$, the $j$-th sample belongs to the foreground.

Regression loss can be formulated as

$$\mathcal{L}_{reg} = \sum \mathbb{1}_{\{y_j=1\}} \left[ \lambda_G \mathcal{L}_{GIoU} \left( b_j, \hat{b} \right) + \lambda_1 \mathcal{L}_1 \left( b_j, \hat{b} \right) \right], \tag{4}$$

which is a linear combination of $\mathcal{L}$1-norm loss $\mathcal{L}_1$ and the generalized IoU loss $\mathcal{L}_{GIoU}$ [19], $b_j$ is the $j$-th predicted bounding box and $\hat{b}$ is ground-truth bounding box. We do not search for these hyper-parameters, and simply set $\lambda_G = 2$ and $\lambda_1 = 5$, following [3].

## 4  Experiment

### 4.1  Implementation Details

The backbone network is initialized with the parameters pretrained on ImageNet [12] and other parameters are initialized with Xavier init [9]. The proposed trackers are trained on the datasets of TrackingNet [18], LaSOT [7], GOT-10k [11] and COCO [16]. The size of the template and the search region as input are 128×128 pixels and 256 × 256 pixels. We train the model with AdamW [17], setting backbone's learning rate to 1e−5, other parameters' learning rate to 1e−4, and weight decay to 1e−4. The network is trained on two Nvidia Titan RTX GPUs with the batch size of 16, for a total of 600 epochs with 1000 iterations per epoch. The learning rate decreases by factor 10 every 250 epochs.

### 4.2  State-of-the-Art Comparison

We compare the proposed CTT with recent state-of-the-art trackers, of which most belong to Siamese tracking or transformer tracking. We report the detailed comparison results on two representative large-scale benchmarks, including the long-term LaSOT [7] dataset and the short-term TrackingNet dataset [18], in Table 1 and Table 2.

**LaSOT.** We conduct experiments on LaSOT [7], which is a large and challenging dataset with long-term video sequences. The LaSOT dataset provides a large-scale, high-quality dense annotations with 1,400 videos in total and 280 videos in the testing set. Since the average video length of LaSOT is more than 2,500 frames, the accumulation of errors could have a huge impact on the results. In that case, the accuracy of feature fusion is crucial to tracking performance.

**Table 1.** Performance comparisons on the LaSOT dataset.

|  | SiamAttn [28] | DTT [27] | STMTracker [8] | SAOT [30] | DualTFR [24] | TrDimp [21] | TREG [5] | TransT [3] | CTT ours |
|---|---|---|---|---|---|---|---|---|---|
| AUC (%) | 56.0 | 60.1 | 60.6 | 61.6 | 63.5 | 63.9 | 64.0 | 64.9 | **65.7** |
| PNorm (%) | 54.8 | – | 69.3 | 70.8 | 72.0 | – | 74.1 | 73.8 | **75.0** |
| P (%) | – | – | 63.3 | – | 66.5 | 61.4 | – | 69.0 | **69.8** |

Area under curve (AUC), precision (P) and normalized precision (PNorm) are calculated for evaluation. Without bells and whistles, the proposed CTT outperforms other state-of-the-art trackers, shown in Table 1. This result proves that our tracker is effective in improving long-term tracking performance.

**Table 2.** Performance comparisons on the TrackingNet dataset.

|           | SiamAttn [28] | TrDimp [21] | TREG [5] | DTT [27] | DualTFR [24] | STMTracker [8] | TransT [3] | CTT ours |
|-----------|------|------|------|------|------|------|------|------|
| AUC (%)   | 75.2 | 78.4 | 78.5 | 79.6 | 80.1 | 80.3 | **81.4** | **81.4** |
| PNorm (%) | 81.7 | 83.3 | 83.8 | 85.0 | 84.9 | 85.1 | **86.7** | 86.4 |

**TrackingNet.** We conduct experiments on TrackingNet [18], a recently released dataset with large amount of sequences. TrackingNet is a popular short-term tracking benchmark. Testing part of TrackingNet contains 511 sequences and the metrics are same with those in LaSOT. The results on TrackingNet are shown in Table 2. Our CTT achieves AUC score of 81.4% and PNorm score of 86.4%. It indicates that our tracker also achieves state-of-the-art performance in short-term tracking.

### 4.3 Ablation Study

**Correlation-based Transformer.** To verify the effectiveness of our designed correlation-based transformer, we firstly present a transformer tracker with traditional transformer architecture, referred as TT-pos, which is shown in Fig. 1(b). Except transformer, the other components of TT-pos is same with CTT. The results are shown in Table 3. Comparing with TT-pos on LaSOT, the proposed CTT has great improvements of 1.7, 1.9 and 2.1% points on AUC, PNorm and P respectively.

**Positional Encoding.** Since positional encoding in transformer significantly contributes to performance in object detection [2], we try to investigate the impact of positional encoding on tracking. The results are shown in Tabel 3. TT denotes the transfomer tracker (TT-pos) without positional encoding in cross-attention and CTT-pos denotes the proposed CTT with positional encoding in cross-correlation. For traditional transformer in our tracking framework, we can find that positional encoding in cross-attention has little effect on the performance. But for our proposed tracker, when there is positional encoding in cross-correlation, the performance of CTT-pos is inferior to TT and TT-pos. After removing positional encoding in cross-correlation, the proposed CTT outperforms TT and TT-pos by a large margin. It indicates that adopting positional encoding in correlation leads to a considerable decline of tracking performance.

From our perspective, the reason why positional encoding is not proper in cross-correlation is perhaps that the process of cross-correlation is not in need

**Table 3.** Ablation study for the impact of correlation-based transformer and positional encoding. TT, PE and CT denote the traditional transformer, the positional encoding and the correlation-based transformer respectively. The suffix "-pos" means the model adopts positional encoding in cross-attention in traditional transformer or cross-correlation in CTT.

| Method | TT | PE | CT | LaSOT | | | TrackingNet | | |
|---|---|---|---|---|---|---|---|---|---|
| | | | | AUC | PNorm | P | AUC | PNorm | P |
| CTT-pos | | ✓ | ✓ | 62.7 | 72.1 | 65.1 | 79.7 | 84.5 | 76.0 |
| TT | ✓ | | | 63.7 | 72.9 | 67.4 | 80 | 85.5 | 78.0 |
| TT-pos | ✓ | ✓ | | 64.0 | 73.1 | 67.7 | 80.5 | 85.4 | 77.9 |
| CTT | | | ✓ | **65.7** | **75.0** | **69.8** | **81.4** | **86.4** | **78.8** |

of sequence information. Viewing tracking as a template matching problem, the process of cross-correlation can be regarded as separate matching processes of patches in the search region and the template. In other words, we can change the order of these matching processes when the result is keeping unchanged. Since the matching processes are independent from each other, positional encoding designed for retaining sequence information [20] will interfere with cross-correlation instead.

## 5    Conclusion

In this paper, we propose a novel transformer tracker with simple network structure, which adopts the correlation-based transformer architecture to capture global contextual information, referred as correlation-based transformer tracking (CTT). Specifically, we present a transformer combined with two-stage pixelwise correlation to realize accurate feature fusion in tracking. This transformer structure takes both advantages of transformer and cross-correlation for global contextual information and precise feature fusion, thus contributes to performance particularly in long-term tracking. The experiments demonstrate that the proposed tracker achieves state-of-the-art performance on large-scale benchmark datasets.

However, the multi-stage pipeline of tracking framework limits further improvements of tracking performance, we plan to integrate the backbone and cross-correlation into one-stage in our future work.

**Acknowledgment.** This work was supported in part by the NSFC fund (No. U1813224, 62031013, 62173113), in part by the Guangdong Basic and Applied Basic Research Foundation under Grant 2019Bl515120055, 2021A1515012528, in part by Guangdong Provincial Key Laboratory of Novel Security Intelligence Technologies under Grant 2022B1212010005, in part by the Shenzhen Key Technical Project under Grant 2020N046, in part by the Shenzhen Fundamental Research Fund under Grant JCYJ20210324132210025, GXWD20201230155427003-20200824164357001, GXWD20201230155427003-20200821173613001 and in part by the Medical Biometrics Perception and Analysis Engineering Laboratory, Shenzhen, China.

# References

1. Bertinetto, L., Valmadre, J., Henriques, J.F., Vedaldi, A., Torr, P.H.S.: Fully-convolutional siamese networks for object tracking. In: Hua, G., Jégou, H. (eds.) ECCV 2016. LNCS, vol. 9914, pp. 850–865. Springer, Cham (2016). https://doi.org/10.1007/978-3-319-48881-3_56

2. Carion, N., Massa, F., Synnaeve, G., Usunier, N., Kirillov, A., Zagoruyko, S.: End-to-end object detection with transformers. In: Vedaldi, A., Bischof, H., Brox, T., Frahm, J.-M. (eds.) ECCV 2020. LNCS, vol. 12346, pp. 213–229. Springer, Cham (2020). https://doi.org/10.1007/978-3-030-58452-8_13

3. Chen, X., Yan, B., Zhu, J., Wang, D., Yang, X., Lu, H.: Transformer tracking. In: Proceedings of the IEEE/CVF Conference on Computer Vision and Pattern Recognition, pp. 8126–8135 (2021)

4. Chen, Z., Zhong, B., Li, G., Zhang, S., Ji, R.: Siamese box adaptive network for visual tracking. In: Proceedings of the IEEE/CVF Conference on Computer Vision and Pattern Recognition, pp. 6668–6677 (2020)

5. Cui, Y., Jiang, C., Wang, L., Wu, G.: Target transformed regression for accurate tracking. arXiv preprint arXiv:2104.00403 (2021)

6. Dosovitskiy, A., et al.: An image is worth $16 \times 16$ words: transformers for image recognition at scale. arXiv preprint arXiv:2010.11929 (2020)

7. Fan, H., et al.: LaSOT: a high-quality benchmark for large-scale single object tracking. In: Proceedings of the IEEE/CVF Conference on Computer Vision and Pattern Recognition, pp. 5374–5383 (2019)

8. Fu, Z., Liu, Q., Fu, Z., Wang, Y.: STMTrack: template-free visual tracking with space-time memory networks. In: Proceedings of the IEEE/CVF Conference on Computer Vision and Pattern Recognition, pp. 13774–13783 (2021)

9. Glorot, X., Bengio, Y.: Understanding the difficulty of training deep feedforward neural networks. In: Proceedings of the Thirteenth International Conference on Artificial Intelligence and Statistics, pp. 249–256. JMLR Workshop and Conference Proceedings (2010)

10. He, K., Zhang, X., Ren, S., Sun, J.: Deep residual learning for image recognition. In: Proceedings of the IEEE Conference on Computer Vision and Pattern Recognition, pp. 770–778 (2016)

11. Huang, L., Zhao, X., Huang, K.: GOT-10k: a large high-diversity benchmark for generic object tracking in the wild. IEEE Trans. Pattern Anal. Mach. Intell. **43**(5), 1562–1577 (2019)

12. Krizhevsky, A., Sutskever, I., Hinton, G.E.: ImageNet classification with deep convolutional neural networks. In: Advances in Neural Information Processing Systems, vol. 25 (2012)

13. Li, B., Wu, W., Wang, Q., Zhang, F., Xing, J., Yan, J.: SiamRPN++: evolution of siamese visual tracking with very deep networks. In: Proceedings of the IEEE/CVF Conference on Computer Vision and Pattern Recognition, pp. 4282–4291 (2019)

14. Li, B., Yan, J., Wu, W., Zhu, Z., Hu, X.: High performance visual tracking with siamese region proposal network. In: Proceedings of the IEEE Conference on Computer Vision and Pattern Recognition, pp. 8971–8980 (2018)

15. Liao, B., Wang, C., Wang, Y., Wang, Y., Yin, J.: PG-net: pixel to global matching network for visual tracking. In: Vedaldi, A., Bischof, H., Brox, T., Frahm, J.-M. (eds.) ECCV 2020. LNCS, vol. 12367, pp. 429–444. Springer, Cham (2020). https://doi.org/10.1007/978-3-030-58542-6_26

16. Lin, Y.-Y., et al.: Microsoft COCO: common objects in context. In: Fleet, D., Pajdla, T., Schiele, B., Tuytelaars, T. (eds.) ECCV 2014. LNCS, vol. 8693, pp. 740–755. Springer, Cham (2014). https://doi.org/10.1007/978-3-319-10602-1_48
17. Loshchilov, I., Hutter, F.: Decoupled weight decay regularization. arXiv preprint arXiv:1711.05101 (2017)
18. Muller, M., Bibi, A., Giancola, S., Alsubaihi, S., Ghanem, B.: TrackingNet: a large-scale dataset and benchmark for object tracking in the wild. In: Proceedings of the European Conference on Computer Vision (ECCV), pp. 300–317 (2018)
19. Rezatofighi, H., Tsoi, N., Gwak, J., Sadeghian, A., Reid, I., Savarese, S.: Generalized intersection over union: a metric and a loss for bounding box regression. In: Proceedings of the IEEE/CVF Conference on Computer Vision and Pattern Recognition, pp. 658–666 (2019)
20. Vaswani, A., et al.: Attention is all you need. In: Advances in Neural Information Processing Systems, vol. 30 (2017)
21. Wang, N., Zhou, W., Wang, J., Li, H.: Transformer meets tracker: exploiting temporal context for robust visual tracking. In: Proceedings of the IEEE/CVF Conference on Computer Vision and Pattern Recognition, pp. 1571–1580 (2021)
22. Wang, X., Girshick, R., Gupta, A., He, K.: Non-local neural networks. In: Proceedings of the IEEE Conference on Computer Vision and Pattern Recognition, pp. 7794–7803 (2018)
23. Wang, Z., Xu, J., Liu, L., Zhu, F., Shao, L.: RANet: ranking attention network for fast video object segmentation. In: Proceedings of the IEEE/CVF International Conference on Computer Vision, pp. 3978–3987 (2019)
24. Xie, F., Wang, C., Wang, G., Yang, W., Zeng, W.: Learning tracking representations via dual-branch fully transformer networks. In: Proceedings of the IEEE/CVF International Conference on Computer Vision, pp. 2688–2697 (2021)
25. Yan, B., Peng, H., Fu, J., Wang, D., Lu, H.: Learning spatio-temporal transformer for visual tracking. In: Proceedings of the IEEE/CVF International Conference on Computer Vision, pp. 10448–10457 (2021)
26. Yan, B., Zhang, X., Wang, D., Lu, H., Yang, X.: Alpha-refine: boosting tracking performance by precise bounding box estimation. In: Proceedings of the IEEE/CVF Conference on Computer Vision and Pattern Recognition, pp. 5289–5298 (2021)
27. Yu, B., et al.: High-performance discriminative tracking with transformers. In: Proceedings of the IEEE/CVF International Conference on Computer Vision, pp. 9856–9865 (2021)
28. Yu, Y., Xiong, Y., Huang, W., Scott, M.R.: Deformable siamese attention networks for visual object tracking. In: Proceedings of the IEEE/CVF Conference on Computer Vision and Pattern Recognition, pp. 6728–6737 (2020)
29. Zhao, M., Okada, K., Inaba, M.: TrTr: visual tracking with transformer. arXiv preprint arXiv:2105.03817 (2021)
30. Zhou, Z., Pei, W., Li, X., Wang, H., Zheng, F., He, Z.: Saliency-associated object tracking. In: Proceedings of the IEEE/CVF International Conference on Computer Vision, pp. 9866–9875 (2021)
31. Zhu, Z., Wang, Q., Li, B., Wu, W., Yan, J., Hu, W.: Distractor-aware siamese networks for visual object tracking. In: Proceedings of the European Conference on Computer Vision (ECCV), pp. 101–117 (2018)

# Deep Graph and Sequence Representation Learning for Drug Response Prediction

Xiangfeng Yan, Yong Liu(✉), and Wei Zhang(✉)

Heilongjiang University, Harbin 150080, China
{2010023,2021110}@hlju.edu.cn

**Abstract.** Drug response prediction plays a crucial role in personalized medicine and drug discovery. Many deep neural networks have been proposed for better drug response prediction. However, these methods only represent drugs as strings or represent drugs as molecular graphs, failing to capture comprehensive information about drugs. To address this challenge, we propose a joint graph and sequence representation learning model for drug response prediction, called DGSDRP. We use convolutional neural networks (CNN) to obtain local chemical context information from the drug sequences and a fusion module based on CNN and Bi-LSTM to capture the features of cell lines. Furthermore, we use graph convolutional networks (GCN) to extract topological structure information from the molecular graphs. Finally, we concatenate all representations through several dense layers and end with a regression layer to predict the response value. Extensive experimental results show that our model outperforms the current state-of-the-art models in terms of RMSE and $CC_p$.

**Keywords:** Drug response prediction · Deep learning · Graph convolutional network · Convolutional neural network

## 1 Introduction

Due to the different genetic backgrounds of individuals, researchers have observed the heterogeneity of immune response induced by the same cancer therapy [1]. Therefore, personalized medicine has attracted extensive attention in discovering the proper therapy for individual patients. However, a recent study suggested that only around 5% of patients benefit from precision oncology [2], which highlights the importance of improving the prediction accuracy of drug response.

With the increasing amount of compound data on cancer patients, several large databases have been established, including The Cancer Genome Atlas (TCGA) and the International Cancer Genome Consortium (ICGC) [3,4]. However, these databases only have a few patient records with drug responses or responses to multiple drugs as these data are collected from patients (donors). On the other hand, there are several large-scale projects on drug response, such as

E. Pimenidis et al. (Eds.): ICANN 2022, LNCS 13529, pp. 97–108, 2022.
https://doi.org/10.1007/978-3-031-15919-0_9

GDSC [5], CCLE [6], and NCI60 [7], which promote the development of computational methods for drug response prediction. Various machine learning-based computational methods have been proposed to predict drug response based on a large number of cell line data. In this trend, deep learning models performed best in predicting drug response, some methods represent drugs as one-dimensional strings to extract the local chemical context from the drug sequences. Others represent drugs as two-dimensional graphs to obtain the topological structure from the molecular graphs. Although these models have achieved promising results, there is no work to integrate the capabilities of both approaches in the drug response prediction task.

In this paper, we propose a novel model for drug response prediction, namely Deep Graph and Sequence representation learning for Drug Response Prediction (DGSDRP). We not only utilize the molecular graph but also utilize the drug sequence to predict drug response. Our model consists of four modules, namely Sequence Representation Learning Module, Graph Representation Learning Module, Cell line Representation Learning Module, and Prediction Module. The Sequence Representation Learning Module consists of three convolutional layers to obtain the features of drug sequences. The Graph Representation Learning Module extracts the features of molecular graphs through the GCN block. The Cell line Representation Learning Module applies one 1D convolutional layer to extract local features of the cell line and two bidirectional long short-term memory (Bi-LSTM) layers to extract global features. Finally, the Prediction Module concatenates all representations through two dense layers to predict the response. The main contributions of this paper are summarized as follows:

- To the best of our knowledge, we are the first to utilize both drug sequence and molecular graph in the drug response prediction task.
- We propose a fusion module, called Cell line Representation Learning Module, which is based on CNN and Bi-LSTM to capture genomic features.
- The performance of the proposed approach is demonstrated by a GDSC dataset, and DGSDRP shows high prediction accuracy among the competing methods.

## 2   Related Work

Drug response prediction methods can divide into two categories. The first one is simply using traditional machine learning-based methods [14–16]. The second one is to employ deep learning-based approachs [8–13]. However, drugs and cell lines are often represented by predefined features such as structural features of drugs and -omics profiles of cell lines. Meanwhile, the sample size is small since nearly thousands of cell lines were tested against hundreds of drugs, thus machine learning methods often face the "small n, large p" challenge and lead to the limitation of their prediction performance.

Compared with traditional machine learning methods, deep learning methods achieved superior performance on many problems in drug development [18–22]. Thus, the prediction of drug response has shifted from traditional machine learning models to deep learning models. Various neural network architectures have been proposed to predict drug response [8–13]. Some methods [12,13] use -omic data without drug representations to predict responses. These models utilized Auto-Encoders and Variational Auto-Encoders techniques, which included encode and decode networks to obtain -omic features as representations to estimate drug response. Compare with [12,13], other models [9–11] used convolutional neural networks (CNN) technology to predict drug response by integrating some omics data of cell line and drug information. tCNNS [9] use one-hot encoding to encode SMILES [28] sequences and cell lines, which obtained the one-hot representations for drugs and the feature vectors for cell lines. They use two CNN branches to process the drug inputs and the cell line inputs, respectively. When they obtained the drug representation and the cell line representation, they concatenated and passed them to a fully connected network for drug response prediction. In summary, previous works either did not use drug information or used drug information in string or numerical representations. Therefore, they cannot utilize the topological structure of drugs.

Graph convolutional networks (GCN) can learn representations of molecular structures, which are already widely used in various other drug discovery prediction tasks. However, only a few works applied this model in drug response prediction task. GraphDRP [8] consists of two modules, a GCN module that captured the features from compound graphs, and a CNN module that learned the features from cell lines. Then the drug representation and cell line representation are concatenated and passed to a fully connected layer to predict the response. However, these deep learning models all have limitations, tCNNS [9] represent drugs as one-dimensional strings, which is not a natural way to describe drugs. GraphDRP [8] only use the topological structure information of drugs, didn't utilize the local chemical context in SMILES sequence.

Enlightened by these works, we utilize the Sequence Representation Learning Module and the Graph Representation Learning Module to simultaneously obtain the local chemical context and the topological structure information to predict the response.

## 3   Model Framework

In this section, we introduce the proposed model for the drug response prediction, namely DGSDRP. Firstly, we convert SMILES sequences into molecular graphs and utilize the Graph Representation Learning Module to learn the graph representation. Secondly, we encode and embed the symbols in the SMILES sequence and use the Sequence Representation Learning Module to obtain the SMILES representation. Thirdly, the cell line is converted to a one-hot format with a vector of 735 dimensions, then we use the Cell line Representation Learning Module to capture the cell line representation. Finally, the Prediction Module concatenates all representations through several dense layers to predict the response. Figure 1 illustrates the framework of our proposed DGSDRP model.

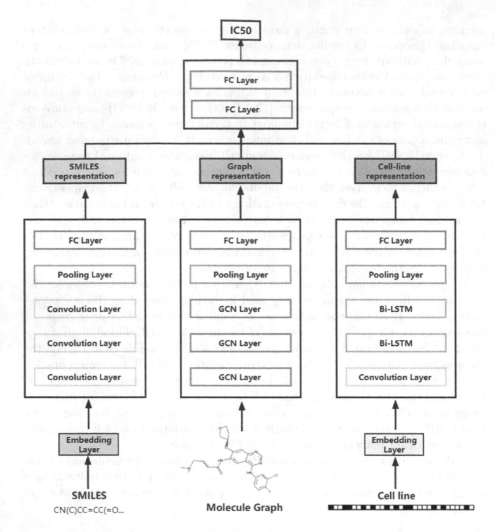

**Fig. 1.** The architecture of DGSDRP. The SMILES sequence is encoded and embedded by the Embedding Layer, then we use the Sequence Representation Learning Module to obtain the SMILES representation. We use the RDKit to convert the SMILES sequence to the molecular graph, then utilize the Graph Representation Learning Module to learn graph representation. The cell line is encoded by one-hot encoding and embedded by the Embedding Layer. Then, we apply the Cell line Representation Learning Module to extract the representation of the cell line. Finally, the three representations are concatenated and passed through several dense fully connected layers to predict the response.

## 3.1   Sequence Representation Learning Module

Drugs are usually presented as SMILES sequence, a specification for explicitly describing molecular structures in ASCII strings. For example, the SMILES string "CN(C)CC=CC(=O..." for a drug in Fig. 1 is a sequence of atoms and chemical bonds. SMILES rules can cover atoms, ions, chemical bonds, valences, chemical reactions, which can accurately express branched, cyclic, tetrahedral, aromatic, and chiral structures, as well as the expression of isomers and isotopes.

CNN can capture local features with the help of filters, and the work of CNN in pattern recognition also shows that as the number of filters increases, the model becomes better at recognition [24]. Therefore, for a SMILES sequence, we first use the Embedding Layer to encode and embed the symbols in the sequence and obtain a two-dimensional representation. Then, we use three consecutive one-dimensional convolutional layers to process the two-dimensional representation. Meanwhile, the number of filters in convolutional layers will increase with the number of CNN layers. The number of filters in convolutional layers will increase with the number of CNN layers. The filters number of the second layer is double of the first layer, and the filters number of the third layer is four times that of the first layer. Each CNN layer is followed by a nonlinear activation function ReLU to capture the nonlinear relationship between the layers. Finally, we obtain the SMILES representation through the max-pooling layer and the fully connected layer.

## 3.2    Graph Representation Learning Module

We use the open-source chemical information software RDKit to construct each input SMILES sequence into a molecular graph. To describe each node in the graph, we adopt an atom feature design based on DeepChem [23]. In detail, the node feature vector consists of the following five atomic features: atom symbol, atomicity-bond neighbor number plus Hydrogen number, the total number of Hydrogen, implicit value of the atom, and whether the atom is aromatic. When we obtain molecular graphs, the problem is to employ an algorithm that can efficiently learn from graph-structured data. GCN is a powerful neural network that can directly process the molecular graph and utilize graph structure information. Recently, a study had theoretically proved that GIN achieved maximum discriminative power among GCNs [27]. Furthermore, GIN was evaluated as the best one in both drug-target affinity prediction, GraphDTA [17], and drug response prediction, GraphDRP [8]. Therefore, we utilize GIN and a combined GAT-GCN architecture as the main component in the GCN block to capture molecular graph features. The details of each GCN model are described as follows.

**GIN Model.** In GIN [27], the node feature is updated by a multi-layer perceptron (MLP) model as Formula (1):

$$MLP((1 + \varepsilon)X_i + \sum_{j \in N(i)} X_j) \tag{1}$$

where $\varepsilon$ is either a learnable parameter or fixed scalar, $X_i \in R^F$ is the node feature vector, and $N(i)$ is the set of nodes adjacent to node $i$.

Our model consists of five GIN layers, each GIN layer is followed by a nonlinear activation function ReLU to capture the nonlinear relationship between the layers. Then a global max-pooling layer is added to aggregate the entire graph representation.

**GAT-GCN Model.** In our model, we investigate the combination of GAT [26] and GCN [25] for learning representations of graphs. Specifically, the graph neural network contains two GAT layers and a GCN layer. Each layer is followed by a nonlinear activation function ReLU to capture the nonlinear relationship between the layers. Finally, the output is passed through the global max-pooling layer and the global average pooling layer to obtain the graph representation. For GAT, in each layer, the node feature can be calculated as:

$$\alpha(WX_i, WX_j) \tag{2}$$

where $X_i \in R^F$, $X_j \in R^F$ are the feature vector of node $i$ and node $j$ and $W \in R^{F' \times F}$ is the weight matrix, $F$ and $F'$ represent the feature dimensions of the input and output nodes, respectively. $\alpha$ is the attention coefficient, which represents the importance of node $j$ to node $i$. These attention coefficients are normalized by a softmax function and then used to calculate the output features for nodes as Formula (3):

$$\sigma(\sum_{j \in N(i)} \alpha_{ij} WX_j) \tag{3}$$

where $\sigma(\cdot)$ denotes the nonlinear activation function, $N(i)$ is the set of neighbors of node $i$ and $\alpha_{ij}$ represents the normalized attention coefficient. For the GCN layer, it will perform a convolution operation through Formula (4):

$$H_i^{l+1} = f(H_i^l, A_i) = \sigma(\hat{D}_i^{-1/2} \hat{A}_i \hat{D}_i^{-1/2} H_i^l W^{l+1}) \tag{4}$$

where $A_i$ is the adjacency matrix of the molecular graph, $\hat{A}_i = A_i + I$, $I$ is the identity matrix, $\hat{D}_i$ is the diagonal node degree matrix calculated by $A_i$, $\hat{D}_i \in R^{N \times N}$, $W^{l+1}$ is the weight matrix of the $l+1$ layer, $H_i^l$ is the output of the $l$ th layer, $H_i^l \in R^{N \times F^l}$, $F^l$ is the output dimension size of the $l$ th layer, and $H_i^0 = X_i$ is the feature vector of nodes.

### 3.3   Cell Line Representation Learning Module

In deep learning models, previous works usually used convolutional neural networks to capture cell line features, which only obtained the local features of the cell line. Different from these models, we propose a fusion module, the Cell line Representation Learning Module, which not only can obtain the local features but also can capture the global features of the cell line.

We first convert each cell line to a one-hot format with a vector of 735 dimensions, where 1 or 0 indicate whether a cell line has or has not had a genomic aberration, respectively. Then the vector is transformed into a two-dimensional representation through an embedding layer. Subsequently, we apply one 1D convolutions layer to extract local features of the cell line. Then the convolutions layer is followed by two Bi-LSTM layers to extract global features. Furthermore, wen use the nonlinear activation function ReLU to capture the nonlinear relationship between the layers. Finally, we obtain the cell line representation through the max-pooling layer and the fully connected layer.

# 4    Experiments and Results

## 4.1    Datasets

Large-scale drug sensitivity screening projects such as GDSC [5] and CCLE [6] generated not only -omics but also drug response data for anti-cancer drugs on thousands of cell lines. The -omics data indicates the amount of RNAs transcribed from DNA and thus the quantity of translated proteins in the cell. Therefore, the expression level of a gene represents the activity level of a gene in a certain state (e.g., disease or normal) in a cell. The drug response is a measure of drug efficiency to inhibit the vitality of cancer cells. More specifically, cell lines are cultured and treated with different doses of drugs. Finally, either an IC50 value, which indicates the dose of a particular drug needed to inhibit the biological activity by half, or an AUC (area under the dose-response curve) value is used as a response measure of a particular drug.

GDSC is the largest database of drug sensitivity for cell lines, which contains 250 drugs tested on 1,074 cell lines in that database. However, only 24 drugs were tested on 504 cell lines in CCLE. Therefore, we selected GDSC as the benchmark dataset for our study. Specifically, as in previous studies tCNNS [9] and GraphDRP [8], we used the GDSC dataset with 223 drugs, 948 cell lines, and drug response values in terms of IC50 normalized in a range (0, 1).

## 4.2    Performance Comparison

**Mixed Test.** This experiment evaluates the performance of models in known drug-cell line pairs. GDSC provides the response for 172,114 pairs [9], these data were shuffled before splitting to help the model remain general and reduce overfitting. The known pairings are divided into 80% as the training set, 10% as the validation set, and 10% as the testing set. In the training phase, the validation set is used to modify the super parameters of the model, while the testing set is used to evaluate the performance of the model.

**Blind Test.** In mixed experiments, drugs that appear in the test set may also appear in the training phase. However, we sometimes need to predict the response of a new drug, such as, a newly invented drug. This experiment was designed to evaluate the prediction performance of unseen drugs. Therefore, drugs are restricted to be present at the same time as training and testing. We randomly selected 90% of the drugs for training, including 80% of drugs used for the training set and 10% are used for the validation set. The remaining 10% of the drugs are used in the test set. Similarly, we also conduct the blind test experiment on unseen cell-lines. We randomly selected 90% of the cell-lines for the training phase and the remaining 10% of the cell-lines are used as the testing set.

## 4.3    Evaluation Metrics

For GDSC [5] dataset, we use the same training/validating/testing data ratio as GraphDRP [8] in our experiments, 80% as the training set, 10% as the validation set, and 10% as the testing set. Besides, we use the same metrics as GraphDRP and tCNNS [9] to measure the performance of models: Root Mean Squared Error(RMSE) and Pearson correlation coefficient ($CC_P$). RMSE is a common metric to measure the difference between the predicted value and the real value, which is calculated as Formula (5):

$$RMSE = \sqrt{\frac{1}{n} \sum_{i=1}^{n} (p_i - y_i)^2} \tag{5}$$

where $p_i$ is the predicted value, $y_i$ is the true value, and $n$ is the number of samples.

Pearson correlation coefficient measures how strong a relationship is between true values $y_i$ and predicted values $p_i$. The $\sigma_p$ and $\sigma_y$ are the standard deviation of the predicted value $p_i$ and true value $y_i$, respectively. $CC_P$ is calculated as Formula (6):

$$CC_p = \frac{\sum_{i=1}^{n} (p_i - y_i)^2}{\sigma_p \sigma_y} \tag{6}$$

## 4.4    Results and Discussion

To examine the competitiveness of our proposed model, we compare our model with the current state-of-the-art models. We conduct experiments to evaluate the performance of our model and the current state-of-the-art models, which include: performance comparison and prediction of unknown drug-cell line response.

**Table 1.** Prediction performance on GDSC dataset in the mixed test experiment, sorted by RMSE. Bold: better than baselines.

| Method | Drug | Cell line | RMSE | $CC_p$ |
|---|---|---|---|---|
| tCNNS | CNN | CNN | 0.0284 | 0.9160 |
| GraphDRP | GCN | | 0.0261 | 0.9201 |
| | GAT | | 0.0252 | 0.9277 |
| | GIN | | 0.0250 | 0.9284 |
| | GAT_GCN | | 0.0249 | 0.9306 |
| DGSDRP (ours) | | | | |
| GIN | CNN+GIN | CNN+Bi-LSTM | **0.0228** | **0.9393** |
| GAT_GCN | CNN+GAT_GCN | CNN+Bi-LSTM | **0.0227** | **0.9402** |

For the mixed experiment (Table 1), the best RMSE for baseline is 0.0249, obtained by GraphDRP. In comparison, our proposed models all outperform GraphDRP and achieve a better RMSE. The best RMSE obtained by our model is 0.0227, which is a reduction of 8.8% over the best baseline. In terms of $CC_p$, our model also has improved in performance, the best $CC_p$ which is obtained by our method is 0.9402.

**Table 2.** Prediction performance on GDSC dataset in the blind test with the unseen drug experiment, sorted by RMSE. Bold: better than baselines.

| Method | Drug | Cell line | RMSE | $CC_p$ |
|---|---|---|---|---|
| tCNNS | CNN | CNN | 0.0763 | 0.0617 |
| GraphDRP | GCN | | 0.0750 | 0.2122 |
| | GIN | | 0.0731 | 0.2277 |
| | GAT | | 0.0699 | 0.2878 |
| | GAT_GCN | | 0.0694 | 0.3280 |
| DGSDRP (ours) | | | | |
| GAT_GCN | CNN+GAT_GCN | CNN+Bi-LSTM | **0.0515** | **0.3652** |
| GIN | CNN+GIN | CNN+Bi-LSTM | **0.0503** | **0.4285** |

**Table 3.** Prediction performance on GDSC dataset in the blind test with the unseen cell-line experiment, sorted by RMSE. Bold: better than baselines.

| Method | Drug | Cell line | RMSE | $CC_p$ |
|---|---|---|---|---|
| tCNNS | CNN | CNN | 0.0576 | 0.3490 |
| GraphDRP | GAT | | 0.0411 | 0.8018 |
| | GCN | | 0.0394 | 0.8091 |
| | GAT_GCN | | 0.0390 | 0.8143 |
| | GIN | | 0.0384 | 0.8224 |
| DGSDRP (ours) | | | | |
| GIN | CNN+GIN | CNN+Bi-LSTM | **0.0368** | **0.8369** |
| GAT_GCN | CNN+GAT_GCN | CNN+Bi-LSTM | **0.0351** | **0.8492** |

For the blind experiment with unseen drugs (Table 2), in terms of RMSE and $CC_p$, our proposed models all outperform GraphDRP and achieve better RMSE and $CC_p$. For GraphDRP, the best RMES is 0.0694 and the best $CC_p$ is 0.3280. Meanwhile, the best RMSE obtained by our model is 0.0503, which is a reduction of 27.5% over GraphDRP and the best $CC_p$ which is obtained by our method is 0.4285.

Similar to the drug blind test, in the blind experiment with unseen cell-lines (Table 3), our proposed models also all outperform other models. The best RMSE obtained by our model is 0.0351, which is a reduction of 8.6% over GraphDRP at 0.0384. In terms of $CC_p$, the best $CC_p$ for GraphDRP is 0.8224, the best $CC_p$ for our proposed models is 0.8492.

From Table 1, Table 2, and Table 3, we can find that our model outperforms tCNNS [9] and GraphDRP [8] in the mixed experiment and the blind experiment. The reason is as follows: (i) compared with tCNNS, we can exploit the topological structure of molecular graphs through the Graph Representation Learning Module; (ii) compared with GraphDRP, we can utilize the local chemical context of the compound by the Sequence Representation Learning Module.

### 4.5    Ablation Experiment

To further validate the effect of the different components in DGSDRP, we conduct ablation experiments on the GDSC dataset with the mixed experiment. Table 4 shows the effectiveness of the Sequence Representation Learning Module and the Graph Representation Learning Module. DGSDRP-SC only uses the Sequence Representation Learning Module and the Cell line Representation Learning Module. DGSDRP-GC only uses the Graph Representation Learning Module and the Cell line Representation Learning Module. DGSDRP-SGC uses the Sequence Representation Learning Module, the Graph Representation Learning Module, and the Cell line Representation Learning Module. When we conduct ablation experiments, the Graph Representation Learning Module is based on the GAT-GCN model.

**Table 4.** Ablation experiments on GDSC dataset with the mixed experiment, sorted by RMSE.

| Model | SMILES | Graph | Cell line | RMSE | $CC_p$ |
|---|---|---|---|---|---|
| DGSDRP-GC | √ | | √ | 0.0249 | 0.9289 |
| DGSDRP-SC | | √ | √ | 0.0241 | 0.9315 |
| DGSDRP-SGC | √ | √ | √ | 0.0227 | 0.9402 |

From Table 4, we can find that in the drug response prediction task, the performance of DGSDRP-GC and DGSDRP-SC are worse than DGSDRP-SGC. The reason is that the topological structure of the molecule graph can reveal the connection relationship between atoms, while the SMILES sequences contains the local chemical context that can uncover the interaction function between atoms. Besides, we can find that our proposed model significantly outperforms other models in the blind test with the unseen drug experiment (Table 2), the fact strongly indicates that the combination of SMILES sequences and molecular graphs applied in DGSDRP are efficient and effective in drug response prediction task. Therefore, in the drug response prediction task, we should consider both the molecular topological structures and the local chemical context, which is beneficial to the performance.

# 5  Conclusion

In this paper, we propose a novel method for drug response prediction, called DGSDRP, which combines the molecular structural features (representation based on molecular graph) and the local chemical context (representation based on SMILES sequence). A GCN model is used to extract the topological structure of the molecular graph, and a CNN model is used to obtain the local chemical context of the SMILES sequence. We also designed a fusion module based on convolutional neural networks and bidirectional long short-term memory (Bi-LSTM) to capture cell line features. We conduct mixed and blind experiments to compare our model with state-of-the-art models, the experimental results indicate that our model outperforms current state-of-the-art models in terms of RMSE and $CC_p$. In the future, we plan to utilize the SMILES representation and the graph representation through an attention mechanism to further improve the performance of our model.

**Acknowledgement.** This work was supported by the National Natural Science Foundation of China (No. 61972135), and the Natural Science Foundation of Heilongjiang Province in China (No. LH2020F043).

# References

1. Hutchinson, L., DeVita, V.: The era of personalized medicine: back to basics. Nat. Rev. Clin. Oncol. **5**, 623 (2008)
2. Marquart, J., Chen, E.Y., Prasad, V.: Estimation of the percentage of US patients with cancer who benefit from genome-driven oncology. Jama Oncol. **4**(8), 1093–1098 (2018)
3. Weinstein, J.N., Collisson, E.A., Mills, G.B., et al.: The cancer genome atlas pancancer analysis project. Nat. Genet. **45**(10), 1113 (2013)
4. Zhang, J., Baran, J., Cros, A., et al.: International cancer genome consortium data portal-a one-stop shop for cancer genomics data. Database (Oxford) **Database**(2011), bar026 (2011)
5. Yang, W., Jorge, S., Patricia, G., et al.: Genomics of drug sensitivity in cancer (GDSC): a resource for therapeutic biomarker discovery in cancer cells. Nucleic Acids Res. **41**(D1), D955–D961 (2012)
6. Barretina, J., Caponigro, G., Stransky, N., et al.: The cancer cell line encyclopedia enables predictive modelling of anticancer drug sensitivity. Nature **483**, 603–607 (2012)
7. Shoemaker, R.: The NCI60 human tumour cell line anticancer drug screen. Nat. Rev. Cancer **6**, 813–823 (2006)
8. Nguyen, T., Nguyen, G.T.T., Nguyen, T., Le, D.-H.: Graph convolutional networks for drug response prediction. IEEE ACM Trans. Comput. Biol. Bioinform. **19**(1), 146–154 (2022)
9. Liu, P., Li, H., Li, S., et al.: Improving prediction of phenotypic drug response on cancer cell lines using deep convolutional network. BMC Bioinform. **20**(1), 408 (2019)
10. Li, M., et al.: DeepDSC: a deep learning method to predict drug sensitivity of cancer cell lines. IEEE ACM Trans. Comput. Biol. Bioinform. **18**(2), 575–582 (2019)

11. Cortés-Ciriano, I., Bender, A.: KekuleScope: prediction of cancer cell line sensitivity and compound potency using convolutional neural networks trained on compound images. J. Cheminform. **11**(1), 1–16 (2019). https://doi.org/10.1186/s13321-019-0364-5
12. Ding, M.Q., Chen, L., Cooper, G.F., Young, J.D., Lu, X.: Precision oncology beyond targeted therapy: combining omics data with machine learning matches the majority of cancer cells to effective therapeutics. Mol. Cancer Res. **16**(2), 269–278 (2018)
13. Rampášek, L., Hidru, D., Smirnov, P., Haibe-Kains, B., Goldenberg, A.: Dr.VAE: improving drug response prediction via modeling of drug perturbation effects. Bioinformatics **35**(19), 3743–3751 (2019)
14. Wang, Y., Fang, J., Chen, S.: Inferences of drug responses in cancer cells from cancer genomic features and compound chemical and therapeutic properties. Sci. Rep. **6**, 32679 (2016)
15. Rahman, R., Matlock, K., Ghosh, S., Pal, R.: Heterogeneity aware random forest for drug sensitivity prediction. Sci. Rep. **7**(1), 11347 (2017)
16. Zhang, N., Wang, H., Fang, Y., Wang, J., Zheng, X., Liu, X.S.: Predicting anti-cancer drug responses using a dual-layer integrated cell line-drug network model. PLoS Comput. Biol. **11**(9), e1004498 (2015)
17. Li, M., et al.: GraphDTA: predicting drug-target binding affinity with graph neural networks. Bioinformatics **37**(8), 1140–1147 (2021)
18. Zeng, Y., Chen, X., Luo, Y., et al.: Deep drug-target binding affinity prediction with multiple attention blocks. Briefings Bioinform. **22**(5), bbab117 (2021)
19. Gonczarek, A., Tomczak, J.M., Zareba, S., Kaczmar, J., Dabrowski, P., Walczak, M.J.: Interaction prediction in structure-based virtual screening using deep learning. Comput. Biol. Med. **100**, 253–258 (2018)
20. Karimi, M., Wu, D., Wang, Z., Shen, Y.: DeepAffinity: interpretable deep learning of compound-protein affinity through unified recurrent and convolutional neural networks. Bioinformatics **38**(18), 3329–3338 (2019)
21. Özt ürk, H., Özg ür, A., Ozkirimli, E.: DeepDTA: deep drug-target binding affinity prediction. Bioinformatics **34**(17), i821–i829 (2018)
22. Wang, L., You, Z.-H., Chen, X., Xia, S.-X., et al.: A computational-based method for predicting drug-target interactions by using stacked autoencoder deep neural network. J. Comput. Biol. **25**(3), 361–373 (2018)
23. Ramsundar, B., Eastman, P., Walters, P.: Deep Learning for the Life Sciences: Applying Deep Learning to Genomics, Microscopy, Drug Discovery, and More, vol. 1, 2nd edn. O'Reilly, New York (2019)
24. Kang, L., Ye, P., Li, Y., et al.: Convolutional neural networks for no-reference image quality assessment. In: Proceedings of the IEEE Conference on Computer Vision and Pattern Recognition (CVPR 2014) (2014)
25. Kipf, T.N., Welling, M.: Semi-supervised classification with graph convolutional networks. In: Proceedings of the International Conference on Learning Representations (ICLR 2017) (2017)
26. Elickovic, P.V., Cucurull, G., Casanova, A.: Graph attention networks. In: Proceedings of the International Conference on Learning Representations (ICLR 2018) (2018)
27. Xu, K., Hu, W., Leskovec, J.: How powerful are graph neural networks. In: Proceedings of the International Conference on Learning Representations (ICLR 2019) (2019)
28. Weininger, D.: SMILES, a chemical language and information system. 1. Introduction to methodology and encoding rules. J. Chem. Inf. Comput. Sci. **28**(1), 31–36 (1988)

# DOT-VAE: Disentangling One Factor at a Time

Vaishnavi Patil[✉], Matthew Evanusa, and Joseph JaJa

University of Maryland, College Park, MD 20740, USA
{vspatil,mevanusa,josephj}@umd.edu

**Abstract.** As we enter the era of machine learning characterized by an overabundance of data, discovery, organization, and interpretation of the data in an *unsupervised* manner becomes a critical need. One promising approach to this endeavour is the problem of *Disentanglement*, which aims at learning the underlying generative latent factors, called the factors of variation, of the data and encoding them in disjoint latent representations. Recent advances have made efforts to solve this problem for synthetic datasets generated by a fixed set of independent factors of variation. Here, we propose to extend this to real-world datasets with a countable number of factors of variations. We propose a novel framework which augments the latent space of a Variational Autoencoders with a disentangled space and is trained using a Wake-Sleep-inspired two-step algorithm for unsupervised disentanglement. Our network learns to disentangle interpretable, independent factors from the data "one at a time", and encode it in different dimensions of the disentangled latent space, while making no prior assumptions about the number of factors or their joint distribution. We demonstrate its quantitative and qualitative effectiveness by evaluating the latent representations learned on two synthetic benchmark datasets; DSprites and 3DShapes and on a real datasets CelebA.

**Keywords:** Deep learning · Representation learning · Unsupervised disentanglement

## 1 Introduction

Deep learning models, which are now widely adopted across multiple Artificial Intelligence tasks ranging from vision to music generation to game playing [16,22,23], owe their success to their ability to learn representations from the data rather than requiring hand-crafted features. However, this self-learning of abstract representations comes at the known cost of the resulting representations being cryptic and inscrutable to human observers [8]. A more comprehensive representation of the data where the essential indivisible, semantic concepts are encoded in structurally disentangled parts could lead to successful domain

Supported by University of Maryland.

E. Pimenidis et al. (Eds.): ICANN 2022, LNCS 13529, pp. 109–120, 2022.
https://doi.org/10.1007/978-3-031-15919-0_10

adaptation and transfer learning [1] and facilitate robust downstream learning more effectively [27]. Learning these latent representations from the data alone without the need of laborious labeling by human observers constitutes the problem of *Unsupervised Disentanglement*. In this work, we attempt to address the problem of unsupervised disentanglement via a novel Variational Autoencoder based framework and training algorithm.

Though there is no commonly accepted formalized notion of disentanglement or validation metrics [11], recent works have characterized disentangled representations, based on natural intuition. This intuition by [1] states that a disentangled representation is a representation of the data which encodes each *factor of variation* in disjoint sets of the latent representation. [21] state further that a change in a single factor of variation produces a change in only a subset of the learned latent representation which corresponds to that factor. Here, a factor of variation is an abstract human defined concept that assumes different values for different examples in the dataset. This intuition is closely related to the independent mechanisms assumption [26] which renders the informative factors as components of a causal mechanism. This assumption allows interventions on one factor without affecting the other factors or the representations corresponding to the other factors and thus can be independently controlled. In our work we use independent interventions on the learned disentangled representations, which encode the different factors, to generate samples and restrict the differences in corresponding representations, of the data and the sample, pertaining to that factor. This process of using interventions and generating new samples resembles the sleep phase of the wake-sleep algorithm.

Most current Variational Autoencoder (VAE) based state-of-the-art (SOTA) make the implicit assumption that there are a fixed number of independent factors, common for all the data points in the dataset. However in real datasets, in addition to the independent factors common to all points in the dataset, there might also be some correlated, noisy factors pertinent to only certain data points. While the approaches based on Generative Adversarial Networks (GAN) do not make an assumption, they learn only a subset of the disentangled factors, whose number is heuristically chosen. We believe however that one of the main goals of disentanglement is to glean insights to the data, and the number of factors of variation is generally one that we do not have access to. To this end, our method augments the entangled latent space of a VAE with a disentangled latent code, and iteratively encodes each factor, common to all the data points, in a single disentangled code using interventions. This process allows our model to learn any number of factors, without prior knowledge or "hardcoding", thus making it better suited for real datasets.

## 1.1   Main Contributions

Our contributions in the proposed work are:

– We introduce a novel, completely unsupervised method for solving disentanglement, which offers the mode-covering properties of a VAE along with the interpretability of the factors afforded by the GANs, to better encode the factors of variations in the disentangled code, while encoding the other informative factors in the entangled representations.

- Our proposed model is the first unsupervised method that is capable of learning an arbitrary number of latent factors via iterative unsupervised interventions in the latent space.
- We test and evaluate our algorithm on two standard datasets and across multiple quantitative SOTA metrics and qualitatively on one dataset. Our qualitative empirical results on synthetic datasets show that our model successfully disentangles independent factors. Across all quantitative metrics, our model generally outperforms existing methods for unsupervised disentanglement[1].

## 2    Disentangling One Factor at a Time Using Interventions

We base our framework on the VAE which assumes that data $x$ is generated from a set of latent features $z \in \mathbb{R}^d$ with a prior $p(z)$. A generator $p_\theta(x|z)$ maps the latent features to the high-dimensional data $x$. The generator, modeled as a neural network, is trained to maximize the total log-likelihood of the data, $\log p_\theta(X)$. However, due to the intractability of calculating the exact log-likelihood, the VAE instead maximizes an evidence lower-bound (ELBO) using an approximate posterior distribution $q_\phi(z|x)$ modeled by an encoder neural network. For given data, this encoder projects the data to a lower-dimensional representation $z$, such that the data can be reconstructed by the generator given only the representation. Without any structural constraints, the dimensions of the inferred latent representation $z$ are informative but entangled. **Disjoint Latent Sets:** To encode the factors of variation in an interpretable way, following [6] we augment the unstructured variables $z$ with a set of structured variables $c = \{c_1, c_2, \cdots, c_K\}$ each of which is tasked with disentangling an independent semantic attribute of the data. We train our network to systematically discern the meaningful latent factors shared across the dataset into $c$, from the entangled representation $z$, both of which are important to maximize the log-likelihood of the data. However, it is only the most informative, common factors of variation encoded in $c$ that we are interested in, as the remaining factors in $z$ are confounded and contain the 'noise' in the dataset, i.e., features that only a few data samples contain.

The generator is now conditioned both on the disentangled latent codes and the entangled latent space $(c, z)$ and describes a causal mechanism [27], where each causal component $c_k$ is independently controllable and a change in a particular index $k$ has no effect on any other index $c_j (j \neq k)$. Manipulating each $c_k$ should correspond to a distinct, semantic change, corresponding to the factor encoded, in the generated sample, without entangling with changes effected by the other factors or with the entangled code $z$. To this end, we perform *interventions* as proposed in [27] (described in detail below) that go into the latent

---

[1] Code available at https://github.com/DOTFactor/DOTFactor.

code, change a single dimension $c_k$ of the disentangled code $c$ while keeping the other dimensions the same. We generate data from this intervened latent and then constrain the model to reconstruct the exact change.

To encourage the generator to make distinct changes for each $c_k$ that is manipulated during interventions, we re-encode the data to recover the manipulated latent representation that was used to generate the data. Thus if the code $c_i$ was manipulated, while keeping the rest $c_j(j \neq i)$ and $z$ unchanged, the encoding of the corresponding generated data must reflect a change only in the manipulated code $c_i$.

**Adversarial Latent Network:** Moreover, in order to ensure that interpretable factors are encoded in the disentangled code $c$, the changes effected by each $c_k$ must correspond to a semantic change in the generated data corresponding to a change which could be effected by a factor of variation. For this, the data generated from the disentangled code manipulation during interventions must lie in the true data distribution. To ensure this we train a discriminator, like in [14], in the latent space such that the latent representations after manipulations continue to lie in the distribution of the encodings of the true data. The encoder is trained to reduce the distance between the distribution of the representations, used by the generator to reconstruct the data, and the distribution of the representations after they have been intervened on. This in effect helps us train a generative model which can be conditioned to generate realistic, new samples with any desired values for the different latent factor. Figure 1 shows the overall framework which is trained with a two step algorithm inspired by the wake-sleep algorithm.

**Model Structure and Learning:** In this section we will detail the training method, and how to combine the architectural components described earlier. We augment the latent space $z$ to include a disentangled set of latent codes $c$ with prior $p(c) = \prod_{i=1}^{K} p(c_i)$, where $p(c_i) \sim \mathcal{N}(0, 1)$. The encoder $q_\phi(c, z|x)$ is split into two to model the distributions of the two latent variables as $q_{\phi_1}(z|x)$ and $q_{\phi_2}(c|x)$ respectively. Under this augmented space the evidence lower-bound of the data log-likelihood is as follows:

$$\mathcal{L}_{\theta,\phi} = -\mathbb{E}_{q(x)}[\mathbb{E}_{q_\phi(c,z|x)}[\log p_\theta(x|c, z)] + KL[q_{\phi_1}(z|x)||p(z)] \\ + KL[q_{\phi_2}(c|x)||p(c)]] \tag{1}$$

where $q(x)$ is the empirical training data distribution. The first term in the above objective function minimizes the error of reconstructing the higher-dimensional data from it's lower-dimensional representations. The KL divergence in the second and the third terms ensure that posterior distribution learned by the model is close to the uninformative prior distribution, and can be sampled from for generating new samples. These three terms together create an information bottleneck in the latent space where only the information relevant to recover the data is encoded in the representations. This ensures that all the informative factors of variations are encoded in the representations either in $z$ or in $c$.

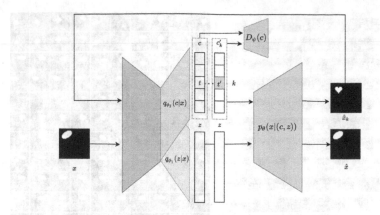

**Fig. 1.** The full architecture of Dot-VAE. Input data is fed into an encoder, which projects the data into two disjoint latent spaces, a disentangled $c$ and entangled $z$. *Interventions* change the value $t$ of a single disentangled latent at index $k$ to a new value $t'$ while keeping the other latents unchanged to get the intervened representation $(c'_k, z)$. The adversarial network ensures that the distribution of the real representations $c$ and the intervened representations $c'_k$ is close to each other. The decoder maps the intervened latents to generated data $\hat{x}_k$. This new generated data is passed back through the encoder to train the generator to make distinct and noticeable changes.

**Learning One Factor at a Time.** Since we want each disentangled latent code $c_k \in c$ to encode a factor of variation, changes in the value of a latent code $c_k$, while keeping the others the same, should bring about semantic changes in the generated samples corresponding *only* to the encoded factor. The changes should be such that when the original data and the generated data (after interventions) are compared, the encoder must be able to discern (1) the index of the changed latent variable, and (2) by how much it was changed. We enforce these conditions by performing interventions on one code at a time and reconstructing the latents of the interventions, sequentially. At the beginning of training, we start with interventions on the first element of the disentangled space $c_1$. Once the objective in Eq. 1 saturates for interventions with $c_1$, we shift the interventions to the next element in the set, $c_2$ along with $c_1$. As the training proceeds, more dimensions of $c$ are intervened upon together and the network learns to encode the confounding information into $z$, while keeping only the disentangled information in $c$. For synthetic datasets with a fixed number of factors of variations, we continue iterating through the elements of $c$ until the entangled part of the representation $z$ encodes no information i.e. $KL(q_{\phi_1}(z|x)||p(z)) = 0$. For real-world datasets we can continue the iteration until we find a desired number of factors.

Formally, given a batch $B$ of examples from the data distribution $\{x^i\}_{i=1}^{B}$, which we write as $\{x^i\}^B$ for brevity, we first encode the batch to find their latent representation $\{(c^i, z^i) \sim q(c, z|x^i)\}^B$. We then select an index $k \in [K]$ and proceed to intervene/change the value of the element $c_k$, which we refer to as $\{t^i\}^B$, of the disentangled code, to $\{t'^i\}^B$ (i.e. to the value of another

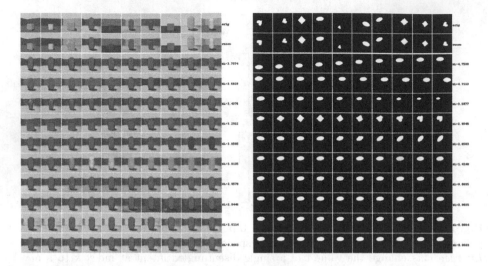

**Fig. 2.** Latent traversals for the disentangled code $c$ for 3Dshapes (Left) and Dsprites dataset (Right). Our method disentangles the informative factors and encodes them in the different dimensions of $c$. The top two rows are the original and reconstructed images, respectively. Each row below the second corresponds to a traversal. *3DShapes (Left):* Each row corresponds to a distinct independent factor. Rows three through ten correspond to orientation, wall hue, size, scale, object hue (two rows), floor color (two rows) respectively. This covers all of the exact factors of variation. In the last row, we can see the model discerned it had discovered all the factors of variation, and need not encode anything. *dSprites: (Right)* Similarly, in dSprites we can also see that the model discerns the factors in rows 3 through 7: x, y coordinate, size, shape, and orientation.

example $t^l(l \neq i)$ at the same dimension $c_k$), for all the representations in the batch, while keeping the other disentangled codes $c_j(j \neq k)$ and the entangled representations $z$ the same. We change the value only for that code to obtain our intervened latent representation $\{c'_k{}^i = (t'^i, c^i_j(j \neq k))\}^B$. We then use these intervened representations to generate a batch of samples $\{\hat{x}^i_k \sim p_\theta(x|c'_k{}^i, z^i)\}^B$.

The generated samples $\{\hat{x}^i_k\}^B$ must differ from the data examples $\{x^i\}^B$ only in the factor corresponding to one encoded in $c_k$. To ensure this, we re-encode the generated samples to reconstruct the intervened latent representation $\{\hat{c}^i_k \sim q_\phi(c, z|\hat{x}^i_k)\}^B$ and optimize the generator to minimize the reconstruction cost as follows:

$$\mathcal{L}_\theta = \frac{1}{B} \sum_{i=1}^{B} \|\hat{c}^i_k - c'_k{}^i\|^2 \tag{2}$$

Since we enforce the model to exactly reconstruct the intervened latent representation, from the generated samples alone, the generator can only make the distinct and noticeable change corresponding to the factor encoded in the intervened disentangled code after converging.

**Fig. 3.** Traversals over latent space $c$ for the *CelebA* real-world celebrity dataset. The dataset consists of cropped headshots of various celebrities. Given a seed image, we perform a traversal across various latents. Our model successfully produces reconstructions that correspond to identifiable factors. Like for synthetic data, some of the latents remain unused; shown are exemplar latents that encoded factors of variation. The model learns many more factors as compared to previous methods such as hair color, skin tone, lighting, etc.

Moreover, we want to ensure that manipulations in the disentangled code $c$ translate to semantic changes in the generated samples thus making them interpretable. To this effect the generator should be constrained to map the intervened representations to examples which lie strictly in the true data manifold. Instead we constrain the encoder to reduce the distance between the posterior distribution $q_{\phi_2}(c)$ and the intervened latent distribution $p(c')$. To this effect we train an adversarial network $D_\psi$ to distinguish between the original representations $c$ and the intervened representations $c'$ by maximizing the following objective:

$$\mathcal{L}_\psi = \mathbb{E}_{p(c')}[\log(D_\psi(c'))] + \mathbb{E}_{c \sim q_{\phi_2}(c|x)}[\log(1 - D_\psi(c))] \tag{3}$$

The encoder is in turn trained to fool the discriminator by making the approximate posterior distribution of $c$ indistinguishable from the intervened representations $c'$ by minimizing the following object:

$$\mathcal{L}_\phi = \mathbb{E}_{c \sim q_{\phi_2}(c|x)}[\log(1 - D_\psi(c))] \tag{4}$$

Since the VAE objective constrains the generator to map the representations to the true data distribution, to minimize the reconstruction cost in the image space, the generator now also maps the intervened representations also to the true data distribution.

We combine the losses in $\{1, 2, 4\}$ linearly to train the encoder and the generator to minimize the following objective:

$$\mathcal{L} = \mathcal{L}_{\theta,\phi} + \lambda \mathcal{L}_\phi + \gamma \mathcal{L}_\theta \tag{5}$$

The latent discriminator $D_\psi$ is trained jointly with the other networks to maximize the objective $\mathcal{L}_\psi$. For the first few epochs, we train the model to maximize the likelihood with the discriminator loss and only start the interventions after a few epochs of training.

**Table 1.** Comparisons of the popular disentanglement metrics on the dSprites dataset. A perfect disentanglement corresponds to 1.0 scores. For all scores, **higher is better**. The scores are averages over 10 runs with different random seeds. The values for the GAN-based models were taken from [19]. Our model outperforms all the VAE-based models while performing comparably with the GAN-based models. DOT-VAE[1] corresponds to the model where intervened values are the values for other samples for the same intervened index whereas DOT-VAE[2] corresponds to the intervened values sampled from the prior distribution.

| Model | FactorVAE | DCI | MIG | BetaVAE | Modularity | Explicitness |
|---|---|---|---|---|---|---|
| $\beta$-VAE (24) | $0.65 \pm .11$ | $0.18 \pm .10$ | 0.11 | $0.83 \pm .30$ | $0.82 \pm .03$ | 0.81 |
| $\beta$-TCVAE | $0.76 \pm .18$ | $0.30 \pm .05$ | 0.18 | $0.88 \pm .18$ | $0.85 \pm .03$ | 0.83 |
| FactorVAE(40) | $0.75 \pm .12$ | $0.26 \pm .04$ | 0.15 | $0.85 \pm .15$ | $0.81 \pm .02$ | 0.80 |
| InfoGAN* | $0.82 \pm .01$ | $0.60 \pm .02$ | 0.22 | $0.87 \pm .01$ | $0.94 \pm .01$ | 0.82 |
| InfoGAN-CR* | $\mathbf{0.88 \pm .01}$ | $\mathbf{0.71 \pm .01}$ | 0.37 | $0.95 \pm .01$ | **0.96** | 0.85 |
| DOT-VAE[1] (ours) | $0.77 \pm .12$ | $0.66 \pm .06$ | **0.38** | $0.95 \pm .13$ | $0.86 \pm .05$ | **0.86** |
| DOT-VAE[2] (ours) | $0.72 \pm .15$ | $\mathbf{0.72 \pm .06}$ | 0.34 | $\mathbf{0.97 \pm .18}$ | $0.82 \pm 0.02$ | 0.84 |

## 3   Related Work

Various authors have attempted to learn unsupervised disentangled representations using generative models in recent years. SOTA for unsupervised disentanglement learning can be broadly classified into two categories based on the type of generative model used; one via Variational Autoencoders (VAE) [15,24], and another via Generative Adversarial Networks (GAN) [9]. Techniques that use VAEs have been modifications of the base VAE architecture to further facilitate a structured latent code. The $\beta$-VAE [10] heavily penalize the KL divergence term thus forcing the learned posterior distribution $q_\phi(z|x)$ to be independent like the prior. AnnealedVAE [2] controls the capacity of the latent encoding to allow for the independent encoding of the factors. Factor-VAE [14] and $\beta$-TCVAE [3] penalize the total correlation of the aggregated posterior $q_\phi(z)$ using adversarial and statistical techniques respectively. DIP-VAE [17] forces the covariance matrix of the aggregated posterior $q(z)$ to be close to the identity matrix by method of moment matching. Other works improved the performance augmenting the latent space to include the discrete factors [5,13], and use optimization techniques based on annealing to encode information effectively in the discrete and continuous factors.

Models based on GANs explicitly condition the generator with a set of independent latent variables $c$ (by concatenation with random noise $z$), and train the generator to generate data which has high mutual information with $c$. The most prominent work is InfoGAN [4] which learns disentangled, semantically meaningful representations by maximizing a lower bound on the intractable mutual information between the conditioning latent variables $c$ and the generated samples $G(z, c)$. InfoGAN-CR [19] add a contrastive regularizer to the InfoGAN model, which is trained to predict the changes in the latent space given only the pairs of images. [29] augment their objective with a similar self-supervised learning

**Table 2.** Quantitative comparisons of the disentanglement metrics on the 3DShapes dataset averaged over 10 runs with different random seeds. The results for other method have been taken from [21]. For all metrics, a higher value indicates a more disentangled latent space. As we can see, DOT-VAE (our model) outperforms most of previous models.

| Model | FactorVAE | DCI | MIG | BetaVAE | Modularity | Explicitness |
|---|---|---|---|---|---|---|
| $\beta$-VAE(32) | 0.82 ± .24 | 0.58 ± .40 | 0.34 | 0.99 ± .06 | 0.94 ± .18 | 0.87 |
| $\beta$-TCVAE | 0.83 ± .20 | 0.68 ± .46 | 0.27 | **1.00 ± .07** | **0.96 ± .23** | 0.92 |
| FactorVAE(20) | 0.81 ± .26 | 0.64 ± .27 | 0.29 | 0.98 ± .07 | 0.95 ± .28 | 0.94 |
| DOT-VAE[1] (ours) | **0.95 ± .18** | **0.80 ± .30** | **0.42** | 1.00 ± .04 | 0.94 ± .19 | **0.95** |

task. In [20], the authors add orthogonal regularization to encourage independent representations. In addition, a major difference between the disjoint sets of InfoGAN and our method is that we explicitly learn the conditioning variables $c$, whereas for the GAN-based methods they are pre-determined. Moreover, we do not need to know the number of factors before-hand and instead learn them as we continue training.

The authors of [27] introduced the concept of interventions to study the robustness of the learned representations under the Independent Mechanisms (IM) assumption [26], while we use the method of interventions while training the model to disentangle common factors from their entangled set. In [18] a VAE is used to disentangle representations and then the representations are passed into a GAN to generate high-fidelity images; our approach instead uses both VAEs and GANs for disentanglement. In [6] the latent space of entangled representations is conditioned with a disentangled code, which is learned in a supervised way using specific attribute discriminators. As far as the authors are aware, we are the first to split the latent dimension into entangled and disentangled in a completely unsupervised way, as well as the first to combine this with interventions, and with incremental learning.

## 4    Empirical Evaluation

For evaluation, we run experiments on three benchmark datasets: two synthetic datasets generated from independent ground truth factors of variation; dSprites [30] and 3DShapes [31]. Each datapoint in these datasets can be exactly described using their factors of generation. For a real-world dataset, with unknown factors of variation, we run our model on the CelebA dataset [32]. This dataset has a copious amount of noise in each sample, and cannot neatly be described as independent factors.

**Qualitative Analysis.** To demonstrate the disentangling ability of our model, we perform *traversals* across the latent space, and plot the resulting reconstruction, in line with the standard methods for disentanglement. A model has better disentanglement capability if a traversal across the latent space matches with a change in a single generative factor. We demonstrate this both for the synthetic datasets (Fig. 2), as well as the real-world sets (Fig. 3).

**Quantitative Analysis.** We also evaluate the learned representations using three kinds of quantitative metrics as described in [28]. Specifically, we use the FactorVAE [14], the BetaVAE [10]; Mutual Information Gap (MIG) [3] and Modularity [25]; and the Disentanglement-Completeness-Informativeness (DCI) [7] and Explicitness [25]. Results for all metrics are found in Table 1 for dSprites Table 2 for 3DShapes. We used the implementation from [21] to calculate all metrics.

### 4.1  Results and Discussion

As we can see in Fig. 2, our model successfully disentangles the dSprites and the 3DShapes dataset, with the traversals showing a change in that latent value corresponds to a change in the true factor of variation. Importantly, the "entangled" latent space $z$ encodes no information, and the model was able to, one at a time, disentangle the relevant factors of variation and encode them in $c$. This is in line with our hypothesis for synthetic datasets as the data can be exactly coded as the independent factors of variation. Our model is able to completely capture all of the factors of variation for dSprites as well as 3DShapes. We believe part of the reason for the success is the iterative, one at a time decomposition, which allows the network itself to discover how many factors there are, contrasted with prior methods that force the network to factorize the data in a given sized latent space. While the latent traversals show near perfect disentanglement, some of the metrics still report a lower value. We believe that this is because the metrics expect each factor to be completely described by a single latent variable. We do not restrict a factor to correspond to be encoded by only one latent variable as doing so amounts to complete unsupervised disentanglement as described in [21] which has been proved to be impossible. Instead we encode it in a subset of the latent variables in $c$. Thus each dimension of $c$ is encodes only one factor while each factor can be encoded in multiple dimensions of $c$. This is a common issue discussed in the community as elaborated by [7]. In Fig. 3, our results for CelebA show that the model can discern the different factors while maintaining a low reconstruction error.

### 4.2  Conclusion

In this work, we present DOT-VAE, or Disentangling One at a Time VAE, a method of disentangling latent factors of variation in a dataset without any *a priori* knowledge of how many factors the dataset contains. We demonstrate that DOT-VAE is on par with or outperforms state of the art methods for disentanglement on standard metrics, and generates crisp, clear and interpretable latent traversal reconstructions for qualitative evaluation. Future directions could be to disentangle multiple datasets together using DOT-VAE while ensuring that the model reuses the learned factors and does not catastrophically forget them when new datasets are introduced.

# References

1. Bengio, Y.: Deep learning of representations: looking forward. In: Dediu, A.-H., Martín-Vide, C., Mitkov, R., Truthe, B. (eds.) SLSP 2013. LNCS (LNAI), vol. 7978, pp. 1–37. Springer, Heidelberg (2013). https://doi.org/10.1007/978-3-642-39593-2_1
2. Burgess, C.P., et al.: Understanding disentangling in $\beta$-VAE. arXiv preprint arXiv:1804.03599 (2018)
3. Chen, R.T., Li, X., Grosse, R.B., Duvenaud, D.K.: Isolating sources of disentanglement in variational autoencoders. In: Advances in Neural Information Processing Systems, vol. 31 (2018)
4. Chen, X., Duan, Y., Houthooft, R., Schulman, J., Sutskever, I., Abbeel, P.: InfoGAN: interpretable representation learning by information maximizing generative adversarial nets. In: Advances in Neural Information Processing Systems, Chicago, vol. 29 (2016)
5. Dupont, E.: Learning disentangled joint continuous and discrete representations. In: Advances in Neural Information Processing Systems, vol. 31 (2018)
6. Hu, Z., Yang, Z., Liang, X., Salakhutdinov, R., Xing, E.P.: Toward controlled generation of text. In: International Conference on Machine Learning, pp. 1587–1596. PMLR (2017)
7. Eastwood, C., Williams, C.K.: A framework for the quantitative evaluation of disentangled representations. In: International Conference on Learning Representations (2018)
8. Geirhos, R., et al.: Shortcut learning in deep neural networks. Nat. Mach. Intell. **2**(11), 665–673 (2020)
9. Goodfellow, I., et al.: Generative adversarial nets. In: Advances in Neural Information Processing Systems, vol. 27 (2014)
10. Higgins, I., et al.: beta-VAE: learning basic visual concepts with a constrained variational framework (2016)
11. Higgins, I., et al.: Towards a definition of disentangled representations. arXiv preprint arXiv:1812.02230 (2018)
12. Hinton, G.E., Osindero, S., Teh, Y.W.: A fast learning algorithm for deep belief nets. Neural Comput. **18**(7), 1527–1554 (2006)
13. Jeong, Y., Song, H.O.: Learning discrete and continuous factors of data via alternating disentanglement. In: International Conference on Machine Learning, pp. 3091–3099. PMLR (2019)
14. Kim, H., Mnih, A.: Disentangling by factorising. In: International Conference on Machine Learning, pp. 2649–2658. PMLR (2018)
15. Kingma, D.P., Welling, M.: Auto-encoding variational bayes. arXiv preprint arXiv:1312.6114 (2013)
16. Krizhevsky, A., Sutskever, I., Hinton, G.E.: ImageNet classification with deep convolutional neural networks. In: Advances in Neural Information Processing Systems, Chicago, vol. 25 (2012)
17. Kumar, A., Sattigeri, P., Balakrishnan, A.: Variational inference of disentangled latent concepts from unlabeled observations. arXiv preprint arXiv:1711.00848 (2017)
18. Lee, W., Kim, D., Hong, S., Lee, H.: High-fidelity synthesis with disentangled representation. In: Vedaldi, A., Bischof, H., Brox, T., Frahm, J.-M. (eds.) ECCV 2020. LNCS, vol. 12371, pp. 157–174. Springer, Cham (2020). https://doi.org/10.1007/978-3-030-58574-7_10

19. Lin, Z., Thekumparampil, K., Fanti, G., Oh, S.: InfoGAN-CR and modelcentrality: Self-supervised model training and selection for disentangling GANs. In: International Conference on Machine Learning, pp. 6127–6139. PMLR (2020)

20. Liu, B., Zhu, Y., Fu, Z., De Melo, G., Elgammal, A.: OOGAN: disentangling GAN with one-hot sampling and orthogonal regularization. In: Proceedings of the AAAI Conference on Artificial Intelligence, vol. 34, no. 04, pp. 4836–4843 (2020)

21. Locatello, F., et al.: Challenging common assumptions in the unsupervised learning of disentangled representations. In: International Conference on Machine Learning, pp. 4114–4124. PMLR (2019)

22. Mnih, V., et al.: Human-level control through deep reinforcement learning. Nature 518(7540), 529–533 (2015)

23. Oord, A.V.D., et al.: WaveNet: a generative model for raw audio. arXiv preprint arXiv:1609.03499. Chicago (2016)

24. Rezende, D.J., Mohamed, S., Wierstra, D.: Stochastic backpropagation and approximate inference in deep generative models. In: International Conference on Machine Learning, pp. 1278–1286. PMLR, Chicago (2014)

25. Ridgeway, K., Mozer, M.C.: Learning deep disentangled embeddings with the f-statistic loss. In: Advances in Neural Information Processing Systems, vol. 31 (2018)

26. Schölkopf, B., Janzing, D., Peters, J., Sgouritsa, E., Zhang, K., Mooij, J.: On causal and anticausal learning. arXiv preprint arXiv:1206.6471 (2012)

27. Suter, R., Miladinovic, D., Schölkopf, B., Bauer, S.: Robustly disentangled causal mechanisms: Validating deep representations for interventional robustness. In: International Conference on Machine Learning, pp. 6056–6065. PMLR (2019)

28. Zaidi, J., Boilard, J., Gagnon, G., Carbonneau, M.A.: Measuring disentanglement: a review of metrics. arXiv preprint arXiv:2012.09276. Chicago (2020)

29. Zhu, X., Xu, C., Tao, D.: Learning disentangled representations with latent variation predictability. In: Vedaldi, A., Bischof, H., Brox, T., Frahm, J.-M. (eds.) ECCV 2020. LNCS, vol. 12355, pp. 684–700. Springer, Cham (2020). https://doi.org/10.1007/978-3-030-58607-2_40

30. Matthey, L., Higgins, I., Hassabis, D., Lerchner, A.: dSprites: disentanglement testing Sprites dataset (2017). github.com/deepmind/dsprites-dataset/

31. Burgess, C., Kim, H.: 3D shapes dataset (2018). github.com/deepmind/3dshapes-dataset/

32. Liu, Z., Luo, P., Wang, X., Tang, X.: Deep learning face attributes in the wild. In: Proceedings of International Conference on Computer Vision (ICCV) (2015)

# DuSAG: An Anomaly Detection Method in Dynamic Graph Based on Dual Self-attention

Weiqin Lin[1], Xianyu Bao[2], Mark Junjie Li[1(✉)], and Zukang Gao[1]

[1] College of Computer Science and Software Engineering, Shenzhen University, Shenzhen, People's Republic of China
{linweiqin2019,2070276158}@email.szu.edu.cn,
jj.li@szu.edu.cn
[2] Shenzhen Academy of Inspection and Quarantine, Shenzhen, People's Republic of China

**Abstract.** Anomaly detection of dynamic graphs, graph stream composed of different graphs, has a wide range of applications. The existing anomaly detection methods of dynamic graph based on random walk did not focus on the important vertices in random walks and did not utilize previous states of vertices, and hence, the extracted structural and temporal features are limited. This paper introduces DuSAG which is a dual self-attention anomaly detection algorithm. DuSAG uses structural self-attention to focus on important vertices, and uses temporal self-attention to utilize the previous and last states of vertices, which improves the ability of structural and temporal features extraction and the ability of anomaly detection. We conducted experiments on three real-world datasets, and the results show that DuSAG outperform the state-of-the-art method.

**Keywords:** Anomaly detection · Dynamic graph · Dual self-attention · Deep learning

## 1 Introduction

A dynamic graph is a graph stream composed of different graphs and it is a powerful way to represent objects and their relationships [13]. The structure or attributes of a dynamic graph will change over time, such as the deletion and addition of edges, the change of vertex attributes, etc. In recent years, the technologies of the dynamic graph have been widely used in various applications, such as financial system [11], social network [17], etc. In these applications, objects and relationships between objects can be effectively represented by a dynamic graph.

Research on the applicability of the model for traceability, early warning and emergency assessment of food risks at ports (No. 2019YFC1605504).

Anomalies usually have negative influence. For example, in a computer network, hackers attack the host computer, steal or destroy the computer's important data, which has a negative impact on the business activities of the enterprise. Dynamic graphs are widely used and anomalies in dynamic graph have negative effects, so it is necessary to detect anomalies in dynamic graphs. The anomalies of a dynamic graph include anomalous vertex, anomalous edge and anomalous subgraph [13]. Specially, in the anomaly detection of a dynamic graph, anomalous edge detection is an indispensable part. Many applications of the dynamic graph use edges to represent complex structural information. Therefore, anomalous edge detection in a dynamic graph has a wide range of applications such as intrusion detection system [8], wildfire detection [4], etc. This paper focuses on the detection of anomalous edge.

The anomalous edge detection needs to consider the structural and temporal features of a dynamic graph. Random walk methods can extract features in an unsupervised manner and extract long-term dependencies compared to traditional machine learning methods [7]. NetWalk [18] generated random walks in a dynamic graph, and used an autoencoder to learn vertex representation on the random walks. Then it applied streaming K-means on vertex representation to detect anomalies. Brochier studies showed that focusing on the important vertices can facilitate feature extraction [3]. Therefore, focusing on more important vertices can improve the ability of extraction of features. However, NetWalk treated all vertices equally, which may learn noise, extract limited features and reduce the performance of anomaly detection.

Based on random walk, how to extract abundant temporal features is another challenge. When the graph is updated, NetWalk [18] regenerated the random walk on the updated vertices, and combined the old random walks into new training sets to fine-tune the autoencoder and update the vertex representation. However, when updating the vertex representation, NetWalk only considered the last vertex states, and did not utilize the previous states of the vertex, which resulted in limited temporal features extracted and further reduced the performance of anomaly detection.

Attention mechanisms have been successfully applied in many sequential learning tasks such as reading comprehension [16]. It focuses on the relevant parts of a context. Self-attention is an attention mechanism that associates different positional element of the same sequence with each other. It was introduced in the Transformer which is an encoder-decoder based model [15]. The self-attention of Transformer has many advantages, it can effectively focus the relevant element in the sequence, capture complex patterns through multi-heads self-attention. In this paper, we propose DuSAG which is a dynamic graph anomaly detection algorithm based on dual self-attention. DuSAG uses structural self-attention to focus on important vertices, and uses temporal self-attention to utilize the previous and last states of vertices, which improves the ability of structural and temporal features extraction and the ability of anomaly detection. Specifically, the contributions of DuSAG are as follows.

- DuSAG uses structural self-attention to focus on the important vertices, which reduces the noise and improves the ability of extracting the complex structural features.
- DuSAG uses temporal self-attention to utilize the previous and last states of vertices, which improves the ability of extracting the temporal features.
- We conducted experiments on three real world datasets, which proves the effectiveness of DuSAG.

The rest of this paper is organized as follows. In Sect. 2, we first describe the related work. In Sect. 3, we propose the DuSAG workflow, including formulas and pseudocode. Then in Sect. 4, we conduct experiment on three real world datasets. Finally, in Sect. 5, we summarize this paper.

## 2   Related Work

Many existing approaches are based on heuristic rules. GOutlier [1] designed a reservoir sampling method to maintain the summaries of a dynamic graph. These summaries can be used to create robust and effective anomaly detection models and define outliers. CM-Sketch [12] used Count-Min Sketch to approximate the global and local properties of a dynamic graph, which can provide constant time and space complexity. StreamSpot [10] designed a similarity function based on relative frequency of local substructures, and realized the constant time and space complexity by sketches. Finally, it used clustering algorithm to find anomalies. Based on sketch, GMicro [2] created micro clusters from a dynamic graph, which can maintain the performance of the method in a limited space. Spotlight [5] calculated a sketch of each graph. In sketch space, the anomalous graph is far from the normal graph. Then the distance gap in sketch space is used to detect anomalies. The above methods are based on heuristic rules, which requires manual feature extraction and are not flexible enough. Some methods use deep neural network to extract the features of a dynamic graph automatically. NetWalk [18] used a vertex reservoir to save summaries of a dynamic graph and used an autoencoder with clique embedding to learn vertex embedding, and find anomalies by streaming k-means. AddGraph [19] combined Graph Convolutional Network (GCN) and Gated Recurrent Unit (GRU) to extract the structural and temporal features of a dynamic graph. These two methods are based on deep learning and have better performance than heuristic rules. However, NetWalk paid equal attention to the vertices of a random walk and did not utilize the past states of vertices, which may learn noise, extract insufficient temporal features and reduce the performance of anomaly detection.

## 3   Proposed Method

In this section, we define the problem and the details of DuSAG.

## 3.1   Problem Definition

A dynamic graph is a series of snapshots, $\mathbb{G} = \{\mathcal{G}^t\}_{t=1}^T$ where $T$ is the number of time steps and $\mathcal{G}^t = (\mathcal{E}^t, \mathcal{V}^t)$ is the $t$-th graph of $\mathbb{G}$. At time step $t$, the edge set in $\mathcal{G}^t$ are denoted by set $E^t$, and vertices in $E^t$ are denoted by set $V^t$. We set entire vertex set $\mathcal{V}^t = \cup_{i=1}^t V^i$, entire edge set $\mathcal{E}^t = \cup_{i=1}^t E^i$ and $n = |\mathcal{V}^t|$. An anomalous edge is defined as an edge that differs from the expected and standard pattern. At time step $t$, our goal is to find the anomalous edges in $E^t$ without using any labeled data.

## 3.2   DuSAG Workflow

In this part, we propose DuSAG which is a dynamic graph anomaly detection algorithm. As shown in the Fig. 1, from top to bottom, the workflow of DuSAG consists of three parts: structural self-attention, temporal self-attention, and anomaly detection. A dynamic graph can be split into many snapshots. Roughly, DuSAG firstly applies structural self-attention on random walks, which allows DuSAG to focus on the important vertices and extract structural features. Secondly, DuSAG uses temporal self-attention to utilize previous and last states of vertices, which allows DuSAG to extract temporal features. Finally, we convert edges into edge embedding and pass it to an anomaly detection method. The details of each part are described in the following.

**Structural Self-attention.** The goal of structural self-attention is to extract the structural features of the graph. DuSAG generates random walks of fixed-length $L$. It extracts structural features by applying self-attention to random walks. By using self-attention, we also can focus the important vertices in the random walk.

Formally, at time step $t$, we generate $\psi$ random walks of fixed-length $L$ for each vertex on the snapshot $\mathcal{G}^t$. The random walks of $\mathcal{G}^t$ are denoted by $\Omega^t$. For each random walk, we convert it to embedding $\mathbf{Q}^t \in \mathbb{R}^{L \times d}$ by initial vertex embedding $\mathbf{H}^t \in \mathbb{R}^{N \times d}$ and $d$ is the dimension of vertex embedding. We pass it to $SelfAttention$ which is given by

$$\mathbf{O}^t = SelfAttention(\mathbf{Q}^t) \tag{1}$$

Here $\mathbf{O}^t \in \mathbb{R}^{L \times \psi d}$ contains structural features. Inspired by [14,15], we use the scaled dot product form of attention. Here, the queries, keys, and values are linear transformation of the input embedding where $\mathbf{W}_q$, $\mathbf{W}_k$, $\mathbf{W}_v$ are linear projection matrices. The $SelfAttention$ is defined by

$$\mathbf{C}^t = \frac{(\mathbf{Q}^t \mathbf{W}_q)(\mathbf{Q}^t \mathbf{W}_k)^T}{\sqrt{d}} \tag{2}$$

$$(\beta^t)_{ij} = \frac{\exp(C^t)_{ij}}{\sum_j \exp(C^t)_{ij}} \tag{3}$$

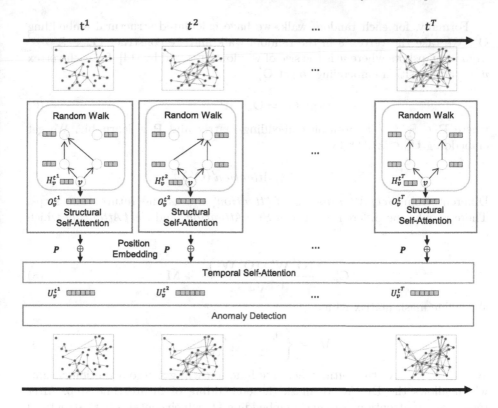

**Fig. 1.** The workflow of DuSAG: the workflow from top to bottom contains the original dynamic graph, structural self-attention, temporal self-attention, anomaly detection, and anomaly edge detection results. The black arrows in Random Walk indicate the direction of random walks.

$$\mathbf{Z}^t = \beta^t \left( \mathbf{Q}^t \mathbf{W}_v \right) \tag{4}$$

where $\beta^t \in \mathbb{R}^{L \times L}$ is the attention weight matrix. We use multi-heads self attention to focus on different subspace of the input, which can capture more complex patterns. It also further enhances the ability of DuSAG to extract structural features of dynamic graphs. By concatenating operator $CAT$, we concatenate the results of $\eta$ heads and $\psi$ random walks for each vertex and get $\mathbf{O}^t$ which contains structural features.

$$\mathbf{O}^t = \mathrm{CAT}\left( \mathrm{CAT}\left( \mathbf{Z}^{t1}, \mathbf{Z}^{t2}, \ldots, \mathbf{Z}^{t\eta} \right)_1, \cdots, \mathrm{CAT}\left( \mathbf{Z}^{t1}, \mathbf{Z}^{t2}, \ldots, \mathbf{Z}^{t\eta} \right)_\psi \right) \tag{5}$$

**Temporal Self-attention.** The goal of temporal self-attention is to utilize the previous and last states of vertices for extracting temporal features of a dynamic graph. As shown in Fig. 1, we get embedding $U_v^t$ by applying temporal self-attention to $\mathbf{O}_v$ of different snapshots.

Formally, for each random walk, we have calculated structural embedding $\mathbf{O}^t$. We take the vertex $v$ in the random walk and we construct $\mathbf{O}_v \in \mathbb{R}^{w \times \psi d}$ from $w$ snapshots where $w$ is the size of window. Inspired by [14], for each vertex $v$, we add position embedding to get $\mathbf{O}'_v$,

$$\mathbf{O}'_v = \mathbf{O}_v + \mathbf{P} \tag{6}$$

where $\mathbf{P} \in \mathbb{R}^{w \times \psi d}$ is position embedding matrix and $\mathbf{P}$ is learnable. We get embedding $\mathbf{U}_v \in \mathbb{R}^{w \times \psi d}$ by

$$\mathbf{U}_v = SelfAttention'(\mathbf{O}'_v) \tag{7}$$

Different from $SelfAttention$, $SelfAttention'$ masks the future time steps. There is only one difference between $SelfAttention'$ and $SelfAttention$ which is

$$\mathbf{C}'_v = \frac{\left(\mathbf{O}'_v \mathbf{W}'_q\right)\left(\mathbf{O}'_v \mathbf{W}'_k\right)^T}{\sqrt{d}} + \mathbf{M} \tag{8}$$

We define mask matrix $\mathbf{M}$ as

$$M_{ij} = \begin{cases} 0, & i \leq j \\ -\infty, & \text{otherwise} \end{cases} \tag{9}$$

When $M_{ij} = -\infty$, the softmax activate function will get zero attention weight, which allows the DuSAG to mask the embedding of future time step. After temporal self-attention, we can get embedding $\mathbf{U}_v$ which contains both structural and temporal features.

**Anomalous Edge Detection.** In this part, the input is the vertex embedding $\mathbf{U}^t$ and edge set $E^t$, and the output is the anomaly probability of each edge. DuSAG uses an edge encoder $\phi$ to transform the vertex embedding and edge set into edge embedded $\mathbf{K}^t$. Inspired by [14], DuSAG assumes that all the edges in the data set are normal edges, DuSAG uses the negative sampled edges as the anomalous edge. The negative sampling method is that given a normal edge $(i, j)$, vertex $i$ is replaced by probability $d_i/(d_i + d_j)$, and vertex $j$ is replaced by probability $d_j/(d_i + d_j)$, where $d_i$ and $d_j$ represent the degree of vertex $i$ and vertex $j$ respectively. DuSAG uses a fully connected network to classify normal and anomalous edges, and uses the sigmoid activation function to represent the probability of abnormal edges. The loss function is cross entropy loss function, and the formula is

$$f_a^t = \sigma\left(\mathbf{K}^t W_a + b_a\right) \tag{10}$$

$$J^t = \sum_{e \in E^t} -\left(y^t \log\left(f_a^t\right) + \left(1 - y^t\right) \log\left(1 - f_a^t\right)\right) \tag{11}$$

---

**Algorithm 1. DuSAG**

---

**Input:** A dynamic graph $\mathbb{G}$ which contains different snapshots $\{\mathcal{G}^t\}_{t=1}^T$
**Parameter:** $d$, $\alpha$, $\eta$, $w$, $b$, and $\phi$
**Output:** Anomalous probability $\{f_a^t\}_{i=1}^T$

1: Define the network structure.
2: Generate random walks $\Omega^t$ for each snapshot.
3: **repeat**
4:    **for** $i = w$ to $T$ **do**
5:        **for** $t = i - w + 1$ to $i$ **do**
6:            Get $\Omega^t$ according to $\mathcal{G}^t$
7:            Get initial vertex embedding $\mathbf{H}^t$
8:            Get $\mathbf{Q}^t$ by $\mathbf{H}^t$ and $\Omega^t$
9:            $\mathbf{O}^t = SelfAttention(\mathbf{Q}^t)$
10:           Get $\mathbf{O}_v$ and $\mathbf{P}$ by $\mathbf{W}_p$
11:           $\mathbf{O}_v' = \mathbf{O}_v + \mathbf{P}$
12:           $\mathbf{U}_v = SelfAttention'(\mathbf{O}_v')$
13:           Sample negative edge
14:           Get edge embedding $K^t$
15:           Minimize $J^t$ (11)
16: **until** Converge
17: **for** $t = 1$ to $T$ **do**
18:    Get $\mathbf{U}^t$
19:    Get edge embedding $\mathbf{K}^t$ by $\mathbf{U}^t$, $\Omega^t$ and $\phi$
20:    $s^t = OCNN(\mathbf{K}^t)$
21:    Calculate anomalous edge probability $f_a^t$ (10)
22: **return** $\{s^i\}_{i=1}^T$

---

where $\sigma(z) = 1/(1 + exp(z))$ is the sigmoid activation function, $W_a$ and $b_a$ are the weight and bias of the full connection layer, respectively. $y^t$ indicates whether $e$ is an abnormal edge under timestamp $t$. If $y = 1$, $e$ is the anomalous edge of negative sampling. If $y = 0$, $e$ is the normal edge.

With learning rate $\alpha$, algorithm DuSAG is summarized in Algorithm 1.

## 4 Experiment

In this section, we describe the experimental setup and compare DuSAG with other methods on three real world datasets.

### 4.1 Experiment Setup

**Dataset.** We conduct experiments on the datasets shown in the Table 1. UCI is the online social graph of the University of California, where each vertex represents a user and each edge represents that a user send a message to another user. DBLP-2010 is an author collaboration graph from the DBLP Computer Science Bibliography in 2010, where each vertex represents an author and each

**Table 1.** Dataset description

| Dataset | #Node | #Edge | Max.Degree | Avg.Degree |
|---------|-------|-------|-----------|-----------|
| UCI message | 1,899 | 13,838 | 255 | 14.57 |
| DBLP-2010 | 300,647 | 807,700 | 238 | 5.37 |
| DARPA | 25,524 | 4,554,344 | 8,063 | 4.80 |

edge represents an author has a collaborative relationship with another user. DARPA [9] is a network dataset which contains various attacks. Each vertex in DARPA represents an unique IP, and each edge represents a communication. The UCI and DBLP-2010 datasets have no anomalies, we use the method in [18] to inject anomalies. The DARPA dataset have ground truth anomalies which represents various attacks.

**Baseline.** The baselines for comparison with DuSAG are as follows.

- CM-Sketch [12]. It uses Count-Min Sketch to approximate the global and local properties of a dynamic graph, and used these properties to define outliers.
- NetWalk [18]. It uses an autoencoder with clique embedding to learn vertex embedding, and uses streaming k-means to find anomalies.
- AddGraph [19]. It uses an GCN and GRU to extract the structural and temporal features, and computes anomalous scores for edges.

**Experimental Design.** We evaluate the performance of DuSAG without and with timestamps. In the experiment without timestamps, we test whether DuSAG could effectively extract structural features of a graph and use them in anomaly detection. In the experiment with timestamps, we divide the test set into several snapshots to simulate the graph update scenario and test whether DuSAG could effectively extract temporal features of a dynamic graph and use structural and temporal features in anomaly detection. We use AUC score as a performance metric.

## 4.2   Experimental Result

**Results on Graphs Without Timestamps.** In the setting without timestamps, we evaluate the anomaly detection performance based on the extracted structural features. We use the first 50% of the data as the training data. For the UCI and DBLP-2010 datasets, we inject 1%, 5% and 10% anomalous edges in the rest 50% of the data as three test sets respectively. The training set are treated as normal data and is used to train the DuSAG. We initialize $H^t$ randomly. For hyperparameters, we set dimension $d$ to 64, the learning rate $\alpha$ is set to 0.0001, the number of heads of self-attention $\eta$ is set to 4, the window size $w$ is set to 3, the margin $b$ is set to 1. The edge embedding is calculated

Table 2. AUC results in the setting without timestamps

| Methods | UCI Messages | | | DBLP-2010 | | | DARPA |
|---------|------|------|------|------|------|------|------|
|         | 1%   | 5%   | 10%  | 1%   | 5%   | 10%  | –    |
| CM-Sketch | 0.7270 | 0.7086 | 0.6861 | 0.7097 | 0.6892 | 0.6332 | 0.6049 |
| Netwalk | 0.7758 | 0.7647 | 0.7226 | 0.7654 | 0.7388 | 0.6858 | 0.7480 |
| AddGraph | 0.8083 | 0.8090 | 0.7688 | 0.7436 | 0.7340 | 0.7299 | 0.7706 |
| DuSAG | **0.9327** | **0.9208** | **0.9194** | **0.8027** | **0.7998** | **0.7876** | **0.9017** |

by Hadamard operator, which is what operator $\phi$ does. We use node2vec [6] to generate random walks and the length $L$ of random walks is 20.

Table 2 shows the results. Because the experiment setup and the UCI dataset are the same as AddGraph, we use the results of the UCI dataset which are reported by AddGraph [19]. As shown in Table 2, DuSAG outperforms all baselines on all datasets. On UCI, DBLP-2010, and DARPA datasets, DuSAG on average has 0.1118, 0.0577, 0.1311 increment compared to AddGraph respectively. The results show that the effectiveness of DuSAG in extract the structural features and DuSAG can apply the structural features in anomaly detection. In addition, For DARPA dataset with ground truth label, we detect anomalous edges only by the edges between vertices, without using other features of vertices, which demonstrates the effectiveness of DuSAG in detecting real-world anomalous edges.

**Results on Dynamic Graphs.** In this settings, we evaluate the anomaly detection performance based on the extracted structural and temporal features. we divided the test sets of UCI, DBLP-2010 and DARPA into 6, 10 and 10 snapshots respectively. With different snapshots, we can simulate the update scenario for the dynamic graph. The hyper parameters of DuSAG are same the as above. We update DuSAG according to Algorithm 1. Figure 2 shows the results of the experiment. We use the results of UCI dataset which are reported by AddGraph [18]. As shown in Fig. 2, DuSAG also outperforms all baselines on all datasets at all snapshots. On UCI, DBLP-2010 and DARPA datasets, DuSAG averagely has 0.1313, 0.0664, 0.151 increment compared to AddGraph respectively. The results show that DuSAG can efficiently extract the updated structural and temporal features and use updated features in dynamic graph anomaly detection.

**Parameter Sensitivity.** In this part, we evaluate the influence of several hyperparameters of DuSAG on AUC results, including $L$ for the length of random walk and training percentage.

First, we evaluate the influence of $L$. The range of $L$ is {3, 4, 5, 6, 7, 10, 15, 20, 25, 30, 35}. We evaluated it on the UCI dataset with 5% anomalous data. The rest parameters are the same as above. As shown in Fig. 3(a), with

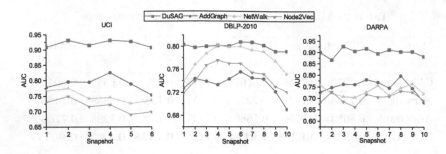

**Fig. 2.** AUC results in dynamic setting with 5% anomalies

the increase of $L$, AUC rises and eventually stabilizes. This means that when the length of random walk is longer, DuSAG can still focus on the important vertices in the walk without degrading performance. Second, we test stability of DuSAG with different training percentages. We use the setting without timestamps, but changed the percentage of the training set. We train the DuSAG with training percentage from 10% to 60%. With 5% anomalous edges in dataset DARPA, we run 20 times to get Fig. 3(b). We can see that the AUC of DuSAG shows an upward trend and more stability as the training percentage increases. AUC increases the most at the 10% to 20% percent training percentage. Then, the AUC steadily increases at 20% to 60% training percentage. This is because DuSAG can learn more structural and temporal features when the training data increases, so the AUC increases steadily.

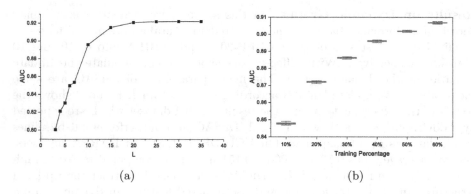

(a)                                    (b)

**Fig. 3.** Parameter sensitivity. (a) AUC results on UCI with different parameters, (b) Stability on DARPA with different training percentages.

## 5    Conclusion

We propose DuSAG, a dynamic graph anomaly detection algorithm based on dual self-attention, which significantly improves the ability of classifying anomalies by applying dual self-attention. Specifically, DuSAG uses structural self-attention to focus on relevant vertices in random walks, and uses temporal self-attention to utilize the previous and last states of vertices, which improves the ability of extracting the structural and temporal features of a dynamic graph and classifying anomalies. We conduct experiments on three real world datasets, and the results show that DuSAG can effectively extract the structural and temporal features of dynamic graph and use them in anomaly detection. It also shows DuSAG outperforms the state of the art method.

# References

1. Aggarwal, C.C., Zhao, Y., Philip, S.Y.: Outlier detection in graph streams. In: 2011 IEEE 27th International Conference on Data Engineering, pp. 399–409. IEEE (2011)
2. Aggarwal, C.C., Zhao, Y., Yu, P.S.: On clustering graph streams. In: Proceedings of the 2010 SIAM International Conference on Data Mining, pp. 478–489. SIAM (2010)
3. Brochier, R., Guille, A., Velcin, J.: Link prediction with mutual attention for text-attributed networks. In: Companion Proceedings of The 2019 World Wide Web Conference, pp. 283–284 (2019)
4. Chen, Z., et al.: Discovery of extreme events-related communities in contrasting groups of physical system networks. Data Min. Knowl. Disc. **27**(2), 225–258 (2013)
5. Eswaran, D., Faloutsos, C., Guha, S., Mishra, N.: SpotLight: detecting anomalies in streaming graphs. In: Proceedings of the 24th ACM SIGKDD International Conference on Knowledge Discovery & Data Mining, pp. 1378–1386 (2018)
6. Grover, A., Leskovec, J.: node2vec: scalable feature learning for networks. In: Proceedings of the 22nd ACM SIGKDD International Conference on Knowledge Discovery and Data Mining, pp. 855–864 (2016)
7. Kazemi, S.M., Goel, R., Jain, K., Kobyzev, I., Sethi, A., Forsyth, P., Poupart, P.: Representation learning for dynamic graphs: a survey. J. Mach. Learn. Res. **21**(70), 1–73 (2020)
8. Lin, P., Ye, K., Xu, C.-Z.: Dynamic network anomaly detection system by using deep learning techniques. In: Da Silva, D., Wang, Q., Zhang, L.-J. (eds.) CLOUD 2019. LNCS, vol. 11513, pp. 161–176. Springer, Cham (2019). https://doi.org/10.1007/978-3-030-23502-4_12
9. Lippmann, R., et al.: Results of the DARPA 1998 offline intrusion detection evaluation. In: Recent Advances in Intrusion Detection, vol. 99, pp. 829–835 (1999)
10. Manzoor, E., Milajerdi, S.M., Akoglu, L.: Fast memory-efficient anomaly detection in streaming heterogeneous graphs. In: Proceedings of the 22nd ACM SIGKDD International Conference on Knowledge Discovery and Data Mining, pp. 1035–1044 (2016)
11. Pourhabibi, T., Ong, K.L., Kam, B.H., Boo, Y.L.: Fraud detection: a systematic literature review of graph-based anomaly detection approaches. Decis. Support Syst. **133**, 113303 (2020)
12. Ranshous, S., Harenberg, S., Sharma, K., Samatova, N.F.: A scalable approach for outlier detection in edge streams using sketch-based approximations. In: Proceedings of the 2016 SIAM International Conference on Data Mining, pp. 189–197. SIAM (2016)

13. Ranshous, S., Shen, S., Koutra, D., Harenberg, S., Faloutsos, C., Samatova, N.F.: Anomaly detection in dynamic networks: a survey. Wiley Interdisc. Rev. Comput. Stat. **7**(3), 223–247 (2015)
14. Sankar, A., Wu, Y., Gou, L., Zhang, W., Yang, H.: Dynamic graph representation learning via self-attention networks. arXiv preprint arXiv:1812.09430 (2018)
15. Vaswani, A., et al.: Attention is all you need. arXiv preprint arXiv:1706.03762 (2017)
16. Yu, A.W., et al.: QANet: combining local convolution with global self-attention for reading comprehension. arXiv preprint arXiv:1804.09541 (2018)
17. Yu, R., Qiu, H., Wen, Z., Lin, C., Liu, Y.: A survey on social media anomaly detection. ACM SIGKDD Explor. Newsl. **18**(1), 1–14 (2016)
18. Yu, W., Cheng, W., Aggarwal, C.C., Zhang, K., Chen, H., Wang, W.: NetWalk: a flexible deep embedding approach for anomaly detection in dynamic networks. In: Proceedings of the 24th ACM SIGKDD International Conference on Knowledge Discovery & Data Mining, pp. 2672–2681 (2018)
19. Zheng, L., Li, Z., Li, J., Li, Z., Gao, J.: AddGraph: anomaly detection in dynamic graph using attention-based temporal GCN. In: IJCAI, pp. 4419–4425 (2019)

# Exploring Deep Learning Architectures
# for Localised Hourly Air Quality Prediction

Sooraj Raj[✉], Jim Smith, and Enda Hayes

University of the West of England, Bristol, UK
sooraj2.rajasekharan@live.uwe.ac.uk, {james.smith,
Enda.Hayes}@uwe.ac.uk

**Abstract.** Air pollution is a global environmental and public health issue, but it is at the local scale that many mitigation measures are implemented. In a human context, we propose that as a decision support tool it is more valuable to provide hourly forecasts at local scales with the following considerations: (1) the system should be designed for rapid and simple human-tuning of different trade-offs; (2) the chosen model and hyper-parameters should maximise consistency of learning given the likelihood of regular retraining with new data; (3) reducing errors when predicting low pollutant values is far less important than accurate prediction of spikes. Target users include local officials deciding whether to enact short-term plans for meeting regulatory objectives or citizens, deciding to change their behaviour or travel patterns to avoid likely exposure. Both groups will also wish to reduce inconvenience and disruption, but the relative importance they will place on these two conflicting factors cannot be pre-determined and hence there is desirability for rapid exploration and tuning of false vs m.sised alarm trade-offs.

Through a series of experiments, we show how Deep Neural architectures can be developed to create an 'early warning' decision support tool, with the ability to personalise the accuracy trade-offs at different time-steps from predicting the possibility of a spike 24 h in advance, to increasingly accurate confirmations that the spike will take place. The results also show that we can significantly improve the prediction accuracy if we could include meteorological prediction values as additional input to the models.

**Keywords:** Air quality · Deep learning · Neural networks · Decision support system

## 1 Introduction

People and governments are increasingly concerned about air pollution, due to its impact on the human health, sensitive habitats and sustainable development. In our urban environments air pollution is a key public health concern with an estimated 7 million premature global deaths annually due to both indoor and ambient pollution [1]. However, the impact of air pollution is not just related to mortality metrics, there is a growing evidence base about the morbidity impact of pollution across multiple human systems including cardio-vascular, respiratory and even a recorded reduction in intelligence, indicating that

© The Author(s), under exclusive license to Springer Nature Switzerland AG 2022
E. Pimenidis et al. (Eds.): ICANN 2022, LNCS 13529, pp. 133–144, 2022.
https://doi.org/10.1007/978-3-031-15919-0_12

the damage to society of toxic air is far deeper than the well-known impacts on physical health. Consequently, it is a vital task to accurately keep track of ambient air pollution levels especially in the urban areas.

Air quality process is inherently complex since the temporal and spatial trends are affected by various factors, and air quality measurement levels are related to complex interaction of different parameters. Population density, city activities such as variation in vehicle traffic volumes, increased heating provision in winter months and meteorological changes can influence the spatial, short-term and long-term variations of ambient concentrations. A successful forecasting model should be able to capture both temporal recurring patterns - short time variations, long term periodicity and spatial correlations for accurate predictions. The conventional methods of air quality measurements and modelling can be mainly classified as Deterministic or Statistical. Deterministic methods involve numerically solving a set of physical equations, driven by the chemistry and the transport of pollutants. They predict more frequent events reasonably accurately but have limitations in accurately predicting extreme events due to the complexity and inherent uncertainty associated with the turbulent flow. Statistical linear methods try to describe the variables based on probability and statistical averages and they are limited by the linear assumptions they make. Hence these models are not reliable for accurate prediction of time series for short and medium time ranges [2].

With the increase in computing power and data availability, more complex Deep Learning models with multiple hidden layers for feature transformation and extraction, have recently gained popularity in the time-series prediction problems. These multi-layer architectures leveraging more and more nonlinear processing units, are found to be good at extracting the inherent features of the data set without any prior knowledge [3]. Since air quality temporal trends and spatial distribution are affected by various factors such as air pollutant emissions, weather conditions, wind direction, traffic flow, industrial activities, Deep Learning algorithms are expected to be useful in learning these complex trends and can lead to achieving a good performance air quality forecasting. The aim of this paper is to achieve a Deep Learning based phased binary 'warning system' for future peak episodes of $PM_{10}$ and $PM_{2.5}$ so that local mitigation and communication strategies can be put in place to avoid these pollution spikes or to manage public exposure better.

In this paper we make the following contributions.

1. We examine the impact of different Deep Learning architectures for Air Quality forecasting on a single site.
2. In contrast to most prior work, and recognizing that a deployed system would likely be regularly re-trained, we focus not just on the mean accuracy (RMSE) across a number of runs, but also on the reliability of learning (expressed as the variance between the runs)
3. Taking extra information into account (predictions for the future period's weather conditions) we demonstrate that we can create a system with low errors for predictions of absolute pollutant values up to 24 h in advance.
4. We demonstrate a novel system that combines these regression predictions to create a binary 'early warning system' where stakeholders can tune the thresholds applied in the run-up to a predicted peak event.

## 2  Models Considered

Deep Learning models have been increasingly applied to Air Quality prediction problems. In a recent study, Reddy et al. [4] used LSTMs to predict pollutant levels 5 to 10 h in advance for Beijing. In another study Huang and Kuo, 2018 [5], used a CNN (Convolutional Neural Networks) - LSTM (Long Short-Term Memory Neural Networks) based Deep Learning model for predicting PM2.5 values 1 h in advance. Another deep learning model analysing spatio-temporal correlations of PM2.5 was proposed by Pak et al. [6] and in this study the authors considered pollution data from 384 monitoring neighboring stations for predicting the daily average PM2.5 values. Though these studies considered using Deep Learning models they are limited by exploring just accurate prediction of the pollutant values. However, local authorities and pollution standard agencies are more interested in reducing the number and severity of peak or high pollutant episodes and predicting the low/background pollutant levels with high accuracy will not have much impact on achieving these pollution standards.

The UK Met office model provides the Daily Air Quality Index calculated as an average of pollutant concentrations over prescribed time periods [7]. The Met Office air pollution forecast is generated from a regional model working on a 12 km grid resolution, and it does not represent the localised increases in pollution that is found close to roads or in urban and industrial centres. The forecast represents the background and regional air quality away from these strong sources of pollution. Though it's helpful for the public to be aware of the daily air quality levels in advance, this model lacks predicting the peak pollutant episodes in the local level therefore won't help in the proactive deployment of targeted mitigation strategies or communication awareness raising campaigns to meet the local air quality objectives and protect public health.

This study aims to predict hourly 24-h rolling average values of PM2.5 and PM10 with the temporal data from one monitoring station, in other words predicting hourly rolling average values in advance. This study focuses on the feasibility of predicting the peak episodes accurately with the available data from one monitoring station and we have also considered the viability of a phased binary warning system for predicting the peak episodes which may be more insightful for local authorities to take measured short-term actions to avoid acute episodes.

We explored the prediction performance of three Deep Learning models based on:

1. LSTM's: Originally introduced by Hochreiter and Schmidhuber [8], they are state-of-the-art RNNs (Recurrent Neural Network) for time series forecasting tasks. LSTM networks are specifically designed to overcome the vanishing and exploding gradient problems of the standard RNNs, while learning long-term and short-term dependencies in the sequence data. With LSTMs each hidden node has a state and three gates (forget, input and output). At each time step the three gates are presented with one element of the sequence and also the output of the memory cell at the previous time step. This information is processed by each of these gates – (i) the forget gate determining which information to remove from the cell state, (ii) the input gate determining which information to add to the cell state and (iii) the output gate determining which information from the cell state to use as output.

2. CNN's: Initially developed for computer vision tasks, they have achieved excellent performance in image classification and object recognition tasks. There have been a few recent studies successfully applying CNNs to time series forecasting tasks, sometimes outperforming the LSTMs [9, 10]. Within CNNs each convolutional layer convolves the input consisting a local region (receptive field) with a weight matrix to compute a feature map. Since these convolutional neurons in same layer also share the same weights, they detect the same pattern but occurring in different parts of the receptive field. The convolutional layers are typically followed by a max pooling layer which computes the maximum value of the selected pool of adjacent neurons from the convolutional layer and this ensures that the output of the max-pooling layer is invariant to any shifts in the input sequence data [11].

3. Wavenets: Originally proposed by Borovykh et al. [12] and they allow the receptive field of the original CNNs to grow exponentially with multiple layers of dilated convolutions allowing the network to access a broad range of history i.e., long term dependencies in the data.

## 3 Methodology

### 3.1 Model Parameters and Hyperparameters

As with most Machine Learning algorithms, the predictive accuracy of the models is affected strongly by choices of hyper-parameters. Thus, we applied grid-search method to examine the impacts of different hyper parameter choices such as the number and size of layers, activation functions, whether to use dropout, batch size, input window size etc. - details are given in Table 1. After exploring all the different combinations of hyper-parameters for each model, we arrived at the following values for each model considered:

• Stacked LSTMs:

– Topology: Input layer with 13 features, 2 LSTM hidden layers with 20 nodes each and an output layer with 1 node predicting a single time step in advance.
– LSTM cell state and hidden state activation: Tanh, Recurrent Activation: Sigmoid
– Input window size: 24, Dropout: 0.2, Batch size: 168

• CNNs:

– Topology – Input layer with 13 features, 4 convolutional layers having 16 filters each with a filter size 3 followed by a max pooling layer with pool size 2 operating on each feature and finally an output layer with 1 node predicting a single time step in advance.
– Convolution layer activation: ReLU
– Input window size: 24, Dropout: 0.2, Batch size:168

- **Wavenets:**

- Topology – Input layer with 13 features, 6 dilated convolutional layers with 16 filters of filter size 3 and dilation rate – 1, 2, 4, 8, 16, 32 operating on each feature and finally followed by an output layer with 1 node predicting a single time step in advance.
- Convolution layer activation: ReLU
- Input window size: 72, Dropout: 0.4, Batch size:168

**Table 1.** Hyper parameters

| Model | Parameters | Tuning range | Chosen optimum value |
|---|---|---|---|
| Stacked LSTMs | Number of nodes | [16, 20, 25, 30] | 20 |
| | Number of layers | [1, 2, 3, 4] | 2 |
| | Dropout | [0.2, 0.3, 0.4, 0.5] | 0.2 |
| | Loss | [MAE, MSE] | MSE |
| | Batch Size | [128, 168, 256, 512] | 168 |
| | Input window size | [24, 72, 168] | 24 |
| CNNs | Number of filters | [8, 16, 32] | 16 |
| | Number of layers | [1, 2, 3, 4] | 4 |
| | Dropout | [0.2, 0.3, 0.4, 0.5] | 0.2 |
| | Loss | [MAE, MSE] | MSE |
| | Batch Size | [128, 168, 256, 512] | 168 |
| | Activation Functions | [Relu, Sigmoid] | Relu |
| | Input window size | [24, 72, 168] | 24 |
| WNs | Number of filters | [8, 16, 32] | 16 |
| | Dropout | [0.2, 0.3, 0.4, 0.5] | 0.4 |
| | Loss | [MAE, MSE] | MSE |
| | Batch Size | [128, 168, 256, 512] | 168 |
| | Activation Functions | [Relu, Sigmoid] | Relu |
| | Input window size | [24, 72, 168] | 72 |

For all models, the Adam optimizer is used with the learning rate set at .0001 and the early stopping on training is done by monitoring the validation loss when no improvements after 5 epochs is observed.

In each of these models it was found experimentally that best results came from averaging the learning updates over batches of 168 h. This experimental result matches the expert's intuition: since industrial activity and traffic flows follow weekly cycles, and training averages the updates over each sample in a batch, it is better if each day is equally represented within each batch.

In terms of how much context is provided for each prediction, the CNN and LSTM models worked best when presented with the values from each of the past 24 h (input window), whereas the Wavenets performed better when given 3 days (72 h) worth of data as an input pattern.

## 3.2  Dataset

The air quality data used for this experimentation is from the Port Talbot Margam monitoring station in the United Kingdom. The Port Talbot suburb of Margam accommodates the UK's largest steelworks and is also near the M4 motorway corridor, hence has both industrial, domestic and transport influences on local PM concentrations. This will help us testing two differing pollution profiles which will also be a more challenging Machine Learning problem.

The dataset from Port Talbot Margam AURN (Automatic Urban and Rural Network) monitoring station site consists of time series data of 10 pollutants and 3 metrological inputs – modelled wind direction, modelled wind speed, modelled temperature for continuous 8 years (spanning from 2011–2019). In this paper we focused on forecasting of the pollution levels of particulate matter – $PM_{2.5}$ and $PM_{10}$.

National air quality objectives for the UK specify the following thresholds for the particulate matter pollutants $PM_{2.5}$ and $PM_{10}$ [13].

- An annual mean of 40 $\mu g/m^3$ for $PM_{10}$
- A 24-h mean of 50 $\mu g/m^3$ more than 35 times in a single year for $PM_{10}$
- An annual average of 25 $\mu g/m^3$ for $PM_{2.5}$

In order to smooth the data and make it relate better to what policy decision makers are interested, a running average of 24 h of PM2.5 and PM10 values is considered for training and prediction. The data from 2011 to 2018 used for training the model, with 10% reserved for cross validation. Data from 2019 is used as test data to estimate the model's performance on the unseen data.

The problem is modelled as Multivariate one step regression to predict future values of one pollutant variable ($PM_{2.5}$ or $PM_{10}$) with other pollutants and metrological values provided as inputs. We have also analysed the binary classification problem of predicting the peak pollution episodes with different set targets for $PM_{2.5}$ and $PM_{10}$ in phases (i.e., 24,12,6 or 3 h in advance), taking as inputs the predicted values from the best performing regression models.

## 3.3  Choice of Comparison Metrics and Hypothesis Tests

We used the RMSE metric to compare the performance of different regression models (and preprocessing/feature set variants), performing 10 runs of each combination with the same train /test split but with different seeds for the initial network weights.

- To compare the *effectiveness* of different algorithms, we used mean differences of RMSE values, calculated over 10 runs for each considered model. We used the Mann

Whitney Wilcoxon test with the Bonferroni correction at 95% level to assess the statistical significance of any observed differences in performance.

- To compare the *reliability* of different algorithms, we used Levene's test for unequal variances, again using the 95% confidence level to assess statistically significant differences.

In contrast to how research results are often presented, we consider both of these metrics to be equally important. This is because in practice, it would be sensible to periodically re-train the system to take into account recently collected data. In this context we prefer a system that reliably learns reasonably accurate models, to one that usually learns slightly more accurate models, but occasionally comes up with very poor predictions.

We have not used the conventional N-fold cross-validation as: (i) the dataset is reasonably large, (ii) there may be underlying long-term patterns in the time series data that an N-fold cross-validation (even using different years for testing) would ignore (iii) for training and testing it is more realistic if the data represents a continuous sequence and (iv) repeating results for the same train/test split allows us to better compare reliability.

RMSE is the most commonly used performance metric in studies predicting air quality. However, it is of course a measure of a model's accuracy across all pollutant levels, whereas in practice low values are of far less concern than high pollutant levels. To analyse the performance of predicting peak episodes we have plotted the ROC curves (Receiver Operating Characteristic curves). They show the performance of classifying peak prediction episodes with different peak thresholds set for PM2.5 and PM10.

## 4    Results When Predicting Absolute Pollutant Values

### 4.1    Which Deep Learning Model is the Most Effective for Air Quality Forecasting?

We structured the air quality forecasting problem as a multi variate time series model to predict the pollution densities of PM2.5 and PM10. The monitoring station records these two pollutants along with other pollutants, and also the modelled current temperature (centigrade), modelled wind speed (m/s) and modelled wind direction (degrees). Since these individual features have different ranges, we used Standard Scaler for pre-processing. Figure 1 shows the results for different algorithms using standardised raw multivariate data to predict PM2.5 (left) and PM10 (right) 24 h in advance.

From the results it can be observed:

- CNN has lower mean values and variability than the other two models when run on Multivariate dataset.
- For both pollutants the LSTM models are again significantly less effective and reliable ($p < 0.001$ for both measures vs CNN or Wavenets).
- Wavenets are significantly more effective ($p < 0.001$) for $PM_{10}$, but not for $PM_{2.5}$.

Wavenets (via dilation) and LSTMs (by maintaining hidden state), are able to capture long-term patterns beyond the size of the input window. However, the results from our experiments for CNNs, is quite counter-intuitive in terms of what we have said earlier about seasonal and medium- term cycles but mostly in line with the time series forecasting results presented by Sayeed et al. [9] on the study using CNNs to predict ozone concentrations and Koprinska et al. [10] on the study using CNNs for energy time series forecasting. Our results suggests that at least for this site, it is not necessary to learn long term dependencies and also for example whether it is a weekday or weekend. Rather, the information is itself captured via different rates of growth and decay in pollutant levels in the temporally neighboring points which are well explored by CNN's.

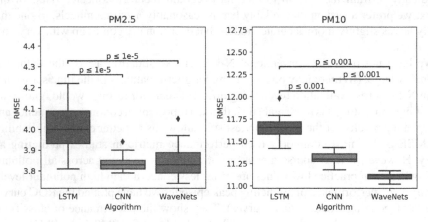

**Fig. 1.** Prediction performance comparison of different deep learning models

### 4.2 Comparison of Neural Approaches with Other Models

The prediction performance of the Deep Learning models is also compared with traditional regression and statistical methods such as Support Vector Regression (SVR) and SARIMAX applied on the same dataset and with the same train-test split to benchmark the performances. For SARIMAX we have tuned the optimal values for the parameters – p (number of autoregressive terms) = 3, d (number of nonseasonal differences needed for stationarity) = 0 and q (number of lagged forecast errors in the prediction equation) = 1 to provide better forecasting. As the Table 2 shows, both these 'conventional' regression approaches were less effective than CNN or Wavenet.

### 4.3 Effect on Prediction Performance if Perfect Weather Prediction is Available as an Auxiliary Input

Given the known impact of weather conditions on pollutants levels [14] we next explored the effect of including features for not just current, but also forecast weather conditions for the future time period being modelled.

In deployment, we would have the weather forecast for the next day and this could be integrated to the model input. But in this study since we were not able to obtain historical forecasts, we have used the actual weather data for the next periods. While this

**Table 2.** Comparison of deep learning and conventional approaches for univariate $PM_{2.5}$ prediction.

| $PM_{2.5}$ | RMSE – Mean | RMSE – Standard deviation | MAPE – Mean |
|---|---|---|---|
| LSTM | 4.1 | 0.09 | 25.23 |
| CNN | 3.82 | 0.02 | 25.64 |
| Wavenet | 3.79 | 0.03 | 24.42 |
| SVR | 4.3 | NA | 28.92 |
| SARIMAX | 5.87 | NA | 28.19 |

necessarily represents an ideal scenario with 'perfect' weather forecasting, in practice modern weather forecasts like from UK Meteorological Office (MET Office) are highly reliable [15].

This is effectively combining our neural models with the huge Monte Carlo simulation-based models used by weather forecasters. In future work we plan to investigate the robustness of the prediction performance as we add increasing amounts of noise to our 'perfect' weather forecasts.

It has been observed if we have perfect weather forecast inputs for – wind direction, wind speed, and the temperature we can further improve the air quality prediction performance (Fig. 2). This illustrates the known close alignment and relationship between air pollution concentrations and meteorological conditions. Figure 2 shows the performance comparisons from our results, between predictions of $PM_{2.5}$ (left) and $PM_{10}$ (right) when the problem is solved as univariate model, multivariate model and multivariate model with weather forecast as auxiliary inputs.

It is worth commenting that although adding this extra information removes any *mean* differences in performance, the LSTM still exhibits worse *reliability* than CNN. In other words, across the ten repetitions with different random seeds, while the best quartile (bottom of blue boxes in Fig. 2) and median (bars within boxes) results are very similar for all three algorithms, the LSTM reaches lower accuracy on some repetitions (top of blue boxes).

### 4.4 Feasibility of an Early Warning System to Predict Peaks

From the experiments conducted in the previous sections, it is clear the deep learning models can significantly improve the air quality prediction performance. We have further explored how effectively the outputs of these prediction models can be used so that local short-term mitigation strategies can be put in place to avoid any possible peak episodes. We considered this as a binary classification problem in which PM2.5 or PM10moving average values crossing a set peak target.

A simplistic binary model would simply predict "Pollutant Value Over X = True" when the predicted level of pollutant exceeds the value X. In practice it is possible to tune the sensitivity and recall of the binary classifier by predicting "Pollutant Value Over X = True" when the predicted level is above some set value Y. Thus, a binary classifier

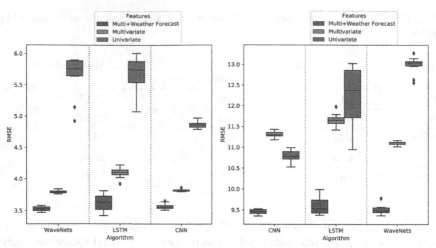

**Fig. 2.** Prediction improvement w.r.t RME values with weather forecast features added for $PM_{2.5}$ (left) and $PM_{10}$ (right)

with $Y < X$ gives a pessimistic prediction of air quality, and $Y > X$ giving an optimistic prediction.

Using this approach, we have plotted Receiver Operating Characteristic (ROC) curves for the prediction performance. These were obtained using four CNN models trained to predict for 24, 12, 6, and 3 h in advance. The points plotted for each curve were then obtained by applying the 'top-level' classifier using different classification peak thresholds (Y) from the range (5 -25 $\mu g/m^3$) for $PM_{2.5}$ and (1–70 $\mu g/m^3$) for $PM_{10}$.

The ROC curves are shown in Fig. 3. As can be seen for $PM_{10}$ it is possible to create a system that correctly warns about impending peaks 24 h in advance, but at the expense of ~50% false warnings. However, by using different thresholds the recall rate (proportion of events warned about) can be kept high while progressively improving the precision (proportion of warnings that result in actual peaks).

We wish to emphasize that the benefits of this approach are that tuning the thresholds does not require any changes to the learned regression models – so it empowers end-users to take advantage of local circumstances without requiring the system designer to 'second- guess' their preferences. Also with this phased binary prediction approach, for example if we encounter a situation in which we get a pessimistic peak episode predicted 24 h in advance or 12 h in advance due to bad weather prediction input or due to other factors affecting the prediction accuracy and then switch to a more accurate prediction in 6 h or 3 h in advance with higher confidence. This helps local authorities to prepare short-term mitigation strategies in advance (24 h/12 h in advance) and then decisions about enactment can be done at 3 h or 6 h in advance when more accurate prediction values are available.

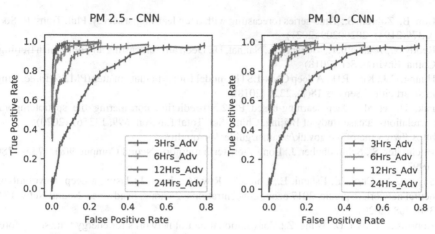

**Fig. 3.** ROC curves for different peak thresholds for $PM_{2.5}$ and $PM_{10}$

# 5  Conclusion

Though LSTMs are considered to be the state of art models to find both long- and short-term dependencies in time series data with memory units, we found our CNN based time series prediction model is more effective, and in particular more reliable in predicting Air Quality data. CNNs take advantage of the data points closer together in time series than data points which are far away for the prediction. We further applied Dilated convolutions (Wavenets) to widen the receptive field enabling the CNN to utilize longer dependencies but still our CNN model was performing better than with the Wavenets. This indicates prediction accuracy does not seem to benefit from the longer dependencies, but rather perform worse with Dilated CNN's and LSTM's. We have also analysed further and proposed the effectiveness of a binary early warning system to predict peak episodes with varying set threshold values for the Pollutants PM2.5 and PM10. In comparison, to the Met Office air pollution forecast which is generated from a regional model working on a 12 km grid resolution, our model represents the very localised increases in pollution that is expected close to roads or in urban/industrial centres. We believe this localized regression predictions combined with the proposed classifier to create the binary 'early warning system' where stakeholders can tune the thresholds applied in the run-up to a predicted peak event is going to be helpful in applying local short-term mitigation and communication strategies effectively in a phased manner that may reduce localized peak pollution episodes, support vulnerable communities in managing their exposure and overall improve public health in our urban environments.

# References

1. https://www.who.int/health-topics/air-pollution
2. Jakeman, A.J., Simpson, R.W., Taylor, J.A.: Modeling distributions of air pollutant concentrations—III. The hybrid deterministic-statistical distribution approach. Atmos. Environ. (1967) **22**(1), 163–174 (1988)

3. Lim, B., Zohren, S.: Time-series forecasting with deep learning: a survey. Phil. Trans. R. Soc. A **379**(2194), 20200209 (2021)
4. Reddy, V., Yedavalli, P., Mohanty, S., Nakhat, U.: Deep air: forecasting air pollution in Beijing, China. Environ. Sci. (2018)
5. Huang, C.J., Kuo, P.H.: A deep CNN-LSTM model for particulate matter (PM2.5) forecasting in smart cities. Sensors **18**(7), 2220 (2018)
6. Pak, U., et al.: Deep learning-based PM2.5 prediction considering the spatiotemporal correlations: a case study of Beijing, China. Sci. Total Environ. **699**, 133561 (2020)
7. https://www.metoffice.gov.uk/weather/guides/air-quality
8. Hochreiter, S., Schmidhuber, J.: Long short-term memory. Neural Comput. **9**(8), 1735–1780 (1997)
9. Sayeed, A., Choi, Y., Eslami, E., Lops, Y., Roy, A., Jung, J.: Using a deep convolutional neural network to predict 2017 ozone concentrations, 24 hours in advance. Neural Netw. **121**, 396–408 (2020)
10. Koprinska, I., Wu, D., Wang, Z.: Convolutional neural networks for energy time series forecasting. In: 2018 International Joint Conference on Neural Networks (IJCNN), pp. 1–8. IEEE (2018)
11. Hinton, G.E., Srivastava, N., Krizhevsky, A., Sutskever, I., Salakhutdinov, R.R.: Improving neural networks by preventing co-adaptation of feature detectors. arXiv preprint arXiv:1207.0580 (2012)
12. Borovykh, A., Bohte, S., Oosterlee, C.W.: Conditional time series forecasting with convolutional neural networks. arXiv preprint arXiv:1703.04691 (2017)
13. https://uk-air.defra.gov.uk/air-pollution/uk-eu-limits
14. Graham, A.M., et al.: Impact of weather types on UK ambient particulate matter concentrations. Atmos. Environ. **5**, 100061 (2020). Walker, History of the Meteorological Office

# Face Super-Resolution with Spatial Attention Guided by Multiscale Receptive-Field Features

Weikang Huang[2] , Shiyong Lan[1,2](✉), Wenwu Wang[3], Xuedong Yuan[1],
Hongyu Yang[1], Piaoyang Li[1], and Wei Ma[1]

[1] College of Computer Science, Sichuan University, Chengdu 610065, China
[2] National Key Laboratory of Fundamental Science on Synthetic Vision,
Sichuan University, Chengdu, China
lanshiyong@scu.edu.cn
[3] University of Surrey, Guildford GU2 7XH, UK
w.wang@surrey.ac.uk

**Abstract.** Face super-resolution (FSR) is dedicated to the restoration
of high-resolution (HR) face images from their low-resolution (LR) counterparts. Many deep FSR methods exploit facial prior knowledge (e.g.,
facial landmark and parsing map) related to facial structure information
to generate HR face images. However, directly training a facial prior estimation network with deep FSR model requires manually labeled data,
and is often computationally expensive. In addition, inaccurate facial priors may degrade super-resolution performance. In this paper, we propose
a residual FSR method with spatial attention mechanism guided by multiscale receptive-field features (MRF) for converting LR face images (i.e.,
$16 \times 16$) to HR face images (i.e., $128 \times 128$). With our spatial attention
mechanism, we can recover local details in face images without explicitly
learning the prior knowledge. Quantitative and qualitative experiments
show that our method outperforms state-of-the-art FSR methods.

**Keywords:** Face super-resolution · Multiscale receptive-field features ·
Spatial attention mechanism · Deep learning

## 1 Introduction

Face super-resolution (FSR), also known as face hallucination, aims to generate
high-resolution (HR) face images from corresponding low-resolution (LR) face
images. In real world scenarios, there are many low-resolution (LR) face images,
generated due to the limitation in an optical imaging system or the program
used for image compression. In LR face images, some details may be lost, thus

---

This work was funded in part by the Key R&D Project of Sichuan Science and Technology Department, China (2021YFG0300), and in part by 2035 Innovation Pilot Program
of Sichuan University, China.

leading to performance degradation for tasks such as face recognition and face landmark prediction. Thus, FSR has attracted increasing interest in a wide range of applications (e.g., face tracking, restoration of old face images).

FSR can be considered a special sub-task of single image super-resolution (SISR) [5]. Compared with SISR which takes images in different scenes as input, FSR only considers face images which are of similar structure. Therefore, FSR methods may offer better results than SISR on enhancing LR face images with higher upscaling factors (e.g., 8×). In recent years, with the rapid development of deep learning techniques, a number of face super-resolution methods have been proposed [2,3,9,16,19,23].

Different from general images, a face image is a highly structured object with facial landmarks and facial parsing maps. Such information has been used by many FSR methods to generate HR face images. For example, Song et al. [19] adopted CNNs to learn basic facial components first, and then synthesized fine-grained details from a high resolution training set to enhance these components. Kim et al. [9] proposed a progressive FSR model that generated multiscale SR results and applied a distilled face alignment network (FAN) to predict face landmark locations. Chen et al. [3] designed an end-to-end FSR network to recover the SR face images using the facial landmarks and parsing maps estimated via the network. Ma et al. [16] developed a FSR method using two recurrent networks for image restoration and landmark estimation, respectively. Although joint training with the facial prior information helps recover the key face structures, there are two major limitations. First, it is labour-intensive to manually label the data required for training the network for estimating the prior information. Second, it is difficult to estimate the prior information precisely for each face image, as each person's face is unique. Inaccurate prior information (e.g. location information) may lead to degraded FSR performance.

In this paper, we propose a multiscale receptive-field residual network (MRR-Net)[1] for face super-resolution, by introducing a spatial attention mechanism within the multiscale receptive-field residual blocks (MRRb). The key idea of our spatial attention mechanism is to obtain multiscale receptive-field features using concurrent convolution operation with different kernel size and then concatenate these features to generate the attention map. The spatial attention mechanism facilitates learning of face components of different size, as well as their outlines, allowing them to be processed at different scales. Our method exploits the advantage of convolution with different receptive-field and the efficiency of a CNN structure.

The main contributions of this paper are summarized as follows:

– We design a deep encoder-decoder residual framework for face super-resolution named MRRNet without explicitly learning facial prior knowledge.
– An improved spatial attention mechanism based on multi-scale receptive fields is used in each embedding layer (i.e., MRRb) of the encoder, for capturing face attributes at different scales for reconstructing the face images.

---

[1] https://github.com/SYLan2019/MRRNet.

Our method achieves state-of-the-art performance in terms of several metrics for image quality evaluation.

## 2   Related Work

Recently, significant progress has been made in face super-resolution using deep learning techniques. Yu et al. [24] introduced a generative adversarial network (GAN) to produce HR face images that are similar to real images. Chan et al. [1] designed an encoder-bank-decoder architecture for FSR using pre-trained GANs. Facial prior guided FSR methods utilize unique facial information to facilitate face reconstruction. Yu et al. [23] developed a convolutional neural network of two branches with one for estimating facial component heatmaps and the other for reconstructing face images aided by the heatmaps. Ma et al. [16] introduced a recursive cooperative FSR method with two recurrent networks that focus on image restoration and landmark estimation. More accurate landmark can be predicted based on better SR face image, which in turn can be recovered based on more precise landmarks. Thus the two recurrent networks can benefit from each other. However, such approaches might generate unnatural face images due to the difficulty in accurately estimating the unique facial information. In addition, building an estimation network requires additional effort for labelling data and training the network.

Attention mechanisms have been widely applied in low-level vision tasks, such as image enhancement and face super-resolution. Zhang et al. [27] proposed a residual channel attention block (RCAN) which generates different attention for each channel-wise feature to improve the discrimination ability of their network. Liu et al. [12] incorporated convolutional block attention module (CBAM) into their UNet-like generator to enhance the representation of regions of interest for anomaly detection. Chen et al. [2] proposed a face attention unit (FAU) that generates an attention map to enlarge the weight of the feature map related to face components. Unlike [27] which is based on channel attention, our attention mechanism utilizes spatial attention which contains more location information of face components. Despite being similar to [2] which takes advantages of multiscale features, our attention map is built from the multiscale receptive-field features corresponding to the face components of different size.

Different from the conventional way for building CNN networks in vision tasks, i.e. stacking many small spatial convolutions (e.g., $3 \times 3$) to enlarge the receptive field [4], several new ideas have emerged recently. In ConvNeXt [14], a Vision Transformers-like pure CNN is designed which outperformed Swin Transformers [13] on detection and segmentation tasks. One of their modifications in ConvNeXt was to use convolution with large kernel size $7 \times 7$. Ding et al. [4] demonstrated that using a few large convolutional kernels instead of using a stack of small kernels could obtain much larger effective receptive field, so as to achieve better performance in low-level vision tasks. Thus, different kernel sizes of convolutions are considered in the design of our spatial attention mechanism.

# 3    Proposed Method

## 3.1    Overview

In face super-resolution task, we aim to convert LR face images $I_{LR}$ to SR counterparts $I_{SR}$ which are close to the ground truth face images $I_{HR}$. In this paper, we propose a residual FSR method with spatial attention mechanism guided by multiscale receptive-filed features. As shown in Fig. 1, our proposed method consists of two networks including a multiscale receptive-field residual network (MRRNet) and an average discriminator. MRRNet works as a generator to generate $I_{SR}$. To recover the face components, MRRNet employs multiscale receptive-field residual (MRR) blocks (which is introduced in Sect. 3.2). In addition, we utilize the average discriminator and other losses (introduced in Sect. 3.3) to recover the face images with additional details.

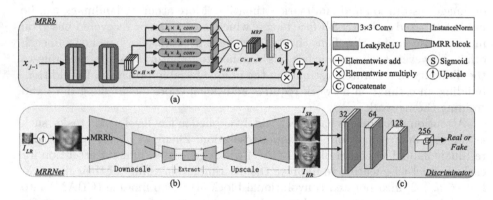

**Fig. 1.** The framework of the proposed method for face super-resolution. (a) is the detailed structure of our multi-scale receptive-field residual block. (b) is our generative network which is composed of MRR block. Rather than recovering low resolution face images directly, we resized them to 128 × 128 first through bicubic. (c) is our proposed average discriminator.

## 3.2    Multiscale Receptive-Field Residual Block

When observing face images, we usually look at the overall outline first, then we pay attention to the key facial components (e.g., eyebrows, eyes, nose, and mouth). This means that a FSR network is expected to not only pay attention to the overall structure, but also the key local details. However, due to the fact that the facial components and overall outline are of different size, it is not trivial to reconstruct the face features at various scales. To address this issue, we propose a spatial attention mechanism guided by multiscale receptive-filed features (MRF) embedded in a residual block. Our MRF is motivated by the Inception module in [20] and ConvNeXt [14]. The Inception module applies convolutions of different kernel size (i.e. 1, 3, 5) for multiscale feature processing, while ConvNeXt uses $7 \times 7$ convolution to simulate shifted window in Swin Transformer [13]. Thus, in our system, we design MRF using convolutions of four different kernel sizes (i.e. 1, 3, 5, 7).

By stacking the MRR blocks, our spatial attention mechanism helps the network to focus on facial features in different size. Denote the feature input of the $j$-th indexed MRR block as $x_{j-1} \in \mathbb{R}^{C_{j-1} \times H_{j-1} \times W_{j-1}}$. The fusion of multiscale receptive-field features can be computed as:

$$f_j^{c_2} = Conv_j^2 \left( Conv_j^1 (x_{j-1}) \right) \tag{1}$$

$$f_j^{fusion} = Concat \left[ Conv_j^{k_1}(f_j^{c_2}), Conv_j^{k_2}(f_j^{c_2}), \right. \\ \left. Conv_j^{k_3}(f_j^{c_2}), Conv_j^{k_4}(f_j^{c_2}) \right] \tag{2}$$

where $Conv_j^{i=1,2}$ is the $i$-th convolutional layer followed by Instance Normalization and Leaky ReLU activation function of the $j$-th MRR block. Features $f_j^{c_2} \in \mathbb{R}^{C_j \times H_j \times W_j}$ extracted by $Conv_j^2$ are passed to four convolutions (e.g., $Conv_j^{k_i}$) of different kernel size (i.e., $k_1, k_2, k_3, k_4$) without using normalization and activation function. Each convolution outputs a feature map where the number of channels is a quarter of $f_j^{c_2}$. We use padding in the four convolutions to ensure the four feature maps to be of same size. Then, we concatenate the four feature maps to get $f_j^{fusion} \in \mathbb{R}^{C_j \times H_j \times W_j}$, where $f_j^{fusion}$ contains multiscale features that can be further utilized for generating the attention map $a_j \in \mathbb{R}^{1 \times H_j \times W_j}$, as follows:

$$a_j = S \left( C_j(f_j^{fusion}) \right) \tag{3}$$

where $C_j$ is a convolution operation that only has one kernel. $S(\cdot)$ denotes the sigmoid function. Finally, the output of the $j$-th MRR block is computed as:

$$x_j = x_{j-1} + a_j \otimes f_j^{c_2} \tag{4}$$

where $\otimes$ is element-wise multiplication, and $a_j$ assigns a value between 0 and 1 to $f_j^{c_2}$ which is passed through the channels.

We design our MRRNet as a hourglass-like network, due to the potential benefits offered by its downscale and upscale layers in improving feature representation. Specifically, we implement the downscale layer by adding a convolution to the residual branch of the MRR block to downscale the feature size, meanwhile in the upscale layer, the feature map is up-sampled by using the nearest neighbor interpolation. Thus, Eq. (4) is changed in downscale and upscale layers to:

$$x_j = Conv^d(x_{j-1}) + a_j \otimes f_j^{c_2} \tag{5}$$

$$x_j = I_n(x_{j-1}) + a_j \otimes f_j^{c_2} \tag{6}$$

where $Conv^d$ denotes downscaling the convolutional layer with stride 2, and $I_n$ is the nearest interpolation where the scale factor is typically chosen as 2 [17].

## 3.3 Objective Functions

**Pixel Loss:** We first train the MRRNet by optimizing the L1 loss with $N$ pairs of LR-HR images as follows

$$\mathcal{L}_{pixel} = \frac{1}{N} \sum_{i=1}^{N} ||I_{HR}^i - \mathcal{F}_{MRRNet}(I_{LR}^i, \Theta)|| \tag{7}$$

where $\mathcal{F}_{MRRNet}$ and $\Theta$ are the MRRNet and its parameters, respectively. $I_{HR}^i$ is the $i$-th HR image, $I_{LR}^i$ is the $i$-th LR image. We then apply other losses including adversarial loss and perceptual loss to train MRRGAN (generative adversarial version of MRRNet) for reconstructing high-fidelity face image.

**Adversarial Loss:** Recently, GAN [6] has been shown to be a powerful method for generating high-fidelity images. Therefore, we introduce Relativistic Average HingeGAN (RAHingeGAN) [8] to generate photo-realistic face images. RAHingeGAN $D$ outputs a matrix as shown in the discriminator in Fig. 1. Each element in this matrix reflects the confidence level on how similar a certain area of the SR images is to that of the HR images. The discriminator $D$ differentiates the ground-truth and $I_{SR}$ by minimizing:

$$\mathcal{L}_D = \mathbb{E}[max(0, 1 - (D(x_h) - \mathbb{E}[D(x_g)]))] \\ + \mathbb{E}[max(0, 1 + (D(x_g) - \mathbb{E}[D(x_h)]))] \tag{8}$$

Meantime, the generator $G$ tries to deceive $D$ by minimizing:

$$\mathcal{L}_G = \mathbb{E}[max(0, 1 + (D(x_h) - \mathbb{E}[D(x_g)]))] \\ + \mathbb{E}[max(0, 1 - (D(x_g) - \mathbb{E}[D(x_h)]))] \tag{9}$$

where $x_h$ and $x_g$ are ground-truth and super-resolved face image, respectively.

**Perceptual Loss:** Perceptual loss [7] encourages $G$ to generate natural results in perception. Perceptual loss here is defined as the $l_1$ norm between the feature maps of the ground-truth and $I_{SR}$ extracted by a pre-trained VGG19 network [18], as follows:

$$\mathcal{L}_{per} = \mathbb{E}\left[\sum_{i=1}^{I} ||\phi_i(x_g) - \phi_i(x_h)||_1\right] \tag{10}$$

where $\phi_i$ extracts feature maps by the $i$-th layer of the VGG network and $I$ is the number of the layers used. Finally, by combining the loss functions with different weights, we get the total loss defined as

$$\mathcal{L}_{total} = \lambda_G \mathcal{L}_G + \lambda_p \mathcal{L}_{per} + \lambda_{pix} \mathcal{L}_{pixel} \tag{11}$$

where $\lambda_G$, $\lambda_p$ and $\lambda_{pix}$ are weights, which are used to adjust the relative importance of $\mathcal{L}_G$, $\mathcal{L}_{per}$, and $\mathcal{L}_{pixel}$, respectively.

# 4  Experiments

## 4.1  Datasets and Metrics

We conduct experiments on two widely used face datasets: CelebA [15] and Helen [11]. For both datasets, we first crop face images roughly according to landmark. Then, we further remove the excess background in the cropped face images by setting a threshold. Finally, we resize the cropped images to $128 \times 128$ as HR (i.e., ground-truth) face images and downsample the HR images to $16 \times 16$ as LR face images. For the CelebA dataset, we use 193K images for training and 1K images for testing. For the Helen dataset, we use 2000 images for training and 50 images for testing. Our test sets are the same as in [16]. We evaluate SR results using performance metrics PSNR, SSIM [21] and LPIPS [26], respectively. PSNR and SSIM are most commonly used evaluation metrics in super-resolution task, calculated on the Y channel of the transformed YCbCr space in our experiments. Learned Perceptual Image Patch Similarity (LPIPS) is a deep features based metric, evaluating the perceptual similarity between two images.

## 4.2  Implementation Details

We set the number of MRRb blocks in the encoder, extractor, decoder to 3, 10, 3, respectively. For training the MRRNet model, we set $\lambda_{pixel} = 1$ and when training the MRRGAN, the parameters $\lambda_G$, $\lambda_{per}$, and $\lambda_{pixel}$ are set as 0.01, 0.01 and 1, respectively. The kernel sizes $k_1, k_2, k_3, k_4$ are set to 1, 3, 5, 7, respectively. The entire network is optimized using Adam [10] with $\beta_1 = 0.9$, $\beta_2 = 0.99$, $\epsilon = 10^{-8}$ and a learning rate 0.0001. For data augmentation, we use random horizontal flipping, and image rescaling. We built our network in Pytorch and trained it on an NVIDIA RTX 3080 GPU.

## 4.3  Results and Analysis

**Comparison with the State-of-the-Art Methods:** We compare our method with state-of-the-art FSR and general SR methods qualitatively and quantitatively on Helen and CelebA test sets provided by [16]. For methods that provide training codes, we retrain these models on our training set. Table 1 shows the PSNR and SSIM results on Helen and CelebA datasets. Different from our method, DIC [16], PFSR [9] and FSRNet [3] applied facial prior knowledge to improve super-resolution performance. It can be observed that our MRRNet outperforms other methods in terms of the PSNR and SSIM metrics. Our MRRGAN has a lower PSNR and SSIM than MRRNet, but gives comparable performance with other methods. This shows that our method offers better performance, achieving balance in perceptual quality and pixel accuracy of super-resolved face image, thanks to the special network design with the attention mechanism and integrated loss function. Apart from PSNR and SSIM, we evaluate our methods and other methods with LPIPS [26] which reflect perceptual similarity based on deep features. Our MRRGAN has achieved best scores on both datasets, which demonstrates that the super-resolved face images generated by our MRRGAN are perceptually more similar to the HR face images.

**Table 1.** Quantitative comparison on CelebA (rows 2 to 4) and Helen (rows 5 to 7) with state-of-the-art FSR methods. The best and second best performance are highlighted in red and blue, respectively.

| Method | Bicubic | PFSR [9] | URDGN [24] | FSRNET [23] | DIC [16] | DICGAN [16] | MRRNET | MRRGAN |
|--------|---------|----------|------------|-------------|----------|-------------|--------|--------|
| PSNR   | 23.73   | 23.97    | 24.73      | 26.29       | 27.22    | 26.38       | 27.27  | 26.64  |
| SSIM   | 0.6261  | 0.6787   | 0.6871     | 0.7518      | 0.7845   | 0.7517      | 0.7873 | 0.7632 |
| LPIPS  | 0.5329  | 0.2716   | 0.2427     | 0.2315      | 0.1974   | 0.0976      | 0.1921 | 0.0930 |
| PSNR   | 24.04   | 23.61    | 24.22      | 25.20       | 26.75    | 26.02       | 26.86  | 26.15  |
| SSIM   | 0.6743  | 0.6486   | 0.6909     | 0.7091      | 0.7894   | 0.7518      | 0.7912 | 0.7614 |
| LPIPS  | 0.5253  | 0.2636   | 0.2449     | 0.2356      | 0.2050   | 0.0966      | 0.2038 | 0.0941 |

In Fig. 2, we visualize some super-resolution results of different methods. We can see that even without face prior information, MRRNet can still correctly generate face key components including eye, nose, and mouth. This is because our spatial attention mechanism exploits feature maps obtained through different receptive fields. Furthermore, compared with DICGAN where a discriminator $D$ is used to differentiate the ground-truth and the super-resolved images. MRRGAN achieved better visual results, i.e. giving clearer textures and more realistic details in eyebrow, teeth and other facial components. The qualitative comparisons demonstrate the powerful ability of our methods for generating human face images.

**Table 2.** Average Euclidean distance between the estimated landmarks and ground truth landmarks.

| Method | DICGAN [16] | MRRGAN |
|--------|-------------|--------|
| AED    | 1.4564      | 1.4126 |

As [3], we conduct facial landmark estimation comparison on Helen between DICGAN and MRRGAN that have the best visual effect in Fig. 2. The more consistent the predictions between super-resolved face images and GT are, the better the generated face images. We use OpenFace [25] to detect 68 facial landmarks of each face image. Then, we calculate the average Euclidean distance (AED) between the 68 landmarks of DICGAN, MRRGAN and GT respectively. We tabulate the results in Table 2. Figure 3 shows a landmark estimation example of DICGAN, MRRGAN and GT. From Fig. 3 we can see the lower AED value, the closer the image is to GT. The comparison demonstrates that MRRGAN has powerful generation ability in recovering facial components of different sizes precisely.

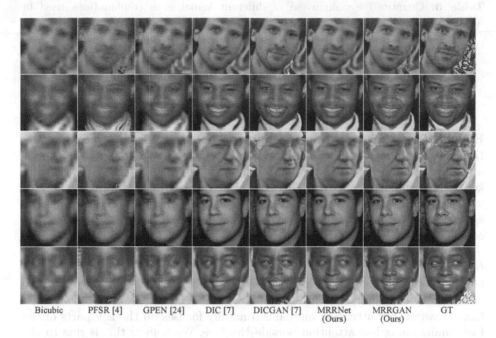

| Bicubic | PFSR [4] | GPEN [24] | DIC [7] | DICGAN [7] | MRRNet (Ours) | MRRGAN (Ours) | GT |

**Fig. 2.** Visual comparison with state-of-the-art methods. The size of low resolution face image is 16 × 16 and magnified by a factor of 8. More details could be observed by zooming into the figures.

| DICGAN | MRRGAN | GT | | DICGAN | MRRGAN | GT |
| 8.9203 | 2.8608 | AED | | 2.1343 | 0.7061 | AED |

**Fig. 3.** Landmark detection comparison between DICGAN and our MRRGAN. For example, the landmark detection accuracy at the nose by the proposed method is significantly higher than that of the baseline.

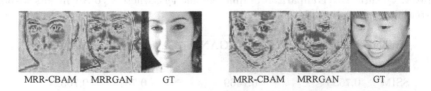

| MRR-CBAM | MRRGAN | GT | | MRR-CBAM | MRRGAN | GT |

**Fig. 4.** Visualization of attention map in MRRGAN and MRR-CBAM.

**Table 3.** Quantitative comparison of different kernel sizes combinations used in MRRGAN on Helen.

| Method | MRRGAN-$k_{1,3}$ | MRRGAN-$k_{5,7}$ | MRRGAN-$k_{1,7}$ | MRRGAN |
|--------|--------|--------|--------|--------|
| PSNR | 26.23 | 26.49 | 26.31 | 26.64 |
| SSIM | 0.7515 | 0.7586 | 0.7530 | 0.7632 |

**Effects of Spatial Attention Mechanism:** In order to demonstrate the effectiveness of the proposed spatial attention mechanism. We conduct an experiment between our spatial attention mechanism and CBAM [22] for extracting key facial components. Specifically, we replace our spatial attention mechanism with CBAM in MRRGAN (denoted as MRR-CBAM) and keep other settings the same. In Fig. 4, we visualize some attention maps, generated in the upscale process of MRRGAN and MRR-CBAM. We can see that: 1) Our spatial attention mechanism can effectively learn to focus on facial components of different sizes (such as eyes, eyebrows, mouths, and facial contours). However, MRR-CBAM lacks attention to the small-scale lip lines in the left image. 2) CBAM pays more attention to the outer contours of the face, and even to the areas outside the face. However, our attention mechanism mainly focuses on the key parts of the face, maintaining low attention outside the face. We believe this is due to the use of convolution in different kernel size in the spatial attention mechanism. This experiment demonstrates that our spatial attention mechanism can guide the generation of HR face images.

**Study of Kernel Size:** To investigate the impact of the convolution in different kernel size used in our spatial attention mechanism. We conducted an experiment by combining convolutions with different kernel sizes pairwise in spatial attention within MRRGAN. In particular, we implement $1 \times 1$ with $3 \times 3$, $5 \times 5$ with $7 \times 7$ and $1 \times 1$ with $7 \times 7$ (denoted as MRRGAN-$k_{1,3}$, MRRGAN-$k_{5,7}$ and MRRGAN-$k_{1,7}$) three combinations, which correspond to small-small, large-large and small-large convolution kernel size paired. We evaluate PSNR and SSIM on CelebA for these three combinations and show the results in Table 3. From this table, it can be observed that MRRGAN which has convolution with four kernels in spatial attention achieves the best performance, while MRRGAN-$k_{5,7}$ is better than other combinations.

**Table 4.** Quantitative comparison of different models, where w/o SA means without the spatial attention module.

| Method | MRRNet w/o SA | MRRGAN w/o SA | MRRNet | MRRGAN |
|--------|--------|--------|--------|--------|
| PSNR | 26.83 | 25.47 | 27.27 | 26.64 |
| SSIM | 0.7585 | 0.7469 | 0.7873 | 0.7632 |

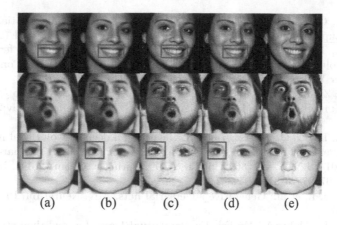

**Fig. 5.** Visual comparison between (a) MRRNet w/o SA. (b) MRRNet. (c) MRRGAN w/o SA. (d) MRRGAN. (e) GT. Better zoom in to see the detail

### 4.4 Ablation Study

We further perform an ablation study to demonstrate the effectiveness of our spatial attention mechanism. In the ablation experiment, we remove the spatial attention mechanism in MRRNet and MRRGAN which are called MRRNet w/o SA and MRRGAN w/o SA. The quantitative comparison results of PSNR and SSIM on Helen are presented in Table 4. It can be observed that, compared with MRRNet w/o SA and MRRGAN w/o SA, MRRNet and MRRGAN achieve better performances in all metrics. In Fig. 5, we visualize SR images generated with and without spatial attention mechanism and GAN. We can see that MRRNet w/o SA and MRRGAN w/o SA produced artifacts in key face components such as the eyes, while MRRGAN generates the best quality face images with the guidance of spatial attention.

## 5 Conclusion

We have presented a multiscale receptive-field residual network for face super-resolution. Specifically, a spatial attention mechanism guided by multiscale receptive field features embedded in a vanilla residual block helps recover the facial components of different size. The qualitative and quantitative experimental results on the CelebA and Helen datasets show the effectiveness of our method, as compared with other state-of-the-art FSR methods.

## References

1. Chan, K.C., Wang, X., Xu, X., Gu, J., Loy, C.C.: GLEAN: generative latent bank for large-factor image super-resolution. In: Proceedings of the IEEE/CVF Conference on Computer Vision and Pattern Recognition, pp. 14245–14254 (2021)

2. Chen, C., Gong, D., Wang, H., Li, Z., Wong, K.Y.K.: Learning spatial attention for face super-resolution. IEEE Trans. Image Process. **30**, 1219–1231 (2020)

3. Chen, Y., Tai, Y., Liu, X., Shen, C., Yang, J.: FSRNet: end-to-end learning face super-resolution with facial priors. In: Proceedings of the IEEE Conference on Computer Vision and Pattern Recognition, pp. 2492–2501 (2018)

4. Ding, X., Zhang, X., Zhou, Y., Han, J., Ding, G., Sun, J.: Scaling up your kernels to 31×31: revisiting large kernel design in CNNs. arXiv preprint arXiv:2203.06717 (2022)

5. Dong, C., Loy, C.C., He, K., Tang, X.: Learning a deep convolutional network for image super-resolution. In: Fleet, D., Pajdla, T., Schiele, B., Tuytelaars, T. (eds.) ECCV 2014. LNCS, vol. 8692, pp. 184–199. Springer, Cham (2014). https://doi.org/10.1007/978-3-319-10593-2_13

6. Goodfellow, I., et al.: Generative adversarial nets. Adv. Neural Inf. Process. Syst. **27** (2014)

7. Johnson, J., Alahi, A., Fei-Fei, L.: Perceptual losses for real-time style transfer and super-resolution. In: Leibe, B., Matas, J., Sebe, N., Welling, M. (eds.) ECCV 2016. LNCS, vol. 9906, pp. 694–711. Springer, Cham (2016). https://doi.org/10.1007/978-3-319-46475-6_43

8. Jolicoeur-Martineau, A.: The relativistic discriminator: a key element missing from standard GAN. arXiv preprint arXiv:1807.00734 (2018)

9. Kim, D., Kim, M., Kwon, G., Kim, D.S.: Progressive face super-resolution via attention to facial landmark. arXiv preprint arXiv:1908.08239 (2019)

10. Kingma, D.P., Ba, J.: Adam: a method for stochastic optimization. arXiv preprint arXiv:1412.6980 (2014)

11. Le, V., Brandt, J., Lin, Z., Bourdev, L., Huang, T.S.: Interactive facial feature localization. In: Fitzgibbon, A., Lazebnik, S., Perona, P., Sato, Y., Schmid, C. (eds.) ECCV 2012. LNCS, vol. 7574, pp. 679–692. Springer, Heidelberg (2012). https://doi.org/10.1007/978-3-642-33712-3_49

12. Liu, G., Lan, S., Zhang, T., Huang, W., Wang, W.: SAGAN: skip-attention GAN for anomaly detection. In: 2021 IEEE International Conference on Image Processing (ICIP), pp. 2468–2472. IEEE (2021)

13. Liu, Z., et al.: Swin transformer: hierarchical vision transformer using shifted windows. In: Proceedings of the IEEE/CVF International Conference on Computer Vision, pp. 10012–10022 (2021)

14. Liu, Z., Mao, H., Wu, C.Y., Feichtenhofer, C., Darrell, T., Xie, S.: A convnet for the 2020s. arXiv preprint arXiv:2201.03545 (2022)

15. Liu, Z., Luo, P., Wang, X., Tang, X.: Deep learning face attributes in the wild. In: Proceedings of the IEEE International Conference on Computer Vision, pp. 3730–3738 (2015)

16. Ma, C., Jiang, Z., Rao, Y., Lu, J., Zhou, J.: Deep face super-resolution with iterative collaboration between attentive recovery and landmark estimation. In: Proceedings of the IEEE/CVF Conference on Computer Vision and Pattern Recognition, pp. 5569–5578 (2020)

17. Odena, A., Dumoulin, V., Olah, C.: Deconvolution and checkerboard artifacts. Distill **1**(10), e3 (2016)

18. Simonyan, K., Zisserman, A.: Very deep convolutional networks for large-scale image recognition. arXiv preprint arXiv:1409.1556 (2014)

19. Song, Y., Zhang, J., He, S., Bao, L., Yang, Q.: Learning to hallucinate face images via component generation and enhancement. arXiv preprint arXiv:1708.00223 (2017)

20. Szegedy, C., et al.: Going deeper with convolutions. In: Proceedings of the IEEE Conference on Computer Vision and Pattern Recognition, pp. 1–9 (2015)
21. Wang, Z., Bovik, A.C., Sheikh, H.R., Simoncelli, E.P.: Image quality assessment: from error visibility to structural similarity. IEEE Trans. Image Process. **13**(4), 600–612 (2004)
22. Woo, S., Park, J., Lee, J.Y., Kweon, I.S.: CBAM: convolutional block attention module. In: Proceedings of the European Conference on Computer Vision (ECCV), pp. 3–19 (2018)
23. Yu, X., Fernando, B., Ghanem, B., Porikli, F., Hartley, R.: Face super-resolution guided by facial component heatmaps. In: Proceedings of the European Conference on Computer Vision (ECCV), pp. 217–233 (2018)
24. Yu, X., Porikli, F.: Ultra-resolving face images by discriminative generative networks. In: Leibe, B., Matas, J., Sebe, N., Welling, M. (eds.) ECCV 2016. LNCS, vol. 9909, pp. 318–333. Springer, Cham (2016). https://doi.org/10.1007/978-3-319-46454-1_20
25. Zadeh, A., Chong Lim, Y., Baltrusaitis, T., Morency, L.P.: Convolutional experts constrained local model for 3D facial landmark detection. In: Proceedings of the IEEE International Conference on Computer Vision Workshops, pp. 2519–2528 (2017)
26. Zhang, R., Isola, P., Efros, A.A., Shechtman, E., Wang, O.: The unreasonable effectiveness of deep features as a perceptual metric. In: Proceedings of the IEEE Conference on Computer Vision and Pattern Recognition (2018)
27. Zhang, Y., Li, K., Li, K., Wang, L., Zhong, B., Fu, Y.: Image super-resolution using very deep residual channel attention networks. In: Proceedings of the European Conference on Computer Vision (ECCV), pp. 286–301 (2018)

# F-Measure Optimization for Multi-class, Imbalanced Emotion Classification Tasks

Toki Tahmid Inan[(✉)], Mingrui Liu, and Amarda Shehu

Department of Computer Science, George Mason University, Fairfax, VA 22030, USA
{tinan,mingruil,ashehu}@gmu.edu

**Abstract.** Recent NLP breakthroughs have significantly advanced the state of emotion classification (EC) over text data. However, current treatments guide learning by traditional performance metrics, such as classification error rate, which are not suitable for the highly-imbalanced EC problems; in fact, EC models are predominantly evaluated by variations of the F-measure, recognizing the data imbalance. This paper addresses the dissonance between the learning objective and the performance evaluation for EC with moderate to severe data imbalance. We propose a series of increasingly powerful algorithms for F-measure improvement. An ablation study demonstrates the superiority of learning an optimal class decision threshold. Increased performance is demonstrated when joint learning is carried out over both the representation and the class decision thresholds. Thorough empirical evaluation on benchmark EC datasets that span the spectrum of number of classes and class imbalance shows clear F-measure improvements over baseline models, with good improvements over pre-trained deep models and higher improvements over untrained deep architectures.

**Keywords:** Emotion classification · Multi-class classification · Class imbalance · F-measure optimization · Transformer models · Deep learning

## 1 Introduction

Emotion classification (EC) is a fundamental task in AI-mediated platforms that track emotional engagement, satisfaction, and interact with employees, consumers, students, patients, etc. [6,15]. Recent NLP breakthroughs due to transformers have significantly advanced EC from text [4]. Existing studies pursue a canonical treatment, where learning is guided by traditional performance metrics, such as classification error rate. These metrics do not address the unique challenges when learning over emotion-annotated text. The number of classes can span from a few to a few dozen, as humans express a variety of emotions. Learning fine-grained emotions rather than coarse sentiments brings the issue of data imbalance to the surface; some emotions are scarce in labeled data.

Recognizing data imbalance as a central challenge, EC models are compared on variations of the F-measure (macro-, weighted, micro-F1). There is a dissonance between the learning objective, which utilizes classification error rates,

E. Pimenidis et al. (Eds.): ICANN 2022, LNCS 13529, pp. 158–170, 2022.
https://doi.org/10.1007/978-3-031-15919-0_14

and the performance evaluation, which utilizes the F-measure. The F-measure is more suitable for imbalanced data. In the binary setting, the F-measure enforces a better balance between performance on the rare versus the dominating class. However, the F-measure is non-decomposable over training examples and is a non-convex function of the model parameters.

In this paper we are inspired by the threshold-based formulation in [9] for optimizing the F-measure. However, work in [9] is restricted to linear models and binary classification. Here, our focus is on complex deep learning transformer models for multi-class classification. Our main contribution in this paper is introducing new practical algorithms which utilize deep learning to maximize F-measure for multi-class classification according to a threshold-based formulation. An important characteristic of the algorithms proposed here is that they can be utilized on any pre-trained model, which facilitates their adoption in a variety of multi-class classification tasks over imbalanced data. Our focus and empirical evaluation is on EC problems which exhibit significant class imbalance.

Driven by practical concerns for the proposed approach to be easily adopted in EC and possibly other multi-class problems beyond EC, we extend a given deep architecture with an additional layer that allows simultaneously estimating the posterior probability and learning the class decision thresholds. An ablation study compares various strategies resulting in different algorithms that are compared and evaluated on several benchmark EC datasets spanning the spectrum of number of classes and class imbalance. The empirical evaluation shows clear, statistically-significant F1-score improvements over baseline models, with good improvements over pre-trained deep models and even higher improvements over untrained deep architectures.

## 2 Related Work

**Class Imbalance Across ML:** Data augmentation is a popular approach to address class imbalance. The Synthetic Minority Oversampling Technique (SMOTE), which generates augmented minority class examples through interpolation [1], and its variants suffer many issues. Oversampling slows down training and leads to overfitting. Undersampling leads a model to miss out on important concepts. Since SMOTE works in feature space, which is very large in NLP tasks, SMOTE is ineffective [11]. More effective text augmentation techniques have emerged [13] that can be clustered into symbolic or neural methods. Symbolic methods use rules or discrete data structures to form synthetic examples, whereas neural augmentations use a deep neural network trained on a different task to augment data. Many of these techniques are very costly for NLP tasks with large training datasets [13]. Other techniques address imbalance by modifying weights in the loss function. The *Class Weights Sampling* (CWS) technique assigns a weight $w_i$ to each class $c_i$ based on the proportion of training samples $n_i$ in $c_i$ [14]. There are variations, but a popular one calculates $w_i = \frac{t}{K*n_i}$; the minority classes get higher weights. In turn, the optimization algorithm focuses on reducing errors for the minority classes.

**Class Imbalance and Methods in EC:** Growth in social media text, crowd-sourcing of emotion annotation, and increased awareness of psychological models have resulted in several benchmark datasets now annotated with fine-grained emotions and in deep EC models. Current state-of-the-art (SOTA) EC models leverage the Bidirectional Encoder Representations from Transformers (BERT) [5] to capture contextual information. Work in [4] debuts a fine-tuned BERT over one benchmark dataset, GoEmotions, yet exposing the class imbalance challenge with very low or 0 F-scores over scarce emotions [4]. Work in[20] targets the improvement of the macro-F1 score via a computationally-costly hyper-parameter optimization on two benchmark datasets, GoEmotions and SemEval-2018 (Task 1). The dissonance is clear; SOTA EC models are trained guided by classification error rates but evaluated by the F-measure.

**F-Measure Optimization in Online Learning:** Direct optimization of the F-measure as part of learning is challenging. F-measure is non-decomposable over training examples and is a non-convex function of the model parameters. There are several efforts in online optimization literature, where F-measure optimization is central due to data imbalance in a changing learning environment. These efforts follow three approaches. The first minimizes a surrogate loss function (or maximizes a surrogate reward function) but has large memory demands; the calibration of the surrogate loss is unclear [10]. The second approach optimizes for F-measure by minimizing a cost-sensitive loss and incurs a large computational cost [17]. A third group of methods achieve an optimal classifier for maximizing the F-measure by thresholding the posterior class probability [9]. F-measure optimization is then reduced to learning the optimal threshold and the posterior probability incrementally.

**F-Measure Optimization to Address Class Imbalance:** Our objective is to optimize F-measure for multi-class, imbalanced EC, and we are inspired by the threshold-based formulation [9], which we extend here beyond a generalized linear model for online binary classification. Specifically, we focus on deep BERT-based models for imbalanced multi-class EC problems and design and evaluate various algorithms. We focus on macro-F1 score as the desired instantiation of the F-measure, as it weights each class-specific F1-score equally and so is a less biased metric for imbalanced data.

## 3   Methodology

**Preliminaries:** Let $(x_1, y_1), \ldots (x_n, y_n)$ be i.i.d. samples from an unknown distribution $\mathcal{P}$. $x_{i \in [n]} \in \mathcal{X}$ are the set of feature vectors, $y_{i \in [n]} \in \{1, 0\}$ are binary class labels, and $\mathcal{Z} = \mathcal{X} \times \mathcal{Y}$ is the domain of the data. We denote the marginal distribution of feature $x \in \mathcal{X}$ by $\mu(x)$; the posterior probability for the true class is $\eta(x) = Pr(y = 1|x)$. The prior distribution of the true class is $\pi = Pr(Y = 1) = \int_{x \in \mathcal{X}} \eta(x) \, d\mu(x)$. Let $\mathcal{C} = \{f : \mathcal{X} \to \{1, 0\}\}$ be the set of all binary classifiers on $\mathcal{X}$. The F-measure for a binary classifier in $\mathcal{C}$ is defined as

$$F(f) = \frac{2 \int_{\mathcal{X}} \eta(x) f(x) \, d\mu(x)}{\int_{\mathcal{X}} f(x) \, d\mu(x) + \int_{\mathcal{X}} \eta(x) \, d\mu(x)} \tag{1}$$

Let $\mathcal{G} = \{g : \mathcal{X} \to [0,1]\}$ be the set of all binary classifiers over $\mathcal{X}$ that assign the probability to a sample $x$ of being the true/positive class. The set of classifiers is induced by thresholding another binary classifier $\mathcal{T} = \{g_\theta(x) = \mathcal{I}_{[g(x) \geq \theta]}\} \subseteq \mathcal{F}$, where $\mathcal{I}$ is the indicator function that is evaluated 1 if its argument is true and 0 otherwise, and $\theta \in [0,1]$ is a threshold.

Minimizing loss does not directly maximize the F-measure. An optimal binary classifier that does so can be obtained by thresholding the true posterior probability $\eta(x)$, i.e., $\eta_\theta = \mathcal{I}_{[\eta(x) \geq \theta]}$ [8,18]. F-measure optimization is so reduced into two sub-problems: a) estimating the true posterior probability and b) estimating the threshold. Work in [21] shows that the optimal threshold $\theta^* \in [0, 0.5]$, which will be used in our approach. (a) The Fast Online F-measure Optimization (FOFO) algorithm [9] learns the posterior probability using a linear model. For a feature vector $\phi(x) \in \mathbf{R}^d$, there exists a good model $w^* \in \mathbf{R}^d$ such that

$$\eta(x) = \Pr(y = 1 | x) = \frac{1}{1 + \exp(-w^{*T}\phi(x))} \tag{2}$$

Model parameter $w^*$ can be estimated by minimizing the expected loss [9]. Specifically, for binary cross entropy,

$$w^* \in \arg\min_{w \in \mathbf{R}^d} L(w) \stackrel{\Delta}{=} \mathbf{E}_{x,y} \log(1 + \exp(-(2y - 1)w^T\phi(x))) \tag{3}$$

(b) In [9] the optimal threshold $\theta^*$ is learned by solving the following strongly convex function

$$\min_{\theta \in [0,0.5]} Q(\theta) \stackrel{\Delta}{=} \frac{1}{2}\mathbf{E}_x[(\eta(x) - \theta)^2] + \frac{1}{2}\theta^2 \tag{4}$$

Work in [9] also shows that, as the decision threshold $\theta$ approaches the optimal threshold $\theta^*$, $F(\eta(\theta))$ moves closer to the optimal F-measure $F^*$, which justifies optimizing the convex function $Q(\theta)$.

### 3.1  Proposed Approach

There are two challenges with adopting the F-measure optimization. First, easily overcome, is the binary classification setting. The second, requiring more care, is extending from linear models in related work to deep, BERT models.

**From Binary to Multi-class Classification:** One-vs-one (OvO) and One-vs-All (OvA) are conventional approaches to build a multi-class classifier from a binary classifier. In OvO, for every pair of $K$ classes, $(K(K-1)/2)$ binary classifiers are introduced; this is impractical for high $K$. We leverage instead OvA, where the classifier consists of $K$ binary classifiers – one for each possible outcome, as illustrated in Fig. 1(a).

**From a Linear Model to a Deep Model:** We are motivated by practical concerns for the proposed F-measure optimization approach to be readily adopted in EC and possibly other multi-class problems. So, we extend a *given* deep architecture with an additional, linear layer, as illustrated in Fig. 1(b). The key idea

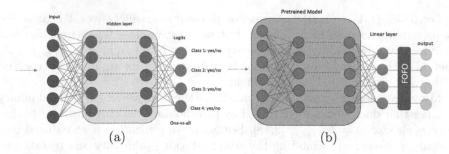

**Fig. 1.** (a) Illustration of the OvA approach we employ to adapt a binary classifier for a multi-class neural network. (b) Schematic of our proposed approach for F-measure optimization for deep multi-class classification models.

is to use a two-stage learning approach. In the first stage, we learn a good feature representation for a problem instance at hand by either a pre-trained model (e.g., a fine-tuned BERT) or by training a model from scratch. In the second stage, we fix all layers except the last and invoke the FOFO algorithm to optimize for F-measure by only updating the last layer. When we only train the last layer, the optimization is strongly-convex; when we train all layers, the problem is not strongly convex.

**F-Measure Optimization for Deep Multi-class Classification:** As shown in Fig. 1(b), the added layer is linear and has an output size equal to the number of classes. The output of each node from the output layer of the pre-trained network is input to the new layer. We obtain the per-class probability by passing the output from each node of the output layer through a sigmoid function. For an output $o_{i \in [K]}$ from a neuron, the class probability, $\Pr(C_i|x) = \frac{1}{1+\exp(-o_i)}$. The FOFO algorithm provides us with the decision threshold for each class, represented by node $\chi(w)$, where $w$ is the node parameter. Conceptually, each individual threshold is data-adaptive: it automatically changes according to the degree of data imbalance. This is in stark contrast to the standard deep learning training, where a fixed threshold (often 0.5) is used and is data-independent. Data-dependent thresholds allow the model to pay more attention to the data in the minority class and improve F-measure.

### 3.2 Algorithmic Instantiations: An Ablation Study

We formulate three algorithms, MCFO-RI, COTE, and MCFO-JL.

**Cross-Fold Threshold Estimation (COTE):** In COTE we investigate whether the FOFO algorithm is essential by removing it. COTE also replaces the output layer of the pre-trained network with a linear layer. While all other layers are kept frozen, the parameters of the new, linear layer are learned via 10-fold cross validation over training data; that is, COTE does *not* use FOFO but learns the per-class decision thresholds via cross validation.

**Multi-class F-Measure Optimization with Randomized Initialization (MCFO-RI):** MCFO-RI retains FOFO, as shown in pseudocode in Algorithm 1. The output layer of a pre-trained network (a fine-tuned BERT for the EC problems we consider here) is replaced with a new linear layer, whose parameters are initialized with values drawn at random in $[0, 1]$. This layer is trained for one epoch over the training data, so the extended model can navigate in the F-measure optimization space. For each node of the linear layer, FOFO is used to estimate the per-class decision threshold.

**Multi-class F-Measure Optimization with Joint Learning (MCFO-JL):** Through MCFO-JL we investigate whether more improvements can be obtained by jointly learning both the data representation and the class decision thresholds. MCFO-JL is shown in pseudocode in Algorithm 2. Its key difference from MCFO-RI is that it conducts *joint* learning of the representation and decision thresholds. MCFO-JL does not just utilize the representation learned from a pre-trained model; instead, a modified network is trained *ab initio*: given a particular given architecture, the output layer is replaced with a new linear layer as in our proposed approach. The entire network is trained for $n$ epochs over the training instances. Then, all layers but the last are frozen, and the last layer is trained for an additional epoch. As in MCFO-RI, the decision threshold for each node of the last layer is obtained via FOFO.

**Pre-trained Models:** Pre-trained models are built using a fine-tuned BERT [5] from hugging-face [16]. The architecture is inspired from [4]. We gradually increase the learning rate for the ADAM optimizer. The modification results in a new baseline; this gives us a slightly higher macro-F1 score (0.50) on the GoEmotions dataset than the model in [4] (0.46). The Adam optimizer [7] is used for all our experiments, with a learning rate of $5e - 5$ on the GoEmotions dataset and $1e - 5$ on the other datasets.

**Enhancements with Traditional Data Imbalance Techniques:** As described in Sect. 2, traditional techniques to address imbalance can be used in conjunction with any of the algorithms proposed here to possibly further improve performance. Since data augmentation comes at high computational cost for NLP tasks with large training datasets, we limit our experimentation to enhancements of the proposed algorithms with CWS.

| **Algorithm 1.** MCFO-RI(w,$\theta$,n,l) | **Algorithm 2.** MCFO-JL(w,$\theta$,n,l) |
|---|---|
| **Require:** pre-trained model $m(w)$ with layers $l \in \{1, \ldots, L\}$ | **Require:** Model $m(w)$ with layers $l \in \{1, \ldots, L\}$ |
| 1: $(h, c) \leftarrow$ dimensions of output layer | 1: $(h, c) \leftarrow$ dimensions of output layer |
| 2: $n \leftarrow$ number of training instances | 2: $n \leftarrow$ number of training instances |
| 3: Replace output layer $L$ with new, linear layer with size $h \times c$ | 3: $e \leftarrow$ number of training epochs |
| 4: Freeze all layers $1, \ldots, L - 1$ | 4: Replace output layer $L$ with new, linear layer $L$ with size $h \times c$ |
| 5: Assign random weight to $w_L \in [0, 1]$ | 5: Train resulting $m(w)$ for $e$ epochs |
| 6: **for** $t = 1, \ldots., n$ **do** | 6: Freeze layers $1, \ldots, L - 1$ |
| 7:     Receive an example $x_t$ | 7: **for** $t = 1, \ldots., n$ **do** |
| 8:     **for** $\tau = 1, \ldots., c$ **do** | 8:     Receive an example $x_t$ |
| 9:       select a node $\chi_\tau$ from layer $L$ | 9:     **for** $\tau = 1, \ldots., c$ **do** |
| 10:      $\hat{\theta}_{t,\tau} = \text{FOFO}(x_t, \chi_\tau)$ | 10:      select a node $\chi_\tau$ from layer $L$ |
| 11:      $w_{t,\tau} \leftarrow \text{Optimizer}(w_{\tau-1}, x_t, y_t)$ | 11:       $\hat{\theta}_{t,\tau} = \text{FOFO}(x_t, \chi_\tau)$ |
| 12: **return** $\hat{\theta}$ | 12:       $w_{t,\tau} \leftarrow \text{Optimizer}(w_{\tau-1}, x_t, y_t)$ |
| | 13: **return** $\hat{\theta}$ |

## 4    Experiments and Results

**Problem Instances and Datasets:** Figure 2 shows the class distributions of the 8 benchmark datasets that span the spectrum in number of classes and data imbalance. In the interest of space, we do not describe these datasets in detail, but relate their class granularity and imbalance in Fig. 2.

### 4.1    Comparison on Macro-F1 Scores

We first compare COTE, MCFO-RI, and MCFO-JL on the macro-F1 scores. Each algorithm is run 10 times on each dataset; the macro-F1 scores obtained are averaged over the 10 runs and reported in Table 1. Column 1 shows the Baseline. Table 1 allows drawing several observations. First, COTE is inferior to MCFO-RI. This is not surprising; the parameters of the last layer are learned independently of the other hidden layers in a single epoch in COTE. Table 1 also suggests that MCFO-RI improves upon the Baseline for most classes; note the ✓ symbol on 6/8 problems. Table 1 also clearly shows that MCFO-JL outperforms both Baseline and MCFO-RI on all problem instances (note the ✓✓ symbol) but one, EmotionLines, which is a highly imbalanced dataset with very few instances for some of the classes. So, it is challenging for the linear layer in MCFO-RI to learn when trained only for one epoch. MCFO-JL achieves a similar performance to the Baseline (0.41 versus 0.42).

**Statistical Significance Analysis:** We use t-tests to evaluate this null hypothesis: the mean macro-F1 score (over 10 runs) of an algorithm is not different from that of the Baseline. We carry out three t-tests, where we compare each algorithm (COTE, MCFO-RI, and MCFO-JL) to the Baseline. The p-values are

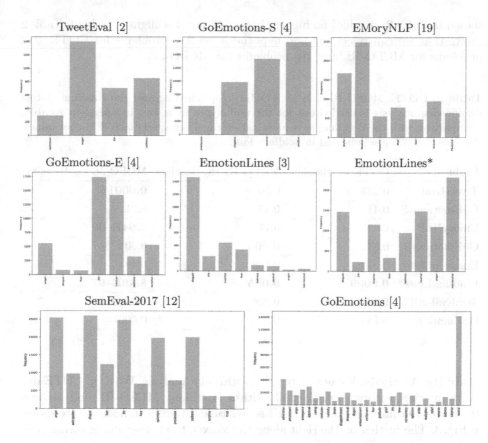

**Fig. 2.** Class distribution over training instances. GoEmotions-S and -E are variations based on the psychological model employed for emotion annotation [4]. Since Emotion-Lines contains only $2K$ training instances, EmotionLines* is augmented with instances sampled from SemEval-2017 and TweetEval.

**Table 1.** Comparison of macro-F1 (averaged over 10 runs). Highest value is shown in boldface font. MCFO-RI outperforming both Baseline and COTE is indicated with a ✓. MCFO-JL outperforming all is indicated with a ✓✓.

| Problem | Baseline | COTE | MCFO-RI | MCFO-JL |
|---|---|---|---|---|
| TweetEval | 0.76 | 0.73 | 0.78 ✓ | **0.8** ✓✓ |
| GoEmotions-S | **0.7** | 0.66 | 0.68 ✓ | **0.7** ✓✓ |
| EmoryNLP | 0.29 | 0.27 | 0.29 ✓ | **0.34** ✓✓ |
| GoEmotions-E | 0.64 | 0.60 | 0.61 | **0.65** ✓✓ |
| EmotionLines | **0.42** | 0.38 | 0.39 | 0.41 |
| EmotionLines* | 0.56 | 0.51 | 0.6 ✓ | **0.63** ✓✓ |
| SemEval-2017 | 0.56 | 0.52 | 0.58 ✓ | **0.61** ✓✓ |
| GoEmotions | 0.5 | 0.48 | 0.51 ✓ | **0.53** ✓✓ |

shown in Table 2; p-values no higher than 0.005 are highlighted in bold. Table 2 shows that we can reject the null hypothesis on 2/8 problems for COTE, 2/8 problems for MCFO-RI, and 4/8 problems for MCFO-JL.

**Table 2.** COTE, MCFO-RI, and MCFO-JL are pitched against the Baseline. T-test significance analysis is carried out for the null hypothesis: two independent samples (comparison with the Baseline) have identical average/expected macro-F1 score values. P-values $\leq 0.005$ are indicated in boldface font.

| Problem | COTE vs. Baseline | MCFO-RI vs. Baseline | MCFO-JL vs. Baseline |
|---|---|---|---|
| TweetEval | 0.233 | 0.56 | **0.00015** |
| GoEmotions-S | 0.41 | 0.83 | 0.01 |
| EmoryNLP | 0.82 | 0.17 | **5.94E−06** |
| GoEmotions-E | 0.88 | **0.005** | 0.001 |
| EmotionLines | 0.0108 | 0.168 | 0.494 |
| EmotionLines* | **0.0009** | **0.005** | **8.46E−07** |
| SemEval-2017 | **0.0004** | 0.006 | **3.21E−05** |
| GoEmotions | 0.185 | 0.039 | 0.0007 |

**Stability Analysis:** We now carry out a stability analysis. We drop COTE due to its inferior performance. Each algorithm (Baseline, MCFO-RI, and MCFO-JL) is run 10 times, and the macro-F1 scores on each problem instance are shown in Fig. 3. The further on the right along the x-axis, the better an algorithm is on a given problem. The wider the distribution of macro-F1 scores on a problem, the more unstable the algorithm.

Figure 3 shows that MCFO-JL outperforms the Baseline, and that MCFO-RI is the most unstable. This is not surprising. MCFO-RI initializes the weights for the last layer at random, and its learning is carried out over one epoch. Its performance is sensitive to the initial

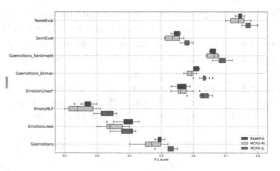

**Fig. 3.** Boxplot of macro-F1 scores over 10 runs of each algorithm on each problem instance.

weights and thus varies more widely over various runs. Altogether, the evaluation suggests that MCFO-JL is a superior algorithm.

**Macro-F1 Score with Class Weight Sampling:** We additionally evaluate the impact of class weight sampling, which we abbreviate as CWS, on MCFO-JL. We also evaluate its impact on the Baseline. Table 3 relates the mean (over 10 runs) macro-F1 scores for Baseline, Baseline+CWS, MCFO-JL, and MCFO-JL+CWS. Table 3 clearly shows that CWS confers more improvement to the Baseline over MCFO-JL on only one problem instance, and that MCFO-JL+CWS outperforms Baseline+CWS in all problems instances.

**Table 3.** Comparisons of Baseline and MCFO-JL with and without CWS on average macro-F1 scores (over 10 independent runs). Highest value per row is highlighted in boldface font. A ✓ symbol indicates the problem instances where MCFO-JL outperforms Baseline+CWS. A ✓✓ symbol indicates the problem instances where MCFO-JL+CWS outperforms all other variants.

| Problem | Baseline | Baseline + CWS | MCFO-JL | MCFO-JL + CWS |
|---|---|---|---|---|
| TweetEval | 0.76 | 0.78 | **0.8**✓ | **0.8**✓✓ |
| GoEmotions-S | 0.7 | 0.68 | **0.7** | **0.7**✓✓ |
| EmoryNLP | 0.29 | 0.35 | 0.34 | **0.41**✓✓ |
| GoEmotions-E | 0.64 | 0.64 | 0.65✓ | **0.66**✓✓ |
| EmotionLines | 0.42 | 0.43 | 0.41 | **0.48**✓✓ |
| EmotionLines* | 0.56 | 0.6 | 0.63✓ | **0.65**✓✓ |
| SemEval-2017 | 0.56 | 0.57 | **0.61**✓ | 0.60 |
| GoEmotions | 0.5 | 0.51 | 0.53✓ | **0.54**✓✓ |

## 4.2   Comparison on Per-Class F1 Scores

In each problem instances, we pitch two algorithms against each-other and count the number of classes in which one of them achieves a higher per-class F1 score. The last row tallies the number of wins. Table 4 supports several conclusions. In agreement with the earlier evaluation on macro-F1 scores, MCFO-RI clearly outperforms COTE; it is indeed more powerful to learn decision thresholds directly from the data. However, it is unclear that MCFO-RI offers an advantage on per-class F1 scores over the Baseline. This is not the case with MCFO-JL, which clearly outperforms all, including the Baseline.

**Comparison of Class Size Proportional F1-Score Improvements:** To evaluate the improvement on the F1 score on a particular class with respect to class size, we devise the following size-proportional F1 score, $spF1$, on a class $c_i$ as follows: $spF1(c_i) = F1(c_i) \cdot n/|n_i|$, where $F1(c_i)$ is the F1 score achieved by an algorithm for class $c_i$, and $n/n_i$ is the proportional class size ($n_i$ samples in a training dataset of size $n$); $spF1$ weighs more F1 score improvements on classes with fewer samples. First, to get a sense of the natural variation between different runs of an algorithm, we record the highest and lowest $spF1$ on a given class over the 10 runs of the Baseline model and calculate $\sum_{i \in [K]} [spF1(c_i)_{\text{Baseline}-\text{Best}} - spF1(c_i)_{\text{Baseline}-\text{Worst}}]$ in order to obtain and report an aggregate score. We refer

**Table 4.** Head-to-head comparison between two algorithms at a time, reporting the number of classes where an algorithm achieves a higher per-class F1 score.

| Problem | COTE vs. Baseline | MCFO-RI vs. Baseline | MCFO-RI vs. COTE | MCFO-JL vs. Baseline | MCFO-JL vs. MCFO-RI |
|---|---|---|---|---|---|
| TweetEval | 1 vs 4 | 2 vs 2 | 4 vs 0 | 4 vs 1 | 4 vs 1 |
| GoEmotions-S | 0 vs 4 | 2 vs 1 | 4 vs 0 | 3 vs 1 | 3 vs 1 |
| EmoryNLP | 1 vs 7 | 3 vs 3 | 7 vs 1 | 5 vs 2 | 4 vs 2 |
| GoEmotions-E | 1 vs 6 | 4 vs 3 | 5 vs 1 | 4 vs 3 | 3 vs 3 |
| EmotionLines | 1 vs 4 | 3 vs 4 | 4 vs 3 | 4 vs 3 | 5 vs 2 |
| EmotionLines* | 1 vs 5 | 4 vs 4 | 5 vs 1 | 5 vs 2 | 5 vs 1 |
| SemEval-2017 | 2 vs 5 | 7 vs 3 | 8 vs 3 | 6 vs 2 | 5 vs 4 |
| GoEmotions | 8 vs 15 | 10 vs 13 | 20 vs 5 | 10 vs 12 | 14 vs 9 |
| **Total** | 15 vs 50 | 35 vs 33 | 57 vs 14 | 41 vs 28 | 43 vs 23 |

to it as Base-Best - Base-Worst in Column 1 in Table 5. Column 2 compares MCFO-JL to the Baseline. In this case, since each algorithm is run 10 times, the per-class F1 score utilized to calculate the spF1 on a given class by a particular algorithm is averaged over the 10 runs.

**Table 5.** Comparison of Baseline and MCFO-JL on aggregate spF1 scores. Problem instances where the aggregate spF1 score of MCFO-JL in comparison to the Baseline model is beyond the normal variation of the Baseline model are highlighted in boldface font.

| Problem | Baseline-Best - Baseline-Worst | MCFO-JL - Baseline |
|---|---|---|
| TweetEval | 0.94 | 0.72 |
| Goemotions-S | 0.61 | 0.24 |
| EmoryNLP | 2.51 | 2.40 |
| Goemotions-E | 5.91 | 1.78 |
| Emotionlines | 14.08 | **41.75** |
| Emotionlines* | 3.81 | **5.78** |
| SemEval-2017 | 4.52 | **6.14** |
| GoEmotions | 94.75 | **770.60 (190.44)** |

Table 5 shows that improvements afforded by MCFO-JL on the aggregate spF1 score over the Baseline are within the normal variations over 10 runs of the Baseline model on half of the problem instances that are characterized by fewer number of classes and not deep imbalance compared to the other problems. On the other half, EmotionLines, EmotionLines*, SemEval-2017, and GoEmotions, MCFO-JL's performance is well outside the normal variation of the Baseline. GoEmotions, the most challenging problem instance, provides an extreme example, where the aggregate spF1 score for MCFO-JL over the Baseline is an order of magnitude more than the expected variation in the Baseline model. A detailed case study analysis on this problem instance, which we do not show here in the interest of space, shows that there is one particular class, *grief*, where the Baseline model yields an F1 score of 0 and MCFO-JL an F1 score of 0.5. This is an underrepresented class. Even if we remove the contribution of this class from the aggregate spF1 score, MCFO-JL 0 Baseline still yields a score of 190.44, more than twice the expected variation in the Baseline model.

## 5   Conclusion

For multi-class, imbalanced EC, F-measure optimization is more suitable. This paper presents several algorithms based on thresholding the posterior class probability. Thorough empirical evaluation on benchmark EC datasets that span the spectrum of number of classes and class imbalance shows clear F1 score improvements, with good improvements on pre-trained deep models and higher improvements on untrained deep architectures when joint learning is carried out over both the representation and per-class thresholds. The macro-F1 and the per-class F1 score evaluations show the superiority of joint learning. No correlation is observed between the per-class F1 score improvements and class size (data not shown). The algorithms proposed here can be utilized on any pre-trained model, which facilitates their adoption over a variety of multi-class, imbalanced data. In the interest of a detailed empirical evaluation, we have focused here on EC tasks across benchmark datasets, but we see opportunities on related problems challenged by imbalanced data across application domains, including medical diagnostics, spam email detection, malicious URL detection, and more.

**Acknowledgement.** All experiments were run on ARGO, a computing cluster provided by the Office of Research Computing at George Mason University, VA (URL: http://orc.gmu.edu).

## References

1. SMOTE for learning from imbalanced data: progress and challenges, marking the 15-year anniversary. J. Artif. Intell. Res. **61**, 863–905 (2018)
2. Barbieri, F., Camacho-Collados, J., Espinosa-Anke, L., Neves, L.: TweetEval: unified benchmark and comparative evaluation for tweet classification. In: Findings of EMNLP (2020)
3. Chen, S.Y., Hsu, C.C., Kuo, C.C., Ku, L.W., et al.: EmotionLines: an emotion corpus of multi-party conversations. arXiv preprint arXiv:1802.08379 (2018)
4. Demszky, D., Movshovitz-Attias, D., Ko, J., Cowen, A., Nemade, G., et al.: GoEmotions: a dataset of fine-grained emotions. In: 58th Annual Meeting of the Association for Computational Linguistics (ACL) (2020)
5. Devlin, J., Chang, M.W., Lee, K., Toutanova, K.: BERT: pre-training of deep bidirectional transformers for language understanding. arXiv preprint arXiv:1810.04805 (2018)

6. Gayed, A., Milligan-Seville, J.S., Nicholas, J., Bryan, B.T., LaMontagne, A.D., et al.: Effectiveness of training workplace managers to understand and support the mental health needs of employees: a systematic review and meta-analysis. Occup. Environ. Med. **75**(6), 462–470 (2017)
7. Kingma, D.P., Ba, J.: Adam: a method for stochastic optimization. arXiv preprint arXiv:1412.6980 (2014)
8. Koyejo, O., Natarajan, N., Ravikumar, P., Dhillon, I.S.: Consistent binary classification with generalized performance metrics. In: NIPS, vol. 27, pp. 2744–2752. Citeseer (2014)
9. Liu, M., Zhang, X., Zhou, X., Yang, T.: Faster online learning of optimal threshold for consistent f-measure optimization. In: Advances in Neural Information Processing Systems, pp. 3893–3903 (2018)
10. Narasimhan, H., Kar, P., Jain, P.: Optimizing non-decomposable performance measures: a tale of two classes. In: International Conference on Machine Learning, pp. 199–208 (2015)
11. Padurariu, C., Breaban, M.E.: Dealing with data imbalance in text classification. Procedia Comput. Sci. **159**, 736–745 (2019)
12. Rosenthal, S., Farra, N., Nakov, P.: SemEval-2017 task 4: sentiment analysis in Twitter. In: International Workshop on Semantic Evaluation, SemEval 2017, Vancouver, Canada. Association for Computational Linguistics (2017)
13. Shorten, C., Khoshgoftaar, T.M., Furht, B.: Text data augmentation for deep learning. J. Big Data **8**, 101 (2021)
14. Singh, K.: How to improve class imbalance using class weights in machine learning (2020). www.analyticsvidhya.com/blog/2020/10/improve-class-imbalance-class-weights/. Accessed 27 Jan 2022
15. Wang, C., Lin, H.: Constructing an affective tutoring system for designing course learning and evaluation. J. Educ. Comput. **55**(8), 1111–1128 (2017)
16. Wolf, T., et al.: Transformers: state-of-the-art natural language processing. In: Conference on Empirical Methods in Natural Language Processing: System Demonstrations, pp. 38–45. Association for Computational Linguistics (2020). www.aclweb.org/anthology/2020.emnlp-demos.6
17. Yan, Y., Yang, T., Yang, Y., Chen, J.: A framework of online learning with imbalanced streaming data. In: AAAI Conference on Artificial Intelligence, pp. 2817–2823 (2017)
18. Ye, L., Xu, R., Xu, J.: Emotion prediction of news articles from reader's perspective based on multi-label classification. In: International Conference on Machine Learning Cybernetics, vol. 5, pp. 2019–2024 (2012)
19. Zahiri, S.M., Choi, J.D.: Emotion detection on tv show transcripts with sequence-based convolutional neural networks. In: Workshops at the Thirty-Second AAAI Conference on Artificial Intelligence (2018)
20. Zahra Rajabi, A.S., Uzuner, O.: Detecting scarce emotions via BERT and hyperparameter optimization. In: International Conference on Artificial Neural Networks (ICANN), pp. 1–12 (2021)
21. Zhao, M.J., Edakunni, N., Pocock, A., Brown, G.: Beyond Fano's inequality: bounds on the optimal F-score, BER, and cost-sensitive risk and their implications. J. Mach. Learn. Res. **14**(1), 1033–1090 (2013)

# F-Transformer: Point Cloud Fusion Transformer for Cooperative 3D Object Detection

Jie Wang, Guiyang Luo, Quan Yuan, and Jinglin Li[✉]

State Key Laboratory of Networking and Switching Technology,
Beijing University of Posts and Telecommunications, Beijing, China
sklab@bupt.edu.cn
http://sklnst.bupt.edu.cn

**Abstract.** We present a novel cooperative detection framework to fuse multi-view point clouds, for accurately detecting hard samples (e.g., partly or fully occluded, or small objects). Building on a two-step communication scheme to transmit the pillar features between views, it is possible to observe the same object from different viewpoints. We then design a feature fusion scheme based on Transformer to fuse the pillar features by discretizing the point clouds. Considering the sparsity of information, we improve Transformer's self-attention mechanism, with Re-Scaled Dot-Product Attention, which allows the sparse information to capture valuable information more effectively. We evaluate the performance of our method by generating synthetic cooperative datasets over multiple complex traffic scenarios. The results show that our method surpasses all other cooperative perception methods with significant margins.

**Keywords:** Feature fusion · Cooperative detection · Self-attention

## 1 Introduction

As a downstream task of the autonomous driving system, the success of decision making and motion planning relies heavily on efficient environmental perception. In autonomous driving, point cloud-based 3D object detection is essential for vehicles to perceive the surrounding environment. Compared with image-based 2D object detection, the vehicle can use reliable depth information that LiDAR provides to locate objects and describe their shape accurately. However, the point cloud data generated by LiDAR is denser in the near and sparse in the distance, and it is difficult to obtain the points of the occluded object. State-of-the-art 3D object detection methods are primarily based on a single LiDAR, and they face a common problem: poor performance on occluded and distant objects. Therefore, in complex road scenes, mainstream 3D object detection algorithms cannot achieve efficient and highly accurate environment perception (see Fig. 1 ego view). To this end, it is possible to improve detection accuracy by aggregating information from other views. As shown in Fig. 1, the other view

© The Author(s), under exclusive license to Springer Nature Switzerland AG 2022
E. Pimenidis et al. (Eds.): ICANN 2022, LNCS 13529, pp. 171–182, 2022.
https://doi.org/10.1007/978-3-031-15919-0_15

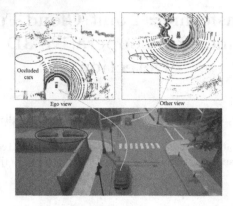

**Fig. 1.** *Below*: RGB image of traffic intersection with multiple cars. *Above*: Lidar point cloud of two vehicles. The ego vehicle's view is on the left, which cannot see objects behind the wall (red circle). The right side shows the view from another vehicle, which can observe objects that ego vehicle can not see. (Color figure online)

can observe the occluded vehicle that the ego view cannot. Therefore, exploiting multiple views' complementary information is important for accurate 3D object detection. There have been some works [1,3,4,16] using V2X networks to help vehicles utilize information from other views. There are two main challenges in this setting: (i) what information should each vehicle transmit to retain the important information while minimizing the transmission bandwidth required? (ii) how to fuse sparse information with different spatial locations? For the first challenge, [1,4] proposed to use raw point cloud as collaborative information. Although it can improve the detection accuracy, it does not consider the limitation of network bandwidth. [3] and [16] took the intermediate features and the compressed intermediate features as collaborative information, respectively, to reduce the data size. It should be noted that due to the increase of channels, the size of the intermediate features is much larger than the raw point cloud, and the compressed data is still difficult to meet the real-time requirements [11–13]. For the second challenge, [3] used maxout as the fusion scheme, which fails to establish inter-view context. [16] used a graph neural network (GNN) to establish the spatial relationship of views, but ignored the effect of sparsity on fusion.

For this purpose, we consider the *vehicle-to-vehicle* (V2V) communication, where each vehicle can transmit and receive information to/from nearby vehicles. Thus, we propose a point cloud fusion Transformer for cooperative 3D object detection, called F-Transformer. It fuses multi-view point clouds by using feature-level fusion for end-to-end 3D object detection to improve detection precision while satisfying the existing transmission bandwidth capabilities. We design a two-step communication scheme to transmit the feature of pillars (1D features), which has a smaller size than the intermediate features. In order to aggregate features from different views, we propose a feature-level fusion scheme based on Transformer (a self-attention based architecture). Considering the sparsity of the point cloud, we improved the Transformer's self-attention mechanism and only use the Transformer encoder to fuse features from different views. To evaluate our method, we require a dataset with multiple sensors at different locations in the same traffic scene to evaluate our method. However, there is no such public dataset available. Therefore, a multi-view dataset containing multiple complex scenes is created by using CARLA [6]. Experiments show that the performance of F-Transformer far exceeds the single-sensor 3D object detection method, and achieves better performance than other cooperative detection methods.

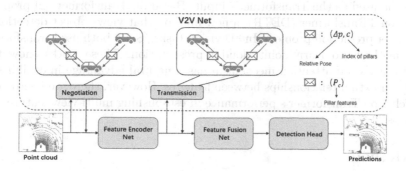

**Fig. 2.** The structure of F-Transformer. The network mainly includes four components: Feature Encoder Net, Feature Fusion Network, Detection Head, and V2V Network. The raw point cloud is converted to a stacked pillar tensor and pillar index tensor. The feature fusion network is used to fuse pillar features from different views and then feed the fused features into the detection head to predict 3D bounding boxes for objects. In addition, V2V Network is responsible for exchanging cooperative information.

## 2    Related Work

### 2.1    Cooperative 3D Object Detection

[1] carried out the work of multi-view cooperative object detection, which proposed three data fusion methods based on different data forms: early fusion, late fusion and hybrid fusion. Similar to [1,4] proposed an early fusion scheme based on coordinate transformation for multi-view cooperative object detection. To reduce the size of data, [3] proposed a feature-based cooperative perception method, which uses the processed features of the raw point cloud for multi-view cooperative detection. And they used maxout as the feature fusion scheme, which highlights the larger values and suppresses the smaller values. [16] used a graph neural network (GNN) as the fusion scheme to establish a spatial relationship between views. The fusion data they used are compressed intermediate features, which waste some bandwidth transmitting redundant data. To evaluate their methods, [3,4] used two frames of the same car at different times in

the KITTI [7] dataset to simulate the data shared between two different views simultaneously. [1] used CARLA, an autonomous driving simulator, deploying several LiDARs at intersections to generate a multi-view dataset for cooperative 3D object detection.

## 2.2  Transformer in Computer Vision

Transformer [15] has achieved great success in natural language processing (NLP). This has inspired the application of Transformer in computer vision [2,5,8,18]. [5] treated pictures as sequences of patches in the 2D classification task to be used as the Transformer's input. Based on Transformer, [2] proposed DEtection TRansformer (DETR), a new method that views object detection as a direct set prediction problem. In 3D vision tasks, [8,18] both used transformer-based methods to learn point cloud representation. These works show that Transformer's self-attention mechanism has a natural advantage in establishing global contextual relationships between features. However, there are microscopic researches on Transformer's performance in establishing multi-view feature relationships.

## 3  Method

Inspired by the success of the cooperative perception algorithm, we propose a novel multi-view cooperative perception framework for 3D Object Detection. Our proposed F-Transformer applies feature-level data as cooperatively transmitted information because it can meet the needs of both speed and accuracy [3,16]. It consists of four main stages (Fig. 2): (1) A feature encoder network that converts point clouds to intermediate features; (2) A feature fusion network fuses features from multiple views; (3) A detection head that detects and regresses 3D boxes; (4) The V2V communication is responsible for transmitting features.

### 3.1  Feature Encoder Network

Each point in the point cloud is represented by a set of fixed-length vectors, i.e., $(x, y, z, I)$, where $(x, y, z)$ represents the coordinates of the point in the three-dimensional space, and $I$ represents the reflectance. On the $x - y$ plane, we divide the three-dimensional space into evenly spaced grids, and each grid represents a regular vertical column with the unlimited spatial extent in the $z$ direction. Suppose there are $W$ pillars in the $x$ direction and $H$ pillars in the $y$ direction. The number of points in each pillar is different due to the sparsity of the point cloud; most pillars are empty. We limit the number of points in each pillar to $N$. If the number of points in a pillar exceeds $N$, the points are randomly sampled. Conversely, zero padding is applied if the number of points in a pillar is less than $N$. Then, all the points in each pillar are encoded into one vector of size $C$ through an encoding network, and we will obtain a tensor of size $(C, H, W)$, named Pillar Feature Map (PFM). We use Pillar Feature Net proposed by PointPillars [9] to extract PFM from point cloud.

## 3.2   Feature Fusion Network

After the ego view has calculated its PFM, it can fuse the PFM of other views to generate an aggregated PFM. Our fusion network is supposed to addressed the following two challenges: 1) features from different views contain different spatial information; 2) the information contained in PFM is sparse due to zero padding.

Towards this goal, we propose a Transformer-based multi-view feature fusion (F-Transformer) scheme to explicitly establish the contextual relationship between PFMs, because the Transformer has a natural advantage in computing the self-attention of different features. As shown in Fig. 3, although the spatial positions of the two LiDARs are different, their sensing ranges have overlapping areas, where pillar 2 from ego view and pillar 4 from other view share the same calibrated 3D space. Here we use Transformer architecture to fuse pillar features (PFs) with the same position. We denote these two pillar features as $\mathbf{p}_1$ and $\mathbf{p}_4$, respectively, and $\mathbf{p}_i \in \mathbb{R}^C$ as the $i$-th PF in the PMF.

$$\mathbf{z}_0 = [\mathbf{p}_i^1; \mathbf{p}_i^2; \cdots ; \mathbf{p}_i^N] \tag{1}$$

$$\mathbf{z}_l' = MSA(LN(\mathbf{z}_{l-1})) + \mathbf{z}_{(l-1)} \qquad l = 1 \cdots L \tag{2}$$

$$\mathbf{z}_l = MLP(LN(\mathbf{z}_l')) + \mathbf{z}_l' \qquad l = 1 \cdots L \tag{3}$$

The standard Transformer receives as input a 1D sequence of token embeddings. In order to use the Transformer to calculate the global self-attention between PFs and establish the contextual relationship between different views, we treat each PF as a token embedding, and features sharing the same location are combined into a 1D sequence $\mathbf{z}_0 \in \mathbb{R}^{(V \times C)}$ as the input of the Transformer, where $V$ is the number of views (Eq. 1). Here we only used the encoder as the multi-view feature fusion network. As shown in Fig. 4 (a), a transformer encoder contains a multi-head self-attention (MSA) module, followed by a 2-layer MLP with GELU nonlinearity in between (Eq. 2, 3). A LayerNorm (LN) layer is applied before each MSA module and MLP, and a residual connection is applied after each module.

Notably, we remove the position embeddings because the spatial position of different views is arbitrary, and there is no ordering relationship between PFs from multiple views. Unlike the language sequence, due to the zero padding, the valuable information contained in each PF is different. This information obtained in dense point cloud areas is higher than in sparse areas. The latter will generate a *Query* with a small value in the attention head, which is not conducive to the PF to fuse information from other PFs through the self-attention mechanism. Therefore, to highlight the PF whose information is greater than the current view during the feature fusion process and suppress the PF whose information is smaller than the current view, we weight the attention scale. Specifically, for each PF, in addition to calculating its *Key*, *Query*, and *Value*, we also introduce *Richness* to indicate the information contained in each PF, where *Key*, *Query*, and *Value* are all vectors, and *Richness* is a number. We call this attention

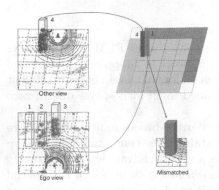

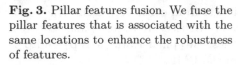

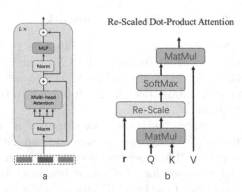

**Fig. 3.** Pillar features fusion. We fuse the pillar features that is associated with the same locations to enhance the robustness of features.

**Fig. 4.** *a*: Transformer encoder. We took the 1D sequence composed of PFs as input and redesigned the self-attention mechanism. *b*: Re-Scaled Dot-Product Attention. *Richness* reflects the sparsity of features, which is used to re-weight the Scaled Dot-Product Attention.

mechanism "Re-Scaled Dot-Product Attention" (Fig. 4 (b)). We use the *Richness* ratio to represent the information scale between any two PFs, then use this scale to weight the dot product of the *Key* and *Query*. We pack *Queries*, *Keys*, *Values* together into matrices $Q$, $K$, $V$, and *Richness* into vector $\mathbf{r}$. We compute the matrix of outputs as:

$$Attention(Q, K, V, \mathbf{r}) = softmax(\frac{QK^T \cdot \mathbf{r}^{-1}\mathbf{r}^T}{\sqrt{d_k}})V \qquad (4)$$

In order to map features from arbitrary viewpoints to the same feature space, parameters of all views are shared when calculating $Q, K, V$ and $\mathbf{r}$. And we use $1 \times 1$ Conv to compute them, which does not introduce large num parameters to the network.

### 3.3  Detection Head and Loss Function

After aggregating information from other views, we generate the final prediction by using the detection head. Similar to [9], we use the Single Shot Detector (SSD) [10] setup to perform 3D object detection. We use 2D Intersection over Union (IoU) to match the prior boxes to the ground truth without height and elevation. The height and elevation become additional regression targets.

We use the same loss functions introduced in [17]. Here use a softmax classification loss to learn the heading because the angle localization loss cannot distinguish flipped boxes.

## 3.4  Communication Scheme

Feature fusion is based on the V2V networks, which transfer information between views. However, there are two problems with the direct transmission of PFM through the V2V network: (i) PFM includes the entire scene feature. The vehicle does not need features from other views to assist in detection for visible objects, so this part of the feature wastes communication resources. (ii) Due to the growth of data dimensions, the size of PFM has not decreased much compared to the raw point cloud. Based on this, we do not directly use PFM as the communication data between views but use a two-step communication scheme to transmit partial features of PFM to reduce the communication bandwidth further and provide important coordination information. Our communication process has two steps: negotiation and transmission.

*Negotiation.* In the feature encoder network, we divide the three-dimensional space into equally spaced pillars, and the number of points that fall on different pillars is different. According to whether the pillar is empty, we divide the area represented by the pillars into two categories: invisible area and visible area. Then, whether it is adjacent to the invisible area, the visible area is divided into partially visible and fully visible areas. We consider invisible areas and partially visible areas to be occluded areas that require auxiliary information from other views. As shown in Fig. 3, pillar 1, pillar 2, and pillar 3 represent the invisible area, the partially occluded area, and the fully visible area, respectively, in the ego view. In the negotiation step, the ego view needs to tell other views which areas need cooperating features. In our V2V settings, the negotiation information includes the relative 6DoF pose $\Delta p$ between two views and the index $c$ of the pillars corresponding to the occluded area of ego view.

*Transmission.* Since the feature encoder network divides the space according to equally divided pillars, each PF in the PFM has a one-to-one correspondence with the pillar. Through the relative position transformation, the other views can find the corresponding PF according to the index $c$. Then other views send it to the ego view through the V2V network without transmitting the entire PFM. In natural scenes, pillars from different views are difficult to match perfectly, and even a tiny deviation between pillars will lead to mismatches. As shown in Fig. 3, we showcase a mismatched situation that one pillar of the ego view falls between the four pillars of the other view. In this case, the other view will transmit these four PFs to the ego view through the V2V network. Then, the PF of the ego view and the four PFs of the other views are combined into a 1D sequence as the input of the feature fusion network.

## 4  Experimental Setup

### 4.1  Large-Scale Cooperative Detection Datasets

Multi-view cooperative 3D object detection requires the support of LiDAR data from different views of the same scene. However, according to our research, there is no publicly available multi-view dataset. Therefore, we use CARLA to generate a multi-view dataset with multiple scenarios (see Fig. 6), aiming to provide a comprehensive dataset that can study dynamic and complex driving scenarios where multiple objects are occluded.

Our dataset is generated in three intersections and two T-junctions, and each intersection contains four LiDARs and cameras with different views. In order to increase the diversity of scenes, we collected data both on urban and rural intersections, simulating traffic intersections with different levels of congestion by setting the total number of vehicles in the scene. Furthermore, we correspond the label format to KITTI so that other methods using the KITTI dataset can use the dataset we made for training and testing without modification. Finally, we generated a total of 39920 frames of labelled data.

## 4.2  Setup

We split our dataset into 23952 training samples and 15968 validation samples for experimental studies. Like KITTI, since only ground truth objects visible in the image will be labelled, we follow the standard convention [19] of only using LiDAR points that project into the image. For our dataset, the detection range in $x, y, z$ is $[(0, 69.1), (-39.68, 39.68), (-2, 1)]$ $m$ respectively, and we use the pillar of size $[0.16\,m, 0.16\,m, \infty]$ to voxelized it on each axis.

We use the same anchors and matching strategy as [19]. Each anchor is described by $[l, h, w, x, y, z, \theta]$, where the size and center position of the object are described by $(l, h, w)$ and $(x, y, z)$ respectively, while $\theta$ is applied at two orientations: 0 and 90°. We use 2D IOU to match ground truth like [9]: A positive match is either the highest with a ground truth box or above the positive match threshold, while a negative match is below the negative threshold. All other anchors are ignored in the loss. In our experiment, we use positive and negative thresholds of 0.6 and 0.45 for vehicles, and positive and negative thresholds of 0.5 and 0.35 are used for matching pedestrians. In the inference stage, we apply NMS with an overlap threshold of 0.7 IoU.

Our F-Transformer uses the ADAM optimizer for end-to-end training. We train our network with batch size 1, learning rate 0.01 for 80 epochs on 1 RTX 2080 Ti GPU. According to [14] suggestion, the cosine annealing learning rate strategy is adopted for the learning rate decay. We use data from four views for cooperative object detection in all experiments unless otherwise specified.

## 5  Results

We use KITTI evaluation detection metrics to evaluate 3D object detection and BEV object detection. Our dataset also divides each category into three levels based on occlusion and truncation: easy, moderate, and hard, the same as KITTI. BEV and 3D detection results are evaluated based on average precision (AP) and mean average precision (mAP) with a 0.7 IoU threshold for Car and 0.5 for Pedestrian.

**Table 1.** Performance comparison in BEV detection: mAP and AP in test dataset.

| Fusion scheme | mAP | | | Car (AP) | | | Pedestrian (AP) | | |
|---|---|---|---|---|---|---|---|---|---|
| | Easy | Mod. | Hard | Easy | Mod. | Hard | Easy | Mod. | Hard |
| Baseline [9] | 82.18 | 74.16 | 72.99 | 96.89 | 90.11 | 89.90 | 67.48 | 58.22 | 56.09 |
| Max Fusion [3] | 79.17 | 78.54 | 75.87 | 98.22 | 98.41 | 98.49 | 60.12 | 58.67 | 53.25 |
| Early Fusion [1,4] | 79.76 | 78.87 | 75.11 | 97.19 | 96.74 | 89.87 | 62.33 | 61.00 | 60.34 |
| F-Transformer | **84.34** | **81.24** | **80.95** | **98.52** | **98.76** | **98.69** | **70.15** | **63.73** | **63.20** |

**Table 2.** Performance comparison in 3D detection: mAP and AP in test dataset.

| Fusion scheme | mAP | | | Car (AP) | | | Pedestrian (AP) | | |
|---|---|---|---|---|---|---|---|---|---|
| | Easy | Mod. | Hard | Easy | Mod. | Hard | Easy | Mod. | Hard |
| Baseline [9] | 60.39 | 56.90 | 53.78 | 84.56 | 83.74 | 77.78 | 36.22 | 30.07 | 29.77 |
| Max Fusion [3] | 72.17 | 74.22 | 69.88 | 88.82 | 97.25 | 88.93 | 55.51 | 51.19 | 50.84 |
| Early Fusion [1,4] | 73.77 | 74.07 | 70.53 | 87.59 | 94.88 | 88.17 | 59.96 | 53.26 | 52.89 |
| F-Transformer | **74.91** | **79.10** | **74.96** | **89.05** | **97.95** | **90.05** | **60.78** | **60.26** | **59.86** |

*Comparative Evaluation of Fusion Schemes.* The purpose of this experiment is to compare the detection performance of different multi-view fusion schemes. We reproduced the fusion scheme in [1,3,4] by designing Early Fusion and Max Fusion as comparative experiments. In addition, we also compared the no fusion method (our baseline PointPillar). Table 1 and Table 2 show the performance of different fusion schemes in 3D object detection and BEV object detection, and it can be seen that our proposed F-Transformer is superior to other fusion schemes in AP and mAP. For 3D object detection, F-Transformer is significantly better than the baseline (no fusion), i.e. increasing the mAP by 14.52%, 22.2%, 21.28% on easy, moderate and hard difficulty levels, respectively. It is worth noting that F-Transformer has outstanding performance in Pedestrian detection, especially in 3D target detection. Pedestrian has more sparse observations, which verifies that our Transformer-based multi-view fusion scheme can effectively capture more accurate spatial context information, improving the quality of fusion features. We present several examples for 3D object detection in Fig. 5, which compared our F-Transformer with other fusion schemes. As can be seen from the examples, the fusion-based scheme significantly outperforms the one without fusion. Notably, F-Transformer achieves better performance on occluded vehicles and pedestrians.

*Effect of Sensors Number.* This experiment evaluates the impact of the number of sensors on object detection performance. The performance is evaluated only for the F-Transformer scheme, and the number of sensors in a set range from one to four. Table 3 reports the AP metric of each set. The results show that the detection performance increases as the number of sensors are increased. In particular, two or more sensors will bring a considerable performance improve-

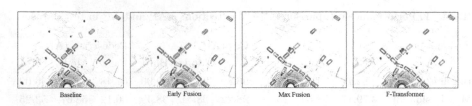

| Baseline | Early Fusion | Max Fusion | F-Transformer |

**Fig. 5.** Qualitative Examples. We show a bird's eye view of the LiDAR point cloud with different fusion schemes in the same scene. We show ground truth (red) and predicted boxes for car (green) and pedestrian (blue). (Color figure online)

**Table 3.** Effect of sensors number.

| Sensors number | 3D(mAP) | | | BEV(mAP) | | |
| --- | --- | --- | --- | --- | --- | --- |
| | Easy | Mod. | Hard | Easy | Mod. | Hard |
| 1 | 60.39 | 56.90 | 53.78 | 82.18 | 74.16 | 72.99 |
| 2 | 69.05 | 68.09 | 65.74 | 77.27 | 75.23 | 73.56 |
| 3 | **76.48** | 78.76 | 74.61 | 84.21 | **81.26** | 80.76 |
| 4 | 74.91 | **79.10** | **74.96** | **84.34** | 81.24 | **80.95** |

**Table 4.** Effect of re-scaled dot-product attention.

| Attention | Benchmark (AP) | Easy | Mod | Hard |
| --- | --- | --- | --- | --- |
| Native | Car (3D) | 88.95 | 97.76 | 89.63 |
| | Car (BEV) | 98.41 | 98.62 | 98.52 |
| | Pedestrian (3D) | 59.78 | 56.89 | 56.23 |
| | Pedestrian (BEV) | 63.86 | 62.45 | 62.53 |
| Re-scaled | Car (3D) | **89.05** | **97.95** | **90.05** |
| | Car (BEV) | **98.52** | **98.76** | **98.69** |
| | Pedestrian (3D) | **60.78** | **60.26** | **59.86** |
| | Pedestrian (BEV) | **70.15** | **63.73** | **63.20** |

ment compared with a single sensor. However, the performance of 4 sensors is similar to the 3 sensors, which shows that the performance gain saturates as the number of sensors increases.

*Effect of Re-Scaled Dot-Product Attention.* We validate the effectiveness of Re-Scaled Dot-Product Attention by comparing it with the native Transformer that uses Scaled Dot-Product Attention. It can be seen from Table 3 and Table 4 that the performance of the two on Vehicle is similar, while the performance of Re-Scaled Dot-Product Attention on Pedestrian is significantly better. This is because *Richness* reflects the amount of information contained in the feature, and the use of the *Richness* ratio to weight the attention scale highlights the more informative views and better fuses multi-view features.

*Runtime Analysis.* The processing time of the model consists of two parts: communication time and inference time. We compare the time of different fusion schemes from these two aspects. In the test, all models are executed on a computer with a GeForce GTX 2080 Ti GPU, and we set the transmission rate of V2V between vehicles to 10 Mbps. The data transmitted by Early Fusion are raw point clouds, while those of Max Fusion and F-Transformer are PFs. All types of data are compressed to further reduce size. In the experimental setting, the size of the PFs will vary in different cases according to the negotiation result, with an average size around 0.6 MB, which can be further reduced to one-tenth by compression. And the compressed raw point clouds are about 0.2 MB. As shown

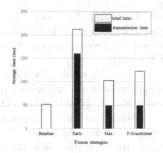

**Fig. 6.** Urban scene. The flags indicate where the sensors are placed.

**Fig. 7.** Comparison on time consuming using different fusion schemes.

in Fig. 7, we show the processing time of different fusion schemes. Note that the complexity of the fusion scheme affects the inference time. F-Transformer used 20 ms over the Max Fusion, a very minimal increase in detection time for a significant increase in performance.

## 6    Conclusion

We propose the F-Transformer framework, a novel multi-view cooperative 3D object detection model. Our method uses the aggregation ability of the Transformer to fuse point cloud features from different views. Due to the sparsity of the information, we improved Transformer's self-attention mechanism to make it more effective to focus on areas with more valuable information. In order to further reduce the communication bandwidth, we propose a two-step V2V communication scheme, which only transmits the features required by the target view. In addition, we used CARLA to create a multi-view dataset containing multiple complex traffic scenes to verify our proposed method. The experimental results verify the superiority of our proposed F-Transformer.

**Acknowledgements.** This paper is supported in part by the National Natural Science Foundation of China under Grant 62102041, Grant 61876023, and Grant 61902035.

## References

1. Arnold, E., Dianati, M., de Temple, R., Fallah, S.: Cooperative perception for 3D object detection in driving scenarios using infrastructure sensors. IEEE Trans. Intell. Transp. Syst. (2020)
2. Carion, N., Massa, F., Synnaeve, G., Usunier, N., Kirillov, A., Zagoruyko, S.: End-to-end object detection with transformers. In: Vedaldi, A., Bischof, H., Brox, T., Frahm, J.-M. (eds.) ECCV 2020. LNCS, vol. 12346, pp. 213–229. Springer, Cham (2020). https://doi.org/10.1007/978-3-030-58452-8_13
3. Chen, Q., Ma, X., Tang, S., Guo, J., Yang, Q., Fu, S.: F-cooper: feature based cooperative perception for autonomous vehicle edge computing system using 3D point clouds. In: Proceedings of the 4th ACM/IEEE Symposium on Edge Computing, pp. 88–100 (2019)

4. Chen, Q., Tang, S., Yang, Q., Fu, S.: Cooper: cooperative perception for connected autonomous vehicles based on 3D point clouds. In: 2019 IEEE 39th International Conference on Distributed Computing Systems (ICDCS), pp. 514–524. IEEE (2019)
5. Dosovitskiy, A., et al.: An image is worth $16 \times 16$ words: transformers for image recognition at scale. arXiv preprint arXiv:2010.11929 (2020)
6. Dosovitskiy, A., Ros, G., Codevilla, F., Lopez, A., Koltun, V.: Carla: an open urban driving simulator. In: Conference on Robot Learning, pp. 1–16. PMLR (2017)
7. Geiger, A., Lenz, P., Stiller, C., Urtasun, R.: Vision meets robotics: the KITTI dataset. Int. J. Robot. Res. **32**(11), 1231–1237 (2013)
8. Guo, M.H., Cai, J.X., Liu, Z.N., Mu, T.J., Martin, R.R., Hu, S.M.: PCT: point cloud transformer. Comput. Vis. Media **7**(2), 187–199 (2021)
9. Lang, A.H., Vora, S., Caesar, H., Zhou, L., Yang, J., Beijbom, O.: PointPillars: fast encoders for object detection from point clouds. In: Proceedings of the IEEE/CVF Conference on Computer Vision and Pattern Recognition, pp. 12697–12705 (2019)
10. Liu, W., et al.: SSD: single shot multibox detector. In: Leibe, B., Matas, J., Sebe, N., Welling, M. (eds.) ECCV 2016. LNCS, vol. 9905, pp. 21–37. Springer, Cham (2016). https://doi.org/10.1007/978-3-319-46448-0_2
11. Luo, G., et al.: Cooperative vehicular content distribution in edge computing assisted 5G-VANET. China Commun. **15**(7), 1–17 (2018). https://doi.org/10.1109/CC.2018.8424578
12. Luo, G., Yuan, Q., Li, J., Wang, S., Yang, F.: Artificial intelligence powered mobile networks: from cognition to decision. IEEE Netw. 1–8 (2021)
13. Luo, G., et al.: Software-defined cooperative data sharing in edge computing assisted 5G-VANET. IEEE Trans. Mob. Comput. **20**(3), 1212–1229 (2021). https://doi.org/10.1109/TMC.2019.2953163
14. Shi, S., Guo, C., Jiang, L., Wang, Z., Shi, J., Wang, X., Li, H.: PV-RCNN: point-voxel feature set abstraction for 3d object detection. In: Proceedings of the IEEE/CVF Conference on Computer Vision and Pattern Recognition, pp. 10529–10538 (2020)
15. Vaswani, A., et al.: Attention is all you need. In: Advances in Neural Information Processing Systems, pp. 5998–6008 (2017)
16. Wang, T.-H., Manivasagam, S., Liang, M., Yang, B., Zeng, W., Urtasun, R.: V2VNet: vehicle-to-vehicle communication for joint perception and prediction. In: Vedaldi, A., Bischof, H., Brox, T., Frahm, J.-M. (eds.) ECCV 2020. LNCS, vol. 12347, pp. 605–621. Springer, Cham (2020). https://doi.org/10.1007/978-3-030-58536-5_36
17. Yan, Y., Mao, Y., Li, B.: Second: sparsely embedded convolutional detection. Sensors **18**(10), 3337 (2018)
18. Zhao, H., Jiang, L., Jia, J., Torr, P.H., Koltun, V.: Point transformer. In: Proceedings of the IEEE/CVF International Conference on Computer Vision, pp. 16259–16268 (2021)
19. Zhou, Y., Tuzel, O.: VoxelNet: end-to-end learning for point cloud based 3D object detection. In: Proceedings of the IEEE Conference on Computer Vision and Pattern Recognition, pp. 4490–4499 (2018)

# How to Face Unseen Defects? UDGAN for Improving Unseen Defects Recognition

Yaxi Chen, Ruimin Hu$^{(\boxtimes)}$, Zheng Wang, and Yuke Li

National Engineering Research Center for Multimedia Software (NERCMS),
School of Computer Science, Wuhan University, Wuhan, China
{chenyaxi,hrm,wangzwhu,sunfreshing}@whu.edu.cn

**Abstract.** The rapid renewal of industrial production lines is accompanied by the emergence of many unseen new defects that are difficult to detect, which may lead to large economic losses. Existing methods focus on the recognition of seen defects, but are powerless against unseen defects. The recognition of unseen defects is a challenging task and has not been widely explored. To our knowledge, we are the first to raise the issue of unseen defect recognition. To tackle this issue, we design an unseen defect generative adversarial network (UDGAN) model. The UDGAN not only explores the similarity between seen and unseen defects by extracting the latent distribution of the images but also represents the difference between these two defects considering the distribution interval. To enhance the understanding of the latent distribution of seen and generated images, we investigate their connection through mutual information optimization, giving some correlation between seen defects and generated images. Meanwhile, the distance between the mean of the seen and unseen defect distributions is expanded to optimize the extraction of latent distributions so that the types of defects in the generated and seen images are as different as possible. Experimental results on the magnetic tile defect dataset show that UDGAN achieves significant improvements over state-of-the-art methods.

**Keywords:** Surface defect recognition · Generative models · Deep learning

## 1 Introduction

The rapid renewal of industrial production lines is a common problem for modern manufacturing. As production lines change, the shape, size, and location of product defects can change unexpectedly, as shown in Fig. 1. How recognize them effectively and accurately is especially important for product quality control.

In recent years, significant progress has been made in surface defect recognition techniques due to the powerful feature extraction capability of convolutional neural networks [17,18,24]. To our knowledge, the existing methods used

Supported by the National Nature Science Foundation of China (U1803262).

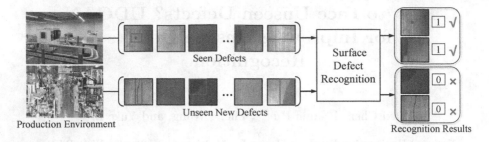

**Fig. 1.** An example of surface defect recognition. The complex and changing production environment leads to the frequent generation of new defects. Existing methods focus on recognizing seen defects, but are powerless against unseen defects.

to work from few shot learning and propose different generative models to solve this problem [14,17,24]. However, applying these existing methods to unseen defect recognition has the following limitations: 1) Few types of defect samples can be collected in industrial scenarios, resulting in a lack of richness in the types of defects among the generated samples as well. 2) Existing methods generate samples that are similar to seen samples and do not capture latent unknown features.

The challenges for the recognition of unseen defects are mainly the following: 1) **Uncertainty**. The uncertainty generated by diverse and highly dynamic new defects leads to difficulties in the generation as well as the recognition of unseen defects. 2) **Automatability**. In real industrial scenarios, the occurrence of unseen defects may cause large economic losses, both in terms of productivity as well as recognition. Existing zero shot learning based methods [4,11,22] need to provide manually labeled semantic information to guide the model, which is undoubtedly more expensive and time-consuming.

In this paper, our key insight is that since unseen defects and seen defects originate from the same product, they are bound to be of some relevance, which is based on the latent distribution of the features to which they correspond. The exploration of latent distribution can provide a richer understanding of possible future defects to some extent: different unseen defects are essentially correlated with the latent distribution. In addition, we believe that the mean of the distribution corresponding to different types of defects is different, while the mean of the distribution corresponding to the same type of defects is more concentrated, so we use this idea to guide learning the latent distribution of defects. Toward this end, we discover the pattern through the seen defects and delve deeper into the characteristics of latent unseen defects to generate different new defects to meet various possible future defects as much as possible.

Thus, we design an Unseen Defect Generative Adversarial Network (UDGAN) model that aims to generate unseen defects from seen defects to enrich the defect samples as much as possible to adapt to the frequently changing recognition tasks in industrial scenarios. The UDGAN not only explores the similarity between seen and unseen defects by extracting the latent distribution of the images but also represent the difference between these two defects considering the distribution interval. Specifically, we generate unseen defects by extracting latent distribution, and investigate the connection between seen defects and generated unseen defects by mutual information optimization, while using triplet loss to optimize the extraction of latent distribution, and using unseen defects to perturb the discriminator to make the generated unseen defects gradually approximate the real unseen defects.

To our knowledge, we are the first to explore unseen defect recognition. In summary, this paper makes the following contributions:

- We propose a new problem: unseen defect recognition. Intelligent recognition of unseen defects can significantly improve the efficiency of the product lines.
- We design the unseen defect generative adversarial network (UDGAN) model, which not only explores the similarity between seen and unseen defects by extracting the latent distribution of the images but also represents the difference between these two defects considering the distribution interval.
- The experimental results show that UDGAN has a strong advantage in unseen defect generation. In addition, our model significantly outperforms the state-of-the-art (SOTA) methods on the public dataset.

## 2   Related Work

In this section, we present the latest research on traditional surface defect recognition and the applications of GAN in surface defect recognition.

### 2.1   Traditional Surface Defect Recognition

Due to the powerful feature extraction capability of CNNs, the use of CNN-based classification networks is becoming the most commonly used model for surface defect recognition nowadays. In general, surface defect recognition usually uses CNN classification networks for feature extraction, followed by classification using connected fully connected layers and softmax structures. Existing surface defect recognition networks usually use the network structures readily available in computer vision, such as VGG [21], AlexNet [16], ResNet [8], etc. In this paper, a ResNet network is applied for defect recognition.

### 2.2   Applications of GAN in Surface Defect Recognition

Goodfellow *et al.* [6] first proposed GAN for image generation, subsequently, the research on GAN has been developed rapidly, and there are more and more derivative networks based on GAN networks [1,3,7,15,19]. DCGAN [19] introduces the convolutional network into the structure of GAN, using the powerful feature extraction ability of the convolutional layer to improve the effect of GAN. WGAN [1] introduces the Wasserstein distance, which has superior smoothing properties relative to KL divergence and JS divergence, and can solve the gradient disappearance problem. WGAN_GP [7] adopts the gradient penalty method to improve the condition of continuity restriction and increase the training speed. LSGAN [15] attempts to build a more stable and faster converging adversarial network using different distance metrics.

In the field of surface defect recognition, GAN can also be used to generate images to enrich the samples. Xu *et al.* [5] trained the generated images based on convolutional self-encoders and Semi-supervised Generative Adversarial Networks (SGAN) to improve the recognition rate of hot-rolled steel sheet defects by 16%. Liu *et al.* [13] proposed a framework for fabric defect recognition based on generative adversarial networks, which can learn existing fabric defect samples and automatically adapt to different fabric textures at different application stages. Niu *et al.* [17] proposed a surface defect generation method, SDGAN, which is capable of generating defects on defect-free images. Zhang *et al.* [24] proposed a Defect-GAN to generate defect samples and recover defects by simulating damage and repair processes.

To sum up, the UDGAN model differs from other models in the following points: 1) Our study focuses on generating unseen defects. 2) Explicit exploration of latent distribution allows our approach to better generate unseen defects rather than utilizing predefined latent variables. 3) Unlike previous studies, UDGAN does not use any semantic information about unseen defects.

## 3   Methodology

In this section, we discuss the method used in this paper. As shown in Fig. 2, our method has two parts: Unseen Defect Generation and Unseen Defect Recognition. The Unseen Defect Generation Model (UDGAN) is used to generate unseen defects, and Unseen Defect Recognition determines whether there are defects in the input image.

### 3.1   Unseen Defect Generation

As mentioned previously, our work focuses on learning and extracting seen defects to generate unseen defects to predict possible unseen defects in the future. Fundamentally, our UDGAN can be viewed as jointly training: 1) an extractor $E$ that learns about a latent distribution, 2) a generator $G$ that generates unseen defect images, 3) an interactor $Q$ that discovers the impact of the extractor $E$ on generated images, and 4) a discriminator $D$ that attempts to differentiate generated images from the real unseen samples. Our objective is to generate unseen defects from seen defects, We express the objective equation as:

$$P(u|s) = \int p(u|s, z)dz \times p(z|s)dz, \tag{1}$$

where $z$ denotes latent distribution, $s$ and $u$ denote seen defect samples and unseen defect samples, respectively. We depict the structure and workflow of our proposed UDGAN framework in Fig. 3. In what follows, we provide detailed descriptions of each part.

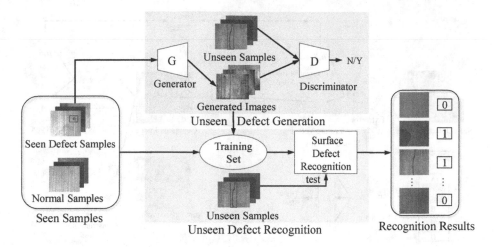

**Fig. 2.** The pipeline of the proposed approach. There are two components: unseen defect generation and unseen defect recognition.

**Latent Distribution Extraction.** We propose the point that the known latent distribution is the key to understanding the unknown. To grasp this point, we propose to first uncover the latent distribution by learning the features of seen defects. This is because there is a correlation between the seen defects and the unseen defects. In practice, we parameterize the distribution of latent features via the extractor $E$.

In the same industrial scenario, the rapid renewal of production lines leads to changes in the shape and type of defects. We believe that although the defect samples of different production lines may have different defect shapes, they must have some correlation. Therefore, we learn a distribution representing the features of seen defects and unseen defects. To achieve this goal, we input the seen defect samples $s$ into a pre-trained convolutional neural network in two parts, obtaining the features of the extracted seen defect samples and generating a two-unit vector, respectively. This two-unit vector is considered a conditional Gaussian distribution with mean $\mu$ and standard deviation $\sigma$, sampled from the latent distribution $z$. It can be formulated as: $\mu, \sigma = Conv(E(s))$, $z \sim p(z|s) = N(\mu, \sigma)$.

We also consider that seen defects and unseen defects differ in defect characteristics, and to capture this idea, we construct triplet loss to constrain them. Triplet loss in Eq. 2, which minimizes the distance between the anchor and the positive, both of which are the seen defect samples $s_i$, and maximize the distance between the anchor and the negative with different identities, which are the seen defect samples $s_i$ and unseen defects samples $u_i$, by which the loss function continuously optimizes the latent distribution $z$ to be able to better generate the unseen defects samples. Triplet loss [20] is being minimized is:

$$\mathcal{L}_{triplet} = \sum_{i}^{N} [\|f(s_i^a) - f(s_i^p)\|_2^2 - \|f(s_i^a) - f(u_i^n)\|_2^2 + \alpha]_+, \qquad (2)$$

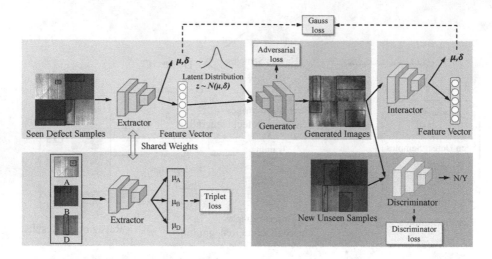

**Fig. 3.** The detailed schematic of UDGAN for generating unseen defect samples. Firstly, the seen defect samples are input to the extractor to extract the latent distribution. Meanwhile, the seen defect samples(A, B) and the unseen defect samples(D) form a triplet and are fed to the extractor to continuously optimize the extraction of latent distribution. Then the generator generates images from the latent distribution and seen defect samples. And interactor reads the generated images and latent distribution to measure the importance of the extractor for generating unseen defect samples. Finally, the discriminator distinguishes the images from the real unseen defect samples.

where $\forall (f(s_i^a), f(s_i^p), f(u_i^n)) \in \mathcal{T}$, $\mathcal{T}$ is the set of all possible triplets in the dataset and has cardinality N. $\alpha$ is a margin that is enforced between positive and negative pairs.

**Generator.** We use the generator $G$ to generate unseen defects. To generate more consistent and real unseen defects images, we adopt adversarial loss to make the generated images $f$ indistinguishable from the real unseen samples $u_n$. The objective of generator [6] is as follows:

$$\mathcal{L}_{adv} = \min_G \max_D \mathbb{E}_u[\log D(u_n)] + \mathbb{E}_f[\log(1 - D(G(z)))]. \tag{3}$$

**Mutual Information Optimization.** In this section, we explicitly delve into the essence that binds latent distribution $z$ to the generator $G$ to gain a clearer insight into the correlation between latent distribution $z$ and generated images $f$. We proceed by optimizing the mutual information between $z$ and $G$ to establish their connection. As a result, we can quantitatively measure the significance of latent distribution on generated images. The mutual information $I(z; G)$ is termed as:

$$I(z; G) = H(z) - H(z|G), \tag{4}$$

where $H(\cdot)$ denotes the Shannon entropy. A larger value of $I(z; G)$ refers to a larger influence on the latent distribution. Optimizing (4) thereby incentivizes $z$ and consolidates its impact on the generated images.

We input the seen defect samples $s$ to the extractor $E$ to obtain the latent distribution $z$, and the generated images $f$ to the interactor $Q$ to obtain the latent distribution $\hat{z}$. The Gauss loss is realized by optimizing the mutual information of $z$ and $\hat{z}$ distributions max. With the help of the mutual information neural estimator [2], optimizing $I(z; G)$ is equivalent to maximizing its lower bound $\mathcal{L}_1$. For this purpose, we introduce an interactor $Q$ to approximate $\mathcal{L}_1$.

$$I(z; G) \geqslant \mathcal{L}_1 = \mathbb{E}_{f \sim G, z \sim p(z|s)} Q(f, z) - \log \mathbb{E}_{f \sim G, \hat{z} \sim p(z|s)} (e^{Q(f,\hat{z})}). \qquad (5)$$

**Discriminator.** We use a discriminator $D$ to distinguish generated images $f$ from unseen samples $u_n$ to guide $G$. The unseen samples $u_n$ are fed to a discriminator $D$ which is continuously perturbed so that the generated images gradually resemble the unseen samples $u_n$ during the training process. As a result, the discriminator can only be fooled if generated images $f$ is consistent with unseen samples $u_n$. The objective of the discriminator is as follows:

$$\mathcal{L}^{\mathcal{D}} = \mathop{\mathbb{E}}_{f \sim P_g} [D(f)] - \mathop{\mathbb{E}}_{u \sim P_r} [D(u_n)] + \lambda \mathop{\mathbb{E}}_{x \sim P_x} [(\|\nabla_x D(x)\|_2 - 1)^2], \qquad (6)$$

$$x = \varepsilon u_n + (1 - \varepsilon) f, \qquad (7)$$

where $[\|\nabla_x D(x)\|_2 - 1]^2$ is the gradient penalty term following Wasserstein GAN with Gradient Penalty (WGAN-GP) [7]. $\lambda$ is a coefficient, and $\epsilon \sim U[0, 1]$ is a random parameter.

### 3.2 Surface Defect Recognition

We use the pre-trained ResNet50 [8] for the anomaly recognition model. We do not modify the backbone framework of ResNet50. We use the unseen defect samples generated by UDGAN and the seen samples as the input to the anomaly recognition model and train the anomaly recognition model. After the training is completed, we test the performance of the model with unseen new defects.

## 4  Experiment

### 4.1  Implementation Detail

**Datasets.** We use the Magnetic tile defect dataset (MT) [9] to validate the performance of our algorithm in the task of generating unseen defects. The dataset is classified into six different types based on the shape of the defects: Blowhole, Crack, Fray, Break, Uneven, and Normal (no defects), as shown in Fig. 4.

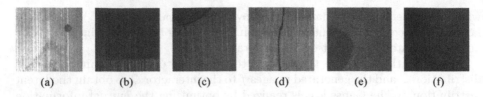

(a)              (b)              (c)              (d)              (e)              (f)

**Fig. 4.** Various defects and normal images in MT. (a) Blowhole. (b) Uneven. (c) Break. (d) Crack. (e) Fray. (f) Normal

To make all the images in the MT of the same size, we cropped the size of all the images to 128 × 128. To express easily, in this experiment, we named the five defect samples as ABCDE, ABC are considered as seen defects and DE are considered as unseen defects. Since in the actual industrial production, we cannot know the actual situation of the samples created by the new production line, so to be closer to real industrial production, our unseen samples are all samples generated by the new production line, *i.e.*, including the unseen defect samples and normal samples (DE + normal samples). In the anomaly recognition part, we simulate the real production environment, and the training set is the samples with labels from the old production line, *i.e.*, the seen defect samples and normal samples (ABC + normal samples), the test set is the samples from the products of the new production line, *i.e.*, the unseen defect samples and normal samples (DE + normal samples).

**Evaluation Metrics.** For surface defect anomaly recognition, it is most important to detect defect samples correctly, avoid missing defect samples as much as possible, and improve product yields. Therefore, we use the **Accuracy Rate** and **Recall Rate** to evaluate the performance of defect image recognition.

**Experimental Settings**

*Unseen Defect Generation.* The proposed unseen defect generation model is validated on the magnetic tile defect dataset and compared with the five state-of-the-art generation method, i.e., GAN, DCGAN, WGAN, WGAN GP, LSGAN, as shown in Table 1. All experiments are carried out with 128 × 128 images on the server, and the batch sizes are 16. The UDGAN uses RMSprop [12] as an optimization method to train $E$ and $Q$ with an initial learning rate of 0.00003 while training $G$ and $D$ with an initial learning rate of 0.00005. The DCGAN, GAN, WGAN_GP, and LSGAN use Adam [10] as the optimization method, while WGAN uses RMSprop [12] as the optimization method, and they are all trained with the initial learning rate of 0.0002. All experiments were done with the same input and output. The experiments were conducted on a server with a Tesla A100 GPU.

*Surface Defect Recognition.* The surface defect recognition network is based on ResNet50, using SGD [12] as the optimization method, and we train the anomaly recognition model using the same hyperparameter settings for comparison. In all experiments, we set the learning rate to 0.01, the batch size to 16, and we train the model for 200 epochs.

## 4.2   Experiment Results

**Surface Defect Recognition.** Table 1 shows the classification accuracy rate, recall rate and relative improvement of the different methods on MT dataset. Our method (UDGAN) improves the accuracy to 85.09% and recall to 76.75%. Compared with the CNN-only baseline, the relative improvement(IMP) of accuracy [23] is 5.59% and IMP of recall is 23.45%. In terms of accuracy, recall and IMP, UDGAN outperforms the state-of-the-art methods, which indicate that UDGAN performs best in generating unseen defect samples.

**Table 1.** Performance of defect anomaly recognition using different generation methods on the MT dataset.

| Method | Acc (%) | Rec (%) | Relative IMP (%) [Acc] | Relative IMP (%) [Rec] |
|---|---|---|---|---|
| CNN-only | 80.59 | 62.17 | – | – |
| GAN [6] | 81.58 | 65.02 | 1.23 | 4.58 |
| DCGAN [19] | 83.11 | 70.83 | 3.13 | 13.93 |
| WGAN [1] | 82.79 | 67.76 | 2.73 | 8.99 |
| WGAN_GP [7] | 82.81 | 67.65 | 2.75 | 8.81 |
| LSGAN [15] | 81.80 | 64.80 | 1.50 | 4.23 |
| UDGAN | **85.09** | **76.75** | **5.59** | **23.45** |

**Sensitivity Analysis.** We analyze the performance of UDGAN with different $\alpha$ parameters when using triplet loss (Eq. 2). When $\alpha$ is more than 1, the model starts to show non-convergence, so we take $\alpha$ maximum of 1. As shown in Fig. 5, it can be seen that the best results are obtained when $\alpha = 1$. The above results indicate that the larger the difference between the distributions of seen and unseen defects, the better the performance of UDGAN in the case of model convergence.

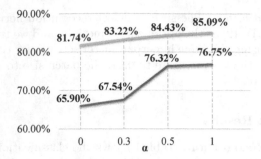

**Fig. 5.** Performance of UDGAN with different parameters $\alpha$ on the MT dataset.

**Ablation Study.** We study the effectiveness of each part of our UDGAN through analyses against the following baselines: 1) **NEGAN:** To highlight the merit of our latent distribution, we use a predefined $z \sim N(0,1)$ rather than inducing the distribution from seen defects. The rest of the framework remains unchanged. 2) **NQGAN:** We evaluate the necessity of mutual information optimization by comparing it with NQGAN. This baseline drops the interactor $Q$ from the UDGAN framework. 3) **NEQGAN:** To test the impact of the extractor on the forecasting of unseen defects, we construct the NEQGAN baseline by discarding both the extractor $E$ and interactor $Q$. 4) **UDGAN-triplet:** To test the effect of the distribution interval of seen defects and unseen defects, we do so by discarding triplet loss.

We did ablation experiments, the results of which are shown in Table 2. The results show that the performance of the model decreases when the latent distribution is removed as well as when the mutual information optimization is removed. However, when the triplet loss is removed, the accuracy rate of the model slightly improves, and the reason for this result deserves to be explored further.

**Table 2.** Performance after removing different parts of UDGAN on the MT dataset.

| Method | Acc (%) | Rec (%) |
|---|---|---|
| NEGAN | 83.11 | 68.53 |
| NQGAN | 82.95 | 67.76 |
| NEQGAN | 81.63 | 66.89 |
| UDGAN-triplet | **85.64** | 74.34 |
| UDGAN | 85.09 | **76.75** |

**Unseen Defect Generation.** As shown in Fig. 6, we show the various unseen defect images generated by UDGAN, from which it can be seen that the generated defects are of various types and different from the seen defects. UDGAN has an excellent ability to generate unseen defects.

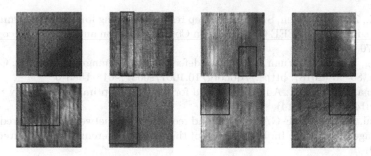

**Fig. 6.** Various unseen defect images are generated by UDGAN.

## 5   Conclusion

In this paper, we design a novel unseen defect generative adversarial network for generating samples of possible future defects. To our knowledge, we are the first to raise the issue of unseen defects recognition. UDGAN can generate latent unseen defect samples from seen defect samples to suit the frequently changing recognition tasks in industrial scenarios. Moreover, UDGAN not only explores the similarity between seen and unseen defects by extracting the latent distribution of the images but also represents the difference between these two defects considering the distribution interval. The experimental results show that the defect samples generated by UDGAN are closer to the real unseen defects, and have a remarkable relative improvement over existing methods. UDGAN can discover the unknown through the known, find out their similarities, and also distinguish their differences, which can help to explore the unknown world better.

## References

1. Arjovsky, M., Chintala, S., Bottou, L.: Wasserstein GAN (2017)
2. Belghazi, M.I., et al.: Mutual information neural estimation. In: International Conference on Machine Learning, pp. 531–540. PMLR (2018)
3. Chen, X., Duan, Y., Houthooft, R., Schulman, J., Sutskever, I., Abbeel, P.: InfoGAN: interpretable representation learning by information maximizing generative adversarial nets. Adv. Neural Inf. Process. Syst. **29** (2016)
4. Chen, Z., et al.: Semantics disentangling for generalized zero-shot learning. In: Proceedings of the IEEE/CVF International Conference on Computer Vision, pp. 8712–8720 (2021)
5. Di, H., Ke, X., Peng, Z., Dongdong, Z.: Surface defect classification of steels with a new semi-supervised learning method. Opt. Lasers Eng. **117**, 40–48 (2019)
6. Goodfellow, I., et al.: Generative adversarial nets. Adv. Neural Inf. Process. Syst. **27** (2014)
7. Gulrajani, I., Ahmed, F., Arjovsky, M., Dumoulin, V., Courville, A.C.: Improved training of Wasserstein GANs. Adv. Neural Inf. Process. Syst. **30** (2017)

8. He, K., Zhang, X., Ren, S., Sun, J.: Deep residual learning for image recognition. In: Proceedings of the IEEE Conference on Computer Vision and Pattern Recognition, pp. 770–778 (2016)
9. Huang, Y., Qiu, C., Yuan, K.: Surface defect saliency of magnetic tile. Vis. Comput. **36**(1), 85–96 (2018). https://doi.org/10.1007/s00371-018-1588-5
10. Kingma, D.P., Ba, J.: Adam: a method for stochastic optimization. arXiv preprint arXiv:1412.6980 (2014)
11. Koksal, A., Lu, S.: RF-GAN: a light and reconfigurable network for unpaired image-to-image translation. In: Proceedings of the Asian Conference on Computer Vision (2020)
12. LeCun, Y., Bengio, Y., Hinton, G.: Deep learning. Nature **521**(7553), 436–444 (2015)
13. Liu, J., Wang, C., Su, H., Du, B., Tao, D.: Multistage GAN for fabric defect detection. IEEE Trans. Image Process. **29**, 3388–3400 (2019)
14. Liu, L., Cao, D., Wu, Y., Wei, T.: Defective samples simulation through adversarial training for automatic surface inspection. Neurocomputing **360**, 230–245 (2019)
15. Mao, X., Li, Q., Xie, H., Lau, R.Y., Wang, Z., Paul Smolley, S.: Least squares generative adversarial networks. In: Proceedings of the IEEE International Conference on Computer Vision, pp. 2794–2802 (2017)
16. Naranjo-Alcazar, J., Perez-Castanos, S., Zuccarello, P., Cobos, M.: Acoustic scene classification with squeeze-excitation residual networks. IEEE Access **8**, 112287–112296 (2020)
17. Niu, S., Li, B., Wang, X., Lin, H.: Defect image sample generation with GAN for improving defect recognition. IEEE Trans. Autom. Sci. Eng. **17**(3), 1611–1622 (2020)
18. Park, J.-K., Kwon, B.-K., Park, J.-H., Kang, D.-J.: Machine learning-based imaging system for surface defect inspection. Int. J. Precis. Eng. Manuf.-Green Technol. **3**(3), 303–310 (2016). https://doi.org/10.1007/s40684-016-0039-x
19. Radford, A., Metz, L., Chintala, S.: Unsupervised representation learning with deep convolutional generative adversarial networks. arXiv preprint arXiv:1511.06434 (2015)
20. Schroff, F., Kalenichenko, D., Philbin, J.: FaceNet: a unified embedding for face recognition and clustering. In: Proceedings of the IEEE Conference on Computer Vision and Pattern Recognition, pp. 815–823 (2015)
21. Simonyan, K., Zisserman, A.: Very deep convolutional networks for large-scale image recognition. arXiv preprint arXiv:1409.1556 (2014)
22. Xian, Y., Sharma, S., Schiele, B., Akata, Z.: F-VAEGAN-D2: a feature generating framework for any-shot learning. In: Proceedings of the IEEE/CVF Conference on Computer Vision and Pattern Recognition, pp. 10275–10284 (2019)
23. Xuan, Q., Chen, Z., Liu, Y., Huang, H., Bao, G., Zhang, D.: Multiview generative adversarial network and its application in pearl classification. IEEE Trans. Industr. Electron. **66**(10), 8244–8252 (2018)
24. Zhang, G., Cui, K., Hung, T.Y., Lu, S.: Defect-GAN: high-fidelity defect synthesis for automated defect inspection. In: Proceedings of the IEEE/CVF Winter Conference on Applications of Computer Vision, pp. 2524–2534 (2021)

# Learning to Generate Textual Adversarial Examples

Xiangzhe Guo, Shikui Tu[✉], and Lei Xu[✉]

Department of Computer Science and Engineering, Shanghai Jiao Tong University,
Shanghai, China
{gggggxz,tushikui,leixu}@sjtu.edu.cn

**Abstract.** Word substitution based textual adversarial attack is actually a combinatorial optimization problem. Existing greedy search methods are time-consuming due to extensive unnecessary victim model calls in word ranking and substitution. In this work, we propose a learnable attack method which uses neural networks to guide the greedy search to reduce victim model calls. Specifically, we use one network to predict the importance of each word, without accessing the victim model. It avoids the victim model calls proportional to the length of the text, which may be in hundreds. Moreover, we use the other network to score each substitute word for a specific substitute position and filter out the attack-inefficient and out-of-context ones, so as to reduce substitution attempts. We evaluate our method on sentiment analysis, natural language inference and paraphrase identification tasks. Experimental results show that our method can achieve higher attack success rate and adversarial example quality than the baseline methods, while requiring less computation overhead. The code is public at https://github.com/CMACH508/PredictiveTextualAttack.

**Keywords:** Textual adversarial attack · Learnable adversarial attack · Adversarial robustness · Deep learning

## 1 Introduction

Deep neural networks (DNNs) have been shown to be vulnerable to adversarial attacks [7,10] which are implemented by small perturbations to the input. The perturbations are imperceptible to humans, but they can cheat models to make mistakes. For example, simply modifying some words in a spam message may make it avoid a DNN based spam detection system, even though the meaning of the message has not changed. On the other hand, using adversarial examples for adversarial training is an effective way to construct robust models. Therefore, research on generating textual adversarial examples has received increasing attention recently.

Black box attack, which does not have access to the victim model's internal architecture and parameters, is usually encountered in the real world scenarios.

E. Pimenidis et al. (Eds.): ICANN 2022, LNCS 13529, pp. 195–206, 2022.
https://doi.org/10.1007/978-3-031-15919-0_17

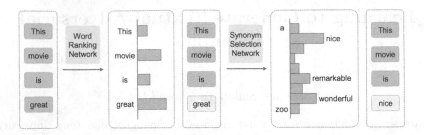

**Fig. 1.** An overview of how our model works with the greedy search. The word ranking network predicts the importance of each word, and words are processed in descending order of predicted importance. For a specific position, the synonym selection network scores all words in the substitute word vocabulary, and selects the synonyms with the highest scores for substitution.

In the field of natural language processing, synonym substitution is an effective black box attack method: it substitutes words in a text with synonyms to deceive the model. It can be formalized as a combinatorial optimization problem [23]: each word in a text is either kept unchanged or replaced with a synonym. Since a word may have multiple synonyms, the number of potential adversarial examples increases exponentially with the length of the text. The greedy search method for this problem has received a lot of attention recently [6,9,11,12,19], which mainly consists of two steps: (1) the *word ranking step* determines the word substitution order so that the words that have a greater impact on the victim model's decision are processed first; (2) the *word substitution step* processes the words in the previously determined order, and selects the synonym with the best attack effect at each position (Fig. 1).

Although the greedy search has made a trade-off between attack performance and efficiency, its computational overhead is still large. For example, it may need to call the victim model hundreds of times to generate one adversarial example on the Yelp [24] dataset. For word ranking step, the greedy search determines the substitution order by evaluating the importance of each word, which requires victim model calls proportional to the length of the text. For word substitution step, the greedy search tries all the synonyms for substitution. Bu in fact, some victim model calls in the two steps can be reduced.

This work focuses on the greedy search and proposes to generates adversarial examples in a predictive way, so as to reduce victim model calls. The motivation is that for a specific victim model: (1) the words that have a greater impact on the model's decision have special patterns. Take part of speech as an example, on SNLI [2] dataset, if words are processed in the order of nouns, verbs, adjectives and adverbs, the attack success rate is 74.7%, while in sequential order, the attack success rate is 56.4%, which suggests that part of speech is a factor that influences the importance of words, and there may be more complex factors; (2) for a specific position, good synonyms have special patterns. Take the sentence "The restaurant service was *poor*" as an example [6], 'terrible' and 'broke' are both synonyms of 'poor', while 'terrible' is more in line with the context. In addition, some synonyms are more likely to deceive the victim model, which may be related to bias or overfitting of the victim model.

To learn more complex patterns, we propose two networks: (1) a *word ranking network* which predicts the words' importance based on the text itself, without accessing the victim model; (2) a *synonym selection network* which predicts the potential of each synonym to deceive the model while maintaining the semantics. Based on the two networks, adversarial examples can be generated in a predictive way, so as to reduce a large number of victim model calls.

We conduct experiments on four datasets of sentiment analysis, natural language inference and paraphrase identification tasks. Compared with the baseline methods, our method can achieve higher attack success rate and adversarial example quality and reduce the number of victim model calls.

## 2  Related Work

Word substitution based attack can be viewed as a combinatorial optimization problem [23], and researchers have proposed some heuristic methods for this problem. One approach is population-based methods like genetic algorithm [1] and discrete particle swarm optimization [23]. Another approach is the greedy search, where the word ranking step determines the substitution order and the word substitution step selects synonyms for substitution for each word, and this type of work includes TextFooler [9], PWWS [19], BERT-Attack [12], etc.

The population-based methods may require tens of thousands of victim model calls to generate one adversarial example [21], which is very time-consuming. The greedy search methods requires fewer victim model calls, but the computation overhead is still large. Some query-efficient methods haven been proposed recently. One is to reduce the number of queries in PWWS word ranking using the attention mechanism and locality sensitive hashing [16], but it only focuses on the word ranking, and still needs to try all synonyms for word substitution. Another attempt is to use reinforcement learning method to generate adversarial examples [3,22], but the quality of generated adversarial examples is poor.

Closest to our work are BERT-Attack [12], BAE [6] and CLARE [11], which use masked language models (BERT [4] and RoBERTa [14]) to predict word at the substitute position and form the synonym set, so that the synonyms are more natural in context. This is similar to our synonym selection network, but in addition to fitting in the context, our network also requires the words to deceive the victim model, that is, the synonym selection network needs to learn some characteristics of the victim model.

## 3  Methodology

### 3.1  Problem Formulation

Given a trained text classification model $f$ and an input text $x = (w_1, w_2, \ldots, w_n)$, the model can predict the probability of each class $f(x) = (p_1, p_2, \ldots, p_C)$, where C is the number of classes.

For each word $w_i$, the synonym set is $\mathcal{S}_i$. Supposing that $y$ is the true label and it can be correctly predicted by $f$, the task is to find $x_{\mathrm{adv}} = (w'_1, w'_2, \ldots, w'_n)$, where $w'_i \in \{w_i\} + \mathcal{S}_i$, and $x_{\mathrm{adv}}$ should satisfy that $\arg\max_{y'} f(x_{\mathrm{adv}})_{y'} \neq y$ and $\mathrm{sim}(x, x_{\mathrm{adv}}) \geq \epsilon$, where $\mathrm{sim}(\cdot, \cdot)$ is a similarity function and $\epsilon$ is the similarity threshold.

## 3.2   Word Ranking Network

For the word ranking step, previous methods score the words one by one and require $\mathcal{O}(n)$ victim model calls, which may involve extensive unnecessary computation. But which words are more important can be inferred from the text itself. We propose the word ranking network, which can *predict* the importance of each word based on the text (Fig. 2).

Given a text $x = (w_1, w_2, \ldots, w_n)$ and the corresponding true label $y$, a pre-trained language model $F_{\mathrm{PLM}}^{\mathrm{wr}}$ (e.g. BERT; [4]) is used to encode each word:

$$e_{\mathrm{wr},i} = F_{\mathrm{PLM}}^{\mathrm{wr}}(x, i) \in \mathbb{R}^{d_{\mathrm{PLM}}^{\mathrm{wr}}}, i = 1, 2, \ldots, n,$$

where $d_{\mathrm{PLM}}^{\mathrm{wr}}$ is the output dimension of $F_{\mathrm{PLM}}^{\mathrm{wr}}$. Pre-trained language models often use subword tokenization and a word may be tokenized into multiple subwords. If there are multiple subwords, we choose the encoding of the first one.

A word may have different importance for different classes. In order to learn different representations for each class, we set a projection matrix $M_\ell^{\mathrm{wr}} \in \mathbb{R}^{d_{\mathrm{wr}} \times d_{\mathrm{PLM}}^{\mathrm{wr}}}$ for each label $\ell \in \{1, 2, \ldots, C\}$, and project $e_{\mathrm{wr},i}$ to a label specific subspace:

$$h_{\mathrm{wr},i} = M_y^{\mathrm{wr}} e_{\mathrm{wr},i} \in \mathbb{R}^{d_{\mathrm{wr}}}.$$

Finally, $h_{\mathrm{wr},i}$ is transformed into scalar by a feedforward neural network $F_{\mathrm{FFN}}^{\mathrm{wr}}$, and then normalized by the sigmoid function to obtain the importance score:

$$p_{\mathrm{wr},i} = \mathrm{sigmoid}(F_{\mathrm{FFN}}^{\mathrm{wr}}(h_{\mathrm{wr},i})) \in \mathbb{R}. \tag{1}$$

Multiple positions can be scored at the same time, and the procedure is denoted as:

$$p_{\mathrm{wr}} = \mathrm{WordRanking}(x, y) \in \mathbb{R}^n,$$

where $p_{\mathrm{wr}}$ is the predicted score of each word in $x$.

**Training.** Since there is no ground truth for word importance, we score the words to construct training examples. Formally, we define a substitution operation:

$$\tilde{x}_{i,z} = (w_1, \ldots, w_{i-1}, z, w_{i+1}, \ldots, w_n).$$

We score the words in a way similar to PWWS [19]. First we evaluate the saliency of each word, i.e., the decrease in the predicted probability after the word is replaced by [UNK]:

$$S_i = f(x)_y - f(\tilde{x}_{i,[\mathrm{UNK}]})_y, i = 1, 2, \ldots, n.$$

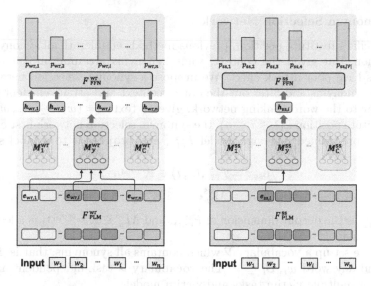

**Fig. 2.** Left: the word ranking network, which first encodes the text with a pre-trained language model, then projects the encoding of each word to a label specific subspace, and finally converts the projected vector to an importance score; Right: the synonym selection network, which first encodes the text with a pre-trained language model, then projects the encoding of the word at the substitute position to a label specific subspace, and finally converts the projected vector to a $|\mathcal{V}|$-dimensional vector, which represents the probability of each word in the synonym vocabulary being selected.

Then attack effect, that is, the maximum possible decrease in predicted probability after word substitution. We exclude some synonyms from $\mathcal{S}_i$ that may reduce text quality, formally, $s \in \mathcal{S}_i$ can be retained if (1) $\mathrm{sim}(\tilde{x}_{i,s}, x) \geq \theta_{\mathrm{wr}}$, (2) the perplexity of $\tilde{x}_{i,s}$ by GPT-2 [17] ranks top $p_{\mathrm{ppl}}^{\mathrm{wr}}\%$ among all synonyms in $\mathcal{S}_i$. Supposing that the retained synonyms form a set $\mathcal{S}_i'$, the attack effect is:

$$\boldsymbol{E}_i = \max_{s \in \mathcal{S}_i'}(f(x)_y - f(\tilde{x}_{i,s})_y) \cdot \mathrm{sim}(\tilde{x}_{i,s}, x) \,, \, i = 1, 2, \ldots, n \,,$$

then, the words are scored by:

$$\mathrm{softmax}(\boldsymbol{S})_i \cdot \boldsymbol{E}_i, \, i = 1, 2, \ldots, n \,.$$

Finally, the words with the highest $p_{\mathrm{pos}}^{\mathrm{wr}}\%$ score are used as positive training examples, and the lowest $p_{\mathrm{neg}}^{\mathrm{wr}}\%$ are negative training examples.

Given a training example $((x, y, i), \, \ell_i)$, the network is optimized by minimizing the binary cross entropy loss of $p_{\mathrm{wr},i}$ in Eq. (1) and label $\ell_i$:

$$loss_{\mathrm{wr}} = -(\ell_i \cdot \log p_{\mathrm{wr},i} + (1 - \ell_i) \cdot \log(1 - p_{\mathrm{wr},i})) \,.$$

**Inference.** During attack, the words are scored and ranked by the word ranking network, and no victim model calls are needed in word ranking.

### 3.3  Synonym Selection Network

For a specific substitute position, previous methods enumerate all synonyms for substitution. But given the context, some synonyms are unnatural and some synonyms have poor attack effect. We propose a synonym selection network to *score* the synonyms and filter out the out-of-context and attack-efficient ones.

Similar to the word ranking network, given a text $x = (w_1, w_2, \ldots, w_n)$ and the substitute position $i$ $(1 \leq i \leq n)$, the synonym selection network first encodes $w_i$ with a pre-trained language model $F_{\mathrm{PLM}}^{\mathrm{ss}}$ and projects it to a label specific subspace:

$$e_{\mathrm{ss},i} = F_{\mathrm{PLM}}^{\mathrm{ss}}(x, i) \in \mathbb{R}^{d_{\mathrm{PLM}}^{\mathrm{ss}}},$$

$$h_{\mathrm{ss},i} = M_y^{\mathrm{ss}} e_{\mathrm{ss},i} \in \mathbb{R}^{d_{\mathrm{ss}}},$$

where $d_{\mathrm{PLM}}^{\mathrm{ss}}$ is the output dimension of $F_{\mathrm{PLM}}^{\mathrm{ss}}$, and $M_y^{\mathrm{ss}} \in \mathbb{R}^{d_{\mathrm{ss}} \times d_{\mathrm{PLM}}^{\mathrm{ss}}}$ is a learnable projection matrix.

Then we set up a vocabulary $\mathcal{V}$ which contains all synonyms, that is, for any text $x$ and any word $w_i$, $\mathcal{S}_i \subseteq \mathcal{V}$. The vocabulary is task-independent and can be used for multiple victim tasks and victim models.

Finally, $h_{\mathrm{ss},i}$ is converted to a $|\mathcal{V}|$-dimensional vector using a feedforward neural network $F_{\mathrm{FFN}}^{\mathrm{ss}}$, and then transformed into the probability of each word in $\mathcal{V}$ being selected by the softmax function:

$$p_{\mathrm{ss},i} = \mathrm{softmax}(F_{\mathrm{FFN}}^{\mathrm{ss}}(h_{\mathrm{ss},i})) = \mathrm{SynonymSelection}(x, y, i) \in \mathbb{R}^{|\mathcal{V}|}. \tag{2}$$

**Training.** Similar to the word ranking network, there is no ground truth for synonym selection, and we evaluate the attack effect of the synonyms to construct training data.

Given a text $x = (w_1, w_2, \ldots, w_n)$, the label $y$ and the substitute position $i$ $(1 \leq i \leq n)$, we substitute $w_i$ with all synonyms in $\mathcal{S}_i$ to get the candidate texts. Similar to the word ranking network, we exclude some candidate texts with low quality. Formally, synonym $s \in \mathcal{S}_i$ can be retained if (1) $\mathrm{sim}(\tilde{x}_{i,s}, x) \geq \theta_{\mathrm{ss}}$, (2) the perplexity of $\tilde{x}_{i,s}$ ranks top $p_{\mathrm{ppl}}^{\mathrm{ss}}\%$ among all candidate texts. Supposing that $\mathcal{S}_i'$ is the retained synonym set, the ground truth for substitution is:

$$s_i^* = \arg\min_{s \in \mathcal{S}_i'} f(\tilde{x}_{i,s})_y.$$

In this way, we construct a training example $(x, y, i, s_i^*)$. Then the synonym selection network is optimized by minimizing the cross entropy of $p_{\mathrm{ss},i}$ in Eq. (2) and $s_i^*$ (for simplicity, $s_i^*$ represents a word or an index in $\mathcal{V}$ according to the context):

$$loss_{\mathrm{ss}} = -\log p_{\mathrm{ss},i,s_i^*}$$

**Inference.** During attack, when substituting a word $w_i$, the synonym selection network predicts the probability of each word in $\mathcal{V}$ being selected, and the words with the top-$K$ highest predicted probability in $\mathcal{S}_i$ are selected for substitution, so as to reduce the number of substitution attempts.

# 4    Experiments

## 4.1    Datasets and Victim Models

We use the following datasets for evaluation:

- **IMDB** [15]. A movie review sentiment classification dataset.
- **Yelp** [24]. A restaurant and hotel review sentiment classification dataset.
- **SNLI** [2]. The Stanford natural language inference benchmark. This task is to determine whether the relationship between a given pair of premise and hypothesis is entailment, neutral or contradiction.
- **QQP**. A paraphrase identification dataset. This task is to determine whether two given questions have the same meaning or not.

In the black box setting, the original training data for the victim model cannot be used. In our experiment, all the data comes from the original test data of each dataset. For evaluation, we randomly select $1,000$ samples that can be correctly predicted by the victim model; For training, we select $20,000$ training samples for IMDB and Yelp, and $30,000$ training samples for SNLI and QQP. The latter two have more training samples because their average text length is shorter.

The victim models are the fine-tuned BERT [4] and BiLSTM [8].

## 4.2    Compared Methods

Previous work usually does not use the same search space, i.e., different synonym sets or different constraints [13,21]. In order to obtain fair comparison, we adopt the same search space for all compared methods, that is, only nouns, verbs, adjectives and adverbs are substituted, and synonym sets are constructed using HowNet [5,23].

In the same search space, the following methods are selected as baselines:

- **TextFooler** (2020) [9]. The words are substituted in the descending order of word importance which is defined as the decrease in the predicted probability of true label when each word is deleted from the text. TextFooler is a strong baseline of greedy search method which well trades off between attack performance and efficiency.
- **LSH** (2021) [16]. The words substitution order is determined by PWWS scoring function, and the number of victim model queries are reduced by attention mechanism and locality sensitive hashing.
- **Reinforce** (2020) [22]. The adversarial examples are generated with a policy trained in a reinforcement learning framework.

All the methods are compared in the same search space. Population based methods [1,23] are not listed because they do not belong to the paradigm of greedy search.

## 4.3   Experiment Settings

For similarity function, we encode the texts using the stsb-mpnet-base-v2 model in SentenceTransformers [18][1] and define the cosine similarity of encoded vectors as the semantic similarity. The threshold is set to 0.9.

The pre-trained language model used in our two networks is BERT-base [4]. The pre-trained model is from Hugging Face Hub [20].[2]

Hyper parameter setting: for the word ranking network, $d_{\mathrm{wr}} = 128$, $\theta_{\mathrm{wr}} = 0.9$, $p_{\mathrm{ppl}}^{\mathrm{wr}} = 80$, $p_{\mathrm{pos}}^{\mathrm{wr}} = 5$, $p_{\mathrm{neg}}^{\mathrm{wr}} = 50$; for the synonym selection network, $d_{\mathrm{ss}} = 128$, $\theta_{\mathrm{ss}} = 0.95$, $p_{\mathrm{ppl}}^{\mathrm{ss}} = 80$, $K = 15$. The two networks are both trained for 5 epochs with learning rate of $10^{-5}$.

## 4.4   Evaluation Metrics

The methods are evaluated with the following metrics:

- **Attack Success Rate**. The percentage of test examples for which an adversarial example can be crafted.
- **Number of Queries**. The average number of queries to the victim model.
- **Semantic Similarity**. The average semantic similarity between the original texts and the adversarial examples.
- **Modification Rate**. The average percentage of words modified.
- **Grammar Correctness**. The average grammar error increase rate of adversarial examples. Following [23], we use LanguageTool[3] to check grammar error.
- **Fluency**. The average perplexity of adversarial examples by GPT-2 [17].

## 4.5   Main Results

Table 1 shows the evaluation results, and we can observe that:

(1) Our method requires fewer victim model queries than the baseline methods and achieves higher attack success rate. Compared with TextFooler, our method substitutes words in a better order with no victim model query in word ranking. For LSH, although it uses attention mechanisms and locally sensitive hash to reduce the computational overhead of PWWS scoring function, the number of model queries required is still proportional to the length of the text. For Reinforce, the attack is efficient, but the trained policy does not have very high attack performance.

(2) In terms of adversarial example quality, our method also achieves better results, which mainly benefits from considering the factor of text quality when constructing the training data of our two attack networks. We show some adversarial examples generated by each method in Table 3, our method makes fewer modifications to the text, and the generated text is more natural.

---

[1] https://www.sbert.net.

[2] https://huggingface.co.

[3] https://languagetool.org.

**Table 1.** The attack results against BERT model. "ASR%" (↑) means the attack success rate, "#VQ" (↓) means the average number of victim model queries. "Sim" (↑) means the average semantic similarity between the original texts and the adversarial examples, "M%" (↓) means the modification rate, "G%" (↓) means the average grammar error increase rate, "PPL" (↓) means the average perplexity. ↑ in the parenthesis means the higher the better, and ↓ means the lower the better.

| Method | IMDB | | | | | | Yelp | | | | | |
|---|---|---|---|---|---|---|---|---|---|---|---|---|
| | ASR% | #VQ | Sim | M% | G% | PPL | ASR% | #VQ | Sim | M% | G% | PPL |
| TextFooler | 92.2 | 255 | 0.946 | 6.7 | 3.9 | 119.9 | 86.8 | 271 | 0.943 | 7.7 | 4.5 | 148.5 |
| LSH | 95.6 | 174 | 0.958 | 3.8 | 3.8 | 91.3 | 90.1 | 198 | 0.953 | 5.9 | 4.5 | 126.3 |
| Reinforce | 91.5 | 62 | 0.951 | 5.1 | 4.0 | 125.3 | 87.8 | 88 | 0.945 | 7.3 | 4.6 | 139.5 |
| Ours | **96.7** | **47** | **0.960** | **3.5** | **3.7** | **84.1** | **91.5** | **70** | **0.958** | **5.6** | **4.4** | **123.8** |
| Method | SNLI | | | | | | QQP | | | | | |
| | ASR% | #VQ | Sim | M% | G% | PPL | ASR% | #VQ | Sim | M% | G% | PPL |
| TextFooler | 81.3 | 44 | 0.934 | 7.9 | 0.7 | 141.1 | 63.7 | 71 | 0.939 | 9.0 | 0.8 | **119.6** |
| LSH | 84.9 | 37 | 0.941 | 6.9 | 0.5 | 129.1 | 62.8 | 58 | 0.940 | 9.2 | 0.6 | 123.3 |
| Reinforce | 78.9 | 32 | 0.936 | 8.3 | 0.6 | 146.4 | **63.9** | 47 | 0.935 | 10.0 | 0.6 | 131.6 |
| Ours | **86.8** | **22** | **0.944** | **6.6** | **0.4** | **123.4** | 63.4 | **41** | **0.943** | **8.5** | **0.5** | 120.9 |

**Table 2.** Attack results against BiLSTM.

| Method | IMDB | | | | | | Yelp | | | | | |
|---|---|---|---|---|---|---|---|---|---|---|---|---|
| | ASR% | #VQ | Sim | M% | G% | PPL | ASR% | #VQ | Sim | M% | G% | PPL |
| TextFooler | 99.5 | 160 | 0.953 | 4.3 | 4.0 | 87.6 | 97.0 | 151 | 0.951 | 5.8 | **4.6** | 117.8 |
| LSH | **99.6** | 87 | 0.959 | 3.7 | 4.0 | 84.2 | 97.8 | 84 | 0.962 | 4.8 | 4.8 | 112.9 |
| Reinforce | 99.5 | 58 | 0.952 | 5.0 | 4.0 | 86.4 | 97.5 | 52 | 0.949 | 5.5 | 4.8 | 121.4 |
| Ours | **99.6** | **40** | **0.963** | **3.5** | **3.9** | **82.3** | **98.0** | **45** | **0.965** | **4.6** | 4.7 | **106.3** |

We also evaluate the attack effect against BiLSTM, and the results on IMDB and Yelp are shown in Table 2. Our method can still achieve very high attack performance among all the methods.

## 4.6 Ablation Study

In this part, we analyze the attack effect of the two proposed attack networks. We compare three settings: (1) **SS**: only the synonym selection network is used and words are substituted in sequential order. (2) **WR**: only the word ranking network is used and all synonyms are tried for substitution. (3) **FULL**: both network are used. In addition, we provide the attack results of processing words in sequential order (**SEQ**) for comparison with SS. The attack results on IMDB and Yelp datasets are shown in Table 4. We can observe that:

(1) Both SS and SEQ process words in sequential order, and the difference is that SS select synonyms guided by the synonym selection network. Compared

**Table 3.** Adversarial examples generated by each method on IMDB dataset.

| | |
|---|---|
| Original | A documentary about a nomadic tribe in Tibet going out to a dry lake to get salt does not sound very appealing. But this is not a popcorn movie but a visual cultural feast whereby you partake of a rapidly vanishing morsel of humanity |
| TextFooler | A documentary about a nomadic tribe in Tibet going out to a dry lake to get salt does either sound very appealing. But this is not a popcorn movie but a visual cultural banquet whereby you partake of a rapidly vanishing morsel of humanity. |
| LSH | A documentary about a nomadic clan in Tibet going outwards to a dry lake to get salt does not screech very appealing. But this is not a popcorn movie but a visual cultural feast whereby you partake of a rapidly vanishing morsel of performance. |
| Reinforce | A documentary about a nomadic clan in Tibet going out to a unsavoury lake to culminate salt does not screech very appealing. But this is not a popcorn movie but a visual cultural banquet whereby you partake of a rapidly vanishing morsel of humanity. |
| Ours | A documentary about a nomadic tribe in Tibet going out to a dry lake to get salt does not sound very appealing. But this assumes not a popcorn flick but a visual cultural feast whereby you partake of a rapidly vanishing morsel of humanity |

with SEQ, SS can achieve similar attack success rate with much fewer victim model queries. In addition, the adversarial example quality of SS is slightly better, which may be because the synonym selection network selects synonyms that fit in the context. Although SEQ has more choices in word substitution and the attack success rate is slightly higher, some synonyms with poor quality are introduced in this process, resulting in worse adversarial example quality.

(2) FULL and WR have similar attack success rate, and WR is slightly higher, indicating that the word substitution order significantly affects the attack performance. The adversarial example quality of FULL is slightly better than that of WR, which may also benefit from the synonym selection network.

### 4.7    Transferability

In this part, we explore the transferability of our model. We train our model with the datasets and victim models of the two sentiment analysis tasks, IMDB and Yelp, respectively, and then attack each other. The attack results are shown in Table 5. When transferred to other victim models, the attack effect will decline to a certain extent, which is in line with our expectations, because the two networks know nothing about the victim model. However, on the whole, the attack effect is still higher than most baseline methods, which indicates that when the accessibility of the victim model is very limited, we can train our attack model on similar tasks and still obtain good attack effect.

**Table 4.** Ablation study for the two proposed attack networks.

| Method | IMDB | | | | | | Yelp | | | | | |
|--------|------|-----|------|-----|-----|-------|------|-----|------|-----|-----|-------|
| | ASR% | #VQ | Sim | M% | G% | PPL | ASR% | #VQ | Sim | M% | G% | PPL |
| SEQ | 90.2 | 292 | 0.931 | 8.8 | 4.0 | 139.8 | 83.9 | 284 | 0.927 | 10.2 | 4.6 | 168.7 |
| SS | 88.1 | 110 | 0.931 | 8.6 | 4.0 | 133.7 | 84.0 | 113 | 0.927 | 10.3 | 4.6 | 168.0 |
| WR | **96.9** | 194 | **0.960** | **3.4** | **3.7** | 84.4 | **91.7** | 283 | **0.958** | **5.6** | **4.4** | 124.7 |
| FULL | 96.7 | **47** | **0.960** | 3.5 | **3.7** | 84.1 | 91.5 | **70** | **0.958** | **5.6** | **4.4** | 123.8 |

**Table 5.** The attack results of our model when transferred to new datasets. "Victim" means the attacked dataset. "Train" means the dataset used to construct training data.

| Victim | Train | ASR% | #VQ | Sim | M% | G% | PPL |
|--------|-------|------|-----|------|-----|-----|-------|
| IMDB | IMDB | 96.7 | 47 | 0.960 | 3.5 | 3.7 | 84.1 |
| | Yelp | 95.5 | 72 | 0.954 | 5.3 | 3.9 | 101.2 |
| Yelp | Yelp | 91.5 | 70 | 0.958 | 5.6 | 4.4 | 123.8 |
| | IMDB | 87.3 | 93 | 0.948 | 7.1 | 4.4 | 131.2 |

# 5 Conclusion

In this work, we propose a learnable textual adversarial attack method, which uses neural networks to guide the greedy search for word substitution based attack. We use a word ranking network to predict the importance of each word and rank the words without accessing the victim model, and use the other synonym selection network to select high-quality synonyms for each substitute position. Our method not only achieves higher attack success rate and adversarial example quality compared with the baseline methods, but also reduces large computation overhead, and further analysis shows the high transferability of our method.

**Acknowledgement.** This work is supported by the National Key R&D Program (2018AAA0100700) of the Ministry of Science and Technology of China, and Shanghai Municipal Science and Technology Major Project (2021SHZDZX0102).

# References

1. Alzantot, M., Sharma, Y., Elgohary, A., Ho, B.J., Srivastava, M., Chang, K.W.: Generating natural language adversarial examples. In: Proceedings of EMNLP (2018)
2. Bowman, S.R., Angeli, G., Potts, C., Manning, C.D.: A large annotated corpus for learning natural language inference. In: Proceedings of EMNLP (2015)
3. Chen, Y., Su, J., Wei, W.: Multi-granularity textual adversarial attack with behavior cloning (2021)

4. Devlin, J., Chang, M.W., Lee, K., Toutanova, K.: BERT: pre-training of deep bidirectional transformers for language understanding. In: Proceedings of NAACL (2019)
5. Dong, Z., Dong, Q.: HowNet and the Computation of Meaning. World Scientific, Singapore (2006)
6. Garg, S., Ramakrishnan, G.: BAE: BERT-based adversarial examples for text classification. In: Proceedings of EMNLP (2020)
7. Goodfellow, I.J., Shlens, J., Szegedy, C.: Explaining and harnessing adversarial examples. In: Proceedings of ICLR (2015)
8. Hochreiter, S., Schmidhuber, J.: Long short-term memory. Neural Comput. **9**(8), 1735–1780 (1997)
9. Jin, D., Jin, Z., Zhou, J.T., Szolovits, P.: Is BERT really robust? A strong baseline for natural language attack on text classification and entailment. In: Proceedings of AAAI (2020)
10. Kurakin, A., Goodfellow, I., Bengio, S.: Adversarial examples in the physical world. ICLR Workshop (2017)
11. Li, D., et al.: Contextualized perturbation for textual adversarial attack. In: Proc. of NAACL (2021)
12. Li, L., Ma, R., Guo, Q., Xue, X., Qiu, X.: BERT-ATTACK: adversarial attack against BERT using BERT. In: Proceedings of EMNLP (2020)
13. Li, Z., et al.: Searching for an effective defender: benchmarking defense against adversarial word substitution (2021)
14. Liu, Y., et al.: Roberta: a robustly optimized BERT pretraining approach (2019)
15. Maas, A.L., Daly, R.E., Pham, P.T., Huang, D., Ng, A.Y., Potts, C.: Learning word vectors for sentiment analysis. In: Proceedings of ACL (2011)
16. Maheshwary, R., Maheshwary, S., Pudi, V.: A strong baseline for query efficient attacks in a black box setting (2021)
17. Radford, A., Wu, J., Child, R., Luan, D., Amodei, D., Sutskever, I.: Language models are unsupervised multitask learners (2019)
18. Reimers, N., Gurevych, I.: Sentence-BERT: sentence embeddings using Siamese BERT-networks. In: Proceedings of EMNLP (2019)
19. Ren, S., Deng, Y., He, K., Che, W.: Generating natural language adversarial examples through probability weighted word saliency. In: Proceedings of ACL (2019)
20. Wolf, T., et al.: Transformers: state-of-the-art natural language processing. In: Proceedings of EMNLP (2020)
21. Yoo, J.Y., Morris, J., Lifland, E., Qi, Y.: Searching for a search method: benchmarking search algorithms for generating NLP adversarial examples. In: Proceedings of the Third BlackboxNLP Workshop on Analyzing and Interpreting Neural Networks for NLP (2020)
22. Zang, Y., Hou, B., Qi, F., Liu, Z., Meng, X., Sun, M.: Learning to attack: towards textual adversarial attacking in real-world situations (2020)
23. Zang, Y., et al.: Word-level textual adversarial attacking as combinatorial optimization. In: Proceedings of ACL (2020)
24. Zhang, X., Zhao, J.J., LeCun, Y.: Character-level convolutional networks for text classification. In: Proceedings of NeurIPS (2015)

# Lymphoma Ultrasound Image Segmentation with Self-Attention Mechanism and Stable Learning

Yingkang Han[1], Dehua Chen[1(✉)], Yishu Luo[1], and Yijie Dong[2]

[1] School of Computer Science and Technology, Donghua University, Shanghai, China
chendehua@dhu.edu.cn
[2] Ruijin Hospital, Shanghai Jiaotong University School of Medicine, Shanghai, China

**Abstract.** Segmentation of lymphoma from ultrasound image has become an important task in the diagnosis of lymphoma. There are two problems in the segmentation of lymphoma ultrasound images: (i) the fuzziness of structural boundaries in the image domain and (ii) the generalization of images scanned by different ultrasonic instruments. To solve these two problems, we propose an segmentation framework based on self-attention mechanism and stable learning, in which self-attention mechanism and stable learning are embedded in the baseline network. Self-Attention mechanism (TSA) learns non-local interaction of encoder coding features to alleviate the problem of information decay caused by multiple sampling. The Stable learning (SA) module uses random Fourier features (RFF) and sample weights to eliminate the dependence between features and solve the problem of false correlation features from images scanned by different instruments. In addition, counterfactual interpretation is used to generate instance level interpretation of our complex model. Experiments show that this method can effectively improve the accuracy and reliability of segmentation.

**Keywords:** Semantic segmentation · Lymphoma ultrasound · Transformer self attention · Stable learning · Counterfactual explanation

## 1 Introduction

Lymphoma is a fatal cancer formed by abnormal mutations of immune system cells, accounting for about 50% of hematologic malignancies [25,29]. In terms of clinical diagnosis and prognosis of lymphoma, ultrasound-guided coarse needle puncture biopsy (US-CNB) is a minimally invasive and convenient way to obtain more tissues. Previous studies have shown that US-CNB has diagnostic significance for lymphoma, especially for the diagnosis of deep lymph nodes [30]. Correct diagnosis and early treatment can effectively improve the cure rate of lymphoma [21]. How to correctly detect and demarcate boundaries is the basis of diagnosis and treatment.

© The Author(s), under exclusive license to Springer Nature Switzerland AG 2022
E. Pimenidis et al. (Eds.): ICANN 2022, LNCS 13529, pp. 207–218, 2022.
https://doi.org/10.1007/978-3-031-15919-0_18

Ultrasound imaging has been widely used in medicine because of its unique nondestructive, real-time and inexpensive properties. However, due to the inherent acoustic characteristics of ultrasonic imaging, the resulting image has high noise, low contrast and poor imaging quality. Image segmentation is the key of ultrasonic image analysis. Generally, such segmentation is performed manually by clinicians, which reduces the objectivity of diagnosis and costs a lot of labor [28,31]. Even experts have slightly different descriptions based on their experience and skills [13]. Therefore, for many medical image applications, correct segmentation of the lesion region by the model is the key to successful application [17,19]. Automatic segmentation models that can accurately obtain region of interest (ROI) from images can provide a basis for clinicians to diagnose or conduct pathological studies.

In the field of deep learning, many semantic segmentation methods based on convolutional neural networks (CNNs) have been proposed. Jonathan Long et al. [15] define a new architecture (FCN) that combines semantic information from deep and coarse layers with superficial and thin layers to produce accurate and detailed segmentation. To solve the problem of a small number of medical data sets, Olaf Ronneberger et al. [18] proposed the application of U-NET to the segmentation of medical images, which effectively improved the accuracy of training detection using a small number of data sets. These semantic segmentation methods ignore some difficulties in medical image segmentation, such as the lack of significant structural boundaries caused by poor image quality, the problem of out-distribution generalization caused by images from different instruments, and the lack of interpretation of segmentation results reduces the reliability of model prediction results.

This paper focuses on the segmentation of lymphoma ultrasound images. This is a very challenging task because lymphoma ultrasound images may not have significant structural boundaries. Lymphoma ultrasound images from different instruments are biased, and changes in data distribution may lead to poor decision making. In addition, deep neural network is a black box model, which usually only provides one result. The lack of explanation for the results of the model reduces the trust of doctors in the model.

To solve the above problems, we propose an ultrasound image segmentation model for lymphoma based on stable learning and attention mechanisms. The model uses Transformer Self Attention mechanism to achieve non-local interaction of semantic features of the encoder to capture richer scene representation to alleviate information degradation and achieve more accurate segmentation. In the training stage, a specific weight is learned for each training sample through stable learning to distinguish environmental features from essential features, and a relatively accurate segmentation result is given according to the essential features. In addition, the counterfactual interpretation method is used to explain our model, which is related to the explainability that can be understood by human beings and can explain complex model decisions [16,24] to improve the credibility of the model.

Our contributions are summarized as follows:

- Non-local interaction between semantic features of the encoder is realized through Transformer Self Attention to obtain richer scene representation to alleviate the problem of information decay.
- Generalization is achieved by distinguishing intrinsic features from environmental features through stable learning.
- Counterfactual interpretation method is used to obtain the interpretability of the model and make the results of the model more credible.

## 2  Related Works

### 2.1  Lymphoma Image Segmentation

Recently, deep neural networks have made some progress in the field of lymphoma image segmentation. Haoming L et al. [14] combined supervised and unsupervised learning and proposed an end-to-end segmentation network(DenseX) for the detection and segmentation of lymphoma. Yuan C et al. [27] designed hybrid learning CNN, which connected the feature maps of 3D positron emission tomography (PET) and computed tomography (CT) encoder branches with the hybrid learning features obtained by 3D convolution fusion operation for lesion segmentation of diffuse large B cell (DLBCL) multimodal images. Huang L et al. [12] proposed an automatic evidence segmentation method based on Dempster-Shafer theory and deep learning to segment lymphoma from PET and CT images. Although these methods have achieved certain results in the segmentation of lymphoma images, they are all targeted at PET and CT images and do not take into account the problems such as blurred ultrasound image boundaries.

### 2.2  Ultrasound Image Segmentation

Due to the problem of ultrasonic image data quality, the task of ultrasonic image segmentation is very complicated. But in recent years, the progress of ultrasonic imaging equipment has promoted the application of image segmentation in ultrasonic images. Lee HJ et al. [9] proposed a new image segmentation method to solve the fuzziness of structural boundaries in medical image domain and the uncertainty of segmentation in the absence of specialized domain knowledge, which performed well in transvaginal ultrasound (TVUS). Mishra D et al. [5] proposed a full convolutional neural network with depth of attention monitoring, which uses FCNN/CNN to infer the high-level background by using low-level image features for automatic and accurate segmentation of ultrasonic images. Amiri M et al. [2] studied the influence of fine-tuning of different layers on ultrasonic image segmentation in pre-trained U-shaped network, and proposed that fine-tuning of shallow layer rather than deep layer plays a better role in ultrasonic image segmentation. However, these methods do not take into account the influence of ultrasonic image background of different instruments on image segmentation results.

## 2.3    Model Interpretability

In recent years, more and more attention has been paid to interpretability. Gu R et al. [8] proposed a comprehensive CNN(CA-NET) based on attention mechanism to achieve more accurate and interpretable medical image segmentation, and at the same time understand the most important spatial position, channel and scale. A Ahmed et al. [1] proposed A model based on generative adversarial network for segmentation of medical images. This model uses hierarchical correlation propagation method to provide interpretation for prediction and specify which input image pixels are related to prediction. Draelos R L et al. [6] proposed a new class-specific interpretation method (HiResCAM), which guarantees to highlight only the locations where the model is used for each prediction, even if these locations are outside the object of interest.But these methods require a retraining of the model and only rank features in importance.

## 3    Lymphoma Ultrasound Image Segmentation Model

Our model trains two identical networks that perform different functions depending on the input. The first network, Net1, inputs the raw image and is used to perform a rough localization to obtain the region of interest of the focal area. The input of the second network, Net2, is a cropped region of interest image, which is used to obtain more accurate boundaries.

Figure 1 shows an overview of the proposed segmentation model framework based on self-attentional mechanisms and stable learning. The feature extraction network extracts features from the original image. Self-attention mechanism is used for non-local interaction of features extracted from encoder to alleviate the problem of information decay caused by multiple sampling. The stable learning module eliminates the dependency between features by means of random Fourier feature (RFF) and sample weighting, so that the model can use a set of independent features to predict, which is used to solve the generalization problem of images scanned by different instruments. The explainable module explains the prediction results of the model by counterfactual explanation method. The following is a detailed description of the proposed ultrasound image segmentation framework for lymphoma.

### 3.1    Feature Extraction Network

The feature extraction network adopts Deeplabv3 + [3] as the network architecture. Deeplabv3 + by spatial pyramid pooling further multi-scale information extraction module, the encoder decoder structure optimization of the border, the encoder samples extracted from low-level features, used to extract spatial information and global information, decoder using sampling returning space information, fusion of encoder to extract feature to capture more clear object boundary. Backbone of Deeplabv3+ is EfficientNetb6 [22].

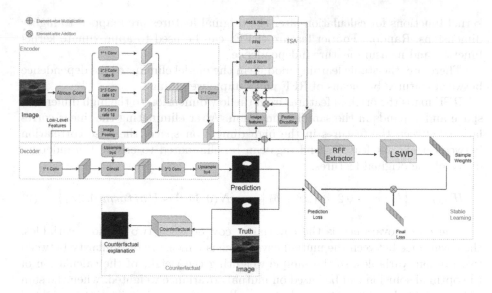

**Fig. 1.** Segmentation framework consists of Transformer Self Attention (TSA), Stable Learning (SA), interpretable and encoder decoder modules. RFF refers to random Fourier features and LSWD refers to weighted de-correlation of learning samples.

## 3.2    Self-Attention Mechanism

TSA mechanism can capture the spatial dependencies of any two positions in the feature graph and obtain long-distance context-dependent information. The encoder decoder structure will have the problem of information decay due to multiple sampling. TSA is added as an attention mechanism to achieve non-local interaction between features extracted by the encoder and obtain richer scene representation. TSA module generates query(Q), key(K) and value(V) vectors through different linear changes of the input feature graph and generated position embedding vectors for attention calculation.

$$TSA(Q, K, V) = softmax(\frac{QK^T}{\sqrt{d_k}})V \tag{1}$$

$QK^T$ in the formula represents the similarity degree between Q and K elements, and softMax normalizes to get context attention graph A, which is multiplied by A and V to get the attention-weighted value.

## 3.3    Stable Learning

The correlation between features is removed so that the model can use a set of independent features to predict and improve the accuracy of the model. Kernel method is used to map features to higher dimensional space, and the nonlinear separable problems in lower dimensional space are transformed into linear separable problems in higher dimensional space. However, it is a problem to define kernel functions for calculation after the original features are mapped to higher dimensions. Random Fourier feature (RFF) can be used to approximate kernel function and measure feature independence.

Therefore, the stable learning module in the model eliminates the dependence between features by means of RFF and sample weighting.

RFF maps the original features from the low dimension to the high dimension space and expands in the sample dimension. After eliminating the linear correlation between the features in the high dimension space, the false correlation between irrelevant features and tags can be eliminated to ensure the independence of the original features.

$$H_{RFF} = \left\{ h : x \rightarrow \sqrt{2}\cos(\omega x + \emptyset) \mid \omega \sim N(0,1), \emptyset \sim Uniform(0,2\pi) \right\} \quad (2)$$

The cross-covariance is the covariance cov between two random variables, the covariance between the mutual covariance is a measure of similarity between two random variables, so the sample weighting the weight of the calculation of the optimal solution can be based on mutual covariance weighted, when the sum of the weighted cross-covariance between all samples is minimized, the weighted weight is the optimal solution of the weight. The weight matrix is calculated as follows:

$$w^* = arg\min \sum_{\substack{1 \leq i < j \leq n}}^{w \in \triangle n} cov(w_i X_i, w_j X_j) \quad (3)$$

In the formula, $\triangle n = \{\sum_{i=1}^n w_i = n\}$, n is the number of input batches, $X_i$ and $X_j$ are characteristic graphs of different samples in the sample space.

In deep learning, it requires huge overhead to use all samples to learn sample weights and features globally, so sample weights need to be stored and reloaded, and a learnable parameter $\alpha_i$ is used to update global weights and features. $X_{Gi}$ is the global sample feature, $X_L$ is the current sample feature, $W_{Gi}$ is the global sample weight, $W_L$ is the current sample weight.

$$X'_{Gi} = \alpha_i X_{Gi} + (1 - \alpha_i) X_L \quad (4)$$

$$W'_{Gi} = \alpha_i W_{Gi} + (1 - \alpha_i) W_L \quad (5)$$

The weight vector $w^*$ of the sample in a batch is obtained by the stable learning module. The loss of the sample was calculated by SoftDiceLoss, and the modified loss was obtained by multiplying $w^*$ and the loss of the sample for model training.

$$loss = SoftDiceLoss(SR, GT).view(1, -1).mm(w^*).view(1) \quad (6)$$

$$SoftDiceLoss = \frac{2\,|SR \cap GT|}{|SR| + |GT|} \quad (7)$$

SR is the predicted value and GT is the true value.

### 3.4    Counterfactual Explanation

Martens and Provost [16] introduced a model-independent search algorithm (SEDC) to find counterfactual explanations of document classifications. An interpretation can be thought of as a set of irreducible features that, the classification of documents will change if they do not exist. In this case, irreducibility means that removing any subset of the interpretation does not change the classification. Vermeire et al. [23] proposed an adapted version based on the above method to generate visual counterfactual interpretation for image classification.

We use a two-dimensional image segmentation algorithm called fast shift image segmentation, which is based on the approximate value of kernel average movement. Split result fragments are used for counterfactual searches.

The goal of applying counterfactual interpretation to semantic segmentation is to find a set of irreducible fragments that will lead to the maximum reduction in IoU score after removal.

$$S \subseteq I(segments\ in\ image) \tag{8}$$

$$T(I \setminus S) < T(I)(IoU\ reduce) \tag{9}$$

I represents the image, S represents the segmented segment, and T represents the model. The fragments with the greatest impact are determined by counterfactual interpretation at the instance level.

## 4    Experiments

### 4.1    Data Description and Preprocessing

The experimental data set included the results of 162 patients with actual lymphoma ultrasound scans from Ruijin Hospital. Each case contained a different number of images, and a total of 296 images were used in the experiment. The ultrasound images were obtained from four different acquisition devices, with a resolution of $1260 \times 910$ from Mindray, $1256 \times 900$ from Sonoscape, and $1024 \times 768$ from Philips. The resolution of ultrasonic images obtained from Esaote Mylab is $800 \times 608$. These images need to be preprocessed before they can be used for model training. The pixel spacing of these images is adjusted to adjust the image resolution to $256 \times 256$. According to the annotation results, the region of interest of the image is cut, and the pixel spacing of the trimmed image is adjusted to adjust the image resolution to $512 \times 512$.

### 4.2    Experimental Settings

Adam was used as the optimizer for the model, and the learning rate was 0.0001. The input size of Net1 is $256 \times 256$, and the batchsize is 10. The input size of Net2 is $512 \times 512$, and the batchsize is 2. Epoch for 305. To quantitatively evaluate our model, we adopted two commonly used segmentation indicators, including Dice coefficient and IoU score. Dice coefficient is a set similarity measure commonly used to calculate the similarity of two samples. IoU score is a standard measure of object class segmentation.

### 4.3   Quantitative Evaluation

To demonstrate the advantages of our lymphoma ultrasound image segmentation framework, we compared our method with other methods. Dice coefficient and IoU score were used as segmentation evaluation indicators.

Table 1 compares the segmentation results of our method with other six methods (Segformer [26], SETR [32], SPNet [10], DANet [7], ISANet [11], Segmenter [20]) on lymphoma ultrasound images. As shown in Table 1, our method reached 92.18% and 86.91% on DICE and IoU respectively, which were 0.37% and 2.06% higher than the best results of the other six methods. Overall, our approach achieved better performance than the other approaches.

In addition to SPNet, the above six methods are implemented by mmsegmentation [4] framework, and their weight files are used for pre-training models.

**Table 1.** Dice and IoU coefficients were compared between our method and six different methods on a lymphoma dataset.

| Method | Dice | IoU |
|---|---|---|
| Segformer | 91.29 | 83.98 |
| SETR | 91.81 | 84.85 |
| SPNet | 80.15 | 66.88 |
| DANet | 91.09 | 83.64 |
| ISANet | 90.17 | 82.11 |
| Segmenterr | 88.01 | 78.58 |
| Net1+Net2+TSA+Stable | 92.18 | 86.91 |

### 4.4   Ablation Studies

In order to prove that the proposed TSA and Stable modules have sufficient effect on improving the segmentation accuracy, we integrate TSA and Stable modules into the basic network respectively.

Figure 2 shows the results of the ablation study in the lymphoma ultrasound dataset. When TSA and Stable are applied to the segmentation network Net1, IoU increases by 2.28% and 2.16% respectively. Backbone(Net1+Net2) IOU increases by 1.44% and 1.13% respectively. Backbone achieved the best IOU score of 86.91% when applying TSA and Stable together.

To further verify the effect of TSA, we also added TSA to different feature layers of the encoder. The experiment was performed on the lymphoma ultrasound dataset with the same Settings except for the location of TSA. TSA(3) indicates that the TSA module is behind the third layer of the encoder

As shown in Fig. 3, when we placed TSA in different layers of the encoder, the performance was different. As the number of layers increases, the encoder extracts more advanced features, and the problem of information degradation caused by multiple sampling also increases. Therefore, the role of TSA becomes more obvious.

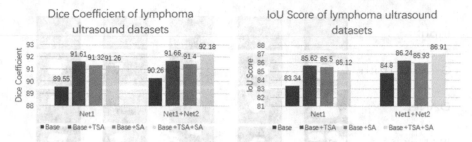

**Fig. 2.** Dice Coefficient and IoU score of ablation experiments on lymphoma dataset.

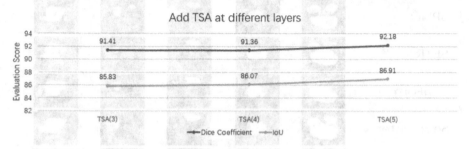

**Fig. 3.** Segmentation performance varies with TSA at different layers of the encoder.

### 4.5   Visualization

In order to prove that TSA and Stable proposed by us optimize the segmentation results in the segmentation process, we visualize the segmentation results.

Figure 4 visually compares the segmentation results of our proposed method with some other methods. The first line is the input image, the second line is the Groud Truth image, and the third to ninth lines are the segmentation results of the other six methods used for comparison and our method. It can be seen that our method can obtain richer scene representation, more accurate target boundary, and effectively improve the segmentation accuracy.

Figure 5 visually show one of our interpretations of image generation, where deleting fragments corresponds to replacing them with the average pixel value of the image. Using fast moving algorithm to create segmented segments.

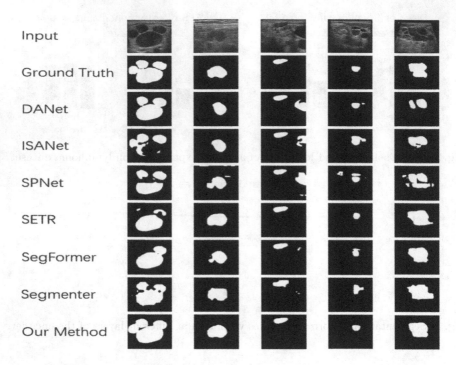

**Fig. 4.** The results of our method were compared with those of other methods for the segmentation of lymphoma ultrasound images

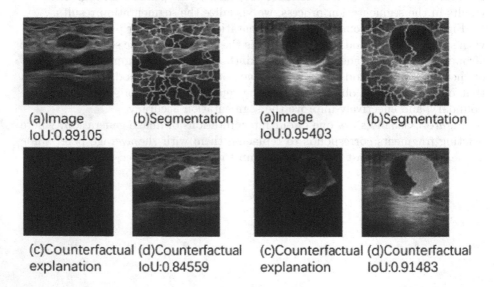

**Fig. 5.** Counterfactual interpretation of lymphoma ultrasound images. (a) is the input image, (b) is the over-segmented segment of, (c) is the counterfactual interpretation result, and (d) is the disturbed image that IoU reduces the most

# 5   Conclusion

In this work, we propose an automatic segmentation model based on self-attention mechanism and stable learning. Through using self-attention mechanism and stable learning module, the structure boundary of segmentation target is optimized, the dependence between features is eliminated, and the reliability of the model is improved. In addition, the reliability of the model is improved by using counterfactual explanation method to explain the model at the instance level. Experimental results show that the performance of our model is superior.

**Acknowledgement.** This work was supported by the National Key R&D Program of China (No. 2019YFE0190500).

# References

1. Ahmed, A., Ali, L.: Explainable medical image segmentation via generative adversarial networks and layer-wise relevance propagation. arXiv e-prints (2021)
2. Amiri, M., Brooks, R., Rivaz, H.: Fine-tuning U-Net for ultrasound image segmentation: different layers, different outcomes. IEEE Trans. Ultrason. Ferroelectr. Freq. Control **67**(12), 2510–2518 (2020)
3. Chen, L.-C., Zhu, Y., Papandreou, G., Schroff, F., Adam, H.: Encoder-decoder with atrous separable convolution for semantic image segmentation. In: Ferrari, V., Hebert, M., Sminchisescu, C., Weiss, Y. (eds.) ECCV 2018. LNCS, vol. 11211, pp. 833–851. Springer, Cham (2018). https://doi.org/10.1007/978-3-030-01234-2_49
4. Contributors, M.: MMSegmentation: openmmlab semantic segmentation toolbox and benchmark (2020). https://github.com/open-mmlab/mmsegmentation
5. Mishra, D., Chaudhury, S., Sarkar, M., Soin, A.S.: Ultrasound image segmentation: a deeply supervised network with attention to boundaries. IEEE Trans. Biomed. Eng. **66**(6), 1637–1648 (2018)
6. Draelos, R.L., Carin, L.: HiResCAM: faithful location representation in visual attention for explainable 3d medical image classification (2020)
7. Fu, J., et al.: Dual attention network for scene segmentation (2020)
8. Gu, R., et al.: CA-Net: comprehensive attention convolutional neural networks for explainable medical image segmentation (2020)
9. Hong, J.L., Kim, J.U., Lee, S., Kim, H.G., Yong, M.R.: Structure boundary preserving segmentation for medical image with ambiguous boundary (2020)
10. Hou, Q., Zhang, L., Cheng, M.M., Feng, J.: Strip pooling: rethinking spatial pooling for scene parsing. IEEE (2020)
11. Huang, L., Yuan, Y., Guo, J., Zhang, C., Chen, X., Wang, J.: Interlaced sparse self-attention for semantic segmentation. IEEE (2019)
12. Huang, L., Ruan, S., Decazes, P., Denoeux, T.: Lymphoma segmentation from 3D PET-CT images using a deep evidential network. arXiv e-prints arXiv:2201.13078 (2022)
13. Park, H., Lee, H.J., Kim, H.G., Ro, Y.M.: Endometrium segmentation on transvaginal ultrasound image using key-point discriminator. Med. Phys. **46**(9), 3974–3984 (2019)
14. Li, H., et al.: DenseX-net: an end-to-end model for lymphoma segmentation in whole-body PET/CT images. IEEE Access **8**, 8004–8018 (2020). https://doi.org/10.1109/ACCESS.2019.2963254

15. Long, J., Shelhamer, E., Darrell, T.: Fully convolutional networks for semantic segmentation. IEEE Trans. Pattern Anal. Mach. Intell. **39**(4), 640–651 (2015)
16. Martens, D., Provost, F.: Explaining documents' classifications. Social Science Electronic Publishing
17. Nie, D., Wang, L., Xiang, L., Zhou, S., Shen, D.: Difficulty-aware attention network with confidence learning for medical image segmentation. In: Proceedings of the AAAI Conference on Artificial Intelligence, vol. 33, pp. 1085–1092 (2019)
18. Ronneberger, O., Fischer, P., Brox, T.: U-Net: convolutional networks for biomedical image segmentation. In: Navab, N., Hornegger, J., Wells, W.M., Frangi, A.F. (eds.) MICCAI 2015. LNCS, vol. 9351, pp. 234–241. Springer, Cham (2015). https://doi.org/10.1007/978-3-319-24574-4_28
19. Sahiner, B., et al.: Deep learning in medical imaging and radiation therapy. Med. Phys. **46**(1), e1–e36 (2019)
20. Strudel, R., Garcia, R., Laptev, I., Schmid, C.: Segmenter: transformer for semantic segmentation (2021)
21. Swerdlow, S.H., Cook, J.R.: As the world turns, evolving lymphoma classifications - past, present and future. Hum. Pathol. **95**, 55–77 (2019)
22. Tan, M., Le, Q.V.: Efficientnet: rethinking model scaling for convolutional neural networks (2019)
23. Vermeire, T., Martens, D.: Explainable image classification with evidence counterfactual (2020)
24. Wachter, S., Mittelstadt, B., Russell, C.: Counterfactual explanations without opening the black box: automated decisions and the GDPR. Social Science Electronic Publishing (2017)
25. Wang, Q., Wang, L., Wang, P.: Analysis of survival and prognostic factors in patients with malignant lymphoma after autologous hematopoietic stem cell transplantation. Pract. J. Cancer **35**(5), 4 (2020)
26. Xie, E., Wang, W., Yu, Z., Anandkumar, A., Alvarez, J.M., Luo, P.: Segformer: simple and efficient design for semantic segmentation with transformers (2021)
27. Yuan, C., et al.: Diffuse large b-cell lymphoma segmentation in PET-CT images via hybrid learning for feature fusion. Med. Phys. **48**, 3665–3678 (2021). https://doi.org/10.1002/mp.14847
28. Zang, X., Bascom, R., Gilbert, C., Toth, J., Higgins, W.: Methods for 2-d and 3-d endobronchial ultrasound image segmentation. IEEE Trans. Biomed. Eng. **63**(7), 1426–1439 (2016)
29. Zeng, Y., Liu, Y.: Prognosis of patients with malignant lymphoma treated by autologous hematopoietic stem cell transplantation. Lab. Med. Clin. **17**(9), 4 (2020)
30. Zhao, H., Liu, D., Zhao, M., Li, Y.: Clinical review of 39 cases of lymphoma diagnosed by percutaneous ultrasound-guided peritoneal mass/lymph node biopsy. Chin. J. Emerg. Med. **28**(6), 3 (2019)
31. Zhao, Y., Rada, L., Chen, K., Harding, S.P., Zheng, Y.: Automated vessel segmentation using infinite perimeter active contour model with hybrid region information with application to retinal images. IEEE Trans. Med. Imaging **34**(9), 1797–1807 (2015)
32. Zheng, S., Lu, J., Zhao, H., Zhu, X., Zhang, L.: Rethinking semantic segmentation from a sequence-to-sequence perspective with transformers (2020)

# MetaAudio: A Few-Shot Audio Classification Benchmark

Calum Heggan[1]([✉]) [ID], Sam Budgett[2] [ID], Timothy Hospedales[1] [ID],
and Mehrdad Yaghoobi[1] [ID]

[1] University of Edinburgh, Edinburgh, Scotland
s1529508@sms.ed.ac.uk
[2] Thales UK, Edinburgh, Scotland

**Abstract.** Currently available benchmarks for few-shot learning
(machine learning with few training examples) are limited in the domains
they cover, primarily focusing on image classification. This work aims to
alleviate this reliance on image-based benchmarks by offering the first
comprehensive, public and fully reproducible audio based alternative,
covering a variety of sound domains and experimental settings. We compare the few-shot classification performance of a variety of techniques on
seven audio datasets (spanning environmental sounds to human-speech).
Extending this, we carry out in-depth analyses of joint training (where
all datasets are used during training) and cross-dataset adaptation protocols, establishing the possibility of a generalised audio few-shot classification algorithm. Our experimentation shows gradient-based meta-
learning methods such as MAML and Meta-Curvature consistently outperform both metric and baseline methods. We also demonstrate that the
joint training routine helps overall generalisation for the environmental
sound databases included, as well as being a somewhat-effective method
of tackling the cross-dataset/domain setting.

## 1 Introduction

To date, the majority of the breakthroughs seen in machine learning have been
in domains or settings where there was an abundance of labelled data, either real
or simulated, for example in [22]. In contrast, the human capability to recognise
and discriminate between classes with few examples, e.g., in visual or acoustic
settings, remains unmatched. The development of techniques that can perform
such Few-shot Learning (FSL) tasks has seen significant interest within modern machine-learning literature, with particular focus on applying meta-learning
(learning to learn) [12]. These approaches aim to address the setting where classes
are rare or labelled data is hard to produce or gather.

Most work on these types of algorithms focuses on the image domain, with
other data modalities and problem settings largely underrepresented. This potentially biases meta-learning algorithmic development towards images, hampering

Supported by EPSRC, UDRC & Thales UK.

the development of general purpose meta-learners, as well as impeding development of high performance few-shot learning for other types of data or task. Compounding this, the most commonly evaluated datasets, e.g., miniImageNet [26], as well as current benchmarks suffer from lack of real-world challenge.

Acoustic classification and event detection have been well studied in conventional fully supervised machine learning [11,19], with public datasets having set evaluation protocols, allowing for fair comparison. This has however not extended to the few-shot equivalent, where the majority of works that exist make little attempt at preserving reproducibility [2,23]. This absence of standardisation poses significant issues when looking to compare novel and existing methods alike. In this work, we look to alleviate this gap by contributing the following: 1) Experimental evaluation of some of the most popular few-shot classifiers on a variety of audio datasets, spanning multiple sub-settings from environmental sounds to speech. 2) A fully reproducible few-shot audio classification benchmark with at least one published evaluation split per dataset along with custom data loading allowing for quick plug and play testing in future works. 3) A generalised prescription for dealing with variable length audio datasets in a few-shot setting. 4) Finally, in-depth analyses and evaluation of the joint training and cross-dataset/domain settings. We include all of our code at https://github.com/CHeggan/MetaAudio-A-Few-Shot-Audio-Classification-Benchmark.

## 2   Few-Shot Classification

### 2.1   Formulation

Generally, few-shot learning involves training, validating and testing a model on pairwise disjoint sets of classes, $C_{train} \notin C_{val} \notin C_{test}$. These sets of classes can be through of as analogous to the similarly named splits in conventional learning, with the added detail that non-overlapping classes are also enforced. The goal of a few-shot classifier is to generalise to a set of $N$ novel classes, given only a few-labelled examples from each class. Meta-learning can either be trained with episodic training [26], where individual few-shot tasks are drawn from $C_{train}$, or non-episodic training [27], where a classifier is trained on all classes contained in $C_{train}$ in order to learn an embedding in the second to last network layer. These episodes (also referred to as tasks throughout) contain a support set $S$ which is used for training and a query set $Q$ where recognition performance is evaluated.

### 2.2   Meta-learners and Other Approaches

Due to the number of learning algorithms posed to solve few-shot tasks within recent literature [12], we restrict our attention to a representative few. Specifically these are; Prototypical Networks [24], Model-Agnostic Meta-Learning [7], Meta-Curvature [18], SimpleShot [27] and Meta-Baseline [1]. This selection covers both metric and gradient-based meta-learning, as well as extensions to simpler baseline methods. We leave the specific details of the algorithms to the original papers and instead offer a very high level overview.

**Prototypical Networks.** The most seminal of the metric learning family of meta-learners, ProtoNets [24] work by calculating class prototypes as the centroid of the embedded support set during learning, followed by applying a nearest-centroid procedure for classifying queries.

**MAML and Meta-curvature.** These gradient-based approaches [7,18] aim to learn a transferable initialisation for any model such that it can quickly adapt to a new task $\tau$ with only a few steps of gradient descent. At training time, the meta-objective is defined as query set performance after a few steps of gradient descent on the $K$ support samples from the model's initial parameters. Meta-curvature expands on MAML by also learning a transform of the inner-optimisation gradients so as to achieve better generalisation on new tasks. In this work, we focus our attention on 1st variants of these algorithms, motivated by initial experimentation which showed similar or degraded performance when using 2nd order variants.

**SimpleShot and Meta-baseline.** SimpleShot [27] and Meta-Baseline [1] were proposed as baseline methods, aimed at lowering computational complexity. Both methods train in a conventional way, outputting logits directly from a linear layer of size $|C_{train}|$, and validate/test using nearest centroid classification. Distinguishing themselves, SimpleShot applies data informed normalisations at test time, while Meta-Baseline undergoes ProtoNet-like fine-tuning.

## 3   Related Work

**Few-Shot Classification.** We review only a small subset of available meta-learners and point the reader to [12] for a more detailed review. MAML [7], Meta-SGD [15] and Meta-Curvature [18] are representative gradient-based meta-learning (GBML) schemes, designed around the idea of fast adaptation to new learning tasks using additional gradient descent steps. The prototypical networks [24] that we evaluate here are metric learners, which aim to learn a strong feature embedding space such that support and queries can be compared using nearest neighbour. All algorithms here have been primarily evaluated in the image domain and their performance in other domains, audio included, is largely unknown.

**Few-Shot Acoustics.** Currently only a handful of studies exist that look at either few-shot audio classification or event detection. Of these, two are set in event detection [2,23] (classification of parts of an audio clip in time) with the other two focused on classification [3,29] (classification of an entire audio clip), the focus of this work. Comparing these works, we see a variety of approaches taken toward dataset processing, split formulation and reproducibility. These variations make comparisons and ranking of the works impossible. Among these, [3] is distinct in that it provides a fully reproducible code base for its experiments. Their main contribution is fitting common metric based learners with an attention similarity module, attached to its purely convolutional backbone. This work is currently state-of-the-art for both the ESC-50 [19] dataset and its proprietary noise injected variant 'noiseESC-50'. As discussed more in Sect. 4, we use this work as a basis for some of our experiments.

**Benchmarks.**    Most relevant to our work are other few-shot and meta-learning benchmarks. Included in this are works such as Meta-Dataset [25] (an aggregation of 10 few-shot image based datasets) and MetaCC [14] (a modifiable set of channel coding tasks). Of the benchmarks currently available for few-shot classifier evaluation, none deal with acoustic classification. This is the primary area that this work aims to fill. Meta-Dataset is of particular relevance to this work as we aim to mimic both the depth and reproducibility achieved. Specifically, both the within and cross dataset evaluations as well as the public leaderboard are components which we find to be useful.

## 4   MetaAudio Setup

### 4.1   Setting and Data

As MetaAudio aims to be a diverse and reproducible benchmark, it covers a variety of experimental settings, algorithms and datasets. Throughout, we mainly consider 5-way 1-shot classification, with some additional analysis of the impact of k-shots and N-ways at test time. We experiment with 7 total datasets, 5 of which are primary datasets which we split for use in training and evaluation, and 2 held-out sets we use exclusively for testing. Among them, 3 have fixed-length and 4 have variable length clips. Additional details about the datasets can be found in Table 1. Due to the highly variable sample size of the original dataset and the issues that it presents with reproducibility, we experiment with a pruned version of BirdClef 2020, where samples longer than 180s are removed along with classes with fewer than 50 samples.

**Splits and Labels.**    For every experiment setup, we apply a 7/1/2 train-validation-testing split ratio over all the classes belonging to an individual dataset. These ratios are chosen to be in line with the majority of machine learning and few-shot works [24]. Any conventional sample based train/val/test splits are ignored, and the class splits are applied to all available data. Outside [3], from which we can obtain a reproducible split of ESC-50, we have no works with prior dataset splits to follow, and so we define our own. Most simply we assign random splits based on the available classes for a given set. However, we also define within-dataset domain-stratification and shift splits for sets that have additional internal structure and/or accompanying meta-data. Extensive experimentation with these more specific splits is not carried out in this work, however we include them in our code repository. Labels for the datasets vary quite significantly with some having time strong (temporally localised) labels like BirdClef2020 [13] and others having only weak (clip-level) labels. In the interest of consistency, we drop the available strong labels for the datasets that have them and operate exclusively with weak labels. The tradeoff of this approach is that for datasets that have access to strong labels, we expect additional label noise to be present during training, possibly hurting final generalisation performance.

**Table 1.** High level details of all datasets considered in MetaAudio

| Name | Setting | N° classes | N° samples | Format | Sample length | Use |
|------|---------|-----------|-----------|--------|---------------|-----|
| ESC-50 [19] | Environmental | 50 | 2,000 | Fixed | 5 s | Meta-train/test |
| NSynth [6] | Instrumentation | 1006 | 305,978 | Fixed | 4 s | Meta-train/test |
| FDSKaggle18 [9] | Mixed | 41 | 11,073 | Variable | 0.3 s–30 s | Meta-train/test |
| VoxCeleb1 [16] | Voice | 1251 | 153,516 | Variable | 3 s–180 s | Meta-train/test |
| BirdCLEF 2020 [13] | Bird Song | 960 | 72,305 | Variable | 3 s–30 m | Meta-train/test |
| BirdCLEF 2020 (Pruned) [13] | Bird Song | 715 | 63,364 | Variable | 3 s–180 s | Meta-train/test |
| Watkins Marine Mammal Sounds [21] | Marine Mammals | 32 | 1698 | Variable | 0.1–150 s | Meta-test |
| SpeechCommandsV2 [28] | Spoken Word | 35 | 105,829 | Fixed | 1 s | Meta-test |

**Pre-processing.** Pre-processing is kept minimal, with only the conversion of raw audio samples into spectrograms and some normalisation factors applied. We fix sample rate and spectrogram parameters over all sets. For normalisation, three techniques were considered; per sample, channel wise and global. Following initial experimentation, global, which uses average statistics across all examples, was used in all experiments due to performance and simplicity.

## 4.2 Sampling Strategies

Throughout MetaAudio, we utilise a variety of sampling strategies for experimentation. The basis of these is our fixed length approach. The steps used for this can be summarised into: 1) Sample a set of N-way classes ($\mathcal{C}_N$) from the necessary split of dataset $\mathcal{D}$ and 2) For each class in $\mathcal{C}_N$, sample both support and query examples, for support the number will be k-shot. In practice, this means that a 5-way 1-shot task would contain a support vector spanning 5 unique classes, each with 1 example, and a query vector containing a balanced number of test examples for each of the classes. During training, batches of these tasks are sampled, with aggregated performance on the query vectors informing a gradient descent step on our model. We extend this fixed length strategy in order to build a method for dealing with variable length sets. Due to how varied sample length is within some of the considered datasets (Table 1), we convert to fixed length representation to avoid the need for specific neural architectures to support variable length inputs and reduce computational requirements. Specifically, we choose to split our variable length samples into $L$ length sub-clips, all sharing the same label. This along with the later conversion of the sub-clips to individual spectrograms is done entirely offline, a decision made to avoid bottlenecking during training. Combining a variety of datasets in a joint training and/or evaluation routine has been advocated for in the image space [25] to evaluate general purpose representation learning, and potentially improve performance through cross-dataset knowledge sharing. We mimic this and expand upon it for the considered acoustic datasets and task. Sampling tasks from the available datasets in this setting can be done in a few distinct ways. We consider this to be an additional area of investigation and compare two variants of task sampling. In **Free Dataset Sampling** the $N$ classes in an episode can be drawn from multiple source datasets. In **Within Dataset Sampling** each episode first randomly chooses a dataset, and then draws $N$ random classes within that dataset. During these sampling strategies, we largely ignore the class sample imbalance seen in the majority of the datasets we experiment with, we do this for a few reasons. The first of these is that recent works, such as [17], suggest it is less detrimental in meta-learning than in conventional learning. The second is that, these imbalances allow algorithms to differentiate themselves with respect to how they handle the more difficult setting. One area in which we do alleviate the effect of this imbalance is in the re-weighting of the loss functions used in teh conventional learning parts of Meta-Baseline and SimpleShot. For this, we employ inverse-frequency class weighting, where the class-wise contribution to the loss function is the inverse of the number of samples present in that class.

## 5    Experiments

### 5.1    Settings

Our experimental design follows prior few-shot works, where after one end-to-end training and evaluation procedure, average classification accuracies are reported along with their 95% confidence intervals using 10,000 tasks drawn from the test set. For all experiments we use Adam with a non-adaptive learning rate. Due to the limited tuning performed, we expect it to be fairly easy to obtain a specific result marginally better than those presented. This does not undermine the results presented here, as we investigate not only dataset specific algorithmic performance but also average expected performance based on original implementation details. Motivated by the performance gap between the commonly used CNNs and other neural architectures currently present in conventional acoustic learning [8,11], we briefly investigated the role of the base neural architecture (the actual parametrised neural network, which is then wrapped by the few-shot protocol). Due to space restriction, we do not report details here, however our best performing model using MAML and ProtoNets on ESC-50 was a lightweight hybrid CRNN. Due to its relatively low computational cost compared to larger models, we opt for this architecture throughout. Specifically, the CRNN contains a 4-block convolutional backbone (1-64-64-64) with an attached 1-layer non-bidirectional RNN containing 64 hidden units. The number of outputs in the final linear layer is either of size N-way or, in the case of metric learning and baseline methods, 64, a value chosen on the basis of hyperparameter search. In the majority of the results presented for variable length datasets, the value of $L$ is set to 5 s. We chose this value based on preliminary experiments where, for Kaggle18, $L = 5s$ performed best when compared against 1 and 10-seconds. Similarly, for the Watkins Mammal Sound Database, $L = 5$ closely resembles the expected value of the dataset's sample length distribution. Setting a common value of $L$ also allows us to more comfortably facilitate joint training and cross-dataset evaluation.

### 5.2    Within-Dataset Evaluation

We first benchmark the algorithms and datasets using a within-dataset protocol: Training and evaluating on datasets independently and further evaluating using the held out testing classes. From Table 2(a), we first remark that on ESC-50 our ProtoNet with a CRNN backbone performs at least as well as the Protonet-CNN considered in [3] with the same split. Comparing the results Table 2(a), we make the following further observations: (i) Out of the two fixed length sets, ESC-50 appears to be the harder problem, with much lower accuracy than NSynth. This is somewhat expected given the very clean NSynth data compared to the noisier ESC-50 data. (ii) The variable length datasets appear to provide a harder setting in general, with significantly lower performance than the fixed-length sets. (iii) Comparing the meta-learners, we see that GBML methods generally perform better, with Meta-Curvature taking first place in 4 out of 5 cases and best average rank; and MAML taking first place on Kaggle18 and second best rank overall. In comparison, our metric and baseline algorithms underperform in accuracy despite their better speed at inference time. We propose that this is due to the GBML methods' adaption mechanism, updating feature representation at each meta-test episode, making them particularly useful for tasks with high inter-class/episode variance. Meanwhile the others must rely on a fixed feature extractor that cannot adapt to each unique episode. Overall the fact that the GMBL methods outperform SimpleShot, in reversal of the widely remarked upon results for miniImageNet in [27], shows the value of an audio-based benchmark as a complement to popular image based benchmarks in drawing conclusions about general purpose and domain-specific meta-learner fitness. (iv) Finally, we observe that Meta-Baseline was the most competitive non-adaptive approach. This confirms that episodic meta-learning provides benefit over the conventional supervised representation learning in SimpleShot [27].

### 5.3   Joint Training and Cross Dataset

In this section we extend our evaluation to joint training, where a single model is learned on the combined training splits of all source datasets (rather than a per-dataset model as in Sect. 5.2), and then evaluated on the testing split of each dataset in turn. Furthermore, we now also test on two held-out datasets that were not included during training (Table 1), to evaluate cross-dataset few-shot learning performance. We report results for both within-dataset and free-dataset episode sampling (as discussed in Sect. 4.2) in Table 2(b) and Table 2(c) respectively. First, we compare the joint training regime results 2(b, c) against the within-dataset evaluation in Table 2(a). For both ESC-50 and Kaggle18 we obtain new SOTA results with MAML and Meta-Curvature respectively, both from the free dataset sampling routine. For all other datasets, we see a degradation of performance compared to within dataset training in Table 2(a). This difference varies in magnitude between datasets and sampling routines. The mixed results here mirror those observed in [25] and reflect the tradeoff between two forces: (1) a positive effect of generally increasing the amount of training data available compared to the within-dataset condition, and (2) a negative effect due to the increased difficulty of learning a single model capable of simultaneous high performance on diverse data domains [20]. This shows that MetaAudio complements [25] in providing a challenging benchmark to test future meta-learners'

**Table 2.** Main Meta Audio benchmark 5-way 1-shot classification results. Table (a) contains the within-dataset results, where models are trained for each dataset individually and then evaluated with that dataset's test split. Tables (b) and (c) contain results from the joint training scenario, where we train meta-learners over all datasets simultaneously and then evaluate on individual test splits. They differ in that in (b) we only allow training tasks to be sampled using classes from one of the datasets per episode, whereas in (c) we allow cross-dataset task creation. In (b) and (c) the bottom group of 'cross' datasets are held out from training and used only for testing.

| a) Baseline Within Dataset Results | | | | | |
|---|---|---|---|---|---|
| Dataset | FO-MAML | FO-Meta-Curvature | ProtoNets | SimpleShot CL2N | Meta-Baseline |
| ESC-50 | 74.66 ± 0.42 | **76.17 ± 0.41** | 68.83 ± 0.38 | 68.82 ± 0.39 | 71.72 ± 0.38 |
| NSynth | 93.85 ± 0.24 | **96.47 ± 0.19** | 95.23 ± 0.19 | 90.04 ± 0.27 | 90.74 ± 0.25 |
| Kaggle18 | **43.45 ± 0.46** | 43.18 ± 0.45 | 39.44 ± 0.44 | 42.03 ± 0.42 | 40.27 ± 0.44 |
| VoxCeleb1 | 60.89 ± 0.45 | **63.85 ± 0.44** | 59.64 ± 0.44 | 48.50 ± 0.42 | 55.54 ± 0.42 |
| BirdClef (Pruned) | 56.26 ± 0.45 | **61.34 ± 0.46** | 56.11 ± 0.46 | 57.66 ± 0.43 | 57.28 ± 0.41 |
| Avg Algorithm Rank | 2.4 | 1.2 | 3.8 | 4.0 | 3.6 |
| b) Joint Training (Within Dataset Sampling) | | | | | |
| Trained  ESC-50 | 68.68 ± 0.45 | **72.43 ± 0.44** | 61.49 ± 0.41 | 59.31 ± 0.40 | 62.79 ± 0.40 |
| NSynth | 81.54 ± 0.39 | 82.22 ± 0.38 | 78.63 ± 0.36 | **89.66 ± 0.41** | 85.17 ± 0.31 |
| Kaggle18 | 39.51 ± 0.44 | **41.22 ± 0.45** | 36.22 ± 0.40 | 37.80 ± 0.40 | 34.04 ± 0.40 |
| VoxCeleb1 | **51.41 ± 0.43** | 51.37 ± 0.44 | 50.74 ± 0.41 | 40.14 ± 0.41 | 39.18 ±0.39 |
| BirdClef (Pruned) | **47.69 ± 0.45** | 47.39 ± 0.46 | 46.49 ± 0.43 | 35.69 ± 0.40 | 37.40 ± 0.40 |
| Cross  Watkins | 57.75 ± 0.47 | **57.76 ± 0.47** | 49.16 ± 0.43 | 52.73 ± 0.43 | 52.09 ± 0.43 |
| SpeechCommands V1 | 25.09 ± 0.40 | **26.33 ± 0.41** | 24.31 ± 0.36 | 24.99 ± 0.35 | 24.18 ± 0.36 |
| Avg Algorithm Rank | 2.0 | 1.6 | 4.0 | 3.4 | 4.0 |
| c) Joint Training (Free Dataset Sampling) | | | | | |
| Trained  ESC-50 | **76.24 ± 0.42** | 75.72 ± 0.42 | 68.63 ± 0.39 | 59.04 ± 0.41 | 61.53 ± 0.40 |
| NSynth | 77.71 ± 0.41 | 83.51 ± 0.37 | 79.06 ± 0.36 | **90.02 ± 0.27** | 85.04 ± 0.31 |
| Kaggle18 | 44.85 ± 0.45 | **45.46 ± 0.45** | 41.76 ± 0.41 | 38.12 ± 0.40 | 35.90 ± 0.38 |
| VoxCeleb1 | 39.52 ± 0.42 | 39.83 ± 0.43 | 40.74 ± 0.39 | **42.66 ± 0.41** | 36.63 ± 0.38 |
| BirdClef (Pruned) | **46.76 ± 0.45** | 46.41 ± 0.46 | 44.70 ± 0.42 | 37.96 ± 0.40 | 32.29 ± 0.38 |
| Cross  Watkins | **60.27 ± 0.47** | 58.19 ± 0.47 | 48.56 ± 0.42 | 54.34 ± 0.43 | 53.23 ± 0.43 |
| SpeechCommands V1 | **27.29 ± 0.42** | 26.56 ± 0.42 | 24.30 ± 0.35 | 24.74 ± 0.35 | 23.88 ± 0.35 |
| Avg Algorithm Rank | 2.1 | 2.1 | 3.4 | 3.0 | 4.3 |

ability to fit diverse audio types, as well as enabling few-shot recognition of new categories. Moving to the other question of interest, we contrast how the joint training episode sampling routines compare. For our main datasets, we observe 3/5 of the top results were obtained using the free sampling method, with the 2 outliers belonging to VoxCeleb and BirdClef - evidence that their tasks require significantly different and specific model parametrisation, as the within dataset task sampling would allow more opportunity to learn these more specialised features. For the held-out cross-dataset tasks (Watkins, SpeechCommands), we also see the strongest performance coming from the free sampling routine, where it outperforms its within dataset counterpart by ~2% in both held-out sets. As for the absolute performances obtained on the held-out sets, we see that our joint training transfers somewhat-effectively, with the model in one case attaining a respectable 50–60% and another obtaining accuracies only 5% above random. Finally, comparing learners, we again see GBML approaches performing best

**Table 3.** Meta Audio benchmark using a variety of pre-trained spectrogram transformers from [11]. Models are trained on ImageNet [4] and AudioSet [10]. Results show 5-way 1-shot performance using simple classifiers on fixed features. We compare these to the results for SimpleShot using dataset specific training and evaluation.

| Dataset | AST ImageNet | | AST ImageNet & AudioSet | | SimpleShot (CL2N) from Table 2 a) |
|---|---|---|---|---|---|
| | SVM | SimpleShot (CL2N) | SVM | SimpleShot (CL2N) | |
| ESC-50 | 61.12 ± 0.41 | 60.41 ± 0.41 | 61.61 ± 0.41 | 64.48 ± 0.41 | **68.82 ± 0.39** |
| NSynth | 64.26 ± 0.41 | 66.68 ± 0.41 | 62.62 ± 0.42 | 63.78 ± 0.42 | **90.04 ± 0.27** |
| Kaggle18 | 34.01 ± 0.40 | 33.52 ± 0.39 | 38.38 ± 0.41 | 38.76 ± 0.41 | **42.03 ± 0.42** |
| VoxCeleb1 | 27.26 ± 0.36 | 28.09 ± 0.37 | 27.45 ± 0.36 | 28.79 ± 0.38 | **48.50 ± 0.42** |
| BirdClef (Pruned) | 30.84 ± 0.37 | 33.04 ± 0.41 | 33.17 ± 0.38 | 36.41 ± 0.42 | **57.66 ± 0.43** |
| Avg Rank | 4.2 | 3.8 | 3.6 | 2.4 | 1.0 |
| Watkins | **55.91 ± 0.42** | 55.40 ± 0.42 | 51.46 ± 0.42 | 51.81 ± 0.42 | N/A |
| SpeechCommands V1 | 26.24 ± 0.36 | 26.46 ± 0.37 | **30.69 ± 0.38** | 30.24 ± 0.38 | N/A |
| Avg Rank | 2.5 | 2.5 | 2.5 | 2.5 | N/A |

overall. However, for this joint training condition, SimpleShot improves to take third place overall by average rank.

## 5.4   External Data and Pretraining

A full meta-learning pipeline for a specific dataset can be expensive. Recent studies in the few-shot and self-supervision communities have debated whether off-the-shelf models pre-trained on large external datasets may provide a better approach to few-shot than meta-learning [27]. Transferring a well-trained representation and training a simple classifier for each task could also be cheaper due to amortizing the cost of large-scale pre-training over multiple downstream tasks. To this end, we also evaluate our MetaAudio benchmark using pre-trained feature models trained on the large scale ImageNet [4] and AudioSet [10] datasets. Specifically, we use the SOTA Audio Spectrogram Transformers(ASTs) from [11]. We experiment with two model variants, the ImageNet only and the ImageNet + AudioSet trained 'base384' transformers provided by the authors, including their suggested AudioSet sample normalisation. We apply both nearest-centroid and SVM linear classification on our output features.

The results in Table 3 show that the features pre-trained on AudioSet and ImageNet unsurprisingly outperforms those pre-trained on ImageNet alone. However, the small size of this margin is perhaps surprising, showing that image-derived features provide most of the information needed to interpret spectrograms.

Comparing these results to in-domain training in Table 2, we see that performance has dropped substantially, with the potential exception of ESC-50 and Kaggle18. In their best cases, NSynth, VoxCeleb and BirdClef all take drops in performance of ~20% due to dataset shift between general purpose pre-training and our specific tasks, such as musical instruments, speech or bird song recognition. While the performance hit due to domain-shift is expected, these results are surprising as AudioSet is a much larger dataset, and the AST transformer is a much larger architecture than the CRNN used in Table 2. In image modality, analogous experiments show a clear win simply applying larger pre-training datasets and larger-models combined with simple readouts, compared to conducting within-domain meta-learning [5]. This confirms the value of Meta-Audio as an important benchmark for assessing meta-learning contributions that cannot easily be replicated by larger architectures and more data. Performance on our held-out sets shows a more mixed set of results, with ImageNet only pre-training favouring Watkins, and ImageNet + AudioSet pre-training setting a new SOTA for SpeechCommands.

## 5.5   N-Way k-Shot Analysis

Although we only trained and evaluated on the task of 5-way 1-shot classification, we are interested in the effect of larger shots and wider ways on algorithm performance. To bridge this gap, we experiment with these components at test time, using our already trained 5-way 1-shot models. We consider all of our primary datasets and algorithms, covering values of N from 5–30, and k from 1–30. Varying N-ways and k-shots are treated separately and not stacked, a decision made to avoid the compounding computational complexity of the problem. For algorithms which have a fixed size output (i.e. GBML methods) we exclude the varying N-ways. Both ESC-50 and Kaggle18 have only 10 and 7 classes belonging to their test sets respectively, and so analysis further than 10/5-way is impossible. We include a sample of our result plots in Fig. 1. Varying the numbers of shots, we observe a clear trend of GBML methods outperforming baseline and metric learning approaches. This is especially true for large k-shots, where the rise in performance also occurs faster. For both fixed length sets, we see some additional distinction between gradient based methods and the others, where methods without adaptation both stagnate and start to decline in performance after 5-shot. Up to 30-shot, we do not observe this same behaviour in variable length sets, however it is possible that this is simply due to the complexity of the problems. Of the three non-gradient-based methods, which algorithm performs best over k-shots appears to be dataset specific, with each outperforming the others in at least one set. Although we are more limited in varying the number of ways we test over, we still observe some interesting trends. All of our tested algorithms show a non-linear decay in performance, with results at 30-way still

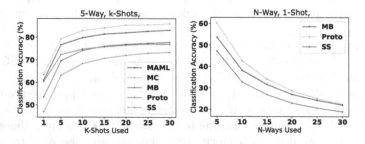

**Fig. 1.** Few-shot learning on VoxCeleb1. Varying test K-shots (left) and N-ways (right).

reaching ∼20–25% for our VoxCeleb and BirdClef sets (approx 7× random). For speed of drop-off, we see a similar story as we saw in increasing k-shot, with all algorithms showing the best performance in at least one set as N-way increases.

## 6   Conclusion

In this work, we presented MetaAudio, a new large-scale and diverse few-shot acoustic classification benchmark covering a variety of algorithms, sound domains and experimental settings.

Our experiments showed that gradient-based meta-learners with feature adaptation capability generally performed better than fixed-representation competitors. This was the case across most of our settings, although the latter algorithms benefitted from faster learning speed.

We also evaluated the ability of meta-learners to span few-shot learning tasks drawn from a heterogeneous variety of datasets, and their ability to generalise across distribution shift between training and testing. Surprisingly, we also showed that in-domain meta-learning led to substantially better performance than transfer learning from larger architectures trained on larger external datasets, a result that is noticeably different to that from computer vision.

Going forward, MetaAudio will provide a substantial complement to influential analogous benchmarks [25] in the vision domain. Besides benefiting few-shot learning in audio domain, we believe that MetaAudio will help to drive meta-learning research overall, ensuring that more generally relevant algorithms and insights are developed, without becoming overly-specific to computer vision (a problem of gaining relevance). This should help ensure meta-learning research benefits data efficient learning demand across society more broadly.

**Acknowledgement.** This work is supported by the Engineering and Physical Sciences Research Council of the UK (EPSRC) Grant number EP/S000631/1 and the UK MOD University Defence Research Collaboration (UDRC) in Signal Processing, EPSRC iCASE account EP/V519674/1 and Thales UK Ltd.

## References

1. Chen, Y., Liu, Z., Xu, H., Darrell, T., Wang, X.: Meta-baseline: exploring simple meta-learning for few-shot learning. In: ICCV (2021)
2. Cheng, K.H., Chou, S.Y., Yang, Y.H.: Multi-label few-shot learning for sound event recognition. In: MMSP (2019)
3. Chou, S.Y., Cheng, K.H., Jang, J.S.R., Yang, Y.H.: Learning to match transient sound events using attentional similarity for few-shot sound recognition. In: ICASSP (2019)
4. Deng, J., Dong, W., Socher, R., Li, L.J., Li, K., Fei-Fei, L.: ImageNet: a large-scale hierarchical image database. In: CVPR (2009)
5. Dumoulin, V., et al.: A unified few-shot classification benchmark to compare transfer and meta learning approaches. In: NIPS Datasets and Benchmarks Track (2021)

6. Engel, J., Cinjon Resnick, A.R., Dieleman, S., Eck, D., Simonyan, K., Norouzi, M.: Neural audio synthesis of musical notes with wavenet autoencoders (2017)
7. Finn, C., Abbeel, P., Levine, S.: Model-agnostic meta-learning for fast adaptation of deep networks. In: ICML (2017)
8. Fonseca, E., Favory, X., Pons, J., Font, F., Serra, X.: Fsd50k: an open dataset of human-labeled sound events. TASLP **30**, 829–852 (2022)
9. Fonseca, E., et al.: General-purpose tagging of freesound audio with audioset labels: task description, dataset, and baseline. In: Proceedings of the DCASE 2018 Workshop (2018)
10. Gemmeke, J.F., et al.: Audio set: an ontology and human-labeled dataset for audio events. In: ICASSP (2017)
11. Gong, Y., Chung, Y.A., Glass, J.: AST: audio spectrogram transformer. In: Interspeech (2021)
12. Hospedales, T.M., Antoniou, A., Micaelli, P., Storkey, A.J.: Meta-learning in neural networks: a survey. TPAMI 1 (2021)
13. Kahl, S., et al.: Overview of BirdCLEF 2020: bird sound recognition in complex acoustic environments (2020)
14. Li, R., et al.: A channel coding benchmark for meta-learning. In: NIPS Datasets and Benchmarks Track (2021)
15. Li, Z., Zhou, F., Chen, F., Li, H.: Meta-SGD: learning to learn quickly for few shot learning. arXiv (2017)
16. Nagrani, A., Chung, J.S., Zisserman, A.: VoxCeleb: a large-scale speaker identification dataset. CoRR (2017)
17. Ochal, M., Patacchiola, M., Storkey, A.J., Vazquez, J., Wang, S.: Few-shot learning with class imbalance. CoRR (2021)
18. Park, E., Oliva, J.B.: Meta-curvature. In: NIPS, vol. 32 (2019)
19. Piczak, K.J.: ESC: dataset for environmental sound classification. In: Proceedings of the 23rd Annual ACM Conference on Multimedia (2015)
20. Rebuffi, S.A., Bilen, H., Vedaldi, A.: Learning multiple visual domains with residual adapters. In: NIPS (2017)
21. Sayigh, L., et al.: The Watkins marine mammal sound database: an online, freely accessible resource, vol. 27, p. 040013 (2016)
22. Senior, A.W., et al.: Improved protein structure prediction using potentials from deep learning. Nature **577**(7792) (2020)
23. Shi, B., Sun, M., Puvvada, K.C., Kao, C.C., Matsoukas, S., Wang, C.: Few-shot acoustic event detection via meta learning. In: ICASSP (2020)
24. Snell, J., Swersky, K., Zemel, R.: Prototypical networks for few-shot learning. In: Advances in Neural Information Processing Systems, vol. 30 (2017)
25. Triantafillou, E., et al.: Meta-dataset: a dataset of datasets for learning to learn from few examples. In: ICLR (2020)
26. Vinyals, O., Blundell, C., Lillicrap, T., Kavukcuoglu, K., Wierstra, D.: Matching networks for one shot learning. In: NIPS (2016)
27. Wang, Y., Chao, W., Weinberger, K.Q., van der Maaten, L.: SimpleShot: revisiting nearest-neighbor classification for few-shot learning. arXiv (2019)
28. Warden, P.: Speech commands: a dataset for limited-vocabulary speech recognition
29. Wolters, P., Careaga, C., Hutchinson, B., Phillips, L.: A study of few-shot audio classification. In: GHC (2020)

# Multi-Knowledge Attention Transfer Framework for Action Recognition

Jiaqiang Zhang(ID), Jinxin Guo(ID), and Ming Ma(✉)(ID)

Inner Mongolia University, Hohhot 010021, Inner Mongolia, China
{32009087,32109117}@mail.imu.edu.cn, csmaming@imu.edu.cn

**Abstract.** Action recognition is a crucial task in computer vision. The Two-Stream Network and 3D ConvNets have achieved outstanding performance. However, due to the enormous amount of computation of optical flow and 3D convolution, they can not be effectively applied to some real-time applications. Therefore, some researchers have used motion vectors and residuals in the compressed video to replace optical flow, but their lack of fine structure leads to decreased model performance, such as noise and inaccurate motion blocks. In this paper, we propose a Multi-Knowledge Attention Transfer (MKAT) framework based on the three-stream network structure, including Multi-Knowledge Enhancement (MKE) module and Feature Loss Enhancement (FLE) module. The MKE module adopts the distillation methods of self-learning and multi-level information fusion, which allow the student network to learn from the decision-making and thinking aspects of the teacher. We use the attention enhancement (AE) module to process the output of each feature layer, so that the FLE module can highlight the differences between the key information of the feature layer. Experimental results on two public benchmarks (i.e., UCF-101, HMDB-51) significantly outperform the current state of the art on the compressed domain.

**Keywords:** Computer vision · Deep learning · Action recognition

## 1 Introduction

Deep learning has been gradually applied to a variety of industries in recent years, and its superior performance made it capable of performing well across a variety of tasks. The purpose of action recognition is to enable the computer to recognize the action in videos. Early approaches consisted of feature extraction, feature encoding and classification steps. Previous studies showed that IDT [12] descriptors and Fisher vector representation had superior performance in some datasets, but the performance of these approaches depended on the hand-crafted features.

This work is supported by the CERNET Innovation Project No. NGII20190625, the Inner Mongolia Natural Science Foundation of China under Grant No. 2021MS06016, and the Inner Mongolia University Postgraduate Research Innovative Project No. 11200-121024.

Some researchers have used deep learning for action recognition, the performance of the model has been dramatically improved. At present, there are two main methods: two-stream network [9,18,23,33] and 3D-CNN network [6,21,25]. The two-stream network converted the original videos into RGB frames and optical flow vector respectively and feed them into the convolutional neural network separately to extract features. The 3D-CNN directly used 3D convolution to extract both temporal and spatial features of the video. However, due to optical flow and 3D convolution, the model has a large calculations and parameters, which cannot be applied to real-time applications.

To reduce the computation of optical flow in two-stream network structure, some studies [30,36] tried to use the information in compressed video. The video compressed by H.264, HEVC, etc. has three main components, I-frames (key frames), P-frames (forward reference frames) and B-frames (bi-directional reference frames). I-frames can also be considered as RGB images used in two-stream networks, which have complete spatial information. P-frames contain motion vectors (MV) and Residuals, and they have rich motion information similar to optical flow and exist directly in compressed video. However, MV and Residual have noise and inaccurate motion patterns, which have difficulty achieving performance comparable to optical flow.

This paper proposes Multi-Knowledge Attention Transfer (MKAT) framework by using the ideas of multimodal learning, knowledge distillation, attention mechanism, and multi-stream networks. Overall, the contributions of this paper are summarized as follows.

- We propose a Multi-Knowledge Attention Transfer (MKAT) framework which includes the FLE module and the MKE module. The MKE module enhances loss representation by fusing different levels of residual block information, and the FLE module improves the learning ability of students' networks based on attention and knowledge distillation methods.
- We conduct experiments on two benchmark datasets to demonstrate the effectiveness of MKAT.

The experiments show that MKAT can achieve outstanding performance in I-frame stream network (Iframe-CNN), Residual stream network (Residual-CNN) and MV stream network (MV-CNN). Our method does not need additional optical flow calculation in the inference, and dramatically improves the accuracy and the inference speed of the model.

## 2   Related Work

### 2.1   Compressed Video Action Recognition

Convolutional Neural Network significantly improves the feature representation. Some researchers proposed two-stream network [23], that is, two different CNNs are used to model the raw video and optical flow separately. TSN [29] in two-stream network was designed to capture long-range temporal structure, TSM

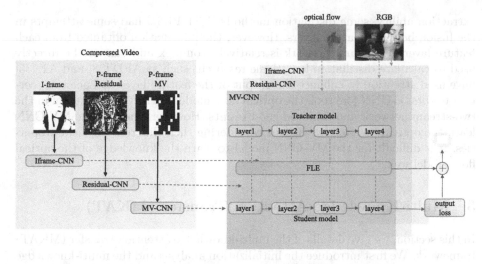

**Fig. 1.** Multi-Knowledge Attention Transfer framework. The red dashed line indicates that different types of inputs are sent to the corresponding student network, and the blue dashed line indicates that different types of inputs are sent to the corresponding teacher network. We build different CNNs for I-frame, Residual, and MV respectively, and for each CNN, we calculate two kinds of losses, one (output loss) for the output of the student model with labels, and one for the FLE module, add them together to get the final loss and use it for the gradient update. (Color figure online)

[20] obtained the approximate 3D-CNN capability through a temporary shift block. Still these methods need to fuse optical flow. On this basis, CoViAR [30] proposed modeling directly in compressed video, they used three CNNs to model I-frame, motion vector (MV) and residual (MV and residual are obtained from P-frame) in compressed domain respectively. The various network is independent of each other in the training process, and fuse the scores after training, which avoid calculating the optical flow explicitly. However, CoViAR used ResNet-152 [10] for I-frame images, so it has many parameters, and MV and residual all have inaccurate motion patterns, so directly using these information can lead to bad performance. TEMSN [19] also used the video compression information and improves temporal modeling structure, but the improved performance is limited. To make the action recognition model better used in the mobile devices, TTP [14] proposed to use the lightweight network (MobileNetV2) as the backbone, and used a multi-modal fuse module to increase the performance of the model, but the performance of the model was decreased.

## 2.2 Knowledge Distillation

Knowledge distillation [11] is a method of model compression, which transfers the knowledge of a large model to another small model. The small model after distillation has more knowledge than the original small model, but it has less complexity and parameters. In order to make the shallow network have strong feature extraction ability, some distillation methods [1,11,13,31] had some attempts in the fusion between feature layers. However, the information obtained from each feature layer of a neural network is relatively complex and can not be directly used to calculate distillation loss. Some researchs such as AFD [28] and AT [35] have used attention to enhance the output of the feature layer and achieved certain results. E-CNN [36] took the optical flow model as the teacher model in the two-stream network and achieved good results. However, they let the MV-CNN learn the optical flow model without considering their different physical properties. It is difficult for the MV-CNN model to learn the knowledge of the optical flow model well.

## 3    Multi-Knowledge Attention Transfer (MKAT)

In this section, we give details of the multi-knowledge attention transfer (MKAT) framework. We first introduce the initialization analysis and the multi-knowledge enhancement (MKE) module. The MKE module introduces the multi-level information distillation fusion methods. Then, the feature loss enhancement (FLE) module uses the attention mechanism to enhance the key information of the feature layer, so as to improve the performance of the MKE module.

### 3.1    Initialization Analysis

In CoViAR [30], MV-CNN adopts the pretrained model of the ResNet-18 [10] on ImageNet [16], which played a specific role in improving the accuracy of the model. However, the input of its pre-trained model contains three-dimensional RGB image information, while the motion vector (MV) contains two-dimensional motion information, so they cannot build up a connection, that is, MV-CNN can not be initialized with the pre-trained model on ImageNet. Therefore, we initialize our model with the help of the two-dimensional optical flow model.

In this paper, we use the same pre-trained model for teacher and student. In this way, the student gets all the knowledge of the teacher, but it should be noted that student can not adopt to these knowledge well, so that we will improve student' learning ability to teacher through multi knowledge enhancement (MKE) module and feature loss enhancement (FLE) module.

$$OF_l^i = S_u^i = T_u^i, i = 1, \ldots, n. \tag{1}$$

$OF_l^i$ is the model of optical flow network in TSN [29] trained on Kinetics [4], $S_u^i$ and $T_u^i$ are student model and teacher model respectively.

### 3.2    Multi-Knowledge Enhancement

Previous work [30] showed that MV and Residual lack fine structural characteristics. For example, as shown in Fig. 1, in the compressed video of "ApplyEye-Makeup" action, the movement of women's make-up hand and make-up position is lost, which makes it difficult for the MV-CNN and Residual-CNN to learn the characteristics of make-up. To compensate for their deficiencies in feature representation, we use knowledge distillation to improve the performance of the network.

Distillation training for MV uses teacher and student output for loss calculation, as in Eq. 2, which does not allow students to fully understand their teachers' thinking abilities. We consider a distillation approach as shown in Fig. 1, loss calculation of output information from different levels of residual blocks for students and teachers. We let the trained optical flow model supervise the training of the network and let them use the same backbone network. The benefits of this processing are computational simplicity and excellent performance.

$$L_{out} = -\log \frac{exp(x[class])}{\sum_{j=1}^{n} exp(x[j])}, j = 1, \ldots, n. \tag{2}$$

$L_{out}$ is the loss between the output of the student model and the target, and $x[class]$ is the classification label.

Since these loss values represent different levels of information, so we use the loss changes in the training process to modify the weight values dynamically, multiplies these weight values with the losses of different semantic levels, and finally fuses them, as in Eq. 3.

$$L_{KD} = \sum_{k} \sum_{i} m_k \cdot w_i (y_i - \hat{y}_i)^2, k = 1, 2, 3; i = 1, \ldots, n. \tag{3}$$

$L_{KD}$ is the output loss between teacher and student feature layers, $m_k$ is the ratio less than 1, which is used to fuse the loss in the way of the weighted summation, and $\sum_i w_i (y_i - \hat{y}_i)^2$ is the MSE function for calculating the output loss of teacher and student. We fuse the output loss $L_{out}$ and distillation loss $L_{KD}$ in the following Eq. 4.

$$L_{loss} = w_1 \cdot L_{out} + w_2 \cdot L_{KD}, (w_1 + w_2 = 1) \tag{4}$$

## 3.3   Feature Loss Enhancement

As shown in Fig. 2, the information obtained from different feature layers is unstable and inaccurate. And we are inspired by [35] to propose Feature Loss Enhancement (FLE) module to make this information more representative.

The core of FLE is attention enhancement (AE), which draws on the idea of attention mechanism and convolutional extraction of main features to establish Eq. 5 to perform feature enhancement on the output of partial residual block, and the enhanced features have a positive effect on the MKE module. This method does not add any computational effort when the model is inferring. According to the results in Table 3, the FLE module can significantly improve the multi-knowledge fusion ability of the MKE module.

$$L_i = MSE \left\{ \frac{(x, y)}{sum(x_s, y_t)^n} \right\} \tag{5}$$

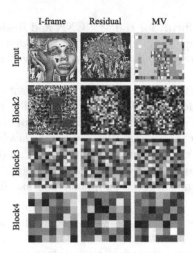

**Fig. 2.** Comparison of the outputs of the network layers under the tensorboard visualization tool. The horizontal row is the type of input data, and the vertical row is the visualization of the output features of the input, second, third, and fourth layers.

## 4  Experiments

In this section, we first describe the relevant datasets and experimental details, then the ablation experiments on different modules of MKAT are presented, and the experimental results are compared with the current mainstream methods.

### 4.1  Datasets

**UCF-101** [24]. This dataset contains 13320 videos from 101 action categories, along with 3 public training/test splits.
**HMDB-51** [17]. This dataset contains 6766 videos from 51 action categories, along with 3 public training/test splits.

### 4.2  Implementation Details

**Training.** For MV-CNN, Iframe-CNN and Residual-CNN, we use the initial learning rates of 0.01, 0.0003 and 0.005 respectively, and the decline periods of learning rate are 40, 80 and 120. We choose Adam [15] as the optimizer. The size of the input feature map is 224 × 224, and the data augmentation uses cropping and flipping. We use MPEG-4 encoded video, TV-L1 [34] is used for extracting optical flow. For the FLE module, we calculate the quadratic power of the feature map to calculate the attention map, and enhance the last dimension of the feature layers in the fusion. Our model is trained on 8 NVIDIA 2080ti GPUs.

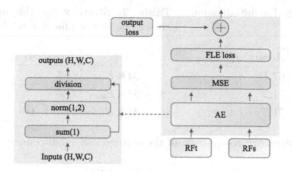

**Fig. 3.** Feature Loss Enhancement. The left half is the AE module, which enhances the information of the input features by the calculation of Eq. 5. The loss value of FLE is summed with the original loss value for gradient update.

**Testing and Fusion.** Each video has 25 frames sampled, each sampled frame has 5 crops augmented with flipping. In the final fusion stage, the test scores of MV-CNN, Iframe-CNN and Residual-CNN are multiplied by the ratio of 1, 2 and 1 respectively.

## 4.3   Ablation Study

In this section, we evaluate the MKAT framework on Split1 of UCF-101 dataset. we first evaluate the effect of multi-knowledge enhancement (MKE) module on MV-CNN, and verify the fusion ability of MKE module to different knowledge. Then we evaluate several strategies of feature loss enhancement (FLE) module.

The experimental results in Table 1 show that using optical flow model on Kinetics [3,4] as the distillation teacher model can better improve the learning ability of MV-CNN, where $MKE_{Im}$ represents the RGB-CNN model as the teacher model, $MKE_{OF}$ represents the optical flow model as the teacher model.

As shown in Table 2, the results show that the loss between teacher and student networks in first three layer can be well used to improve students' learning ability, and the accuracy of the model can be improved by 0.8%.

As shown in Table 3, the results show that the first three layers of the network are processed by the AE module to obtain different semantic loss values respectively, and then the loss values are averaged, which can significantly improve the student' learning ability, and the accuracy can be improved by 1.8%. The weighted average method ($FLE_{1,2,3}^{w_\psi}$ and $FLE_{1,2,3}^{w_\mu}$) can not effectively fuse the losses of each layer, as shown in Table 3, their improvement in accuracy is not obvious. $w_\psi$ represents that the $w$ is 0.5, 0.3, 0.2, $w_\mu$ represents that the $w$ is 0.2, 0.3, 0.5.

**Table 1.** Strategy for initialization analysis.

|  | Accuracy (%) |
|---|---|
| Baseline [30] | 67.1 |
| $MKE_{Im}$ | 71.2 |
| $MKE_{OF}$ | 71.5 |

**Table 2.** Strategy for the multi-knowledge enhancement module.

|  | Accuracy (%) |
|---|---|
| $MKE_{OF}$ | 71.5 |
| $MKE_0$ | 71.6 |
| $MKE_{1,2,3}$ | **72.3** (+0.8) |

**Table 3.** Strategy comparison of the feature loss enhancement module.

|  | Accuracy (%) |
|---|---|
| $MKE_{1,2,3}$ | 72.3 |
| $FLE_1$ | 73.3 |
| $FLE_{1,2,3}$ | **74.1** (+1.8) |
| $FLE_{1,2,3,4}$ | 72.9 |
| $FLE_{1,2,3}^{w_\psi}$ | 72.4 |
| $FLE_{1,2,3}^{w_\mu}$ | 72.3 |

## 4.4  Comparison of Fusion Accuracy

As shown in Table 4. We apply the MKAT framework to UCF-101 dataset, and the accuracies of MV-CNN, Iframe-CNN and Residual-CNN are improved by 10.2%, 4.9% and 8.1% respectively. The accuracy after fusion is 95.5%, 4.7% higher than CoViAR [30], and 1% higher than that after adding optical flow [30]. In HMDB-51 dataset, the accuracy after fusion is 73.2%, 12.8% higher than CoViAR, and 3% higher than that after adding optical flow.

**Table 4.** Accuracy(%) comparison of MKAT and CoViAR [30] on UCF-101 and HMDB-51.

| Datasets | Methods | I-frame | MV | Residual | Fusion |
|---|---|---|---|---|---|
| UCF-101 | CoViAR | 88.4 | 63.9 | 79.9 | 90.8 |
|  | MKAT(ours) | 93.3 | 74.1 | 88.0 | **95.5** |
| HMDB-51 | CoViAR | 54.1 | 37.8 | 44.6 | 60.4 |
|  | MKAT(ours) | 68.0 | 46.7 | 59.2 | **73.2** |

## 4.5  Computation Evaluation

As mentioned earlier, minimizing the cost of computation is the key to the model in some real-time applications. As shown in Table 5. We evaluate the method through the average calculation quantity index $\mathbf{R}_{GFlops}^\alpha$, as in Eq. 6 (t includes

Table 5. Flops comparison of MKAT and CoViAR.

|                | I-frame | MV   | Residual | $R^\alpha_{Flops}(G)$ |
|----------------|---------|------|----------|-----------------------|
| **CoViAR**     | 11.57   | 1.78 | 1.82     | 5.06                  |
| **MKAT**(*ours*) | 4.12  | 4.08 | 4.12     | 4.10                  |
| $\Delta_{cost}$ | −7.5   | +2.3 | +2.3     | −0.96                 |

Table 6. Compressed video based methods. We achieved the best results in terms of the accuracy of the model.

|                           | UCF-101 | HMDB-51 |
|---------------------------|---------|---------|
| EMV + RGB-CNN [36]        | 86.4    | –       |
| DTMV-CNN [37]             | 87.5    | 55.3    |
| TTP [14]                  | 87.2    | 58.2    |
| TEMSN [19]                | 91.8    | 61.1    |
| DMC-Net [22]              | 92.3    | 71.8    |
| Two-Stream fusion [9]     | 92.5    | 65.4    |
| MFCD-Net [2]              | 93.2    | 66.9    |
| I3D [4]                   | 93.4    | 66.4    |
| ST-ResNet [5]             | 93.4    | 66.4    |
| ST-Mult [8]               | 94.2    | 68.9    |
| TSN [29]                  | 94.2    | 69.4    |
| CoViAR [30]               | 90.4    | 59.1    |
| CoViAR + optical flow [30]| 94.9    | 70.2    |
| MV IF-TTN [32]            | 94.5    | 70.0    |
| **MKAT** (ours)           | **95.5**| **73.2**|

Iframe, MV, Residual). Our MKAT is 0.96 lower than CoViAR, which verifies that our method reduces computational effort while improving accuracy.

$$\mathbf{R}^\alpha_{GFlops} = \sum_{i=1}^{3} l_i^r \times CNN_t \qquad (6)$$

## 4.6  Comparison with State-of-the-Art

As shown in Table 6, IDT+FT [27] was designed based on manual features, but it has been defeated by deep learning based methods. EMV + RGB-CNN [36] improved the feature fusion ability of MV-CNN by using optical flow and simple knowledge distillation, but their distillation method was too simple to achieve good results. Since FULL IF-TTN [32] is supplemented by the prediction score of optical flow, we do not make reference, but only compare MV IF-TTN [32].

In the field of two-stream network in the compressed domain, there are three leading models: CoViAR [30], DMC-Net [22] and TTP [14], they have made great contributions to model compression and accuracy, but they did not fully utilize the multimodal compression information and optical flow information. Our MKAT is superior to the previous methods of two-stream network structure based on compressed domain.

## 5    Conclusions

This paper present a multi-knowledge attention transfer (MKAT) framework which can enhance the accuracy and speed of action recognition. Using the compressed domain information as the input of the temporal stream network can greatly reduce the cost of calculating the model, but they contains noise and inaccurate motion patterns, resulting in a decrease in model performance. We have devised a method to alleviate this problem by using multi-information fusion and attention enhancement techniques to significantly improve the recognition ability of the model. Meanwhile, since our methods only continuously add multiple supervised knowledge to the feature representation during training without affecting the model inference, our model does not add any additional computation during inference. The accuracy on UCF-101 and HMDB-51 datasets achieve 95.5% and 73.2%, which exceeds the current two-stream network structure based on the video compression domain.

## References

1. Ba, L.J., Caruana, R.: Do deep nets really need to be deep? arXiv preprint arXiv:1312.6184 (2013)
2. Battash, B., Barad, H., Tang, H., Bleiweiss, A.: Mimic the raw domain: accelerating action recognition in the compressed domain. In: Proceedings of the IEEE/CVF conference on computer vision and pattern recognition workshops, pp. 684–685 (2020)
3. Carreira, J., Noland, E., Hillier, C., Zisserman, A.: A short note on the kinetics-700 human action dataset. arXiv preprint arXiv:1907.06987 (2019)
4. Carreira, J., Zisserman, A.: Quo vadis, action recognition? a new model and the kinetics dataset. In: proceedings of the IEEE Conference on Computer Vision and Pattern Recognition, pp. 6299–6308 (2017)
5. Christoph, R., Pinz, F.A.: Spatiotemporal residual networks for video action recognition. Adv. Neural Inf. Process. Syst. 3468–3476 (2016)
6. Diba, A., et al.: Temporal 3d convnets: new architecture and transfer learning for video classification. arXiv preprint arXiv:1711.08200 (2017)
7. Donahue, J., et al.: Long-term recurrent convolutional networks for visual recognition and description. In: Proceedings of the IEEE Conference on Computer Vision and Pattern Recognition, pp. 2625–2634 (2015)
8. Feichtenhofer, C., Pinz, A., Wildes, R.P.: Spatiotemporal multiplier networks for video action recognition. In: Proceedings of the IEEE Conference on Computer Vision and Pattern Recognition, pp. 4768–4777 (2017)

9. Feichtenhofer, C., Pinz, A., Zisserman, A.: Convolutional two-stream network fusion for video action recognition. In: Proceedings of the IEEE Conference on Computer Vision and Pattern Recognition, pp. 1933–1941 (2016)

10. He, K., Zhang, X., Ren, S., Sun, J.: Deep residual learning for image recognition. In: Proceedings of the IEEE Conference on Computer Vision and Pattern Recognition, pp. 770–778 (2016)

11. Hinton, G., Vinyals, O., Dean, J.: Distilling the knowledge in a neural network. arXiv preprint arXiv:1503.02531 (2015)

12. Huang, S., Zhao, X., Niu, L., Zhang, L.: Static image action recognition with hallucinated fine-grained motion information. In: 2021 IEEE International Conference on Multimedia and Expo (ICME), pp. 1–6. IEEE (2021)

13. Huang, Z., Wang, N.: Like what you like: Knowledge distill via neuron selectivity transfer. arXiv preprint arXiv:1707.01219 (2017)

14. Huo, Y., Xu, X., Lu, Y., Niu, Y., Lu, Z., Wen, J.R.: Mobile video action recognition. arXiv preprint arXiv:1908.10155 (2019)

15. Kingma, D.P., Ba, J.: Adam: a method for stochastic optimization. arXiv preprint arXiv:1412.6980 (2014)

16. Krizhevsky, A., Sutskever, I., Hinton, G.E.: Imagenet classification with deep convolutional neural networks. Adv. Neural. Inf. Process. Syst. **25**, 1097–1105 (2012)

17. Kuehne, H., Jhuang, H., Garrote, E., Poggio, T., Serre, T.: HMDB: a large video database for human motion recognition. In: 2011 International Conference on Computer Vision, pp. 2556–2563. IEEE (2011)

18. Lan, Z., Zhu, Y., Hauptmann, A.G., Newsam, S.: Deep local video feature for action recognition. In: Proceedings of the IEEE Conference on Computer Vision and Pattern Recognition Workshops, pp. 1–7 (2017)

19. Li, B., Kong, L., Zhang, D., Bao, X., Huang, D., Wang, Y.: Towards practical compressed video action recognition: a temporal enhanced multi-stream network. In: 2020 25th International Conference on Pattern Recognition (ICPR), pp. 3744–3750. IEEE (2021)

20. Lin, J., Gan, C., Han, S.: Temporal shift module for efficient video understanding. 2019 IEEE. In: CVF International Conference on Computer Vision (ICCV), pp. 7082–7092 (2019)

21. Qiu, Z., Yao, T., Mei, T.: Learning spatio-temporal representation with pseudo-3d residual networks. In: proceedings of the IEEE International Conference on Computer Vision, pp. 5533–5541 (2017)

22. Shou, Z., et al.: Dmc-net: generating discriminative motion cues for fast compressed video action recognition. In: Proceedings of the IEEE/CVF Conference on Computer Vision and Pattern Recognition, pp. 1268–1277 (2019)

23. Simonyan, K., Zisserman, A.: Two-stream convolutional networks for action recognition in videos. arXiv preprint arXiv:1406.2199 (2014)

24. Soomro, K., Zamir, A.R., Shah, M.: Ucf101: a dataset of 101 human actions classes from videos in the wild. arXiv preprint arXiv:1212.0402 (2012)

25. Tran, D., Bourdev, L., Fergus, R., Torresani, L., Paluri, M.: Learning spatiotemporal features with 3d convolutional networks. In: Proceedings of the IEEE International Conference on Computer Vision, pp. 4489–4497 (2015)

26. Tran, D., Ray, J., Shou, Z., Chang, S.F., Paluri, M.: Convnet architecture search for spatiotemporal feature learning. arXiv preprint arXiv:1708.05038 (2017)

27. Wang, H., Schmid, C.: Action recognition with improved trajectories. In: Proceedings of the IEEE International Conference on Computer Vision, pp. 3551–3558 (2013)

28. Wang, K., Gao, X., Zhao, Y., Li, X., Dou, D., Xu, C.Z.: Pay attention to features, transfer learn faster CNNs. In: International Conference on Learning Representations (2019)
29. Wang, L., et al.: Temporal segment networks: towards good practices for deep action recognition. In: European Conference on Computer Vision (2016)
30. Wu, C.Y., Zaheer, M., Hu, H., Manmatha, R., Smola, A.J., Krähenbühl, P.: Compressed video action recognition. In: Proceedings of the IEEE Conference on Computer Vision and Pattern Recognition, pp. 6026–6035 (2018)
31. Wu, M.C., Chiu, C.T.: Multi-teacher knowledge distillation for compressed video action recognition based on deep learning. J. Syst. Archit. **103**, 101695 (2020)
32. Yang, K., Qiao, P., Li, D., Dou, Y.: If-TTN: Information fused temporal transformation network for video action recognition. arXiv preprint arXiv:1902.09928 (2019)
33. Yue-Hei Ng, J., Hausknecht, M., Vijayanarasimhan, S., Vinyals, O., Monga, R., Toderici, G.: Beyond short snippets: deep networks for video classification. In: Proceedings of the IEEE Conference on Computer Vision and Pattern Recognition, pp. 4694–4702 (2015)
34. Zach, C., Pock, T., Bischof, H.: A duality based approach for realtime TV-$L^1$ optical flow. In: Hamprecht, F.A., Schnörr, C., Jähne, B. (eds.) DAGM 2007. LNCS, vol. 4713, pp. 214–223. Springer, Heidelberg (2007). https://doi.org/10.1007/978-3-540-74936-3_22
35. Zagoruyko, S., Komodakis, N.: Paying more attention to attention: improving the performance of convolutional neural networks via attention transfer. arXiv preprint arXiv:1612.03928 (2016)
36. Zhang, B., Wang, L., Wang, Z., Qiao, Y., Wang, H.: Real-time action recognition with enhanced motion vector CNNs. In: Proceedings of the IEEE Conference on Computer Vision and Pattern Recognition, pp. 2718–2726 (2016)
37. Zhang, B., Wang, L., Wang, Z., Qiao, Y., Wang, H.: Real-time action recognition with deeply transferred motion vector CNNs. IEEE Trans. Image Process. **27**(5), 2326–2339 (2018)

# Multi-level Metric Learning for Few-Shot Image Recognition

Haoxing Chen⬤, Huaxiong Li(✉)⬤, Yaohui Li⬤, and Chunlin Chen⬤

Nanjing University, Nanjing, China
{haoxingchen,yaohuili}@smail.nju.edu.cn,
{huaxiongli,clchen}@nju.edu.cn

**Abstract.** Few-shot learning devotes to training a model on a few samples. Most of these approaches learn a model based on a pixel-level or global-level feature representation. However, using global features may lose local information, and using pixel-level features may lose the contextual semantics of the image. Moreover, such works can only measure their relations on a single level, which is not comprehensive and effective. And if query images can simultaneously be well classified via three distinct level similarity metrics, the query images within a class can be more tightly distributed in a smaller feature space, generating more discriminative feature maps. Motivated by this, we propose a novel Part-level Embedding Adaptation with Graph (PEAG) method to generate task-specific features. Moreover, a Multi-level Metric Learning (MML) method is proposed, which not only calculates the part-level similarity but also considers the similarity of pixel-level and global-level metrics. Extensive experiments on popular few-shot image recognition datasets prove the effectiveness of our method compared with the state-of-the-art methods. Our code is available at: https://github.com/chenhaoxing/M2L.

**Keywords:** Few-shot learning · Multi-level metic learning · Image recognition

## 1 Introduction

Humans can learn novel concepts and objects with just a few samples. Recently, many methods were proposed to learn new concepts with limited labeled data, such as semi-supervised learning [16,29,32], zero-shot learning [3,30,35], and few-shot learning [2,9,17,24,25,27]. Facing the problem of data scarcity, these three paradigms propose solutions from different perspectives. Semi-supervised learning aims to train a model with few labeled data and many unlabeled data. Zero-shot learning is devoted to identifying unseen categories with no labeled data. In contrast, few-shot learning focuses on learning new concepts with few labeled data. We propose a novel few-shot learning method to address this data scarcity problem.

The few-shot learning methods can be roughly classified into two categories: meta-learning based methods [9,26,36,37] and metric-learning based methods

© The Author(s), under exclusive license to Springer Nature Switzerland AG 2022
E. Pimenidis et al. (Eds.): ICANN 2022, LNCS 13529, pp. 243–254, 2022.
https://doi.org/10.1007/978-3-031-15919-0_21

[2,17,24,25,27]. Metric-based few-shot learning methods have achieved remarkable success due to their fewer parameters and effectiveness. In this work, we focus on this branch.

The basic idea of the metric-learning based few-shot learning method is to learn a good metric to calculate the similarity between query images and the support set. Therefore, learning good feature embedding representation and similarity metrics are the key problem of the metric-learning based few-shot learning method. For feature embedding representation, ProtoNets [25] and Relation-Nets [27] adopt global-level feature representations. However, due to the scarcity of data, it is not sufficient to measure the relation at the global-level [25,27]. Recently, CovaMNet [18], DN4 [17] and MATANet [2] introduced pixel-level representations into few-shot learning and utilized these representations to represent the image features, which can achieve better recognition results.

For similarity metrics, these existing methods calculate similarities by different metrics. For example, Relation Networks [27] proposes a network to learn the most suitable global-level similarity metric functions. DN4 [17] proposes a cosine-based image-to-class metric to measure the similarity on the pixel-level.

However, global-level features lose local semantic information, and pixel-level features lose contextual semantics. Thus all methods mentioned above are not effective for few-shot learning. Moreover, these methods only calculate similarities on a single level, i.e., pixel-level or global-level, which is not effective enough. Intuitively, the features obtained by adopting a single similarity measure are not comprehensive under the few-shot learning setting. The single similarity measure may lead to a specific similarity deviation, thus reducing the model's generalization ability. It is necessary to adopt a multi-level similarity metric, generating more discriminative features than a single measure.

To this end, we propose part-level embedding adaptation with the graph (PEAG) method and multi-level metric learning method (MML). In PEAG, we divide each image into patches and get part-level features. Since directly using part-level features for similarity calculation may be misled by the background [8], we utilize Graph Convolutional Network (GCN) [13] to generate task-specific features. Finally, we adopt a nearest neighbor matching module to get part-level similarity. In MML, we use global-level and pixel-level metrics to provide complementary information, and images within a class can be more tightly distributed in a smaller feature space.

The main contributions are summarized as follows:

(1) We propose a novel part-level embedding adaptation with the graph method, which can generate task-specific part-level features and capture the part-level semantic similarity between query images and support images.
(2) We propose a novel multi-level metric learning method by simultaneously computing the semantic similarities on pixel-level, part-level, and global-level, aiming to find more comprehensive semantic similarities.
(3) We conduct sufficient experiments on popular benchmark datasets to verify the advancement of our model and the performance of our model achieves the state-of-the-art.

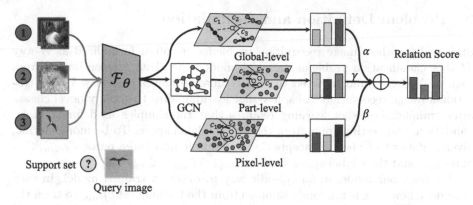

**Fig. 1.** The framework of MML under the 3-way 2-shot image classification setting. (Best view in color.)

## 2 Related Works

In this section, we focus on related works on metric-learning based few-shot learning model.

### 2.1 Learning Feature Embedding Representation

Koch et al. [14] used a Siamese Neural Network to tackle the one-shot learning problem, in which the feature extractor is of VGG styled structure, and $L_1$ distance is used to measure the similarity between query images and support images. Snell et al. [25] proposed ProtoNets, in which the Euclidean distance is used to compute the distance between class-specific prototypes. Li et al. [17] proposed an image-to-class mechanism to find the relation at the pixel-level, in which the image features are represented as a local descriptor collection.

### 2.2 Learning Similarity Metric

Sung et al. [27] replaced the existing metric with the Relation Network, which measures the similarity between each query instance and support classes. Li et al. [17] proposed a Deep Nearest Neighbor Neural Network (DN4) to learn an image-to-class metric by measuring the cosine similarity between the deep local descriptors of a query instance and its neighbors from each support class. Li et al. [18] explored the distribution consistency-based metric by introducing local covariance representation and deep covariance metric. Unlike these methods, the proposed MML measures the similarity at three different feature levels, i.e., pixel-level, part-level, and global-level.

## 3    Problem Definition and Formulation

Standard few-shot image recognition problems are often formalized as $N$-way $M$-shot classification problems, in which models are given $M$ seen images from each of $N$ classes and required to classify unseen images correctly. Unlike traditional image recognition tasks, few-shot learning aims to classify novel classes after training. Few-shot learning requires that the samples used for training, validation, and testing come from the disjoint label space. To be more specific, given a dataset of visual concepts $\mathcal{C}$, we divide it into three parts: $\mathcal{C}_{train}$, $\mathcal{C}_{val}$ and $\mathcal{C}_{test}$, and their label space satisfy $\mathcal{L}_{train} \cap \mathcal{L}_{val} \cap \mathcal{L}_{test} = \emptyset$.

We train our model in an episodic way to obtain a trained model. In each episode, a new task is randomly sampled from the training set $\mathcal{C}_{train}$ to train the current model. Each task consists of two subsets, including support set $\mathcal{A}_S$ and query set $\mathcal{A}_Q$. The $\mathcal{A}_S$ contains $\mathcal{N}$ previously unseen classes, with $\mathcal{M}$ samples for each class. We focus on training our model to determine each image correctly belongs to which category in the $\mathcal{A}_Q$. Similarly, we randomly sample tasks from $\mathcal{C}_{val}$ and $\mathcal{C}_{test}$ for meta-validation and meta-testing scenarios.

## 4    Multi-level Metric Learning

As shown in Fig. 1, our MML is mainly composed of two modules: a feature extractor $\mathcal{F}_\theta$, a multi-level metric-learning module. All images are first fed into the $\mathcal{F}_\theta$ to get feature embeddings. Then, the multi-level metric-learning module simultaneously calculates similarities on part-level, pixel-level, and global-level. Finally, we fuse these three similarities. All the modules can be trained jointly in an end-to-end manner.

### 4.1    Part-Level Metric

To obtain features containing contextual and local information, we divide each image into $H \times W$ patches evenly and input each patch into $\mathcal{F}_\theta$ separately to generate part-level descriptors. We adopt a pyramid structure to enhance the representation ability of features further. Thus, under $N$-way $M$-shot few-shot learning setting, given a query image $q$ and support class $\mathcal{S}_n, n = \{1, ..., N\}$, through $\mathcal{F}_\theta$ and global-average pooling (GAP) layer, we can get the part-level descriptors: $\mathcal{X}_q^{\mathrm{part}} \in \mathbb{R}^{C \times K}$ and $\mathcal{X}_{\mathcal{S}_n}^{\mathrm{part}} \in \mathbb{R}^{C \times MK}$. Specifically, we adopt two image patch division strategies of size $2 \times 2$ and $3 \times 3$ to obtain 13 part-level descriptors.

However, using the obtained part-level descriptors for similarity calculation may be misled by background patches [11,33]. We propose a novel part-level embedding adaptation with the graph (PEAG) method to generate task-specific support features. Specifically, we concatenate all support features and get $\mathcal{X}_{\mathcal{S}}^{\mathrm{part}} \in \mathbb{R}^{C \times NMK}$. Then, we construct the degree matrix $A \in \mathbb{R}^{NMK \times NMK}$ to represent the similarity between patches in the support set. If two patches $p_i$

and $p_j$ have the same semantics, then we set the corresponding element $A_{ij}$ to 1, otherwise to 0. Based on $A$, we build the adjacency matrix $S$:

$$S = D^{-\frac{1}{2}}(A + I)D^{-\frac{1}{2}}, \tag{1}$$

where $I \in \mathbb{R}^{NMK \times NMK}$ is the identity matrix and $D$ is the diagonal matrix ($D_{ii} = \sum_j A_{ij} + 1$). Let $\Psi^0 = \mathcal{X}_{\mathcal{S}}^{\text{part}}$, the relationship between patches could be propagated based on $S$:

$$\Psi^{t+1} = \text{ReLU}(S\Psi^t W), t = \{0, ..., T-1\}, \tag{2}$$

where $W$ is a learned feature transformation matrix. After propagate the embedding set $T$ times, we can get the final propagated embedding set $\Psi^T = \mathcal{X}_{\mathcal{S}'}^{\text{part}}$.

Then, for each class $\mathcal{X}_{\mathcal{S}_n}^{\text{part}}$, we calculate the correlation matrix $R^{\text{part}} \in \mathbb{R}^{K \times MK}$ between the query image and the support class $n$ on part-level:

$$\mathcal{R}^{\text{part}} = \frac{(\mathcal{X}_q^{\text{part}})^\top \mathcal{X}_{\mathcal{S}'_n}^{\text{part}}}{\left\|\mathcal{X}_q^{\text{part}}\right\| \cdot \left\|\mathcal{X}_{\mathcal{S}_n}^{\text{part}}\right\|}, \tag{3}$$

$\mathcal{R}_{i,j}^{\text{part}}$ is $(i, j)$ element of $\mathcal{R}^{\text{part}}$ reflecting the distance between the $i$-th descriptor of the query image and the $j$-th descriptor of support class $n$. Each row in $\mathcal{R}^{\text{part}}$ represents the semantic relation of each descriptor in the query image to all descriptors in the support class. For each patch of the query image $q$, we find its most similar descriptor. Then, we sum $K$ selected part-level descriptors as the part-level similarity between the query image and the support class $n$:

$$\mathcal{D}_{\text{part}}(q, \mathcal{S}_n) = \sum_{i=1}^{K} \text{Top1}(\mathcal{R}_i^{\text{part}}), \tag{4}$$

where $\text{Top1}(\cdot)$ means selecting the largest elements in each row of the $R^{\text{part}}$.

## 4.2  Pixel-Level Metric

Following [2,17,18], given a query image $q$ and a certain support class $\mathcal{S}_n$, through feature extractor $\mathcal{F}_\theta$, we can get the feature representation $\mathcal{F}_\theta(q) \in \mathbb{R}^{C \times H \times W}$ and $\mathcal{F}_\theta(\mathcal{S}_n) \in \mathbb{R}^{M \times C \times H \times W}$, respectively. The $\mathcal{F}_\theta(q)$ can be regard as a set of $H \times W$ $C$-dimensional pixel-level features:

$$\mathcal{L}_q^{\text{pixel}} = [u_1^{\text{pixel}}, ..., u_{HW}^{\text{pixel}}] \in \mathbb{R}^{C \times HW}, \tag{5}$$

Also, the $\mathcal{F}_\theta(\mathcal{S}_n)$ can be regards as

$$\mathcal{L}_{\mathcal{S}_n}^{\text{pixel}} = [v_1^{\text{pixel}}, ..., v_{MHW}^{\text{pixel}}] \in \mathbb{R}^{C \times MHW}. \tag{6}$$

In common with part-level metrics, we calculate the correlation matrix $R^{\text{pixel}} \in \mathbb{R}^{HW \times MHW}$ between the query image and the support class on pixel-level and select the largest element in each row of the correlation matrix:

$$\mathcal{R}^{\text{pixel}} = \frac{(u_i^{\text{pixel}})^\top v_j^{\text{pixel}}}{\left\|u_i^{\text{pixel}}\right\| \cdot \left\|v_j^{\text{pixel}}\right\|}, \tag{7}$$

$$\mathcal{D}_{\text{pixel}}(q, \mathcal{S}_n) = \sum_{i=1}^{HW} \text{Top1}(\mathcal{R}_i^{\text{pixel}}). \tag{8}$$

### 4.3 Global-Level Metric

We adopt ProtoNets [25] as a global-level similarity metric. ProtoNets computes the empirical mean of global convolution embeddings as the prototype representation of each category $n$:

$$c_n = \frac{1}{M} \sum_{M}^{i=1} \text{GAP}(\mathcal{F}_\theta(\mathcal{S}_n^i)), \tag{9}$$

where $c_n \in \mathbb{R}^C$. Similarly, given a query image $Q$, we can get its global convolution embeddings $\mathcal{X}_Q^{\text{global}} \in \mathbb{R}^K$. Then, ProtoNets utilized Euclidean distance as the distance metric and assigns a probability over class $n$:

$$\mathcal{D}_{\text{global}}(q, \mathcal{S}_n) = -||\mathcal{X}_Q^{\text{global}} - c_n||^2. \tag{10}$$

### 4.4 Fusion Layer

Since three different level similarities have been calculated, we need to design a fusion module to integrate them. Specifically, the final similarity and probability over any class $n$ can be obtained by the following equation:

$$P_{part}(y = n|q) = \frac{\mathcal{D}_{part}(q, \mathcal{S}_n)}{\sum_{i=1}^{N} \mathcal{D}_{part}(q, \mathcal{S}_n)}, \tag{11}$$

$$P_{pixel}(y = n|q) = \frac{\mathcal{D}_{pixel}(q, \mathcal{S}_n)}{\sum_{i=1}^{N} \mathcal{D}_{pixel}(q, \mathcal{S}_n)}, \tag{12}$$

$$P_{global}(y = n|q) = \frac{\mathcal{D}_{global}(q, \mathcal{S}_n)}{\sum_{i=1}^{N} \mathcal{D}_{global}(q, \mathcal{S}_n)}, \tag{13}$$

$$P(y = n|q) = \alpha P_{part}(y = n|q) + \beta P_{global}(y = n|q) + \gamma P_{pixel}(y = n|q), \tag{14}$$

where $y$ is the label of $q$, $\alpha$, $\beta$ and $\gamma$ are superparameters. If $y = n'$, then we can define the loss function as follows:

$$\mathcal{L} = -\alpha log(p_{part}(y = n'|q)) - \beta log(p_{pixel}(y = n'|q)) - \gamma log(p_{global}(y = n'|q)). \tag{15}$$

**Table 1.** Comparison with other state-of-the-art methods with 95% confidence intervals on miniImageNet and tieredImageNet. (Top two performances are in bold font.)

| Model | Backbone | miniImageNet | | tieredImageNet | |
|-------|----------|--------------|------------|----------------|------------|
| | | 1-shot | 5-shot | 1-shot | 5-shot |
| MatchingNets [28] | ResNet-12 | $63.08 \pm 0.80$ | $75.99 \pm 0.60$ | $68.50 \pm 0.92$ | $80.60 \pm 0.71$ |
| ProtoNets [25] | ResNet-12 | $62.59 \pm 0.85$ | $78.60 \pm 0.16$ | $68.37 \pm 0.23$ | $83.43 \pm 0.16$ |
| CAN [11] | ResNet-12 | $63.85 \pm 0.48$ | $79.44 \pm 0.34$ | $\mathbf{69.89 \pm 0.51}$ | $84.23 \pm 0.37$ |
| DN4 [17] | ResNet-12 | $64.84 \pm 0.82$ | $77.74 \pm 0.61$ | $69.60 \pm 0.89$ | $83.41 \pm 0.67$ |
| TADAM [20] | ResNet-12 | $58.50 \pm 0.30$ | $76.70 \pm 0.30$ | - | - |
| MeaOptNet [15] | ResNet-12 | $62.64 \pm 0.61$ | $78.63 \pm 0.46$ | $65.99 \pm 0.72$ | $81.56 \pm 0.53$ |
| AM3 [31] | ResNet-12 | $65.30 \pm 0.49$ | $78.10 \pm 0.36$ | $69.08 \pm 0.47$ | $82.58 \pm 0.31$ |
| TAPNet [34] | ResNet-12 | $61.65 \pm 0.15$ | $76.36 \pm 0.10$ | $63.08 \pm 0.15$ | $80.26 \pm 0.12$ |
| DSN-MR [24] | ResNet-12 | $64.60 \pm 0.72$ | $79.51 \pm 0.50$ | $67.39 \pm 0.82$ | $82.85 \pm 0.56$ |
| FEAT [33] | ResNet-12 | $66.78 \pm 0.20$ | $\mathbf{82.05 \pm 0.14}$ | $67.39 \pm 0.82$ | $82.85 \pm 0.56$ |
| GLoFA [19] | ResNet-12 | $66.12 \pm 0.42$ | $81.37 \pm 0.33$ | $69.75 \pm 0.33$ | $83.58 \pm 0.42$ |
| Meta-baseline [4] | ResNet-12 | $63.17 \pm 0.23$ | $79.26 \pm 0.17$ | $68.62 \pm 0.27$ | $83.74 \pm 0.18$ |
| Fine-tuning [9] | WRN-28-10 | $57.73 \pm 0.62$ | $78.17 \pm 0.49$ | $66.58 \pm 0.70$ | $\mathbf{85.55 \pm 0.48}$ |
| AWGIM [10] | WRN-28-10 | $63.12 \pm 0.08$ | $78.40 \pm 0.11$ | $67.69 \pm 0.11$ | $82.82 \pm 0.13$ |
| PSST [5] | WRN-28-10 | $64.16 \pm 0.44$ | $80.64 \pm 0.32$ | - | - |
| **PEAG** | ResNet-12 | $\mathbf{67.29 \pm 0.23}$ | $78.49 \pm 0.21$ | $68.89 \pm 0.25$ | $82.08 \pm 0.21$ |
| **MML** | ResNet-12 | $\mathbf{67.58 \pm 0.23}$ | $\mathbf{81.41 \pm 0.20}$ | $\mathbf{71.38 \pm 0.25}$ | $\mathbf{84.65 \pm 0.20}$ |

## 5   Experiments

In this section, we perform extensive experiments to verify the advance and effectiveness of MML.

### 5.1   Datasets

To verify the advance and effectiveness of our proposed MML, we performed experiments on four benchmark datasets.

**ImageNet Derivatives:** Both miniImageNet dataset and tieredImageNet dataset are subsets of ImageNet [6]. The miniImageNet [28] dataset consists 100 classes, each of which contains 600 samples. We follow the standard partition settings [25], where there are 64/16/20 categories for training, validation and evaluation. tieredImageNet [23] contains 608 classes. All 608 categories are grouped into 34 broader categories. Following the same partition settings [11], we use 20/6/8 broader categories for training, validation, and evaluation respectively.

**CIFAR Derivatives:** Both CIFAR-FS [1] dataset and FC100 [20] dataset are subsets of CIFAR-100. Both of them consist of 100 classes. The CIFAR-FS is divided into 64, 16, and 20 for training, validation, and evaluation. And the FC100 uses a split similar to tieredImageNet, where train, validation, and test splits contain 60, 20, and 20 classes.

**Table 2.** Experimental results compared with other methods on CIFAR-FS and FC100. (Top two performances are in bold font.)

| Model | Backbone | CIFAR-FS | | FC100 | |
|---|---|---|---|---|---|
| | | 1-shot | 5-shot | 1-shot | 5-shot |
| ProtoNets [25] | Conv-64F | $55.50 \pm 0.70$ | $72.00 \pm 0.60$ | $35.30 \pm 0.60$ | $48.60 \pm 0.60$ |
| RelationNets [27] | Conv-256F | $55.00 \pm 1.00$ | $69.30 \pm 0.80$ | - | - |
| R2D2 [1] | Conv-512F | $65.30 \pm 0.20$ | $79.40 \pm 0.10$ | - | - |
| ProtoNets [25] | ResNet-12 | $72.20 \pm 0.70$ | $83.50 \pm 0.50$ | $37.50 \pm 0.60$ | $52.50 \pm 0.60$ |
| ShotFree [22] | ResNet-12 | $69.20 \pm 0.00$ | $84.7 \pm 0.00$ | - | - |
| TEAM [21] | ResNet-12 | $64.07 \pm 0.00$ | $79.05 \pm 0.00$ | - | - |
| TADAM [20] | ResNet-12 | - | - | $40.10 \pm 0.40$ | $56.10 \pm 0.40$ |
| MeaOptNet [15] | ResNet-12 | $72.60 \pm 0.70$ | $84.30 \pm 0.50$ | $41.10 \pm 0.60$ | $55.50 \pm 0.60$ |
| MABAS [12] | ResNet-12 | $73.51 \pm 0.92$ | $85.49 \pm 0.68$ | $42.31 \pm 0.75$ | $57.56 \pm 0.78$ |
| Fine-tuning [7] | WRN-28-10 | $\mathbf{76.58 \pm 0.68}$ | $\mathbf{85.79 \pm 0.50}$ | $43.16 \pm 0.59$ | $\mathbf{57.57 \pm 0.55}$ |
| **PEAG** | ResNet-12 | $74.27 \pm 0.23$ | $83.89 \pm 0.20$ | $\mathbf{43.99 \pm 0.21}$ | $56.47 \pm 0.24$ |
| **MML** | ResNet-12 | $\mathbf{75.28 \pm 0.23}$ | $\mathbf{85.95 \pm 0.19}$ | $\mathbf{44.43 \pm 0.21}$ | $\mathbf{59.56 \pm 0.25}$ |

## 5.2 Implementation Details

**Backbone.** In order to make a fair comparison with other works, we adopt the ResNet-12 network [15] as our feature extractor $\mathcal{F}_\theta$. ResNet-12 has four residual blocks, each residual block has three convolutional layers with $3 \times 3$ kernel, and a $2 \times 2$ max-pooling layer is added in the first residual block.

**Patching Dividing Details.** We select various grids and their combinations (see Fig. 2). To generate dense pyramid features, we add a global average pooling layer at the end of the backbone, such that the backbone generates a vector for each input image patch. Moreover, we slightly expand the area of the local patches in the grid twice to merge the context information, which helps generate the local representations.

**Training Details.** We conduct our experiments on a series of $N$-way $M$-shot tasks, i.e., 5-way 1-shot and 5-way 5-shot. Following [33], we first pre-trained $\mathcal{F}_\theta$ with an MLP consisting of a single hidden layer. Then we meta-train the whole model by momentum SGD for 40 epochs. In each epoch, we randomly sampled 200 tasks. Our batch size is set to 4, and the initial learning rate is $5 \times 10^{-4}$, multiplied by 0.5 every ten epochs. We report the average accuracy and the corresponding 95% confidence interval during the test stage over these 10,000 tasks.

## 5.3 Comparison Against Related Approaches

**Results on ImageNet Derivatives.** As seen from Table 1, our MML achieves the highest accuracy on miniImageNet with 67.58% and 81.41% on 5-way 1-shot and 5-way 5-shot tasks, respectively, which make a great improvement compared

**Table 3.** Ablation study on miniImageNet and tieredImageNet.

| $\alpha$ | $\beta$ | $\gamma$ | miniImageNet | | tieredImageNet | |
|---|---|---|---|---|---|---|
| | | | 1-shot | 5-shot | 1-shot | 5-shot |
| 1 | 0 | 0 | $67.29 \pm 0.23$ | $78.49 \pm 0.21$ | $71.04 \pm 0.24$ | $81.59 \pm 0.21$ |
| 0 | 1 | 0 | $64.12 \pm 0.23$ | $78.55 \pm 0.21$ | $68.02 \pm 0.24$ | $82.67 \pm 0.23$ |
| 0 | 0 | 1 | $61.86 \pm 0.24$ | $79.03 \pm 0.21$ | $65.95 \pm 0.23$ | $82.39 \pm 0.21$ |
| 1 | 1 | 0 | $66.85 \pm 0.23$ | $80.52 \pm 0.20$ | $69.73 \pm 0.23$ | $83.47 \pm 0.20$ |
| 1 | 0 | 1 | $61.65 \pm 0.24$ | $78.87 \pm 0.21$ | $66.82 \pm 0.23$ | $82.20 \pm 0.20$ |
| 0 | 1 | 1 | $61.95 \pm 0.24$ | $78.85 \pm 0.21$ | $67.35 \pm 0.23$ | $82.05 \pm 0.20$ |
| 1 | 1 | 1 | $64.77 \pm 0.23$ | $79.93 \pm 0.20$ | $69.86 \pm 0.22$ | $83.02 \pm 0.19$ |
| 1 | 0.5 | 0.5 | $66.72 \pm 0.23$ | $81.01 \pm 0.20$ | $70.54 \pm 0.22$ | $84.19 \pm 0.19$ |
| 1 | 0.1 | 0.1 | $\mathbf{67.58 \pm 0.23}$ | $\mathbf{81.41 \pm 0.20}$ | $\mathbf{71.38 \pm 0.25}$ | $\mathbf{84.65 \pm 0.20}$ |

to the previous single-level metric-learning based methods. For example, our MML is 4.6% and 8.0% better than DSN-MR [24] and ProtoNets [25] on the 5-way 1-shot task, respectively. And our MML achieves 71.38% and 84.65% on tieredImageNet under 5-way 1-shot and 5-way 5-shot few-shot learning settings, respectively, achieving competitive performance.

**Results on CIFAR Derivatives.** Table 2 evaluates our method on two CIFAR derivatives, i.e., CIFAR-FS and FC100. It can be seen that the proposed MML obtains significant improvements compared with previous state-of-the-art methods. Specifically, compared with global-level metric-learning based methods (i.e., Relation Networks [27], ProtoNets [25] and Fine-tuning [7]), MML is 20.3% and 3.5% better than the best one of them on CIFAR-FS and FC100 under 5-way 5-shot setting.

Moreover, we can also see that the proposed PEAG achieved competitive results. For example, our PEAG is 0.8% and 1.8% better than FEAT [33] and GLoFA [19] on miniImageNet under the 5-way 1-shot setting, respectively.

The reason why our MML can achieve these state-of-the-art performances is that MML can measure the semantic similarities on multiple levels, i.e., part-level, pixel-level, and global-level.

# 6 Discussion

## 6.1 Ablation Study

To explore the effect of the multi-level metric learning module, we prune any of three similarity branches in the multi-level metric-learning module. Specifically, we change the values of $\alpha$, $\beta$, and $\gamma$, and experiment on miniImageNet and tieredImageNet.

As seen in Table 3, each part of the MML is indispensable. It can be observed that the accuracy of few-shot image recognition using only one level of features is very low. The results were significantly improved when two or three levels of features were used together, and the results were best when all three levels were used together. Specifically, compared with the method that only uses pixel-level features, our MML gains 5.4%/4.4% and 3.7%/2.4% improvements on miniImageNet and tieredImageNet under 1-shot/5-shot settings, respectively. Note that it is essential to choose the appropriate hyperparameters. When $\beta$ and $\gamma$ become larger, the accuracy of the model will become worse. Appropriate $\beta$ and $\gamma$ can provide useful auxiliary information for part-level metrics.

**Table 4.** Computation time.

| Method | Time (s) |
|---|---|
| ProtoNets [25] | 0.065 |
| CAN [11] | 0.069 |
| FEAT [33] | 0.092 |
| DN4 [33] | 0.060 |
| MML | 0.227 |
| MML* | 0.082 |

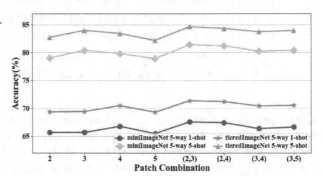

**Fig. 2.** Influence of patch combination.

## 6.2 Time Complexity

$10^4$ forward inferences average the computation time on miniImageNet under the 5-way 1-shot setting. As shown in Table 4, the training and inference of MML come with more computation costs. After the experiment, we found that most of our time was spent on the step of dividing the image into patches, so we pre-divided the image into patches (see MML*).

## 6.3 Influence of Patch Combination

While dividing input images into patches, we have to define the grid for patches. We select various grids and their combinations and conduct analysis experiments on miniImageNet and tieredImageNet. As shown in Fig. 2, it is better to use a combination of grids of different sizes. A possible explanation is that the size of the main object in different images is different, and using a single size may lose context information, making it challenging to generate high-level semantic representations.

## 7 Conclusion

In this paper, we revisit the metric-learning based method and proposed novel Part-level Embedding Adaptation with Graph (PEAG) method and Multi-level

Metric Learning (MML) method for few-shot image recognition, aiming to capture more comprehensive semantic similarities. Specifically, PEAG can generate task-specific part-level features and capture the part-level semantic similarity between query images and support images. MML can measure semantic similarities on multiple levels and produce more discriminative features. Extensive experiments show the effectiveness and the superiority of both PEAG and MML.

**Acknolewdgement.** This work was partially supported by the National Natural Science Foundation of China (Nos. 62176116, 62073160, 71732003), and the Natural Science Foundation of the Jiangsu Higher Education Institutions of China, No. 20KJA520006.

# References

1. Bertinetto, L., Henriques, J.F., Torr, P.H.S., Vedaldi, A.: Meta-learning with differentiable closed-form solvers. In: ICLR (2019)
2. Chen, H., Li, H., Li, Y., Chen, C.: Multi-scale adaptive task attention network for few-shot learning. In: ICPR (2022)
3. Chen, S., et al.: MSDN: mutually semantic distillation network for zero-shot learning. In: CVPR (2022)
4. Chen, Y., Liu, Z., Xu, H., Darrell, T., Wang, X.: Meta-baseline: exploring simple meta-learning for few-shot learning. In: ICCV, pp. 9042–9051 (2021)
5. Chen, Z., Ge, J., Zhan, H., Huang, S., Wang, D.: Pareto self-supervised training for few-shot learning (2021)
6. Deng, J., Dong, W., Socher, R., Li, L., Li, K., Li, F.: ImageNet: a large-scale hierarchical image database. In: CVPR, pp. 248–255 (2009)
7. Dhillon, G.S., Chaudhari, P., Ravichandran, A., Soatto, S.: A baseline for few-shot image classification. In: ICLR (2020)
8. Dong, B., Zhou, P., Yan, S., Zuo, W.: Self-promoted supervision for few-shot transformer
9. Finn, C., Abbeel, P., Levine, S.: Model-agnostic meta-learning for fast adaptation of deep networks. In: ICML, vol. 70, pp. 1126–1135 (2017)
10. Guo, Y., Cheung, N.: Attentive weights generation for few shot learning via information maximization. In: CVPR, pp. 13496–13505 (2020)
11. Hou, R., Chang, H., Ma, B., Shan, S., Chen, X.: Cross attention network for few-shot classification. In: NeurIPS, pp. 4005–4016 (2019)
12. Kim, J., Kim, H., Kim, G.: Model-agnostic boundary-adversarial sampling for test-time generalization in few-shot learning. In: Vedaldi, A., Bischof, H., Brox, T., Frahm, J.-M. (eds.) ECCV 2020. LNCS, vol. 12346, pp. 599–617. Springer, Cham (2020). https://doi.org/10.1007/978-3-030-58452-8_35
13. Kipf, T.N., Welling, M.: Semi-supervised classification with graph convolutional networks. In: ICLR (2017)
14. Koch, G., Zemel, R., Salakhutdinov, R.: Siamese neural networks for one-shot image recognition. In: ICML Workshops, vol. 2 (2015)
15. Lee, K., Maji, S., Ravichandran, A., Soatto, S.: Meta-learning with differentiable convex optimization. In: CVPR, pp. 10657–10665 (2019)
16. Li, J., Xiong, C., Hoi, S.C.H.: Comatch: semi-supervised learning with contrastive graph regularization. In: ICCV, pp. 9455–9464 (2021)

17. Li, W., Wang, L., Xu, J., Huo, J., Gao, Y., Luo, J.: Revisiting local descriptor based image-to-class measure for few-shot learning. In: CVPR, pp. 7260–7268 (2019)
18. Li, W., Xu, J., Huo, J., Wang, L., Gao, Y., Luo, J.: Distribution consistency based covariance metric networks for few-shot learning. In: AAAI, pp. 8642–8649 (2019)
19. Lu, S., Ye, H., Zhan, D.: Tailoring embedding function to heterogeneous few-shot tasks by global and local feature adaptors. In: AAAI, pp. 8776–8783 (2021)
20. Oreshkin, B.N., López, P.R., Lacoste, A.: TADAM: task dependent adaptive metric for improved few-shot learning. In: NeurIPS, pp. 719–729 (2018)
21. Qiao, L., Shi, Y., Li, J., Tian, Y., Huang, T., Wang, Y.: Transductive episodic-wise adaptive metric for few-shot learning. In: ICCV, pp. 3602–3611 (2019)
22. Ravichandran, A., Bhotika, R., Soatto, S.: Few-shot learning with embedded class models and shot-free meta training. In: ICCV, pp. 331–339 (2019)
23. Ren, M., et al.: Meta-learning for semi-supervised few-shot classification. In: ICLR (2018)
24. Simon, C., Koniusz, P., Nock, R., Harandi, M.: Adaptive subspaces for few-shot learning. In: CVPR, pp. 4135–4144 (2020)
25. Snell, J., Swersky, K., Zemel, R.S.: Prototypical networks for few-shot learning. In: NeurIPS, pp. 4077–4087 (2017)
26. Sun, Q., Liu, Y., Chua, T., Schiele, B.: Meta-transfer learning for few-shot learning. In: CVPR, pp. 403–412 (2019)
27. Sung, F., Yang, Y., Zhang, L., Xiang, T., Torr, P.H.S., Hospedales, T.M.: Learning to compare: relation network for few-shot learning. In: CVPR, pp. 1199–1208 (2018)
28. Vinyals, O., Blundell, C., Lillicrap, T., Kavukcuoglu, K., Wierstra, D.: Matching networks for one shot learning. In: NeurIPS, pp. 3630–3638 (2016)
29. Wang, Y., Khan, S., Gonzalez-Garcia, A., van de Weijer, J., Khan, F.S.: Semi-supervised learning for few-shot image-to-image translation. In: CVPR, pp. 4452–4461 (2020)
30. Wu, J., Zhang, T., Zha, Z., Luo, J., Zhang, Y., Wu, F.: Self-supervised domain-aware generative network for generalized zero-shot learning. In: CVPR, pp. 12764–12773 (2020)
31. Xing, C., Rostamzadeh, N., Oreshkin, B.N., Pinheiro, P.O.: Adaptive cross-modal few-shot learning. In: NeurIPS, pp. 4848–4858 (2019)
32. Xu, M., et al.: End-to-end semi-supervised object detection with soft teacher. In: ICCV, pp. 3040–3049 (2021)
33. Ye, H.J., Hu, H., Zhan, D.C., Sha, F.: Few-shot learning via embedding adaptation with set-to-set functions. In: CVPR, pp. 8808–8817 (2020)
34. Yoon, S.W., Seo, J., Moon, J.: TapNet: neural network augmented with task-adaptive projection for few-shot learning. In: ICML, vol. 97, pp. 7115–7123 (2019)
35. Yu, Y., Ji, Z., Han, J., Zhang, Z.: Episode-based prototype generating network for zero-shot learning. In: CVPR, pp. 14032–14041 (2020)
36. Zhang, C., Ding, H., Lin, G., Li, R., Wang, C., Shen, C.: Meta navigator: search for a good adaptation policy for few-shot learning. In: ICCV, pp. 9415–9424 (2021)
37. Zhang, X., Meng, D., Gouk, H., Hospedales, T.M.: Shallow Bayesian meta learning for real-world few-shot recognition. In: ICCV, pp. 631–640 (2021)

# Multistage Diagnosis of Alzheimer's Disease Based on Slice Attention Network

Xiaolai Huo[1], Chung-Ming Own[1(✉)], Yue Zhou[1], Nannan Wu[1],
and Jianwen Sun[2]

[1] Tianjin University, Tianjin, China
chungming.own@tju.edu.cn
[2] Tianjin University of Technology, Tianjin, China

**Abstract.** Alzheimer's disease (AD) is a latent progressive neurodegenerative disease. Early detection can prevent further damage to patient's health. We proposed a 3D abnormal perception depth residual network based on the squeeze and excitation module (RSE) and recurrent slice attention module (RSA). In our model, RSE captures the importance of different channels by integrating extrusion and excitation modules into residual blocks, while RSA aims to model 3D MRI images as slice sequences to capture the long-term dependence of different slices in different directions. Our model combine the context information of the abnormal area with local and spatial information. Experimental results show that the accuracy of our method is 87.5%, which is better than the most advanced model in terms of normal cognition (NC), early mild cognitive impairment (EMCI), late mild cognitive impairment (LMCI) and Alzheimer's disease (AD) on the ADNI dataset. The CAM visualization results also show that our method can successfully highlight the most contributing regions of 3D MRI images.

**Keywords:** Alzheimer's disease · Deep learning · Attention mechanism

## 1 Introduction

Alzheimer's Disease (AD) is one of the most common chronic neurodegenerative diseases characterized by memory decay and other neurological impairment. Early intervention can effectively slow the progression of AD [4]. Traditional AD's classification method which is based on the 2D slicing method often causes CNN to ignore the spatial 3D information. Therefore, some studies focus on 3D processing rather than 2D CNN. For example, the 3D patch-based approach divides the whole brain image into several patches [7,9,35]. However, the weaknesses are slow to train and ignoring the entire brain structure information. Furthermore, the whole-brain-based 3D CNN claims to capture consecutive slices' dependencies [3,33].

In our study, we design an abnormal-aware 3D deep CNN incorporating the original data's structural features to classify four stages of AD, including cognitively normal (NC), early mild cognitive impairment (EMCI), late mild cognitive impairment (LMCI), and AD on the ADNI dataset. The main contributions of this paper are as follows:

(1) We designed the 3D squeeze and excitation residual blocks for AD classification to capture the interdependencies between feature channels.
(2) The slice attention module can effectively capture long-range dependencies among slices from different orientations [37].
(3) Our model only uses 600 sMRI data for training. The proposed model can classify different stages of AD and exceeds the existing deep learning methods.

The rest of the manuscript is organized as follows: Sect. 2 review the related works; Sect. 3 illustrates the system model. The experiments are testified and concluded in Sect. 4, finally, Sect. 5 summarizes the content and discusses the future researches.

## 2    Related Work

The most commonly used feature extraction methods for neuroimaging data can divide into the following four categories: 1) Voxel-based methods; 2) Regions of interest-based methods; 3) Patch-based methods; 4) Deep learning methods.

### 2.1    Voxel-Based Methods

Ashburner et al. formally proposed the voxel-based approach, which is a morphometric method in voxels to detect localized brain features and differences in brain composition [2]. In addition to voxel-based methods (VBM), other methods such as deformation-based morphometry (DBM) and tensor-based morphometry (TBM) have shown to be effective in AD classification [2].

### 2.2    Regions of Interest-Based Methods

Region of interest-based methods in [24], most of these methods are based on a prior knowledge [5,29]. Liu et al. proposed a multimodal neuroimaging feature learning algorithm based on SAE to learn feature representations from ROI-based features for AD diagnosis [29]. However, the expressive power of features by ROI is limited.

### 2.3    Patch-Based Methods

Patch-based method decomposed brain regions into small 3D patches and extracted features from each selected patch separately [22]. Suket et al. used a multimodal depth-constrained Boltzmann machine (RBM) to learn features from huge 3D patches [30]. Besides, Payan and Montana combined sparse autoencoders and convolutional neural networks to learn feature representations from local patches for AD prediction [27]. However, the features extracted by these patch-based methods ignore that other regions are also affected.

## 2.4   Deep Learning Methods

**CNN-Based Methods.** Recently deep learning methods are popular in the medical field. Ali Nawaz et al. proposed a 2D CNN to diagnose AD using an imbalanced 3D MRI dataset [26]. Besides, Maqsood et al. used transfer learning to classify images by fine-tuning the pre-trained AlexNet [25]. Juan et al. proposed three 3D DenseNet with different hyper parameters to classify MR images [28]. Finally, used a probability-based fusion method to obtain the final classification $\alpha$, which is defined as follows,

$$a = \arg\max \left( \prod_{i=1}^{c} \beta_1^i, \prod_{i=1}^{c} \beta_2^i, \prod_{i=1}^{c} \beta_4^i, \prod_{i=1}^{c} \beta_4^i \right), \tag{1}$$

where $\beta_n^i$ indicates the probabilities of the class $n$.

**Self Attention to Complement CNNs.** Recently, researchers have tried to apply the attention modules to CNN to improve the model's performance. These attention modules mainly include channel attention module [14,17,20], spatial attention module [34], and self-attention module [15]. Meanwhile, some studies use visualization to explain the model. Class activation mapping (CAM) and gradient-weighted class activation mapping (Grad-CAM) are two popular explainable method for CNN [38]. They can identify the image areas with the most relevance to a particular category.

   The self-attention function can describe as mapping queries, keys, and values to inputs, and the self-attention map can derive as follows:

$$\text{Key: } f(x) = W_f x,$$
$$\text{Query: } g(x) = W_g x, \tag{2}$$
$$\text{Value: } h(x) = W_h x,$$

and

$$a_{i,j} = \frac{\exp\left( f(x_i)^T g(x_j) \right)}{\sum_{i=1}^{n} \exp\left( f(x_i)^T g(x_j) \right)}, \tag{3}$$

where $a_{i,j}$ denotes the degree of relevant attention between each region $i$ and all other regions. Although the application of the attention mechanism on CNN improves the accuracy, the limit is that such kind of model does not consider the characteristics of MRI data and the relationships between slices.

## 3   Method

This section aims to build a tool for automatically performing AD diagnosis. Figure 1 represents the overall framework of our proposed model. Given a 3D sMRI image, depth features are extracted by four residual blocks with residual connection. We integrate 3D squeeze and activation structure [17] in the residual block. The sizes of the feature maps in the four Residual SE are $64 \times 64 \times 64$, $32 \times 32 \times 32$, $16 \times 16 \times 16$, and $8 \times 8 \times 8$. Then slice attention is inserted to capture the importance between different slices. Finally, global average pooling was performed to compress the features into vectors for the next classification step. The classification includes four categories: normal healthy control group (NC), early MCI (EMCI), late MCI (LMCI) and Alzheimer's disease (AD).

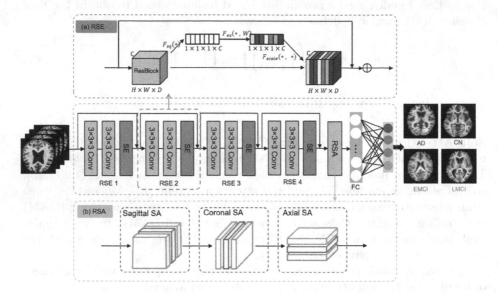

**Fig. 1.** The architecture of 3D residual deep Neural Network with Slice attention. (a) RSE: 3D Residual Squeeze-and-Excitation Block (b) RSA: Recurrent Slice Attention block.

### 3.1  3D Residual Squeeze-and-Excitation Block (RSE)

Traditional neural networks have the problem of gradient explosion or gradient disappearance as the network level deepens. We use 3D ResNet to solve this problem [16]. The Attention Mechanism can focus on essential regions and suppress unnecessary information by learning a weight matrix throughout the image. The channel attention SE is initially helpful in this study. Our proposed 3D RSE model includes the following two layers,
1) Residual network layer:
A residual network can be defined as follows:

$$x^{res} = x + F_{res}(x),\tag{4}$$

where $x^{res}$ is the output of the residual module, $x$ is the input and $F_{res}(x)$ is the residual function. This layer includes two Conv3D blocks consisting of $3 \times 3 \times 3$ 3D convolution layers, 3D batch normalization and rectified-linear-unit nonlinearity layer (ReLU).

2) SE layer:

The SE layer is appended to each residual block. As shown in Fig. 1(a), the SE layer can be described as a three-step compression operation, the first step $F_{sq}$ compresses the spatial dimension of the feature map of with a size of $C \times W \times H \times D$ after $1 \times 1 \times 1 \times 1$ convolution to obtain a $1 \times 1 \times 1 \times 1$ feature vector, that is,

$$U = F_{sq}(x^{res}) = \frac{1}{D \times H \times W} \sum_{i=1}^{D} \sum_{j=1}^{H} \sum_{k=1}^{W} x^{res}(i, j, k), \qquad (5)$$

where $U = [u_1, u_2, ..., u_c]$. $D$, $H$ and $W$ represent the number of slices, height and width respectively. Furthermore, the second step $F_{ex}$ is an activation operation to perform a series of nonlinear operators on the obtained feature maps to get the corresponding weights for each channel. Thus, the operator is

$$s = F_{ex}(u, W) = \sigma(W_2 \delta(W_1 u)), \qquad (6)$$

where $\sigma(.)$ denotes the sigmoid activation function, $\delta(.)$ represents the ReLU function, and $W_1$, $W_2$ denote the weights. Finally, there is a reweight operation $F_{scale}$,

$$x^{se} = F_{scale}(u_i, s_i) = u_i s_i, \qquad (7)$$

that is, the weight of the output of Excitation is considered as the importance of each feature channel after feature selection, then a channel-wised multiplication between each excitation scalar and the feature map is to generate the final rescaling feature output.

The final output of the RSE Block Y is given by:

$$Y = \delta(x^{se} + x), \qquad (8)$$

## 3.2   Slice Attention Block (SA)

Our proposed slice attention module can learn the correlation between slices in different directions and highlight the features of key regions. The SA block is divided into three branches. In these three branches, the input features are gathered into three feature spaces $f$, $g$, and $h$ as shown in Eq. 2 and the channels of feature maps $f(x)$, $g(x)$, and $h(x)$ are the same. Accordingly, the feature maps are arranged into $f'(x) \in \mathbb{R}^{CHW \times D}$ and $g'(x) \in \mathbb{R}^{D \times CHW}$ by transposing and deforming the matrix. After that, a matrix multiplication between $f'(x)$ and $g'(x)$ is applied to get the slice-wise attention map $A$, that is,

$$A_{ij} = \frac{\exp(g'(x_i) f(x_j))}{\sum_{k=1}^{D} \exp(g'(x_i) f'(x_k))}, \qquad (9)$$

where $A_{ij} \in \mathbb{R}^{D \times D}$ represents the influence of $j^{th}$ slices on $i^{th}$ slices. In the last branch, feature map $h'(x)$ is attended to $A$ by the other matrix multiplication, followed by a reshape-transpose operation and an element-wise sum operation with original input feature $x$ to get the final SA module output $x^{sa}$ as shown in the following equation,

$$x^{sa} = x + \alpha RT \left( Ah'(x) \right), \tag{10}$$

where $\alpha \in [0, 1]$ is a scaling parameter that will be updated through back propagation, $RT()$ denoted as reshape-transpose operation. Accordingly, the SA block aggregates the different contextual information of each slice. Compared with the self-attention mechanism, our model enhances the abnormal regions and suppresses the noise in the rest/normal regions by capturing the dependencies between slices.

### 3.3   Recurrent Slice Attention Block

The overall recurrent slice attention (RSA) block is shown in the Fig. 1(b). The RSA block consists of three SA blocks with three different directions (sagittal, coronal, and axial). Our study proposes a recurrent slice attention block which repeats the SA block in three directions, and each SA block shares the same convolution kernel parameters, however, the parameters of each SA are updated independently.

## 4   Experimentation and Evaluation

### 4.1   Dataset

The training data used in our experiment comes from ADNI2 and ADNIGO (http://adni.loni.usc.edu), and computes after a series of preprocessing, such as masking, intensity normalization, redirection, and spatial normalization. For all the experiments, the dataset was divided into 80% for training and 20% for validation.

### 4.2   Implementation Details

Our study implemented the proposed model by Pytorch, and 3D-ResNet18 is the backbone network. NVIDIA GeForce RTX 3090 GPU is used for the training acceleration. The initial learning rate is 1e−4, the weight decay is also 1e−4, the batch size is 4, and the epoch is 100. The cross entropy is selected as the loss function.

### 4.3   Quantitative and Qualitative Results

To evaluate our model's performance and versatility, three experiments are listed as follows: (1) Comparative study of AD diagnosis with state-of-the-art deep learning methods, (2) Ablation experiment on the various module of the network, (3) Evaluation of the generalizability of the proposed model using a realistic clinical dataset (Table 1).

**Table 1.** Performance of different methods of four-classification task

| Model | Dataset(n) | | | | Accuracy(%) |
|---|---|---|---|---|---|
| | CN | [s/E]MCI | [p/c/L]MCI | AD | |
| 3D-SAE [23] | 52 | 56 | 42 | 51 | 47.42 |
| RF [8] | 60.2 | 60 | 60 | 60 | 60 |
| MSDNN [24] | 360 | 409 | 217 | 238 | 75.44 |
| 3D-ResNet [1] | 237 | 245 | 189 | 157 | 83.01 |
| 3D-DenseNet [28] | 120 | 120 | 120 | 120 | 83.33 |
| U-Net [11] | 213 | 261 | 163 | 108 | 86.47 |
| Our Proposed | 120 | 120 | 120 | 120 | **87.5** |

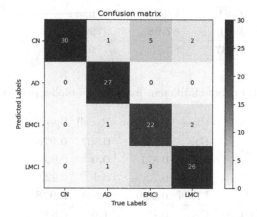

**Fig. 2.** Confusion matrix for CN vs. AD vs. EMCI vs. LMCI

Accordingly, we visualized the classification performance through the confusion matrix in Fig. 2. Clearly, our proposed model distinguished better on the AD class with more distinct pathological features.

In addition to the four-classification task of AD diagnosis, we also perform additional binary-classification tasks. From Table 2, we can see that the proposed model achieves the highest accuracy on AD vs. NC, EMCI vs. LMCI and LMCI vs. AD with 96.67%, 91.67% and 98.33% respectively.

Table 3 demonstrated the effectiveness of the proposed RSE and RSA with several state-of-the-art models. The three metrics of precision, recall, and specificity are higher than the original ResNet with the addition of the SE module to the residual block, indicating that channel attention emphasizes the characteristics of essential channels. The RSA module improved the classification precision on CN and AD categories and achieves a specificity of 96.7% in the AD category. Moreover, the combination of SE and RSA module allowed the model to achieve optimal performances.

**Table 2.** Performance of different methods of binary-classification task

| Approach | AD vs. NC | NC vs. EMCI | EMCI vs. LMCI | LMCI vs. AD |
|---|---|---|---|---|
| VoxCNN [19] | 80 | 56 | 56 | 62 |
| k-NN [31] | 74.73 | n/a | n/a | n/a |
| CAE [10] | 88.31 | n/a | n/a | n/a |
| DNN [13] | 89.6 | 68.0 | 68.2 | 68.4 |
| CNN [6] | 89.64 | n/a | n/a | n/a |
| CNN + SAE [32] | 91.1 | n/a | n/a | n/a |
| DBN [12] | 91.76 | n/a | n/a | n/a |
| ELM [18] | 91.76 | n/a | n/a | n/a |
| D2ML [21] | 93.7 | n/a | n/a | n/a |
| SRNN [36] | 94.63 | n/a | n/a | n/a |
| U-Net [11] | 95.71 | **87.98** | 90.14 | 90.05 |
| **Our Proposed** | **96.67** | 86.67 | **91.67** | **98.33** |

**Table 3.** Impact of different modules on model performance

| Model | Class | Precision | Recall | Specificity | Accuracy |
|---|---|---|---|---|---|
| 3D-ResNet18 | CN | 0.703 | 0.867 | **0.978** | 0.8 |
| | AD | 0.871 | **0.9** | 0.956 | |
| | EMCI | 0.72 | 0.6 | 0.922 | |
| | LMCI | **0.926** | 0.833 | **0.978** | |
| 3D-SE-ResNet18 | CN | 0.75 | **1.0** | 0.889 | 0.8417 |
| | AD | 0.9 | 0.9 | 0.967 | |
| | EMCI | **0.905** | 0.633 | **0.978** | |
| | LMCI | 0.862 | 0.833 | 0.956 | |
| 3D-RSA-ResNet18 | CN | 0.812 | 0.867 | 0.933 | 0.8333 |
| | AD | **0.903** | **0.933** | **0.967** | |
| | EMCI | 0.769 | 0.667 | 0.933 | |
| | LMCI | 0.839 | 0.867 | 0.944 | |
| Our Proposed | CN | 0.789 | **1.0** | 0.911 | 0.875 |
| | AD | **1.0** | 0.9 | **1.0** | |
| | EMCI | 0.88 | 0.733 | 0.967 | |
| | LMCI | 0.867 | 0.867 | 0.956 | |

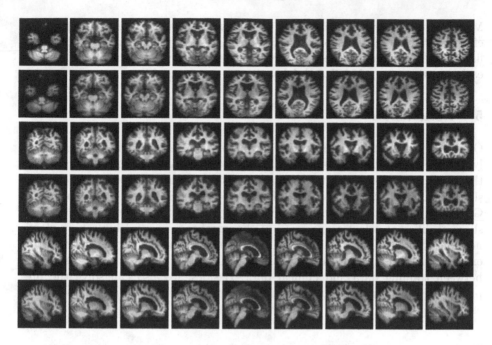

**Fig. 3.** Slices of an MRI scan of an AD patient, from top to bottom: in axial view, coronal view, sagittal view and their corresponding attention maps.

Accordingly, Fig. 3 showed the attention maps of brain MRI. The RSA module can color feature maps with highlight abnormal regions on different slices in different directions successfully.

**Table 4.** Summary of clinical data

| Class | Amount | Accuracy(%) |
|-------|--------|-------------|
| AD    | 12     | 75%         |
| CN    | 9      | 55.56%      |

In the final experiment, a set of clinical data was provided by Tianjin Hospital, Tianjin, China. All patients' samples were in the AD category and CN category due to the efficiency needed for reality situation Table 4, which included twenty-one patients with twelve AD and nine CN. The clinical data uses FSE sequence to obtain thick layer images by the direct scanning of the axial plane with a layer thickness of 5 mm and 1.5 mm interval between layers, while the ADNI data used in this experiment was a GRE sequence. Due to the different scanning methods, the sagittal and coronal planes are very blurred, which dramatically affects the experimental results. However, the final results are still improvable. It could be an accessible solution for the clinical doctor since cranial

MRI is a relatively easy and non-invasive screening method. According to the classification results, in-depth research on high-risk groups can assist in establishing the early diagnosis of Alzheimer's disease and play a positive role in the early identification of MCI and delay the occurrence of AD.

## 5 Conclusion

Our study used a deep residual network based on slice attention module to analyze and evaluate different stages of Alzheimer's disease, which was inspired by the attention mechanism and residual learning method. We also considered the slices in different directions and different effects on classification performance. Generally, our model is capable of capturing long-range dependencies between slices of different orientations, sensing abnormal regions, and improving classification accuracy. The experimental results show that our model outperforms existing methods. In future work, we will address the problem of mismatch between training data and clinical data. Besides, we also can solve the preprocessing problem of sagittal and coronal blurring using generation model such as GANs.

## References

1. Abrol, A., Bhattarai, M., Fedorov, A., Du, Y., Plis, S., Calhoun, V., Alzheimer's Disease Neuroimaging Initiative: Deep residual learning for neuroimaging: an application to predict progression to Alzheimer's disease. J. Neurosci. Methods **339** (2020)
2. Ashburner, J., Friston, K.J.: Voxel-based morphometry-the methods. Neuroimage **11**(6), 805–821 (2000)
3. Backstrom, K., Nazari, M., Gu, Y.H., Jakola, A.S.: An efficient 3D deep convolutional network for Alzheimer's disease diagnosis using MR images, pp. 149–153 (2018)
4. Bahar-Fuchs, A., Clare, L., Woods, B.: Cognitive training and cognitive rehabilitation for persons with mild to moderate dementia of the Alzheimer's or vascular type: a review. Alzheimer's Res. Ther. **5**(4), 35 (2013)
5. Cheng, B., Zhong, J., Jiang, X.: Multimodal ensemble classification of Alzheimer's disease and mild cognitive impairment. J. Integr. Technol. (2013)
6. Cheng, D., Liu, M.: CNNs based multi-modality classification for ad diagnosis. In: International Congress on Image and Signal Processing, Biomedical Engineering and Informatics, pp. 1–5 (2017)
7. Cheng, D., Liu, M., Fu, J., Wang, Y.: Classification of MR brain images by combination of multi-CNNs for ad diagnosis. In: Ninth International Conference on Digital Image Processing (ICDIP 2017) (2017)
8. Dimitriadis, S.I., Liparas, D., Tsolaki, M.N., Alzheimer's Disease Neuroimaging Initiative: Random forest feature selection, fusion and ensemble strategy: combining multiple morphological MRI measures to discriminate among healthy elderly, MCI, CMCI and Alzheimer's disease patients: from the Alzheimer's disease neuroimaging initiative (ADNI) database. J. Neurosci. Methods 14–23 (2017)

9. Li, F., Liu, M., Alzheimer's Disease Neuroimaging Initiative: Alzheimer's disease diagnosis based on multiple cluster dense convolutional networks. Computerized Medical Imaging and Graphics: The Official Journal of the Computerized Medical Imaging Society (2018)
10. Fan, L., Cheng, D., Liu, M.: Alzheimer's disease classification based on combination of multi-model convolutional networks, pp. 1–5 (2017)
11. Fan, Z., et al.: U-Net based analysis of MRI for Alzheimer's disease diagnosis. Neural Comput. Appl. 1–13 (2021)
12. Faturrahman, M., Wasito, I., Hanifah, N., Mufidah, R.: Structural MRI classification for Alzheimer's disease detection using deep belief network. In: 2017 11th International Conference on Information & Communication Technology and System (ICTS) (2018)
13. Forouzannezhad, P., Abbaspour, A., Li, C., Cabrerizo, M., Adjouadi, M.: A deep neural network approach for early diagnosis of mild cognitive impairment using multiple features. In: IEEE International Conference on Machine Learning and Applications, pp. 1341–1346 (2018)
14. Ghosal, P., Nandanwar, L., Kanchan, S., Bhadra, A., Nandi, D.: Brain tumor classification using ResNet-101 based squeeze and excitation deep neural network. In: 2019 Second International Conference on Advanced Computational and Communication Paradigms (ICACCP) (2019)
15. Guo, X., Yuan, Y.: Triple ANet: adaptive abnormal-aware attention network for WCE image classification. In: Shen, D., et al. (eds.) MICCAI 2019. LNCS, vol. 11764, pp. 293–301. Springer, Cham (2019). https://doi.org/10.1007/978-3-030-32239-7_33
16. He, K., Zhang, X., Ren, S., Sun, J.: Deep residual learning for image recognition. In: 2016 IEEE Conference on Computer Vision and Pattern Recognition (CVPR) (2016). https://doi.org/10.1109/CVPR.2016.90
17. Jie, H., Li, S., Gang, S., Albanie, S.: Squeeze-and-excitation networks. IEEE Trans. Pattern Anal. Mach. Intell. **PP**(99) (2017)
18. Kim, J., Lee, B.: Automated discrimination of dementia spectrum disorders using extreme learning machine and structural T1 MRI features. In: International Conference of the IEEE Engineering in Medicine and Biology Society, pp. 1990–1993 (2017)
19. Korolev, S., Safiullin, A., Belyaev, M., Dodonova, Y.: Residual and plain convolutional neural networks for 3D brain MRI classification. In: IEEE International Symposium on Biomedical Imaging 2017 (2017)
20. Li, Y., Fan, Y.: DeepSEED: 3D squeeze-and-excitation encoder-decoder convolutional neural networks for pulmonary nodule detection. In: 2020 IEEE 17th International Symposium on Biomedical Imaging (ISBI) (2019)
21. Liu, M., Zhang, J., Adeli, E., Shen, D.: Joint classification and regression via deep multi-task multi-channel learning for Alzheimer's disease diagnosis. IEEE Trans. Biomed. Eng. **66**(5), 1195–1206 (2019)
22. Liu, M., Zhang, D., Shen, D.: Hierarchical fusion of features and classifier decisions for Alzheimer's disease diagnosis. Hum. Brain Mapp. **35**(4), 1305–1319 (2014)
23. Liu, S., Liu, S., Cai, W., Pujol, S., Feng, D.: Early diagnosis of Alzheimer's disease with deep learning. In: IEEE International Symposium on Biomedical Imaging (2014)
24. Lu, D., Popuri, K., Ding, G.W., Balachandar, R., Beg, M.F., Initiative, A.D.N.: Multimodal and multiscale deep neural networks for the early diagnosis of Alzheimer's disease using structural MR and FDG-PET images. Sci. Rep. **8**(1), 5697 (2018)

25. Maqsood, M., et al.: Transfer learning assisted classification and detection of Alzheimer's disease stages using 3D MRI scans. Sensors (Basel, Switzerland) **19**(11) (2019)

26. Nawaz, A., Anwar, S.M., Liaqat, R., Iqbal, J., Majid, M.: Deep convolutional neural network based classification of Alzheimer's disease using MRI data (2021)

27. Payan, A., Montana, G.: Predicting Alzheimer's disease: a neuroimaging study with 3D convolutional neural networks. Comput. Sci. (2015)

28. Ruiz, J., Mahmud, M., Modasshir, Md., Shamim Kaiser, M., Alzheimer's Disease Neuroimaging Initiative: 3D DenseNet ensemble in 4-way classification of Alzheimer's disease. In: Mahmud, M., Vassanelli, S., Kaiser, M.S., Zhong, N. (eds.) BI 2020. LNCS (LNAI), vol. 12241, pp. 85–96. Springer, Cham (2020). https://doi.org/10.1007/978-3-030-59277-6_8

29. Liu, S., et al.: Multimodal neuroimaging feature learning for multiclass diagnosis of Alzheimer's disease (2015)

30. Suk, H.I., Lee, S.W., Shen, D.: Hierarchical feature representation and multimodal fusion with deep learning for AD/MCI diagnosis. Neuroimage **101**, 569–582 (2014)

31. Telagarapu, P., Mohanty, B., Anandh, K.R.: Analysis of Alzheimer condition in T1-weighted MR images using texture features and K-NN classifier, pp. 331–334 (2018)

32. Vu, T.D., Yang, H.J., Nguyen, V.Q., Oh, A.R., Kim, M.S.: Multimodal learning using convolution neural network and sparse autoencoder. In: IEEE International Conference on Big Data and Smart Computing, pp. 309–312 (2017)

33. Wang, H., et al.: Ensemble of 3D densely connected convolutional network for diagnosis of mild cognitive impairment and Alzheimer's disease. Neurocomputing **333**, 145–156 (2019)

34. Woo, S., Park, J., Lee, J.-Y., Kweon, I.S.: CBAM: convolutional block attention module. In: Ferrari, V., Hebert, M., Sminchisescu, C., Weiss, Y. (eds.) ECCV 2018. LNCS, vol. 11211, pp. 3–19. Springer, Cham (2018). https://doi.org/10.1007/978-3-030-01234-2_1

35. Wu, G., Kim, M., Sanroma, G., Wang, Q., Munsell, B.C., Shen, D.: Hierarchical multi-atlas label fusion with multi-scale feature representation and label-specific patch partition. Neuroimage **106**, 34–46 (2015)

36. Xin, Y., Qiang, W., Hong, D., Zou, J.: Spatial regularization for neural network and application in Alzheimer's disease classification. In: 2016 Future Technologies Conference (FTC) (2017)

37. Zhang, H., et al.: RsaNet: recurrent slice-wise attention network for multiple sclerosis lesion segmentation (2020)

38. Zhou, B., Khosla, A., Lapedriza, A., Oliva, A., Torralba, A.: Learning deep features for discriminative localization. In: CVPR (2016)

# Multi-stream Information-Based Neural Network for Mammogram Mass Segmentation

Zhilin Li[1], Zijian Deng[1], Li Chen[2(✉)], Yu Gui[2], Zhigang Cai[1(✉)],
and Jianwei Liao[1]

[1] School of Computer and Information Science, Southwest University,
Chongqing, China
czg@swu.edu.cn
[2] Breast Disease Center, Southwest Hospital of Chongqing, Chongqing, China
lichen20021522@163.com

**Abstract.** Mass segmentation is the first step in computer-aided detection (CAD) systems for classification of breast masses as malignant or benign, and it greatly impacts the accuracy of CAD systems. This paper proposes a model called region-based graph convolution and the atrous spatial pyramid pooling network (*RGC-ASPP-Net*), by considering mass context information, such as the features of location and size of mammogram masses, to yield better segmentation results for the CAD systems of mammogram diagnosis. Specifically, it introduces *ASPP* module in its skip-connection layer, to capture multi-scale mass context information. Then, it constructs a graph convolution module based on the clustering results of mass positions, for taking factors of the location of mammogram masses into account during the process of segmentation. We evaluated our model on the *CBIS-DDSM* dataset for conducting segmentation tasks, and the results demonstrate that our model *RGC-ASPP-Net* outperforms *PSPNet*, *DeepLabV3+*, *AUnet* and *ASPP-FC-DenseNet* by a large margin in terms of segmentation performance.

**Keywords:** Breast mass segmentation · Deep learning · Convolutional neural network · Graph convolutional network

## 1 Introduction

Breast cancer has a high risk and mortality rate among the women population [1]. According to the survey conducted by the World Health Organization, there are 2.3 million women diagnosed with breast cancer and more than half of a million deaths globally in 2020 [1]. On the other side, it is verified that breast cancer treatment can be highly effective, achieving survival probabilities of 90% or higher particularly when the disease is early diagnosed [2]. For example, the risk of death decreases by 28% to 36% after the mammogram screening program was introduced [3].

© The Author(s), under exclusive license to Springer Nature Switzerland AG 2022
E. Pimenidis et al. (Eds.): ICANN 2022, LNCS 13529, pp. 267–278, 2022.
https://doi.org/10.1007/978-3-031-15919-0_23

Digital mammography is a non-invasive, tissue-based technique, so it is widely used to give early detection of breast cancer or detect a patient's condition [4]. In other words, the results of mammography can be used to determine the possible presence of breast cancer including lesion, calcification and masses [6]. This time-consuming task requires not only a number of specialized radiologists, but also acceptable accuracy on checks. However, approximately 25% to 33% of visible cancers may be missed during a mammographic interpretation because of overlying dense breast tissue, or variability in radiologist experience [7]. To reduce the number of cancers from being overlooked, computer-aided detection (CAD) methods are introduced to assist the radiologist to locate potentially associated with breast cancer, such as masses, and regions of architectural distortion [7].

In a CAD system, mass segmentation is the first step for classification of breast masses as malignant or benign, so it greatly affects the accuracy of CAD systems [5]. Different from traditional segmentation algorithms (e.g. thresholding), the modern deep learning models, such as convolutional neural networks (*CNN*) and fully convolution network (*FCN*) can significantly boost the segmentation performance of CAD systems [8]. Specifically, *Unet* has been specially proposed for medical segmentation in CAD systems based on *FCN*, by following the architecture of encoder, decoder and skip-connection [9].

Although the modern deep learning models of *UNet*, and its variants of *AUNet* and *DenseNet* have been practically used in many medical CAD systems, they cannot work well on multi-scale information extraction and reduction when carrying out mass segmentation tasks [13,14]. From the perspective of physiological structure, it has been proven that the distribution of breast cancer masses does have regional features [15]. However, the factors of region and distribution information of mass in breast have not been considered in existing segmentation models of CAD systems.

To address the aforementioned issues in existing deep learning models for mass segmentation of mammography, we propose a multi-stream information-based model called region-based graph convolution and the atrous spatial pyramid pooling networks (*RGC-ASPP-Net*). Similar to *U-Net*, the overall structure of our proposed model consists of the encoder, the decoder and skip-connection.

Different from the previous studies that process mass size and distribution separately, this paper couples them together when carrying out breast mass segmentation. In brief, the following three contributions are made:

– We analyze the mass distribution of digital mammography in the *DDSM* dataset, and improve the graph convolutional neural network by feeding the summarized information of mass distribution.
– We count the mass size in the *CBIS-DDSM* dataset, then use the *ASPP* in skip-connection layers considering the different size of masses for capturing multi-scale mass context.
– The proposed *RGC-ASPP-Net* achieves superior results than other related encoder-decoder architectures by integrating the distribution and size information.

## 2    Background and Related Work

### 2.1    Graph Neural Networks

Graph convolutional neural network ($GCN$) is effective in processing non-euclidean structure data [19], and it is then used in object detection, classification, semantic segmentation and other relevant fields [16]. Especially, Zhang et al. [18] proposed a breast cancer classification network based on $GCN$. They constructed a graph convolution network by clustering similar pixels, and then added it to the convolution network for classifying benign and malignant breast cancer. However, they used k-nearest neighbor to cluster pixels by referring to their values, and did not take the macroscopic region information into account.

Liu et al. [17] proposed a novel target detection model using the Bipartite Graph convolutional Network ($BGN$) for cross reasoning, to improve the performance of breast mass detection. Their approach has good cross-view region-based reasoning ability which can perform reasoning about cross-view correspondences. The model, however, has geometric limitations. This is because it manually uses pseudo landmarks to define the regions of breasts, and it lacks the distribution of pathological features. Additionally, the graph convolution cannot be applied if patients have only one mammography in single-view.

### 2.2    Mammograms Mass Segmentation

Deep learning has developed rapidly in the field of computer vision, among which $FCN$ is the most widely used in CAD systems and performs especially well in the task of breast mass segmentation [8]. However, most implementations are trained by extracting patches instead of the original mammogram image during completing segmentation tasks [10–12]. Though their method can yield high segmentation performance on local patches, it requires more manual efforts on labeling patches of mammogram before segmentation, which is "a tedious and difficult work for radiologists" [13].

Hai et al. [14] has summarized the range of mass size and proposed a multi-scale fully convolution network for breast tumor segmentation. Similarly, Sun et al. [13] proposed $AUNet$ for mass segmentation in whole mammograms, but it lacks multi-scale information in the skip-connection layer. More importantly, both of them did not take account of the distribution of mass location.

Consequently, we propose a new model structure (called $RGC\text{-}ASPP\text{-}Net$) on the basis of $BGN$ for better directing breast tumor segmentation, by merging the multi-information over the region and size of the mass.

## 3    Methods

### 3.1    Overall Architecture

The proposed model is built on top of the encoder-decoder architecture, Fig. 1, (a) shows the overview of our model. Specifically, the backbone of the encoder

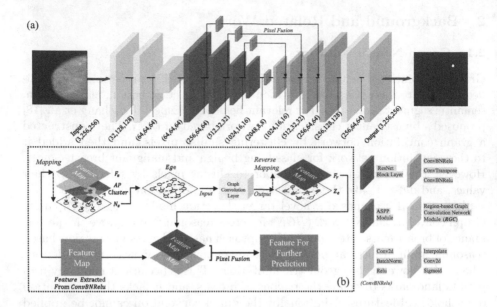

**Fig. 1.** Multi-stream information-based networks (*RGC-ASPP-Net*). (a) High level architectural overview with specific feature information. (b) Region-based graph convolution process (RGC).

is *ResNet-50*. Region-based graph convolution (*RGC*) and the atrous spatial pyramid pooling (*ASPP*) are built to learn the multi-information of mass at the macroscopic level. In the decoder phase, each layer is composed of two *ConvBNRelu* blocks and one *Transopose* convolution. The *ConvBNRelu* block is composed of a $3 \times 3$ convolution, batch normalization and *ReLU*. Besides, the *ASPP* module is added in the skip-connection layer to extract and restore the feature of mass at different scales. In the end, *Interpolate* is the *upsampling* layer followed by the *ConvBNRelu* block. After that, *Conv2d* and *Sigmoid* are utilized to adjust channels and predict the label.

**Skip-Connection with ASPP.** Segmentation has difficulty on recovering the details of information and building multi-scale contexts especially in various mass sizes. We add the *ASPP* module into the skip-connection to restore the details of mass at multiple scales during the decoding process. The *ASPP* module consists of three $3 \times 3$ convolutions with different atrous ratios, a $1 \times 1$ convolution, and an average pooling layer. In brief, the atrous convolution is an effective way to expand the receptive field without increasing extra parameters [21].

**Region-Based Graph Convolution (*RGC*).** In order to learn the relationships between different regions of mammograms, we construct *RGC* in the case of a single view by referring to *BGN* [17], and Fig. 1(b) presents its architecture. Based on *BGN*, we make the following modifications for better fitting pathological features of mammograms in the single view. **(1)** Improve the nodes mapping strategy to cluster similar regions better; **(2)** Adjust the definition of edges to fit the correlation of mammogram regions; **(3)** Construct a two-layer *GCN* to better learn the relationship between the nodes and the edges. The details are showed as follows:

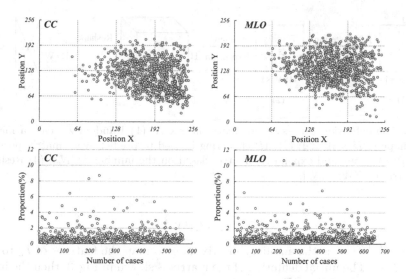

**Fig. 2.** First row is statistical results of breast mass central locations on *DDSM*. Because the left or right breast screen direction is adverse, we flip the left and right breast images to the same direction under the same view, to facilitate statistics of the distribution under different views. Note that each point represents the coordinates of mass position in mammograms; Second row shows *CBIS-DDSM* mass size distribution in two views computed at original mammogram resolution. The X-axis represents the sequential number of patients, and the Y-axis means the proportion of the mass in the whole mammogram.

**Step 1.** Breast region definition. To match the breast structure and regional features, we improve the manner of pseudo landmark. First, we count the mass positions of mammograms in the *DDSM* dataset by calculating the centroid of the mask which representing the ground truth of mammography. The obtained scatter plot is shown in Fig. 2. After that, the process of affinity propagation (*AP*) clustering that has a lower average error is performed on all mass coordinates of locations in both craniocaudal (*CC*) and mediolateral oblique (*MLO*) views. Figure 4 a) and b) show the clustering outcome in two views, each area represents a region or a mapping cell, and the background area locates at the edge of the image while the mass tends to gather in the center.

**Step 2.** Region graph node mapping. The node mapping exposes the relation between graph nodes and all the pixel features. We embed the extracted low-dimensional features into the region graph nodes through a mapping process, which is defined as:

$$\phi_{\text{AP}}(F_e, N_e) = \left(F_e \cdot Q^f\right)^T \tag{1}$$

where $\phi_{AP}$ maps the features of $F_e$ to the nodes of $N_e$, and $F_e \in \mathbb{R}^{C \times HW}$ is a feature extracted and reshaped from $CNN$, $N_e \in \{\nu\}$ are node sets that stand for region information.

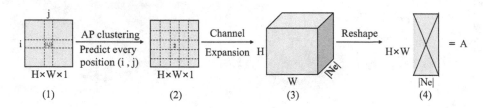

(1)    (2)    (3)    (4)

**Fig. 3.** The definition process of auxiliary matrix A. (1) Randomly create a matrix with shape of $H \times W \times 1$; (2) $AP$ clustering is used to predict every matrix position like (i,j); (3) Copy and expand the matrix based on the number of $|N_e|$. (4) Reshape the matrix to $HW \times |N_e|$.

$$Q^f = A \cdot (\Lambda^f)^{-1} \tag{2}$$

$A \in \mathbb{R}^{HW \times |N_e|}$ is the auxiliary matrix used to map the features of $F_e$ to the nodes of $N_e$. The initial definition of the matrix is shown in Fig. 3, then the inner computation way follows Eq. 3.

$$A_{ij} = \begin{cases} 1, & \textit{if the value of } i \textit{ belongs to } j \textit{ node} \\ 0, & \textit{otherwise} \end{cases} \tag{3}$$

$\Lambda^f \in \mathbb{R}^{|N_e| \times |N_e|}$ is a diagonal matrix, where $\Lambda^f_{jj} = \sum\limits_{i=1}^{HW} A_{ij}$. $Q^f \in \mathbb{R}^{HW \times |N_e|}$ is normalized to $A$.

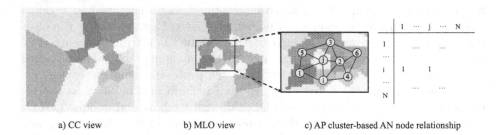

a) CC view            b) MLO view            c) AP cluster-based AN node relationship

**Fig. 4.** a) and b) show the visualization of affinity propagation ($AP$) clustering in two views based on mass distribution; c) is the illustration of $AP$ clustering-based adjacency matrix definition. The ellipses mean omission which is uncertain values.

**Step 3.** Region graph edges definition. There are some relationships among different nodes in the graph, we define them as $E \in \mathbb{R}^{|N_e| \times |N_e|}$. To simulate distinct ties between the breast regions and represent edge links $(v_i, v_j)$, and area neighbor $(AN)$ can be defined expressing an adjacency region corresponding to the node in the mapping matrix. If two different areas are neighboring in Fig. 4, they must have an $AN$ relationship. Thus, we can obtain the correlation between different regions at the macroscopic level, by following Eq. 4:

$$E_{ij} = \begin{cases} 1, & if\ node\ i\ is\ AN\ node\ j \\ 0, & otherwise \end{cases} \tag{4}$$

**Step 4.** Two-layer graph convolution. Two-layer $GCN$ defined in Eq. 5 is used to update and learn the graph, which constructs the breast area relationship with $E$ and $N_e$. By the way, $GCN$ has $P$ probability to dropout.

$$Z_e = \delta \cdot (E \cdot \delta(E \cdot X \cdot W_1) \cdot W_2) \tag{5}$$

where $W_1 \in \mathbb{R}^{C \times D_0}$, $W_2 \in \mathbb{R}^{D_0 \times D_1}$, and $X \in \mathbb{R}^{|N_e| \times C}$ is the feature resulted from $\phi_{AP}$, and $\delta$ is the $ReLU$ function.

**Step 5.** Region graph reverse mapping. The reverse mapping is consistent with $BGN$. Specifically, $\psi_{AP}$ is used to map node information back to the original spatial feature, where $\Lambda^r \in \mathbb{R}^{HW \times HW}$, $\Lambda_{ii}^r \in \sum\limits_{j=1}^{|N_e|} A_{ij}$ and $Q^r \in \mathbb{R}^{HW \times |N_e|}$ is reverse mapping matrix and defined as following:

$$\psi_{AP}(Z_e, N_e) = Q^r \cdot Z_e \tag{6}$$

$$Q^r = (\Lambda^r)^{-1} \cdot A \tag{7}$$

$F_{final}$ is the enhanced feature for further prediction where $F_e \in \mathbb{R}^{C \times HW}$ is feature extracted and reshaped from the $CNN$ feature of $F \in \mathbb{R}^{C \times H \times W}$.

$$F_{final} = F + RGC(F_e) \tag{8}$$

## 3.2  Loss Function

The combination of $Dice$ and cross-entropy $(CE)$ loss is the basic loss function in binary semantic segmentation. As shown in Fig. 2, the size of mass does not exceed 10% of the whole mammogram, which will lead to the class-imbalance problem. To overcome this problem, we use the $Focal$ loss combined with $Dice$ as loss function for our model training, as defined in Eq. 9.

$$L = L_{DICE} + L_{Focal} \tag{9}$$

# 4 Experiments

## 4.1 Datasets

In this study, all of the mammograms are collected from public datasets of Digital Database for Screening Mammography (*DDSM*) and Curated Breast Imaging Subset of *DDSM* (*CBIS-DDSM*) [22,23] in which two views of mammograms (*CC* and *MLO*) are provided. We use the *DDSM* dataset for counting the mass locations, and the *CBIS-DDSM* for model training, testing and size counting. Specifically, the *DDSM* dataset includes 2620 patient cases, and each case contains four mammograms and the corresponding ground truth labels. To disclose the mass distribution over the breasts, we analyze 1784 mammograms. Figure 2 shows the distribution results. As seen, it comprises 895 images in *CC* view, 889 images in *MLO* view. For the training and testing dataset, i.e. *CBIS-DDSM*, there exist 522 images in *CC* view and 620 images in *MLO* view. We analyze 1142 mammograms for disclosing mass size characteristics, Fig. 2 presents the statistical results of the mass size. According to the results, the size of most tumors does not exceed 4% of the entire picture.

**Preprocessing.** Mammograms normally contain a certain amount of noises and irrelevant regions [24], thus we preprocess the mammograms as follows:(1) Removing the background noise such as the metal plate. (2) Using the bilateral filter to denoise the image. (3) Applying the homomorphic filter to process the mammography. (4) Removing the irrelevant black margin. Considering medical datasets (including our selected ones) typically have a small number of samples, augmentation is carried out to minimize over-fitting and increase the generalization ability of our proposed model [25]. The images with pixel-level annotation are randomly dispatch into three sets according to the mass size proportion, the dataset are divided into 60% for training, 20% for validation and 20% for testing purposes.

## 4.2 Implementation Details

Our experimental models are constructed on the Pytorch framework, and we use a *NVIDIA RTX* 3060 *GPU*(12 *G*) for training. *ResNet*-50 pretrained on *ImageNet* is taken as a backbone network, and the numbers of *ResNet* blocks in layers are{3,4,6,3}. The image size of the training model is 256×256. The whole training procedure takes 200 epochs. The optimizer of the model uses stochastic gradient descent(*SGD*) and the parameters are set as: $lr = $ 5e-3, momentum $=$ 0.9, weight decay $=$1e-4. The numbers of graph nodes are $|N_e|$=20 in *CC* view and 22 in the *MLO* view resulted from the *AP* clustering. Hyper-parameters is set as: $D_0 = D_1 = 64$, the batch size is 8.

## 4.3 Results and Analysis

**Ablation Studies.** To verify the effectiveness and performance of different proposed components, ablation experiment is used for validation under distinct settings. Table 1 shows the consequences of the different components. Compared to basic model (*ResUnet*), It can be seen that when the performance of models combining either *ASPP* in skip-connection or *RGC* raises about 5% in the field of Dice. And the integration of these three components can bring further improvements.

**Table 1.** Ablation experiments of Skip-connection with *ASPP* and *RGC*

| Models | ASPP | RGC | Dice (%) | PPV (%) | Recall (%) | RAD (%) |
|--------|------|-----|----------|---------|------------|---------|
| Basic  | ×    | ×   | 56.46    | 58.80   | 58.58      | 37.60   |
| Basic  | ✓    | ×   | 61.48    | 66.71   | 59.96      | 31.72   |
| Basic  | ×    | ✓   | 61.87    | 62.85   | 63.23      | 28.64   |
| Ours   | ✓    | ✓   | **67.36** | **67.41** | **67.98** | **17.75** |

**Comparison with Existing Models.** Since the information shown in two views (*CC* and *MLO*) are distinct, mammography are divided into two views for model training and comparison. In order to verify the performance of our proposal. And test the performance of our model, we employ the pyramid scene parsing network *PSPNet* [20] and *DeepLabV3+* [21], both of them can capture multi-scale contexts and their backbones are *ResNet-50*. In addition, we re-implemented *AUnet*, *ASPP-FC-DenseNet*, and *ResUnet* as the three comparison counterparts. The overall average performance of mass segmentation is evaluated by Dice coefficient (*Dice*), *Recall*, positive predictive value (*PPV*) and relative area difference (*RAD*).

**Table 2.** Results in CC and MLO view

| Models | Backbone | View | Dice (%) | PPV (%) | Recall (%) | RAD (%) |
|--------|----------|------|----------|---------|------------|---------|
| ResUnet | ResNet-50 | CC | 56.46 | 58.80 | 58.58 | 37.60 |
| PSPNet | ResNet-50 | CC | 57.98 | 64.40 | 54.32 | 42.22 |
| DeepLabV3+ | ResNet-50 | CC | 61.30 | 64.25 | 61.19 | 31.67 |
| ASPP-FC-DenseNet | - | CC | 46.92 | 47.36 | 49.92 | 31.86 |
| AUnet | - | CC | 56.96 | 57.26 | 59.78 | 34.80 |
| **Ours** | ResNet-50 | CC | **67.36** | **67.41** | **67.98** | **17.75** |
| ResUnet | ResNet-50 | MLO | 53.62 | 56.50 | 53.77 | 38.09 |
| PSPNet | ResNet-50 | MLO | 61.48 | 63.38 | 59.98 | 45.72 |
| DeepLabV3+ | ResNet-50 | MLO | 61.79 | 66.12 | 58.70 | **28.71** |
| ASPP-FC-DenseNet | - | MLO | 47.48 | 49.24 | 48.26 | 31.51 |
| AUnet | - | MLO | 58.95 | 65.45 | 55.32 | 34.32 |
| **Ours** | ResNet-50 | MLO | **65.28** | **70.23** | **62.66** | 31.67 |

Table 2 presents the comparison of performance while using various models. Clearly, in the *CC* view, our approach achieves the best segmentation performance compared with the established networks. More exactly, it shows our model increases 6.06% in *Dice*, 3.01% in *PPV*, 6.79% in *Recall* and decreases 14.1% in *RAD*. Similarly, our model can increase more than 3.49% in *Dice* 4.11% in *PPV*, 2.68% in *Recall* in contrast to other networks when the view is *MLO*. It is worth to mention that the two re-implemented models of *AUnet* and *ASPP-FC-DenceNet* do not perform as well as the results reported in the original papers. This is because their experiments were running on the private dataset or only selective samples from the public datasets in the original scenarios. To guarantee the consistency of the verification, we input mammography to the models with the same preprocessing and image augmentation.

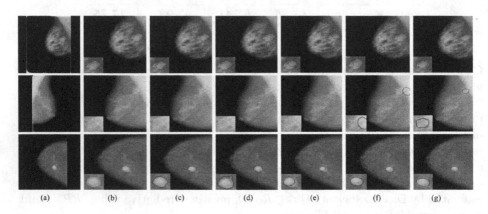

(a)          (b)          (c)          (d)          (e)          (f)          (g)

**Fig. 5.** The segmentation results of the *CBIS-DDSM* dataset with different models, and each row represents a case. Specifically, the first three rows are cases in the *MLO* view and the last three rows are in the *CC* view. Column (a) is the original mammograms with noises. (b) refers to the images after preprocessing and the ground truth labels (Green Line). (c)-(e) show the boundary consequences predicted from *AUnet*, *DeepLabV3+*, *PSPNet* and *ASPP-FC-DenseNet*, (g) is the mass segmentation result from our proposal networks (Red Line).

Figure 5 shows the example of the visualization results of mass segmentation of different networks. Clearly, our approach of *RGC-ASPP-Net* can yield a better segmentation performance in both two views. Moreover, our approach can also outperform other networks at mass boundary details and could always give more accurate results.

## 5    Conclusions

This paper proposed and evaluated a novel model *RGC-ASPP-Net* for mammography mass segmentation task, consisting of the encoder, the decoder and skip-connection. To be specific, we employed *ResNet-50* as the backbone network for feature extraction, two *ConvBNRelu* blocks and one *Transpose* convolution as the decoder. In order to capture multi-scale mass context information, the *ASPP* module was used in the skip-connection layer. At last, we built a graph convolution based on the clustering results of mass positions of mammograms. The extensive results showed that our method (*RGC-ASPP-Net*) outperformed *PSPNet, DeepLabV3+, AUnet* and *ASPP-FC-DenseNet* by a large margin in terms of segmentation performance in both *CC* and *MLO* views of mammograms.

# References

1. Wild, C., Weiderpass, E., Stewart, B.W.: World Cancer Report: Cancer Research for Cancer Prevention. IARC Press (2020)
2. DeSantis, C.E., et al.: International variation in female breast cancer incidence and mortality rates. Cancer Epidemiol. Prev. Biomarkers **24**(10), 1495–1506 (2015). https://doi.org/10.1158/1055-9965.EPI-15-0535
3. Oeffinger, K.C., Fontham, E.T., et al.: Breast cancer screening for women at average risk: 2015 guideline update from the American cancer society. JAMA **314**(15), 1599–1614 (2015). https://doi.org/10.1001/jama.2015.12783
4. Pisano, E.D., Yaffe, M.J.: Digital mammography. Radiology **234**(2), 353–362 (2005). https://doi.org/10.1148/radiol.2342030897
5. Sahiner, B., Petrick, N., et al.: Computer-aided characterization of mammographic masses: accuracy of mass segmentation and its effects on characterization. IEEE Trans. Med. Imaging **20**(12), 1275–1284 (2001). https://doi.org/10.1109/42.974922
6. Chang, J.M., Moon, W.K., Cho, N., Kim, S.J.: Breast mass evaluation: factors influencing the quality of us elastography. Radiology **259**(1), 59–64 (2011). https://doi.org/10.1148/radiol.10101414
7. Schwartz, T.M., Hillis, S.L., et al.: Interpretation time for screening mammography as a function of the number of computer-aided detection marks. J. Med. Imaging **7**(2), 022408 (2020). https://doi.org/10.1117/1.JMI.7.2.022408
8. Long, J., Shelhamer, E., Darrell, T.: Fully convolutional networks for semantic segmentation. In: Proceedings of the IEEE Conference on Computer Vision and Pattern Recognition, pp. 3431–3440 (2015)
9. Ronneberger, O., Fischer, P., Brox, T.: U-Net: convolutional networks for biomedical image segmentation. In: Navab, N., Hornegger, J., Wells, W.M., Frangi, A.F. (eds.) MICCAI 2015. LNCS, vol. 9351, pp. 234–241. Springer, Cham (2015). https://doi.org/10.1007/978-3-319-24574-4_28
10. Caballo, M., Pangallo, D.R., Mann, R.M., Sechopoulos, I.: Deep learning-based segmentation of breast masses in dedicated breast CT imaging: radiomic feature stability between radiologists and artificial intelligence. Comput. Biol. Med. **118**, 103629 (2020). https://doi.org/10.1016/j.compbiomed.2020.103629
11. Kooi, T., Litjens, G., et al.: Large scale deep learning for computer aided detection of mammographic lesions. Med. Image Anal. **35**, 303–312 (2017). https://doi.org/10.1016/j.media.2016.07.007
12. Zeiser, F.A., et al.: Segmentation of masses on mammograms using data augmentation and deep learning. J. Digit. Imaging **33**(4), 858–868 (2020). https://doi.org/10.1007/s10278-020-00330-4

13. Sun, H., Li, C., et al.: AUNet: attention-guided dense-upsampling networks for breast mass segmentation in whole mammograms. Phys. Med. Biol. **65**(5), 055005 (2020). https://orcid.org/0000-0002-0575-6523

14. Hai, J., Qiao, K., et al.: Fully convolutional DenseNet with multiscale context for automated breast tumor segmentation. J. Healthcare Eng. **2019** (2019). https://doi.org/10.1155/2019/8415485

15. Marongiu, F., Bertozzi, N., et al.: "Bifidus pedicle", the use of bilobed supero-medial pedicle for breast reshaping following upper outer quadrantectomy: a new oncoplastic breast surgery technique. Aesthetic Plastic Surgery **45**(3), 866–874 (2021). https://doi.org/10.1007/s00266-020-01982-x

16. Zhou, J., Cui, G., Hu, S., et al.: Graph neural networks: a review of methods and applications. AI Open **1**, 57–81 (2020). https://doi.org/10.1016/j.aiopen.2021.01.001

17. Liu, Y., Zhang, F., et al.: Cross-view correspondence reasoning based on bipartite graph convolutional network for mammogram mass detection. In: Proceedings of the IEEE/CVF Conference on Computer Vision and Pattern Recognition, pp. 3812–3822 (2020)

18. Zhang, Y.D., Satapathy, S.C., Guttery, D.S., Górriz, J.M., Wang, S.H.: Improved breast cancer classification through combining graph convolutional network and convolutional neural network. Inf. Process. Manag. **58**(2), 102439 (2021). https://doi.org/10.1016/j.ipm.2020.102439

19. Li, Y., Gupta, A.: Beyond grids: learning graph representations for visual recognition. In: Advances in Neural Information Processing Systems, vol. 31 (2018)

20. Zhao, H., Shi, J., Qi, X., Wang, X., Jia, J.: Pyramid scene parsing network. In: Proceedings of the IEEE Conference on Computer Vision and Pattern Recognition, pp. 2881–2890 (2017)

21. Chen, L.C., Zhu, Y., et al.: Encoder-decoder with atrous separable convolution for semantic image segmentation. In: Proceedings of the European Conference on Computer Vision (ECCV), pp. 801–818 (2018)

22. Heath, M., Bowyer, K., et al.: Current status of the digital database for screening mammography. In: Karssemeijer, N., Thijssen, M., Hendriks, J., van Erning, L. (eds.) Digital Mammography, pp. 457–460. Springer, Cham (1998). https://doi.org/10.1007/978-94-011-5318-8_75

23. Lee, R.S., Gimenez, F., Hoogi, A., Miyake, K.K., Gorovoy, M., Rubin, D.L.: A curated mammography data set for use in computer-aided detection and diagnosis research. Sci. Data **4**(1), 1–9 (2017). https://doi.org/10.1038/sdata.2017.177

24. Gøtzsche, P.C., Jørgensen, K.J.: Screening for breast cancer with mammography. Cochrane Database Syst. Rev. (6) (2013). https://doi.org/10.1002/14651858.CD001877.pub5

25. Eaton-Rosen, Z., Bragman, F., Ourselin, S., Cardoso, M.J.: Improving data augmentation for medical image segmentation (2018)

# MUST Augment: Efficient Augmentation with Multi-stage Stochastic Strategy

Qingrui Li[✉], Song Xie, Anil Oymagil, Ziyin Zhang, Mustafa Eseoglu, and Choonmeng Lee

Huawei Technologies Co., Ltd., Shenzhen, China
{liqingrui,xiesong5,anil.oymagil,zhangziyin1,mustafa.furkan.eseoglu, lee.choonmeng}@huawei.com

**Abstract.** Data augmentation has been widely used for enhancing data diversity and deep-learning model generalization. Recent research achieved better accuracies on image classification tasks by introducing automated search for optimal augmentation policies, but incurred high computation cost and long search time because of large search spaces and complex searching algorithms. In this paper, we present an augmentation method called MUST (MUlti-Stage sTochastic) Augment which completely skips policy searching. Instead of searching, our method applies a multi-stage augmentation strategy on top of a simple stochastic augmentation mechanism. This multi-stage complexity driven augmentation strategy ensures the whole training process converges smoothly to a good quality model; and within individual stages, it applies augmentation in a stochastic manner and provides both scalability and diversity by introducing more augmentation operations without extra search cost. Our extensive experiments with state-of-the-art results show that our method has advantages in both accuracy and efficiency compared to search-based augmentation methods. Besides image classification, we also examine the general validity of MUST on Face Recognition and Text Detection tasks, and demonstrate the effectiveness of our method across various CV tasks.

**Keywords:** Data augmentation · Multi-stage · Stochastic

## 1 Introduction

Data is an essential and dominant factor for learning AI models, especially in deep learning era where deep neural networks normally require large data volume for training. Data augmentation techniques artificially create new samples to increase the diversity of training data and in turn the generalization of AI models. For example, different image transformation operations, such as rotation,

---

Q. Li and S. Xie—Equal Contribution.

---

**Supplementary Information** The online version contains supplementary material available at https://doi.org/10.1007/978-3-031-15919-0_24.

flip, shear etc., have been used to generate variations on original image samples in image classification and other computer vision tasks. More intricate augmentation operations have also been implemented, such as Cutout [9], Mixup [25], Cutmix [23], Sample Pairing [15], and so on. How to formulate effective augmentation strategies with these basic augmentation methods becomes the crucial factor to the success of data augmentation.

Recent research [4,13,18] introduced automated searching or optimization techniques in augmentation policy search. Though these methods achieved accuracy breakthroughs on image classification tasks, they lead to high computational cost in general, due to large search space and extra training steps.

Our method of data augmentation aims to avoid policy search and cost, while maintaining or improving model performance in terms of both accuracy and training efficiency. Inspired by the idea of Curriculum Learning (CL) [1], which presents training samples in an increasing order of difficulties, our method defines various complexity levels of augmentation strategies and applies them on phased training stages. To avoid the confounding overfitting problem of the original Curriculum Learning in practice, our method applies the inverted CL order, which presents the hardest augmentation strategies from the beginning and decreases the complexity level when training goes from one stage to the next. Within each stage, we simply apply stochastic augmentation policies instead of searched ones for efficiency purpose. Besides efficiency, the more important advantage of stochastic policy is scalability, because introducing more operations in the augmentation pool does not bring additional search cost. In contrast, with search-based methods, more operations in the pool causes exponential increase of the search space. Therefore, our method is able to introduce more operations for better data diversity. Figure 1 describes our method and the difference compared to search-based methods.

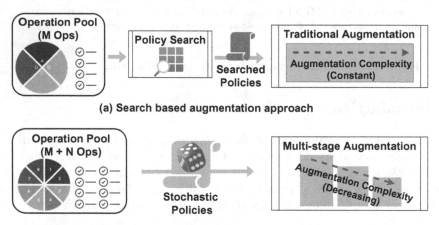

(a) Search based augmentation approach

(b) Multi-stage stochastic (MUST) augmentation without policy search

**Fig. 1.** MUST Augment vs Search-based Augment.

## 2   Related Work

AutoAugment [4] uses an RNN controller to propose an augmentation strategy, based on which the model is trained and the validation results are used for updates of the RNN controller. Search cost of AutoAugment is prohibitively huge, for instance, 5000 GPU (NVIDIA Tesla P100) hours on the CIFAR-10 dataset and Pyramid-Net+ShakeDrop model. Fast AutoAugment (Fast AA) [18] ameliorates AutoAugment's huge search cost by applying density matching with Bayesian Optimization based method [2] and avoiding repeated model retraining. Adversarial Augment (Adv AA) [26] reduces the huge computational cost of AutoAugment through the adversarial policy framework, which generates data samples that maximizes the training loss of the target network. PBA [13] introduces the idea of non-stationary policy schedules instead of the fixed augmentation policy proposed in AutoAugment, where non-stationary policy schedules refers to how the policy evolves with the training epochs; the evolving process for PBA is in nature a search process and has the corresponding cost. RandAugment [5] started to simplify the parameters and scale down the search space defined by AutoAugment [4], but their method still relied on grid search for iterative optimization of the simplified parameters. Our work targets at solving the same problem but belongs to the no-search based augmentation strategy and stands diametrically opposite to the AutoAugment series of methods, in which the best data augmentation policy is derived through a search.

## 3   Method

We describe the three key components of our proposed method in this section. Section 3.1 proposes our multi-stage complexity driven policy that helps to resolve the tension between augmented data diversity and data distribution fidelity. Section 3.2 puts forward a stochastic-based method as opposed to the search-based paradigm and provides our insights into stochastic augmentation policies. Section 3.3 capitalizes on our proposed stochastic-based method by proposing additional operations which can further enrich the data diversity.

### 3.1   Multi-stage Complexity Driven Augmentation

CL puts forward the view that learning progressively harder tasks may improve training performance. Drawing inspiration from their work, we manipulate the overall augmentation complexity in different training stages instead of controlling the creation of augmentation policies. Here augmentation complexity refers to the distortion produced by the augmentation operations and the result of successively applying these operations. In our work, these augmentation operations are first grouped into three categories: 1) baseline operations such as flip, random crop, and cutout which are frequently used as fundamental augmentations for image-related tasks; 2) mix-based operations such as mixup, cutmix, and augmix; 3) transformation-based operations such as rotate, shear, sharpness etc.,

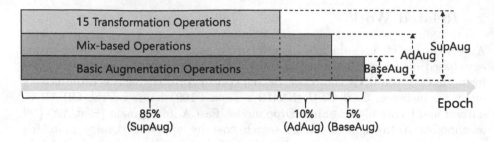

**Fig. 2.** Three stages with different augmentation complexities

which have been used in experiments of related works [4,5,18,26]. Our method then divides the complexity of augmentation into multiple levels that map to various combinations of the above three categories, and apply them in different training stages. Starting from the simplest, three complexity levels are defined as follows. First, baseline augmentation (BaseAug), exactly the same baseline augmentation used in AutoAugment; depending on the specific datasets, BaseAug may consist of flip, random crop, or cutout operations in the baseline category. Second, advanced augmentation (AdAug), which introduces the category of mix-based operations upon BaseAug. Third, super augmentation (SupAug), which additionally applies 15 transformation operations upon AdAug. Except for baseline augmentations which are applied with 100% probability, mix-based and transformation augmentations are selected in a stochastic manner when the corresponding augmentation category is applied at the designated augmentation stage. Figure 2 shows the above 3 stages with different augmentation complexities; while Table 1 describes the detailed augmentation operations applied in each of the stages.

**Table 1.** Details of augmentation operations for each stage.

| BaseAug | | | AdAug (BaseAug + mix_based ops) | | | SupAug (AdAug + 15 transformation ops) | | |
|---|---|---|---|---|---|---|---|---|
| op_pool | magnitude | probability | mix_based op_pool | magnitude | probability | op_pool | magnitude | probability |
| Cutout | size:16 | 100% | Cutmix | random | random | ShearX/Y, TranslateX/Y, Rotate, AutoContrast, Invert, Equalize, Solarize, Posterize, Contrast, Color, Brightness, Sharpness, Cutout | random | random |
| RandomCrop | crop_size:32 | 100% | Mixup | | | | | |
| RandomHorizontalFlip | 180 | 50% | Augmix | | | | | |

For the overall augmentation strategy, we first tried applying augmentation complexity in ascending order while the training proceeded, as per CL. However, the result was not ideal and we noticed apparent trend of over-fitting in training. Our interpretation of the phenomenon is that the over-fitting is due to insufficient diversity of training data. When this insufficiency takes place in early training stages of a deep neural network (DNN), it is prone to over-fit because the relatively smaller amount of data with limited diversity cannot support learning DNNs with large sizes and complex structures.

The above-mentioned observation led us to apply the inverted CL order of augmentation complexities, which trains the network with sufficiently diversified data in the early stage and gradually adapts the network to the original data distribution without augmentation. Specifically, our method removes one augmentation category going from one stage to the next, for instance the transformation category is removed going from stage 1 to stage 2. Note that our method does not tune or search the optimal epoch allocation during this process, it has a common setting of epoch allocation for a three-phase augmentation strategy across all datasets. Here the first stage is set to have the highest complexity and the majority of the epochs, it is necessary to maintain the high complexity and enough epochs to obtain sufficient data diversity and to prevent overfitting. Details of phase definition are further described in Sect. 4, and our experiments verified our hypothesis and confirmed the effectiveness of this method. Figure 3 shows example curves of training loss and test accuracy with a three-stage augmentation strategy obtained in practice.

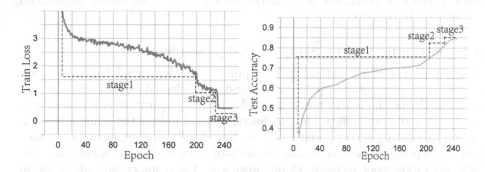

**Fig. 3.** Training loss and test accuracy with Phased Augmentation

We can also explain the need for data diversity vs. fidelity to the original data distribution in terms of the data augmentation theoretical foundation constructed in [6]. In this work, data augmentation is regarded as a perturbation about the original data. Thus, using a Taylor expansion about the original data, the first order effect of data augmentation is given in (1). From (1), we can therefore understand data augmentation as *feature averaging* over the data augmentation operations. This is precisely the reason why towards the end of training, we want to keep only data augmentation operations that introduce minimum distortion, thus allowing convergence to a model that can best learn the original data distribution, instead of the augmented distribution.

$$g(w) \approx \hat{g}(w) := \frac{1}{n} \sum_{i=1}^{n} l(w^T \, \mathbb{E}\, [\phi(t_i)]; y_i) \tag{1}$$

where $\mathbb{E}\,[.] = \mathbb{E}_{t_i \sim T(x_i)}\,[.]$ is the expectation taken over the sampled augmented data, $g(.)$ is the loss function after data augmentation, $l(.)$ is the original loss function, $w$ are the weights to be learned, $t_i$ is the data augmentation operation sampled from the operation pool $T$, $\hat{g}(.)$ is the expansion at any data point not dependent on $t_i$, $\phi$ is the feature map and $y_i$ is the label.

The second order expansion is given in (2). The squared term in (2) gives a clear indication of the role of data augmentation towards *variance regularization*, helping to prevent over-fitting. This gives strong justification to why we chose higher complexity data augmentation operations in the early part of the training, which serves to provide strong regularization effect for preventing choosing $w$ that will lead to over-fitting in the latter part of training.

$$g(w) \approx \hat{g}(w) + \frac{1}{2n} \sum_{i=1}^{n} \mathbb{E}\left[\left(w^T \phi(t_i) - \psi(t_i)\right)^2 \eta; y_i\right] \tag{2}$$

where $\mathbb{E}\left[.\right] = \mathbb{E}_{t_i \sim T(x_i)}\left[.\right]$ is the expectation taken over the sampled augmented data, $\eta = l''(\zeta_i(w^T \phi(t_i)))$, $\psi(x_i) = \mathbb{E}_{t_i \sim T(x_i)}[\phi(t_i)]$ is the expectation over the feature map applied on the augmented data and $l''(.)$ is the remainder function from Taylor's theorem. For more mathematical details, we highly recommend the readers to refer to [6].

## 3.2   Stochastic Policy - Skipping Policy Search

This component of our method removes policy searching completely and applies a stochastic augmentation policy with randomly selected operations and magnitudes. Unlike the search-based methods, once an operation is selected, it is used with 100% probability. Our stochastic method follows the same policy definition as existing search-based methods. Specifically, one augmentation policy has 5 sub-policies; each sub-policy consists of 2 augmentation operations. The base operation pool includes 15 operations as listed under SupAug stage in Table 1, each operation has 11 uniformly discretized magnitudes which is randomly selected upon each use.

We provide an abstract analysis for stochastic policy through a data deficiency complement point of view. It expects a relatively slower accuracy increase for stochastic method in early stage of training, while as training carries on, the amount of data for deficient dimensions and the corresponding performance of random approach may gradually get close to or even go beyond search-based methods. More detailed intuitions are provided in Sect. 1 of the supplementary document.

Though this stochastic policy alone is not expected to outperform the search-based augmentation policies, it provides a good foundation for us to build upon; it allows us to further incorporate the multi-stage complexity augmentation strategy and additional operations with very little or no extra cost compared to search-based methods.

## 3.3   Additional Augmentation Operations

To further boost the advantages of stochastic policies, our approach adds more augmentation operations in the operation pool for introducing further data diversity. Various augmentation operations bring specific data variations and diversities. Theoretically, enlarging the pool of augmentation operations benefits model learning as more data are produced and learned. With policy search based augmentation methods, increasing the number of operations has its price because it will cause exponential grow of the search space and associated search cost. While in our approach, these additional operations bring no extra overhead or cost as far as the stochastic method is concerned.

Building upon stochastic policies, mix-based operations such as Mixup, Cutmix, and Augmix are introduced into our method. Augmix is applied on individual images when selected, same as existing operations in the pool; while Mixup and Cutmix are randomly applied on individual batches due to the inherent pairing logic of these operations. These operations are added into the operation pool with the basic image transformation operations used by AutoAugment series of works. RandAugment showed certain operation (e.g. posterize) brought consistent negative effect to augmentation result regardless of the number of operations in the pool; while some (e.g. rotate) had consistent positive effect. We also observed some operations might harm the augmentation performance when directly applied on top of the stochastic policy; however, an interesting finding is that the negative influence could be weakened or even turned back to positive when these operations were used together with our complexity driven strategy.

Each of the above-mentioned three sub-methods may benefit augmentation individually; however the best result is achieved by combining them together as one solution, MUST augment, whose performance is demonstrated with our experiments presented as follows.

## 4 Experiments and Results

In this section, we first evaluate the performance of MUST augment in terms of accuracy and efficiency on various datasets and compare our method with our baseline and existing search-based methods described in Sect. 2. We then present our extensive experiments on sub-methods of MUST and ablation studies. Besides image classification tasks, we further conduct experiments on Face Recognition and Text Detection tasks, which further demonstrate the transferability of our method across domains. All experiments are conducted three times and the average performances of the experiments are reported.

### 4.1 Overall Experiment Setup

We follow AutoAugment and successive related works for baseline settings, we provide our reproduced baseline results together with those reported by AutoAugment in Table 2.

## 4.2 Experiments on Accuracy

As shown in Table 2, our method achieves SOTA accuracies on many datasets or models, and competitive ones on the rest. In particular, MUST obtains 0.56% SOTA improvement with Wide-ResNet-40-2 on CIFAR-10 [17], while on CIFAR-100 it obtains 0.87% SOTA increment with Wide-ResNet-40-2 and 0.44% SOTA increment with Wide-ResNet-28-10. Also, for all models trained on reduced CIFAR-10, MUST achieves the highest scores when compared to AutoAugment, PBA and RandAugment (with 1.78% increment on Wide-ResNet-28-2, 1.48% increment on Wide-ResNet-28-10). On ImageNet [7], MUST achieves 1.16% accuracy increment with ResNet50 compared to most search-based methods (AutoAugment, Fast AA, RandAugment) except Adv AA.

**Table 2.** Top1 test accuracy(%) on various datasets and models. Our baseline follows the same baseline settings of AutoAugment; the first two columns show our reproduced baseline results and the ones reported by AutoAugment respectively. We apply standard random crops and horizontal flips for our baseline experiments. The models used in our experiments are: Wide-ResNet (40-2, 28-2, 28-10) [24], Shake-Shake (26 2x32d, 26 2x96d, 26 2x112d) [10], PyramidNet+ShakeDrop [11,21], ResNet-50 and ResNet-200 [12].

| DataSet | Model | Baseline(our) | Baseline(AA) | AA | PBA | FastAA | RA | AdvAA | Ours |
|---|---|---|---|---|---|---|---|---|---|
| CIFAR-10 | Wide-ResNet-40-2 | 94.52 | 94.70 | 96.30 | - | 96.30 | - | - | **96.86** |
| | Wide-ResNet-28-10 | 95.43 | 96.10 | 97.40 | 97.40 | 97.30 | 97.30 | **98.10** | 97.97 |
| | Shake-Shake(26 2x32d) | 95.78 | 96.40 | 97.50 | 97.50 | 97.50 | - | **97.64** | 97.54 |
| | Shake-Shake(26 2x96d) | 96.65 | 97.10 | 98.00 | 98.00 | 98.00 | 98.00 | 98.15 | **98.3** |
| | Shake-Shake(26 2x112d) | 96.68 | 97.20 | 98.10 | 98.00 | 98.10 | - | 98.22 | **98.31** |
| | PyramidNet+ShakeDrop | 97.34 | 97.30 | 98.50 | 98.50 | 98.30 | 98.50 | **98.64** | 98.57 |
| Reduced CIFAR-10 | Wide-ResNet-28-2 | 80.10 | - | 85.60 | - | - | 85.30 | - | **87.38** |
| | Wide-ResNet-28-10 | 81.17 | 81.20 | 87.70 | 87.18 | - | 86.80 | - | **89.18** |
| | Shake-Shake(26 2x96d) | 80.26 | 82.90 | **89.98** | 89.25 | - | - | - | **89.98** |
| CIFAR-100 | Wide-ResNet-40-2 | 74.18 | 74.00 | 79.30 | - | 79.40 | - | - | **80.27** |
| | Wide-ResNet-28-10 | 80.79 | 81.20 | 82.90 | 83.30 | 82.70 | 83.30 | 84.51 | **84.95** |
| | Shake-Shake(26 2x96d) | 80.54 | 82.90 | 85.70 | 84.70 | 85.40 | - | **85.90** | 85.31 |
| SVHN (core set) | Wide-ResNet-28-10 | 96.57 | 96.90 | 98.10 | - | - | **98.30** | - | 98.06 |
| IMAGENET | ResNet50 | 76.32 | 76.30 | 77.60 | - | 77.60 | 77.60 | **79.40** | 78.76 |
| | ResNet200 | 77.75 | 78.5 | 80.00 | - | 80.60 | - | **81.32** | 80.62 |

## 4.3 Experiments on Efficiency

This experiment examines the efficiency of MUST augment and compares the results with search-based methods. The computation cost in this context has two major components: searching (or tuning) and training cost. For the searching part, the cost of a search-based method is normally proportional to some factors such as model size, dataset size, number of the operations in augmentation pool etc. For example, Fast AA's policy-search cost is 3.5 GPU-hours for WResNet 40-2 with reduced Cifar-10, but 780 GPU-hours for Pyramid-Net+ShakeDrop on full Cifar-10 dataset. Table 3 shows the searching costs of different augmentation methods.

Here, Adv AA claimed its search cost close to 0 as it does not have a separate policy search phase, but its training cost is much higher than our method, which is further explained as follows. For the training part, MUST augment has similar cost with the majority of search-based methods like AutoAugment and Fast AA, which process the training samples in one round. Suppose the training cost is a constant value $C$, which is affected by the dataset size and the number of total training epochs. For Adv AA, the training cost is at least 8 times $C$, because it augments more data in one epoch (number of batches is 8 times compared to MUST, AutoAugment, and Fast AA). Rand Augment has significantly reduced the search space to $10 \times 10$, but it still relies on grid search with training and has a relatively higher training cost than MUST augment. In general, our method demonstrates overwhelming advantage in terms of overall efficiency as it bypasses policy search completely and does not increase training cost with any tuning or optimization logic.

**Table 3.** Efficiency on various dataset. Unit: GPU hour; hardware: Fast AA - Tesla V100, AutoAugment - Tesla P100, PBA - Titan XP. Dashes indicate unavailable figures; despite the unavailability, the advantage of our method in terms of search cost is apparent.

| Search cost | | | | |
|---|---|---|---|---|
| Method | Search Space | Reduced CIFAR-10 | Full CIFAR-10 | Reduced ImageNet |
| AA | $10^{32}$ | 5000 | - | 15000 |
| FastAA | $10^{32}$ | 3.5 | 780 | 450 |
| PBA | $10^{61}$ | 5 | - | - |
| Our | 0 | 0 | 0 | 0 |

### 4.4 Experiments on Multi-stage Strategy

As described in Sect. 3.1, our data augmentation consists of three stages: stage 1 (SupAug), stage 2 (AdAug), stage 3 (BaseAug). We first look at the effect of two stages vs. three stages. The two stage strategy is constructed by choosing two of the three stages. From Table 4, we see that our 3-stage augmentation strategy offers better overall performance in comparison with 2-stage strategies. Note that the small differences between Table 2 and Table 4 on CIFAR experiments are due to smaller epoch setting in this experiment; a 200-epoch setting of this experiment is made to keep consistent with other ablation experiments.

**Table 4.** Accuracy of 2-stage vs. 3-stage augmentation, with Wide-ResNet-28-10 and Wide-ResNet-40-2 respectively.

|  | Stage 1,2 | Stage 1,3 | Stage 2,3 | Stage 1,2,3 |
|---|---|---|---|---|
| CIFAR-10 | 97.47 | 97.44 | 96.94 | **97.75** |
| CIFAR100 | 79.49 | 79.33 | 77.78 | **79.89** |

**Table 5.** Accuracy on CIFAR-100 with different epoch allocations for stages.

| Stage1 | Stage2 | Stage3 | Accuracy |
|---|---|---|---|
| 50 | 100 | 50 | 75.99 |
| 50 | 50 | 100 | 74.94 |
| 70 | 70 | 60 | 77.69 |
| 170 | 20 | 10 | **79.89** |

Next we look at the epoch allocation for each stage. We vary the number of epochs for each stage on the CIFAR-100 dataset. From Table 5, we derive an overall principle for epoch allocation: stage 1 has the majority (about 85%) of the total epochs; while stage 2 and 3 are set as 10% and 5% respectively. This is used as common strategy and one-time setting for all cases; no tuning or searching is used in our method for epoch allocation. The total number of epochs for all experiments in this section is set to 200. We also justify the need for an inverted CL by comparing with the standard CL, where the latter shows a performance drop. Detailed results can be found in the Sect. 3.3 of supplementary document.

### 4.5   Experiments on Face Recognition

We apply our method on face recognition task. The face recognition model is trained on MobileFaceNet [3] architecture with ArcFace loss [8], using the CASI-AWebFace [22] dataset. We integrate our training backbone with Fast AA implementation and the training is conducted with the same settings described in Fast AA. The experiments are performed on the following test datasets: LFW [14], AgeDB-30 [19] and CFP-FP [20]. As shown in Table 6 our method surpasses the baseline model and shows similar accuracy results compared to Fast AA, but without the high cost of policy search used in Fast AA. Please refer to the Sect. 4.1 of the supplementary document for more training details.

### 4.6   Experiments on Text Detection

We conduct experiments on text detection task to test the generality of our method. With ICDAR 2015 dataset [16], we train EAST [27] model (our own implementation) by using default baseline augmentations same as [27], the augmentation policies searched by Fast AA, and our proposed multi-stage augmentation strategy, respectively. We perform several independent runs and average the results which are shown in Table 7. The results demonstrate our augmentation method outperforms the default augmentation approach and search-based method Fast AA, and confirm it can be applied in a larger domain. Please refer to the Sect. 4.2 of the supplementary document for more training details.

**Table 6.** Face recognition accuracy on the standard benchmark

|          | Default | Fast AA | Ours      |
|----------|---------|---------|-----------|
| LFW      | 99.20   | 99.27   | **99.28** |
| AgeDB-30 | 91.82   | 91.88   | **91.95** |
| CFP-FP   | 94.31   | **95.53** | 95.41   |

**Table 7.** Text detection results on the ICDAR 2015 dataset.

|           | Default | Fast AA | Ours      |
|-----------|---------|---------|-----------|
| F1        | 80.43   | 80.98   | **82.24** |
| Precision | 80.71   | 82.56   | **83.56** |
| Recall    | 80.16   | 79.47   | **80.97** |

## 4.7   Ablation Experiments

We design ablation studies to explore the benefits brought by individual components of our proposed method. The first control experiment evaluates stochastic policy ("Stoch. + Base"), in which transformation augmentations are applied randomly on top of baseline augmentations while mix-based operations and stage concept are removed. The second control experiment evaluates phased augmentation strategy without mix-based augmentations ("Stoch. + 2-stage"), where the first stage consists of stochastic transformations on top of baseline augmentations and the second stage with only the baseline augmentations. Note that 2-stage but not 3-stage is used here because removing mix-based augmentations removes the corresponding phase, stochastic augmentations have to be kept otherwise there will be only one stage left. The third control experiment evaluates the mix-based operations on top of stochastic transformations without phased augmentation strategy ("Stoch. + mix-based"). As we can see from Table 8, using partially selected components of our proposed method results in apparent accuracy drops in all cases, thus validating that our method as a whole is greater than the sum of its parts.

**Table 8.** Ablation study result. In "Stoch. + 2-stage", the first stage consists of stochastic transformations on top of baseline augmentations and only the baseline augmentations for the second stage.

| Dataset   | Model         | Stoch.+Base | Stoch.+2-stage | Stoch.+mix-based | Ours      |
|-----------|---------------|-------------|----------------|------------------|-----------|
| CIFAR-10  | WResNet-40-2  | 96.28       | 96.3           | 96.17            | **96.64** |
|           | WResNet-28-10 | 97.43       | 97.51          | 97.56            | **97.75** |
| CIFAR-100 | WResNet-40-2  | 79.12       | 79.34          | 79.01            | **79.89** |
|           | WResNet-28-10 | 82.61       | 83.11          | 84.18            | **85.17** |

## 5   Conclusion

In this paper, we present an automated augmentation method without policy search. Building upon stochastic policies, our method introduces more augmentation methods without extra search cost; by further applying a multi-stage complexity driven augmentation strategy, our method achieves state-of-the-art accuracies for image classification task on most datasets and absolute advantage on efficiency as policy search is skipped. We also apply this method on face recognition and text detection tasks, thereby demonstrating the generality of our method.

# References

1. Bengio, Y., Louradour, J., Collobert, R., Weston, J.: Curriculum learning. In: ICML 2009 (2009)
2. Bergstra, J., Bardenet, R., Bengio, Y., Kégl, B.: Algorithms for hyper-parameter optimization. In: NIPS (2011)
3. Chen, S., Liu, Y., Gao, X., Han, Z.: MobileFaceNets: efficient CNNs for accurate real-time face verification on mobile devices. In: Zhou, J., et al. (eds.) CCBR 2018. LNCS, vol. 10996, pp. 428–438. Springer, Cham (2018). https://doi.org/10.1007/978-3-319-97909-0_46
4. Cubuk, E., Zoph, B., Mané, D., Vasudevan, V., Le, Q.V.: AutoAugment: learning augmentation strategies from data. In: 2019 IEEE/CVF Conference on Computer Vision and Pattern Recognition (CVPR), pp. 113–123 (2019)
5. Cubuk, E.D., Zoph, B., Shlens, J., Le, Q.V.: RandAugment: practical automated data augmentation with a reduced search space. In: 2020 IEEE/CVF Conference on Computer Vision and Pattern Recognition Workshops (CVPRW), pp. 3008–3017 (2020)
6. Dao, T., Gu, A., Ratner, A.J., Smith, V., Sa, C.D., Ré, C.: A kernel theory of modern data augmentation. In: Proceedings of Machine Learning Research, vol. 97, pp. 1528–1537 (2019)
7. Deng, J., Dong, W., Socher, R., Li, L., Li, K., Fei-Fei, L.: ImageNet: a large-scale hierarchical image database. In: CVPR 2009 (2009)
8. Deng, J., Guo, J., Zafeiriou, S.: ArcFace: additive angular margin loss for deep face recognition. CoRR abs/1801.07698 (2018)
9. Devries, T., Taylor, G.W.: Improved regularization of convolutional neural networks with cutout. arXiv abs/1708.04552 (2017)
10. Gastaldi, X.: Shake-shake regularization. arXiv abs/1705.07485 (2017)
11. Han, D., Kim, J., Kim, J.: Deep pyramidal residual networks. In: 2017 IEEE Conference on Computer Vision and Pattern Recognition (CVPR), pp. 6307–6315 (2017). https://doi.org/10.1109/CVPR.2017.668
12. He, K., Zhang, X., Ren, S., Sun, J.: Deep residual learning for image recognition. In: 2016 IEEE Conference on Computer Vision and Pattern Recognition (CVPR), pp. 770–778 (2016). https://doi.org/10.1109/CVPR.2016.90
13. Ho, D., Liang, E., Stoica, I., Abbeel, P., Chen, X.: Population based augmentation: efficient learning of augmentation policy schedules. In: ICML (2019)
14. Huang, G.B., Mattar, M., Berg, T., Learned-Miller, E.: Labeled faces in the wild: a database for studying face recognition in unconstrained environments (2008)
15. Inoue, H.: Data augmentation by pairing samples for images classification. arXiv abs/1801.02929 (2018)
16. Karatzas, D., et al.: ICDAR 2015 competition on robust reading. In: ICDAR, pp. 1156–1160. IEEE Computer Society, relocated from Tunis, Tunisia
17. Krizhevsky, A.: Learning multiple layers of features from tiny images (2009)
18. Lim, S., Kim, I., Kim, T., Kim, C., Kim, S.: Fast autoaugment. In: Advances in Neural Information Processing Systems, vol. 32, pp. 6665–6675 (2019)

19. Moschoglou, S., Papaioannou, A., Sagonas, C., Deng, J., Kotsia, I., Zafeiriou, S.: AgeDB: the first manually collected, in-the-wild age database. In: Proceedings of the IEEE Conference on Computer Vision and Pattern Recognition Workshops, pp. 51–59 (2017)
20. Sengupta, S., Chen, J.C., Castillo, C., Patel, V.M., Chellappa, R., Jacobs, D.W.: Frontal to profile face verification in the wild. In: IEEE Conference on Applications of Computer Vision (2016)
21. Yamada, Y., Iwamura, M., Akiba, T., Kise, K.: Shakedrop regularization for deep residual learning. IEEE Access **7**, 186126–186136 (2019)
22. Yi, D., Lei, Z., Liao, S., Li, S.Z.: Learning face representation from scratch. CoRR abs/1411.7923 (2014). http://arxiv.org/abs/1411.7923
23. Yun, S., Han, D., Oh, S.J., Chun, S., Choe, J., Yoo, Y.: CutMix: regularization strategy to train strong classifiers with localizable features. In: 2019 IEEE/CVF International Conference on Computer Vision (ICCV), pp. 6022–6031 (2019)
24. Zagoruyko, S., Komodakis, N.: Wide residual networks. In: Richard, C., Wilson, E.R.H., Smith, W.A.P. (eds.) Proceedings of the British Machine Vision Conference (BMVC), pp. 87.1-87.12. BMVA Press (2016). https://doi.org/10.5244/C.30.87
25. Zhang, H., Cissé, M., Dauphin, Y., Lopez-Paz, D.: Mixup: beyond empirical risk minimization. arXiv abs/1710.09412 (2018)
26. Zhang, X., Wang, Q., Zhang, J., Zhong, Z.: Adversarial autoaugment. In: International Conference on Learning Representations (2020)
27. Zhou, X., et al.: EAST: an efficient and accurate scene text detector. CoRR abs/1704.03155 (2017)

# Neural-Gas VAE

Jan-Ole Perschewski[(✉)] [iD] and Sebastian Stober [iD]

AILab, Otto-von-Guericke University, Magdeburg, Germany
{jan-ole.perschewski,stober}@ovgu.de

**Abstract.** Most deep learning models are known to be black-box models due to their overwhelming complexity. One approach to make models more interpretable is to reduce the representations to a finite number of objects. This can be achieved by clustering latent spaces or training models which include quantization by design such as the Vector Quantised-Variational AutoEncoder (VQ-VAE). However, if the architecture is not chosen carefully, a phenomenon called index collapse can be observed. Here, a large part of the codebook containing the prototypes is not used decreasing the possible performance. Approaches to circumvent this either rely on data-depending initialization or decreasing the dimensionality of the codebook vectors. In this paper, we present a novel variant of the VQ-VAE, the Neural-Gas VAE, which adapts the codebook loss inspired by neural-gas to avoid index collapse. We show that the Neural-Gas VAE achieves competitive performance on CIFAR and Speech Commands for different codebook sizes and dimensions. Moreover, we show that the resulting architecture learns a meaningful latent space and topology for both features or objects.

**Keywords:** Index collapse · Vector quantization

## 1  Introduction

Deep learning models are often seen as black boxes that are hard to understand but achieve State-of-the-Art performance in almost all domains. However, the lack of understanding can diminish trust in a system. Hence, there are a multitude of approaches to explain model predictions [2,22] or find model features [19]. Unfortunately, this cannot be seen as full explainability due to the continuous representations paired with a high number of non-linearities.

One approach is to use models with a discrete latent space that can be analyzed due to the limited number of different states in the latent space [4,15]. These models became popular with the VQ-VAE [20] that set off a wave of research into the domain of models with quantized latent spaces. The idea behind these models is to quantize the latent space using vectors from the codebook. This leads to the challenge of training the codebook and the encoder since the gradient is only available with respect to the quantized representation. In the original paper [20], the authors propose to copy the gradient from the codebook to the encoder and train the codebook either with an additional loss term or

E. Pimenidis et al. (Eds.): ICANN 2022, LNCS 13529, pp. 292–303, 2022.
https://doi.org/10.1007/978-3-031-15919-0_25

batch-wise expectation-maximization. However, this approach leads to the phenomenon of index collapse [11] where only a small subset of the codebook is
used.

To solve this issue there are currently four main approaches. First, there is
the idea to split the latent dimensions into multiple slices of lower dimensions
[3,11,25]. These adaptations can be seen as parallel to the cartesian product k-
means approach [18]. Even though models with this construction are successful
in image generation and retrieval, they increase the number of discrete units
by introducing more possible quantizations so that interpretability is not easily
given anymore.

Second, the Gumbel-softmax approach allows the selection of discrete codebook entries [3,10] by using an approximation of the categorical distribution
during training. During testing, the closest codebook vector is used. However,
this results in slightly different behavior between training and testing.

The third idea is to combine the codebook with a grid structure between
the codebook vectors to adapt vectors in a small neighborhood simultaneously
[7]. This resulted in the SOM-VAE. However, this approach in combination with
the introduced grid structure assumes that the data is on a two-dimensional
manifold which is not necessarily the case.

The fourth idea is to re-initialize codebook vectors depending on the input
data if they were not used for a certain number of steps [14]. This approach
can effectively circumvent the problem of index collapse but adds additional
complexity in form of the collection of representative encodings and applications
of clustering algorithms during training.

Due to the weaknesses of the existing approaches, we introduce the Neural-
Gas VAE[1] to combat the index collapse without a combinatorial explosion or
assumptions about the data manifold. This is done by incorporating the ideas
from neural-gas [17] into the current VQ-VAE framework. Hence, our main contributions are the introduction of the Neural-Gas VAE, the search for useful
hyperparameters for audio and image data sets, the comparison to the VQ-VAE,
and the demonstration of the learned manifolds for interpretability.

## 2   Background

### 2.1   Neural-Gas

The neural-gas network is a vector quantization technique that learns a topology
between the codebook vectors [17]. For that, a codebook vector $c$, which is a row
of the codebook $C \in \mathbb{R}^{S \times F}$, the age matrix $T \in \mathbb{N}^{S \times S}$ and a connection matrix
$A \in \{0, 1\}^{S \times S}$ are iteratively updated. Here, $S$ is the number of codebook vectors
and $F$ is the feature size.

A codebook vector is updated depending on its position in the ranking
$(c_{i_0}, c_{i_1}, c_{i_2}, ...)$ with respect to a training example $v$ where $||c_{i_0} - v|| \leq ||c_{i_1} - v|| \leq ||c_{i_2} - v|| \leq ...$ holds:

---

[1] Code available at https://github.com/perschi/Neural-Gas-VAE.

$$c_{i_r}^{new} = c_{i_r}^{old} + \varepsilon e^{-\frac{r}{\lambda}} \cdot (v - c_{i_r}^{old}) \tag{1}$$

As the equation shows, the strength of the update decays with rank $r$. Additionally, the adaption is regulated by the influence $\lambda$ which determines how many ranks are effectively updated and the learning rate $\varepsilon$. Afterwards, $T$ is updated by increasing the age of all outgoing edges except the edge between the first two codebook vectors $c_{i_0}$ and $c_{i_1}$ in the distance ranking whose age is set to zero.

$$T_{i,j}^{new} = \begin{cases} 0 & i = i_0, j = i_1 \\ T_{i,j}^{old} + 1 & i = i_0, j \neq i_1 \\ T_{i,j}^{old} & else \end{cases} \tag{2}$$

Next, the connection matrix $A$ is updated. This matrix represents the final graph that is used to display the topology.

$$A_{i,j}^{new} = \begin{cases} 1 & i = i_0, j = i_1 \\ 0 & i = i_0, j \neq i_1, T_{i,j}^{new} > L \\ A_{i,j}^{old} & else \end{cases} \tag{3}$$

Here, we add the edge from $i_0$ to $i_1$. All other outgoing edges from $i_0$ are removed if their age exceeds the lifetime $L$. The remaining adjacency matrix stays the same. Applying this algorithm results in a subgraph of the Delauney triangulation that includes all edges where data is present. [16]. This is especially interesting in the context of deep representation learning since there is the hypothesis that data is situated on a low-dimensional manifold [6,21] and the learned graph is a more meaningful representation of this manifold.

## 2.2   VQ-VAE

The VQ-VAE [20] was introduced to avoid posterior collapse of variational autoencoders and learns a discrete representation of the data set. For that, we consider an encoder $z_e : \mathbb{R}^{Ch \times D} \rightarrow \mathbb{R}^{F \times \tilde{D}}$ where $Ch$ is the number of input channels, $D$ the dimensionality of the input data, and $\tilde{D}$ is the reduced dimensionality. If we consider RGB-images we have $Ch = 3$ and $D = W \times H$ representing the width- and height-resolution. After applying the encoder, the representation is quantized by replacing the feature vectors at each position $p \in \tilde{D}$ with the closest vector $c_p$ regarding the Euclidean distance from the codebook $C \in \mathbb{R}^{S \times F}$ where $S$ is the number of codebook vectors. Afterwards, the decoder $z_q : \mathbb{R}^{F \times \tilde{D}} \rightarrow \mathbb{R}^{Ch \times D}$ reconstructs the input data. To train this model, the loss in Eq. (4) is used, where the $sg(\cdot)$ function stops the gradient computation.

$$\log p(x|z_q(z_e(x))) + \frac{1}{|D|} \sum_{p \in D} (||sg(z_e(x)_p) - c_p||^2 + \beta||z_e(x)_p - sg(c_p)||^2) \tag{4}$$

This first term is the reconstruction loss so that the decoder learns to recreate the input data. The second term is the codebook loss which adapts the codebook

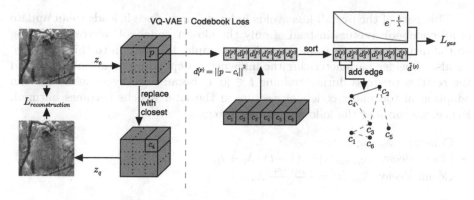

**Fig. 1.** Training the Neural-Gas VAE includes the VQ-VAE forward pass on the left. On the right, $L_{gas}$ is evaluated as a weighted average of the sorted distances and edges are added between the two closest codebook vectors.

vectors by pulling them towards the encoding. The last term is the commitment loss which forces the encoder to map the input to a certain codebook vector. Additionally, $\beta$ weights the loss terms. Since we replace the continuous representation with a vector from the codebook, there is no direct gradient for the encoder. To resolve this, the gradient from the decoder is copied to the encoder.

In the following, we combine neural-gas and the VQ-VAE to counter the phenomenon of index collapse and add a more detailed representation of the data manifold.

## 3 Method

The main idea in the combination of neural-gas and the VQ-VAE is to adapt the codebook loss of the VQ-VAE and include the mechanism for creating the graph from neural-gas.

For that, we consider analogously to the VQ-VAE a codebook $C$, an encoder $z_e$, and a decoder $z_q$. In addition to that, we introduce the adjacency matrix $A \in \{0, 1\}^{S \times S}$ and the age matrix $T \in \mathbb{N}^{S \times S}$ from the neural-gas.

During training, as seen in Fig. 1, we consider each position $p \in \tilde{D}$ in the encoding $z_e(x)$ and calculate the distances $d_i^{(p)}$ to each codebook vector such that:

$$d_i^{(p)} = ||sg(z_e(x)_{:,p}) - C_{i,:}||^2$$

Next, we sort distances $d^{(p)}$ at each position $p$ ascending resulting in $\tilde{d}^{(p)}$. With this, we can calculate the new codebook loss $L_{gas}$ inspired by the adaptation of neural-gas.

$$L_{gas} = \frac{1}{|D| \cdot S} \sum_{p \in D} \sum_{i=0}^{S} e^{-\frac{i}{\lambda}} \cdot \tilde{d}_i^{(p)} \tag{5}$$

This part of the overall loss avoids index collapse since it leads to an update of all codebook vectors instead of only the closest codebook vector depending on the distance ranking from the training sample. In addition to this adaption, we also consider parameterizing the influence $\lambda$ depending on an initial $\lambda_0$ and the relative progress during training $t \in [0,1]$ because we hypothesize that an adaption of too many codebook vectors in the later epochs becomes harmful. Hence, we consider the following three strategies:

- Constant: $\lambda_{constant}(t) = \lambda_0$
- Linear decay: $\lambda_{linear}(t) = (1-t) \cdot \lambda_0 + t\varepsilon$
- Cosine decay: $\lambda_{cos}(t) = \frac{cos(t\pi)+1}{2}\lambda_0 + t\varepsilon$

The linear and cosine decay are chosen such that $\lambda$ becomes almost $\epsilon(0 < \epsilon \ll 1)$ in the final epoch which then results in an adaption that is similar to the VQ-VAE. The remaining terms in the loss are analogical to the VQ-VAE resulting in an overall loss of:

$$\log p(x|z_q(z_e(x))) + L_{gas} + \beta\frac{1}{|D|}\sum_{p \in D} ||z_e(x)_p - sg(c_p)||^2 \tag{6}$$

In addition to the differentiable loss, we also want to use the heuristic from neural-gas to create a topology between the codebook vectors. For this, we can either use the algorithm from Sect. 2.1 and apply it in parallel over all positions or a post-hoc method that was introduced in [16]. The advantage of the post-hoc approach is that it can also be applied to any other vector quantization. For that purpose, we create an adjacency matrix $A$ for a data set $X$ such that $A_{i,j} = 1$ if there is one encoding $z_e(x)_{:,p}$ for $x \in X$ that is closest to $c_i \in C$ and second closest to $c_j \in C$.

# 4 Experiments

## 4.1 Finding Good Hyper-parameters

To find a set of good hyper-parameters for the algorithm, we focus on models trained on CIFAR-10 [13] and Speech Commands [24] to determine if there are different ideal hyper-parameters for different data modalities within a reasonable time-frame. Even though the data sets have a small dimensionality within their respective domain, the approach scales analogous to the VQ-VAE [20] due to the same general setup.

**CIFAR.** On CIFAR, we compare the performance of convolutional models, where the encoder consists of two blocks of convolution, Batch Normalization [9], and ReLU [1] with each block producing 256 channels with a kernel size of four and a stride two. This is followed by two Residual Blocks [8,23] (Branch: ReLU, Conv3x3, ReLU, Conv1x1) and finally a Conv1x1 layer producing $F$ many channels. The decoder starts with a Conv1x1 layer producing 256 channels that are followed by two residual blocks, two layers of transposed convolution with kernel size four and stride two, and Conv1x1 which reproduces the input channels. As the reconstruction loss, we use the Mean-Squared-Error (MSE). This architecture is the same as in the paper [20] except for the inner layers. All models are trained with the Adam optimizer with the default parameters [12] for 100 epochs with a batch size of 64. Here, we analyze the performance regarding the following parameters by training one model for each combination of codebook sizes $S \in \{256, 512\}$ codebook dimensions $F \in \{2, 16, 32, 64\}$, initial influence parameters $\lambda_0 \in \{0.25, 0.5, 1, 2, 4, 8\}$, decay strategies $\lambda(x) \in \{\lambda_{constant}, \lambda_{linear}, \lambda_{cos}\}$, and loss weight $\beta \in \{0.25, 0.5, 1\}$. For the evaluation, we consider the best MSE on the test set.

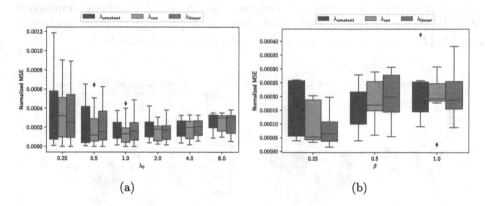

(a)    (b)

**Fig. 2.** Performance of different $\lambda_0$ and *beta* values regarding MSE normalized by subtracting the minimum for each set of $(S, F)$. In (a) each box plot contains the performance of the 24 combinations of $S, F, \beta$. In (b) each box plot contains 8 samples since only runs where $\lambda_0 = 2$ are considered.

Figure 2a shows the distribution of the normalized MSE depending on the initial influence $\lambda_0$ and the selected decay strategy. The MSE is normalized by subtracting the minimum of the loss for the values grouped by $(S, F)$. This removes the influence of these parameters on the lowest possible loss. In the figure, we see that the performance is expected to be best if $\lambda_0 = 2$. Furthermore, we see that with decreasing influence the normalized MSE increases in average magnitude and variance. In this case, the approach degenerates into the normal VQ-VAE showing that the Neural-Gas VAE can lead to an improvement. In addition, we see that the differences between the loss values are small, showing that the choice of $\lambda_0$ is robust. Next, we look for a fitting $\beta$ assuming that $\lambda_0 = 2$ in Fig. 2b. Here, we see that the influence of the parameter is insignificant only appearing in the third significant digit. However, $\beta = 0.25$ provides marginally better results. Moreover, we can say that we would prefer $\lambda_{constant}$ or $\lambda_{linear}$ depending on $\beta$.

**Speech Commands.** The Speech Commands [24] data set, consists of 105829 utterances from 2618 speakers with a length of up to one second sampled at 16 kHz. We are working with the raw audio using an encoder that consists of six blocks of convolution, batch normalization [9] and ReLU [1], where each layer has a kernel of size six and a stride of two with zero-padding of one on each size. Each layer produces 256 channels. The last layer of the encoder is a convolutional layer with a kernel size of one reducing the dimensions to $S$. The decoder consists of a convolutional layer with a kernel size of one followed by 6 transposed convolution blocks reverting the sequence reduction in the encoder. Finally, there is a convolutional layer with a kernel size of one reducing the channels to one. The model is trained with the same optimizer as Sect. 4.1 but only for 20 epochs and with the multiscale spectral loss proposed in [5]. Informed by the previous experiment, we use a codebook size $S$ of 512, codebook dimensions $F \in \{2, 16, 32\}$, initial influence parameters $\lambda_0 \in \{0.5, 1, 2, 4\}$, decay strategies $\lambda(x) \in \{\lambda_{constant}, \lambda_{linear}, \lambda_{cos}\}$, and loss weight $\beta \in \{0.1, 0.25, 0.5\}$.

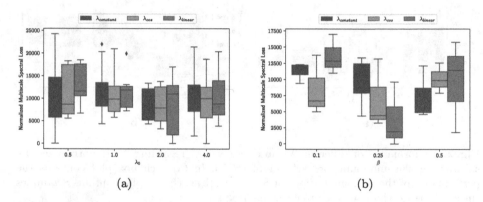

**Fig. 3.** Performance of different $\lambda_0$ and *beta* values regarding multiscale spectral loss normalized by subtracting the minimum for each set of $(S, F)$. In (a) each box plot contains the performance of the 9 combinations of $S, F, \beta$. In (b) each box plot contains 3 samples since only runs where $\lambda_0 = 2$ are considered.

Following the same protocol as before, we see in Fig. 3a that the best performance regarding the normalized loss is at $\lambda_0 = 2$. However, the increase in test loss for the smaller $\lambda_0$ is less pronounced than in the case of the previous experiment. Looking at the performance assuming that we select $\lambda_0 = 2$ in Fig. 3b, we observe that $\beta = 0.25$ seems to be the best choice for reliable good performance. Furthermore, we see that in this case $\lambda_{linear}$ is the preferable choice.

To summarize these results, we suggest to select $\lambda_0 = 2$, $\lambda_{linear}$ and $\beta = 0.25$ for good results in different settings. The next question is whether this approach improves upon the VQ-VAE.

## 4.2    Comparison with the VQ-VAE

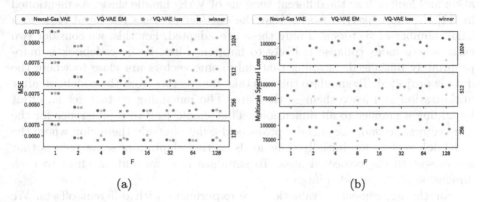

(a)                                                                (b)

**Fig. 4.** Performance of VQ-VAEs trained with a codebook loss or expectation-maximization and Neural-Gas VAE for different combinations of feature sizes $F$ and codebook sizes $S$ on (a) CIFAR and (b) Speech Commands.

For the comparison with the VQ-VAE, we use the same architectures as in Sect. 4.1, but substitute the bottleneck with either the Neural-Gas VAE, the VQ-VAE trained with codebook loss, or the VQ-VAE with the codebook trained with expectation-maximization [20]. Every model is trained with the default parameters from the corresponding papers and the same optimizer as previously. These models are trained over varying codebook sizes and feature sizes. For CIFAR, we the codebook sizes $S \in \{128, 256, 512, 1024\}$ and codebook dimensions $F \in \{1, 2, 4, 8, 16, 32, 64, 128\}$. Figure 4a shows the performance of the models for each combination. We can see that the Neural-Gas VAE performs better or similar to both VQ-VAE models. Surprisingly, the VQ-VAE with expectation-maximization performs worse in almost all cases. In addition, we did the analogous experiment on the Speech Commands data set but left out $S = 128$ since there was close to no difference in performance between the models. The results can be found in Fig. 4b. Here, we see that Neural-Gas VAE is outperformed by the VQ-VAE with expectation-maximization. However, the reconstruction performance is better than the performance of the VQ-VAE with codebook loss. This discrepancy is due to the convergence speed of the different models. The models training the codebook with a loss function have more influences and seem to need more time for convergence.

Surprisingly, we did not observe a single case of index collapse even though it was observed by [11]. This is most likely due to either the architecture that was taken from [20] or the used initialization for the codebook which we initialized by sampling from a normal distribution and division by $F$ whereas the original VQ-VAE is initialized by sampling from a uniform distribution between $[-\sqrt{3/F}, \sqrt{3/F}]$. Hence, we need to investigate where index collapse appears.

### 4.3   Avoiding Index Collapse

As index collapse is a hard-to-predict phenomenon, we artificially create the situation and look at how the different versions of VAEs handle these. As mentioned in [11] the most likely reason is that the encoder projects the input close to a small number of vectors and only these are adapted. For this, we consider two cases where index collapse is likely to happen. First, if the codebook is inappropriately initialized, meaning that only some vectors are close to where the data is projected. To simulate this, we take five vectors from the codebook after initialization and leave them as they are. The remaining vectors get an offset by adding a number to all dimensions. This should lead to a preference for the five vectors. Second, the encoder projects the data outside the region where the codebook vectors are initially. This leads to the adaption of some vectors that are closest to the projected area. To simulate this, we add an offset to each dimension of the encoded input.

For the experimental evaluation, we experiment with different offsets. We take the same setup as in Sect. 4.1 with a codebook size of 512, codebook dimensions of 2, which is the best case for the VQ-VAE to avoid index collapse, and 50 epochs of training. The results of these runs can be seen in Fig. 5.

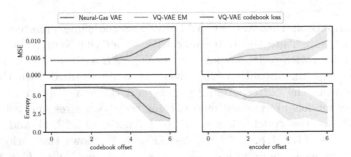

**Fig. 5.** Behavior of vector quantization processes with respect to artificial index collapse by inducing offsets aggregated over three runs.

The VQ-VAE performance decreases for expectation-maximization with an encoder offset whereas the codebook loss version gets worse with a codebook offset. In contrast, the Neural-Gas VAE can recover in both cases and use the complete notebook. The VQ-VAE codebook loss version can handle the encoder offset since the commitment loss and codebook loss can counteract this by meeting somewhere in the middle. However, if there are codebook vectors in the general area of the data, they are preferred and the rest is ignored as seen in the codebook offset performance. The performance with expectation-maximization is the other way around. In the case of the encoder offset only some vectors are adapted and the rest stays close to the origin. The better performance with a codebook offset is explainable since all vectors where no data is assigned move slowly towards the origin, where they can later participate in the expectation-maximization process.

## 4.4    Neural-Gas VAE Topology

Next, we evaluate the topologies that are created with the neural-gas method. As mentioned in the original neural-gas paper [17], the resulting graph is a subgraph of a Delauney triangulation keeping edges where the data in the distribution appears. This can especially help the visualization if we chose the $F$ as two. In this case, we can trivially reuse the codebooks for the layout. However, we can also ignore the codebook values and choose an arbitrary graph layout which can allow to display the graph in 2D even though the points are higher dimensional.

**Feature Manifolds.** In the usual setting of the VQ-VAE, the quantized vectors are on a feature level since they only describe parts of the image. If we take the setup from Sect. 4.1 with a codebook size of 512 and a lifetime of 2, we can see the manifold in Fig. 6a. The lifetime is selected such that all updates in the final epoch are incorporated.

In the feature manifold, we see several trends in the reconstruction of the codebook vectors. From top to bottom, we see a change in brightness with high brightness at the bottom. Furthermore, there are multiple vertical stripes with the outer ones being complementary edges. In the center, we find stripes for blue-ish, green-ish, and red-ish prototypes. In this situation, it is still open how the model encodes more fine-grained features. For instance, brighter colors require combinations of codebook vectors.

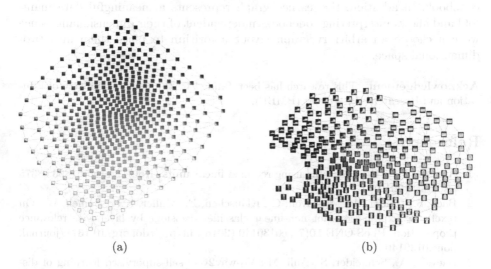

(a)                                                              (b)

**Fig. 6.** (a) Feature manifold of a Neural-Gas VAE model trained on CIFAR. (b) Object manifold of a Neural-Gas VAE trained on Fashion-MNIST. Both manifold's layout is according to the 512 two-dimensional codebook vectors. The edges are drawn according to the adjacency matrix $A$. The nodes are a representation of individually decoded codebook vectors.

**Object Manifolds.** Next, we take a look at a possible graph resulting from a Neural-Gas VAE in the object domain. Using the Fashion-MNIST data set [26]. The idea is to reduce the latent space of the encoder to a single vector. In this experiment, we take a similar setup to Sect. 4.1 but the last layer in the encoder and the first layer in the decoder are replaced with convolution with a kernel size of 7 and a transposed convolution with the same kernel size. This model is trained for 5 epochs with the Adam optimizer. Figure 6b shows the different kinds of clothing are well clustered in different regions of the latent space. Furthermore, we see that trousers and sneakers are less connected demonstrating that the edges are helpful to see an absence of a smooth transition. Additionally, we see the transitions between different types of shoes and shirts.

## 5 Conclusion

We introduced the Neural-Gas VAE which is a novel variant of the VQ-VAE. The Neural-Gas VAE adapts the codebook loss by incorporating the adaption of vectors corresponding to their rank with respect to the distance. Furthermore, we apply the graph learning algorithm from neural-gas and propose to also use it with arbitrary vector quantization methods. In the evaluation, we discovered default parameters that allow stable training so that the model achieves competitive performance. Moreover, we showed that the Neural-Gas VAE is robust against index collapse that is due to a mismatch between the encoder and the codebook. In addition, the learned graph represents a meaningful data manifold and allows interpreting codebooks independent of their dimensionality since we can choose an arbitrary graph layout algorithm to place them in a two-dimensional space.

**Acknowledgement.** This research has been funded by the Federal Ministry of Education and Research of Germany (BMBF).

## References

1. Agarap, A.F.: Deep learning using rectified linear units (ReLU). arXiv:1803.08375 [cs, stat] (2019)
2. Bach, S., Binder, A., Montavon, G., Klauschen, F., Müller, K.R., Samek, W.: On pixel-wise explanations for non-linear classifier decisions by layer-wise relevance propagation. PLoS ONE **10**(7), e0130140 (2015). https://doi.org/10.1371/journal.pone.0130140
3. Baevski, A., Schneider, S., Auli, M.: Vq-wav2vec: self-supervised learning of discrete speech representations. arXiv:1910.05453 [cs] (2020)
4. Chorowski, J., Weiss, R.J., Bengio, S., van den Oord, A.: Unsupervised speech representation learning using WaveNet autoencoders. IEEE/ACM Trans. Audio Speech Lang. Process. **27**(12), 2041–2053 (2019). https://doi.org/10.1109/TASLP.2019.2938863
5. Engel, J., Hantrakul, L.H., Gu, C., Roberts, A.: DDSP: differentiable digital signal processing. In: International Conference on Learning Representations (2019)

6. Fefferman, C., Mitter, S., Narayanan, H.: Testing the manifold hypothesis. arXiv:1310.0425 [math, stat] (2013)

7. Fortuin, V., Hüser, M., Locatello, F., Strathmann, H., Rätsch, G.: SOM-VAE: interpretable discrete representation learning on time series. arXiv:1806.02199 [cs, stat] (2019)

8. He, K., Zhang, X., Ren, S., Sun, J.: Deep residual learning for image recognition. arXiv:1512.03385 [cs] (2015)

9. Ioffe, S., Szegedy, C.: Batch normalization: accelerating deep network training by reducing internal covariate shift. arXiv:1502.03167 [cs] (2015)

10. Jang, E., Gu, S., Poole, B.: Categorical reparameterization with gumbel-softmax. arXiv:1611.01144 [cs, stat] (2017)

11. Kaiser, L., et al.: Fast decoding in sequence models using discrete latent variables. arXiv:1803.03382 [cs] (2018)

12. Kingma, D.P., Ba, J.: Adam: a method for stochastic optimization. arXiv:1412.6980 [cs] (2017)

13. Krizhevsky, A.: Learning multiple layers of features from tiny images. Technical report (2009)

14. Łańcucki, A., et al.: Robust training of vector quantized bottleneck models. arXiv:2005.08520 [cs, stat] (2020)

15. Liao, C.F., Tsao, Y., Lu, X., Kawai, H.: Incorporating symbolic sequential modeling for speech enhancement. arXiv:1904.13142 [cs, eess, stat] (2019)

16. Martinetz, T.: Competitive Hebbian learning rule forms perfectly topology preserving maps. In: Gielen, S., Kappen, B. (eds.) ICANN 1993, pp. 427–434. Springer, London (1993). https://doi.org/10.1007/978-1-4471-2063-6_104

17. Martinetz, T., Schulten, K.: A "Neural-Gas" network learns topologies. Artif. Neural Netw. **1**, 397–402 (1991)

18. Norouzi, M., Fleet, D.J.: Cartesian K-Means. In: 2013 IEEE Conference on Computer Vision and Pattern Recognition, Portland, OR, USA, pp. 3017–3024. IEEE (2013). https://doi.org/10.1109/CVPR.2013.388

19. Olah, C., Mordvintsev, A., Schubert, L.: Feature visualization. Distill **2**(11), e7 (2017). https://doi.org/10.23915/distill.00007

20. van den Oord, A., Vinyals, O., Kavukcuoglu, K.: Neural discrete representation learning. arXiv:1711.00937 [cs] (2018)

21. Roweis, S.T., Saul, L.K.: Nonlinear dimensionality reduction by locally linear embedding. Science (New York, N.Y.) **290**(5500), 2323–2326 (2000). https://doi.org/10.1126/science.290.5500.2323

22. Selvaraju, R.R., Cogswell, M., Das, A., Vedantam, R., Parikh, D., Batra, D.: Grad-CAM: visual explanations from deep networks via gradient-based localization. Int. J. Comput. Vis. **128**(2), 336–359 (2019). https://doi.org/10.1007/s11263-019-01228-7

23. Srivastava, R.K., Greff, K., Schmidhuber, J.: Highway networks. arXiv:1505.00387 [cs] (2015)

24. Warden, P.: Speech commands: a dataset for limited-vocabulary speech recognition. arXiv:1804.03209 [cs] (2018)

25. Wu, H., Flierl, M.: Learning product codebooks using vector quantized autoencoders for image retrieval. arXiv:1807.04629 [cs, eess] (2019)

26. Xiao, H., Rasul, K., Vollgraf, R.: Fashion-MNIST: a novel image dataset for benchmarking machine learning algorithms. arXiv:1708.07747 [cs, stat] (2017)

# Opemod: An Optimal Performance Selection Model for Prediction of Non-stationary Financial Time Series

Zichao Xu[1], Hongying Zheng[2], and Jianyong Chen[1(✉)]

[1] Department of Computer Science and Software Engineer, Shenzhen University, Shenzhen, China
jychen@szu.edu.cn
[2] Sino-German Robotics School, Shenzhen Institute of Information Technology, Shenzhen, China

**Abstract.** It is a critical challenge in financial time series analysis to reduce noise and forecast future stock prices. In this paper, we propose Opemod, an optimal performing selection model to predict and adaptively select prediction modes based on performance. Opemod is designed with three parts: two-ends extension mode decomposition (TEEMD) algorithm, attention based encoder and decoder (AED) model, and optimal performing selection (OPS) algorithm. Firstly, we propose TEEMD algorithm to restrain the end effect of sequence decomposition by differently extending and truncating both two ends of the sequence, and the original financial time series are decomposed into intrinsic mode functions (IMFs) more accuracy by TEEMD. Secondly, we design a novel encoding and decoding model based on both LSTM and multi-head attention mechanism (AED) to capture both long-term and short-term dependence information. Thus the trends of IMFs can be predicted separately. Finally, after the processes of decomposition and prediction, OPS is used to select modes with the best performance. Extensive experiments have been carried out on CSI 300 index and Dow Jones index (DJI) datasets, and the results show that Opemod can get better investment return than other state-of-the-art methods.

**Keywords:** Financial time series · Forecasting · Empirical mode decomposition · Deep learning

## 1 Introduction

Multi-step stock price prediction is crucial to value investment in stock market as they can reduce the risk of decision-making by appropriately determining the future movement of an investment asset. However, stock price series are non-linear, non-stationary and chaotic. They can be affected by many factors, such as interest rates, inflation rates, trader's expectation, catastrophe, political events and economic environments [1]. If the noise and anomalies cannot be effectively detected, the stock prices can not be predicted accuracy.

© The Author(s), under exclusive license to Springer Nature Switzerland AG 2022
E. Pimenidis et al. (Eds.): ICANN 2022, LNCS 13529, pp. 304–315, 2022.
https://doi.org/10.1007/978-3-031-15919-0_26

Traditional LSTM [2] has limited ability to predict one step stocks prices because short-term stock prices are noisy and unstable. In contrast, LSTM is more suitable for multi-step prediction since it has memory cell and can retain the pattern of the sequence. However, the prediction errors will accumulate step by step. In [3], the Mid-LSTM is proposed to predict midterm stocks prices. It uses the hidden Markov model (HMM) to detect hidden states in markets and trading volumes to reduce risks and avoid anomalies. N-BEATS in [4] is designed based on backward and forward residual links and a very deep stack of fully-connected layers to solve the forecasting problem of univariate time series points. Although the architectural details of models [5, 6] vary, they show that deep learning approaches are effective in finding non-linear patterns in stock market.

The prediction of financial time series exhibits less success due to a high noise-to-signal ratio [7], and none of the methods mentioned above concerns the impact of noise in signals. Noise is an important source of disturbances that could mislead the detection of main patterns from the series. However, in the presence of noisy time series, it is difficult to filter out the signal in some cases where the noise shares fundamental harmonics with the series [8]. Moreover, in some situations, the noise does not come from any external source, and the erratic behavior is part of the sequence. The discrimination between signal and noise is not only unsuitable but also undesired since some important elements from the signal could be removed. Therefore, instead of handling the problem as a pure series and random noise, the signal is considered as a sequence of stable and irregular patterns [9], and how to distinguish them is a very difficult and important problem.

The empirical mode decomposition (EMD) [10] is developed as an iterative algorithm that decomposes the series in a set of orthogonal signals called intrinsic mode functions, or IMFs. EMD is appropriate for non-stationary sequences since it decomposes the signal based on a local time scale representation without a pre-setting function nor the use of any harmonic. However, EMD has the end effect [11] problem which leads to error accumulation of IMFs.

This paper aims at predicting the multi-step stock prices and proposes a unique optimal performance selection model (Opemod), which are presented in the following section.

## 2  Opemod

In this section, Opemod is first presented in details. It consists of three components: TEEMD, AED, and OPS. The "min-max" normalization method and the training details are then provided.

### 2.1  Opemod Architecture

Opemod aims at multi-step (5 days) stock price prediction. Different from other methods which use composite sequence for forecasting, Opemod divides decomposition and composition into two separate parts. We think that financial series,

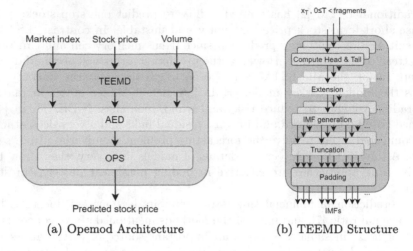

(a) Opemod Architecture          (b) TEEMD Structure

**Fig. 1.** Architecture and structure

such as stock prices, contain information in different frequency domains, and it is a more reasonable method to use high-frequency signals to predict high-frequency signals and use low-frequency signals to predict low-frequency signals. The architecture of Opemod is shown in Fig. 1 (a). First, we propose TEEMD, a data processing method which can be used to decompose the original signal $x(t)$ (which includes daily stock closing price, market index and volume) into IMFs. Afterwards, the IMFs are fed into AED for prediction. The output of AED is the prediction result of the IMFs. Finally, we design OPS which is oriented by investment income to handle the problem of signals composition, so as to get the final predicted result $y(t)$.

## 2.2 TEEMD

We propose TEEMD to decompose the original signal $x(T)$ into several IMFs. These IMFs are differentiated by frequencies from high to low, and each IMF has mode characteristics with different frequencies. The architecture of TEEMD is shown in Fig. 1 (b). First, we use the original sequence ahead of $x(T)$ as left extension of $x(T)$. Then we calculate the maximum sequence and the minimum sequence of $x(T)$, and calculate a new pair of the maximum and the minimum points based on statistics. After that, the two points are used to do the right extension of $x(T)$. Second, the extended $x(T)$ is fed into IMF generation [12], and the head and tail of IMFs are truncated. TEEMD effectively restrains the end effect in the process of mode decomposition by extending and truncating both two ends of the orignal $x(T)$, thus to get more accuracy result. Finally, we pad the truncated IMFs to adapt to the training process of the model. Futhermore, considering the additivity of signal, we use 0 to fill the missing dimension. All details of computing procedure can be found in Algorithm 1.

---

**Algorithm 1:** TEEMD Algorithm

---

**Input:** original series $x(T), 0 \leq T < frags$, amount of data fragments $frags$,
the predicted sequence lengths $seqlen$

**Output:** IMFs

1   Let $i = 0, maxshape = 0, \alpha = 1.5$.

2   **while** $i < frags$ **do**

3      **if** $i < seqlen$ **then**

4          Get maximum points series of $x(i)$: $peaks_{max}$.

5          Get minimum points series of $x(i)$: $peaks_{min}$.

6          Compute the maximum of right extension:

7             $maxP = mean(peaks_{max}) + \alpha std(peaks_{max})$.

8          Compute the minimum of right extension:

9             $minP = mean(peaks_{min}) - \alpha std(peaks_{min})$.

10         Add $maxP$ and $minP$ (Tail) to the end of $x(i)$.

11         Generate IMF from $x(i)$ and get $IMFs_{extension}$.

12         Truncate $IMFs_{extension}$, and cut off the right extension to get $IMFs$.

13      **else**

14          Get $seqlen$ points (Head) before $x(i)$.

15          Put Head in front of $x(i)$.

16          Get the maximum points of $x(i)$: $peaks_{max}$.

17          Get the minimum points of $x(i)$: $peaks_{min}$.

18          Compute the maximum of right extension:

19             $maxP = mean(peaks_{max}) + \alpha std(peaks_{max})$.

20          Compute the minimum of right extension:

21             $minP = mean(peaks_{min}) - \alpha std(peaks_{min})$.

22          Add $maxP$ and $minP$ (Tail) to the end of $x(i)$. Generate IMF from $x(i)$
and get $IMFs_{extension}$.

23          Truncate $IMFs_{extension}$, and cut off both the left and right extension
to get $IMFs$.

24      Record max shape of the $IMFs$ for padding:

25         $maxshape = max(maxshape, shape(IMFs))$.

26      $i = i + 1$

27   **while** $i < frags$ **do**

28      Pad $IMFs(i)$ with 0 on both time axis and feature axis.

29      $i = i + 1$

30   **return** $IMFs$

---

## 2.3   AED

As presentation above, different from other methods which use composite
sequence for forecasting, Opemod divides decomposition and composition into
two separate parts. AED is designed to handle the prediction task. The original
series is composed into several IMFs by TEEMD. As shown is Fig. 2 (a), these

IMFs (signed as IMFx) are fed into the encoder of AED to obtain intermediate hidden states vectors. Then, the multi-head attention layer is used to aggregate temporal hidden states vectors through dynamic weights. After that, the Add and LayerNorm layer is used to add the hidden states vectors and the output of multi-head attention layer, and then the layer normalization is processed to get the vector as the input of the decoder. Finally, the predicted IMFs (signed as IMFy) are obtained by the decoder. Here, both the encoder and the decoder use LSTM.

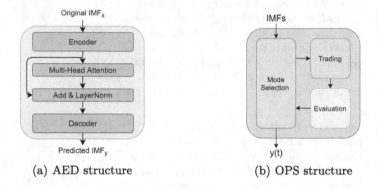

(a) AED structure              (b) OPS structure

**Fig. 2.** AED and OPS

## 2.4   OPS

Signal composition is another crucial and difficult problem. Here, OPS is created to solve the problem of signal composition. As mentioned above, we can get the predicted IMFs signals through AED model, and these signals will be composed in OPS model to get composite series. By backtesting the composite forecasted series on the training set, and calculating its actual rate of return, we choose the best composition mode based on profit performance. In this way, our model is changed from precision-oriented to profit-oriented. We record this best composition mode and migrate it to the test set to achieve the best results. All the calculation details of OPS can be found in Algorithm 2.

## 2.5   Opemod Training

**Data Process.** We use "max-min" normalization to reform dataset. In addition, in order to avoid any data leakage, the training set data and the test set data are strictly separated. Then we calculate"max" and "min" on the training set to complete the normalization process of the training set data. We transfer them directly to the testing set to complete the normalization operation. After that, all data will be packed into fragments by using a roling window. Finnaly, the normalized data is fed into Opemod to process the multi-step prediction task.

---

**Algorithm 2:** OPS Algorithm

---

**Input:** predicted $IMFs$, number of $IMFs$' components $maxshape$, status,
number of selected components $K$

**Output:** predicted sequence $y(t)$

1  Let $y(t) = 0$.

2  Add all predicted IMFs: $x(t) = sum(IMFs)$.

3  Do IMF generation for $x(t)$ to get frequency accurated $IMFs$.

4  **if** $status='train'$ **then**

5      Let $k = 1, maxincome = 0$.

6      **while** $k < maxshape$ **do**

7          Let $i = 0$.

8          **for** $i = 0$ $to$ $k - 1$ **do**

9              $y(t) = y(t) + IMFs(maxshape - 1 - i)$

10         Trade and get total income rate $income$ of $y(t)$.

11         **if** $income > maxincome$ **then**

12             $maxincome = income$

13             Record $K = k$

14         $k = k + 1$

15 **else**

16     **for** $k = 0$ $to$ $K - 1$ **do**

17         $y(t) = y(t) + IMFs(maxshape - 1 - k)$.

18 **return** $y(t)$

---

**Network Training.** In Opemod, only AED needs to be trained. AED in Fig. 2 (a) has four layers (a LSTM layer for Encoder, a Multi-Head Attention layer, an Add & LayerNorm layer, a LSTM layer for Decoder, respectively). The loss function is MSE. The optimizer of our network is Adam. The explanation and numerical values of the neural network parameters we use are shown in Table 1.

## 3 Performance Evaluation

In this section, we validate our Opemod based on the CSI 300 index and Dow Jones index (DJI). First, data preprocessing with rolling window and iterative forecasting method are provided. Then, the price sequence processed by TEEMD is demonstrated. Finally, we propose a simple trading strategy and demonstrate automatic trading results based on price sequences, which are predicted by both our models and other methods.

### 3.1 Data Preprocessing with Rolling Window and Iterative Forecasting Method

The price data for this project are the historical CSI 300 index and DJI. CSI 300 is composed of the most representative stocks from the shanghai and shenzhen

**Table 1.** Layer parameters.

| Layer | Parameter | Value |
|---|---|---|
| LSTM (Encoder) | Input size | 3 |
| | Hidden size | 54 |
| Multi-head attention | Head | 2 |
| | Embedding dimension | 54 |
| LSTM (Decoder) | Input size | 54 |
| | Output size | 3 |

stock market, and shanghai stock market index is used as the market index data. DJI is composed of the most representative stocks from newyork stock market, and S&P 500 index is used as the market index data.

We use the data over the period of about 15 years (from 04/20/2005 to 07/30/2021, including 3960 trading days for CSI 300). About 89% of the dataset (including 3540 trading days) are used as the training data, and the remainders (including 420 trading days) are used as the test data. On the other hand, DJI dataset (from 02/03/2011 to 01/20/2022, including 2760 trading days) is also uesd in our experiments. About 85% of DJI data (including 2340 trading days) are used as the training data, and the remainders (including 420 trading days) are used as the test data. A rolling window is used to pack data, and the size of window is set as 60. According to the size of rolling window, the training data is divided into many training input sets (each set length 59) and training output sets (each set length 1). The test data is divided into input data and output data of 72 windows.

We focus on multi-step forecasting of stock price (5 days) in the project. Unlike the point-by-point prediction processing, the multi-step forecasting predicts several days price based on the data that predicted in the previous predictions, so we choose iterative forecasting method. In particular, the window is first initialized with all real data, and we slide the window back one step and add the first predicted point to the last point of window. Then the new window is fed into the model to predict the next point. In our experiments, the above process is iterated 5 times, and a 5-day prediction sequence is obtained.

## 3.2   TEEMD Results

In order to show the outstanding performance of TEEMD algorithm in restraining end effect, we randomly select two pairs of experimental results, which are shown in Fig. 3. Figure 3 shows the divergence at the end of the sequence when the classical EMD is used. However, it has been has been effectively restrained by TEEMD. Futhermore, IMF generation is an iterative process, the errors at the end of sequence will accumulate due to the defects of EMD, and the errors of TEEMD will be much smaller by comparison. Therefore, more accurate IMFs can be obtained through TEEMD algorithm.

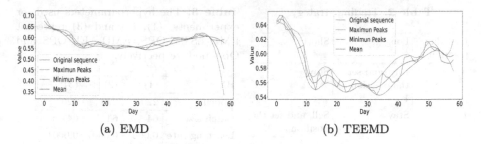

(a) EMD                                    (b) TEEMD

**Fig. 3.** Cubic spline interpolation curves of (a) EMD and (b) TEEMD on CSI 300

## 3.3   Trading Strategy and Evaluation Indicators

We consider the forecasting issue in discrete time, and denote $\hat{x}_t$ the forecast of $x_t$. sMAPE defined as:

$$sMAPE = \frac{200}{T} \sum_{t=1}^{T} \frac{|x_t - \hat{x}_t|}{|x_t| + |\hat{x}_t|} \tag{1}$$

is introduced to evaluate our model. The direction accuracy (DA) is defined as:

$$DA = \frac{T}{100} \sum_{t=1}^{T} d_t \tag{2}$$

Here, $d_t$ is given by

$$d_t = \begin{cases} 1, & (\hat{x}_t - \hat{x}_{t-1})(x_t - x_{t-1}) \geq 0 \\ 0, & (\hat{x}_t - \hat{x}_{t-1})(x_t - x_{t-1}) < 0 \end{cases} \tag{3}$$

where $\hat{x}_t$ corresponds to the forecasted value produced by the proposed Opemod. In addition, we have designed a simple trading strategy, which calculates the trading signal according to the series predicted by the model. We use the position situation to reflect the decision of buying, selling or keeping unchanged (Stay). The position is calculated as:

$$position_t = \begin{cases} position_{t-1}, & position_{t-1} = 0 \ and \ \hat{x}_t \leq \hat{x}_{t-1} \\ 1, & position_{t-1} = 0 \ and \ \hat{x}_t > \hat{x}_{t-1} \\ position_{t-1}, & position_{t-1} = 1 \ and \ \hat{x}_t \geq \hat{x}_{t-1} \\ 0, & position_{t-1} = 1 \ and \ \hat{x}_t < \hat{x}_{t-1} \end{cases} \tag{4}$$

and details of the trading signals are shown in Table 2.

In order to evaluate how effective of models intuitively, we calculate the cumulative return (CR), annualized rate of return (AR), Sharpe ratio (SR) and max drawdown (MDD) based on the transaction results on the test set data. To start with, the daily asset $Asset_t$ is defined. We initialize $Asset_0 = 1.0$ and

**Table 2.** Trading strategy.

| Last day position | Long | Short |
|---|---|---|
| 0 | Buy, and set the position as 1 | Stay |
| 1 | Stay | Sell, and set the position as 0 |

**Table 3.** The hyperparameters used for experiments. (1), (2) and (3) represent EMD-LSTM-OPS, EMD-AED-OPS and Ope-mod, respectively.

| HYP | (1) | (2) | (3) |
|---|---|---|---|
| Epochs | 220 | 220 | 220 |
| Batch size | 64 | 64 | 64 |
| Learning rate | 0.0001 | 0.0001 | 0.0001 |

[1] HYP refers to the hyperparameters.

$Asset_t, t \in [1, T-1]$ is computed based on the position above. The cumulative return is defined as:

$$CR = \prod_{t=1}^{T-1} (R_t + 1) \tag{5}$$

where

$$R_t = \frac{Asset_t}{Asset_{t-1}} - 1, t = 1, ..., T - 1 \tag{6}$$

is the daily return rate. And annualized rate of return can be computed as:

$$AR = 252 \times \frac{CR - 1}{T} \times 100\% \tag{7}$$

In order to consider the benefits and risks comprehensively, SR and MDD are also introduced to evaluate our model. The risk-free rate $R_f$ is set as 1.5%.

## 3.4   Trading Results and Discussion

In the experiments, we compare the performance of our models with traditional LSTM, Mid-LSTM and N-BEATS. In order to show the mechanism of the proposed Opemod in details, we also carry out ablation experiments. Firstly, we combine EMD with LSTM to build EMD-LSTM. Secondly, we use the proposed AED to repalce LSTM and build EMD-AED. Finally, we use TEEMD to replace EMD to build TEEMD-AED. Futhermore, in order to show the advantages of performance, these three models all adopt our proposal, i.e., separating decomposition from composition process. Thus, combining with our OPS, we develop two new models, i.e., EMD-LSTM-OPS and EMD-AED-OPS. They as well as Opemod are compared each other in the following experiments. At the same time, these new models can be compared with other methods. Besides, the hyperparameters of these models are listed in Table 3.

In the experiments of CSI 300 and DJI, we calculate direction accuracy of the prediction result. We also compute the cumulative return, annual return, Sharpe ratio and max drawdown based on the trading results of models. These experiment results are presented in Table 4, and Table 5. From these results,

**Table 4.** Performance evaluation indexes on CSI 300. (a), (b), (c), (1), (2) and (3) represent LSTM, Mid-LSTM, N-BEATS, EMD-LSTM-OPS, EMD-AED-OPS and Opemod, respectively.

| Method | sMAPE | DA | CR | AR | SR | MDD |
|--------|-------|-----|-----|-----|-----|-----|
| (a) | 2.8721 | 46.24% | 1.0981 | 6.77% | 0.4635 | −14.49% |
| (b) | 5.8941 | 52.37% | 1.2698 | 18.20% | 0.9897 | −16.08% |
| (c) | **2.2911** | 52.09% | 1.3905 | 25.95% | 1.9840 | **−6.30%** |
| (1) | 4.0558 | 53.20% | 1.5513 | 35.98% | 2.0353 | −7.16% |
| (2) | 3.7241 | 55.71% | 1.6329 | 40.95% | **2.2733** | −7.16% |
| (3) | 2.8614 | **57.94%** | **1.6338** | **41.01%** | 2.1348 | −7.17% |

**Table 5.** Performance evaluation indexes on DJI. (a), (b), (c), (1), (2) and (3) represent LSTM, Mid-LSTM, N-BEATS, EMD-LSTM-OPS, EMD-AED-OPS and Opemod, respectively.

| Method | sMAPE | DA | CR | AR | SR | MDD |
|--------|-------|-----|-----|-----|-----|-----|
| (a) | 3.2374 | 46.52% | 1.0028 | 0.2% | −0.1356 | **−4.39%** |
| (b) | 4.9807 | 49.03% | 1.0018 | 0.12% | −0.0392 | −9.58% |
| (c) | 4.0631 | 52.09% | 1.1017 | 7.01% | 0.6200 | −6.09% |
| (1) | 6.1332 | 53.20% | 1.2162 | 14.68% | 1.4316 | −5.03% |
| (2) | 4.7609 | 53.48% | 1.2378 | 16.11% | 1.4800 | −8.54% |
| (3) | **2.7137** | **57.66%** | **1.3121** | **20.94%** | **1.6210** | −8.93% |

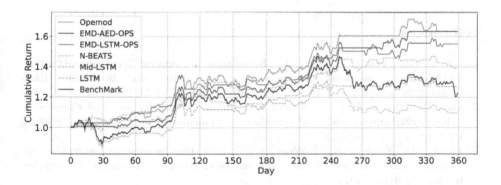

**Fig. 4.** Cumulative returns of Opmod and other models on CSI 300 (360 days)

we can observe that our proposed model have better performance than other models. In addition, we can notice that EMD-AED-OPS has higher direction accuracy than EMD-LSTM-OPS, which leads to higher returns. It indicates that the proposed AED can evidently benefit the accuracy of prediction. Furthermore, the proposed Opemod has better performance than EMD-AED-OPS, proving that TEEMD restrains the end effect and reduces the error of IMFs.

The cumulative returns of models are shown in Fig. 4. In order to reflect market situation and demonstrate the performance more objectively, we also add CSI 300 index as benchmark for comparison. In Fig. 4, we can find that the cumulative return of EMD-AED-OPS is higher than that of EMD-LSTM-OPS, and the cumulative return of Opemod is the highest. It is noteworthy that our three models can predict the corrected trend before the market fell sharply. Therefore, the trader we set can sell stocks at right time and avoids huge loss. As a result, we obtain excess returns on the whole test period.

## 4   Conclusion

In this paper, we first propose a new novel algorithm to restrain the end effect of sequence decomposition by differently extending and truncating two ends of the sequence. Secondly, we design AED to capture a large amount of both long-term and short-term dependence information in these separated IMFs output by TEEMD. Finally, after decomposing and predicting process, OPS is used to complete the process of modes selection and signal composition. Extensive experiment results based on CSI 300 and DJI datasets show that the proposed Opemod has better performance in predicting financial time series.

**Acknowledgement.** This work was supported in part by the National Nature Science Foundation of China under Grant U2013201 and in part by the Pearl River Talent Plan of Guangdong Province under Grant 2019ZT08X603.

## References

1. Chang, P.C., Fan, C.Y., Liu, C.H.: Integrating a piecewise linear representation method and a neural network model for stock trading points prediction. IEEE Trans. Syst. Man Cybern. Part C Appl. Rev. **39**(1), 80–92 (2009)
2. Bao, W., Yue, J., Rao, Y.: A deep learning framework for financial time series using stacked autoencoders and long-short term memory. PloS One **12**(7), e0180944 (2017)
3. Li, X., Li, Y., Liu, X.Y., Wang, C.D.: Risk management via anomaly circumvent: mnemonic deep learning for midterm stock prediction. arXiv preprint arXiv:1908.01112 (2019)
4. Oreshkin, B.N., Carpov, D., Chapados, N., Bengio, Y.: N-beats: neural basis expansion analysis for interpretable time series forecasting. arXiv preprint arXiv:1905.10437 (2020)
5. Selvin, S., Vinayakumar, R., Gopalakrishnan, E.A., Menon, V.K., Soman, K.P.: Stock price prediction using LSTM, RNN and CNN-sliding window model. In: 2017 International Conference on Advances in Computing, Communications and Informatics (ICACCI), pp. 1643–1647. IEEE (2017)
6. Hongfeng, X., Chai, L., Luo, Z., Li, S.: Stock movement prediction via gated recurrent unit network based on reinforcement learning with incorporated attention mechanisms. Neurocomputing **467**, 214–228 (2022)

7. Wu, G.G.R., Hou, T.C.T., Lin, J.L.: Can economic news predict Taiwan stock market returns? Asia Pac. Manag. Rev. **24**(1), 54–59 (2019)
8. Wu, Z., Huang, N.E.: A study of the characteristics of white noise using the empirical mode decomposition method. Proc. R. Soc. Lond. Ser. A: Math. Phys. Eng. Sci. **460**(2046), 1597–1611 (2004)
9. Chacón, H.D., Kesici, E., Najafirad, P.: Improving financial time series prediction accuracy using ensemble empirical mode decomposition and recurrent neural networks. IEEE Access **8**, 117133–117145 (2020)
10. Huang, N.E., et al.: The empirical mode decomposition and the Hilbert spectrum for nonlinear and non-stationary time series analysis. Proc. R. Soc. Lond. Ser. A: Math. Phys. Eng. Sci. **454**(1971), 903–995 (1998)
11. He, Z., Wang, Q., Shen, Y., Jin, J., Wang, Y.: Multivariate gray model-based BEMD for hyperspectral image classification. IEEE Trans. Instrum. Meas. **62**(5), 889–904 (2013)
12. Cao, J., Li, Z., Li, J.: Financial time series forecasting model based on CEEMDAN and LSTM. Phys A: Stat. Mech. Appl. **519**, 127–139 (2019)

# PSP-MVSNet: Deep Patch-Based Similarity Perceptual for Multi-view Stereo Depth Inference

Leiping Jie[1,2] and Hui Zhang[2(✉)]

[1] Department of Computer Science, Hong Kong Baptist University,
Hong Kong SAR, China
`cslpjie@comp.hkbu.edu.hk`
[2] Guangdong Key Laboratory of Interdisciplinary Research and Application
for Data Science, BNU-HKBU United International College, Zhuhai, China
`amyzhang@uic.edu.cn`

**Abstract.** This paper proposes PSP-MVSNet for depth inference problem in multi-view stereo (MVS). We first introduce a novel patch-based similarity perceptual (PSP) module for effectively constructing 3D cost volume. Unlike previous methods that leverage variance-based operators to fuse feature volumes of different views, our method leverages a cosine similarity measure to calculate matching scores for pairs of deep feature vectors and then treats these scores as weights for constructing the 3D cost volume. This is based on an important observation that many performance degradation factors, *e.g.*, illumination changes or occlusions, will lead to pixel differences between multi-view images. We demonstrate that a patch-based cosine similarity can be used as explicit supervision for feature learning and can help speed up convergence. Furthermore, To adaptively set different depth ranges for different pixels, we extend an existing dynamic depth range searching method with a simple yet effective improvement. We can use this improved searching method to train our model in an end-to-end manner and further improve the performance of our method. Experimental results show that our method achieves state-of-the-art performance on the DTU dataset and comparative results on the intermediate set of Tanks and Temples dataset.

**Keywords:** Depth estimation · Patch-based similarity · Dynamic depth range · Multi-view stereo

## 1 Introduction

Multi-view Stereo (MVS) is one of the most important problems in computer vision and has been studied for decades [5,7,8,10,11,18,20,21]. It takes a couple of images containing the same object or scene from different viewpoints as input and outputs an estimated corresponding 3D representation. Benefiting from the vigorous development of deep convolutional neural networks (CNN), learning-based approaches [3,22–24] show better performance than traditional methods.

E. Pimenidis et al. (Eds.): ICANN 2022, LNCS 13529, pp. 316–328, 2022.
https://doi.org/10.1007/978-3-031-15919-0_27

State-of-the-art learning-based MVS methods typically consist of three steps: constructing a 3D cost volume using warped deep features on each discrete depth hypothesis, regularizing the 3D cost volumes by 3D convolutions, and performing depth regression for each pixel.

Despite the powerful representative ability of deep perceptual features, a core issue is how to construct the 3D cost volume considering different lighting, occlusion or visibility. We believe that all these factors, undermining the 3D cost volume construction performance, will lead to photo inconsistency. Recent state-of-the-art approaches follow [27] to leverage the variance-based metric to construct 3D cost volume. The advantage of this metric is that it can operate on an arbitrary number of input images. However, it has two major drawbacks. First, it processes each pixel individually, ignoring useful spatial information. Second, it does not consider factors such as illumination changes or occlusions when constructing the 3D cost volume. Inspired by the patch-based similarity in the traditional MVS methods, we propose a novel *Patch-based Similarity Perception* (PSP) module for 3D cost volumes construction. In other words, the constructed 3D cost volume considers all factors leading to photo inconsistency and further suppresses the noise in it. Furthermore, we explicitly impose PSP module to learn similarities of learned feature vectors. This explicit guidance brings less disturbance and speeds up the convergence of the training.

Recently, it has been proved that a coarse-to-fine network architecture [4,9, 25] with iteratively decreasing number of depth hypothesis can reduce the huge GPU memory consumption problem, which is caused by the 3D convolution operators for regularizing raw 3D cost volume. Therefore, another concern is how to dynamically set the depth range for finer stages. Specifically, the entire possible depth range is considered for plane sweeping for the first stage. We only consider the adjacent depth range of the estimated depth map from previous stage for finer stages instead of the entire possible depth range. However, an end-to-end training framework with a learned dynamic depth range always suffers from instability and a longer training time. As shown in [25], dynamic depth range searching can only be applied in the testing phase rather than the training. To the best of our knowledge, [4] is the only feasible solution that can be trained to learn the depth range. Nevertheless, their model requires more training time than other learning-based methods. In contrast, based on [25], we propose a simple yet efficient *dynamic depth range searching* (DDRS) strategy to effectively learn reasonable depth range for different pixels at different stages. The main contributions of this paper are summarized as follows:

1. We propose a novel 3D cost volume construction algorithm based on cosine similarity, which explicitly supervises the feature learning and suppresses noise.
2. Our end-to-end framework can be trained with learned dynamic depth ranges and achieves better performance.
3. Compared with state-to-the-art MVS methods, our approach achieve the best overall performance on the DTU benchmark [1]. It can also achieves competitive scores on the Tanks and Temples dataset [13].

## 2    Methodology

### 2.1    Overview

Given a reference image $I_0$ and $N-1$ source images, our network predicts the reference depth map $D_0$ at the same resolution as $I_0$. In particular, our network first uses a weight-shared 2D CNN to extract multi-scale features of the reference image and all source images. The corresponding source image features will be warped for each scale to align with the reference image feature at each depth hypothesis. Then, the reference-source feature pair is fed into the proposed patch-based similarity perceptual module (Sect 2.3) that outputs the similarity score used for 3D cost volume construction, followed by 3D cost volume regularization and depth map regression in a coarse-to-fine manner. In order to achieve the depth range for the finner stage, dynamic depth range searching (Sect 2.4) is applied in finer stages. While in the coarsest stage, depth hypotheses between the smallest and largest possible depth value are uniformly sampled. The overview architecture of our proposed PSP-MVSNet is shown in Fig. 1.

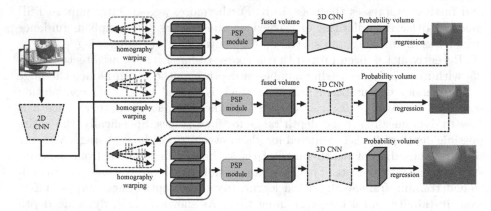

**Fig. 1.** PSP-MVSNet network architecture. Our model operates in a coarse-to-fine manner with multi-scale input features and outputs dense depth estimations. Please refer to Sect 2 for more details.

### 2.2    Multi-Scale Feature Pyramid

In order to prepare multi-scale features for each stage in our coarse-to-fine refinement structure, we adopt the 9-layer 2D feature extractor from [25]. In particular, it takes an image of resolution $H \times W \times 3$ as input and outputs feature pyramid with three different resolutions. The shape of these feature pyramids are $\frac{H}{4} \times \frac{W}{4} \times C$, $\frac{H}{2} \times \frac{W}{2} \times C$ and $H \times W \times C$, where $H$, $W$ and $C$ represents height, width and channel respectively. In contrast to [4,9,27], each pyramid contains only high-level CNN features. As shown in [29], low-level features encode edges, colours, and corners, while high-level features encode semantic information. For depth estimation, cues such as edge are less favorable as the flat regions with rich textures bring more noise.

## 2.3   Patch-Based Similarity Perceptual Module

Most current methods follow MVSNet [27], which uses a variance-based operator to fuse the warped source feature volumes with the reference feature volume. This allows their models to be scalable with any number of input views. However, different pixels are treated equally without considering any spatial information. In contrast, we propose to use patch-based similarity measure to calculate matching scores for building 3D cost volume more effectively. In particular, for each view $i$, given its camera intrinsic $K_i$ and extrinsic parameters $E_i$, the $4 \times 4$ homography warping matrix between the reference image and source image $i$ at depth $d$ can be formulated as:

$$H_i(d) = K_i E_i E_0^{-1} K_0^{-1}. \tag{1}$$

We can then project a pixel in the reference image to the source image by:

$$P_i = H_i(d)[dx \quad dy \quad d \quad 1]^T, \tag{2}$$

where $[dx \quad dy \quad d \quad 1]^T$ is the homogeneous coordinate of a pixel in the reference image $I_0$, and $P_i$ refers to the corresponding homogeneous coordinate in the source image $I_i$. Next, we can use this differentiable homography to warp the 2D source feature maps at each depth hypothesis under the reference camera and build source feature volumes aligned with the reference feature volume.

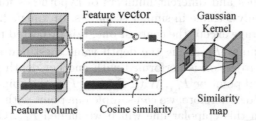

**Fig. 2.** PSP module. Cosine similarity is used to measure the similarity of the feature vectors of two corresponding pixels. The Gaussian kernel is fixed with non-learnable parameters.

Instead of using the variance-based operator to fuse all feature volumes, we propose to calculate the patch-based similarity scores for each reference-source feature pair, as shown in Fig. 2. Let the $k$th feature volume be $F_k$ of shape $D \times C \times H \times W$, where $D, C, H, W$ represents the number of depth hypothesis, the number of channels, height and width of the feature volume respectively. For a reference-source feature pair $(F_0, F_k)$, the patch-based similarity score of pixel $p(x,y)$ at depth $d$ can be calculate by:

$$W(x,y,d,k) = \sum_{i=-\frac{w}{2}}^{\frac{w}{2}} \sum_{j=-\frac{h}{2}}^{\frac{h}{2}} \omega_{ij}[F_{x+i,y+j,d,k} \odot F_{x+i,y+j,d,k}], \tag{3}$$

where $[\odot]$ denotes the similarity measure used to calculate the similarity score, $w$, $h$, $\omega_{ij}$ are the width, height and Gaussian kernel-based weight of the patch window. In our paper, we adopt the cosine similarity measure, which explicitly guides the network to learn high scores for similar features and low scores for different features that may be caused by occlusion or visibility. Since the range of the original cosine similarity measure is between $-1$ and $1$, we rescale it to $[0, 1]$ by first plus 1 and then halve it. It is worth noting that the weights of the patch window $\omega$ are non-learnable parameters and are initialized with fixed normalized values. After obtaining all the reference-source pair similarity scores for all depth planes, we construct the raw 3D cost volume $C$ with these scores as weights as follows:

$$V = \frac{\sum_{i=0}^{N-1} F_i \circ W_i}{\sum_{i=0}^{N-1} W_i}, \tag{4}$$

where $W_0$ is the weight matrix (all its entities to 1) for the reference feature volume and $\circ$ is element-wise multiplication. This formula can effectively consider the similarity scores when constructing the 3D cost volume, thereby suppressing the noise degrading the overall performance.

## 2.4 Dynamic Depth Range Searching Module

Most existing approaches manually tune the depth range by setting different depth interval values and different numbers of hypotheses for different stages, which are empirically feasible in similar scenarios. In Yang's [25] work, for each pixel $P_{i,j}$ of each stage except the coarsest one, it is projected to the corresponding source image point $P'_{i,j}$ using the depth value $d$ estimated in the previous stage. The same projection is performed with another depth value, e.g., $d + 1$, and let its projected point be $P^*_{i,j}$. With $P'_{i,j}$ and $P^*_{i,j}$, the epipolar line in source image is determined. Therefore, we can sample one point with a certain distance $m$ far from $P'_{i,j}$ on this epipolar line which we named $P^s_{i,j}$. Once $P'_{i,j}$ and $P^s_{i,j}$ are projected back to 3D space, different depth ranges for different pixels can be obtained. In [25], $m$ is fixed to 1. In contrast, we set different values of $m$ for different stages, which is reasonable and robust under the coarse-to-fine architecture. In addition, another variance-based dynamic depth range searching strategy is proposed in [4]. In the experimental section, Cheng's method [4] is compared with ours in terms of performance and convergence.

## 2.5 Cost Volume Regularization

Although our proposed PSP module can suppress noise by being aware of occlusions and illumination changes when constructing the raw 3D cost volume $V$, it is still necessary to conduct a further regularization for higher performance. Similar to previous works, we use a 3D U-Net [17] like network as our regularization module. In contrast to the four-scale network used in [4,27,28], we use a two-scale 3D CNN in our model since our PSP module already suppresses the noise caused by photo inconsistency. In particular, our 3D CNN module downsamples twice with increasing channel numbers and upsamples twice with decreasing channel numbers. Afterwards, we apply the *softmax* operator for probability normalization along the depth direction to convert the regularized 3D cost volume into the probability volume $P$.

## 2.6 Depth Regression and Loss Function

Based on the probability volume $P$, considering each pixel in a stage, we obtain its depth by following:

$$d(x,y) = \sum_{i=1}^{K_i} p_i(x,y)d_i(x,y), \tag{5}$$

where $d_i(x,y)$ and $p_i(x,y)$ are the depth value of the *ith* hypothesis plane and the corresponding probability. At each stage in our coarse-to-fine network, a depth map is estimated. Therefore, we impose supervision to each estimated depth map and the total loss is defined as:

$$Loss = \sum_{i=1}^{N} \lambda_i L_i, \tag{6}$$

where $L_i$, $\lambda_i$ represent to the loss and the corresponding weight at stage $i$ respectively. We choose smoothed L1 loss as the loss function for each $L_i$. Empirically, we set $\lambda_i = 1$ for all stages.

## 3 Experiments

In this section, we evaluate our proposed PSP-MVSNet on the indoor DTU and the outdoor Tanks and Temples dataset, followed by ablation studies to demonstrate the effectiveness of our proposed PSP and DDRS modules.

**Datasets.** DTU [1] Dataset is a large-scale MVS dataset consisting of 124 diverse scenes captured from 49 or 64 locations under 7 different lighting conditions. For each scan, it provides the captured RGB image, corresponding camera parameters and point cloud. The Tanks and Temples dataset [13] contains two subsets: intermediate and advanced. In order to verify the generalization of our model, we evaluate on its intermediate set. More specifically, the intermediate set consists of 8 collections of realistic indoor or outdoor scenes including *Family, Francis, Horse, Lighthouse, M60, Panther, Playground*, and *Train*.

### 3.1 Implementation

**Training.** We implement our PSP-MVSNet with PyTorch [16] and train it on the DTU training set from scratch. During training, the number of source views is 2. Since our PSP-MVSNet is equipped with the dynamic depth range search, different numbers of depth hypotheses are used in different stages. In particular, 48 uniform depth hypotheses are sampled from the initial depth range for the coarsest stage. Since the depth range is dynamically reduced for the finer stage, we only set 8 uniformly sampled depth planes. The learning rate is initially set to 0.001 and then halved at the $10^{th}$, $12^{th}$, $14^{th}$ and $20^{th}$ epoch as shown in [27]. Adam optimizer [12] is used with batch size 16. The entire model is trained for 21 epochs using an NVIDIA TITAN RTX GPU. During the training phase, we follow [25] to train with low-resolution input images to achieve a lightweight and fast training process.

**Evaluation Details.** At this phase, the number of source views is set to 5 following MVSNet [27], while the number of depth hypothesis at the coarsest stage is changed to 96. Similar to existing state-of-the-art methods, we follow the method in [27] to fuse all predicted depth maps into point cloud. For a fair comparison, we directly use the MATLAB code provided in [1] and report the accuracy, completeness and overall scores, repectively.

### 3.2   Benchmarking on DTU Dataset

We first evaluate our model on DTU testing set following the configuration in [27]. Specifically, a reference view with four source views is used to estimate the depth map of the reference view. Each test image has a resolution of $1600 \times 1184$ and the initial depth range is approximately [425 mm, 905 mm] according to values provided by the DTU dataset.

**Table 1.** Quantitative results on DTU testing set [1].

| Type | Method | Acc. | Comp. | Overall |
|---|---|---|---|---|
| Geometric | Camp [2] | 0.835 | 0.554 | 0.695 |
| | Furu [6] | 0.613 | 0.941 | 0.777 |
| | Tola [21] | 0.342 | 1.190 | 0.766 |
| | Gipuma [7] | **0.283** | 0.873 | 0.578 |
| | Colmap [19, 20] | 0.400 | 0.664 | 0.532 |
| Learning | MVSNet [27] | 0.396 | 0.527 | 0.462 |
| | R-MVSNet [26] | 0.383 | 0.452 | 0.417 |
| | Point-MVSNet [3] | 0.342 | 0.411 | 0.376 |
| | AttMVS [15] | 0.383 | **0.329** | 0.356 |
| | CasMVSNet [9] | 0.325 | 0.385 | 0.355 |
| | CVP-MVSNet [25] | 0.296 | 0.406 | 0.351 |
| | UCSNet [4] | 0.338 | 0.349 | 0.344 |
| | **Ours** | 0.341 | **0.329** | **0.335** |

We compare our method with both traditional methods and learning-based approaches. As shown in Table 1, our proposed PSP-MVSNet achieves the best completeness and overall performance, while Gipuma [7] is the best in terms of accuracy. Quantitatively, our method achieves superior performance over other methods. Moreover, as shown in Fig. 3, our model predicts better results than

CasMVSNet [9]. In particular, our predicted surfaces are smoother and cleaner in the first, third and last columns. In the second column, our results contain more details about the surface.

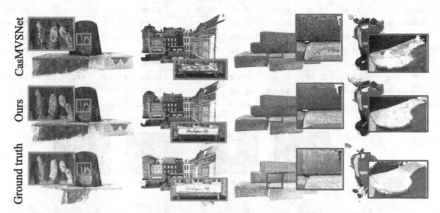

(a) Point cloud reconstruction on DTU testing set [1]. We compare our results with CasMVSNet [9].

(b) Point cloud reconstruction on the intermediate set of Tanks and Template dataset [13].

**Fig. 3.** Qualitative results on two benchmark datasets. Best viewed on screen.

### 3.3 Benchmarking on Tanks and Temples Dataset

We now evaluate the generalization ability of our PSP-MVSNet on the intermediate set of Tanks and Temples dataset [13]. As shown in Fig. 3, our performance is visually acceptable. Moreover, we compare with state-of-the-art methods [4,9,23,25] in terms of *f-score*. Detailed results are summarized in Table 2. Our method achieves the best performance on scene *Horse* and *M60*. Additionally, we are the second best on scene *Francis*, *Panther* and *Train*.

**Table 2.** Quantitative results on the intermediate set of Tanks and Temples [13]. The best and the second best results are shown in bold and underlined, respectively.

| Method | Mean | Family | Francis | Horse | Lighthouse | M60 | Panther | Playground | Train |
|---|---|---|---|---|---|---|---|---|---|
| COLMAP [20] | 42.14 | 50.41 | 22.25 | 25.63 | <u>56.43</u> | 44.83 | 46.97 | 48.53 | 42.04 |
| MVSNet [27] | 43.48 | 55.99 | 28.55 | 25.07 | 50.79 | 53.96 | 50.86 | 47.90 | 34.69 |
| R-MVSNet [26] | 48.40 | 69.96 | 46.65 | 32.59 | 42.95 | 51.88 | 48.80 | 52.00 | 42.38 |
| Fast-MVSNet [28] | 47.39 | 65.18 | 39.59 | 34.98 | 47.81 | 49.16 | 46.20 | 53.27 | 42.91 |
| CVP-MVSNet [25] | 54.03 | **76.50** | 47.74 | 36.34 | 55.12 | <u>57.28</u> | 54.28 | 57.43 | 47.54 |
| UCSNet [4] | 54.83 | 76.09 | 53.16 | 43.03 | 54.00 | 55.60 | 51.49 | 57.38 | 47.89 |
| P-MVSNet [14] | 55.62 | 70.04 | 44.64 | 40.22 | **65.20** | 55.08 | **55.17** | 60.37 | **54.29** |
| CasMVSNet [9] | **56.84** | <u>76.37</u> | **58.45** | <u>46.26</u> | 55.81 | 56.11 | 54.06 | <u>58.18</u> | 49.51 |
| Ours | <u>56.02</u> | 73.99 | <u>53.56</u> | **47.56** | 53.82 | **58.42** | <u>54.39</u> | 56.45 | <u>49.98</u> |

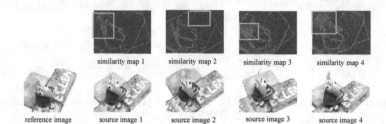

**Fig. 4.** Visualization of similarity maps of scan4 in DTU testing set. When wrapping from the source view to the reference view, the red area is the valid area after differentiable homography. The brighter the area, the greater the dissimilarity. (Color figure online)

### 3.4   Visualization of Similarity Maps

Recall that in Sect 2.3, the similarity maps are learned in the proposed PSP module. We now visualize the intermediate similarity maps of scan4 in the DTU testing set. As shown in Fig. 4, different regions show different activation values, which means the similarity score between the warped source image feature and the reference image feature. Higher activation values always appear around object boundaries, where the depth value changes rapidly. This phenomenon is reasonable since these regions are more likely to be occluded if the camera's viewpoint changes. It is worth noting that not all object boundaries have high activation values. The green box in similarity map 2 indicates that the boundaries between two bottom objects do not have high activate values. In addition to these boundary regions, higher activation values cluster in the occluded regions. For instance, in the similarity map 1, 3 and 4, since the head of the toy occludes some visible regions in the reference image, the similarity map corresponding to these visible regions shows higher dissimilarity. An interesting observation is that in the green box region in similarity map 2, the intensity is much brighter than its corresponding region in the reference image. Despite their different intensities, the similarity map can still treat these two regions as matched regions and assign smaller activation values. By assigning different similarity maps to different warped source image features, our proposed PSP module can construct the 3D cost volume more reasonably and effectively and simultaneously suppress noise.

**Table 3.** Ablation study on the DTU testing set. All models are trained on the entire DTU training set with the same training and testing settings.

| Model | epochs | Acc. | Comp. | Overall |
|---|---|---|---|---|
| Model A | 21 | 0.421 | 0.504 | 0.462 |
| Model B | 21 | 0.354 | 0.383 | 0.369 |
| Model B | 50 | **0.332** | 0.350 | 0.341 |
| Model C | 21 | 0.347 | 0.332 | 0.339 |
| Model D | 21 | 0.341 | **0.329** | **0.335** |

**Table 4.** Impact of different gaussian kernel sizes and pixel interval settings.

| Kernel size | Acc. | Comp. | Overall |
|---|---|---|---|
| $3 \times 3$ | 0.350 | 0.337 | 0.343 |
| $5 \times 5$ | 0.341 | **0.329** | **0.335** |
| $7 \times 7$ | **0.337** | 0.342 | 0.340 |
| $9 \times 9$ | 0.339 | 0.343 | 0.341 |

| Pixel interval | Acc. | Comp. | Overall |
|---|---|---|---|
| $[2, 1.5]$ | 0.353 | 0.341 | 0.347 |
| $[1.5, 1]$ | 0.345 | 0.331 | 0.338 |
| $[1, 0.5]$ | 0.341 | **0.329** | **0.335** |
| $[0.5, 0.25]$ | 0.361 | 0.372 | 0.367 |

## 3.5   Ablation Studies

**Evaluation on the PSP and DDRS Module.** In this section, we evaluate our PSP module using different variants. In particular, we denote the dynamic depth range searching module in [25] as *DDRS1*, the dynamic depth search module in [4] as *DDRS2* and our modified version as *DDRS-Ours*. Several variant models are trained: (a) Model A, which uses the variance-based fusion method as in [27] and *DDRS1*. (b) Model B adopts the proposed PSP module and *DDRS2*. (c) Model C is trained with PSP module and *DDRS1*. (d) Model D is the proposed model equipped with the PSP module and *DDRS-Ours*. Our experiments show that training model B requires much more epochs than other models. Therefore, for model B, we train it twice with different epochs, 21 and 50, respectively. As can be seen from Table 3, our proposed PSP module can significantly boost the overall performance, and our modified version of the dynamic depth range searching module in [25] is slightly better than the original one. Furthermore, training with the dynamic depth range searching module in [4] takes more time to converge. A possible reason might be the variance measure since different probability distributions may lead to similar variance. Nonetheless, our PSP module can still improve the performance and reduce the training time when trained with their strategy.

**Evaluation on Gaussian Kernel Sizes.** Since we use a Gaussian kernel in the PSP module, we also evaluate the impact of different Gaussian kernel sizes. In our experiment, we try four different values: $3 \times 3$, $5 \times 5$, $7 \times 7$, and $9 \times 9$. As shown in Table 4, the mean accuracy increases with larger kernel size but with worse mean completeness. In addition, the $3 \times 3$ kernel performs worse while $5 \times 5$ has the best overall performance. This is reasonable since patch-based similarity measures are difficult to handle smooth textureless regions with smaller kernels. Meanwhile, larger kernels show a more distinguishable ability, but suffer from over-smoothing problems.

**Evaluation on Pixel Intervals.** We now evaluate different interval settings for the DDSR module. We choose four different groups $[2, 1.5]$, $[1.5, 1]$ $[1, 0.5]$ and $[0.5, 0.25]$ for training. As shown in Table 4, $[1, 0.5]$ performs the best. Setting the pixel interval too large or too small both lead to performance degradation, which is consistent with results in [25]. Moreover, pixel pairs with the same distance on epipolar line will result in different depth range under the reference camera. Therefore, the pixel interval values still need to be tuned for very large or very small scenes in terms of high performance.

## 4   Conclusion

In this work, we propose PSP-MVSNet, an end-to-end coarse-to-fine network for multi-view stereo depth inference. Specifically, we introduce a patch-based similarity perceptual (PSP) module that produces matching scores for 3D volume construction. We leverage the cosine similarity metric as explicit supervision in the process of feature learning. The PSP module can suppress noise and accelerate convergence. In addition, a simple yet effective extension of the existing dynamic depth range searching method is presented. This extension can automatically infer different depth ranges for different pixels at different stages. Experimental results demonstrate that, compared with various start-of-the-art approaches, our proposed PSP-MVSNet achieves superior performance on the DTU dataset and competitive results on the Tanks and Temples dataset.

**Acknowledgement.** This work was supported by the National Natural Science Foundation of China (62076029), the Natural Science Foundation of Guangdong Province (2022B1212010006, 2017A030313362) and internal funds of the United International College (R202012, R201802, UICR0400025-21).

## References

1. Aanæs, H., Jensen, R.R., Vogiatzis, G., Tola, E., Dahl, A.B.: Large-scale data for multiple-view stereopsis. Int. J. Comput. Vis **120**(2), 153–168 (2016). https://doi.org/10.1007/s11263-016-0902-9
2. Campbell, N.D.F., Vogiatzis, G., Hernández, C., Cipolla, R.: Using multiple hypotheses to improve depth-maps for multi-view stereo. In: Forsyth, D., Torr, P., Zisserman, A. (eds.) ECCV 2008. LNCS, vol. 5302, pp. 766–779. Springer, Heidelberg (2008). https://doi.org/10.1007/978-3-540-88682-2_58
3. Chen, R., Han, S., Xu, J., Su, H.: Point-based multi-view stereo network. In: ICCV, pp. 1538–1547 (2019)

4. Cheng, S., et al.: Deep stereo using adaptive thin volume representation with uncertainty awareness. In: CVPR, pp. 2524–2534 (2020)
5. Furukawa, Y., Hernández, C.: Multi-view stereo: a tutorial. Found. Trends Comput. Graph. Vis **9**(1–2), 1–148 (2015)
6. Furukawa, Y., Ponce, J.: Accurate, dense, and robust multiview stereopsis. TPAMI **32**(8), 1362–1376 (2010)
7. Galliani, S., Lasinger, K., Schindler, K.: Massively parallel multiview stereopsis by surface normal diffusion. In: ICCV, pp. 873–881 (2015)
8. Goesele, M., Curless, B., Seitz, S.M.: Multi-view stereo revisited. In: CVPR. vol. 2, pp. 2402–2409 (2006)
9. Gu, X., Fan, Z., Zhu, S., Dai, Z., Tan, F., Tan, P.: Cascade cost volume for high-resolution multi-view stereo and stereo matching. In: CVPR, pp. 2495–2504 (2020)
10. Hannah, M.J.: Computer matching of areas in stereo images. Ph.D. thesis (1974)
11. Kanade, T., Yoshida, A., Oda, K., Kano, H., Tanaka, M.: A stereo machine for video-rate dense depth mapping and its new applications. In: CVPR, pp. 196–202 (1996)
12. Kingma, D., Ba, J.: Adam: a method for stochastic optimization. In: ICLR (2015)
13. Tanks and temples: Knapitsch, A., Park, J., Zhou, Q.Y., Koltun, V.: Benchmarking large-scale scene reconstruction. In: TOG. vol. 36, pp. 2651–2660 (2017)
14. Luo, K., Guan, T., Ju, L., Huang, H., Luo, Y.: P-mvsnet: learning patch-wise matching confidence aggregation for multi-view stereo. In: ICCV, pp. 10452–10461 (2019)
15. Luo, K., Guan, T., Ju, L., Wang, Y., Chen, Z., Luo, Y.: Attention-aware multi-view stereo. In: CVPR, pp. 1590–1599 (2020)
16. Paszke, A., et al.: Automatic differentiation in pytorch. In: NeurIPS Workshop (2017)
17. Ronneberger, O., Fischer, P., Brox, T.: U-net: convolutional networks for biomedical image segmentation. vol. 9351, pp. 234–241 (2015)
18. Scharstein, D., Szeliski, R.: A taxonomy and evaluation of dense two-frame stereo correspondence algorithms. IJCV **47**(1–3), 7–42 (2002)
19. Schönberger, J.L., Frahm, J.M.: Structure-from-motion revisited. In: CVPR, pp. 4104–4113 (2016)
20. Schönberger, J.L., Zheng, E., Frahm, J.-M., Pollefeys, M.: Pixelwise view selection for unstructured multi-view stereo. In: Leibe, B., Matas, J., Sebe, N., Welling, M. (eds.) ECCV 2016. LNCS, vol. 9907, pp. 501–518. Springer, Cham (2016). https://doi.org/10.1007/978-3-319-46487-9_31
21. Tola, E., Strecha, C., Fua, P.: Efficient large-scale multi-view stereo for ultra high-resolution image sets. Mach. Vis. Appl. **23**(5), 903–920 (2012). https://doi.org/10.1007/s00138-011-0346-8
22. Wang, Y., Guan, T., Chen, Z., Luo, Y., Luo, K., Ju, L.: Mesh-guided multi-view stereo with pyramid architecture. In: CVPR, pp. 2039–2048 (2020)
23. Xu, Q., Tao, W.: Multi-scale geometric consistency guided multi-view stereo. In: CVPR, pp. 5483–5492 (2019)
24. Yan, J., Wei, Z., Yi, H., Ding, M., Zhang, R., Chen, Y., Wang, G., Tai, Y.-W.: Dense hybrid recurrent multi-view stereo net with dynamic consistency checking. In: Vedaldi, A., Bischof, H., Brox, T., Frahm, J.-M. (eds.) ECCV 2020. LNCS, vol. 12349, pp. 674–689. Springer, Cham (2020). https://doi.org/10.1007/978-3-030-58548-8_39
25. Yang, J., Mao, W., Alvarez, J.M., Liu, M.: Cost volume pyramid based depth inference for multi-view stereo. In: CVPR, pp. 4877–4886 (2020)

26. Yao, Y., Luo, Z., Li, S., Shen, T., Quan, T.F.L.: Recurrent mvsnet for high-resolution multiview stereo depth inference. In: CVPR, pp. 5525–5534 (2019)
27. Yao, Y., Luo, Z., Li, S., Tian, F., Long, Q.: Mvsnet: depth inference for unstructured multi-view stereo. In: ECCV, pp. 767–783 (2018)
28. Yu, Z., Gao, S.: Fast-mvsnet: sparse-to-dense multi-view stereo with learned propagation and gauss-newton refinement. In: CVPR, pp. 1949–1958 (2020)
29. Zeiler, M.D., Fergus, R.: Visualizing and understanding convolutional networks. In: ECCV, pp. 818–833 (2014)

# R2P: A Deep Learning Model from mmWave Radar to Point Cloud

Yue Sun[1], Honggang Zhang[2]([✉]), Zhuoming Huang[2], and Benyuan Liu[3]

[1] The Department of Computer Science, UMass, Boston, USA
Yue.Sun001@umb.edu
[2] The Department of Engineering, UMass, Boston, USA
{Honggang.Zhang,Zhuoming.Huang001}@umb.edu
[3] The Department of Computer Science, UMass, Lowell, USA
bliu@cs.uml.edu

**Abstract.** Recent research has shown the effectiveness of mmWave radar sensing for object detection in low visibility environments, which makes it an ideal technique in autonomous navigation systems. In this paper, we introduce Radar to Point Cloud (R2P), a deep learning model that generates smooth, dense, and highly accurate point cloud representation of a 3D object with fine geometry details, based on rough and sparse point clouds with incorrect points obtained from mmWave radar. These input point clouds are converted from the 2D depth images that are generated from raw mmWave radar sensor data, characterized by inconsistency, and orientation and shape errors. R2P utilizes an architecture of two sequential deep learning encoder-decoder blocks to extract the essential features of those radar-based input point clouds of an object when observed from multiple viewpoints, and to ensure the internal consistency of a generated output point cloud and its accurate and detailed shape reconstruction of the original object. We implement R2P to replace the Stage 2 of our recently proposed 3DRIMR (3D Reconstruction and Imaging via mmWave Radar) system. Our experiments demonstrate the significant performance improvement of R2P over the popular existing methods such as PointNet, PCN, and the original 3DRIMR design.

**Keywords:** 3D reconstruction · Point cloud · Deep learning · mmWave radar

## 1 Introduction

Recently the advantage of Millimeter Wave (mmWave) radar in object sensing in low visibility environment has been actively studied and applied in autonomous vehicles [5] and search/rescue in high risk areas [10]. However, further application of mmWave radar in object imaging and reconstruction is quite difficult because of the characteristics of mmWave radar signals such as low resolution, sparsity, and large noise due to multi-path and specularity. Recent work [3,5,10] attempts to design deep learning systems to generate 2D depth images based on mmWave

E. Pimenidis et al. (Eds.): ICANN 2022, LNCS 13529, pp. 329–341, 2022.
https://doi.org/10.1007/978-3-031-15919-0_28

radar signals. 3DRIMR [20] further introduces an architecture that generates 3D object shapes based on mmWave radar, but there is still room for significant improvement in order to produce more satisfactory end results.

In this paper, we introduce Radar to Point Clouds (R2P), a deep learning model that generates 3D objects in the format of dense and smooth point clouds that accurately resemble the 3D shapes of original objects with fine details. The inputs to R2P are simply some rough and sparse point clouds with possibly many inaccurate points due to the imperfect conversion from raw mmWave radar data. For example, they can be directly converted from those 2D depth images generated from radar data, using systems such as [5] or the Stage 1 of 3DRIMR [20]. R2P can be used to replace the generator network in Stage 2 of 3DRIMR. Recall that 3DRIMR's Stage 1 takes 3D radar intensity data as input and generates 2D depth images of an object, which are then combined and converted to a rough and sparse point cloud to be used as the input to Stage 2. The generator network of Stage 2 outputs the 3D shape of the object in the form of dense and smooth point cloud. Even though 3DRIMR can give some promising results, its Stage 2's generator network design is still not quite satisfactory. Specifically, the edges of generated point clouds are still blurry and their points tend to be evenly distributed in space and thus do not give a clear sharp shape structure. We introduce R2P in this paper to replace the Stage 2 of the original 3DRIMR, and we find that R2P significantly outperforms 3DRIMR both quantitatively and visually.

Our major contributions are summarized as follows. We propose Radar to Point Cloud (R2P), a deep neural network model, to generate smooth, dense, and highly accurate point cloud representation of a 3D object with fine geometry details, based on rough and sparse point clouds with incorrect points. These input point clouds are directly converted from the 2D depth images of an object that are generated from raw mmWave radar sensor data, and thus characterized by mutual inconsistency and orientation/shape errors, due to the imperfect process to generate them. R2P utilizes an architecture of two sequential deep learning encoder-decoder blocks to extract the essential features of those input point clouds of an object when observed from various viewpoints, and to ensure the internal consistency of a generated output point cloud and its detailed shape reconstruction of the original object. We further demonstrate with extensive experiments the importance of loss function design in the training of models for reconstructing point clouds. We also show the limitations of Chamfer Distance (CD) and Earth Mover's Distance (EMD), the two state-of-the-art point clouds evaluation metrics, in the evaluation of the shape similarity of two point clouds.

In the rest of the paper, we discuss related work and preliminaries in Sections 2 and 3, and then the design of R2P in Sect. 4. Experiment results are given in Sect. 5. Finally the paper concludes in Sect. 6.

## 2   Related Work

Frequency Modulated Continuous Wave (FMCW) Millimeter Wave (mmWave) radar sensing has been an active research area in recent years, especially in applications such as person/gesture identification [25,29], car detection/imaging [5], and environment sensing [3,10]. Usually Synthetic Aperture Radar (SAR) is used in data collection for high resolution, e.g., [4,11,15,17]. This paper is built on our recent work [20] on applying mmWave radar for 3D object reconstruction, in which we proposed 3DRIMR. The deep neural network model proposed in this paper can replace the model in the Stage 2 of 3DRIMR, and this new model significantly outperforms the original 3DRIMR. There have been a few recent work on mmWave radar based imaging, mapping, and 3D object reconstruction [3,5,10,13,30]. Our work is inspired by their promising research results, especially PointNet [13,14] and PCN [30]. Due to the low cost and small form factor of commodity mmWave radar sensors, we plan to develop a simple 3D reconstruction system with fast data collection to be attached in our UAV SLAM system [21] for search and rescue in dangerous environment. Besides radar signals, vision community has also been working on learning-based 3D object shape reconstruction [1,16,18,28], most of which use voxels to represent 3D objects. Our proposed neural network model uses point cloud as a format for 3D objects to capture detailed geometric information with efficient memory and computation performance. Our proposed R2P significantly outperforms the existing methods such as PointNet [13], PointNet++ [14], PCN [30], and 3DRIMR [20].

## 3 Preliminaries

### 3.1 FMCW Millimeter Wave Radar Sensing and Imaging

Similar to [20], we use FMCW mmWave radar sensor [23] signals to reconstruct 3D object shapes. Fast Fourier Transform (FFT) along three directions are conducted on received waveforms to generate 3D intensity maps of a space that represent the energy or radar intensity per voxel in the space, written as $x(\phi, \theta, \rho)$. Note that $\phi$, $\theta$, and $\rho$ represent azimuth angle, elevation angle, and range respectively. We use IWR6843ISK [24] operating at 60 GHz frequency, and for high resolution radar signals, we adopt SAR operation. Unlike data from LiDAR and camera sensor, mmWave radar sensors can only give us sparse, low resolution, and highly noisy data. Incorrect ghost points in radar signals can be generated due to multi-path effect. References [3,5,10] give more detailed discussion on FMCW mmWave radar sensing.

### 3.2 Representation of 3D Objects

We adopt point cloud format to represent 3D objects. Even though point cloud is a standard representation of 3D objects and it is used in learning-based 3D reconstruction, e.g., [2,13,14], the convolutional operation of Convolutional Neural Network (CNN) cannot be directly applied to a point cloud set as it is essentially an unordered point set. Furthermore, the point cloud of an object that is directly generated by raw radar signals is not a good choice to represent the shape of an object because of radar signal's low resolution, sparsity, and incorrect ghost points due to multi-path effect. Besides point clouds, voxel-based representations can also be used in 3D reconstruction [7, 8, 12, 27], and the advantage of such representation is that 3D CNN convolutional operations can be applied. In addition, mesh representations of 3D objects are also used in existing work [9, 26]. However these two representation formats are limited by memory and computation cost.

### 3.3 Review of 3DRIMR Architecture

This paper introduces R2P as a generator network to replace the Stage 2 of 3DRIMR in order to generate smooth and dense point clouds. For completeness, we now briefly review 3DRIMR's architecture. 3DRIMR consists of two back-to-back generator networks $\mathbf{G_{r2i}}$ and $\mathbf{G_{p2p}}$. In Stage 1, $\mathbf{G_{r2i}}$ receives a 3D radar energy intensity map of an object and outputs a 2D depth image of the object. We let a mmWave radar sensor scans an object from multiple viewpoints to get multiple 3D energy maps. Then $\mathbf{G_{r2i}}$ generates the corresponding 2D depth images of the object. The Stage 2 of 3DRIMR first pre-processes these images to get multiple coarse point clouds of the object, which are used as the input to $\mathbf{G_{p2p}}$ to generate a single point cloud of the object. A conditional generative adversarial network (GAN) architecture is designed for 3DRIMR's training. That is, two discriminator networks $\mathbf{D_{r2i}}$ and $\mathbf{D_{p2p}}$ that are jointly trained together with their corresponding generator networks. Let $m_r$ denotes a 3D radar intensity map of an object captured from a viewpoint, and let $g_{2d}$ be a ground truth 2D depth image of the same object captured from the same viewpoint. $\mathbf{G_{r2i}}$ generates $\hat{g}_{2d}$ that predicts or estimates $g_{2d}$ given $m_r$. If there are $k$ different viewpoints $v_1, ..., v_k$, generator $\mathbf{G_{r2i}}$ predicts their corresponding 2D depth images $\{\hat{g}_{2d,i}|i = 1, ..., k\}$. Each $\hat{g}_{2d,i}$ can be directly converted to a coarse and sparse 3D point cloud. Then we can have $k$ coarse point clouds $\{P_{r,i}|i = 1, ..., k\}$ of the object. The Stage 2 of 3DRIMR unions the $k$ coarse point clouds to form an initial estimated coarse point cloud of the object, denoted as $P_r$, which is a set of 3D points $\{p_j|j = 1, ..., n\}$. Generator $\mathbf{G_{p2p}}$ takes $P_r$ as input, and outputs a dense and smooth point cloud $P_o$. Note that since the generation process of $\mathbf{G_{r2i}}$ is not perfect, a coarse $P_r$ may likely contain many missing or even incorrect points. Next we will discuss our proposed R2P.

## 4    R2P Design

### 4.1    Overview

R2P is a generative model that generates a smooth and dense 3D point cloud of an object from the union of multiple coarse point clouds, which are directly converted from the 2D depth images of the object observed from different viewpoints. Since those 2D depth images are generated from raw radar energy maps, the union of their converted point clouds may contain many inconsistent and incorrect points due to the imperfect image generation process. R2P network model is able to extract the essential features of those input point clouds, and to ensure the internal consistency of a generated output point cloud and its detailed, accurate shape reconstruction of the original object. R2P can be used to replace the generator network of the Stage 2 of 3DRIMR, and it can also be used as an independent network that works on any rough and sparse input point clouds that contain incorrect points. The architecture of R2P is shown in Fig. 1. Let $P_r$ denote a union of $k$ separate coarse point clouds observed from $k$ viewpoints of the object $\{P_{r,i}|i = 1, ..., k\}$. R2P aims at generating a point cloud of an object with continuous and smooth contour $P_o$ from $P_r$. In our design we also include a discriminator network to train the generator under GAN framework. Due to space limitations, we do not discuss the discriminator here.

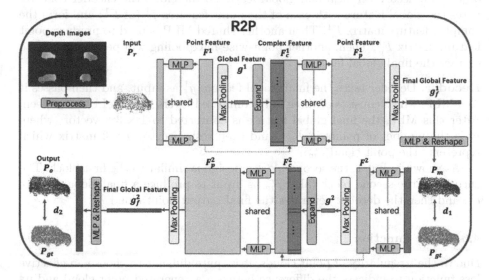

**Fig. 1.** R2P network architecture. The system first pre-processes multiple 2D depth images of an object to get multiple coarse and sparse point clouds, which may contain many incorrect points. These depth images are generated for the same object but viewed from four different viewpoints. Combining those coarse point clouds we can derive a single coarse point cloud, which is used as the input of R2P. Then R2P outputs a dense, smooth, and accurate point cloud representation of the object.

## 4.2   R2P Architecture

R2P's input $P_r$ and output $P_o$ are 3D point clouds represented as $n \times 3$ matrices, where $n$ is the number of points in the point cloud, and each row represents the 3D Cartesian coordinate $(x, y, z)$ of a point. Note that the output point cloud generated from our network has a larger number of points than the input point cloud, i.e., our network can reconstruct a dense and smooth point cloud from a sparse one. R2P consists of two sequential processing blocks, and both blocks share the same encoder-decoder network design. The first block takes the raw input point cloud $P_r$ to produce an intermediate point cloud $P_m$, and then the second block processes $P_m$ to generate the final output $P_o$. In each block, the encoder takes its input point cloud and converts it to a high dimensional feature vector, and the decoder takes this feature vector and converts it to an intermediate or a final output point cloud.

**Encoder.** As shown in Fig. 1, in the first block, the encoder gets $P_r$ as input, and passes it to a shared multilayer perceptron (MLP) to extend every point $p_i$ in $P_r$ to a high dimensional feature vector $f_i$ and form the point feature matrix $F^1$. This shared MLP is a network with two linear layers with BatchNorm and ReLU in between. Then, the encoder applies a point-wise maxpooling on $F^1$ and extracts a global feature vector $g^1$. To produce a complete point cloud for an object, we need both local and global features, therefore, the encoder concatenates the global feature with each of the point features $f_i^1$ (of $F^1$) and form the complex feature matrix $F_c^1$. Then another shared MLP is used to produce point feature matrix $F_p^1$. Then, another point-wise maxpooling will perform on $F_p^1$ to extract the final global feature $g_f^1$.

**Decoder.** Decoder takes the final global feature $g_f^1$ as input, and then passes it to a MLP, which consists of three fully-connected layers with ReLU in between. After this MLP, the final global feature is converted to $1 \times 3m$ vector (where $m$ is the number of points in $P_m$), and then reshaped to $m \times 3$ matrix which represents the point cloud $P_m$.

As shown in Fig. 1, the second block's design is similar to the first block. The encoder of the second block takes $P_m$ as input to produce a final global feature $g_f^2$, and then the decoder generates the final output point cloud $P_o$.

### 4.3   Loss Function

Due to the irregularity of point clouds, it is quite difficult to choose an effective loss function to indicate the difference between a generated point cloud and its corresponding ground truth point cloud. There are two popular metrics to evaluate the difference between two point clouds: Chamfer Distance (CD) [30] and Earth Mover's Distance (EMD) [30]. CD calculates the average closest distance between two point clouds $S_1$ and $S_2$. The symmetric version of CD is defined as:

$$CD(S_1, S_2) = \frac{1}{|S_1|} \sum_{x \in S_1} \min_{y \in S_2} \|x - y\|_2 + \frac{1}{|S_2|} \sum_{y \in S_2} \min_{x \in S_1} \|y - x\|_2 \tag{1}$$

EMD can find a bijection $\phi : S_1 \to S_2$, which can minimize the average distance between each pair of corresponding points in two point clouds $S_1$ and $S_2$. EMD is calculated as:

$$EMD(S_1, S_2) = \min_{\phi : S_1 \to S_2} \frac{1}{|S_1|} \sum_{x \in S_1} \|x - \phi(x)\|_2 \tag{2}$$

In our system, R2P generates the intermediate point cloud $P_m$ after its first encoder-decoder block, and then generates the final output point cloud $P_o$ after the second block. Hence, we design our loss function to evaluate both generated point clouds. That is, R2P's loss function is defined as a weighted sum of the loss of the first block $d_1(P_m, P_{gt})$ and the loss of the second block $d_2(P_o, P_{gt})$.

$$L(R2P) = d_1(P_m, P_{gt}) + \alpha d_2(P_o, P_{gt}) \tag{3}$$

Both $d_1$ and $d_2$ can be either CD or EMD, or some weighted combination of them. $\alpha$ is a hand-tuned parameter, and in our experiments, we find it performs well when set to 0.1. Note that unlike CD, EMD needs to find a bijection relationship between two point clouds, which is a optimization problem and hence computationally expensive, especially when the point clouds have large amounts of points. Moreover, this bijection also requires these two evaluated point clouds have the same number of points.

## 5  Implementation and Experiments

We implement our proposed R2P network and use it as the generator network of 3DRIMR system's Stage 2. The system first generates 2D depth images from 3D radar intensity maps from multiple views of an object, and then passes these output depth images to R2P to produce a 3D point cloud of the object.

### 5.1  Datasets

We conduct experiments on a dataset including 5 different categories of objects, namely industrial robot arms, cars, chairs, desks, and L-shape boxes. This dataset consists of both synthesized data and real data collected from experiments. The input point clouds to R2P are the output depth images produced by 3DRIMR's Stage 1. We follow a procedure that is similar to [20] to generate ground truth point clouds. In order to obtain enough amount of data required to train our deep neural network models, we modified HawkEye's data synthesizer [6] to synthesize 3D radar intensity maps and 2D depth images from 3D CAD point-cloud models, with configurations matching TI's mmWave radar sensor IWR6843ISK with DCA1000EVM [22], and Stereolabs' ZED mini camera [19]. In our experiments and when generating synthesized data, we determine the space setup to capture the views of various objects in a 3D environment. Four pairs of mmWave radar sensors and depth camera sensors are placed at the centers of the four edges of a square area, pointing towards the center of the square area where objects are randomly placed.

### 5.2  Model Training and Testing

We use the 2D depth images generated in the Stage 1 of 3DRIMR to form a dataset of coarse and sparse input point clouds for the 5 different categories of objects. Each input point cloud has 1024 points and an intermediate/final output point cloud has 4096 points. We train our proposed network model for each category independently. For each object category, we train the model based on 1400 pairs of point clouds for 200 epochs with batch size 2. The learning rate for the first 100 epochs is $2 \times 10^{-4}$ and linearly decreases to 0 in the rest 100 epochs. Then we test the model using the remaining 100 point clouds.

### 5.3   Evaluation Results

To the best of our knowledge, except for our previous work 3DRIMR, there are no other point cloud-based networks to reconstruct smooth, dense, and accurate point clouds from *point clouds with many incorrect and inconsistent points*, e.g., the union of multiple coarse point clouds which are converted from various 2D depth images of an object that are possibly inaccurate and inconsistent between themselves in terms of orientation and shape structure details. For example, a generated 2D depth image from radar data [5, 20] can possibly have a car's left and right sides switched, or it can be shaped like a similar but different car with different shape details. Note that the existing works (e.g., [30]) on this subject usually do not have such strong inaccuracy assumption on their inputs except missing points. Nevertheless we compare our proposed architecture against five related baseline methods. They are popular point cloud-based generative models, mainly designed for the purposes of classification, segmentation, and point clouds completion, assuming input data is either sparse or there are missing points. To ensure fair comparison, we train all six models (including baselines and ours) based on the same training and testing datasets. These baseline methods include: (1) **PointNet**. It is introduced in [13]. We choose 1024 as the dimension of global feature of Point-Net. The loss function is a combination of CD and EMD. (2) **PointNet++**. We use the same encoder architecture of PointNet++ [14] for classification with three Set Abstraction (SA) modules to get a 1024-dimension global feature, followed by a decoder consists of 3 fully-connected layers. The loss function is also a combination of CD and EMD. (3) **PCN_CD**. We use the same architecture of PCN [30], and set the grid size as 2. The number of points in the coarse and detailed output point clouds are 1024 and 4096 respectively. Note that in this method, both $d_1$ and $d_2$ are CD. (4) **PCN_EMD**. In this method, the architecture of the network is same as PCN_CD, but $d_1$ is EMD. (5) **3DRIMR**. This is the only architecture designed for point clouds reconstruction from inaccurate input point clouds among the 5 baselines. To ensure fair comparison, we use the combination of CD and EMD as its loss function. We compare the performance of the two variants of our proposed R2P, labeled as R2P_CD (both $d_1$ and $d_2$ use CD) and R2P_EMD (both $d_1$ and $d_2$ use EMD), with the five baseline methods mentioned above in terms of CD and EMD. The results are shown in Fig. 2. We can see that except the case of robot arms, our methods always have the smallest CD or EMD loss among all the methods. Even for the robot arms, the performance of our methods are similar to the other five methods.

We further compare the results of all six methods by visually examining their output points clouds, and some of them are shown in Fig. 3. We can see that all the output point clouds are coarser than the ground truth point clouds and some

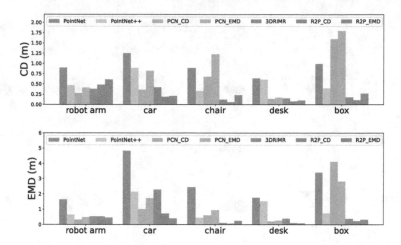

**Fig. 2.** Quantitative comparison on datasets of 5 different objects using baseline methods and our method. Top: Chamfer Distance of the output point cloud and the ground truth. Bottom: Earth Mover's Distance of the output point cloud and the ground truth.

of them lose many detailed shape characteristics. However, R2P_EMD can give the best shape reconstruction among all the methods, keeping most geometry characteristics. Especially for some small objects with fine shape details like chairs, only our method R2P_EMD can reconstruct an object with accurate shape.

## 5.4    Performance of Different Loss Functions

Loss function plays a quite important role in model training. A well-designed loss function can not only speed up the training process, but also affect the performance of a deep learning model. On the other hand, a bad loss function may not converge even with a well-designed network model. Hence, we need to carefully design our loss function used when training our model. However, existing popular evaluation metrics to compare point clouds are CD and EMD, which can only evaluate the overall distance between a pair of point clouds but cannot effectively capture the similarity of their shapes.

To search for a good loss function for R2P, we conduct a series of experiments with different combinations of these two metrics. Except the loss functions used in training are different, all other settings are all the same for these experiments. The quantitative results are shown in Fig. 4. We can see that if we only use EMD in the loss function, which is L2 in the figure, the CD between output and ground truth point clouds will be large; and except in the box experiment, if we only use CD in the loss function, which is L1 in the figure, the EMD between output and ground truth point clouds will also be large. Hence, it makes sense to use the combination of CD and EMD, which is L3 in the figure, which gives both small CD and EMD. However, since calculating EMD is very expensive

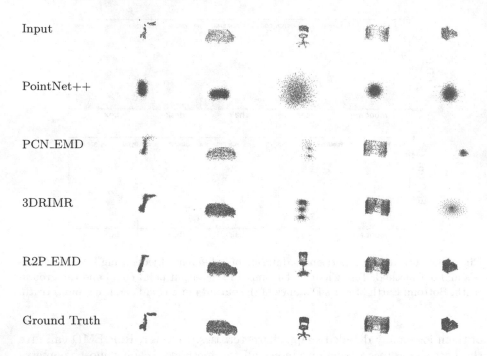

**Fig. 3.** Comparison of generated point clouds of different objects using different methods. The output point clouds of PointNet, PCN_CD, R2P_CD are very similar to those of PointNet++, PCN_EMD, R2P_EMD, respectively. They are not shown here due to space limitations.

and time-consuming, using CD to evaluate intermediate output $P_m$ and EMD to evaluate final output $P_o$, which is L4 in the figure, is also a good choice for the sake of efficiency.

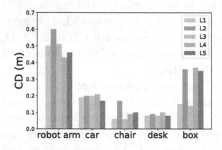
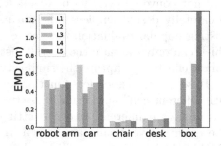

**Fig. 4.** Comparison of different loss functions. L1: both $d_1$ and $d_2$ are CD; L2: both $d_1$ and $d_2$ are EMD; L3: both $d_1$ and $d_2$ are CD+EMD; L4: $d_1$ is CD and $d_2$ is EMD; L5: $d_1$ is EMD and $d_2$ is CD.

**Remarks.** (1) CD and EMD are important metrics to evaluate the difference between two point clouds. Generally speaking, small CD/EMD value means better reconstruction performance, and vice versa. However, due to the irregular format and lack-of-order information of point clouds, these two metrics are quite limited in terms of accurately indicating the shape difference between two point clouds, and hence cannot accurately describe the performance of a point cloud reconstruction method. Sometimes, a reconstructed point cloud may have larger CD or EMD though its shape is more similar to the ground truth point cloud. For example, as we can see in Fig. 2, the EMD of chair using 3DRIMR is smaller than R2P_EMD, but from Fig. 3, we can see that the output of R2P_EMD has more accurate shape of a chair. Hence, we should not focus only on the values of CD or EMD when evaluating a method's reconstruction performance. (2) We have also conducted a series of experiments to explore different designs of our network architecture, e.g., using different pooling methods to extract global features, applying discriminators during the training process, and deeper network architecture with more layers. Nevertheless we find that the architecture shown in Fig. 1 performs the best and is efficient.

## 6    Conclusions and Future Work

We have proposed R2P, a deep learning model that generates 3D objects in the form of smooth, dense, and highly accurate point clouds with fine geometry details. The inputs to R2P are directly converted from the 2D depth images that are generated from raw mmWave radar sensor data, and thus characterized by mutual inconsistency or errors in terms of orientation and shape. We have demonstrated with extensive experiments that R2P significantly outperforms existing methods such as PointNet/PointNet++, PCN, and 3DRIMR. In addition, we have shown the importance of loss function design in the training of models for reconstructing point clouds. For future work, we will further improve our design and test it with large scale experiments in more practical environments and with more object categories.

## References

1. Dai, A., Ruizhongtai Qi, C., Nießner, M.: Shape completion using 3D-encoder-predictor CNNS and shape synthesis. In: IEEE CVPR (2017)
2. Fan, H., Su, H., Guibas, L.J.: A point set generation network for 3D object reconstruction from a single image. In: IEEE CVPR (2017)
3. Fang, S., Nirjon, S.: Superrf: enhanced 3D RF representation using stationary low-cost mmwave radar. In: Proceedings of 2020 International Conference on EWSN (2020)
4. Ghasr, M.T., Horst, M.J., Dvorsky, M.R., Zoughi, R.: Wideband microwave camera for real-time 3-D imaging. IEEE Trans. Antennas Propag. **65**(1), 258–268 (2016)
5. Guan, J., Madani, S., Jog, S., Gupta, S., Hassanieh, H.: Through fog high-resolution imaging using millimeter wave radar. In: IEEE CVPR (2020)

6. Guan, J., Madani, S., Jog, S., Gupta, S., Hassanieh, H.: Hawkeye dataset and radar data synthesizer (2020). https://github.com/JaydenG1019/HawkEye-Data-Code
7. Ji, M., Gall, J., Zheng, H., Liu, Y., Fang, L.: SurfaceNet: an end-to-end 3D neural network for multiview stereopsis. In: Proceedings of the IEEE ICCV (2017)
8. Kar, A., Häne, C., Malik, J.: Learning a multi-view stereo machine. In: Proceedings of the 31st International Conference on NeurIPS, pp. 364–375 (2017)
9. Kong, C., Lin, C.H., Lucey, S.: Using locally corresponding cad models for dense 3D reconstructions from a single image. In: IEEE CVPR (2017)
10. Lu, C.X., et al.: See through smoke: robust indoor mapping with low-cost mmWave radar. In: ACM MobiSys (2020)
11. Mamandipoor, B., Malysa, G., Arbabian, A., Madhow, U., Noujeim, K.: 60 GHZ synthetic aperture radar for short-range imaging: theory and experiments. In: The 48th Asilomar Conference on Signals, Systems and Computers. IEEE (2014)
12. Paschalidou, D., Ulusoy, O., Schmitt, C., Van Gool, L., Geiger, A.: Raynet: learning volumetric 3D reconstruction with ray potentials. In: IEEE CVPR (2018)
13. Qi, C.R., Su, H., Mo, K., Guibas, L.J.: Pointnet: deep learning on point sets for 3D classification and segmentation. arXiv preprint arXiv:1612.00593 (2016)
14. Qi, C.R., Yi, L., Su, H., Guibas, L.J.: Pointnet++: deep hierarchical feature learning on point sets in a metric space. arXiv preprint arXiv:1706.02413 (2017)
15. National Academies of Sciences, E., Medicine, et al.: Airport Passenger Screening Using Millimeter Wave Machines: Compliance with Guidelines. National Academies Press, Washington (2018)
16. Sharma, A., Grau, O., Fritz, M.: VConv-DAE: deep volumetric shape learning without object labels. In: Hua, G., Jégou, H. (eds.) ECCV 2016. LNCS, vol. 9915, pp. 236–250. Springer, Cham (2016). https://doi.org/10.1007/978-3-319-49409-8_20
17. Sheen, D.M., McMakin, D.L., Hall, T.E.: Near field imaging at microwave and millimeter wave frequencies. In: 2007 IEEE/MTT-S International Microwave Symposium, pp. 1693–1696. IEEE (2007)
18. Smith, E.J., Meger, D.: Improved adversarial systems for 3D object generation and reconstruction. In: Conference on Robot Learning, pp. 87–96. PMLR (2017)
19. STEREOLABS: Zed mini datasheet 2019 rev1. https://cdn.stereolabs.com/assets/datasheets/zed-mini-camera-datasheet.pdf
20. Sun, Y., Huang, Z., Zhang, H., Cao, Z., Xu, D.: 3drimr: 3D reconstruction and imaging via mmWave radar based on deep learning. In: IEEE IPCCC (2021)
21. Sun, Y., Xu, D., Huang, Z., Zhang, H., Liang, X.: Lidaus: localization of IoT device via anchor UAV slam. In: IEEE IPCCC (2020)
22. Texas-Instruments: Dca1000evm. https://www.ti.com/tool/DCA1000EVM
23. Texas-Instruments: Introduction to mmwave radar sensing: Fmcw radars. https://training.ti.com/node/1139153
24. Texas-Instruments: Iwr6843isk, 2021. https://www.ti.com/tool/IWR6843ISK
25. Vandersmissen, B., et al.: Indoor person identification using a low-power FMCW radar. IEEE Trans. GRSS 56(7), 3941–3952 (2018)
26. Wang, N., Zhang, Y., Li, Z., Fu, Y., Liu, W., Jiang, Y.G.: Pixel2mesh: generating 3D mesh models from single RGB images. In: Proceedings of the ECCV, pp. 52–67 (2018)
27. Wu, J., Zhang, C., Xue, T., Freeman, W.T., Tenenbaum, J.B.: Learning a probabilistic latent space of object shapes via 3D generative-adversarial modeling. arXiv preprint arXiv:1610.07584 (2016)
28. Yang, B., Wen, H., Wang, S., Clark, R., Markham, A., Trigoni, N.: 3D object reconstruction from a single depth view with adversarial learning. In: IEEE ICCV Workshops (2017)

29. Yang, X., Liu, J., Chen, Y., Guo, X., Xie, Y.: Mu-id: multi-user identification through gaits using millimeter wave radios. In: IEEE INFOCOM (2020)
30. Yuan, W., Khot, T., Held, D., Mertz, C., Hebert, M.: PCN: point completion network. In: 2018 International Conference on 3D Vision (3DV), pp. 728–737. IEEE (2018)

# Sim-to-Real Neural Learning with Domain Randomisation for Humanoid Robot Grasping

Connor Gäde[✉], Matthias Kerzel, Erik Strahl, and Stefan Wermter

Knowledge Technology, Department of Informatics, University of Hamburg,
Vogt-Koelln-Street 30, 22527 Hamburg, Germany
{connor.gaede,matthias.kerzel,erik.strahl,stefan.wermter}@uni-hamburg.de
http://www.knowledge-technology.info

**Abstract.** Collecting large amounts of training data with a real robot to learn visuomotor abilities is time-consuming and limited by expensive robotic hardware. Simulators provide a safe, distributable way to collect data, but due to discrepancies between simulation and reality, learned strategies often do not transfer to the real world. This paper examines whether domain randomisation can increase the real-world performance of a model trained entirely in simulation without additional fine-tuning. We replicate a reach-to-grasp experiment with the NICO humanoid robot in simulation and develop a method to autonomously create training data for a supervised learning approach with an end-to-end convolutional neural architecture. We compare model performance and real-world transferability for different amounts of data and randomisation conditions. Our results show that domain randomisation improves the transferability of a model and can mitigate negative effects of overfitting.

**Keywords:** Sim-to-real transfer · Domain randomisation · Humanoid robot grasping · Deep learning

## 1 Introduction

A humanoid robot assisting humans in a complex environment needs a set of visuomotor abilities, such as grasping, to properly manipulate and interact with its surroundings. Learning these skills requires the collection of large amounts of training data. Collecting data with a real robot is time-consuming and can wear out or damage the expensive hardware [10,13]. Parallelising this process to speed it up requires multiple copies of the same robot [10]. Therefore, it is often beneficial to use a simulator, which allows for easy distribution and avoids safety

---

The authors gratefully acknowledge support from the German Research Foundation DFG for the projects CML TRR169, LeCAREbot and IDEAS.

The original version of this chapter was revised: this chapter was previously published non-open access. The correction to this chapter is available at
https://doi.org/10.1007/978-3-031-15919-0_63

E. Pimenidis et al. (Eds.): ICANN 2022, LNCS 13529, pp. 342–354, 2022.
https://doi.org/10.1007/978-3-031-15919-0_29

concerns. However, simulated environments are not a fully accurate representation of the real robot and its environment, often making additional fine-tuning necessary to transfer a policy to the real world [1]. A way to reduce this *reality gap* is domain randomisation [14]. By altering aspects of the simulation such as dynamics and visual features, learned strategies become more robust to changes in the environment, allowing an easier transfer to the real world.

We examine how domain randomisation affects the transferability of a grasping approach from simulation to a real-world setup. We develop a simulated approach to autonomously generate data for end-to-end training of a deep convolutional architecture, replicating a real-world reach-to-grasp experiment [7] with the NICO (Neuro-Inspired COmpanion) humanoid robot [6], and create three datasets with varying degrees of randomisation which we compare to a real-world dataset. First, we test whether our simulated data is suitable to solve the task. We show that models trained with our simulated data can reach a target object with similar accuracy in simulation as a model trained with real data could in the real world. We then evaluate whether a model trained on simulated data can solve the task in the real world and if domain randomisation affects it. For this, we compare the performance of models trained on canonical simulation data to ones trained with either randomised colours or camera angles when evaluated with real-world data. Our randomised samples reach a better real-world performance than the unaltered ones. We discover that an increasing amount of canonical training data leads to overfitting, which hurts the transferability of the model. Domain randomisation can mitigate this effect.

## 2   Related Work

### 2.1   Robot Grasping

Developing robotic grasping and manipulation agents is an important challenge in research [9]. Many approaches are trying to solve this task. Pinto and Gupta [13] developed a multistage learning algorithm to train a Convolutional Neural Network (CNN) to predict the probability of a grasp at a given position and angle. Each resulting model was used to collect additional data for subsequent training iterations. Levine et al. [10] used a CNN architecture to predict the likelihood of a given image and motion to produce a successful grasp. The robot could then choose the path with the highest predicted probability. In the method proposed by Kerzel and Wermter [7], a CNN is used to predict the motor positions to reach an object in a given image. A NICO robot produced training data autonomously by placing an object on a table and recording the motor values of the arm as well as an image of the object. Our work expands this approach by Kerzel and Wermter by replicating their experiment in a simulated environment and evaluating its transferability to the real world.

### 2.2   Domain Randomisation for Physical Manipulation

Domain randomisation has been shown to improve the transferability of physical manipulation tasks. James et al. [3] produced training data in simulation by calculating a set of trajectories with inverse kinematics to have a robotic arm pick up a cube and put it into a basket. Images of the scene and motor velocities were recorded to train a neural model to predict velocities from images. They showed that by randomising colours, textures, light sources, and object sizes as well as introducing additional clutter, they could significantly improve the performance of the transferred model in the real environment. Similarly, Matas et al. [11] utilised domain randomisation to train a set of cloth manipulation tasks entirely on a simulated robotic arm and transfer it to a real-world setup. They altered textures, lighting, and camera orientation as well as the location and size of objects and starting position of the arm. These results show, that domain randomisation can greatly increase the transferability of a model.

## 3   Approach

To analyse the real-world applicability of a strategy learned in simulation, we recreate a reach-to-grasp experiment with the NICO humanoid robot in a simulated environment. We develop an approach to autonomously collect training data with a simulated NICO robot placing the target object at random positions on a table, which we use to create three datasets. One of them serves as a canonical baseline, without domain randomisation, while the others have either the colours or the camera angle altered for each image. As a real-world comparison and test of transferability, we use a fourth dataset, collected with a physical NICO robot. We implement a deep convolutional architecture and optimise its hyperparameters for each dataset under the same conditions to ensure comparability. The resulting models are first evaluated within their domain to see how the simulated and real data compare to each other. We then evaluate the sim-to-real transfer through their performance on our real-world data.

(a) real

(b) simulation

**Fig. 1.** Real and simulated NICO robot seated at a table with the target object on top.

### 3.1   Experimental Setup

We examine the same reach-to-grasp task as presented by Kerzel and Wermter [7]. A NICO humanoid robot has to grab a cylindrical object that is randomly placed on the table in front of it by performing a side grasp with its left arm. We also use a NICO humanoid robot in our experiments. Both of its arms offer four degrees of freedom to control the shoulder and elbow angles. Each arm also has a three-fingered SeedRobotics RH4D hand attached with two wrist motors to adjust the hand's rotation as well as another two actuators to open and close the fingers. The head of the robot can be positioned with another two motors and contains two cameras within its eye sockets.

We replicate the experimental setup within the CoppeliaSim simulator[1] with a simulated NICO robot (see Fig. 1). Both the environment and the robot are controlled using the PyRep [4] library, which allows manipulation of the simulation with the Python programming language. The free, open-source software API[2] of the NICO robot provides an integrated PyRep mode, which allows for the same controls as the real robot.

### 3.2 Dataset Recording

With our simulated setup, we generate three datasets of 2000 samples each. One set maintains a canonical visual representation for all trials, whereas the others are randomised for each sample. The canonical images serve as a baseline to analyse the benefits of domain randomisation. Additionally, we use a fourth dataset consisting of 1100 samples collected with the real NICO robot. The purpose of this set is to test the transferability of our approach. Each sample consists of an image of the target object from the robot's perspective (see Fig. 2), as well as the associated angles of each of the six motors of the left arm.

(a) real

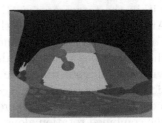

(b) simulation

The real-world dataset was collected with the same method as proposed by Kerzel and Wermter [7]. Grasping can be viewed as the inversion of putting an object onto the table. Accordingly, training samples are produced by the robot placing the target object at a random position on the table and memorizing the motor angles of the arm which were used to reach that position. After removing the arm, a picture of the target object on the table is taken with the robot's eye cameras.

**Fig. 2.** Sample image taken with the right eye camera of a real and a simulated NICO robot.

The object is then moved to a new location to repeat the process. An experimenter initially demonstrates reachable positions to the robot by manually moving its arm over the table. The robot memorises the motor angles, which it then randomly reproduces to generate training data autonomously.

In our simulated approach, rather than demonstrating valid poses to the robot, we define ranges for each actuator to randomly generate motor configurations, such that $-75.38° \leq l\_shoulder\_z \leq -9.45°$, $-39.69° \leq l\_shoulder\_y \leq$

---

[1] https://coppeliarobotics.com/.

[2] https://github.com/knowledgetechnologyuhh/NICO-software.

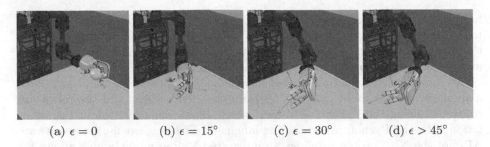

(a) $\epsilon = 0$        (b) $\epsilon = 15°$        (c) $\epsilon = 30°$        (d) $\epsilon > 45°$

**Fig. 3.** Increasing hand orientation difference $\epsilon$ between the baseline (a) and the respective pose. Poses with $\epsilon > 45°$ are rejected as the hand is rotated too much (d).

$20.35°$, $-3.91° \leq l\_arm\_x \leq 36.79°$, $35.30° \leq l\_elbow\_y \leq 102.90°$, $0.0° \leq l\_wrist\_z \leq 22.44°$ and $-50.0° \leq l\_wrist\_x \leq -8.84°$. These limits were obtained from the minimum and maximum values recorded on the real robot.

Additionally, we ensure with a set of constraints that the generated motor values result in a valid side grasping pose. Before executing a pose, we calculate its forward kinematics with the kinematic model provided by *gaikpy* [5] to obtain the position and orientation of the hand. First, we define positional boundaries around the size of an A4 sheet of paper, such that $0.2037 \leq x \leq 0.4231$, $-0.2060 \leq y \leq 0.1454$ and $0.5773 \leq z \leq 0.6674$, to ensure that the hand is within the target area on the table at the correct height to grasp the object. After that, we confirm whether the orientation approximates a valid side grasp. For this, we define a baseline pose in which the arm is forming an L-shape and the palm faces right towards the centre of the table (see Fig. 3a). Only poses with a total angle difference of less than $45°$ between their end-effector orientation and our baseline are accepted. This angle is calculated between the rotation axes of the quaternion representation of both orientations. Thus, it measures the combined rotation along all three dimensions. As depicted in Fig. 3, the constraint is chosen such that it still accepts side grasps towards the right side of the robot, while poses with a strongly rotated hand are rejected.

Once these constraints are met, the simulated robot executes the pose. Rather than physically moving the object across the table, it is directly placed at the final location of the hand. The angles of the arm motor are then saved, and the robot returns to its default pose, leaving the object in the robot's view to take an image with its simulated eye cameras.

### 3.3    Domain Randomisation

To increase robustness and allow transferability to the real world, we randomise visual features of the scene for two of our simulated datasets. Due to changing lighting conditions in a real environment, the colours in the simulation do not match perfectly. This difference could provide difficulties for a trained model. Randomising the colours of the scene should make the resulting model more robust to changes in colour and lighting. Therefore, in our first randomised

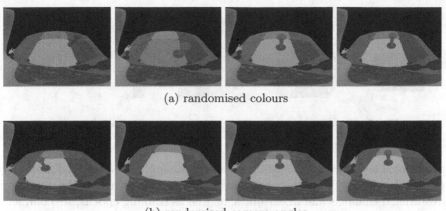

(a) randomised colours

(b) randomised camera angles

Fig. 4. Sample images from our randomised colour and camera angle datasets

dataset, we alter the colours of the chair and table elements, the target object, and the floor for each recorded sample (see Fig. 4a). Colours within CoppeliaSim are defined as an $[r, g, b]$ triple, with each value having a range of $[0, 1]$. We randomise these colours by sampling each channel from a normal distribution with a mean corresponding to the canonical colour values and a standard deviation of 0.1.

As the robot is not completely fixed to the table and the head angle is influenced by its motion, the position of the camera and thus the distortion of the image does not align perfectly between simulation and real setup. By changing the angle of the camera for each sample, the model predictions should be less dependent on the accurate camera perspective and more on the position of the object relative to the table. Previous works have shown that randomisation of the camera position was crucial to successfully transfer a task into the real world [3,11]. Therefore, in the second randomised dataset, we alter the angles of head motors and thus the camera angle for each recorded sample (see Fig. 4b). By default, our data collection positions the $head\_y$ motor, which rotates around the y-axis (pitch), at 55° and leaves the $head\_z$ motor, which rotates around the z-axis (yaw), at 0° before taking an image. Our randomisation instead chooses a pitch between 40° and 60° and a yaw of up to 10° in either direction.

## 3.4   Network Architecture

We use a Convolutional Neural Network to predict motor positions for a given image (see Fig. 5), similar to the one proposed by Kerzel and Wermter [7]. Our models are implemented using the Pytorch library [12]. As input, the model is given an 80 × 60 RBG image, which was downsampled from a 320 × 240 crop of the original sample image. Our output layer consists of 6 units to predict the motor configuration for a given image. The hidden layers are comprised of two

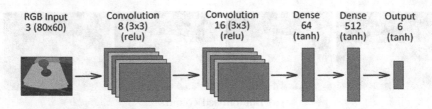

**Fig. 5.** Optimised model architecture for the canonical dataset

convolutional layers with rectified linear activation and a $3 \times 3$ kernel, followed by two dense layers with hyperbolic tangent activation. To determine the number of convolutional channels and linear units, as well as training epochs, we conduct a hyperparameter optimisation for each dataset using Hyperopt [2] (see Sect. 4.2). Each model is trained using mean squared error as our loss function and the Adam optimiser [8] with a default learning rate of 0.001 as well as an additional L2 penalty of 0.001 to prevent overfitting.

## 4    Experiments and Results

First, we optimise the hyperparameters of our deep convolutional architecture for each of our datasets and evaluate them separately. The canonical set serves as a baseline to observe if either of our randomisations affects the performance. Additionally, we analyse the influence of the dataset size on the performance. To evaluate the transferability of our models, we train each architecture with its respective dataset while using the real-world data as a test set.

### 4.1    Metrics

To determine the capabilities of our trained models, we define some additional metrics. We measure the distance between the prediction and the target object, by computing the forward kinematics of both the predicted and target motor configuration and calculating the Euclidean distance between the respective end-effector positions. Additionally, we verify whether our models generate valid side grasping poses by utilising the same constraints we defined for our data generation (see Sect. 3.2). We calculate the percentage of test cases where the predicted pose is within the height boundaries and deviates less than a total of $45°$ in orientation from our baseline pose.

### 4.2    Hyperparameter Optimisation

We conduct a hyperparameter optimisation of 100 trials for each model, choosing epochs in $\{10 \cdot n \in \mathbb{N} \mid n \leq 12\}$, convolutional filters in $\{2^n, n \in \mathbb{N} \mid 3 \leq n \leq 7\}$ for the first and $n \leq 6$ for the second layer, as well as $\{2^n, n \in \mathbb{N} \mid 6 \leq n \leq 9\}$ units for both dense layers. The models are evaluated on 1000 samples of the respective dataset with 5-fold cross-validation. The best model configurations and their respective test loss are listed in Table 1.

**Table 1.** Final model parameters and test performance for each examined dataset

| Data | Conv | | Dense | | Epochs | Loss ($\mu \pm \sigma$) |
|------|------|------|-------|------|--------|-------------------------|
| Canonical | 8 | 16 | 64 | 512 | 110 | $7.3940 \times 10^{-4} \pm 6.0177 \times 10^{-5}$ |
| Randomised colour | 64 | 32 | 64 | 256 | 110 | $7.1711 \times 10^{-4} \pm 5.2067 \times 10^{-5}$ |
| Randomised angles | 8 | 8 | 64 | 512 | 100 | $8.8976 \times 10^{-4} \pm 5.7630 \times 10^{-5}$ |
| Real | 128 | 32 | 128 | 128 | 90 | $5.2640 \times 10^{-4} \pm 7.8630 \times 10^{-5}$ |

Notably, the architectures for the canonical and randomised-angle dataset feature a minimal number of convolutional filters, with 8 on the first as well as 16 and 8 on the second layer, whereas the randomised-colour and real dataset feature 64 and 128 filters on the first and 32 on the second layer. This could reflect the higher visual complexity of the latter two sets. For the dense units, the simulated datasets result in similar architectures with 64 units on the first and 512 on the second layer for the canonical and randomised-angle datasets or 256 for the colour dataset. The real-world dataset differs from this with 128 units on both layers. The number of epochs is also similar, with 110 for the canonical and colour datasets, 100 for randomised angles, and 90 for the real data.

## 4.3   Dataset Performance

Before analysing the transferability of our datasets, we establish how they perform on their own. We train each optimised architecture with the full 2000 samples of the respective dataset for the number of epochs determined by our hyperparameter optimisation and evaluate them with 5-fold cross-validation. We analyse the influence of the dataset size by training reduced versions of the canonical dataset with 500 and 1000 samples in the same manner. To maintain consistency throughout all of our datasets, we apply our orientational constraint of 45° (see Sect. 3.2) to the real-world data, reducing it to 1073 samples.

**Table 2.** Test loss and percentage of valid generated poses for each examined dataset

| Dataset | # Samples | Loss ($\mu \pm \sigma$) | Valid poses ($\mu \pm \sigma$) |
|---------|-----------|-------------------------|--------------------------------|
| Canonical | 500 | $7.7718 \times 10^{-4} \pm 9.3450 \times 10^{-5}$ | $100.0\% \pm 0.00$ |
| | 1000 | $8.2458 \times 10^{-4} \pm 1.7685 \times 10^{-4}$ | $96.4\% \pm 7.20$ |
| | 2000 | $7.6861 \times 10^{-4} \pm 1.0146 \times 10^{-4}$ | $100.0\% \pm 0.00$ |
| Colours | 2000 | $1.2258 \times 10^{-3} \pm 2.7900 \times 10^{-4}$ | $100.0\% \pm 0.00$ |
| Angles | 2000 | $1.0962 \times 10^{-3} \pm 2.5002 \times 10^{-4}$ | $93.8\% \pm 8.23$ |
| Real | 1073 | $5.5526 \times 10^{-4} \pm 4.3983 \times 10^{-5}$ | $100.0\% \pm 0.00$ |

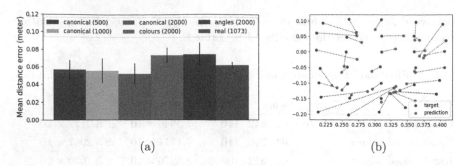

**Fig. 6.** Mean distance error after evaluating each dataset with 5-fold cross-validation (a) and a selection of actual and predicted positions for the best-performing model (b)

Table 2 shows the training results for all examined datasets. The model trained on real-world samples reaches the best overall performance, with an average loss of $5.5526 \times 10^{-4}$. The results of our simulated datasets span from $7.6861 \times 10^{-4}$ loss for the full canonical dataset, to $1.2258 \times 10^{-3}$ for the randomised-colour set. Our full canonical dataset, as well as its subset of 500 samples, both perform slightly better than their 1000-sample counterpart, although still within each other's standard deviations, with the full dataset achieving the better score but also a higher standard deviation than the smaller subset. The randomised datasets achieve the worst performances. However, as indicated by the higher standard deviations, their best models are closer to the canonical ones. This difference could be due to the higher difficulty of learning more randomised data. Yet, during hyperparameter optimisation, the randomised-colour data performed better than the other simulated datasets.

All models generate valid poses as defined in Sect. 4.1 for more than 90% of their test cases. Most architectures achieve 100%, barring the ones trained on 1000 canonical samples and randomised camera angles (see Table 2).

By looking at the average distance between the target object and end-effector position, as depicted in Fig. 6a, we can see that the loss does not fully represent the ability to reach the target. As the reached position depends on the combination of all angles, the errors of different motors seem to be able to compensate for each other. All models trained with canonical data reach the object at a closer average distance than the real robot. The smallest subset reaches the target pose around 5 mm closer at 5.68 cm than the real data with 6.19 cm. An increase of samples improves this to 5.59 cm for the 1000 sample subset and 5.21 cm for the full set, though they are also more inconsistent between the different runs at 11.2 mm, 14.1 mm, and 12.3 mm standard deviation respectively. The randomised sets perform about 1 cm worse than the real-world samples with an average distance of 7.35 cm for randomised colours and 7.45 cm for angles, but also have a higher standard deviation of 13.1 mm and 8.5 mm respectively.

The distance error is not evenly distributed across the samples. As seen in Fig. 6b, all predictions gravitate towards the centre of the workspace. For targets closer to the edge of the reachable space, the inaccuracy of the prediction increases. One explanation for this could be that the edges of the reachable space contain fewer samples than the centre. This would coincide with the findings by Kerzel et al. [5] who showed that predictions on the fringes of a workspace converge towards its centre unless the data is sampled from a larger area.

While neither of the models are accurate enough to reliably grasp the target object throughout the entire workspace, we can see that our simulated data can reach similar or better results than the real-world data.

## 4.4  Sim-to-Real Transfer

After confirming that our simulated datasets can produce models with comparable performance to the real-world data, we analyse how well their success transfers into the real-world application. We train each optimised architecture on the full 2000 samples of the respective simulated dataset for the optimised number of epochs while using our 1073 real-world samples as test set. Each model is evaluated five times to account for deviations between individual runs. As in Sect. 4.3, we also examine reduced subsets at 500 and 1000 samples of our datasets to analyse the influence of the amount of data on the result.

**Table 3.** Test loss and percentage of valid generated side grasping poses for each examined dataset when tested on real-world data.

| Dataset | # Samples | Loss ($\mu \pm \sigma$) | Valid poses ($\mu \pm \sigma$) |
|---|---|---|---|
| Canonical | 500 | $\mathbf{2.6830 \times 10^{-3} \pm 2.7898 \times 10^{-4}}$ | $\mathbf{91.50\% \pm 10.16}$ |
| | 1000 | $3.6398 \times 10^{-3} \pm 1.1927 \times 10^{-3}$ | $50.93\% \pm 32.72$ |
| | 2000 | $8.6718 \times 10^{-3} \pm 9.7359 \times 10^{-3}$ | $59.81\% \pm 37.95$ |
| Colours | 500 | $\mathbf{2.1284 \times 10^{-3} \pm 2.3500 \times 10^{-4}}$ | $\mathbf{100.00\% \pm\ 0.00}$ |
| | 1000 | $2.6896 \times 10^{-3} \pm 2.9349 \times 10^{-4}$ | $94.63\% \pm 10.74$ |
| | 2000 | $3.0234 \times 10^{-3} \pm 1.6071 \times 10^{-3}$ | $87.42\% \pm 25.14$ |
| Angles | 500 | $\mathbf{2.2035 \times 10^{-3} \pm 2.1958 \times 10^{-4}}$ | $\mathbf{100.00\% \pm\ 0.00}$ |
| | 1000 | $2.6528 \times 10^{-3} \pm 1.8045 \times 10^{-4}$ | $92.59\% \pm 10.89$ |
| | 2000 | $2.5690 \times 10^{-3} \pm 2.7915 \times 10^{-4}$ | $100.00\% \pm\ 0.00$ |
| Real | 1073 | $\mathbf{5.5526 \times 10^{-4} \pm 4.3983 \times 10^{-5}}$ | $\mathbf{100.00\% \pm\ 0.00}$ |

Table 3 shows that the test losses of our models increase by an order of magnitude for most datasets when evaluated on real-world data. Our smallest subset of canonical data reaches an average loss of $2.6830 \times 10^{-3}$. Increasing the amount of data seems to negatively affect the transferability of the model, as the average loss increases with larger datasets up to $8.6718 \times 10^{-3}$ for the full canonical set. The standard deviation also becomes incrementally worse. This could be caused by the model overfitting on aspects specific to the simulation which it does not discover when trained with fewer, less redundant samples. Domain randomisation seems to mitigate this effect. Our randomised datasets achieve similar or better results as the small canonical dataset between $2.1284 \times 10^{-3}$ and $2.6896 \times 10^{-3}$, barring the full colour set, which performs slightly worse due to an outlier, as indicated by the higher standard deviation.

The rate of valid generated poses seems to support our overfitting hypothesis. While the smallest subset of 500 canonical samples reaches 91.50%, the bigger datasets only generate an average of less than 60% valid grasp poses for the real-world test samples. The full randomised-colour dataset performs slightly worse than the smallest canonical subset with 87.42% valid poses, whereas the other randomised sets outperform it, with the three best ones reaching 100%.

A similar pattern emerges in the resulting distances between the end-effector of generated poses and the target position. Models trained on the smallest subset of canonical data reach a mean distance of 12.54 cm, further than 6 cm away from the target than within its own domain or the model trained on the real dataset at 6.19 cm. The distance increases to 17.34 cm ± 4.96 cm with 1000 samples and 21.91 cm ± 13.24 cm for 2000 samples. Models trained on our full

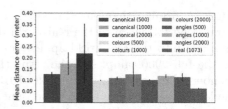

**Fig. 7.** Mean distance between the real-world target and the predicted hand position for each model. Each dataset was evaluated five times.

randomised-colour dataset achieve a similar result to the small canonical subset, approaching the target at an average 12.60 cm with a higher standard deviation of 5.5 cm, whereas the other randomised sets reach better performances, coming as close as 9.84 cm average distance for the smallest colour subset.

Overall, our randomised datasets show a higher transferability than the canonical data. Larger amounts of canonical data result in lower performance due to overfitting, whereas domain randomisation mitigates this effect.

## 5   Conclusion

We explored the effects of domain randomisation on the transferability of a robotic reach-to-grasp task trained entirely in simulation without additional fine-tuning. Our approach recreated a real-world experiment conducted by Kerzel and Wermter [7] with the NICO robot in a simulated environment. We developed a data collection method similar to the real-world approach, which utilised the advantages of a simulation to create three datasets of 2000 samples each. A fourth dataset of 1100 samples collected in the same way as the original experiment served as a real-world comparison. Each sample consisted of an image of the target object on the table from the robot's perspective and the angles of the six motors of the left arm required to reach it.

Our simulated data reached a similar or better performance within simulation than the real-world dataset. However, when evaluating the models trained on simulated data with real-world samples, the sim-to-real gap becomes apparent through lower accuracy. Contrary to the general expectation, simply adding more training data decreased the transferability of the resulting models. We demonstrated, however, that randomising individual visual features of the simulation mitigates this loss of transferable behaviour for larger amounts of simulated training data and improves the real-world performance of a transferred model.

In future work, we could explore randomising multiple features at once and improve the accuracy of the model to deploy it on a physical robot.

# References

1. van Baar, J., Sullivan, A., Cordorel, R., Jha, D., Romeres, D., Nikovski, D.: Sim-to-real transfer learning using robustified controllers in robotic tasks involving complex dynamics. In: 2019 International Conference on Robotics and Automation (ICRA), pp. 6001–6007. IEEE (2019)
2. Bergstra, J., Yamins, D., Cox, D.D., et al.: Hyperopt: a python library for optimizing the hyperparameters of machine learning algorithms. In: Proceedings of the 12th Python in Science Conference, vol. 13, p. 20. Citeseer (2013)
3. James, S., Davison, A.J., Johns, E.: Transferring end-to-end visuomotor control from simulation to real world for a multi-stage task. In: Conference on Robot Learning, pp. 334–343. PMLR (2017)
4. James, S., Freese, M., Davison, A.J.: Pyrep: bringing v-rep to deep robot learning. arXiv preprint arXiv:1906.11176 (2019)
5. Kerzel, M., Spisak, J., Strahl, E., Wermter, S.: Neuro-genetic visuomotor architecture for robotic grasping. In: Farkaš, I., Masulli, P., Wermter, S. (eds.) ICANN 2020. LNCS, vol. 12397, pp. 533–545. Springer, Cham (2020). https://doi.org/10.1007/978-3-030-61616-8_43
6. Kerzel, M., Strahl, E., Magg, S., Navarro-Guerrero, N., Heinrich, S., Wermter, S.: Nico-neuro-inspired companion: A developmental humanoid robot platform for multimodal interaction. In: 2017 26th IEEE International Symposium on Robot and Human Interactive Communication (RO-MAN), pp. 113–120. IEEE (2017)
7. Kerzel, M., Wermter, S.: Neural end-to-end self-learning of visuomotor skills by environment interaction. In: Lintas, A., Rovetta, S., Verschure, P.F.M.J., Villa, A.E.P. (eds.) ICANN 2017. LNCS, vol. 10613, pp. 27–34. Springer, Cham (2017). https://doi.org/10.1007/978-3-319-68600-4_4
8. Kingma, D.P., Ba, J.: Adam: a method for stochastic optimization. arXiv preprint arXiv:1412.6980 (2014)
9. Kleeberger, K., Bormann, R., Kraus, W., Huber, M.F.: A survey on learning-based robotic grasping. Curr. Robot. Rep. 1(4), 239–249 (2020). https://doi.org/10.1007/s43154-020-00021-6
10. Levine, S., Pastor, P., Krizhevsky, A., Ibarz, J., Quillen, D.: Learning hand-eye coordination for robotic grasping with deep learning and large-scale data collection. Int. J. Robot. Res. 37(4–5), 421–436 (2018)
11. Matas, J., James, S., Davison, A.J.: Sim-to-real reinforcement learning for deformable object manipulation. In: Conference on Robot Learning, pp. 734–743. PMLR (2018)

12. Paszke, A., et al.: Pytorch: an imperative style, high-performance deep learning library. In: Advances in Neural Information Processing Systems 32 (2019)

13. Pinto, L., Gupta, A.: Supersizing self-supervision: learning to grasp from 50 k tries and 700 robot hours. In: 2016 IEEE International Conference on Robotics and Automation (ICRA), pp. 3406–3413. IEEE (2016)

14. Tobin, J., Fong, R., Ray, A., Schneider, J., Zaremba, W., Abbeel, P.: Domain randomization for transferring deep neural networks from simulation to the real world. In: 2017 IEEE/RSJ International Conference on Intelligent Robots and Systems (IROS), pp. 23–30 (2017). https://doi.org/10.1109/IROS.2017.8202133

# Systematic Comparison of Incomplete-Supervision Approaches for Biomedical Image Classification

Sayedali Shetab Boushehri[1,2,3,4]📷, Ahmad Bin Qasim[2,3]📷,
Dominik Waibel[1,2,3]📷, Fabian Schmich[4]📷, and Carsten Marr[1,2(✉)]📷

[1] Institute of AI for Health, Helmholtz Munich, Munich, Germany
carsten.marr@helmholtz-muenchen.de
[2] Institute of Computational Biology, Helmholtz Munich, Munich, Germany
[3] Technical University of Munich, Munich, Germany
[4] Data Science, Pharmaceutical Research and Early Development Informatics
(pREDi), Roche Innovation Center Munich (RICM), Munich, Germany

**Abstract.** Deep learning based classification of biomedical images requires expensive manual annotation by experts. Incomplete-supervision approaches including active learning, pre-training, and semi-supervised learning have thus been developed to increase classification performance with a limited number of annotated images. In practice, a combination of these approaches is often used to reach the desired performance for biomedical images.

Most of these approaches are designed for natural images, which differ fundamentally from biomedical images in terms of color, contrast, image complexity, and class imbalance. In addition, it is not always clear which combination to use in practical cases.

We, therefore, analyzed the performance of combining seven active learning, three pre-training, and two semi-supervised methods on four exemplary biomedical image datasets covering various imaging modalities and resolutions. The results showed that the ImageNet (pre-training) in combination with pseudo-labeling (semi-supervised learning) dominates the best performing combinations, while no particular active learning algorithm prevailed. For three out of four datasets, this combination reached over 90% of the fully supervised results by only adding 25% of labeled data. An ablation study also showed that pre-training and semi-supervised learning contributed up to 25% increase in F1-score in each cycle. In contrast, active learning contributed less than 5% increase in each cycle.

Based on these results, we suggest employing the correct combination of pre-training and semi-supervised learning can be more efficient than active learning for biomedical image classification with limited annotated images. We believe that our study is an important step towards annotation-efficient model training for biomedical classification challenges.

**Keywords:** Incomplete-supervision · Biomedical imaging · Deep learning · Active learning · Pre-training · Transfer learning · Self-supervised learning · Semi-supervised

E. Pimenidis et al. (Eds.): ICANN 2022, LNCS 13529, pp. 355–365, 2022.
https://doi.org/10.1007/978-3-031-15919-0_30

# 1    Introduction

Recent successes of deep learning methods rely on large amounts of well-annotated training data [1]. However, annotations for biomedical images are often scarce as they crucially depend on the availability of trained experts, whose time is expensive and limited. Many biomedical image classification tasks can be categorized as incomplete-supervision approaches, where labeled data is limited while unlabeled data is abundant [6,10]. From this perspective, there are three directions to take when facing an incomplete-supervision problem:

(i) Active learning algorithms address the issue by finding the most informative instances for further annotation [8,14,24] and have been benchmarked extensively on natural image datasets [13,20,23,27,30,33,36,40].

(ii) Pre-training methods such as transfer learning and self-supervised learning can help to optimize the network performance with small number of labeled images [9,19,25,32]. In transfer learning, a neural network uses the representation from another model, ideally trained on a similar dataset. A common transfer learning approach, also used in many biomedical applications, is to initialize a model with pre-trained ImageNet weights [5,28]. In self-supervised learning, a representation based on the underlying structure of the characterisitcs of the data and without any labels is learned [7]. Pre-training based on self-supervised learning for medical image analysis recently has been studied by [41,42], where a variety of methods are compared.

(iii) Semi-supervised learning leverages unlabeled data in addition to labeled data during training, to increase the performance as well as the stability of predictions [15,22].

Methodological improvements of these three approaches are mostly benchmarked on natural image datasets. Biomedical image datasets however differ from natural images: They are often strongly imbalanced, typically less diverse in terms of shapes and color range, and classes are often distinguished by only small feature variations, e.g., in texture and size [4,18]. Besides that, biomedical images are different among different domains as well as experiments.

In this paper, we address the following questions: Do approaches that perform well on natural image datasets show the same performance on biomedical image datasets? Which one of the three incomplete-supervision approaches work best on biomedical images? What is the best combination of these approaches which work on biomedical images?

Thus we performed a systematic comparison on different incomplete-supervision approaches, including seven active learning algorithms (plus random sampling), three pre-training methods (plus random initialization), and two training strategies (plus supervised learning), on four exemplary biomedical imaging datasets. We compared each approach as well as their combinations on each dataset. Then we analyzed the contribution of each approach for the top combinations. Finally, we recommended a combination of approaches for dealing with similar biomedical classification tasks.

## 2   Biomedical Imaging Datasets

We have selected four exemplary, publicly available, and fully annotated datasets from the biomedical imaging field to evaluate the efficiency and performance of active learning algorithms, pre-training methods, and training strategies (see Fig. 1):

(a) The white blood cell dataset contains 18,395 microscopic images of single stained human leukocyte cells in ten classes ($128 \times 128 \times 3$ pixels) [4,34,35].

(b) The skin lesion dataset contains 25,339 dermoscopy images from eight skin cancer classes, which can be used for melanoma diagnosis ($128 \times 128 \times 3$ pixels) [12,16,39].

(c) The cell cycle dataset comprises 32,273 images of Jurkat cells in seven different cell cycle stages created by imaging flow cytometry ($64 \times 64 \times 3$ pixels) [31].

(d) The diabetic retinopathy dataset consists of 3,672 color fundus retinal photography images classified into five stages of diabetic retinopathy ($128 \times 128 \times 3$ pixels) [37]

## 3   Results

### 3.1   Experimental Setup

To perform the experiments, we used ResNet18 architecture [29]. Also, we selected a series of active learning algorithms ( BADGE [30], learning loss [33], augmentation-based [11], Monte Carlo dropout [40], entropy-based [24], margin confidence [38], least confidence [26], plus random sampling), pre-training methods (ImageNet [3], autoencoder [21], SimCLR [9], plus random initialization) and training strategies (FixMatch [22], pseudo-labeling [17], plus supervised learning).

These approaches were selected in such a way that they cover a wide range of methodologies. Among active learning algorithms there are different ways of estimating uncertainty (in BADGE via gradients of the network and clustering; in learning loss via separate loss function; in Augmentation-based via input perturbation; in MC-dropout via model perturbation, Margin sampling, and least confidence; and in entropy based via softmax output). For the pre-training methods, the weights are calculated differently in each method (ImageNet: pre-training on natural images; autoencoder: learning efficient codings of unlabeled data by attempting to regenerate the input; SimCLR: using positive and negative samples to train a network with a contrastive loss function). For the semi-supervised learnings the same applies (FixMatch: using strong and weak augmentations and using a contrastive loss function; pseudo-labeling: using the softmax values for generating pseudo-labels).

In each experiment, we first selected a combination of aforementioned active learning algorithm, pre-training method and training strategy. Then we randomly selected 1% of data from each dataset as our initial annotated set. The

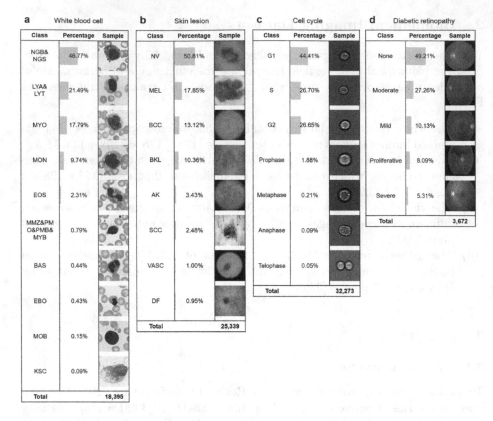

**Fig. 1.** The four selected biomedical image datasets exhibit strong class imbalance, little color variance and high similarity among classes. (Color figure online)

selected pre-training method was used to initialize the model. Next the model was trained based on the selected training strategy. After the training, we added 5% of annotated data as suggested by the selected active learning algorithm. This process was repeated eight times leading to eventually adding 40% (and using 41%) of annotated data in total. Using a 4 fold-cross validation, this ended up in $4 \times 8 \times 4 \times 3 \times 4 \times 9 = 13,824$ independent experiments (see Fig. 2). We calculated macro F1-score, accuracy, precision, and recall. The macro F1-score was used as our main metric of comparison, defined as the average F1-score over all classes, thus accounting for the imbalanced nature of the datasets. To quantitatively compare different combinations, we looked at the average macro F1-score across all cycles. Moreover, every combination is reported in the form of "active learning algorithm + pre-training method + training strategy".

## 3.2    Experiments

Learning loss + SimCLR + pseudo-labeling on the white blood cell dataset (see Fig. 3a) achieved the highest average macro F1-score of $0.71 \pm 0.07$ (mean $\pm$

standard deviation on n = 8 cycles). BADGE + ImageNet + pseudo-labeling on the skin lesion dataset achieved the highest average macro F1-score (0.56 ± 0.09). BADGE + ImageNet + pseudo-labeling on the cell cycle dataset achieved the highest average macro F1-score (0.54 ± 0.08). Augmentation-based + ImageNet + FixMatch on the diabetic retinopathy dataset achieved the highest average macro F1-score (0.54 ± 0.08). (see Fig. 3).

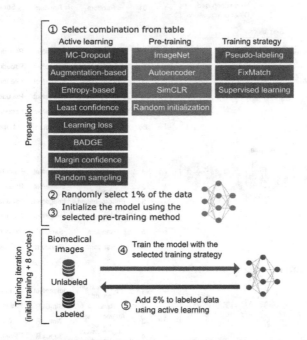

**Fig. 2.** We systematically compared combinations of different incomplete-supervision approaches on biomedical imaging datasets. Specifically, we ran $4 \times 8 \times 4 \times 3 \times 4 \times 9 = 13,824$ independent experiments (4 datasets, 7 active learning algorithms + 1 baseline, 3 pre-training methods + 1 baseline, 2 training strategies + 1 baseline, 4-fold cross-validation and 1 initial step + 8 active learning cycles) to identify the best out of 96 possible combinations.

In almost all cases (17 out of 20), the top-5 combinations were the ones that performed well from the first cycle where no active learning is involved. ImageNet and SimCLR pre-training, as well as pseudo-labeling, were always in the top combinations. Furthermore, no active learning algorithm showed up in the best combinations consistently. Finally, BADGE+ImageNet+pseudo-labeling was the top combination on two different dataset.

### 3.3   Ablation Study

To better understand each approach's contribution to the performance, we selected the top combination for each dataset (see Fig. 3) and conducted a systematic ablation study. We define the contribution to the performance of each

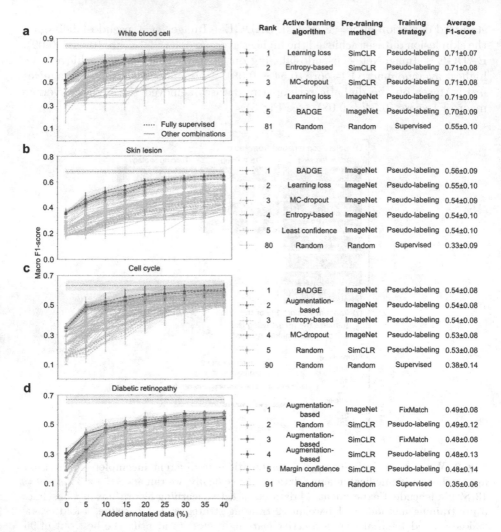

**Fig. 3.** ImageNet and SimCLR as pre-training methods and pseudo-labeling as the training strategy dominate the best performing combinations, while no particular active learning algorithm prevails. In each panel (a–d) the upper bound of performance is fully supervised learning (black dotted line). The grey lines are combinations which did not achieve the top-5 rank. The baseline is plotted in light blue. (Color figure online)

incomplete-supervision approach by calculating the difference in F1-score if that approach was substituted with its baseline: active learning algorithms were substituted with random sampling, pre-training methods with the random initialization, and training strategies with supervised learning. The analysis showed that the contribution of pre-training and semi-supervised learning can reach up to 25% increase in macro F1-score. In contrast, the active learning algorithms contributed up to only 5% increase in macro F1-score in each cycle (see Fig. 4).

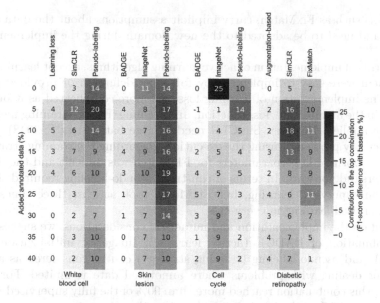

**Fig. 4.** Semi-supervised learning and pre-training contribute stronger to the top performing combination in comparison to active learning. For every dataset, the top combination of active learning algorithm, pre-training method, and training strategy is used (see Fig. 3). The contribution to performance of each approach is calculated by substituting it with its baseline and subtracting the obtained macro F1-score from the original.

## 4 Discussion

We have investigated how incomplete-supervision approaches can increase performance on sparsely labeled biomedical datasets. With a systematic study over seven active learning algorithms, three pre-training methods, and two training strategies, as well as their baselines, we have studied how these approaches work on biomedical imaging datasets.

As expected, the results showed that combining active learning algorithms, pre-training methods, and semi-supervised learning strategies leads to superior performance as compared to their baselines for every biomedical imaging datasets. However, the interesting finding was that the contribution of pre-training and semi-supervised learning could reach up to 25% increase in macro F1-score. In contrast, we observed that the state-of-the-art active learning algorithms contributed only up to 5% increase in macro F1-score in each cycle. Therefore, we recommend investing in time and resources on semi-supervised learning strategy and pre-training methods as the identified best approaches, instead of finding the appropriate active learning while working on biomedical imaging datasets.

In addition, we found that high performance on natural images does not guarantee the same quality on biomedical images. This can be due to the fact that algorithms such as FixMatch, carry implicit assumptions about the data distribution, and need to be adapted to the new domain during the implementation phase.

In terms of implementation of active learning algorithms, except learning loss, all of them were easy to implement by following definition or provided public codes. The implementation of learning loss was more complicated as it brought changes in the architecture, loss function, and training. For pre-training methods, the same applied. However, SimCLR needed large batch sizes (>2048), which led to memory problems during the execution. Regarding the training strategies, tuning the optimal hyperparameters for FixMatch was difficult and the default parameters did not work. In terms of run-time, pseudo-labeling required slightly more than supervised learning, but FixMatch took at least three times more than supervised learning in every case.

Based on the implementation and numerical considerations, we suggest that the combination of BADGE (active learning), ImageNet initialization (pre-training), and pseudo-labeling (training strategy) can be considered as a good choice for dealing with problems where annotated data is limited. For three datasets, this combination reached more than 90% of the fully supervised results by only using 25% of the labeled data (see Fig. 5).

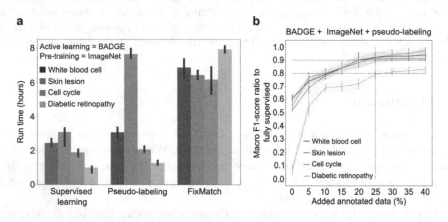

**Fig. 5.** The annotation and resource-efficient combination, BADGE + ImageNet + pseudo-labeling, reaches above 90% of the fully supervised result in three out of four biomedical datasets by using only 25% of annotated data.

Due to the computational costs, we used a fixed architecture and a fixed set of parameters. While this choice might not lead to the best fully supervised performance for each dataset (e.g., compared to much bigger architectures or series of ensemble learners used for white blood cell [[34] $ROC = 0.99$], cell cycle [[31] $accuracy = 0.99$], and diabetic retinopathy [APTOS 2019 $\kappa^2 = 0.93$]), it provides a framework to systematically analyze the combination of incomplete-supervision approaches. Based on the work of [2], we also suggest testing bigger architectures to figure out if there is a correlation between the architecture size and the performance for biomedical data. Finally, based on the recent findings [42], another question to answer in upcoming works would be to compare self-supervised learning pre-training on natural images vs. biomedical images.

We believe that our study is an important step towards helping bioinformaticians working on annotation-scarce and resource-efficient model training of biomedical image classification challenges.

**Acknowledgment.** We thank Björn Menze, Tingying Peng, Christian Matek, Melanie Schulz, Rudolf Matthias Hehr, Lea Schuh, Valerio Lupperger, and Ario Sadafi (Munich) for discussions and for contributing their ideas.

**Funding Information.** SSB has received funding by F. Hoffmann-la Roche LTD and supported by the Helmholtz Association under the joint research school "Munich School for Data Science - MUDS". CM has received funding from the European Research Council (ERC) under the European Union's Horizon 2020 research and innovation program (Grant agreement No. 866411).

**Data Availability Statement.** All scripts and how to access and process the data can be found here: https://github.com/marrlab/Med-AL-SSL.

# References

1. Tan, C., Sun, F., Kong, T., Zhang, W., Yang, C., Liu, C.: A survey on deep transfer learning. In: Kůrková, V., Manolopoulos, Y., Hammer, B., Iliadis, L., Maglogiannis, I. (eds.) ICANN 2018. LNCS, vol. 11141, pp. 270–279. Springer, Cham (2018). https://doi.org/10.1007/978-3-030-01424-7_27
2. Chen, T., Kornblith, S., Swersky, K., et al.: Big self-supervised models are strong semi-supervised learners (2020). http://arxiv.org/abs/2006.10029
3. Raghu, M., Zhang, C., Kleinberg, J., et al.: Transfusion: understanding transfer learning for medical imaging. In: Wallach, H., Larochelle, H., Beygelzimer, A., et al. (eds.) Advances in Neural Information Processing Systems 32, pp. 3347–3357. Curran Associates Inc (2019)
4. Matek, C., Schwarz, S., Marr, C., Spiekermann, K.: A single-cell morphological dataset of leukocytes from AML patients and non-malignant controls [Data set]. Cancer Imaging Arch. (2019). https://doi.org/10.7937/tcia.2019.36f5o9ld
5. Wang, X., Peng, Y., Lu, L., et al.: ChestX-ray8: Hospital-scale Chest X-ray Database and Benchmarks on Weakly-Supervised Classification and Localization of Common Thorax Diseases (2017). http://arxiv.org/abs/1705.02315
6. Blasi, T., Hennig, H., Summers, H.D., et al.: Label-free cell cycle analysis for high-throughput imaging flow cytometry. Nat. Commun. **7**, 10256 (2016)
7. Jing, L., Tian, Y.: Self-supervised visual feature learning with deep neural networks: a survey. IEEE Trans. Pattern Anal. Mach. Intell. **43**(11), 4037–4058 (2020)
8. Joshi, A.J., Porikli, F., Papanikolopoulos, N.: Multi-class active learning for image classification. In: 2009 IEEE Conference on Computer Vision and Pattern Recognition, pp. 2372–2379 (2009)

9. Chen, T., Kornblith, S., Norouzi, M., et al.: A simple framework for contrastive learning of visual representations (2020). http://arxiv.org/abs/2002.05709

10. Zhou, Z.-H.: A brief introduction to weakly supervised learning. Natl. Sci. Rev. **5**, 44–53 (2017)

11. Sadafi, A., et al.: Multiclass deep active learning for detecting red blood cell subtypes in brightfield microscopy. In: Shen, D., et al. (eds.) MICCAI 2019. LNCS, vol. 11764, pp. 685–693. Springer, Cham (2019). https://doi.org/10.1007/978-3-030-32239-7_76

12. Combalia, M., Codella, N.C.F., Rotemberg, V., et al.: BCN20000: dermoscopic lesions in the wild (2019). http://arxiv.org/abs/1908.02288

13. Holub, A., Perona, P., Burl, M.C.: Entropy-based active learning for object recognition. In: 2008 IEEE Computer Society Conference on Computer Vision and Pattern Recognition Workshops, pp. 1–8 (2008)

14. Ren, P., Xiao, Y., Chang, X., et al.: A Survey of Deep Active Learning (2020). http://arxiv.org/abs/2009.00236

15. Tarvainen, A., Valpola, H.: Mean teachers are better role models: weight-averaged consistency targets improve semi-supervised deep learning results (2017). http://arxiv.org/abs/1703.01780

16. Tschandl, P., Rosendahl, C., Kittler, H.: The HAM10000 dataset, a large collection of multi-source dermatoscopic images of common pigmented skin lesions. Sci. Data **5**, 180161 (2018)

17. van Engelen, J.E., Hoos, H.H.: A survey on semi-supervised learning. Mach. Learn. **109**(2), 373–440 (2019). https://doi.org/10.1007/s10994-019-05855-6

18. Esteva, A., Kuprel, B., Novoa, R.A., et al.: Dermatologist-level classification of skin cancer with deep neural networks. Nature (2017)

19. Newell, A., Deng, J.: How Useful is Self-Supervised Pretraining for Visual Tasks? (2020). http://arxiv.org/abs/2003.14323

20. Ducoffe, M., Precioso, F.: QBDC: query by dropout committee for training deep supervised architecture (2015). http://arxiv.org/abs/1511.06412

21. Goodfellow, I., Bengio, Y., Courville, A.: Deep Learning. MIT Press (2016)

22. Sohn, K., Berthelot, D., Li, C.-L., et al.: FixMatch: Simplifying Semi-Supervised Learning with Consistency and Confidence (2020). http://arxiv.org/abs/2001.07685

23. Wei, K., Iyer, R., Bilmes, J.: Submodularity in data subset selection and active learning. In: Bach, F., Blei, D. (eds.) Proceedings of the 32nd International Conference on Machine Learning, pp. 1954–1963 PMLR, Lille, France (2015)

24. Settles, B.: Active Learning Literature Survey, University of Wisconsin-Madison Department of Computer Sciences (2009)

25. Sagheer, A., Kotb, M.: Unsupervised pre-training of a deep LSTM-based stacked autoencoder for multivariate time series forecasting problems. Sci. Rep. **9**, 19038 (2019)

26. Culotta, A., McCallum, A.: Reducing labeling effort for structured prediction tasks. In: Veloso, M.M., Kambhampati, S. (eds.) Proceedings, The Twentieth National Conference on Artificial Intelligence and the Seventeenth Innovative Applications of Artificial Intelligence Conference, July 9–13, 2005, Pittsburgh, Pennsylvania, USA, pp. 746–751. AAAI Press / The MIT Press (2005)

27. Sener, O., Savarese, S.: Active Learning for Convolutional Neural Networks: A Core-Set Approach (2017). http://arxiv.org/abs/1708.00489

28. Rajpurkar, P., Irvin, J., Zhu, K., et al.: CheXNet: Radiologist-Level Pneumonia Detection on Chest X-Rays with Deep Learning (2017). http://arxiv.org/abs/1711.05225

29. He, K., Zhang, X., Ren, S., et al.: Deep residual learning for image recognition. In: 2016 IEEE Conference on Computer Vision and Pattern Recognition (CVPR), pp. 770–778 (2016)
30. Ash, J.T., Zhang, C., Krishnamurthy, A., et al.: Deep batch active learning by diverse, uncertain gradient lower bounds (2019). http://arxiv.org/abs/1906.03671
31. Eulenberg, P., Köhler, N., Blasi, T., et al.: Reconstructing cell cycle and disease progression using deep learning. Nat. Commun. **8**, 463 (2017)
32. van Oord, A,D., Li, Y., Vinyals, O.: Representation Learning with Contrastive Predictive Coding (2018). http://arxiv.org/abs/1807.03748
33. Yoo, D., Kweon, I.S.: Learning loss for active learning. In: Proceedings of the IEEE Conference on Computer Vision and Pattern Recognition, pp. 93–102 (2019)
34. Matek, C., Schwarz, S., Spiekermann, K., et al.: Human-level recognition of blast cells in acute myeloid leukaemia with convolutional neural networks. Nat. Mach. Intell. **1**, 538–544 (2019). https://doi.org/10.1038/s42256-019-0101-9
35. Clark, K., et al.: The cancer imaging archive (TCIA): maintaining and operating a public information repository. J. Digit. Imaging **26**(6), 1045–1057 (2013). https://doi.org/10.1007/s10278-013-9622-7
36. Killamsetty, K., Sivasubramanian, D., Ramakrishnan, G., et al.: GLISTER: generalization based data subset selection for efficient and robust learning (2020). http://arxiv.org/abs/2012.10630
37. APTOS 2019 Blindness Detection. https://www.kaggle.com/c/aptos2019-blindness-detection/
38. Zhou, J., Sun, S.: Improved margin sampling for active learning. In: Li, S., Liu, C., Wang, Y. (eds.) CCPR 2014. CCIS, vol. 483, pp. 120–129. Springer, Heidelberg (2014). https://doi.org/10.1007/978-3-662-45646-0_13
39. Codella, N.C.F., Gutman, D., Celebi, E.M., et al.: Skin lesion analysis toward melanoma detection: a challenge at the 2017 international symposium on biomedical imaging (isbi), hosted by the international skin imaging collaboration (ISIC) (2017). http://arxiv.org/abs/1710.05006
40. Gal, Y., Islam, R., Ghahramani, Z.: Deep bayesian active learning with image data (2017). http://arxiv.org/abs/1703.02910
41. Ericsson, L., Gouk, H., Hospedales, T.M.: How well do self-supervised models transfer? (2020). http://arxiv.org/abs/2011.13377
42. Taher, M.R.H., Haghighi, F., Feng, R., et al.: A Systematic Benchmarking Analysis of Transfer Learning for Medical Image Analysis (2021). https://doi.org/10.1007/978-3-030-87722-4_1, http://arxiv.org/abs/2108.05930

# Time Series Forecasting Models Copy the Past: How to Mitigate

Chrysoula Kosma[1]([✉]), Giannis Nikolentzos[1], Nancy Xu[2],
and Michalis Vazirgiannis[1,2]

[1] École Polytechnique, Palaiseau, France
kosma@lix.polytechnique.fr
[2] KTH Royal Institute of Technology, Stockholm, Sweden

**Abstract.** Time series forecasting is at the core of important application domains posing significant challenges to machine learning algorithms. Recently neural network architectures have been widely applied to the problem of time series forecasting. Most of these models are trained by minimizing a loss function that measures predictions' deviation from the real values. Typical loss functions include mean squared error (MSE) and mean absolute error (MAE). In the presence of noise and uncertainty, neural network models tend to replicate the last observed value of the time series, thus limiting their applicability to real-world data. In this paper, we provide a formal definition of the above problem and we also give some examples of forecasts where the problem is observed. We also propose a regularization term penalizing the replication of previously seen values. We evaluate the proposed regularization term both on synthetic and real-world datasets. Our results indicate that the regularization term mitigates to some extent the aforementioned problem and gives rise to more robust models.

**Keywords:** Time-series forecasting · Deep learning · Loss functions

## 1 Introduction

Time series are ubiquitous in several application domains including quantitative finance, seismology and meteorology, just to name a few. Due to this abundance of time series data, the problem of time series forecasting has recently emerged as a very important task with applications ranging from traffic forecasting to financial investment. Indeed, accurate forecasting is of great importance since it can improve future decisions which is the main objective in a number of scenarios. For example, traffic forecasting seeks to predict future web traffic to make decisions for better congestion control [11]. Moreover, forecasting the spread of COVID-19 is of paramount importance to governments and policymakers in order to impose measures to combat the spread of the disease [6].

With the advent of deep learning, deep neural networks have become the dominant approach to the problem of time series forecasting. For instance, models and layers such as Long Short-Term Memory [12], Gated Recurrent Units [7]

© The Author(s), under exclusive license to Springer Nature Switzerland AG 2022
E. Pimenidis et al. (Eds.): ICANN 2022, LNCS 13529, pp. 366–378, 2022.
https://doi.org/10.1007/978-3-031-15919-0_31

and Temporal Convolution Networks [2] have proven to be very successful in temporal modeling. Specifically, these models have demonstrated great success in capturing complex nonlinear dependencies between variables and time, while they usually operate on raw time series data, thus requiring considerably less human effort than traditional approaches. However, as these architectures make fewer structural assumptions, they typically require larger training datasets to learn accurate models, while they also lack robustness and are very sensitive to noise and perturbations. A common problem in time series forecasting with deep neural networks is the one where the model just replicates the last observed value of the time series. This is quite common in the case of noisy datasets, and is a problem of paramount importance since most real-world datasets contain noise. In fact, this problem which we refer to as "mimicking" also depends on the nature of the employed loss function (e. g., MSE).

In this paper, our goal is to formally define the aforementioned problem such that practitioners can identify whether their models replicate previous values instead of making predictions. Therefore, we provide a definition of "mimicking" in time series forecasting and a methodology to quantify the extent to which a model suffers from it. Furthermore, we present examples of forecasts where this phenomenon is clearly observed. The key technical contribution of this work is a carefully designed regularization term which can be added to the loss function and mitigate the drawbacks of "mimicking" which might occur in models trained by minimizing common loss functions. The proposed regularization term is evaluated on a range of different datasets. Our results suggest that the proposed term mitigates "mimicking" and reduces its impact on the model's performance. The main contributions of this paper are summarized as follows:

- To the best of our knowledge, we are the first to formally define the problem of "mimicking" in time series forecasting.
- We designed a regularization term that, when added to the loss function, mitigates to some degree the effect of "mimicking". This term is general for all neural network architectures and does not make any assumptions.
- We specifically investigate and deal with the phenomenon of "mimicking" on three standard deep neural networks (LSTM, TCN and Transformer) which are some of the most widely used and effective models in time series forecasting and sequence modeling.
- The proposed regularization term improves the movement predictive performance of the vanilla models on 6 public time series benchmark datasets and one stock dataset. On average, it leads to absolute improvements of 3.33% in accuracy (considered for the three models), while MSE increases slightly.

## 2   Related Work

*Time Series Forecasting.* Before the advent of deep learning, the Auto-Regressive Integrated Moving Average (ARIMA) model [4] and exponential smoothing [13] were among the most popular and widely used methods for time series forecasting. However, these approaches have some drawbacks (e. g., ARIMA assumes stationarity, while most real-world time series are not stationary), and thus have been replaced recently with neural network architectures [16]. Different instances of recurrent neural networks such as Long Short Term Memory Networks (LSTMs) [12] and Gated Recurrent Units (GRUs) [7] have become the dominant approaches for time series forecasting mainly due to their ability to model complex patterns and long term dependencies, and to extract useful features from raw data. Besides recurrent neural networks, convolutional neural networks have also been recently investigated in the task of time series forecasting. The Temporal Convolution Network (TCN) [2] is perhaps the most prominent example from this family of models. Attention mechanisms have proven very successful in many tasks and have also been applied to the problem of time series forecasting [15,18]. Different neural network components such as recurrent, convolutional and attention layers have been combined with autoregressive components to make predictions [14]. The potential of residual connections along with a very deep stack of fully-connected layers in the context of time series forecasting has also been explored recently [17]. Matrix factorization methods have achieved prominent results in the case of high-dimensional time series data [22,24]. Some recent works have combined neural networks and state space models [19,23]. Probabilistic forecasting, for predicting the distribution of possible future outcomes, has also recently started to receive increasing attention [5,21].

*Loss Functions.* Besides the traditional functions (MSE, MAE, etc.), other measures that capture different time series properties have been proposed. However, in most cases, these evaluation metrics are not differentiable, thus they cannot be directly employed as loss functions. Examples of such measures include the dynamic time warping algorithm which captures the shape of the time series, and standard evaluation metrics of supervised learning algorithms (e. g., accuracy, f1-score) in the context of change point detection algorithms [1]. The need for measures alternatives to MSE has recently led to the development of new differentiable loss functions which capture different meaningful statistical properties of time series such as shape and time, including differentiable variants of dynamic time warping [3,8]. These differentiable dynamic time warping terms can also be combined with terms that penalize temporal distortions for more accurate temporal localization [9], while they have also been generalized to nonstationary time series [10] and binary series [20].

## 3   The Phenomenon of "Mimicking" and How to Mitigate

We first introduce some key notations for time series forecasting. Let $x_{1:\tau} = (x_1, x_2, \ldots, x_\tau)$ be a univariate time series where $x_t \in \mathbb{R}$ denotes the value of the time series at time $t$. The goal of a forecasting model is to predict the future values of the time series $z_{1:n} = (z_1, z_2, \ldots, z_n) = (x_{\tau+1}, x_{\tau+2}, \ldots, x_{\tau+n})$. Let $\hat{z}_{1:n} = (\hat{z}_1, \hat{z}_2, \ldots, \hat{z}_n)$ denote the predictions of the forecasting model. Neural network models for time series forecasting are typically trained to minimize the MSE which is defined as the sum of squared distances between the target variable and predicted values, i. e., MSE $= 1/n \sum_{i=1}^{n} (\hat{z}_i - z_i)^2$. Similar metrics, that measure the difference between the forecast and the actual value per time-step, such as MAE, are also employed in various applications.

## 3.1   "Mimicking" in Time Series Forecasting

Even though MSE and related functions enjoy some nice properties (e. g., MSE is convex on its input), when dealing with real-world data with multiple co-occurring patterns and noisy components, these functions might become sensitive to noise. This might result into the problem of predicting previously seen values (usually the last seen observation in the time series), rather than making predictions based on long-term extracted patterns. We next formalize the problem described above. The following analysis focuses on the MSE loss, but it also applies to other loss functions that are commonly employed in time series forecasting (e. g., MAE). To investigate whether the model just replicates the last observed value of the time series, we can examine if the MSE between the forecast in time-step $t$ and the real value in time-step $t$ is greater than the MSE between the forecast in time-step $t$ and the real value in time-step $t - 1$.

**Definition 1 ("Mimicking" in Time Series).** *We say that the phenomenon of "mimicking" in time series forecasting occurs if the following inequality holds*

$$\sum_{i=1}^{n} (z_i - \hat{z}_i)^2 > \sum_{i=1}^{n} (z_{i-1} - \hat{z}_i)^2 \tag{1}$$

*We can quantify the amount of "mimicking" as follows (the larger the (positive) value of MIM, the larger its severity): MIM $= \sum_{i=1}^{n} \left[ (z_i - \hat{z}_i)^2 - (z_{i-1} - \hat{z}_i)^2 \right]$.*

To demonstrate that "mimicking" is related to the level of noise present in a dataset, we generated a synthetic dataset that corresponds to a sum of sinusoidal series with added random Gaussian noise (more details are given in Sect. 4). A linear term is also added to the above terms. Table 1 illustrates the MSE achieved by an LSTM and a TCN model along with the amount of "mimicking" as a function of the level of noise (i. e., increasing variance). We observe that the LSTM model is more prone to "mimicking" than the TCN model, while the greater the value of the variance of the Gaussian noise, the greater the impact of "mimicking" on the models' performance. We also need to mention that the TCN model does not suffer from "mimicking" for $\sigma = 0$ and $\sigma = 0.01$.

## 3.2   Proposed Regularization Term

To mitigate the effects of mimicking in time series forecasting, we begin our analysis from the definition provided above. Specifically, we would like the second term of inequality (1) to be greater or at least equal to the first term, i. e., we would like the following to hold

$$\sum_{i=1}^{n} \left[ (z_i - \hat{z}_i)^2 - (z_{i-1} - \hat{z}_i)^2 \right] \le 0 \tag{2}$$

**Table 1.** MSE and "mimicking" as a function of the level of noise added to a synthetic dataset.

| $\sigma$ | MSE ($\times 10^{-3}$) | MIM ($\times 10^{-3}$) |
|---|---|---|
| LSTM | | |
| 0 | 6.191 | 0.048 |
| 0.01 | 3.225 | 0.035 |
| 0.1 | 9.765 | 0.052 |
| 0.25 | 10.446 | 0.066 |
| 0.5 | 13.357 | 0.069 |
| TCN | | |
| 0 | 0.024 | −0.006 |
| 0.01 | 0.007 | −0.003 |
| 0.1 | 0.046 | 0.002 |
| 0.25 | 0.068 | 0.004 |
| 0.5 | 0.182 | 0.008 |

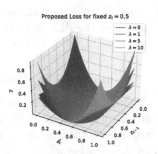

**Fig. 1.** A visualization of the proposed loss $\mathcal{L}$ of Eq. (7) for different values of $\lambda$, $\hat{z}_t$ and $z_{t-1}$.

By introducing the above term into the loss function, we directly punish "mimicking" to some extent. However, incorporating solely the above term into the loss function gives rise to an unbounded function. Indeed, in case $\sum_{i=1}^{n}(z_i - z_{i-1}) < 0$, setting $\hat{z}_i \to +\infty$ can drive the loss to negative infinity. Likewise, if $\sum_{i=1}^{n}(z_i - z_{i-1}) > 0$, setting $\hat{z}_i \to -\infty$ also leads to a loss function that is unbounded from below. Hence, since the loss is not bounded, there is no admissible estimator, and this will render the model to be of no practical use.

Note that a perfect model would achieve an MSE equal to 0, i.e., $\sum_{i=1}^{n}(z_i - \hat{z}_i) = 0$. In such a scenario, we would like the loss function to take its lowest value. If we replace the term that corresponds to the MSE in Eq. (2) with 0, we obtain $0 - \sum_{i=1}^{n}(z_{i-1} - \hat{z}_i)^2 = -\sum_{i=1}^{n}(z_{i-1} - z_i)^2$ The equality is due to the fact that the model is perfect, i.e., $z_i = \hat{z}_i \; \forall i \in 1, \ldots, n$ holds. We would like the above term to be the lower bound of the proposed loss function (since the model is perfect). Therefore, we have

$$- \sum_{i=1}^{n}(z_{i-1} - z_i)^2 \leq \sum_{i=1}^{n}(z_i - \hat{z}_i)^2 - \sum_{i=1}^{n}(z_{i-1} - \hat{z}_i)^2 \qquad (3)$$

By combining Eqs. (2) and (3), we obtain the following inequality

$$- \sum_{i=1}^{n}(z_{i-1} - z_i)^2 \leq \sum_{i=1}^{n}(z_i - \hat{z}_i)^2 - \sum_{i=1}^{n}(z_{i-1} - \hat{z}_i)^2 \leq 0$$

$$\iff 0 \leq \sum_{i=1}^{n} 2(z_i - z_{i-1})(z_i - \hat{z}_i) \leq \sum_{i=1}^{n}(z_{i-1} - z_i)^2 \qquad (4)$$

$$\iff 0 \leq \sum_{i=1}^{n}(z_i - z_{i-1})(z_i - \hat{z}_i) \leq \frac{1}{2}\sum_{i=1}^{n}(z_{i-1} - z_i)^2$$

Ideally, we would like the above inequality to hold. That would mean that the phenomenon of mimicking does not occur. However, the middle term is still not bounded, thus we cannot directly minimize that term. Note that all the terms are nonnegative. Hence, we can square all the sides of the inequality as follows

$$0 \leq \sum_{i=1}^{n} \left[ (z_i - z_{i-1})(z_i - \hat{z}_i) \right]^2 \leq \frac{1}{4} \sum_{i=1}^{n} (z_{i-1} - z_i)^4 \tag{5}$$

Now, the middle term is nonnegative by construction, and we can thus safely minimize it. Interestingly, the above function is continuous and differentiable which are both desirable properties for loss functions. For instance, the first and second derivatives of the function are shown below:

$$\frac{d}{d\hat{z}_i} \sim \sum_{i=1}^{n} 2(z_{i-1} - z_i)^2 (\hat{z}_i - z_i), \qquad \frac{d^2}{d\hat{z}_i^2} \sim \sum_{i=1}^{n} 2(z_{i-1} - z_i)^2 \tag{6}$$

From the above, it is also clear that the second derivative of the function is nonnegative on its entire domain, thus the function is convex. However, we need to mention that even though the function is convex in $\hat{z}_i$, in case neural networks are employed (or other non-linear models), we have $\hat{z}_i = f(z_{i-1}, \dots, z_{i-k}; \theta)$ and the function is not convex in $\theta$.

Our proposed loss function for a sequence of $n$ time-steps is defined as

$$\mathcal{L} = \sum_{i=1}^{n} (z_i - \hat{z}_i)^2 + \lambda \sum_{i=1}^{n} \left[ (z_i - z_{i-1})(z_i - \hat{z}_i) \right]^2 \tag{7}$$

where $\lambda$ is a parameter which controls the importance of the regularization term, i. e., how much penalty needs to be imposed to alleviate "mimicking". The two factors $(z_i - z_{i-1})$, $(z_i - \hat{z}_i)$ that constitute the penalty term above can be interpreted as a discrete-time cross-correlation measure function between the difference of the series at $i$ and $i - 1$ and the predicted error at $i$. If we expand the term for a specific $i$, we derive $[(z_i - z_{i-1})z_i - (z_i - z_{i-1})\hat{z}_i]^2$. The closer the prediction $\hat{z}_i$ is to $z_{i-1}$ and the farther $z_i$ is from $z_{i-1}$, the larger the imposed penalty term will be. Figure 1 illustrates how the proposed loss function varies as a function of $z_{t-1}$ and $\hat{z}_t$ for different values of $\lambda$ (for $z_t$ fixed to 0.5).

In some cases, the model might not replicate solely the last observed value of the time series $x_\tau$, but also observations that occurred farther in the past, e. g., $x_{\tau-1}, x_{\tau-2}$, etc. We next generalize the proposed penalty term to account for such kind of scenarios. To prevent a neural network model from replicating the last $K$ observations, we can use the following loss function

$$\mathcal{L} = \sum_{i=1}^{n} (z_i - \hat{z}_i)^2 + \lambda \sum_{i=1}^{n} \sum_{k=1}^{K} \left[ (z_i - z_{i-k})(z_i - \hat{z}_i) \right]^2 \tag{8}$$

The proposed loss of Eq. (7) can also be generalized to the case of multi-step ahead forecasting. Specifically, it can be directly applied to iterative 1-step methods [16], while in the case of direct multi-horizon forecasting (vector output/Seq2Seq architectures), we need to consider vectors $(\hat{z}_1, \hat{z}_2, \dots, \hat{z}_h)$ of length $h$ which refer to the desired horizon. Direct multi-horizon strategies have been recently preferred, despite the flexibility of iterative ones.

# 4   Experimental Evaluation

## 4.1   Datasets

**Synthetic.** This synthetic dataset corresponds to a sum of sinusoidal series with added random noise: $y(t) = \sin(t) + \sin\left(\frac{\pi}{2}t\right) + \sin\left(\frac{-3\pi}{2}t\right) + \epsilon(t)$, where $\epsilon(t)$ is a Gaussian distribution with mean $\mu$ and variance $\sigma^2$ ($\mu = 0$, $\sigma = 0.5$).

**Monthly Sunspots.** This dataset describes a monthly count of the number of observed sunspots from 1749 to 1983, a total of $2,820$ observations.

**Electricity.** It contains electricity consumption measurements (kWh) from 321 clients, recorded every 15 min from 2012 to 2014. We utilize the first univariate series of length $26,304$.

**Beijing PM2.5.** This hourly dataset contains the PM2.5 data of the US Embassy in Beijing. It is a multivariate dataset that consists of eight variables, including the PM2.5 concentration and a total number of $43,824$ observations. The task is to predict the future hourly concentration given the other variables.

**Solar Energy.** It contains the solar power production data from photovoltaic plants in Alabama in 2006. We utilize the first univariate series of length $26,304$.

**Exchange Rate.** It includes the exchange rates of eight foreign countries (Australia, Britain, Canada, China, Japan, New Zealand, Singapore, and Switzerland) from 1990 to 2016. We utilize the first univariate series of length $7,588$.

## 4.2   Evaluation Metrics

In order to evaluate the performance of our proposed loss function in the experiments that follow, we employ the following metrics:

**Mean Squared Error (MSE) and Shifted Mean Squared Error (s-MSE).** MSE compares the predictions $\hat{z}_t$ against the targets $z_t$. Shifted MSE compares $\hat{z}_t$ against the last values $z_{t-1}$, i.e., s-MSE $= 1/n \sum_{i=1}^{n}(\hat{z}_i - z_{i-1})^2$.

**Accuracy (Acc) and Shifted Accuracy (s-Acc).** To compute these two metrics, we turn the forecasting problem into a classification one. Let $v$ be a $n$-dimensional vector such that its $i$-th element is defined as $v_i = \text{change}(z_i, z_{i-1})$ where $\text{change}(a, b) = \text{sign}(a - b)$. Let also $\hat{v}$ be a $n$-dimensional vector such that $\hat{v}_i = \text{change}(\hat{z}_i, \hat{z}_{i-1})$. Then, Acc is defined as the accuracy between the above two vectors. s-Acc is defined as the accuracy between the vector $\hat{v}$ and the vector $v$ shifted by 1 step to the left. Predicting whether the value of a time series will increase or decrease is a task of high importance for many applications such as stock price prediction. Indeed, successful predictions would enable hedge funds or investors lay a successful strategy for buying and selling stocks.

We should note here that MSE and accuracy are two metrics orthogonal to each other. A time series forecasting model ideally would achieve a low value of MSE and a high accuracy. Models that suffer from "mimicking" can yield low

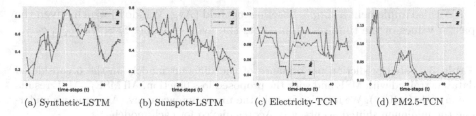

(a) Synthetic-LSTM     (b) Sunspots-LSTM     (c) Electricity-TCN     (d) PM2.5-TCN

**Fig. 2.** 1-step predictions of models trained with MSE on part of the test set.

**Table 2.** 1-step prediction performance of the different models, and the baseline on the 6 considered datasets. All MSE/s-MSE results are in scale $(\times 10^{-3})$.

| Methods | | Synthetic | | Sunspots | | Electricity | | Beijing PM2.5 | | Solar | | Exchange rate | |
|---|---|---|---|---|---|---|---|---|---|---|---|---|---|
| | | MSE | s-MSE | MSE | s-MSE | MSE | s-MSE | MSE | s-MSE | MSE | s-MSE | MSE | s-MSE |
| Avg. window | 1 | 9.759 | 0.0 | 6.825 | 0.0 | 5.063 | 0.0 | 0.489 | 0.0 | 1.803 | 0.0 | 0.248 | 0.0 |
| | 3 | 12.398 | 4.524 | 6.881 | 3.03 | 4.766 | 2.15 | 0.905 | 0.30 | 3.531 | 1.150 | 0.244 | 0.103 |
| | 5 | 18.378 | 9.791 | 7.541 | 4.54 | 4.851 | 3.05 | 1.358 | 0.72 | 5.654 | 2.918 | 0.292 | 0.171 |
| | 7 | 22.896 | 15.382 | 8.642 | 5.91 | 5.066 | 3.62 | 1.793 | 1.16 | 7.998 | 4.998 | 0.348 | 0.235 |
| | 9 | 24.883 | 19.127 | 9.737 | 7.22 | 5.363 | 4.11 | 2.192 | 1.57 | 10.485 | 7.291 | 0.407 | 0.298 |
| LSTM | | 4.742 | 4.778 | 5.739 | 3.572 | 3.594 | 1.49 | 0.421 | 0.08 | 1.358 | 0.463 | 0.388 | 0.236 |
| TCN | | 3.784 | 5.650 | 6.043 | 3.485 | 3.582 | 2.22 | 0.506 | 0.12 | 1.489 | 0.397 | 0.270 | 0.122 |
| Transf. | | 5.422 | 5.128 | 12.21 | 11.21 | 4.299 | 2.659 | 0.560 | 0.18 | 1.802 | 0.391 | 3.811 | 3.747 |

values of MSE, thus achieving solely a low MSE might not be a clear indicator of the model's predictive power. On the other hand, a model that yields solely high accuracy captures the shape and the change points of the time series, but the predicted values might significantly deviate from the actual values of the series.

## 4.3   Experimental Setup

We divide the sequence into multiple samples, where $T$ observations are given as input and the expected output is the actual value of $n$ observations that follow each one of those $T$ observations. We choose $T$ from $\{32, 64, 128, 256, 512\}$.

We choose parameters as follows. For the LSTM model, we use a single LSTM layer. We use the hidden state of the last time step of the LSTM layer as the vector representation of the time series. The generated vector representations are then fed into a two layer MLP with a ReLU activation function. For the TCN model, we adjust the parameters to capture the different history lengths $T$ that we test, from the equation $R_{field} = 2^{D-1} \cdot K_{size}$, for $K_{size} = 2$ and $D$ the number of dilation layers. Each layer has dilation rate of $2^{N_l - 1}$, where $N_l = \{1, 2, ..., D\}$. We also implement a model consisting of two stacked encoders of the Transformer architecture followed by a fully-connected layer for the final prediction. The hidden-dimension size of the LSTM, TCN and Transformer layers is chosen from $\{32, 64, 128, 256\}$. For all the three models, we use the Adam optimizer with an initial learning rate of $10^{-3}$ and decay the learning rate by 0.1 every 10 epochs. We choose the batch size from $\{32, 64, 128\}$. We set the number of epochs to 100, and we retrieve the model that achieves the lowest validation loss. The regularization parameter $\lambda$ is chosen from $\{0.1, 0.5, 1, 5, 10, 20, 50, 100, 200, 500, 800, 1000\}$.

We also implement a simple baseline method (Avg. Window) which, given the past $n$ values of the time series, predicts the average value: $\hat{z}_t = 1/n \sum_{i=1}^{n} z_{t-i}$.

**Table 3.** 1-step prediction performance of the different models on the 6 considered datasets trained with MSE and with the proposed loss function. All MSE/s-MSE results are in scale $(\times 10^{-3})$. We mention in bold the maximum accuracy (Acc) and we underline the minimum shifted accuracy (s-Acc) achieved for each model.

| Methods | Synthetic | | | | Sunspots | | | | Electricity | | | |
|---|---|---|---|---|---|---|---|---|---|---|---|---|
| | MSE | s-MSE | Acc | s-Acc | MSE | s-MSE | Acc | s-Acc | MSE | s-MSE | Acc | s-Acc |
| LSTM | 4.742 | 4.778 | 0.616 | 0.695 | 5.739 | 3.572 | 0.388 | 0.739 | 3.594 | 1.490 | 0.278 | 0.702 |
| LSTM+reg. | 5.747 | 9.767 | **0.657** | <u>0.586</u> | 8.857 | 8.033 | **0.440** | <u>0.628</u> | 28.97 | 29.79 | **0.440** | <u>0.122</u> |
| TCN | 3.784 | 5.650 | 0.677 | 0.636 | 6.043 | 3.485 | 0.439 | 0.725 | 3.582 | 2.220 | 0.366 | 0.497 |
| TCN+reg. | 4.491 | 9.335 | **0.685** | <u>0.569</u> | 7.554 | 6.207 | **0.529** | <u>0.631</u> | 26.01 | 27.32 | **0.442** | <u>0.319</u> |
| Transf | 5.422 | 5.128 | 0.603 | 0.713 | 12.21 | 11.21 | 0.447 | 0.659 | 4.299 | 2.659 | 0.350 | 0.509 |
| Transf.+reg. | 6.467 | 8.780 | **0.636** | <u>0.610</u> | 22.05 | 21.99 | **0.479** | <u>0.488</u> | 15.86 | 16.73 | **0.417** | <u>0.337</u> |
| Methods | Beijing PM2.5 | | | | Solar | | | | Exchange rate | | | |
| | MSE | s-MSE | Acc | s-Acc | MSE | s-MSE | Acc | s-Acc | MSE | s-MSE | Acc | s-Acc |
| LSTM | 0.421 | 0.080 | 0.547 | 0.846 | 1.358 | 0.463 | **0.262** | 0.352 | 0.388 | 0.236 | 0.427 | 0.685 |
| LSTM+reg. | 1.605 | 1.263 | **0.553** | <u>0.661</u> | 3.638 | 3.250 | 0.257 | <u>0.313</u> | 0.524 | 0.414 | **0.436** | <u>0.594</u> |
| TCN | 0.506 | 0.120 | 0.540 | 0.822 | 1.489 | 0.397 | **0.269** | 0.364 | 0.270 | 0.122 | 0.430 | 0.643 |
| TCN+reg. | 0.518 | 0.140 | **0.542** | <u>0.809</u> | 3.855 | 3.240 | 0.255 | <u>0.304</u> | 0.494 | 0.379 | **0.443** | <u>0.586</u> |
| Transf | 0.560 | 0.180 | **0.559** | 0.791 | 1.802 | 0.391 | **0.266** | 0.363 | 3.811 | 3.747 | 0.454 | <u>0.444</u> |
| Transf.+reg | 0.890 | 0.510 | 0.545 | <u>0.696</u> | 3.927 | 2.834 | 0.254 | <u>0.320</u> | 9.320 | 9.321 | **0.471** | 0.453 |

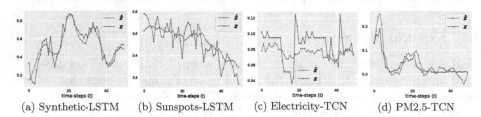

(a) Synthetic-LSTM    (b) Sunspots-LSTM    (c) Electricity-TCN    (d) PM2.5-TCN

**Fig. 3.** Predictions as in Fig. 2 but after training with the proposed loss.

## 4.4    Results

**Examples of "Mimicking".** We next provide some examples of forecasts where the LSTM model and the TCN model just learn to replicate the last seen observations. Figure 2 illustrates such examples for some of the considered datasets. The first 2 plots (i.e., (a) and (b)) correspond to predictions of the LSTM model, while the last 2 plots (i.e., (c) and (d)) to predictions of the TCN model. On the synthetic dataset, the LSTM model learns to infer quite accurately the future values of the time series. This is mainly due to the simplistic nature of that dataset. On the other hand, on the real-world datasets, the two models fail to generalize, replicating previously observed data. This is especially true for plots

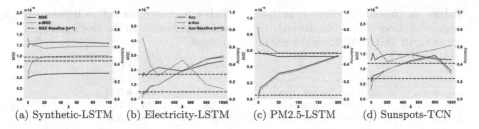

(a) Synthetic-LSTM     (b) Electricity-LSTM     (c) PM2.5-LSTM     (d) Sunspots-TCN

**Fig. 4.** 1-step prediction performance of different models, trained to minimize the proposed loss, as a function of $\lambda$ and the baseline (Avg. Window ($n = 1$)).

(b) and (d). Specifically, on the Beijing PM2.5 dataset, "mimicking" is observed to a very large extent, probably due to the complexity of the dataset.

Besides the above qualitative results, we also present some quantitative results in Table 2. We can see that on the 5 real-world datasets, the LSTM, TCN and Transformer models suffer from "mimicking" since s-MSE is smaller than MSE in all cases. Interestingly, s-MSE can even be an order of magnitude smaller than MSE (see LSTM on Beijing PM2.5 and all three models on Solar). On the other hand, on the synthetic dataset both the LSTM and the TCN model achieve a smaller MSE than s-MSE. Thus, on this dataset, the two models are more robust. Indeed, this dataset is less noisy, while its trend is more predictable than that of the real-world datasets. With regards to the baselines, in most cases, they also achieve low values of MSE (especially when $n = 1$). In fact, on the Beijing PM2.5 dataset, the Avg. Window ($n = 1$) outperforms the TCN model since it yields a smaller MSE than TCN. This interesting result indicates that a simplistic baseline may outperform a sophisticated model on this dataset.

**Regularization Term.** In this set of experiments, we train the models to minimize the loss function of Eq. (7) and we report the 1-step forecasting results in Table 3. We also provide some examples of the predictions of the models in Fig. 3. We observe that the proposed regularization term mitigates to some extent the effects of "mimicking", however, it does not eliminate it completely. In most cases, the models trained with the proposed loss function result into a slight increase in MSE compared to the vanilla models, but also into a larger increase in s-MSE. We also observe that even though the proposed function incurs a very small increase in MSE, it improves the generalization ability of the base models since they achieve higher accuracy in the task of predicting whether the value of the time series will increase or decrease. The increase in the achieved accuracy of the binary problem is in some cases significant. The proposed loss offers LSTM a relative increase of 16.2% in accuracy and Transformer an increase of 6.7% on the Electricity dataset, while TCN's accuracy increases by 9.0% on Sunspots.

**Table 4.** 5-step prediction performance of models on the Electricity dataset. All MSE/s-MSE results are in scale ($\times 10^{-3}$).

| Methods | MSE | s-MSE | Acc | s-Acc |
|---|---|---|---|---|
| Seq2Seq | 5.495 | 0.522 | 0.375 | 0.605 |
| Seq2Seq+reg. | 5.410 | 0.477 | **0.383** | 0.547 |
| LSTM | 5.534 | 0.502 | 0.380 | 0.646 |
| LSTM+reg. | 5.561 | 0.328 | **0.385** | 0.614 |
| TCN | 5.546 | 0.621 | 0.398 | 0.626 |
| TCN+reg. | 5.541 | 0.745 | **0.401** | 0.610 |
| Transf | 5.845 | 0.3819 | 0.373 | 0.659 |
| Transf.+reg. | 5.346 | 0.3850 | **0.387** | 0.592 |

**Table 5.** 1-step prediction performance of models on the stock price dataset.

| Methods | Acc | F1 |
|---|---|---|
| LSTM | 0.552 | 0.398 |
| LSTM+reg. | **0.570** | **0.520** |
| TCN | 0.545 | 0.184 |
| TCN+reg. | **0.586** | **0.360** |

**Sensitivity Analysis.** We next study how the performance of the proposed loss varies as a function of hyperparameter $\lambda$. We expect the effect of "mimicking" to be inversely proportional to $\lambda$. Figure 4 illustrates how the performance of the different models on 4 datasets varies with respect to $\lambda$. We observe that both MSE and s-MSE increase as the value of $\lambda$ increases. This is not surprising since the objective of the regularization term is to make s-MSE as large as possible without hurting MSE much. In most cases, the increase of s-MSE is larger than that of MSE, which is the desired behavior. In many cases, large values of $\lambda$ result into MSEs that are even greater that of the baseline (Avg. Window ($n = 1$)). In terms of accuracy, we observe that in most cases, increasing the value of $\lambda$ leads to a slight increase of Acc and a slight decrease of s-Acc.

**Multi-step Ahead Predictions.** We present in Table 4 results of the multi-step ahead forecasting experiments performed on Electricity. We employ a sequence-to-sequence model of LSTM encoder and decoder, as well as LSTM, TCN, and Transformer encoders followed by fully connected layers for direct predictions. In most cases, when trained to minimize the proposed loss function, the different models achieve slightly larger values of Acc and in some cases significantly smaller values of s-Acc. In terms of MSE, quite surprisingly in the case of all models except LSTM, MSE decreases when the proposed loss is employed.

**Case Study: Predicting Stock Prices Trends.** We also experiment with a dataset recording high-frequency bids for the TSLA stocks. Due to the class imbalance, besides accuracy, we also report F1-scores in Table 5. The proposed term leads to slight improvements in accuracy, but significant ones in F1-score.

## 5 Conclusion

In this paper, we deal with "mimicking" in time series forecasting. Our results indicate that the proposed regularization term partially mitigates this phenomenon, constituting a first approach towards this research direction. We plan to further study its properties along with potential improvements in the future.

Also, investigating the exact conditions under which a model replicates the last observed values of the time series is on our agenda for future work.

# References

1. Aminikhanghahi, S., Cook, D.J.: A survey of methods for time series change point detection. Knowl. Inf. Syst. **51**(2), 339–367 (2016). https://doi.org/10.1007/s10115-016-0987-z
2. Bai, S., Kolter, J.Z., Koltun, V.: An empirical evaluation of generic convolutional and recurrent networks for sequence modeling. arXiv:1803.01271 (2018)
3. Blondel, M., Mensch, A., Vert, J.P.: Differentiable divergences between time series. In: AISTATS 2021, pp. 3853–3861 (2021)
4. Box, G.E., Jenkins, G.M., Reinsel, G.C., Ljung, G.M.: Time Series Analysis: Forecasting and Control. Wiley, New York (2015)
5. Chen, Y., Kang, Y., Chen, Y., Wang, Z.: Probabilistic forecasting with temporal convolutional neural network. Neurocomputing **399**, 491–501 (2020)
6. Chimmula, V.K.R., Zhang, L.: Time series forecasting of COVID-19 transmission in Canada using LSTM networks. Chaos Solitons Fractals **135**, 109864 (2020)
7. Cho, K., et al.: Learning phrase representations using RNN encoder-decoder for statistical machine translation. In: EMNLP 2014, pp. 1724–1734 (2014)
8. Cuturi, M., Blondel, M.: Soft-DTW: a differentiable loss function for time-series. In: ICML 2017, pp. 894–903 (2017)
9. Guen, V.L., Thome, N.: Shape and time distortion loss for training deep time series forecasting models. In: NeurIPS 2019, pp. 4189–4201 (2019)
10. Guen, V.L., Thome, N.: Probabilistic time series forecasting with shape and temporal diversity. In: NeurIPS 2020, pp. 4427–4440 (2020)
11. Hamed, M.M., Al-Masaeid, H.R., Said, Z.M.B.: Short-term prediction of traffic volume in urban arterials. J. Transp. Eng. **121**(3), 249–254 (1995)
12. Hochreiter, S., Schmidhuber, J.: Long short-term memory. Neural Comput. **9**(8), 1735–1780 (1997)
13. Holt, C.C.: Forecasting seasonals and trends by exponentially weighted moving averages. Int. J. Forecast. **20**(1), 5–10 (2004)
14. Lai, G., Chang, W.C., Yang, Y., Liu, H.: Modeling long- and short-term temporal patterns with deep neural networks. In: SIGIR 2018, pp. 95–104 (2018)
15. Li, S., et al.: Enhancing the locality and breaking the memory bottleneck of transformer on time series forecasting. In: NeurIPS 2019, pp. 5243–5253 (2019)
16. Lim, B., Zohren, S.: Time-series forecasting with deep learning: a survey. Phil. Trans. R. Soc. A **379**(2194), 20200209 (2021)
17. Oreshkin, B.N., Carpov, D., Chapados, N., Bengio, Y.: N-beats: neural basis expansion analysis for interpretable time series forecasting. In: ICLR 2020 (2020)
18. Qin, Y., Song, D., Cheng, H., Cheng, W., Jiang, G., Cottrell, G.W.: A dual-stage attention-based recurrent neural network for time series prediction. In: IJCAI 2017, pp. 2627–2633 (2017)
19. Rangapuram, S.S., Seeger, M.W., Gasthaus, J., Stella, L., Wang, Y., Januschowski, T.: Deep state space models for time series forecasting. In: NeurIPS 2018, pp. 7785–7794 (2018)
20. Rivest, F., Kohar, R.: A new timing error cost function for binary time series prediction. IEEE TNNLS **31**(1), 174–185 (2019)

21. Salinas, D., Flunkert, V., Gasthaus, J., Januschowski, T.: DeepAR: probabilistic forecasting with autoregressive recurrent networks. Int. J. Forecast. **36**(3), 1181–1191 (2020)
22. Sen, R., Yu, H.F., Dhillon, I.S.: Think globally, act locally: a deep neural network approach to high-dimensional time series forecasting. In: NeurIPS 2019, pp. 4837–4846 (2019)
23. Wang, Y., Smola, A., Maddix, D., Gasthaus, J., Foster, D., Januschowski, T.: Deep factors for forecasting. In: ICML 2019, pp. 6607–6617 (2019)
24. Yu, H.F., Rao, N., Dhillon, I.S.: Temporal regularized matrix factorization for high-dimensional time series prediction. In: NeurIPS 2016, pp. 847–855 (2016)

# Towards Both Accurate and Robust Neural Networks Without Extra Data

Faqiang Liu[ID] and Rong Zhao[✉][ID]

Center for Brain-Inspired Computing Research, Department of Precision Instrument,
Tsinghua University, Beijing, China
lfq18@mails.tsinghua.edu.cn, r_zhao@mail.tsinghua.edu.cn

**Abstract.** Deep neural networks have achieved remarkable performance in various applications but are extremely vulnerable to adversarial perturbation. The most representative and promising methods that can enhance model robustness, such as adversarial training and its variants, substantially degrade model accuracy on benign samples, limiting practical utility. Although incorporating extra training data can alleviate the trade-off to a certain extent, it remains unsolved to achieve both robustness and accuracy under limited training data. Here, we demonstrate the feasibility of overcoming the trade-off, by developing an adversarial feature stacking (AFS) model, which combines multiple independent feature extractors with varied levels of robustness and accuracy. Theoretical analysis is further conducted, and general principles for the selection of basic feature extractors are provided. We evaluate the AFS model on CIFAR-10 and CIFAR-100 datasets with strong adaptive attack methods, significantly advancing the state-of-the-art in terms of the trade-off. The AFS model achieves a benign accuracy improvement of ∼6% on CIFAR-10 and ∼10% on CIFAR-100 with comparable or even stronger robustness than the state-of-the-art adversarial training methods.

**Keywords:** Adversarial robustness · Deep networks · Adversarial training

## 1 Introduction

With the assistance of big data and powerful parallel computing platforms, deep neural networks (DNNs) [6,7,9,12] have achieved significant success in computer vision and natural language processing. However, DNNs are extremely vulnerable to adversarial perturbation, which is imperceptible by humans but can fool the state-of-the-art deep models to give wrong predictions [14]. The poor robustness of DNNs hinders applications of DNNs in security-critical scenarios. Till now, a large body of work has been proposed to enhance model robustness [1,8,16]. From a comprehensive consideration of feasibility and effectiveness, adversarial training based on projected gradient descent (PGD-AT) [10] remains one of the most promising and popular methods to improve model robustness. Unfortunately, PGD-AT and its variants [17,17,20] substantially degrade model accuracy

E. Pimenidis et al. (Eds.): ICANN 2022, LNCS 13529, pp. 379–390, 2022.
https://doi.org/10.1007/978-3-031-15919-0_32

on benign samples, which limits their value for tasks in practice. Remarkably, augmenting the training set with extra data can mitigate the trade-off to some extent [2]. However, additional training data is not always available due to the heavy cost of data collecting and labeling. This motivates us to explore the following question: **can we obtain both accurate and robust models at the same time without extra training data?**

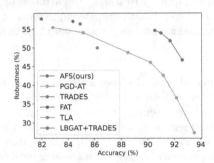

**Fig. 1.** Comparison of PGD-AT [13], TRADES [19], FAT [20], TLA [11], LBGAT+TRADES [4], and AFS. The robustness is evaluated on CIFAR-10 using PGD attack under the perturbation budget of 8/255. Our model significantly improves the trade-off.

To answer this question, we first investigate the influence of the features extracted by the networks with different training algorithms on the model accuracy and robustness. For convenience, we refer to the accurate features as the features that are highly correlated to the labels, and the robust features as the features that remain almost unchanged with adversarially perturbed inputs. Adversarial training with large perturbation budgets can hinder the network from learning non-robust but predictive features [5,15], which are important for accurate predictions of benign samples. From this perspective, the trade-off between accuracy and robustness can be interpreted as it is difficult to train a single network to extract both robust features and non-robust but accurate features.

To solve this dilemma, we develop an adversarial feature stacking (AFS) model with a two-stage training paradigm. The AFS model combines the features extracted by multiple separately trained networks with varied levels of robustness and accuracy. Then, we adopt a linear merger to fuse the useful features to give final predictions. Due to the availability of accurate features and robust features, the AFS model can facilitate predictions with both accuracy and robustness. We analyze the AFS model theoretically and evaluate it on CIFAR-10 and CIFAR-100 datasets with advanced adaptive attack methods, which significantly improves the trade-off between accuracy and robustness as presented in Fig. 1. The experimental results indicate that **it is feasible to obtain a model with high accuracy and strong robustness under limited training data.** Our key contributions are summarized as follows:

1 A stacking model is developed to fuse the features extracted by multiple networks with different levels of robustness and accuracy. The stacking model is further analyzed theoretically and general principles are derived for selecting the basic feature extractors.

2 The AFS model is verified on CIFAR-10 and CIFAR-100 datasets with advanced attack methods. The experimental results demonstrate the feasibility to achieve both high accuracy and strong robustness without extra data.

3 We conduct extensive ablation experiments and analyze the characteristics of the linear merger, verifying the effectiveness of the AFS model.

## 2    Methods

In this section, we will introduce the overall architecture and the training methods of the proposed AFS model. In this work, we focus on the norm bounded adversarial perturbation for classification tasks. The AFS model can be generalized to other tasks and the adversarial perturbation with other constraints.

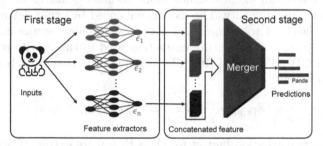

**Fig. 2.** The schematic of the AFS model. The AFS model fuses the features extracted by multiple networks with a learnable linear merger. These networks are adversarially trained with varied perturbation budgets. The classifier is optimized to select useful features for both accurate and robust predictions.

### 2.1    Overall Architecture

The AFS model consists of two parts: several pre-trained feature extractors with varied levels of robustness and accuracy and a linear merger to fuse the features, whose overall architecture is illustrated in Fig. 2. Generally, as discussed above, there are two types of feature extractors. For a given benign input, some of these pre-trained extractors can extract accurate features, thus contributing more accurate predictions. The others of these pre-trained extractors can extract more robust features that are not easily affected by the adversarial perturbation. The robustness and accuracy of pre-trained feature extractors can be determined by the strength of the defense methods. The processing procedure of the AFS model can be formulated as follows:

$$z = w^T G(x; \Theta) + b, \tag{1}$$

where $x$ and $z$ denote the input and the prediction, respectively. $w$ and $b$ are the trainable parameters of the linear merger. $G(x; \Theta)$ is formed by concatenating the features generated by the pre-trained extractors along the feature dimension. $\Theta$ denotes the set of parameters of all the extractors, which is presented as the following equation:

$$G(x; \Theta) = \left[ g_1(x; \theta_1)^T, g_2(x; \theta_2)^T, ..., g_n(x; \theta_n)^T \right]^T , \qquad (2)$$

where $g_i$ is the $i$-th feature extractor parameterized by $\theta_i$, whose outputs are high dimensional vectors. These feature vectors are concatenated together to feed into the linear merger.

## 2.2 Adversarially Trained Feature Extractor

In this work, we use the networks that are adversarially trained with different perturbation budgets as the feature extractors. The perturbation budgets should range from small values to large values. These networks trained with different perturbation levels can extract either more accurate features or more robust features with a large diversity. The models enhanced by other defense methods with different levels of robustness and accuracy can also be the candidates of the feature extractors. The feature extractors used in this work are separately trained with PGD-AT method [10]. The training objective of each extractor is formulated as follows:

$$\min_{\theta_i, w_i, b_i} \mathbb{E}_{(x,y) \in \mathcal{D}} \max_{\|\hat{x} - x\|_p \leq \epsilon_i} \mathcal{L} \left[ w_i^T g_i(\hat{x}; \theta_i) + b_i, y \right] , \qquad (3)$$

where $\epsilon_i$ is the perturbation budget for the $i$-th feature extractor and $w_i, b_i$ are the parameters of the corresponding linear classifier. $\mathcal{D}$ is the data distribution and $y$ is the true label. The inner maximization is solved by PGD method, whose iterative formula is presented as follows:

$$\begin{aligned} \hat{x}_0 &= x + \text{Uniform}(-\epsilon_i, \epsilon_i) \\ \hat{x}_{k+1} &= P_S \left( \hat{x}_k + \eta \cdot \text{sgn} \left( \nabla_x \mathcal{L} \left[ w_i^T g_i(\hat{x}_k; \theta_i) + b_i, y \right] \right) \right) , \end{aligned} \qquad (4)$$

where $\eta$ is the step size and $\text{sgn}(\cdot)$ is the sign function. $P_S$ is an operator to project $\hat{x}_k$ into the image space.

## 2.3 Linear Merger

A naive approach to fuse the features is to take the average of the outputs of the original corresponding classifiers. However, this approach cannot adaptively select features. To address this issue, we propose a learnable linear merger to fuse the diverse features to give final predictions, which can balance the total accuracy and robustness when considering all the features. After obtaining a group of feature extractors, the linear merger is trained on the generated features. To balance the final accuracy and robustness of the whole stacking model, the features of both benign samples and adversarially perturbed samples are used to train the merger. The training objective of the linear merger is presented as follows:

$$\min_{w,b} \mathbb{E}_{(x,y)\in\mathcal{D}}\{\alpha\mathcal{L}\left[w^T G(x;\Theta) + b, y\right]$$

$$+ \max_{\|\hat{x}-x\|_p \leq \epsilon} (1-\alpha)\mathcal{L}\left[w^T G(\hat{x};\Theta) + b, y\right]\}, \tag{5}$$

where $\alpha$ is the ratio ranging in $[0,1]$. $\alpha$ can balance the loss for accuracy and robustness. $\epsilon$ denotes the perturbation budget for training the merger. The crafting method of the adversarial perturbation for adversarial training is the same as the Eq. 4 except for targeting the whole model. A small $\alpha$ encourages the merger to use more robust features to give robust predictions. On the contrary, a large $\alpha$ encourages the merger to use more accurate features to give accurate predictions.

## 2.4   Theoretical Analysis

To understand why fusing multiple networks can improve performance, we conduct a brief theoretical analysis of the stacking model to explore the underneath mechanism. In addition, a general principle for the selection of the perturbation budgets is derived. Without loss of generality, we consider a binary classification problem with $y \in \{\pm 1\}$ and stacking three networks trained with perturbation budgets $\epsilon_1 < \epsilon_2 < \epsilon_3$. The error rate of each single network under the evaluation attack strength of $\Delta$ can be calculated as follows:

$$\mathrm{err}_i = \mathbb{E}_{(x,y)\in\mathcal{D}} \max_{\|\hat{x}-x\|_p \leq \Delta} \left[1 - \mathrm{sgn}(w_i^T g_i(\hat{x};\theta_i) + b_i) \cdot y\right]/2,$$

$$= \mathbb{E}_{(x,y)\in\mathcal{D}} \max_{\|\hat{x}-x\|_p \leq \Delta} \left[1 - \mathrm{sgn}(\hat{z}_i) \cdot y\right]/2, \tag{6}$$

where $\hat{z}_i$ is the logit of the network $i$ under the input perturbation:

$$\hat{z}_i = w_i^T g_i(\hat{x};\theta_i) + b_i \tag{7}$$

The maximum perturbation of $\hat{z}_i$, denoted by $\Delta_{z_i}$, is strongly correlated to the error rate of the network under the adversarial perturbation, which is presented as following equation:

$$\Delta_{z_i} = \max_{\|\hat{x}-x\|_p \leq \Delta} \|\hat{z}_i - z_i\|_p. \tag{8}$$

$\Delta_{z_i}$ decreases with training perturbation budgets, which can be validated empirically. The error rate of the stacking model with the weighted average of logits of single networks can be calculated as follows:

$$\mathrm{err} = \mathbb{E}_{(x,y)\in\mathcal{D}} \max_{\|\hat{x}-x\|_p \leq \Delta} \left[1 - \mathrm{sgn}(\Sigma_i\lambda_i\hat{z}_i) \cdot y\right]/2, \tag{9}$$

where $\lambda_i > 0$ and $\Sigma_i\lambda_i = 1$. As an instance, to make the error rate of the stacking model lower than the single network such as the second network, a sufficient condition is to make the maximum perturbation of the logit of the stacking model smaller than that of the single network, which can be presented as the following equation:

$$\Sigma_i \lambda_i \Delta_{z_i} < \Delta_{z_2}. \tag{10}$$

To make the above equation hold, one solution is to make $\Delta_{z_i}$ concave with respect to the perturbation budget $\epsilon$ used to train the single network. This condition is a practical standard for the selection of perturbation budgets. Note that in the derivation, the evaluation attack strength $\Delta$ is not fixed as a specific value. Therefore, lower error rates under a range of $\Delta$ show improved trade-off. As a general case of the above logit averaging model, the proposed feature stacking model uses a learnable merger to fuse features, which is more adaptive. In practical applications, to reduce computation overhead, we can train multiple networks with evenly-spaced perturbation budgets to calculate $\Delta_{z_i}$, and then filter the candidates according to the above standard.

## 3   Experiments

In this section, we conduct a series of experiments to verify the effectiveness of the AFS model. The effects of different parameter settings on the performance are also extensively studied. Without loss of generality, we evaluate the AFS model with the adversarial perturbation bounded by infinity norm. Our code is available at https://github.com/anonymous1s8f2o/afs_code. The experimental settings are summarized as follows.

**Dataset.** We conduct experiments on widely adopted CIFAR-10 and CIFAR-100 datasets for evaluating adversarial robustness. We train feature extractors on the standard training set without extra training data.

**Network.** Unless otherwise indicated, we adopt the prevalent wide ResNet backbone with 28 layers and a width factor of 10 (WRN-28-10) [18] as the feature extractor. We use a linear classifier as the merger.

**Training.** The training setting of CIFAR-10 is the same as CIFAR-100. The training settings of feature extractors follow the prevalent PGD model with early stopping [13]. We train the linear merger 5 epochs. The perturbation budget for training the merger is set to 8/255. Other settings are the same as those of training extractors.

**Evaluation Protocol.** We evaluate the model robustness with PGD method [10]. We denote PGD-10 and PGD-20 for PGD with 10 steps and 20 steps, respectively. Stronger attack such as auto attack (AA) [3] is also applied, which ensembles multiple gradient-based and black-box attack methods. For simplicity, we refer to the model robustness as the model accuracy on samples with a perturbation budget of 8/255. When evaluating the stacking model, the adversarial perturbation is generated for the whole model.

## 3.1   Selection and Analysis of Basic Feature Extractors

To form the stacking model, we firstly train multiple WRN-28-10 with evenly-spaced perturbation budgets from 0/255 to 9/255, which are named network-0 to network-9. The accuracy and robustness of these networks are summarized in Table 1. It can be seen that the network trained with a larger perturbation budget has lower accuracy and stronger robustness. According to the selection standard, $\Delta_{z_i}$ should be concave with respect to the training perturbation. As shown in Fig. 3, $\Delta_{z_i}$ of the network trained with perturbation budgets less than 3/255 is not concave. Thus, these networks should not be fused. We select the networks trained with the perturbation budgets less than 9/255 and larger than 2/255 as the candidates of the feature extractors.

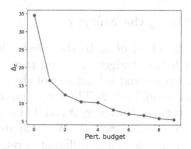

**Fig. 3.** The plot of $\Delta_z$ under the evaluation attack strength of 8/255 versus the training perturbation budget. $\Delta_{z_i}$ of the network trained with perturbation budgets less than 3/255 is not concave.

**Table 1.** Accuracy and robustness of basic extractors (%)

| Network Pert. | 0 | 1 | 2 | 3 | 4 | 5 | 6 | 7 | 8 | 9 |
|---|---|---|---|---|---|---|---|---|---|---|
| | 0/255 | 1/255 | 2/255 | 3/255 | 4/255 | 5/255 | 6/255 | 7/255 | 8/255 | 9/255 |
| Clean | 94.62 | 93.92 | 93.50 | 92.16 | 91.17 | 90.21 | 88.52 | 87.30 | 85.15 | 83.85 |
| PGD-10 | 0 | 15.10 | 31.48 | 39.12 | 44.63 | 47.76 | 50.16 | 52.88 | 54.76 | 55.02 |
| PGD-20 | 0 | 10.71 | 27.41 | 36.64 | 42.65 | 46.12 | 48.76 | 51.74 | 54.06 | 54.37 |

As a preliminary analysis of the features extracted by these candidates, we visualize the 2-dimensional embeddings of some benign test samples using t-SNE method. As shown in Fig. 4, we present the t-SNE embeddings of the features generated by the network-3 and the network-8, and the embeddings of the concatenation, respectively. The features extracted by the network trained with small perturbation budgets are separated well, but the robustness of these networks is lower. In contrast, the robustness of the network trained with large perturbation budgets is stronger, but the features extracted by these networks are not well separated, thus leading to lower accuracy on benign samples. Notably, the features formed by simply concatenating these two types of features are also separated well, indicating improved accuracy.

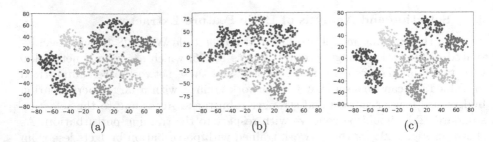

(a)                    (b)                    (c)

**Fig. 4.** Visualization of t-SNE embeddings. Different colors denote different classes. (a)–(c) The embeddings of the features extracted by the network-3, the network-8, and the concatenation of these two features.

## 3.2 Effect of $\alpha$ in Training the Merger

In this section, we study the effect of $\alpha$. In these experiments, we select 6 networks trained with perturbation budgets ranging from 3/255 to 8/255 as the feature extractors. The accuracy and robustness of the stacking models trained with varied $\alpha$ are summarized in Table 2. The larger the $\alpha$, the higher the accuracy and the lower the robustness. However, it should be noted that the trade-off is significantly improved than single models. We evaluate the robustness of the stacking model with an $\alpha$ of 0.5 under different levels of perturbation budgets, and compare it with several single networks. The experimental results are depicted in Fig. 5(a). The AFS model significantly improves the accuracy without sacrificing robustness. Practically, the $\alpha$ can be set to 0.5 for a better trade-off.

**Table 2.** Accuracy and robustness of stacking models with different $\alpha$ (%)

| $\alpha$ | 0.0 | 0.2 | 0.4 | 0.6 | 0.8 | 1.0 |
|---|---|---|---|---|---|---|
| Clean | 90.06 | 90.55 | 90.80 | 91.01 | 91.70 | 92.60 |
| PGD-10 | 56.16 | 55.74 | 55.21 | 54.61 | 53.18 | 48.20 |
| PGD-20 | 54.94 | 54.65 | 53.79 | 53.33 | 51.89 | 46.76 |

To investigate how the features of different extractors influence the performance, we analyze the characteristic of the weight matrix of the linear merger trained with different $\alpha$. The weight matrix can be divided into several sub-matrices. The sum of the absolute values of each sub-matrix reflects the importance of the feature generated by the corresponding extractor. Thus, we calculate the normalized sum as the importance ratio and plot it versus the stacked single model under different settings of $\alpha$ in Fig. 5(b). These results demonstrate that the AFS model indeed utilizes diverse features generated by different extractors to give predictions.

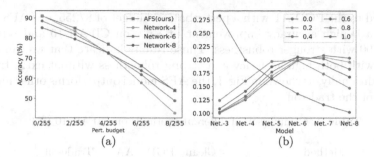

**Fig. 5.** (a) Robustness of different models under different perturbation budgets. (b) The importance ratio of each stacked network under different $\alpha$.

## 3.3 Effect of Stacking Different Extractors

In this section, we study the effect of the number of different networks to be stacked. In this experiment, we select 9 basic networks (network-0 to network-8) as the candidates to be stacked. We use a 9-dimensional binary vector to denote whether a single network is adopted. For example, '100000001' denotes the setting that network-0 and network-8 are adopted. The accuracy and robustness of different settings are summarized in Table 3. Generally, the more networks are stacked, the higher accuracy and the stronger robustness are. As the results show, stacking network-0, network-1 or network-2 contributes marginally to the total performance, which is consistent with the proposed selection standard. From the both consideration of performance and cost, we choose to stack the 6 networks (network-3 to network-8) as the default setting.

**Table 3.** Accuracy and robustness of stacking different networks (%)

| Setting | 100000001 | 100010001 | 101010101 | 111111111 |
|---------|-----------|-----------|-----------|-----------|
| Clean   | 86.25     | 90.00     | 90.79     | 91.08     |
| PGD-10  | 53.30     | 53.01     | 53.77     | 54.90     |
| PGD-20  | 52.44     | 51.96     | 52.44     | 53.38     |

## 3.4 Comparison with State-of-the-Art Methods

The default AFS model is evaluated on CIFAR-10 and CIFAR-100 with advanced attacks such as AA, and compared with state-of-the-art defense methods, whose results are summarized in Table 4 and Table 5. The trade-off is measured by the mean of the clean accuracy and the robustness evaluated by AA. The results listed at the bottom part of the table are our implementations. Other results are cited from original papers. All the methods are evaluated with the WRN-34-10 network architecture. The AFS model in this work is based on PGD-AT.

Compared to the PGD-AT with a perturbation budget of 8/255, our AFS model achieves a benign accuracy improvement of ∼6% on CIFAR-10 and ∼10% on CIFAR-100 with stronger robustness. These results indicate that we can obtain a model with both high accuracy and strong robustness without extra training data. Additionally, as shown in Fig. 1, the AFS model outperforms other methods in terms of the trade-off.

**Table 4.** Comparison of different methods on CIFAR-10 (%)

| Method | Clean | PGD | AA | Trade-off |
|---|---|---|---|---|
| FAT [20] | 84.39 | 57.12 | **53.51** | 68.95 |
| TLA [11] | 86.21 | 50.03 | 47.41 | 66.81 |
| TRADES [19] | 84.92 | 56.43 | 53.08 | 69 |
| LBGAT+TRADES [4] | 81.98 | **57.78** | 53.14 | 67.56 |
| PGD-AT [13] | 85.77 | 55.53 | 52.08 | 68.92 |
| AFS(ours) | **90.93** | 54.70 | 53.05 | **71.99** |

**Table 5.** Comparison of different methods on CIFAR-100 (%)

| Method | Clean | PGD | AA | Trade-off |
|---|---|---|---|---|
| LBGAT+TRADES [4] | 60.43 | **35.50** | **29.34** | 44.88 |
| PGD-AT [13] | 60.68 | 30.45 | 26.59 | 43.63 |
| AFS(ours) | **70.54** | 29.03 | 27.36 | **48.95** |

### 3.5   Ablation Study

To investigate the key points that make AFS model work, we conduct several ablation experiments on CIFAR-10. The parameters, computational costs, and performance, are presented in Table 6. The baseline model is a WRN-28-10 trained with a perturbation budget of 8/255. For comparison, we train a single WRN-28-10 with random perturbation budgets ranging from 3/255 to 8/255. The accuracy of this model improves about 4% at the cost of the same level robustness degradation, thus failing to improve the trade-off between accuracy and robustness than the baseline model. The results indicate that training a single network with different perturbation budgets cannot alleviate the trade-off.

To investigate the effect of the model capacity on the trade-off, we train a large WRN-28–30 model, whose depth is the same as the default AFS model. With large width, the parameters and computational costs of the large model are 1.5 times larger than the default AFS model. The accuracy of this large model improves about 2.5% without degrading robustness. The results demonstrate that increasing model capacity can improve the trade-off within certain limits but the improvement is not remarkable. In contrast, with even fewer parameters and smaller computational costs than the above mentioned large model, the AFS model can significantly improve the accuracy about 6% without degrading robustness.

**Table 6.** Comparison of different ablation settings

| Setting | Para. (M) | MACs (G) | Clean | PGD-20 |
|---|---|---|---|---|
| Baseline | 36.47 | 5.24 | 85.15 | 54.06 |
| Rand.pert. | 36.47 | 5.24 | 89.02 | 49.73 |
| Large model | 328 | 47.04 | 87.67 | 54.08 |
| AFS | 218.82 | 31.44 | 91.01 | 53.94 |

### 3.6 Weight Analysis

We present the histogram of the weight matrix of the AFS model with the default setting (Fig. 6(c)), of the classifier of the network-1 and the network-8 (Fig. 6(a),(b)). The weight matrices of the network-1 and the network-8 are relatively sparse and have a small part of larger values, indicting that the corresponding classifier heavily depends on a few key features to give predictions. In contrast, the weight matrix of the linear merger of the AFS model is distributed more evenly, demonstrating that the AFS model uses more diverse features.

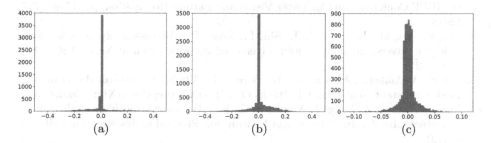

(a) (b) (c)

**Fig. 6.** Histograms of the weight matrix of linear classifiers. (a)–(c) The histogram of the network-1, the network-8, and the AFS model with the default setting.

## 4 Conclusion

In this work, we propose the AFS model that deploys a linear merger to fuse the features extracted by multiple networks adversarially pre-trained with different levels of perturbation budgets. The AFS model is verified on CIFAR-10 and CIFAR-100 datasets with advanced attack methods, which significantly outperforms the state-of-the-art methods. The experimental results demonstrate the feasibility to obtain models with both high accuracy and strong robustness without extra training data. In the future, the AFS model is expected to be combined with more advanced defense methods and trained on more data to further improve the accuracy and robustness.

**Acknowledgements.** This work was partly supported by the National Key Research and Development Program of China (No. 2021ZD0200300) and the National Nature Science Foundation of China (No. 61836004).

# References

1. Athalye, A., Carlini, N., Wagner, D.: Obfuscated gradients give a false sense of security: Circumventing defenses to adversarial examples, pp. 274–283 (2018)
2. Carmon, Y., Raghunathan, A., Schmidt, L., Duchi, J.C., Liang, P.S.: Unlabeled data improves adversarial robustness. In: Advances in Neural Information Processing Systems, pp. 11192–11203 (2019)
3. Croce, F., Hein, M.: Reliable evaluation of adversarial robustness with an ensemble of diverse parameter-free attacks, pp. 2206–2216 (2020)
4. Cui, J., Liu, S., Wang, L., Jia, J.: Learnable boundary guided adversarial training, pp. 15721–15730 (2021)
5. Ilyas, A., Santurkar, S., Tsipras, D., Engstrom, L., Tran, B., Madry, A.: Adversarial examples are not bugs, they are features. In: Advances in Neural Information Processing Systems, pp. 125–136 (2019)
6. LeCun, Y., Bengio, Y., Hinton, G.: Deep learning. Nature **521**(7553), 436–444 (2015)
7. Li, H., Li, G., Shi, L.: Super-resolution of spatiotemporal event-stream image. Neurocomputing **335**, 206–214 (2019)
8. Liao, F., Liang, M., Dong, Y., Pang, T., Hu, X., Zhu, J.: Defense against adversarial attacks using high-level representation guided denoiser. In: Proceedings of the IEEE Conference on Computer Vision and Pattern Recognition, pp. 1778–1787 (2018)
9. Liu, F., Xu, M., Li, G., Pei, J., Shi, L., Zhao, R.: Adversarial symmetric gans: Bridging adversarial samples and adversarial networks. Neural Netw. **133**, 148–156 (2021)
10. Madry, A., Makelov, A., Schmidt, L., Tsipras, D., Vladu, A.: Towards deep learning models resistant to adversarial attacks (2017). arXiv preprint arXiv:1706.06083
11. Mao, C., Zhong, Z., Yang, J., Vondrick, C., Ray, B.: Metric learning for adversarial robustness. In: Advances in Neural Information Processing Systems, pp. 480–491 (2019)
12. Pei, J., et al.: Towards artificial general intelligence with hybrid Tianjic chip architecture. Nature **572**(7767), 106–111 (2019)
13. Rice, L., Wong, E., Kolter, Z.: Overfitting in adversarially robust deep learning. In: International Conference on Machine Learning, pp. 8093–8104. PMLR (2020)
14. Szegedy, C., et al.: Intriguing properties of neural networks. In: ICLR 2014: International Conference on Learning Representations (ICLR) 2014 (2014)
15. Tsipras, D., Santurkar, S., Engstrom, L., Turner, A., Madry, A.: Robustness may be at odds with accuracy (2018)
16. Wong, E., Kolter, Z.: Provable defenses against adversarial examples via the convex outer adversarial polytope. In: International Conference on Machine Learning, pp. 5286–5295. PMLR (2018)
17. Wu, D., Xia, S.T., Wang, Y.: Adversarial weight perturbation helps robust generalization. In: Advances in Neural Information Processing Systems 33 (2020)
18. Zagoruyko, S., Komodakis, N.: Wide residual networks. arXiv preprint arXiv:1605.07146 (2016)
19. Zhang, H., Yu, Y., Jiao, J., Xing, E., El Ghaoui, L., Jordan, M.: Theoretically principled trade-off between robustness and accuracy, pp. 7472–7482 (2019)
20. Zhang, J., Xu, X., Han, B., Niu, G., Cui, L., Sugiyama, M., Kankanhalli, M.: Attacks which do not kill training make adversarial learning stronger, pp. 11278–11287 (2020)

# Using Orientation to Distinguish
# Overlapping Chromosomes

Daniel Kluvanec[(✉)] [iD], Thomas B. Phillips[iD], Kenneth J. W. McCaffrey[iD],
and Noura Al Moubayed[iD]

Durham University, Durham, UK
`Daniel.Kluvanec@Durham.ac.uk`

**Abstract.** A difficult step in the process of karyotyping is segmenting chromosomes that touch or overlap. In an attempt to automate the
process, previous studies turned to Deep Learning methods, with some
formulating the task as a semantic segmentation problem. These models treat separate chromosome instances as semantic classes, which we
show to be problematic, since it is uncertain which chromosome should
be classed as #1 and #2. Assigning class labels based on comparison
rules, such as the shorter/longer chromosome alleviates, but does not
fully resolve the issue. Instead, we separate the chromosome instances
in a second stage, predicting the orientation of the chromosomes by the
model and use it as one of the key distinguishing factors of the chromosomes. We demonstrate this method to be effective. Furthermore, we
introduce a novel Double-Angle representation that a neural network can
use to predict the orientation. The representation maps any direction and
its reverse to the same point. Lastly, we present a new expanded synthetic dataset, which is based on Pommier's dataset, but addresses its
issues with insufficient separation between its training and testing sets.

**Keywords:** Karyotyping · Deep learning · Semantic segmentation ·
Instance segmentation · Representation · Invariance

## 1 Introduction

There are numerous defects that can be identified by visually inspecting chromosomes, such as genetic abnormalities [4] or cancer [18]. Chromosomes are
separated and ordered by size from a metaphase image in a process called karyotyping [16], which is commonly done by hand and is not yet fully automated.
One of the difficulties with karyotyping is that the chromosomes are positioned
randomly in the image and can touch or overlap. It is often simpler to prepare
multiple images of chromosomes from the same patient and search for ones without overlaps [1,24] than to segment overlapping chromosomes. Numerous image
processing algorithms have been proposed to separate overlapping chromosomes

---

Our code and dataset is available on Github:
https://github.com/KluvaDa/Chromosomes.

E. Pimenidis et al. (Eds.): ICANN 2022, LNCS 13529, pp. 391–403, 2022.
https://doi.org/10.1007/978-3-031-15919-0_33

[2, 9, 13, 15, 17, 25], however the task remains an open problem. Deep Learning [12], which has advanced many areas of image processing and computer vision, promises to aid with this task as well.

Semantic segmentation and instance segmentation are two approaches that seem particularly appropriate for the separation of chromosomes. Semantic segmentation classifies every pixel in an image into one of many semantic categories, while instance segmentation additionally classifies multiple instances of the same class separately. We argue that using semantic segmentation to separate overlapping chromosomes is inappropriate, since the chromosome instances are semantically identical. If a category was created for each of the overlapping chromosomes the model would not be able to tell which chromosome should be assigned to which category. We criticise existing methods that chose this approach in Sect. 2. It is possible that assigning a category to the chromosomes based on a rule, such as the longer/shorter chromosome or the more/less vertical chromosome, is sufficient to distinguish the categories. We demonstrate an improvement with such comparison rules, but find that the performance is lacking in comparison to a single semantic category in Sect. 5.

Highlighting separate instances is done in a variety of ways [23], but the methods commonly classify images semantically and use bounding boxes [19] to separate instances. However, bounding boxes rely on different instances being localised differently. This is not necessarily the case for overlapping chromosomes, which may mostly occupy the same space. We argue that a key assumption can be made about chromosomes, which is that in order for two chromosomes to overlap, they must lie in different directions, have different orientations. The only exception to this rule is when two parallel chromosomes touch end-to-end or side-by-side, where knowing their area of intersection is sufficient to segment them. It is for this reason that we explore ways in which a deep learning model can predict the orientation of chromosomes and demonstrate that this information can be used to separate chromosomes in Sect. 6.

We define the orientation of the chromosome as the direction along its arms, however it does not matter what the top and the bottom of the chromosome is. If a chromosome is rotated by 180° we treat it as having the same orientation. This makes it difficult to represent the orientation in a way that a neural network can predict. For this purpose we propose a novel Double-Angle representation in Sect. 6, which maps any vector and its negative to the same point in space, and train a model to predict it.

We use Pommer's dataset[1], which consists of 13434 synthetically generated images of overlapping chromosomes, generated from a pool of only 46 chromosomes. This means that the images are not independent, which means that it cannot easily be separated into independent subsets for training and testing. We criticise the dataset in Sect. 3 and papers that used the dataset in this form in Sect. 2. To address the issue, we modify the dataset, reusing Pommier's method

---

[1]  Pommier, J.P. (2016) Overlapping chromosomes dataset
https://www.kaggle.com/jeanpat/overlapping-chromosomes
https://github.com/jeanpat/DeepFISH.

to create the synthetic images, but ensure that training and testing subsets don't reuse the same chromosomes. In addition, we annotate the chromosomes with the orientation and expand the set of source images from 46 chromosomes to 620, all of which are based on data provided by Pommier.

In summary, our contributions in this paper are the following:

- We present a new bigger synthetic dataset based on Pommier's data, which can be split into independent subsets and contains annotations for the orientation of chromosomes.
- We demonstrate that chromosome instances cannot be separated effectively as semantic categories.
- We propose a novel representation of orientation called Double-Angle, which maps any vector and its inverse to the same point.
- We demonstrate that orientation can be used to separate overlapping chromosomes.

## 2 Related Work

[5] and [22] both used Pommier's dataset and a semantic segmentation method. They classify the pixels in the image into four categories: background, chromosome 1 (ch1), chromosome 2 (ch2), and overlap. The segmentation result would also be valid if the labels ch1 and ch2 were reversed for any given image. Nevertheless, they train the model to predict the specific category that was assigned to every image in Pommier's dataset. [22] identify that the performance of their system is better if the two chromosomes categories are merged. However, we believe all of the reported metrics to be unreliable because of a design error in Pommier's dataset, which allows superficial performance gains achieved through overfitting to improve performance on the test set. This means that the model would not generalise not only to other datasets, but also to completely unseen images created the same way. We further criticise the dataset in Sect. 3.

[14] also treated the task as semantic segmentation, however, they addressed the issue of the arbitrary class labels using a cGAN [7] to calculate an additional adversarial loss term using the discriminator network. This loss is agnostic to which class label is assigned to which chromosome, since it is not directly compared against the label.

[3] adopted a two-stage method. In the first stage they use a deep learning method to perform a 3-category semantic segmentation with the classes background, chromosome and overlap. In the second stage they separate the chromosomes instances using an image processing algorithm. On top of segmenting where the individual chromosomes are, [3] also reconstructs an image of the separated chromosomes.

## 3    Dataset

Pommier's dataset is created from a single image of a human metaphase stained using 4', 6-diamidino-2-phenylindole together with a Cy3 fluorescent telomeric probe [11]. The image contains 46 individual chromosomes that do not overlap or touch. The synthetic dataset is created by taking pairs of chromosomes, rotating, translating, and averaging them. The synthetic images are then labelled with the categories: ch1, ch2, overlap and background, where any pair of chromosomes will always have the same labels regardless of their rotation and translation. The model could therefore recognise a pair of chromosomes in the test set and recall their class labels, having seen them before, albeit rotated and translated differently. In other words, the dataset cannot be split into independent subsets, which would allow overfitting on one subset to benefit the performance on the other. As with all models trained on synthetic datasets, the extent to which they generalise to other datasets is questionable, however, when using Pommier's training and testing sets, even the extent to which the model generalises to the synthetic images is uncertain.

To address this issue, we propose that the chromosome source images are separated into subsets, before selecting pairs to create synthetic images with. Pommier also published 14 other human metaphase images that were not used to create the dataset, some of which contain overlapping chromosome pairs and larger clusters. We manually segmented all 15 metaphase images, which contained 620 separate chromosomes, while also annotating their orientation. In our experiments, 20% of the data is reserved for testing, while the remaining 80% is split into training and validation sets using 4-fold cross validation [20]. The synthetic images are created in a similar way to Pommier's method.

The methaphase images also contained 30 images of overlapping chromosome pairs and larger clusters. We use these to tell how well the model generalises from synthetic to real data, while minimising the domain shift that would occur when comparing against other datasets, which we use in equal proportion for validation and testing. Our orientation-based segmentation can work effectively with clusters, however the semantic segmentation can only separate pairs of chromosomes. To test the semantic segmentation, we separated the larger clusters into a total of 41 smaller images that are cropped around each pair of chromosomes, expecting the model to only classify the chromosome pair and ignore the other chromosomes that might be visible in the image (Fig. 2).

## 4    Model

We ran our experiments with both U-net [21] network variations used by [5] and by [22]. We found that the larger network performs marginally better and report on its results. To adapt the architecture to the different task definitions, we only modify the number of output channels and the loss function used. The network architecture is illustrated in Fig. 1.

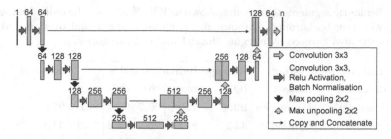

**Fig. 1.** The U-net-style neural network architecture used, where the numbers in the image represent the number of channels.

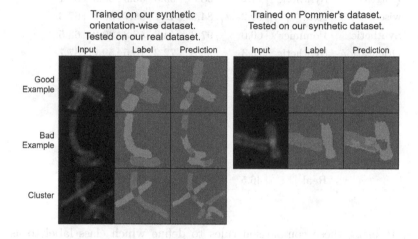

**Fig. 2.** Semantic segmentation result examples.

We use 4-fold cross validation [20], where we train the model independently 4 times, using a different quarter of the training set for validation. All metrics are averaged across the 4 runs.

We train the model using an Adam optimizer [10], with a learning rate of 0.001 and betas of 0.9 and 0.999.

# 5   Semantic Segmentation

We argue that separating chromosome instances using a semantic segmentation with the classes: background, ch1, ch2 and overlap is an inappropriate approach, because the chromosome instances aren't semantically different. This is problematic because it is uncertain which chromosomes should be assigned which class label. We hypothesise that this issue could be addressed by applying comparison rules for determining the class label, even though the chromosomes remain semantically similar. We tested the following properties for comparing the chromosomes: length-wise (longer/shorter), orientation-wise (more/less vertical), position-wise (rightmost/leftmost), and randomly as a control.

**Table 1.** Semantic segmentation results, shown as IOU % scores. The individual semantic categories are: background, chromosome 1, chromosome 2 and overlap. ch1+ch2 represents the area covered by merging the ch1 and ch2 categories.

| Training dataset | Testing dataset | Average IOU | Individual IOUs | | | | ch1+ch2 |
|---|---|---|---|---|---|---|---|
| | | | back. | ch1 | ch2 | over. | |
| Pommier's | Pommier's | **92.4** | 100 | 90.7 | 96.4 | 82.6 | 97.7 |
| | Synthetic | 43.2 | 86.6 | 26.1 | 25.2 | 34.9 | 44.4 |
| | Real | 35.9 | 66.5 | 25.8 | 22.3 | 29.0 | 51.4 |
| Synthetic | Pommier's | 51.1 | 92.4 | 33.1 | 48.3 | 30.5 | 55.2 |
| Length- | Synthetic | 71.2 | 98.8 | 69.5 | 56.9 | 59.8 | 88.1 |
| wise | Real | 50.2 | 84.3 | 42.1 | 38.7 | 35.8 | 67.3 |
| Synthetic | Pommier's | 60.0 | 97.3 | 44.8 | 58.8 | 39.2 | 63.5 |
| Orientation- | Synthetic | 75.3 | 98.8 | 72.2 | 70.5 | 59.7 | 87.7 |
| wise | Real | **56.8** | 84.2 | 49.8 | 53.4 | 39.8 | 67.7 |
| Synthetic | Pommier's | 55.2 | 97.5 | 38.7 | 47.9 | 36.6 | 62.2 |
| Position- | Synthetic | **77.3** | 98.8 | 74.2 | 76.2 | 60.0 | 88.0 |
| wise | Real | 52.7 | 84.5 | 43.9 | 43.3 | 39.2 | 67.9 |
| Synthetic | Pommier's | 50.9 | 95.5 | 29.5 | 46.3 | 32.1 | 61.3 |
| Random | Synthetic | 64.6 | 98.7 | 53.4 | 52.1 | 54.0 | 87.5 |
| | Real | 46.5 | 82.3 | 35.6 | 34.9 | 33.5 | 65.1 |

Despite using these comparison rules to define which class label to assign during training, it does not matter if the labels were switched during evaluation. We therefore switch the predicted classes for ch1 and ch2 if it yields better metrics. The metrics that we track are the intersection over union (IOU) scores, also known as the Jaccard Index [8]. These are calculated for every predicted class separately and averaged to get an overall performance metric. For comparison with our orientation-based segmentation, we also report the IOU scores averaged over the two chromosome categories, ch1 and ch2, only.

Table 1 presents the results of the semantic segmentation. Example images of good and bad results can be seen in Fig. 2. The following are our key observations:

- When training and evaluating on Pommier's dataset, we achieve a semantic IOU score of 92.4%, which is comparable to 94.7% reported by [5] and the range of 90.63%–99.94% reported by [22].
- There remains a sizeable domain shift between Pommier's synthetic dataset and ours despite their similar approach. Transitioning from Pommier's to our synthetic dataset yields a 49.2% reduction in average IOU, while the opposite yields a reduction of at least 13.7%.
- The average IOU score when trained and evaluated on our synthetic dataset is at least 15.1% lower than when trained and evaluated on Pommier's dataset. This suggests that either our synthetic dataset is more difficult to solve, or

that the performance metrics on Pommier's dataset are unreliable due to overfitting improving testing performance.

– To compare the rules for assigning class labels, we look at their average IOU on the synthetic and real datasets. Orientation-wise assignment yielded the best performance on the real dataset, while position-wise assignment yielded the best performance on the synthetic dataset. Notably, all three rules performed better than the control with random assignment, with an improvement of 6.6%, 10.7% and 12.7% for the synthetic dataset and an improvement of 3.7%, 10.3% and 6.2% for the real dataset, respectively for length-wise, orientation-wise and position-wise assignment.

– Another way of comparing how well the assignment rules work is to compare the IOU score for the two chromosome classes with the IOU score if the categories were merged. For the synthetic dataset we find a difference of 16.6%, 9.4%, 6.2% and 25.2%, and for the real data 20.3%, 10.7%, 17.6% and 23.4%, respectively for length-wise, orientation-wise, position-wise and random assignment. Larger values suggest that the model is more confused with which of the two chromosome labels to assign. These results similarly show that position-wise assignment performed best on the synthetic dataset, while orientation-wise assignment performed best on the real dataset.

Despite the improvement that the class assignment rules offer, we believe that the approach is still fundamentally problematic. Firstly, there are instances where the properties used for the assignment rules are very similar for both chromosomes. Two chromosomes can have the same length, orientation or position. In these cases the assignment is still a source of uncertainty. Secondly, using a semantic segmentation in this way requires the image to be cropped around the pair of overlapping chromosomes. This could be done with a separate model, however it also causes the issues with larger clusters, where more than two chromosomes are visible in the cropped image, which the model wasn't trained to deal with. This can also be seen in Fig. 2, where the model is expected to only highlight two chromosomes in the cluster, but struggles to tell which chromosomes cropped around. We would therefore recommend only using the semantic segmentation to distinguish the semantic categories: background, unique-chromosome and overlap, which can be applied to images with any amount of chromosomes, and rely on other methods to separate chromosome instances.

## 6   Orientation-Based Segmentation

In order to segment chromosome instances, we argue that knowing their orientation is an important distinguishing feature, since most overlapping chromosomes will have different orientations. The only exception being parallel chromosomes that partially overlap, either side-to-side or end-to-end. In this case the overlapping area should fully separate the two chromosome instances. The key utility provided by knowing the orientation of the chromosomes is, that it can be used to match multiple separate chromosome areas that are divided by overlapping

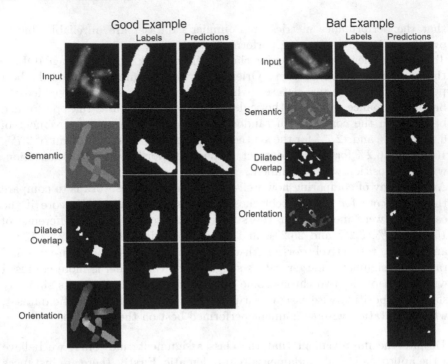

**Fig. 3.** Orientation-based segmentation result examples. The labels and predictions are the separated chromosomes, while semantic, dilated overlap and orientation are the network outputs.

areas. Assuming that chromosomes don't bend very sharply, the orientation of the chromosome before and after an overlap will be mostly the same.

We define the orientation of the chromosome as a direction vector along the length of the chromosome. However, it does not matter what the top and the bottom of the chromosome is. If the chromosome is rotated by 180° it will still have the same orientation. Equivalently, any direction vector and its negative represent the same orientation. Equivalently, the orientation could be represented as an angle in the range [0°, 180°). Getting a neural network to predict such an orientation is non-trivial, which led us to develop a novel Double-Angle representation.

Getting a neural network to predict the value of an angle directly is difficult, because of its cyclical nature and a discontinuity at 0° and 360°. Angles close to the discontinuity are very similar, yet their angle values can be very different. Instead one can represent an angle $\theta$ using $\sin(\theta)$ and $\cos(\theta)$, which is effectively a unit vector positioned $\theta$ degrees anticlockwise from the x-axis. This definition avoids the issues of discontinuity. In our case, with angles restricted to 180°, the resulting representation would effectively be a unit vector with a positive y-axis component, which would still contain a discontinuity near values of $(1, 0)$ and $(-1, 0)$. Instead let us define the Double-Angle representation that maps any vector and its negative onto the same point as follows:

$$[0°, 180°) \longrightarrow \mathbb{R}^2$$
$$\theta \longmapsto (\cos(2\theta), \sin(2\theta)), \tag{1}$$

with its inverse:

$$\mathbb{R}^2 \longrightarrow [0°, 180°)$$
$$(d_0, d_1) \longmapsto \frac{1}{2} \arctan 2(d_1, d_0) \mod 180°. \tag{2}$$

Our proposed instance segmentation model outputs a total of six channels: two for the Double-Angle representation, which is trained using the Huber loss [6] and masked out in pixels that do not belong to a unique chromosome. The third channel is used to predict a dilated overlap, which is defined as the overlap dilated by two pixels. This allows us to separate chromosomes that are very close to each other but do not overlap. It is trained using a binary cross-entropy loss (with logits). The last three channels are used as a semantic segmentation with the classes: background, chromosome and overlap, which is trained using a cross-entropy loss. These predictions are used by our instance segmentation post-processing algorithm, which uses image-processing to separate the chromosome instances. Its intended purpose is to demonstrate the utility of the Double-Angle representation and its use for segmenting chromosome instances. The algorithm is defined in Algorithm 1 and explained below:

In order to separate the chromosome instances we first analyse the prediction and identify unique chromosome segments. These segments are then merged to create the predicted chromosome instances based on their orientation and relative location to the areas of overlap.

To avoid issues with noisy network outputs, we remove any areas of overlap that are too small. We then subtract the dilated overlap prediction from the chromosome class to spatially separate chromosome segments from each other. Nonetheless, the segments may not be fully disjointed, so we perform the following operation to identify them. First we determine seeding points as the maxima of a distance transform applied to the segments. These will be the points in which the chromosome segments are the widest. We then iteratively grow these segments to cover the whole segment area. Crucially, due to fluctuations in chromosome widths, multiple seeding points may exist in a single chromosome segment. We therefore merge two segments if either of their seeding points was barely a local maximum, raised only 1 pixel over the neighbouring area. Finally we grow the segments over the areas of the dilated overlap until they cover the whole chromosome areas. We further consider merging two adjacent segments if their orientation is sufficiently similar in the area where they touch. We do not apply this operation near areas of overlap where two distinct chromosomes must be present. Next we determine which chromosome segments belong to the same chromosome. We assume that every area of overlap is created by overlapping exactly two chromosomes. We therefore merge the chromosome segments with

---

**Algorithm 1:** Orientation-Based Instance Segmentation

---

**Input:** *orientation, dilated_overlap, background, chromosome, overlap*
1  remove small areas from *overlap*
2  *distance_image* ← distance transform of (*chromosome - dilated_overlap*)
3  *segments* ← local maxima of (*distance_image*)
4  **for** *distance* in max(*distance_image*) to 0 **do**
5      dilate *segments* until they fill the area where *distance_image* ≥ *distance*
6      **if** two *segments* touch and maximum distance in either *segment* ≤ *distance*+1 **then**
7        | merge the two *segments*
8  dilate *segments* until they fill the area of *chromosome*
9  **for** all pairs of *segments* **do**
10     *neighbouring_pixels* ← intersection of (pair of *segments* dilated by 1 pixel)
11     **if** *neighbouring_pixels* are not near an overlap and their *orientation* is sufficiently similar **then**
12       | merge the two *segments*
13 remove small *segments*
14 **for** all *overlaps* **do**
15     **while** there are more than two *segments* adjacent to the *overlap* **do**
16       | merge the *segments* with the most similar *orientation*
17 *separate_chromosomes* ← *segments* merged with adjacent areas of *overlap*

---

the most similar orientation until only two chromosome instances are present near every overlap. Finally we add the adjacent overlap areas to all chromosome instances.

This algorithm uses the output of a model that achieved the following results: backround IOU: 98.8%, chromosome IOU: 88.3%, overlap IOU: 58.6%, dilated overlap IOU: 70.4%, average orientation difference: 70.4%. After separating the chromosomes using the post-processing algorithm, we compare the labelled chromosomes with the best matching predicted chromosome and average their IOU values. Note that any extra predicted chromosomes that did not get matched are ignored. These metrics can be seen in Table 2. The instance segmentation performs 3.6% better on the synthetic data and 20.8% better on the real data than the semantic segmentation trained on the orientatino-wise synthetic dataset. When qualitatively evaluating the results in Fig. 3, we find that the model can correctly separate some examples, but fails on others. When it does fail, the network prediction is very noisy, suggesting that the neural network failed to generalise well. We suspect that the issue stems from the synthetic dataset, which does not perfectly resemble real chromosome images. Moreover, the dataset is of limited size and sample variety, owing to its source of only 15 human metaphase images, nine of which were used for training.

**Table 2.** The average IOU scores over the best-matching separated chromosomes.

| Testing dataset | Semantic segmentation (orientation-wise) | Orientation-Based segmentation |
|---|---|---|
| Pommier's | 61.5 | 66.4 |
| Synthetic | 78.3 | 85.4 |
| Real | 57.0 | 77.8 |

# 7  Conclusion

In this paper we address the task of segmenting overlapping chromosomes. When using an existing synthetic dataset, we warn of its images not being independent and therefore not appropriate for splitting into training and testing subsets. We present an alternative synthetic dataset based on the same source images that has proper separation between training, validation and testing sets.

We demonstrate that segmenting chromosome instances as separate semantic classes is problematic. This is especially true when class labels for ch1 and ch2 are randomly assigned. Applying comparison rules to assign the class improves performance, but remains problematic in cases where the overlapping chromosomes are too similar. Moreover this method only works well for pairs of overlapping chromosomes and not clusters.

Instead, we propose separating the chromosome instances out in a post-processing step, which relies on predicted features from the deep learning model. We propose a novel Double-Angle representation for the orientation of the chromosomes, that is predicted by the neural network. The Double-Angle representation maps any direction vector in 2D and its negative onto the same point in a continuous and smooth manner. We demonstrate the effectiveness of separating the chromosomes based on their orientation and encourage readers to incorporate orientation as one of the distinguishing factors in their approaches.

For future work we suggest focusing on improving the deep learning model's performance by improving the data used to train the model. Larger datasets that include real images of overlapping chromosomes in the training sets could make the model generalise better. Data augmentation, which would add noise and distortions to the images, could also serve to make the model more robust.

**Acknowledgments.** This work was supported by Durham University, the European Regional Development Fund-Intensive Industrial Innovation Programme Grant No. 25R17-P01847 and GeoTeric Ltd.

# References

1. Arora, T., Dhir, R.: A review of metaphase chromosome image selection techniques for automatic karyotype generation. Med. Biol. Eng. Comput. **54**(8), 1147–1157 (2015). https://doi.org/10.1007/s11517-015-1419-z
2. Cao, H., Deng, H.W., Wang, Y.P.: Segmentation of M-FISH images for improved classification of chromosomes with an adaptive fuzzy C-means clustering algorithm. IEEE Trans. Fuzzy Syst. **20**(1), 1–8 (2011)
3. Cao, X., Lan, F., Liu, C.M., Lam, T.W., Luo, R.: Chromseg: two-stage framework for overlapping chromosome segmentation and reconstruction. In: 2020 IEEE International Conference on Bioinformatics and Biomedicine (BIBM), pp. 2335–2342. IEEE (2020)
4. Gardner, R.M., Amor, D.J.: Chromosome Abnormalities and Genetic Counseling. Oxford University Press (2018)
5. Hu, R.L., Karnowski, J., Fadely, R., Pommier, J.P.: Image segmentation to distinguish between overlapping human chromosomes. arXiv preprint arXiv:1712.07639 (2017)
6. Huber, P.J.: Robust estimation of a location parameter. Ann. Math. Stat. **35**, 492–518 (1964)
7. Isola, P., Zhu, J.Y., Zhou, T., Efros, A.A.: Image-to-image translation with conditional adversarial networks. In: Proceedings of the IEEE Conference on Computer Vision and Pattern Recognition, pp. 1125–1134 (2017)
8. Jaccard, P.: The distribution of the flora in the alpine zone. 1. New Phytol. **11**(2), 37–50 (1912)
9. Ji, L.: Fully automatic chromosome segmentation. Cytometry J. Int. Soc. Anal. Cytol. **17**(3), 196–208 (1994)
10. Kingma, D.P., Ba, J.: Adam: a method for stochastic optimization. arXiv preprint arXiv:1412.6980 (2014)
11. Lansdorp, P.M., et al.: Heterogeneity in telomere length of human chromosomes. Hum. Mol. Genet. **5**(5), 685–691 (1996)
12. LeCun, Y., Bengio, Y., Hinton, G.: Deep learning. Nature **521**(7553), 436–444 (2015). https://doi.org/10.1038/nature14539
13. Li, Y., Knoll, J.H., Wilkins, R.C., Flegal, F.N., Rogan, P.K.: Automated discrimination of dicentric and monocentric chromosomes by machine learning-based image processing. Microsc. Res. Tech. **79**(5), 393–402 (2016)
14. Mei, L., et al.: Adversarial multiscale feature learning for overlapping chromosome segmentation. arXiv preprint arXiv:2012.11847 (2020)
15. Nair, R.M., Remya, R., Sabeena, K.: Karyotyping techniques of chromosomes: a survey. Int. J. Comput. Trends Technol. **22**(1), 30–34 (2015)
16. O'Connor, C.: Karyotyping for chromosomal abnormalities. Nat. Educ. **1**(1), 27 (2008)
17. Popescu, M., Gader, P., Keller, J., Klein, C., Stanley, J., Caldwell, C.: Automatic karyotyping of metaphase cells with overlapping chromosomes. Comput. Biol. Med. **29**(1), 61–82 (1999)
18. Pui, C.H., Crist, W.M., Look, A.T.: Biology and clinical significance of cytogenetic abnormalities in childhood acute lymphoblastic leukemia. Blood **76**(8), 1449–63 (1990)
19. Redmon, J., Divvala, S., Girshick, R., Farhadi, A.: You only look once: unified, real-time object detection. In: Proceedings of the IEEE Conference on Computer Vision and Pattern Recognition, pp. 779–788 (2016)

20. Refaeilzadeh, P., Tang, L., Liu, H.: Cross-Validation, pp. 532–538. Springer, US, Boston, MA (2009). https://doi.org/10.1007/978-0-387-39940-9_565
21. Ronneberger, O., Fischer, P., Brox, T.: U-net: convolutional networks for biomedical image segmentation. In: Navab, N., Hornegger, J., Wells, W.M., Frangi, A.F. (eds.) MICCAI 2015. LNCS, vol. 9351, pp. 234–241. Springer, Cham (2015). https://doi.org/10.1007/978-3-319-24574-4_28
22. Saleh, H.M., Saad, N.H., Isa, N.A.M.: Overlapping chromosome segmentation using u-net: convolutional networks with test time augmentation. Procedia Comput. Sci. **159**, 524–533 (2019)
23. Van de Sande, K.E., Uijlings, J.R., Gevers, T., Smeulders, A.W.: Segmentation as selective search for object recognition. In: 2011 International Conference on Computer Vision, pp. 1879–1886. IEEE (2011)
24. Shen, X., Qi, Y., Ma, T., Zhou, Z.: A dicentric chromosome identification method based on clustering and watershed algorithm. Sci. Rep. **9**(1), 1–11 (2019)
25. Somasundaram, D., Kumar, V.V.: Separation of overlapped chromosomes and pairing of similar chromosomes for karyotyping analysis. Measurement **48**, 274–281 (2014)

# 3DLaneNAS: Neural Architecture Search for Accurate and Light-Weight 3D Lane Detection

Ali Zoljodi[1]([✉])[ID], Mohammad Loni[1][ID], Sadegh Abadijou[1][ID], Mina Alibeigi[2][ID], and Masoud Daneshtalab[1,3][ID]

[1] School of Innovation, Design and Engineering, Mälardalen University, Västerås, Sweden
{ali.zoljodi,mohammad.loni,masoud.daneshtalab}@mdu.se
s.abadijou@gmail.com
[2] Zenseact AB, Gothenburg, Sweden
mina.alibeigi@zenseact.com
[3] Department of Computer Systems, Tallinn University of Technology, Tallinn, Estonia

**Abstract.** Lane detection is one of the most fundamental tasks for autonomous driving. It plays a crucial role in the lateral control and the precise localization of autonomous vehicles. Monocular 3D lane detection methods provide state-of-the-art results for estimating the position of lanes in 3D world coordinates using only the information obtained from the front-view camera. Recent advances in Neural Architecture Search (NAS) facilitate automated optimization of various computer vision tasks. NAS can automatically optimize monocular 3D lane detection methods to enhance the extraction and combination of visual features, consequently reducing computation loads and increasing accuracy. This paper proposes 3DLaneNAS, a multi-objective method that enhances the accuracy of monocular 3D lane detection for both short- and long-distance scenarios while at the same time providing a fair amount of hardware acceleration. 3DLaneNAS utilizes a new multi-objective energy function to optimize the architecture of feature extraction and feature fusion modules simultaneously. Moreover, a transfer learning mechanism is used to improve the convergence of the search process. Experimental results reveal that 3DLaneNAS yields a minimum of 5.2% higher accuracy and ≈1.33× lower latency over competing methods on the synthetic-3D-lanes dataset. Code is at https://github.com/alizoljodi/3DLaneNAS

**Keywords:** Autonomous vehicles · 3D lane detection · Neural architecture search

## 1 Introduction

To operate safely, an autonomous vehicle needs a precise understanding of the road perspective. Lane detection is the task of estimating lane markings' positions, which is a crucial part of road understanding [33]. The majority of prior works focused on improving the lane detection accuracy on 2D images [5,12,18,31,36]. 2D lane detection methods work as follows: first, they perform lane segmentation on a 2D image; then, extracted lanes are mapped on a 3D coordination space. Despite 2D lane detection's simplicity, lanes should be projected into 3D. The detected lanes in the image plane are commonly projected to the 3D world using the flat earth assumption, which can lead to erroneous elevation and lane curvature estimates on hilly, banked, or curving roadways. (up to 14% accuracy loss [10]). Multi-sensor 3D lane detection methods aim to overcome this limitation by exploiting images with 3D shapes obtained from stereo-vision cameras or LiDAR sensors. However, multi-sensor 3D lane detection methods suffer from (i) expensive sensor configuration and (ii) erroneous prediction over long distances. Monocular 3D lane detection methods have been proposed to tackle these challenges [10,11]. The monocular 3D lane detection methods work as follows: first, they extract scene features with various scales from a 2D image; then, the extracted features are transformed into a top-view (bird's eye view) since lanes are parallel in the top-view, which helps in their detection precision. Next, using Convolutional Neural Networks (CNNs), top-view features are fused to construct a unified representation. Note that CNNs are known to provide the best results for accurate lane detection [10,11,33]. Finally, the fused features are classified using the fully-connected layer(s) to detect lane markings' positions. Figure 1 shows the overview of state-of-the-art monocular 3D lane detection methods. The monocular 3D lane detection methods benefit from (i) a cost-efficient sensor configuration and (ii) accurate estimations over long distances compared to multi-sensor 3D lane detection methods (Sect. 5). Despite the success of monocular 3D lane detection methods, they suffer from inefficient feature extraction and feature fusion modules causing inaccurate predictions.

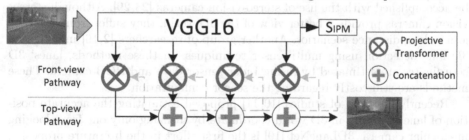

**Fig. 1.** The overview of the state-of-the-art 3DLaneNet [10] architecture. The feature extraction module is fed a front-view image. The VGGNet-16 [32] architecture is used extract features. Using the sampling information provided by $S_{IPM}$, the projective transformation layers project features to the top-view. To estimate 3D lane coordinations, top-view features are concatenated and processed via a fully-connected network.

Neural Architecture Search (NAS) advances the design procedure in CNNs [21,24,25]. Inspired by NAS's success, we designed a high-performance CNN architecture for monocular 3D lane detection. To this aim, we propose 3DLaneNAS, a multi-objective NAS method that designs an accurate yet efficient monocular 3D lane detection architecture. 3DLaneNAS uses multi-objective simulated annealing (MOSA) to explore the search space since it quickly finds the optimal solution [25]. While state-of-the-art methods provide excellent results in detecting short-distance lanes, our analysis indicates that they are not sufficient for detecting long-distance objects (Sect. 5). 3DLaneNAS considers short- and long-distance errors and the network inference time in its objective function. 3DLaneNAS also devises a transfer learning mechanism to expedite the search procedure in a large search space.

According to our experiments on the synthetic-3D-lanes dataset [10], 3DLaneNAS outperforms the state-of-the-art monocular 3D lane detection methods by achieving up to 17.5% higher accuracy and 1.2× lower inference time on NVIDIA® RTX A4000. 3DLaneNAS generates similar results with 2.74% standard deviation demonstrating our results are reproducible. To the best of our knowledge, 3DLaneNAS is the first attempt in the literature that successfully develops a NAS method for the 3D lane detection task.

## 2    Related Work

### 2.1    Lane Detection

Convolutional Neural Networks (CNNs) provide the most accurate results for the lane detection task [2,3,5,10–12,16,17,28,29,31]. Earlier studies attempted to improve the accuracy of CNN-based lane detection on 2D images. 2D lane detection methods are based on either image classification [12] or image segmentation [5,31]. Some studies on 2D lane detection methods transform front-view to top-view as the post-processing module to provide a precise perception of 3D coordination space [3,17]. A group of researchers proposed that 3D lane detection be accomplished with the use of stereo-vision cameras [28,29]. Although stereo-vision cameras provide a better view of the 3D world, they suffer from accuracy loss in long-distance scenarios. Another group of researchers [2,16] investigated 3D lane detection using multi-sensor techniques. In these methods, lanes' 3D coordinates are estimated by fusing Lidar sensor data and RGB camera. These methods are still costly regarding the sensor configuration.

Recently, a group of studies [10,11] proposed estimating the accurate position of lane markings in 3D world coordinate by utilizing only one front-looking monocular camera. 3DLaneNet [10] is the first effort in the literature proposing intra-network inverse-perspective mapping (IPM) [27] to remove road geometry assumptions. The architecture of 3DLaneNet is shown in Fig. 1. The IPM is front-view to top-view transformation with anisotropic scaling. The transformation is applied by utilizing a fixed set of parameters that specify top-view region boundaries and anisotropic scaling. The transformation parameters are estimated by an additional head directly connected to the feature extraction module. Inspired by [15], $S_{IPM}$ samples the front-view image pixels that aim to assign a new position in the top-view image. To improve the interaction between CNN feature extraction and feature map transformation, 3DLaneNet designed a dual-pathway architecture. 3DLaneNet has improved the lane fitting accuracy by integrating the transformation mechanism in the lane detection architecture. 3DLaneNet leveraged VGGNet-16 [32] pre-trained on the ImageNet dataset [6]. Despite the success of 3DLaneNet, it suffers from (i) inefficient feature extraction/fusion modules and (ii) bounded coordination system used to represent anchors. GenLaneNet [11] proposed an improved anchor representation by decoupling the learning of image encoding and 3D geometry reasoning. However, GenLaneNet still suffers from requiring significant computing resources for the learning process (up to 3M parameters) and inaccurate long-distance estimations.

## 2.2  Neural Architecture Search

Automated machine learning (AutoML) advances the capability of intelligent systems by tweaking hyper-parameters of learning models [13]. Neural Architecture Search (NAS), as a subset of AutoML, aims to design efficient neural networks for complex learning tasks [8]. Early proposed NAS methods employed Reinforcement Learning (RL) [14,37] or evolutionary-based algorithms [23,26] to search through the search space. However, these methods require remarkable computing capacity, for example, 500 NVIDIA® P100 GPUs to evaluate 20,000 neural architectures over four days [38]. Recently, differentiable NAS methods provide state-of-the-art results for various learning tasks [20–22]. DARTS [21] is a differentiable NAS method that uses the gradient descent algorithm to search and train neural architecture cells jointly. Despite the success of differentiable NAS methods in various domains [22], they suffer from inefficient training due to interfering with the training of different sub-networks each other [4]. Moreover, it has been proved that with equal search spaces and training setups, differentiable NAS methods converge to similar results [7].

Meta-heuristic-based NAS methods [24,25,35] benefit from fast and flexible algorithms to search a discrete search space. FastStereoNet [25] is a state-of-the-art meta-heuristic method that designs an accurate depth estimation pipeline. Inspired by FastStereoNet, we propose 3DLaneNAS for 3D lane detection. 3DLaneNAS advantages from meta-heuristic NAS approaches' quick convergence search. In addition, we decoupled search space into two modules to have a more efficient search. The results (Sect. 5) show that the 3DLaneNAS method outperforms two of the most well-known 3D lane detection benchmark models, 3DLaneNet [10] and GenLaneNet [11].

# 3  3DLaneNAS

## 3.1  Search Space

The 3DLaneNAS search space contains feature extraction, projective transformation, and feature fusion modules (Fig. 2). First, the feature extraction module extracts feature maps from the front-view image in four resolution scales. Second, the front-view feature maps are passed throw the projective transformation layers to construct the top-view feature maps. The projective transformation layers estimate input picture pixels' new position on the target image via bilinear interpolation. We set the parameters of the projective transformation layers according to [15]. Next, the feature fusion module concatenates top-view feature maps of multiple resolutions into a single feature space. Finally, a fully-connected layer classifies the output of the feature fusion module to estimate lane positions in 3D world coordinate. In this paper, we used NAS to optimize the architecture of feature extraction (Sect. 3.1) and feature fusion modules (Sect. 3.1).

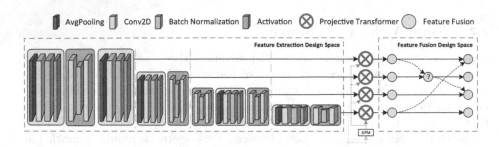

**Fig. 2.** The overview of 3DLaneNAS architecture. The search space of feature extraction is a stack of `ConvBnAct` and `Squeeze Blocks`. The search space of feature fusion is the combination of projective transformation outputs.

**Feature Extraction Search Space.** The feature extraction module computes a hierarchy of feature maps in a certain number of resolutions. Each resolution level has been extracted by a stack of atomic blocks. In this paper, we define two simple atomic blocks, including `ConvBnAct` and `Squeeze Block`. The `ConvBnAct` is a convolution layer followed by batch-normalization and an activation function. `Squeeze Block` works as a light-weight encoder-decoder function to augment the features that have a higher impact on 3D lane detection performance. Each `Squeeze Block` is built by a $1 \times 1$ average-pooling layer followed by two convolution layers with reversed input/output sizes and a batch-normalization in between. Five different output channels are available for `ConvBnAct` and `Squeeze Block`, including 16, 32, 64, 128, 256. We insert or remove an atomic block of feature extraction in each search iteration. The size of the feature extraction search space is proportional to the current state of the feature extraction stack. The minimum size of the feature extraction stack is set to 4 and is limited to 50 blocks. Thus, the maximum size of feature extraction search space is $10^{50}$.

**Feature Fusion Search Space.** Figure 3 represents feature fusion module. The feature fusion module consists of concatenation nodes, where each node can be active or inactive. An active node modifies a feature map by concatenating it with another feature map from a different resolution group. If the feature map should be concatenated with a higher resolution feature map, a max-pooling operation should be used to decrease the additional layer's resolution (down-sampling layer). On the other hand, if the feature map should be concatenated with a lower resolution feature map, an up-sampler operation should be used to increase the additional layer's resolution (up-sampling layer). In each search iteration, one concatenation node swaps from/to active/inactive. The maximum number of active nodes for feature fusion is 20, and the minimum is zero. Each concatenation node can have 12 distinct input combinations. Thus, the size of search space for the feature fusion module is $12 \times 2^{20}$.

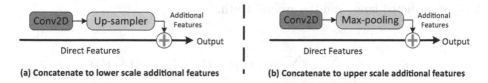

(a) Concatenate to lower scale additional features     (b) Concatenate to upper scale additional features

**Fig. 3.** (a) The Up-sampler is used for concatenating the additional features with lower resolution. (b) The Max-pooling is used for concatenating the additional features with higher resolution.

## 3.2   Search Algorithm

We use multi-objective simulated annealing (MOSA) [1] algorithm to find the near-optimal architecture for 3D lane detection. MOSA's search convergence is faster than genetic programming [25]. MOSA selects candidates with the probability of $min(1, exp(-\Delta/T))$. $\Delta$ is the difference in energy between the present and the newly generated candidate. $T$ is the regulating parameter for annealing temperature. $T$ starts from a big value ($T_{Max}$) that is gradually decreases to a small value ($T_{Min}$). Early on, $T_{Max}$ must be large enough to choose non-optimal choices. (exploration). On the other hand, $T_{Min}$ should be small enough to only give the maximum selection chance to optimal candidates (exploitation).

We consider a multi-objective energy function (Eq. 1) to improve the 3D lane detection accuracy in addition to reducing the network inference time. The energy function ($E$) is the multiplication of the network inference time ($t$) and the average value of lateral ($LatE$) and longitudinal ($LongE$) errors. $n$ indicates the number of test samples in each batch. We do not use any proxy such as Floating-Point-Operations-per-Second (FLOPs) for the inference time estimation. Instead, we run the network directly on the target hardware (NVIDIA® RTX A4000) to measure the exact inference time. We also consider a penalty coefficient ($\alpha=10$) to find the best error-latency trade-off.

$$E = \frac{1}{2n} \sum_{i=1}^{n} ((LatE_i + LongE_i)t_i) \times \max(1, \frac{1}{n} \sum_{i=1}^{n} (t_i - \alpha)) \qquad (1)$$

## 3.3  Training Procedure

The training procedure for 3D lane detection is time-consuming ($\approx$ 10 GPU hours for training one candidate). Inspired by [25], we partially train each candidate with fewer epochs to reduce the search time. After achieving 5× reduction search cost, our search process takes $\approx$ 130 GPU hours on a single NVIDIA® RTX A4000. In addition, 3DLaneNAS leverages the idea of the transferred weights mechanism [25] to expedite the search process.

The loss function is a combination of two equal-weighted terms (Eq. 2): The cross-entropy of lane detection (first term) and least absolute deviations ($\mathcal{L}$1-loss) of predicted lanes and the ground truth.

$$
\begin{aligned}
\mathcal{L} \ = - &\sum_{t\in\{c_1,c_2,d\}} \sum_{i=1}^{N}(p_t^i \ log \ p_t^i + (1 - \hat{p}_t^i) \ log \ (1 - p_t^i)) \\
+ &\sum_{t\in\{c_1,c_2,d\}} \sum_{i=1}^{N} \hat{p}_t^i.(\|x_t^i + \hat{x}_t^i\| + \|z_t^i + \hat{z}_t^i\|)
\end{aligned}
\tag{2}
$$

The $p_t^i$ indicates the confidentiality of detecting the i-th lane section, represented by an anchor. $x$ and $z$ indicate lanes' coordination.

## 4  Experimental Setup

### 4.1  Dataset

To evaluate our proposed method, we use the synthetic-3D-lanes dataset [10]. The dataset has been synthesized by the Blender graphic engine [9]. synthetic-3D-lanes contains more than 300 K training samples and 5k validation samples for different illumination and weather conditions. In this dataset, the scene terrains are modeled by a mixture of Gaussian distribution.

### 4.2  Configuration Setup

Hardware specification as well as training and search parameters are summarized in Table 1.

### 4.3  Evaluation Metrics

The performance of lane detection methods is evaluated using the average precision (AP) metric, which is the average percentage of the matched predicted lanes [30]. We also report $lateral(x)$ and $longitudinal(z)$ errors for near (0–40 m) and far distances (40–100 m). Additionally, we report the maximum F-score to indicate the application's optimal operation point.

**Table 1.** Summarizing hardware specification, train, and search parameters.

| Train/Test hardware device | Specification |
|---|---|
| GPU | NVIDIA® RTX A4000 |
| GPU compiler | CUDA v11.3 & cuDNN v8.2.0 |
| DL framework | PyTorch v1.9.1 |
| Training and search parameters | Value |
| Full-training epochs | 30 |
| Search epochs | 5 |
| Batch size | 8 |
| Learning rate | $5 \times 10^{-4}$ |
| Optimizer | Adam |
| $T_{Max}$ / $T_{Min}$ | 2500/2.5 |

# 5 Experimental Results

## 5.1 3D Lane Detection Performance Metrics

Table 2 presents a comparison of the results obtained by 3DLaneNAS with Gen-LaneNet [11] and 3DLaneNet [10] as the cutting-edge 3D lane detection methods. The inference time for GPU is measured with batch size set to 1. 3DLaneNAS yields 5.2% and 17.5% higher accuracy compared to GenLaneNet and 3DLaneNet, respectively. Compared to GenLaneNet and 3DLaneNet, 3DLaneNAS reduces inference time by 1.33× and 1.2×, respectively. 3DLaneNAS predicts lane positions with 41.9% and 50.4% lower longitudinal error, and 44% and 59% lower lateral error in comparison with GenLaneNet and 3DLaneNet, respectively. Figure 4 compares the visualization results of 3DLaneNAS with state-of-the-art on three different road scenarios. 3DLaneNAS performs better in curvy, downhill, and uphill road settings with partially visible lanes.

**Table 2.** Comparing the performance of 3DLaneNAS with the states-of-the-art.

| Architecture | AP | F-score | Lateral error (cm) | | Longitudinal error (cm) | | #Params | Inference |
|---|---|---|---|---|---|---|---|---|
| | (%) | (%) | 0–40 m | 40–100 m | 0–40 m | 40–100 m | (M) | Time (ms) |
| 3DLaneNet [10] | 74.9 | 77.7 | 11.5 | 60.1 | 3.2 | 23.0 | 20.8 | 14.5 |
| GenLaneNet [11] | 87.2 | 83 | 7.4 | 53.8 | 1.5 | 23.2 | 3.36 | 16 |
| 3DLaneNAS | 92.4 | 92.1 | 3.7 | 35.8 | 0.5 | 19.2 | 1.75 | 12 |

## 5.2 Analyzing Search Methods

Figure 5a shows the variation of the energy function (Eq. 1) during the search process for 3DLaneNAS, random search, and a local search method [34]. Note that random search is selected as the comparison baseline since it can find the

**Fig. 4.** Illustrating the performance of 3DLaneNet [10], GenLaneNet [11] and 3DLaneNAS in three different road scenarios. Blue lines are ground-truth, red lines are network predictions. Left column: curvy roads' results. Middle column: downhill sample results. Right column: uphill road sample. Yellow circles show low-confidence estimations. (Color figure online)

optimal architecture in several applications [19]. 3DLaneNAS provides a continuous reduction in energy function during the search procedure, indicating the proposed NAS method's potential for learning the best architecture. On the other hand, random search and local search methods could not find many improved architectures, which means that our proposed search space is not the only reason behind the efficiency of 3DLaneNAS. Figure 5b shows the error-latency trade-off for the best-discovered architectures proposed by different lane detection methods. Results show that 3DLaneNAS provides a higher error-latency trade-off compared to state-of-the-art lane detection methods.

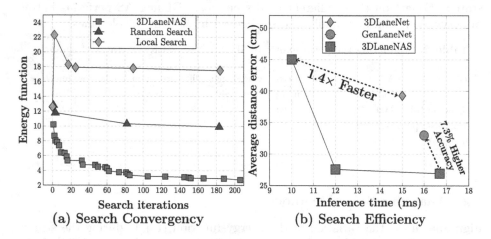

**Fig. 5.** (a). Convergency of energy function (b). Error-latency trade-off of 3DLaneNAS in comparison with 3DLaneNet and GenLaneNet.

### 5.3   Statement of Reproducibility

A common issue in many NAS studies is to demonstrate reproducibility
[19]. To prove the reproducibility of
the results, we re-run the 3DLane-
NAS five more times with different
random seeds. Then, we plot the average energy function for the improved
solutions for five times running with
the shades to denote the confidence
intervals (Fig. 6). According to the
Results, while the confidence interval is wide in some iterations, all
search runs converge to a similar
energy value. The standard deviation
(STDEV) is 2.74%. Finally, 3DLane-
NAS is an open-source project. The
code will be made public upon accep-
tance.

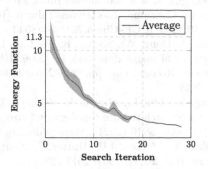

**Fig. 6.** Demonstrating the reproducibility of results. The solid line shows the average energy value of five runs with different random seeds. The shade is a representation of the STDEV.

## 6   Conclusion

This paper proposes 3DLaneNAS, a multi-objective NAS method for designing a fast and accurate monocular 3D lane detection architecture. 3DLaneNAS
improves the performance of monocular 3D lane detection by employing multi-
objective simulated annealing as the search method to optimize feature extraction and feature fusion modules. According to experimental results, 3DLaneNAS
yields a minimum of 5.2% higher Average Precision and ≈1.33× lower inference
time over counterparts. These results suggest that 3DLaneNAS is an effective
method that paves the way for designing efficient lane detection methods.

**Acknowledgement.** This work was supported by Sweden's Innovation Agency (VIN-
NOVA) within the AutoDeep project, and KKS within the DPAC project. This work
has been also partially conducted in the project ICT programme which was supported
by the European Union through the European Social Fund.

## References

1. Amine, K.: Multiobjective simulated annealing: principles and algorithm variants.
   Adv. Oper. Res. **2019** (2019)
2. Bai, M., Mattyus, G., Homayounfar, N., Wang, S., Lakshmikanth, S.K., Urtasun,
   R.: Deep multi-sensor lane detection. In: 2018 IEEE/RSJ International Conference
   on Intelligent Robots and Systems (IROS), pp. 3102–3109. IEEE (2018)
3. Borji, A.: Vanishing point detection with convolutional neural networks. arXiv
   preprint arXiv:1609.00967 (2016)

4. Cai, H., Gan, C., Wang, T., Zhang, Z., Han, S.: Once-for-all: train one network and specialize it for efficient deployment. arXiv preprint arXiv:1908.09791 (2019)

5. Chen, P.Y., Lee, C.M., Yeh, H.Z., Huang, Y.C.: Design and implementation for a vision-guided wheeled mobile robot system. In: 2018 IEEE International Conference on Consumer Electronics-Taiwan (ICCE-TW), pp. 1–5 (2018). https://doi.org/10.1109/ICCE-China.2018.8448543

6. Deng, J., Dong, W., Socher, R., Li, L.J., Li, K., Fei-Fei, L.: Imagenet: a large-scale hierarchical image database. In: 2009 IEEE Conference on Computer Vision and Pattern Recognition, pp. 248–255 (2009). https://doi.org/10.1109/CVPR.2009.5206848

7. Dong, X., Liu, L., Musial, K., Gabrys, B.: Nats-bench: benchmarking nas algorithms for architecture topology and size. IEEE Trans. Pattern Anal. Mach. Intell. **44**(7), 3634–3646 (2021). https://doi.org/10.1109/TPAMI.2021.3054824

8. Elsken, T., Metzen, J.H., Hutter, F.: Neural architecture search: a survey. J. Mach. Learn. Res. **20**(1), 1997–2017 (2019)

9. Foundation, B.: Home of the blender project - free and open 3D creation software. https://www.blender.org/

10. Garnett, N., Cohen, R., Pe'er, T., Lahav, R., Levi, D.: 3d-lanenet: end-to-end 3d multiple lane detection. In: Proceedings of the IEEE/CVF International Conference on Computer Vision, pp. 2921–2930 (2019)

11. Guo, Y., et al.: Gen-lanenet: a generalized and scalable approach for 3D lane detection. In: Vedaldi, A., Bischof, H., Brox, T., Frahm, J.-M. (eds.) ECCV 2020. LNCS, vol. 12366, pp. 666–681. Springer, Cham (2020). https://doi.org/10.1007/978-3-030-58589-1_40

12. Gurghian, A., Koduri, T., Bailur, S.V., Carey, K.J., Murali, V.N.: Deeplanes: end-to-end lane position estimation using deep neural networks. In: 2016 IEEE Conference on Computer Vision and Pattern Recognition Workshops (CVPRW), pp. 38–45 (2016). https://doi.org/10.1109/CVPRW.2016.12

13. He, X., Zhao, K., Chu, X.: Automl: a survey of the state-of-the-art. Knowl.-Based Syst. **212**, 106622 (2021)

14. Hsu, C.H., et al.: Monas: multi-objective neural architecture search using reinforcement learning. arXiv preprint arXiv:1806.10332 (2018)

15. Jaderberg, M., Simonyan, K., Zisserman, A., et al.: Spatial transformer networks. In: Advances in Neural Information Processing Systems 28 (2015)

16. Jung, J., Bae, S.H.: Real-time road lane detection in urban areas using lidar data. Electronics **7**(11), 276 (2018)

17. Kheyrollahi, A., Breckon, T.P.: Automatic real-time road marking recognition using a feature driven approach. Mach. Vis. Appl. **23**(1), 123–133 (2012). https://doi.org/10.1007/s00138-010-0289-5

18. Lee, S., et al.: Vpgnet: vanishing point guided network for lane and road marking detection and recognition. In: Proceedings of the IEEE International Conference on Computer Vision, pp. 1947–1955 (2017)

19. Lindauer, M., Hutter, F.: Best practices for scientific research on neural architecture search. J. Mach. Learn. Res. **21**(243), 1–18 (2020)

20. Liu, C., et al.: Auto-deeplab: hierarchical neural architecture search for semantic image segmentation. In: Proceedings of the IEEE/CVF Conference on Computer Vision and Pattern Recognition, pp. 82–92 (2019)

21. Liu, H., Simonyan, K., Yang, Y.: Darts: differentiable architecture search. arXiv preprint arXiv:1806.09055 (2018)

22. Loni, M., Mousavi, H., Riazati, M., Daneshtalab, M., Sjödin, M.: Tas: ternarized neural architecture search for resource-constrained edge devices. In: Design, Automation & Test in Europe Conference & Exhibition DATE 2022, 14 March 2022, Antwerp, Belgium. IEEE (2022). http://www.es.mdh.se/publications/6351-

23. Loni, M., Sinaei, S., Zoljodi, A., Daneshtalab, M., Sjödin, M.: Deepmaker: a multi-objective optimization framework for deep neural networks in embedded systems. Microprocess. Microsyst. **73**, 102989 (2020)

24. Loni, M., et al.: Densedisp: resource-aware disparity map estimation by compressing siamese neural architecture. In: 2020 IEEE Congress on Evolutionary Computation (CEC), pp. 1–8 (2020). https://doi.org/10.1109/CEC48606.2020.9185611

25. Loni, M., et al.: Faststereonet: a fast neural architecture search for improving the inference of disparity estimation on resource-limited platforms. IEEE Trans. Syst. Man Cybern. Syst. **52**(8), 1–13 (2021). https://doi.org/10.1109/TSMC.2021.3123136

26. Loni, M., Zoljodi, A., Sinaei, S., Daneshtalab, M., Sjödin, M.: NeuroPower: designing energy efficient convolutional neural network architecture for embedded systems. In: Tetko, I.V., Kůrková, V., Karpov, P., Theis, F. (eds.) ICANN 2019. LNCS, vol. 11727, pp. 208–222. Springer, Cham (2019). https://doi.org/10.1007/978-3-030-30487-4_17

27. Mallot, H.A., Bülthoff, H.H., Little, J., Bohrer, S.: Inverse perspective mapping simplifies optical flow computation and obstacle detection. Biol. Cybern. **64**(3), 177–185 (1991)

28. Nedevschi, S., Oniga, F., Danescu, R., Graf, T., Schmidt, R.: Increased accuracy stereo approach for 3D lane detection. In: 2006 IEEE Intelligent Vehicles Symposium, pp. 42–49. IEEE (2006)

29. Nedevschi, S., et al.: 3D lane detection system based on stereovision. In: Proceedings. The 7th International IEEE Conference on Intelligent Transportation Systems (IEEE Cat. No. 04TH8749), pp. 161–166. IEEE (2004)

30. Padilla, R., Netto, S., da Silva, E.: A survey on performance metrics for object-detection algorithms (2020). https://doi.org/10.1109/IWSSIP48289.2020

31. Pizzati, F., García, F.: Enhanced free space detection in multiple lanes based on single cnn with scene identification. In: 2019 IEEE Intelligent Vehicles Symposium (IV), pp. 2536–2541 (2019). https://doi.org/10.1109/IVS.2019.8814181

32. Simonyan, K., Zisserman, A.: Very deep convolutional networks for large-scale image recognition. arXiv preprint arXiv:1409.1556 (2014)

33. Tang, J., Li, S., Liu, P.: A review of lane detection methods based on deep learning. Pattern Recogn. **111**, 107623 (2021)

34. White, C., Nolen, S., Savani, Y.: Exploring the loss landscape in neural architecture search. In: Uncertainty in Artificial Intelligence, pp. 654–664. PMLR (2021)

35. Xu, H., Wang, S., Cai, X., Zhang, W., Liang, X., Li, Z.: CurveLane-NAS: unifying lane-sensitive architecture search and adaptive point blending. In: Vedaldi, A., Bischof, H., Brox, T., Frahm, J.-M. (eds.) ECCV 2020. LNCS, vol. 12360, pp. 689–704. Springer, Cham (2020). https://doi.org/10.1007/978-3-030-58555-6_41

36. Zhang, W., Mahale, T.: End to end video segmentation for driving: lane detection for autonomous car. arXiv preprint arXiv:1812.05914 (2018)

37. Zoph, B., Le, Q.V.: Neural architecture search with reinforcement learning. arXiv preprint arXiv:1611.01578 (2016)

38. Zoph, B., Vasudevan, V., Shlens, J., Le, Q.V.: Learning transferable architectures for scalable image recognition. In: Proceedings of the IEEE Conference on Computer Vision and Pattern Recognition, pp. 8697–8710 (2018)

# A Coarse-to-Fine Training Paradigm
# for Dialogue Summarization

Zhiyue Liu[1,2], Zhaoyang Wang[2], and Jiahai Wang[2(✉)]

[1] School of Computer, Electronics and Information, Guangxi University,
Nanning, China
[2] School of Computer Science and Engineering, Sun Yat-sen University,
Guangzhou, China
{liuzhy93,wangzhaoy22}@mail2.sysu.edu.cn, wangjiah@mail.sysu.edu.cn

**Abstract.** Pre-trained language models (PLMs) have achieved promising results on dialogue summarization. Previous works mainly encode semantic features from wordy dialogues to help PLMs model dialogues, but extracting those features from the original dialogue text is costly. Besides, the resulting semantic features may be also redundant, which is harmful for PLMs to catch the dialogue's main idea. Without searching for dispensable features, this paper proposes a coarse-to-fine training paradigm for dialogue summarization. Instead of directly fine-tuning PLMs to obtain complete summaries, this paradigm constructs a coarse-grained summarizer which automatically infers the key information to annotate each dialogue. Further, a fine-grained summarizer would generate detailed summaries based on the annotated dialogues. Moreover, to utilize the knowledge from out-of-domain pre-training, a meta learning mechanism is adopted, which could cooperate with our training paradigm and help the model pre-trained on other domains adapt to the dialogue summarization. Experimental results demonstrate that our method could outperform competitive baselines.

**Keywords:** Dialogue summarization · Pre-trained language models · Training paradigm

## 1 Introduction

Abstractive dialogue summarization is a challenging task, which aims at distilling the essential parts of a human dialogue into short and informative natural text [17]. Automatic dialogue summarization brings benefits to many scenarios, such as meetings and online chats [27,28]. With universal semantic knowledge, pre-trained language models (PLMs) have obtained satisfactory results on most text summarization tasks [7,13,15], and thus they are also investigated for dialogue summarization [3].

Previous works mostly rely on sophisticated strategies to obtain auxiliary information which helps PLMs understand dialogues. Various features are utilized to identify the dialogue's main idea, such as key utterances [14], topics [10,18,26], and entities [19]. Chen and Yang [1] model dialogue structures

E. Pimenidis et al. (Eds.): ICANN 2022, LNCS 13529, pp. 416–427, 2022.
https://doi.org/10.1007/978-3-031-15919-0_35

from four different views. However, those features are extracted by human annotation from the dialogue text, which is quite expensive [4]. In addition, DialoGPT [25] is employed to automatically annotate three types of features for each dialogue [4], but performing DialoGPT on all dialogues is still time-consuming. The above methods search the whole wordy dialogue text, containing inessential content, for auxiliary information, and thus their resulting features may be also redundant, which does not benefit PLMs in catching the dialogue's core part.

To alleviate the above problem, this paper proposes a coarse-to-fine training paradigm without extracting massive features from dialogues. We utilize the semantic information in human-annotated summaries (i.e., golden summaries) as training supervision for both keyword inference and summary generation. In detail, our training paradigm first uses concise keywords to build coarse-grained targets which are informative and easy for a pre-trained model (i.e., the coarse-grained summarizer) to acquire. Previous works discover redundant and noisy text from dialogues as keywords [4], while ignoring utilizing human-annotated summaries which contain most likely keywords to express the dialogue's main idea. Thus, we extract keywords from human-annotated summaries and combine those keywords with textual prompts as the coarse-grained targets, where prompting is a practice of adding phrases to transform a downstream task closer to the pre-training task [12,20]. After fine-tuning, the coarse-grained summarizer automatically infers key information and annotates each dialogue, which is less costly than re-searching for dialogue features in most existing methods. The annotated dialogues aid another model (i.e., the fine-grained summarizer) to focus on the key information and generate the complete summaries. Moreover, this paper employs a meta learning mechanism to utilize the knowledge from out-of-domain pre-training. Given a model pre-trained on other domains (e.g., the news domain), directly fine-tuning it on dialogue data is not ideal [29] because dialogues have inherent differences from conventional documents. Through meta learning, the parameters after the update on other domains tend to fit the dialogue domain, offering the model's knowledge a smooth transfer. The meta learning mechanism would cooperate with the fine-grained summarizer's training to further enhance summarization performance.

In summary, our contributions are as follows:

- Without sophisticated strategies to extract dispensable features, a coarse-to-fine training paradigm is introduced for dialogue summarization.
- A meta learning mechanism is employed to help the out-of-domain knowledge accommodate the summarization of dialogues.
- Experimental results indicate the superiority of our method on two standard dialogue summarization datasets, including SAMSum [6] and DIALOG-SUM [2].

**Fig. 1.** Overview of our training paradigm. The keywords (in red) are extracted from the human-annotated summary, and then combined with the textual prompt (in blue) as a simple and informative target. The coarse-grained summarizer would learn the target and obtain a coarse-grained summary to annotate the original dialogue. The fine-grained summarizer receives the annotated dialogue to generate the detailed summary. (Color figure online)

## 2    Method

As shown in Fig. 1, our training paradigm twice employs the pre-trained model, BART [9], to construct the coarse-grained and fine-grained summarizers, respectively. Given a dataset $\mathbb{D}^{\text{dialog}} = \{(\mathbf{x}, \mathbf{y})\}$ that includes pairs of the dialogue $\mathbf{x}$ and the human-annotated summary $\mathbf{y}$, the coarse-grained summarizer receives the keywords from $\mathbf{y}$ and learns to obtain the coarse-grained summary which annotates the original dialogue. Further, the fine-grained summarizer would utilize the annotated dialogue to generate the detailed summary.

### 2.1    Coarse-to-Fine Summarization

**Coarse-Grained Summarization.** For utilizing the pre-trained model's knowledge to conclude the key information in the dialogue, the training paradigm produces a coarse-grained target based on the human-annotated summary. Previous works [4,19] show that the entities extracted from the original dialogue text are more crucial than other words for summarization, but those entities may be also redundant. By contrast, the human-annotated summary $\mathbf{y}$ is always concise, and its entities are more expressive and very likely to exhibit the dialogue's main idea. Thus, we extract entities from the summary $\mathbf{y}$ rather than the original dialogue $\mathbf{x}$ as keywords. For simplicity, based on part-of-speech tagging, the nouns and noun phrases are extracted from $\mathbf{y}$ as the entities utilized to build the coarse-grained target. Note that the speakers are removed from the keywords, since we expect the model to focus on the dialogue's content.

Recent studies on prompt-based learning show that the appropriate prompt profits the utilization of the pre-trained model's knowledge [12]. The prefix "In summary" added in the target summary is an efficient prompt for summarization [20,23]. Hence, we combine keywords and a textual prompt as follows:

$$\mathbf{z} = \text{``In summary, they talk about: [KEY].''}, \tag{1}$$

where [KEY] = [key$_1$,key$_2$,$\cdots$] should be filled with the keywords extracted from the summary $\mathbf{y}$. The text "they talk about" is added to $\mathbf{z}$, which could keep semantic fluency. $\mathbf{z}$ could be viewed as a coarse-grained but informative target. Then, the probability of $\mathbf{z}$ given $\mathbf{x}$ is computed for obtaining the optimal model which minimizes the negative log-likelihood as follows:

$$l_{\beta}^{\text{coarse}} = \mathop{\mathbb{E}}_{\mathbf{x},\mathbf{y}\sim\mathbb{D}^{\text{dialog}}} \left[ -\log[P_{\beta}(\mathbf{z}|\mathbf{x})] \right], \qquad (2)$$

where $\beta$ is the parameters of the coarse-grained summarizer BART$_\beta$. By taking $\mathbf{z}$ as supervision, BART$_\beta$ could infer the prompted keywords for dialogues, aiding the fine-grained summarization.

**Fine-Grained Summarization.** The inferred information $\hat{\mathbf{z}} = \text{BART}_\beta[\mathbf{x}]$ would annotate the original dialogue. That is, the dialogue $\mathbf{x}$ and $\hat{\mathbf{z}}$ are concatenated as the annotated dialogue $[\mathbf{x};\hat{\mathbf{z}}]$. With the help of $\hat{\mathbf{z}}$, the fine-grained summarizer could better capture the dialogue's main idea to generate the detailed summary. Formally, the negative log-likelihood is minimized to reconstruct the complete summary $\mathbf{y}$ given $[\mathbf{x};\hat{\mathbf{z}}]$ as follows:

$$l_{\theta}^{\text{fine}} = \mathop{\mathbb{E}}_{\mathbf{x},\mathbf{y}\sim\mathbb{D}^{\text{dialog}}} \left[ -\log[P_{\theta}(\mathbf{y}|\mathbf{x};\hat{\mathbf{z}})] \right], \qquad (3)$$

where $\theta$ is the parameters of the fine-grained summarizer BART$_\theta$. Given an unseen dialogue, it is first annotated with BART$_\beta$. Then, BART$_\theta$ is able to distill the annotated dialogue into a concise and informative summary. Without complicated strategies to extract auxiliary information from the dialogue text, our training paradigm automatically infers keywords, assisting BART in catching the main idea of dialogues.

## 2.2 Meta Optimization

This paper attempts to utilize the model pre-trained on the news domain and transfer this model's knowledge to dialogue summarization, since the news domain's data is abundant. Due to the gap between news articles and dialogues, directly fine-tuning the model on the dialogue data may lead to unsatisfactory performance [27,29]. This paper applies the model-agnostic meta-learning algorithm [5] to help the model pre-trained on the news domain better fit the fine-grained summarization of our training paradigm.

Specifically, BART$_\theta$ is initial with the parameters pre-trained on the news domain. Then, the model updated on the news data is viewed as a standard model for fast adapting to the new task that optimizes the performance on the dialogue data. BART$_\theta$ is fine-tuned using a gradient-based learning rule on $l_{\theta}^{\text{fine}}$. Formally, one gradient update is implemented as the meta gradient update which adopts the news data through:

$$\theta' = \theta - \alpha\nabla_{\theta}l_{\theta}^{\text{news}}, \qquad (4)$$

**Table 1.** Statistics for the SAMSum and DIALOGSUM (i.e., DIALOG) datasets. "Avg.Turns", "Avg.Tokens", and "Avg.Sum" mean the average of dialogue's turns, dialogue's tokens, and summary's tokens, respectively.

|        |            | Train  | Valid  | Test   |
|--------|------------|--------|--------|--------|
| SAMSum | Dialogues  | 14,732 | 818    | 819    |
|        | Avg.Turns  | 11.17  | 10.83  | 11.25  |
|        | Avg.Tokens | 128.72 | 125.48 | 131.04 |
|        | Avg.Sum    | 22.88  | 22.87  | 22.54  |
| DIALOG | Dialogues  | 12,460 | 500    | 500    |
|        | Avg.Turns  | 9.49   | 9.38   | 9.71   |
|        | Avg.Tokens | 163.46 | 161.23 | 167.72 |
|        | Avg.Sum    | 25.10  | 23.04  | 20.55  |

where $l_\theta^{\text{news}} = \mathbb{E}_{\mathbf{x},\mathbf{y}\sim\mathbb{D}^{\text{news}}} [-\log[P_\theta(\mathbf{y}|\mathbf{x})]]$, $\alpha$ is the meta learning rate, and $\mathbb{D}^{\text{news}}$ indicates the news dataset. The resulting model $\text{BART}_{\theta'}$ is expected to perform well on a meta objective $l_{\theta'}^{\text{fine}}$, making $\theta'$ fits the dialogue data simultaneously. This objective is added to Eq. 3 to update $\theta$ as follows:

$$\mathcal{L}_\theta = l_\theta^{\text{fine}} + l_{\theta'}^{\text{fine}}, \tag{5}$$

where $\theta$ could be updated by $l_{\theta'}^{\text{fine}}$ as

$$\nabla_\theta l_{\theta'}^{\text{fine}} = \frac{\partial l_{\theta'}^{\text{fine}}}{\partial \theta'} \frac{\partial \theta'}{\partial \theta}$$
$$= \mathbb{E}_{\mathbf{x},\mathbf{y}\sim\mathbb{D}^{\text{dialog}}} \left[ -\frac{\partial \log[P_{\theta'}(\mathbf{y}|\mathbf{x};\hat{\mathbf{z}})]}{\partial \theta'} \right] \frac{\partial \theta'}{\partial \theta}. \tag{6}$$

$l_{\theta'}^{\text{fine}}$ provides the model a smooth migration from the news domain to the dialogue domain. On the right-hand side of Eq. 5, the first term ensures the optimization on the dialogue data, while the second term assists in transferring the news domain's knowledge to dialogue summarization. Our meta learning mechanism could help the fine-grained summarizer collect out-of-domain knowledge for better generating the dialogue summary.

In summary, $\text{BART}_\beta$ relies on the BART's universal semantic knowledge for keyword inference, while $\text{BART}_\theta$ could leverage the out-of-domain knowledge and inferred keywords for summary generation.

## 3   Experiments

### 3.1   Datasets and Baselines

Experiments are conducted on two standard dialogue summarization datasets, SAMSum and DIALOGSUM, which have 16,369 samples and 13,460 samples,

**Table 2.** Automatic evaluation results on SAMSum and DIALOGSUM. "C2F" is short for the proposed coarse-to-fine training paradigm. ↑ means higher is better. The two best results are in bold.

| Method | SAMSum | | | DIALOGSUM | | |
|---|---|---|---|---|---|---|
| | R-1 (↑) | R-2 (↑) | R-L (↑) | R-1 (↑) | R-2 (↑) | R-L (↑) |
| PGNet | 40.08 | 15.28 | 36.63 | 39.11 | 13.53 | 37.92 |
| Transformer | 37.20 | 10.86 | 34.69 | 35.91 | 8.74 | 33.50 |
| DialoGPT | 40.39 | 15.37 | 37.31 | 35.69 | 10.07 | 33.79 |
| MV-BART | 53.42 | 27.98 | 49.97 | - | - | - |
| PLMA | 53.70 | 28.79 | **50.81** | 45.07 | 19.67 | 42.96 |
| BART | 53.24 | 28.04 | 49.95 | 44.92 | 19.36 | 42.33 |
| BART (CNNDM) | 53.44 | 28.20 | 50.03 | 45.14 | 19.53 | 42.73 |
| Ours | | | | | | |
| BART (Meta) | **53.81** | 28.61 | 50.35 | 45.32 | 19.73 | 43.07 |
| BART (C2F) | 53.46 | 28.51 | 50.30 | 45.56 | 19.70 | 43.01 |
| BART (C2F w/ CNNDM) | 53.65 | **28.95** | 50.42 | **45.75** | **20.04** | **43.28** |
| BART (C2F w/ Meta) | **54.16** | **29.01** | **50.60** | **45.95** | **20.51** | **43.53** |

respectively. The dataset's statistics are listed in Table 1. This paper compares our method with some competitive dialogue summarization models, including PGNet [21], Transformer [22], MV-BART [1], PLMA [4], and popular pre-trained models (i.e., DialoGPT and BART).

### 3.2 Experiment Settings

The ROUGE-1/2/L (**R-1/2/L**) [11] and BERTScore (**BS**) [24] scores are employed to evaluate summaries, as in previous works [1,4]. Without the meta learning mechanism, both $BART_\beta$ and $BART_\theta$ are initialized with *bart.large*[1] which is the conventional parameters of BART. This paper leverages the news domain's knowledge for dialogue summarization, and the CNNDM [8] dataset is used as the external news data for meta learning. Hence, with meta learning, $BART_\theta$ is initialized with *bart.large.cnn*[1] which is pre-trained on CNNDM. For SAMSum and DIALOGSUM, the learning rate is set to 3e−5, and the meta learning rate $\alpha$ is set to 3e−7. Other hyperparameters follow the same settings in *bart.large* and PLMA [4]. The same hyperparameters are used for both coarse-grained and fine-grained summarization. We utilize the NLTK[2] package to extract entities from the human-annotated summary, and those entities are the essential part of the coarse-grained target. The Py-rouge[3] package is implemented to calculate the ROUGE scores. The experiments run on the equipment with four NVIDIA GeForce RTX 3090 graphics cards.

---

[1] https://github.com/pytorch/fairseq.
[2] https://www.nltk.org.
[3] https://github.com/Diego999/py-rouge.

**Table 3.** BERTScore results.

| Method | SAMSum | DIALOGSUM |
|--------|--------|-----------|
|  | BS (↑) | BS (↑) |
| BART | 89.53 | 92.09 |
| PLMA | 90.04 | 92.51 |
| BART (C2F w/ Meta) | **90.06** | **92.76** |

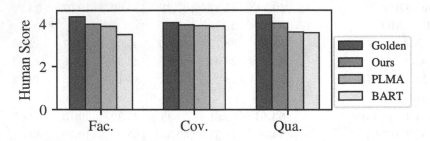

**Fig. 2.** Human evaluation. "Golden" indicates the scores on human-annotated summaries.

### 3.3 Experimental Results

Automatic evaluation results are shown in Table 2. Due to the gap between different domains, BART (CNNDM) directly employs dialogue data to fine-tune the model pre-trained on CNNDM but cannot achieve obvious improvement. The proposed meta learning mechanism could be employed in the fine-tuning procedure of BART (CNNDM). BART (Meta) only introduces the meta learning mechanism into the training of BART (CNNDM) and boosts all ROUGE scores, illustrating that this mechanism helps to transfer the news domain's knowledge. Through our coarse-to-fine training paradigm (i.e., C2F), prompted keywords are utilized by the model to catch the dialogue's main idea. Thus, both BART (C2F) and BART (C2F w/ CNNDM) increase the summarization performance in contrast to their models without C2F. BART (C2F w/ Meta) obtains the best results on most ROUGE scores over two datasets, showing the effectiveness of the cooperation between the training paradigm and the meta learning mechanism. Note that, compared with PLMA which expensively annotates various types of features and uses DialoGPT to extract information, BART (C2F), which only takes inferred keywords as annotation, still achieves competitive performance. It illustrates the validity of our coarse-grained summarization. Besides, BART (C2F w/ Meta) consistently outperforms baseline models on the embedding-based metric, BERTScore, as shown in Table 3. In general, our method could generate valid keywords and efficiently exploit out-of-domain knowledge, resulting in the superior performance for dialogue summarization.

**Table 4.** Automatic evaluation results. "C2F$_{key}$" is short for the coarse-to-fine training paradigm only using keywords.

| Method | SAMSum | | | DIALOGSUM | | |
|---|---|---|---|---|---|---|
| | R-1 ($\uparrow$) | R-2 ($\uparrow$) | R-L ($\uparrow$) | R-1 ($\uparrow$) | R-2 ($\uparrow$) | R-L ($\uparrow$) |
| BART (C2F$_{key}$) | 53.35 | 28.24 | 50.01 | 45.40 | 19.64 | 42.82 |
| BART (C2F) | 53.46 | 28.51 | 50.30 | 45.56 | 19.70 | 43.01 |
| BART (C2F$_{key}$ w/ Meta) | 53.82 | 28.47 | 50.39 | 45.72 | 19.86 | 43.15 |
| BART (C2F w/ Meta) | **54.16** | **29.01** | **50.60** | **45.95** | **20.51** | **43.53** |

**Table 5.** Results of using various methods for annotation.

| Method | R-1 ($\uparrow$) | R-2 ($\uparrow$) | R-L ($\uparrow$) |
|---|---|---|---|
| TextRank | 53.29 | 27.66 | 49.33 |
| Entities | 53.36 | 27.71 | 49.69 |
| Nouns & Verbs | 52.75 | 27.48 | 48.82 |
| Topics | 53.28 | 27.76 | 49.59 |
| PLMA$_{KEY}$ | 53.43 | 28.03 | 49.93 |
| BART (C2F) | **53.46** | **28.51** | **50.30** |

## 3.4 Analysis

**Human Evaluation.** In addition to the automatic metrics, the human evaluation is conducted on SAMSum to evaluate the generated summaries. This paper randomly selects 100 dialogues in test data for each method to summarize. Then, each summary is rated by three recruited human workers from 1 to 5 (higher is better) in terms of three criteria. The facticity (**Fac.**) measures the factual consistency between the summary and the dialogue. The coverage (**Cov.**) measures how well the summary covers the dialogue's content. The quality (**Qua.**) measures the conciseness and fluency of the generated summary. The average scores are shown in Fig. 2, illustrating that our method achieves the best performance. Specially, compared with BART, our method gets much better summaries with 14.08% higher facticity and 11.91% higher quality.

**Validity of Prompt-Based Learning.** To illustrate the validity of employing the textual prompt, the results of our training paradigm only using keywords (i.e., C2F$_{key}$) are listed in Table 4. Without the prompt, only keywords are learned and inferred by BART$_\beta$. The performance of BART (C2F$_{key}$) and BART (C2F$_{key}$ w/ Meta) drops, showing that using our designed prompt for learning benefits the utilization of the pre-trained model's knowledge. Besides, compared with BART (C2F$_{key}$), BART (C2F$_{key}$ w/ Meta) significantly improves ROUGE scores, which also illustrates the effectiveness of our meta learning mechanism.

**Table 6.** Quantitative evaluation for keywords.

| Method | TextRank | Entities | PLMA$_{KEY}$ | BART (C2F) |
|---|---|---|---|---|
| Precision (↑) | 47.74% | 60.42% | 33.20% | **65.58%** |

**Table 7.** Case study.

**Dialogue**

Lorenna : Girls, Im sorry, I cant come to the party tomorrow Lorenna : Emma has a fever and I need to take her to the doctor. Ann : Oh Im so sorry about her Shirley : . Shirley : how's she feeling? Lorenna : not too bad, but I need to stay at home with her for a few days. Lorenna : she's sleeping now. Ann : give her a kiss from auntie Anna! Shirley : and from me too! Lorenna : thanks!

**Golden**

Lorenna is not coming to the party because her daughter is ill. She is going to see a doctor with her. Ann and Shirley send kisses to the kid.

**BART**

Emma has a fever and Lorenna needs to take her to the doctor. She needs to stay at home with her for a few days.

**PLMA**

**Extracted keywords**: Shirley Ann Lorenna Girls Im sorry I cant come to the party tomorrow fever Im she feeling stay sleeping Anna

**Summary**: Lorenna can't come to the party tomorrow as she needs to take Emma to the doctor. She needs to stay at home with her for a few days.

**Ours**

**Inferred information**: In summary, they talk about : **fever party Emma tomorrow doctor**

**Summary**: Lorenna can't come to the **party tomorrow** because **Emma** has a **fever** and she needs to take her to the **doctor**

**Validity of Coarse-Grained Summarization.** To further verify the validity of our inferred keywords, this paper fine-tunes BART on SAMSum with the annotation from different keyword extraction methods, such as TextRank [16], Entities [19], Nouns & Verbs [19], Topics [18], and PLMA$_{KEY}$ [4]. Those methods would search the whole dialogue text for auxiliary keywords, and thus their keywords may not be concise. As shown in Table 5, our method achieves the best ROUGE scores, showing that the annotation from our coarse-grained summarization better assists the summary generation. For the quantitative evaluation, we calculate the precision by viewing human-annotated summary words as golden keywords [4], and the results are shown in Table 6. It demonstrates that the keywords inferred by our method obtain the highest precision, and thus contain fewer redundant words.

**Case Study.** A case generated by different methods for an example dialogue in the SAMSum dataset is shown in Table 7. BART does not capture the key information well without annotation, and omits the important content about "not coming to the party". PLMA cannot generate the content about "ill" or "fever". The reason may be that PLMA extracts redundant keywords from the original dialogue text, and those keywords make it hard for BART to catch the main idea. By contrast, the concise keywords containing "party" and "fever" are inferred by our coarse-grained summarizer as annotation, and our summary better covers the dialogue's semantics with a shorter text length. However, all three generated summaries miss the content about "send kisses to the kid". The reason may be that this content has few descriptions in the dialogue.

## 4   Conclusion

This paper proposes a coarse-to-fine training paradigm for abstractive dialogue summarization without searching wordy dialogues for massive features. The key information inferred by the coarse-grained summarizer would assist the fine-grained summarizer in distilling the dialogue into a brief and precise summary. Besides, a meta learning mechanism is introduced to adapt the out-of-domain knowledge to the summarization of dialogues. Experimental results demonstrate the superiority of our method. In the future, we would explore the proposed method for other summarization tasks.

**Acknowledgements.** This work is supported by the National Key R&D Program of China (2018AAA0101203), and the National Natural Science Foundation of China (62072483).

## References

1. Chen, J., Yang, D.: Multi-view sequence-to-sequence models with conversational structure for abstractive dialogue summarization. In: Proceedings of EMNLP, pp. 4106–4118. Association for Computational Linguistics (2020)
2. Chen, Y., Liu, Y., Chen, L., Zhang, Y.: DialogSum: a real-life scenario dialogue summarization dataset. In: Findings of ACL, pp. 5062–5074. Association for Computational Linguistics (2021)
3. Feng, X., Feng, X., Qin, B.: A survey on dialogue summarization: recent advances and new frontiers. arXiv preprint arXiv:2107.03175 (2021)
4. Feng, X., Feng, X., Qin, L., Qin, B., Liu, T.: Language model as an annotator: exploring DialoGPT for dialogue summarization. In: Proceedings of ACL-IJCNLP, pp. 1479–1491. Association for Computational Linguistics (2021)
5. Finn, C., Abbeel, P., Levine, S.: Model-agnostic meta-learning for fast adaptation of deep networks. In: Proceedings of ICML. Proceedings of Machine Learning Research, vol. 70, pp. 1126–1135. PMLR (2017)
6. Gliwa, B., Mochol, I., Biesek, M., Wawer, A.: SAMSum corpus: a human-annotated dialogue dataset for abstractive summarization. In: Proceedings of the 2nd Workshop on New Frontiers in Summarization, pp. 70–79. Association for Computational Linguistics, Hong Kong, China (2019)

7. Hardy, H., Vlachos, A.: Guided neural language generation for abstractive summarization using Abstract Meaning Representation. In: Proceedings of EMNLP, pp. 768–773. Association for Computational Linguistics, Brussels, Belgium (2018)
8. Hermann, K.M., et al.: Teaching machines to read and comprehend. In: Proceedings of NeurIPS, vol. 28. Curran Associates, Inc. (2015)
9. Lewis, M., et al.: BART: denoising sequence-to-sequence pre-training for natural language generation, translation, and comprehension. In: Proceedings of ACL, pp. 7871–7880. Association for Computational Linguistics (2020)
10. Li, M., Zhang, L., Ji, H., Radke, R.J.: Keep meeting summaries on topic: Abstractive multi-modal meeting summarization. In: Proceedings of ACL, pp. 2190–2196. Association for Computational Linguistics, Florence, Italy (2019)
11. Lin, C.Y.: ROUGE: a package for automatic evaluation of summaries. In: Text Summarization Branches Out, pp. 74–81. Association for Computational Linguistics, Barcelona, Spain (2004)
12. Liu, P., Yuan, W., Fu, J., Jiang, Z., Hayashi, H., Neubig, G.: Pre-train, prompt, and predict: a systematic survey of prompting methods in natural language processing. arXiv preprint arXiv:2107.13586 (2021)
13. Liu, Y., Liu, P.: SimCLS: a simple framework for contrastive learning of abstractive summarization. In: Proceedings of ACL-IJCNLP, pp. 1065–1072. Association for Computational Linguistics (2021)
14. Liu, Z., Chen, N.: Reading turn by turn: hierarchical attention architecture for spoken dialogue comprehension. In: Proceedings of ACL, pp. 5460–5466. Association for Computational Linguistics, Florence, Italy (2019)
15. Maynez, J., Narayan, S., Bohnet, B., McDonald, R.: On faithfulness and factuality in abstractive summarization. In: Proceedings of ACL, pp. 1906–1919. Association for Computational Linguistics (2020)
16. Mihalcea, R., Tarau, P.: TextRank: bringing order into text. In: Proceedings of EMNLP, pp. 404–411. Association for Computational Linguistics, Barcelona, Spain (2004)
17. Murray, G., Renals, S., Carletta, J., Moore, J.: Incorporating speaker and discourse features into speech summarization. In: Proceedings of NAACL, pp. 367–374. Association for Computational Linguistics, New York City, USA (2006)
18. Narayan, S., Cohen, S.B., Lapata, M.: Don't give me the details, just the summary! topic-aware convolutional neural networks for extreme summarization. In: Proceedings of EMNLP, pp. 1797–1807. Association for Computational Linguistics, Brussels, Belgium (2018)
19. Qi, P., Zhang, Y., Zhang, Y., Bolton, J., Manning, C.D.: Stanza: a python natural language processing toolkit for many human languages. In: Proceedings of ACL, pp. 101–108. Association for Computational Linguistics (2020)
20. Schick, T., Schütze, H.: Few-shot text generation with pattern-exploiting training. arXiv preprint arXiv:2012.11926 (2020)
21. See, A., Liu, P.J., Manning, C.D.: Get to the point: summarization with pointer-generator networks. In: Proceedings of ACL, pp. 1073–1083. Association for Computational Linguistics, Vancouver, Canada (2017)
22. Vaswani, A., et al.: Attention is all you need. In: Proceedings of NeurIPS, vol. 30. Curran Associates, Inc. (2017)
23. Yuan, W., Neubig, G., Liu, P.: BARTScore: evaluating generated text as text generation. arXiv preprint arXiv:2106.11520 (2021)
24. Zhang, T., Kishore, V., Wu, F., Weinberger, K.Q., Artzi, Y.: BERTScore: Evaluating text generation with BERT. In: Proceedings of ICLR (2020)

25. Zhang, Y., et al.: DIALOGPT : large-scale generative pre-training for conversational response generation. In: Proceedings of ACL, pp. 270–278. Association for Computational Linguistics (2020)
26. Zhao, L., Xu, W., Guo, J.: Improving abstractive dialogue summarization with graph structures and topic words. In: Proceedings of COLING, pp. 437–449. International Committee on Computational Linguistics, Barcelona, Spain (2020)
27. Zhu, C., Xu, R., Zeng, M., Huang, X.: A hierarchical network for abstractive meeting summarization with cross-domain pretraining. In: Findings of EMNLP, pp. 194–203. Association for Computational Linguistics (2020)
28. Zou, Y., et al.: Topic-oriented spoken dialogue summarization for customer service with saliency-aware topic modeling. In: Proceedings of AAAI, pp. 14665–14673 (2021)
29. Zou, Y., Zhu, B., Hu, X., Gui, T., Zhang, Q.: Low-resource dialogue summarization with domain-agnostic multi-source pretraining. arXiv preprint arXiv:2109.04080 (2021)

# A Comparison of Neural Network Architectures for Malware Classification Based on Noriben Operation Sequences

Rajchada Chanajitt[✉], Bernhard Pfahringer, and Heitor Murilo Gomes

Department of Computer Science, University of Waikato, Hamilton, New Zealand
rajchada.ch@gmail.com

**Abstract.** Behavior-based machine learning plays a vital role in malware classification, as it potentially overcomes the limitations of signature-based methods. This paper explores the use of dynamic call sequences as extracted by the open source Noriben tool, which employs dynamic analysis in a virtualized environment. Call sequences of a length of up to 5000 operations are generated for a total of 2000 benign and malware samples. Seven malware families are recognized: ransomware, trojan, backdoor, rootkit, virus, miner, and other. An empirical comparison analyzes five different classifiers: fully connected neural networks, GRU and LSTM, Transformer, and two combination approaches. The overall best performing approach is a concatenation of a GRU with a Transformer architecture, yielding the highest F1-score. This best model achieves accuracy and F1-score values of up to 97%.

**Keywords:** Noriben · GRU · Transformer

## 1 Introduction

The proliferation of the runtime packers and obfuscation techniques easily facilitates the creation of malware variants which can disguise themselves to avoid detection by antivirus software. Noriben [4] is a python-based script analysis tool that allows to not only run applications automatically within a guest virtual machine by executing a script itself but also collect and log the applications' activities. This will be useful for generating report later. In this study, we propose a malware detection method based on a consecutive sequence of Noriben operations using a concatenation of GRU and Transformer architecture. Although Noriben is beneficial for security analysis, using it to represent meaningful features and be learned by model approaches for malware classification is not done publicly. In the Noriben log file, it records all running processes. However, we focus on the output of the activity of our application process in an ascending timing order, and the first 5000 operations are extracted and learned by machine learning approaches. A few types of application files: MSI files (an installer package file format), EXE files (an executable file format), AppxBundle files (a Windows 8.1 App Bundle Package format), and DOC/DOCX file are analyzed.

© The Author(s), under exclusive license to Springer Nature Switzerland AG 2022
E. Pimenidis et al. (Eds.): ICANN 2022, LNCS 13529, pp. 428–440, 2022.
https://doi.org/10.1007/978-3-031-15919-0_36

The main contributions of the paper are as follows: (i) We show how text vectorization mapping features to integer sequences can be used to characterize and predict malware categories. (ii) We analyze the frequency of Noriben operations for each malware category (iii) We benchmark different machine learning approaches using our sequences. The experiments highlight that using a combination of GRU and Transformer yields highly accurate classifier.

The remaining of the paper is organized as follows: Sect. 2 is related works. The data collection and preprocessing of Noriben sequences are explained in Sect. 3. Section 4 describes how machine learning models are created and fine-tuned, followed by the empirical experiments presented in Sect. 5. Finally, Sect. 6 provides conclusions, limitations, and directions for future work.

## 2 Related Work

This section describes prior work on malware classification based on behavior-based analysis. These research efforts are divided into (i) binary classification, and (ii) multi-class classification.

### 2.1 Binary Classification

The work of [14] tries to discover explicit sub-sequences, or episodes, by investigating n-grams of the API call sequences. They achieve high accuracies using some specialised online algorithms, but these accuracies might be misleading given that their dataset is very unbalanced, with more than 90% of the samples being malware.

Joshua Saxe [16] proposed the eXpose deep neural network to work on short character strings, and evaluated it against an n-gram model and manual feature extraction on three different problems. These problems included predicting malicious URLs, or unique file paths, or specific registry key paths as used in malware applications. A standard convolutional network architecture is used in the eXpose system.

A two-dimensional feature extraction method together with a sliding local attention mechanism model (SLAM) was proposed in [5]. These inputs are then processed by a standard convolutional backbone network. They use the data that was collected for Alibaba's 3rd Security Algorithm Challenge [2]. API calls are preprocessed using the word2vec [9] embedding approach. They specify a maximum sequence length of 2000. Their reported accuracies lie in the high 90s, but they rely on some specialised sampling to deal with the imbalanced nature of their data source.

### 2.2 Multiclass Classification

Kolosnjaji [10] proposed a deep hybrid architecture of convolutional and recurrent neural networks to process API call sequences into malware families. The convolutional network part only counts the presence and relationship of n-grams in system calls, regardless of the actual position in the input data, whereas the recurrent part utilizes the full sequence information. The dataset is obtained from three primary sources: Virus Share [8], Maltrieve [11], and some private collections. Regarding experimental results, using this combination of a convolution of n-grams with a fully sequential modeling architecture results in a significant improvement over HMMs or SVMs for malware classification. They achieve accuracy, precision, and recall values of over 90% for most malware families they are considering.

A very innovative approach to malware classification was proposed in Qian [15]. They turn application binaries into artificial images and then use standard deep learning methods to classify malware into nine different families. Their dataset is well balanced, with 1000 samples in each family. Images are generated such that pixels represent different subsets of API calls, with the pixels' brightness encoding call frequencies. The resulting images are then processed by a standard convolutional neural network. They achieve very high performance on their specific dataset, with an F1-score of 99% and a false positive rate of only 0.085%.

Other previous research [3] has explored the use file event streams using both LSTM and GRU architectures for malware detection. Their best performing model was an LSTM network trained with temporal max-pooling using a logistic regression classifier (LR-LSTM-MAX) that achieved a better than 80% TPR at a 2% FPR.

## 3   Data Collection and Feature Preprocessing

Around 2000 samples for malware and benign applications are collected from publicly available sources. Precisely, the dataset contains 1244[1] malicious files and 756[2] benign samples. The labels are obtained from two primary sources: submitting the files to VirusTotal [19] by using at least five or more anti-virus engines to assign a class label and retrieving threat names from the Windows Defender/Operational event log. If an application is not in the seven categories mentioned before, it will be assigned to the "other" class. To keep our systems safe, the collection of dynamic behaviour is performed in a virtualized environment, where Windows Defender has been disabled, to allow the malware full reign over the virtual machine.

The extracted call sequences are treated like a string of words, and are therefore preprocessed in a similar way, utilizing Tensorflow's [1] TextVectorization tool. This tool is set to "count" mode, with an dictionary size of 500. Any missing values after this preprocessing step are replaced with a constant default value using Scikit-Learn's *SimpleImputer* [13]. An example of the first ten Noriben operations with no repetition of occurrences is given in Fig. 1. Table 1 provides some statistics for the top-10 most frequently occurring Noriben operation. The first number is the average number of times an operation is being called an

---

[1] Downloads from VirusShare [8] and VirusSign [18].
[2] Downloads from FileHorse [7].

application in a family. Only applications that call the operation at least once are being considered for the average. The second number is the total number of applications in that family that use this operation at least once.

Regarding the applications, it is not surprising to see the less frequent families being more uniform, with *Virus* at the extreme, where each of the 11 samples uses almost all of the top 10 operations, with the notable exception of "RgQuery KeySecurity", which is never called at all. The *Virus* family is also an outlier with regard to the averages, with each operation being called only a few times, except for "WriteFile", which features a very average call count. The highest average call count is associated with the "ReadFile" action in the *Miner* family, followed by three operation counts that are all featured in the *Ransom* family: "RegQueryValue", "WriteFile", and "ReadFile". When looking at the averages for any of the operations for the *Benign* family, unfortunately there are no obvious simple patterns present: all these averages lie somewhere in the middle of all the values for any operation, when viewed across families. This absence of simple to exploit patterns for malware detection justifies the application of more complex machine learning methods as described below.

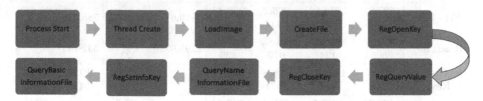

**Fig. 1.** The first 10 unique Noriben operations in sequence order, for some sample application

## 4    Model Architectures

Five state of the art Machine Learning algorithms are evaluated here for their malware detection performance: a fully connected neural network (FCNN), gated recurrent unit (GRU) and long short-term memory (LSTM), Transformer, and two combination approaches. Our choices were inspired by the various approaches described above in the related work section, with the exception of the Transformer approach, which to the best of our knowledge, has not been used before in malware sequence prediction tasks.

All models are implemented using TensorFlow [1]. Furthermore, in order to obtain a good performance, all hyperparameters were tuned by utilizing Keras-Tuner's [12] RandomSearch. For proper estimation 10-fold cross-validation was employed, together with a scheduled decrease of the learning rate. More details will be given in the following subsections.

### 4.1    FCNN

The architecture of the fully connected network follows a standard setup using nonlinear activations, and employing BatchNormalization, Dropout and other

**Table 1.** Top-10 frequently occurrences of Noriben sequences classified by two numeric values: (1) maximum number for each category and (2) the number of applications for each and every operation-category pair.

| Noriben Operations/Total | Benign (756) | Ransom (139) | Trojan (980) | Miner (43) | Rootkit (10) | Backdoor (23) | Virus (11) | Other (38) |
|---|---|---|---|---|---|---|---|---|
| Query Standard Information File | 48.4/ 602 | 590.5/ 122 | 2920.6 /964 | 82.7 / 40 | 19.7/10 | 3.0/23 | 2.2/11 | 315.9/ 38 |
| RegQuery Value | 95.6 / 748 | 4185.4/ 124 | 200.9 /971 | 1955.9 / 40 | 331.9/10 | 164.1 / 23 | 7.5 /11 | 2546.5/ 38 |
| RegQuery KeySecurity | 62.2/86 | 2542.7 / 110 | 2196.7 /202 | 845.4 / 39 | 1118.4/8 | 161.5/ 21 | 0/0 | 416.2 / 9 |
| RegQuery Key | 224.7/ 613 | 2273.9 / 123 | 457.9 /969 | 2456.7 / 40 | 894.7/10 | 181.7 / 23 | 13.1/11 | 2299.6 / 38 |
| Query Directory | 143.4/ 373 | 1029.6 / 98 | 562.2 /754 | 135.5/ 30 | 10657.3 /8 | 3.2/20 | 1.9/11 | 203.2 / 25 |
| WriteFile | 507.9/ 498 | 3774.1/ 98 | 236.2 /447 | 200.4/ 35 | 819.6/7 | 4.3/16 | 585.0/4 | 49.4/ 31 |
| ReadFile | 453.5/ 605 | 2926.5/ 124 | 110.8 / 970 | 5373.1 /39 | 1195.6/10 | 60.2/ 23 | 34.8/11 | 308.6/ 38 |
| RegOpen Key | 99.4/ 748 | 1292.0/ 124 | 308.8 /971 | 2081.8/ 40 | 564.8/10 | 131.1 / 23 | 19.3 /11 | 2445.3/ 38 |
| CreateFile | 172.6/ 602 | 2239.5 /124 | 255.3 /966 | 787.6/ 40 | 2592.8/10 | 30.7 /23 | 16.0/11 | 500.5/ 38 |
| CloseFile | 114.4 / 745 | 1807.3 / 124 | 245.8 /971 | 785.3/ 40 | 2591.7/10 | 22.5/23 | 13.6/11 | 436.4 / 38 |

regularizers to avoid overfitting. The details of the architecture and the best values for the various hyperparameters have been determined by RandomSearch. The setup for this search, and the selected best values are listed in Table 2, whereas Fig. 2 depicts the final best architecture for the FCNN, as determined by RandomSearch.

## 4.2  GRU and LSTM

Both LSTM and GRU [6] are standard approaches for sequence learning. Here we experiment with Bidirectional CuDNNGRU and CuDNNLSTM architectures, where the embedded input is first processed by a convolutional layer. Again, the best configurations were determined by RandomSearch in Keras, with the setup and outcomes provided in Table 3 and Fig. 3.

## 4.3  Transformer

Transformer [17] is an attention-based encoder-decoder architecture. The attention mechanism focuses on different tokens while generating words to model

```
Layer (type)                    Output Shape          Param #
==================================================================

input_1 (InputLayer)            [(None, 77)]          0

dense (Dense)                   (None, 288)           22464

sequential (Sequential)         (None, 256)           795904

dropout (Dropout)               (None, 256)           0

batch_normalization (BatchN     (None, 256)           1024
ormalization)

dense_8 (Dense)                 (None, 448)           115136

dense_9 (Dense)                 (None, 224)           100576

dense_10 (Dense)                (None, 160)           36000

dropout_1 (Dropout)             (None, 160)           0

batch_normalization_1 (Batc     (None, 160)           640
hNormalization)

dense_11 (Dense)                (None, 8)             1288

==================================================================
```

**Fig. 2.** The best FCNN as determined by RandomSearch in Tensorflow.

**Table 2.** FCNN hyperparameter tuning setup and outcome

| Name | Initial value | Tuning ranges | Best value |
|---|---|---|---|
| batch_size | 15 | ranges(10, 50, 5) | 40 |
| epochs | 100 | ranges(100, 600, 50) | 300 |
| optimizer | RMSprop | ['Adam','RMSprop', 'Adadelta', 'Adagrad'] | Adam |
| learning_rate | 0.0002 | [0.0001, 0.001, 0.01, 0.0002, 0.002, 0.02] | 0.0001 |
| Neurons | [256, 256, 128, 128] | range(256, 512, 32) | [288, 448, 224, 160] |
| Hidden Layers | 5 | range(2,10) | 7 |
| Hidden Neurons | [256, 256, 256, 256, 256] | range(128, 512, 32) | [512, 448, 480, 160, 320, 128, 256] |
| bias_regularizer | [0.002, 0.02, 0.002, 0.002, 0.002] | [0.0001, 0.001, 0.01, 0.0002, 0.002, 0.02] | [0.02, 0.0002, 0.002, 0.02,0.0001] |
| kernel_regularizer | [0.01,0.02,0.01, 0.01,0.01] | [0.0001, 0.001, 0.01, 0.0002, 0.002, 0.02] | [0.001, 0.01, 0.01, 0.02, 0.002] |
| kernel_constraint | [2.0, 1.5, 1.5, 1.5, 1.0] | range(1, 3, 0.5) | [1.0, 3.0, 1.0, 2.5, 1.5] |
| activity_regularizer | [0.0001,0.001,0.0001, 0.0001,0.001] | [0.0001, 0.001, 0.01, 0.0002, 0.002, 0.02] | [0.0002, 0.001, 0.001, 0.01, 0.0002] |

Noriben sequences. To configure the model, the standard transformer architecture as described in [17] is applied. The setup for the RandomSearch, and the selected best values are listed in Table 4.

### 4.4   Combination of GRU and Transformer

This classifier is created as a combination of a GRU and a Transformer network. It is a simple concatenation of the outputs of the penultimate layers of

```
Layer (type)                   Output Shape          Param #
=================================================================
embedding (Embedding)          (None, None, 448)      527296

conv1d (Conv1D)                (None, None, 256)      459008

max_pooling1d (MaxPooling1D    (None, None, 256)      0
)

bidirectional (Bidirectiona    (None, None, 576)      943488
l)

dropout (Dropout)              (None, None, 576)      0

bidirectional_1 (Bidirectio    (None, 896)            2757888
nal)

batch_normalization (BatchN    (None, 896)            3584
ormalization)

dense (Dense)                  (None, 8)              7176

=================================================================
```

**Fig. 3.** The best GRU as determined by RandomSearch in Tensorflow.

**Table 3.** Hyperparameter tuning for GRU and LSTM

| Name | Initial value | Tuning ranges | GRU best value | LSTM best value |
|---|---|---|---|---|
| batch_size | 15 | range(10, 50, 5) | 25 | 25 |
| epochs | 200 | range(50, 550, 50) | 600 | 600 |
| optimizer | RMSprop | ['Adam','RMSprop', 'Adadelta', 'Adagrad'] | Adam | Adam |
| learning_rate | 0.0001 | [0.0001, 0.001, 0.01, 0.0002, 0.002, 0.02] | 0.0002 | 0.0002 |
| embedding | 128 | ranges(256, 1024, 32) | 544 | 544 |
| embedding regularizer | 0.0001 | [0.0001, 0.001, 0.01, 0.0002, 0.002, 0.02] | 0.02 | 0.02 |
| gru/lstm units | [512, 256] | ranges(128, 512, 32) | [288, 448] | [288, 448] |
| recurrent regularizer | [0.0001, 0.001] | [0.0001, 0.001, 0.01, 0.0002, 0.002, 0.02] | [0.01, 0.001] | [0.01, 0.001] |
| kernel regularizer | [0.001, 0.001] | [[0.0001, 0.001, 0.01, 0.0002, 0.002, 0.02] | [0.002, 0.01] | [0.002, 0.01] |
| bias regularizer | [0.01, 0.02] | [0.0001, 0.001, 0.01, 0.0002, 0.002, 0.02] | [0.01, 0.01] | [0.01, 0.01] |
| kernel constraint | [2.0, 1.5] | range(1, 3, 0.5) | [1.5, 2.0] | [1.5, 2.0] |
| activity regularizer | [0.0001, 0.0002] | [0.0001, 0.001, 0.01, 0.0002, 0.002, 0.02] | [0.02, 0.002] | [0.02, 0.002] |

both networks. In particular, the output of the last BatchNormalization layer of the GRU, and the output of the final GlobalAveragePooling1D layer of the Transformer are concatenated and passed to a final softmax layer. The tuning information for this combination is provided in Table 5

**Table 4.** Hyperparameter tuning for Transformer

| Name | Initial value | Tuning ranges | Best value |
|---|---|---|---|
| batch_size | 10 | range(10, 50, 5) | 25 |
| epochs | 100 | range(50, 500, 50) | 600 |
| optimizer | Adam | ['Adam','RMSprop', 'Adadelta', 'Adagrad'] | Adam |
| learning_rate | 0.0001 | [0.0001, 0.001, 0.01, 0.0002, 0.002, 0.02] | 0.0002 |
| trans_dim | 512 | ranges(512, 2048, 32) | 704 |
| num_heads | 12 | ranges(6, 20, 2) | 12 |
| feed_forward_dim | 1024 | ranges(1024, 3172, 32) | 2048 |
| enc_layer | 5 | ranges(2, 10) | 2 |
| dec_layer | 5 | ranges(1, 10) | 2 |
| embedding regularizer | [0.001, 0.001] | [0.0001, 0.001, 0.01, 0.0002, 0.002, 0.02] | [0.002. 0.01] |
| kernel regularizer | [0.001, 0.001] | [0.0001, 0.001, 0.01, 0.0002, 0.002, 0.02] | [0.02, 0.01] |
| bias regularizer | [0.01, 0.02] | [0.0001, 0.001, 0.01, 0.0002, 0.002, 0.02] | [0.001, 0.001] |
| kernel constraint | [2.0, 1.5] | range(1, 3, 0.5) | [2.5, 2.0] |
| activity regularizer | [0.001, 0.001] | [0.0001, 0.001, 0.01, 0.0002, 0.002, 0.02] | [0.001, 0.002] |

### 4.5   Combination of FCNN and Transformer

This classifier is created as a hybrid architecture of a fully connected neural network and a transformer. Effectively, the FCNN simply replaces the GRU in the previous combination approach. The details of the hyperparameter tuning are shown in Table 6.

## 5   Experimental Results

In this section, we present results for the five algorithms when applied to Noriben sequences. Accuracy is used to measure predictive performance. In addition information theoretic measures like precision, recall, and F1-measure, as well as Area Under the receiver operating characteristic Curve (AUC) and Mean Absolute Error (MAE) are also provided.

Table 7 lists results for running all algorithms with their default parameter settings. Overall, GRU performs best out of all five classifiers, achieving an accuracy of 76.4%.

Table 8 shows the substantial improvements achievable by proper tuning of the essential hyperparameters. The overall performance increases for all classi-

**Table 5.** Hyperparameter tuning for combining GRU and Transformer

| Name | Initial value | Tuning ranges | Best value |
|------|---------------|---------------|------------|
| batch_size | 15 | ranges(10,50,5) | 25 |
| epochs | 100 | ranges(100,600,50) | 300 |
| optimizer | RMSprop | ['Adam','RMSprop', 'Adadelta', 'Adagrad'] | Adam |
| learning_rate | 0.002 | [0.0001, 0.001, 0.01, 0.0002, 0.002, 0.02] | 0.0001 |
| embedding | 256 | range(256, 1024, 32) | 448 |
| embedding regularizer | [0.001, 0.001, 0.001] | [0.0001, 0.001, 0.01, 0.0002, 0.002, 0.02] | [0.0001, 0.002, 0.01] |
| gru units | [512, 256] | ranges(128, 512, 32) | [224, 384] |
| recurrent regularizer | [0.0001, 0.001] | [0.0001, 0.001, 0.01, 0.0002, 0.002, 0.02] | [0.0001, 0.002] |
| kernel regularizer | [0.001, 0.001, 0.001, 0.001, 0.01] | [0.0001, 0.001, 0.01, 0.0002, 0.002, 0.02] | [0.002, 0.01, 0.01, 0.002, 0.01] |
| bias regularizer | [0.01, 0.02, 0.01, 0.01, 0.001] | [0.0001, 0.001, 0.01, 0.0002, 0.002, 0.02] | [0.002, 0.002, 0.0002, 0.01, 0.002] |
| kernel constraint | [2.0, 1.5, 1.5, 2.0, 1.0] | range(1, 3, 0.5) | [3.0, 3.0, 2.0, 1.5, 3.0] |
| activity regularizer | [0.001, 0.001, 0.001, 0.001, 0.0001] | [0.0001, 0.001, 0.01, 0.0002, 0.002, 0.02] | [0.01, 0.0001, 0.01, 0.01, 0.0002] |
| trans_dim | 128 | ranges(512, 1024, 32) | 864 |
| num_heads | 4 | ranges(6, 20, 2) | 20 |
| feed_forward _dim | 1024 | ranges(1024, 3172, 128) | 2944 |
| enc_layer | 3 | ranges(2, 10) | 4 |
| dec_layer | 2 | ranges(1,10) | 6 |

fication models compared to the default performances from Table 7. The combination of GRU with a transformer exhibits the best performance, reaching an accuracy at 97%, and also achieving the overall best F1, MAE and AUC results.

Regarding separate performance measures for each class, Table 9 lists per-class precision, recall, and F1 scores. The majority of the samples are correctly classified into their respective families.

In addition to the evaluation metrics reported, we also present the total elapsed time on the training default configuration and hyperparameter tuning with ten maximum trials for each estimator. We used stratified 10-Folds cross-validation using the GPU. Although RandomSearch considers not all possible combinations, a combination of GRU and Transformer takes the most prolonged hours for optimization as represented in Table 10.

We also analyze the confusion matrix as depicted in Fig. 4 which compares between actual and predictive values. As expected, the diagonal values dominate,

**Table 6.** Hyperparameter tuning for combining FCNN and Transformer

| Name | Initial value | Tuning ranges | Best value |
|---|---|---|---|
| batch_size | 15 | ranges(10, 50, 5) | 30 |
| epochs | 100 | ranges(100, 600, 50) | 150 |
| optimizer | RMSprop | ['Adam','RMSprop', 'Adadelta', 'Adagrad'] | RMSprop |
| learning_rate | 0.0002 | [0.0001, 0.001, 0.01, 0.0002, 0.002, 0.02] | 0.0001 |
| Neurons | [256, 256, 128, 128] | range(128, 512, 32) | [704, 224, 288, 320] |
| Hidden Layers | 5 | range(2, 10) | 7 |
| Hidden Neurons | [256, 256, 256, 256,256] | range(128, 512, 32) | [192, 288, 480, 352, 480, 320, 288] |
| bias_ regularizer | [0.001, 0.002, 0.002, 0.001, 0.001, 0.001] | [0.0001, 0.001, 0.01, 0.0002, 0.002, 0.02] | [0.0001, 0.02, 0.01, 0.02, 0.0001, 0.002] |
| kernel_ regularizer | [0.01, 0.02, 0.02, 0.01, 0.01, 0.001] | [0.0001, 0.001, 0.01, 0.0002, 0.002, 0.02] | [0.002, 0.01, 0.02, 0.001, 0.002, 0.002] |
| kernel_ constraint | [2.0, 1.5, 1.5, 1.5, 1.0, 1.0] | range(1, 3, 0.5) | [1.5, 1.5, 2.5, 1.5, 2.0, 2.0] |
| activity_ regularizer | [0.0001, 0.001, 0.0001, 0.0001, 0.001, 0.001] | [0.0001, 0.001, 0.01, 0.0002, 0.002, 0.02] | [0.0002, 0.0002, 0.001, 0.01, 0.001, 0.0001] |
| trans_dim | 512 | ranges(512, 1024, 32) | 608 |
| num_heads | 8 | ranges(6, 20, 2) | 10 |
| feed_forward_ dim | 1024 | ranges(1024, 3172, 128) | 2176 |
| enc_layer | 6 | ranges(2, 10) | 6 |
| dec_layer | 6 | ranges(1, 10) | 4 |
| embedding regularizer | [0.001, 0.001] | [0.0001, 0.001, 0.01, 0.0002, 0.002, 0.02] | [0.01, 0.01] |

with most off-diagonal values being very close to zero. The classifier has the best classification capability for miners, followed by the virus.

Finally, Fig. 5 presents ROC curves for all malware category predictions produced by the combination of a GRU with and a Transformer. Almost perfect prediction is achieved across all classes of malware.

**Table 7.** Cross-validation results for default hyperparameter values

| Algorithm | ACC | F1 | MAE | AUC |
|---|---|---|---|---|
| LSTM | $0.597 \pm 0.11$ | $0.601 \pm 0.12$ | $0.107 \pm 0.03$ | $0.880 \pm 0.03$ |
| GRU | $\mathbf{0.764 \pm 0.03}$ | $\mathbf{0.765 \pm 0.03}$ | $\mathbf{0.063 \pm 0.03}$ | $0.952 \pm 0.02$ |
| Transformer | $0.749 \pm 0.04$ | $0.749 \pm 0.04$ | $0.066 \pm 0.03$ | $0.941 \pm 0.02$ |
| FCNN | $0.653 \pm 0.03$ | $0.646 \pm 0.03$ | $0.114 \pm 0.01$ | $0.923 \pm 0.01$ |
| GRU + Transformer | $0.754 \pm 0.05$ | $0.759 \pm 0.04$ | $0.066 \pm 0.03$ | $\mathbf{0.954 \pm 0.02}$ |
| FCNN + Transformer | $0.704 \pm 0.05$ | $0.705 \pm 0.04$ | $0.095 \pm 0.03$ | $0.941 \pm 0.03$ |

**Table 8.** Cross-validation results after hyperparameter tuning

| Algorithm | Avg. ACC | Avg. F1 | Avg. MAE | Avg. AUC |
|---|---|---|---|---|
| LSTM | $0.939 \pm 0.07$ | $0.941 \pm 0.06$ | $0.020 \pm 0.02$ | $0.989 \pm 0.02$ |
| GRU | $0.941 \pm 0.06$ | $0.942 \pm 0.06$ | $0.021 \pm 0.02$ | $0.990 \pm 0.02$ |
| Transformer | $0.935 \pm 0.06$ | $0.936 \pm 0.06$ | $0.029 \pm 0.02$ | $0.986 \pm 0.02$ |
| FCNN | $0.882 \pm 0.06$ | $0.878 \pm 0.06$ | $0.049 \pm 0.01$ | $0.967 \pm 0.04$ |
| GRU + Transformer | $\mathbf{0.970 \pm 0.06}$ | $\mathbf{0.970 \pm 0.06}$ | $\mathbf{0.012 \pm 0.02}$ | $\mathbf{0.995 \pm 0.02}$ |
| FCNN + Transformer | $0.928 \pm 0.06$ | $0.929 \pm 0.06$ | $0.021 \pm 0.02$ | $0.989 \pm 0.02$ |

**Table 9.** Precision, recall, and F1 score per class, for 10-fold cross-validation of the GRU+Transformer setup.

| | Precision | Recall | f1_score |
|---|---|---|---|
| Benign | $0.99 \pm 0.04$ | $0.96 \pm 0.06$ | $0.97 \pm 0.04$ |
| Backdoor | $1.00 \pm 0.00$ | $0.96 \pm 0.15$ | $0.98 \pm 0.09$ |
| Miner | $1.00 \pm 0.30$ | $0.90 \pm 0.30$ | $0.95 \pm 0.30$ |
| Ransom | $0.93 \pm 0.16$ | $0.93 \pm 0.20$ | $0.93 \pm 0.18$ |
| Rootkit | $0.90 \pm 0.05$ | $0.90 \pm 0.04$ | $0.90 \pm 0.04$ |
| Trojan | $0.97 \pm 0.23$ | $0.98 \pm 0.00$ | $0.98 \pm 0.17$ |
| Virus | $0.79 \pm 0.15$ | $1.00 \pm 0.22$ | $0.88 \pm 0.20$ |
| Other | $0.97 \pm 0.30$ | $0.92 \pm 0.30$ | $0.95 \pm 0.30$ |

**Table 10.** Elapsed time used for training for each algorithm

| Algorithm | LSTM | GRU | NN | Transformer | GRU+Transformer | NN+ Transformer |
|---|---|---|---|---|---|---|
| Default | 1 h:41 m | 1 h:39 m | 16 m | 10 h:48 m | 10 h:58 m | 10 h:35 m |
| Tuning | 3 h:45 m | 3 h:08 m | 1h:49 m | 12 h:30 m | 12 h:59 m | 12 h:41 m |

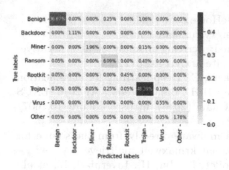

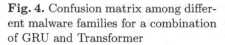

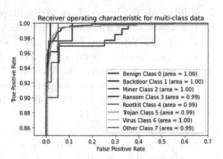

**Fig. 4.** Confusion matrix among different malware families for a combination of GRU and Transformer

**Fig. 5.** ROC Curve for a combination of GRU and Transformer

# 6 Conclusions and Future Work

In this paper, we use dynamic analysis to extract Noriben sequences and then use five classifiers to predict malware categories. Combining a GRU network with a Transformer outperforms all other approaches investigated in this paper. Despite the excellent predictions achievable with this setup, there are still some shortcomings to be addressed in future work. Most importantly, some ransomware applications encrypt Noriben outputs during runtime, which renders operation extraction impossible. Therefore, besides Noriben operations, alternative behavioral features from dynamic analysis will need to be investigated. We also intend to collect more malware samples to apply our methods to a larger dataset, to verify its effectiveness.

# References

1. Abadi, M., Agarwal, A., Barham, P., Brevdo, E., et al.: Tensorflow: Large-scale machine learning on heterogeneous distributed systems (2016)
2. Alibaba: Alitianchi contest (2021). https://tianchi.aliyun.com/competition/introduction.htm?spm=5176.11409106.5678.1.4354684cI0fYC1?raceId=231668s
3. Athiwaratkun, B., Stokes, J.W.: Malware classification with lstm and gru language models and a character-level cnn. In: 2017 IEEE International Conference on Acoustics, Speech and Signal Processing (ICASSP), pp. 2482–2486 (2017). https://doi.org/10.1109/ICASSP.2017.7952603
4. Baskin, B.: Noriben malware analysis sandbox (2015). https://github.com/Rurik/Noriben
5. Chen, J., Guo, S., Ma, X., Li, H., Guo, J., Chen, M., Pan, Z.: Slam: a malware detection method based on sliding local attention mechanism. Secur. Commun. Networks **2020**, 6724513:1–6724513:11 (2020)
6. Cho, K., van Merrienboer, B., Gulcehre, C., Bahdanau, D., Bougares, F., Schwenk, H., Bengio, Y.: Learning phrase representations using rnn encoder-decoder for statistical machine translation (2014)

7. FileHorse: Filehorse, June 2020, https://fileHorse.com
8. Forensics, C.: Virusshare, June 2020, https://virusshare.com/
9. Goldberg, Y., Levy, O.: word2vec explained: deriving mikolov et al'.s negative-sampling word-embedding method (2014). cite arxiv:1402.3722
10. Kolosnjaji, B., Zarras, A., Webster, G., Eckert, C.: Deep learning for classification of malware system call sequences. In: Kang, B.H., Bai, Q. (eds.) AI 2016. LNCS (LNAI), vol. 9992, pp. 137–149. Springer, Cham (2016). https://doi.org/10.1007/978-3-319-50127-7_11
11. Maxwell, K.: Maltrieve: a tool to retrieve malware directly from the source for security researchers (2015). https://github.com/krmaxwell/maltrieve
12. O'Malley, T., Bursztein, E., Long, J., Chollet, F., Jin, H., Invernizzi, L., et al.: Keras Tuner (2019). https://github.com/keras-team/keras-tuner
13. Pedregosa, F., et al.: Scikit-learn: machine learning in python. JMLR **12**, 2825–2830 (2011)
14. Pektas, A., Acarman, T.: Malware classification based on api calls and behaviour analysis. IET Inf. Secur. **12**, 107–117 (2018)
15. Qian, Q., Tang, M.: Dynamic api call sequence visualization for malware classification. IET Inf. Secur. **13**, October 2018
16. Saxe, J., Berlin, K.: expose: a character-level convolutional neural network with embeddings for detecting malicious urls, file paths and registry keys (2017)
17. Vaswani, A., et al.: Attention is all you need (2017)
18. VirusSign: Virussign, June 2020. https://samples.virussign.com/samples/
19. VirusTotal: Virustotal, June 2020. http://www.virustotal.com

# A Knowledge-Driven Enhanced Module for Visible-Infrared Person Re-identification

Shihao Shan, Enyuan Xiong, Xiang Yuan, and Song Wu[✉]

College of Computer and Information Science, Southwest University,
Chongqing, China
songwuswu@swu.edu.cn

**Abstract.** Visible-infrared person re-identification (VI-ReID) is a task in computer vision that has gained increasing importance in today's social surveillance systems. VI-ReID suffers from additional cross-modality variance caused by the inherent heterogeneous gap between the visible and infrared modality compared with previous person re-identification. This paper aims to reduce the difficulty of cross-modality shared feature learning through a knowledge-driven modality. From a novel perspective, we focus on explicitly modeling an appropriate knowledge-driven modality to narrow the cross-modality difference. Specifically, we propose a Knowledge-driven Enhanced Module (KDEM) to synthesize the feature of the knowledge-driven modality and help the model accumulate transitional knowledge. The synthetic feature distribution is controlled by two modality influencing factors generated by KDEM. To this end, for better characterizing knowledge-driven modality in a diverse way, we enforce a diversity loss on the two modality influence factors, which is instrumental in the knowledge accumulation of the model. Meanwhile, the Consistency loss is proposed to maintain the similarity between the knowledge-driven modality and the other two modalities, thereby can avoid knowledge accumulation of the knowledge-driven modality impacts on the performance of the model. In all the common VI-REID tasks, Our proposed method performs state-of-the-art. The code will be announced at https://github.com/SWU-CS-MediaLab/KDEM.

**Keywords:** Cross-modality re-identification · Computer vision · Neural network model

## 1 Introduction

Person re-identification (Re-ID), which aims at associating the same pedestrian images across disjoint camera views, has attracted increasing attention from the computer vision community [10,17,18]. With the high semantic abstraction capability of deep convolutional neural networks (CNNs) [5], the recent

Supported by organization Southwest University.

CNNs based Re-ID methods have obtained encouraging performance in the visible spectrum images. However, the visible cameras capture the visible spectrum images, which cannot provide sufficient discriminate information in the dark environment. Generally, the surveillance system will automatically be converted to infrared modal under poor lighting or dark conditions in real-life applications. Thus, the cross-modal matching task of Visible-Infrared Person Re-identification (VI-ReID) is proposed to match any one modality data with the corresponding person's another modality data [20]. Specifically, in the task of VI-ReID, since the images are captured by different wavelength ranges of visible and infrared cameras, as shown in Fig. 1, the intra-modality variance involved in single-modality Re-ID and the cross-modal discrepancies resulting from the natural difference between the reflectivity of the visible modality and the emissivity of the infrared modality, both increase the challenge for VI-ReID task. In summary, the most challenging issue in VI-ReID is how to learn high discriminative features to reduce the intra-domain and cross-domain discrepancy between the infrared and visible for effective cross-modality matching.

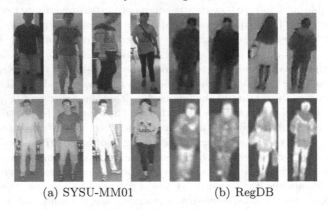

(a) SYSU-MM01          (b) RegDB

**Fig. 1.** Difference between the visible modality and infrared modality, and images in each column are from the same identity. (a) examples from the SYSU-MM01 dataset. (b) examples from the RegDB dataset.

Common representation space learning and metric learning are usually used to overcome the cross-modal discrepancy [8,16]. The existing methods based on common representation space learning mainly focus on how to design a reasonable deep network architecture for extracting robust and discriminative features shared by two modality data, minimizing the semantic gap between different modalities, and effectively comparing their semantic similarity. The methods based on metric learning aim to design a reasonable metric or loss function to effectively preserve the semantic similarity of different modalities during the deep network training and the loss function optimization. However, an insurmountable gap between visible and infrared modalities makes preserving the semantic similarity of different modalities exceedingly tricky.

However, most existing VI-ReID methods ignore the corresponding relationships of intrinsic property knowledge inside different modality data. From the perspective of neuroscience, the human brain's cognitive process of knowledge discovering and matching is firstly to parse the perceived raw multi-modality data. Then the specific expression pattern inside each modality data will be generated, and the high-level semantic knowledge will be abstracted for each specific expression pattern. The matching process will be completed by comparing the significant or noticeable semantic information in the high-level semantic knowledge. Inspired by this, in this paper, a novel Knowledge-driven Enhance Module (KDEM) is proposed, which is designed to imitate the cognitive process of the human brain, to achieve the effective matching of cross modalities. Specifically, the backbone deep neural network is first used to extract specific feature representations for visible and infrared modalities. The modality-specific feature representations of the visible and infrared modalities are then taken as the input of the KDEM. In the proposed KDEM, the high-level semantic knowledge representations will be generated by the followed several convolution operations. Meanwhile, the function of modality influence factors is designed in the KDEM to determine the high discriminative semantic information in the high-level semantic knowledge representations. The high discriminative semantic information extracted from each modality is further integrated into a new modality to supervise common representation space learning. Thus, the generated new modality could learn the significant or noticeable semantic knowledge of both the positive and negative pair-wise samples from intra-modality and cross-modality, effectively reducing the semantic gap between the visible and infrared modalities.

Additionally, in the KDEM, a novel diversity loss is designed to make the generated new modality exclude redundant knowledge as much as possible and preserve the variety of semantic knowledge as much as possible. The diversity loss is designed by maximizing the standard deviation of the modality influence factors to enforce the KDEM better accumulate the diverse knowledge of visible and infrared modalities. Moreover, the consistency loss is also designed to preserve the semantic correlation of the generated new modality similar to visible and infrared modalities. Benefiting from imitating the cognitive process of the human brain, the proposed KDEM, the designed diversity loss, and the proposed consistency loss could effectively discover and integrate a variety of high distinguish semantic knowledge with the consist of preserving the semantic correlation among different modalities. The main contributions of this paper are summarized below:

**Firstly**, a Knowledge-driven Enhance Module (KDEM) is proposed to imitate the cognitive process of the human brain. It could discover and integrate the significant semantic pattern from cross-modality data and supervise the learning of common representation space.

**Secondly**, the designed diversity loss could effectively exclude redundant knowledge and preserve the variety of semantic knowledge as much as possible from cross-modality. Meanwhile, the consistency loss could also preserve the semantic correlation among different modalities.

**Thirdly**, the evaluation results on two popular VI-ReID datasets show the effectiveness of our proposed KDEM. Meanwhile, compared with the existing state-of-the-art baseline, our KDEM achieves better gain in terms of Rank-k accuracy and mAP.

## 2    Related Work

Given an image of a specific query person in one modality, i.e., a visible image or an infrared image, VI-ReID is a person re-identification task whose goal is to retrieve the query image's counterpart from a gallery set of another modality [19]. The wavelength difference between visible and infrared lights results in a semantic gap in the cross-modality [13]. Thus, extracting cross-modal invariant discriminative knowledge in an advisable way contributes significantly to the task of VI-ReID. Most of the existing VI-ReID methods can be generally divided into two categories. The first category focuses on learning the modality-shared feature representations and aggregating the specific visible and infrared feature representations for better performance. For example, Wu et al. [16] proposed a deep zero-padding network learning feature in a common space and constructed the first large-scale visible-infrared dataset named SYSU-MM01. Ye et al. [20] proposed a dual-path network and a bi-directional dual-constrained top-ranking loss. Moreover, this network was introduced to learn modality alignment feature representations. Park et al. [8] use dense alignment to gain modality-shared discriminating local features. The secondary category methods mainly compensate for the lack of each modality's information, such as GAN-based approaches. Wang et al. [12] leverage GANs to transfer stylistic properties of infrared images to their visible counterparts. In essence, the methods mentioned above aim to overcome the semantic gap and improve the robustness of the model.

## 3    Proposed Method

### 3.1    Overview

A dual-path deep neural network is designed for the VI-ReID, which learns the modality-specific feature representations and optimizes similarity metrics in an end-to-end manner [19]. The detailed architecture of our proposed method is shown in Fig. 2, which includes a feature extractor $f(\cdot)$, a classifier $c(\cdot)$, and a modality generator by the designed KDEM. The ResNet-50 [5] is utilized as the backbone for feature extracting, which includes a total of five stages of ResNet-50. The KDEM is designed to discover high discriminative semantic patterns from modality-specific feature representations, and integrate them into a new modality to supervise the network optimization. The KDEM, as shown in Fig. 2(b), is plugged after stage-0 of ResNet-50. Moreover, in order to avoid modeling unknown redundant knowledge and preserve the variety of semantic knowledge during the knowledge accumulation process, meanwhile, to preserve the semantic correlation among different modalities, a diversity loss and a consistency loss are designed and detail is shown in Fig. 2(c).

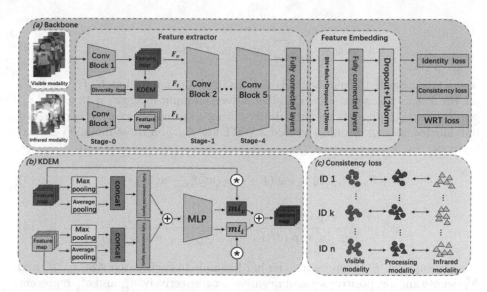

**Fig. 2.** (*a*) Illustration of our method. The visible and infrared modality features are mixed with KDEM to compose the feature of the transitional modality. The shared identity loss and WRT loss are enforced to help the model converge. (*b*) The detailed structure of KDEM. (*c*) The consistency loss is targeted at preserving the semantic correlation of the transitional modality similar to visible and infrared modalities. The circles and triangles represent the characteristic distribution of visible modality and infrared modality, respectively.

## 3.2   Feature Extractor

The modality-specific features of the data samples are extracted through the stage-0 of the network, in which the weights are not shared. Moreover, the modality-shared features of the three modalities are extracted by the remaining stages of the weights-sharing network. In the architecture, the data samples of $n$ visible and $n$ infrared of the same identity are combined into $n$ pairs in a mini-batch and fed into the network. For the sample pair $(x_v, x_i)$, their modality-specific features is obtained by the stage-0 of feature extractor: $F_v$ and $F_i$,

$$F_v = f_0(x_v) \, ; F_i = f_0(x_i) \tag{1}$$

$f_0(\cdot)$ represents the stage-0 of ResNet-50. $x_v$ and $x_i$ are data samples from visible and infrared modalities. The $F_v$ and $F_i$ are mixed in KDEM (in Sect. 3.3) for the purpose of obtaining the knowledge-driven modality feature $F_t$. Then, the feature representations of all the visible, infrared, and the knowledge-driven modality are fed into the following stage of the network. Furthermore, For each modality, the identity loss $\mathcal{L}_{id}$ and weight regularization triplets (WRT) loss $\mathcal{L}_{wrt}$ [19] are applied to help the model effectively converge.

$$\mathcal{L}_{id} = -\frac{1}{n} \sum_{i=1}^{n} \log \left( p \left( y_i \mid C(f(x_i)) \right) \right) \tag{2}$$

where $n$ represents the number of training samples in a mini-batch, $f(\cdot)$ and $c(\cdot)$ are the feature extractor and a classifier. Given an input image $x_i$ with a label $y_i$, $p(y_i | C(f(x_i)))$ represents the probability of that a sample $x_i$ is correctly classified into labeled class $y_i$. Besides, we add a WRT loss $\mathcal{L}_{wrt}$ on three-modality-shared features.

$$\mathcal{L}_{wrt}(i,j,k) = \log \left( 1 + \exp \left( w_i^p d_{ij}^p - w_i^n d_{ik}^n \right) \right) \tag{3}$$

$$w_{ij}^p = \frac{\exp \left( d_{ij}^p \right)}{\sum_{d_{ij}^p \in \mathcal{P}_i} \exp \left( d_{ij}^p \right)}, w_{ik}^n = \frac{\exp \left( -d_{ik}^n \right)}{\sum_{d_{ik}^n \in \mathcal{N}_i} \exp \left( -d_{ik}^n \right)} \tag{4}$$

The tuple $(i, j, k)$ represents the hard sample in each batch size. $i_y$, $\mathcal{P}_i$ and $\mathcal{N}_i$ denote anchor, positive set and negative set respectively. $d_{ij}^p$ and $d_{ik}^n$ represent the distance between anchor and the positive and negative samples, respectively.

### 3.3   Knowledge-Driven Enhance Module

In this section, we exceedingly elaborate on how the KDEM works. The modality-specific features $F_v$ and $F_i$ from stage-0 of the network are used as input for the KDEM, and synthesize the feature $F_p$ of knowledge-driven modality with the assistance of modality influence factors. As shown in Fig. 2($b$), the modality influence factors are obtained by the following formula:

$$\alpha = \delta \left( MLP \left( \sum_{m \in \{v,i\}} FC \left( [F_m^{avg}; F_m^{max}] \right) \right) \right) \tag{5}$$

$\delta$ is the binary softmax function. After the Average-pooling and Max-pooling operations on the $F_v$ and $F_i$, the features are concatenated for each modality. $[F_v^{avg}; F_v^{max}]$ and $[F_i^{avg}; F_i^{max}]$ are defined for the visible modality and infrared modality, respectively. The aforementioned two pooling operations are combined to exclude redundant knowledge. After the followed fully connected operations, these vectors are sent to MLP to calculate their influence factors.

Aforementioned procedures are designed to obtain the modality influence factors $\alpha = (mi_v, mi_i)$, where $mi_v + mi_i = 1$. $mi_v$ and $mi_i$ are the modality influence factors for the visible modality and the infrared modality, respectively. The feature of the knowledge-driven modality is obtained by mixing the visible and infrared modality-specific features with two modality influence factors. The feature of knowledge-driven modality $F_t$ is formulated by:

$$F_t = mi_v \cdot F_v + mi_i \cdot F_i \tag{6}$$

Here $F_v$ and $F_i$ are the modality-specific features from stage-0 of ResNet-50, which are obtained by Eq. 1. The synthesis of $F_t$ can represent the newly generated knowledge-driven. By using adaptive modality influence factors, a suitable knowledge-driven modality can be generated, which can help the model decrease the pressure of the modal-shared feature learning and accumulate high distinguish semantic knowledge of two completely different modalities. The knowledge-driven modality only exists in the training stage and is deleted in the test stage.

Additionally, the characteristic of the knowledge-driven modality should be diversified as much as possible so that the network can better accumulate knowledge from the two modalities. To this end, diversity loss is designed to enlarge the standard deviation of the two modality influence factors in a mini-batch. The diversity loss $L_{div}$ is defined as follows:

$$L_{div} = -[\phi(mi_v)_{i=1}^n + \phi(mi_i)_{i=1}^n] \qquad (7)$$

$n$ represents the number of training samples in a mini-batch. $\phi$ means calculating the standard deviation of the modality influence factors in a mini-batch. By minimizing $L_{div}$, the feature of the knowledge-driven modality becomes as diverse as possible, which can be more conducive to the knowledge-driven modality and modal-shared feature learning.

## 3.4    Consistency Loss

Features of the modeled knowledge-driven modality should maintain semantic similarity between visible and infrared modalities to avoid the accumulation of redundant knowledge. Thus, we propose a consistency loss, as shown in Fig. 2(c). For the features of the same identity, the feature distributional similarity between the knowledge-driven modality and the other two modalities should be preserved. The loss is as follows,

$$L_{con} = \frac{1}{n} \sum_{i=1}^n \sum_{m \in \{v,i\}} mi_m \cdot \|f(F_m) - f(F_t)\|_2 \qquad (8)$$

The modality influence factors $mi_m$ are the weights of the consistency loss function. $\|:\|_2$ is L2-norm which is used to measure the distance of features. $F_m$ is obtained by Eq. 1. $F_t$ is the feature of knowledge-driven modality and obtained in Eq. 6. The $f(\cdot)$ is the mapping from stage-1 to stage-4 of the backbone. The gradients of $L_{con}$ for feature $F_m$ and $F_p$ can be directly concluded as follows.

*Proof.* This subsection proves that $L_{con}$ can find the derivative.

$$\frac{\partial L_{con}}{\partial F_t} = \frac{\partial L_{con}}{\partial f(F_p)} \cdot \frac{\partial f(F_t)}{\partial F_t} \qquad (9)$$

$$= \{-2 \cdot mi_v \cdot [f(F_v) - f(F_t)] - 2 \cdot mi_i \cdot [f(F_i) - f(F_t)]\} \cdot f'(F_t)$$

$$= \{-2[mi_v \cdot f(F_v) + mi_i \cdot f(F_i) - f(F_t)]\} \cdot f'(F_t)$$

$$\frac{\partial L_{con}}{\partial F_m} = \frac{\partial L_{con}}{\partial f(F_m)} \cdot \frac{\partial f(F_m)}{\partial F_m} \tag{10}$$

$$= \{2 \cdot mi_m \cdot [f(F_m) - f(F_t)]\} \cdot f'(F_m)$$

### 3.5 Overall Training

The overall training loss $L_{all}$ is represented as follows:

$$\mathcal{L}_{all} = \lambda_1 \mathcal{L}_{id} + \lambda_2 \mathcal{L}_{wrt} + \lambda_3 \mathcal{L}_{div} + \lambda_4 \mathcal{L}_{con} \tag{11}$$

where $\lambda_1, \lambda_2$ , $\lambda_3$ and $\lambda_4$ are the weights of the overall loss function. The algorithm flow of KDEM are given in Algorithm 1

---

**Algorithm 1:** algorithm of KDEM.

**Input: Input:** Visible sample $x_v$ and infrared sample $x_i$ with their labels;
**Output: Output:** The trained feature extractor $f(\cdot)$ and classifier $c(\cdot)$;
1 **Initialization:** Initialize the network $f(\cdot)$ in ImageNet-pretrained ResNet-50, set iteration number *epoch*, learning rate and other hyper-parameters.
2 **for** $i = 1$ *to epoch* **do**
3    ·Use stage-0 of ResNet-50 to extract features $F_v$ and $F_i$ for the visible and infrared
4    modalities;
5    ·Calculate the knowledge-driven modality feature $F_p$ by Eq.6;
6    ·Feed forward the batch into the following network
7    ·Calculate the overall loss by Eq.11 .
8    ·Update the network $f(\cdot)$ and classifier $c(\cdot)$ by SGD to descending gradients of
9      Eq.11.
10   **end**
11 **end**
12 **Until** model convergence or the fixed *epoch*;

---

## 4    Experiments

### 4.1    Datasets and Settings

Two available datasets are used to evaluate the performance of our proposed KDEM: RegDB [3] and SYSU-MM01 [16]. The experiments follow the evaluation protocol as described in Ye et al. [19]. The RegDB dataset is divided into 206 training identities and 206 test identities, and the number of both visible and infrared images is ten for each identity. SYSU-MM01 is split into 395 identities and 96 identities. The former of each dataset is used for training, while the latter is used for testing.

The proposed method is implemented with PyTorch. Furthermore, the initial learning rate and optimization method are 0.1 and SGD. The $\lambda_1, \lambda_2$ and $\lambda_3$ from Eq. 11 are set to be 1 and $\lambda_4$ is set to be 0.1. The batch size for each modality is set to be eight on one single TITAN Xp GPU. The training epoch is set to be 80. The evaluation protocol adopts the Rank-1, 10, 20 accuracy, mean Average Precision (mAP), and mean Inverse Negative Penalty (mINP).

## 4.2   Comparison with State-of-the-Art Methods

As shown in Table 1 and Table 2, we made a objective comparison of our method with the state-of-the-art. The Rank-1, 10, 20 accuracy(%) and mean average precision (mAP)(%), and mean Inverse Negative Penalty (mINP)(%) are reported in each table.

**Table 1.** Comparison with the state-of-the-art methods on RegDB dataset.

| Method | Venue | Visible to infrared | | | | | Infrared to visible | | | | |
|---|---|---|---|---|---|---|---|---|---|---|---|
| | | Rank-1 | Rank-10 | Rank-20 | mAP | mINp | Rank-1 | Rank-10 | Rank-20 | mAP | mINp |
| BDTR [18] | IJCAI (2018) | 33.56 | 58.61 | 67.43 | 32.76 | – | 32.92 | 58.46 | 68.43 | 31.96 | – |
| D²RL [14] | CVPR (2019) | 43.4 | 66.1 | 76.3 | 44.1 | – | – | – | – | – | – |
| AlignGAN [13] | ICCV (2019) | 57.9 | – | – | 53.6 | – | 56.3 | – | – | 53.4 | – |
| Xmodal [6] | AAAI (2020) | 62.21 | 83.13 | 91.72 | 60.18 | – | – | – | – | – | – |
| DDAG [20] | ECCV (2020) | 69.34 | 86.19 | 91.49 | 63.46 | 49.24 | 68.06 | 85.15 | 90.31 | 61.80 | 48.62 |
| Hi-CMD [1] | CVPR (2020) | 70.93 | 86.39 | – | 66.04 | – | – | – | – | – | – |
| AGW [19] | TAPMI (2021) | 70.05 | 86.21 | 91.55 | 66.37 | 50.19 | 70.04 | 87.12 | 91.84 | 65.90 | 51.24 |
| FBP-AL [15] | TNNLS (2021) | 73.98 | **89.71** | **93.69** | 68.24 | – | 70.05 | **89.22** | **93.88** | 66.61 | – |
| cmAlign [8] | ICCV (2021) | 74.17 | – | – | 67.64 | – | 72.43 | – | – | 65.46 | – |
| KDEM (Ours) | – | **77.33** | 88.25 | 91.70 | **70.32** | **56.08** | **76.26** | 87.62 | 90.92 | **67.77** | **52.38** |

**Performance Analysis on RegDB.** The evaluation results on RegDB show that KDEM achieves the most advanced performance in terms of Rank-1 accuracy, mAP, and mINP. Although the FBP-AL [15] shows better results in terms of Rank-10, 20 accuracy, the FBP-AL [15] needs to segment the body structure additionally, which is not efficient for model training. Compared to cmAlign [8], under the test mode of Visible to Infrared, the performance of KDEM is improved by 3.16% and 2.68% in terms of Rank-1 and mAP, respectively. As for the test mode of Infrared to Visible, our KDEM can also increase by 3.83% and 2.31% in performance. The performance improvement indicates that our model can effectively reduce the semantic gap in cross modalities by the generated knowledge-driven modality.

**Performance Analysis on SYSU-MM01.** It can be seen from the Table 2 that KDEM achieves a new state-of-the-art performance on SYSU-MM01 in both all search and indoor search modes. Compared to cmAlign [8] in All search mode, our KDEM gains 2.68% and 1.38% in Rank-1 and mAP. As for the Indoor search, the performance of KDEM can also be improved by 3.72% and 1.97% on Rank-1

**Table 2.** Comparison with the state-of-the-art methods on SYSU-MM01 dataset.

| Method | Venue | All search | | | | | Indoor search | | | | |
|---|---|---|---|---|---|---|---|---|---|---|---|
| | | Rank-1 | Rank-10 | Rank-20 | mAP | mINp | Rank-1 | Rank-10 | Rank-20 | mAP | mINp |
| cmGAN [9] | IJCAI (2018) | 27.0 | 67.5 | 80.6 | 27.8 | – | 31.6 | 77.2 | 89.2 | 42.2 | – |
| D$^2$RL [14] | CVPR (2019) | 28.9 | 70.6 | 82.4 | 29.2 | – | – | – | – | – | – |
| AlignGAN [13] | ICCV (2019) | 42.40 | 85.0 | 93.7 | 40.7 | – | 45.9 | 87.6 | 94.4 | 54.3 | – |
| Xmodal [6] | AAAI (2020) | 49.92 | 89.79 | 95.96 | 50.73 | – | – | – | – | – | – |
| DDAG [20] | ECCV (2020) | 54.75 | 90.39 | 95.81 | 53.02 | 39.62 | 61.02 | 94.06 | 98.40 | 67.98 | 62.61 |
| Hi-CMD [1] | CVPR (2020) | 34.94 | 77.58 | – | 35.94 | – | – | – | – | – | – |
| AGW [19] | TAPMI (2021) | 47.50 | 84.39 | 62.14 | 47.65 | 35.30 | 54.17 | 91.14 | 95.98 | 62.97 | 59.23 |
| FBP-AL [15] | TNNLS (2021) | 54.14 | 86.04 | 93.03 | 50.20 | – | – | – | – | – | – |
| cmAlign [8] | ICCV (2021) | 55.41 | – | – | 54.14 | – | 58.46 | – | – | 66.33 | – |
| KDEM (Ours) | – | **58.09** | **91.19** | **96.63** | **55.52** | **40.69** | **62.18** | **94.38** | **98.64** | **68.30** | **64.11** |

and mAP. The class activation mapping [11] of our model is shown in Fig. 3. We can notice that our model mainly focuses on cross-modal invariant features, such as the face, clothing logos, backpacks, and gait, which are significant or noticeable indicators of one pedestrian's identity.

## 4.3  Ablation Study

Ablation experiments are performed on the RegDB dataset to verify the effectiveness of KDEM. As shown in Table 3, superior results have been achieved by the proposed KDEM, diversity loss, and consistency loss. A remarkable improvement in performance is obtained by KDEM, which shows that the KDEM can effectively overcome the cross-modal semantic gap by accumulating the high distinguish knowledge from cross modalities. Moreover, the improvement of the loss functions is prominent. The diversity loss can help the model accumulate diverse knowledge and exclude redundant knowledge of visible and infrared modalities. The consistency loss aims to preserve the distribution and semantic similarity between the knowledge-driven modality and the other modalities. Both of $L_{div}$ and $L_{con}$ achieved good results.

**Table 3.** Ablation study on RegDB dataset.

| Baseline | KDEM | $L_{div}$ | $L_{con}$ | Rank-1 | Rank-10 | Rank-20 | mAP | mINP |
|---|---|---|---|---|---|---|---|---|
| √ | – | – | – | 70.05 | 86.21 | 91.55 | 66.37 | 50.19 |
| √ | √ | – | – | 73.69 | 86.84 | 91.61 | 68.36 | 54.59 |
| √ | √ | √ | – | 76.41 | 87.55 | 91.68 | 69.40 | 54.85 |
| √ | √ | – | √ | 75.29 | 87.33 | 91.65 | 69.08 | 55.19 |
| √ | √ | √ | √ | **77.33** | **88.25** | **91.70** | **70.32** | **56.08** |

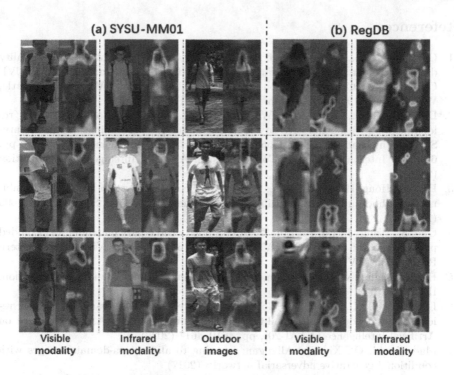

**(a) SYSU-MM01**        **(b) RegDB**

| Visible | Infrared | Outdoor | Visible | Infrared |
| modality | modality | images | modality | modality |

**Fig. 3.** Class activation mapping of our model. It can be seen that our model focuses on the cross-modal invariant image region. Images from each row are from the same identity.

## 5  Conclusion

This paper proposes a Knowledge-driven Enhance Module (KDEM) to tackle the problem of VI-ReID, which can help the model to accumulate transitional natural knowledge. From a novel perspective, our proposed KDEM can generate an appropriate knowledge-driven modality to better bridge the visible and infrared modalities. The distribution of knowledge-driven modality is modified by two modality influence factors generated by KDEM. With the proposed knowledge-driven modality, we propose the diversity loss to make the modality as diverse as possible and retain the complete helpful information of the original data. Moreover, we propose a consistency loss to promote the similarity between knowledge-driven modality and the other two modalities. With the assistance of KDEM, semantic gap can be narrowed. The effectiveness of our method in shown in ample experiments.

**Acknowledgment.** This work was supported by the Fundamental Research Funds for the Central Universities (SWU-KT22032).

# References

1. Choi, S., Lee, S., Kim, Y., Kim, T., Kim, C.: Hi-cmd: hierarchical cross-modality disentanglement for visible-infrared person re-identification. In: 2020 IEEE/CVF Conference on Computer Vision and Pattern Recognition, CVPR 2020, Seattle, WA, USA, 13–19 June 2020, pp. 10254–10263. IEEE (2020)
2. Dai, P., Ji, R., Wang, H., Wu, Q., Huang, Y.: Cross-modality person re-identification with generative adversarial training. In: Proceedings of the Twenty-Seventh International Joint Conference on Artificial Intelligence, IJCAI-18, pp. 677–683. International Joint Conferences on Artificial Intelligence Organization (2018)
3. Dat, N., Hong, H., Ki, K., Kang, P.: Person recognition system based on a combination of body images from visible light and thermal cameras. Sensors 17(3), 605 (2017)
4. Gao, S., Wang, J., Lu, H., Liu, Z.: Pose-guided visible part matching for occluded person reid. In: 2020 IEEE/CVF Conference on Computer Vision and Pattern Recognition (CVPR) (2020)
5. He, K., Zhang, X., Ren, S., Sun, J.: Deep residual learning for image recognition. IEEE (2016)
6. Li, D., Wei, X., Hong, X., Gong, Y.: Infrared-visible cross-modal person re-identification with an x modality. In: The Thirty-Fourth AAAI Conference on Artificial Intelligence (AAAI-20), pp. 4610–4617 (2020)
7. Mao, X., Li, Q., Xie, H.: Aligngan: learning to align cross-domain images with conditional generative adversarial networks (2017)
8. Park, H., Lee, S., Lee, J., Ham, B.: Learning by aligning: visible-infrared person re-identification using cross-modal correspondences (2021)
9. Pingyang, D., Ji, R., Wang, H., Wu, Q., Huang, Y.: Cross-modality person re-identification with generative adversarial training, pp. 677–683 (2018)
10. Pu, N., Chen, W., Liu, Y., Bakker, E.M., Lew, M.S.: Dual Gaussian-Based Variational Subspace Disentanglement for Visible-Infrared Person Re-Identification, pp. 2149–2158. Association for Computing Machinery, New York, NY, USA (2020)
11. Selvaraju, R.R., Cogswell, M., Das, A., Vedantam, R., Parikh, D., Batra, D.: Grad-cam: visual explanations from deep networks via gradient-based localization. In: IEEE International Conference on Computer Vision (2017)
12. Wang, G.A., Yang, T., Cheng, J., Chang, J., Liang, X., Hou, Z.: Cross-modality paired-images generation for rgb-infrared person re-identification. In: Proceedings of the AAAI Conference on Artificial Intelligence (2020)
13. Wang, G., Zhang, T., Cheng, J., Liu, S., Yang, Y., Hou, Z.: Rgb-infrared cross-modality person re-identification via joint pixel and feature alignment. In: 2019 IEEE/CVF International Conference on Computer Vision, ICCV 2019, Seoul, Korea (South), October 27 - November 2 2019, pp. 3622–3631. IEEE (2019)
14. Wang, Z., Wang, Z., Zheng, Y., Chuang, Y.Y., Satoh, S.: Learning to reduce dual-level discrepancy for infrared-visible person re-identification. In: 2019 IEEE/CVF Conference on Computer Vision and Pattern Recognition (CVPR) (2019)
15. Wei, Z., Yang, X., Wang, N., Gao, X.: Flexible body partition-based adversarial learning for visible infrared person re-identification. IEEE Trans. Neural Netw. Learn. Syst. 1–12 (2021)
16. Wu, A., Zheng, W.S., Yu, H.X., Gong, S., Lai, J.: Rgb-infrared cross-modality person re-identification. In: 2017 IEEE International Conference on Computer Vision (ICCV) (2017)

17. Xu, X., Wu, S., Liu, S., Xiao, G.: Cross-modal based person re-identification via channel exchange and adversarial learning. In: Mantoro, T., Lee, M., Ayu, M.A., Wong, K.W., Hidayanto, A.N. (eds.) ICONIP 2021. LNCS, vol. 13108, pp. 500–511. Springer, Cham (2021). https://doi.org/10.1007/978-3-030-92185-9_41

18. Ye, M., Lan, X., Wang, Z., Yuen, P.C.: Bi-directional center-constrained top-ranking for visible thermal person re-identification. IEEE Trans. Inf. Forensics Secur. **15**, 407–419 (2020)

19. Ye, M., Shen, J., Lin, G., Xiang, T., Hoi, S.: Deep learning for person re-identification: a survey and outlook. IEEE Trans. Pattern Anal. Mach. Intell. **44**(6), 2872–2893 (2021)

20. Ye, M., Shen, J., J. Crandall, D., Shao, L., Luo, J.: Dynamic dual-attentive aggregation learning for visible-infrared person re-identification. In: Vedaldi, A., Bischof, H., Brox, T., Frahm, J.-M. (eds.) ECCV 2020. LNCS, vol. 12362, pp. 229–247. Springer, Cham (2020). https://doi.org/10.1007/978-3-030-58520-4_14

# A New Model for Artificial Intuition

Marcello Trovati[1]($\boxtimes$) (iD), Olayinka Johnny[1] (iD), Xiaolong Xu[2] (iD),
and Nikolaos Polatidis[3] (iD)

[1] Department of Computer Science, Edge Hill University,
Ormskirk, UK
`trovatim@edgehill.ac.uk`
[2] Jiangsu Key Laboratory of Big Data Security and Intelligent Processing,
Nanjing University of Posts and Telecommunications, Nanjing 210023, China
[3] School of Architecture Technology and Engineering, University of Brighton,
Brighton, UK

**Abstract.** The ability to inform and facilitate data-driven decisions is at
the core of Data Science, AI, and general Machine Learning techniques.
To achieve this, all possible scenarios must be considered, and their outcomes must be assessed logically and systematically to obtain accurate
and applicable methods for knowledge discovery. There is compelling evidence from the cognitive sciences that intuition plays an important role
in intelligence extraction and the associated decision-making process. As
a consequence, the embedding of Artificial Intuition within AI would
provide novel ways to identify and process information.

**Keywords:** Artificial intuition · Artificial intelligence · Network
theory · Decision algorithms

## 1 Introduction

Artificial Intuition is becoming an increasingly relevant area in Computer Science as it could potentially lead to more efficient and fast problem-solving and
decision-making approaches [4]. Artificial Intuition is the ability of a system
to assess a problem context and identify novel links among the corresponding
knowledge components to facilitate the decision process in an automated manner. Furthermore, intuition is dependent on past knowledge and experience for
better recall of solutions to the given problems or normal logical process [2].
In this work, Artificial Creativity and Artificial Intuition refer to different, yet
overlapping concepts. The former is associated with the automated creation and
design of artefacts, objects, ideas, etc. which are regarded as (primarily) cre-
atively 'beautiful'. They could, of course, be useful and have various applications.
On the other hand, Artificial Intuition involves the automated identification of
innovative solutions.

In this article, a rigorous approach to artificial intuition is proposed. The
aim is to facilitate a comprehensive theory and subsequent implementations of

The authors declare that they have no conflict of interest.

Artificial Intuition to provide a better decision system, which mimics the agile and efficient intuitive processes extensively used by human agents.

The structure of the article is as follows: in Sect. 2, the state-of-the-art technology, methods and approaches of Artificial Intuition are presented and discussed, and Sect. 3 focuses on the necessary background information, which is at the core of the approach introduced in this article. Sections 4 and 5 provide the details of the Artificial Intuition model, and its development with respect to a decision system. The experimental evaluation is discussed in Sects. 6 and 6.2. Finally, Sect. 7 concludes the article and prompts future research directions.

## 2 Related Work

The multi-disciplinary nature of Artificial Intuition is reflected by the extensive research carried out in several fields, such as Neuroscience, Business, Psychology and Computer Science, to name but a few.

In [4], a computational model of artificial intuition and decision making is discussed, which is achieved via the recognition of significant patterns and properties that are made available by prior knowledge and experience, given the domain of the problem.

From a cognitive research perspective, [9] presents a descriptive research on managerial decision-making and problem solving where insights into the nature of intuition are provided. It is argued that business executives who focus on real-time information aided by intuition, can react quickly and accurately to changing stimuli in their firm or its environment. Even though the available data is limited, executives who based their decision policies on real-time information were also most frequently described as being intuitive.

In [5], the authors have identified two fundamental and distinct modes of intuition based decision-making and reasoning, which are labelled as *System 1* (intuition) and *System 2* (logical reasoning). System 1 is an automated, fast and often unconscious way of thinking. It is autonomous and efficient, requiring little energy or attention and is dependent on some known information. System 2 is an effortful, slow and deliberately controlled way of thinking. Despite System 1 is likely to be affected by models of pattern recognition, System 2 is based on rational choices where humans use logic in its best sense to perform a cost/benefit analysis that will provide the best possible choice. Studies have shown that human beings do not have the natural ability to perform more than one cognitive process at the same time, hence it is argued that System 2 (rational and logic based reasoning) is less significant than System 1 (subconsciousness and intuition) [11]. However, this requires the agent/human to acquire considerable skills and experiences over a specific time period.

## 3 General Definitions and Background

The problems (or scenarios) which need to be assessed to reach a given solution will be referred to as *queries*.

**Definition 1.** *A* query *is a collection of semantically-linked concepts, which defines the main scenario or objective to be assessed. The* solution of a query *is a set of paths linking the query with suitably identified concepts.*
*The concepts at the end of a path connected to a query are called the* query leaf nodes.

Knowledge must be at the core of any Artificial Intuition approach, and the model proposed in this article will be based on three different types of knowledge as introduced in Definition 2.

**Definition 2.** *We define*

- Existing knowledge *as the information associated with specific and well-known (prior) knowledge,*
- Intuitive knowledge *as the information associated with more general (and potentially overlapping) knowledge, which might complement the above,*
- Contextualised knowledge *as the information associated with individual experience and knowledge, if applicable.*

In this section, we shall describe the main mathematical concepts and algorithms, which will be evaluated and assessed in Sect. 6.

## 3.1 Network Theory

Let $G = G(V, E)$ be an undirected network, where $V = \{v_i\}_{i=1}^n$ is the *node set* and $E = \{e_{w_{i,j}}(v_i, v_j)\}_{v_i \neq v_j \in V}$ is the *edge set*. Note that each edge $e_{w_{i,j}}(v_i, v_j)$ is weighted by the parameter $w_{i,j} \in (0, 1]$, which is related to the type of relationship linking the two nodes $v_i$ and $v_j$. We say that two nodes are *adjacent* if they are connected by an edge, and two edges are *incident* if they have a node in common. We define a *path* $P(v_a, v_b)$ between two nodes $v_a$ and $v_b$ a sequences of incident edges

$$e_{w_{a,k_1}}(v_a, v_{k_1}), e_{w_{k_1,k_2}}(v_{k_1}, v_{k_2}), \ldots, e_{w_{k_{n-1},k_n}}(v_{k_{n-1}}, v_{k_n}), e_{w_{k_n,b}}(v_{k_n}, v_b)$$

joining the two nodes. Note that if a network is not acyclic, then more than a path might exist between any two nodes.
In this article, as discussed in Definition 2, we shall consider the network generated by the union of three (usually overlapping) following networks

$$G = G_k \cup G_i \cup G_c \tag{1}$$

where

- $G_k$ is the (semantic) network associated with existing knowledge within a specific setting,
- $G_i$ is the (semantic) network associated with intuitive knowledge and
- $G_c$ is the (semantic) network associated with contextualised knowledge.

As discussed above, each node is associated with a specific concept and the overall topology of the network $G$ governs the way information is propagated across the network. More specifically, the overall information captured by the above (union of) networks must include

- The (perceived) probability of occurrence of each concept,
- Types of relationships associated with each edge, and
- Influence weight of each of them, which loosely speaking refers to the 'strength' of the corresponding relation.

## 4   Description of the Model

The mutual interactions within knowledge systems can be efficiently described as networks, where concepts correspond to nodes, linked by suitably defined edges. These contain the relevant information on the relationships joining any two nodes, which is assume to include the observed, estimated, or defined level of influence, as formalised in Definition 3.

**Definition 3.** *Each edge joining two nodes* $x, y \in V$ *has an associated* activation value $\alpha(x, y) \in (0, 1]$, *which is associated with the influence that* $x$ *exerts on* $y$.

In this article, the activation value is deliberately defined in general terms. In fact, it should be learnt automatically based on the topology and the properties of the overall knowledge system. Future research will focus on a more comprehensive and robust investigation of its properties. The concepts and their mutual relations within a query are identified either manually, or via automated methods. In this article, only the former will be considered. This will create a semantic network which will be embedded into a suitably defined network generated by the corresponding existing, intuitive and contextualised knowledge. The topology of such network will be subsequently used to identify novel and potentially innovative solutions to a given query.

Each node $v \in V$ will be associated with a value $p(v) \in (0, 1]$. This can be interpreted as the (observed) probability of occurrence of the corresponding concept, which might refer to an actual or estimated assessment. Note that probability is closely related to the concept of information. In this article, the level of information captured by a node is regarded by its (observed) probability of occurrence. The authors are aware that this might not be appropriate in all theoretical scenarios. However, in line with this work, such distinction is deemed not to be significant. In the following definition, the *information propagation* will be introduced, which will be explicitly formulated in the following sections.

**Definition 4.** *The information propagation* $I(x, y)$ *between two nodes* $x$ *and* $y \in V$ *is defined as a map*

$$I : V \times V \to [0, 1]. \tag{2}$$

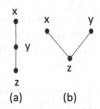

**Fig. 1.** Two simple networks as discussed in Sect. 4.1.

An important observation is that the information propagation from $x$ to $y$ might not necessarily coincide with the (observed) probability of $y$. Therefore, we define the *post node probability* of a node $v$ with respect to one of its neighbours $w$ as

$$\tilde{p}(v) = \min\{I(w,v), p(v)\}, \tag{3}$$

where $p(v)$ is the (observed) probability of $v$.

## 4.1  Combination of Edge Attributes

The information propagated along the edges feeds into the nodes in the corresponding paths. However, their topology can be interpreted in different ways. Consider, for example Fig. 1 which depicts two very simple networks consisting of 3 nodes, namely $x, y$ and $z$. These simple configurations might be associated with the following possibilities:

- Both $x$ and $y$ directly influence $z$, as depicted by Fig. 1(a). In other words, they need to co-exist in order to have $z$.
- Fig. 1(b) depicts a cumulative influence of $x$ and $y$ on $z$.

The above cases are formally written as

$$x \oplus y \to z \tag{4}$$

$$x \odot y \to z \tag{5}$$

$$x \not\leftrightarrow y \to z, \tag{6}$$

where '$\oplus$', '$\odot$' and '$\not\leftrightarrow$' refer to the disjoint, joint as information independence relationships. Note that the above expressions also include '$\to z$'. This refers (with a slight abuse of notation) to the fact that we are considering the information propagation of the nodes $x$ and $y$ into the node $z$. This notation will be dropped when such influence does not need to be emphasised.

**Lemma 1.** *Let $x$ and $y$ be two nodes. Then*

$$x \oplus y \to z \equiv x \not\leftrightarrow y \to z$$

*if either $I(x,z) = 1$, or $I(y,z) = 1$*

*Proof.* This is can be easily observed from the above. In fact, is the disjoint relationship yields the same influence on $z$ as the information independence, then either the influence propagation $I(x, z) = 1$, or $I(y, z) = 1$.    □

## 4.2   Explicit Calculation of the Edge Attributes

Since the activation value associated with each edge joining two nodes $x$ and $y$ governs the information propagation, it will be an important parameter in the explicit formulation of Eqs. 4 and 5.

More specifically, for three nodes $x, y, z$ we define $x \odot y (\rightarrow z)$ as

$$x \odot y = p(x)p(y)W_{x,y}W_{y,z},   \tag{7}$$

where

$$W_{x,y} = \tanh\left(\frac{k\,\alpha(x, y)}{2}\right),   \tag{8}$$

where the choice of $k$ depends on the required steepness of $W_{x,y}$. In this article, we shall assume that $k = 4$. Equation 8 is motivated by the sigmoid activation function widely used in Artificial Neural Networks [4].

Similarly, the disjoint relationship operation $x \oplus y \rightarrow z$ is defined as

$$x \oplus y = \begin{cases} p(x)W_{x,z} + p(y)W_{y,z}, & \text{if } p(x)W_{x,z} + p(y)W_{y,z} \leq 1 \\ 1, & \text{otherwise.} \end{cases}   \tag{9}$$

Finally, we define the information independence relationship operation as

$$x \not\rightarrow y = \max\{p(x)W_{x,z}, p(y)W_{y,z}\}   \tag{10}$$

## 5   The Assessment of Potential Solutions

In this work a solution is assumed to be based on the paths joining a set of nodes starting from a query and connecting all its neighbouring concepts. However, any such path needs to be assessed to determine whether it provides a viable solution.

Loosely speaking, an intuitive problem-solving process focuses on finding *different paths* to a solution, which might lead to a better solution compared to a 'conventional' one. In this section we will address the assessment and identification of the most suitable set of solutions via the *intuition* and *propagation indices*. In the rest of this section, for brevity we shall refer to a path $P(x_1, x_n) = \bigodot_{i=1}^{n} x_i$ as a vector $\underline{x} = [x_1, \ldots, x_n]$.

### 5.1   Intuition Index

Recall that knowledge is associated with the union of three different (knowledge) networks

$$G = G_k \cup G_i \cup G_c   \tag{11}$$

where

- $G_k$ is the (semantic) network associated with existing (prior) knowledge within a specific setting,
- $G_i$ is the (semantic) network associated with intuitive knowledge and
- $G_c$ is the (semantic) network associated with contextualised knowledge.

We can assume that a 'conventional' solution is embedded in $G_k$.

**Definition 5.** *We define the* innovation index *between the nodes $x_s$ and $x_e$ following the path $\underline{x}$, as*

$$i(\underline{x}) = \frac{|E(G \setminus G_k)(\underline{x})|}{|E_p(G)(\underline{x})|}, \tag{12}$$

*where $E_p(G \setminus G_k)(\underline{x})$ and $E(G)(\underline{x})$ are the set of edges in $G \setminus G_k$ (that is the edges not in the 'common' knowledge) and the set of edges in $G$ for a path $\underline{x}$ between the nodes $x_s$ and $x_e$, respectively.*

Hence, based on Eq. 12, the overall innovation index between the nodes $x_s$ and $x_e$, assuming there are $n$ paths between them is

$$i(x_s, x_e) = \frac{1}{n} \sum_{j=1}^{n} i_{\underline{x}_j} \tag{13}$$

### 5.2  Propagation Index

As discussed in Sect. 4.2, the information is propagated based on specific rules, such as Eq. 7 and more specifically, Eq. 8. We define the *propagation index* associated with a path $\underline{x}$ as

$$\alpha(\underline{x}) = \prod_{x_i \in \underline{x}} \alpha(x_i). \tag{14}$$

The propagation index simply estimates how well information can spread along a specific path $\underline{x}$ and it will be used in conjunction with the innovation index to assess the suitability of paths related to a solution.

### 5.3  Edge Entropy

A network with very strong edge relations is optimal for reasoning as information is propagated more reliably and as such, the corresponding scenario can be modelled more efficiently. Therefore, we can use the concept of entropy to explore and assess how well a network with respect to a specific query-concept can be used to reason and find a solution. Note that high entropy values are also associated with very sparse networks. However, this corresponds to a trivial case, which will not be discussed in this article.

**Definition 6.** *Let $\underline{x}_t$ be a path at time $t$ that is a sequence of incident edges $x_{i_1}, x_{i_2}, \ldots, x_{i_t}$. We define its entropy $H(\underline{x}_t)$ as*

$$H(\underline{x}_t) = -\alpha(\underline{x}_t) \log \alpha(\underline{x}_t). \tag{15}$$

*The overall entropy from $x_s$ is given by*

$$H(x_s) = -\sum_{j=1}^{k} \alpha(\underline{x}_t^j) \log \alpha(\underline{x}_t^j), \tag{16}$$

*for all the paths $\underline{x}_t^1, \ldots, \underline{x}_t^k$ originating from $x_s$.*

The concept of entropy defined in Definition 6 will be used as an exploratory tool to assess whether a specific query (defined by one or more concepts) can be investigated based on a specific (knowledge) network and determine viable solutions. In other words, this will allow us to identify:

- Whether a given network can be used to identify one or more solutions from a query;
- How far we need to navigate into the network (by following paths originating from the query/concepts) to obtain a feasible solution.

It is straightforward to prove the following lemma.

**Lemma 2.** *Let $H(x_s)$ be defined as in Eq. 16. If $\alpha(\underline{x}_t^j) = 1/e$ for all the paths $\underline{x}_t^1, \ldots, \underline{x}_t^k$ originating from $x_s$, then $H(x_s)$ is at its maximum value.*

The rest of the section will focus on defining a discovery algorithm to identify the best solution(s) for a query. The aim is to approximate the value of the entropy of the different paths, which are incrementally expanded during the discovery process as per the iteration time $t$. This will allow to automatically assess the most appropriate solution based on the edge properties of the corresponding paths.

As discussed above, it is clear that the best outcome in assessing a path $\underline{x}$ is when all the edges are associated with an activation index equal, or very close to 1. Let $0 \leq \epsilon \leq 1$ and consider the values of $H(\underline{x})$ for $\alpha(\underline{x}) = 1 - \epsilon$. In other words, $\epsilon$ can be regarded as a perturbation of $\alpha(\underline{x})$ for values close to 1.

**Proposition 1.** *Let $0 \leq \epsilon_i \leq 1$ for $i = 1, \ldots, k$. We have that the entropy of the path $\underline{x}_k$ is*

$$H(x_s) = \sum_{i=1}^{k} H(\underline{x}_t^i) \approx \sum_{i=1}^{k} \left( \epsilon_i - \frac{\epsilon_i^2}{2} - \frac{\epsilon_i^3}{6} - \frac{\epsilon_i^4}{12} - \frac{\epsilon_i^5}{20} \right) \tag{17}$$

$$\leq k \left( \bar{\epsilon} - \frac{\bar{\epsilon}^2}{2} - \frac{\bar{\epsilon}^3}{6} - \frac{\bar{\epsilon}^4}{12} - \frac{\bar{\epsilon}^5}{20} \right) \text{ where } \bar{\epsilon} = \max_{i=1}^{k} \{\epsilon_i\}.$$

*Proof.* The above can be obtained via Taylor's expansion of $x \log x$ at $x = 0.5$ and by substituting $x = 1/2 - \epsilon$, namely

$$\sum_{n \geq 2} \frac{(-1)^{1+n} 2^{-1+n} (-0.5 + \epsilon)^n}{(-1 + n)n} + (\epsilon - 0.5)(\log(2) - 1) + \frac{\log(2)}{2} \qquad (18)$$

Therefore, for all the paths discovered at time $t$, which originate at the node $x_1$, the result follows from Eq. 16.                                                                  □

Note that if $\bar{\epsilon}$ is close to 0, then all the $\epsilon_i$ are also close to 0. When this happens, we say that the query has a *strong solution space* at time $t$.

Based on Definition 6, the overall entropy can be used to explore the query space. From Lemma 2, we therefore need to consider the entropy in the interval $[1/e, 1]$, which is equivalent to having $\alpha_k > 1/(ke)$

---

**Algorithm 1** Solution Assessment

---
1: Let $t = 1$ and $D \leq 1$ be the threshold for the maximum entropy
2: Let $\underline{x}_t$ be a path connecting a query concept with one of its leaves leaf($\underline{x}$)
3: **for** path $\underline{x}$ **do**
4:     **if** $\alpha(\underline{x}_t) \geq 1/(t\,e)$ **and** $H(\underline{x}_t) \leq D$ **then**
5:         Continue
6:     **else**
7:         Stop
8:     **end if**
9:     **if** $\underline{x}_t! =$ leaf($\underline{x}$) **then**
10:         $t = t + 1$
11:     **else**
12:         Stop
13:     **end if**
14: **end for**
15: **return** path $\underline{x}_t, H(\underline{x}_t)$

---

Algorithm 1 returns a path $\underline{x}_t$ and its entropy based on a query. However, it does not guarantee to identify the shortest path between the concept and leaf nodes which, based on the different parameters associated with the path, might not be reached by $x_t$. Despite such limitations, Algorithm 1 formalises an effective exploratory tool to assess a query. This will be further discussed in Sect. 6.2.

# 6    Experimental Results

This section presents an evaluation of the method introduced in this article based on semantic networks, generated by ConceptNet [6] and Wikipedia [7] as a corpus. Section 6.1 provides a description of their use in the context of this article [8].

## 6.1   ConceptNet and Wikipedia Datasets

ConceptNet is a semantic network of knowledge that consist of assertions of common sense knowledge encompassing the spatial, physical, social, temporal, and psychological aspects of everyday life. ConceptNet consists of information collected from many sources, including expert created resources and open Mind Common Sense corpus [6], a crowd-sourced knowledge project.

In this article, ConceptNet is used to identify suitable semantic networks as part of the validation process, via the following steps:

1. Identify specific concepts contained in a query;
2. Extract the relevant network defined by the main concepts related to the query and mutual relationships;
3. Merge the network with any other (semantic) network previously defined;
4. Navigate across the network to discover knowledge related to the query.

An important decision to make when building a knowledge graph from ConceptNet, is on what a node should represent, as this has significant effects on the graph that is retrieved and how the graph is used. Moreover, it also has implications on making linking and importing other resources non-trivial, as different resources are associated with different decisions about their representation [10]. Statements contain concepts, which are linked by a positive or negative weight. The higher values of the weights, the more likely that the assertion is reliable and true. On the other hand, a negative weight implies that the assertion may not be true [10].

Wikipedia is a multilingual online encyclopaedia created and maintained as an open collaboration project by a community of volunteer editors using a wiki-based editing system [7]. It is the largest and most popular general reference work on the World Wide Web and it features exclusively free content. SpaCy [1] was used to build an appropriate graph representation of knowledge from Wikipedia pages. See [12] for more technical details used in this work.

## 6.2   Evaluation Details

The validation process presented in this article, focuses on a query 'weather forecast'. We retrieved the assertions associated with the following concepts: *weather, rain, rainfall, wind, temperature, cloud, cloudy, modelling, maths, statistics, sunshine, hot_weather, weather_forecast, weather_prediction predict_rainfall, wind_forecast, maths_statistics.*

More specifically, a total of 5495 relations from ConceptNet database were extracted. The lowest weight in the relations retrieved was 0.1 while the highest weight was 10.472. We noticed there were some repeating assertions which are due to data originating from various sources. In this work, this issue was addressed by ignoring all assertions with weight less than 1. The weights were subsequently normalised and grouped into 10 discrete categories

$$[0, 0.1), [0.1, 0.2), \ldots [0.9, 1].$$

This query identified the concepts: *aircraft, climate change, statistics* and *cattle*, as shown in Table 1. Note that despite a low propagation index for *aircraft*, its innovation index is the highest. Interestingly, aircraft technology does contribute to weather forecast [3], despite not been fully captured in the dataset created for this validation. This suggests that using aircraft for weather forecast is a novel and intuitive solution with respect to the knowledge related to this context.

**Table 1.** The validation results as discussed in Sect. 6.2

|  | Path length | Propagation Index | Innovation Index |
|---|---|---|---|
| Aircraft | 9 | 0.077 | 0.72 |
| Climate Change | 5 | 0.39 | 0.63 |
| Statistics | 3 | 0.64 | 0.39 |
| Cattle | 11 | 0.20 | 0.45 |

The validation discussed in this section has demonstrated the potential of this approach introduced in this article. In fact, this is far from being a comprehensive evaluation due to some obvious reasons. First of all, innovative and novel solutions can be complex to precisely pinpoint as this would require a manual comparison based on data that is currently either limited or non existent. Furthermore, ConceptNet and Wikipedia do not offer full semantic properties to create a fully implementable semantic network for artificial intuition.

## 7    Conclusion

Despite artificial intuition has drawn considerable attention from the research community, there has been limited effort in the creation of defining and investigating its mathematical concepts and properties. This work has addressed this by introducing a rigorous model to model and implement artificial intuition. The preliminary experimental results demonstrate the potential of this approach and motivate further work in this field. More specifically, future research will focus on a comprehensive mathematical analysis of the dynamical and algebraic properties of information aggregation and propagation. This will provide an in-depth analysis critical aspects and properties which can be applied to artificial intuition and its integration with AI systems. Furthermore, a collaborative research effort will focus on the creation a large (semantic) dataset to complement and enhance the state-of-the-art data, which is currently available. This will enable a more comprehensive evaluation tools as well as training datasets to automatically identify some of the most important parameters related to artificial intuition.

# References

1. Choi, J.D., Tetreault, J., Stent, A.: It depends: Dependency parser comparison using a web-based evaluation tool. In: Proceedings of the 53rd Annual Meeting of the Association for Computational Linguistics and the 7th International Joint Conference on Natural Language Processing (Volume 1: Long Papers), pp. 387–396. Association for Computational Linguistics, Beijing, China (2015). https://doi.org/10.3115/v1/P15-1038. https://www.aclweb.org/anthology/P15-1038
2. Dundas, J., Chik, D.: Implementing human-like intuition mechanism in artificial intelligence. ArXiv abs/1106.5917 (2011)
3. Hewage, P., Behera, A., Trovati, M., Pereira, E., Ghahremani, M., Palmieri, F., Liu, Y.: Temporal convolutional neural (TCN) network for an effective weather forecasting using time-series data from the local weather station. Soft. Comput. **24**(21), 16453–16482 (2020). https://doi.org/10.1007/s00500-020-04954-0
4. Johnny, O., Trovati, M., Ray, J.: Towards a computational model of artificial intuition and decision making. In: Barolli, L., Nishino, H., Miwa, H. (eds.) INCoS 2019. AISC, vol. 1035, pp. 463–472. Springer, Cham (2020). https://doi.org/10.1007/978-3-030-29035-1_45
5. Kahneman, D., Frederick, S.: Representativeness revisited: attribute substitution in intuitive judgment. In: T. Gilovich, D. Griffin, D. Kahneman (eds.) Heuristics & Biases: The Psychology of Intuitive Judgment, pp. 49–81. Cambridge University Press, New York (2002)
6. Liu, H., Singh, P.: Conceptnet – a practical commonsense reasoning tool-kit. BT Technol. J. **22**(4), 211–226 (2004). https://doi.org/10.1023/B:BTTJ.0000047600.45421.6d. http://portal.acm.org/citation.cfm?id=1031373
7. McNeill, A.: A corpus of learner errors: making the most of a database. In: Flowerdew and A. Tong (eds.), pp. 114–125 (1994)
8. Olayinka, J., Marcello, T.: Knowledge-based networks for artificial intuition. In: Advances in Intelligent Networking and Collaborative Systems - The 12th International Conference on Intelligent Networking and Collaborative Systems (INCoS-2020) (2020)
9. Simon, H.: Making management decisions: the role of intuition and emotion. Acad. Manag. Exec. **1**(1), 57–64 (1987)
10. Speer, R., Havasi, C.: Representing general relational knowledge in ConceptNet 5. In: Proceedings of the Eighth International Conference on Language Resources and Evaluation (LREC'12), pp. 3679–3686. European Language Resources Association (ELRA), Istanbul, Turkey (2012)
11. Stanovich, K.E., West, R.F.: Individual differences in reasoning: implications for the rationality debate? Behav. Brain Sci. **23**(5), 645–665 (2000). https://doi.org/10.1017/S0140525X00003435
12. Trovati, M., Hayes, J., Palmieri, F., Bessis, N.: Automated extraction of fragments of bayesian networks from textual sources. Appl. Soft Comput. **60**(Supplement C), 508–519 (2017). https://doi.org/10.1016/j.asoc.2017.07.009

# A Novel LSTM-CNN Architecture to Forecast Stock Prices

Amol Dhaliwal[1], Nikolaos Polatidis[1]([✉]), and Elias Pimenidis[2]

[1] School of Architecture, Technology and Engineering, University of Brighton, BN2 4GJ
Brighton, UK
{A.Dhaliwal,N.Polatidis}@Brighton.ac.uk
[2] Department of Computer Science and Creative Technologies, University of the West of
England, BS16 1QY Bristol, UK
Elias.Pimenidis@uwe.ac.uk

**Abstract.** With stock market participation increasing worldwide due to a variety of factors such as the prospect of earning dividend income or poor interest rates being offered by banks, there has been an increased focus by investors to get ahead of the curve by trying to predict the movement of stocks. Due to the nature of stock prices having characteristics of time series data, a range of Deep Learning algorithms can be used to analyze the underlying patterns of stocks. This paper proposes a novel LSTM-CNN architecture to predict the closing prices of stocks. An LSTM layer is used to learn the long-term dependencies of the stock data whilst a one-dimensional convolutional layer is used to extract local features. The stock history of Tesla and American Express from June 2010 to August 2020 are utilized in this paper to train the model where the model predicts the closing prices. More traditional approaches such as LSTM, CNN, MLP and CNN-LSTM have also been used as baselines where the regression metrics Root Mean Squared Error (RMSE) and Mean Absolute Percentage Error (MAPE) were used for the evaluation. The findings have shown that the proposed LSTM-CNN method outperforms the other architectures in terms of forecasting accuracy. This novel architecture not only provides a guide for investors to maximize their gains but an opportunity for researchers to conduct further analysis of hybrid architectures within the stock market.

**Keywords:** Stock · Forecast · Deep learning · Neural networks

## 1 Introduction

The stock market is a collection of exchanges where the purchases and sales of shares of public companies occur. These transactions can take place through institutionalized exchanges, or even heavily regulated over-the-counter marketplaces. Over recent years, the stock market has seen a surge in activity with the public more willing to invest in stocks and shares. A survey in 2020 found that 33% of people within Britain said they owned stocks and shares which equates to a 50% increase in involvement since 2018. A variety of factors such as saving account interest rates being perceived as poor and greater

E. Pimenidis et al. (Eds.): ICANN 2022, LNCS 13529, pp. 466–477, 2022.
https://doi.org/10.1007/978-3-031-15919-0_39

accessibility of investing platforms are among the leading justifications for stepping foot into the stock market. However, stocks remain volatile due to the deviation in investment methodologies as well as the continuous flow of news and announcements. This has left many people questioning if changes to the most analyzed economic data over the past 50 years, stock market prices, can even be forecasted.

With advancements in artificial intelligence over recent years, researchers have tried to forecast stocks by proposing a wide range of solutions involving deep learning algorithms such as Long Short-Term Memory (LSTM) and Convolutional Neural Networks (CNN). Neural networks are trainable algorithms which aim to emulate aspects of the human brain by being able to self-train and make forecasts based on the data provided. These algorithms have already seen great success within many sectors where they are considered the leaders for fraud detection and risk assessment. However, they are also suitable for forecasting stocks since stock data can be treated as a discrete-time series model. This is because a set of numerical data items, the closing stock price in this instance, are collected at successive points at regular time intervals.

This paper delivers a novel LSTM-CNN hybrid neural network architecture that improves the performance of stock forecasting compared to more traditional neural network approaches. Creating this model enables keen investors to have a guide on what decision they want to make on assets whether it's buying shares or selling assets that are currently present within their portfolio. The model can predict the closing price of a stock for a day by a sliding window approach where it analyses the previous 60 days for any trends and makes a prediction based on this. This also saves the time of investors as the algorithm allows to make automated predictions rather than the investor having to take time to analyze the market fully.

The rest of the paper is organized as follows: Sect. 2 is the related work, Sect. 3 delivers the proposed method, Sect. 4 presents the experimental evaluation and Sect. 5 contains the conclusions.

## 2 Related Work

This section reviews the related works that are used in stock forecasting.

The efficient market hypothesis states that stock prices reflect all available information which implies that it is impossible to predict the fluctuations within the stock market as prices only ever react to new information [1]. Despite this, several researchers believe that some models are acceptable if predictions can be formed with a considerable degree of accuracy. The most common models for stock forecasting are artificial neural networks (ANN) and ARIMA. The ARIMA model has been considered a very successful prediction technique within finance where results are formed from the values of input variables and error terms. However, ARIMA is limited as it is a linear regression model where it often suffers from deviations when facing complex scenarios that are nonlinear. Meanwhile, ANN forms predictions based on the observation of results from the original data where the model can make inferences. The ANN model is effective in solving nonlinear problems which suit the fluctuations within the stock market meaning that it's a better solution than ARIMA for stock forecasting. However, the two models cannot measure the frame of evolving price trends within the stock market. LSTM has been introduced as a variation of recurrent neural network where it contains a feedback connection that makes it easy to find development trends via back propagation of previous and current prices unlike the other two methods. The LSTM model can be deemed as a viable algorithm for stock prediction over ANN and ARIMA as it solves the problem of gradient disappearance that occurs easily within other recurrent neural networks, ultimately making it more capable of learning long term dependencies within time series data [2].

Further to this study, Siami-Namini et al., investigated how LSTM compared to Auto-Regressive Integrated Moving Average (ARIMA), a popular mathematical algorithm within finance. in terms of forecasting time series data. The results showed that the LSTM based algorithm improved the prediction by 85% on average in comparison to ARIMA, ultimately advocating the benefits of applying deep learning algorithms over more traditional methods when it comes to forecasting financial data [3]. These two papers have shown how LSTM is a more viable model for stock forecasting than the most used algorithms within the finance sector. However, the first paper also concludes that further research on LSTM is needed as it has rarely been used in previous studies and the true performance of this recurrent neural network cannot be demonstrated as many institutions do not conduct thorough pre-processing of data. This has motivated the inclusion of the LSTM model over ANN and ARIMA within this line of research to improve stock forecasting performance. Pawar et al., utilized an LSTM based model to forecast the stock prices of Tesla, Google, and Apple. The results of this model were compared against more traditional machine learning algorithms such as Random Forest and Support Vector Machine (SVM). It was concluded that the LSTM model produced a higher forecasting accuracy than the other two models [4]. This was influential on the project as it has shown how LSTM is superior to traditional machine learning models for analyzing the temporal features of time series data and supports the decision to exclude traditional machine learning algorithms from the focus of this project.

Since the stock market is a noisy, complex, and nonlinear environment, extracting features that provide enough information to form predictions remains a difficult task. The CNN algorithm has been touted as a promising solution for the feature extraction problem. In a study, four deep learning architectures were utilized by M et al., to predict the stock prices of NSE and NYE. The results showed that the deep learning architectures in general and not just LSTM can identify underlying dynamics within time series data that more traditional algorithms such as ARIMA fail to do due to its nonlinear nature. In addition to this, CNN outperformed LSTM, MLP and RNN due to the study using a particular window for predicting the next instant. This study outlined the ability of CNN to capture abrupt changes in the system making it a great candidate for feature extraction. The possibility of a hybrid network is also discussed where two models could be combined to form stock predictions [5]. Furthermore, the paper has supported the inclusion of deep learning architectures over more traditional methods within this line of study whilst also being open to a hybrid network architecture such as LSTM-CNN or CNN-LSTM. This hybrid architecture can be advantageous as CNN has been proven to be great at extracting features from a dataset. For further proof of the capabilities of a CNN architecture, Selvin et al. also utilized CNN, RNN and LSTM to predict the stocks of companies within the IT and pharmaceutical sectors. It was concluded that CNN was the best model as it captured abrupt changes that the other models could not beyond a certain period [6].

In 2020, Lu et al., proposed a CNN-LSTM hybrid architecture for forecasting the Shanghai Composite Index and found that it had the highest forecasting accuracy and performance compared to other algorithms such as LSTM, CNN, Multilayer Perceptron (MLP), Recurrent Neural Network (RNN) and CNN-RNN [7]. The hybrid model had the lowest RMSE and MAE values which indicated that the model formed more accurate predictions than the traditional neural network approaches for stock forecasting. This study displayed the potential benefits of utilizing a CNN-LSTM architecture within this line of study but also created an opportunity for further research on this architecture. The data preparation included data standardization which assumes that the data fits a Gaussian distribution for the best possible results. As stocks are not normally distributed, the CNN-LSTM architecture has been included in this project to see if the model could be optimized by altering the data preparation steps. The data would only be normalized using Min-Max scaling and no standardization would take place. The benefits of utilizing a CNN-LSTM model were also demonstrated by Liu et al., by including the hybrid architecture within a training strategy. When the LSTM predictive value for a stock was equal to 1, the stock would be purchased and then held for 5 days where a variable for the number of held days was updated to 5. If the LSTM predictive value is −1, the variable for held days would be decreased by 1 and if the value for the held days was 0 then the stock share would be sold. It was found that the CNN-LSTM led to returns 2.5 times as large as the benchmark index, ultimately demonstrating the strength of this hybrid architecture and providing an opportunity to include the architecture for further analysis within this project [8]. Further to this, Kim and Kim introduced a feature fusion LSTM-CNN model to forecast stock prices by using different representations of the same data. The LSTM was used to extract the temporal features of stock data by analyzing the closing prices and trading volume. Meanwhile, the CNN in this model was used to extract the features of chart images for the stock where each of the layers underwent joint training to analyze the SPDR S&P 500 ETF Trust ticker data. This study found that the feature fusion LSTM-CNN model outperformed the single LSTM and CNN models in terms of MAPE and RMSE. On the other hand, this study motivated the inclusion of an LSTM-CNN model but with only one type of data representation. This is since a one-dimensional convolutional layer is capable of processing data such as closing stock prices and not just images. This opens the opportunity to see if the forecasting accuracy could be improved by implementing a LSTM-CNN model that works to extract the features from a dataset containing the closing prices of the stock where the CNN takes the outputs of the LSTM layer as an input [9]. Further to this study, the LSTM-CNN architecture has also enjoyed success in forecasting gold prices. He et al., utilized the LSTM to extract temporal features whilst the CNN was responsible for capturing the local patterns. Their study found that it produced the highest forecasting accuracy compared to other models such as CNN-LSTM, LSTM, ARIMA, CNN and Support Vector Regression (SVR) [10]. Despite the study focusing on gold prices, the results are still valid for stock prediction as the data is still treated as a time series problem. This study was influential on the project as it is one of very few papers to compare the difference in performance between the LSTM-CNN and CNN-LSTM models for time series data. The study has shown how a LSTM-CNN model results in lower feature loss than a CNN-LSTM and provides an opportunity for further analysis on the two models within this project. In another study, Naeini et al., utilized a three-layer MLP model to predict the stock price changes of the Tehran Stock Exchange Corporation. It was found that the MLP model outperformed Elman network and linear regression models by having lower scores for metrics such as MAPE. This has motivated the inclusion of a three-layer MLP model within this study to see how it would compare against other neural networks [11]. Hota, Handa and Shivas explored utilizing an ANN technique to predict the prices of BSE30 index data where it was concluded that the prediction of a next day close price on a basis of the current price was not deemed viable. Instead, they aimed to predict the close price of the stock by utilizing a sliding window approach using different window sizes varying between 5, 10 and 15 and 20 days. Within the example provided, the sliding window with a window size of 5 accumulates all the stock data between days 1 to 5 and is then used to predict the close price of the next day. Once a prediction has been made, the window slides across one day where it covers days 2 to 6 and then utilizes that stock data to predict the close price of day 7. Within this study, it was found that increasing the window size resulted in a decrease of MSE for both the training and testing phase. Meanwhile, there was a decrease in the MAPE for the training phase as the window size increased [12]. This motivated the decision to include a sliding window approach as having a set number of days to base a prediction off helps to lower the error metrics and avoids utilizing the analysis of irrelevant data points from months back which could skew the prediction. In 2020, Kamalov constructed LSTM, CNN and MLP models to forecast the significant price changes of stocks. The performance of these models was compared against benchmark models such as Random Forest and relative strength index methods. It was concluded that LSTM could provide superior results than the other models in certain scenarios, despite the training time. However, the main reason that this study is influential on this project is that it found that utilizing a 60-day window for stock predictions provided the optimal results [13]. Moghar and Hamiche utilized a LSTM model to predict the stock prices of Google and Apple based off data ranging from January 2010 to December 2019. Their study concluded that the precision of their model increased significantly as more epochs were included for training [14]. This has motivated this study to analyze the effects of epochs and deem if the stock forecasting of the five models could be improved. However, this will be done without changing the size of the training dataset which was a feature of the study. Ding and Xin attempted to predict the stock prices of the Shanghai Stock Index by utilizing a LSTM based deep recurrent neural network model. This study was significant as it mentions the benefits of data normalization by min-max scaling where normalizing the values tackled the problems of differing scales and sped up the gradient descent process which improved the accuracy of their results [15]. As a result of this, this project will also include data normalization within the data preparation steps to ensure the best possible results are obtained. Pai and Ilango utilized an LSTM model to analyze the case of feature selection within stock forecasting. The LSTM model was used in three different scenarios where one only utilized the prices for a stock and the other two were a combination of indicators where only one of the two included the stock prices [16]. Results of this study showed that the LSTM model with only the stock prices performed the best. This paper was influential as it shows that feature elimination techniques should be used to only keep relevant features than maintaining those that do not.

# 3 Proposed Method

## 3.1 Data Preparation

The stock ticker data for Tesla and American Express have been extracted from the Yahoo Finance website to create a dataset containing 2561 days' worth of trading data covering the period between 29 June 2010 to 28 August 2020. The Yahoo Finance website contains a multitude of information such as opening price, closing price, high, low, volume and stock symbol. However, only the day-wise closing stock price is extracted and used for the dataset as the closing price is considered the most accurate valuation of a stock until the next trading day resumes. This makes it the reference point that an investor often uses to evaluate the performance of stock and whether they want to purchase or remove it from their portfolio. It was also crucial to ensure there is a large amount of data as the algorithms in question are nonlinear and high variance where predictions vary on the data that is used to train them. Therefore, the current amount of data ensures there is enough training data which can allow the deep learning methods to improve in skill. The datasets wer created by using the functionality of the Pandas library to store these values within a two-dimensional data structure called a DataFrame. Following the creation of the dataset, the data underwent normalization using min-max scaling. This is when the values for a feature, the closing prices of Tesla and American Express in this case, are transformed into a range between 0 and 1 where the minimum and maximum values for the closing prices will be 0 and 1. This process can be found in the Eq. 1 below where x represents a single feature with min and max referring to the minimum and maximum values for that feature.

$$x_{scaled} = \frac{x - \min(x)}{\max(x) - \min(x)} \tag{1}$$

Normalizing the data attempts to give every attribute equal weighting so that there is no dependence on the choice of units such as differing currencies. If there was a difference in scale between input variables it would result in large weight values which would make the model unstable as it would suffer during the learning phase ultimately producing a higher generalization error. Using smaller value inputs generated by normalization helps to mitigate against this issue as the features would avoid a large spread [17]. Data normalization is also key for neural networks that utilize the backpropagation function as using normalized values for training tuples would speed up the learning phase and lead to faster convergence. Most deep learning models construct a loss function which calculates the difference between the actual and predicted outputs. Following this, the gradients of this cost function and weights are calculated and propagated back between layers. The derivative of this loss function L with respect to a weight $w_i$ can be seen in the equation below where a is the predicted value, y is the true value and $x_i$ is the input feature. Equation 2 shows that the speed of the learning process is proportional to the magnitude of the inputs as a bigger input $x_i$ would result in a larger update.

If the inputs were of differing scales, the weights connected to certain outputs would be updated at a much slower pace than other weights which could affect the learning process. Normalizing the data prevents this by ensuring that the inputs remain small and are within the same scale.

$$\frac{dL}{dw_i} = x_i * (a - y) \tag{2}$$

## 3.2  The Proposed LSTM-CNN Architecture

An LSTM-CNN hybrid neural network architecture was implemented where a tuple containing the timesteps and target value are inputted into the LSTM layer. The hidden states for all these timesteps are outputted by the LSTM layer as 'return_sequences' has been set to true. This is to ensure that the CNN layer receives the required input which is the hidden states returned by the LSTM layer. Following this, a max-pooling layer is implemented to reduce the dimensionality of the feature map generated by the previous CNN layer so that there are less parameters and overfitting is prevented. There is then a flatten layer which flattens the output of the max-pooling layer so that the fully connected layers receive one dimensional data to output a prediction. The structure of this model can be seen in Fig. 1 below where the features of LSTM and CNN discussed earlier within this section make them suitable for working together on analyzing time series data. LSTM has the feature of extended memory in terms of gated cells where it can discard irrelevant information and CNN has been proven to be great at local feature extraction. For this reason, the LSTM architecture is used within the proposed model to

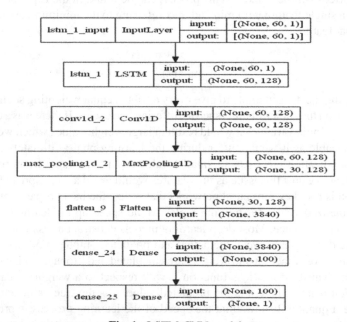

**Fig. 1.** LSTM-CNN model.

learn the long-term dependencies whilst the CNN layer uses the output of the LSTM to form a tensor of outputs by convolving the input over a temporal dimension where local features are extracted.

## 4 Experimental Evaluation

### 4.1 Evaluation Details

The Python programming language and the Keras library has been used for the development and evaluation of all algorithms, including the proposed method. Furthermore, to evaluate the performance of these algorithms over predicting the closing stock price of Tesla and American Express, the performance metrics mean absolute percentage error (MAPE) and root mean squared error (RMSE) are used while 80% of each dataset has been used for training and 20% for testing. MAPE measures the percentage error of the forecast by the algorithm in relation to the actual value. This evaluation metric is popular within a sector like finance due to its intuitive nature. Furthermore, gains and losses are measured in relative values which supports the use of a relative metric such as MAPE. The calculation for MAPE can be found in Eq. 3 below where x_t represents the actual value, x^_t is the value predicted by the algorithm and n is the number of data points.

$$MAPE = \frac{1}{n} \sum_{t=1}^{n} \left| \frac{x_t - \hat{x}_t}{x_t} \right| \tag{3}$$

Meanwhile, RMSE measures the standard deviation of residuals which show how far from the regression line these algorithmic predictions are. This is also a popular metric for forecasting as individuals within hedge funds are interested to see how concentrated the predicted values are around the actual trends for stock prices. Equation 2 represent RMSE where n is the number of data points, x_is the actual value and x^ is the predicted value by the algorithm.

$$RMSE = \sqrt{\frac{\sum_{i=0}^{n}(x_i - \hat{x}_i)^2}{n}} \tag{4}$$

### 4.2 Results

This section delivers the evaluation results. For the results presented in Tables 1 and 2 the proposed method has been compared with alternative methods as described below.

**Comparisons with alternative methods**
**LSTM-CNN:** The proposed method.
**LSTM:** Standard LSTM algorithm utilized from Keras library.
**CNN:** Standard CNN algorithm utilized from Keras library.
**MLP:** Reference [11].
**CNN-LSTM:** Reference [7].

The specific settings of all algorithms are available in Fig. 2 for the LSTM, Fig. 3 for the CNN, Fig. 4 for the MLP and Fig. 5 for the CNN-LSTM.

**Table 1.** RMSE and MAPE results for TESLA

| Algorithm | RMSE | MAPE |
|---|---|---|
| LSTM | 14.27 | 5.16 |
| CNN | 17.85 | 7.14 |
| MLP | 27.57 | 14.58 |
| LSTM-CNN (proposed) | **9.07** | **4.20** |
| CNN-LSTM | 9.58 | 4.64 |

**Table 2.** RMSE and MAPE results for American Express

| Algorithm | RMSE | MAPE |
|---|---|---|
| LSTM | 3.74 | 2.89 |
| CNN | 4.53 | 3.16 |
| MLP | 9.52 | 7.69 |
| LSTM-CNN (proposed) | **3.23** | **2.15** |
| CNN-LSTM | 3.37 | 2.33 |

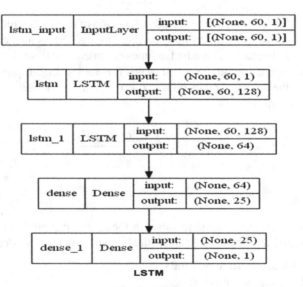

**Fig. 2.** LSTM

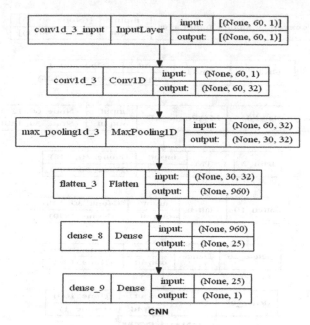

**Fig. 3.**  CNN

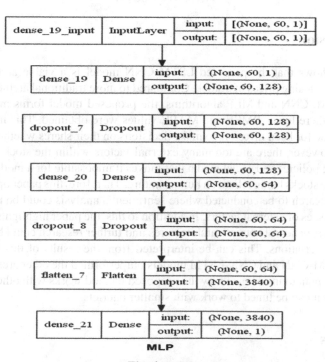

**Fig. 4.**  MLP

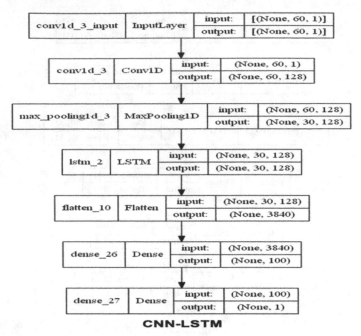

**CNN-LSTM**

Fig. 5. CNN-LSTM

## 5   Conclusions

This paper shows that the proposed LSTM-CNN model is a viable architecture for predicting the closing prices of a stock. Compared to more traditional architectures such as pure LSTM, CNN and MLP algorithms, the proposed model forms more accurate predictions where lower RMSE and MAPE values were obtained. This model can be used as a guide for keen investors to make decisions on their shares whether it's buying or selling. However, there are too many external factors within the stock market such as developing policies and social media that makes it impossible for a model to be fully reliable due to stocks being reliant on human nature. Therefore, this paper opens the door for further research to be conducted where sentimental analysis could be implemented to solve the issues of external factors. In addition to this, the paper highlights the benefits of creating hybrid neural network architectures and further research could be conducted into possible variations. This can be interpreted from the results of this paper where both the LSTM-CNN and CNN-LSTM models outperformed the other architectures. In the future we plan to investigate how the proposed method works with other stocks and examine how it can be tuned to work with smaller datasets.

## References

1. Fama, E.F.: Efficient capital markets: a review of theory and empirical work. J. Financ. **25**(2), 383–417 (1970)

2. Ma, Q.: Comparison of ARIMA, ANN and LSTM for stock price prediction. In: E3S Web of Conferences, Vol. 218, no. 01026 (2020)
3. Siami-Namini, S., Tavakoli, N., Siami Namin, A.: A comparison of ARIMA and LSTM in forecasting time series. In: 2018 17th IEEE International Conference on Machine Learning and Applications (ICMLA) (2018)
4. Pawar, K., Jalem, R.S., Tiwari, V.: Stock market price prediction using LSTM RNN. In: Rathore, V., Worring, M., Mishra, D., Joshi, A., Maheshwari, S. (eds.) Emerging Trends in Expert Applications and Security, vol. 841, pp. 493–503. Springer, Cham (2018). https://doi.org/10.1007/978-981-13-2285-3_58
5. Hiransha, M., Gopalakrishnan, E.A., Menon, V.K., Soman, K.P.: NSE stock market prediction using deep-learning models. Procedia Comput. Sci. **132**, 1351–1362 (2018)
6. Selvin, S., Vinayakumar, R., Gopalakrishnan, E.A., Menon, V.K., Soman, K.P.: Stock price prediction using LSTM, RNN and CNN-sliding window model. In: 2017 International Conference on Advances in Computing, Communications and Informatics (ICACCI) (2017)
7. Lu, W., Li, J., Li, Y., Sun, A., Wang, J.: A CNN-LSTM-based model to forecast stock prices. Complexity **2020**, 1–10 (2020)
8. Liu, S., Zhang, C., Ma, J.: CNN-LSTM neural network model for quantitative strategy analysis in stock markets. In: Liu, D., Xie, S., Li, Y., Zhao, D., El-Alfy, E.S. (eds.) Neural Information Processing, vol. 10635, pp. 198–206. Springer, Cham (2017). https://doi.org/10.1007/978-3-319-70096-0_21
9. Kim, T., Kim, H.Y.: Forecasting stock prices with a feature fusion LSTM-CNN model using different representations of the same data. PLoS ONE **14**(2), e0212320 (2019)
10. Ji, L., Zou, Y., He, K., Zhu, B.: Carbon futures price forecasting based with ARIMA-CNN-LSTM model. Procedia Comput. Sci. **162**, 33–38 (2019)
11. Naeini, M.P., Taremian, H., Hashemi, H.B.: Stock market value prediction using neural networks. In: 2010 International Conference on Computer Information Systems and Industrial Management Applications (CisIM) (2010)
12. Hota, H., Handa, R., Shrivas, A.: Time series data prediction using sliding window based RBF neural network. Int. J. Comput. Intell. Res. **13**(5), 1145–1156 (2017)
13. Kamalov, F.: Forecasting significant stock price changes using neural networks. Neural Comput. Appl. **32**(23), 17655–17667 (2020). https://doi.org/10.1007/s00521-020-04942-3
14. Moghar, A., Hamiche, M.: Stock market prediction using LSTM recurrent neural network. Procedia Comput. Sci. **170**, 1168–1173 (2020)
15. Ding, G., Qin, L.: Study on the prediction of stock price based on the associated network model of LSTM. Int. J. Mach. Learn. Cybern. **11**(6), 1307–1317 (2019). https://doi.org/10.1007/s13042-019-01041-1
16. Pai, N., Ilango, V.: LSTM neural network model with feature selection for financial time series prediction. In: 2020 Fourth International Conference on I-SMAC (IoT in Social, Mobile, Analytics and Cloud) (I-SMAC), pp. 672–677. IEEE (2020)
17. Han, J., Kamber, M., Pei, J.: Data Mining: Concepts and Techniques. Elsevier, Burlington (2012)

# A Taxonomy of Recurrent Learning Rules

Guillermo Martín-Sánchez[1] , Sander Bohté[2] , and Sebastian Otte[1]([✉])

[1] Neuro-Cognitive Modeling, University of Tübingen,
Sand 14, 72076 Tübingen, Germany
`sebastian.otte@uni-tuebingen.de`
[2] Machine Learning Group, CWI, Science Park 123,
1098XG Amsterdam, The Netherlands
`S.M.Bohte@cwi.nl`

**Abstract.** Backpropagation through time (BPTT) is the de facto standard for training recurrent neural networks (RNNs), but it is non-causal and non-local. Real-time recurrent learning is a causal alternative, but it is highly inefficient. Recently, e-prop was proposed as a causal, local, and efficient practical alternative to these algorithms, providing an approximation of the exact gradient by radically pruning the recurrent dependencies carried over time. Here, we derive RTRL from BPTT using a detailed notation bringing intuition and clarification to how they are connected. Furthermore, we frame e-prop within in the picture, formalising what it approximates. Finally, we derive a family of algorithms of which e-prop is a special case.

**Keywords:** Recurrent neural networks · Backpropagation through time · Real-time recurrent learning · Forward propagation · E-prop

## 1  Introduction

*Backpropagation through time* (BPTT) [6] is currently the most used algorithm for training *recurrent neural networks* (RNNs) and is derived from applying the chain rule (backpropagation) to the computational graph of the RNN unrolled in time. It suffers however from undesired characteristics both in terms of biological plausibility and large scale applicability: (i) it is *non-causal*, since at each time step it requires future activity to compute the current gradient of the loss with respect to the parameters; and (ii) it is *non-local*, since it requires reverse error signal propagating across all neurons and all synapses. An equivalent algorithm is *real-time recurrent learning* (RTRL) [8]. It uses eligibility traces that are computed at each time step recursively in order to be causal, and can therefore be computed online. However, this comes at the cost of very high computational and memory complexity, since all temporal forward dependencies have to be maintained over time. RTRL is, hence, also non-local. Recently, a new online learning algorithm, called *e-prop* [2] has been proposed, which is tailored for training *recurrent spiking neural networks* (RSNNs) with local neural dynamics.

E. Pimenidis et al. (Eds.): ICANN 2022, LNCS 13529, pp. 478–490, 2022.
https://doi.org/10.1007/978-3-031-15919-0_40

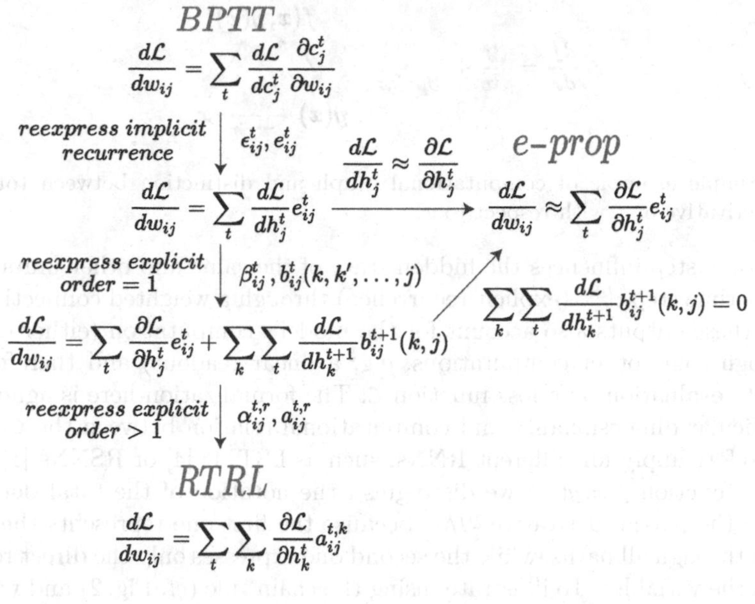

$$BPTT$$
$$\frac{d\mathcal{L}}{dw_{ij}} = \sum_t \frac{d\mathcal{L}}{dc_j^t} \frac{\partial c_j^t}{\partial w_{ij}}$$

*reexpress implicit* $\Big\downarrow$ $\epsilon_{ij}^t, e_{ij}^t$
*recurrence*

$$\frac{d\mathcal{L}}{dw_{ij}} = \sum_t \frac{d\mathcal{L}}{dh_j^t} e_{ij}^t \qquad \xrightarrow{\quad \frac{d\mathcal{L}}{dh_j^t} \approx \frac{\partial \mathcal{L}}{\partial h_j^t} \quad} \qquad \frac{d\mathcal{L}}{dw_{ij}} \approx \sum_t \frac{\partial \mathcal{L}}{\partial h_j^t} e_{ij}^t$$

$$e\text{-}prop$$

*reexpress explicit* $\Big\downarrow$ $\beta_{ij}^t, b_{ij}^t(k, k', \dots, j)$
*order = 1*

$$\frac{d\mathcal{L}}{dw_{ij}} = \sum_t \frac{\partial \mathcal{L}}{\partial h_j^t} e_{ij}^t + \sum_k \sum_t \frac{d\mathcal{L}}{dh_k^{t+1}} b_{ij}^{t+1}(k, j) \qquad \sum_k \sum_t \frac{d\mathcal{L}}{dh_k^{t+1}} b_{ij}^{t+1}(k, j) = 0$$

*reexpress explicit* $\Big\downarrow$ $\alpha_{ij}^{t,r}, a_{ij}^{t,r}$
*order > 1*

$$RTRL$$
$$\frac{d\mathcal{L}}{dw_{ij}} = \sum_t \sum_k \frac{\partial \mathcal{L}}{\partial h_k^t} a_{ij}^{t,k}$$

**Fig. 1.** Overview of all the algorithms and how they relate to each other.

The aim was to find an alternative to BPTT (and RTRL) that is causal, local, but also computational and memory efficient.

In this paper, we look in depth into the formalisation of BPTT and RTRL and formalise e-prop into the picture. To do so, we use the computational graph and notation of the architecture in the e-prop paper [2] to understand how these three algorithms relate to each other. Furthermore, in a posterior paper [9], it was shown that e-prop was an approximation of RTRL. Here, by formalising also RTRL in the same framework we indeed confirm the connection and make it more explicit (cf. Fig. 1). In the process, we uncover a family of algorithms determined by the level of approximation allowed to benefit from causality and locality. The main focus of this paper is to give intuition and understanding of all of these gradient computation rules.

## 1.1   Background

The most common way to train a model in supervised learning is to compute the gradient of a given loss $\mathcal{L}$ with respect to the parameters $\theta$, $d\mathcal{L}/d\theta$, and use this gradient in some gradient descent scheme of the form $\theta(\tau + 1) = \theta(\tau) - f(d\mathcal{L}/d\theta)$, where $\tau$ refers to the current update iteration and $f$ is some gradient postprocessing. Therefore, we here focus on the algorithms for the computation (or approximation) of this gradient.

In particular, we focus on a general class of RNN models where we have $n$ computational units. These units have hidden states at each time step $c_i^t$ that influence the hidden state at the next time step $c_i^{t+1}$ (implicit recurrence) as well as the output of the unit at the current time step $h_i^t$. The output $h_i^t$ of a unit at

$$\frac{df}{dx} = \frac{\partial f}{\partial x} + \frac{\partial f}{\partial y}\frac{\partial y}{\partial x}$$

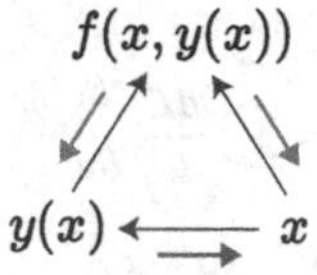

$$f(x, y(x))$$

$$y(x) \longleftrightarrow x$$

**Fig. 2.** Simple example of computational graph and distinction between total and partial derivative of $f$ with respect to $x$.

a given time step influences the hidden state of the same and other units at the following time step $c_j^{t+1}$ (explicit recurrence) through a weighted connection $w_{ij}$. Finally, these outputs also account for the model's computation (either directly or through some other computations, e.g. a linear readout) and therefore are subject to evaluation by a loss function $\mathcal{L}$. The formalization here is agnostic to the particular dimensionality and computational relation between the variables and therefore apply for different RNNs, such as LSTMs [4] or RSNNs [1].

For a function $f(x, y(x))$ we distinguish the notation of the total derivative $df/dx$ and the partial derivative $\partial f/\partial x$ because the first one represents the whole gradient through all paths, while the second one expresses only the direct relation between the variables. To illustrate: using the chain rule (cf. Fig. 2) and with the example $y = 2x$ and $f(x, y(x)) = xy$, the total derivative is calculated as:

$$\frac{df}{dx} = \frac{\partial f}{\partial x} + \frac{\partial f}{\partial y}\frac{\partial y}{\partial x} = y + x \cdot 2 = 4x \tag{1}$$

## 2 Backpropagation Through Time

In RNNs, since previous states affect the current state, the trick to applying the chain rule is to unroll the RNN in time, obtain a virtual feed-forward architecture and apply to this computational graph error-backpropagation [7]. The resulting algorithm is BPTT [6] and it is the currently most used algorithm to compute $d\mathcal{L}/dw_{ij}$ since it reuses many previous computations to be highly efficient. Here, we focus our attention on the role of the recurrences dividing the algorithm into the following steps:

**Explicit Recurrences:** Compute $d\mathcal{L}/dh_j^t$ using the recursive definition given by the explicit recurrences (cf. Fig. 3A):

$$\frac{d\mathcal{L}}{dh_j^t} = \frac{\partial \mathcal{L}}{\partial h_j^t} + \frac{d\mathcal{L}}{dc_j^{t+1}}\frac{\partial c_j^{t+1}}{\partial h_j^t} + \sum_{k \neq j}\frac{d\mathcal{L}}{dc_k^{t+1}}\frac{\partial c_k^{t+1}}{\partial h_j^t}$$

$$= \frac{\partial \mathcal{L}}{\partial h_j^t} + \sum_k \frac{d\mathcal{L}}{dc_k^{t+1}}\frac{\partial c_k^{t+1}}{\partial h_j^t} \tag{2}$$

**Implicit Recurrences:** Compute $d\mathcal{L}/dc_j^t$ using the value of the previous step and the recursive definition given by the implicit recurrence (cf. Fig. 3B):

$$\frac{d\mathcal{L}}{dc_j^t} = \frac{d\mathcal{L}}{dh_j^t}\frac{\partial h_j^t}{\partial c_j^t} + \frac{d\mathcal{L}}{dc_j^{t+1}}\frac{\partial c_j^{t+1}}{\partial c_j^t} \tag{3}$$

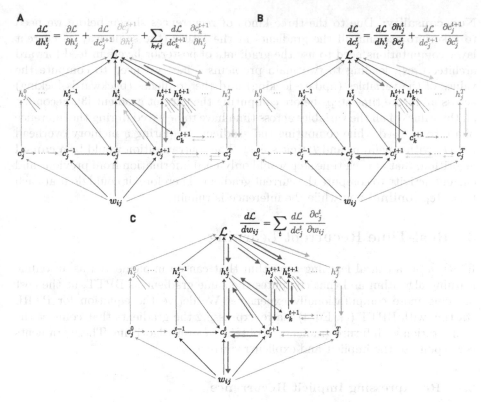

**Fig. 3.** Computational graph for A) explicit recurrences gradients, B) implicit recurrence gradients and C) final computation of BPTT.

**BPTT:** Finally, compute $d\mathcal{L}/dw_{ij}$ using the values obtained in the previous two steps for all time steps (cf. Fig. 3C):

$$\frac{d\mathcal{L}}{dw_{ij}} = \sum_t \frac{d\mathcal{L}}{dc_j^t} \frac{\partial c_j^t}{\partial w_{ij}} \qquad (4)$$

We use explicit and implicit recurrences from the maximum time $T$ backwards and for all $t \leq T$, and finally, sum all the results from Eq. 3. The existence of these recurrences makes BPTT present the following problems [2,5]:

**Non-locality:** Due to the explicit recurrences, we need to take into account how the current synaptic strength $w_{ij}$ between the neurons $i$ and $j$ affects the future value of the postsynaptic neuron: $\partial c_k^{t+1}/\partial h_j^t$ for all $k \neq j$ (cf. Eq. 2). This means that to compute the weight change for synapse magnitude $w_{ij}$ we need information of the hidden variables $c_k^{t+1}$ for all $k$. Moreover, this chain of dependencies continues at each time step, such that at the next time step we need information of the variables $c_q^{t+2}$ for all $q$ (including $q \neq j$) and so forth. The contraposition would be a **local** algorithm that does not require messages passing from every neuron to every synapse to compute the gradients, but rather only need information close to the given synapse.

**Non-causality:** Due to the three kinds of recurrences shown before we need to take into account all the gradients in the future (the same way as current layer computations need to use the gradients of posterior layers in feed-forward architectures), leading to two main problems. First, we need to compute the values of the variables (update locking) and the gradients (backwards locking) across all future time steps before computing the current gradient [3]. Secondly, all the values of all the variables across time have to be saved during the inference phase to be used while computing the gradients, requiring a memory overhead ($O(nT)$ with $n$ neurons and $T$ time steps). The contraposition would be a **causal** algorithm, that at each time step would only need information from previous and current activity to compute the current gradient. Therefore, it could do it at each time step (**online**) and while the inference is running.

## 3    Real-Time Recurrent Learning

RTRL [8] is a causal learning algorithm that can be implemented as an online learning algorithm and that computes the same gradient as BPTT, at the cost of being more computationally expensive. We derive the equation for RTRL starting with BPTT (cf. Eq. 4) via re-expressing the gradients that connect the computation with future gradients to obtain a causal algorithm. These gradients correspond to the implicit and explicit recurrences.

### 3.1    Re-expressing Implicit Recurrence

First, we re-express the implicit recurrence gradient $\partial c_j^{t+1}/\partial c_j^t$.

**Unrolling the Recursion:** To unroll, we plug the equation of implicit recurrence Eq. 3 into Eq. 4:

$$
\begin{aligned}
\frac{d\mathcal{L}}{dw_{ij}} &= \sum_{t'} \left( \frac{d\mathcal{L}}{dh_j^{t'}} \frac{\partial h_j^{t'}}{\partial c_j^{t'}} + \frac{d\mathcal{L}}{dc_j^{t'+1}} \frac{\partial c_j^{t'+1}}{\partial c_j^{t'}} \right) \frac{\partial c_j^{t'}}{\partial w_{ij}} \\
&= \sum_{t'} \left( \frac{d\mathcal{L}}{dh_j^{t'}} \frac{\partial h_j^{t'}}{\partial c_j^{t'}} + \left( \frac{d\mathcal{L}}{dh_j^{t'+1}} \frac{\partial h_j^{t'+1}}{\partial c_j^{t'+1}} + (\cdots) \frac{\partial c_j^{t'+2}}{\partial c_j^{t'+1}} \right) \frac{\partial c_j^{t'+1}}{\partial c_j^{t'}} \right) \frac{\partial c_j^{t'}}{\partial w_{ij}} \quad (5) \\
&= \sum_{t'} \sum_{t \geq t'} \frac{d\mathcal{L}}{dh_j^t} \frac{\partial h_j^t}{\partial c_j^t} \frac{\partial c_j^t}{\partial c_j^{t-1}} \cdots \frac{\partial c_j^{t'+1}}{\partial c_j^{t'}} \frac{\partial c_j^{t'}}{\partial w_{ij}}
\end{aligned}
$$

**Flip Time Indices:** The derived formula is non-causal since it requires future gradients (for each $t'$ we sum products of gradients with factors starting from $t \geq t'$). To make it causal, we change the indices as follows:

$$
\frac{d\mathcal{L}}{dw_{ij}} = \sum_t \frac{d\mathcal{L}}{dh_j^t} \frac{\partial h_j^t}{\partial c_j^t} \sum_{t' \leq t} \frac{\partial c_j^t}{\partial c_j^{t-1}} \cdots \frac{\partial c_j^{t'+1}}{\partial c_j^{t'}} \frac{\partial c_j^{t'}}{\partial w_{ij}} \quad (6)
$$

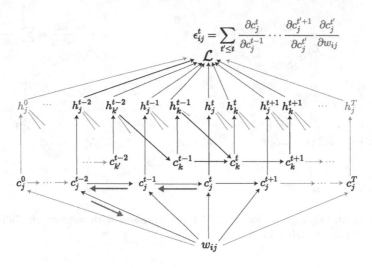

$$\epsilon_{ij}^t = \sum_{t' \le t} \frac{\partial c_j^t}{\partial c_j^{t-1}} \cdots \frac{\partial c_j^{t'+1}}{\partial c_j^{t'}} \frac{\partial c_j^{t'}}{\partial w_{ij}}$$

**Fig. 4.** Computational graph for the implicit variable $\epsilon_{ij}^t$ with $t' = t - 2$.

**Definition (Implicit variable).** *We define the* implicit variable $\epsilon_{ij}^t$ *as:*

$$\epsilon_{ij}^t := \sum_{t' \le t} \frac{\partial c_j^t}{\partial c_j^{t-1}} \cdots \frac{\partial c_j^{t'+1}}{\partial c_j^{t'}} \frac{\partial c_j^{t'}}{\partial w_{ij}} \tag{7}$$

*Backwards Interpretation:* Starting at $c_j^t$, the implicit variable represents the sum over all the paths going backwards through the implicit recurrence until $c_j^{t'}$ and from there to the synaptic weight $w_{ij}$ (cf. Fig. 4).

*Forwards Interpretation:* The implicit variable represents how the hidden variable of neuron $j$ has been affected by the synapse weight $w_{ij}$ through time, i.e. taking into account also how the hidden variables at previous time steps have affected the variables at the current time step through the implicit recurrence.

*Incremental Computation:* Importantly, there is a recursive relation to this variable that allows it to be updated at each time step:

$$\epsilon_{ij}^t = \frac{\partial c_j^t}{\partial c_j^{t-1}} \epsilon_{ij}^{t-1} + \frac{\partial c_j^t}{\partial w_{ij}} \tag{8}$$

**Definition (Implicit eligibility trace).** *Given the implicit variable $\epsilon_{ij}^t$, we define the* implicit eligibility trace $e_{ij}^t$ *as:*

$$e_{ij}^t := \frac{\partial h_j^t}{\partial c_j^t} \epsilon_{ij}^t \tag{9}$$

Since $\partial h_j^t / \partial c_j^t$ is causal and local, and so is the implicit variable $\epsilon_{ij}^t$ (can be computed at each time step and is specific for each synapse), then the implicit eligibility trace $e_{ij}^t$ is also **causal** and **local**.

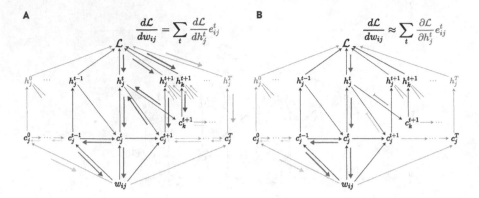

**Fig. 5.** Computational graph for A) BPTT re-expressed with implicit eligibility trace (cf. Eq. 10) B) symmetric e-prop.

**Final Equation with Re-expressed Implicit Recurrence:** With all of this combined, BPTT (cf. Eq. 4) has become (substituting Eq. 7 in Eq. 6) the following (cf. Fig. 5A):

$$\frac{d\mathcal{L}}{dw_{ij}} = \sum_t \frac{d\mathcal{L}}{dh_j^t} \frac{\partial h_j^t}{\partial c_j^t} e_{ij}^t = \sum_t \frac{d\mathcal{L}}{dh_j^t} e_{ij}^t \tag{10}$$

Even though $e_{ij}^t$ is causal and local, this equation as a whole is not, since the factor $d\mathcal{L}/dh_j^t$ still includes explicit recurrences. E-prop will simply ignore these recurrences to solve this problem (cf. Fig. 5B, Sect. 4).

## 3.2  Re-expressing Explicit Recurrences of Order 1

Now we re-express the explicit recurrences' gradient $\partial c_k^{t+1}/\partial h_j^t$ analogously to the implicit recurrence in the previous section. First, we plug Eq. 2 (explicit recurrences) into Eq. 10 (re-expressed implicit recurrence):

$$\begin{aligned}
\frac{d\mathcal{L}}{dw_{ij}} &= \sum_{t'} \left( \frac{\partial \mathcal{L}}{\partial h_j^{t'}} + \sum_k \frac{d\mathcal{L}}{dc_k^{t'+1}} \frac{\partial c_k^{t'+1}}{\partial h_j^{t'}} \right) e_{ij}^{t'} \\
&= \sum_{t'} \frac{\partial \mathcal{L}}{\partial h_j^{t'}} e_{ij}^{t'} + \sum_k \sum_{t'} \frac{d\mathcal{L}}{dc_k^{t'+1}} \frac{\partial c_k^{t'+1}}{\partial h_j^{t'}} e_{ij}^{t'}
\end{aligned} \tag{11}$$

The first factor of this sum is already causal since it only requires the direct derivative and the implicit eligibility trace introduced in Eq. 7. Focusing on the second factor, this term represents the gradient until $c_k^{t'+1}$, the jump to $h_j^{t'}$ and the implicit eligibility trace $e_{ij}^{t'}$ stored there that represents the sum over all of the paths from there to $w_{ij}$.

$$\beta_{ij}^t(k, k', ..., j) = \sum_{t' \leq t-1} \frac{\partial c_k^t}{\partial c_k^{t-1}} \cdots \frac{\partial c_k^{t'+2}}{\partial c_k^{t'+1}} \frac{\partial c_k^{t'+1}}{\partial h_{k'}^{t'}} \frac{\partial h_{k'}^{t'}}{\partial c_{k'}^{t'}} \beta_{ij}^{t'}(k', k'', ..., j)$$

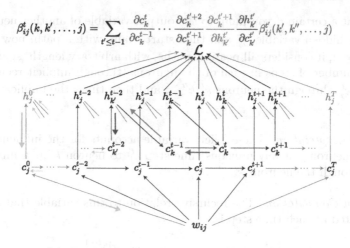

**Fig. 6.** Computational graph for the explicit variable $\beta_{ij}^t(k, k', ..., j)$ with $t' = t - 1$.

**Unrolling the Recursion:** We can now unroll the recursion by plugging the equation of explicit recurrences Eq. 2 into the second term of Eq. 11:

$$\sum_{t'} \frac{d\mathcal{L}}{dc_k^{t'+1}} \frac{\partial c_k^{t'+1}}{\partial h_j^{t'}} e_{ij}^{t'} = \sum_{t'} \left( \frac{d\mathcal{L}}{dh_k^{t'+1}} \frac{\partial h_k^{t'+1}}{\partial c_k^{t'+1}} + \frac{d\mathcal{L}}{dc_k^{t'+2}} \frac{\partial c_k^{t'+2}}{\partial c_k^{t'+1}} \right) \frac{\partial c_k^{t'+1}}{\partial h_j^{t'}} e_{ij}^{t'}$$

$$= \sum_{t'} \left( \frac{d\mathcal{L}}{dh_k^{t'+1}} \frac{\partial h_k^{t'+1}}{\partial c_k^{t'+1}} + \left( \frac{d\mathcal{L}}{dh_k^{t'+2}} \frac{\partial h_k^{t'+2}}{\partial c_k^{t'+2}} + (\dots) \frac{\partial c_k^{t'+3}}{\partial c_k^{t'+2}} \right) \frac{\partial c_k^{t'+2}}{\partial c_k^{t'+1}} \right) \frac{\partial c_k^{t'+1}}{\partial h_j^{t'}} e_{ij}^{t'}$$

$$= \sum_{t'} \sum_{t \geq t'} \frac{d\mathcal{L}}{dh_k^{t+1}} \frac{\partial h_k^{t+1}}{\partial c_k^{t+1}} \frac{\partial c_k^{t+1}}{\partial c_k^t} \cdots \frac{\partial c_k^{t'+2}}{\partial c_k^{t'+1}} \frac{\partial c_k^{t'+1}}{\partial h_j^{t'}} e_{ij}^{t'} \tag{12}$$

**Flip Time Indices:** We flip the indices again to have a causal formula:

$$\sum_{t'} \frac{d\mathcal{L}}{dc_k^{t'+1}} \frac{\partial c_k^{t'+1}}{\partial h_j^{t'}} e_{ij}^{t'} = \sum_{t} \frac{d\mathcal{L}}{dh_k^{t+1}} \frac{\partial h_k^{t+1}}{\partial c_k^{t+1}} \sum_{t' \leq t} \frac{\partial c_k^{t+1}}{\partial c_k^t} \cdots \frac{\partial c_k^{t'+2}}{\partial c_k^{t'+1}} \frac{\partial c_k^{t'+1}}{\partial h_j^{t'}} e_{ij}^{t'} \tag{13}$$

**Definition (Explicit variable).** *We define the* explicit variable $\beta_{ij}^t(k, k', ..., j)$ *as:*

$$\beta_{ij}^t(k, k', ..., j) := \sum_{t' \leq t-1} \frac{\partial c_k^t}{\partial c_k^{t-1}} \cdots \frac{\partial c_k^{t'+2}}{\partial c_k^{t'+1}} \frac{\partial c_k^{t'+1}}{\partial h_{k'}^{t'}} \frac{\partial h_{k'}^{t'}}{\partial c_{k'}^{t'}} \beta_{ij}^{t'}(k', k'', ..., j) \tag{14}$$

*with* $\beta_{ij}^t(j) = \epsilon_{ij}^t$.

*Backwards Interpretation:* The explicit variable represents the idea of starting at $c_k^t$, moving an arbitrary number of steps through the implicit recurrence $c_k^t \rightarrow$

$h_k^{t-1}$ until at a certain $t'$ you jump to the output variable of another neuron $h_{k'}^{t'}$, down to its hidden variable $c_{k'}^{t'}$ and then start again, with a path, now starting at $c_{k'}^{t'}$. In total, it considers all possible paths, with arbitrary length, spending an arbitrary number of steps in each of the neurons (through implicit recurrences) from $c_k^t$ to $c_j^{t'}$ through the neurons $k', k'', ...$ and then times the implicit variable $\epsilon_{ij}^{t'}$ (cf. Fig. 6).

*Forwards Interpretation:* The explicit variable accounts for the influence of the activity of neuron $j$ at any previous time step $c_j^{t'}$ to neuron $k'$ at a future time step $c_{k'}^t$ through the neurons $k', k'', ...$.

*Incremental Computation:* The recursive relation to this variable that allows it to be updated at each time step is:

$$\beta_{ij}^t(k, k', ..., j) = \frac{\partial c_k^t}{\partial c_k^{t-1}} \beta_{ij}^{t-1}(k, k', ..., j) + \frac{\partial c_k^t}{\partial h_{k'}^{t-1}} \frac{\partial h_{k'}^{t-1}}{\partial c_{k'}^{t-1}} \beta_{ij}^{t-1}(k', ..., j) \qquad (15)$$

**Definition (Explicit eligibility trace).** *Given the explicit variable* $\beta_{ij}^t(k, k', ..., j)$, *we define the* explicit eligibility trace $b_{ij}^t(k, k', ..., j)$ *as:*

$$b_{ij}^t(k, k', ..., j) := \frac{\partial h_k^t}{\partial c_k^t} \beta_{ij}^t(k, k', ..., j) \qquad (16)$$

*with* $b_{ij}^t(j) = e_{ij}^t$.

Since $\partial h_k^t / \partial c_k^t$ is causal and local, and the explicit variable $\beta_{ij}^t(k, k', ..., j)$ is causal but only partially local (it requires message passing from the presynaptic neuron $k'$ to the postsynaptic neuron $k$), then the explicit eligibility trace $b_{ij}^t(k, k', ..., j)$ is also **causal** but only **partially local**.

**Final Equation with Re-expressed Explicit Recurrence of Order 1:** Substituting the explicit variable Eq. 14 in Eq. 13 yields:

$$\sum_k \sum_t \frac{d\mathcal{L}}{dc_k^{t+1}} \frac{\partial c_k^{t+1}}{\partial h_j^t} e_{ij}^{t'} = \sum_k \sum_t \frac{d\mathcal{L}}{dh_k^{t+1}} b_{ij}^{t+1}(k, j) \qquad (17)$$

And substituting this back to the original equation (cf. Eq. 11):

$$\begin{aligned} \frac{d\mathcal{L}}{dw_{ij}} &= \sum_t \frac{\partial \mathcal{L}}{\partial h_j^t} e_{ij}^t + \sum_k \sum_t \frac{d\mathcal{L}}{dc_k^{t+1}} \frac{\partial c_k^{t+1}}{\partial h_j^t} e_{ij}^t \\ &= \sum_t \frac{\partial \mathcal{L}}{\partial h_j^t} e_{ij}^t + \sum_k \sum_t \frac{d\mathcal{L}}{dh_k^{t+1}} b_{ij}^{t+1}(k, j) \end{aligned} \qquad (18)$$

Here it becomes clear how setting this second factor to 0 is what gives us e-prop (cf. the right arrow in Fig. 1), since we forcefully ignore the influence of a neuron on other neurons (and itself) through the explicit recurrences.

## 3.3    Re-expressing Explicit Recurrences of Order $> 1$

Now that we have seen how the explicit eligibility connects the activity of neuron $j$ with other neurons through explicit recurrences, we can use it to re-express higher-order explicit recurrences.

**Unroll the Recursion:** Starting from the equation with one order of explicit recurrence already re-expressed (cf. Eq. 18), and alternatively using the definition of explicit recurrences (cf. Eq. 2) and the action of the explicit eligibility trace (cf. Eq. 17), we can repeat the previous steps for higher orders:

$$
\frac{d\mathcal{L}}{dw_{ij}} = \sum_t \frac{\partial \mathcal{L}}{\partial h_j^t} e_{ij}^t + \sum_{k_1} \sum_t \left( \frac{\partial \mathcal{L}}{\partial h_{k_1}^{t+1}} + \sum_{k_2} \frac{d\mathcal{L}}{dc_{k_2}^{t+2}} \frac{\partial c_{k_2}^{t+2}}{\partial h_{k_1}^{t+1}} \right) b_{ij}^{t+1}(k_1, j)
$$

$$
= \sum_t \frac{\partial \mathcal{L}}{\partial h_j^t} e_{ij}^t + \sum_t \sum_{k_1} \frac{\partial \mathcal{L}}{\partial h_{k_1}^{t+1}} b_{ij}^{t+1}(k_1, j) + \sum_t \sum_{k_1, k_2} \frac{d\mathcal{L}}{dc_{k_2}^{t+2}} \frac{\partial c_{k_2}^{t+2}}{\partial h_{k_1}^{t+1}} b_{ij}^{t+1}(k_1, j)
$$

$$
= \sum_t \frac{\partial \mathcal{L}}{\partial h_j^t} e_{ij}^t + \sum_t \sum_{k_1} \frac{\partial \mathcal{L}}{\partial h_{k_1}^{t+1}} b_{ij}^{t+1}(k_1, j) + \sum_t \sum_{k_1, k_2} \frac{d\mathcal{L}}{dh_{k_2}^{t+2}} b_{ij}^{t+2}(k_2, k_1, j)
$$

$$
= \sum_t \sum_{t' \geq t} \sum_{k_0 = j, k_1, .., k_{t}} \frac{\partial \mathcal{L}}{\partial h_{k_t}^{t'}} b_{ij}^{t'}(k_t, \cdots, k_1, k_0 = j) \tag{19}
$$

This gives us a high overview of separating the different levels of explicit recurrences which will lead to the definition of the m-order e-prop (Sect. 4).

**Flip Time Indices:** As before we change the time indices and reorganise to allow for causality,

$$
\frac{d\mathcal{L}}{dw_{ij}} = \sum_t \sum_k \frac{\partial \mathcal{L}}{\partial h_k^t} \frac{\partial h_k^t}{\partial c_k^t} \sum_{t' \leq t} \sum_{k_0 = j, k_1, .., k_{t'-1}} \beta_{ij}^t(k, k_{t'-1}, \cdots, k_1, k_0 = j) \tag{20}
$$

**Definition (Recurrence variable).** *We define the* recurrence variable $\alpha_{ij}^{t,r}$ *as:*

$$
\alpha_{ij}^{t,r} = \sum_{t' \leq t} \sum_{k_0 = j, k_1, .., k_{t'-1}} \beta_{ij}^t(r, k_{t'-1}, \cdots, k_1, k_0 = j) \tag{21}
$$

*Backwards Interpretation:* Starting at current time $t$ in neuron $r$, the recurrence variable represents all combinations of paths through any combination of neurons $k_{t'-1}, .., k_1$ ending in neuron $j$.

*Forwards Interpretation:* The recurrence variable accounts for the influence of the activity of neuron $j$ at any previous time step to neuron $r$ at the current timestep $t$ through all possible paths through all neurons.

$$\frac{d\mathcal{L}}{dw_{ij}} = \sum_t \sum_k \frac{\partial \mathcal{L}}{\partial h_k^t} a_{ij}^{t,k}$$

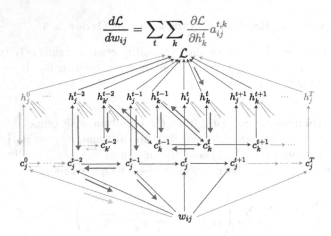

**Fig. 7.** Computational graph for final computation of RTRL.

*Incremental Computation:* Once again, importantly, we have a recursive equation for computing the recurrence variable:

$$\alpha_{ij}^{t,r} = \frac{\partial c_r^t}{\partial c_r^{t-1}} \alpha_{ij}^{t-1,r} + \sum_k \frac{\partial c_r^t}{\partial h_k^{t-1}} \frac{\partial h_k^{t-1}}{\partial c_k^{t-1}} \alpha_{ij}^{t-1,k} \tag{22}$$

**Definition (Recurrence eligibility trace).** *Given the recurrence variable* $\alpha_{ij}^{t,r}$, *we define the* recurrence eligibility trace $a_{ij}^{t,r}$ *as:*

$$a_{ij}^{t,r} := \frac{\partial h_r^t}{\partial c_r^t} \alpha_{ij}^{t,r} \tag{23}$$

Since $\partial h_r^t / \partial c_r^t$ is causal and local, but the recurrence variable $\alpha_{ij}^{t,r}$ is causal but non-local, the recurrence eligibility trace $a_{ij}^{t,r}$ is also **causal** but **non-local**. It is non-local in an equivalent way as BPTT is not: each synapse $ij$ requires to store a variable representing how the activation in the past of any other neuron $r$ would affect its computation in the present, even if $r \neq i, j$ and through all possible paths of synapses. The recursive computation of $\alpha_{ij}^{t,r}$ requires of the summation of the recurrence variables of all the neurons requiring non-local communication.

**Final Equation of RTRL:** Eq. 20 transforms into (by substituting Eq. 21 into Eq. 20) the final equation for RTRL (cf. Fig. 7):

$$\frac{d\mathcal{L}}{dw_{ij}} = \sum_t \sum_k \frac{\partial \mathcal{L}}{\partial h_k^t} \frac{\partial h_k^t}{\partial c_k^t} \alpha_{ij}^{t,k} = \sum_t \sum_k \frac{\partial \mathcal{L}}{\partial h_k^t} a_{ij}^{t,k} \tag{24}$$

We now have a causal but still non-local gradient computation algorithm.

# 4   E-prop

The e-prop algorithm approximates the gradient by not considering the explicit recurrences in RNNs. E-prop was originally formulated for RSNNs, since it is considered more biologically plausible than BPTT and RTRL due to its characteristics of being causal and local [2]. The approximation of the gradient that defines e-prop is:

$$\frac{d\mathcal{L}}{dw_{ij}} \approx \sum_t \frac{\partial \mathcal{L}}{\partial h_j^t} e_{ij}^t \tag{25}$$

Through the derivation of RTRL from BPTT, e-prop has arisen naturally in three different places. This allows us for equivalent interpretations of the approximation, each more detailed than the previous one.

First, and as originally proposed [2], we can understand e-prop from the equation that arises after re-expressing the implicit eligibility trace (cf. Eq. 10):

$$\frac{d\mathcal{L}}{dw_{ij}} = \sum_t \frac{d\mathcal{L}}{dh_j^t} e_{ij}^t$$

Here we approximate the non-causal and non-local total derivative by the causal and local partial derivative, i.e. $d\mathcal{L}/dh_j^t \approx \partial\mathcal{L}/\partial h_j^t$ (cf. Fig. 5).

Second, we can understand it from the equation after re-expressing the explicit recurrences of order 1 (cf. Eq. 18):

$$\frac{d\mathcal{L}}{dw_{ij}} = \sum_t \frac{\partial \mathcal{L}}{\partial h_j^t} e_{ij}^t + \sum_k \sum_t \frac{d\mathcal{L}}{dh_k^{t+1}} b_{ij}^{t+1}(k,j)$$

Here we see explicitly what we are ignoring in the approximation, since ignoring this non-causal and non-local second term, i.e. $\sum_k \sum_t \frac{d\mathcal{L}}{dh^{t+1}} b_{ij}^{t+1}(k,j) = 0$, defines e-prop. Ignoring these future dependencies to other neurons through explicit recurrences leads to a gradient computing algorithm that treats each neuron as producing an output only for the network's computation and not to communicate to other neurons. Therefore, synapses arriving at neurons that are not directly connected to the readout of the RNN, are not modified by e-prop (e-prop does not compute through additional feed-forward layers).

Finally, the most expressive of the interpretations comes from the equation that shows how to apply the re-expressing of the explicit recurrences of order 1, recursively, to re-express higher orders (cf. Eq. 19):

$$\frac{d\mathcal{L}}{dw_{ij}} = \sum_t \frac{\partial \mathcal{L}}{\partial h_j^t} e_{ij}^t + \sum_k \sum_t \frac{d\mathcal{L}}{dh_k^{t+1}} b_{ij}^{t+1}(k,j)$$

$$= \sum_t \frac{\partial \mathcal{L}}{\partial h_j^t} e_{ij}^t + \sum_t \sum_{k_1} \frac{\partial \mathcal{L}}{\partial h_{k_1}^{t+1}} b_{ij}^{t+1}(k_1,j) + \sum_t \sum_{k_1,k_2} \frac{d\mathcal{L}}{dh_{k_2}^{t+2}} b_{ij}^{t+2}(k_2,k_1,j)$$

$$= \cdots$$

Here we define the *m-order e-prop* as the approximation resulting from setting in the above equation $\sum_t \sum_{k_0=j,k_1,\ldots,k_m} \frac{d\mathcal{L}}{dh_{k_m}^{t+m}} b_{ij}^{t+m}(k_m,\cdots,k_1,k_0=j) = 0$.

By increasing the order $m$ we better approximate the gradient at the cost of needing the activities of other neurons $m$ time steps ahead to compute the current gradient of the loss. Under this scope, standard e-prop [2] is just the 1-order e-prop (fully causal and local but the most inaccurate approximation). On the other extreme, the T-order e-prop (nothing is approximated or set to 0) corresponds to the full gradient computation, in a middle form between BPTT and RTRL (the exact computation of the gradient but completely non-causal and non-local). Moreover, synapses arriving into neurons connected to the readout through up to $m-1$ synapses will be modified by the m-order e-prop (m-order e-prop computes through up to $m-1$ additional feed-forward layers).

## 5    Conclusion

In this paper, we formally explored how BPTT, RTRL, and e-prop relate to each other. We extended the general scheme for re-expressing recurrences as eligibility traces from [2] and applied it iteratively to go from BPTT to RTRL. In the process, we found intermediate expressions that allow for better intuition of these algorithms. Moreover, we showed how e-prop can be seen as an extreme case of a series of approximation algorithms, which we coin m-order e-prop.

## References

1. Bellec, G., Salaj, D., Subramoney, A., Legenstein, R., Maass, W.: Long short-term memory and learning-to-learn in networks of spiking neurons (2018)
2. Bellec, G., et al.: A solution to the learning dilemma for recurrent networks of spiking neurons. Nat. Commun. **11**, 1–15 (2020)
3. Czarnecki, W.M., Świrszcz, G., Jaderberg, M., Osindero, S., Vinyals, O., Kavukcuoglu, K.: Understanding synthetic gradients and decoupled neural interfaces (2017)
4. Hochreiter, S., Schmidhuber, J.: Long short-term memory. Neural Comput. **9**(8), 1735–1780 (1997)
5. Marblestone, A., Wayne, G., Kording, K.: Toward an integration of deep learning and neuroscience. Front. Comput. Neurosci. **10** (2016)
6. Werbos, P.: Backpropagation through time: what it does and how to do it. Proc. IEEE **78**, 1550–1560 (1990)
7. Werbos, P., John, P.: Beyond regression: new tools for prediction and analysis in the behavioral sciences (1974)
8. Williams, R.J., Zipser, D.: A learning algorithm for continually running fully recurrent neural networks. Neural Comput. **1**, 270–280 (1989)
9. Zenke, F., Neftci, E.O.: Brain-inspired learning on neuromorphic substrates. CoRR abs/2010.11931 (2020)

# Adaptive Online Domain Incremental Continual Learning

Nuwan Gunasekara[✉], Heitor Gomes, Albert Bifet, and Bernhard Pfahringer

AI Institute, University of Waikato, Hamilton, New Zealand
ng98@students.waikato.ac.nz, {heitor.gomes,abifet,bernhard}@waikato.ac.nz

**Abstract.** Continual Learning (CL) problems pose significant challenges for Neural Network (NN)s. Online Domain Incremental Continual Learning (ODI-CL) refers to situations where the data distribution may change from one task to another. These changes can severely affect the learned model, focusing too much on previous data and failing to properly learn and represent new concepts. Conversely, if a model constantly forgets previously learned knowledge, it may be deemed too unstable and unsuitable. This work proposes Online Domain Incremental Pool (ODIP), a novel method to cope with catastrophic forgetting. ODIP also employs automatic concept drift detection and does not require task ids during training. ODIP maintains a pool of learners, freezing and storing the best one after training on each task. An additional Task Predictor (TP) is trained to select the most appropriate NN from the frozen pool for prediction. We compare ODIP against regularization methods and observe that it yields competitive predictive performance.

**Keywords:** Continual learning · Online domain incremental continual learning

## 1 Introduction

Though modern Neural Network (NN)s have shown great success in image classification and natural language processing, they assume training data to be Independent and Identically Distributed (IID). Due to this assumption, once confronted with a distribution shift in the input data, the model may undergo costly retraining to preserve old knowledge while adjusting to the new distribution. Without retraining, an NN receiving non-IID data forgets its past knowledge when confronted with a distribution shift. This phenomenon is identified as "catastrophic forgetting" in literature [6,9,17,20].

Continual Learning (CL) currently attempts to minimize this catastrophic forgetting in NNs via replay and regularization methods [17]. Though current replay methods outperform regularization methods in terms of performance, they may not be suitable for situations with memory and privacy constraints on the replay buffer [2,17]. Even though offline CL methods have been proposed, current research mainly focuses on online methods to solve catastrophic forgetting. This allows one to develop continually learning agents which are adaptive. But resilient to catastrophic forgetting.

© The Author(s), under exclusive license to Springer Nature Switzerland AG 2022
E. Pimenidis et al. (Eds.): ICANN 2022, LNCS 13529, pp. 491–502, 2022.
https://doi.org/10.1007/978-3-031-15919-0_41

Online Domain Incremental Continual Learning (ODI-CL) focuses on CL models, which learn from one input distribution to another with minimum catastrophic forgetting. Here the class distribution remains the same. There are many practical applications of this scenario in the modern IoT world. For example, one could use an ODI-CL approach to avoid costly retraining of an X-ray image classification model after a distribution shift in the incoming data due to some hardware changes in the X-ray machine [22]. The same scenario could be valid for many NN models that rely on hardware sensor inputs. Also, on certain ODI-CL settings, replay approaches may be less preferred due to constraints on having a replay buffer.

Considering the practical importance of non-replay ODI-CL, this work proposes an ODI-CL method that alleviates catastrophic forgetting in NNs. But superior to regularization methods. Here a tiny pool of small Convolutional Neural Network (CNN)s are trained online. Once confronted with concept drift, it freezes the best CNN for a given concept, considering the estimated loss of all CNNs. Task Predictor (TP) is trained to pick the best CNN from the frozen pool for prediction. This approach is further extended to automatically detect concept drifts in incoming data using a Task Detection (TD) instead of relying on an external task id signal. Experiment results reveal that both the proposed methods: with and without automatic TD, surpass the performance of current popular regularization methods.

The main contributions of this paper are the following:

1. Online Domain Incremental Pool (ODIP): we introduce a novel method to alleviate catastrophic forgetting for Online Domain Incremental Continual Learning without using instance replay. Here, a small pool of tiny CNNs is trained, and the best one is frozen at the end of each task. Task Predictor is trained to predict the best frozen CNN for evaluation for a given instance. The experiment results reveal that ODIP yields superior accuracy than regularization baselines. Furthermore, an in-depth investigation is done to better understand the effectiveness of different TPs on three ODI-CL datasets.
2. Instead of relying on an external task id signal during prediction, ODIP uses an automatic Task Detection mechanism to detect tasks in the incoming data. This allows ODIP to select the most appropriate frozen network to produce predictions for each instance. ADaptive sliding WINdow (ADWIN) is used to detect drifts in CNN's loss to determine a new task. To the best of our knowledge, this automatic Task Detection for Online Domain Incremental Continual Learning has not been proposed before.

The rest of the paper is organized as follows. The following section presents the current developments in Online Domain Incremental Continual Learning, including some practical use cases. The next section presents the proposed Online Domain Incremental Pool for ODI-CL. The experiments section explains the experimental setup where the proposed method is compared against popular ODI-CL methods on three datasets. It also provides insights into the effectiveness of different Task Predictors. The final section provides conclusions and directions for future research.

## 2   Related Work

The literature has thoroughly documented that an NN receiving non-IID data forgets past knowledge when confronted with a concept shift [6,9,17,20]. Continual Learning (CL) attempts to continually learn with minimal forgetting of past concepts [9,17]. In Online Domain Incremental Continual Learning (ODI-CL), this learning happens online, and the data stream comprises different concepts (distributions) with the same label distribution [17].

To avoid catastrophic forgetting in NNs, CL algorithms use two popular approaches: regularization and replay. Regularization algorithms like Elastic Weight Consolidation (EWC) [9] and Learning without Forgetting (LwF) [13] adjust the weights of the network in such a way that it minimizes the overwriting of the weights for the old concept. Elastic Weight Consolidation (EWC) uses a quadratic penalty to regularize updating the network parameters related to the past concept. It uses the diagonal of the Fisher Information Matrix to approximate the importance of the parameters [9]. EWC has some shortcomings: 1) Fisher Information Matrix needs to be stored for each task, 2) requires an extra pass over each task's data at the end of the training [17]. Though different versions of EWC address these concerns [4,14,21], [4] seems to be the one suitable for online CL by keeping a single Fisher Information Matrix calculated by a moving average. Learning without Forgetting (LwF) uses knowledge distillation to preserve knowledge from past tasks. Here, the model related to the old task is kept separate, and a separate model is trained on the current task. When the LwF receives data for a new task $(X_n, Y_n)$, it computes the output $(Y_o)$ from the old model for new data $X_n$. During training, assuming that $\hat{Y}_o$ and $\hat{Y}_n$ are predicted values for $X_n$ from the old model and new model, LwF attempts to minimize the loss: $\alpha L_{KD}(Y_o, \hat{Y}_o) + L_{CE}(Yn, \hat{Y}_n) + R$. Here $L_{KD}$ is the distillation loss for the old model, and $\alpha$ is the hyper-parameter controlling the strength of old model against the new one. $L_{CE}$ is the cross-entropy loss for the new task. $R$ is the general regularization term. Due to this strong relation between old and new tasks, it may perform poorly in situations where there is a huge difference between old and new tasks distributions [17].

Replay methods present a mix of instances from the old and current concepts to the Neural Network (NN) based on a given policy while training. This reduces the forgetting as the training instances from the old concepts avoid complete overwriting of past concepts' weights. GDUMB [19], Experience Replay (ER) [5], and Maximally Interfered Retrieval (MIR) [1] are some of the most popular CL replay methods. Replay Using Memory Indexing (REMIND) [7] takes this approach to another level by storing the internal representations of the instances by the initial frozen part of the network and using a randomly selected set of these internal representations to train the last unfrozen layers of the network. Here, REMIND can store more instances' representations using internal low-dimensional features. In general, these replay approaches are motivated by how the hippocampus in the brain stores and replays high-level representations of the memories to the neocortex to learn from them [12].

Recent research has focused on using ODI-CL methods to avoid costly retraining in practical situations where the model is confronted with concept drift. ODI-CL has been used in X-ray image classification to avoid costly retraining on distribution shifts due to unforeseen shifts in hardware's physical properties [22]. Also, it has been used to mitigate bias in facial expression and action unit recognition across different demographic groups [8]. Furthermore, ODI-CL was used to counter retraining on concept drifts for multi-variate sequential data of critical care patient recordings [2]. The authors highlight some replay methods' infeasibility due to strong privacy requirements in clinical settings. This concern is further highlighted in [17] empirical study as well.

Most of the current ODI-CL methods rely on an explicit end-of-task signal during training. EWC and LwF use this signal to optimize weights, while replay methods like ER use it to update their replay buffer. However, GDUMB does not rely on this signal for replay buffer updates. Though [17] identifies ODI-CL as training without the end of the task signal. Practical implementations such as [8] and [2] use the end of the task signal to employ CL methods such as EWC and LWF. However, on the other hand, practical implementation in [22] assumes a gradual distribution shift in the input data distribution where instances from both the new and old tasks could appear in the stream for a certain period.

Our approach (ODIP) initially assumes the presence of an end-of-task signal at training and later proposes a method to detect it automatically. When confronted with concept drift, the proposed method freezes the best NN from a small pool of little networks, and a predictor is trained to choose the best network from the frozen pool for a given evaluation instance. As it avoids using a replay buffer, it is a good candidate for settings with higher privacy requirements.

## 3    Online Domain Incremental Pool

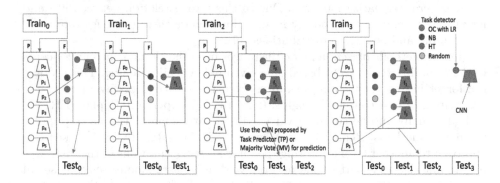

**Fig. 1.** Proposed Online Domain Incremental Pool (ODIP)

The ODI-CL is defined as the training set composed of multiple concepts of non-IID data, where each concept has a different input distribution with the

---
**Algorithm 1.** TRAIN OC WITH LR
---
**Input:** Task Predictor $TP$: One Class Classifier with Logistic Regression , $z$: extracted
   features
 1: *score, in_class* ← TRAIN $OC(z)$
 2: TRAIN $LR(score, in\_class)$

---

same label distribution [17]. The goal of the learning algorithm is to minimize catastrophic forgetting of the past concepts while performing well on the current concept [7,17]. Initially, at training, we assume that the task id that signals the end of a concept is available to the learning model. However, this information is not available to the model during evaluation. Later, the proposed method(ODIP) is extended to discard this external task id signal.

---
**Algorithm 2.** ODIP TRAINING ALGORITHM
---
**Input:** $P$: pool of training CNNs, $F$: pool of frozen CNNs, $T$: task set, $X_t$: training
   set for task $t$, $TP$: TP
 1: Initialize pool $F = \{\}$
 2: **for** all task $t \in T$ **do**
 3:     **for** all mini-batch $b_t$ in training set $X_t$ for task $t$ **do**
 4:         $z$ ← features from mini-batch $b_t$ for task $t$
 5:         **for** all learner $p \in P$ **do**
 6:             Compute loss $L_p$ of mini-batch $b_t$ and train $CNN_p$
 7:             Update $ADWIN_p$ with $L_p$
 8:             **if** task predictor $TP_p$ is One Class Classifier with LR **then**
 9:                 TRAIN OC WITH LR$(TP_p, z)$
10:             **end if**
11:         **end for**
12:         **if** task predictor $TP$ is Naive Bayes or HoeFFding Tree **then**
13:             TRAIN $TP(z, t)$
14:         **end if**
15:     **end for**
16:     Append the CNN with lowest loss estimated using ADWIN to F
17: **end for**

---

We propose an Online Domain Incremental Pool (ODIP), where $P$ pool of tiny CNNs are trained for each concept $t$ with a given Task Predictor. The Task Predictors could be None, Naive Bayes (NB), Hoeffding Tree (HT), and One Class Classifier (OC) with Logistic Regression (LR). The Task Predictor is trained for mini-batch $b_t$ using extracted features from a static feature extractor. At the end of each task's training, CNN with the lowest estimated loss is frozen and added into the frozen pool $F$. In the special case of OC with LR, the relevant OC with the LR is also part of the frozen CNN. Algorithm 2, along with Fig. 1, further explains this training approach.

**Algorithm 3.** PREDICT OC WITH LR

**Input:** Task Predictor $TP$: One Class Classifier with Logistic Regression, $z$: extracted features.
1: $score, in\_class \leftarrow$ PREDICT $OC(z)$
**Output:** PREDICT $LR(score)$

In ODIP, there are two vote aggregation methods for prediction: Weighted Voting (WV) or votes from the best CNN ($CNN_{best}$). For Weighted Voting (WV), the probabilities of the Task Predictor are used as weights. In the $CNN_{best}$ case, it is either selected randomly from the $F$ pool or the one predicted by Task Predictor. Algorithm 4 further explains this. Recently proposed ODI-CL algorithms rely on an explicit end of the task signal (task id) to identify the start of a new task. ODIP is also relying on these explicit task ids to distinguish different tasks. This reliance on an explicit task id may preclude one from employing current ODIP algorithms in real-life settings where it may be challenging to identify such a signal explicitly.

**Algorithm 4.** ODIP PREDICTION ALGORITHM

**Input:** $x_t$: instance of task $t$, $F$: pool of frozen CNNs, $TP$: Task Predictor, useWeightedVoting
1: $z \leftarrow$ features from instance $x_t$ of task $t$
2: **if** useWeightedVoting **then**
3:     **if** $TP$ is WeightedVoting **then**
4:         $votes \leftarrow 1/|F| \sum_{f=1}^{|F|}$ PREDICT$(f, x_t)$
5:     **else if** $TP$ is One Class Classifier with LR **then**
6:         $votes \leftarrow 1/|F| \sum_{f=1}^{|F|}$ PREDICT OC WITH LR$(TP_f, z) \times$ PREDICT$(f, x_t)$
7:     **else**
8:         $votes \leftarrow 1/|F| \sum_{f=1}^{|F|}$ PREDICT$(TP, z) \times$ PREDICT$(f, x_t)$
9:     **end if**
10: **else**
11:     **if** $TP$ is Random **then**
12:         Select $CNN_{selected}$ randomly from pool $F$
13:     **else if** $TP$ One Class Classifier with LR **then**
14:         $CNN_{selected} \leftarrow \arg\max_{f \in F}$ PREDICT OC WITH LR$(TP_f, z)$
15:     **else**
16:         $CNN_{selected} \leftarrow \arg\max_{f \in F}$ PREDICT$(TP_f, z)$
17:     **end if**
18:     $votes \leftarrow$ PREDICT$(CNN_{selected}, x_t)$
19: **end if**
**Output:** $votes$

**Algorithm 5.** ODIP TRAINING ALGORITHM WITH AUTO TASK DETECTION

**Input:** $P$: pool of training CNNs, $F$: pool of frozen CNNs, $T$: task set, $X_t$: training set for task $t$, $TP$: Task Predictor

1: Initialize pool $F = \{\}$
2: Initialize $taskId = 0$
3: **for** all task $t \in T$ **do**
4:    **for** all mini-batch $b_t$ in training set $X_t$ for task $t$ **do**
5:       $taskEnd \leftarrow false$
6:       $z \leftarrow$ features from mini-batch $b_t$ for task $t$
7:       **for** all learner $p \in P$ **do**
8:          Compute the loss $L_p$ of mini-batch $b_t$ and train $CNN_p$
9:          Update $ADWIN_p$ with $L_p$
10:          **if** $ADWIN_p$ detects change **then**
11:             $taskEnd \leftarrow true$
12:          **end if**
13:          **if** task predictor $TP_p$ is One Class Classifier with LR **then**
14:             TRAIN OC WITH LR($TP_p$, $z$)
15:          **end if**
16:       **end for**
17:       **if** task predictor $TP$ is Naive Bayes or Hoeffding Tree **then**
18:          TRAIN $TP(z, taskId)$
19:       **end if**
20:       **if** $taskEnd$ **then**
21:          $taskId \leftarrow taskId + 1$
22:          Append the CNN with lowest loss estimated using ADWIN to F
23:       **end if**
24:    **end for**
25: **end for**

ODIP is extended to identify concept drifts in the incoming stream automatically. ADaptive sliding WINdow (ADWIN) [3] is used as a task detector. ADWIN has nice properties where it uses exponential histograms for memory efficiency and discards the buffer related to the previous concept once confronted with a drift. Every CNN in $P$ pool has its ADWIN. They are updated with each CNN's loss after training. Once updated, a new task is identified if any ADWIN detects a drift in the loss. Here a drift in the loss is assumed to be related to the drift in the input stream. Algorithm 5 explains this training with automatic Task Detection in detail. In the experiments, the effectiveness of ODIP was compared against popular regularization baselines.

**Table 1.** Datasets

| Dataset | Number of tasks | Number of classes | Channels, H, W |
|---|---|---|---|
| CORe50 | 11 | 10 | 3, 32, 32 |
| RotatedCIFAR10 | 4 | 10 | 3, 32, 32 |
| RotatedMNIST | 4 | 10 | 1, 28, 28 |

# 4   Experiments

The experiments attempt to understand the effectiveness of ODIP against popular regularization baselines. They also attempt to identify the effectiveness of Task Predictors. Lastly, they attempt to determine the effectiveness of ODIP with automatic Task Detection against regularization baselines.

Different versions of ODIP were compared against regularization baselines: LWF and EWC. The replay methods were not considered in the baselines as the setting avoids using a replay buffer. The baselines use CNNs with 4.3 times the parameters (144234) than in ODIP experiments (33450). For ODIP, ResNet-18 was used as the static feature extractor and flattened last layer features were used to train the TPs. Five types of TPs were used in the experiments: random, Majority Vote (MV), NB, HT[1], and OC[2] with LR. Also, two types of vote aggregation methods were considered in the experiments: WV and the use of votes from $CNN_{best}$. Furthermore, two variants of automatic Task Predictor were considered in the experiments: $\alpha$) include the best training CNN for prediction when the frozen pool is empty, $\beta$) include the best training CNN for prediction when the frozen pool is empty OR when the predicted network is related to the current concept. $P$ pool size for ODIP was set to 6 CNNs. In the experiments, we also considered a hypothetical scenario of ODIP, where the task id is available at evaluation, and it is used to determine the correct frozen CNN. This is presented as the "Tid known" in the results. This allows one to determine the hypothetical upper bound of ODIP.

As shown in Table 1, three datasets were used in the experiments: CORe50 [15], RotatedCIFAR10, and RotatedMNIST. With RotatedCIFAR10 and RotatedMNIST, 90° rotations (0°, 90°, 180°, −90°) of the original images from CIFAR10 [10] and MNIST [11] were considered separate tasks. Altogether there were four tasks in those two datasets. With CORe50, 11 distinct sessions (8 indoor and 3 outdoor) of the same object were considered separate tasks: tasks 0–2, 4–8 indoor, tasks 3, 9, and 10 outdoor. Here 10 object categories were considered as the class labels. In the above datasets, all classes were presented in all the tasks. Such rearranging was done to the original datasets to adhere to the ODI-CL definition described in [17].

---

[1] Use skmultiflow [18] online versions of NB and HT.
[2] Online One-Class SVM. ODIP source code available at github.

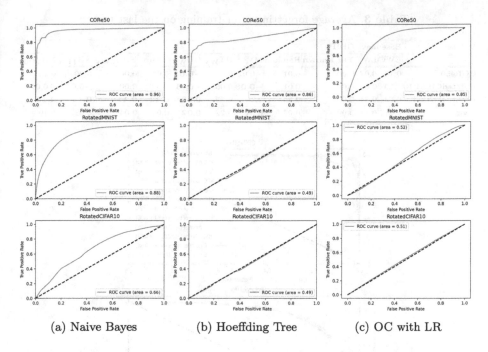

(a) Naive Bayes          (b) Hoeffding Tree          (c) OC with LR

**Fig. 2.** Effectiveness of Task Predictors. ROC curves for predicted task id and AUC scores for all the Task Predictors

**Table 2.** Average accuracy after training on the last task

| Dataset | Baselines | | | ODI-CL | | | | | | | | |
|---|---|---|---|---|---|---|---|---|---|---|---|---|
| | EWC | LWF | Tid known | Random | MV | HT$_{WV}$ | OC$_{WV}$ | NB$_{WV}$ | NB$_{NoWV}$ | NB$_{TD\alpha}$ | NB$_{TD\beta}$ |
| CORe50 | 0.41 | 0.41 | 0.69 | 0.42 | 0.53 | 0.63 | 0.56 | **0.66** | 0.61 | 0.44 | 0.47 |
| RotatedCIFAR10 | 0.44 | **0.48** | 0.48 | 0.38 | 0.45 | 0.44 | 0.46 | 0.43 | 0.40 | 0.40 | 0.42 |
| RotatedMNIST | 0.51 | 0.72 | 0.97 | 0.48 | 0.66 | 0.53 | 0.65 | **0.79** | 0.78 | **0.79** | **0.79** |
| **Avg** | 0.45 | 0.54 | 0.72 | 0.42 | 0.55 | 0.53 | 0.56 | **0.63** | 0.60 | 0.54 | 0.56 |

All experiments were run using Avalanche [16] Continual Learning platform. Average accuracy and forgetting defined in [17] are used in the evaluation. All experiments were run three times, and relevant averages and standard deviations were considered in the evaluation. The standard deviations were omitted from this manuscript due to space constraints.

Table 2 contains the average accuracy of each method after training on the last task. As one can see from the table, ODIP NB$_{WV}$ produces the best results. ODIP Random and EWC seem to yield poor results. In general, all methods with Weighted Voting produced good results compared to the two baselines. However, weights from a good Task Predictor seem to boost the performance significantly. Also, ODIP NB$_{TD\beta}$, which has automatic Task Detection, yields better results than regularization baselines. It is also on-par or better than the other ODIP methods, which use task ids, except for NB. Considering the hypothetical "Tid

**Table 3.** Average forgetting after training on the last task

| Dataset | Baselines | | ODIP | | | | | | | | |
|---|---|---|---|---|---|---|---|---|---|---|---|
| | EWC | LWF | Tid known | Random | MV | HT$_{WV}$ | OC$_{WV}$ | NB$_{WV}$ | NB$_{NoWV}$ | NB$_{TD\alpha}$ | NB$_{TD\beta}$ |
| CORe50 | 0.10 | 0.07 | 0.00 | 0.01 | −0.02 | 0.02 | **−0.03** | 0.01 | 0.00 | 0.00 | 0.20 |
| RotatedCIFAR10 | 0.10 | 0.00 | 0.00 | 0.01 | **−0.03** | 0.05 | −0.03 | −0.01 | 0.00 | −0.03 | −0.01 |
| RotatedMNIST | 0.63 | 0.24 | 0.00 | 0.20 | 0.16 | 0.59 | **0.12** | **0.12** | **0.12** | **0.12** | **0.12** |
| **Avg** | 0.28 | 0.11 | 0.00 | 0.07 | 0.04 | 0.22 | **0.02** | 0.04 | 0.04 | 0.03 | 0.10 |

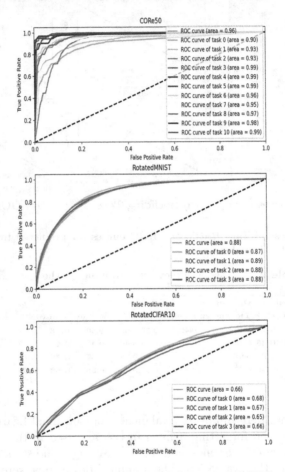

**Fig. 3.** Effectiveness of Naive Bayes as a TP. ROC curves and AUC scores for predicted task id for each task.

known" scenario, it is evident that just selecting the correct frozen CNN is sufficient to outperform current baselines by a considerable margin. This is further evident in Table 3, with "Tid known" having a zero average forgetting across all datasets after training on the last task. Note here that a smaller average forgetting is better.

To further understand the effectiveness of the Task Predictors, the predicted task id was compared against the true task id in non-auto-TD mode against all datasets. This comparison was made for all evaluation instances after training on the last task. Figure 2 shows the ROC curves for predicted task id and the relevant AUC scores for each TP on each dataset. According to the figure, it is clear that NB is a better Task Predictor for all datasets. This further strengthens the overall strong NB results in Table 2. Figure 3 further explains the effectiveness of NB as a Task Predictor when predicting each task in a given dataset. From the per-task ROC curves and AUC scores, it is clear that NB performs similarly on all the tasks for a given dataset. Nevertheless, it does perform slightly better on certain tasks. This is evident in CORe50, with NB performing slightly better for tasks 3, 4, 5, 9, and 10. This suggests, in general, that NB is a good Task Predictor.

## 5   Conclusion

The proposed ODIP produces competitive results for ODI-CL in comparison to regularization-based approaches. The extended version can detect tasks in ODI-CL automatically. ODIP with and without automatic Task Detection produces competitive results compared to current popular regularization baselines: LWF and EWC. This makes ODIP as a good replacement for regularization methods in the ODI-CL setting. It could be further improved to have a fixed frozen pool size. Then information from the Task Predictor could be used to identify the CNN to train and then replace when the frozen pool is full.

## References

1. Aljundi, R., et al.: Online continual learning with maximally interfered retrieval. arXiv preprint arXiv:1908.04742 (2019)
2. Armstrong, J., Clifton, D.: Continual learning of longitudinal health records. arXiv preprint arXiv:2112.11944 (2021)
3. Bifet, A., Gavalda, R.: Learning from time-changing data with adaptive windowing. In: Proceedings of the 2007 SIAM International Conference on Data Mining, pp. 443–448. SIAM (2007)
4. Chaudhry, A., Dokania, P.K., Ajanthan, T., Torr, P.H.: Riemannian walk for incremental learning: understanding forgetting and intransigence. In: Proceedings of the European Conference on Computer Vision (ECCV), pp. 532–547 (2018)
5. Chaudhry, A., et al.: On tiny episodic memories in continual learning. arXiv preprint arXiv:1902.10486 (2019)
6. French, R.M.: Catastrophic forgetting in connectionist networks. Trends Cogn. Sci. **3**(4), 128–135 (1999)
7. Hayes, T.L., Kafle, K., Shrestha, R., Acharya, M., Kanan, C.: REMIND your neural network to prevent catastrophic forgetting. In: Vedaldi, A., Bischof, H., Brox, T., Frahm, J.-M. (eds.) ECCV 2020. LNCS, vol. 12353, pp. 466–483. Springer, Cham (2020). https://doi.org/10.1007/978-3-030-58598-3_28

8. Kara, O., Churamani, N., Gunes, H.: Towards fair affective robotics: continual learning for mitigating bias in facial expression and action unit recognition. arXiv preprint arXiv:2103.09233 (2021)
9. Kirkpatrick, J., et al.: Overcoming catastrophic forgetting in neural networks. Proc. Natl. Acad. Sci. **114**(13), 3521–3526 (2017)
10. Krizhevsky, A., Hinton, G., et al.: Learning multiple layers of features from tiny images (2009)
11. LeCun, Y., Bottou, L., Bengio, Y., Haffner, P.: Gradient-based learning applied to document recognition. Proc. IEEE **86**(11), 2278–2324 (1998)
12. Lewis, P.A., Durrant, S.J.: Overlapping memory replay during sleep builds cognitive schemata. Trends Cogn. Sci. **15**(8), 343–351 (2011)
13. Li, Z., Hoiem, D.: Learning without forgetting. IEEE Trans. Pattern Anal. Mach. Intell. **40**(12), 2935–2947 (2017)
14. Liu, X., Masana, M., Herranz, L., Van de Weijer, J., Lopez, A.M., Bagdanov, A.D.: Rotate your networks: better weight consolidation and less catastrophic forgetting. In: International Conference on Pattern Recognition (ICPR). IEEE (2018)
15. Lomonaco, V., Maltoni, D.: CORe50: a new dataset and benchmark for continuous object recognition. In: Conference on Robot Learning, pp. 17–26. PMLR (2017)
16. Lomonaco, V., et al.: Avalanche: an end-to-end library for continual learning. In: Proceedings of IEEE Conference on Computer Vision and Pattern Recognition. 2nd Continual Learning in Computer Vision Workshop (2021)
17. Mai, Z., Li, R., Jeong, J., Quispe, D., Kim, H., Sanner, S.: Online continual learning in image classification: an empirical survey. Neurocomputing **469**, 28–51 (2022). https://doi.org/10.1016/j.neucom.2021.10.021, https://www.sciencedirect.com/science/article/pii/S0925231221014995
18. Montiel, J., Read, J., Bifet, A., Abdessalem, T.: Scikit-multiflow: a multi-output streaming framework. J. Mach. Learn. Res. **19**(72), 1–5 (2018). http://jmlr.org/papers/v19/18-251.html
19. Prabhu, A., Torr, P.H.S., Dokania, P.K.: GDumb: a simple approach that questions our progress in continual learning. In: Vedaldi, A., Bischof, H., Brox, T., Frahm, J.-M. (eds.) ECCV 2020. LNCS, vol. 12347, pp. 524–540. Springer, Cham (2020). https://doi.org/10.1007/978-3-030-58536-5_31
20. Ratcliff, R.: Connectionist models of recognition memory: constraints imposed by learning and forgetting functions. Psychol. Rev. **97**(2), 285 (1990)
21. Schwarz, J., et al.: Progress & compress: a scalable framework for continual learning. In: International Conference on Machine Learning, pp. 4528–4537. PMLR (2018)
22. Srivastava, S., Yaqub, M., Nandakumar, K., Ge, Z., Mahapatra, D.: Continual domain incremental learning for chest X-Ray classification in low-resource clinical settings. In: Albarqouni, S., et al. (eds.) DART/FAIR -2021. LNCS, vol. 12968, pp. 226–238. Springer, Cham (2021). https://doi.org/10.1007/978-3-030-87722-4_21

# Associative Memory Networks
# with Multidimensional Neurons

Roseli S. Wedemann[1]([⊠]) [iD] and Angel R. Plastino[2,3] [iD]

[1] Instituto de Matemática e Estatística, Universidade do Estado do Rio de Janeiro,
Rua São Francisco Xavier 524, Rio de Janeiro, RJ 20550-900, Brazil
`roseli@ime.uerj.br`
[2] CeBio y Departamento de Ciencias Básicas, Universidad Nacional del Noroeste
de la Provincia de Buenos Aires, UNNOBA, Conicet, Roque Saenz Peña 456,
Junin, Argentina
`arplastino@unnoba.edu.ar`
[3] Centro Brasileiro de Pesquisas Físicas (CBPF), Rua Xavier Sigaud 150,
Rio de Janeiro, RJ 22290-180, Brazil

**Abstract.** Neural networks normally used to model associative memory can be regarded as consisting of dissipative units (the neurons) that interact in such a way that the network itself admits a global energy or Liapunov function. The network's global dynamics is such that the system always evolves "downhill" in the energy landscape. In most models for associative memory, the individual neurons are described as one-dimensional, dynamical systems. In the present contribution, we explore the possibility of extending the structural scheme of associative memory neural networks to more general scenarios, where the units (that is, the neurons) are modeled as multi-dimensional, dissipative systems. With that aim in mind, we advance a coupling scheme for dissipative, multi-dimensional units, that generates dynamical features akin to those required when modeling associative memory.

**Keywords:** Neural networks · Associative memory · Liapunov functions · Multidimensional neurons

## 1 Introduction

In 1943, McCulloch and Pitts argued that the discrete, binary activity of neurons connected by a network of synapses produces events that can be mathematically represented by propositional logic [20]. Logical expressions and memory functioning can then be reproduced by the behavior of these kinds of networks, and they are therefore powerful computational devices. Hopfield later proposed a model where the states of neurons assume continuous values and these types of interconnected neurons behave as an associative memory [12,13], similarly to the network model composed of McCulloch-Pitts neurons. Artificial neurons with continuous state values more closely resemble biological neurons. In these models, neurons are characterized by a real state variable adopting a continuous

© The Author(s), under exclusive license to Springer Nature Switzerland AG 2022
E. Pimenidis et al. (Eds.): ICANN 2022, LNCS 13529, pp. 503–514, 2022.
https://doi.org/10.1007/978-3-031-15919-0_42

range of values that determine whether a neuron fires at a certain time or not. The Hopfield associative memory model has been used to represent an approximation of human memory functioning, and also as an artificial storage device, a content-addressable memory [2,12,13].

The capacity of human memory to store and retrieve information is central to many mental processes, be they normal, pathological, conscious or unconscious and these have been widely studied by the fields of psychiatry, psychoanalysis, neuroscience and computational science [4–6,10,14,22,28,29]. As examples of the application of associative memory neural networks to the study of mental phenomena, we can mention our own efforts in recent years, devoted to develop schematic simulation models that represent aspects of some mental processes such as neurosis, creativity, and the interaction between consciousness and unconsciousness, as described by psychoanalysis, in terms of associative memory functioning [25,33,38,39]. Hopfield-like networks and generalizations such as the Boltzmann Machine [1,2] and Generalized Simulated Annealing (GSA) [31] have been also used in many artificial intelligence tasks [1,17,24,26]. These considerations have motivated us to investigate basic aspects of artificial associative memory models [19,34,35,37,40,41], which we continue to develop in the present work.

Most of the fundamental models in theoretical biology exhibit a dynamics that is dissipative. By continuous dynamical systems with a dissipative, or a nonconservative dynamics, we mean dynamical systems that do not preserve the volume in phase space. Important examples are given by the Lotka-Volterra models in biological population dynamics [18], the continuous, Hopfield, neural network models [12,13], the Cohen-Grossberg network models, and various mathematical models for biological, evolutionary processes [21]. In particular, all biologically inspired models supporting universal computation are nonconservative or, in the case of discrete models, nonreversible. A paradigmatic example (within the class of discrete systems) is Conway's celebrated "Game of Life" cellular automata.

The continuous models mentioned above, besides being non-conservative, exhibit a modular structure. They consist of a set of interacting units, each one characterized by an intrinsic dissipative dynamics. This is certainly the case with the continuous Hopfield model. In this model the units are the neurons, each one represented by a simple, one-dimensional, dissipative dynamics. Real biological neurons are certainly more complex than those appearing in the Hopfield model. It is generally believed, however, that the Hopfield model captures some essential aspects of real biological neural networks. Nervous systems over all the biological kingdom *Animalia* consist of neurons exhibiting similar, basic features. Intriguing theoretical arguments have been advanced suggesting that this remarkable feature of animal life might hold even within astrobiological scenarios [8]. In spite of the notable uniformity of biological, neuronal systems, there exist valid motivations to investigate new or alternative biologically-inspired, mathematical models of computation. First, it would be naive to expect that the already known models exhaust all the richness and complexity of biological computation (even if neurons are everywhere more or less alike). Second, there are also a variety of theoretical reasons for the exploration of other models of computation. For instance, the Cohen-Grossberg family of models are closely related to mathematical models in other areas of biology. The Cohen-Grossberg models include, as particular cases, various mathematical models in population dynamics. It is very natural to consider extensions of these models where the basic interacting units are characterized by multi-dimensional, dynamical systems. For instance, effects of time-delay lead to multidimensional dynamics. Within this context, it is theoretically appealing to formulate a family of neural network models, with multi-dimensional neurons, encompassing other biological models with nonconservative dynamics, and a modular structure based on multi-dimensional units. The study of networks with multi-dimensional units opens new theoretical possibilities, such as that of implementing dynamical thermostatting schemes for neural networks [23]. Generalized models with multi-dimensional neurons might also be relevant in connection with the intriguing recent works by Vanchurin, exploring the possibility that neural networks might provide the most fundamental description of physical reality (see [32] and references therein).

In the case of continuous models for associative memory, the Hopfield model has, from the biological point of view, some unrealistic features. First, as already mentioned, real neurons are more complex than the Hopfield ones. Second, even if neurons are quite uniform, real neurons in an animal's nervous system are not all strictly identical. An important step towards removing these simplifying features was done by Cohen and Grossberg, who proposed a rich family of continuous neural networks, admitting more general and varied types of neurons [7]. In the Cohen-Grossberg models, however, individual neurons are still modeled as one-dimensional, dissipative, dynamical systems. It is a plausible assumption that, in order to represent the complexity of real biological neurons, one would need to describe the neurons with dynamical systems with two or more dimensions. Indeed, in the literature there are models where neurons are described by two-dimensional systems (see, for instance, [27] and references therein). The aim of the present effort is to explore a general framework for constructing modular, dynamical systems, akin to associative memory, neural networks, that consist of $N$ interacting units, each one described by a multi-dimensional, dissipative, dynamical system. Within this general context, we shall show that it is possible to implement an interaction scheme leading to the kind of dynamical behavior that characterizes an associative memory, neural network. The family of generalized networks we advance here admit, as particular cases, the continuous, neural models of Cohen and Grossberg, as well as the continuous, Hopfield model.

## 2    A Continuous Network with Multidimensional Neurons

We thus advance a continuous, associative memory, neural network model constituted by multidimensional neurons. The network consists of $N$ neurons. The $i$-th neuron $(i = 1, \ldots, N)$ is modeled as an $n_i$-dimensional, dissipative, dynamical system. The points in the concomitant phase-space, describing the possible states of the neuron, are given by an $n_i$-dimensional vector $\boldsymbol{X}_i$. Note that the dimension $n_i$ depends on the neuron: in our model, we allow for different neurons to have different dimensions. There are two scalar functions $W_i(\boldsymbol{X}_i)$ and $a_i(\boldsymbol{X}_i)$, and two $n_i$-dimensional vector functions $\boldsymbol{B}_i(\boldsymbol{X}_i)$ and $\boldsymbol{D}_i(\boldsymbol{X}_i)$ associated with each neuron $i$. In addition, there is an $n_i \times n_i$ positive-definite, symmetric square matrix $\boldsymbol{M}_i(\boldsymbol{X}_i)$, which is also a function of the neuron's state $\boldsymbol{X}_i$. The function $a_i$ is assumed to be positive: $a_i > 0$. As we shall soon explain, the functions $W_i$, $a_i$, $\boldsymbol{B}_i$, $\boldsymbol{D}_i$, and $\boldsymbol{M}_i$ are related to the intrinsic dynamics of neuron $i$, and with the output signals through which this neuron affects the dynamics of other neurons. The vectorial function $\boldsymbol{B}_i$, and the matrix-valued function $\boldsymbol{M}_i$ are introduced only for notational convenience, since they are not independent of the other functions characterizing the $i$-th neuron. The independent functions that characterize the dynamics of the $i$-th neuron are the scalar functions $a_i$ and $W_i$, and the vector-valued function $\boldsymbol{D}_i$. The vector $\boldsymbol{B}_i$ is determined by $W_i$ and $\boldsymbol{M}_i$, through

$$\boldsymbol{B}_i = -\boldsymbol{M}_i \nabla W_i, \tag{1}$$

and the matrix-valued function $\boldsymbol{M}_i$ is determined by $\boldsymbol{D}_i$, through

$$\left(\boldsymbol{M}_i^{-1}\right)^T = \frac{\partial \boldsymbol{D}_i}{\partial \boldsymbol{X}_i}. \tag{2}$$

For a matrix $\boldsymbol{A}$, $\boldsymbol{A}^T$ denotes the transpose of $\boldsymbol{A}$. The $n_i \times n_i$ square matrix $\frac{\partial \boldsymbol{D}_i}{\partial \boldsymbol{X}_i}$ is the Jacobian matrix associated with the vector function $\boldsymbol{D}_i(\boldsymbol{X}_i)$,

$$\frac{\partial \boldsymbol{D}_i}{\partial \boldsymbol{X}_i} = \begin{bmatrix} \frac{\partial D_{i;1}}{\partial X_{i;1}} & \cdots & \frac{\partial D_{i;1}}{\partial X_{i;n_i}} \\ \cdots & \cdots & \cdots \\ \cdots & \cdots & \cdots \\ \frac{\partial D_{i;n_i}}{\partial X_{i;1}} & \cdots & \frac{\partial D_{i;n_i}}{\partial X_{i;n_i}} \end{bmatrix}. \tag{3}$$

Here, $\boldsymbol{X}_{i;j}$ stands for the $j$-th component of the vector $\boldsymbol{X}_i$, and $\boldsymbol{D}_{i;j}$ for the $j$-th component of the vector $\boldsymbol{D}_i$. The positive-definite character of the matrix $\boldsymbol{M}_i$ means that, for any vector $\boldsymbol{V} \in \Re^{n_i}$, one has

$$\boldsymbol{V}^T \boldsymbol{M}_i \boldsymbol{V} > 0. \tag{4}$$

In the above equation, as in similar equations appearing in this work, it is useful to think of $\boldsymbol{V}$ as an $n_i$-dimensional column vector, and of $\boldsymbol{V}^T$ as an $n_i$-dimensional row vector.

The interactions between the neurons are codified in an $N \times N$ square matrix array $\boldsymbol{C}$, with elements $C_{ik}, i = 1, \ldots, N$ and $k = 1, \ldots, N$. Each element $C_{ik}$, which describes the interaction between neuron $i$ and neuron $k$, is itself an $n_i \times n_k$ rectangular matrix whose elements are real numbers. The elements of the matrices $C_{ik}$ are constants, not depending on the neurons' states. We shall assume that the rectangular matrix $C_{ki}$ describing the effect of neuron $i$ on neuron $k$ is equal to the transpose of the matrix $C_{ik}$ describing the effect of neuron $k$ on neuron $i$. That is, we assume that the matrices $C_{ik}$ satisfy the relation

$$C_{ki} = C_{ik}{}^T. \tag{5}$$

The intrinsic dynamics of a single neuron $i$ is governed by the equations of motion

$$\frac{d\boldsymbol{X}_i}{dt} = a_i \boldsymbol{B}_i = -a_i \boldsymbol{M}_i \boldsymbol{\nabla} W_i, \tag{6}$$

where $\boldsymbol{\nabla} W_i = (\partial W_i / \partial X_{i;1}, \ldots, \partial W_i / \partial X_{i;n_i})^T$. Here we adopt the usual convention that, when acting on a scalar function defined on an $n_i$-dimensional space, $\boldsymbol{\nabla}$ represents the gradient operator on that space. Notice that we are not using Einstein's convention here: repeated indices in an expression do not mean summation.

The scalar function $W_i$ plays the role of a potential energy (or Liapunov) function. Indeed, let us consider the time derivative of $W_i$,

$$\frac{dW_i}{dt} = (\boldsymbol{\nabla} W_i)^T \cdot \frac{d\boldsymbol{X}_i}{dt} = -a_i (\boldsymbol{\nabla} W_i)^T \boldsymbol{M}_i (\boldsymbol{\nabla} W_i) < 0, \tag{7}$$

where, to obtain the last inequality, we used the fact that $\boldsymbol{M}_i$ is a positive-definite matrix (in the above equation and according to our previous convention, it is convenient to consider $\boldsymbol{X}_i$ and $\boldsymbol{\nabla} W_i$ as column vectors, and to think of $(\boldsymbol{\nabla} W_i)^T$ as a row vector). We see that an isolated, individual neuron always evolves downhill in the $W_i$, multi-dimensional landscape. The vector $d\boldsymbol{X}_i/dt$ does not, in general, point exactly in the direction opposite to the gradient $\boldsymbol{\nabla} W_i$, but it always has a negative projection on the direction of $\boldsymbol{\nabla} W_i$.

We now consider a network of $N$ interacting neurons. The basic equations of motion of our network are

$$\frac{d\boldsymbol{X}_i}{dt} = a_i \left[ \boldsymbol{B}_i - \sum_{k=1}^{N} \boldsymbol{C}_{ik} \boldsymbol{D}_k \right], \quad i = 1, \ldots, N. \tag{8}$$

In the above equation, the first term within the square bracket corresponds to the intrinsic dynamics of the $i$-th neuron, while the second term describes the effects of the other neurons on the dynamics of the $i$-th neuron. The strengths of the interactions between the different neurons are given by the matrices $\boldsymbol{C}_{ik}$. We emphasize that the effects of the $k$-th neuron on the $i$-th are given by the elements of the matrix $\boldsymbol{C}_{ik}$, and not by a single coefficient, as in a standard Hopfield neural network.

## 3  Liapunov Function

We are now going to prove that our neural network model admits a Liapunov, or energy function. Let us consider the function

$$\Omega(\boldsymbol{X}_1, \ldots, \boldsymbol{X}_N) = \left[ \sum_{i=1}^{N} W_i(\boldsymbol{X}_i) \right] + \frac{1}{2} \left[ \sum_{i,k=1}^{N} \boldsymbol{D}_i^T \boldsymbol{C}_{ik} \boldsymbol{D}_k \right]. \tag{9}$$

Notice that $\Omega$ is a function of the total state of the network, which is given by the set of vectors $(\boldsymbol{X}_1, \ldots, \boldsymbol{X}_N)$. We shall now compute the time derivative of the function $\Omega$,

$$\frac{d\Omega}{dt} = \left\{ \sum_{i=1}^{N} (\boldsymbol{\nabla}W_i)^T \cdot \frac{d\boldsymbol{X}_i}{dt} \right\} + \frac{1}{2} \sum_{i,k=1}^{N} \left[ \frac{d\boldsymbol{D}_i^T}{dt} \boldsymbol{C}_{ik}\boldsymbol{D}_k + \boldsymbol{D}_i^T \boldsymbol{C}_{ik} \frac{d\boldsymbol{D}_k}{dt} \right]. \quad (10)$$

Substituting time derivatives $\frac{d\boldsymbol{X}_i}{dt}$ by the right hand sides of the equations of motion (8), yields

$$\frac{d\Omega}{dt} = \left\{ \sum_{i=1}^{N} a_i (\boldsymbol{\nabla}W_i)^T \cdot \left[ \boldsymbol{B}_i - \sum_{k=1}^{N} \boldsymbol{C}_{ik}\boldsymbol{D}_k \right] \right\}$$
$$+ \frac{1}{2} \sum_{i,k=1}^{N} \left[ \frac{d\boldsymbol{D}_i^T}{dt} \boldsymbol{C}_{ik}\boldsymbol{D}_k + \boldsymbol{D}_i^T \boldsymbol{C}_{ik} \frac{d\boldsymbol{D}_k}{dt} \right]. \quad (11)$$

Using now the expression (1) for the vectors $\boldsymbol{B}_i$, and the symmetry property (5) of the matrices $\boldsymbol{C}_{ik}$, one gets,

$$\frac{d\Omega}{dt} = - \left[ \sum_{i=1}^{N} a_i \boldsymbol{B}_i^T \cdot \left(\boldsymbol{M}_i^{-1}\right)^T \boldsymbol{B}_i \right] + \left\{ \sum_{i=1}^{N} a_i \boldsymbol{B}_i^T \cdot \left(\boldsymbol{M}_i^{-1}\right)^T \left[ \sum_{k=1}^{N} \boldsymbol{C}_{ik}\boldsymbol{D}_k \right] \right\}$$
$$+ \frac{1}{2} \sum_{i,k=1}^{N} \left[ \frac{d\boldsymbol{D}_i^T}{dt} \boldsymbol{C}_{ik}\boldsymbol{D}_k + \boldsymbol{D}_i^T \boldsymbol{C}_{ik} \frac{d\boldsymbol{D}_k}{dt} \right]$$
$$= - \left[ \sum_{i=1}^{N} a_i \boldsymbol{B}_i^T \cdot \left(\boldsymbol{M}_i^{-1}\right)^T \boldsymbol{B}_i \right] + \left\{ \sum_{i=1}^{N} a_i \boldsymbol{B}_i^T \cdot \left(\boldsymbol{M}_i^{-1}\right)^T \left[ \sum_{k=1}^{N} \boldsymbol{C}_{ik}\boldsymbol{D}_k \right] \right\}$$
$$+ \frac{1}{2} \sum_{i,k=1}^{N} \left[ \frac{d\boldsymbol{D}_i^T}{dt} \boldsymbol{C}_{ik}\boldsymbol{D}_k + \frac{d\boldsymbol{D}_k^T}{dt} \boldsymbol{C}_{ik}^T \boldsymbol{D}_i \right]$$
$$= - \left[ \sum_{i=1}^{N} a_i \boldsymbol{B}_i^T \cdot \left(\boldsymbol{M}_i^{-1}\right)^T \boldsymbol{B}_i \right] + \left\{ \sum_{i=1}^{N} a_i \boldsymbol{B}_i^T \cdot \left(\boldsymbol{M}_i^{-1}\right)^T \left[ \sum_{k=1}^{N} \boldsymbol{C}_{ik}\boldsymbol{D}_k \right] \right\}$$
$$+ \frac{1}{2} \sum_{i,k=1}^{N} \left[ \frac{d\boldsymbol{D}_i^T}{dt} \boldsymbol{C}_{ik}\boldsymbol{D}_k + \frac{d\boldsymbol{D}_k^T}{dt} \boldsymbol{C}_{ki}\boldsymbol{D}_i \right]$$
$$= - \left[ \sum_{i=1}^{N} a_i \boldsymbol{B}_i^T \cdot \left(\boldsymbol{M}_i^{-1}\right)^T \boldsymbol{B}_i \right] + \left\{ \sum_{i=1}^{N} a_i \boldsymbol{B}_i^T \cdot \left(\boldsymbol{M}_i^{-1}\right)^T \left[ \sum_{k=1}^{N} \boldsymbol{C}_{ik}\boldsymbol{D}_k \right] \right\}$$
$$+ \left[ \sum_{i,k=1}^{N} \frac{d\boldsymbol{D}_i^T}{dt} \boldsymbol{C}_{ik}\boldsymbol{D}_k \right]. \quad (12)$$

We want to prove that the time derivative $d\Omega/dt$ is always a non-positive number. In order to do that, we need first to consider the time derivative of the vectors $\boldsymbol{D}_i = \boldsymbol{D}_i(\boldsymbol{X}_i)$. We have that

$$\frac{d\boldsymbol{D}_i}{dt} = \frac{\partial \boldsymbol{D}_i}{\partial \boldsymbol{X}_i} \frac{d\boldsymbol{X}_i}{dt}$$

$$= \frac{\partial \boldsymbol{D}_i}{\partial \boldsymbol{X}_i} a_i \left[ \boldsymbol{B}_i - \sum_{j=1}^{N} \boldsymbol{C}_{ij} \boldsymbol{D}_j \right], \tag{13}$$

implying that

$$\frac{d\boldsymbol{D}_i^{T}}{dt} = a_i \left[ \boldsymbol{B}_i^{T} - \sum_{j=1}^{N} \boldsymbol{D}_j^{T} \boldsymbol{C}_{ji} \right] \left( \frac{\partial \boldsymbol{D}_i}{\partial \boldsymbol{X}_i} \right)^{T}, \tag{14}$$

where $\frac{\partial \boldsymbol{D}_i}{\partial \boldsymbol{X}_i}$ is the Jacobian matrix of the vector-valued function $\boldsymbol{D}_i(\boldsymbol{X}_i)$ (see equation (3)). Using relation (2), one then obtains

$$\frac{d\boldsymbol{D}_i^{T}}{dt} = a_i \left[ \boldsymbol{B}_i^{T} - \sum_{j=1}^{N} \boldsymbol{D}_j^{T} \boldsymbol{C}_{ji} \right] \boldsymbol{M}_i^{-1}. \tag{15}$$

Substituting now, in the last line of (12), $\frac{d\boldsymbol{D}_i^{T}}{dt}$ by the expression in the right hand side of (15), one gets

$$\begin{aligned}
\frac{d\Omega}{dt} &= - \left[ \sum_{i=1}^{N} a_i \boldsymbol{B}_i^{T} \cdot (\boldsymbol{M}_i^{-1})^{T} \boldsymbol{B}_i \right] + \left[ \sum_{i=1}^{N} a_i \boldsymbol{B}_i^{T} \cdot (\boldsymbol{M}_i^{-1})^{T} \left( \sum_{k=1}^{N} \boldsymbol{C}_{ik} \boldsymbol{D}_k \right) \right] \\
&\quad + \left[ \sum_{i,k=1}^{N} a_i \left( \boldsymbol{B}_i^{T} - \sum_{j=1}^{N} \boldsymbol{D}_j^{T} \boldsymbol{C}_{ji} \right) \boldsymbol{M}_i^{-1} \boldsymbol{C}_{ik} \boldsymbol{D}_k \right] \\
&= - \left[ \sum_{i=1}^{N} a_i \boldsymbol{B}_i^{T} \cdot (\boldsymbol{M}_i^{-1})^{T} \boldsymbol{B}_i \right] + \left[ \sum_{i=1}^{N} a_i \boldsymbol{B}_i^{T} \cdot (\boldsymbol{M}_i^{-1})^{T} \left( \sum_{k=1}^{N} \boldsymbol{C}_{ik} \boldsymbol{D}_k \right) \right] \\
&\quad + \left[ \sum_{i,k=1}^{N} a_i \boldsymbol{D}_k^{T} \boldsymbol{C}_{ik}^{T} (\boldsymbol{M}_i^{-1})^{T} \left( \boldsymbol{B}_i - \sum_{j=1}^{N} \boldsymbol{C}_{ji}^{T} \boldsymbol{D}_j \right) \right] \\
&= - \left[ \sum_{i=1}^{N} a_i \boldsymbol{B}_i^{T} \cdot (\boldsymbol{M}_i^{-1})^{T} \boldsymbol{B}_i \right] + \left[ \sum_{i=1}^{N} a_i \boldsymbol{B}_i^{T} \cdot (\boldsymbol{M}_i^{-1})^{T} \left( \sum_{k=1}^{N} \boldsymbol{C}_{ik} \boldsymbol{D}_k \right) \right] \\
&\quad + \left[ \sum_{i=1}^{N} a_i \left( \sum_{k=1}^{N} \boldsymbol{C}_{ik} \boldsymbol{D}_k \right)^{T} (\boldsymbol{M}_i^{-1})^{T} \boldsymbol{B}_i \right] \\
&\quad - \left[ \sum_{i=1}^{N} a_i \left( \sum_{k=1}^{N} \boldsymbol{C}_{ik} \boldsymbol{D}_k \right)^{T} (\boldsymbol{M}_i^{-1})^{T} \left( \sum_{j=1}^{N} \boldsymbol{C}_{ij} \boldsymbol{D}_j \right) \right]. 
\end{aligned} \tag{16}$$

It follows from the above equation that

$$\frac{d\Omega}{dt} = - \sum_{i=1}^{N} a_i \boldsymbol{V}_i^{T} (\boldsymbol{M}_i^{-i})^{T} \boldsymbol{V}_i \leq 0, \tag{17}$$

where

$$V_i = B_i - \left( \sum_{j=1}^{N} C_{ij} D_j \right). \tag{18}$$

The inequality in (17) follows from the fact that the quantities $a_i(X_i)$ are positive and that the matrices $M_i$ are positive-definite. We see that our network model exhibits a dynamics admitting an energy, Liapunov function $\Omega$. The Liapunov function $\Omega$ can be neatly decomposed as the sum of two terms: one inherited from the gradient-like character of the constituting units' intrinsic dissipative dynamics, and one arising from the networks' architecture describing the interactions between the basic units (that is, the interactions between the neurons). The system, as a whole, always evolves downhill in the energy landscape, tending to the landscape's local minima, and therefore complying with the basic behavior typical of an associative memory neural network [7].

## 4    Connection with the Cohen-Grossberg Neural Network Model

In this section, we show that the neural network models proposed by Cohen and Grossberg [7] constitute a particular instance of the general models described by the equations of motion (8). We shall consider the particular instance of the dynamical system (8), where the behavior of individual neurons are all determined by one-dimensional, dynamical systems. In other words, we shall now consider the particular case where $n_i = 1$, $i = 1, \ldots, N$. In this case, the state of each neuron is described by a single number $x_i$, the functions $a_i(X_i)$, $B_i(X_i)$ and $D_i(X_i)$ become the single-variable, real-valued functions $a_i(x_i)$, $b_i(x_i)$ and $d_i(x_i)$, and each of the matrices $C_{i,j}$ becomes a single numerical coefficient $c_{ij}$ (the weights). The neural network's equations of motion (8) then reduce to those of the neural network model proposed by Cohen and Grossberg [7], which are

$$\frac{dx_i}{dt} = a_i(x_i) \left[ b_i(x_i) - \sum_{k=1}^{N} c_{ik} d_k(x_k) \right], \quad i = 1, \ldots, N, \tag{19}$$

where the functions $a_i(x_i)$ and $d_i(x_i)$ comply with $a_i(x_i) > 0$ and $d_i'(x_i) > 0$. Different forms of the functions $a_i(x_i)$'s, $b_i(x_i)$'s, and $d_i(x_i)$'s give rise to different instances of the Cohen-Grossberg model. The condition (5) reduces to the symmetric requirement for the weights, $c_{ij} = c_{ji}$. The model's energy (Liapunov) function is then given by [7]

$$\Omega = \sum_{i=1}^{N} W_i(x_i) + \frac{1}{2} \sum_{i,k=1}^{N} c_{ik} d_i(x_i) d_k(x_k), \tag{20}$$

where

$$W_i(x_i) = - \int_0^{x_i} b_i(z) d_i'(z) dz. \tag{21}$$

For the particular case of one-dimensional neurons, the energy function coincides with the one derived by Cohen-Grossberg [7].

The equations of motion (19) can be recast in terms of the partial derivative of the Liapunov function $\Omega$, as

$$\frac{dx_i}{dt} = - \left[ \frac{a_i(x_i)}{d_i'(x_i)} \right] \frac{\partial \Omega}{\partial x_i}. \tag{22}$$

These equations govern the dynamics of the network's state, which at each instant is represented by the $N$ phase-space variables $\{x_1, x_2, \cdots, x_N\}$.

The celebrated Hopfield model for continuous neural networks constitutes a particular realization of the Cohen-Grossberg model. In fact, when $a_i(x_i) = -1/\tau_i$, $b_i(x_i) = x_i$, and $d_i(x_i) = g(x_i)$, where all the $\tau_i$'s are constant parameters, the equations of motion (19) become

$$\tau_i \frac{dx_i}{dt} = -x_i + \sum_{j=1}^{N} c_{ij}\, g(x_j), \tag{23}$$

which have the same form as the equations governing the continuous Hopfield model [12].

# 5    Concluding Remarks

Mathematical models for associative memory are usually implemented as networks of neurons, interacting in such a way that the network's dynamics is characterized by a global energy or Liapunov function. The network's behavior is such that it always moves "downhill" in the energy landscape. In most models for associative memory, the individual neurons are modeled as simple, one-dimensional, dynamical systems. In the present contribution, we investigated an extension of the structural scheme of associative memory, neural networks to more general settings, where the network's units (that is, the neurons) are described by multi-dimensional, dissipative, dynamical systems. We advanced a coupling scheme for dissipative, multi-dimensional units, that leads to dynamical features akin to those required when modeling associative memory. The family of network systems that we have proposed admits an energy (Liapunov) function, such that the network always evolves downhill in the energy landscape. Our general scheme includes, as particular instances, the continuous neural networks advanced by Cohen and Grossberg, as well as the continuous version of the celebrated Hopfield model.

The present developments suggest various possible lines for future research. Our proposal follows the general trend in mathematical biology, according to which fundamental models are described by non-conservative, dynamical systems (see [36] for a recent discussion). There have been, however, interesting attempts at alternative approaches in terms of conservative, dynamical systems, admitting a Lagrangean or Hamiltonian formalism [9,11,15,16] (or, in the case of discrete dynamical systems, in terms of reversible dynamics [3]). It would be interesting to explore the implications of our present model, with respect to the tension between conservative and nonconservative dynamical models in biology. It would also be worth to investigate possible relations between our approach to networks of multi-dimensional neurons, and intriguing recent developments on the theory of quantum mechanical neural networks [30].

**Acknowledgments.** We acknowledge financial support from the Brazilian funding agencies: Conselho Nacional de Desenvolvimento Científico e Tecnológico (CNPq), Fundação Carlos Chagas Filho de Amparo à Pesquisa do Estado do Rio de Janeiro (FAPERJ) and Coordenação de Aperfeiçoamento de Pessoal de Nível Superior - Brasil (CAPES). The authors are also grateful for the kind hospitality of the Centro Brasileiro de Pesquisas Físicas (CBPF), where part of this research was conducted.

# References

1. Aggarwal, C.C.: Neural Networks and Deep Learning. Springer, Cham, Switzerland (2018)
2. Barbosa, V.C.: Massively Parallel Models of Computation: Distributed Parallel Processing in Artificial Intelligence and Optimisation. Ellis Horwood, River (1993)
3. Berto, F., Tagliabue, J., Rossi, G.: There's plenty of Boole at the bottom: a reversible CA against information entropy. Mind. Mach. **26**(4), 341–357 (2016). https://doi.org/10.1007/s11023-016-9401-6
4. Cabessa, J., Villa, A.E.P.: Attractor dynamics of a Boolean model of a brain circuit controlled by multiple parameters. Chaos: Interdisc. J. Nonlinear Sci. **28**(10), 106318 (2018)
5. Carhart-Harris, R.L., Friston, K.J.: Free-energy and Freud: an update. In: Fotopoulou, A., Pfaff, D., Conway, M.A. (eds.) From the couch to the lab: Trends in psychodynamic neuroscience, pp. 219–229. Oxford Univ. Press, Oxford (2012)
6. Cleeremans, A., Timmermans, B., Pasquali, A.: Consciousness and metarepresentation: a computational sketch. Neural Netw. **20**, 1032–1039 (2007)
7. Cohen, M.A., Grossberg, S.: Absolute stability of global pattern formation and parallel memory storage by competitive neural networks. IEEE Trans. Syst. Man Cybern. **13**, 815–826 (1983)
8. Cranford, J.L.: Astrobiological Neurosystems: Rise and Fall of Intelligent Life Forms in the Universe. Springer, Cham (2015)
9. De Wilde, P.: Class of Hamiltonian neural networks. Phys. Rev. E **47**(2), 1392–1396 (1993)
10. Edalat, A., Mancinelli, F.: Strong attractors of Hopfield neural networks to model attachment types and behavioural patterns. In: Angelov, P., Levine, D., Apolloni, B. (eds.) Proceedings of the 2013 International Joint Conference on Neural Networks (IJCNN), Red Hook, NY, pp. 14027190-1-10. IEEE (2013)
11. Fagerholm, E.D., Foulkes, W.M.C., Friston, K.J., Moran, R.J., Leech, R.: Rendering neuronal state equations compatible with the principle of stationary action. J. Math. Neurosci. **11**(1), 1–15 (2021). https://doi.org/10.1186/s13408-021-00108-0
12. Hertz, J.A., Krogh, A., Palmer, R.G.: Introduction to the Theory of Neural Computation. Lecture Notes, vol. 1. Perseus Books, Cambridge, MA, USA (1991)

13. Hopfield, J.J.: Neurons with graded responses have collective computational properties like those of two-state neurons. Proc. Natl. Acad. Sci. **81**, 3088–3092 (1984)
14. Kandel, E.: Psychiatry, Psychoanalysis, and the New Biology of Mind. American Psychiatric Publishing Inc, Washington D.C. (2005)
15. Kerner, E.H.: A statistical mechanics of interacting biological species. Bull. Math. Biophys. **19**, 121–146 (1957). https://doi.org/10.1007/BF02477883
16. Kerner, E.H.: Note on Hamiltonian format of Lotka-Volterra dynamics. Phys. Lett. A **151**(8), 401–402 (1990)
17. Knoblauch, A., Palm, G.: Iterative retrieval and block coding in autoassociative and heteroassociative memory. Neural Comput. **32**(1), 205–260 (2020)
18. Lotka, A.J.: Elements of Mathematical Biology. Dover, New York (1956)
19. de Luca, V.T.F., Wedemann, R.S., Plastino, A.R.: Neuronal asymmetries and Fokker-Planck dynamics. In: Kůrková, V., Manolopoulos, Y., Hammer, B., Iliadis, L., Maglogiannis, I. (eds.) ICANN 2018. LNCS, vol. 11141, pp. 703–713. Springer, Cham (2018). https://doi.org/10.1007/978-3-030-01424-7_69
20. McCulloch, W.S., Pitts, W.: A logical calculus of the ideas immanent in nervous activity. Bull. Math. Biophys. **5**(4), 115–133 (1943). https://doi.org/10.1007/BF02478259
21. Nowak, M.A.: Evolutionary Dynamics. Harvard University Press, Cambridge (2006)
22. Palm, G.: Neural Assemblies, An Alternative Approach to Artificial Intelligence. Studies of Brain Function, Springer-Verlag, Berlin, Heidelberg (1982)
23. Plastino, A.R., Anteneodo, C.: A dynamical thermostatting approach to nonextensive canonical ensembles. Ann. Phys. **255**(2), 250–269 (1997)
24. Salakhutdinov, R.R., Hinton, G.E.: Replicated softmax: an undirected topic model. In: Bengio, Y., Schuurmans, D., Lafferty, J., Williams, C., Culotta, A. (eds.) Advances in Neural Information Processing Systems (NIPS 2009), vol. 22. Curran Associates, Inc. (2009)
25. Siddiqui, M., Wedemann, R.S., Jensen, H.J.: Avalanches and generalized memory associativity in a network model for conscious and unconscious mental functioning. Phys. A **490**, 127–138 (2018)
26. Srivastava, N., Salakhutdinov, R.R., Hinton, G.: Modeling documents with deep Boltzmann machines. In: Nicholson, A., Smyth, P. (eds.) Proceedings of the Twenty-Ninth Conference on Uncertainty in Artificial Intelligence (UAI2013), pp. 616–624. UAI 2013, AUAI Press, Arlington, Virginia, USA (2013)
27. Stewart, I., Golubitsky, M.: Symmetric networks with geometric constraints as models of visual illusions. Symmetry **11**(6), 799 (2019)
28. Taylor, J.G., Villa, A.E.P.: The "Conscious I": a neuroheuristic approach to the mind. In: Baltimore, D., Dulbecco, R., Francois, J., Levi-Montalcini, R. (eds.) Frontiers of Life, vol. 3, pp. 349–368. Academic Press (2001)
29. Taylor, J.G.: A neural model of the loss of self in schizophrenia. Schizophrenia Bull. **37**(6), 1229–1247 (2011)
30. Torres, J.J., Manzano, D.: A model of interacting quantum neurons with a dynamic synapse. New J. Phys. **24**, 073007 (2022)
31. Tsallis, C., Stariolo, D.A.: Generalized simulated annealing. Phys. A **233**, 395–406 (1996)
32. Vanchurin, V.: The world as a neural network. Entropy **22**(11), 1210 (2020)
33. Wedemann, R.S., Donangelo, R., de Carvalho, L.A.V.: Generalized memory associativity in a network model for the neuroses. Chaos 19(1), 015116-(1–11) (2009)

34. Wedemann, R.S., Plastino, A.R.: $q$-Maximum entropy distributions and memory neural networks. In: Lintas, A., Rovetta, S., Verschure, P.F.M.J., Villa, A.E.P. (eds.) Artificial Neural Networks and Machine Learning - ICANN 2017. LNCS, vol. 10613, pp. 300–308. Springer, Cham (2017). https://doi.org/10.1007/978-3-319-68600-4_35

35. Wedemann, R.S., Plastino, A.R.: A nonlinear Fokker-Planck description of continuous neural network dynamics. In: Tetko, I.V., Kurková, V., Karpov, P., Theis, F. (eds.) ICANN 2019. LNCS, vol. 11727, pp. 43–56. Springer, Cham (2019). https://doi.org/10.1007/978-3-030-30487-4_4

36. Wedemann, R.S., Plastino, A.R.: Nonlinear Lagrangean neural networks. In: Farkaš, I., Masulli, P., Otte, S., Wermter, S. (eds.) ICANN 2021. LNCS, vol. 12894, pp. 163–173. Springer, Cham (2021). https://doi.org/10.1007/978-3-030-86380-7_14

37. Wedemann, R.S., Plastino, A.R., Tsallis, C.: Curl forces and the nonlinear Fokker-Planck equation. Phys. Rev. E **94**(6), 062105 (2016)

38. Wedemann, R.S., de Carvalho, L.A.V., Donangelo, R.: Complex Networks in Psychological Models. Prog. Theor. Phys. Suppl. **162**, 121–130 (2006)

39. Wedemann, R.S., de Carvalho, L.A.V., Donangelo, R.: Network properties of a model for conscious and unconscious mental processes. Neurocomputing **71**(16), 3367–3371 (2008)

40. Wedemann, R.S., Plastino, A.R.: Nonlinear, nonequilibrium landscape approach to neural network dynamics. In: Farkaš, I., Masulli, P., Wermter, S. (eds.) ICANN 2020. LNCS, vol. 12397, pp. 180–191. Springer, Cham (2020). https://doi.org/10.1007/978-3-030-61616-8_15

41. Wedemann, R.S., Plastino, A.R.: Nonlinear Fokker-Planck approach to the Cohen-Grossberg model. In: Lintas, A., Enrico, P., Pan, X., Wang, R., Villa, A. (eds.) Advances in Cognitive Neurodynamics (VII), pp. 61–72. Springer, Singapore (2021)

# Collaborative Multiple-Student Single-Teacher for Online Learning

Alaa Zain[✉], Yang Jian, and Jinjia Zhou

Graduate School of Science and Engineering, Hosei University, Tokyo, Japan
alaa.marouf.7@stu.hosei.ac.jp

**Abstract.** Knowledge distillation is a popular method where a large trained network (teacher) is implemented to train a smaller network (student). To decrease the need for training a much larger network (teacher) for real time application, one student self-knowledge distillation was introduced as a solid technique for compressing neural networks specially for real time applications. However, most of the existing methods consider only one type of knowledge and apply one-student one-teacher learning strategy. This paper presents a collaborative multiple-student single-teacher system (CMSST). The proposed approach is based on real time applications that contain temporal information, which play an important role in understanding. We designed a backbone old student network with target complexity for deployment, during training, once the old student provides high-quality soft labels to guide the hierarchical new student, it also offers the opportunity for the new student to make meaningful improvements based on the students' revised feedback via the shared intermediate representations. Moreover, we introduced soft target label smoothing technique to the CMSST. Experimental results showed that the accuracy can be improved on newly developed teacher knowledge distillation by 1.5% on the UCF-101. Also the accuracy was improved by 1.15% compared to normal huge teacher knowledge distillation on CIFAR100 dataset.

**Keywords:** Knowledge distillation · Deep convolutional model compression · Transfer learning · Label smoothing

## 1 Introduction

Compared to traditional methods, Machine Learning (ML) has demonstrated superior performance when applied to several challenging computer vision and image processing applications. The idea behind Knowledge distillation, is to enhance the learning output of student network by using teacher's model transfer learning method [1]. Recently Deep Neural Networks (DNNs) have shown impressive performance on a wide range of complex machine learning tasks [2]. However, models are computationally costly and memory overloading, which hinder their deployment in portable devices with limited memory resources, or for

E. Pimenidis et al. (Eds.): ICANN 2022, LNCS 13529, pp. 515–525, 2022.
https://doi.org/10.1007/978-3-031-15919-0_43

applications with specific latency requirements [3]. Several methods were introduced for model compression, and learn compact models with fewer number of parameters, but with much reduced accuracy [2].

As the most potent learners in the real world, humans can improve themselves by accumulating a lot of learning skills, such as learning through experiments, self-explanation, active recalling, interleaving learning, reading, and reviewing. These learning skills and methodologies enhance the humans ability to learn new topics effectively and efficiently. Therefore, we present the Collaborative multiple-student single-teacher learning for online knowledge distillation model (CMSST) for online knowledge distillation, based on inspiration from the above-mentioned learning skills. Algorithms based on Convolutional Neural Networks (CNNs) have been particularly applied in solving image and video classification and object detection problems. The proposed method also helps in overcoming regression problems including image segmentation, super-resolution and restoration [4].

Improving and developing the effective and accurate image and video compression algorithms has been an attractive research topic recently. The difficulties related to image and video compression algorithms remain essential, because of the gradual increase in display and sensor resolution, and the urge for a higher-quality media for consumers and professional applications [5].

We propose a novel old student-helping- new student approach. Specifically, we designed a backbone old student network with target complexity for deployment. During training, the old student provides high-quality soft labels to guide the hierarchical new students, which offers the opportunity for the new student to make meaningful improvements based on students' revised feedback via the shared intermediate representations. The most of the important information is stored in the first frame [6], so when the old student is trained given the first farm, that improves the accuracy of and video recognition. Also for the images the learned fetcher by the old student improve the dark knowledge.

Our proposed method introduced a teacher-free practical method, in addition to this we overcame the obstacles in the issues related to the tuning parameter of Tf-KD. Therefore, we proposed CMSST with label smoothing approach (CMSST-LS) which improved the generalization of a two components based model; Improving the teacher capability and Label Smoothing. Thus this approach redesigned the LSR method in the CMSST-LS expression, instead of manually reformulating directly the teacher as Tf-KD.

## 2   Related Works

The term Knowledge Distillation refers to transfer the learning between neural networks, strong learning capacity with higher performance (teacher) to another (student) as shown in Fig. 1. As was first proposed by Hinton et al. [9]. The Knowledge distillation techniques can be sub-grouped into two main categories; an offline knowledge distillation (Offline-KD), and an online knowledge distillation (Online-KD). The Offline-KD mainly contains two stages, first a heavy teacher network is trained then preserved, and utilized to output the knowledge to guide the light student network. However, a capacity gap between offline (trained teacher network) and a smaller (student network) always exists, and causes limitation in the Offline-KD approach.

When there is a huge gap between the student and teacher, the student network performance degrades. In addition, a two-step training in Offline-KD will extend both the training cost, and the pipeline complexity [4]. Unlike Offline knowledge distillation, Online-KD is an end-to-end training scheme using only one-phase. In Online-KD, both the teacher network and the student network are updated together.

Although, Online-KD was introduced to overcome the Offline-KD's disadvantages with a modern teacher, it still needs a teacher network, and the large teacher network needs to be continuously trained. Recently, Self-knowledge distillation (Self-KD), which is a special case from the Online-KD approach, has been introduced to overcome the need to expensive and large teacher network. In Self-KD, the student network is improved without the need for a teacher network [7,8].

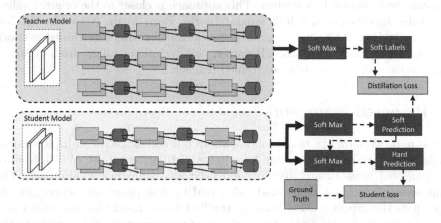

**Fig. 1.** General teacher student model

Conventional Knowledge Distillation methods address knowledge from a better performing teacher model to invent soft predictions for a student network. Several researchers have tried to use the student network solely as a teacher network, This approach was named self-knowledge distillation (self-KD) [4]. The response-based distillation is based on learning the last prediction of the teacher model and was generally used in different applications [9]. Given a vector of logits(z) as the outputs of the final fully connected layer of a deep model [9], the distillation loss for knowledge can be formulated as (1):

$$L_{\text{ResD}}(z_t, z_s) = L_R(z_t, z_s) \tag{1}$$

Soft targets are the estimations that the input belongs to the classes and can be predicted by a softmax function as (2):

$$P(z_i, \ T) = \frac{\exp(\frac{z_i}{T})}{\sum_j \exp(\frac{z_j}{T})} \tag{2}$$

The class, and a temperature factor is introduced to represent the importance of each soft target. Hinton et al. [9], stated that soft targets contains the informative dark knowledge from the teacher model. The distillation loss for soft logits can be viewed as (3):

$$L_{\mathrm{ResD}}(p(z_t, \ T), \ p(z_s, \ T)) \ = \ L_R(p(z_t, \ T), \ p(z_s, \ T)) \tag{3}$$

Self-KD has mainly two approaches the first approach is to reduce the distance between features inputs and it use only one network. This approach is similar to progressive self-knowledge distillation (PS-KD) [4] and [10] class-wise predictions (CS-KD) [10] which focuses on distilling knowledge among each samples in one class. The main problem for this approach is the possibility of overfitting.

The second approach is to transfer the learning from a teacher network with the same architecture to a student. This approach is closer to the original online knowledge distillation and it is similar to the Born-Again Networks (BANs) proposed in [15]. BANs first train a network and use this pre-trained network as a teacher for next generation.However, this technique suffers from accuracy degradation and still needs a pre-trained teacher.

## 3   Proposed Framework

In this part, we showed a brief proposal about our collaborative multiple-student single-teacher learning for online knowledge distillation model. Will introduce the proposed network architecture, and used algorithm in our approach. The proposed approach for image and video real time applications, where the old student as the expert-teacher knowing the first frame mark the best model performance as checkpoint and guides training of the new student according to the last output layer, and the current student indicates the training model at the new epoch. Algorithm 1 presents the training technique given a set of N training samples.

CMSST proposes an old student helping new student formula. Specifically, we designed a backbone old student network with target to reduce complexity for deployment, during training, once the old student provides high-quality soft labels to guide the hierarchical new students, it also offers the opportunity for the new student to make meaningful improvements based on students' revised feedback via the shared intermediate representations.

We believe that most of the important information is found in first frame so when we train the old student given the first farm it improves the accuracy of images and video recognition.

**Algorithm 1**

**Input:** $(F^S, \alpha^S)$
\# $(F^S, \alpha^S)$ The old student model
S is the set of trained parameters.
\# $(F^T, \alpha^T)$: The old student models
$\alpha^T$ is the set of frozen parameters
$N$: numbers of epochs.
$\tau$ : temperature factor.
**Output:** Return $\alpha^*$
\# $\alpha^*$is optimal weights
**for** *epoch* $= 1....N$ **do**
$\quad Z^T = F^T$
$\quad P^T = SoftMax\left(Z^T, \tau\right)$
$\quad P^S = SoftMax\left(Z^S, \tau\right)$
Calculate the back propagation and update $S^\alpha$
if Val_Accuracy$(F^S, \alpha^S) >$ Val_Accuracy$(F^T, \alpha^T)$
**then**
$$\alpha^S = \alpha^T$$
**else**
$$\alpha^S = \alpha^*$$
**End**

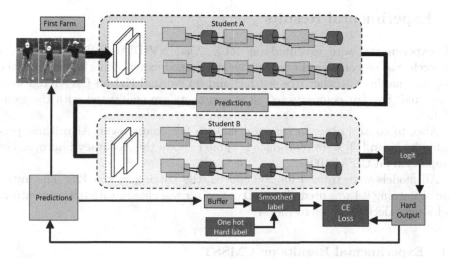

**Fig. 2.** Overview of collaborative multiple-student single-teacher learning approach with Label smoothing

## 3.1 CMSST: Collaborative Multiple-Student Single-Teacher Learning

CMSST was proposed to solve the offline and online distillation constrains by avoiding the necessity for larger teacher and decreasing the gap between teachers and students. The proposed method is generalizing the capability by distilling the knowledge from the student network itself. Particularly, the student becomes the teacher as well, and take advantage of old student previous predictions to have extra guidance within training as can be seen in Fig. 2.

The proposed CMSST overcome the following problems:

1) Offline knowledge distillation where gap between teacher (large network) and student (small network) always remains, and student usually depends on teacher.2) Online knowledge distillation where often fails to overcome the high-capacity teacher in settings. 3) Moreover, using the same network structure will be easier in hardware implementation.

### 3.2   CMSST with Label Smoothing

In order to improve the proposed model CMSST the second proposed approach Collaborative Multiple-Student Single-Teacher learning with Label Smoothing (CMSST-LS) was introduced.

The label smoothing was used to avoid the over-confidence in our model. The model is said to be scaled if its predicted probabilities of outcomes reflect their accuracy. We load the model at previous epoch on buffer, when current epoch began so that the previous predictions for softening targets are also calculated in forward passes. The CMSST-LS model is seen in Fig. 2.

## 4   Experimental Results

All experiments were executed on RTX 2080 NVIDIA GPU system with PyTorch. For our empirical analysis, we performed experiments to evaluate the proposed method, teacher free self-KD and on Normal KD on CIFAR100 were conducted. For fair comparisons, all experiments are conducted with the same setting.

Also, to control other factors and make a fair comparison, Algorithms presented by Yuan [13] were reproduced. Table 1 shows the Accuracy improvement comparison on CIFAR100.

All models were trained for 200 epochs, the batch size was 128. The initial rate of learning 0.1 was used.The SGD optimizer was chosen with 0.9 momentum, and weight decay was set to (5e−4).

### 4.1   Experimental Results on CMSST

In this section, the effectiveness of our collaborative multiple-student single-teacher learning for online knowledge distillation along a multiple tasks is presented. The experimental tasks include image classification, image recognition, and video recognition.

The test accuracy of the six models is shown in Table 1. As shown in Table 1, the present online Collaborative multiple-student single-teacher learning for online knowledge distillation model consistently outperforms the baselines.

**Table 1.** Accuracy improvement comparison on CIFAR100

| Model | Accuracy% | | | No. of parameters (model size) | | |
|---|---|---|---|---|---|---|
| | Teacher KD [7] | TF KD [11] | CMSST | Teacher KD [7] | TF KD [11] | CMSST |
| MobileNet-V2 | 70.96 | 70.46 | **73.13** | 3.4 M | **1.6 M** | 1.6 M |
| ShuffleNet-V2 | 72.23 | 71.84 | **73.75** | 5.4 M | **2.49 M** | 2.5 M |
| ResNet-18 | 77.10 | 76.98 | **78.17** | 11.4 M | **5.11 M** | 5.13 M |
| GoogLeNet | 80.17 | 79.83 | **81.22** | 20.87 M | **9.6 M** | 9.62 M |
| DenseNet-121 | 80.26 | 80.52 | **81.67** | 34 M | **15.8 M** | 15.8 M |
| ResNet-29 | 82.08 | 82.39 | **83.51** | 20.87 M | **9.6 M** | 9.62 M |

**Table 2.** Accuracy improvement comparison CMSST on UCF-101

| Model | Accuracy% | | | No. of parameters (model size) | | |
|---|---|---|---|---|---|---|
| | Teacher KD [7] | TF KD [11] | CMSST | Teacher KD [7] | TF KD [11] | CMSST |
| 3D ResNet-29 | 46.5 | 68.4 | **69.8** | 60.2 M | **18.9 M** | 18.9 M |
| 3D ResNet-50 | 52.1 | 71.1 | **72.6** | 46.4 M | **14.8 M** | 14.8 M |

For example, as a powerful model DenseNet-121 with 34.52M parameters, improves itself by 1.15% compared to normal huge teacher knowledge distillation also it improves itself by 1.41% on the teacher free self KD.

Figure 3, presents the test accuracy of the proposed CMSST model consistently outperforms the baselines on ResNet-29. In addition to testing the accuracy improvement of the proposed model on an image recognition application, the model was tested on video data set UCF-101 to verify the accuracy on the video recognition applications. The test accuracy of the proposed model and baseline models are shown in Table 2. It can be shown that the presented CMSST consistently outperforms the baselines. For example, as a powerful model with 25.6M parameters, ResNet-50 improves itself by 1.5% with CMSST (Proposed).

**Table 3.** Comparison between Top-1 test accuracy on UCF-101

| Method | Backbone | Pretraining data set | UCF-101 |
|---|---|---|---|
| Random Init | 3D ResNet-18 | None | 46.5% |
| Random Init | C3D | None | 45.9% |
| Random Init | 3D ResNet-50 | None | 59.2% |
| VCP [14] | 3D ResNet-18 | UCF-101 | 66.0% |
| TCE [16] | 3D ResNet-18 | K400 | 68.8% |
| DPC [13] | 3D ResNet-18 | K400 | 68.2% |
| CMSST-LS (ours) | 3D ResNet-18 | None | **69.8%** |
| CMSST-LS (ours) | 3D ResNet-50 | None | **72.6%** |

**Table 4.** Comparison result between accuracy error results on CIFAR100 compared to other methods with popular architecture

| Model + Method | Parameters | Top-1 Error % | Top-5 Error % |
|---|---|---|---|
| ResNet-18 (Teacher KD) | 11.4 M | 24.18 | 6.90 |
| ResNet-18 + Label Smoothing [11] | 11 M | 20.94 | 6.02 |
| ResNet-18 + CS-KD [10] | - | 22.31 | 5.70 |
| ResNet-18 + TF-KD [11] | **5.11 M** | 22.88 | 6.01 |
| ResNet-18 + PS-KD [4] | 5.34 M | 20.82 | 5.10 |
| ResNet-18 + CMSST (ours) | 5.13 M | **21.83** | **5.23** |
| ResNet-18 + CMSST-LS (ours) | 5.13 M | **21.67** | **5.09** |
| DenseNet-121 (Teacher KD) | 34.52 M | 20.05 | 4.99 |
| DenseNet-121 + Label Smoothing [11] | 34 M | 19.08 | 5.64 |
| DenseNet-121 + CS-KD [10] | - | 20.47 | 6.21 |
| DenseNet-121 + TF-KD [11] | **15.8 M** | 19.88 | 5.10 |
| DenseNet-121 + PS-KD [4] | 17.3 M | 18.73 | 3.90 |
| DenseNet-121 + CMSST (ours) | **15.8 M** | **18.24** | **3.96** |
| DenseNet-121 + CMSST-LS (ours) | **15.8 M** | **18.73** | **3.53** |
| ResNet-29 (Teacher KD) | 20.87 M | 18.65 | 4.47 |
| ResNet-29 + Label Smoothing [11] | 20 M | 17.60 | 4.23 |
| ResNet-29 + CS-KD [10] | - | 18.26 | .37 |
| ResNet-29 + TF-KD [11] | **9.6 M** | 17.33 | 3.87 |
| ResNet-29 + PS-KD [4] | 11.2 M | 17.28 | 3.60 |
| ResNet-29 + CMSST (ours) | 9.62 M | **16.94** | **3.50** |
| ResNet-29 + CMSST-LS (ours) | 9.62 M | **16.72** | **3.13** |

As shown in Table 3, the presented technique obtains the SOTA performance, more accurate on the UCF-101 dataset compared to the previous methods with several backbone networks and different pre-training dataset. As shown in Fig. 4, the test accuracy of the proposed CMSST model outperforms the baselines on 3D ResNet-50.

## 4.2  Experimental Results on CMSST with Label Smoothing Approach

The previous epoch had an essential role for training the current epoch. The past predictions could be obtained using two main techniques.

The first technique is to upload the model at previous epoch on buffer at the time the current epoch start so that the previous predictions aused for softening targets are also calculated in forward passes. The second technique is to keep the previous predictions executed from the previous epoch on buffer in advance, and read this information to calculate the soft targets.

**Table 5.** Comparison results with multi students algorithms on CIFAR100

| Model | Accuracy% | | | No. of parameters (model size) | | |
|---|---|---|---|---|---|---|
| | BANs [15] | CMSST | CMSST-LS | BANs [15] | CMSST | CMSST-LS |
| ResNet-56 | 74.15 | 75.21 | **75.68** | 25.85 M | **11.79 M** | **11.79 M** |
| ResNet-110 | 75.33 | 76.49 | **76.83** | 24.67 M | **12.51 M** | 12.51 M |

**Table 6.** Top-1 error rate (%) on various image classification tasks and model architectures

| Model ResNet-18 | | | | |
|---|---|---|---|---|
| Method | MIT67 | TinyImageNet | Stanford Dogs | CUB-200-2011 |
| Cross-entropy [19] | 44.75 | 43.53 | 36.29 | 46.00 |
| AdaCos [17] | 42.66 | 42.61 | 32.66 | 35.47 |
| Virtual-softmax [20] | 42.86 | 42.41 | 31.48 | 35.03 |
| Maximum-entropy [18] | 42.63 | 41.77 | 32.41 | 39.86 |
| Label-smoothing [11] | 44.40 | 43.09 | 35.30 | 42.99 |
| CS-KD [10] | 40.45 | 41.62 | 30.85 | 33.28 |
| CMSST (ours) | **39.77** | **40.93** | **28.56** | **30.79** |
| CMSST-LS (ours) | **39.02** | **40.12** | **28.01** | **29.96** |
| Model DeseNet-121 | | | | |
| Cross-entropy [19] | 41.79 | 39.22 | 33.39 | 42.30 |
| AdaCos [17] | 40.25 | 38.76 | 27.87 | 30.84 |
| Virtual-softmax [20] | 43.66 | 41.58 | 30.55 | 33.85 |
| Maximum-entropy [18] | 43.48 | 38.39 | 29.52 | 37.5 |
| Label-smoothing [11] | 42.24 | 38.75 | 31.39 | 40.63 |
| CS-KD [10] | 40.02 | 37.96 | 27.81 | 30.83 |
| CMSST (ours) | **38.98** | **37.44** | **26.87** | **29.21** |
| CMSST-LS (ours) | **38.63** | **37.03** | **26.65** | **28.65** |

These two approaches have advantages and disadvantages. The first technique needs more GPU memory. On the other hand, the second technique does not require extra GPU memory but requires more vacancy to store previous predictions.

In our study, we address an efficient technique according to the task. Table 4 shows that our result is improved compared to the baseline from the first approach of self-knowledge distillation with reduction the fetchers between the inputs and usage of only one students network. CMSST shows better accuracy while efficiently enhancing the performance on confidence estimation, such as; it improves accuracy by 1.21% from TF-KD. To approve the validity of the proposed approaches: CMSST and CMSST-LS, we compared them with recent work

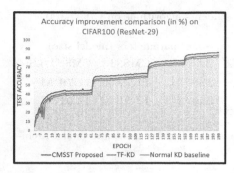 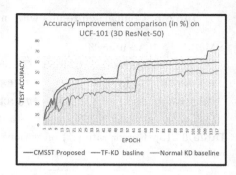

**Fig. 3.** Accuracy improvement CIFAR100 (ResNet29)

**Fig. 4.** Accuracy improvement UCF-101 (3D ResNet50)

that used multiple students like BANs[15] and with variety of image classification tasks using wide range of datasets as shown in Table 6. BANs related to the second self-knowledge distillation approach that depends on transfer knowledge from a teacher network. As shown in Table 5 that our result is improved compared to the BANs. Although the proposed approaches CMSST and CMSST-LS have a 50% number of parameters compared to BANs, CMSST and CMSST-LS improved the accuracy on Resnet-110 by 1.16% and 1.5% respectively.

## 5    Conclusion

CMSST and CMSST-LS are proposed techniques inspired from the human learning skills to enhance the performance and improve the generalization capability of DNNs, which transfers the knowledge from the model itself to reproduce more informative targets for training. We used the old student to teach the new student. The previous predictions about data from the model at the past epoch was used to soften the target.

The experimental results among diverse tasks, show that the proposed method is effective to enhance the generalization capability of DNNs. The improvement is noticeable on video recognition applications because most of the important data is located in the first frame. The conducted experiments also indicated that this model can be applied in both images and video recognition applications.

## References

1. Bhat, P., Arani, E., Zonooz, B.: Distill on the go: online knowledge distillation in self-supervised learning. In: Proceedings of the IEEE/CVF Conference on Computer Vision and Pattern Recognition (2021)

2. Gou, J., et al.: Knowledge distillation: a survey. Int. J. Comput. Vis. **129**(6), 1789–1819 (2021)
3. Berthelier, A., Chateau, T., Duffner, S., Garcia, C., Blanc, C.: Deep model compression and architecture optimization for embedded systems: a survey. J. Signal Process. Syst. **93**(8), 863–878 (2021)
4. Kim, K., et al.: Self-knowledge distillation with progressive refinement of targets. In: Proceedings of the IEEE/CVF International Conference on Computer Vision (2021)
5. Wang, L., Yoon, K.-J.: Knowledge distillation and student-teacher learning for visual intelligence: a review and new outlooks. IEEE Trans. Pattern Anal. Mach. Intell. (2021)
6. Pan, B., et al.: Spatio-temporal graph for video captioning with knowledge distillation. In: Proceedings of the IEEE/CVF Conference on Computer Vision and Pattern Recognition (2020)
7. Vu, D.-Q., Le, N., Wang, J.-C.: Teaching yourself: a self-knowledge distillation approach o action recognition. IEEE Access **9**, 105711–105723 (2021)
8. Cho, J.H., Hariharan, B.: On the efficacy of knowledge distillation. In: Proceedings of the IEEE/CVF International Conference on Computer Vision (2019)
9. Hinton, G., Vinyals, O., Dean, J.: Distilling the knowledge in a neural network. arXiv preprint arXiv:1503.02531, vol. 2, no. 7 (2015)
10. Yun, S., Park, J., Lee, K., Shin, J.: Regularizing class-wise predictions via self-knowledge distillation. In: Proceedings of the IEEE/CVF Conference on Computer Vision and Pattern Recognition, pp. 13876–13885 (2020)
11. Yuan, L., et al.: Revisiting knowledge distillation via label smoothing regularization. In: Proceedings of the IEEE/CVF Conference on Computer Vision nd Pattern Recognition (2020)
12. Knights, J., et al.: Temporally coherent embeddings for self-supervised video representation learning. In: 2020 25th International Conference on Pattern Recognition (ICPR). IEEE (2021)
13. Han, T., Xie, W., Zisserman, A.: Video representation learning by dense predictive coding. In: Proceedings of the IEEE/CVF International Conference on Computer Vision Workshops (2019)
14. Luo, D., et al.: Video cloze procedure for self-supervised spatio-temporal learning. In: Proceedings of the AAAI Conference on Artificial Intelligence, vol. 34. no. 7 (2020)
15. Furlanello, T., et al.: Born again neural networks. In: International Conference on Machine Learning. PMLR (2018)
16. Patrick, M., et al.: Multi-modal self-supervision from generalized data transformations. arXiv preprint arXiv:2003.04298 (2020)
17. Zhang, X., et al.: Adacos: adaptively scaling cosine logits for effectively learning deep face representations. In: Proceedings of the IEEE/CVF Conference on Computer Vision and Pattern Recognition (2019)
18. Dubey, A., et al.: Maximum-entropy fine grained classification. In: Advances in Neural Information Processing Systems, vol. 31 (2018)
19. Haarnoja, T., et al.: Soft actor-critic: off-policy maximum entropy deep reinforcement learning with a stochastic actor. In: International Conference on Machine Learning. PMLR (2018)
20. Wang, F., et al.: Additive margin softmax for face verification. IEEE Signal Process. Lett. **25**(7), 926–930 (2018)

# D-TRACE: Deep Triply-Aligned Clustering

Ding-Hua Chen[1], Dong Huang[1,2(✉)], Haiyan Cheng[1],
and Chang-Dong Wang[3,4]

[1] College of Mathematics and Informatics, South China Agricultural University,
Guangzhou, China
dhchen@stu.scau.edu.cn, huangdonghere@gmail.com
[2] Key Laboratory of Smart Agricultural Technology in Tropical South China,
Ministry of Agriculture and Rural Affairs, Guangzhou, China
[3] School of Computer Science and Engineering, Sun Yat-sen University,
Guangzhou, China
[4] Guangdong Key Laboratory of Information Security Technology,
Guangzhou, China

**Abstract.** Deep clustering has recently emerged as a promising direction in clustering analysis, which aims to leverage the representation learning power of deep neural networks to enhance the clustering of highly-complex data. However, most of the existing deep clustering algorithms tend to utilize a single layer (typically the last fully-connected layer) of representation to build the clustering, yet cannot well exploit the rich and diverse information hidden in multiple layers. In view of this, this paper proposes a **deep triply-aligned clustering** (D-TRACE) approach, which is able to jointly explore three types of representations from multiple layers in the neural network. Specifically, we incorporate the contrastive learning into the first-stage network training, where three modules (i.e., the backbone network, the instance contrastive head, and the cluster contrastive head) are simultaneously optimized. By fusing the three types of representations from the three modules, we further propose the concept of the triply-aligned representation, based on which a unified neural network with a reconstruction loss and a Kullback-Leibler (KL) divergence based clustering loss is trained and thus the final clustering can be achieved in an unsupervised manner. Experiments on multiple image datasets demonstrate the superiority of our D-TRACE approach over the state-of-the-art deep clustering approaches.

**Keywords:** Deep clustering · Deep neural network · Contrastive learning · Feature representations

## 1 Introduction

Clustering analysis is a fundamental yet challenging research topic in the field of data mining and machine learning [13–15]. Traditional clustering algorithms aim to partition unlabeled data into several clusters with some similarity/dissimilarity metrics based on handcrafted features, which may be unsuitable

E. Pimenidis et al. (Eds.): ICANN 2022, LNCS 13529, pp. 526–537, 2022.
https://doi.org/10.1007/978-3-031-15919-0_44

for very complex high-dimensional data (such as image data and video data) due to its limitation in feature representation.

Recently the deep learning based clustering (i.e., deep clustering) has been attracting a considerable amount of attention due to its capability of exploiting the representation learning power of deep neural networks for unsupervised learning. In recent years, many deep clustering methods have been designed, which can be divided into two main categories, i.e., the single-stage methods [3,9,10,16,18,30,31] and the two-stage methods [8,27]. As a classical single-stage deep clustering method, the deep embedding clustering (DEC) method [30] exploits the deep neural network to jointly learn feature representations and cluster assignments. To extend the DEC method, Guo et al. [10] proposed the improved deep embedded clustering (IDEC) method, which applies an under-complete autoencoder to maintain the local structure of data. Ji et al. [18] developed the invariant information clustering (IIC) method, which aims to discover clusters by maximizing mutual information between the cluster assignments of each data pair. Huang et al. [16] presented the partition confidence maximization (PICA) method by learning the most semantically plausible data separation with a partition uncertainty index to quantify the global confidence of the clustering assignment. Different from the single-stage (end-to-end) learning methods [3,9,10,16,18,30,31], Van Gansbeke et al. [27] devised a two-stage deep clustering method named semantic clustering by adopting nearest neighbors (SCAN), where a pretext task is employed in the first stage to obtain the semantically meaningful nearest neighbors from the learned representation and a further learning and clustering process based on the nearest neighbors is performed in the next stage.

These deep clustering methods have achieved significant success for unsupervised representation learning and clustering. However, a critical limitation to them is that they mostly rely on a single layer of representation (typically the last fully-connected layer) to construct the clustering result, but cannot well exploit the rich information hidden in multiple layers. More recently, Li et al. proposed the contrastive clustering (CC) method [22], which utilizes the contrastive samples to improve the clustering performance. Though the CC method performs the representation learning in both the instance contrastive head and the cluster contrastive head, yet its cluster assignments are generated merely by the single-layer representation in the cluster contrastive head, which still lacks the ability to jointly leverage multiple types of representations from multiple layers in the deep neural network.

To tackle the above-mentioned limitation, this paper presents a deep triply-aligned clustering (D-TRACE) method, which is capable of jointly utilizing multiple types of feature representations from multiple network layers in a unified deep clustering framework (as illustrated in Fig. 1). Specifically, a convolutional neural network (i.e., the backbone network) is first trained via an instance contrastive head and a cluster contrastive head, with the contrastive learning paradigm exploited at the instance-level and the cluster-level, respectively. Though the learning process simultaneously involves the backbone, the instance

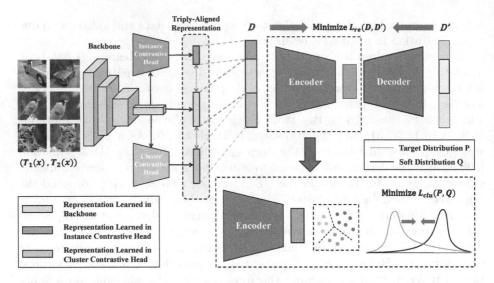

**Fig. 1.** The pipeline of the proposed D-TRACE method. The data pairs constructed by different data augmentations are first used to train the contrastive clustering network. Based on the trained network, three types of feature representations learned in different layers are fused into a triply-aligned representation. The unified representation is then fed to a unified neural network, through which the clustering result can be achieved via a reconstruction loss and a KL divergence-based clustering loss.

contrastive head, and the cluster contrastive head, yet the previous attempt [22] is only able to utilize a single layer of representation in the cluster contrastive head for the final clustering. In this paper, we argue that the joint modeling of multiple types of representations can substantially benefit the deep clustering performance. In particular, we integrate the representations learned in the backbone, the instance contrastive head, and the cluster contrastive head into a triply-aligned representation, which is further fed into a unified neural network. By training the unified neural network with a reconstruction loss and iteratively refining the cluster distributions with a Kullback-Leibler (KL) divergence-based clustering loss, the final clustering result can be obtained in a purely unsupervised manner. Experiments on several benchmark datasets demonstrate the effectiveness of the proposed D-TRACE method.

The rest of the paper is organized as follows. The proposed D-TRACE framework is described in Sect. 2. The experimental results are reported in Sect. 3. Finally, the paper is concluded in Sect. 4.

## 2   Proposed Framework

In this section, we describe the proposed D-TRACE framework, which is a two-stage deep clustering framework with the ability to jointly leverage multiple types of representations from multiple layers for enhancing the deep clustering performance. Specifically, the contrastive clustering network as a pretext task is introduced in Sect. 2.1. The triply-aligned representation and the unsupervised network training for the final clustering are described in Sect. 2.2.

## 2.1 Contrastive Clustering Network

In the proposed framework, we first utilized the contrastive clustering as a pre-task. Instead of merely utilizing a single layer of representation for final clustering [22], we aim to fuse the multiple representations from three modules (i.e., the backbone, the instance contrastive head, and the cluster contrastive head) into a triply-aligned representation. Before the fusion, we will describe the details of the three module in the contrastive clustering network in the following.

**Backbone Network.** The contrastive learning has been an important self-supervised learning technique in recent years [6,11,22], which aims to train the neural network by maximizing the similarity between positive pairs and minimizing that between negative pairs. Similar to the SimCLR method [22] and its extension (termed the CC method) for the clustering task [22], we adopt the ResNet34 [12] as the backbone, and exploit data augmentations to generate positive pairs and negative pairs. Specifically, given a sample image $x_i$, two augmentations $T^a$, $T^b$ are randomly selected from the augmentation group to build the two views $x_i^a$ and $x_i^b$ of this image. In this work, five types of augmentation methods are used independently with a certain probability, including resized-crop, horizontal-flip, color-jitter, grayscale-blur, and Gaussian-blur. With two random augmentations for each image, a weight-sharing network is used for feature extraction, leading to the two representations $h_i^a$ and $h_i^b$, which will then be fed to the instance contrastive module and the cluster contrastive module.

**Instance Contrastive Head.** The instance contrastive head takes the representations $h_i^a$ and $h_i^b$ (from the backbone) as input, and trains the network with an instance-level contrastive loss [22]. Formally, let $\mathcal{X}$ denote a dataset with $M$ sample images. Given a mini-batch of size $N$, a total of $2 \cdot N$ samples can be obtained after two random data augmentations. In particular, two augmented views $x_i^a$ and $x_i^b$ for the same sample $x_i$ are defined as its positive pairs, while considering the remaining $2 \cdot (N-1)$ sample pairs are as the negative pairs. The similarity between samples is measured by the cosine similarity, i.e., $sim(u, v) = (u^\top v)/(\|u\| \|v\|)$. Further, based on $h_i^a$ and $h_i^b$ extracted by the backbone for sample $x_i$, the corresponding representations $z_i^a$ and $z_i^b$ can be obtained through the instance contrastive head, which is a two-layer fully connected multi-layer perceptron (MLP). In order to optimize the instance-level similarity between sample pairs, the loss for sample $x_i^a$ is defined as

$$l_i^a = -log \frac{e^{sim(z_i^a, z_i^b)/\tau_I}}{\sum_{j=1}^{N} (e^{sim(z_i^a, z_j^b)/\tau_I} + e^{sim(z_i^a, z_j^a)/\tau_I})}, \tag{1}$$

where $\tau_I$ is a temperature parameter. By traversing all $2N$ augmented samples, the instance-level contrastive loss $L_I$ is defined as

$$L_I = \frac{1}{2N} \sum_{i=1}^{N} (l_i^a + l_i^b). \tag{2}$$

**Cluster Contrastive Head.** Besides the instance-level contrastiveness, we proceed to employ the cluster-level contrastive learning [22] via the cluster contrastive head. Specifically, when a sample is mapped to a feature vector whose dimension equals the number of clusters, this vector can reflect its probability of belonging to each cluster as soft label. Thereby, if $N$ probability vectors are stacked into matrix $W \in \mathbb{R}^{N \times K}$, where $K$ denotes the number of clusters, each column of $W$ can be regarded as a representation of the corresponding cluster. Formally, for a given sample $x_i$, based on $h_i^a$ and $h_i^b$ generated by the backbone, the feature vector $w_i^a$ and $w_i^b$ are obtained through the cluster contrastive head (which is a two-layer MLP with the dimension of the last layer being equal to the number of clusters). We stack the $N$ representations corresponding to the $N$ samples into a matrix $W^a$ under the first augmentation $T^a$, and form matrix $W^b$ with the other $N$ representations under the second augmentation $T^b$. The cluster-level contrastive loss is computed from $W^a$ and $W^b$ in terms of columns. Let $y_i^a$ denote the $i$-th column of $W^a$ (i.e., the representation of cluster $i$ under the first augmentation), which is coupled with $y_i^b$ to construct a positive pair $(y_i^a, y_i^b)$, while leaving the other $2 \cdot (K-1)$ pairs to be the negative pairs. To optimize the cluster-level similarity, the loss for cluster $y_i^a$ is defined as

$$\tilde{l}_i^a = -log \frac{e^{sim(y_i^a, y_i^b)/\tau_C}}{\sum_{j=1}^{K} (e^{sim(y_i^a, y_j^b)/\tau_C} + e^{sim(y_i^a, y_j^a)/\tau_C})}, \tag{3}$$

where $\tau_C$ is a temperature parameter. Then the cluster-level contrastive loss $L_C$ can be computed over all clusters, that is

$$L_C = \frac{1}{2K} \sum_{i=1}^{K} (\tilde{l}_i^a + \tilde{l}_i^b) - L_E, \tag{4}$$

To avoid assigning most samples to a single cluster, an entropy term $L_E$ is further incorporated, denoted as $L_E = -\sum_{i=1}^{K} [\Phi(y_i^a)log\Phi(y_i^a) + \Phi(y_i^b)log\Phi(y_i^b)]$, where $\Phi(y_i^t) = \sum_{v=1}^{N} W_{vi}^t / \|W^t\|_1, t \in \{a, b\}$ is the cluster assignment probability under each data augmentation.

The backbone, the instance contrastive head, and the cluster contrastive head are optimized simultaneously in the learning process, thus the overall objective function of the contrastive clustering network is defined as:

$$L_{cc} = L_I + L_C. \tag{5}$$

## 2.2    Deep Triply-Aligned Clustering

With the contrastive clustering network trained, three types of representations can be learned in the three modules (i.e., the backbone, the instance contrastive head, and the cluster contrastive head), respectively. In this section, we will jointly leverage these three representations into a second-stage neural network for the final clustering.

**Triple Alignment of Representations.** Though the three modules in the contrastive clustering network are simultaneously trained, which lead to three types of representations, the previous CC [22] method merely utilizes a single layer of representation in the cluster contrastive head to build the clustering result, which ignores the potential benefits hidden in multiple representations from multiple modules. In view of this, we seek to fuse the representations from the three modules in the contrastive clustering network into a more discriminative representation.

We define an alignment operation $\mathbb{A}$, where multiple representations are concatenated in sequence. For a specific sample $x_i$, a new representation $d_i$ can be obtained as

$$d_i = \mathbb{A}(h_i, z_i, w_i), \tag{6}$$

where $h_i$, $z_i$, and $w_i$ denote the representations learned in the backbone, the instance contrastive head, and the cluster contrastive head, respectively. As illustrated in Fig. 1, three types of representations are fused in a contiguous manner in D-TRACE. Taking $d_i$ as a representative of the original sample $x_i$, a representation set for all $M$ samples can be formed as

$$D = \{d_1, d_2, ..., d_M\}. \tag{7}$$

Then, $D$ will be served as the input for a unified deep clustering network in the later stage, which further improves the clustering performance in an unsupervised manner.

**From Aligned Representations to Deep Clustering.** With the triply-aligned representations obtained, our D-TRACE method further performs feature learning and clustering optimization with the help of the reconstruction loss and the KL divergence-based clustering loss.

To obtain a parameterized encoder, we train a stacked fully connected autoencoder by minimizing a reconstruction loss that is defined as the mean squared error (MSE) between its input and output over all samples, that is [30]

$$L_{re} = \sum_{i=1}^{N} \|g'(g(d_i)) - d_i\|_2^2, \tag{8}$$

where $d_i$ is the triply-aligned representation of sample $x_i$, and $g$ and $g'$ are the encoder and decoder mappings, respectively. The encoder can project an input sample into a low-dimensional embedding whose dimension is equal to the number of clusters.

After the training of the autoencoder, we only retain the encoder and stack the clustering layer behind it to incorporate the cluster centers $\{\mu_j\}_{j=1}^K$ as trainable weights. The initial cluster centers $\{\mu_j\}_{j=1}^K$ can be obtained by employing $K$-means on the overall embeddings $\{g(d_i)\}_{i=1}^M$. Then, the encoder network is finetuned by optimizing the KL divergence-based clustering loss:

$$L_{clu} = KL(P||Q) = \sum_{i=0}^N \sum_{j=0}^K p_{ij} log \frac{p_{ij}}{q_{ij}}, \tag{9}$$

where $q_{ij}$ indicates the probability of $g(d_i)$ belonging to the cluster center $\mu_j$ and $p_{ij}$ is the target distribution. Note that $q_{ij}$ is measured by the Student's $t$-distribution [23], that is

$$q_{ij} = \frac{(1 + ||g(d_i) - \mu_j||^2)^{-1}}{\sum_{j'=0}^K (1 + ||g(d_i) - \mu_{j'}||^2)^{-1}}. \tag{10}$$

It can be observed that the clustering layer maps the embedding $g(d_i)$ into the soft label $q_i$, in which $q_{ij}$ is the $j$-th entry. And the target distribution $p_{ij}$ is defined as:

$$p_{ij} = \frac{q_{ij}^2/\sum_{i=0}^M q_{ij}}{\sum_{j'=0}^K (q_{ij'}^2/\sum_{i=0}^M q_{ij'})}. \tag{11}$$

In particular, the clustering loss $L_{clu}$ based on the KL divergence makes the soft distribution $Q$ close to the target distribution $P$, which focuses more on the highly-confident samples in the latent space and may strengthen the clustering predictions. The target distribution $P$ which serves as the "true soft label" is derived from the soft distribution $Q$, so minimizing the clustering loss $L_{clu}$ is a form of self-training [25]. Specifically, we update the target distribution $P$ with all samples every $\sigma$ iterations. The training process will be stopped if the change of the label assignment between two consecutive updates for the target distribution is less than a threshold $\xi$.

Finally, the clustering result of D-TRACE can be obtained according to the label assigned to each sample $x_i$, that is

$$c_i = arg \max_j q_{ij}, \tag{12}$$

where $q_{ij}$ is the probability of $x_i$ belonging to the $j$-th cluster.

## 3   Experiments

In this section, we evaluate the effectiveness of the proposed D-TRACE method against other deep clustering methods on multiple datasets.

**Table 1.** Statistics of the datasets.

| Dataset | Images | Clusters | Image size |
|---|---|---|---|
| STL-10 [7] | 13,000 | 10 | $96 \times 96 \times 3$ |
| CIFAR-10 [21] | 60,000 | 10 | $32 \times 32 \times 3$ |
| CIFAR-100 [21] | 60,000 | 20 | $32 \times 32 \times 3$ |
| ImageNet-10 [22] | 13,000 | 10 | $224 \times 224 \times 3$ |

## 3.1 Datasets and Evaluation Metrics

We conduct experiments on four challenging image datasets for deep unsupervised learning and clustering. For a fair comparison, we adopt the same setting as that in [22], where the entire set of samples is used for the STL-10 [7], CIFAR-10 [21], and CIFAR-100 [21] datasets, while only the training set is used for the ImageNet-10 dataset [22]. For CIFAR-100, the 20 super-classes rather than 100 classes are considered as the true label in the experiments. In addition, the 100,000 unlabeled samples in STL-10 are used to train the instance-level contrastive head. The statistics of these datasets are summarized in Table 1.

All deep clustering methods are evaluated by normalized mutual information (NMI), clustering accuracy (ACC), and adjusted Rand index (ARI), which are three widely-used evaluation metrics in the clustering task. Higher values of these metrics indicate better clustering results.

## 3.2 Implementation Details

In the first-stage training, all input images are resized to the size of $224 \times 224$ for ResNet34 [12] as the dual weight sharing backbone network. The temperature parameter $\tau_I$ and $\tau_C$ are fixed to 0.5 and 1.0 in all experiments. The batch size is set to 256, and the network trained for 1,000 epochs as [22].

In the second stage, we fuse the three types of feature representations into a triply-aligned representation. The dimension of the last layer in backbone is 512, and that of the instance contrastive head is 128. Especially, we use the representation from the first 512-dimensional layer of the cluster contrastive head instead of the last softmax layer, in order to obtain richer feature information. Thus the dimension of the triply-aligned representation is 1,152. The following encoder network is set as a fully connected MLP with dimensions 1152-500-500-2000-$K$ for all datasets, where $K$ is the number of classes of the dataset. And the decoder network is a mirror of encoder, i.e. a MLP with dimensions $K$-2000-500-500-1152. Then, the autoencoder is pretrained for 100 epochs using the Adam optimizer [19] with default parameters. Then only the encoder is trained with the KL-divergence based clustering loss, with the convergence threshold set to $\xi = 0.1\%$ and the update intervals set to $\sigma = 30$ for all experiments without dataset-specific hyper-parameter-tuning. To rule out the factor of getting lucky occasionally, we run our method 10 times and report the average score in each experiment.

**Table 2.** The clustering performance of different conventional and deep clustering methods on four image datasets. The best score in each column is in **Bold**.

| Dataset | STL-10 | | | CIFAR-10 | | | CIFAR-100 | | | ImageNet-10 | | |
|---|---|---|---|---|---|---|---|---|---|---|---|---|
| Eval. Metric | NMI | ACC | ARI | NMI | ACC | ARI | NMI | ACC | ARI | NMI | ACC | ARI |
| $K$-means [17] | 0.125 | 0.192 | 0.061 | 0.087 | 0.229 | 0.049 | 0.084 | 0.130 | 0.028 | 0.119 | 0.241 | 0.057 |
| SC [24] | 0.098 | 0.159 | 0.048 | 0.103 | 0.247 | 0.085 | 0.090 | 0.136 | 0.022 | 0.151 | 0.274 | 0.076 |
| AC [17] | 0.239 | 0.332 | 0.140 | 0.105 | 0.228 | 0.065 | 0.098 | 0.138 | 0.034 | 0.138 | 0.242 | 0.067 |
| NMF [2] | 0.096 | 0.180 | 0.046 | 0.081 | 0.190 | 0.034 | 0.079 | 0.118 | 0.026 | 0.132 | 0.230 | 0.065 |
| AE [1] | 0.250 | 0.303 | 0.161 | 0.239 | 0.314 | 0.169 | 0.100 | 0.165 | 0.048 | 0.210 | 0.317 | 0.152 |
| DAE [28] | 0.224 | 0.302 | 0.152 | 0.251 | 0.297 | 0.163 | 0.111 | 0.151 | 0.046 | 0.206 | 0.304 | 0.138 |
| DCGAN [26] | 0.210 | 0.298 | 0.139 | 0.265 | 0.315 | 0.176 | 0.120 | 0.151 | 0.045 | 0.225 | 0.346 | 0.157 |
| DeCNN [32] | 0.227 | 0.299 | 0.162 | 0.240 | 0.282 | 0.174 | 0.092 | 0.133 | 0.038 | 0.186 | 0.313 | 0.142 |
| VAE [20] | 0.200 | 0.282 | 0.146 | 0.245 | 0.291 | 0.167 | 0.108 | 0.152 | 0.040 | 0.193 | 0.334 | 0.168 |
| JULE [31] | 0.182 | 0.277 | 0.164 | 0.192 | 0.272 | 0.138 | 0.103 | 0.137 | 0.033 | 0.175 | 0.300 | 0.138 |
| DEC [30] | 0.276 | 0.359 | 0.186 | 0.257 | 0.301 | 0.161 | 0.136 | 0.185 | 0.050 | 0.282 | 0.381 | 0.203 |
| DAC [5] | 0.366 | 0.470 | 0.257 | 0.396 | 0.522 | 0.306 | 0.185 | 0.238 | 0.088 | 0.394 | 0.527 | 0.302 |
| DDC [4] | 0.371 | 0.489 | 0.267 | 0.424 | 0.524 | 0.329 | - | - | - | 0.433 | 0.577 | 0.345 |
| DCCM [29] | 0.376 | 0.482 | 0.262 | 0.496 | 0.623 | 0.408 | 0.285 | 0.327 | 0.173 | 0.608 | 0.710 | 0.555 |
| PICA [16] | 0.611 | 0.713 | 0.531 | 0.591 | 0.696 | 0.512 | 0.310 | 0.337 | 0.171 | 0.802 | 0.870 | 0.761 |
| CC [22] | 0.764 | 0.850 | 0.726 | 0.705 | 0.790 | 0.637 | 0.431 | 0.429 | 0.266 | 0.859 | 0.893 | 0.822 |
| **D-TRACE** | **0.782** | **0.864** | **0.752** | **0.745** | **0.815** | **0.686** | **0.477** | **0.461** | **0.311** | **0.882** | **0.921** | **0.854** |

## 3.3   Comparison Against State-of-the-Art Clustering Methods

The clustering performances of the proposed D-TRACE method and the baseline methods are presented in Table 2. These baseline methods not only include the traditional clustering methods, such as $K$-means [17], spectral clustering (SC) [24], agglomerative clustering (AC) [17], and the nonnegative matrix factorization (NMF) based clustering [2], but also include the deep clustering methods, such as auto-encoder (AE) [1], denoising auto-encoder (DAE) [28], deep convolutional generative adversarial networks (DCGAN) [26], deconvolutional networks (DeCNN) [32], variational autoencoding (VAE) [20], jointly unsupervised learning (JULE) [31], deep embedding clustering (DEC) [30], deep adaptive image clustering (DAC) [5], deep discriminative clustering (DDC) [4], deep comprehensive correlation mining (DCCM) [29], partition confidence maximization (PICA) [16], and contrastive clustering (CC) [22].

As shown in Table 2, the proposed D-TRACE method, which jointly utilizes three types of representations learned from multiple layers in deep network, outperforms the baselines on the benchmark datasets. Especially, our method achieves a further improvement over CC [22]. On the CIFAR-100 dataset, the score of D-TRACE is 4.6% and 3.2% higher than that of CC in terms of NMI and ACC, respectively. For ARI, the gain of D-TRACE is 4.9% over CC on the CIFAR-10 dataset. The experimental results demonstrate the effectiveness of our proposed framework.

**Table 3.** The clustering performances of different configurations on STL-10. The best score in each column is in **Bold**.

| Method | Representation type | | | Metric | | |
|---|---|---|---|---|---|---|
| | $f_{Backbone}$ | $f_{ICH}$ | $f_{CCH}$ | NMI | ACC | ARI |
| D-TRACE with different components | ✓ | | | 0.772 | 0.821 | 0.726 |
| | | ✓ | | 0.755 | 0.812 | 0.703 |
| | | | ✓ | 0.768 | 0.852 | 0.729 |
| | ✓ | ✓ | | 0.754 | 0.813 | 0.703 |
| | ✓ | | ✓ | 0.763 | 0.838 | 0.717 |
| | | ✓ | ✓ | 0.775 | 0.851 | 0.741 |
| | ✓ | ✓ | ✓ | **0.782** | **0.864** | **0.752** |

## 3.4  Effect of Triply-Aligned Representation

Previous deep clustering methods mostly use single-layer feature information for clustering, such as the CC method [22] which only uses the feature output from the cluster contrastive head to obtain the final clustering. Instead of investigating a single layer for clustering, the proposed D-TRACE method jointly leverages the feature representations from multiple layers in the network, which are fused in the second-stage network training and further improve the clustering performance. In this section, we conduct ablation study to analyze the contributions of the three types of representations, namely, the representation learned in the backbone $f_{Backbone}$, the representation learned in the instance contrastive head $f_{ICH}$, and the representation learned in the cluster contrastive head $f_{CCH}$. As shown in Table 3, the triple alignment of $\mathbb{A}(f_{Backbone}, f_{ICH}, f_{CCH})$, which corresponds to the joint use of the three types of representations, leads to better performance than using a single layer or two layers of representations, which confirms the benefits brought in by multiple feature representations for the clustering task.

## 4  Conclusion

In this paper, we propose a novel deep clustering approach termed D-TRACE, which is able to take advantage of the feature representations learned in multiple layers of the deep neural network. Specifically, the contrastive clustering network is first utilized, where three modules, namely, the backbone, the instance contrastive head, and the cluster contrastive head, are simultaneously trained. Then the representations learned in the three modules are jointly integrated into the triply-aligned representation, which is further fed to a unified neural network that is trained with a reconstruction loss and a KL-divergence based clustering loss to achieve the final clustering. Experiments on multiple image datasets have demonstrated the superior performance of the D-TRACE approach when compared with the state-of-the-art deep clustering approaches.

**Acknowledgments.** This work was supported by the Science and Technology Program of Guangzhou, China (202201010314), the NSFC (61976097 & 61876193), and the Natural Science Foundation of Guangdong Province (2021A1515012203).

# References

1. Bengio, Y., Lamblin, P., Popovici, D., Larochelle, H.: Greedy layer-wise training of deep networks. In: Advances in Neural Information Processing Systems, vol. 19 (2006)
2. Cai, D., He, X., Wang, X., Bao, H., Han, J.: Locality preserving nonnegative matrix factorization. In: Proceedings of International Joint Conference on Artificial Intelligence (2009)
3. Caron, M., Bojanowski, P., Joulin, A., Douze, M.: Deep clustering for unsupervised learning of visual features. In: Proceedings of European Conference on Computer Vision, pp. 132–149 (2018)
4. Chang, J., Guo, Y., Wang, L., Meng, G., Xiang, S., Pan, C.: Deep discriminative clustering analysis. arXiv preprint arXiv:1905.01681 (2019)
5. Chang, J., Wang, L., Meng, G., Xiang, S., Pan, C.: Deep adaptive image clustering. In: Proceedings of IEEE International Conference on Computer Vision, pp. 5879–5887 (2017)
6. Chen, T., Kornblith, S., Norouzi, M., Hinton, G.: A simple framework for contrastive learning of visual representations. In: Proceedings of International Conference on Machine Learning, pp. 1597–1607 (2020)
7. Coates, A., Ng, A., Lee, H.: An analysis of single-layer networks in unsupervised feature learning. In: Proceedings of International Conference on Artificial Intelligence and Statistics, pp. 215–223 (2011)
8. Dang, Z., Deng, C., Yang, X., Wei, K., Huang, H.: Nearest neighbor matching for deep clustering. In: Proceedings of IEEE/CVF Conference on Computer Vision and Pattern Recognition, pp. 13693–13702 (2021)
9. Dizaji, K.G., Herandi, A., Deng, C., Cai, W., Huang, H.: Deep clustering via joint convolutional autoencoder embedding and relative entropy minimization. In: Proceedings of IEEE International Conference on Computer Vision, pp. 5736–5745 (2017)
10. Guo, X., Gao, L., Liu, X., Yin, J.: Improved deep embedded clustering with local structure preservation. In: Proceedings of International Joint Conference on Artificial Intelligence, pp. 1753–1759 (2017)
11. He, K., Fan, H., Wu, Y., Xie, S., Girshick, R.: Momentum contrast for unsupervised visual representation learning. In: Proceedings of IEEE/CVF Conference on Computer Vision and Pattern Recognition, pp. 9729–9738 (2020)
12. He, K., Zhang, X., Ren, S., Sun, J.: Deep residual learning for image recognition. In: Proceedings of IEEE Conference on Computer Vision and Pattern Recognition, pp. 770–778 (2016)
13. Huang, D., Wang, C., Peng, H., Lai, J., Kwoh, C.: Enhanced ensemble clustering via fast propagation of cluster-wise similarities. IEEE Trans. Syst. Man Cybern. Syst. **51**(1), 508–520 (2021)
14. Huang, D., Wang, C.D., Wu, J.S., Lai, J.H., Kwoh, C.K.: Ultra-scalable spectral clustering and ensemble clustering. IEEE Trans. Knowl. Data Eng. **32**(6), 1212–1226 (2020)

15. Huang, D., Wang, C.D., Lai, J.H., Kwoh, C.K.: Toward multidiversified ensemble clustering of high-dimensional data: from subspaces to metrics and beyond. IEEE Trans. Cybern. (2021, in press)
16. Huang, J., Gong, S., Zhu, X.: Deep semantic clustering by partition confidence maximisation. In: Proceedings of IEEE/CVF Conference on Computer Vision and Pattern Recognition, pp. 8849–8858 (2020)
17. Jain, A.K.: Data clustering: 50 years beyond k-means. Pattern Recogn. Lett. **31**(8), 651–666 (2010)
18. Ji, X., Henriques, J.F., Vedaldi, A.: Invariant information clustering for unsupervised image classification and segmentation. In: Proceedings of IEEE/CVF International Conference on Computer Vision, pp. 9865–9874 (2019)
19. Kingma, D.P., Ba, J.: Adam: a method for stochastic optimization. arXiv preprint arXiv:1412.6980 (2014)
20. Kingma, D.P., Welling, M.: Auto-encoding variational Bayes. arXiv preprint arXiv:1312.6114 (2013)
21. Krizhevsky, A., Hinton, G., et al.: Learning multiple layers of features from tiny images (2009)
22. Li, Y., Hu, P., Liu, Z., Peng, D., Zhou, J.T., Peng, X.: Contrastive clustering. In: Proceedings of AAAI Conference on Artificial Intelligence (2021)
23. Van der Maaten, L., Hinton, G.: Visualizing data using t-SNE. J. Mach. Learn. Res. **9**(11) (2008)
24. Ng, A.Y., Jordan, M.I., Weiss, Y.: On spectral clustering: analysis and an algorithm. In: Advances in Neural Information Processing Systems, pp. 849–856 (2002)
25. Nigam, K., Ghani, R.: Analyzing the effectiveness and applicability of co-training. In: Proceedings of International Conference on Information and Knowledge Management, pp. 86–93 (2000)
26. Radford, A., Metz, L., Chintala, S.: Unsupervised representation learning with deep convolutional generative adversarial networks. arXiv preprint arXiv:1511.06434 (2015)
27. Van Gansbeke, W., Vandenhende, S., Georgoulis, S., Proesmans, M., Van Gool, L.: Scan: learning to classify images without labels. In: Proceedings of European Conference on Computer Vision, pp. 268–285 (2020)
28. Vincent, P., Larochelle, H., Lajoie, I., Bengio, Y., Manzagol, P.A., Bottou, L.: Stacked denoising autoencoders: learning useful representations in a deep network with a local denoising criterion. J. Mach. Learn. Res. **11**(12) (2010)
29. Wu, J., et al.: Deep comprehensive correlation mining for image clustering. In: Proceedings of IEEE/CVF International Conference on Computer Vision, pp. 8150–8159 (2019)
30. Xie, J., Girshick, R., Farhadi, A.: Unsupervised deep embedding for clustering analysis. In: Proceedings of International Conference on Machine Learning, pp. 478–487 (2016)
31. Yang, J., Parikh, D., Batra, D.: Joint unsupervised learning of deep representations and image clusters. In: Proceedings of IEEE Conference on Computer Vision and Pattern Recognition, pp. 5147–5156 (2016)
32. Zeiler, M.D., Krishnan, D., Taylor, G.W., Fergus, R.: Deconvolutional networks. In: Proceedings of IEEE Conference on Computer Vision and Pattern Recognition, pp. 2528–2535 (2010)

# Infering Boundary Conditions in Finite Volume Neural Networks

Coşku Can Horuz[1](ID), Matthias Karlbauer[1](ID), Timothy Praditia[2](ID),
Martin V. Butz[1](ID), Sergey Oladyshkin[2](ID), Wolfgang Nowak[2](ID),
and Sebastian Otte[1(✉)](ID)

[1] Neuro-Cognitive Modeling, University of Tübingen, Tübingen, Germany
{matthias.karlbauer,martin.butz,sebastian.otte}@uni-tuebingen.de
[2] Department of Stochastic Simulation and Safety Research for Hydrosystems,
University of Stuttgart, Stuttgart, Germany
{timothy.praditia,sergey.oladyshkin,wolfgang.nowak}@iws.uni-stuttgart.de

**Abstract.** When modeling physical processes in spatially confined domains, the boundaries require distinct consideration through specifying appropriate boundary conditions (BCs). The finite volume neural network (FINN) is an exception among recent physics-aware neural network models: it allows the specification of arbitrary BCs. FINN is even able to generalize to modified BCs not seen during training, but requires them to be known during prediction. However, so far even FINN was not able to handle unknown BC values. Here, we extend FINN in order to infer BC values on-the-fly. This allows us to apply FINN in situations, where the BC values, such as the inflow rate of fluid into a simulated medium, is unknown. Experiments validate FINN's ability to not only infer the correct values, but also to model the approximated Burgers' and Allen-Cahn equations with higher accuracy compared to competitive pure ML and physics-aware ML models. Moreover, FINN generalizes well beyond the BC value range encountered during training, even when trained on only one fixed set of BC values. Our findings emphasize FINN's ability to reveal unknown relationships from data, thus offering itself as a process-explaining system.

**Keywords:** Physics-aware neural networks · Boundary conditions ·
Retrospective inference · Partial differential equations · Inductive biases

## 1 Introduction

Physics-informed machine learning incorporates physical knowledge as inductive biases [1], providing significant advantages in terms of generalization and data

This work was partially funded by German Research Foundation (DFG) under Germany's Excellence Strategy - EXC 2075 - 390740016 as well as EXC 2064 - 390727645. We acknowledge the support by the Stuttgart Center for Simulation Science (SimTech). Moreover, we thank the International Max Planck Research School for Intelligent Systems (IMPRS-IS) for supporting Matthias Karlbauer.

E. Pimenidis et al. (Eds.): ICANN 2022, LNCS 13529, pp. 538–549, 2022.
https://doi.org/10.1007/978-3-031-15919-0_45

efficiency when contrasted with pure machine learning systems (ML) applied to physical domains [8,15]. Moreover, inductive biases often help ML models play down their "technical debt" [16], reducing model complexity while improving model explainability. Several recently proposed approaches augment neural networks with physical knowledge [5,9,10,17,18]. But these models do neither allow including or structurally capturing explicitly defined physical equations, nor do they generalize to unseen initial and boundary conditions [15]. The recently introduced finite volume neural network (FINN) [7,14] accounts for both: it combines the learning abilities of artificial neural networks with physical and structural knowledge from numerical simulations by modeling partial differential equations (PDEs) in a mathematically compositional manner. So far, FINN is the only physics-aware neural network that can handle boundary conditions that were not considered during training.

Nonetheless, the boundary conditions (BCs) need to be known and presented to all these networks explicitly. To date, not even FINN can predict processes, where the boundary conditions are completely unknown. In realistic application scenarios, however, a quantity of interest is measured for a specific, limited region only. The amount of the quantity that flows into the observed volumes through boundaries are notoriously unknown and impossible to predict. One example is weather forecasting: a prediction system observes e.g. precipitation or cloud density for a limited area. Incoming weather dynamics from outside of the observed region that strongly control the processes inside the domain cannot be incorporated, turning into one of the main error sources in the numerical simulations.

Here, we present an approach to infer the explicitly modeled BC values of FINN on-the-fly, while observing a particular spatiotemporal process. The approach is based on a retrospective inference principle [2,13], which applies a prediction error-induced gradient signal to adapt the BC values of a trained FINN model. Only very few data points are required to find boundary conditions that best explain the recently observed process dynamics and, moreover, to predict the process henceforth with high accuracy in closed-loop. We compare the quality of the inferred boundary conditions and the prediction error of FINN with two state-of-the-art architectures, namely, DISTANA [6] and PhyDNet [5]. Our results indicate that FINN is the only architecture that reliably infers BC values and outperforms all competitors on predicting non-linear advection-diffusion-reaction processes when the BC values are unknown.

## 2  Finite Volume Neural Network

The finite volume neural network (FINN) introduced in [7,14] is a physics-aware neural network model that combines the well-established finite volume method (FVM) [11] as an inductive bias with the learning abilities of deep neural networks. FVM discretizes a continuous partial differential equation (PDE) spatially into algebraic equations over a finite number of control volumes. These volumes have states and exchange fluxes via a clear mathematical structure.

The enforced physical processing within the FVM structure constrains FINN to implement (partially) known physical-laws, resulting in an interpretable, well generalizing, and robust method.

## 2.1   Architecture

FINN solves PDEs that express non-linear spatiotemporal advection-diffusion-reaction processes, such as formulated in [7] as

$$\frac{\partial u}{\partial t} = D(u)\frac{\partial^2 u}{\partial x^2} - v(u)\frac{\partial u}{\partial x} + q(u), \tag{1}$$

where $u$ is the state or the unknown function of time $t$ and spatial coordinate $x$. The objective of a PDE solver (if the PDE was fully known) is to find the value of $u$ in all time steps and spatial locations. However, Eq. 1 is composed by three, often unknown functions of $u$, i.e. $D$, $v$, and $q$. $D$ is the diffusion coefficient, which controls the equilibration between high and low concentrations, $v$ is the advection velocity, which represents the movement of concentration due to the bulk motion of a fluid, and $q$ is the source/sink term, which increases or decreases the quantity of $u$ locally. These unknown functions are approximated by neural network modules, which imitate the structure of Eq. 1 applying it to a set of spatially discretized control volumes. Figure 1 and Eq. 2 illustrate how FINN models the PDE for a single control volume $i$. The first- and second-order spatial derivatives $\left(\frac{\partial u}{\partial x}, \frac{\partial^2 u}{\partial x^2}\right)$, for example, can be approximated with a linear layer, $\varphi_{\mathcal{N}}$, aiming to learn the FVM stencil, i.e. the exchange terms between adjacent volumes. Furthermore, and in order to account for the structure of Eq. 1, FINN introduces two kernels that are applied on each control volume with index $i$— similar to how convolution kernels are shifted over an input image. First, the flux kernel $\mathcal{F} = f_- + f_+$ models both the diffusive $D(u)\frac{\partial^2 u}{\partial x^2}$ and the advective flux $v(u)\frac{\partial u}{\partial x}$, respectively, via the feedforward network modules $\varphi_{\mathcal{D}}$ and $\varphi_{\mathcal{A}}$. Second, the state kernel $\mathcal{S}$ models the source/sink term $q$ for each volume. All modules' outputs are summed up to conclude in $\frac{\partial u}{\partial t}$, which results in a system of ODEs with respect to time that is solved by NODE [3]. Accordingly, FINN predicts $u$ in time step $(t+1)$, that is $\hat{u}^{(t+1)}$, and the error is computed via $\mathcal{L}(\hat{u}_i^{(t+1)}, u_i^{(t+1)})$, where $i$ corresponds to the discretized spatial control volume index and $\mathcal{L}$ is the mean squared error. FINN operates entirely in a closed-loop manner, i.e. only $u^{(t=0)}$ is fed into the model to unroll a prediction $\hat{u}^{(1:T)}$ into the future, with sequence length $T$. The connection scheme of the different kernels and modules ensures compliance with fundamental physical rules, such that advection can spatially propagate exclusively to the left *or* to the right. Note that we only consider one-dimensional problems in this work, although FINN can also be applied to higher-dimensional equations. The reader is referred to [7] and [14] for an in-depth depiction of the model.

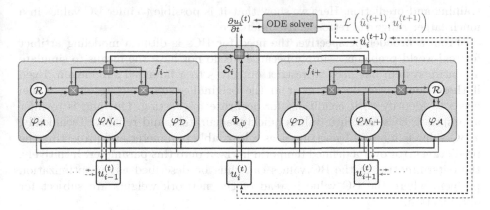

**Fig. 1.** The composition of the modules to represent and learn different parts of an advection-diffusion equation. Figure from [7].

$$\frac{\partial u_i}{\partial t} = \overbrace{D\left(u_i\right) \frac{\partial^2 u_i}{\partial x^2}}^{\substack{\varphi_{\mathcal{N}_{i-}} \\ + \\ \varphi_{\mathcal{D}} \;\; \varphi_{\mathcal{N}_{i+}}}} - \overbrace{v\left(u_i\right) \frac{\partial u_i}{\partial x}}^{\substack{\varphi_{\mathcal{N}_{i-}} \\ \text{or} \\ \mathcal{R}(\varphi_{\mathcal{A}}) \, \varphi_{\mathcal{N}_{i+}}}} + \overbrace{q\left(u_i\right)}^{\Phi_\psi} \tag{2}$$

$$\underbrace{\underbrace{\qquad\qquad\qquad\qquad\qquad\qquad}_{\mathcal{F}_i = f_{i-} + f_{i+}}}_{\mathcal{S}_i}$$

## 2.2   Boundary Condition Inference

The specification of boundary conditions (BCs) is required to obtain a unique solution of a PDE. Common BCs are Dirichlet (fixed values for $u$), periodic (quantity leaving the field on the left enters on the right side), or Neumann (the derivative of $u$ is specified at the boundary). In contrast to state-of-the-art physics-aware neural networks [5,10,15,19], FINN allows the explicit formulation of a desired BC. Thus, FINN can deal with not only simple boundary conditions (Dirichlet or periodic) but also more complicated ones (e.g. Neumann) [7]. This study applies constant Dirichlet BCs, while we leave the in-depth exploration of other BCs for future research.

FINN uses the boundary conditions strictly. The solid implementation of a BC type (Dirichlet, periodic, Neumann) paves the way for the model to *read out* an unknown/unseen BC value of a given dataset. So far, however, it was unfeasible not to use an explicit BC for solving a PDE. However, novel ML models reinforced by inductive biases can extract essential information from data. FINN is an ML model that is predestined for this purpose, as it is tailored to conveniently implement various BC types and values for different PDEs. Accordingly, it is able to learn which BC values best describe a specific dataset—during both training and prediction. Here we show that it is possible to infer BC values in a much larger range via retrospective inference.

From a broader perspective, the need for BCs is often a modeling artifact for real-world problems—simply because we do not have the means to simulate an entire system but need to restrict ourselves to a bounded subdomain. Even if these boundaries do not exist in the original system, our resulting model needs to identify their conditions for accurate forecasting. Our aim is to infer appropriate BCs and their values quickly, accurately, and reliably. Technically, a BC value is inferred by setting it as a learnable parameter and projecting the prediction error over a defined temporal horizon onto this parameter. Intuitively, the determination of the BC values can thus be described as an optimization problem where the BC value instead of the network weights are subject for optimization.

## 3    Equations

We performed experiments on two different PDEs and will first introduce these equations to later report the respective experiments and results.

### 3.1    Burgers' Equation

Burgers' equation is frequently used in different research fields to model e.g. fluid dynamics, nonlinear acoustics, or gas dynamics [4,12], and is a practical toy example formulated as a 1D equation in this work as

$$\frac{\partial u}{\partial t} = -v(u)\frac{\partial u}{\partial x} + D\frac{\partial^2 u}{\partial x^2}, \tag{3}$$

where $u$ is the unknown function and $v(u)$ is the advective velocity, which is defined as an identity function $v(u) = u$. The diffusion coefficient $D$ is set to $0.01/\pi$ in data generation. During training, Burgers' equation has constant values on the left and right boundaries defined as $u(-1,t) = u(1,t) = 0$. However, these were modified to take different symmetric values at inference in order to assess the ability of the different models to cope with such variations. The initial condition is defined as $u(x,0) = -\sin(\pi x)$.

### 3.2    Allen-Cahn Equation

Allen-Cahn is chosen and also defined as a 1D equation that could have periodic or constant boundary conditions. It is typically applied to model phase-separation in multi-component alloy systems and has also been used in [15] to analyse the performance of their physics-informed neural network (PINN). The equation is defined as

$$\frac{\partial u}{\partial t} = D\frac{\partial^2 u}{\partial x^2} + R(u), \tag{4}$$

where the reaction term takes the form $R(u) = 5u - 5u^3$. The diffusion coefficient is set to $D = 0.05$, which is significantly higher than in [7] where it was set to $D = 10^{-4}$. The reason for this decision is to scale up the diffusion relative to the reaction, such that a stronger effect of the BCs is more apparent.

## 4    Experiments

We have conducted two different experiments. First, the ability to learn BC values during training is studied in Sect. 4.1. Afterwards, we analyze the ability of the pre-trained models to infer unknown BC values in Sect. 4.2. Data was generated with numerical simulation using the Finite Volume Method, similarly to [7].

### 4.1    Learning with Fixed Unknown Boundary Conditions

This experiment is conducted in order to discover whether it is possible for the model to approximate the boundary conditions of the given dataset. It can be utmost useful in real-world-datasets to determine the unknown BC values simultaneously while training the model.

The learnt BC values shown in Table 1 suggest that it is not even slightly possible for DISTANA and PhyDNet to infer reasonable BC values. Also for FINN, the problem is non-trivial. The complex nature of the equations combined with large-range BC values yield a challenging optimization problem, in which gradient-based approaches can easily end-up in local minima. Additionally, the fact that FINN uses NODE [3] to integrate the ODE, may, for example, lead to the convergence into a stiff system. In preliminary experiments, we have realized that the usage of shorter sequences actually helped identifying the correct BC values. Moreover, a sufficiently large learning rate was advantageous. The shape of the generated training data was $(256, 49)$, where $N_x = 49$ specifies the discretized spatial locations and $N_t = 256$ the number of simulation steps. To train FINN, we only used the first 30 time steps of a sequence. As a result, FINN identifies the correct BCs and—although this was not necessarily the goal—even yields a lower test error for the entire 256 time steps of the sequence, even though it was trained on only the first 30. Neither PhyDNet nor DISTANA offer the option to meaningfully implement boundary conditions. Accordingly, they are simply fed into the model on the edges of the simulation domain. The missing inductive bias of how to use these BC values prevent the models to determine the correct BC values (c.f. Table 1). Nevertheless, both PhyDNet and DISTANA can approximate the equation fairly correct (albeit not reaching FINN's accuracy), even when the determined BC values deviate from the true values. The learnt BC values by the two models do not converge to any point and persist around the initial values which are $[0.5, -0.5]$ for Burgers' and $[-0.5, 0.5]$ for Allen-Cahn. Similarly, they remain around 0 when we set the initial BC values to 0. This suggests that PhyDNet and DISTANA did not consider the BC values at all. On the other hand, FINN appears to benefit from the structural *knowledge* about

**Table 1.** Comparison of the training errors and the learnt BC values of all models. For each trial the average results over 5 repeats are presented. Burgers' dataset BC = $[1.0, -1.0]$ and Allen-Cahn dataset BC = $[-1.0, 1.0]$.

| Eqn. | Model | Training error | Learnt BC |
|---|---|---|---|
| Burgers' | DISTANA | $(4.14 \pm 2.07) \times 10^{-5}$ | $[0.61 \pm 0.05, -0.61 \pm 0.03]$ |
| | PhyDNet | $1.04 \times 10{-4} \pm 6.68 \times 10^{-5}$ | $[0.51 \pm 0.18, -0.40 \pm 0.26]$ |
| | FINN | $(9.58 \pm 9.94) \times 10^{-8}$ | $[1.0004 \pm 0.0002, -1.0004 \pm 0.0002]$ |
| Allen-Cahn | DISTANA | $1.64 \times 10^{-5} \pm 7.93 \times 10^{-6}$ | $[-0.54 \pm 0.02, 0.53 \pm 0.02]$ |
| | PhyDNet | $(4.50 \pm 2.17) \times 10^{-5}$ | $[-0.59 \pm 0.11, 0.44 \pm 0.07]$ |
| | FINN | $(3.42 \pm 4.48) \times 10^{-7}$ | $[-0.99 \pm 0.004, 0.99 \pm 0.0006]$ |

BCs when determining their values. The BC values in Table 1 converged from $[4.0, -4.0]$ to $[1.0, -1.0]$, well-maintaining them for the rest of the training (see first row of Fig. 2). As it can be seen on the second row of Fig. 2, FINN also manages to infer BC values for Allen-Cahn in a larger range. In Fig. 2, FINN shows its ability to neither overshoot nor undershoot. As we used synthetic data in this study, we knew what the true BC values were. However, it would be possible to trust FINN, even when the BC values are unknown to the researcher—as the correct BC values are learnt, the gradients of the boundary conditions converge to 0, maintaining the accurate BC well (see the right plots of Fig. 2).

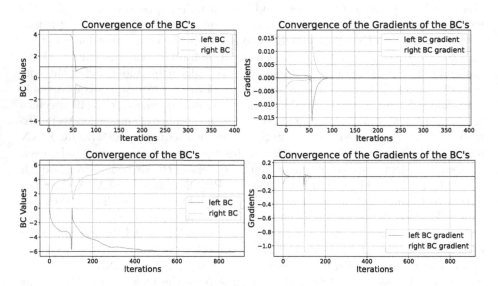

**Fig. 2.** Convergence of the boundary conditions and their gradients during training in FINN. The dataset BC = $[1.0, -1.0]$ for Burgers' on the first row. On the second row for Allen-Cahn with BC = $[-6.0, 6.0]$.

**Table 2.** Comparison of *multi-batch training* and prediction errors along with the inferred BC values by the corresponding models. The experiments were repeated 5 times for each trial and the average results are presented. Burgers' dataset BC = [3.0, −3.0] and Allen-Cahn dataset BC = [−1.0, 1.0].

| Eqn. | Model | Training error | Test error | Inferred BC |
|---|---|---|---|---|
| Burgers' | DISTANA | $(3.9 \pm 1.2) \times 10^{-5}$ | $3.19 \pm 0.14$ | $[4.4 \pm 1.12, -4.0 \pm 1.27]$ |
| | PhyDNet | $(1.9 \pm 1.0) \times 10^{-4}$ | $4.04 \pm 0.29$ | $[3.6 \pm 2.03, -4.4 \pm 2.49]$ |
| | FINN | $(1.5 \pm 1.3) \times 10^{-7}$ | $0.05 \pm 0.02$ | $[3.1 \pm 0.06, -3.1 \pm 0.06]$ |
| Allen-Cahn | DISTANA | $(7.6 \pm 4.4) \times 10^{-5}$ | $0.05 \pm 0.02$ | $[-1.0 \pm 0.18, 3.2 \pm 2.30]$ |
| | PhyDNet | $1 \times 10^{-4} \pm 6 \times 10^{-5}$ | $0.09 \pm 0.07$ | $[-1.2 \pm 0.52, 0.2 \pm 0.45]$ |
| | FINN | $(2.6 \pm 3.7) \times 10^{-6}$ | $(8 \pm 8) \times 10^{-6}$ | $[-0.99 \pm 0.006, 0.99 \pm 0.005]$ |

## 4.2  Boundary Condition Inference with Trained Models

The main purpose of this experiment is to investigate the possibility to infer an unknown BC value after having trained a model on a particular BC value. In accordance with this purpose, we examined two different training algorithms, while applying the identical inference process when evaluating the BC inference ability of the trained models.

**Multi-batch Training and Inference.** Ten different sequences with randomly sampled BC values from the ranges [−1, 1] for Burgers' and [−0.3, 0.3] for Allen-Cahn equation were used as training data. Thus, the models have the opportunity to learn the effect of different BC values, allowing the weights to be adjusted accordingly.

During inference, the models had to infer BC values outside of the respective ranges when observing 30 simulation steps. The rest of the dataset, that is, the remaining 98 time steps, was used for simulating the dynamics in closed-loop. As can be seen in Table 2, FINN is superior in this task compared to DISTANA and PhyDNet. All three models have small training errors, but DISTANA and PhyDNet mainly fail to infer the correct BC values as well as to predict the equations accurately. FINN, however, manages to find the correct BC values with high precision and significantly small deviations. After finding the correct BC values, FINN manages to predict the equations correctly. Figure 3 shows how the prediction error changes in different models as the BC range drifts away from the BC range of the training set. On the other hand, Fig. 4 depicts the predictions of the multi-batch trained models after inference presenting once again the precision of FINN.

**One-Batch Training and Inference.** In this experiment, the models receive only one sequence with $t = [0, 2]$, $N_t = 256$ and $N_x = 49$. The BC values of the dataset are constant and set to [0.0, 0.0]. Hence the models do not see how the equations behave under different BC values. This is substantially harder

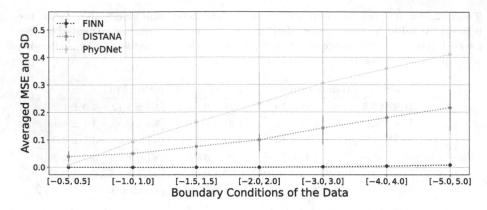

**Fig. 3.** Average prediction errors of 5 multi-batch trained models for Allen-Cahn-Equation. Standard deviations of FINN's averaged errors range from $4 \times 10^{-6}$ to $1 \times 10^{-3}$. Hence it is not possible to see them in the plot.

**Table 3.** Comparison of *one-batch training* and prediction errors after inference along with the BCs inferred by the corresponding models. The experiments were repeated 5 times for each trial and the average results are presented. Burgers' dataset BC = $[3.0, -3.0]$ and Allen-Cahn dataset BC = $[-1.0, 1.0]$.

| Eqn. | Model | Training error | Test error | Inferred BC |
|---|---|---|---|---|
| Burgers' | DISTANA | $(8.4 \pm 1.7) \times 10^{-7}$ | $4.14 \pm 0.82$ | $[-2.5 \pm 3.41, 3.0 \pm 7.31]$ |
|  | PhyDNet | $1 \times 10^{-4} \pm 9 \times 10^{-5}$ | $5.12 \pm 0.47$ | $[4.1 \pm 3.24, 2.5 \pm 8.36]$ |
|  | FINN | $(1.7 \pm 1.5) \times 10^{-7}$ | $0.17 \pm 0.16$ | $[3.0 \pm 0.01, -3.0 \pm 0.01]$ |
| Allen-Cahn | DISTANA | $1 \times 10^{-5} \pm 4 \times 10^{-6}$ | $0.09 \pm 0.03$ | $[-3.8 \pm 3.18, 0.1 \pm 11.2]$ |
|  | PhyDNet | $(4.8 \pm 2.2) \times 10^{-5}$ | $0.08 \pm 0.04$ | $[-1.3 \pm 1.23, 1.9 \pm 1.61]$ |
|  | FINN | $(2.9 \pm 4.2) \times 10^{-6}$ | $(1 \pm 1) \times 10^{-5}$ | $[-0.99 \pm 0.01, 0.99 \pm 0.006]$ |

compared to the previous experiment and the results clearly exhibit this (see Table 3). Despite low training errors, DISTANA and PhyDNet fail to infer correct BC values. The prediction errors when testing in closed-loop after BC inference also indicate that these models have difficulties solving the task. FINN manages to infer the correct BC values, but also its prediction error increases significantly when compared to the training error. Nonetheless, FINN still infers the correct BC values and produces the lowest test error. These results demonstrate that the networks largely benefit from sequences with various BC values, enabling them to infer and predict the same equations over a larger range of novel BCs. While we only report the results of one set of boundary conditions for each experiment, due to space constraints, we have conducted these experiments with several other BC values, which all show the same result pattern.

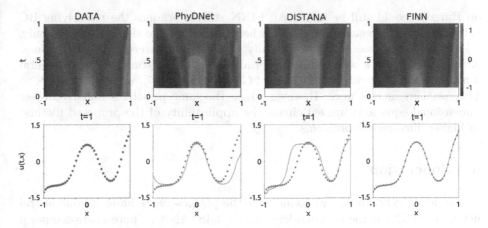

**Fig. 4.** The predictions of the Allen-Cahn dynamics after inference. First row shows the models' predictions over space and time. The respective white columns on the left side of the model predictions are the 15 simulation steps that were used for inference and subtracted before the prediction. Second row shows the predictions over $x$ and $u(x, t = 1)$, i.e. $u$ in the last simulation step. Best models were used for the plots.

## 5 Discussion

The aim of our first experiment (see Sect. 4.1) was to assess whether FINN, DISTANA, and PhyDNet are able to learn the fixed and unknown Dirichlet BC values of data generated by Burgers' and Allen-Cahn equations. This was achieved by setting the value of the BC as a learnable parameter to optimize it along with the models' weights during training. The results, as detailed in Table 1, suggest two conclusions: First, all models can satisfactorily approximate the equations by achieving error rates far below $10^{-1}$. Second, only FINN can infer the BC values underlying the data accurately. Although DISTANA and PhyDNet simulate the process with high accuracy, they apparently do not exhibit an explainable and interpretable behavior. Instead, they treat the BC values in a way that does not reflect their true values and physical meaning. This is different in FINN, where the inferred BC value can be extracted and interpreted directly from the model. This is of great value for real-world applications, where data are given with an unknown BC, such as in weather forecasting or traffic forecasting in a restricted simulation domain.

In the second experiment (see Sect. 4.2), we addressed the question of whether the three models can infer an unknown BC value when they have already been trained on a (set of) known BC values. Technically, this is a traditional test for generalization. The results in Table 2 suggest that both DISTANA and PhyDNet decently learn the effect of the different BC values on the data when being trained on a range of BC values. Once the models are trained on one single BC value only (c.f. Table 3), however, the inferred BC values of DISTANA and PhyDNet are far off the true values. This is different for FINN: although the test error on Burgers' could still be improved, FINN still determines the underlying BC values in both cases accurately, even when trained on one single BC value only.

Our main aim was to infer physically plausible and interpretable BC values. Although FINN is a well tested model and it has been compared with several models such as ConvLSTM, TCN, and CNN-NODE in [7], we applied FINN to 1D equations in this work. However, since the same principles underlie higher dimensional equations, we anticipate the applicability of the proposed method to higher dimensional problems.

## 6   Conclusion

In a series of experiments, we found that the physics-aware finite volume neural network (FINN) is the only model—among DISTANA (a pure spatiotemporal processing ML approach) and PhyDNet (another physics-aware model)—that can determine an unknown boundary condition value of data generated with two different PDEs with high accuracy. Once the correct BC values are found, it can predict the equation depending on them with high precision. So far, the universal pure ML models stay too general to solve the problem studied in this work. State-of-the-art physics-aware networks (e.g. in [5,8]) are likewise not specific enough. Instead, this work suggests that a physically structured model that can be considered as an application-specific inductive bias is indispensable and should be paired with the learning abilities of neural networks. FINN integrates these two aspects by implementing multiple feedforward modules and mathematically composing them to satisfy physical constraints. This structure allows FINN to determine unknown boundary condition values both during training and inference, which, to the best of our knowledge, is a unique property under physics-aware ML models.

In future work, we will investigate how different BC types (Dirichlet, periodic, Neumann, etc.)—and not only their values—can be inferred from data. Moreover, an adaptive and online inference scheme that can deal with dynamically changing BC types and values is an exciting direction to further advance the applicability of FINN to real-world problems. Finally, the further evaluation of FINN on real-world data is imminent.

## References

1. Battaglia, P.W., et al.: Relational inductive biases, deep learning, and graph networks. arXiv preprint arXiv:1806.01261 (2018)
2. Butz, M.V., Bilkey, D., Humaidan, D., Knott, A., Otte, S.: Learning, planning, and control in a monolithic neural event inference architecture. Neural Netw. **117**, 135–144 (2019)
3. Chen, R.T.Q., Rubanova, Y., Bettencourt, J., Duvenaud, D.: Neural ordinary differential equations (2019)
4. Fletcher, C.A.: Generating exact solutions of the two-dimensional burgers' equations. Int. J. Numer. Meth. Fluids **3**, 213–216 (1983)

5. Guen, V.L., Thome, N.: Disentangling physical dynamics from unknown factors for unsupervised video prediction. In: Proceedings of the IEEE/CVF Conference on Computer Vision and Pattern Recognition, pp. 11474–11484 (2020)
6. Karlbauer, M., Otte, S., Lensch, H.P., Scholten, T., Wulfmeyer, V., Butz, M.V.: A distributed neural network architecture for robust non-linear spatio-temporal prediction. In: 28th European Symposium on Artificial Neural Networks (ESANN), Bruges, Belgium, pp. 303–308, October 2020
7. Karlbauer, M., Praditia, T., Otte, S., Oladyshkin, S., Nowak, W., Butz, M.V.: Composing partial differential equations with physics-aware neural networks. In: International Conference on Machine Learning (ICML) (2022)
8. Karniadakis, G.E., Kevrekidis, I.G., Lu, L., Perdikaris, P., Wang, S., Yang, L.: Physics-informed machine learning. Nat. Rev. Phys. **3**(6), 422–440 (2021)
9. Li, Z., et al.: Fourier neural operator for parametric partial differential equations. arXiv preprint arXiv:2010.08895 (2020)
10. Long, Z., Lu, Y., Ma, X., Dong, B.: PDE-net: learning PDEs from data. In: International Conference on Machine Learning, pp. 3208–3216. PMLR (2018)
11. Moukalled, F., Mangani, L., Darwish, M.: The Finite Volume Method in Computational Fluid Dynamics: An Advanced Introduction with OpenFOAM and Matlab. FMIA, vol. 113. Springer, Cham (2016). https://doi.org/10.1007/978-3-319-16874-6
12. Naugolnykh, K.A., Ostrovsky, L.A., Sapozhnikov, O.A., Hamilton, M.F.: Nonlinear wave processes in acoustics (2000)
13. Otte, S., Karlbauer, M., Butz, M.V.: Active tuning. arXiv preprint arXiv:2010.03958 (2020)
14. Praditia, T., Karlbauer, M., Otte, S., Oladyshkin, S., Butz, M.V., Nowak, W.: Finite volume neural network: modeling subsurface contaminant transport. In: International Conference on Learning Representations (ICRL) - Workshop Deep Learning for Simulation (2021)
15. Raissi, M., Perdikaris, P., Karniadakis, G.E.: Physics-informed neural networks: a deep learning framework for solving forward and inverse problems involving nonlinear partial differential equations. J. Comput. Phys. **378**, 686–707 (2019)
16. Sculley, D., et al.: Hidden technical debt in machine learning systems. In: Proceedings of the 28th International Conference on Neural Information Processing Systems - Volume 2, NIPS 2015, pp. 2503–2511. MIT Press, Cambridge (2015)
17. Seo, S., Meng, C., Liu, Y.: Physics-aware difference graph networks for sparsely-observed dynamics. In: International Conference on Learning Representations (2019)
18. Sitzmann, V., Martel, J., Bergman, A., Lindell, D., Wetzstein, G.: Implicit neural representations with periodic activation functions. Adv. Neural. Inf. Process. Syst. **33**, 7462–7473 (2020)
19. Yin, Y., et al.: Augmenting physical models with deep networks for complex dynamics forecasting. J. Stat. Mech: Theory Exp. **2021**(12), 124012 (2021)

# Layer-Specific Repair of Neural Network Classifiers

Shuo Sun[1,3] (iD), Jun Yan[2,3(✉)], and Rongjie Yan[2,3]

[1] Technology Center of Software Engineering, Institute of Software,
Chinese Academy of Sciences, Beijing, China
sunshuo20@otcaix.iscas.ac.cn
[2] State Key Laboratory of Computer Science, Institute of Software,
Chinese Academy of Sciences, Beijing, China
{yanjun,yrj}@ios.ac.cn
[3] University of Chinese Academy of Sciences, Beijing, China

**Abstract.** Deep neural networks (DNNs) become increasingly popular. However, the vulnerability of DNNs can lead to a performance decrease when they cannot correctly predict the given samples. We propose a repair method for DNN-based classifiers to solve this problem, such that the accuracy can be improved by modifying the parameters of a DNN. First, we transform the DNN repair problem into a linear programming model, by encoding the constraints and the objective in linear programming. Second, to reduce the scale of the LP model, we repair the DNN by considering the parameters in the last layer. Third, to enhance the accuracy on the previously wrongly predicted samples without sacrificing the accuracy on the previously correctly predicted samples, we adopt these two types of samples in the optimization process. The evaluation on two popular datasets shows that our method outperforms the state-of-the-art methods and improves the accuracies by 25.4% points in the adversarial attacking scenario and 67.6% points in the backdooring attacking scenario. Meanwhile, our method can avoid obvious accuracy decreasing on standard test sets, which is at most 0.5%. The extensive experimentation demonstrates that the proposed method is effective and efficient in repairing DNN based classifiers.

**Keywords:** Neural network repair · Linear programming · Bug fixing

## 1 Introduction

Deep neural networks (DNNs) have been widely applied in various fields such as facial recognition [12], computer vision [9], and malware detection [17]. However, DNNs may be vulnerable thus performing unexpectedly. For example, DNNs may provide wrong outputs when small or unnoticeable perturbations are integrated into inputs that can be handled correctly [3]. Meanwhile, DNNs may also make wrong decisions due to the *poisoned* training data [4]. These phenomena have motivated numerous research branches in enhancing the robustness and accuracy of DNNs.

Supported by the Key Research Program of Frontier Sciences, CAS under grant No. QYZDJSSW-JSC036 and the National Natural Science Foundation of China (NSFC) under grant number 62132020.

In this paper, we focus on how to *repair* a DNN to increase its accuracy when it makes mistakes. In practice, retraining and fine-tuning are candidate solutions to enhance the accuracy of a DNN when defects are detected. The former adopts the original dataset and the *buggy samples* (that trigger the defects of the DNNs) to retrain the networks. This process can be inefficient because training a large-scale DNN can take days or weeks on state-of-the-art hardware. Meanwhile, retraining may arbitrarily change the parameters of the DNN and introduce new defects into the DNN. The latter mainly adopts the buggy samples for parameter modification. The fine-tuned DNNs gain higher accuracy on buggy samples but significantly increases the risk of decreasing the accuracy of the original dataset.

Different from those solutions, repairing considered here is to modify a subset of parameters to enhance the accuracy of a DNN. For example, the repair method PRDNN guarantees that by modifying the parameters in one layer, the repaired DNNs can correctly classify all the wrongly predicted samples [14]. However, this method is memory-consuming and not suitable for repairing a DNN with a large set of wrongly predicted samples. NNRepair [15] can repair the DNNs by locating the faulty parameters and modifying the parameters to remedy the defects. However, it provides no guarantee of the accuracy of repaired DNNs on the original test set. The main challenge in repairing is how to increase the accuracy of a DNN towards the augmented samples efficiently without sacrificing the accuracy on the original samples.

In this paper, we present a *linear programming* (LP) based approach to repair neural networks for classification tasks. To reduce the modification degree and increase the scale of the repairable networks, we focus on repairing the parameters of the last layer. Based on the structure feature of the last layer, we build a linear model for finding new weights and biases of the neurons in the last layer. To avoid sacrificing the accuracy of the repaired DNN on the original samples, we introduce additional constraints requiring that the original samples should be correctly classified and the new parameters should be close to the original parameters.

The contributions of this paper are as follows. First, we provide RIPPLE (Repair with linear Programming concerning Positive samplEs), an effective and efficient method to repair DNN-based classifiers using the original dataset augmented buggy samples. The effectiveness is achieved by considering both the original dataset and the buggy samples. Meanwhile, the efficiency is achieved by adopting the last layer for repairing. Second, to enhance the accuracy of the repaired DNNs on buggy samples without scarifying the accuracy on the original dataset, we adopt linear programming to encode the constraints and the accuracy as the objective to compute the feasible parameters. Third, we have conducted a series of experimentation to validate the effectiveness and efficiency of RIPPLE. Meanwhile, we have also compared RIPPLE with state-of-the-art repairing methods. The experimental results demonstrate that our method outperforms the others in most cases.

## 2   Preliminaries

In this paper, we focus on DNN-based classifiers, each of which can be considered as a function $Net$ that takes an input and outputs the label of the input. A DNN consists of an input layer, multiple hidden layers, and an output layer. Each layer contains a set of neurons. Except for the input layer, in each layer, every node is connected with neurons in the previous layer. Each edge connected to a node is assigned with a weight $w$. Meanwhile, each neuron is assigned with a bias $b$. Given an input $x$, the value of a neuron $n$ in layer $l$ is $Node_l(x, n) = \sigma(\sum_{i \in [1,m]} w_i \cdot Node_{l-1}(x, n_i) + b)$, where $m$ is the number of neurons in the previous layer, $n_i$ is the $i$th neuron in the previous layer, $w_i$ is the weight of the edge between neurons $n$ and $n_i$, $b$ is the bias of neuron $n$, and $\sigma$ is an activation function (e.g., rectified linear unit (ReLU), or sigmoid and hyperbolic tangent (Tanh)). For DNN-based classifiers, the last layer is usually a linear classifier which outputs its confidence for classifying the input in each category. Therefore, the output of a network is the index of the highest confidence representing the predicted label of the input.

We use an indicator function $Ind$ as a mapping from Boolean values to integers. That is, let $expr$ be a Boolean expression, $Ind(expr) = 1$ if $expr$ is true. Otherwise, $Ind(expr) = 0$. Let $S = \{(x_1, y_1), (x_2, y_2), ... (x_n, y_n)\}$ be a set of labeled samples where $x_i$ is a sample and $y_i$ is the correct label of $x_i$ for all $i \in [1, n]$. Then the accuracy of a classifier $Net$ on dataset $S$ is

$$Acc(Net, S) = \frac{1}{|S|} \sum_{(x,y) \in S} Ind(Net(x) = y). \tag{1}$$

The repaired DNNs are expected to have higher accuracy on the erroneous example set and perform well on the original test set. Formally, we define the DNN repair problem as follows.

**Definition 1 (The DNN repair problem).** *Given a DNN $Net$, let $T_o$ be the standard test set of $Net$, let $T_b$ be a set of labeled samples. The DNN repair problem is to find a new DNN $Net'$ such that $Acc(Net', T_b) > Acc(Net, T_b)$ and $Acc(Net, T_o) - Acc(Net', T_o)$ is at most $\delta$ where $\delta$ is a positive constant.*

Note that $T_o$ and $T_b$ can be the same set. In this case, the goal of repair is to improve the accuracy of $Net$ on the standard test set.

## 3   The Linear Programming Based Method

In Definition 1, the test sets $T_o$ and $T_b$ are to test the accuracy of $Net$ and $Net'$ on general examples. Therefore, they should not be used in the repairing process. With this consideration, we divide the set of buggy samples $E$ into two subsets $E_a$ and $E_r$, where $E_a$ is for computing the accuracy of the repaired DNN, and $E_r$ is for exposing the fault and guiding the repair process. The original training set without buggy samples $O$ and the subset of buggy sample $E_r$ are adopted for repairing. The union of the two sets is denoted by $R = O \cup E_r$.

In the rest of the paper, we abuse the notation and adopt $R_p = O$ to represent the samples that can be correctly predicted (denoted as *positive samples*) in the original DNN, and $R_n = E_r$ for the buggy samples. Obviously, we have $Acc(Net, R_p) = 1.0$ and $Acc(Net, R_n) = 0.0$. Let DNN $Net'$ be the repaired network, we expect that $Acc(Net', R_p) = 1.0$ and $Acc(Net', R_n) = 1.0$.

An overview of RIPPLE is illustrated in Fig. 1. With the structure of the DNN to be repaired, we can construct the linear model which encodes the constraints on the structure of the DNN and the expected objectives. With the provided dataset, we can calculate the new parameters and repair the DNN.

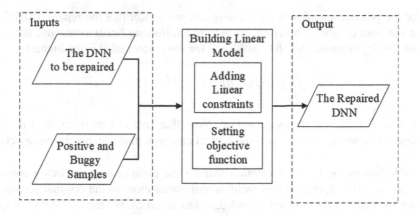

**Fig. 1.** Overview of RIPPLE

## 3.1 Construction of the Linear Model

Our method focuses on the repair of the output layer. The input to the output layer is the feature vector provided by the last hidden layer. For a sample $x$, the feature vector of the last hidden layer $l$ is denoted by $v(x) = (v_1(x), \ldots, v_m(x))$, where $m$ is the number of neurons in the last hidden layer, and $v_i(x) = Node_l(x, n_i)$. For every sample in the dataset, we need to obtain the feature vector provided by the last hidden layer. As previously discussed, when we transform a DNN repair problem into an optimization problem, we need to find a set of weights between the neurons in the last hidden layer and the output layer, and a set of biases such that the following goal can be obtained:

$$Maximize \sum_{(x,y)\in R} Ind(\arg\max_{i\in[1,n]}(\sum_{j\in[1,m]} w_{i,j} \cdot v_j(x) + b_i) = y) \qquad (2)$$

where $n$ is the number of neurons in the output layer, and $m$ is the number of neurons in the last hidden layer. Informally speaking, we expect that the repaired DNN can correctly classify as many samples as possible.

**Linear Constraints.** Let $W = \{w_{i,j}\}_{i\in[i,n],j\in[1,m]}$ and $B = \{b_i\}_{i\in[i,n]}$ be the sets of new weights and biases of the output layer, respectively, where $w_{i,j}$ is weights of edges connected between the $i$th neuron in the output layer and the $j$th neuron in the last hidden layer, $b_i$ is the bias of the $i$th neuron in the output layer, and $n$ and $m$ are the numbers of neurons in the output layer and the last hidden layer, respectively. The confidence of classifying sample $x$ into class $i$ is a function of $x$ and $i$.

$$Conf(x, i) = \sum_{j \in [1,m]} (w_{i,j} \cdot v_j(x) + b_i) \tag{3}$$

For the positive samples in the training set, we expect that the repaired DNN can output the correct label. Therefore, we add the following linear constraint for every sample $x \in R_p$ to ensure that the confidence for the correct label is the highest.

$$\bigwedge_{i \neq y} Conf(x, y) - Conf(x, i) \geq \epsilon \tag{4}$$

where $0 < \epsilon < 1$ is a positive constant. Note that setting $\epsilon$ as 0 can lead to equal confidence in a wrong category and the correct category thus causing the wrong classification.

In addition to the basic expectation that all the positive samples being correctly classified, we also require the new weights and biases close to the original parameters in order to maintain the original knowledge and avoid overfitting on buggy samples. Therefore, we add constraints for new weights and biases.

$$\|W - W_{origin}\|_\infty \leq tolerance$$
$$\|B - B_{origin}\|_\infty \leq tolerance \tag{5}$$

where $W_{origin}$ and $B_{origin}$ are original parameters and $tolerance \geq 0$ is a non-negative constant. $Tolerance$ indicates the maximal allowed distance between the new and original parameters. Note that setting $tolerance$ to 0 will result in the new parameters equal to original parameters and introducing no influence on accuracy. This fact also shows that RIPPLE is always able to find a solution for any given input.

**Objective Function.** We expect that DNN $Net'$ can correctly classify examples in $R_n$ as many as possible. Therefore, the optimization objective should be

$$Maximize \sum_{(x,y) \in R_n} Ind(Net'(x) = y) \tag{6}$$

With this objective function, the model is a *mixed integer linear programming* (MILP) problem, which is NP-hard. To improve the efficiency and scalability of our method, we propose a new objective function to replace Eq. 6.

$$Maximize \sum_{(x,y) \in R_n} \sum_{i \neq y} (Conf(x, y) - Conf(x, i)) \tag{7}$$

In Eq. 7, we adopt the sum of the differences between the confidences of the correct label and other labels as the objective function.

# 4 Evaluation

In this section, we consider the following research questions to validate our method:

**RQ1:** Do the selection of parameters and encoding formats influence the repair performance?

**RQ2:** Is it effective to adopt the training set as a subset of dataset for repairing to achieve the expected accuracy on the targeted test set?

**RQ3:** Can RIPPLE improve the accuracy of repaired DNNs on buggy samples efficiently?

To answer RQ1, we first compare the time consumption of the repairing process and the obtained accuracy of the repaired DNN between two kinds of encoding for the objective. Moreover, we compare the performance of RIPPLE with various assignments for constant *tolerance*. To answer RQ2, we compare the accuracy of the training set and the test set on the repaired DNNs and check their difference. To answer RQ3, we compare RIPPLE with the state-of-the-art techniques in accuracy improvement and time consumption.

## 4.1 Setup

All experiments are carried out on a workstation with an Intel® Xeon® CPU E5-2680 v4 @ 2.40 GHz and 64GB memory. We adopt Gurobi [6] as our LP solver. We set the lower bound $\epsilon$ to $1e-5$. Empirically, we set the lower bound *tolerance* to 0.5.

We mainly adopt two popular datasets MNIST and CIFAR-10 in the experimentation, where MNIST is a massive handwritten digit dataset and CIFAR-10 is a collection of images with ten different classes.

## 4.2 Benchmarks Description

To answer RQ1, we compare the repair performance on the same DNN with two different encodings of the objective function. We adopt the MNIST model used by NNRepair [15] as the target model to repair. This model is a convolutional neural network(CNN) and has an accuracy of 96.34% on the standard test set. This model contains 10 layers of convolutional, dense, max-pooling, softmax, and other typical structures. In this experiment, the purpose of repair is to enhance the accuracy of the DNN on the standard test set.

To answer RQ2, we improve the accuracy of two DNNs on the training set with RIPPLE and check the change of accuracy of modified DNNs on the test set. We adopt the MNIST model and CIFAR10 model used by NNRepair [15] as the target model to repair, with the original dataset and the adversarial attacked dataset. FGSM adversarial attacking is applied to generate the buggy training set and test set. We improve the accuracy of DNN on the buggy training set and expect the accuracy on the buggy test set also improved.

To answer RQ3, we compare the performance of RIPPLE with state-of-the-art techniques, we consider two repair techniques NNRepair [15] and PRDNN [14] and conduct the comparison on their DNNs and the corresponding datasets. All of the DNNs and datasets used in our experiment are provided by the author of the two techniques and the detailed description can be found in their papers. The benchmarks are constructed based on 3 public datasets and 4 different scenarios, and totally 12 benchmarks are used for the comparison.

NNRepair adopts six DNN structures in its experimentation: MNIST, MNIST-Pois, MNIST-Adv, CIFAR10, CIFAR10-Pois and CIFAR10-Adv, for repair in the cases of low accuracy, with poison data, or with adversarial examples. For classification tasks, PRDNN considers two datasets ImageNet and MNIST with two network structures SqueezeNet [8] and MNIST ReLU-3–100 [13] (MNIST-C for short), respectively. The former has a dataset of natural adversarial examples datasets as the buggy samples [7]. The latter contains corrupted images as buggy samples [11]. As PRDNN is memory-consuming, we always meet out-of-memory problems with 64 GB memory. Consequently, we randomly select 800 buggy samples for the repair with PRDNN in the comparison.

As the two techniques consider three cases of repair with various variations on the available datasets, and the datasets adopted in repair and accuracy calculation are different, we consider two types of benchmarks: samples for computing the accuracy on standard samples and buggy samples are both available, i.e., $T_o \neq T_b$ as defined in Definition 1, and benchmarks that only contain samples to compute the accuracy on standard samples, i.e., $T_o = T_b$.

### 4.3 Experimental Results

**RQ1: Comparison on the Encoding of the Objective Function and Parameter Selection**

*Comparison on the Encoding Format.* We compare the repair performance on the same DNN with two different encodings of the objective function. The accuracy of repaired DNN and the time consumption results are shown in Fig. 2.

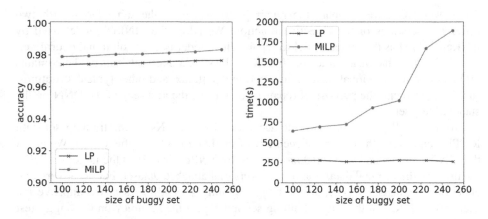

**Fig. 2.** The comparison on the objective function encoding

In Fig. 2, we can observe that though the accuracy of the solution provided by the MILP model is higher than that of the LP model, the LP model can be solved quickly and the accuracy is still higher than 97%. Therefore, as the accuracy difference between the two encoding is acceptable, we regard the encoding with LP as feasible, for the benefit of time-saving and scalability increases.

*Comparison on the Parameter Selection.* We evaluate the influence of different assignments for *tolerance* on two datasets MNIST and CIFAR10 against FGSM adversarial attacking [3]. The MNIST model has an accuracy of 97.9% on the standard test set and an accuracy of 28.7% on the attacking sample set. The CIFAR10 model has accuracies of 72.3% and 15.9% on standard and attacking sample sets, respectively. With the results of RQ1, we encode the objective function as a linear function.

The results are shown in Fig. 3. The green and red lines show results on MNIST and CIFAR10 models respectively. The lines with dots are the change of accuracy on attacking sets, and the lines with crosses are the change of accuracy on standard test sets.

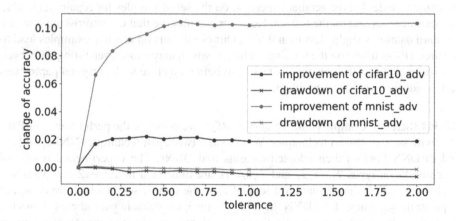

**Fig. 3.** The influence of different assignments of *tolerance* (Color figure online)

In Fig. 3, we observe that the drawdown of accuracy on standard test set of the two models are slight, benefited from the requirements that all the positive samples should be corrected predicted. Meanwhile, the improvements in accuracy on the attacking sample set of the two models increase rapidly and then maintain stable after a point around 0.5. Therefore, we conclude that if *tolerance* is large enough, the difference in the assignment does not result in various performances.

**RQ2: The Effectiveness of Repair with Training Set.** To evaluate the effectiveness of using training data in repair to achieve the high accuracy of the repaired DNN on the test data, we provide the training and test accuracy on dataset MNIST and CIFAR-10. Between the accuracy on the training set and the test set, we repair the DNNs provided in method NNRepair to improve the accuracy of DNNs in MNIST and CIFAR10 datasets with RIPPLE and evaluated the accuracy on test sets. We list the original accuracy and the improvement in Table 1.

**Table 1.** Comparison of accuracy change on Training set and Test set

|  | Training set | | Test set | |
|---|---|---|---|---|
|  | Original acc | Improvement | Original acc | Change of acc |
| MNIST | 96.58% | 0.88% | 96.34% | +0.49% |
| CIFAR10 | 87.24% | 2.22% | 81.04% | +0.22% |
| MNIST-Adv | 29.92% | 10.09% | 28.37% | +10.11% |
| CIFAR10-Adv | 34.39% | 1.99% | 35.96% | +2.05% |

In Table 1, MNIST and CIFAR10 indicate the change of accuracy on standard training and test sets, and MNIST-Adv and CIFAR10-Adv show the results on attacked training and test sets. The results show that for standard and buggy sample sets, the accuracies on both the training set and test set are increased for the repaired DNN. Therefore, we can conclude that the accuracy increase on the set of samples for repair can lead to the accuracy increase on the test set. However, we observe that the improvement on the standard dataset is slight (less than 0.5%). Our constraints on positive examples lead to repaired DNNs fitting on the training set better, which may cause over-fitting. However, *tolerance* prevents the new parameters from being too close to the original parameters and avoids the over-fitting problem.

**RQ3: Efficiency Comparison.** To answer RQ3, we compare the performance of RIPPLE with state-of-the-art techniques. We consider two repair techniques NNRepair [15] and PRDNN [14] on their adopted datasets and DNNs. The experimental results of benchmarks on types $T_o = T_b$ and $T_o \neq T_b$ are illustrated in Tables 2 and 3 respectively, where $T_o$ is the standard test set and $T_b$ is the sample set on which we expect to improve the accuracy of the DNN. In Tables 2 and 3, the value in parentheses shows the original accuracy before the repair, the other columns provide the change of accuracy. NNRepair and PRDNN can repair both hidden layers and the last layer. We show the results of the layers that perform best. As the source code of NNRepair is not available, the executing time and the results for the two DNNs adopted in PRDNN are not available (N/A).

*Efficiency Comparison with Repair Accuracy.* From the experimental results on the five models, we can observe that RIPPLE can achieve higher increased accuracy on the buggy samples and a smaller accuracy drawdown on the test sets. We can observe the negative accuracy increase of two DNNs for PRDNN. The reason is that the distribution of the selected buggy samples for repair may be different from those for accuracy calculation. Consequently, the accuracy on the buggy samples may decrease. The accuracy increase for buggy samples with NNRepair is lower in most cases. Therefore, the performance of RIPPLE is better than the other two techniques in most cases.

However, compared with PRDNN, the time consumption of our method is larger in most cases (except for DNN MNIST-C). The reason is that PRDNN only adopts buggy samples in DNN repair and the considered number of samples is much smaller than that considered in our method. Consequently, though the increased accuracy on buggy

Table 2. Comparison on both test and repair accuracy

|  |  | RIPPLE | NNRepair | PRDNN |
|---|---|---|---|---|
| MNIST-Adv | $T_b$ (28.7%) | 10.1% | 10.4% | 46.4% |
|  | $T_o$ (97.9%) | −0.1% | −3.1% | −19.4% |
|  | Time(s) | 155.99 | N/A | 1.4 |
| MNIST-Pois | $T_b$ (10.4%) | 67.6% | 47.4% | 80.3% |
|  | $T_o$ (98.6%) | −0.5% | −3.1% | −9.0% |
|  | Time(s) | 207.83 | N/A | 1.1 |
| CIFAR10-Adv | $T_b$ (36.0%) | 2.1% | 0.3% | -4.1% |
|  | $T_o$ (81.0%) | −0.3% | −0.1% | −18.6% |
|  | Time(s) | 1435.93 | N/A | 1.1 |
| CIFAR10-Pois | $T_b$ (15.9%) | 25.4% | 3.8% | -0.5% |
|  | $T_o$ (72.3%) | +0.3% | −0.6% | −4.3% |
|  | Time(s) | 532.46 | N/A | 980.5 |
| MNIST-C | $T_b$ (19.5%) | 21.9% | N/A | 42.9% |
|  | $T_o$ (96.5%) | +0.3% | N/A | −2.4% |
|  | Time(s) | 313.7 | N/A | 655.7 |

samples may be higher, the accuracy drawdown is always larger. For DNN MNIST-C, the highest accuracy increase is achieved by repairing the hidden layers, which is time-consuming for the structure complexity. Therefore, its time consumption is higher.

For DNNs MNIST and CIFAR10, without additional samples, as shown in Table 3, it is hard to improve the accuracy on the standard test set. Therefore, accuracy improvement for all the three techniques is less than 5%. Even though, RIPPLE achieves the highest accuracy improvement in the shortest time for the first two DNNs. For the third DNN, as the images in ImageNet and NAE have different data distribution, fixing all the buggy samples in NAE leads to an accuracy drawdown on ImageNet. For this DNN, we take more time than PRDNN but fix all the buggy samples with lower cost of accuracy because of the use of training set. PRDNN performs well on the last DNN. But for DNNs MNIST and CIFAR10, it takes more time and results in a larger accuracy drawdown.

## 5 Related Work

DNNs can be regarded as a special type of software. Automated Program Repair (APR) techniques automatically provide a patch to a program that makes the program meet a specification of the expected behavior. For example, AllRepair [16] combines an SAT solver and an SMT solver to search in mutation space and provides repair on C programs. DeepFix [5] build a multi-layered sequence-to-sequence neural network to assist the repair of the buggy program.

For DNN repair, one branch of research aims to fix all the known buggy samples and provide the theoretical guarantee [1,2,14]. The goal of this research branch is to

**Table 3.** Experimental results on datasets in TN

|          |              | RIPPLE | NNRepair | PRDNN   |
|----------|--------------|--------|----------|---------|
| MNIST    | $T_o$ (96.3%) | 0.5%   | 0.2%     | −1.3%   |
|          | Time(s)      | 236.9  | N/A      | 740.2   |
| CIFAR10  | $T_o$ (81.0%) | 0.2%   | 0.2%     | −19.9%  |
|          | Time(s)      | 1029.2 | N/A      | 2625.5  |
| SqueezeNet | $T_o$ (93.6%) | −1.6% | N/A      | −5.3%   |
|          | Time(s)      | 742.3  | N/A      | 508.1   |

modify the weights and biases of a DNN such that it can correctly predict all the buggy samples. PRDNN [14] is the latest method that can provide a theoretical guarantee on the repaired DNN. It provides various types of repairs for various types of specifications and is not limited to the repair of the last layer.

Another branch of research is scenario-driven [10, 15]. For example, the test accuracy of a given test set on a DNN trained with limited data is low. We expect to apply the existing training data for repair to improve the test accuracy. Meanwhile, we also expect that the original accuracy can be maintained. NNRepair [15] is the latest method capable of improving accuracy in different scenarios. It needs to locate the faulty neurons and consider the activation pattern of neurons as an oracle when repairing intermediate layers.

Similar to NNRepair, we apply both positive and buggy samples for repair, and cannot provide any guarantees on the repaired DNN. However, NNRepair has to construct a network for every class, and collect all the results for the final decision. For PRDNN, though the number of samples required in repair is small, it has to duplicate the network. Therefore, the memory consumption is high. Compared with NNRepair and PRDNN, our method only considers the last layer for repair. Therefore, the time consumption of our method is relatively low. The constraints in linear programming can achieve a tighter approximation on the ideal parameters than the heuristics adopted in NNRepair. Consequently, our method outperforms NNRepair and PRDNN.

## 6    Conclusion

In this paper, we propose RIPPLE, a method to encode the DNN repair problem into an LP problem. To increase the scalability of the method, we only consider the repair of the last layer, which can reduce the considered parameters and simplify the complexity of the constraints. To improve the accuracy on the buggy samples while maintaining the accuracy before DNN repair, we consider both the positive and buggy samples to optimize the parameters. Though the time consumption may increase with the increased number of considered samples, the time consumption is still acceptable compared with state-of-the-art techniques. We have conducted extensive experimentation to validate the effectiveness and efficiency of our method. The experimental results demonstrate that our method outperforms the two existing techniques.

In comparison with the existing techniques, we cannot guarantee that all samples in $T_b$ are correctly classified by the repaired DNN. Meanwhile, when the original DNN is already well-fitting, we may fail to achieve any accuracy improvement on buggy samples. As the future work, we will investigate on how to overcome these limitations.

# References

1. Dong, G., Sun, J., Wang, J., Wang, X., Dai, T.: Towards repairing neural networks correctly. arXiv preprint arXiv:2012.01872 (2020)
2. Goldberger, B., Katz, G., Adi, Y., Keshet, J.: Minimal modifications of deep neural networks using verification. In: LPAR, vol. 2020, p. 23rd (2020)
3. Goodfellow, I.J., Shlens, J., Szegedy, C.: Explaining and harnessing adversarial examples. arXiv preprint arXiv:1412.6572 (2014)
4. Gu, T., Liu, K., Dolan-Gavitt, B., Garg, S.: BadNets: evaluating backdooring attacks on deep neural networks. IEEE Access 7, 47230–47244 (2019)
5. Gupta, R., Pal, S., Kanade, A., Shevade, S.: DeepFix: fixing common c language errors by deep learning. In: 31st AAAI Conference on Artificial Intelligence (2017)
6. Gurobi Optimization, LLC: Gurobi optimizer reference manual (2021). https://www.gurobi.com
7. Hendrycks, D., Zhao, K., Basart, S., Steinhardt, J., Song, D.: Natural adversarial examples. In: Proceedings of the IEEE Computer Society Conference on CVPR, pp. 15262–15271 (2021)
8. Iandola, F.N., Han, S., Moskewicz, M.W., Ashraf, K., Dally, W.J., Keutzer, K.: SqueezeNet: alexnet-level accuracy with 50x fewer parameters and <0.5 mb model size. arXiv preprint arXiv:1602.07360 (2016)
9. Krizhevsky, A., Sutskever, I., Hinton, G.E.: ImageNet classification with deep convolutional neural networks. Commun. ACM 60(6), 84–90 (2017)
10. Ma, S., Liu, Y., Lee, W.C., Zhang, X., Grama, A.: Mode: automated neural network model debugging via state differential analysis and input selection. In: Proceedings of the 2018 26th ACM Joint Meeting ESEC/FSE, pp. 175–186 (2018)
11. Mu, N., Gilmer, J.: MNIST-C: a robustness benchmark for computer vision. arXiv preprint arXiv:1906.02337 (2019)
12. Schroff, F., Kalenichenko, D., Philbin, J.: FaceNet: a unified embedding for face recognition and clustering. In: Proceedings of the IEEE Conference CVPR, pp. 815–823 (2015)
13. Singh, G., Gehr, T., Püschel, M., Vechev, M.: An abstract domain for certifying neural networks. Proc. ACM Program. Lang. 3(POPL), 1–30 (2019)
14. Sotoudeh, M., Thakur, A.V.: Provable repair of deep neural networks. In: Proceedings of the 42nd ACM SIGPLAN International Conference PLDI, pp. 588–603 (2021)
15. Usman, M., Gopinath, D., Sun, Y., Noller, Y., Pasareanu, C.: NNrepair: constraint-based repair of neural network classifiers. arXiv preprint arXiv:2103.12535 (2021)
16. Wei, Y., et al.: Automated fixing of programs with contracts. In: Proceedings of the 19th ISSTA, pp. 61–72 (2010)
17. Yuan, Z., Lu, Y., Wang, Z., Xue, Y.: Droid-sec: deep learning in android malware detection. In: Proceedings of the 2014 ACM conference SIGCOMM, pp. 371–372 (2014)

# Learning Trajectories of Hamiltonian Systems with Neural Networks

Katsiaryna Haitsiukevich[(✉)] and Alexander Ilin

Aalto University, Espoo, Finland
{katsiaryna.haitsiukevich,alexander.ilin}@aalto.fi

**Abstract.** Modeling of conservative systems with neural networks is an area of active research. A popular approach is to use Hamiltonian neural networks (HNNs) which rely on the assumptions that a conservative system is described with Hamilton's equations of motion. Many recent works focus on improving the integration schemes used when training HNNs. In this work, we propose to enhance HNNs with an estimation of a continuous-time trajectory of the modeled system using an additional neural network, called a deep hidden physics model in the literature. We demonstrate that the proposed integration scheme works well for HNNs, especially with low sampling rates, noisy and irregular observations.

**Keywords:** Conservative systems · Deep hidden physics models · Dynamical systems · Hamiltonian neural networks · Physics-informed neural networks

## 1 Introduction

Many physical systems are modeled using (partial) differential equations which are derived from the laws of physics [9,31,32]. This modeling approach has the benefits that one can build a functional model using a small amount of data and the model may generalize well outside of the training data distribution (provided that the modeling assumptions are correct). However, building the model from the first principles requires deep understanding of the modeled process and often results in a tedious procedure when various modeling assumptions are tested in how well they can explain the data. The data-driven approach is therefore an attractive alternative: one can fit a generic model like neural networks [13] to training data without much effort on the model design and the derivations of the learning and inference procedures. The downside is, however, that the accuracy of this model depends greatly on the amount of available data: too little data may result in models that do not generalize well. Thus, there is clear demand for combining two modeling approaches: using neural networks models for better flexibility while also constraining the solutions with laws of physics can greatly improve sample efficiency. The laws of conservation (of energy/mass/momentum) are among very common modeling assumptions made for describing physical systems. Many physical systems can be modeled as

© The Author(s), under exclusive license to Springer Nature Switzerland AG 2022
E. Pimenidis et al. (Eds.): ICANN 2022, LNCS 13529, pp. 562–573, 2022.
https://doi.org/10.1007/978-3-031-15919-0_47

closed and therefore conservative systems [27]. Combining the conservation laws with neural networks (see, e.g., [7,14,18,19,23]) is therefore a promising line of research with many potential applications.

One prominent research direction that emerged recently in the literature is modeling Hamiltonian systems with neural networks [14]. In Hamiltonian neural networks (HNNs), the law of the energy conservation is in-built in the structure of the dynamics model and therefore it is automatically satisfied. The idea of utilizing Hamilton's equations was successfully used to predict the dynamics of Hamiltonian systems from pixel observations [17,35,40], to build representations of molecular data [25] and it was extended to control tasks [38,40] and meta-learning [24]. The original HNN model [14] had the limitation of assuming the knowledge of the state derivatives with respect to time or approximating those using finite differences. Many recent works have used numerical integrators for modeling the evolution of the system state and several improvements of the integration procedure have been proposed [5,8,10,20,34,37].

In this paper, we propose to model the evolution of the system state by adding another neural network instead of relying on traditional numerical integrators for ordinary differential equations (ODEs). This alternative to numerical integration is known in the literature under the name *deep hidden physics models* [29]. Our approach provides a continuous-time approximation of system states without relying on additional assumptions such as Hamiltonian separability. Hamiltonian preservation is encoded as a soft constraint through an extra loss term rather than being in-built in the architecture itself. We experimentally show that the proposed approach can improve the modeling accuracy in the presence of observation noise and for measurements with low sampling rates or irregularly-sampled observations.

## 2 Modeling Hamiltonian Systems

### 2.1 Hamiltonian Neural Networks

The modeling assumption of Hamiltonian neural networks [14] is that the observed state $s = (q, p)$ of a dynamical system evolves according to Hamilton's equations:

$$\frac{d\mathbf{q}}{dt} = \frac{\partial \mathcal{H}}{\partial \mathbf{p}}, \qquad \frac{d\mathbf{p}}{dt} = -\frac{\partial \mathcal{H}}{\partial \mathbf{q}}, \tag{1}$$

where $\mathcal{H}$ is the Hamiltonian (total energy) of the system, $q$ is the position and $p$ is the momentum part of the system state $s = (q, p)$. Although Hamiltonian $\mathcal{H}(q, p)$ is modeled with a generic neural network with inputs $q$ and $p$, using (1) to describe the system dynamics guarantees that the total energy is conserved:

$$\frac{\partial \mathcal{H}}{\partial t} = \frac{\partial \mathcal{H}}{\partial \mathbf{p}} \frac{d\mathbf{p}}{dt} + \frac{\partial \mathcal{H}}{\partial \mathbf{q}} \frac{d\mathbf{q}}{dt} = 0. \tag{2}$$

The original HNN model [14] was trained by minimizing the loss

$$\mathcal{L}_{\text{HNN}} = \frac{1}{N} \sum_{i=1}^{N} \left( \frac{d\boldsymbol{q}_i}{dt} - \frac{\partial \mathcal{H}_i}{\partial \boldsymbol{p}} \right)^2 + \left( \frac{d\boldsymbol{p}_i}{dt} + \frac{\partial \mathcal{H}_i}{\partial \boldsymbol{q}} \right)^2 \qquad (3)$$

where $\frac{\partial \mathcal{H}_i}{\partial \boldsymbol{p}}, \frac{d\boldsymbol{p}_i}{dt}, \frac{\partial \mathcal{H}_i}{\partial \boldsymbol{q}}, \frac{d\boldsymbol{q}_i}{dt}$ are partial derivatives computed at the locations of $N$ training examples $\boldsymbol{q}(t_i), \boldsymbol{p}(t_i)$. The derivatives $\frac{\partial \mathcal{H}_i}{\partial \boldsymbol{p}}, \frac{\partial \mathcal{H}_i}{\partial \boldsymbol{q}}$ are calculated by differentiating the neural network which models the Hamiltonian, while the derivatives $\frac{d\boldsymbol{p}_i}{dt}, \frac{d\boldsymbol{q}_i}{dt}$ are either assumed to be known (from the simulator) or approximated with finite differences. Using finite differences to approximate the derivatives $\frac{d\boldsymbol{p}}{dt}$ and $\frac{d\boldsymbol{q}}{dt}$ is essentially equivalent to Euler integration with a time step being equal to the sampling interval, which limits the accuracy of the trained model [8].

Many extensions of HNNs [5,10,34,35] use more advanced numerical integrators combined with the Neural ODE approach [3] to model the evolution of the system state in time. Several works [5,10,20,34,37] use symplectic integrators which preserve the conserved quantity and therefore are natural options for Hamiltonian systems. The analysis [41] of several numerical integrators when applied to HNNs shows that non-symplectic integrators cannot guarantee the recovery of true Hamiltonian $\mathcal{H}$ and the prediction accuracy obtained with a symplectic integrator depends on the integrator accuracy order. In addition to the use of a symplectic integrator, SympNets [20] have the network architecture that guarantees zero energy loss by network design. Some symplectic integration schemes [5,10,34] make additional assumptions such as the separability of the Hamiltonian.[1] A recent model called Non-separable Symplectic Neural Networks (NSSNN) [37] releases this assumption by an improved symplectic integrator which works well for both separable and non-separable Hamiltonians.

One potential problem in applying model in (1) to real-world data is the fact that the system dynamics in (1) is written for clean states $\boldsymbol{p}$ and $\boldsymbol{q}$ while in practice state measurements typically contain noise. Working with noisy states leads to inaccurate modeling due to the compounding error problem. Therefore the states should be denoised both at training and inference times. Many existing HNN models were trained with noisy observations but they do not have in-built techniques for handling observation noise in initial states at inference time. Some works directly address this issue: for example, [5] which proposes an initial state optimization procedure.

## 2.2  Physics-Informed Neural Networks as an Integrator for HNN

Physics-informed neural networks (PINNs) [22,30] is a mesh-free method of solving given differential equations using neural networks. The method can be used to approximate a solution of an initial value problem defined by an ODE with a *known* function $\boldsymbol{f}$

$$\frac{d\boldsymbol{s}(t)}{dt} = \boldsymbol{f}(t, \boldsymbol{s}(t)) \qquad (4)$$

---

[1] Hamiltonian $\mathcal{H}(\boldsymbol{q}, \boldsymbol{p}) = V(\boldsymbol{q}) + K(\boldsymbol{p})$ where $V$ and $K$ are potential and kinetic energies is separable.

and initial conditions $s_0 = s(t_0)$. The solution $s(t)$ of the ODE is approximated by a neural network with time $t$ as input trained by minimizing a composite loss function. The loss function for the network training can be represented as a weighted sum of the supervised learning loss for the initial conditions

$$\mathcal{L}_{\text{init}} = ||s(t_0) - s_0||^2 \tag{5}$$

and the loss forcing the network to satisfy the ODE in (4):

$$\mathcal{L}_{\text{ode}} = \frac{1}{K} \sum_{k=1}^{K} \left( \frac{ds_k}{dt} - f(t_k) \right)^2 \tag{6}$$

where $\frac{ds_k}{dt}$ denotes derivatives computed at locations $t_k$. The locations $t_k$ can be sampled randomly on the interval on which the ODE is solved.

In case a sequence of observations $\{(t_0, s_0), ..., (t_N, s_N)\}$ from the modelled system in (4) is available, PINNs allow to easily include the observations in the model training procedure in which case the loss in (5) is replaced with the following supervision loss:

$$\mathcal{L}_{\text{fit}} = \frac{1}{N} \sum_{i=1}^{N} ||s(t_i) - s_i||^2. \tag{7}$$

The PINN method can be viewed as a supervised learning method with the ODE-based regularizer given in (6). Unlike traditional numerical solvers PINNs can handle ill-posed problems, e.g. with unknown initial conditions but with measurements for other time points.

Deep hidden physics models (DHPMs) [29] extend the PINNs approach to the case of an *unknown* function $f$ in (4). Function $f$ is approximated with another neural network which is trained by minimizing the loss in (6). Thus, DHPMs contain two neural networks: one defines the differential equation and the other one approximates its solution.

**Deep Hidden Hamiltonian.** In this paper, we propose to use physics-informed neural networks as an integrator when learning HNNs. This means that we use an additional neural network $s(t)$ to model the solution of Hamilton's equations in (1) which describe the system dynamics. This additional neural network outputs the two components $q$, $p$ of the system state as a function of input $t$.

The solution network $s(t)$ is trained to fit the available observations $s_i = (q_i, p_i)$ at time instances $t_i$ by minimizing the loss in (7) and to satisfy Hamilton's equations by minimizing the loss in (3). The value of Hamiltonian $\mathcal{H}$ is approximated by an HNN which is jointly trained with the solution network $s(t)$. Note that the derivatives $\frac{dq_i}{dt}$, $\frac{dp_i}{dt}$ required in the loss term in (3) can be computed by differentiating the neural network $s(t)$ with respect to its input $t$. The locations of points $t_i$ used to compute that loss do not have to coincide with the locations of the training samples: they are sampled randomly on the solution interval.

We found it beneficial to include in the loss an additional term which forces the energy values to stay constant throughout a trajectory:

$$\mathcal{L}_{\text{extra}} = \frac{1}{M} \sum_{ij} \left( \mathcal{H}(s(t_i)) - \mathcal{H}(s(t_j)) \right)^2, \tag{8}$$

where pairs of points $t_i, t_j$ are sampled randomly and $M$ is the number of sampled pairs in a mini-batch. Thus, the total loss minimized during training is the weighted sum of the losses in (3), (7) and (8).

We call our algorithm Deep Hidden Hamiltonian (DHH) in analogy to DHPMs: we assume that Hamiltonian $\mathcal{H}$ is unknown and should be learned from data.

## 3    Related Work

Recently many improvements to the original HNN architecture have been proposed in the literature. The proposed improvements include the use of symplectic integrators [5,10,20,34,37], hard constraints on energy conservation [20] as well as modifications to the soft constraints, for example, by switching to the Cartesian coordinates [12]. More details on the comparison of different methods for Hamiltonian systems can be found in survey [39]. In contrast to many existing works, our method does not rely on traditional numerical integrators but instead utilizes an extra neural network for learning of the system trajectory. Another alternative to the approaches listed above is a method called generating function neural network or GFNN [2] that learns modified generating functions as a symplectic map representation instead of approximating a vector field directly. Thus, the method does not require finite difference approximations of the vector field. However, GFNN requires solving a system of non-linear equations for prediction of one step evolution which might be a computational bottleneck.

When modelling physical systems one should take into account the measurement noise in the observations. In general, neural network regularization techniques [16,33] can be applied to prevent overfitting to the training data and to make the model more robust to noise. For modelling of physical systems in particular, previous works have a separate denoising step, for example, by basis functions approximations [36] or an optimization procedure for the initial step [5]. In comparison, the proposed algorithm relies on the solution network that finds a continuous-time approximation of the system state trajectory from noisy observations together with the regularization loss term in (8).

Several recent works [11,19,26,28] utilize physics-informed neural networks for modelling of conservative systems. The closest to ours is work [26] that applies PINNs for solving Hamilton's differential equations with a *known* Hamiltionian $\mathcal{H}$. In contrast, we learn the Hamiltonian from the data following the DHPMs methodology.

## 4    Experiments

We test our method on the following four physical systems from [14]:

– mass-spring

$$\mathcal{H} = \frac{1}{2}kq^2 + \frac{p^2}{2m} \tag{9}$$

with $m = \frac{1}{2}$ and $k = 2$;
– pendulum

$$\mathcal{H} = 2mgl(1 - \cos q) + \frac{l^2 p^2}{2m} \tag{10}$$

with $l = 1$, $m = \frac{1}{2}$ and $g = 3$;
– 2-body and 3-body systems

$$\mathcal{H} = \sum_{i=0}^{N} \frac{\|\mathbf{p}_i\|^2}{2m_i} - \sum_{1 \le i < j \le N} \frac{Gm_i m_j}{\|\mathbf{q}_i - \mathbf{q}_j\|} \tag{11}$$

with $G = 1$, $m_i = 1$, $i = 1, \ldots, N$ and $N \in \{2, 3\}$.

We generate training data by randomly sampling the initial state and numerically solving differential equations in (1) using the fourth-order Runge-Kutta method with $\mathcal{H}$ given in (9)–(11) for a given number of time steps. We use 80% of sequential time steps from the generated time series as a training set and the remaining 20% as a test set. To test the robustness of the proposed method to noise in observations, the generated data points are corrupted with additive Gaussian noise with zero mean and 0.1 standard deviation.

In all the experiments, Hamiltonian $\mathcal{H}$, solutions $s(t)$ and dynamics $f$ (for a DHPM baseline) are modeled with multi-layer perceptron networks. The models are optimized using the Adam optimizer [21] with learning rates of 0.0001 for HNN and dynamics $f$ and 0.01 for the solution network. We normalize the modeling interval of $t$ to be $[-1, 1]$. Points $t_k$ required for computing the loss terms in (3) and (6) for the DHPM baseline (described in Sect. 2.2) are sampled uniformly from the interval $[-1, 1]$ for each optimization step. Similarly, pairs of points $(t_i, t_j)$ for the extra loss term in (8) are sampled at each optimization step such that $t_i \in [-1, 0]$ and $t_j \in [0, 1]$. In our experiments, the training loss is the weighted sum of the supervision loss in (7) (with weight 1), the loss in (3) (with weight 0.1 for the mass-spring system and the pendulum and 1 for the 2-body and 3-body systems) and the loss in (8) (with weight 0.01).

In Fig. 1, we compare the trajectories for the mass-spring system estimated with the proposed DHH approach and with the HNN from [14] in which the derivatives are estimated using finite differences. Figures 1a-c shows the results for three settings: 1) clean regularly-sampled observations 2) noisy regularly-sampled observations 3) clean irregularly-sampled observations. In the experiment with noisy observations (Fig. 1b), we additionally show a trajectory obtained by the baseline HNN when we assume access to the clean state observation for the last time step in the training set. The results show that the proposed

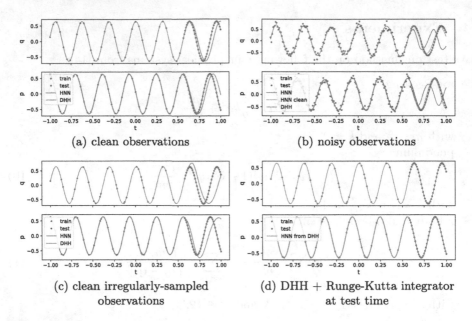

(a) clean observations       (b) noisy observations

(c) clean irregularly-sampled       (d) DHH + Runge-Kutta integrator

        observations                         at test time

**Fig. 1.** (a)–(c): Estimated state trajectories for the mass-spring system with DHH (green) and HNN (blue). (d): The trajectory obtained by integrating the system Eqs. 1 with the Runge-Kutta integrator using the Hamiltonian $\mathcal{H}$ learned by DHH for the data from Fig. 1c. (Color figure online)

method performs well under low sampling rates and it tolerates noise in the data. Additionally, the system trajectory can be obtained by integrating equations in (1) with, for example, the Runge-Kutta integrator using the Hamiltonian $\mathcal{H}$ learned by DHH (see Fig. 1d). The results show that the Hamiltonian $\mathcal{H}$ found by DHH is very accurate and the model works well even when changing the integration scheme at test time.

The proposed algorithm can also be used when some of the state variables are not observed (see Fig. 2). In this experiment, we model the mass-spring system using only noisy measurements of the position variable $q$ while $p$ is assumed unobserved. The only change in the training procedure is the calculation of the supervision loss in (7) just for $q$ measurements. As the results show, the proposed method is able to reconstruct the missing coordinate (up to an additive constant).

Next, we quantitatively compare the proposed approach against the following baselines: 1) HNN [14] with derivatives calculated as finite differences, 2) HNN [14] with derivatives provided by the simulator, 3) NSSNN [37], 4) Neural ODE [3] and 5) DHPMs [29]. The implementations of NSSNN and HNN are taken from the original papers. For Neural ODE, we use the same implementation as in [37] with the second-order Runge-Kutta integrator. DHPMs estimate the system dynamics in (4) by modeling $f$ with a multi-layer perceptron and by minimizing the sum of the losses in (6) and (7).

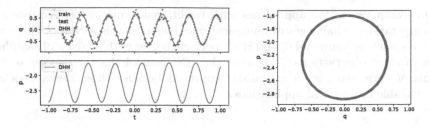

**Fig. 2.** Estimated trajectories and the corresponding vector field by DHH for the mass-spring system with noisy observations of $q$ and no observations of $p$.

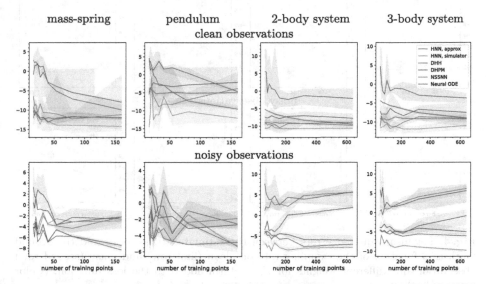

**Fig. 3.** Log-mean-squared errors between the estimated trajectories and the ground truth as a function of the sampling rate on clean (first row) and noisy (second row) observations.

In Fig. 3, we present the effect of the sampling rate on the log mean-squared error (log-MSE) of the estimated trajectories compared to the ground truth. We show the average log-MSE for each model across five runs with a solid line, while the shaded interval represent the minimum and maximum log-MSEs among the five runs.[2] The $x$-axis corresponds to the number of points in the training set: smaller number of points in the training set corresponds to a lower sampling rate. As can be seen from the results, the proposed method performs similarly to the baselines on clean observations and it outperforms the baselines on noisy observations. We attribute the improvement to the energy conservation bias inbuilt in the model and to the noise filtration capabilities of the solution network. The performance of DHH and DHPMs is more stable in the low sampling rate

---

[2] Minimum and maximum errors are used to emphasize extreme cases (e.g., failed runs).

regime compared to the approaches with traditional numerical integrators due to computational challenges of numerical integration in this scenario. However, methods, such as Neural ODE and HNN perform better with increase of sampling rates of clean observations. Note that the HNN model that has access to the simulator derivatives is an unrealistic approach because those derivatives are not available in practical applications.

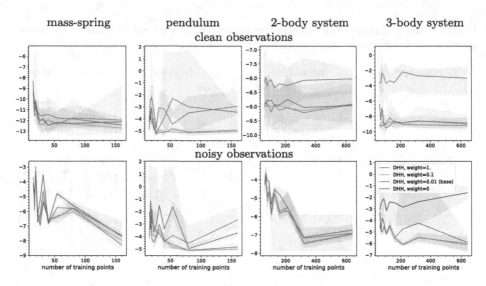

**Fig. 4.** Log-mean-squared errors between the estimated trajectories and the ground truth as a function of the sampling rate on clean (first row) and noisy (second row) observations for different weights for $\mathcal{L}_{\mathrm{extra}}$ term added to the loss function. (Color figure online)

Additionally, the use of the extra loss term in (8) has a positive effect on the training of the proposed model. In Fig. 4, we report the results for four studied systems trained with the term in (8) added to the loss function with different weights. Even though the model is quite robust to small variations in the weight (e.g., orange and green lines), stronger regularization (e.g., with weight equal to 1 in blue) or no regularization (in red) hurts the performance.

## 5    Conclusion and Future Work

In this work, we proposed to learn a continuous-time trajectory of a modeled Hamiltonian system using an additional neural network. The time derivatives provided by this network can replace the finite-difference estimates of the derivatives used as the targets in the original HNN model. We showed experimentally that the proposed approach can outperform existing alternatives, especially in the case of low sampling rates and presence of noise in the state measurements.

A big limitations of the HNN methodology is its applicability only to conservative systems described by Hamilton's equations and observed in the canonical coordinates. These assumptions may be restrictive in many practical applications. Addressing this limitation is an important line for future research with many promising results obtained recently (see, e.g., [4,6,7,18]).

Another important research question is to identify the most efficient way to incorporate inductive biases from physics into modeling of dynamical systems, which is a topic of active debate at the moment [1,15].

**Acknowledgments.** We thank CSC (IT Center for Science, Finland) for computational resources and the Academy of Finland for the support within the Flagship programme: Finnish Center for Artificial Intelligence (FCAI).

# References

1. Botev, A., Jaegle, A., Wirnsberger, P., Hennes, D., Higgins, I.: Which priors matter? Benchmarking models for learning latent dynamics. arXiv preprint arXiv:2111.05458 (2021)
2. Chen, R., Tao, M.: Data-driven prediction of general Hamiltonian dynamics via learning exactly-symplectic maps. In: Meila, M., Zhang, T. (eds.) Proceedings of the 38th International Conference on Machine Learning. Proceedings of Machine Learning Research, vol. 139, pp. 1717–1727. PMLR (2021)
3. Chen, R.T.Q., Rubanova, Y., Bettencourt, J., Duvenaud, D.K.: Neural ordinary differential equations. In: Bengio, S., Wallach, H., Larochelle, H., Grauman, K., Cesa-Bianchi, N., Garnett, R. (eds.) Advances in Neural Information Processing Systems, vol. 31. Curran Associates, Inc. (2018)
4. Chen, Y., Matsubara, T., Yaguchi, T.: Neural symplectic form: learning Hamiltonian equations on general coordinate systems. In: Beygelzimer, A., Dauphin, Y., Liang, P., Vaughan, J.W. (eds.) Advances in Neural Information Processing Systems (2021)
5. Chen, Z., Zhang, J., Arjovsky, M., Bottou, L.: Symplectic recurrent neural networks. In: International Conference on Learning Representations (2020)
6. Choudhary, A., Lindner, J.F., Holliday, E.G., Miller, S.T., Sinha, S., Ditto, W.L.: Forecasting Hamiltonian dynamics without canonical coordinates. Nonlinear Dyn. **103**(2), 1553–1562 (2021)
7. Cranmer, M., Greydanus, S., Hoyer, S., Battaglia, P., Spergel, D., Ho, S.: Lagrangian neural networks. arXiv preprint arXiv:2003.04630 (2020)
8. David, M., Méhats, F.: Symplectic learning for Hamiltonian neural networks. arXiv preprint arXiv:2106.11753 (2021)
9. Davis, M.E., Davis, R.J.: Fundamentals of chemical reaction engineering. Courier Corporation (2012)
10. DiPietro, D., Xiong, S., Zhu, B.: Sparse symplectically integrated neural networks. In: Larochelle, H., Ranzato, M., Hadsell, R., Balcan, M.F., Lin, H. (eds.) Advances in Neural Information Processing Systems, vol. 33, pp. 6074–6085. Curran Associates, Inc. (2020)
11. Fang, Y., Wu, G.Z., Wen, X.K., Wang, Y.Y., Dai, C.Q.: Predicting certain vector optical solitons via the conservation-law deep-learning method. Optics Laser Technol. **155**, 108428 (2022)

12. Finzi, M., Wang, K.A., Wilson, A.G.: Simplifying Hamiltonian and Lagrangian neural networks via explicit constraints. In: Larochelle, H., Ranzato, M., Hadsell, R., Balcan, M.F., Lin, H. (eds.) Advances in Neural Information Processing Systems, vol. 33, pp. 13880–13889. Curran Associates, Inc. (2020)

13. Goodfellow, I., Bengio, Y., Courville, A., Bengio, Y.: Deep Learning, vol. 1. MIT Press (2016)

14. Greydanus, S., Dzamba, M., Yosinski, J.: Hamiltonian neural networks. In: Advances in Neural Information Processing Systems, vol. 32 (2019)

15. Gruver, N., Finzi, M.A., Stanton, S.D., Wilson, A.G.: Deconstructing the inductive biases of Hamiltonian neural networks. In: International Conference on Learning Representations (2022)

16. Hinton, G.E., Srivastava, N., Krizhevsky, A., Sutskever, I., Salakhutdinov, R.R.: Improving neural networks by preventing co-adaptation of feature detectors. arXiv preprint arXiv:1207.0580 (2012)

17. Hochlehnert, A., Terenin, A., Saemundsson, S., Deisenroth, M.: Learning contact dynamics using physically structured neural networks. In: Banerjee, A., Fukumizu, K. (eds.) Proceedings of the 24th International Conference on Artificial Intelligence and Statistics. Proceedings of Machine Learning Research, vol. 130, pp. 2152–2160. PMLR (2021)

18. Hoedt, P., et al.: MC-LSTM: mass-conserving LSTM. In: Meila, M., Zhang, T. (eds.) Proceedings of the 38th International Conference on Machine Learning, ICML 2021. Proceedings of Machine Learning Research, vol. 139, pp. 4275–4286. PMLR (2021)

19. Jagtap, A.D., Kharazmi, E., Karniadakis, G.E.: Conservative physics-informed neural networks on discrete domains for conservation laws: applications to forward and inverse problems. Comput. Methods Appl. Mech. Eng. **365**, 113028 (2020)

20. Jin, P., Zhang, Z., Zhu, A., Tang, Y., Karniadakis, G.E.: SympNets: intrinsic structure-preserving symplectic networks for identifying Hamiltonian systems. Neural Netw. **132**, 166–179 (2020)

21. Kingma, D.P., Ba, J.: Adam: a method for stochastic optimization. arXiv preprint arXiv:1412.6980 (2014)

22. Lagaris, I.E., Likas, A., Fotiadis, D.I.: Artificial neural networks for solving ordinary and partial differential equations. IEEE Trans. Neural Netw. **9**(5), 987–1000 (1998)

23. Lee, K., Carlberg, K.T.: Deep conservation: a latent-dynamics model for exact satisfaction of physical conservation laws. In: Proceedings of the AAAI Conference on Artificial Intelligence, vol. 35, no. 1, pp. 277–285 (2021)

24. Lee, S., Yang, H., Seong, W.: Identifying physical law of Hamiltonian systems via meta-learning. In: International Conference on Learning Representations (2021)

25. Li, Z., Yang, S., Song, G., Cai, L.: HamNet: conformation-guided molecular representation with Hamiltonian neural networks. In: International Conference on Learning Representations (2021)

26. Mattheakis, M., Sondak, D., Dogra, A.S., Protopapas, P.: Hamiltonian neural networks for solving differential equations. arXiv preprint arXiv:2001.11107 (2020)

27. Noether, E.: Invariant variation problems. Transp. Theory Stat. Phys. **1**(3), 186–207 (1971)

28. Patel, R.G., et al.: Thermodynamically consistent physics-informed neural networks for hyperbolic systems. J. Comput. Phys. **449**, 110754 (2022)

29. Raissi, M.: Deep hidden physics models: deep learning of nonlinear partial differential equations. J. Mach. Learn. Res. **19**(1), 932–955 (2018)

30. Raissi, M., Perdikaris, P., Karniadakis, G.E.: Physics-informed neural networks: a deep learning framework for solving forward and inverse problems involving nonlinear partial differential equations. J. Comput. Phys. **378**, 686–707 (2019)
31. Rubinstein, I., Rubinstein, L.: Partial Differential Equations in Classical Mathematical Physics. Cambridge University Press, Cambridge (1994)
32. Taylor, J.R.: Classical Mechanics. University Science Books (2005)
33. Tibshirani, R.J.: Regression shrinkage and selection via the lasso. J. Roy. Stat. Soc.: Ser. B (Methodol.) **58**(1), 267–288 (1996)
34. Tong, Y., Xiong, S., He, X., Pan, G., Zhu, B.: Symplectic neural networks in Taylor series form for Hamiltonian systems. J. Comput. Phys. **437**, 110325 (2021)
35. Toth, P., Rezende, D.J., Jaegle, A., Racanière, S., Botev, A., Higgins, I.: Hamiltonian generative networks. In: International Conference on Learning Representations (2020)
36. Wu, K., Qin, T., Xiu, D.: Structure-preserving method for reconstructing unknown Hamiltonian systems from trajectory data. SIAM J. Sci. Comput. **42**(6), A3704–A3729 (2020)
37. Xiong, S., Tong, Y., He, X., Yang, S., Yang, C., Zhu, B.: Nonseparable symplectic neural networks. In: International Conference on Learning Representations (2021)
38. Zhong, Y.D., Dey, B., Chakraborty, A.: Symplectic ode-net: learning Hamiltonian dynamics with control. In: International Conference on Learning Representations (2020)
39. Zhong, Y.D., Dey, B., Chakraborty, A.: Benchmarking energy-conserving neural networks for learning dynamics from data. In: Proceedings of the 3rd Conference on Learning for Dynamics and Control. Proceedings of Machine Learning Research, vol. 144, pp. 1218–1229. PMLR (2021)
40. Zhong, Y.D., Leonard, N.: Unsupervised learning of Lagrangian dynamics from images for prediction and control. In: Larochelle, H., Ranzato, M., Hadsell, R., Balcan, M.F., Lin, H. (eds.) Advances in Neural Information Processing Systems, vol. 33, pp. 10741–10752. Curran Associates, Inc. (2020)
41. Zhu, A., Jin, P., Tang, Y.: Deep Hamiltonian networks based on symplectic integrators. arXiv preprint arXiv:2004.13830 (2020)

# MLPPose: Human Keypoint Localization via MLP-Mixer

Biao Guo, Kun Liu, and Qian He[✉]

School of Computer Science and Information Security,
Guilin University of Electronic Technology, Guilin, China
{guob,heqian}@guet.edu.cn, 20032303077@mails.guet.edu.cn

**Abstract.** Although existing methods have made great progress in human pose estimation, there are still a lot of challenging situations not well-handled, such as occluded limbs, invisible body parts or complex scenarios. In this work, we propose a novel approach called MLPPose, which combining the MLP-Mixer layers with the convolutional token embedding for human pose estimation. The MLP-Mixer layers are consisted of two types of MLP blocks, one concerns the global receptive field and the other mixes the channel feature at each location. This composition can not only obtain the association between different keypoints, but also efficiently capture the global dependency relationships between keypoints and scenes. Thus, it allows our model to efficiently locate the keypoints, despite that some of them are occluded, invisible or in complex scenarios. Meanwhile, it is able to simplify the progress of extracting the global dependency relationships compared to the attentional mechanism which is widely used in transformer models. Experiments show that our model achieves competitive results with state-of-the-art methods on the MS-COCO and MPII human pose estimation benchmarks. Moreover, our model is more lightweight and faster than other best performance methods.

**Keywords:** Computer vision · Neural network · Human pose estimation

## 1 Introduction

Vision-based 2D human pose estimation(HPE), as one of the most fundamental and challenging problems in computer vision, aims to obtain the human keypoints of interest in an input image. It plays an important role in many computer vision tasks such as action/activity recognition [1] or detection [2], human tracking [3] and sport motion analysis [4], etc.

Deep convolutional neural networks have achieved impressive performance on human pose estimation due to their powerful capacity to capture local visual representation. For example, HRNet [5] constructed based on convolutional neural network can extract and fuse local semantic information of different scales in parallel, which can effectively locate the keypoints in normal situation and

(a) HRNet      (b) MLPPose      (c) HRNet      (d) MLPPose

**Fig. 1.** Human pose prediction results based on HRNet and MLPPose on obscured limbs(a)(b), and complex scenes(c)(d).

enhance the robustness of keypoints estimation when visual scale changes. However, local visual information captured by convolutional-based networks is not enough to effectively deal with the complex situations such as occluded keypoints and high similarity of limbs. As shown in Fig. 1, the occluded positions of legs (in the red box in Fig. 1a) and the keypoints with high similarity (in the red box in Fig. 1c) cannot be effectively detected by HRNet.

The work [6] has proved that the global dependency is crucial for accurately and effectively locating keypoints in complex situations. As shown in Fig. 2a, the keypoint of the adult in the red box is invisible due to occluded. But the location of such keypoint can be refined by obtaining the global dependency relationships between the keypoint and scene, which is through getting larger receptive fields, as shown in Fig. 2b and Fig. 2c. Although convolutional neural networks could extract features of larger receptive fields by stacking multiple convolutional layers, they are still insufficient to adequately express global dependencies. It is because that the static convolution kernels used by CNN are limited to represent variables [7].

Recently, transformer [8] models have been used to solve human keypoint localization problems with effective results due to their outstanding performance in the visual domain [9, 10]. The structure of transformer can also model global dependencies. However, because that it focuses more on attention mechanism, it is not efficient enough to extract global dependencies. The work [11] demonstrates that the transformer model is more effective in its structure than in its attention mechanism.

Inspired by works [12,13], in this paper, we propose MLPPose model to solve the problem of human pose estimation. The MLPPose is composed of the MLP-Mixer layers [12] and the convolutional token embedding module [13], as shown in Fig. 3. The MLP-Mixer layer contains two types MLP block: one token-mixing MLP block to merge global information, other channel-mixing MLP block to mix per-location channel information. Convolutional token embedding module makes the model not only reduce the dimension of MLP-Mixer input but also obtain tokens with higher semantics, which helps MLP-Mixer to better establish global dependency. Thus, this composition can not only obtain the association between different keypoints, but also efficiently capture the global dependency relationships between keypoints and scenes. It is also able to simplify the progress

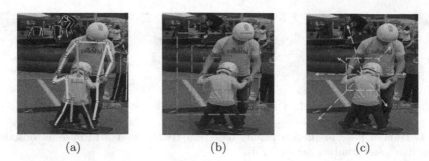

(a)                          (b)                          (c)

**Fig. 2.** (a) The keypoint in the red frame is obscured. (b) Keypoints can be located by expanding the local receptive field to obtain a larger receptive field. (c) Gather information from global receptive fields to locate keypoints.

of extracting the global dependency relationships compared to the attentional mechanism.

In summary, we introduce MLP-Mixer to predict heatmap-based keypoints positions, which can efficiently capture the global dependency relationships between human keypoints. And to our knowledge, the proposed MLPPose is the first to apply MLP-Mixer for 2D human pose estimation. And our work shows that this structure is effective in locating human keypoints. The experimental results on two widely-used benchmark datasets: MS-COCO keypoint detection [14] and MPII Human Pose dataset [15] demonstrate our model can achieves competitive performance compared with existing state-of-the-art counterparts while being more lightweight and faster.

## 2   Related Work

**Human Pose Estimation.** Deep convolutional neural networks have been applied to human pose estimation and heatmap-based pose estimation methods perform the state-of-the-art performance in human pose estimation. A lot of excellent work [5, 16–18, 25] has proved the effectiveness of convolutional neural network in human pose estimation. However, for the occluded keypoints and the keypoints in complex scenes, high-level feature maps with large receptive are needed to infer such kind of keypoints. Therefore, most common solutions are to enlarge the receptive field, e.g. by downsampling the resolution, increasing the depth of the network or expanding the kernel size. It also includes some complex strategies including multi-scale fusion [16,17], high-resolution representation [5,18]. For instance, cascaded pyramid network [16] design a RefineNet to explicitly handle the difficult keypoints by integrating all levels of feature representations. HRNet [5] connects high-to-low resolution subnet in parallel to maintain high-resolution representation in order to advance precise heatmap estimation. But the locality nature of convolution makes it impossible to capture long-term dependencies. In contrast, our model can effectively locate human keypoint from global dependencies.

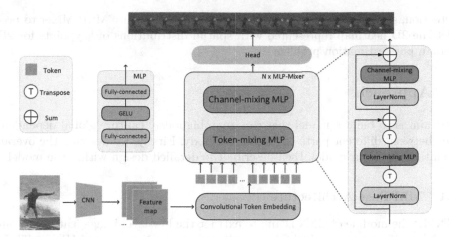

**Fig. 3.** MLPPose consists of CNN extractor, Convolutional token embedding, MLP-Mixer layer and a predict head. Firstly, the feature maps are extracted by a CNN extractor and flattened into a sequence by a Convolutional token embedding. Then the global dependencies were captured by token-mixing MLP block and channel-mixing MLP block build in MLP-Mixer layer. Finally adopt a simple head to predict the human keypoints heatmap.

**Vision Transformer.** Transformer [8] relys entirely on an attention mechanism to learn global dependencies between input and output, and achieves impressive performances in natural language processing(NLP). Recently, transformer has achieved excellent results both in combination with convolutional neural networks and as a substitute for convolutional neural networks in computer vision tasks [9,10,19,26,27].

Recently, transformer-based model has been applied to human pose estimation with effective results. TransPose [20] introduce transformer to predict heatmap-based keypoints positions and enhance the explainability for human pose estimation. TokenPose [21] propose a novel approach based on token representation to learn constraint relationships and appearance cues from images for human pose estimation. Although transformer-based model have achieved competitive performance on human pose estimation, but the overall algorithm complexity also increase due to the calculation of self-attention. In this work, we introduce MLP-Mixer instead of self-attention to locate human keypoints, which is able to simplify the progress of extracting the global dependency relationships.

**MLP-Mixer Architecture.** Recently, MLP-Mixer [12] showed competitive performance in image classification tasks. MLP has again attracted extensive research in the computer vision community. Because of the high performance and global receptive field of the MLP-Mixer, it becomes a new choice in other computer vision fields. For example, AS-MLP [22], makes the pure MLP architecture have local receptive through by moving characteristic information of axial. It is also the first MLP architecture for downstream task, such as target detection, semantic segmentation. But in this paper, we use MLP-Mixer to predict the 2D heatmap represented with spatial distributions of keypoints for 2D human pose estimation problem.

# 3   Approach

Our aim is to build a model that can unambiguously capture global dependencies between different parts of the human body. Firstly, we describe the overall architecture of our model, then describe the detailed design within the model.

## 3.1   MLPPose Architecture

**CNN.** The module of CNN is aim to extract the low-level image feature. In our model we choose two typical CNN architectures: ResNet [18] and HRNet [5]. In order to decrease the parameter we only choose the several part of the original ImageNet pretrained CNNs to extract feature from images.

**Convolutional Token Embedding.** In our model, we use convolutional token embedding to replace the position embedding. Due to the standard MLP expects a 1D sequence of token embedding as input. An input image $I \in R^{3 \times H_I \times W_I}$. we assume that the CNN outputs a 2D spatial structure image feature $F \in R^{d \times H \times W}$, then through a convolution layer with kernel size $= P$, stride $= P$. The output image feature is $X \in R^{C \times H^* \times W^*}$. Finally, the output feature is then flattened into size $L \in R^{T \times C}$, $T = H^* \times W^*$.

**MLP-Mixer.** MLP-Mixer include multiple layers of identical size, each layer contains two types MLP block:token-mixing MLP block and channel-mixing MLP block. Given an sequence $L \in R^{T \times C}$. The first Token-mixing MLP block act on columns of $L$(i.e.it is applied to a transposed input table $L^T$) in order to merge global information from all token. The second channel-mixing MLP block act on the rows of $L$ in order to mix spatial information of each token. Each MLP Block contains two fully-connected layers and GELU [23]. Each MLP-Mixer layer takes an input and output of the same size. In addition, MLP-Mixer layer also use skip-connections and layer normalization.

**Head.** In order to obtain the 2D heatmap of keypoints with size $K \times H_{out} \times W_{out}$ of from output of MLP-Mixer layer $L \in R^{T \times C}$. We firstly reshape $L \in R^{T \times C}$ back to $X \in R^{C \times H^* \times W^*}$. Then we use 1*1 convolution to reduce the channel dimension $C$ of from to $K$. If $H^*$, $W^*$ are not equal $H_{out}$, $H_{out}$, an additional 4 * 4 transposed convolution layer is used to do upsampling before 1 * 1 convolution.

## 3.2   Resolution Settings

Due to that the computational complexity of per MLP-Mixer is $O(H^2W^2C)$, we adopt $r\times$ downsampling rate of the original input resolution as the input of the MLP-Mixer, $H = H_I/r, W = W_I/r$. In the common human pose estimation architectures, such as [16], 32× downsampling is usually adopted as a standard setting to obtain a very low-resolution maps with global information. In contrast, in this work, we adopt r = 4 setting for Small-RestNet and Small-HRNet, which are beneficial to the trade-off between the memory footprint for MLP-Mixer and the loss in detailed information. Thus, our model directly captures higher resolution remote interaction while preserving fine-grained local feature information. As shown in Table 1, through experiments, we designed two MLPPose structures: MLPPose-B and MLPPose-H.

**Table 1.** Architecture configurations for different MLPPose models. The number of parameters and GFLOPs are reported for an input resolution of 256 × 192.

| Specification | MLPPose-B | MLPPose-H |
|---|---|---|
| Backbone | HRNet-Small-W32 | HRNet-Small-W48 |
| Patch resolution $P \times P$ | $4 \times 4$ | $4 \times 4$ |
| Token hidden dim | 384 | 384 |
| Token mlp dim | 192 | 192 |
| Channels hidden dim | 192 | 192 |
| Channels mlp dim | 384 | 576 |
| Parameters (M) | 11.9 | 21.0 |
| GFLOPs | 6.8 | 10.9 |

# 4  Experiments

## 4.1  COCO Keypoint Detection

**Dataset.** The COCO dataset [14] consists of over 200,000 images and 250,000 person instances labeled with 17 keypoints. The COCO dataset contains three datasets-train2017/val2017/test-dev2017, cover 27 K, 5 K and 20 K images individually. We only use train2017 dataset to train out model. The models are evaluated on the val2017 and test-dev2017.

**Evaluation Metric.** The standard average precision (AP) as out model evaluation metric on the COCO dataset. The average precision (AP) based on Object Keypoint Similarity (OKS): $OKS = \frac{\sum_i exp(-d_i^2/2s^2 k_i^2)\sigma(v_i>0)}{\sum_i \sigma(v_i>0)}$, Here $d_i$ is the Euclidean distance between the predicted keypoint and the corresponding groundtruth, $v_i$ is the visibility flag of the keypoint, $s$ is the object scale, and $k_i$ is a keypoint constant.

**Train.** We use data augmentation with random rotation ([−45°, +45°]), random scale ([0.65, 1.35]), and flipping. In this paper, we follow the standard two stage top-down human pose estimation paradigm. In the paradigm, the training samples are the images with single person from a person detector and then keypoints are predicted. We adopt the person detectors result provided by SimpleBaseline [18] on the validation set and test-dev set. In our work, we use the Adam [24] as the optimizer of our model. The base learning rate is set as 1e-3, and is dropped to 1e-4 and 1e-5 at the 170th and 200th epochs respectively. The total training process is terminated within 210 epochs.

**Comparison with State-of-the-Art Methods.** As the Table 2 shown, Our model achieves competitive performance compared with the other state-of-the-art methods via much fewer model GFLOPs and parameters. Compared to HRNet-W32 [5] and HRNet-W48 [5], our MLPPose-B and MLPPose-H achieves similar result with less than 50% model parameters, respectively. Compared with TransPose-H-S [20], our MLPPose-B model improves AP by 0.4 points with significant reduction in model GFLOPs(↓33%). Compared with TransPose-H-A6 [20], our MLPPose-H model achieves competitive result with less than 50% model GFLOPs. Besides, we test all models on a single NVIDIA Tesla M10 GPU with the same experimental conditions to compute the average FPS. Under the input size - 256 × 192, our model has much higher speed (↑50%). In particular, as shown in Table 3, input image size is 256 × 192, our model achieves competitive performance compare exists state-of-the-art methods on MS-COCO test-dev dataset.

**Table 2.** Results on MS-COCO validation set, all provided with the same detected human boxes. Pretrain means pre-training the corresponding parts on the ImageNet classification task. MLPPose-B and MLPPose-H achieve competitive results to Simplebaseline [18], HRNet [5] and TransPose [20] respectively, with much fewer parameters & GFLOPs.

| Model | Pretrain | Input size | AP | AR | #Param | GFLOPs | FPS |
|---|---|---|---|---|---|---|---|
| SimpleBaseline-Res50 [18] | Y | 256 × 192 | 70.4 | 76.3 | 34.0 M | 8.9 | 25 |
| SimpleBaseline-Res101 [18] | Y | 256 × 192 | 71.4 | 76.3 | 53.0 M | 12.4 | 22 |
| SimpleBaseline-Res152 [18] | Y | 256 × 192 | 72.0 | 77.8 | 68.6 M | 15.7 | 19 |
| HRNet-W32 [5] | Y | 256 × 192 | 74.4 | 79.8 | 28.5 M | 7.1 | 17 |
| HRNet-W48 [5] | Y | 256 × 192 | 75.1 | 80.4 | 63.6 M | 14.6 | 6 |
| TransPose-H-S [20] | Y | 256 × 192 | 74.2 | 78.0 | 8.0 M | 10.2 | 13 |
| TransPose-H-A6 [20] | Y | 256 × 192 | 75.8 | 80.8 | 17.5 M | 21.8 | 10 |
| MLPPose-B | Y | 256 × 192 | 74.6 | 79.8 | 11.9 M | 6.8 (↓33%) | 29 (↑55%) |
| MLPPose-H | Y | 256 × 192 | 75.3 | 80.4 | 21.0 M | 10.9 (↓50%) | 20 (↑50%) |

## 4.2 MPII Human Pose Estimation

**Dataset and Evaluation Metric.** The MPII Human Pose dataset [15] contains images with full-body pose annotations from real-world activities. There are 40 K person samples with 16 joints label, where 12 K person samples as the testing set and the remaining person samples for the training set. The data augmentation is same to MS-COCO, expect that the input images size are cropped to 256 × 256.

**Table 3.** Comparisons with state-of-the-art CNN-based models on the MS-COCO test-dev set. Tested on smaller input resolution 256 × 192, our models achieve comparable performances with the others.

| Model | Input size | #Param | GFLOPs | $AP$ | $AP^{50}$ | $AP^{75}$ | $AP^M$ | $AP^L$ | $AR$ |
|---|---|---|---|---|---|---|---|---|---|
| CPN [17] | 384 × 288 | 58.8 M | 29.2 | 72.1 | 91.4 | 80.0 | 68.7 | 77.2 | 78.5 |
| SimpleBaseline-Res152 [18] | 384 × 288 | 68.6 M | 35.6 | 73.7 | 91.9 | 81.8 | 70.3 | 80.0 | 79.0 |
| HRNet-W32 [5] | 384 × 288 | 28.5 M | 16 | 74.9 | 92.5 | 82.8 | 71.3 | 80.9 | 80.1 |
| HRNet-W48 [5] | 256 × 192 | 63.6 M | 14.6 | 74.2 | 92.4 | 82.4 | 70.9 | 79.7 | 79.5 |
| HRNet-W48 [5] | 384 × 288 | 63.6 M | 32.9 | 75.5 | 92.5 | 83.3 | 71.9 | 81.5 | 80.5 |
| TransPose-H-S [20] | 256 × 192 | 8.0 M | 10.2 | 73.4 | 91.6 | 81.1 | 70.1 | 79.3 | 78.0 |
| TransPose-H-A6 [20] | 256 × 192 | 17.5 M | 21.8 | 75.0 | 92.2 | 82.3 | 71.3 | 81.1 | 80.1 |
| MLPPose-B | 256 × 192 | 11.9 M | 6.8 | 74.1 | 91.9 | 81.7 | 70.6 | 80.1 | 79.2 |
| MLPPose-H | 256 × 192 | 21.0 M | 10.9 | 74.7 | 92.1 | 82.2 | 71.3 | 80.6 | 79.8 |

The PCKh [15] (head-normalized probability of correct keypoint) score is the standard metric.

**Results on the Validation Set.** We follow the testing procedure in Token-Pose [21]. The PCK@0.5 results of some top performed methods are presented in Table 4. The input image size is 256 × 256. As shown in Table 4, our proposed MLPPose-B achieves similar result compare to Simplebaseline [18], HRNet-W32 [5] and TokenPose-L/D24 [21] model with less parameters.

**Table 4.** Results on the MPII validation set (PCK@0.5). The input image size is 256 × 256

| Model | Hea | Sho | Elb | Wri | Hip | Kne | Ank | Mean | #Param |
|---|---|---|---|---|---|---|---|---|---|
| SimpleBaseline-Res50 [18] | 96.4 | 95.3 | 89.0 | 83.2 | 88.4 | 84.0 | 79.6 | 88.5 | 34.0 M |
| SimpleBaseline-Res101 [18] | 96.9 | 95.9 | 89.5 | 84.4 | 88.4 | 84.5 | 80.7 | 89.1 | 53.0 M |
| SimpleBaseline-Res152 [18] | 97.0 | 95.9 | 90.0 | 85.0 | 89.2 | 85.3 | 81.3 | 89.6 | 68.6 M |
| HRNet-W32 [5] | 96.9 | 96.0 | 90.6 | 85.8 | 88.7 | 86.6 | 82.6 | 90.1 | 28.5 M |
| TokenPose-D/L24 [21] | 97.1 | 95.9 | 90.4 | 86.0 | 89.3 | **87.1** | 82.5 | 90.2 | 28.1 M |
| MLPPose-B | 97.2 | 96.2 | 91.0 | 86.7 | 89.3 | 86.4 | 82.6 | 90.4 | 12.0 M |
| MLPPose-H | **97.3** | **96.2** | **91.2** | **87.2** | **89.6** | 87.0 | **83.9** | **90.8** | 21.3 M |

### 4.3  Ablation Study

**The Different CNN Extractors for Model Accuracy.** To make comparisons between RestNet-Small and HRNet-Small based models, we use the RestNet-Small and HRNet-Small as the CNN extractors respectively. As shown in Table 5, at the same image size, we adopts HRNet-Small-W32 as the backbone, the model increase 4.4 performance compare to adopt RestNet-Small as the backbone. When adopt HRNet-Small-W48 as the backbone, our model increase 0.4 performance compare to adopt HRNet-Small-W32 as the backbone. We think the main reason is that the multi-scale fusion of HRNet led to the quality of feature maps better than RestNet. It make our model to better capture global dependencies.

**Table 5.** MLPPose performance on MPII valid set under different CNN extractors.

| Model | Backbone | Image size | Mean | #Param |
|---|---|---|---|---|
| MLPPose-S | RestNet-Small | $256 \times 256$ | 86.0 | 5.6 M |
| MLPPose-B | HRNet-Small-W32 | $256 \times 256$ | 90.4 | 12.3 M |
| MLPPose-H | HRNet-Small-W48 | $256 \times 256$ | 90.8 | 21.3 M |

**The Importance of Convolutional Embedding.** In order to explore the importance of different embedding method. We conduct experiments on MLPPose-B models with two embedding strategies: convolutional token embedding, linear embedding. As Table 6 shown, when we replace the non-overlapping convolutional token embedding with overlapping convolutional token embedding, the performance of mean drops 1% (Table 6a vs Table 6c). When linear embedding is used, the performance drops of mean 0.4% (Table 6b vs Table 6c). These results validate the non-overlapping convolution embedding is the most efficient way for our model.

**Table 6.** Abliations on different token embedding. Result on MPII benchmark valid set.

| Method | Convolutional | Overlapping convolutional | Linear | Mean | Mean@0.1 |
|---|---|---|---|---|---|
| A | | ✓ | | 88.7 | 38.0 |
| B | | | ✓ | 90.0 | 39.3 |
| C | ✓ | | | 90.4 | 41.5 |

**The Layers of MLP-Mixer.** We study how performance scales with the size of MLP-Mixer, as shown in Table 7. For MLPPose-B, with the number of layers increasing to 8, the performance improvements gradually tend to saturate or degenerate.

**Table 7.** Ablation study on the size of MLP-Mixer. Result on MPII benchmark valid set.

| Method | Layers | Mean | Mean@0.1 |
|---|---|---|---|
| A | 4 | 89.4 | 39.9 |
| B | 6 | 89.9 | 40.7 |
| C | 8 | 90.4 | 41.5 |
| D | 10 | 89.0 | 39.5 |

**Fig. 4.** Qualitative of some example images in the MS-COCO datasets: containing viewpoint and appearance change, occlusion, multiple person.

### 4.4 Qualitative Results

We present example outputs of our model in Fig. 4: contains viewpoint and appearance change, occlusion, multiple persons, and common imaging artifacts.

## 5 Conclusion

Recently, transformer-based models have achieved state-of-the-art performance in the human pose estimation. In this work, we demonstrate that while self-attention is sufficient for good performance, it is not necessary. We propose a model called MLPPose, by introducing MLP-Mixer for human pose estimation. The MLP-Mixer can make our model to capture global spatial dependencies efficiently and simply. This allows our model to better handle keypoints of occlusion or complex scenes. With lightweight architectures, MLPPose achieves competitive result compare to state-of-the-art methods with less parameters on COCO and MPII human pose estimation benchmarks. Furthermore, we expect the proposed method to be a new choice for human pose estimation. And because of the high performance and global receptive field of MLP-Mixer, we believe it will perform even better in human pose estimation tasks.

**Acknowledgments.** This work was supported in part by the National Natural Science Foundation of China (62162018, 61967005), the Natural Science Foundation of Guangxi (2019GXNSF- GA245004, AA17202024,), the Science and Technology Base and Talent Project of Guangxi (No. AD21220097), Guangxi Key Laboratory of cryptography and information security Found (GCIS201701), Guangxi Collaborative Innovation Center of Cloud Computing and Big Data Found (YD1901), CETC Key Laboratory of Aerospace Information Applications Found, Young and middle-aged backbone teacher of Guangxi colleges and universities Found, Basic Ability Improvement Project for Young and Middle-aged Teachers in Colleges And Universities In Guangxi (No. 2021KY0202).

# References

1. Li, B., Dai, Y., Cheng, X., Chen, H., Lin, Y., He, M.: Skeleton based action recognition using translation-scale invariant image mapping and multi-scale deep CNN. In: ICMEW, pp. 601–604, July 2017
2. Li, B., Chen, H., Chen, Y., Dai, Y., He, M.: Skeleton based action recognition using translation-scale invariant image mapping and multi-scale deep CNN. In: ICMEW, pp. 613–616, July 2017
3. Insafutdinov, E., et al.: Arttrack: articulated multi-person tracking in the wild. In: CVPR, pp. 6457–6465 (2017)
4. Kulkarni, K.M., Shenoy, S.: Table Tennis stroke recognition using two-dimensional human pose estimation. In: CVPR, pp. 4576–4584 (2021)
5. Sun, K., Xiao, B., Liu, D., Wang, J.: Deep high-resolution representation learning for human pose estimation. In: CVPR, pp. 5693–5703 (2019)
6. Papandreou, G., Zhu, T., Chen, L.C., Gidaris, S., Tompson, J., Murphy, K.: Personlab: person pose estimation and instance segmentation with a bottom-up, part-based, geometric embedding model. In: ECCV, pp. 269–286 (2018)
7. Graves, A., et al.: Hybrid computing using a neural network with dynamic external memory. In: Nature, pp. 471–476 (2016)
8. Vaswani, A., et al.: Attention is all you need. In: NeurIPS, pp. 5998–6008 (2017)
9. Dosovitskiy, A., et al.: An image is worth $16 \times 16$ words: transformers for image recognition at scale. In: ICLR (2020)
10. Carion, N., Massa, F., Synnaeve, G., Usunier, N., Kirillov, A., Zagoruyko, S.: End-to-end object detection with transformers. In: ECCV, pp. 213–229, August 2020
11. Yu, W., et al.: MetaFormer is actually what you need for vision. arXiv preprint arXiv:2111.11418 (2021)
12. Tolstikhin, I.O., et al.: MLP-mixer: an all-MLP architecture for vision. In: NeurIPS (2017)
13. Wu, H., et al.: CVT: introducing convolutions to vision transformers. In: ICCV (2021)
14. Lin, T.-Y., Maire, M., Belongie, S., Hays, J., Perona, P., Ramanan, D., Dollár, P., Zitnick, C.L.: Microsoft COCO: common objects in context. In: Fleet, D., Pajdla, T., Schiele, B., Tuytelaars, T. (eds.) ECCV 2014. LNCS, vol. 8693, pp. 740–755. Springer, Cham (2014). https://doi.org/10.1007/978-3-319-10602-1_48
15. Andriluka, M., Pishchulin, L., Gehler, P., Schiele, B.: 2D human pose estimation: new benchmark and state of the art analysis. In: CVPR, pp. 3686–3693 (2014)
16. Newell, A., Yang, K., Deng, J.: Stacked hourglass networks for human pose estimation. In: Leibe, B., Matas, J., Sebe, N., Welling, M. (eds.) ECCV 2016. LNCS, vol. 9912, pp. 483–499. Springer, Cham (2016). https://doi.org/10.1007/978-3-319-46484-8_29
17. Chen, Y., Wang, Z., Peng, Y., Zhang, Z., Yu, G., Sun, J.: Cascaded pyramid network for multi-person pose estimation. In: CVPR, pp. 7103–7112 (2018)
18. Xiao, B., Wu, H., Wei, Y.: Simple baselines for human pose estimation and tracking. In: ECCV, pp. 466–481 (2018)
19. Zheng, S., et al.: Rethinking semantic segmentation from a sequence-to-sequence perspective with transformers. In: CVPR, pp. 6881–6890 (2021)
20. Yang, S., Quan, Z., Nie, M., Yang, W.: Transpose: keypoint localization via transformer. In: ICCV, pp. 11802–11812 (2021)
21. Li, Y., et al.: TokenPose: learning keypoint tokens for human pose estimation. arXiv preprint arXiv:2104.03516 (2021)

22. Lian, D., Yu, Z., Sun, X., Gao, S.: AS-MLP: an axial shifted MLP architecture for vision. arXiv preprint arXiv:2107.08391 (2021)
23. Hendrycks, D., Gimpel, K.: Gaussian error linear units (GELUs). arXiv preprint arXiv:1606.08415 (2016)
24. Kingma, D.P., Ba, J.: Adam: a method for stochastic optimization. arXiv preprint arXiv:1412.6980 (2014)
25. Cheng, B., Xiao, B., Wang, J., Shi, H., Huang, T. S., Zhang, L.: Higherhrnet: scale-aware representation learning for bottom-up human pose estimation. In: CVPR, pp. 5386–5395 (2020)
26. Wang, W., Xie, E., Li, X., Fan, D.P., Song, K., Liang, D., Shao, L.: Pyramid vision transformer: a versatile backbone for dense prediction without convolutions. In: ICCV, pp. 568–578 (2021)
27. Yue, X., et al.: Vision transformer with progressive sampling. In: ICCV, pp. 387–396 (2021)

# Nesterov Adam Iterative Fast Gradient Method for Adversarial Attacks

Cheng Chen[1,2] , Zhiguang Wang[1,2]([✉]), Yongnian Fan[1,2], Xue Zhang[1,2],
Dawei Li[3], and Qiang Lu[1,2]

[1] Beijing Key Laboratory of Petroleum Data Mining,
China University of Petroleum, Beijing, China
cwangzg@cup.edu.cn, leedw@petrochina.com.cn
[2] Department of Computer Science and Technology, China University of Petroleum,
Beijing, China
[3] PetroChina Research Institute of Petroleum Exploration and Development,
Beijing, China

**Abstract.** Deep Neural Networks (DNNs) are vulnerable to adversarial
examples that mislead DNNs with imperceptible perturbations. Existing
adversarial attacks often exhibit weak transferability under the black-box
setting, especially when attacking the models with defense mechanisms.
In this work, we regard the adversarial example generation problem as
the problem of optimizing DNNs, and propose Nesterov Adam Iterative
Fast Gradient Method (NAI-FGM) which applies Nesterov accelerated
gradient and Adam to iterative attacks to improve the transferability of
the gradient-based attack method so as to adjust the attack step size by
itself and avoid local optimum more effectively. Empirical results on ImageNet dataset demonstrate that NAI-FGM could improve transferability
of adversarial examples. Under the setting of ensemble model, the integrated method of NAI-FGM with various input transformations could
achieve an average attack success rate of 91.88% against six advanced
defense models, 1.78%–3.3% higher than the benchmarks. Code is available at https://github.com/NinelM/NAI-FGM.

**Keywords:** Adversarial examples · Nesterov accelerated gradient ·
Adam optimization algorithm

## 1 Introduction

Deep Neural Networks (DNNs) have been known to be vulnerable to adversarial
examples generated by adding imperceptible perturbations to the original input,
which will mislead predictions of the DNNs [3,18]. At the same time, adversarial
examples have certain transferability in that adversarial examples crafted by the
current model that can also affect the prediction of other unknown models [11,

---

Supported by National Natural Science Foundation of China (No. 61972414), National
Key R&D Program of China (NO. 2019YFC0312003) and Beijing Natural Science
Foundation (No. 4202066).

E. Pimenidis et al. (Eds.): ICANN 2022, LNCS 13529, pp. 586–598, 2022.
https://doi.org/10.1007/978-3-031-15919-0_49

18]. Adversarial examples can not only identify the robustness of DNNs, but also help improve the robustness and accuracy of DNNs by training on adversarial examples [3,18,21]. Therefore, learning how to generate adversarial examples with high transferability has gained increasing academic attention.

A variety of gradient-based methods to generate adversarial examples have been proposed. Under the white-box setting, existing methods can achieve high attack success rates with the architecture and parameters of the current model. However, most of them fail to exhibit high transferability for black-box attacks, and there is still a big gap of performance between black-box attacks and white-box attacks.

In this work, by considering the adversarial examples' generation process as the optimization process of DNNs, we apply Nesterov accelerated gradient (NAG) [13] and Adam optimization algorithm [7] to gradient-based iterative attacks, and propose Nesterov Adam Iterative Fast Gradient Method (NAI-FGM) to improve the transferability of adversarial examples for black-box attack. NAI-FGM combines the advantages of NAG and Adam optimization algorithm, which can not only effectively avoid local optimum, but also adaptively adjust the attack step size to reach the global optimum fast.

Extensive experiments on the ImageNet dataset [15] show that NAI-FGM could achieve higher attack success rates than the benchmarks in the setting of black-box, including MI-FGSM [2], NI-FGSM [10] and AI-FGM [25], and maintain attack success rates similar to that of the benchmarks for white-box models. To further demonstrate the effectiveness of NAI-FGM, we integrate NAI-FGM with various input transformations and conduct a large number of comparative experiments. The results indicate that NAI-FGM could be effectively combined with various input transformations, and our integrated method exhibit higher transferability than the benchmarks. We generate adversarial examples for ensemble models [11] using our integrated method, which achieve an average attack success rate of 94.6%, 2.47%–4.33% higher than the benchmarks. Finally, we compare our attack method with the benchmarks against six advanced defense methods [4,9,12,22,24]. Our integrated method yields an average attack success rate of 91.88%, which outperforms the benchmarks by 1.78%–3.3%.

## 2   Related Work

Let $x$ and $y$ denote a clean image and corresponding label, and $f(x; \theta)$ denote the prediction result of classifier with parameters $\theta$. Let $J(x, y)$ be the loss function of the classifier (e.g. the cross-entropy loss), let $x^{adv}$ be an adversarial example of clean image $x$. The goal of adversarial attack is to find an adversarial example $x^{adv}$ that satisfies $f(x; \theta) \neq f(x^{adv}; \theta)$ and $\|x^{adv} - x\|_p \leq \epsilon$, where $p$ could be $0, 1, 2, \infty$, $\| \cdot \|_p$ is $p$-norm distance, $\epsilon$ is the size of adversarial perturbations.

### 2.1   Adversarial Attacks

In this work, we mainly concentrate on the transferability of attack. We are going to introduce some existing adversarial attacks based on transferability. These adversarial attacks can be roughly divided into two categories.

**Gradient-Based Attacks.** The first category focuses on advancing gradient calculation to improve the transferability of gradient-based attacks.

*Fast Gradient Sign Method (FGSM).* FGSM [3] finds an adversarial example $x^{adv}$ by maximizing the loss function $J(x^{adv}, y)$ using the gradient one-step update. The fast gradient method (FGM) is a generalization of FGSM that uses $L_2$ norm to restrict the distance between $x^{adv}$ and $x$.

*Iterative Fast Gradient Sign Method (I-FGSM).* I-FGSM [8] extends FGSM to an iterative version by applying FGSM in iterations with a small step size $\alpha$.

*Momentum Iterative Fast Gradient Sign Method (MI-FGSM).* MI-FGSM [2] has higher transferability than I-FGSM by integrating the momentum into the iterative attack.

*Nesterov Iterative Fast Gradient Sign Method (NI-FGSM).* NI-FGSM [10] adopts Nesterov accelerated gradient into I-FGSM because of the fact that Nesterov accelerated gradient is superior to momentum in optimization.

*Adam Iterative Fast Gradient Method (AI-FGSM).* AI-FGM [25] applies the idea of Adam optimization algorithm to generate adversarial examples, integrating Adam optimization algorithm into FGM, which uses $L_2$ norm to limit the distance between $x^{adv}$ and $x$ to satisfy $\|x^{adv} - x\|_2 \leq \epsilon$.

**Input Transformations.** The second category focuses on adopting various input transformations to enhance the attack transferability.

*Diverse Input Method (DIM).* DIM [23] improves the transferability of adversarial examples by applying random resizing and random padding to the inputs at each iteration with a fixed probability, and then feeding the transformed images into the classifier to calculate the gradient.

*Translation-Invariant Method (TIM).* TIM [1] uses a specific convolution kernel to translate a set of images to calculate gradients, so that it can obtain a better gradient direction to improve the success rates of black-box attacks.

*Scale-Invariant Method (SIM).* Taking the scale-invariant property of the neural network into consideration, SIM [10] enhances the transferability of adversarial attack by computing the gradient of a set of scaled images, which is achieved by $x/2^i$, where $i$ is a hyper-parameter.

## 2.2   Adversarial Defenses

In order to deal with the impact of adversarial examples on the prediction of DNNs, many defense methods have been proposed. Existing defense methods can be roughly divided into two branches. One is adversarial training, the other is input-modified.

**Adversarial Training.** GoodFellow et al. [3] use adversarial examples to augment training data to enhance model robustness during the training process. Tramr et al. [19] attack multiple models simultaneously to generate adversarial examples, then augment the training data with adversarial examples to increase the robustness against the black-box attacks.

**Input Modification.** Liao et al. [9] purify the input image by training a high-level representation denoiser named HGD. Guo et al. [4] exploit a set of image transformation methods to enhance the defense capabilities of the model, including JPEG compression, total variance minimization. Xie et al. [22] mitigate the effects of adversarial attacks by randomly padding and modifying the picture size (P&R). Liu et el. [12] have proposed a feature extraction method based on the JPEG defensive compression framework to defend against adversarial examples. Xu et al. [24] have proposed two feature compression methods, bit reduction and spatial smoothing, to detect adversarial examples.

# 3  Methodology

In this section, we first introduce the motivation, then we provide a detailed description of the proposed idea and analyze the proposed method.

## 3.1  Motivation

Given a classifier $f$ with parameters $\theta$, the goal of adversarial attack is to find an image $x^{adv}$ that satisfies:

$$f(x, \theta) \neq f(x^{adv}, \theta) \quad s.t. \quad \|x^{adv} - x\| \leq \epsilon \tag{1}$$

For classification problems, Eq. (1) can also be transformed into:

$$x^{adv} = \underset{\|x-x'\|_p}{\arg\max}(J(x', y; \theta) \tag{2}$$

Equation (2) indicates that adversarial attacks can be regarded as an optimization process to maximize the loss function value of the classifier by continuously optimizing $x'$ in the neighborhood of $x$. For the adversarial example generation problem, the input $x$ of the classifier can be regarded as the parameter that needs to be optimized, and the process of finding the adversarial examples $x^{adv}$ can be regarded as the training process. The white-box models are equivalent to the training sets, and the black-box models can be regarded as the testing sets. The transferability of adversarial examples is equivalent to the generalization ability of the models [10], that is, the same model can show similar performance on different distribution datasets.

To improve the generalization ability of the model, it can be done in the following two ways: (i) better optimization algorithm, and (ii) data augmentation. Correspondingly, these two methods can also be used to improve the transferability of adversarial examples.

---

**Algorithm 1.** NAI-FGM

---

**Input:** A classifier $f$ with loss function $J$, a clean example $x$ and ground-truth label $y$, the size of perturbation $\epsilon$, the number of iteration $T$, decay factor of momentum $\mu$, decay factor of Adam optimization algorithm $\beta_1$ and $\beta_2$, image dimension $N$, denominator stability coefficient $\delta$

**Output:** An adversarial example $x^{adv}$ with $\|x^{adv} - x\|_2 \leq \epsilon$

1: $\alpha_1 = \epsilon/T$, $\alpha_2 = \epsilon/\sqrt{N}$, $m_0 = 0$, $v_0 = 0$, $g_0 = 0$, $x_0^{adv} = x$
2: Calculate the coefficient of attack step normalization

$$nc = \sum_{i=0}^{T-1} \frac{\sqrt{1-\beta_2^{t+1}}}{1-\beta_1^{t+1}} \qquad (3)$$

3: **for** $t = 0 \rightarrow T - 1$ **do**
4:      Input $x_t^{adv}$ to $f$ and obtain the gradient $\nabla_x J(x_t^{adv}, y)$
5:      Make a jump in the direction of previous accumulated gradient

$$x_t^{nes} = x_t^{adv} + \alpha_1 \cdot \mu \cdot g_t \qquad (4)$$

6:      Calculate the future gradient $g_{t+1} = \frac{\nabla_x J(x_t^{nes}, y)}{\|\nabla_x J(x_t^{nes}, y)\|_1}$
7:      Calculate the first and second momentum estimate

$$m_{t+1} = \beta_1 \cdot m_t + (1-\beta_1) \cdot g_{t+1}$$
$$v_{t+1} = \beta_2 \cdot v_t + (1-\beta_2) \cdot g_t^2 \qquad (5)$$

8:      Make NAI-FGM to be adaptive by

$$S_{t+1} = \frac{m_{t+1}}{\delta + \sqrt{v_{t+1}}} \qquad (6)$$

9:      Normalize the size step of attack

$$\alpha_t = \alpha_2 \cdot \frac{\sqrt{1-\beta_2^{t+1}}}{1-\beta_1^{t+1}} / nc \qquad (7)$$

10:      Update $x^{adv}$ by $x_{t+1}^{adv} = Clip_x^{\epsilon}(x_t^{adv} + \alpha_t \cdot \frac{S_{t+1}}{\|S_{t+1}\|_2})$

11: $x^{adv} = x_T^{adv}$
12: **return** $x^{adv}$

---

Both MI-FGSM [2] and NI-FGSM [10] successfully apply optimization algorithm to improve the transferability of adversarial examples, and NI-FGSM exhibits higher transferability than MI-FGSM. These facts suggest that applying optimization algorithm to generation of adversarial examples is effective, and the performance of optimizing algorithm may affect the transferability of adversarial examples. However, both MI-FGSM and NI-FGSM perturb the original example with a fixed step size, and their attack effect may be weakened by an unreasonable fixed step size. For example, when the fixed step size is set too large, it may miss the global optimal, and when it is too small, more times of attack are required to reach the global optimal.

**Table 1.** The success rates (%) of MI-FGSM, NI-FGSM, AI-FGM and NAI-FGM on seven models in the single model setting. The adversarial examples are crafted on Inc-v3, Inc-v4, IncRes-v2, and Res-v2. * indicates the white-box model.

| | Inc-v3 | Inc-v4 | IncRes-v2 | Res-v2 | Inc-v3$_{ens}$ | Inc-v4$_{ens}$ | IncRes-v2$_{ens}$ |
|---|---|---|---|---|---|---|---|
| MI-FGSM | **100.0*** | 46.1 | 42.5 | 36.7 | 12.5 | 12.5 | 6.5 |
| NI-FGSM | **100.0*** | 51.5 | 50.8 | 40.0 | 13.0 | 12.9 | 6.1 |
| AI-FGM | **100.0*** | 48.6 | 44.6 | 36.7 | 15.0 | 14.5 | 6.1 |
| NAI-FGM | **100.0*** | **58.3** | **56.5** | **44.8** | **15.9** | **15.3** | **7.2** |
| MI-FGSM | 55.9 | 99.8* | 45.8 | 41.6 | 16.5 | 15.7 | 7.5 |
| NI-FGSM | 64.7 | **100.0*** | 52.7 | 46.5 | 16.1 | 12.7 | 7.0 |
| AI-FGM | 58.0 | 99.8* | 48.3 | 43.2 | 19.3 | **16.6** | 8.8 |
| NAI-FGM | **68.4** | **100.0*** | **57.0** | **49.1** | **20.6** | 16.0 | **8.9** |
| MI-FGSM | 59.7 | 51.2 | 97.9* | 45.2 | 22.3 | 16.7 | 11.4 |
| NI-FGSM | 62.1 | 55.6 | **99.1*** | 45.6 | 19.3 | 14.7 | 10.0 |
| AI-FGM | 61.0 | 53.0 | 98.5* | 43.0 | 24.5 | 18.6 | 13.4 |
| NAI-FGM | **67.1** | **57.7** | 97.7* | **49.0** | **24.8** | **19.6** | **13.7** |
| MI-FGSM | 57.4 | 52.5 | 49.6 | 99.3* | 24.3 | 21.3 | 12.2 |
| NI-FGSM | 65.2 | 59.2 | 56.2 | **99.4*** | 23.7 | 22.2 | 11.7 |
| AI-FGM | 58.6 | 53.7 | 51.1 | 99.3* | 26.9 | 25.0 | 15.5 |
| NAI-FGM | **69.2** | **63.8** | **61.2** | **99.4*** | **29.4** | **25.1** | **16.7** |

The Adam optimization algorithm [7] is adaptive and can adjust the learning rate by itself to solve the problems that may be caused by the fixed step size. However, in some cases, Adam optimization algorithm may miss the global optimal solution [6,20]. For example, when the Adam optimization algorithm overfits the features that appear in the early training period, the features that appear in the later training period are difficult to correct the impact of overfitting in the early stage. At this time, the Adam optimization algorithm will miss the global optimal solution.

Considering that momentum method [14] is used in Adam [7], and NAG [13] is effective to improve momentum method, we can use NAG to improve the momentum part of Adam optimization algorithm. Improved method can avoid local optimum and maintain the adaptivity of Adam optimization algorithm. Based on above consideration, we design the Nesterov Adam Iterative Fast Gradient Method (NAI-FGM) to improve the transferability of adversarial examples.

## 3.2    Nesterov Adam Iterative Fast Gradient Method

We integrate NAG and Adam optimization algorithm into the iterative gradient-based attack to build an adversarial attack with high transferability, which is named NAI-FGM (Nesterov Adam Iterative Fast Gradient Method). The algorithm details of NAI-FGM are shown in Algorithm 1, where the $\alpha_1$ is the attack step size for NAG, the $\alpha_2$ is the attack step size for Adam, the $m_0$ and $v_0$ are the initial first and second momentum estimate for Adam, and $g_0$ is the initial gradient.

We first calculate the coefficient of step size normalization $nc$ by Eq. (3) that is used to normalize the attack step size in Eq. (7), and $nc$ is only related to the total number of attack iterations $T$, $\beta_1$ and $\beta_2$. Then we integrate NAG with FGM by Eq. (4), which could know the future gradient in advance. If the future gradient is larger, then the update range of $x_{t+1}^{adv}$ will be larger, when the future gradient is smaller, $x_{t+1}^{adv}$ will also have smaller update amplitudes, which is helpful for avoiding local optimum. Therefore $x_{t+1}^{adv}$ could both leave the local optimum fast without oscillating around the local optimum.

The idea of Adam optimization algorithm [7] is applied in Eq. (5), Eq. (6) and Eq. (7). The first momentum estimate and the second momentum estimate of Adam optimization algorithm are used in Eq. (5), $\beta_1 = 0.99$ and $\beta_2 = 0.999$ in ours work. $S_{t+1}$ in Eq. (6) could adaptively adjust the step size of adversarial attack, so NAI-FGM does not need to fix the step size of each attack, which can avoid unreasonable setting of the step size, resulting in weaking transferability of generated adversarial examples. The role of Eq. (7) is to calculate the bias-corrected in Adam optimization algorithm and normalize the attack step size by $nc$. In addition, $S_{t+1}$ could control $x_{t+1}^{adv}$ update direction of adversarial examples adaptively, so NAI-FGM uses the $L_2$ norm in FGM to limit the distance between $x_{adv}$ and $x$, instead of the $sign(\cdot)$ function. Finally NAI-FGM uses the $Clip$ function to limit the gap between $x_{adv}$ and $x$, limiting the adversarial examples to $[0, 1]$.

The NAI-FGM could be integrated with SIM [10], SI-TIM (the combination of SIM and TIM [1]) and CT [10] (the combination of DIM [23], TIM and SIM) as NAI-SI-FGM, NAI-SI-TI-FGM, NAI-CT-FGM, respectively, to further improve the transferability of NAI-FGM. In Sect. 4.3, we design comparative experiments to illustrate the performance of NAI-FGM that is integrated with input transformations.

## 4    Experiments

In this section, we conduct extensive experiments on the ImageNet dataset to verify the effectiveness of our proposed adversarial attack. In Sect. 4.1, we introduce the experimental setup, including dataset, models selected, benchmarks, and hyper-parameters. Then in Sect. 4.2, we conduct experiments of adversarial attack in the single model setting and show the results. In Sect. 4.3, we demonstrate that NAI-FGM could be combined with various input transformations effectively. In Sect. 4.4, we show the results in the multi-models. In Sect. 4.5, we quantify the effectiveness of NAI-FGM on 6 defense models.

### 4.1    Experimental Setup

We randomly select 1000 clean images from 1000 classes in the ILSVRC 2012 validation set [15], which are almost correctly classified by the model selected in this work.

**Table 2.** The success rates (%) of MI-SI-FGSM, NI-SI-FGSM, AI-SI-FGM and NAI-SI-FGM on seven models in the single model setting. The adversarial examples are crafted on Inc-v3. * indicates the white-box model.

|            | Inc-v3  | Inc-v4 | IncRes-v2 | Res-v2 | Inc-v3$_{ens}$ | Inc-v4$_{ens}$ | IncRes-v2$_{ens}$ |
|------------|---------|--------|-----------|--------|----------------|----------------|-------------------|
| MI-SI-FGSM | **100.0*** | 69.6   | 66.6      | 62.7   | 32.0           | 31.2           | 16.9              |
| NI-SI-FGSM | **100.0*** | 76.9   | 75.0      | 67.2   | 32.2           | 29.1           | 16.7              |
| AI-SI-FGM  | **100.0*** | 72.6   | 70.4      | 62.5   | 36.4           | 33.9           | 19.4              |
| NAI-SI-FGM | **100.0*** | **81.2** | **78.9**  | **70.4** | **38.4**       | **36.3**       | **20.8**          |

**Table 3.** The success rates (%) of MI-SI-TI-FGSM, NI-SI-TI-FGSM, AI-SI-TI-FGM and NAI-SI-TI-FGM on seven models in the single model setting. The adversarial examples are crafted on Inc-v3. * indicates the white-box model.

|               | Inc-v3  | Inc-v4 | IncRes-v2 | Res-v2 | Inc-v3$_{ens}$ | Inc-v4$_{ens}$ | IncRes-v2$_{ens}$ |
|---------------|---------|--------|-----------|--------|----------------|----------------|-------------------|
| MI-SI-TI-FGSM | **100.0*** | 71.9   | 68.8      | 63.0   | 49.2           | 47.2           | 31.6              |
| NI-SI-TI-FGSM | **100.0*** | 78.5   | 75.9      | 67.7   | 50.5           | 47.2           | 32.8              |
| AI-SI-TI-FGM  | **100.0*** | 71.5   | 68.8      | 61.8   | 50.8           | 49.7           | 34.8              |
| NAI-SI-TI-FGM | **100.0*** | **82.8** | **78.7**  | **71.5** | **58.2**       | **55.4**       | **39.3**          |

**Table 4.** The success rates (%) of MI-CT-FGSM, NI-CT-FGSM, AI-CT-FGM and NAI-CT-FGM on seven models in the single model setting. The adversarial examples are crafted on Inc-v3. * indicates the white-box model.

|            | Inc-v3  | Inc-v4 | IncRes-v2 | Res-v2 | Inc-v3$_{ens}$ | Inc-v4$_{ens}$ | IncRes-v2$_{ens}$ |
|------------|---------|--------|-----------|--------|----------------|----------------|-------------------|
| MI-CT-FGSM | 98.9*   | 84.8   | 82.7      | 76.9   | 67.3           | 64.6           | 46.4              |
| NI-CT-FGSM | **99.4*** | 83.8   | 81.1      | 75.3   | 61.4           | 55.8           | 40.7              |
| AI-CT-FGM  | 99.0*   | 83.8   | 80.3      | 74.8   | 65.9           | 63.7           | 48.1              |
| NAI-CT-FGM | 99.1*   | **88.0** | **85.5**  | **80.1** | **69.1**       | **66.1**       | **51.0**          |

The model selection in this work is consistent with NI-FGSM [10] and MI-FGSM [2], and seven different models are selected. Four of them are normally trained models, including Inception-v3 (Inc-v3) [16], Inception-v4 (Inc-v4), Inception-Resnet v2 (IncRes-v2) [17], Resnet-v2 (Res-v2) [5], and the others are models trained on adversarial examples, including Inc-v3$_{ens}$, Inc-v4$_{ens}$, IncRes-v2$_{ens}$. Besides, we selected six defense models to defend against adversarial examples including JPEG [4], R&P [22], HGD [9], Bit-Red [24], FD [12], NIPS-r3[1].

This study uses two momentum iteration-based adversarial attack, *i.e.* MI-FGSM [2], NI-FGSM [10] and an Adam-based adversarial attack AI-FGM [25] as benchmarks. In addition, we integrate the proposed adversarial attack with various input transformations, *i.e.* SIM [10], SI-TIM and CT [10], denoted as NAI-SI-FGM, NAI-SI-TI-FGM, NAI-CT-FGM, respectively, to further validate the effectiveness of our method.

---

[1] https://github.com/anlthms/nips-2017/tree/master/mmd.

We follow the attack setting in [10] with the maximum perturbation of $\epsilon = 16$, number of iteration $T = 10$ and step size $\alpha_1 = 1.6$. We set the decay factor of MI-FGSM and NI-FGSM $\mu = 1.0$. For AI-FGM, set the decay factor of Adam optimization algorithm $\beta_1 = 0.99, \beta_2 = 0.999$, image dimension $N = 299 \times 299 \times 3$, which $299 \times 299$ is the image size and 3 is the number of image channels. For DIM, the transformation probability is set to 0.5. For TIM, the Gaussian kernel size is $7 \times 7$. For SIM, the number of scale copies is $5(i.e.i = 0, 1, 2, 3, 4)$.

### 4.2    Attacking a Single Model

Attacking a single model, *i.e.* performing adversarial attacks on a single neural network. We first generate adversarial examples on four normally trained models, and test them on all the seven neural networks we choose. We take the attack success rates of adversarial attack as the evaluation indicators, which are the misclassification rates of the corresponding model on the adversarial examples. The attack success rates of MI-FGSM [2], NI-FGSM [10], AI-FGM [25], and NAI-FGM are shown in Table 1.

We can observe that in almost all black-box attacks, NAI-FGM performs better than the benchmarks, while it could also achieve attack success rates close to the benchmarks in the white-box attacks. For instance, if adversarial examples are crafted on Inc-v3 model, all the attacks can achieve 100% success rates in the white-box setting, but NAI-FGM could achieve higher attack success rates than the benchmarks under the black-box setting. The average attack success rate of NAI-FGM can reach 42.57%, while the average attack success rates of MI-FGSM [2], NI-FGSM [10], AI-FGM [25] can reach 36.69%, 39.23%, 37.93%, which fully demonstrates the effectiveness of our proposed method.

### 4.3    Attacking with Input Transformations

Attacking with input transformations utilizing image transformations on images first and then calculate the gradient. In this subsection, we combine NAI-FGM with SIM [10], SI-TIM and CT [10] as NAI-SI-FGM, NAI-SI-TI-FGM, NAI-CT-FGM, demonstrating that NAI-FGM can further improve transferability. The results are shown in Table 2, Table 3 and Table 4.

Table 2 shows the attack success rates of NAI-SI-FGM on seven models. From Table 2, we can see that the attack success rate of NAI-SI-FGM in the white-box attack could reach 100%, and the performance in the black-box attacks is also better than the benchmarks. The average attack success rate of NAI-SI-FGM could reach 60.86%, while the average attack success rates of MI-SI-FGSM, NI-SI-FGSM and AI-SI-FGM are 54.14%, 56.73%, and 56.46%. The results indicates that NAI-FGM could further improve the transferability by integrating with input transformation, and still perform better than the benchmarks.

As shown in Table 3, NAI-FGM could also be combined with SI-TIM to improve transferability and perform better than the benchmarks. Table 4 presents the results of the combination of NAI-FGM and CT. From Table 3 and Table 4, we observe that NAI-FGM could be integrated with various input

**Table 5.** The success rates (%) of MI-CT-FGSM, NI-CT-FGSM, AI-CT-FGM and NAI-CT-FGM on seven models in the multi-model setting. The adversarial examples are generated on the ensemble models, i.e. Inc-v3, Inc-v4, IncRes-v2 and Res-v2.

|            | Inc-v3 | Inc-v4 | IncRes-v2 | Res-v2  | Inc-v3$_{ens}$ | Inc-v4$_{ens}$ | IncRes-v2$_{ens}$ |
|------------|--------|--------|-----------|---------|----------------|----------------|-------------------|
| MI-CT-FGSM | 99.7*  | 98.9*  | 98.2*     | 100.0*  | 92.3           | 91.4           | 88.0              |
| NI-CT-FGSM | 99.8*  | 99.8*  | **99.8***  | 99.9*   | 93.6           | 90.90          | 86.3              |
| AI-CT-FGM  | 99.7*  | 99.4*  | 98.8*     | 100.0*  | 93.5           | 92.1           | 90.8              |
| NAI-CT-FGM | **99.9*** | **99.9*** | 99.6*  | **100.0*** | **95.7**    | **95.0**       | **93.1**          |

**Table 6.** The success rates (%) of MI-CT-FGSM, NI-CT-FGSM, AI-CT-FGM and NAI-CT-FGM on six models with advanced defense mechanism. The adversarial examples are generated on the ensemble models, i.e. Inc-v3, Inc-v4, IncRes-v2 and Res-v2.

|            | HGD    | R&P    | NIPS-r3 | Bit-Red | JEPG   | FD     | Average |
|------------|--------|--------|---------|---------|--------|--------|---------|
| MI-CT-FGSM | 91.5   | 89.3   | 91.0    | 77.0    | 94.7   | 89.5   | 88.8    |
| NI-CT-FGSM | 92.6   | 88.2   | 90.8    | 73.3    | 96.2   | 90.4   | 88.6    |
| AI-CT-FGM  | 94.2   | 90.9   | 92.0    | 77.4    | 95.7   | 90.4   | 90.1    |
| NAI-CT-FGM | **95.9** | **93.2** | **94.2** | **78.3** | **97.2** | **92.5** | **91.9** |

transformations to achieve higher attack success rates and consistently outperform the benchmarks.

### 4.4 Attacking an Ensemble of Models

According to the work of Liu et al. [10], attacking the ensemble model can greatly improve the success rate of black-box attacks. In this section, we use the ensemble attack method in [2], which simultaneously attack the Inc-v3 [16], Inc-v4, IncRes-v2 [17], Res-v2 [5], and fuses the logic outputs of Inc-v3, Inc-v4, IncRes-v2, and Res-v2 by averaging, to demonstrate that our NAI-FGM could further improve the transferability of adversarial attacks in the multi-model setting.

As shown in Table 5, the attack success rates achieved by our method, is 1.1%–6.8% higher than the benchmarks. The average attack success rate of NAI-CT-FGM is 94.6%, compared with 90.57% for MI-CT-FGSM, 90.27% for NI-CT-FGSM, and 92.13% for AI-CT-FGM in the setting of black-box, while NAI-FGM can also maintain attack success rates similar to the benchmarks in white-box setting.

### 4.5 Attacking Advanced Defense Models

The defense model eliminates the interference of adversarial examples by defense algorithms, which eliminates the perturbations before input. To further demonstrate the effectiveness of NAI-FGM in practical applications, we evaluate NAI-

FGM on 6 defense methods, including JPEG [4], R&P [22], HGD [9], Bit-Red [24], FD [12], NIPS-r3.

We first generate adversarial examples for the ensemble models, including Inc-v3, Inc-v4, IncRes-v2, and Res-v2, by using MI-CT-FGSM, NI-CT-FGSM, AI-CT-FGM, NAI-CT-FGM, respectively. Then, we evaluate the adversarial examples by attacking the six defense models.

As shown in Table 6, our method could achieve higher attack success rates than the benchmarks on various defense models, and the average attack success rate can reach 91.88%, 1.78%–3.3% higher than the benchmarks. The results show that our method can attack not only the adversarial trained models successfully, but also the advanced defense models.

## 5    Conclusion

In this paper, we propose the Nesterov Adam Iterative Fast Gradient Method (NAI-FGM) for adversarial attack to improve the transferability of adversarial examples. Specifically, NAG is used to improve the momentum part of Adam optimization algorithm. NAI-FGM could retain the adaptability of Adam optimization algorithm and adjust the step size of the adversarial attack by itself to avoid the problems caused by unreasonable fixed step size settings. For example, if the fixed step size is too large, the global optimum will be missed. If the fixed step size is too small, the numbers of iterations will increase. Meanwhile, NAG-FGM could avoid the local optimum and approach to the global optimum fasterly.

Extensive experiments demonstrate that NAI-FGM generates adversarial examples efficiently. NAI-FGM could achieve higher attack success rates with the higher transferability of adversarial examples than the benchmarks. At the same time, NAI-FGM could be well integrated with varieties input transformations in the setting of ensemble models to achieve the most advanced attack success rates. Results on six advanced defense models show that our integrated method could achieve a higher attack success rate than the benchmarks, with an average attack success rate of 91.88%, exceeding the benchmarks by 1.78%–3.3%.

## References

1. Dong, Y., Pang, T., Su, H., Zhu, J.: Evading defenses to transferable adversarial examples by translation-invariant attacks. In: 2019 IEEE/CVF Conference on Computer Vision and Pattern Recognition (CVPR) (2020)
2. Dong, Y., Liao, F., Pang, T., Su, H., Zhu, J., Hu, X., Li, J.: Boosting adversarial attacks with momentum. In: Proceedings of the IEEE Conference on Computer Vision and Pattern Recognition, pp. 9185–9193 (2018)
3. Goodfellow, I.J., Shlens, J., Szegedy, C.: Explaining and harnessing adversarial examples. Comput. Sci. (2014)

4. Guo, C., Rana, M., Cisse, M., Van Der Maaten, L.: Countering adversarial images using input transformations. arXiv preprint arXiv:1711.00117 (2017)
5. He, K., Zhang, X., Ren, S., Sun, J.: Deep residual learning for image recognition. In: Proceedings of the IEEE Conference on Computer Vision and Pattern Recognition, pp. 770–778 (2016)
6. Keskar, N.S., Socher, R.: Improving generalization performance by switching from Adam to SGD. arXiv preprint arXiv:1712.07628 (2017)
7. Kingma, D., Ba, J.: Adam: a method for stochastic optimization. Comput. Sci. (2014)
8. Kurakin, A., Goodfellow, I.J., Bengio, S.: Adversarial examples in the physical world. In: Artificial Intelligence Safety and Security, pp. 99–112. Chapman and Hall/CRC (2018)
9. Liao, F., Liang, M., Dong, Y., Pang, T., Hu, X., Zhu, J.: Defense against adversarial attacks using high-level representation guided denoiser. In: Proceedings of the IEEE Conference on Computer Vision and Pattern Recognition, pp. 1778–1787 (2018)
10. Lin, J., Song, C., He, K., Wang, L., Hopcroft, J.E.: Nesterov accelerated gradient and scale invariance for adversarial attacks. arXiv preprint arXiv:1908.06281 (2019)
11. Liu, Y., Chen, X., Liu, C., Song, D.: Delving into transferable adversarial examples and black-box attacks. arXiv preprint arXiv:1611.02770 (2016)
12. Liu, Z., et al.: Feature distillation: DNN-oriented JPEG compression against adversarial examples. In: 2019 IEEE/CVF Conference on Computer Vision and Pattern Recognition (CVPR), pp. 860–868. IEEE (2019)
13. Nesterov, Y.: A method for unconstrained convex minimization problem with the rate of convergence o $(1/k\hat{~}2)$. In: Doklady an USSR, vol. 269, pp. 543–547 (1983)
14. Polyak, B.T.: Some methods of speeding up the convergence of iteration methods. USSR Comput. Math. Math. Phys. **4**(5), 1–17 (1964)
15. Russakovsky, O., Deng, J., Su, H., Krause, J., Satheesh, S., Ma, S., Huang, Z., Karpathy, A., Khosla, A., Bernstein, M., et al.: Imagenet large scale visual recognition challenge. Int. J. Comput. Vision **115**(3), 211–252 (2015). https://doi.org/10.1007/s11263-015-0816-y
16. Szegedy, C., Vanhoucke, V., Ioffe, S., Shlens, J., Wojna, Z.: Rethinking the inception architecture for computer vision, pp. 2818–2826. IEEE (2016)
17. Szegedy, C., Ioffe, S., Vanhoucke, V., Alemi, A.A.: Inception-v4, inception-resnet and the impact of residual connections on learning. In: Thirty-first AAAI Conference on Artificial Intelligence (2017)
18. Szegedy, C., et al.: Intriguing properties of neural networks. In: ICLR (2014)
19. Tramèr, F., Kurakin, A., Papernot, N., Goodfellow, I., Boneh, D., McDaniel, P.: Ensemble adversarial training: attacks and defenses. arXiv preprint arXiv:1705.07204 (2017)
20. Wilson, A.C., Roelofs, R., Stern, M., Srebro, N., Recht, B.: The marginal value of adaptive gradient methods in machine learning. Adv. Neural Inf. Process. Syst. **30** (2017)
21. Xie, C., Tan, M., Gong, B., Wang, J., Yuille, A.L., Le, Q.V.: Adversarial examples improve image recognition. In: Proceedings of the IEEE/CVF Conference on Computer Vision and Pattern Recognition, pp. 819–828 (2020)
22. Xie, C., Wang, J., Zhang, Z., Ren, Z., Yuille, A.: Mitigating adversarial effects through randomization. arXiv preprint arXiv:1711.01991 (2017)

23. Xie, C., Zhang, Z., Zhou, Y., Bai, S., Wang, J., Ren, Z., Yuille, A.L.: Improving transferability of adversarial examples with input diversity. In: Proceedings of the IEEE/CVF Conference on Computer Vision and Pattern Recognition, pp. 2730–2739 (2019)
24. Xu, W., Evans, D., Qi, Y.: Feature squeezing: detecting adversarial examples in deep neural networks. arXiv preprint arXiv:1704.01155 (2017)
25. Yin, H., Zhang, H., Wang, J., Dou, R.: Boosting adversarial attacks on neural networks with better optimizer. Secur. Commun. Netw. **2021**, 1–9 (2021)

# Perceiver Hopfield Pooling for Dynamic Multi-modal and Multi-instance Fusion

Dominik Rößle[1,2]([✉]), Daniel Cremers[2], and Torsten Schön[1]

[1] Technische Hochschule Ingolstadt, Esplanade 10, 85049 Ingolstadt, Germany
{dominik.roessle,torsten.schoen}@thi.de
[2] Technische Universität München, Boltzmannstr. 3, 85748 Garching, Germany
cremers@tum.de

**Abstract.** Deep network architectures are usually based on domain-specific assumptions and are specialized to the modalities under consideration. This conceptual behavior also applies to multimodal networks, leading to modality-specific subnetworks. In this paper, we introduce a novel dynamic multi-modal and multi-instance (MM-MI) network based on Perceiver and Hopfield pooling which can learn intrinsic data fusion. We further introduce a novel composite dataset for evaluating MM-MI problems. We successfully show that our proposed architecture outperforms the late fusion baseline in all multi-modal setups by more than 40% accuracy on noisy data. Our simple, generally applicable, yet efficient architecture is a novel generalized approach for data fusion with high potential for future applications.

**Keywords:** Perceiver · Hopfield pooling · Attention · Data fusion · Multi-modal · Multi-instance

## 1 Introduction

Modern autonomous systems are equipped with various sensors for environment perception to ensure safe operation. For example, self-driving cars often use multiple RGB cameras, LiDAR and radar systems to perceive information at different scales and distances [24]. Extracting and combining information from diverse sources requires sensor data fusion before or after processing [22]. For perception tasks, Deep Learning has become state of the art in many applications and offers a third option for fusion based on the feature level of the neural networks [7]. Although Deep Learning based sensor fusion has proven successful in many applications, it suffers from three major problems: First, architectural decisions for processing multi-modal inputs are highly influenced and targeted by the modality used, leading to good results in the considered domain, but very specific architectures and thus limited flexibility. A specialized network architecture for object detection in images can often not be applied directly to 3D data generated by LiDAR sensors nor to time series data of audio signals. Second, the sensor fusion level must be determined and optimized for each problem individually. Based on the involved modalities and the number of their instances, early

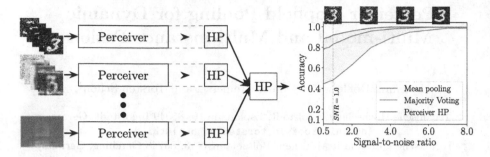

**Fig. 1.** Our novel Perceiver Hopfield pooling architecture enables intrinsic data fusion for dynamic multi-modal and multi-instance (MM-MI) data using a simple, generally applicable, yet efficient architecture. Modalities and their instances are processed by Perceiver blocks, and the resulting features are fused using Hopfield pooling, which increases accuracy by up to 40% on challenging noisy data.

or deep fusion has to be developed and tuned individually for each application, while late fusion suffers from learning joint sensor information [19]. Third, the sensor setup for fusion architectures is static, requiring significant updates of the network architecture when adding or removing modalities or instances. While many autonomous systems are equipped with a static sensor set, the interconnection between the systems themselves and their environment leads to highly dynamic availabilities of.different sensors during operation. A car passing a crossroad could utilize sensors from the infrastructure and from other nearby vehicles, using the latest communication standards like 5G (Fig. 1).

We propose an adaptive network architecture that can solve all of these problems, using a Perceiver [10] architecture which can process different sensor modalities and modern Hopfield pooling [20] to dynamically fuse a varying number of inputs across modalities and instances without relying on modality-specific architectural elements. Our contributions are summarized as follows:

1. We combine Perceivers of diverse modalities using Hopfield pooling, which can individually prioritize inputs to build a dynamically fused feature vector.
2. We demonstrate that our proposed architecture can handle dynamically changing multi-modal and multi-instance (MM-MI) data during training as well as at inference time using a novel MM-MI dataset composed of MNIST [13], SVHN [18], and AudioMNIST [1].
3. We compare our approach to majority voting and demonstrate that we outperform the baseline, especially when increasing noise on the data. Code is available at: https://github.com/cvims/perceiver_hp.

## 2   Related Work

Sensor fusion is a promising approach in the presence of multiple modalities and multiple instances per modality to increase the prediction results in a wide range of applications [7,9,14,15]. However, the fusion technique as well as the fusion architecture decision depends on the considered modalities [3,10,11]. This creates a change in the overall architecture when adding or removing new modalities or when the modality itself changes.

Processing data using a modality-independent concept is possible through the Transformer attention of Vaswani et al. [21]. However, this approach has the disadvantage that the self-attention module depends quadratically on the modality input size and therefore requires a high computational cost for large inputs. Therefore, Dosovitskiy et al. [6] as well as Carion et al. [2] project their inputs to smaller representations using modality-specific architectural elements before processing them with the attention mechanism. Strong modality independence in the processing of uni and multi-modal inputs was recently presented by the Perceiver architecture of Jaegle et al. [10] and achieved comparable results to modality-specific networks, e.g. on ImageNet [5] and video + audio fusion [8]. The Perceiver handles the quadratic complexity of self-attention by introducing a cross-attention module and decoupling input size and network depth. In our approach, we exploit the elimination of a conception of individual modality-dependent architectures by the Perceiver and design a fusion network that allows the integration of any modality.

The fusion method of multi-modal data is based on the problem statement and considered modalities [19]. Three fusion techniques are generally considered for deep learning architectures: Early-, Deep- and Late-Fusion. Early Fusion cannot be used in our case because we consider a varying number of modalities and instances. Late Fusion represents the fusion of the prediction results from different modalities and provides a simple multi-modal solution, especially for highly heterogeneous modalities, while suffering from learning joint sensor information. Deep Fusion models concatenate feature representations in one or more intermediate stages of a multi-modal network. A sophisticated deep fusion operation for individually weighting modalities according to the expressiveness of their features is Attention Fusion. Chumachenko et al. [4] consider multi-modal inputs (video + audio) and use attention fusion to learn representations where each modality attends to every other modality, which results in a high computational cost when fusing a large modality set. A multi-modal fusion transformer was introduced by Nagrani et al. [17] where patches of modalities can exchange information via attention bottlenecks. The bottleneck tokens are updated so that the first modality shares important features and the second modality uses the extracted features of the first modality and extends the tokens with its features, and so on. Therefore, for the consideration of a dynamic number of modalities, it is not possible to specify a predefined order for updating the attention bottlenecks, nor is it possible to ensure that the modalities considered at the beginning contain valuable information at all and focus on the features that important in all following modalities. Hang et al. [9] use an attention-based instance aggregation for multi-instance processing to assign individual weights to the considered instances. Subsequently, these weights are used to create a summary vector that contains more information from highly representative instances. The mentioned multi-modal and MM-MI applications use different feature extractors for the modalities and thus differ from our idea of a universal, modality-independent and easily extensible fusion network. Considering a dynamic number of modalities and instances, we also need pooling mechanisms that accept and aggregate dynamic amounts of inputs. Besides the pooling methods such as mean or max pooling [14,15,23], we are inspired by the calculation of individual weights by attention fusion [9]. Hopfield pooling [20] provides an attention pooling procedure of arbitrarily many sequences and is related to the Transformer self-attention [21]. Our approach can benefit from Hopfield pooling not only because of the individual weighting of feature representations but also because of the flexibility in processing a variable number of modalities and instances.

In contrast to previous approaches, we present a fully modality-independent and attention-based fusion network for highly dynamic MM-MI applications.

## 3    Perceiver Hopfield Pooling

Our network architecture builds upon two major components: **Perceiver** [10] and **Hopfield pooling** [20] and thus fully related to the Transformer Attention of Vaswani et al. [21]. It is designed to provide processing of a dynamic number of instances per modality as well as a fusion of multiple modalities and can even handle varying numbers during training and inference time. An overview of the architectural concepts is given in Fig. 2 and described in the following sections.

### 3.1    Processing Instances and Modalities

We use a Perceiver followed by a single Hopfield pooling layer for feature extraction of instances per modality. Each modality $m \in \{m_1, m_2, \ldots, m_M\}$ where $M$ is the number of modalities has an individual Perceiver $P_m$ that sequentially processes instances $i_m \in \{i_1, i_2, \ldots, i_{I_m}\}$, where $I_m$ is the number of instances of $m$. The representation of $i_m$ is $B_m \times C_m$, with $B_m$ as index dimension (e.g. for image data $B_m = $ width $\times$ height) and $C_m$ as the channel dimension of $m$. The Perceiver $P_m$ projects each $i_m$ onto a representation $N_m \times D_m$, with $N_m$ as latent index dimension and $D_m$ as latent projection dimension of $m$, with $N_m \ll B_m$ [10]. We average each instance representation $i_m$ in this process analogously to Jaegle et al. [10] and produce a summary instance vector $D_m$.

After processing all $i_m$, we stack $I_m \times D_m$ feature vectors and pool them to a summary feature sequence $S_m$ using a Hopfield pooling layer $HP_m$, where the size of $S_m$ is a hyperparameter across all considered modalities. Thus, each instance $i_m$ processed by the Perceiver $P_m$ can be individually weighted and dynamically set into a summary instance pooling sequence $S_m$. Note that the Perceiver parameters $N_m$ and $D_m$ can be defined individually for each modality $m$. Therefore, the depth of the modality-internal Hopfield pooling layer $HP_m$ depends on the input dimension $D_m$ but outputs an equally sized pooling sequence $S_m$ across all modalities $m$. Contrary to our approach, Jaegle et al.

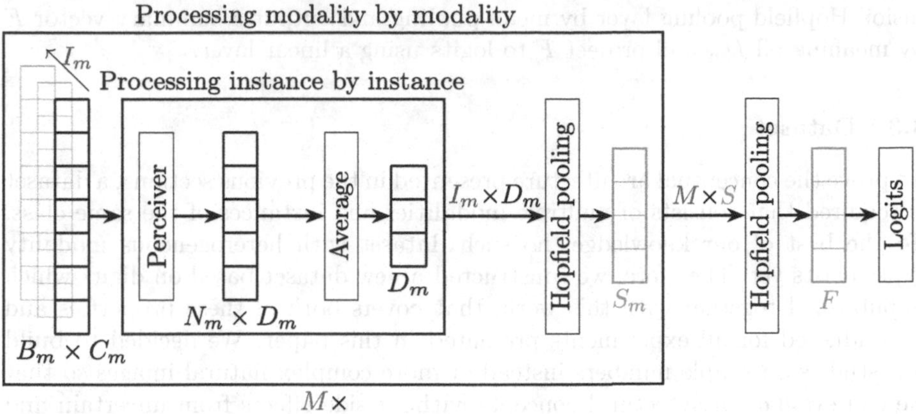

**Fig. 2.** When processing modalities $m \in \{m_1, m_2, \ldots, m_M\}$ with $M$ as the number of modalities, all instances of a modality $I_m$ are processed sequentially by modality-assigned Perceivers and Hopfield pooling layers. An additional Hopfield pooling layer is then used for cross-modality information fusion.

[10] use early fusion by combining modalities at the input level while considering one instance per modality. We decided for two reasons against early fusion because it would limit the ability to process dynamic numbers of modalities and instances due to the input layer size. First, the input layer size is static and has a maximum input limit which breaks the dynamic data amount property. Second, a small number of available modalities and instances leads to a strong representation of missing values in the input layer, making feature learning and generation difficult.

After extracting feature representations of all individual modalities, the resulting equally sized pooling sequences $S_m$ are stacked $(M \times S)$ and processed by a modality-fusion Hopfield pooling layer. Thus, the network learns the contributions of each modality sequence $S_m$ and projects them onto a summary modality pooling sequence $F$. We chose Hopfield pooling to learn the contributions of individual modalities, which is especially important once a modality delivers uncertain information. We study and verify this robustness in Sect. 4. At last, we use a linear layer to project $F$ to the output vector with the size of the number of target classes. Our architecture thus follows straight and easy principles, allowing adding modalities and a dynamic instance amount per modality.

## 3.2 Mean Pooling

We create a second approach by replacing the Hopfield pooling layers with standard mean pooling. To replace the modality-internal Hopfield pooling layer $HP_m$, we use mean pooling over the instance dimension $I_m$ of feature vectors $I_m \times D_m$ of modality $m$ resulting in a summary vector $D_m$. We project $D_m$ using a linear layer to the same output size as $HP_m$. We also replace the modality-fusion Hopfield pooling layer by mean pooling and output a summary vector $F$ by meaning all $D_m$ and project $F$ to logits using a linear layer.

### 3.3  Dataset

To prove the conceptual architecture presented in the previous sections, a dataset is required that consists of multiple modalities and instances of the same class. To the best of our knowledge, no such dataset with heterogeneous modality types exists yet. Therefore, we constructed a new dataset based on digits which is published together with this work, that covers both of these properties and is conducted for all experiments presented in this paper. We decided to build our studies on simple numbers instead of more complex natural images so that we can evaluate architectural concepts without side effects from uncertain and more difficult data distributions. The generated dataset consists of two image datasets (MNIST [13] and cropped and centred SVHN [18]) as well as one audio dataset (AudioMNIST [1]). All datasets represent ten classes by the numbers from 0 to 9. We downsample data from AudioMNIST from 48 kHz to 8 kHz but do not preprocess data from MNIST and SVHN.

We follow the predefined training and test splits for MNIST and SVHN, resulting in 60k train data and 10k test data for MNIST and ≈73k train data and ≈26k test data for SVHN. For AudioMNIST, we divide the data into 80% training data (24k) and 20% test data (6k). We split the training splits into 80% training data and 20% validation data. We sample MM-MI bags so that a sample represents an MM-MI bag where all instances of all modalities have the same class label, and each modality composes a dynamic number of instances. Thus, MM-MI bags can differ in their number of instance representations. The instances of an MM-MI bag are randomly sampled from the data split under consideration. The overall label of each bag is the same as the label of all containing instances.

## 4  Experiments

Our approach aims to extract information by dynamically prioritizing modalities to maximize the prediction result. Thus, the goal is to classify an MM-MI bag, as described in Sect. 3.3 with its corresponding label, even if some of the modalities or instances are absent or deliver corrupted or uncertain information.

### 4.1  Implementation Details

We follow the authors' implementation details for creating the individual Perceivers for each modality and adapt the input sizes and network depths according to the used dataset modalities [10]. We do not use data augmentation as we explicitly study the influence of noise on the prediction stability later on in more detail. The attention mechanism itself has the property of permutation invariance and cannot extract relations of temporal or spatial information, contrary to convolutional networks [12]. However, temporal and spatial information is valuable for the considered modalities in our experimental setup. Therefore, we follow the approach of [10,21] and use Fourier feature position encodings. We generate position encodings with 16 bands for each instance of each modality.

We use 25k and 5k MM-MI bags for training and validation, respectively. We always use five randomly sampled instances per modality in the training bags. We use the cross-entropy loss function for the classification task, set the batch size to 32, train for 50 epochs, and use an initial learning rate of $1e^{-4}$ with a decay factor of 10 at epochs $28, 34$ and 38. We normalize all modalities to the range from $-1$ to 1 and convert the $1 \times 8192$ raw AudioMNIST samples into $64 \times 128$-d vectors before passing them to the corresponding Perceiver.

## 4.2   Analysis of the Modality Weights

We can calculate attention weights for sequences by using Hopfield pooling, as shown in Fig. 3. Furthermore, we introduce a modality dropout concept to allow the network to reasonable predict even with a fluctuating number of available modalities and set the dropout equally to 0.5 (50%) for all modalities. If a modality is affected by the dropout mechanism, all instances are excluded and not traversed to the associated network.

We found that both a static instance amount and modality dropouts are essential to tweak the weights of all modality-associated Perceivers to avoid intrinsic preferences for individual (simple) modalities. A dynamic number of instances or the absence of modality dropouts resulted in only using the simplest modality (MNIST) for the predictions, as the Hopfield pooling attention weights for all other modalities tended toward 0 and had no effect on pooling and the final feature vector.

## 4.3   Baseline

We aim to prove that our approach can successfully extract information across various modalities and instances leading to an intrinsic data fusion. To show that our model can deliver state of the art results, we compare it to a standard data fusion method. For dynamic processing of modalities and instances, early fusion is not suitable, as mentioned in Sect. 3.1, so we use late fusion as a baseline. Late fusion runs classification networks on single instances of each modality independently. We apply Majority Voting to decide on a class for the whole training bag. For the baseline network, we project the outputs of the individual Perceiver models to logits using a linear layer with the input size of the latent projection dimension $D_m$ of the modality-assigned Perceiver $P_m$. This results in 96.4% (MNIST), 96.3% (SVHN) and 98.3% (AudioMNIST) of the number of trainable parameters of the models compared to our Hopfield pooling approach. The individual models predict instance by instance for each modality and decide on a final prediction based on the majority.

We use the same Perceiver architecture and configurations for the baseline as for our approaches and train all models from scratch using the same data splits. Our mean pooling approach, as proposed in Sect. 3.2 contains 99.3% (MNIST),

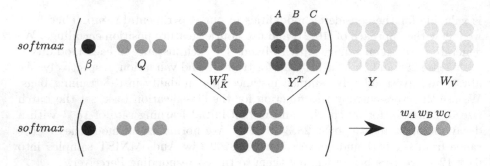

**Fig. 3.** Attention (association) weights calculated by Hopfield pooling. Matrices $W$ are projection matrices, $\beta$ is a scaling factor, $Q$ is the query pattern (static but learnable) and $Y$ are the processed features of the considered modalities. (adapted from [20])

98.4% (SVHN) and 98.9% (AudioMNIST) of the number of trainable parameters of the models compared to our Hopfield pooling approach.

### 4.4    Results and Analysis

For the baseline, we assume to get highly accurate results as especially the images from MNIST dataset are easy to classify. Nevertheless, classifying SVHN as well as AudioMNIST is more challenging. Majority voting yields better results compared to our approaches when considering only one modality and one instance ($I = 1$) as the strength of intrinsic data fusion in our architecture does not yet apply. In that scenario we get for majority voting, Perceiver Hopfield pooling and Perceiver mean pooling $(98.90\%, 86.18\%, 84.35\%)$ for MNIST, $(86.53\%, 73.40\%, 72.04\%)$ for SVHN and $(81.55\%, 71.48\%, 71.84\%)$ for AudioM-NIST, respectively. Considering the same setup where $I \geq 2$, the accuracies of our Hopfield pooling and mean pooling approaches are close to or even surpass those of majority voting. However, both pooling architectures outperform majority voting when considering more than one modality, as shown in Table 1.

**Table 1.** Accuracies of modality combinations of the baseline and our approaches with **noise-free** instances. Variable $I$ represents the number of instances per modality.

|  | Majority voting | | | Mean pooling | | | Hopfield pooling | | |
|---|---|---|---|---|---|---|---|---|---|
|  | $I = 1$ | $I = 2$ | $I = 3$ | $I = 1$ | $I = 2$ | $I = 3$ | $I = 1$ | $I = 2$ | $I = 3$ |
| MNIST + AudioMNIST | 89.68 | 97.67 | 99.18 | 92.87 | **99.22** | **99.78** | 94.87 | 98.76 | 99.72 |
| MNIST + SVHN | 92.70 | 98.01 | 99.34 | 92.73 | **99.10** | 99.80 | 93.92 | 99.09 | **99.84** |
| SVHN + AudioMNIST | 84.29 | 92.54 | 95.61 | **86.91** | **96.27** | 98.57 | 85.86 | 96.05 | **98.91** |
| All 3 modalities | 96.98 | 98.63 | 99.76 | 96.71 | 99.64 | **99.96** | **97.43** | **99.74** | 99.93 |

## 4.5  Adaptability

Our proposed architecture promises to learn an intrinsic data fusion based on a dynamic number of modalities and instances. In the previous section, we have successfully shown that our model keeps its promise under easy conditions. It is left to analyse the performance under more difficult circumstances where our approach can consistently outperform the baseline. To do so, we artificially add uncertainty to the data bags by applying two different noise methods *Additive White Gaussian Noise* (AWGN) and *Random Noise* (RN) to the test data.

**AWGN** We define the severity of AWGN by the signal-to-noise ratio (SNR) expressed in dB. Noise is sampled over a normal distribution $\mathcal{N}(0, \sigma)$ with mean $= 0$ and standard deviation

$$\sigma = \sqrt{\frac{\frac{1}{N}\sum_{n=0}^{N-1}|x_i|^2}{10^{\frac{SNR}{10}}}} \qquad (1)$$

where $N$ is the length of input $x$. The sampled noise is added to the input $x$ and clipped to the initial limits of $x$, respectively.

**RN** Puts random values at arbitrary positions where the intensity of this procedure depends on a percentage value. The random values cannot exceed the initial value limits of the input data.

Examples of both noise methods under different configurations are illustrated and compared in Fig. 4. Note that the applied method for AWGN adds a kind of background noise whereas RN adds strong information losses to the inputs.

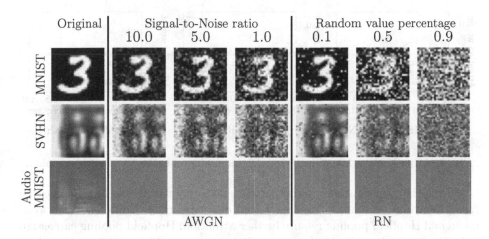

**Fig. 4.** Example data under the different influence of added noise. The first row shows an example from MNIST, the second row from SVHN and the last row from MNISTAudio, all sharing class three.

For all following experiments, we use all modalities with an instance count per modality of 1. Results with added noise are given in Fig. 5. It is noticeable that our approach consistently outperforms mean pooling and the baseline. Especially for higher noise intensities, the benefits of our architecture to fusing information from diverse sources come to light. Applying AWGN with an SNR of 1.0 (vertical line in Fig. 5 a), the Perceivers combined with Hopfield pooling (Perceiver HP) reach an accuracy of 91.2% compared to mean pooling 82.9% and majority voting 48.0%. For RN, e.g. applying 50% RN to the inputs, our approach yields 61.9% compared to mean pooling 52.1% and majority voting 25.0%.

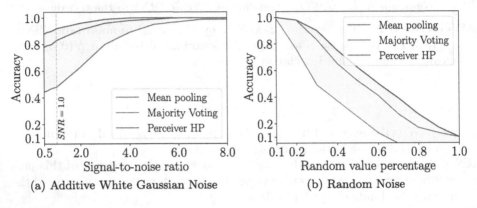

(a) Additive White Gaussian Noise            (b) Random Noise

**Fig. 5.** Accuracies for our approaches with Hopfield pooling and mean pooling and the majority voting baseline in the presence of noisy inputs of different intensity levels.

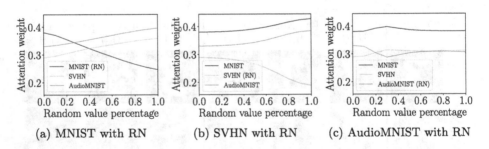

(a) MNIST with RN        (b) SVHN with RN        (c) AudioMNIST with RN

**Fig. 6.** Attention weights adjustment with increasing noise (RN) on each modality.

While the gain in accuracy compared to majority voting can be explained by fusing information of all modalities within our network, the differences between mean and Hopfield pooling require further attention. Hopfield pooling can assign individual weights to inputs for its pooling operation. We can thus analyze how Hopfield pooling adjusts its attention to the output feature vectors of the modalities while adding noise to the modalities. Figure 6 shows the average attention weightings for the considered modalities when constantly adding different RN levels per modality. Once all instances are noise-free, attention to the MNIST modality is the highest. Note that we performed the network training on noise-free data only. One can easily see that attention consistently decreases for noisy modalities, and thus more attention is directed to the noise-free modalities. This attention behavior is particularly noticeable when considering noisy MNIST inputs, as shown in Fig. 6 (a), where Hopfield pooling dynamically reduces the attention weight from 0.38 (noise-free) to 0.25 (full RN). The same applies to noisy SVHN, whereas the adjustments for noisy AudioMNIST are not as distinctive as the other two.

## 5    Conclusion

We have introduced a novel, fully attention-based architecture based on Perceiver [10] and Hopfield pooling [20] which is capable of extracting and fusing information from a dynamic number of instances over different modalities. Our architecture clearly outperforms a majority voting based late fusion baseline in all conducted experiments and is especially beneficial when adding uncertainty to the input data. To perform these experiments, we present a new composite dataset that includes MNIST, SVHN, and AudioMNIST datasets for training and evaluation, from which we sample MM-MI bags that contain a dynamic number of instances per modality. We have successfully shown that our approach can prioritize the considered modalities depending on their representative value. Prioritization helped reduce the impacts of weak feature representations, such as noisy modality instances, to ensure high accuracies.

Although we demonstrated that Hopfield pooling is more stable than mean pooling under noise conditions, its impact on the overall network performance compared to mean pooling needs further investigation. While the architectural concept has been proven to work, it is left to future work to evaluate it on more challenging datasets such as ImageNet [5] or COCO [16]. We assume that the greatest benefit of our approach is with information that is no longer available in single instances but has to be combined over multiple instances of different modalities. Future work may consider scenarios where each modality contains only a piece of the information needed for the final prediction, such as in autonomous driving, where each camera or 3D sensor of the vehicle perceives only specific directions.

## References

1. Becker, S., Ackermann, M., Lapuschkin, S., Müller, K.R., Samek, W.: Interpreting and explaining deep neural networks for classification of audio signals. arXiv preprint arXiv:1807.03418 (2018)
2. Carion, N., Massa, F., Synnaeve, G., Usunier, N., Kirillov, A., Zagoruyko, S.: End-to-end object detection with transformers. In: Vedaldi, A., Bischof, H., Brox, T., Frahm, J.-M. (eds.) ECCV 2020. LNCS, vol. 12346, pp. 213–229. Springer, Cham (2020). https://doi.org/10.1007/978-3-030-58452-8_13
3. Chen, S., Jin, Q.: Multi-modal conditional attention fusion for dimensional emotion prediction. arXiv preprint arXiv:1709.02251 (2017)
4. Chumachenko, K., Iosifidis, A., Gabbouj, M.: Self-attention fusion for audiovisual emotion recognition with incomplete data. arXiv preprint arXiv:2201.11095 (2022)

5. Deng, J., Dong, W., Socher, R., Li, L.J., Li, K., Fei-Fei, L.: ImageNet: a large-scale hierarchical image database. In: 2009 IEEE Conference on Computer Vision and Pattern Recognition (2009)

6. Dosovitskiy, A., et al.: An image is worth 16x16 words: transformers for image recognition at scale. In: ICLR (2021)

7. Fung, M.L., Chen, M.Z.Q., Chen, Y.H.: Sensor fusion: a review of methods and applications. In: 29th Chinese Control And Decision Conference (CCDC) (2017)

8. Gemmeke, J.F., et al.: Audio set: an ontology and human-labeled dataset for audio events. In: 2017 IEEE International Conference on Acoustics, Speech and Signal Processing (ICASSP) (2017)

9. Hang, C., Wang, W., Zhan, D.C.: Multi-modal multi-instance multi-label learning with graph convolutional network. In: International Joint Conference on Neural Networks (IJCNN) (2021)

10. Jaegle, A., Gimeno, F., Brock, A., Vinyals, O., Zisserman, A., Carreira, J.: Perceiver: general perception with iterative attention. In: International Conference on Machine Learning. PMLR (2021)

11. Kaiser, L., et al.: One model to learn them all. arXiv preprint arXiv:1706.05137 (2017)

12. LeCun, Y., Bottou, L., Bengio, Y., Haffner, P.: Gradient-based learning applied to document recognition. Proc. IEEE **86**(11), 2278–2324 (1998)

13. LeCun, Y.: The MNIST database of handwritten digits (1998). http://yann.lecun.com/exdb/mnist/

14. Li, H., et al.: Multi-modal multi-instance learning using weakly correlated histopathological images and tabular clinical information. In: International Conference on Medical Image Computing and Computer-Assisted Intervention (2021)

15. Li, X., et al.: Multi-modal multi-instance learning for retinal disease recognition. arXiv preprint arXiv:2109.12307 (2021)

16. Lin, T.-Y., et al.: Microsoft COCO: common objects in context. In: Fleet, D., Pajdla, T., Schiele, B., Tuytelaars, T. (eds.) ECCV 2014. LNCS, vol. 8693, pp. 740–755. Springer, Cham (2014). https://doi.org/10.1007/978-3-319-10602-1_48

17. Nagrani, A., Yang, S., Arnab, A., Jansen, A., Schmid, C., Sun, C.: Attention bottlenecks for multimodal fusion. arXiv preprint arXiv:2107.00135 (2021)

18. Netzer, Y., Wang, T., Coates, A., Bissacco, A., Wu, B., Ng, A.Y.: Reading digits in natural images with unsupervised feature learning. In: NIPS Workshop on Deep Learning and Unsupervised Feature Learning 2011 (2011)

19. Ramachandram, D., Taylor, G.W.: Deep multimodal learning: a survey on recent advances and trends. IEEE Signal Process. Mag. **34**(6), 96–108 (2017)

20. Ramsauer, H., et al.: Hopfield networks is all you need. arXiv preprint arXiv:2008.02217 (2020)

21. Vaswani, A., et al.: Attention is all you need. In: Advances in Neural Information Processing Systems (2017)

22. Wang, Z., Wu, Y., Niu, Q.: Multi-sensor fusion in automated driving: a survey. IEEE Access **8**, 2847–2868 (2019)

23. Yang, Y., Wu, Y.F., Zhan, D.C., Liu, Z.B., Jiang, Y.: Complex object classification: a multi-modal multi-instance multi-label deep network with optimal transport. In: Proceedings of the 24th ACM SIGKDD International Conference on Knowledge Discovery and Data Mining (2018)

24. Yurtsever, E., Lambert, J., Carballo, A., Takeda, K.: A survey of autonomous driving: common practices and emerging technologies. IEEE Access **8**, 58443–58469 (2020)

# PlAA: Pixel-level Adversarial Attack on Attention for Deep Neural Network

Huailin Liu and Jing Liu[✉]

College of Computer Science, Inner Mongolia University, Hohhot, China
32009005@mail.imu.edu.cn, liujing@imu.edu.cn

**Abstract.** Deep Neural Networks (DNNs) have demonstrated excellent performance in many fields. However, existing studies have shown that deep neural networks are very susceptible to well-designed adversarial samples. Adversarial samples cause the system to make incorrect classifications or predictions and may lead to security risks in the real world. Many adversarial attacks methods for making adversarial samples have been proposed. However, the excessive perturbation of most attack methods causes adversarial perturbations to be visible in human vision. In this paper, we proposed pixel-level adversarial attack on attention, named PlAA, which aims to attack a very few pixels in the attention area of DNNs to generate adversarial samples to achieve a high attack success rate and better hide adversarial disturbance. The experimental results show that in the single-pixel attack scenario, our PlAA attack method has an improvement up to 34.16% in the attack success rate compared with the existing one-pixel attack methods. In the multi-pixel attack scenario, compared with the existing attack on attention (AoA) methods, PlAA can better hide the adversarial disturbance while ensuring the same high attack success rate.

**Keywords:** Adversarial attack · Attention mechanism · Pixel-level attack

## 1 Introduction

Deep neural networks play an indispensable role in image recognition, natural language processing, speech processing and other significant application fields. Especially, DNN-based methods have outperformed traditional image processing techniques and even better than human in the domain of image recognition [1]. However, current studies have shown that DNNs are very susceptible to adversarial samples [2]. The adversarial samples are so similar to the clean ones that they are almost indistinguishable in human vision, but adversarial samples are able to cheat the DNNs to produce incorrect predictions in high confidence [3]. Due to the vulnerability of DNN to adversarial attacks, it may be affected by adversarial attacks in practical applications and produce undesirable consequences. For example, adversarial attacks can defraud autonomous driving

© The Author(s), under exclusive license to Springer Nature Switzerland AG 2022
E. Pimenidis et al. (Eds.): ICANN 2022, LNCS 13529, pp. 611–623, 2022.
https://doi.org/10.1007/978-3-031-15919-0_51

systems, facial recognition systems, etc. Many adversarial attacks methods for making adversarial samples have been proposed, such as FGSM [4], C&W [5], PGD [6], One-pixel Attack [7], AoA [8] and so on. Hence, the development of efficient adversarial attack algorithms is of great significance for testing the security of DNNs, developing adversarial defense algorithms, and finally improving the robustness of DNN models.

The basic idea of creating adversarial samples is adding as little perturbation as possible to make DNNs classify the samples incorrectly. The previous work was to add perturbation to the whole picture, but there is no guarantee that the perturbation is completely invisible. Su et al. propose one-pixel attack [7], which modifies one pixel in image to attack image classification model. They utilize the differential evolution algorithm to select the best pixel and optimal perturbation imposed on the pixel. On the ImageNet dataset, only modifying one pixel on BVLC can be to achieve 16.04% success rate. This method effectively hides adversarial perturbation. Specifically, it limits the number of pixels that can be modified to measure the minimum perturbation, instead of restricting $L_2$ or $L_\infty$ distance between the original sample and the adversarial sample. Most of one-pixel attack methods have an unsatisfactory attack success rate on large-size images. The possible reason is that the search for sensitive pixels is not accurate, but more iterations may increase the success rate of the attack.

In this paper, we propose pixel-level attack on attention for neural networks, named PlAA, which utilizes the attention mechanism to search for sensitive pixels more accurately and quickly. For large-size images in ImageNet, modifying a very few pixels can achieve a high attack success rate, and look almost the same as the original images in human perception. The contributions of our PlAA method are given as below:

1. We proposed pixel-level attack on attention method. This method can disturb a very few pixels in a short time to achieve adversarial attacks. The adversarial samples looks no different from the original samples in human vision.
2. Regarding the extremely limited one-pixel attack scenario, the attack success rate of our method on VGG19 is 50.2%, VGG16 is 43.5%, and InceptionV3 is 56.8%. PlAA significantly improves the attack success rate compared with the existing one-pixel attack.
3. On the ImageNet dataset, the success rate of non-targeted attacks on common deep neural networks can be over 90%, and the average number of disturbed pixels is 1.863. Moreover, compared with the existing AoA methods, PlAA achieves a similar attack success rate and effectively hides adversarial disturbances.

## 2   Related Work

Adversarial attacks and defenses against deep neural networks have attracted widespread attention, and the robustness issues of DNNs have become a critical topic [9]. Currently, attack methods are mainly divided into white-box attacks and black-box attacks. White-box attacks mean that the attacker can access the internal structure and parameters of the model. However, black-box attacks mean that the attacker has no knowledge of the internal information of the model. Recent studies have proposed pixel-level attack methods, which can generate adversarial samples by perturbing a very few pixels. Experimental results show that pixel-level attack is promising adversarial attack method.

As for white-box attacks, Szegedy et al. [10] first revealed the existence of adversarial samples and proposed to find the minimum disturbance by using the box-constrained L-BFGS method, adding the perturbation to the image to generate adversarial samples. Goodfellow et al. [4] proposed fast gradient sign method, named FGSM, which is a method to quickly and effectively generate adversarial samples by increasing the loss function of network training. Kurakin et al. [11] proposed basic & least-likely-class iterative method, named BIM, which is an iterative method of adding small perturbation to the sample to generate adversarial samples. Carlini et al. [5] introduced three adversarial attacks by restricting $l_2$, $l_\infty$ and $l_0$ norms respectively, named C&W, these attacks make perturbations difficult to be perceived by human vision and it is shown that defensive distillation almost completely fails against.

Currently, there are two main types of black-box attacks, based on query [12] or transferability [13]. C Guo et al. [14] proposed a simple and effective black-box adversarial attack, which is to randomly select a vector perturbation image from a set of predefined orthogonal bases. This method achieves a success rate similar to that of the most advanced black-box attack algorithm, but the number of black-box queries is unprecedentedly low. S Chen et al. [8] proposed universal adversarial attack on attention which is to change the attention heat map of the sample, and utilize similar attention heat maps between different DNNs to improve the transferability of adversarial samples.

As for pixel-level adversarial attacks, Su et al. proposed one-pixel attack [7] which is can achieve a good attack success rate by only modifying one pixel of the sample in the CIFAR-10 dataset. They utilize differential evolution algorithm to select sensitive pixel and optimal perturbation. However, their method has an attack success rate of only 16.04% on large-size images in the ImageNet dataset. Papernot et al. [15,16] proposed JSMA attack method which perturbs images with the limitation of $l_0$ distance. They utilize the Jacobian matrix to construct an adversarial saliency map to select the pixels that have the greatest impact on the target class, and increase or decrease the pixel value to generate adversarial samples. It is worth mentioning that JSMA performs poorly on large-size images, so it cannot be used on the ImageNet dataset. N Narodytska et al. [17] proposed LocSearchAdv attack algorithm which is based on the idea of greedy local search (an iterative search process). In each iteration, the local neighborhood of the pixel that reduces the maximum confidence of the sample is used to perturb the image to generate adversarial samples.

In a word, most pixel-level adversarial attack methods are only suitable for small-size images, while the attack success rate on large-size images is unsatisfactory. In this paper, we aim to propose a pixel-level adversarial attack on attention method, which can achieve a high attack success rate on large-size images.

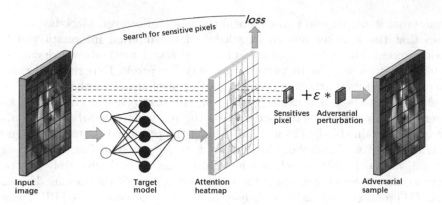

**Fig. 1.** The workflow of PlAA method

## 3  Methodology

Inspired by the attention mechanism, we found that the pixels in the area concerned by DNN have a greater influence on image classification. Therefore, we propose a pixel-level attack on attention for deep neural networks. As shown in Fig. 1, PlAA has two major related parts. First, the loss function is constructed through the attention heat map of the sample. Second, the adversarial sample is generated by perturbing a single pixel iteratively.

### 3.1  Loss Function Construction

The construction of the loss function is inspired by the suppression loss function of AoA. Suppressing the magnitude of attention heat maps for the correct class of input sample, the DNN's attention degree on the other classes will eventually exceed the correct one, causing the DNN to make incorrect classifications. Therefore, the proposed method needs to utilize the SGLRP to calculate the attention heat map, which is good at distinguishing the attention for the target class from the others, and it can effectively calculate the gradient of the attention heat map on the input sample. Let $x_{ori}$ be a benign sample, $y_{ori}$ is the corresponding class label of the sample, $h(x_{ori}, y_{ori})$ represents the attention heat map of the input sample, $h(x_{ori}, y_{ori})$ is a tensor with the same dimension as the input sample $x_{ori}$. The loss function $Loss$ of the proposed method is designed by combining the logarithmic suppression loss function $L_{log}$ and the cross-entropy loss function $L_c$. The logarithmic suppression loss function $L_{log}$ is shown in Eq. 1.

$$L_{log}(x) = log(\|h(x, y_{ori})\|_1) \tag{1}$$

The logarithmic suppression loss function can suppress the DNN's attention to the correct class, causing the DNN to make incorrect classifications. The cross-entropy loss function $L_c$ is shown in Eq. 2.

$$L_c(x) = -\sum_{i=1}^{n} p(x^i) log(q(x^i)) \tag{2}$$

$p(x^i)$ represents the true probability distribution of sample $x$ on class $i$, $q(x^i)$ represents the predicted probability distribution of sample $x$ on class $i$. The cross-entropy loss function can improve the confidence of adversarial samples, causing the DNN to classify adversarial samples as incorrect classes with high confidence. At last, the loss function $Loss(x)$ is shown in Eq. 3.

$$Loss(x) = L_{log}(x) + \alpha L_c(p, q) \tag{3}$$

where $\alpha$ is a trade-off between logarithmic suppression loss function $L_{log}$ and cross-entropy loss function $L_c$. In this paper, $\alpha = 1000$ such that the two items have similar variance for different inputs. The combination of the two items makes the selection of the pixels to be disturbed more accurately, and the DNN will judge the adversarial samples as the wrong class with high confidence.

## 3.2   Adversarial Sample Generation

Basically, the adversarial samples are generated by iterative disturbing a single pixel in the process of minimizing the loss function $Loss(x)$. First, we calculate the derivative of the loss function $Loss$ to the original sample to obtain the gradient matrix $M$. Then according to the gradient matrix $M$, the pixel with the largest gradient value is disturbed. This pixel has a significant influence on suppressing the magnitude of attention heat map. Specifically, we set $x^0_{adv} = x_{ori}$, the gradient matrix can be described as Eq. 4.

$$M = \frac{\partial Loss(x^k_{adv})}{\partial x^k_{adv}} \tag{4}$$

The gradient matrix $M$ is a tensor with the dimension consistent to input $x_{ori}$, each element in $M$ represents the gradient value of the pixel at that position to suppress the attention heat map. Our method is to select the pixel with the largest gradient value to perturbation to generate adversarial samples. Since a pixel is formed by superimposing the brightness values of the RGB three channels, the gradient matrix needs to be summed in rows, that is to sum the gradient values of the RGB three channels, obtain the gradient matrix $M_{sum}$ of pixel, and then select the pixel with the largest gradient value to perturbation to generate adversarial samples. The disturbance procedure could be generally described as the following Eq. (5) to (7).

$$M_{sum} = sum(M, reduction\_indices = 2) \tag{5}$$

$$index = argmax(M_{sum}) \tag{6}$$

$$x^{k+1}_{adv} = x^k_{adv}[index] - \epsilon * M[index] \tag{7}$$

The parameter $reduction\_indices = 2$ refers to the summation of the gradient matrix $M$ by rows. Parameter $\epsilon$ represents the intensity of the perturbation to the pixel. Since only one pixel is perturbed in each iteration, the distortion caused to the overall picture is very small, so no necessary to limit the perturbation

**Algorithm.** *PlAA  Attack*

---

**Input:**

    Loss, $Loss(x)$; Iterator threshold, $\theta$;

    Origin sample, $(x_{ori}, y_{ori})$;

    Attack step length, $\epsilon$;

**Output:**

    Adversarial sample, $x_{adv}$;

 1: set $x_{adv}^0 = x_{ori}$

 2: set $k = 0$

 3: **while** $k < \theta$ **do**

 4:    $M = \frac{\partial Loss(x_{adv}^k)}{\partial x_{adv}^k}$;

 5:    $M_{sum} = sum(M, reduction\_indices = 2)$;

 6:    $index = argmax(M_{sum})$;

 7:    $x_{adv}^{k+1} = x_{adv}^k[index[0:2]] - \epsilon * M[index[0:2]]$;

 8:    $k = k + 1$

 9:    **if** $F(x_{adv}^k) \neq y_{ori}$ **then**

10:       *break*;

11:    **end if**

12: **end while**

13: return $x_{adv}^k$

---

intensity to the pixel. Let $F$ be the DNN image classifier, that can classify the sample $x_{ori}$ into the correct class $y_{ori}$. The procedure of attack is summarized in Algorithm *PlAA Attack*.

When the number of disturbed pixels is greater than $\theta$ or the sample prediction class changes, the iteration stops. The method in this paper improves the search efficiency of sensitive pixels and further verifies the vulnerability of deep neural networks.

The existing AoA mainly takes the overall constraint of cumulative modification strength as the constraint condition, and then disturbs all pixels of the image to generate adversarial samples. Different from the existing attention attack method (AoA), PlAA aims to modify a very few pixels in a short period of time, but does not limit the intensity of the modification to generate adversarial samples, and the overall distortion caused to the image is very small. We illustrate one example in Fig. 2. It can be seen that the adversarial samples generated by the AoA have obvious wavy patterns. The adversarial sample generated by our method looks no different from the original one. For Fig. 2, we adopt lpips [18] as the perceptual metric, which measures how similar the two images are in a way that coincides with human judgment. The value of lpips denotes the perceptual loss, the lower, the better.

We summarize the results in Fig. 3, the perceptual loss of adversarial samples generated by AoA is 0.185, while the perceptual loss of the adversarial samples generated by PlAA is 0.0004. This indicates that the adversarial samples generated by PlAA are more perceptually aligned with clean images compared with AoA. As shown in Fig. 3a, the adversarial examples generated by AoA have sig-

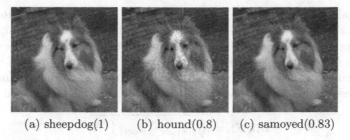

(a) sheepdog(1)        (b) hound(0.8)        (c) samoyed(0.83)

**Fig. 2.** The figure (a) is original sample. The figure (b) is the generated adversarial sample by AoA and the figure (c) is generated by our method. The predicted class label and their corresponding confidence are given below.

nificant differences in the contours of objects compared to the original sample. However, as shown in Fig. 3b, the adversarial samples generated by PlAA only have very few pixels changed. Therefore, the lpips perception metric further proves that PlAA effectively hides adversarial perturbations.

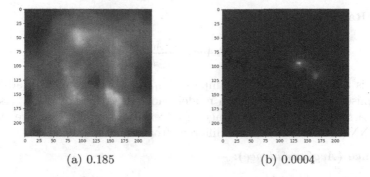

(a) 0.185                                      (b) 0.0004

**Fig. 3.** The figure (a) is the perceptual distance space map between the original sample and the adversarial sample generated by AoA. The figure (b) is the perceptual distance space map between the original sample and the adversarial sample generated by PlAA. The perceptual loss is given below.

## 4 Experiments and Results Analysis

In this section, we discuss the experimental setup and the evaluation indicators of the experimental results. Then based on the two experimental scenarios, we show and analyze the experimental results of the PlAA attack on the deep neural networks. Since our method only modifies a very few pixels of the original image, it provides adversarial samples that can effectively hide adversarial perturbation.

### 4.1 Experiments Setup

The experiments are conducted on the ImageNet [19] validation set. For attack and verify, several well-trained models in Keras Applications [20] are used, including VGG19 and VGG16, InceptionV3, ResNet50 and ResNet152, DenseNet121 and DenseNet201. Keras preprocessing function, central cropping, and resizing (to 224) are used. The experiments are implemented in TensorFlow, Keras with NVIDIA Tesla V100-SXM2 GPU.

The change of the adversarial sample $x_{adv}$ compared to the original sample $x_{ori}$ is measured by the Root Mean Square Error ($RMSE$), as shown in Eq. 8.

$$RMSE = \sqrt{\|x_{adv} - x_{ori}\|_2^2 / N}. \tag{8}$$

In the experiments, one thousand images are randomly selected from the ImageNet validation set and the samples incorrectly predicted by the victim model are skipped. The number of iterations is $\theta = 20$ and perturbation intensity for each pixel is $\epsilon = 155$.

## 4.2   Evaluation Indicators

In order to evaluate the effectiveness of our method, we have designed several evaluation indicators as follows.

**Success Rate ($AttackAcc$):**

$$AttackAcc = \frac{N_{Att\_suc}}{N} \tag{9}$$

where $N$ is the total number of samples, $N_{Att\_suc}$ is the number of adversarial samples misclassified by the victim model under the attack of PlAA. As shown in Eq. 9, $AttackAcc$ is the percentage of adversarial samples that are classified by the DNN into any target class different from the original class.

**Confidence ($AvgConfidence$):**

$$AvgConfidence = \frac{\sum_{i=1}^{N_{Att\_suc}} P_i}{N_{Att\_suc}} \tag{10}$$

where $N_{Att\_suc}$ is the number of adversarial samples misclassified by the victim model, $P_i$ is the confidence when sample $i$ is misclassified. As shown in Eq. 10, $AvgConfidence$ is the average confidence of the DNN classifying adversarial samples.

**Time Complexity ($AvgTime$):**

$$AvgTime = \frac{\sum_{i=1}^{N_{Att\_suc}} T_i}{N_{Att\_suc}} \tag{11}$$

where $N_{Att\_suc}$ is the number of adversarial samples misclassified by the victim model, $T_i$ is the time spent in generating adversarial sample $i$. As shown in Eq. 11, $AvgTime$ is the average time for PlAA to generate adversarial examples.

**Number of Disturbed Pixels ($AvgPixels$):**

$$AvgPixels = \frac{\sum_{i=1}^{N_{Att\_suc}} Pix_i}{N_{Att\_suc}} \tag{12}$$

where $N_{Att\_suc}$ is the number of adversarial samples misclassified by the victim model, $Pix_i$ is the number of pixels disturbed when generating adversarial sample $i$. As shown in Eq. 12, $AvgPixels$ is the average number of disturbed pixels for generating adversarial samples.

## 4.3   Results Analysis of Adversarial Attack

In this section, we performed single-pixel attack and multi-pixel attack scenario to show advantages of our method.

**Single-Pixel Attack Scenario.** The results of single-pixel attack on seven commonly used DNNs are shown in Table 2.

**Success Rate (AttackAcc) and Confidence (AvgConfidence):** It can be seen from Table 2 that the success rate of single-pixel attack is affected by the depth of the DNN. For example, for shallow neural networks, the attack success rate for VGG19 (layer 19) is 50.2%, VGG16 (layer 16) is 43.5%, and InceptionV3 (layer 47) is 56.8%. However, the success rate of single-pixel attack on deep neural networks is relatively unsatisfactory. For example, the success rate of ResNet50 (50 layers) is 16.7%, ResNet152 (152 layers) is 23.3%, DenseNet121 (121 layers) is 13.1% and DenseNet201 (201 layers) is 15.2%. On average, VGG19, VGG16, ResNet50, ResNet152, DenseNet121 and DenseNet201 classify the adversarial samples generated by the single-pixel attack into the incorrect class with high confidence. The average confidence of InceptionV3 is only 20.833, which may be related to its generalization performance and network structure. On the ImageNet dataset, the success rates of single-pixel attack on seven different networks show the effectiveness of PlAA on different network structures.

**Time Complexity (AvgTime) and AvgRMSE:** As shown in Table 2, single-pixel attack on shallow networks only take a few seconds on average. For example, the average time complexity of VGG19 is 2.4s, VGG16 is 1.5s, InceptionV3 is 6.0s and Resnet50 is 6.4s. However, the deep neural networks require more time cost. The average time complexity of the deep neural networks ResNet152 is 14.8s, DenseNet121 is 35.7s and DenseNet201 is 48.1s. On all networks, the root mean square error of the adversarial samples generated by the single-pixel attack and the original sample is about 15.

In the limited single-pixel attack scenario, the PlAA method can generate adversarial samples by modifying only one pixel in a short period of time. It has achieved a very impressive attack success rate on seven deep neural networks, and the DNN can classify the adversarial samples into the incorrect class with high confidence. From the comparison of Table 1 and Table 2, it can be seen that our method improves attack success rate and average confidence on large-size images compared with the existing one-pixel attack methods [7], and fully verifies the effectiveness and efficiency of the PlAA.

**Table 1.** Results of the 'One-pixel attack [7]'

| Indicators | Victim |
|---|---|
| | BVLC |
| AttackAcc | 16.04% |
| AvgConfidence | 22.91 |
| AvgRMSE | - |
| AvgTime (sec) | - |

**Table 2.** Single-pixel attack results of PlAA on different networks

| Indicators | Victim | | | | | | | |
|---|---|---|---|---|---|---|---|---|
| | BVLC | VGG19 | VGG16 | IncV3 | RN50 | RN152 | DN121 | DN201 |
| AttackAcc | 43.2% | 50.2% | 43.5% | 56.8% | 16.7% | 23.3% | 13.1% | 15.2% |
| AvgConfidence | 69.552 | 68.987 | 69.650 | 20.833 | 45.710 | 55.465 | 45.461 | 49.898 |
| AvgRMSE | 16.437 | 16.534 | 16.310 | 12.433 | 18.434 | 18.839 | 18.116 | 18.977 |
| AvgTime (sec) | 1.4 | 2.4 | 1.5 | 6.0 | 6.4 | 14.8 | 35.7 | 48.1 |

**Multi-pixel Attack Scenario.** The results of multi-pixel attack on seven commonly used deep neural networks are shown in Table 3.

**Success Rate (AttackAcc) and Confidence (AvgConfidence):** In the multi-pixel attack scenario, only DenseNet121 has an attack success rate of 75.1%, and the other networks have an attack success rate of more than 90%. Similar to the situation in the single-pixel attack scenario, InceptionV3 has the lowest average confidence, only 21.054, and the average confidence of the other networks is above 40.

**Time Complexity (AvgTime) and AvgRMSE:** The time complexity is similar to the single-pixel attack scenario. The shallow neural networks only take a few seconds to attack. For example, VGG19 is 3.3s, VGG16 is 3.5s, while the deep networks take tens of seconds, for example, DenseNet121 is 43.7s, DenseNet201 is 59.5s. InceptionV3 has the lowest AvgRMSE of 14.446, while DenseNet121 has the highest AvgRMSE of 36.724.

**Number of Disturbed Pixels (AvgPixels):** It can be seen from Table 3 that all networks can generate adversarial samples by modifying no more than 10 pixels on average. Specifically, the shallow neural network VGG19 is 2.415,

**Table 3.** Results of multi-pixel attacks on different networks

| Indicators | Victim | | | | | | |
|---|---|---|---|---|---|---|---|
| | VGG19 | VGG16 | IncV3 | RN50 | RN152 | DN121 | DN201 |
| AoA [8] | 99.99% | 99.85% | 89.84% | 93.94% | 86.78% | 96.14% | 93.44% |
| AttackAcc | 98.8% | 98.5% | 99.9% | 97.6% | 94.6% | 75.1% | 91.0% |
| AvgPixels | 2.415 | 2.561 | 1.918 | 5.231 | 4.448 | 7.347 | 5.692 |
| AvgConfidence | 69.940 | 70.260 | 21.054 | 43.977 | 58.185 | 54.876 | 44.870 |
| AvgRMSE | 20.143 | 20.158 | 14.446 | 28.970 | 30.744 | 36.724 | 28.888 |
| AvgTime (sec) | 3.3 | 3.5 | 8.2 | 18.9 | 32.1 | 43.7 | 59.5 |

VGG16 is 2.561, InceptionV3 is 1.918, all only need to modify about 2 pixels on average to generate adversarial samples, while the deep neural network only needs to modify 5 to 7 pixels on average to generate adversarial samples.

## 5 Conclusion

How to effectively hide the adversarial disturbance of the adversarial sample and ensure a high attack success rate is very important for an efficient adversarial attack algorithm. In this paper, we proposed a pixel-level attack on attention method, named PlAA, which attacks the attention of deep neural networks. By perturbing a very few pixels in the attention area of DNNs, the adversarial disturbance can be better hidden while ensuring high attack success rate. We conducted experiments on seven neural networks and two attack scenarios. Experimental results show that in single-pixel attack scenario, the attack success rate of shallow neural networks is about 50%, and that of deep neural networks is about 15%. All networks can generate adversarial samples in a short period of time and classify them into the incorrect category with high confidence. Compared with the existing one-pixel attack methods, our method achieves a higher success rate of single-pixel attacks on large-size images. In the multi-pixel attack scenario, all neural networks have achieved a high attack success rate. Moreover, the adversarial samples are generated in a short time when 2–7 pixels are modified on average. And compared with the existing AoA methods, PlAA can better hide the adversarial disturbance while ensuring the success rate of the attack. In addition, PlAA can be used as a tool to measure the robustness of the system on tiny disturbance samples, and we will explore the transferability of adversarial samples generated by PlAA in the future work.

**Acknowledgements.** This work was supported in part by the Inner Mongolia Science and Technology Plan Project (No. 2020GG0187), the Self-funding Project of Engineering Research Center of Ecological Big Data, Ministry of Education, and Inner Mongolia Engineering Laboratory for Cloud Computing and Service Software, Inner Mongolia Key Laboratory of Social Computing and Data Processing.

# References

1. Taigman, Y., Yang, M., Ranzato, M., Wolf, L.: DeepFace: closing the gap to human-level performance in face verification. In: Proceedings of the IEEE Conference on Computer Vision and Pattern Recognition (CVPR), pp. 1701–1708 (2014)
2. Akhtar, N., Mian, A.: Threat of adversarial attacks on deep learning in computer vision: a survey. IEEE Access 6(1), 14410–14430 (2018)
3. Moosavi-Dezfooli, S.M., Yang, M., Wolf, L.: DeepFool: a simple and accurate method to fool deep neural networks. In: Proceedings of the IEEE Conference on Computer Vision and Pattern Recognition (CVPR), pp. 2574–2582 (2016)
4. Goodfellow, I., Shlens, J., Szegedy, C.: Explaining and harnessing adversarial examples. In: Proceedings of the IEEE Conference on International Conference on Pattern Recognition (ICPR), pp. 676–681 (2015)
5. Carlini, N., Wagner, D.: Towards evaluating the robustness of neural networks. In: Proceedings of the IEEE Symposium on Security and Privacy (SP), pp. 39–57 (2017)
6. Madry, A., Makelov, A., Schmidt, L., Tsipras, D., Vladu, A.: Towards deep learning models resistant to adversarial attacks. In: Proceedings of the International Conference on Learning Representations (ICLR), pp. 35–53 (2018)
7. Su, J., Vargas, D.V., Kouichi, S.: One pixel attack for fooling deep neural networks. IEEE Trans. Evol. Comput. 23(5), 828–841 (2019)
8. Chen, S., He, Z., Sun, C., Huang, X.: Universal adversarial attack on attention and the resulting dataset DAmageNet. IEEE Trans. Pattern Anal. Mach. Intell. 44, 2188–2197 (2020)
9. Barreno, M., Nelson, B., Joseph, A.D., Tygar, J.D.: The security of machine learning. Mach. Learn. 81(2), 121–148 (2010). https://doi.org/10.1007/s10994-010-5188-5
10. Szegedy, C., et al.: Intriguing properties of neural networks. In: Proceedings of the International Conference on Learning Representations (ICLR), pp. 1–9 (2014)
11. Kurakin, A., Goodfellow, I., Bengio, S.: Adversarial examples in the physical world. In: Proceedings of the International Conference on Learning Representations (ICLR), pp. 1–11 (2017)
12. Yan, Z., Guo, Y., Zhang, C.: Subspace attack: exploiting promising subspaces for query-efficient black-box attacks. In: Proceedings of the Advances in Neural Information Processing Systems, pp. 3820–3829 (2019)
13. Dong, Y., Pang, T., Zhu, J.: Evading defenses to transferable adversarial examples by translation-invariant attacks. In: Proceedings of the IEEE Conference on Computer Vision and Pattern Recognition (CVPR), pp. 4312–4321 (2019)
14. Guo, C., Gardner, J.R., You, Y., Wilson, A.G., Weinberger, K.Q.: Simple black-box adversarial attacks. In: Proceedings of the International Conference on Machine Learning (ICML), pp. 2484–2493 (2019)
15. Papernot, N., Mcdaniel, P., Jha, S., Fredrikson, M., Swami, A., Celik, Z.B.: The limitations of deep learning in adversarial settings. In: Proceedings of the IEEE European Symposium on Security and Privacy (EuroS&P), pp. 372–387 (2016)
16. Combey, T., Loison, A., Faucher, M., Hajri, H.: Probabilistic Jacobian-based saliency maps attacks. Mach. Learn. Knowl. Extract. 2(12), 558–578 (2020)
17. Narodytska, N., Kasiviswanathan, S.: Simple black-box adversarial attacks on deep neural networks. In: Proceedings of the IEEE Conference on Computer Vision and Pattern Recognition (CVPR), pp. 1310–1318 (2017)

18. Zhang, R., Isola, P., Efros, A.A., Wang, O.: The unreasonable effectiveness of deep features as a perceptual metric. In: Proceedings of the IEEE Conference on Computer Vision and Pattern Recognition (CVPR), pp. 586–595 (2018)
19. Jia, D., Wei, D., Socher, R., Li, L.J., Kai, L., Li, F.F.: ImageNet: a large-scale hierarchical image database. In: Proceedings of the IEEE Conference on Computer Vision and Pattern Recognition, pp. 248–255 (2009)
20. Chollet, F.: Keras: the Python deep learning library. In: Proceedings of the Astrophysics Source Code Library (ASCL), pp. 1806–1807 (2018)

# Robust Logo Detection Across Large Style Variations

Zhiyuan Zhao and Qingjie Liu[✉]

State Key Laboratory of Virtual Reality Technology and Systems,
Beihang University, Beijing, China
{zhaozhiyuan,qingjie.liu}@buaa.edu.cn

**Abstract.** Style variation of logo refers to changes in the logo's visual characteristics during the evolution of the logo, which is a common yet easily overlooked phenomenon. However, conventional logo detection methods suffer from severe performance degradation once the visual characteristics of the logo change, because they fail to establish a relation between different styles due to their lack-of-interaction learning procedure. In this paper, we attend to address this detection failure by learning a transferable and flexible cross-style relation under the meta-learning policy. Our proposed method contains one more sibling branch except for the vanilla Faster-RCNN pipeline, which creates a pair-wise comparing environment. Meanwhile, the classification head of the detector is remodeled into a matching module which meta-learns how to classify regions through pair-wise matching. This pair-wise matching mechanism gives matching module the ability to establish deep transferable relations across styles. Additionally, two logo detection datasets are proposed to support research on logo detection across style variations. Experiments revealed the superior performance of our proposed method.

**Keywords:** Logo detection · Style variations · Meta-learning · Cross-style relation

## 1 Introduction

Logo detection is an important task and has many applications such as brand exposure mining [1] and commodity logo retrieval [2]. Over the past few years, benefitting from deep neural networks (DNNs) based object detection methods, logo detection has gained remarkable progress. However, logo detection in the real world remains an open problem with many challenges.

This paper focuses on an interesting yet challenging problem that has not received attention from the community: detecting logos across evolution. A logo is imperative to a company. It is the signature of a company and a bridge between the company and the public. Meanwhile, a strong logo has to be adjusted to keep up with shifts and changes in the company. Therefore, the logo evolves with the development of the corporation. Design elements such as color, shape, and

E. Pimenidis et al. (Eds.): ICANN 2022, LNCS 13529, pp. 624–634, 2022.
https://doi.org/10.1007/978-3-031-15919-0_52

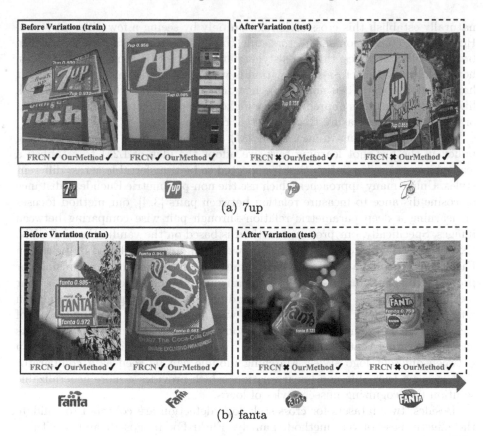

(a) 7up

(b) fanta

**Fig. 1.** An illustration of style variations of 7up (a) and fanta (b). Detection results of baseline Faster-RCNN (green) and our proposed method (red) are given. The solid box denotes logo before style variation, and the dashed box denotes logo after style variation. Checkmark (✔) denotes successful detection and cross (✘) denotes detection failure. We can see that (1) conventional detection method will fail quickly when style changes while our method will not. (2) there is a strong relation across these styles in the evolution of logo. (Color figure online)

typology (collectively called style variations for convenience) of a logo change over time, as illustrated in Fig. 1. However, as we can see, style variations bring great challenges to logo detectors and lead to performance degradation of many detection models. Current logo detectors may perform well under the same logo style while facing a significant challenge when the logo evolves.

Although the style of the logo has constantly been changing and updating, due to the principle of longevity in the area of logo designing, this change will not be so drastic that one cannot recognize it after logo changes. This results in a strong relation between different styles of the logo, as shown in Fig. 1. In fact, this cross-style relation is the key to recognizing unseen logo styles. For example, humans can easily recognize unseen logo styles because they can naturally establish this cross-style relation only by seeing a few different styles. However, in conventional detectors, due to the lack of interaction mechanism between different styles, this cross-style relation can not be learned well. Besides, how to leverage this cross-style relation is very challenging since logos are built hand-crafted and we can not foresee how logos evolve and what they will look like in the future. This unpredictability makes it impossible to learn a pre-defined or fixed metric to measure this cross-style relation.

Inspired by learning-to-measure (L2M) approaches under the meta-learning policy in the few-shot learning task, we adopt the idea of L2M to establish a learnable cross-style relation that is expected to be transferrable across different styles. Unlike many approaches which use the non-parametric Euclidean distance or cosine distance to measure relation between pairs [3,4], our method focuses on learning a deep parametric relation through pair-wise comparing between images. Specifically, our proposed method is based on the vanilla Faster-RCNN. Except from the Faster-RCNN pipeline, we design a weight-shared branch upon Faster-RCNN to create pair-wise matching. This new branch is responsible for providing information of each class. Meanwhile, the classification head of our method is remodeled into a matching module, in which categories of regions in query image are determined through pair-wise matching with the deep feature of each class. In this manner, the classification head in our proposed method works as a meta-learner that learns to establish a parametric and flexible deep relation between different logo styles. Matching module can be seen as a comparator that learns a learnable non-linear relation, which provides a more generalizable solution to recognizing unseen styles of logos.

Besides, two datasets for cross-style logo detection are collected to validate the effectiveness of our method, namely, Flickr-FoodLogos-10 and YouTube-TVLogos-10. Compared to other logo detection datasets, our proposed datasets with multiple styles for each logo are highly diverse in visual characteristics of the logo.

Our contribution is threefold. First, we reveal a challenge that exists in real-world logo detection under the style variation scenario, that is, cross-style logo detection. Besides, two logo detection datasets called Flickr-FoodLogos-10 and YouTube-TVLogos-10 are collected to facilitate the research in this field. Second, we propose a novel logo detection method which can locate and identify unseen styles of a logo accurately. Third, experiments on our proposed datasets and benchmark dataset FlickrLogos-32 are conducted to verify the superior performance of our proposed method on both cross-style logo detection and conventional logo detection tasks.

## 2   Related Work

### 2.1   Logo Detection

Traditional logo detection methods employ human-designed features such as SIFT [5,6], HOG [7], and other hand-crafted features [8–10] to represent logos. Classifiers such as SVM [7] are employed to recognize a logo. With the popularity of CNN-based object detectors, most logo detection methods are constructed based on state-of-the-art object detection frameworks like Faster-RCNN [11–14]. In recent years, application scenario of logo detection has been broadened. New logo detection scenarios such as universal logo detection [15] and open set logo retrieval [16] have been proposed. Notably, these logo detection methods may perform well on the conventional logo detection task while their performance under corss-style scenario is severely compromised. Meanwhile, there are several logo datasets built for logo detection, such as BelgaLogos [6] and FlickrLogos-32 [17]. However, existing datasets lack diversity in logo styles.

**Meta-learning.** Meta-learning represents one kind of learning system that learns a task-agnostic model on the level of tasks, which allows the model to adapt to unseen and novel tasks quickly [18,19]. Learn-to-Measure (L2M) is an important branch of meta-learning, which adopts the meta-learning policy to learn similarities between support and query samples, which might be a parameter-free distance metric (e.g., Euclidean distance, cosine distance) [3,4], or learnable metric [19]. Recent studies [20,21] propose meta-learning-over-RoI, which brings meta-learning into the few-shot object detection task. These works suggest that the information of possible objects and background can be separated in RCNN-based detectors thanks to its two-stage design. Because of this advantage, meta-learning on detection models is possible.

# 3   Approach

## 3.1   Problem Definition

The goal of cross-style logo detection is to locate and classify unseen styles of logos in an image only using limited styles of logos. Images of each class of logo are divided into two parts: **seen** styles and **unseen** styles. The seen styles of all classes are used in training and the unseen styles are used in testing. An example of seen/unseen split is illustrated in Fig. 1.

## 3.2   Network Overview

Our proposed method is built on top of the vanilla Faster-RCNN. Figure 2 shows the overall architecture of our proposed method. During training, images in mini-batch $B$ are fed into the Faster-RCNN backbone. Then RoI features are produced after RPN and RoIAlign. Except for the training mini-batch, a meta-batch $B_{meta}$ containing images of each class is constructed. For meta-batch, a weight-shared branch is proposed to generate class-specific features. Then class-specific features and RoI features are fused and fed into the classification head of the Faster-RCNN. Finally, the classification head is remodeled into a matching module which classifies RoI regions by pair-wise matching, working as a meta-learner $f(B, B_{meta}; \theta)$, instead of a conventional learner $f(B; \theta)$.

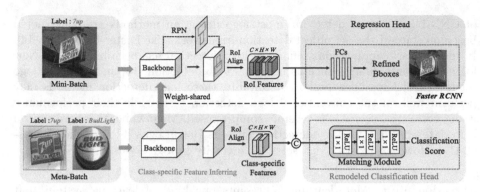

**Fig. 2.** Illustration of our proposed cross-style logo detection method. Our proposed method is built on Faster-RCNN. Faster-RCNN receives images (the figure represents the case where the mini-batch contains only one image) in the current mini-batch ($B$) and outputs RoI features of all regions. Besides, a weight-shared branch is proposed to infer class-specific features for each class in meta-batch ($B_{meta}$). The classification head of Faster-RCNN is remodeled into a matching module which classify RoIs through pair-wise matching. Pair-wise matching enables the matching module to learn a robust relation between different styles. In this manner, classification head of Faster-RCNN is remodeled into a meta-learner $f(B, B_{meta}; \theta)$ instead of $f(B; \theta)$.

### 3.3   Class-Specific Features Inferring

During training, images in mini-batch $B$ are processed by the Faster-RCNN backbone, and RoI features $r_i$ are output through RPN and RoIAlign. Except for this pipeline, we add one more branch onto Faster-RCNN, which handles meta-batch $B_{meta}$ and outputs deep features for each class, namely class-specific features. This additional branch disentangles information of each class and creates a comparing paradigm so that model can measure relation between different styles of logos.

Specifically, $B_{meta}$ is composed of $N$ images, where each image corresponds to one class. Formally, the backbone network, which is weight-shared with the backbone in Faster-RCNN, is utilized to extract features of images in $B_{meta}$. Then class-specific features $\{r_j^{meta}\}$ of ground truth objects in the image are inferred using RoIAlign, $j$ stands for the class label. Class-specific features output by this process contain information of each class of logos. After inferring class-specific features, class-specific features $\{r_j^{meta}\}$ are fed into the classification head for classifying RoI into each single class through pair-wise matching. Images of class $k$ in $B_{meta}$ are randomly sampled from the training set. The same class of logos in $B$ and $B_{meta}$ must be different in style in the training stage to encourage the model to learn a depth-wise transferrable relation between different styles.

### 3.4   Classification Head Remodeling

After class-specific features and RoI features are extracted, respectively, they are pair-wise combined and fed into the matching module which eventually produces a scalar in the range of 0 to 1 representing the similarity between $r_i$ and $r_j^{meta}$, called matching score. In this way, class-specific features are used to assist classifying RoIs and the classification head is remodeled into a meta-learner $f(B, B_{meta}; \theta)$ instead of $f(B; \theta)$. In this manner, the remodeled classification head is responsible for classifying RoI into a single class rather than outputting class probability. Formally, there is:

$$s_{i,j} = f(r_i, B_{meta}; \theta) = f(r_i, r_j^{meta}; \theta) = f(g([r_i, r_j^{meta}]); \theta) \qquad (1)$$

where $g$ denotes the matching module, [ ] indicates channel-wise concatenation and $\theta$ denotes the parameter of Faster-RCNN. Specifically, after all class-specific features $\{r_j^{meta}\}$ and all RoI features $\{r_i\}$ are fed into the matching module, they are fused by channel-wise concatenation in a pair-wise manner. Assuming there are $N$ classes and $M$ RoIs output by RPN and RoIAlign, this fusion process leads to $M \times N$ matching pairs $[r_i, r_j^{meta}]_{i,j}$. Regarding the design of the matching module, we consider that (1) the style variation of the logo mostly happens on the overall logo instead of some parts of the original logo, and (2) most logos have a hollow appearance and noise may misguide the matching. Thus, a simple but effective design is adopted for the matching module. Matching module is composed of two successive $1 \times 1$ convolution layers followed by a ReLU activation layer. Next, an average pooling layer is utilized to reduce the dimension of the feature maps. Finally, a fully-connected layer is employed to output the matching score $s_{i,j}$. Classification loss used in training is the binary cross-entropy loss. During testing, this RoI is considered a background if the highest matching score of all classes is lower than a threshold, which is experimentally set to 0.45.

## 4    Experiments

### 4.1    Datasets

Two datasets are proposed for cross-style logo detection: Flickr-FoodLogos-10 and YouTube-TVLogos-10. Flickr-FoodLogos-10 consists of images crawled from *Flickr.com*. It contains logos of 10 famous food brands. Youtube-TVLogos-10 consists of 10 popular media on YouTube. Each logo contains at least 3 styles. Except for conventional object detection annotations, an additional style label is provided to split data into training and testing set. Particularly, Youtube-TVLogos-10 and Flickr-FoodLogos-10 are sufficient for not only cross-style logo detection but also for the conventional logo detection task.

### 4.2    Experiment Setup

Our method is trained using stochastic gradient descent (SGD) with an initial learning rate of 0.01. All comparison methods are trained to achieve their best results. All methods adopt ResNet-50 pre-trained on ImageNet as the backbone network. Input images are resized to allow the shorter side to have a length of 800 pixels. Due to GPU memory limits, our method is tested using 2-way splits, which is the same for our method and all comparison methods. Training is conducted on 4 RTX2080Ti GPUs. The mean Average Precision (mAP) of VOC protocol is used as the main evaluation metric.

**Table 1.** Results of cross-style logo detection on Flickr-FoodLogos-10 and YouTube-TVLogos-10. "Flickr" denotes Flickr-FoodLogos-10 and "YouTube" represents YouTube-TVLogos-10.

| Type | Method | mAP | |
|---|---|---|---|
| | | Flickr | YouTube |
| Two-stage | Faster-RCNN [22] | 0.491 | 0.507 |
| | Libra-RCNN [23] | 0.517 | 0.537 |
| | Cascade-RCNN [24] | 0.437 | 0.425 |
| | Double-Head RCNN [25] | 0.512 | 0.455 |
| Single-stage | SSD300 [26] | 0.422 | 0.347 |
| | Yolov3 [27] | 0.344 | 0.357 |
| | Retinanet [28] | 0.449 | 0.488 |
| Anchor-free | FCOS [29] | 0.325 | 0.542 |
| | Reppoints [30] | 0.452 | 0.399 |
| Meta-learning | Meta-RCNN [20] | 0.509 | 0.561 |
| | Attention-RPN [21] | 0.432 | 0.576 |
| | **Our Method** | **0.548** | **0.621** |

## 4.3   Cross-Style Logo Detection

In this section, experiments are conducted on cross-style logo detection. Comparison methods include state-of-the-art object detection methods and two meta-learning-based object detection methods. Following the setup of cross-style logo detection, only two styles of logos are used in the training phase, and all other unseen styles are used in the test phase. The proposed Flickr-FoodLogos-10 and Youtube-TVLogos-10 are used for evaluation.

**Experiments on Flickr-FoodLogos-10.** As revealed in Table 1, our method significantly outperforms comparison methods with remarkable improvements. Our proposed method obtains 0.548 mAP, which is the best result. The second-best method is Libra-RCNN, which achieves 0.517 mAP, and our method is +3% higher. Compared with single-stage detectors, our method has an improvement of +10%. For base Faster-RCNN, our method surpasses it by about +5% mAP.

The performance of meta-learning-based detectors (Meta-RCNN and Attention-RPN) are also suboptimal. This is probably because it is not feasible to directly transplant the relation-learning module in a few-shot object detection method into a new scenario. For meta-RCNN, images in meta-batch are also resized to $224 \times 224$, which is quite a small size. This leads to insufficient knowledge for relation-learning, which makes it difficult for model to learn the relation between images. As for Attention-RPN, we notice that the complex relation module design leads to poor results. The reason may be that logos in images are mostly hollowed, and complex relation learning operations may bring much noise and fail to learn a robust cross-style relation.

**Fig. 3.** Visualization of detection results and class-activation-map (CAM) on two test styles of 7up, correspond respectively to our method and Faster-RCNN. From detection results (solid box), we can see that our method can rescue many unseen styles of the logo. Through framed part by dashed box, we can see that feature learned by our method have a much higher response for other unseen styles.

**Experiments on YouTube-TVLogos-10.** As indicated in Table 1, our method achieves the best performance: 0.621 mAP. The second-highest-ranking method is Libra-RCNN, which obtains 0.537 mAP and our method is about +9% higher. Compared with vanilla Faster-RCNN, our method presents an improvement of +12%. Besides, our method outperforms Meta-RCNN and Attention-RPN by about 6% and 4.5%, respectively, which is a significant performance gap. This further demonstrates the robust recognition ability of our proposed matching module. In conclusion, experimental results on two different types of logos (brand logo and TV logo) validate that our proposed method has an outstanding performance in recognizing unseen styles of logos.

**Visualization Results.** Detection results and class-activation-map (CAM) on learned feature maps of our method and Faster-RCNN are visualized for comparison to further explore the effectiveness of our proposed method (see Fig. 3). It can be observed that our method can rescue unseen styles of logo foregrounds that are treated as background in Faster-RCNN. Meanwhile, from CAM it can be obviously seen that feature learned by our method is much more sensitive to unseen styles. However, features learned by Faster-RCNN is less sensitive to unseen styles. This reveals that matching module can learn a strong relation between different styles under pair-wise matching paradigm, and this relation is transferrable across unseen styles.

### 4.4 Conventional Logo Detection

Our method is compared with general object detection methods and logo detection methods to verify the performance of our method on conventional logo detection task. Experiments are conducted on **FlickrLogos-32**. Experimental results are presented in Table 2. Our method achieves a new SOTA performance: 0.870 mAP. Compared to logo detection methods, our method surpasses the second best method by about 2%. Moreover, some of these logo detection methods use images of much higher resolution or synthetic images that can significantly boost logo detection performance [13], while our method is trained without these tricks.

**Table 2.** Results on FlickrLogos-32. "Logo Detectors" refers to logo detection methods. "Object Detectors" refers to general object detection methods.

| Type | Method | mAP |
|------|--------|-----|
| Logo detectors | Deep-Logo-AlexNet [31] | 0.735 |
|  | Deep-Logo-VGG16 [31] | 0.744 |
|  | Fast [12] | 0.746 |
|  | Fast-M [12] | 0.842 |
|  | Faster-L [12] | 0.812 |
|  | BD-FRCN-M [32] | 0.735 |
|  | ME-FRCN [1] | 0.786 |
|  | SCL [13] | 0.811 |
|  | MI [33] | 0.722 |
|  | LogoNet [14] | 0.820 |
| Object detectors | Retinanet [28] | 0.783 |
|  | FCOS [28] | 0.762 |
|  | Reppoints [28] | 0.818 |
|  | Cascade-RCNN [24] | 0.853 |
|  | Libra-RCNN [23] | 0.859 |
|  | Double-Head RCNN [25] | 0.863 |
|  | **Our Method** | **0.870** |

## 5 Conclusion

In this paper an unnoticed yet challenging task, namely cross-style logo detection, is elaborated. Two logo detection datasets are proposed to facilitate research on this task, that is, Flickr- FoodLogo-10 and YouTube-TVLogo-10. We believe that these two logo datasets will drive the development of logo detection. Besides, a novel logo detection method is designed for cross-style logo detection. This method can effectively detect unseen styles of logos using only a few limited styles. The experiments demonstrate the effectiveness of our method on both cross-style logo detection and conventional logo detection. However, cross-style logo detection needs further research and attention. Our future work mainly includes but is not limited to the accurate localization of unseen styles of logos and the improvement of the computational efficiency of our proposed method to meet the needs of practical use.

**Acknowledgements.** This work is supported by National Natural Science Foundation of China (Grant No. 62176017 and No. 41871283).

# References

1. Liao, Y., Lu, X., Zhang, C., et al.: Mutual enhancement for detection of multiple logos in sports videos. In: ICCV (2017)
2. Gandhi, S., Kokkula, S., Chaudhuri, A, et al.: Scalable detection of offensive and non-compliant content/logo in product images. In: WACV (2020)
3. Snell, J., Swersky, K., Zemel, R.: Prototypical networks for few-shot learning. In: NIPS (2017)
4. Vinyals, O., Blundell, C., Lillicrap, T., et al.: Matching networks for one shot learning. In: NIPS (2016)
5. Constantinopoulos, C., Meinhardt-Llopis, E., Liu, Y., et al.: A robust pipeline for logo detection. In: ICME (2011)
6. Joly, A., Buisson, O.: Logo retrieval with a contrario visual query expansion. In: ACM Multimedia (2009)
7. Li, K.W., Chen, S.Y., Su, S., et al.: Logo detection with extendibility and discrimination. In: MTA (2014). https://doi.org/10.1007/s11042-013-1449-1
8. Wang, J., Duan, L., Li, Z., et al.: A robust method for TV logo tracking in video streams. In: ICME (2006)
9. Gao, K., Lin, S., Zhang, Y., et al.: Logo detection based on spatial-spectral saliency and partial spatial context. In: ICME (2009)
10. Natarajan, P., Wu, Y., Saleem, S., et al.: Large-scale, real-time logo recognition in broadcast videos. In: ICME (2011)
11. Hoi, S.C., Wu, X., Liu, H., et al.: Logo-net: large-scale deep logo detection and brand recognition with deep region-based convolutional networks: arXiv (2015)
12. Bao, Y., Li, H., Fan, X., et al.: Region-based CNN for logo detection. In: ICIMCS (2016)
13. Su, H., Zhu, X., Gong, S.: Deep learning logo detection with data expansion by synthesising context. In: WACV (2017)
14. Jain, R.K., Watasue, T., Nakagawa, T., et al.: LogoNet: layer-aggregated attention centernet for logo detection. In: ICCE (2021)
15. Fehérvári, I., Appalaraju, S.: Scalable logo recognition using proxies. In: WACV (2019)
16. Tüzkö, A., Herrmann, C., Manger, D., et al.: Open set logo detection and retrieval: arXiv (2017)

17. Romberg, S., Pueyo, L.G., Lienhart, R., et al.: Scalable logo recognition in real-world images. In: ICMR (2017)
18. Ravi, S., Larochelle, H.: Optimization as a model for few-shot learning. In: ICLR (2017)
19. Sung, F., Yang, Y., Zhang, L., et al.: Learning to compare: relation network for few-shot learning. In: CVPR (2018)
20. Yan, X., Chen, Z., Xu, A., et al.: Meta r-cnn: towards general solver for instance-level low-shot learning. In ICCV (2019)
21. Fan, Q., Zhuo, W., Tang, C.K., et al.: Few-shot object detection with attention-RPN and multi-relation detector. In: CVPR (2020)
22. Ren, S., He, K., Girshick, R., et al.: Faster r-cnn: towards real-time object detection with region proposal networks. In: NIPS (2015)
23. Pang, J., Chen, K., Shi, J., et al.: Libra r-cnn: towards balanced learning for object detection. In: CVPR (2019)
24. Cai, Z., Vasconcelos, N.: Cascade r-cnn: delving into high quality object detection. In: CVPR (2018)
25. Wu, Y., Chen, Y., Yuan, L., et al.: Rethinking classification and localization for object detection. In: CVPR (2020)
26. Liu, W., Anguelov, D., Erhan, D., et al.: Ssd: single shot multibox detector. In: ECCV (2016). https://doi.org/10.1007/978-3-319-46448-0_2
27. Redmon, J., Farhadi, A.: Yolov3: an incremental improvement: arXiv (2018)
28. Lin, T.Y., Goyal, P., Girshick, R., et al.: Focal loss for dense object detection. In: ICCV (2017)
29. Tian, Z., Shen, C., Chen, H., et al.: Fcos: fully convolutional one-stage object detection. In: ICCV (2019)
30. Yang, Z., Liu, S., Hu, H., et al.: Reppoints: point set representation for object detection. In: ICCV (2019)
31. Iandola, F.N., Shen, A., Gao, P., et al.: Deeplogo: hitting logo recognition with the deep neural network hammer: arXiv (2015)
32. Oliveira, G., Frazão, X., Pimentel, A., et al.: Automatic graphic logo detection via fast region-based convolutional networks. In: IJCNN (2016)
33. Tang, P., Peng, Y.: Exploiting distinctive topological constraint of local feature matching for logo image recognition. Neurocomputing **236**, 113–122 (2017)

# Self-organization of a Dynamical Orthogonal Basis Acquiring Large Memory Capacity in Modular Reservoir Computing

Yuji Kawai[1]([✉]) [iD], Jihoon Park[1,2] [iD], Ichiro Tsuda[3] [iD],
and Minoru Asada[1,2,3,4] [iD]

[1] Symbiotic Intelligent Systems Research Center, Open and Transdisciplinary Research Initiatives, Osaka University, 1-1 Yamadaoka, Suita, Osaka 565-0871, Japan
{kawai,jihoon.park,asada}@otri.osaka-u.ac.jp
[2] Center for Information and Neural Networks, National Institute of Information and Communications Technology, 1-4 Yamadaoka, Suita, Osaka 565-0871, Japan
[3] Center for Mathematical Science and Artificial Intelligence, Chubu University Academy of Emerging Sciences, 1200 Matsumoto-cho, Kasugai, Aichi 487-8501, Japan
tsuda@isc.chubu.ac.jp
[4] International Professional University of Technology in Osaka, 3-3-1 Umeda, Kita-ku, Osaka 530-0001, Japan

**Abstract.** The ability of the brain to generate complex spatiotemporal patterns with a specific timing is essential for motor learning and time series prediction. An approach that tries to replicate this ability using the self-sustained neural activity of a randomly connected recurrent neural network (reservoir) meets the difficulty of orbital instability. We propose a novel system that learns an arbitrary time series as the linear sum (readout) of stable trajectories produced by numerous small network modules. Our experimental results show that the trajectories of the module outputs are orthogonal to each other, that is, the reservoir self-organizes an orthogonal basis. Furthermore, the system can learn the timing of extremely long intervals, say tens of seconds for a millisecond computation unit and the complex time series of the Lorenz system.

**Keywords:** Reservoir computing · Recurrent neural network · Orthogonal basis · Timing learning

## 1 Introduction

Generating an arbitrary time series is an essential ability required in various tasks that have been considered to be difficult to accomplish, such as timing learning and motor learning. In motor timing learning, a system is trained to emit an output after a specific interval from an onset signal. During this interval, no input is received. To realize such a function with a recurrent neural network, the neural activity induced by the onset input signal must be sustained within the network for at least the interval [1]. In addition, a set of time series of the neural activity should have sufficient representational capability to synthesize the desired time series; that is, they should create an orthogonal basis, whereby any trajectories can be represented or, at least, approximated.

We address this issue of time series generation in the framework of reservoir computing (RC) using random neural networks (RNNs) as reservoirs. In the standard RC, the recurrent weights of the reservoir are fixed, and only the weights of the linear sum (readout) of the unit outputs are trained using linear regression [2, 3]. Large recurrent weights put the reservoir into the high-gain regime, in that the units are spontaneously activated even without any external inputs. The self-sustained trajectories exhibit a chaotic nature, which may have great computational power because they are complex and differ from each other. However, they cannot be used for learning because they exhibit orbital instability in which slight differences in initial values or noise are magnified over time. By contrast, the trajectories in low-gain reservoirs decay to zero in the absence of an input.

Several methods have been proposed to inhibit chaos in reservoirs, such as providing output feedback to all units [4] and introducing a small-world topology into reservoirs [5]. Laje and Buonomano [6] proposed "innate training" as a model for learning motor timing and patterns, where each unit in a high-gain reservoir learns to output its own past noiseless trajectory. As a result, the reservoir generates self-sustained stable complex trajectories, which enables it to learn not only the timing of intervals of a few seconds, but also arbitrary complex time series of a few seconds. However, the computational cost of innate training is much greater than that of standard RC because it modulates the recurrent weights, and it is difficult to generate time series longer than several tens of seconds because the duration it can suppress the orbital instability is limited.

Therefore, instead of an approach that suppresses chaos, we take an approach that places the reservoir in an intermediate state between a stable equilibrium state and a chaotic state. An RNN has a parameter region in which the system exhibits limit cycles or tori, and it is known that such regions expand as the network size decreases [7, 8]. Hence, non-chaotic stable self-sustained trajectories can be obtained when the network size is small and the parameter is adequately set. However, such a small network makes the trajectories of the unit outputs similar to each other, which reduces the orthogonality between the trajectories. Therefore, a sufficiently large network size is chosen for the standard RC.

In this study, we propose a novel system in which many modules, that is, small size RNNs, are connected independently and in parallel to achieve both their orthogonality and stability. Through simulation, we evaluated the inner products between the trajectories of the module outputs to confirm orthogonality and the local Lyapunov exponents of the trajectories to confirm instability. Because the proposed modular reservoir creates a dynamical orthogonal basis, we refer to it as the reservoir of basal dynamics (reBASICS). We evaluated the performance of reBASICS in timing learning and verified that it can generate more complex time series, such as the Lorenz system.

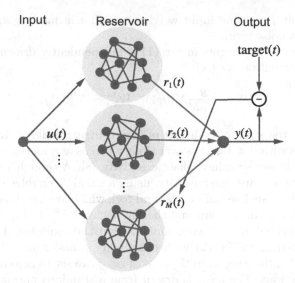

Input          Reservoir          Output

**Fig. 1.** Configuration of the proposed reservoir of basal dynamics (reBASICS). The reservoir layer consists of $M$ modules of RNNs. The system output $y(t)$ is computed as the linear sum of the module outputs $r_k(t)$ ($k = 1, 2, \ldots, M$) (red arrows), and the readout weights are sequentially modulated by the recursive least squares to minimize the error between $y(t)$ and a target signal, target$(t)$.

## 2   reBASICS

reBASICS consists of an input layer, output layer, and reservoir layer that is composed of $M$ RNN modules (Fig. 1). At time $t$, all units in the reservoir layer receive a signal $u(t)$ from the input layer and inputs from other units in the same module, and they update their states. The output signal of a unit $r_k(t)$ ($k = 1, 2, \ldots,$ or $M$) that is randomly chosen from each module is supposed to be the module output, and the outputs are combined as a system output $y(t)$ at a readout unit, shown as red arrows in Fig. 1. Ideally, the time series of the module outputs $\{r_1(t), r_2(t), \ldots, r_M(t)\}$ should be orthogonal to each other. The randomness of the weights in the modules is expected to contribute to the generation of diverse trajectories. Only the readout weights are trained to minimize the error between $y(t)$ and a target signal, target$(t)$, and the other parameters are fixed through learning.

The dynamics of the state $x_{k,i}(t)$ of unit $i$ ($i = 1, 2, \ldots, N$) in module $k$ are given as a rate model using tanh as the activation function:

$$\tau \frac{dx_{k,i}(t)}{dt} = -x_{k,i}(t) + \sum_{j=1}^{N} W_{k,ij}^{\text{Rec}} r_{k,j}(t) + W_{k,i}^{\text{In}} u(t) + I_{k,i}^{\text{noise}}(t), \qquad (1)$$

where $r_{k,i}(t) = \tanh(x_{k,i}(t))$, $\tau$ denotes the time constant, $N$ denotes the network size, that is, the number of units in a module, $W_{k,ij}^{\text{Rec}}$ and $W_{k,i}^{\text{In}}$ denote recurrent weights from unit $j$ to $i$ and input weights to unit $i$ in module $k$, respectively, and $I_{k,i}^{\text{noise}}(t)$ is a noise term.

Each element of the weights in Eq. (1) is independently drawn from a standard normal distribution $\mathcal{N}(0,1)$:

$$W_{k,ij}^{\text{Rec}} \sim \frac{g}{\sqrt{pN}} \mathcal{N}(0,1), \quad W_{k,i}^{\text{In}} \sim \mathcal{N}(0,1), \tag{2}$$

where $g$ denotes the scaling coefficient of the recurrent weights. In general, the activity of RNNs with $g < 1$ decays over time, whereas as $g$ increases beyond one, the RNNs exhibit self-sustained chaotic activity [8]. Although reBASICS sets $g > 1$ to generate self-sustained activity, using a small $N$ enables its modules to output stable orbits, such as limit cycles and tori, which are intermediate between convergence to a zero fixed point and chaotic behavior [7]. In Eq. (2), $p$ denotes the connection probability between units within the modules. Thus, $W_{k,ij}^{\text{Rec}}$ is determined according to Eq. (2) with probability $p$ and zero with probability $1 - p$. Additionally, the weights in the case of $i = j$ are set to zero to remove self-recurrent connections. The noise is drawn from a standard normal distribution with amplitude $I_0$: $I_{k,i}^{\text{noise}}(t) \sim I_0 \mathcal{N}(0,1)$.

The system output is given by

$$y(t) = \sum_{k=1}^{M} W_k^{\text{Out}}(t) r_k(t), \tag{3}$$

where $W_k^{\text{Out}}(t)$ denotes the output weights, which are trained with the recursive least squares (RLS) [9]. The initial values are $W_k^{\text{Out}}(0) = 0$. Note that the recurrent weights of the modules whose outputs converge to a fixed point are resampled because such trajectories are unnecessary for learning. In other words, $W_{k,ij}^{\text{Rec}}$ is given according to Eq. (2) again if the difference between the maximum and minimum values of the module outputs from 5 (s) to 10 (s) is less than 0.01.

The RLS modulates $W_k^{\text{Out}}$ such that $y(t)$ matches target$(t)$ in an online manner, which has been used in previous RC methods [4,6]. At time $t$, $W_k^{\text{Out}}(t)$ is updated based on the error $e(t)$ between the system output and target$(t)$:

$$W_k^{\text{Out}}(t) = W_k^{\text{Out}}(t - \Delta t) - e(t) \sum_l P_{kl}(t) r_l(t), \tag{4}$$

$$e(t) = \sum_k W_k^{\text{Out}}(t - \Delta t) r_k(t) - \text{target}(t), \tag{5}$$

where $P_{kl}(t)$ ($\mathbf{P}(t)$, an $M \times M$ matrix) corresponds to the running estimate of the inverse sample covariance matrix of $r_k(t)$ [9], and is updated according to

$$P_{kl}(t) = P_{kl}(t - \Delta t) - \frac{\sum_m \sum_n P_{lm}(t - \Delta t) r_m(t) r_n(t) P_{nl}(t - \Delta t)}{1 + \sum_m \sum_n r_m(t) P_{mn}(t - \Delta t) r_n(t)}. \tag{6}$$

The initial value of $\mathbf{P}(t)$ is given as $\mathbf{P}(0) = (1/\alpha)\mathbf{I}$, where $\mathbf{I}$ denotes an identity matrix and $\alpha$ is a constant.

**Table 1.** Parameter settings

| Parameter | Description | Value |
|-----------|-------------|-------|
| $M$ | Number of modules | 800 |
| $N$ | Network size (the number of units) of a module | 100 |
| $g$ | Scaling coefficient of recurrent weights | 1.2 |
| $p$ | Connection probability | 0.1 |
| $\tau$ | Time constant | 10 (ms) |
| $I_0$ | Noise amplitude | 0.001 |
| $\alpha$ | Initial value for recursive least squares | 1.0 |

## 3    Experimental Evaluation

Unless otherwise noted, the parameter values in Table 1 were used in the experiments, and the numerical solutions of Eq. (1) were obtained with a simulation step size of 1 (ms). During the training period, RLS was applied once every two steps, and $\Delta t$ in Eqs. (4)–(6) were set to 2 (ms). The simulation began at time $-250$ (ms) with a uniform random value in the range $[0, 1]$ as the initial state of each unit. The input $u(t)$ was a single pulse with a magnitude of five between $-50$ and $-1$ (ms) and zero in other periods (orange line in Fig. 2).

First, we evaluated the orthogonality and stability of the trajectories of unit outputs in a single module to clarify the utility of using numerous small modules. The temporal vectors of trajectories $r_{k,i}(t)$ from $t = 1$ to 10 (s) were normalized to unit vectors, and the absolute inner products between all combinations of vectors within the same module were computed to evaluate the orthogonality between unit trajectories within a module. The inner products were averaged over $i$ and then over 100 modules. The smaller this value is, the higher the orthogonality of the unit trajectories is. To evaluate the instability of unit trajectories with a module, we obtained the local Lyapunov exponent of a trajectory set $\mathbf{r}_k(t) = \{r_{k,1}(t), r_{k,2}(t), \ldots, r_{k,N}(t)\}$ from $t = 1$ to 10 (s) and averaged the values over ten times with different initial network states. The number of unstable modules with values greater than 0.05 was counted for 100 modules. We used a perturbation method in which minute perturbations are given to all units at $t = 0$, and subsequent orbital deviations are measured to compute the local Lyapunov exponent. These analyses were performed using different values of $N$ and $g$. In addition, for reBASICS, the absolute inner product between module outputs $r_k(t)$ and the number of modules with orbital instability were computed.

Second, we evaluated the performance of reBASICS for timing learning using a benchmark timer task [1,6]. In this task, the system receives a single pulse of length 50 (ms) and should output a single Gaussian pulse with a peak after a specific interval from the end of the input pulse (Fig. 2). The Gaussian pulse magnitude and standard deviation were one and 30 (ms), respectively. The interval was set from 1 to 120 (s) in the experiments. The training period was defined as the interval $+$ 150 (ms) from time 0, which is shown as the shaded period

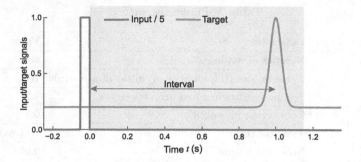

**Fig. 2.** Timer task. The input signal (orange) is a single pulse of length 50 (ms), and the target signal (green) is a single Gaussian pulse with a peak after a certain interval from the end of the input pulse. The shaded region indicates the training period. (Color figure online)

in Fig. 2. reBASICS was trained on ten trials (a trial is a run to the end of the training period), and then its learning performance was evaluated by using ten untrained trials. We used the squared Pearson correlation coefficient $R^2$ between $y(t)$ and target$(t)$, which was averaged over ten trials and then over ten networks. For comparison, we also evaluated the learning performance of innate training with a network size of 800, for which the weights of 480 units were trained. Its parameter settings followed those used by Laje and Buonomano [6]. Innate training uses all unit outputs for the readout; therefore, its learning cost for the readout is the same as that of reBASICS with 800 modules. However, the learning cost of the entire system is much higher than that of reBASICS because of the learning inside the reservoir.

Finally, we evaluated the learning ability of reBASICS for chaotic time-series using the Lorenz system. The use of the Lorenz system is effective to numerically prove the predominance of reBASICS for analyses of complex time series, because the Lorenz system typically yields complex and unpredictable time series by its low-dimensional deterministic equations:

$$\frac{dx(t)}{dt} = -px(t) + py(t),$$
$$\frac{dy(t)}{dt} = -x(t)z(t) + rx(t) - y(t), \qquad (7)$$
$$\frac{dz(t)}{dt} = x(t)y(t) - bz(t),$$

where $p = 10$, $r = 28$, and $b = 8/3$, and we set $x(0) = 0.1$, $y(0) = 0$, and $z(0) = 0$. A numerical solution of Eqs. (7) was obtained using the fourth-order Runge–Kutta method, with a step size of 0.001. Then, it was downsampled to 1/5 of its length and normalized to $[-1, 1]$ in magnitude to create a 20 (s) three-dimensional target signal, where one step is regarded as 1 (ms).

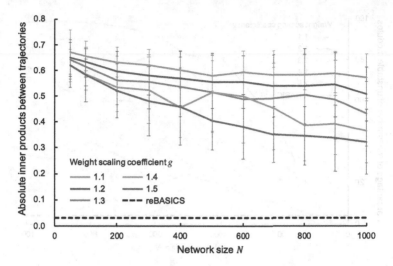

**Fig. 3.** Orthogonality (absolute inner products) between unit trajectories within a single RNN (solid curves) and between module trajectories in reBASICS (broken line). The colors indicate the values of $g$. Mean $\pm$ s.d. across 100 networks.

## 4   Result

### 4.1   Orthogonality and Stability

Figures 3 and 4 show the orthogonality between the unit trajectories of a module and their orbital instability, respectively. Figure 3 shows the large inner products, that is, low orthogonality for a small $N$, while the orthogonality increased moderately as $N$ and/or $g$ increased. However, as shown in Fig. 4, the orbital instability also increased when $N$ and/or $g$ were large. Therefore, RC using an RNN has a tradeoff between the orthogonality and stability.

Using several small modules allows reBASICS to overcome this tradeoff. Figure 5 shows a histogram of the absolute inner products between the trajectories of the module outputs. Most combinations resulted in inner products of zero, averaging 0.038, which is shown as the broken line in Fig. 3. In addition, the percentage of unstable modules for reBASICS was the same as that for $N = 100$ and $g = 1.2$, as indicated by the broken line in Fig. 4. These results indicate that reBASICS can exhibit high orthogonality and stability.

### 4.2   Timer Task

Figure 6 shows the results of the timer task. The red and black curves indicate the learning performance of reBASICS and innate training [6], respectively. reBASICS was found to be capable of learning, even for very long intervals of one minute or more. The defined memory capacity (MC) is the area under the curve; the MC of reBASICS was 90.0, which was more than 20 times larger than that of innate training (4.4). In this simulation, the recurrent weights for

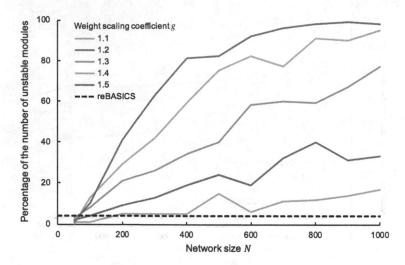

**Fig. 4.** Instability of unit trajectories within a single RNN. The local Lyapunov exponents of 100 modules were computed, and the percentage of unstable modules with a value greater than 0.05 is shown. The broken line indicates the percentage for reBA-SICS ($N = 100$, $g = 1.2$). The colors indicate the values of $g$.

an average of 45% of the modules that converged at a fixed point were resampled. The performance of reBASICS without this resampling is shown by the orange curve in Fig. 6, which indicates that the performance decreased because fixed-point attractors were unnecessary for learning.

Figure 7 shows the learning performance for different values of $g$, indicating that the best performance was obtained for $g = 1.1$ and 1.2, and it decreased as $g$ increased. This was because the trajectories became unstable when $g$ was large (see Fig. 4). Although orbital stability appeared for small $g$, the number of modules converging at a fixed point increased and, therefore, when $g = 1.0$ and 1.1, 91% and 62% of the modules were resampled, respectively. This indicates that $g$ should be determined by considering the computational cost of resampling the modules.

Figure 8 shows the learning performance for different values of $N$ when $M = 400$. The performance for $N = 200$ was the best; interestingly, as $N$ increased, it decreased because a large $N$ tended to cause orbital instability (see Fig. 4).

## 4.3 Learning of the Lorenz System

Figure 9 shows an example of the learning results for the Lorenz system. The green and red curves indicate the target signal and the system output, respectively. The performance values for $x$, $y$, and $z$ in the Lorenz system were $R^2 = 0.98$, 0.96, and 0.95, respectively. This result indicates that reBASICS is capable of learning for non-periodic complex time series such as the Lorenz system.

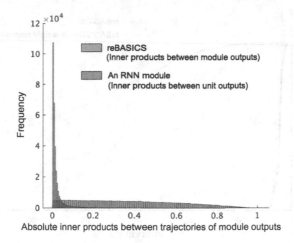

**Fig. 5.** Histograms of the absolute inner products between module outputs for reBA-SICS (magenta) and between unit outputs in a module ($N = 800$, $g = 1.2$; cyan).

## 5 Discussion

Here, we first elucidated the tradeoff between the orthogonality and stability of self-sustained trajectories in an RNN with $g \geq 1$ (see Figs. 3 and 4). The large network size resulted in high orthogonality but orbital instability, whereas the small network size resulted in orbital stability but low orthogonality, which reduced the representational capability of the system. To overcome this, we proposed reBASICS, which consists of many small RNN modules. Modularization of RNNs with different weights made their outputs orthogonal to each other (see Fig. 5) and also expressed orbital stability. Considering that any functions can be represented by an orthonormal basis, such as Fourier series, we assert that the genesis of an orthogonal basis inside the reservoir assures the high computing power of reBASICS.

Classical studies on the behavior of RNNs [7,8] have reported that for a finite network size, the unit trajectories converging to a zero fixed point bifurcate trajectories converging to a non-zero fixed point or limit cycles, and then reach chaotic behavior as $g$ increases. Furthermore, the parameter region generating such intermediate behavior expands as the network size decreases. The present experiments showed that the small modules produced intermediate stable trajectories that created a dynamic orthogonal basis, enabling the system to learn time series on a scale of tens of seconds (see Figs. 6 and 9). Because of this property, as not only $g$ but also the network size increased, learning performance was reduced due to orbital instability (see Figs. 7 and 8).

The computational complexity for the learning by reBASICS is extremely low because it modulates only the readout weights, as in standard RC. It retains the advantages of conventional RC in that the recurrent weights do not need

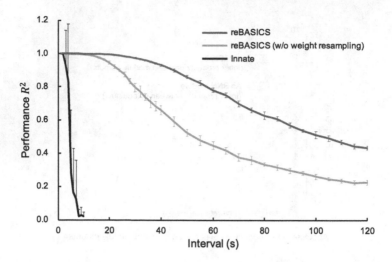

**Fig. 6.** Learning performance $R^2$ for reBASICS (the red curve) in the timer task. The orange curve indicates reBASICS where the recurrent weights for the modules converging at a fixed point were not resampled. The black curve indicates the performance of innate training [6] with the size of 800. Mean ± s.d. across 10 networks. (Color figure online)

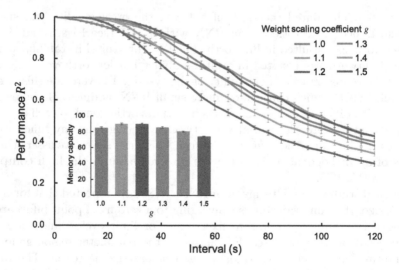

**Fig. 7.** Learning performance $R^2$ for the different values of the weight scaling coefficient $g$. The bottom-left bars show the memory capacity. Mean ± s.d. across 10 networks.

to be trained, making it easy to implement with physical materials, including analog circuits [10]. Such physical RC is promising as a future energy-saving computer, which should be a small size, by applying reBASICS.

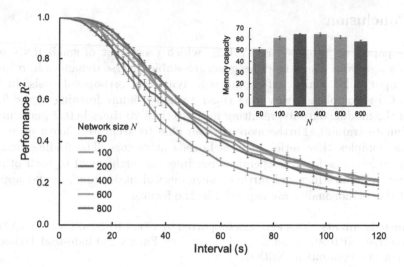

**Fig. 8.** Learning performance $R^2$ for the different values of the network size $N$. The number of modules was 400. The top-right bars show the memory capacity. Mean ± s.d. across 10 networks.

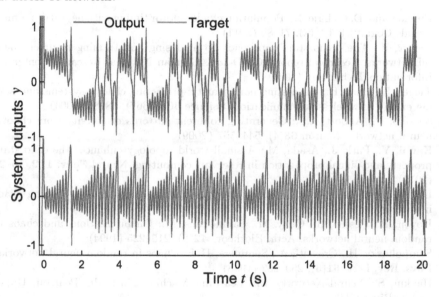

**Fig. 9.** Learning results for the Lorenz system. The green and red curves indicate the target signal and system output, respectively. Top and bottom indicate the results for $x$ and $z$ of the Lorenz system, respectively. The result for $y$ was omitted because of the result being similar to that for $x$. (Color figure online)

# 6    Conclusion

In this paper, we proposed reBASICS, which uses a set of small RNN modules as a reservoir. These modules generate stable diverse dynamics in response to an input pulse, which self-organizes a dynamical orthogonal basis. In fact, reBASICS accomplished very long timer tasks by online learning of the linear sum of the module outputs, resulting in more than 20 times better performance than innate training. Furthermore, it was able to accurately learn even non-periodic complex time series such as Lorenz attractors. The finding that the output trajectories from independent modules are orthogonal to each other is particularly interesting, and further mathematical understanding and application of this orthogonality are expected in the future.

**Acknowledgements.** This work was supported by JST, CREST (JPMJCR17A4) and the project, JPNP16007, commissioned by the New Energy and Industrial Technology Development Organization (NEDO).

# References

1. Buonomano, D.V., Laje, R.: Population clocks: motor timing with neural dynamics. Trends Cogn. Sci. **14**(12), 71–85 (2011)
2. Jaeger, H.: The "echo state" approach to analysing and training recurrent neural networks. Technical report, GMD-148, German National Research Center for Information Technology (2001)
3. Jaeger, H., Haas, H.: Harnessing nonlinearity: predicting chaotic systems and saving energy in wireless communication. Science **304**(5667), 78–80 (2004)
4. Sussillo, D., Abbott, L.F.: Generating coherent patterns of activity from chaotic neural networks. Neuron **63**(4), 544–557 (2009)
5. Kawai, Y., Park, J., Asada, M.: A small-world topology enhances the echo state property and signal propagation in reservoir computing. Neural Netw. **112**, 15–23 (2019)
6. Laje, R., Buonomano, D.V.: Robust timing and motor patterns by taming chaos in recurrent neural networks. Nat. Neurosci. **16**(7), 925–933 (2013)
7. Doyon, B., Cessac, B., Quoy, M., Samuelides, M.: On bifurcations and chaos in random neural networks. Acta. Biotheor. **42**(2), 215–225 (1994)
8. Sompolinsky, H., Crisanti, A., Sommers, H.J.: Chaos in random neural networks. Phys. Rev. Lett. **61**(3), 259–262 (1988)
9. Haykin, S.: Neural Networks and Learning Machines, 3rd edn. Pearson, Upper Saddle River (2009)
10. Tanaka, G., et al.: Recent advances in physical reservoir computing: a review. Neural Netw. **115**, 100–123 (2019)

# Targeted Aspect-Based Sentiment Analysis by Utilizing Dynamic Aspect Representation

Siqi Miao and Meilian Lu[✉]

State Key Laboratory of Networking and Switching Technology, School of Computer Science (National Pilot Software Engineering School), Beijing University of Posts and Telecommunications, Beijing 100876, China
{miaosiqi,mllu}@bupt.edu.cn

**Abstract.** Aspect-Based Sentiment Analysis (ABSA) task can analyze the sentiment of social reviews on different aspects. On the basis of ABSA, Targeted Aspect-Based Sentiment Analysis (TABSA) task additionally takes into account target entities. However, current studies on these tasks usually represent aspects based on word-level vectors, as static aspects and may not strongly correlated with review semantics, thus the effectiveness of sentiment prediction may be affected. Based on pre-trained BERT, we propose a sentiment analysis model using dynamic aspect representation. Specifically, we supplement external knowledge for limited review information, and integrate dynamic review features into static aspect. We also build a hierarchical interactive attention to fully explore the relationship among target, context and aspect. Several experiments are conducted on SentiHood dataset (for TABSA) and SemEval-2014 dataset (for ABSA). Our model has the best results in aspect detection and sentiment classification subtasks. Especially in contrast with BERT-pair, the accuracy of our model improves 1.2% and 0.6% in two subtasks on SentiHood dataset, and 1.9% and 1.4% on SemEval dataset.

**Keywords:** TABSA · Dynamic aspect representation · Hierarchical interactive attention

## 1 Introduction

Traditional sentiment analysis predicts an overall sentiment polarity for a document or a sentence, and it's feasible when the entire comment expresses a single emotion. While if there're several target entities and aspects which may present opposite attitudes, it's insufficient to predict just one polarity. Therefore traditional method is regarded as coarse-grained. With the emergence of fine-grained sentiment analysis, multiple aspects and targets can be analyzed. Fine-grained task consists of ABSA [1] and TABSA [2]. ABSA predicts sentiment for aspects, like *"The salmon is tasty while the waiter is very rude."*, *"salmon"* is abstracted to *"food"* category with positive polarity. TABSA is the most fine-grained task at present. It predicts the sentiment of (target entity, aspect category), like *"The salmon of Restaurant1 is tasty, while in Restaurant2 the waiter is very rude."* is positive on (Restaurant1, food) and negative on (Restaurant2, service).

© The Author(s), under exclusive license to Springer Nature Switzerland AG 2022
E. Pimenidis et al. (Eds.): ICANN 2022, LNCS 13529, pp. 647–659, 2022.
https://doi.org/10.1007/978-3-031-15919-0_54

Early sentiment analysis [3–6] usually adopt RNN (Recurrent Neural Network) including LSTM (Long Short Term Memory) and GRU (Gate Recurrent Unit) as encoder. Henceforth, (T)ABSA researches [7–11] have used pre-trained models to encode sentence. Then the review representation is fed into a sentiment classifier. Prepared with RNN methods, pre-trained method fine-tunes (T)ABSA task in downstream, which accelerates convergence and also has good effect on small datasets. However, there are two problems in current Aspect-Category based Sentiment Analysis methods:

1. Lack of semantic correlation between aspect category and review. When representing aspect, existing studies [3,5,12] commonly use context-free embedding (aspect vector is static), ignoring semantic between aspect and review. While dynamic aspect vector emphasizes this relation, integrating the review feature into aspect. A few researches have considered such correlation. [13] employs Context2Aspect attention, and [11] sets a context-aware layer to refine aspect vector. However, these methods don't fully extract the semantic of context (lack of connections between words), and may lead to less information in dynamic aspect vector and eventually affect prediction.
2. Limited length of review with less semantic information. [8,14] believe that the length and quantity of ABSA reviews are both limited. Similarly, TABSA reviews, as well as practical reviews, are constrained in short statement with multiple target entities and emotional words. While common sense, concepts and other understandable knowledge, is usually not explained.

Aimed at above, we propose DynamicAspect based on dynamic aspect representation. In this model, pre-trained BERT (Bidirectional Encoder Representations from Transformers) is applied for encoding. Firstly, we integrate dynamic review feature into static aspect representation, enhancing the semantic relation between aspect and review. Secondly, we employ two sources of external knowledge when extracting dynamic review feature. We also put forward a hierarchical attention layer for target, context and dynamic aspect. Experiments are performed on TABSA task and aspect-category based ABSA task. Results show that our model has obvious effects on improving the accuracy of sentiment classification. The contribution of this paper includes three parts:

1. Propose a dynamic aspect representation method. Dynamic review feature is extracted from extended review to fuse with static aspect vector.
2. Integrate two sources of external knowledge for constructing dynamic aspect vector, namely, utilizing document-level sentiment analysis knowledge and similar concepts from sentiment dictionary.
3. Propose a hierarchical interactive attention mechanism to focus on the regional and interactive semantics in target, context and dynamic aspect.

## 2    Related Work

### 2.1    ABSA Methods

ABSA approaches include RNN methods, pre-trained methods and dynamic aspect methods.

RNN methods generally use RNN to encode the sequence, and finally use a sentiment classifier to predict. AGDT [3] utilizes GRU, and H-LSTM [12] apply hierarchical LSTM. The other kind of researches adopt attention-based RNN, which allocates different weights to review words, such as ATAE-LSTM [5] and ASBL-RL [15]. Ma et al. [6] (IAN) firstly apply interactive attention mechanism; on this basis, [16,17] propose PBAN and AEN respectively.

Pre-trained models (like [18]), not only use multi-layer network, but also have pre-trained corpus knowledge. Li et al. [14] set up a variety of specific task layers on BERT; FastText+CNN [19] uses pre-trained word embeddings. BERT-PT proposed by Xu et al. [8] adopts a joint post-training technique to supplement external knowledge. Ke et al. [20] propose SentiLR by introducing SentiWordNet to add prior sentiment polarity.

Above researches all use context-free embedding for aspect. This static vector is identical under different reviews, with low dependency on reviews and will affect sentiment prediction. A few studies have adopted dynamic aspect. MGAN [13] adopts Context2Aspect attention to focus on more essential words of aspect and construct context-aware aspect vectors. Li et al. [21] propose TNet by dynamically associating aspect representation with each review word. [22] apply a capsule network and a dynamic routing algorithm to select context information highly related to aspect.

## 2.2  TABSA Methods

Similarly, we divide TABSA approaches into non-pretrained methods, pretrained methods and dynamic aspect methods.

Non-pretrained methods usually adopt RNN and CNN (Convolutional Neural Network). Ma et al. [23] (SenticLSTM) add a hierarchical attention layer in LSTM. The first layer uses self-attention inside target, and the second layer represents the whole sentence with aspect and target.

In pre-trained TABSA methods, Zhang et al. [9] (SNAT) use BERT as an embedding layer and apply layered self-attention mechanism to jointly model aspect and target. Sun et al. [10] propose BERT-pair to transform TABSA task into sentence-pair classification task.

At present, the only dynamic aspect-based TABSA method is GBCN proposed by Li et al. [11]. In GBCN, a context-aware layer is employed to learn context feature, and refine target and aspect vectors. In this layer, a step function and a feed forward layer are used to select highly relevant words in context.

# 3  DynamicAspect Methodology

## 3.1  Task Definition and Framework

**Definition 1. *ABSA* [1]:** *Given a review sequence $S$, consisting of $L$ words: $S = \{w_1, w_2, \cdots, w_L\}$. Jointly execute aspect detection and sentiment classification subtasks through "None" label. For aspect category $a \in A$ (A is predefined as set of aspects), predict the sentiment polarity $y \in \{Negative, Positive, None\}$ of $S$ on aspect $a$.*

**Definition 2.** *TABSA [2]: Given a review sequence $S = \{w_1, w_2, \cdots, w_L\}$.*
*Where $M$ words are pre-labeled as a target entity $t = \{w_{t_1}, w_{t_2}, \cdots, w_{t_M}\}$*
*$\in \{w_1, w_2, \cdots, w_L\}$, and other words are defined as context $c = \{w_{c_1}, w_{c_2}, \cdots, w_{c_N}\}$, $L = M + N$. For aspect category $a \in A$, predict the sentiment polarity*
*$y \in \{Negative, Positive, None\}$ of $S$ on aspect $a$ and corresponding target entity $t$.*

To approach these tasks by utilizing dynamic aspect, we propose **Dynamic-icAspect** model, including a BERT-pair embedding layer, a dynamic aspect layer, a hierarchical interactive attention layer and a sentiment classification layer. Figure 1 shows its framework. Specifically, in dynamic aspect layer, we propose a method of constructing dynamic aspect representation, which extracts feature from extended review and fuses it with static aspect vector. Besides, we set up two forms of attention in the third layer, Context-Target interactive attention and Aspect-Review attention, respectively.

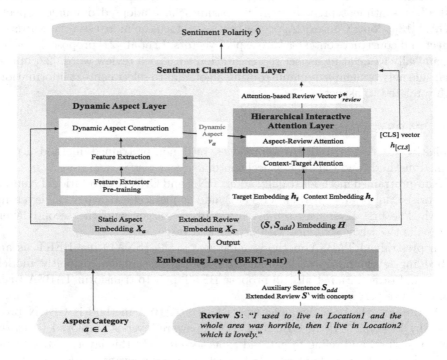

**Fig. 1.** Overall framework of DynamicAspect

## 3.2 BERT-Pair Embedding Layer

Firstly, BERT-pair generates an auxiliary sentence for each review, denote as
$S_{add} = \{w_{add_1}, \cdots, w_{add_p}\}$. Then combine the review and auxiliary sentence into a sentence pair (starts with [CLS], separates with [SEP], where [CLS] is the key vector for classification). The joint sequence embedding matrix $H$ is:

$$H = \{h_{[CLS]}, h_{w_1}, h_{w_2}, \cdots, h_{w_L}, h_{[SEP]}, h_{add_1}, \cdots, h_{add_p}, h_{[SEP]}\} \quad (1)$$

$h_w$ contains target entity embedding $h_t = \{h_{t_1}, h_{t_2}, \cdots, h_{t_M}\}$ and context embedding $h_c = \{h_{c_1}, h_{c_2}, \cdots, h_{c_N}\}$. Since dynamic aspect layer (Subsect. 3.3) requires concepts-extended review embedding and aspect embedding, we directly input extended review $S^\backslash$ and aspect $a$ into BERT. Embedding of sequence $S^\backslash$:

$$X_{S^\backslash} = \{x_{w_1}, x_{w_2}, \cdots, x_{w_{L^\backslash}}\} \tag{2}$$

For aspect embedding, we calculate the average of word embeddings. Denote aspect $a$ with $d$ words ($d \in \{1, 2, \cdots, K\}$), aspect embedding is:

$$X_a = \text{mean}(x_{a_1}, \cdots, x_{a_d}) \tag{3}$$

## 3.3   Construction of Dynamic Aspect Vector

To incorporate dynamic review semantics into aspect, we design a dynamic aspect layer shown in Fig. 2. We consider that a feature extractor could not be directly applied to extract review feature. Firstly, it has not been trained on sentiment classification task, cannot effectively generate the feature of review. Besides, review often contains a variety of emotional words without specific explanation. In consequence, we propose two methods to supplement external knowledge, including extending review with common sense and pre-training feature extractor with coarse-grained task. The whole method includes four steps.

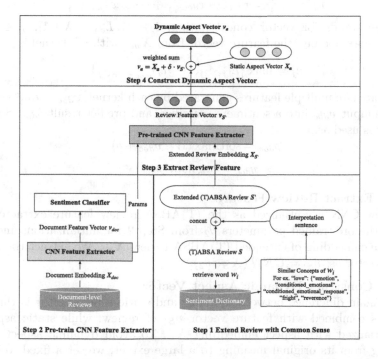

**Fig. 2.** Dynamic aspect layer with external knowledge

## Step 1. Extend Review with Common Sense

For each review word $w_i$ in review $S$, we retrieve SenticNet Dictionary for its similar concepts $\{w_{i_1}, w_{i_2}, \cdots, w_{i_5}\}$. Then we generate an interpretation statement "*(it is $w_{i_1}$, $w_{i_2}$, $\cdots$ and $w_{i_5}$)*" for the concepts and add it to the original review. The extended (T)ABSA review will have more specific semantics, and the feature vector extracted will more fully represent the review.

## Step 2. Pre-train CNN Feature Extractor

We adopt CNN as a feature extractor, which is less likely to produce gradient disappearance and gradient explosion. Firstly, use a document-level dataset to pre-train CNN, and add a sentiment classifier for prediction. Then, pre-trained CNN is used to learn review representation, which provides task-related knowledge, and also sets appropriate neural parameters.

We have Glove embedding $X_{doc} = \{x_{doc_1}, x_{doc_2}, \cdots, x_{doc_n}\}$. Assume the random initialization parameter of CNN is $\theta_1$, and the feature vector generated for document is:

$$v_{doc} = CNN\left(X_{doc}; \theta_1\right) \tag{4}$$

Above, $CNN()$ represents for adopting multiple convolution kernels (denote as $z$ kernels) with stride 1. When conduct convolution in $i^{th}$ word window $\{x_{doc_i}, x_{doc_{i+1}}, \cdots, x_{doc_{i+\lambda-1}}\}$, with $j^{th}$ kernel of size $\lambda$, the generated feature is:

$$c_{ij} = RELU\left(w_j^\top x_{doc_{i:i+\lambda-1}} + b_j\right) \tag{5}$$

$$x_{doc_{i:i+\lambda-1}} = x_{doc_i} \oplus x_{doc_{i+1}} \oplus \cdots \oplus x_{doc_{i+\lambda-1}} \tag{6}$$

Above, $\oplus$ stands for vector concatenating, $i \in [1, L_{doc} - \lambda + 1]$, $j \in [1, z]$. Through max pooling, the feature vector from $X_{doc}$ with $j^{th}$ kernel is:

$$c_j = \max\left\{c_{1j}, c_{2j}, \cdots, c_{(L_{doc}-\lambda+1)j}\right\} \tag{7}$$

We concatenate multiple features generated by each kernel: $v_{doc} = c_1 \oplus \cdots \oplus c_z$. Then we input $v_{doc}$ into a sentiment classifier, and predict result $\hat{y}_{doc}$. Softmax classifier is used as:

$$p_{doc} = \text{softmax}\left(W \cdot v_{doc} + b\right) \tag{8}$$

$$\hat{y}_{doc} = \arg\max\left(p_{doc}\right) \tag{9}$$

## Step 3. Extract Review Feature

A new CNN is initialized as the (T)ABSA review feature extractor. We employ the pre-trained parameters $\theta_2$ from Step 2 for initialization, and then input the embedding of extended (T)ABSA review $X_{S'}$. We extract the review feature vector as: $v_{S'} = CNN\left(X_{S'}; \theta_2\right)$.

## Step 4. Construct Dynamic Aspect Vector

The main difference between dynamic and static aspect vector is that, the former is combined with feature vector $v_{S'}$ of review, while static aspect is only initialized with aspect embedding $X_a$. To avoid dynamic aspect vector deviating from its original meaning to a large extent, we set a fixed weight $\delta$. Then construct dynamic aspect vector: $v_a = X_a + \delta \cdot v_{S'}$.

## 3.4   Hierarchical Interactive Attention Layer

We find recent TABSA researches [9,23] apply self-attention in target and context respectively, ignoring the interaction between target and context. To fully model the relationship of internal and external review, we employ an interactive attention [6] on target entity and context, and a general attention on aspect, then propose a hierarchical interactive attention mechanism for TABSA task.

### 1. Target-Context Interactive Attention

(1) Context $\rightarrow$ Target Attention: Firstly, we obtain the pooling vector of context: $\bar{h}_c = \frac{1}{N} \sum_{j=1}^{N} h_{c_j}$. Then calculate attention $\alpha$ between $\bar{h}_c$ and target entity vector $h_t$:

$$\alpha_i = \frac{\exp\left(\text{score}\left(h_{t_i}, \bar{h}_c\right)\right)}{\sum_{k=1}^{M} \exp\left(\text{score}\left(h_{t_k}, \bar{h}_c\right)\right)} \tag{10}$$

$$\text{score}\left(h_{t_k}, \bar{h}_c\right) = h_{t_k}^{\top} W_{\alpha} \bar{h}_c \tag{11}$$

Above, $\alpha_i$ represents the attention of $\bar{h}_c$ to the $i^{th}$ target vector $h_{t_i}$. And the weighted target vector is obtained as: $v_{target} = \sum_{i=1}^{M} \alpha_i h_{t_i}$

(2) Target $\rightarrow$ Context Attention: We obtain the pooling vector of target: $\bar{h}_t = \frac{1}{M} \sum_{i=1}^{M} h_{t_i}$. Then calculate attention $\beta$ between $\bar{h}_t$ and context vector $h_c$:

$$\beta_j = \frac{\exp\left(\text{score}\left(h_{c_j}, \bar{h}_t\right)\right)}{\sum_{k=1}^{N} \exp\left(\text{score}\left(h_{c_k}, \bar{h}_t\right)\right)} \tag{12}$$

$$\text{score}\left(h_{c_k}, \bar{h}_t\right) = h_{c_k}^{\top} W_{\beta} \bar{h}_t \tag{13}$$

Above, $\beta_j$ represents the attention of $\bar{h}_t$ to the $j^{th}$ context vector $h_{c_j}$. And the weighted target vector matrix is obtained as: $v_{context} = \sum_{j=1}^{N} \beta_j h_{c_j}$

We merge the weighted target vector and context vector, then we have inner-review vector: $v_{\text{review}} = [v_{\text{target}}; v_{\text{context}}]$.

### 2. Aspect-Review Attention

The second level focuses on review and aspect category. We calculate attention $\gamma$ based on the output vector of first attention layer and dynamic aspect vector $v_a$. Weighted review vector is obtained as $v_{\text{review}}^* = \sum_{k=1}^{M+N} \gamma_k v_{\text{review}_k}$:

$$\gamma_k = \frac{\exp\left(\text{score}\left(v_{\text{review}_k}, v_a\right)\right)}{\sum_{m=1}^{M+N} \exp\left(\text{score}\left(v_{\text{review}_m}, v_a\right)\right)} \tag{14}$$

$$\text{score}\left(v_{\text{review}_m}, v_a\right) = v_{\text{review}_m}^{\top} W_{\gamma} v_a \tag{15}$$

## 3.5   Sentiment Classification

The output vector comes from two parts:

1. The [CLS] vector generated by embedding layer. According to BERT's Next Sentence Prediction task, $h_{[CLS]}$ is regarded as the output vector of sentiment classification.

2. The review vector generated by hierarchical interactive attention layer. Through such attention, BERT is fine-tuned to (T)ABSA, and $v^*_{review}$ is also used as the output vector.

We combine the above vectors and input into sentiment classifier. The category with the highest probability $p$ is the predicted polarity $\hat{y} = \mathrm{argmax}(p)$:

$$p = \mathrm{softmax}\left(W\left[h_{[CLS]}; v^*_{review}\right] + b\right) \tag{16}$$

# 4    Experiments

## 4.1    Dataset and Experiment Settings

Table 1. Statistics of SentiHood and SemEval dataset. SemEval-2014 dataset is only split into train-set and test-set.

| Dataset | Positive | | | Negative | | |
|---|---|---|---|---|---|---|
| | Train | Val | Test | Train | Val | Test |
| SentiHood | 1626 | 406 | 810 | 834 | 204 | 406 |
| SemEval | 2178 | - | 657 | 839 | - | 222 |

We conduct experiments on two kinds of sentiment analysis datasets (see in Table 1), SentiHood dataset[1] (for TABSA task) and SemEval-2014 Task 4 Restaurant dataset[2] (for ABSA task). For SentiHood dataset, we reserve aspects of {*general, price, safety, transit-location*}. DynamicAspect model also adopts Amazon Electronic dataset[3] (document-level dataset) and SenticNet dictionary for external knowledge.

We use BERT-pair as embedding layer, including 12 Transformer layers, and hidden dimension $d_{hid}$ is 768, the head number of self-attention is 12. In dynamic aspect layer, the convolution layer of CNN has three types of filter sizes "3, 4, 5", each with 100 filters, and we set the dynamic coefficient $\delta$ to 0.3. The maximum text length is 256, train batch size is 24, and validation batch size is 8. We use 2e-5 learning rate, and adopt Adam optimizer in training. In this paper, we select Accuracy, Macro-F1 and Auc for model evaluation.

## 4.2    Model Comparisons and Ablations

We select some aspect-level sentiment analysis methods to compare with. To evaluate the effect of dynamic aspect, we set up three ablations.

**SenticLSTM** [23]: As TABSA comparison. A hierarchical self-attention model based on LSTM, including target-level and sentence-level attentions.

---

[1] http://annotate-neighborhood.com/download/download.html.
[2] http://alt.qcri.org/semeval2014/task4/data/uploads/.
[3] https://nijianmo.github.io/amazon/index.html.

**Table 2.** Comparison and Ablation Results (%). All models are evaluated in their best settings. SenticLSTM is only applied in TABSA, and ATAE-LSTM is only applied in ABSA, besides it doesn't have aspect detection, their unavailable results are labeled as "-". The best scores are in **bold**.

| Models | TABSA (SentiHood) | | | | ABSA (SemEval) | | | |
|---|---|---|---|---|---|---|---|---|
| | Aspect detection | | Sentiment classification | | Aspect detection | | Sentiment classification | |
| | Accuracy | Macro-F1 | Accuracy | Auc | Accuracy | Macro-F1 | Accuracy | Macro-F1 |
| SenticLSTM | 66.2 | 76.5 | 87.5 | 90.5 | - | - | - | - |
| ATAE-LSTM | - | - | - | - | - | - | 76.7 | 64.1 |
| BERT | 75.0 | 81.0 | 90.5 | 94.7 | 67.9 | 90.8 | 82.0 | 68.0 |
| BERT-pair | 79.0 | 83.5 | 93.4 | 96.4 | 70.4 | 91.4 | 84.9 | 73.0 |
| GBCN | 78.7 | 85.1 | 92.0 | 95.0 | 70.4 | 91.4 | 83.0 | 72.1 |
| SNAT | 78.5 | 85.8 | 93.1 | 96.8 | 70.9 | 91.8 | 85.0 | 73.2 |
| DynamicAspect | **80.2** | **86.3** | **94.0** | **97.6** | **72.3** | **92.4** | **86.3** | **74.3** |
| NoneDA | 78.5 | 85.0 | 93.2 | 96.6 | 70.9 | 91.9 | 85.5 | 71.8 |
| Semantic-DA | 79.8 | 86.1 | 93.3 | 97.1 | 72.0 | 91.6 | 85.7 | 73.0 |
| Document-DA | 79.0 | 85.7 | 93.6 | 97.4 | 71.5 | 91.8 | 85.9 | 73.5 |

**ATAE-LSTM** [5]: As ABSA comparison. LSTM model based on single-hop attention. It combines aspect category into reviews by concatenating and aspect attention.

**BERT** [18]: As (T)ABSA comparisons. A baseline model with Softmax classifier. If TABSA reviews have at most $m$ target entities and $n$ aspects, $m \times n$ classifiers are needed.

**BERT-pair** [10]: As (T)ABSA comparisons. It constructs auxiliary sentences (NLI-M method) for reviews, which contains targets and aspects. BERT-pair is the basis of DynamicAspect.

**SNAT** [9]: As (T)ABSA comparisons. A hierarchical self-attention model based on BERT-pair.

**GBCN** [11]: As (T)ABSA comparisons. A dynamic aspect model based on BERT-pair.

**NoneDA:** As (T)ABSA ablations. Drop the dynamic aspect layer.

**Semantic-DA:** As (T)ABSA ablations. Only use SenticNet dictionary in dynamic aspect layer.

**Document-DA:** As (T)ABSA ablations. Only use document-level dataset in dynamic aspect layer.

As can be seen in Table 2, LSTM-based models have lower effect, while pre-trained models perform better in two tasks. Compared with pre-trained methods, DynamicAspect achieves the best results. Among them, BERT has the lowest value indicating that it isn't adapt to sentiment classification properly. As for BERT-pair, our model has a few improvements in (T)ABSA than this base model. And in contrast to GBCN, which also adopts dynamic aspect, results show that our model has higher accuracy. As a result, our model based on dynamic aspect better combines BERT-pair embedding and provides richer semantics. Also, the results of DynamicAspect fully exceed its ablation models. Specifically, NoneDA has the lowest values indicating that dynamic aspect layer can significantly improve the accuracy. Compared with Semantic-DA and Document-DA, DynamicAspect has higher values. Deleting any external knowledge in dynamic aspect layer will lead to degradation of its overall performance.

### 4.3   Training Process Analysis

To visually display the different performances of DynamicAspect and contrast models in training process, a prediction test is performed after each epoch training in this paper. We record the test results of the first 10 or 8 training epochs. By calculating the accuracy under different epochs, we draw the accuracy-epoch curves of different models on (T)ABSA, shown in Fig. 3.

It can be seen that, in two subtasks of (T)ABSA, DynamicAspect model has superior results than contrast methods. After the first iteration, DynamicAspect has the first-rank performance in aspect detection, and has apparent advantages

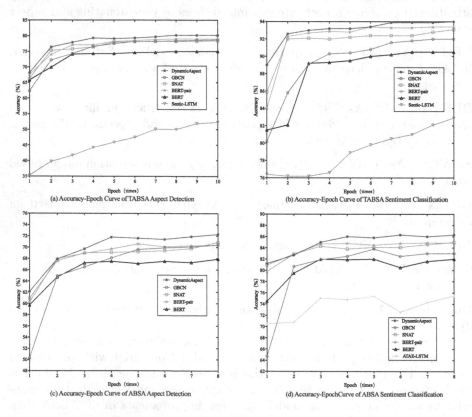

(a) Accuracy-Epoch Curve of TABSA Aspect Detection

(b) Accuracy-Epoch Curve of TABSA Sentiment Classification

(c) Accuracy-Epoch Curve of ABSA Aspect Detection

(d) Accuracy-EpochCurve of ABSA Sentiment Classification

**Fig. 3.** Accuracy-epoch curves of (T)ABSA model comparisons

**Table 3.** Results of DynamicAspect on SentiHood dataset

| ID | Review | Target & Aspect | Label | Predict |
|---|---|---|---|---|
| 1005 | I live in location-1 and I **like** the area with always something to do if you want to and also provides real calm places when you want it | location-1 general | Positive | Positive✓ |
| 1138 | location-1 mainly has sizeable houses, most of which have been converted into flats, and the cost of renting or purchasing is favourable compared with most of london because the area isn't regarded as fashionable | location-1 general | None | None✓ |
| 1334 | The cheap parts of london are **location-2** and **location-1** and they are all poor, crime ridden and crowded with immigrants | location-2 general | Negative | Negative✓ |
| 1013 | Rare lane, inchicore dublin, ireland 085.760.5190 email: fwa training is in the uk location-1 has the high-speed link to london and to the kent coast and france (via chunnel), it has some beautiful villages around | location-1 general | Positive | None✗ |

compared with other methods (except SNAT in ABSA task) in sentiment classification. When the accuracies of most models tend to be stable, the eventual accuracies of DynamicAspect model in two tasks are higher than others. Based on the results of (T)ABSA, DynamicAspect proposed by us has the optimal performance.

### 4.4 Case Study and Analysis

We perform case study on SentiHood dataset (see Table 3), and analyze the reasons of correct and false classifications. From Table 3, when reviews directly express sentiment (such as ID = 1005 implies positive sentiment on *"like"*), or not mention some aspect (review ID = 1138 doesn't refer to *"general"* aspect), and even with multiple targets (ID = 1134), the proposed DynamicAspect accurately detects aspect and makes correct prediction. While in some complex semantics with irrelevant information (in sample ID = 1013), this model does have difficulties in comprehension.

# 5   Conclusion

In this paper, we propose DynamicAspect based on BERT-pair, integrating dynamic review semantics into static aspect. When extracting review feature, we utilize two methods to fuse external knowledge, namely, extending review with similar common sense, and pre-training feature extractor with document-level task knowledge. We evaluate DynamicAspect and other methods on (T)ABSA tasks, and DynamicAspect acquires the best experiment results. In addition, we prove that both of external knowledge contribute to the generation of dynamic aspect vectors through ablation experiment. We also find that DynamicAspect has the greatest initial effect in training process on (T)ABSA.

# References

1. Pontiki, M., Galanis, D., Pavlopoulos, J., et al.: SemEval-2014 task 4: aspect based sentiment analysis. In: Proceedings of the 8th International Workshop on Semantic Evaluation (SemEval 2014), pp. 27–35 (2014)
2. Saeidi, M., Bouchard, G., Liakata, M., Riedel, S.: SentiHood: targeted aspect based sentiment analysis dataset for urban neighbourhoods. In: Proceedings of the 26th COLING 2016, pp. 1546–1556 (2016)
3. Liang, Y., Meng, F., Zhang, J., et al.: A novel aspect-guided deep transition model for aspect based sentiment analysis. In: Proceedings of the 24th EMNLP, pp. 5572–5584 (2019)
4. Zhang, M., Zhang, Y., Vo, D.T.: Gated neural networks for targeted sentiment analysis. In: Proceedings of the AAAI Conference on Artificial Intelligence, pp. 3087–3093 (2016)
5. Wang, Y., Huang, M., Zhu, X., Zhao, L.: Attention-based LSTM for aspect-level sentiment classification. In: Proceedings of EMNLP, pp. 606–615 (2016)
6. Ma, D., Li, S., Zhang, X., Wang, H.: Interactive attention networks for aspect-level sentiment classification. In: Proceedings of the 26th International Joint Conference on Artificial Intelligence, pp. 421–423 (2017)
7. He, R., Lee, W.S., Ng, H.T., Dahlmeier, D.: Exploiting document knowledge for aspect-level sentiment classification. In: The 56th ACL, pp. 579–585 (2018)
8. Xu, H., Liu, B., Shu, L., Yu, P.S.: BERT post-training for review reading comprehension and aspect-based sentiment analysis. In: Proceedings of Conference of the North American Chapter of the Association for Computational Linguistics (NAACL), pp. 1–12 (2019)
9. Zhang, Z., Hang, C.W., Singh, M.P.: Would you like Sashimi even if it's sliced too thin? Selective neural attention for aspect targeted sentiment analysis (SNAT). arXiv (2020). https://arxiv.org/abs/2004.13150
10. Sun, C., Huang, L.Y., Qiu, X.P.: Utilizing BERT for aspect-based sentiment analysis via constructing auxiliary sentence. In: Proceedings of Conference of the North American Chapter of the Association for Computational Linguistics (NAACL), pp. 380–385 (2019)
11. Li, X., Fu, X., Xu, G., et al.: Enhancing BERT representation with context-aware embedding for aspect-based sentiment analysis. IEEE Access **8**, 46868–46876 (2020)
12. Ruder, S., Ghaffari, P., J.G.: A hierarchical model of reviews for aspect-based sentiment analysis. In: Proceedings of EMNLP, pp. 999–1005 (2016)

13. Li, Z., Wei, Y., Zhang, Y., et al.: Exploiting coarse-to-fine task transfer for aspect-level sentiment classification. In: Proceedings of the AAAI Conference on Artificial Intelligence, pp. 1–8 (2019)
14. Li, X., Bing, L., Zhang, W., Lam, W.: Exploiting BERT for end-to-end aspect-based sentiment analysis. In: Proceedings of the 5th Workshop on Noisy User-Generated Text (W-NUT), pp. 34–41 (2019)
15. Li, M.-F., Zhou, K., Wang, H., et al.: Aspect-based sentiment classification with reinforcement learning and local understanding. In: Proceedings of 30th ICANN, pp. 662-674 (2021)
16. Gu, S., Zhang, L., Hou, Y., Song, Y.: A position-aware bidirectional attention network for aspect-level sentiment analysis. In: Proceedings of the 27th COLING 2018, pp. 774–784 (2018)
17. Song, Y., Wang, J., Jiang, T., et al.: Targeted sentiment classification with attentional encoder network. In: Proceedings of 28th ICANN, pp. 93–103 (2019)
18. Devlin, J., Chang, M.W., Lee, K., Toutanova, K.: BERT: pre-training of deep bidirectional transformers for language understanding. In: Proceedings of Conference of the North American Chapter of the Association for Computational Linguistics (NAACL), pp. 4171–4186 (2019)
19. Schmitt, M., Steinheber, S., Schreiber, K., Roth, B.: Joint aspect and polarity classification for aspect-based sentiment analysis with end-to-end neural networks. In: Proceedings of EMNLP, pp. 1109–1114 (2018)
20. Ke, P., Ji, H., Liu, S., et al.: SentiLR: linguistic knowledge enhanced language representation for sentiment analysis. arXiv (2019). https://arxiv.org/abs/1911.02493
21. Li, X., Bing, L., Lam, W., Shi, B.: Transformation networks for target-oriented sentiment classification. In: Proceedings of the 56th ACL, pp. 946–956 (2018)
22. Jiang, M., Wang, J.J., Zhang, M., et al.: Fine-grained sentiment analysis method based on context-aware embedding. Chinese Patent: CN111506700A (2020)
23. Ma, Y.K., Peng, H.Y., Cambria, E.: Targeted aspect-based sentiment analysis via embedding commonsense knowledge into an attentive LSTM. In: Proceedings of the AAAI Conference on Artificial Intelligence, pp. 5876–5883 (2018)

# To Tree or Not to Tree? Assessing the Impact of Smoothing the Decision Boundaries

Anthea Mérida[✉], Argyris Kalogeratos, and Mathilde Mougeot

Centre Borelli, ENS Paris-Saclay, Université Paris-Saclay, Gif-sur-Yvette, France
{anthea.merida,argyris.kalogeratos,mathilde.mougeot}@ens-paris-saclay.fr

**Abstract.** When analyzing a dataset, it can be useful to assess how smooth the decision boundaries need to be for a model to better fit the data. This paper addresses this question by proposing the quantification of how much should the 'rigid' decision boundaries, produced by an algorithm that naturally finds such solutions, be relaxed to obtain a performance improvement. The approach we propose starts with the rigid decision boundaries of a seed Decision Tree (seed DT), which is used to initialize a Neural DT (NDT). The initial boundaries are challenged by relaxing them progressively through training the NDT. During this process, we measure the NDT's performance and decision agreement to its seed DT. We show how these two measures can help the user in figuring out how expressive his model should be, before exploring it further via model selection. The validity of our approach is demonstrated with experiments on simulated and benchmark datasets.

**Keywords:** Decision trees · Neural decision trees · Neural networks · Model family selection · Model selection · Interpretability · Data exploration

## 1 Introduction

During the exploratory phase of data analysis, and before choosing a model to fit it to the data, it is interesting to know whether the data can be sufficiently summarized with decision boundaries composed of a set of 'hard' or 'rigid' rules, which can be interpreted by humans. Rejecting this assumption would mean that it is necessary to have a certain degree of smoothness to the decision boundaries in order to capture better the structure of the dataset. Typically, one would simply compare members of different model families and select one through a procedure such as cross-validation (CV). In machine learning, where it is more usual to focus on the prediction capacity of models, CV is a widespread procedure both for model and algorithm selection [6]. Indeed, CV is easy to implement and simplifies the comparison of different models based on the variability of a chosen performance metric.

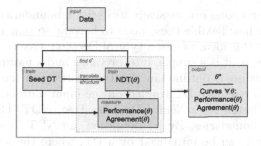

**Fig. 1.** Outline of the proposed method.

From a higher level point-of-view, automated machine learning (auto-ML) or meta-learning methods can be used to first decide which type of algorithm can be suitable for a dataset, and then to train the final model on it. Indeed, packages such as Auto-WEKA [8] and Auto-sklearn [7] provide tools to automate the algorithm and model selection process. They apply Bayesian optimization and meta-learning procedures [7,13] to select the most appropriate algorithm and its parametrization according to a metric, and within a user-defined budget. Other methods aim to use data characterizations to obtain insights into what kind of data mining algorithm is suitable for a dataset. These characterizations can be statistical and information-theoretical measures to be employed as input, and then the aim is to learn their association with the algorithms' performance for the data. Users can interpret these methods, e.g. by producing decision rules using the C5.0 algorithm [1], or a self-organizing map to cluster various datasets according to their characteristics [14]. Other, more complex, data characterizations (or meta-features) have been proposed to describe the problem at hand [9,12]. Closer to our work, the approach of [11] extracts meta-features from a dataset's inducted decision tree, which attempt to capture learning complexity of the dataset. These methods, however, require a database of use-cases (datasets and their associated preferred algorithms) whose clustering would provide general guidance on model selection, and might need to be retrained when adding new use-cases.

The aforementioned existing methods aim mostly at deciding among candidate models, and eventually train a good performing final model. In this sense, they do not provide the user with direct insights regarding the complexity of the underlying structure of the data itself, which is something generally less studied in the literature, and it is exactly the main point of focus of this work. Specifically, we propose an exploratory procedure to help the user assessing the expressive power needed for producing efficient classification boundaries for a given dataset. This procedure is meant to be followed to better understand the dataset, prior to selecting the set of models to be further explored through model selection techniques. The procedure can be directly applied to a dataset and does not require prior knowledge for the input data or processing of external data.

More specifically, our idea for assessing the expressive power needed for a dataset is to challenge the decision boundaries produced by a rigid trained model.

This is achieved by relaxing progressively its decision boundaries, and evaluating in a controlled way how flexible these need to become so that they fit better to the data. To realize this idea, we use a typical Decision Tree (DT) for the initial decision boundaries, as it is a simple, interpretable, and a naturally rigid model. The proposed procedure is outlined in Fig. 1: it starts with the decision boundaries produced by a reference DT trained on the input dataset, also called seed DT. The seed DT initializes a Neural Decision Tree (NDT) [3], which inherits the DT's decision boundaries. By its definition, an NDT is a special type of Neural Network that can be initialized by a DT, where the smoothness of the activation functions can be controlled. What we put forward is the idea that, by training an NDT, it becomes possible to measure two things: its 'departure' from the seed DT in terms of disagreement at the decision level, and the evolution of any performance metric as a function of the allowed smoothness of the decision boundaries. We show with experiments on real and synthetic data that the indicators provided by our data exploration procedure are meaningful for the classification task, and we illustrate with examples how users can interpret them in practice.

## 2    Background

In this section, we present the tools we use to build our procedure. First, the core of the proposed method is the gradual relaxation of the decision boundaries produced by a rigid model. The algorithm to be used to perform this relaxation needs to offer the possibility of controlling the expressive power of the final model by tuning a small number of parameters. We propose this to be done using a Neural Decision Tree [3], which will be presented in Subsect. A. Once a model with more flexible decision boundaries is obtained, we can measure its 'departure' from the initial rigid one. Subsection B describes metrics to evaluate the difference between two models.

*A. Neural Decision Trees (NDTs).* An NDT is a neural network (NN) whose architecture and weights initialization are obtained directly from an input DT [2,3,10], which we call here 'seed DT'. The NDT variant we use is the one from [3], which we extend to classification tasks. The hyperparameters of this NDT type allow us to control the smoothness of its activation functions, which in fact is a proxy for controlling the smoothness of the decision boundaries.

An important NDT feature is that there is no need for the user to search for the right network architecture for each dataset, i.e. the number of layers or the number of neural units in each layer. Its generally shallow architecture may be too restrictive for complex problems, but this feature is seen as an advantage for our purpose. An NDT is always formed by four layers: an input layer, two hidden layers, and an output layer. The connections between the layers encode the information extracted from the seed DT. For a dataset with $d$ features and a seed DT with $K$ leaves, we get the following architecture and weights initialization:

- *Input layer*. As usual, it has $d$ neurons corresponding to the data features.
- *First hidden layer*: It consists of $K - 1$ neurons, each one representing a split node of the seed DT. A split condition of a node refers to a feature and a threshold on its value. The NDT encodes this information in the weight and bias matrices of the connections between this layer and the input layer.
- *Second hidden layer*: It consists of $K$ neurons, one for each leaf of the DT. Then, the connections between the neurons of this layer and those of the previous layer encode the positions of the leaves with respect to each split node. The elements of the weight and bias matrices encode the root-to-leaves paths present in the DT structure.
- *Output layer*: For a classification task, this layer contains the observed probability of an instance belonging to a class, according to its leaf membership.
- *Activation functions*: In a DT, the splits, as well as the instance-to-leaf memberships, are crisp. For an NDT to behave like a DT, its activation functions have to be crisp as well. However, a crisp function is not differentiable, and hence it would not be possible to train the NDT using backpropagation. To mitigate this problem, it is proposed to approximate each crisp threshold function of the trees with the function (see [3]):

$$\sigma : \ x \mapsto \tanh(\gamma x).$$

The parameter $\gamma$ allows controlling the smoothness of the $\sigma$ function: the higher the value of $\gamma$, the steeper the curve of $\sigma$ gets. Moreover, the same $\sigma$ form is used as an activation function for both NDT hidden layers, but with a different value of the $\gamma$ parameter in each case, which we denote by $\gamma_1$ and $\gamma_2$ that have the index of the respective hidden layer.

As depicted in Fig. 2, these parameters adjust the flexibility of the trained NDT model, which concerns its ability to learn smoother decision boundaries. Starting from a single DT, several models of variable flexibility can be generated by fixing the seed DT and then training NDTs that differ only in their $\gamma_1$ and $\gamma_2$ parameter values.

**B. Metrics.** One way to compare two classification models is with respect to their prediction capacity. This can be measured in various ways according to the kind of classification error that is minimized. We denote this performance measure by $\mathcal{M}$. Nevertheless, two models can have the same performance on a dataset, even though they may use a decision boundary of different structure. Measuring the distance between two models based on their decision structure is a challenging problem, especially when comparing models from different families, since that would require a meaningful representation for distance calculation. On the other hand, comparing the behavior of two models can be model-agnostic, that is when one quantifies how much the models agree or disagree on their predictions on the same dataset. For classification tasks, in particular, several metrics have been introduced for pairwise model comparison [16]. We specifically measure the decision agreement, denoted by $\mathcal{A}$, between two models as a proxy to measure what we term in this work as the 'departure' of one model from the other. Finally, the average value of the metrics over a number of experiments are denoted by $\overline{\mathcal{A}}$ and $\overline{\mathcal{M}}$.

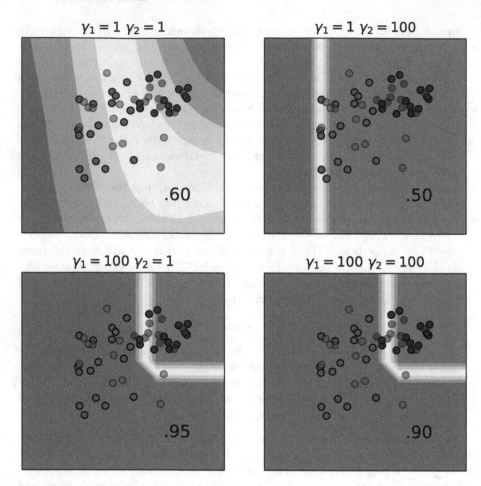

**Fig. 2.** Decision boundaries for data classification, obtained with NDTs that are all initialized with the same seed DT, whereas with different parameter values $\gamma_1$ and $\gamma_2$ that influence the smoothness and precision of the boundaries of the trained models. For parameter values, the NDT decision boundaries coincide with those of its seed DT.

## 3  Proposed Method

**A. Outline.** The main idea of the proposed data exploration procedure is to start from a DT whose training hyperparameters have been tuned (e.g. using CV). This is taken as a seed DT, and its structure is transferred to an NDT with a parameter set $\theta$ (see Fig. 1), including the batch size, the number of training epochs, type of optimizer, and the $\gamma_1$ and $\gamma_2$ values. During the procedure, the latter two are the only hyperparameters of the NDT that are not fixed. Therefore, finding $\theta^*$ in our case means finding the values of $\gamma_1$ and $\gamma_2$ for which the best average performance is observed.

$\gamma_1$ and $\gamma_2$ control the smoothness of the NDT activation functions: for higher values (e.g. 100) the NDT behaves very similarly to the seed DT, while for lower values it gets closer to an NN with hyperbolic tangent activation functions (see Fig. 2c). Varying progressively $\gamma_1$ and $\gamma_2$ from higher to lower values *causes a progressive departure of the NDT model*: from the initial DT to an altered model that is relaxed and closer to an NN model. It is then possible to detect the point where better performance is obtained with respect to $\mathcal{M}$, and also to measure using the metric $\mathcal{A}$ how far from a DT is the best NDT model obtained with $\theta^*$, which we also denote by $NDT^* := NDT(\theta^*)$. Note that while we can measure the departure from a specific seed DT, we cannot (as of yet) conclude that the NDT is departing from all the DTs that could be induced from the dataset. Hence the need of repeating the procedure with different seed DTs and evaluating the average behavior of DTs and NDTs, as well as the differences in their distributions, with statistical tests. The proposed method searches for $\theta^*$ and its subsequent interpretation, as well as that of $\overline{\mathcal{M}}(NDT^*)$ and $\overline{\mathcal{A}}(NDT^*)$. This is facilitated by graphical plots depicting the evolution of the metrics as a function of the values of the NDT parameters, over $n$ repetitions.

**B. Relationship Between $\gamma_1$ and $\gamma_2$.** As $\gamma_1$ has a bigger impact on the global shape of the decision boundaries, and in order to simplify the procedure and provide easy-to-interpret results, we link the value of $\gamma_2$ to that of $\gamma_1$ such that $\gamma_2 = f(\gamma_1)$. In the work [3] that originally presented the type of NDT we use, the general rule suggested is to use $\gamma_1 \gg \gamma_2$, since a smoother activation function in the second hidden layer allows for stronger weight corrections in the first hidden layer during backpropagation. An example of how having $\gamma_1 < \gamma_2$ can cause the loss of the initial information obtained from the seed DT and prevent the correct training of an NDT, can be seen in Fig. 2b.

Our particular goal is to start with an NDT that coincides with its seed DT, and then progressively relax the produced NDT's decision boundaries through training. This translates to $\gamma_2$ being of the same order of magnitude as $\gamma_1$. This is because if a much lower value of $\gamma_2$ is used, it would mean that, while the parts of the NDT corresponding to the information of the seed DT's inner nodes (first NDT layer) would progressively be adjusted, the paths between them would be able to be updated in an unconstrained way. However, this is not desired.

Note that there is no known optimal function relating $\gamma_1$ and $\gamma_2$. To present our proof of concept, we decided to link the hyperparameters with the function $f : x \mapsto \sqrt[q]{x}$, which allows us to respect the conditions stated previously. In what follows, we use $\gamma$ to actually refer to $\gamma_1$, and then $\gamma_2$ is computed internally by:

$$\gamma_2 = f(\gamma_1) = \sqrt[q]{\gamma_1}, \text{ with } q = 1.1. \tag{1}$$

**C. The Algorithm of the Procedure.** Equation 1 reduces the process of finding $\theta^*$ to that of estimating the optimal $\gamma^*$. As we are interested in a progressive departure from any given DT, we can produce multiple seed DTs, and for each one of those to build several NDTs by decreasing gradually the value of $\gamma$. The 36 tested values are in the ordered set $\Gamma = \{9000, 8000, ..., 1000\} \cup$

---

**Algorithm 1:** Pseudocode of the proposed method

---

**Input:** a dataset $D$, a set $\Gamma$ of values to test for $\gamma$
**Output:** the optimal $\gamma^*$ value of $\gamma$, the mean agreement $\overline{\mathcal{A}}(NDT, DT)$, and the and mean
     respective performance $\overline{\mathcal{M}}(NDT)$ and $\overline{\mathcal{M}}(DT)$

1   find the hyperparameters $h$ of a DT model for the dataset
2   **for** $i = 1, ...n$ times **do**
3      form the $D_{\text{train}}$, $D_{\text{test}}$, and $D_{\text{valid}}$ sets from $D$
4      build the new $DT_i := DT_i(h)$ with $D_{\text{train}}$
5      measure $\mathcal{M}(DT_i)$ on $D_{\text{test}}$
6      **foreach** $\gamma \in \Gamma$ **do**
7         initialize $NDT_{i,\gamma} := NDT(\gamma)$ using $DT_i$
8         fit $NDT_{i,\gamma}$ to $D_{\text{train}}$ and regularize it with $D_{\text{valid}}$
9         measure $\mathcal{A}(NDT_{i,\gamma}, DT_i)$, $\mathcal{M}(NDT_{i,\gamma})$ on $D_{\text{test}}$
10     **end**
11 **end**
12 $\overline{M_{DT}} = \frac{1}{n} \sum_{i=1}^{n} \mathcal{M}(DT_i)$
13 $\overline{M} = \left[ \frac{1}{n} \sum_{i=1}^{n} \mathcal{M}(NDT_{i,\gamma}) \right]_{\gamma \in \Gamma}$
14 $\overline{A} = \left[ \frac{1}{n} \sum_{i=1}^{n} \mathcal{A}(NDT_{i,\gamma}, DT_i) \right]_{\gamma \in \Gamma}$
15 $\gamma^* = \text{argmax}_{\gamma \in \Gamma} \, \overline{M}_\gamma$
16 **return** $\gamma^*$, $\overline{A}$, $\overline{M}$, $\overline{M_{DT}}$

---

$\{900, 800, ..., 100\} \cup \{90, 80, ..., 10\} \cup \{9, 8, ..., 1\}$. For each trained NDT, we measure the chosen performance metric $\mathcal{M}$ and the agreement $\mathcal{A}$ (see Sect. 2 – B). The overall procedure is detailed in Algorithm 1.

As we mainly aim to show a proof of our concept, we use a simple way to optimize $\gamma$: by testing $n$ times the performance of $NDT(\gamma)$ for $\gamma \in \Gamma$, and then by selecting the value that provides the best average performance. Algorithm 1 can be computationally expensive for a large $\Gamma$ set, as that would lead to the training of $n \times |\Gamma|$ NNs. However, by using NDTs and by relating $\gamma_2$ to $\gamma_1$ (Eq. 1), there is no need to also search for the optimal NN architecture, and hence we reduce the parameter space to be searched. Note also that the initialization of the NDT weights by a seed DTs provides a warm start, which makes the NDT training to be less sensitive to randomness and generally to converge faster compared to usual initialization techniques (e.g. random uniform weights).

**D. Using Comparative Metrics Between Models.** Given a trained NDT that was initialized by a specific seed DT, we measure its departure with respect to its seed DT as the decision agreement $\mathcal{A}$ between the two models.

More specifically, the agreement metric used for the considered classification task is Cohen's $\kappa$ statistic [5], which calculates the extent to which the class predicted by two classifiers agree while also taking into account the probability for them to agree by chance: $\kappa = \frac{p_o - p_e}{1 - p_e}$, where $p_o$ is the probability that the two classifiers do agree, and $p_e$ the probability that they agree by chance. When the models agree completely, $\kappa = 1$; when they agree by chance, $\kappa = 0$; if their agreement is less than what is expected by chance, then $\kappa < 0$. By abusing the notation, we write as $\mathcal{A}(NDT(\gamma))$ the agreement evaluation for an NDT and its seed DT. Finally, the performance metric $\mathcal{M}$ that is used to measure and compare the performance of different models is their classification accuracy.

# 4   Experiments

***Datasets.*** The proposed method is tested on 8 datasets, 1 synthetic and 7 containing real data taken from the UCI repository. The characteristics of these datasets are summarized in Table 1. Some of them were chosen because either rule-based models (such as DTs) or more expressive models (such as NNs) are better suited for them. First, the synthetic sim_1000_3 dataset contains two non-linearly separable classes, each of them generated by a Gaussian distribution. Regarding real data, the Gastrointestinal Lesions in Regular Colonoscopy dataset (lesions) was chosen as it is high-dimensional and in such cases DTs can be better in selecting only the most informative features [4]. The mushroom dataset is interesting as it can be accurately modeled using simple rules. The rest of the datasets used are cases where the underlying structure is not as clear as above: the Spambase (spam), the Congressional Voting Records (votes), Student Performance (student-math), and the Wine (wine) datasets, as well as a part of the Vehicle Silhouettes dataset (xab). The last three datasets were transformed into binary classification problems. The implementation of the compared methods, and the datasets used, are available online[1].

**Table 1.** Datasets used to obtain the experimental results.

| Dataset | #Feats | #Inst. | DT depth |
|---|---|---|---|
| sim_1000_3 | 3 | 1000 | 4 |
| wine | 13 | 178 | 3 |
| votes | 16 | 435 | 2 |
| xab | 18 | 94 | 6 |
| mushroom | 23 | 8124 | 5 |
| student-math | 31 | 395 | 3 |
| spam | 58 | 4601 | 5 |
| lesions | 371 | 152 | 4 |

***Experimental Pipeline.*** For each dataset, we first used CV to determine the depth of the DTs to be used as seeds (reported in Table 2), which was found to be the hyperparameter with the biggest impact on DT performance. Aside from removing the categorical variables (except for mushroom, where all its variables are categorical and were encoded, similarly to student-math) and the instances with missing data, no other preprocessing preceded.

For the NDTs, for all datasets, we set the number of training epochs to 100 and the batch size to 32. We use the Adam optimizer with default parameters, and for regularization we use early stopping with a patience of 10 epochs.

---

[1] See: https://kalogeratos.com/material/DTvsNDT.

**Table 2.** Summary of the experimental results. The results are the average of 30 iterations, and 'Imp.' indicates whether an NDT achieved (on average) an improvement over the performance of its seed DT.

| Dataset | $\gamma^*$ | $\overline{\mathcal{M}}(DT)$ | $\overline{\mathcal{M}}(NDT(\gamma^*))$ | $\overline{\mathcal{M}}$ diff. | Imp. | $\overline{\mathcal{A}}(NDT(\gamma^*))$ | $\overline{\mathcal{M}}(NN)$ |
|---|---|---|---|---|---|---|---|
| sim_1000_3 | 3 | 0.906 (0.008) | 0.989 (0.008) | −0.083 (0.010) | ✓ | 0.821 (0.020) | 0.990 (0.009) |
| wine | 8000 | 0.962 (0.017) | 0.956 (0.024) | 0.007 (0.016) | | 0.976 (0.034) | 0.627 (0.076) |
| votes | 50 | 0.977 (0.008) | 0.971 (0.020) | 0.006 (0.019) | | 0.974 (0.060) | 0.748 (0.138) |
| xab | 60 | 0.871 (0.041) | 0.865 (0.047) | 0.006 (0.018) | | 0.982 (0.035) | 0.532 (0.066) |
| mushroom | 4 | 0.983 (0.002) | 1.000 (0.000) | −0.016 (0.002) | ✓ | 0.967 (0.003) | 0.969 (0.015) |
| student-math | 5 | 0.735 (0.014) | 0.721 (0.022) | 0.014 (0.027) | | 0.601 (0.266) | 0.675 (0.010) |
| spam | 1 | 0.916 (0.004) | 0.941 (0.006) | −0.025 (0.006) | ✓ | 0.845 (0.021) | 0.920 (0.059) |
| lesions | 8000 | 0.891 (0.025) | 0.889 (0.037) | 0.003 (0.028) | | 0.892 (0.127) | 0.719 (0.111) |

To generate the training, validation, and test sets we use repeated random subsampling with proportions 50%/25%/25% respectively, which we repeat 30 times (i.e. $n = 30$). We use stratification to ensure that classes are in the same proportions in the sets.

We additionally compare the results obtained with the performance of an NN architecture chosen via a typical CV procedure. The parameters we investigated are: the depth ($D = \{1, 2, 3\}$), the width for all layers ($W = \{2, 3, 4, 5, 6, 7\}$), and the activation function to be used for all hidden layers (tanh or ReLU). This corresponds to training 36 NNs for each dataset, hence the computational budget is comparable to that used by our method when $|\Gamma| = 36$.

Finally, we evaluate the significance of the differences of the observed performance using statistical tests. We use Wilcoxon's signed rank test [15] (to which we refer to as Wilcoxon's test in the following sections), since the paired samples we compared can not be assumed to be normally distributed (as per Shapiro-Wilk's test). The null hypothesis we test is: the median of the population of differences between the paired data to be zero ($H_0$), and the two-sided alternative hypothesis is: the median of the population of differences to be different from zero ($H_a$). These hypotheses are tested with a risk $\alpha = 0.05$.

*Results.* The method outputs $\gamma^*$, $\overline{\mathcal{M}}(NDT^*)$, and $\overline{\mathcal{A}}(NDT^*)$. These values are then to be interpreted so that we get insights whether the dataset would need more flexible decision boundaries than those of a hard set of rules. We present here detailed examples of this interpretation for three datasets (sim_1000_3, lesions and spam). We also present the results of tests that measure the statistical significance of the obtained results, and how they compare to a CV done in a limited set of NNs.

*Examples.* Figure 3a shows the average performance of the NDT with respect to $\gamma$, and compares it to that of the initial seed DT. It tells us that, as expected, for higher values of $\gamma$ the NDT has an average performance that is close to that of its seed DT, and as $\gamma$ decreases the performance of the NDT varies. In this case, the accuracy increases monotonically and reaches its maximum for $\gamma = 3$. For this value, $\sigma$ is closer to a tanh function and thus the NDT decision boundaries are smooth. This is a case where the specific needs of the user will

**Table 3.** Results from statistical Wilcoxon's signed rank tests comparing pairwise the accuracies of the models NDTs, DTs, and NNs.

| Dataset | $\gamma^*$ | NDTs vs. DTs | | NDTs vs. NNs | | NNs vs. DTs | |
|---|---|---|---|---|---|---|---|
| | | $p$-value | Reject $H_0$ | $p$-value | Reject $H_0$ | $p$-value | Reject $H_0$ |
| sim_1000_3 | 3 | 1.65e−06 | ✓ | 5.49e−01 | | 1.64e−06 | ✓ |
| wine | 8000 | 8.38e−02 | | 1.63e−06 | ✓ | 1.55e−06 | ✓ |
| votes | 50 | 4.89e−01 | | 2.29e−06 | ✓ | 1.66e−06 | ✓ |
| xab | 60 | 2.15e−01 | | 1.65e−06 | ✓ | 1.62e−06 | ✓ |
| mushroom | 4 | 1.56e−06 | ✓ | 1.73e−06 | ✓ | 2.36e−05 | ✓ |
| student-math | 5 | 1.81e−02 | ✓ | 1.89e−06 | ✓ | 1.61e−06 | ✓ |
| spam | 1 | 1.72e−06 | ✓ | 2.70e−05 | ✓ | 5.53e−05 | ✓ |
| lesions | 8000 | 1.49e−01 | | 1.61e−06 | ✓ | 1.66e−06 | ✓ |

determine which should be the next steps to take. Indeed, the high agreement between $NDT(\gamma^*)$ and the DT (0.821, see Table 2) indicates that a DT and a more flexible model may not differ much decision-wise, so the latter can be more promising to explore if one is interested in obtaining better performance at the cost of sacrificing the explainability. Nevertheless, if one can afford to sacrifice a bit in terms of model accuracy to gain understanding, the former can suffice.

Figure 3b shows both the performance and the agreement decreasing as the value of $\gamma$ decreases. Here, the best average accuracy for the NDT is reached when $\gamma^* = 8000$. In this case, the function $\sigma$ is practically a threshold function, and hence the NDT will behave similarly to a DT. In contrast, there is no improvement over the seed DT, even for $NDT^*$. Our interpretation of these results is that the dataset can be described by a model with rigid decision boundaries, such as a set of decision rules or a DT.

Similar reasoning can be used for the rest of the datasets, based on the results of Table 2. Similar graphs can be drawn for all the datasets, however, their interpretation might be less straightforward than for the examples of Fig. 3a. The data preprocessing can also greatly affect the shape of the plots.

Figure 3c is an example where the interpretation is more complex. In this figure, the agreement and the classification performance do not have a monotonic evolution, but their curves follow similar trends. This can be explained by the fact that the agreement measure we use evaluates the proportion of the instances where an NDT and its seed DT make the same decisions, and this is influenced by the quality of the models being compared. In Fig. 3c, we can see that the seed DTs have a good average accuracy, and so when the derived NDTs are more accurate, they are bound to make similar decisions, and vice-versa. When the NDTs are less accurate, it is natural that these models make different predictions for a significant part of the dataset. When $\gamma$ is lower ($<100$), we observe an increase in the accuracy of the NDTs, with the best accuracy being reached when $\gamma^* = 1$. In this case, the information we have at hand indicates that the dataset can be modeled using a DT, but its accuracy is sensitive to changes in its structure. When $\gamma$ is low enough, it is easier for the NDT to adapt to these changes, since its decision boundaries get sufficiently flexible. It can thus

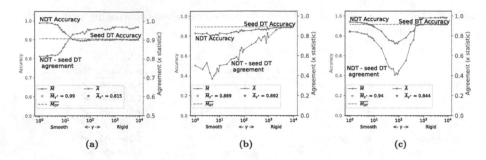

**Fig. 3.** Progressive relaxation (right-to-left along x-axis, as $\gamma$ reduces) of the NDT decision boundaries with respect to its seed DT. No data scaling is used; the training set is 50% of each dataset. **(a)** sim_1000_3 dataset – As the boundaries are getting relaxed, the NDT performs better, but agrees less with the seed DT, suggesting that a more flexible model might be more adapted. **(b)** lesions dataset – Both the agreement and the accuracy of the NDT decrease with the value of $\gamma$, meaning that a relaxation of the initial DT's boundaries is not beneficial. **(c)** spam dataset – As the boundaries get relaxed, the NDT performs better, and also agrees more with the seed DT, which means that the relaxation is beneficial when the rigid boundaries ($\gamma$ is high) are sensitive to small changes to which it is hard for them to adapt through training.

progressively approach a better local minimum of the loss function. In conclusion, a model with a higher expressive power is worth exploring in this case, although the agreement with a DT might be high (it is 0.845 as shown in Table 2).

***Testing for Statistical Significance.*** In support of our experimental results, we performed statistical tests to confirm the significance of the difference in the median performance of the seed DTs and the $NDT(\gamma^*)$ for each dataset. We also present tests to show the significance of the difference between DTs and NNs, and between NNs and $NDT(\gamma^*)$.

Table 3 reports the results of Wilcoxon's tests, which show that when $\gamma^*$ is low, the hypothesis $H_0$ that the median difference in the performance of the two models that are compared is 0. $H_0$ is rejected when the $p$-value is lower than 0.05. We observe that we can reject $H_0$ and accept $H_a$ for half of the datasets. These are the datasets where $\gamma^*$ is the lowest, meaning that even though NDTs are initialized by the DTs, a statistically significant gain (or loss) is achieved by the departure of the NDT from the DT. The cases where we cannot reject $H_0$ are those where $\gamma^*$ is higher, and $\mathcal{A}$ is very high, as shown in Table 2. The need for departure from a DT structure by relaxing its decision boundaries is reflected by the $\mathcal{A}$ and $\gamma^*$ values.

Furthermore, when NNs and NDTs are compared, our tests show that $H_0$ can be rejected in most cases, except for the sim_1000_3, where $\gamma^*$ is low and $\mathcal{A}$ is relatively low. Notice also that in most cases the performance of the NDT is better than that of the NN found via CV.

Simply comparing the performances of DTs and NNs leads to significantly different performance for all datasets, confirming that indeed the DT and NN model spaces are clearly separated for the datasets we use. However, this comparison, is not in itself very informative for the datasets.

*Note on the Computational Complexity.* As here we mainly presented a proof of concept, there are aspects that can be further optimized. One of them is the search strategy for $\gamma^*$. Although performing an exhaustive search makes the curves of $\mathcal{A}$ and $\mathcal{M}$ easier to understand by the user, we have observed that these curves evolve monotonically in certain subranges of $\Gamma$. For example, reading right-to-left Fig. 3c, there is first a plateau when $\gamma \in [700, 9000]$, then there is a monotonic decrease of the metric values when $\gamma \in [90, 600]$, and finally there is a monotonic increase when $\gamma < 90$. Interestingly, the monotonicity of the observed behaviors is preserved in the range of the same order of magnitude of $\gamma$. This implies that the general behavior of the metrics over $\Gamma$ could be inferred from fewer points, and hence use the presented method more efficiently.

## 5 Conclusion

The data exploration procedure we presented in this work allows us to determine how flexible should be the decision boundaries should be for a given classification task, in comparison to those of a rigid model. We propose a controlled way to investigate this by using NDTs initialized by a seed DT, and then progressively relax the NDTs' decision boundaries through training their weights. Furthermore, the agreement metric provides insights about how far it is necessary to depart from the seed DT to achieve a performance gain (if there is one). We demonstrated that our data exploration procedure is meaningful for analyzing the properties of a given dataset, and how the computed metric can be used as indicators by the user. The analysis of the statistical soundness of the results support our findings.

In the future, we plan to work on the optimization of $\gamma_1$, $\gamma_2$ and the enrichment of the experimental results. Even more important is to investigate further other concrete uses of our procedure that can be beneficial for practitioners.

**Acknowledgements.** This work was funded by the Île-de-France Region and additionally by the IdAML Chair hosted at ENS Paris-Saclay. The authors are thankful to Atos for providing an Atos Edge machine to perform numerical experiments.

## References

1. Ali, S., Smith, K.A.: On learning algorithm selection for classification. Appl. Soft Comput. **6**(2), 119–138 (2006)
2. Balestriero, R.: Neural decision trees. arXiv preprint (2017). https://doi.org/10.48550/arXiv.1702.07360
3. Biau, G., Scornet, E., Welbl, J.: Neural random forests. Sankhya A **81**(2), 347–386 (2018)
4. Brown, D.E., Corruble, V., Pittard, C.L.: A comparison of decision tree classifiers with backpropagation neural networks for multimodal classification problems. Pattern Recogn. **26**(6), 953–961 (1993)

5. Cohen, J.: A coefficient of agreement for nominal scales. Educ. Psychol. Measur. **20**(1), 37–46 (1960)
6. Ding, J., Tarokh, V., Yang, Y.: Model selection techniques: an overview. IEEE Signal Process. Mag. **35**(6), 16–34 (2018)
7. Feurer, M., Klein, A., Eggensperger, K., Springenberg, J., Blum, M., Hutter, F.: Efficient and robust automated machine learning. In: Cortes, C., Lawrence, N.D., Lee, D.D., Sugiyama, M., Garnett, R. (eds.) Advances in Neural Information Processing Systems 28, pp. 2962–2970. Curran Associates, Inc. (2015)
8. Kotthoff, L., Thornton, C., Hoos, H.H., Hutter, F., Leyton-Brown, K.: Auto-WEKA: automatic model selection and hyperparameter optimization in WEKA. In: Hutter, F., Kotthoff, L., Vanschoren, J. (eds.) Automated Machine Learning. TSSCML, pp. 81–95. Springer, Cham (2019). https://doi.org/10.1007/978-3-030-05318-5_4
9. Lindner, G., Studer, R.: AST: support for algorithm selection with a CBR approach. In: Żytkow, J.M., Rauch, J. (eds.) PKDD 1999. LNCS (LNAI), vol. 1704, pp. 418–423. Springer, Heidelberg (1999). https://doi.org/10.1007/978-3-540-48247-5_52
10. Lu, Y.L., Wang, C.: Validation of an alternative neural decision tree. In: IEEE International Conference on Big Data, pp. 3682–3691 (2020)
11. Peng, Y., Flach, P.A., Soares, C., Brazdil, P.: Improved dataset characterisation for meta-learning. In: Lange, S., Satoh, K., Smith, C.H. (eds.) DS 2002. LNCS, vol. 2534, pp. 141–152. Springer, Heidelberg (2002). https://doi.org/10.1007/3-540-36182-0_14
12. Pimentel, B.A., de Carvalho, A.C.P.L.F.: A new data characterization for selecting clustering algorithms using meta-learning. Inf. Sci. **477**, 203–219 (2019)
13. Reif, M., Shafait, F., Dengel, A.: Meta-learning for evolutionary parameter optimization of classifiers. Mach. Learn. **87**(3), 357–380 (2012)
14. Smith, K.A., Woo, F., Ciesielski, V., Ibrahim, R.: Matching data mining algorithm suitability to data characteristics using a self-organizing map. In: Abraham, A., Köppen, M. (eds.) Hybrid Information Systems, vol. 14, pp. 169–179. Physica, Heidelberg (2002). https://doi.org/10.1007/978-3-7908-1782-9_13
15. Wilcoxon, F.: Individual comparisons by ranking methods. Biom. Bull. **1**(6), 80–83 (1945)
16. Zhou, Z.H.: Ensemble Methods: Foundations and Algorithms. Chapman & Hall/CRC, Boca Raton (2012)

# Towards Robust Uncertainty Estimation in the Presence of Noisy Labels

Chao Pan[1,2](✉), Bo Yuan[1,2], Wei Zhou[3], and Xin Yao[1,2]

[1] Research Institute of Trustworthy Autonomous System,
Southern University of Science and Technology (SUSTech), Shenzhen 518055, China
11930665@mail.sustech.edu.cn
[2] Guangdong Provincial Key Laboratory of Brain-inspired Intelligent Computation,
Department of Computer Science and Engineering,
Southern University of Science and Technology (SUSTech), Shenzhen 518055, China
{yuanb,xiny}@sustech.edu.cn
[3] Trustworthiness Theory Research Center, Huawei Technology Co., Ltd.,
Shenzhen, China
zhouwei203@huawei.com

**Abstract.** In security-critical applications, it is essential to know how confident the model is in its predictions. Many uncertainty estimation methods have been proposed recently, and these methods are reliable when the training data do not contain labeling errors. However, we find that the quality of these uncertainty estimation methods decreases dramatically when noisy labels are present in the training data. In some datasets, the uncertainty estimates would become completely absurd, even though these labeling noises barely affect the test accuracy. We further analyze the impact of existing label noise handling methods on the reliability of uncertainty estimates, although most of these methods focus only on improving the accuracy of the models. We identify that the data cleaning-based approach can alleviate the influence of label noise on uncertainty estimates to some extent, but there are still some drawbacks. Finally, we propose a robust uncertainty estimation method under label noise. Compared with other algorithms, our approach achieves a more reliable uncertainty estimates in the presence of noisy labels, especially when there are large-scale labeling errors in the training data.

**Keywords:** Uncertainty estimation · Noisy label · Out-of-distribution data · Mis-classification detection

This work was supported by the Research Institute of Trustworthy Autonomous Systems, the Guangdong Provincial Key Laboratory (Grant No. 2020B121201001), the Program for Guangdong Introducing Innovative and Entrepreneurial Teams (Grant No. 2017ZT07X386), the Shenzhen Science and Technology Program (Grant No. KQTD2016112514355531) and Huawei project on "Fundamental Theory and Key Technologies of Trustworthy Systems".

# 1    Introduction

Estimating the predictive uncertainty of neural networks is essential in security-critical areas. Despite the impressive performance achieved by deep neural networks in a variety of tasks, it is particularly important to know how reliable their predictions are when applied to real-world scenarios, especially in safety-critical applications like medical diagnostics, autonomous driving, etc. In these areas, overconfident incorrect predictions may cause serious consequences [1].

Several approaches have been proposed to estimate the uncertainty of neural network models. Uncertainty estimation methods for deep neural networks include Bayesian and non-Bayesian methods [4,5]. When the training data are all labeled correctly, these methods can achieve promising performance [3,6], that is, the uncertainty estimation is trustworthy at this point.

However, we find that many uncertainty estimation methods will become untrustworthy when label noise is present in the training data. As shown in Fig. 1, the test accuracy of the neural network model is almost constant when we add 20% noisy labels to the MNIST dataset. But the performance of Monte Carlo Dropout-based uncertainty estimates for mis-classification detection and out-of-distribution (OOD) data detection is dramatically reduced, and in some scenarios is even worse than a random classifier.

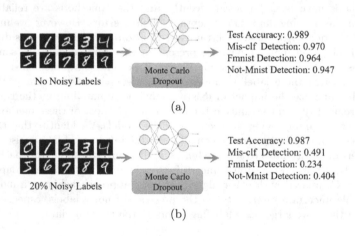

(a)

(b)

**Fig. 1.** (a): When the MNIST dataset contains no label noise, the Monte Carlo Dropout-based predictive uncertainty estimation for both misclassification detection and OOD data detection works remarkably well. (b): When 20% noisy labels are present in the MNIST dataset, the test accuracy of the LeNet5 model remains almost identical, but the Monte Carlo Dropout-based uncertainty estimates become completely unreliable: the AUROC for misclassification detection is close to the result of random guessing, and the performance of OOD data detection is even much worse than a random detector.

To the best of our knowledge, current approaches to address label noise are aimed at improving the test accuracy of the model without focusing on how to improve the reliability of uncertainty estimation [14–16]. In this paper, we compare different label noise handling strategies and find that the strategy based on data cleaning is superior to obtaining reliable uncertainty estimates. Further, we propose an iterative sample selection algorithm based on Monto Carlo Dropout, which can significantly improve the reliability of uncertainty estimates when noisy labels are present in the training data without reducing the accuracy of the model.

The primary contributions of this paper are as follows:

- This paper reveals that many uncertainty estimation methods, including Bayesian methods (e.g., Monte Carlo Dropout) and non-Bayesian methods (e.g., Deep Ensemble), will become unreliable when label noise is present in the training data. To our best knowledge, no relevant literature has previously identified this problem.
- This paper compares and analyzes the impact of different types of label noise handling approaches on the reliability of uncertainty estimation methods.
- We propose a simple but effective robust uncertainty estimation method under noisy labels. Compared with other label noise processing methods, our algorithm not only obtains similar or superior accuracy but also can significantly improve the reliability of uncertainty estimates in the presence of massive label noise.

This paper is organized in the following order: In Sect. 2, we present the problem definition and background information on uncertainty. In Sect. 3, we analyze the effect of noisy labels on the reliability of uncertainty estimates. We compare the impact of different label noise handling methods on uncertainty estimates in Sect. 4. Section 5 proposes a robust uncertainty estimation method in the presence of label noise. Section 6 is the experimental settings and results, and Sect. 7 provides the conclusions.

## 2 Preliminaries

### 2.1 Problem Definition

Lets consider a classification problem with training set $\mathcal{D} = \{(x_1, y_1), ..., (x_n, y_n)\}$, where $x_i \in \mathcal{R}^d$ is a d-dimensional feature and $y_i \in \{1, ..., c\}$ denotes the observed label of $x_i$. There are some noisy labels in $\mathcal{D}$, and the true label of $x_i$ is $y_i^*$.

The classifier learns a function $f : \mathcal{X} \rightarrow \mathcal{Y}$ that maps the input space to the label space. The uncertainty estimation method learns a function $g : \mathcal{X} \rightarrow \mathcal{R}$ that represents the confidence on the prediction. Suppose there is a series of uncertainty reliability evaluation methods $\mathcal{E} = \{e_1, ..., e_k\}$. We expect the uncertainty estimation method $g$ to obtain the highest possible score in $\mathcal{E}$ when label noise is present in $\mathcal{D}$.

## 2.2  Reliability of Uncertainty Estimation Methods

Since the definition of uncertainty varies from field to field, it is necessary to explain what is meant by uncertainty in this paper. In machine learning, uncertainty is usually denoted as the model's confidence score in its prediction, that is, how confident the neural network model is that its output is correct [7,8].

Analyzing the reliability of uncertainty estimation methods is challenging because we usually do not have ground truth uncertainty estimates [6]. In this paper, we focus on the performance of applying predictive uncertainty to misclassification detection and OOD data detection [9–11]. The performance of these two tasks can, to some extent, reflect the reliability of the uncertainty estimates.

**Misclassification Detection.** One application of predictive uncertainty is misclassification detection, which is knowing which predictions are more likely to be incorrect. Trustworthy uncertainty estimation methods are supposed to give higher uncertainty to samples that are mis-predicted. Therefore, when the predictive uncertainty for a given sample is quite large, this result should be discarded.

**Out-of-Distribution Data Detection.** The data with the same distribution as the training data is referred to as in-distribution (ID) data. In contrast, data that differ significantly from the training data are called out-of-distribution (OOD) data. In real scenarios, OOD data are inevitable, and neural network models cannot provide correct predictions for them. For example, for a model of cat and dog classification, when the input is a rabbit, it is absurd to predict whether it is a cat or a dog when the input is a rabbit. At this point, the best approach for the neural network model is to say I don't know, that is, to give a high predictive uncertainty for this sample. A reliable uncertainty estimation method is expected to assign higher uncertainty to OOD data and lower uncertainty to ID data.

## 3  Impact of Noisy Labels on Reliability of Uncertainty Estimates

Many researches have shown that label noise has a negative impact on the practical applications of neural network models, such as transfer learning, facial attribute recognition, etc. However, to the best of our knowledge, no studies have revealed the influence of label noise on predictive uncertainty. In this section, we analyze the effect of label noise on different predictive uncertainty estimation methods on two popular datasets, MNIST and CIFAR10.

We chose representatives of Bayesian and non-Bayesian methods, Monte Carlo Dropout [2] and Deep Ensemble [6], as uncertainty estimation methods. All experimental settings, such as neural network architectures, optimization methods, types of labeling noise, etc., remain consistent throughout this paper and will be described in detail in Sect. 6. We take the performance of the two

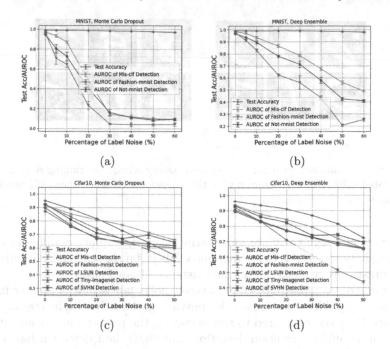

**Fig. 2.** (a): Test accuracy of models trained on MNIST datasets with different proportions of noisy labels, and AUROC of Monte Carlo Dropout-based predictive uncertainty for misclassification detection and OOD data detection. (b): Similar to (a), but using Deep Ensemble to estimate uncertainty. (c) (d): Similar to (a) and (b), but with the Cifar10 dataset.

applications of predictive uncertainty presented in Sect. 2 to compare the reliability of uncertainty estimates under different proportions of label noise. Since OOD detection may not be consistent between datasets [12], we use as many OOD datasets as possible.

On the MNIST dataset, even without additional processing of label noise, it does not have much influence on the test accuracy (Fig. 2(a), (b)). More specifically, a 50% noisy labeling only reduces the test accuracy of Monte Carlo Dropout by 1.18% and that of Deep Ensemble by 0.69%. One reason for this is that the Monte Carlo Dropout spars the neural network and is capable of providing some robustness against noisy labels [17].

However, we find that even a small amount of label noise can significantly affect the reliability of uncertainty estimates and even make the outcomes absurd (Fig. 2(a), (b)). Monte Carlo Dropout will fail completely when 20% of label noise is present in the MNIST dataset. As the proportion of label noise is further increased, the AUROC of the Monte Carlo Dropout-based uncertainty estimation method for both misclassification detection and OOD data detection is even less than 0.5, which means it is worse than a random detector. Although Deep Ensemble's robustness against noisy labels is somewhat better, it also becomes completely unreliable when the proportion of noisy labels reaches 40%. This

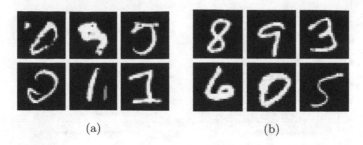

(a)                          (b)

**Fig. 3.** (a): The samples with the largest uncertainty when the training data does not contain label noise. (b): The samples with the largest uncertainty when 30% label noise is present in the training data.

implies that although there are some variations in the ability of different uncertainty estimation methods to tolerate noisy labels, but in general, their reliability will be drastically reduced due to the existence of label noise.

On the more complex CIFAR10 dataset, noisy labels have a greater impact on test accuracy. The test accuracy declines almost linearly with increasing labeling errors. However, compared to test accuracy, the performance of uncertainty estimation for misclassification detection and OOD data detection has a more substantial reduction. Under 40% label noise, Monte Carlo Dropout maintains a test accuracy of over 60%, while AUROC for several OOD detections is already close to 0.5, which is the expected AUROC value for a random detector.

In addition, a reliable uncertainty estimation method ought to give higher uncertainty to anomalous or odd samples in the trained ID data. As shown in Fig. 3, when the training data does not include labeling errors, the samples with the highest uncertainty are all relatively peculiar. However, when there are 30% noisy labels in the training data, the samples with the highest uncertainty are all normal samples, that is, the uncertainty estimation method loses the ability to identify exotic samples at this time. This also illustrates from another perspective that label noise has an impact on the reliability of uncertainty estimates.

## 4    Comparison of Different Label Noise Handling Methods

Several techniques have been proposed in the literature to make the model more robust to label noise, but most of these strategies focus on how to improve the test accuracy of the model under noisy labels. As we describe in Sect. 3, noisy labels have a more significant impact on predictive uncertainty than test accuracy. The quality of uncertainty estimates for two models with similar test accuracies may differ significantly. Therefore, in this section, we will analyze the effect of different label noise processing strategies on the improvement of uncertainty reliability.

Label noise processing methods can be classified into several categories including data re-weighting, data cleaning, robust losses, etc. The objective of data re-weighting is to assign lower weights to training data that are more likely to be mislabeled, and one of the most common methods is to weight them according to the loss and uncertainty [13,20,21]. Label cleaning, also often called sample selection, refers to using training data that are more likely to be correctly labeled or fixing the labels of the training data [22,23]. Robust losses are to use loss functions that are robust to label noise. For example, recent literature suggests that mean absolute error (MAE) and generalized cross entropy loss (GCE) are more robust to label noise than cross entropy [18,19].

Deep Ensemble relies on training multiple models, which makes it not very convenient to calculate predictive uncertainty during the training process. Therefore, although we show that the Deep Ensemble-based uncertainty estimates are more robust to label noise in Sect. 3, we still choose Monte Carlo Dropout as the uncertainty estimation method after comprehensive consideration.

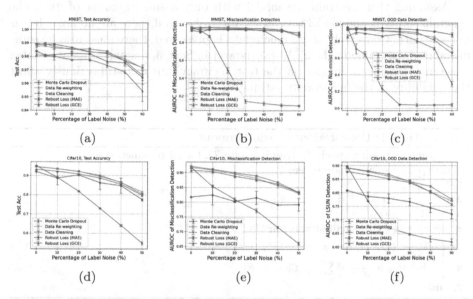

**Fig. 4.** (a) (d): Test accuracy of Monte Carlo Dropout model with multiple label noise processing methods under different proportions of noisy labels. (b) (e): AUROC of Monte Carlo Dropout uncertainty for misclassification detection. (c) (f): AUROC of Monte Carlo Dropout uncertainty for OOD data detection.

As can be observed from Fig. 4, when the training data does not contain labeling errors, the utilization of two categories of label noise processing methods, data re-weighting and data cleaning, does not affect the test accuracy compared to the normally trained Monte Carlo Dropout model. And robust loss function, both in terms of MAE and GCE, the test accuracy is reduced to some extent, which is consistent with the results of other literature [18].

As long as there is a certain percentage of labeling error in the training data, using any of the label noise handling methods can significantly improve the performance of predictive uncertainty for misclassification detection and OOD data detection, with very few exceptions. Comparing the three label noise processing methods, we can notice that GCE has the least improvement in uncertainty reliability. The effectiveness of data cleaning and data re-weighting is similar, but overall, data cleaning provides the best reliability improvement for uncertainty.

## 5   Robust Monte Carlo Dropout

Although the data cleaning strategy has been able to significantly improve the reliability of uncertainty estimates, it still has some drawbacks: since label noise has a greater impact on the reliability of uncertainty estimates than test accuracy, how much of the data that is more likely to be mislabeled should be discarded?

Assuming that we train the model with only a small amount of data, the generalizability of the model is severely affected even if there are no noisy labels in these data. Conversely, if too much data is preserved, there must also be some mislabeled data among them. As we showed in Sect. 3, a small amount of label noise may have little impact on the test accuracy, but can still seriously affect the reliability of the uncertainty estimates.

---

**Algorithm 1:** Robust Monte Carlo Dropout

**Input**   : Training epoch $T$. Training data $\mathcal{D}$. Initial parameters $\theta$.
**Output:** Updated parameters $\theta$.

1   $k = \frac{|\mathcal{D}|}{T}$ ;
2   **for** $t \leftarrow 0$ **to** $T - 1$ **do**
3   $\quad$ $W \leftarrow P(y|x) \cdot U(x)$ ;
4   $\quad$ $s \leftarrow (k \cdot t)$th smallest value in $W$ ;
5   $\quad$ $\mathcal{D}' \leftarrow \{(x_i, y_i) | (x_i, y_i) \in \mathcal{D} \cap W_i > s\}$ ;
6   $\quad$ $\theta \leftarrow \theta - \alpha \frac{1}{|\mathcal{D}'|} \nabla \sum_{i=1}^{|\mathcal{D}'|} \mathcal{L}(x_i, y_i; \theta);$
7   **end**

---

Therefore, one strategy is to dynamically adjust the amount of training data. Specifically, as training proceeds, less but cleaner data is applied to train the model. In this way, a sufficient amount of training data in the early stages ensures the generalization of the model, and clean data in the later stages enhances the reliability of the uncertainty estimates. As shown in Algorithm 1, we first calculate the number of samples $k$ to be discarded for each epoch (line 1). Then we find the threshold of weight $s$ for the current epoch (line 4). We select training samples with weights greater than the threshold and update the model parameters with these samples only (lines 5 and 6).

Besides, the trustworthy uncertainty estimation method would assign low uncertainty to the ID data and large uncertainty to the OOD data. One way to reduce the uncertainty of the training ID data is to focus more on the samples with high predictive uncertainty in the training set during the training process. Unlike other studies that treat the historical variation in sample loss or probability as uncertainty [13], we directly use the uncertainty obtained from the Monte Carlo Dropout in the training phase. The purpose of doing so is to maintain consistency, in addition to paying more attention to samples that are more likely to be on the decision boundary. Since we finally adopt Monte Carlo Dropout for OOD data detection, it is advisable to reduce the Monte Carlo Dropout uncertainty of ID data as much as possible during the training process. Therefore, we assign larger weights to samples with low loss (more likely to be correctly labeled) and high Monte Carlo Dropout uncertainty (line 3). Since a low cross-entropy loss corresponds to a high softmax probability for a given label, we directly used $P(y|x)$.

# 6 Experiments

## 6.1 Experimental Setting

We evaluate our approach on two ID datasets, including MNIST and CIFAR10. Since OOD detection results may be inconsistent among datasets [12], we will take several OOD datasets. To avoid the data imbalance problem, we set the samples of each OOD dataset to be the same as the test set of ID data.

We trained the LeNet5 model on the MNIST dataset using SGD with a learning rate of 0.01 and a momentum of 0.9. For the CIFAR10 dataset, we followed the settings in [13]. We trained the ResNet18 model using SGD with an initial learning rate of 0.1, the momentum of 0.9, and weight decay of $5 * 10^{-4}$ [24]. All data are normalized to a standard normal distribution. In the training process, we adopt cosine decay as the learning rate schedule, with a batch size of 128 and a total training epoch of 100.

We consider Monte Carlo Dropout as the baseline for uncertainty estimates and apply the classical methods for tackling label noise in the three categories mentioned in Sect. 4, including FOCI [13], MAE [19] and GCE [18], to improve the reliability of Monte Carlo Dropout uncertainty under label noise. We compare the reliability of Robust Monte Carlo Dropout and these algorithms under different proportions of label noise by the performance of misclassification detection and multiple OOD data detections.

Based on Monte Carlo Dropout and Deep Ensemble, several approaches can be applied to quantify uncertainty, such as entropy, mutual information, and variance. In this paper, we use variance to extract uncertainty estimates [25].

## 6.2 Experimental Results

On the simple dataset of MNIST, the label noise has only a slight effect on the test accuracy, and thus all methods have similar test accuracies. Due to the limitation of space, we do not present the test accuracies of various methods

**Table 1.** Experimental results on mnist. Bold face indicates that this value is within 0.01 of the maximum value.

| % | AUROC of misclassification detection | AUROC of Not-MNIST detection | AUROC of fashion-MNIST detection |
|---|---|---|---|
| | MC-dropout/data re-weighting/data cleaning/robust loss (MAE)/robust loss (GCE)/ours | | |
| 0 | **0.970**/0.966/**0.967**/0.937/0.952/**0.970** | **0.947**/0.922/0.927/0.903/0.903/**0.939** | **0.964**/0.934/0.950/0.941/0.855/0.952 |
| 5 | 0.933/**0.963**/**0.968**/0.918/0.948/**0.967** | 0.804/0.930/**0.941**/0.888/**0.934**/**0.935** | 0.708/**0.944**/**0.953**/**0.943**/0.905/**0.950** |
| 10 | 0.871/**0.964**/**0.969**/0.945/0.947/**0.968** | 0.728/0.922/**0.943**/0.920/0.917/0.928 | 0.647/0.934/**0.950**/0.947/0.891/**0.958** |
| 20 | 0.491/0.958/**0.968**/0.945/0.949/**0.975** | 0.404/0.924/0.928/0.912/0.907/**0.939** | 0.234/0.923/0.923/**0.955**/0.862/**0.947** |
| 30 | 0.142/**0.955**/**0.962**/0.943/0.951/**0.962** | 0.161/0.906/**0.928**/0.904/0.910/**0.933** | 0.045/0.907/0.918/**0.948**/0.883/0.934 |
| 40 | 0.118/0.951/**0.957**/0.937/0.932/**0.963** | 0.111/**0.913**/0.899/0.903/0.873/**0.915** | 0.040/0.884/0.904/**0.937**/0.806/0.928 |
| 50 | 0.098/0.937/0.945/0.929/0.822/**0.955** | 0.086/0.886/0.870/0.902/0.782/**0.917** | 0.039/0.846/0.813/**0.915**/0.712/0.905 |
| 60 | 0.093/0.871/0.882/0.909/0.310/**0.947** | 0.094/0.778/0.778/0.858/0.381/**0.900** | 0.041/0.711/0.653/**0.877**/0.290/**0.887** |
| avg | 0.465/0.946/0.952/0.933/0.851/**0.963** | 0.417/0.898/0.902/0.899/0.826/**0.926** | 0.340/0.885/0.883/**0.933**/0.775/**0.933** |

on the MNIST dataset in Table 1. The performance of Robust Monte Carlo Dropout for misclassification detection is similar to Monte Carlo Dropout with data cleaning and outperforms other algorithms. On two OOD data detection tasks, our algorithm performs best, especially when the proportion of label noise is large enough.

**Table 2.** Experimental results on cifar10. Bold face indicates that this value is within 0.01 of the maximum value.

| % | Testing accuracy | AUROC of misclassification detection | AUROC of fashion-MNIST detection |
|---|---|---|---|
| | MC-dropout/data re-weighting/data cleaning/robust loss (MAE)/robust loss (GCE)/ours | | |
| 0 | **0.951**/0.946/0.945/0.920/0.931/**0.941** | **0.918**/0.917/**0.921**/0.817/0.908/**0.915** | 0.919/**0.926**/0.916/0.905/**0.920**/0.910 |
| 10 | 0.890/**0.934**/**0.934**/0.887/0.921/**0.935** | 0.853/**0.909**/**0.911**/0.824/**0.903**/**0.906** | 0.831/**0.912**/**0.912**/**0.910**/**0.906**/0.904 |
| 20 | 0.818/**0.920**/**0.921**/0.903/0.907/**0.923** | 0.809/**0.896**/**0.900**/0.803/0.888/**0.894** | 0.742/0.897/**0.915**/**0.905**/0.903/0.903 |
| 30 | 0.729/**0.901**/0.896/0.862/0.887/**0.909** | 0.771/**0.881**/**0.889**/0.815/0.876/**0.885** | 0.665/**0.884**/**0.888**/0.883/**0.886**/**0.889** |
| 40 | 0.640/0.862/0.864/0.847/0.854/**0.883** | 0.715/0.856/**0.867**/0.791/**0.861**/**0.866** | 0.585/0.837/**0.867**/**0.875**/0.846/0.861 |
| 50 | 0.548/0.814/0.803/0.774/0.796/**0.852** | 0.660/0.830/0.833/0.792/0.833/**0.851** | 0.500/0.783/0.815/**0.853**/0.833/0.843 |
| avg | 0.763/0.896/0.894/0.865/0.883/**0.907** | 0.788/**0.881**/**0.887**/0.807/**0.878**/**0.886** | 0.707/0.873/**0.886**/**0.888**/0.882/0.885 |

On the CIFAR10 dataset, our algorithm performs no worse than other algorithms in terms of test accuracy when there are relatively few labeling errors, but has superior performance when labeling errors are more frequent. This is because our algorithm gradually discards more and more data, and no matter what percentage of label noise there is, the remaining data is mostly clean in the later stages of training. As seen in Tables 2 and 3, our algorithm is competitive for both misclassification detection and OOD data detection, especially in the presence of large-scale labeling errors, which also implies that Robust Monte Carlo Dropout is a reliable uncertainty estimation method in the presence of labeling noise.

**Table 3.** Experimental results on cifar10. Bold face indicates that this value is within 0.01 of the maximum value.

| % | AUROC of LSUN detection | AUROC of tiny-ImageNet detection | AUROC of SVHN detection |
|---|---|---|---|
| | MC-dropout/data re-weighting/data cleaning/robust loss (MAE)/robust loss (GCE)/ours | | |
| 0 | **0.898**/0.890/**0.892**/0.808/0.878/0.880 | **0.874**/0.868/**0.864**/0.764/0.855/0.854 | **0.924**/**0.919**/0.911/0.834/0.876/0.910 |
| 10 | 0.769/**0.878**/**0.879**/0.786/0.865/**0.870** | 0.759/**0.852**/**0.857**/0.746/0.840/0.844 | 0.811/**0.915**/0.895/0.821/0.849/**0.909** |
| 20 | 0.670/**0.860**/**0.867**/0.779/0.851/0.854 | 0.679/**0.833**/**0.841**/0.752/0.828/0.829 | 0.711/**0.888**/**0.897**/0.840/0.870/0.879 |
| 30 | 0.647/**0.842**/**0.841**/0.766/**0.837**/**0.844** | 0.636/**0.818**/**0.822**/0.733/**0.813**/**0.820** | 0.670/**0.871**/0.853/0.806/0.829/0.847 |
| 40 | 0.630/0.804/**0.824**/0.745/0.803/**0.816** | 0.612/0.783/**0.800**/0.735/0.780/**0.800** | 0.696/**0.826**/0.800/0.750/0.789/**0.821** |
| 50 | 0.619/0.769/0.775/0.721/0.757/**0.792** | 0.605/0.750/0.758/0.714/0.733/**0.780** | 0.643/0.741/0.746/0.726/0.731/**0.761** |
| avg | 0.705/**0.841**/**0.846**/0.768/0.832/**0.843** | 0.694/**0.817**/**0.824**/0.741/0.808/**0.821** | 0.742/**0.860**/**0.850**/0.796/0.824/**0.854** |

# 7    Conclusion

In this paper, we first analyze the negative impact of label noise on different uncertainty estimation methods. We reveal that label noise has a stronger impact on the reliability of uncertainty estimates compared to test accuracy. In particular, on simple datasets, even a small percentage of noisy labels can have a devastating effect on uncertainty estimates. Next, we compare the enhancement of the reliability of uncertainty estimation methods by different categories of label noise processing methods. We find that the method based on label cleaning performs the best but still has some drawbacks. Finally, we propose a simple but effective method for reliable uncertainty estimates under label noise. Compared with other algorithms, our algorithm achieves competitive results for both misclassification detection and OOD data detection, especially when large-scale labeling errors are present in the training data.

# References

1. Amodei, D., Olah, C., Steinhardt, J., Christiano, P., Schulman, J. Mané, D.: Concrete problems in AI safety. CoRR. abs/1606.06565 (2016). http://arxiv.org/abs/1606.06565
2. Gal, Y., Ghahramani, Z.: Dropout as a Bayesian approximation: representing model uncertainty in deep learning. International Conference on Machine Learning, pp. 1050–1059 (2016)
3. Kendall, A., Gal, Y.: What uncertainties do we need in Bayesian deep learning for computer vision? Adv. Neural Inf. Process. Syst. **30** (2017)
4. Abdar, M., et al.: A review of uncertainty quantification in deep learning: techniques, applications and challenges. Inf. Fusion **76**, 243–297 (2021)
5. Gawlikowski, J., et al.: A survey of uncertainty in deep neural networks. ArXiv. abs/2107.03342 (2021)
6. Lakshminarayanan, B., Pritzel, A., Blundell, C.: Simple and scalable predictive uncertainty estimation using deep ensembles. Adv. Neural Inf. Process. Syst. **30** (2017)
7. Seoh, R.: Qualitative analysis of Monte Carlo dropout. ArXiv Preprint ArXiv:2007.01720 (2020)

8. Valdenegro-Toro, M.: I find your lack of uncertainty in computer vision disturbing. In: Proceedings Of The IEEE/CVF Conference on Computer Vision and Pattern Recognition, pp. 1263–1272 (2021)

9. Schwaiger, A., Sinhamahapatra, P., Gansloser, J., Roscher, K.: Is uncertainty quantification in deep learning sufficient for out-of-distribution detection? In: AISafety@ IJCAI (2020)

10. Salvador, T., Voleti, V., Iannantuono, A., Oberman, A.: Improved predictive uncertainty using corruption-based calibration. STAT **1050**, 7 (2021)

11. Hendrycks, D., Gimpel, K.: A Baseline for detecting misclassified and out-of-distribution examples in neural networks. In: Proceedings of International Conference on Learning Representations (2017)

12. Tajwar, F., Kumar, A., Xie, S., Liang, P.: No true state-of-the-art? OOD detection methods are inconsistent across datasets. ArXiv Preprint ArXiv:2109.05554 (2021)

13. Shin, W., Ha, J., Li, S., Cho, Y., Song, H., Kwon, S.: Which strategies matter for noisy label classification? Insight into loss and uncertainty. ArXiv. abs/2008.06218 (2020)

14. Cordeiro, F., Carneiro, G.: A survey on deep learning with noisy labels: how to train your model when you cannot trust on the annotations? In: 2020 33rd SIBGRAPI Conference on Graphics, Patterns and Images (SIBGRAPI), pp. 9–16 (2020)

15. Algan, G., Ulusoy, I.: Image classification with deep learning in the presence of noisy labels: a survey. Knowl.-Based Syst. **215**, 106771 (2021)

16. Karimi, D., Dou, H., Warfield, S., Gholipour, A.: Deep learning with noisy labels: exploring techniques and remedies in medical image analysis. Med. Image Anal. **65**, 101759 (2020)

17. Goel, P., Chen, L.: On the robustness of Monte Carlo dropout trained with noisy labels. In: Proceedings of the IEEE/CVF Conference on Computer Vision and Pattern Recognition, pp. 2219–2228 (2021)

18. Zhang, Z., Sabuncu, M.: Generalized cross entropy loss for training deep neural networks with noisy labels. Adv. Neural Inf. Process. Syst. **31** (2018)

19. Ghosh, A., Kumar, H., Sastry, P.: Robust loss functions under label noise for deep neural networks. In: Proceedings of the AAAI Conference on Artificial Intelligence, vol. 31 (2017)

20. Han, B., et al.: Co-teaching: robust training of deep neural networks with extremely noisy labels. Adv. Neural Inf. Process. Syst. **31** (2018)

21. Chen, P., Liao, B., Chen, G., Zhang, S.: Understanding and utilizing deep neural networks trained with noisy labels. In: International Conference on Machine Learning, pp. 1062–1070 (2019)

22. Northcutt, C., Wu, T., Chuang, I.: Learning with confident examples: rank pruning for robust classification with noisy labels. In: Proceedings of the Thirty-Third Conference on Uncertainty in Artificial Intelligence (2017). http://auai.org/uai2017/proceedings/papers/35.pdf

23. Song, H., Kim, M., Lee, J.: SELFIE: refurbishing unclean samples for robust deep learning. In: International Conference on Machine Learning, pp. 5907–5915 (2019)

24. He, K., Zhang, X., Ren, S., Sun, J.: Deep residual learning for image recognition. In: Proceedings of the IEEE Conference on Computer Vision and Pattern Recognition, pp. 770–778 (2016)

25. Feinman, R., Curtin, R., Shintre, S., Gardner, A.: Detecting adversarial samples from artifacts. ArXiv Preprint ArXiv:1703.00410 (2017)

# Transfer Learning Approach Towards a Smarter Recycling

Nermeen Abou Baker(✉) [iD], Jonas Stehr [iD], and Uwe Handmann [iD]

Ruhr West University of Applied Sciences, 46236 Bottrop, Germany
nermeen.baker@hs-ruhrwest.de
https://www.hochschule-ruhr-west.de

**Abstract.** The increasing consumption of electrical and electronic devices is alarming. Therefore, the transition from linear to circular economy becomes essential. The key solution to support this transformation is artificial intelligence. This work presents a transfer learning approach to support the recycling of electrical and electronic waste (Ewaste). We emphasize the use of transfer learning technique, particularly, to classify Ewaste. In this approach, we design a hybrid model of residual nets and inception modules that can classify features of a source domain (smartphones in our case) and leverage this knowledge to another device (electric screwdrivers, as an example). Using our model, we achieve an overall accuracy of 94.27% and 97.22%, respectively. These are comparable to the popular pre-trained models, which use similar network topologies. We use a web crawler program for collecting images from search engines to build the datasets with less efforts. We show that transfer learning is more robust and performs better than training from scratch. It avoids duplication and waste of computational resources. As a result, with the benefits of transfer learning, we can provide detailed information about the devices that need to be recycled. Ultimately, this would greatly support the overall recycling process.

**Keywords:** Transfer learning · Classification · Ewaste · Circular economy

## 1 Introduction

According to the Organization of Electronic Cooperation and Development (OECD) [5], all products that contain a Printed Circuit Board (PCB) and use electricity are called electrical and electronic devices. When this appliance reaches end-of-life, it is called Ewaste. Middle to high-income countries are more likely to consume more technology that will sooner become Ewaste [18]. This paper is organized as follows: It starts by introducing the motivation and challenges, state of the art of automated Ewaste management, and the reason for

This work has been funded by the Ministry of Economy, Innovation, Digitization, and Energy of the State of North Rhine-Westphalia within the project Prosperkolleg.

using smartphones recycling as a case study, in the Introduction in Sect. 1. Section 2 presents the research gap. Section 3 describes our transfer learning approach, which is designing an Ewaste classifier as an efficient method for Ewaste classification. Finally, the conclusion of the work is given in Sect. 4.

### 1.1    Motivation and Challenges

Recently, many initiatives foster the transformation from linear to a circular economy. However, only a few studies mention this transformation of Ewaste. Other studies attempted to recover electrical components (ECs) and materials using conventional methods such as acid burning, melting, and shredding to reduce metal and materials recovery. Informal recovery of lead from PCBs also emits dioxin and other chlorine compounds [5].

A survey of literature reviews [16] conducted from 2004 to 2019, found that there are six fundamental Artificial Intelligence (AI) applications in Solid Waste Management (SWM), which are: waste dumpster level detection, forecasting of waste characteristics, process parameters prediction, process output prediction, vehicle routing, and SWM planning. The field of Ewaste classification for recycling is still emerging.

### 1.2    State of the Art of Using Artificial Intelligence in Related Works

A review of the state-of-the-art is presented by [15] to dismantle and sort ECs. They found that Convolution Neural Networks (CNN) combined with physical separation and spectroscopy techniques play a vital role in classifying ECs because of their low cost. It shows that machine learning can detect the Tantalum capacitors on PCBs, then scrap them using a robot arm. ECs from a PCB image could be identified using CNN with high accuracy [11].

ZenRobotics Recycler (ZRR) utilizes a combination of AI, robots, and sensors [22]. It is a robot system that features two robot arms with multiple sensors, including High Definition (HD) RGB cameras, Near InfraRed (NIR) sensors, and metal detectors. With the support of deep learning software, it can sort 13 different materials or waste streams. This robot has an average purity 97% for tested waste streams. The study emphasizes the importance of digitalization as an "instrument" for achieving sustainability and future competitiveness efforts.

In addition, our review of [4], shows that transfer learning is a promising technology that supports object classification. It has significant advantages in achieving high performance while saving training time, memory, and effort in network design. They also proved that weight freezing is an effective method to reduce network complexity and eliminate overfitting.

### 1.3    Case Study: Smartphones

Smartphone recycling will be used as a case study because it faces many challenges. Due to their rapid production and low recycling rates, smartphones are the fastest-growing Ewaste stream. Additionally, traditional recycling can be challenging due to the complexity of recycling hazardous substances and contamination with other materials and metals. Moreover, the technical lifespan of the device is short, almost two years [3]. According to Nordmann et al. [1], between 65–80% of smartphones are recyclable. They found that smartphones are made of 60 different substances. Approximately 56% of a smartphone is made of plastic, 28% of metal (of which 15% copper, 0.35 g silver, 0.034 g gold, 0.015 g palladium, and 0.00034 g platinum) are used for the cables, the contacts, the circuit board, and the battery, 16% of glass and ceramics are used for displays, and 3% are other substances. The major problem with these substances is that they are mined in different countries. The research on automated smart waste management is still in its infancy due to the lack of datasets and the slow move towards AI-based smart waste management.

## 2   Research Gap

AI and robotics can be used to support the transition from linear to smarter Ewaste recycling. This study aims to bridge the gap between Ewaste recycling and AI by emphasizing the role of transfer learning as a promising method to leverage knowledge gained from training a specific device into other devices, rather than training each device from scratch.

## 3   Our Approach

Our goal is to process small and medium-sized electronic devices that need to be recycled. The suggested technique is: designing an artificial intelligence (transfer learning specifically) system. We aim to maximize material recovery rates and to classify objects reliably with the least amount of human intervention. Eventually, this will be a black box classifier for many future devices.

### 3.1   Design an Artificial Intelligence System

Besides negative health impacts, human intuition is imprecise when dealing with repeated patterns in waste streams. Hence, intelligent systems are imperative, especially when dealing with complicated tasks with small datasets.

**Why Artificial Intelligence.** In the waste stream, there are repeated patterns that play a fundamental role in dealing with complicated tasks that have incomplete or uncertain datasets. This makes it impossible for humans to process them precisely. Thus, an intelligent system is essential. Machine learning is a promising method because of its lower cost and distinctive features of ECs. Although research in this domain could be costly at the beginning, it is a smart investment if it is designed to be modular, and extensible in the long term. Since there is a high need to structure, analyze and evaluate a large stream of patterned data, including AI in waste management is essential.

Using artificial neural networks to mimic human brains is an efficient method to process Ewaste classification with minimal human interventions. In addition, deep learning can be applied to recognize recycling devices in a way that is more accurate than human performance. Theoretically, increasing the number of images per category can boost the accuracy of recognition. On the other hand, this, in turn, increases training time and memory consumption, which are undesirable in the industry. Our approach suggests a trade-off between accuracy, training time, and memory by using the transfer learning technique. It will reduce the computational burden and surpass the accuracy of training from scratch. To ensure this point, in a previous study [2], we used an AlexNet as a pre-trained model to focus on the transfer learning technique as a promising solution for object classification and the benefits of applying previously gained knowledge from a source domain and transferring it to a target domain via deep neural networks.

**Creating Datasets.** The web contains a huge amount of data that could enrich the data sources for building a useful dataset. A web crawler is a program or a script that retrieves useful information according to an algorithm. It navigates the web and downloads a document in an automated and methodical way. It fetches the HTML pages, parses them, and extracts the related data [26].

Training CNNs requires huge datasets used as training images. To our knowledge, no previous study has published a public dataset for Ewaste. Therefore, we use a web crawler program that is designed for collecting garbage datasets by [12]. This web crawler is written to capture images from Google images and Baidu images. It is relatively easy to crawl here because it doesn't require a login, authentication, or dynamic load. The only concern is the time between requests should be long enough to prevent floods of queries to the web page that could block the IP requests because the source may consider these requests as malicious or suspicious and cause a denial-of-service attack [23]. We use a keyword-based web crawler as a starting point to collect data from the web. Using keywords, we can construct our dataset for each class, such as "iPhone 6" + "backside". We can also set the maximum number of images that we want to download. The resolution of the images could also be identified.

It is difficult to collect appropriate images from the Internet to train a CNN directly. For example, searching for a specific keyword doesn't just crawl images we want, it also retrieves noisy images. The keyword "iPhone 6" leads to images that are not suitable for learning, such as the charger, the packaging of the device, or non-related photos taken with the device. This happens because it uses keyword-based metadata for the searched image [8]. The dataset should be homogeneous and should not contain anomalous objects. In this case, manual pre-processing is essential to filter the data and focus on the object in the center region-of-interest. Thus, data pre-processing should be completed before training, and removing irrelevant images manually is an important step, as shown in Fig. 1. After data cleaning, we apply deep learning models to classify smart-phones, and electric screwdrivers, as example, to test transfer learning method. With this crawler, we create the source dataset (smartphones) that contain 8 classes with 150 images per each as, Gigaset GX290_plus, HTC One M8, Huawei P20 Pro, iPhone 6, Samsung Galaxy A20, Sony XA Dual, Sony XZ1, and Xiaomi Redmi Note 8, with a balanced dataset of about 1200 images in total. For the target dataset (electric screwdrivers), it consists of 4 balanced classes as, Bosch_IXO, Hitachi_DS_12DVF3, Makita_DDF481, and Parkside_PAS_3.6_A1 with 240 images in total.

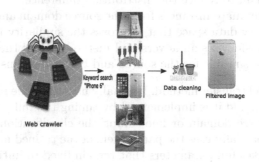

**Fig. 1.** The web crawler and pre-processing of a smartphone device.

**Transfer Learning.** Humans leverage previous knowledge gained from experience and reuse them to tackle new but related problems. CNN tries to mimic the human brain employing a concept called, transfer learning. Transfer learning is the process that uses the information gathered from a previous task to improve the performance of a new but related task [6]. Therefore, transfer learning by definition contains two basic components, which are: the domain and the task, as follows [17]:

- The domain $D$ has two elements, namely, the feature space $X$, and a marginal probability distribution $P(x)$ i.e. $D = \{X, P(x)\}$, where $x \in X$.
- The task $T$ has two elements, namely, a label source Y and the prediction function $f(\cdot)$ denoted by $T = \{Y, f(\cdot)\}$.

By using the notations of: $D_S$ for source domain, $T_S$ for source task, $D_T$ for target domain, and $T_T$ for target task, where $y \in Y$ and $y$, is the corresponding label of $x$ in $D_T$ using the knowledge in $D_S$ and $T_S$, where $D_S \neq D_T$, or $T_S \neq T_T$. Transfer learning could be defined as follows: Transfer learning aims to help improve the learning of the target predictive function that is used to predict the corresponding label, i.e. $f(x) = P(y|x)$, which is the probability distribution.

Choosing the source should be well defined because it should provide two requirements: The source distribution should be similar to the target distribution i.e. it has similar features, and source data (in our case as images) should provide useful information to classify. Therefore, the source data should have a high accuracy rate.

Transfer learning has four techniques, which are: Model transfer, instance transfer, mapping transfer, and adversarial transfer [21]:

- Model transfer uses the learned knowledge from the base model to predict the target model.
- Instance transfer chooses partial instances from the source domain and assigns suitable weights as supplements to the training set in the target domain. This approach focuses on giving less importance to samples who are irrelevant in the source domain to reduce the distribution difference.
- Mapping transfer maps instances from the source domain and a target domain and creates a new data space that improves the similarity between them.
- Adversarial transfer uses an adversarial method to find the transferable features, which are suitable for the source and target domains.

We apply the model transfer method. It usually uses the same model architecture as a trained model, and it is implemented by tuning the full layers of the model trained on the source domain or fine-tuning the classification layers only. The former approach partially uses the parameters of the trained model, whereas the latter approach takes full parameters that remain fixed to initialize the training process [13].

The similarity of data distribution between source and target domain has a huge impact on the efficiency of transfer learning [24]. In addition, the backpropagation in CNN may decrease when the model becomes very deep. Therefore, the skip-connections approach can overcome this problem by skipping inactive levels and reusing the activation from previous levels. Recently, transfer learning and domain adaptation have gained attention in many applications. Most of recent domain adaptation research focuses on learning the domain invariant features. This is done by mapping the source and target domains in the same latent space or adapting one or more layers in the network structure. Domain adaptation methods such as the Central Moment Discrepancy (CMD) [25], Maximum Mean Discrepancy (MMD) [9], and Residual Transfer Network (RTN) [14] employ residual layers. Therefore, we will use RTN as a method to control domain adaptation. The model transfer design of our approach is shown in Fig. 2.

**Implementation.** We propose a hybrid model that is inspired by a combination of two concepts, namely, residual nets and inception module with dimension reductions. This model consists of four parts, and 67 layers, as illustrated in Fig. 3:

- The input image size is [224 224 3]. It starts with stacking three convolutional layers (followed by a RELU as activation function and channel normalization layer). These layers are as follows; the first convolutional layer has a $7 \times 7$ filter size to reduce the input image directly without losing spatial information. Then two consecutive convolution layers are added with $1 \times 1$ and $3 \times 3$ filter

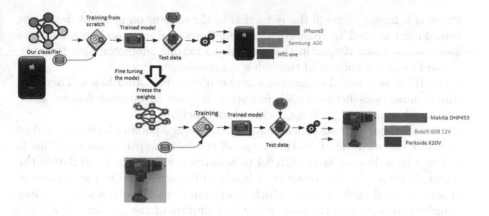

**Fig. 2.** The model transfer design of our approach.

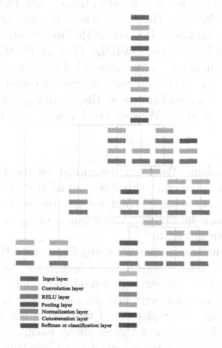

**Fig. 3.** Our classifier model.

sizes to generate a large number of feature maps. These layers are used to enable the model to learn global features.

- Stacking three inception modules on top of each other. Inception blocks with dimension reductions play a major role in reducing computation costs. This module has four branches that are $1 \times 1$, $3 \times 3$, and $5 \times 5$ convolutional kernels size in parallel, with one branch that has a max-pooling layer. It is used to down-sample the input when it is fed-forward through the network, which is achieved through the reduction of the dimension of input data. The convolution is used to compute the reductions. We increase the number of filters when going deeper in the network to extract more complex features. These blocks are connected through a concatenation layer.

- Using RTN as residual connections between each inception block. There are three connections between each inception module to increase feature reuse and avoid vanishing gradients, as mentioned before.
- It ends with output task-specific layers. An average pooling layer is added to calculate the mean of all feature maps of the last inception module. This is followed by a dropout layer with 0.4 to enhance regularization and flatten the layers. Then a fully connected layer is added to correspond to the number of classes in the domain dataset, which is 4 in our case. Finally, a softmax layer is utilized to calculate the probability distribution of the prediction vector.

The implementation environment is MATLAB, and the following training options are chosen, as follows: The batch size is 64, and the maximum epochs is 320, and Stochastic Gradient Descent with Momentum (SGDM) optimizer. To accelerate the training, we use NVIDIA Quadro P4000. The learning rate is $10^{-3}$ for the source domain and we scheduled the learning rate for the task domain, with a decay factor of 0.5 for each 20 epoch to detect local features. This technique maintains the global features at the beginning and drops the learning rate to detect the local features. We split the labels as 80% for training and 20% for validation sets.

**Results and Discussion.** We train the model on the training set and test it on the validation set. We train this base model from scratch for the source domain (the smartphones dataset), and we got the accuracy of 94.27% with generalization, as shown in Fig. 4a. An example of the tested images of the source dataset is shown in Fig. 4b.

Then, training a small target dataset using fine-tuning the base model. First, it freezes the network parameters for the whole base model except the task-specific layers. This means preserving (not changing) the model parameters, including weights and biases for every neuron, rather than training using random initialization. This process is implemented by setting the learning rate to zero for the frozen layers. Next, training the result by backpropagation the network parameters instead of random initialization. We fine-tune this model for the target domain (the electric screwdriver dataset), hence, we get the accuracy of 97.22% with generalization. Although it is achieved with about 75 epochs, we unify the testing for fair evaluation, with very short training time compared to training the source domain, as shown in Fig. 4c.

An example of the tested images of the target dataset is shown in Fig. 4d.

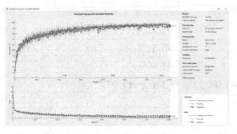

(a) Example of accuracy performance for testing source domain (smartphones dataset).

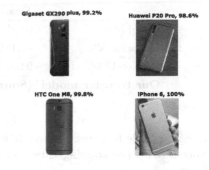

(b) Example of accuracy performance for testing source domain (smartphones dataset).

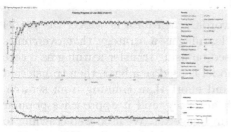

(c) Model performance for target domain (electric screwdriver dataset).

(d) Example of accuracy performance for testing target domain (electric screwdriver dataset).

Fig. 4. The performance of the suggested model

We evaluate our classifier with three popular trained models that use similar design methods, such as GoogLeNet [19] and Inception-V3 [20] that use the inception module concept, and ResNet-18 that uses the residual method [7]. From the confusion matrix, the diagonal elements represent the samples that were correctly classified. To calculate the overall accuracy, is the percentage of the correctly classified samples over the total number of samples. Table 1 shows the overall accuracy values of the tested models.

We find that, our suggested model approaches the popular pre-trained models with the advantage that training the network can leverage features related to Ewaste rather than images like ImageNet (a benchmark dataset that is used for training the popular models). These results are also confirmed by [10], that pre-training on ImageNet provides fewer benefits and does not transfer well to small fine-grained tasks. Therefore, training off-the-shelf models, like GoogLeNet, Inception-V3, and ResNet-18, in our case, can be a starting point to extract features, but transferring weights from related source tasks can learn

**Table 1.** Evaluation of our approach

| Tested models | Tested datasets | |
| --- | --- | --- |
| | *Smartphones* | *Electric screwdriver* |
| GoogLeNet | 94.3% | 93.33% |
| Inception-V3 | 96.11% | 95.52% |
| ResNet-18 | 94.97% | 94.59% |
| **Our transfer model** | **(Source)** 94.27% | **(Target)** 97.22% |

better adaptable features. Figures 4a and 4b proves the transfer learning benefits of speeding up the training time and overcoming the small-scale related target dataset.

## 4    Conclusion

Deep learning is data-hungry. In other words, when data is scarce, the model will perform poorly. Therefore, transfer learning is a strategy that overcomes this limitation. In our approach, we focused on using transfer learning as a core technique for object classification. Our model is used as a base, then transferred to another task. This would save time and effort than training from scratch. We proved that our model achieves high accuracy, and it approaches popular pre-trained models that are applied to train ImageNet. We used web crawling to extract images automatically from web pages to build our datasets. We show that web crawling is a powerful tool for retrieving any information from a seed URL, usually from search engines. Finally, we can transfer all the detailed information to the next phase of material processing to support the overall recycling process with minimum human intervention, but with higher accuracy. A more extensive comparison with other object classification models (e.g. other artificial neural networks topologies) can be performed as a future work.

## References

1. Nordmann, J., Oettershagen: Factsheets zum Thema Mobiltelefone und Nachhaltigkeit December 2013. https://wupperinst.org/uploads/tx_wupperinst/mobiltelefone_factsheets.pdf
2. Abou Baker, N., Szabo-Müller, P., Handmann, U.: A feature-fusion transfer learning method as a basis to support automated smartphone recycling in a circular smart city. In: Paiva, S., Lopes, S.I., Zitouni, R., Gupta, N., Lopes, S.F., Yonezawa, T. (eds.) SmartCity360° 2020. LNICST, vol. 372, pp. 422–441. Springer, Cham (2021). https://doi.org/10.1007/978-3-030-76063-2_29
3. Abou Baker, N., Szabo-Müller, P., Handmann, U.: Transfer learning-based method for automated e-waste recycling in smart cities. EAI Endors. Trans. Smart Cities **5**(16) (2021). https://doi.org/10.4108/eai.16-4-2021.169337

4. Abou Baker, N., Zengeler, N., Handmann, U.: A transfer learning evaluation of deep neural networks for image classification. Mach. Learn. Knowl. Extract. **4**(1), 22–41 (2022). https://doi.org/10.3390/make4010002, https://www.mdpi.com/2504-4990/4/1/2

5. Ari, V.: A review of technology of metal recovery from electronic waste. E-Waste in transition–from pollution to resource (2016)

6. Chakraborty, H., Samanta, P., Zhao, L.: Sequential data imputation with evolving generative adversarial networks. In: 2021 International Joint Conference on Neural Networks (IJCNN), pp. 1–8 (2021). https://doi.org/10.1109/IJCNN52387.2021.9534108

7. He, K., Zhang, X., Ren, S., Sun, J.: Deep residual learning for image recognition. In: 2016 IEEE Conference on Computer Vision and Pattern Recognition (CVPR), pp. 770–778 (2016). https://doi.org/10.1109/CVPR.2016.90

8. Hwang, K.H., Lee, M.J., Ha, Y.G.: A befitting image data crawling and annotating system with CNN based transfer learning. In: 2020 IEEE International Conference on Big Data and Smart Computing (BigComp), pp. 165–168 (2020). https://doi.org/10.1109/BigComp48618.2020.00-81

9. Koniusz, P., Tas, Y., Porikli, F.: Domain adaptation by mixture of alignments of second- or higher-order scatter tensors (2017)

10. Kornblith, S., Shlens, J., Le, Q.V.: Do better ImageNet models transfer better? In: Proceedings of the IEEE/CVF Conference on Computer Vision and Pattern Recognition (CVPR) (2019)

11. Kuo, C.W., Ashmore, J., Huggins, D., Kira, Z.: Data-efficient graph embedding learning for PCB component detection (2018)

12. di Liao, Y.: A web-based dataset for garbage classification based on Shanghai's rule. Int. J. Mach. Learn. Comput. **10**, 599–604 (2020)

13. Liu, Z., Sabar, N., Song, A.: Partial transfer learning for fast evolutionary generative adversarial networks. In: 2021 International Joint Conference on Neural Networks (IJCNN), pp. 1–7 (2021). https://doi.org/10.1109/IJCNN52387.2021.9533384

14. Long, M., Zhu, H., Wang, J., Jordan, M.I.: Unsupervised domain adaptation with residual transfer networks (2017)

15. Maurice, A.A., Dinh, K.N., Charpentier, N.M., Brambilla, A., Gabriel, J.C.P.: Dismantling of printed circuit boards enabling electronic components sorting and their subsequent treatment open improved elemental sustainability opportunities. Sustainability **13**(18) (2021). https://doi.org/10.3390/su131810357, https://www.mdpi.com/2071-1050/13/18/10357

16. Neirotti, P.: Adapting market proposition of a waste management system to customers' needs. Master's thesis, Politecnico di Torino (2021). https://webthesis.biblio.polito.it/18449/

17. Pan, S.J., Yang, Q.: A survey on transfer learning. IEEE Trans. Knowl. Data Eng. **22**(10), 1345–1359 (2010). https://doi.org/10.1109/TKDE.2009.191

18. Sarc, R.: The "rewaste4.0" project–a review. Processes **9**(5) (2021). https://www.mdpi.com/2227-9717/9/5/764

19. Szegedy, C., et al.: Going deeper with convolutions. In: 2015 IEEE Conference on Computer Vision and Pattern Recognition (CVPR), pp. 1–9 (2015). https://doi.org/10.1109/CVPR.2015.7298594

20. Szegedy, C., Vanhoucke, V., Ioffe, S., Shlens, J., Wojna, Z.: Rethinking the inception architecture for computer vision. In: 2016 IEEE Conference on Computer Vision and Pattern Recognition (CVPR), pp. 2818–2826 (2016). https://doi.org/10.1109/CVPR.2016.308

21. Tiwari, M., Sanodiya, R.K., Mathew, J., Saha, S.: Multi-source based approach for visual domain adaptation. In: 2021 International Joint Conference on Neural Networks (IJCNN), pp. 1–7 (2021). https://doi.org/10.1109/IJCNN52387.2021.9534305

22. Wilts, H., Garcia, B.R., Garlito, R.G., Gómez, L.S., Prieto, E.G.: Artificial intelligence in the sorting of municipal waste as an enabler of the circular economy. Resources **10**(4) (2021). https://doi.org/10.3390/resources10040028, https://www.mdpi.com/2079-9276/10/4/28

23. Yang, Z., Cao, S.: Job information crawling, visualization and clustering of job search websites. In: 2019 IEEE 4th Advanced Information Technology, Electronic and Automation Control Conference (IAEAC), vol. 1, pp. 637–641 (2019). https://doi.org/10.1109/IAEAC47372.2019.8997713

24. Yi, C., Wang, J., Cheng, N., Zhou, S., Xu, B.: Transfer ability of monolingual wav2vec2.0 for low-resource speech recognition. In: 2021 International Joint Conference on Neural Networks (IJCNN), pp. 1–6 (2021). https://doi.org/10.1109/IJCNN52387.2021.9533587

25. Zellinger, W., Grubinger, T., Lughofer, E., Natschläger, T., Saminger-Platz, S.: Central moment discrepancy (CMD) for domain-invariant representation learning (2019)

26. Zhao, L., Kong, W., Wang, C.: Electricity corpus construction based on data mining and machine learning algorithm. In: 2020 IEEE 5th Information Technology and Mechatronics Engineering Conference (ITOEC), pp. 1478–1481 (2020). https://doi.org/10.1109/ITOEC49072.2020.9141559

# Addressing Contradiction Between Reconstruction and Correlation Maximization in Deep Canonical Correlation Autoencoders

Qixing Sun[1], Xiaodong Jia[1], and Xiao-Yuan Jing[1,2,3]($\boxtimes$)

[1] School of Computer Science, Wuhan University, Wuhan 430072, China
`jingxy_2000@126.com`
[2] Guangdong University of Petrochemical Technology, Maoming 525000, China
[3] State Key Laboratory for Novel Software Technology, Nanjing University, Nanjing 210023, China

**Abstract.** Canonical correlation analysis (CCA) and its nonlinear extensions have shown promising performance in multi-view representation learning. One of the most representative methods is Deep Canonical Correlation Analysis Autoencoders (DCCAE), which combines CCA with a reconstruction loss to reserve more information in representations. However, the contradiction between reconstruction and correlation maximization hinders the optimization of them. Here we propose a multi-view representation learning method named Full Reconstruction based Deep Canonical Correlation Analysis (FR-DCCA), which not only addresses this contradiction but also enables the reconstructing and correlation maximization to benefit from each other. In FR-DCCA, Split Encoder models the information in each view as shared information and specific information; CCA layer maintains consistency through maximizing the canonical correlation between shared information of views; Full Reconstruction module guarantees completeness and complementarity by reconstructing each view with both the shared and specific information. In FR-DCCA, reconstructing and correlation maximization mutually improve each other and yield complete, compact, and discriminative view representations. Experiments and analysis on multiple datasets demonstrate: 1) FR-DCCA significantly outperforms the comparison methods. 2) FR-DCCA effectively addresses the contradiction between reconstruction and correlation maximization. To facilitate future research, we release the codes at https://github.com/FR-DCCA/FR-DCCA.

**Keywords:** Multi-view · Correlation maximization · DCCAE · Reconstruction

## 1 Introduction

In various real-world applications, data are collected from different domains or in different measurements. These data can be viewed as distinct views which exhibit

E. Pimenidis et al. (Eds.): ICANN 2022, LNCS 13529, pp. 697–708, 2022.
https://doi.org/10.1007/978-3-031-15919-0_58

different statistical characteristics [12,15]. For example, in speech recognition, record audio and articulation are regarded as different views which represent the speaker's acoustic characteristics on different aspects [22]. In web page classification, the description of a web page consists of page text and hyperlinks [4,18], which are regarded as two distinct views. In multi-view datasets, consistency and complementarity are two significant principles [6,19]. Consensus principle aims to maximize the agreement between multiple distinct views. Complementary principle states that each view contains some knowledge unique to itself. Effective exploitation of these two principles improves the performance of multi-view learning methods [3,20,25].

In recent years, various multi-view learning methods have been proposed. Canonical correlation analysis (CCA) [9] and its nonlinear extensions are representative methods among them. Canonical correlation analysis, finding the mapping vectors of two views through maximizing the correlation between them, is a basic technique in multi-view learning. However, CCA is limited to linear transformations [1,2,8,21] and most of real-world data is nonlinear. To overcome this limitation, some nonlinear CCA based methods have been proposed, such as Kernel Canonical Correlation Analysis (KCCA) [1], Deep Canonical Correlation Analysis (Deep CCA) [2] and Category-Based Deep CCA(C-DCCA) [24]. KCCA corresponds to performing linear CCA in a kernel-induced feature space by introducing the kernel trick [11,15]. Deep CCA and C-DCCA are deep extensions of canonical correlation analysis. They extract nonlinear features from two views separately with DNNs and then maximizes the canonical correlation between them [2,6,15]. However, the methods above suffer from a common drawback that they discount the complementary information between the two views [6,15,20]. These methods align representations of different views by maximizing the canonical correlation between them. This alignment forces representations to exclude view-specific information, which can't be aligned but is beneficial to discriminating between different samples [12,26,27]. Deep Canonical Correlation Autoencoders (DCCAE), which combines CCA and reconstruction objective [10], is a trade-off between reserving complete view information and maximizing canonical correlation [15,21]. Nonetheless, when applied on the same representation, these two objectives contradict each other. Essentially, reconstruction reserves complete view information, which includes view-specific information, but CCA inclines to discard the view-specific information in aligning two views. The contradiction leads to that DCCAE performs weakly in extracting features and preserving the consistency and complementarity of multiple views. Motivated by the limitations above, we aim to propose a method that can address the contradiction between reconstruction and correlation maximization in CCA and reconstruction based methods.

In this paper, we propose a novel multi-view representation learning method, named Full Reconstruction based Deep Canonical Correlation Analysis (FR-DCCA). The framework of FR-DCCA is shown in Fig. 1. In Split Encoder, we employ the shared encoder to extract information shared between two views (shared information) and employ the specific encoder to extract view-specific

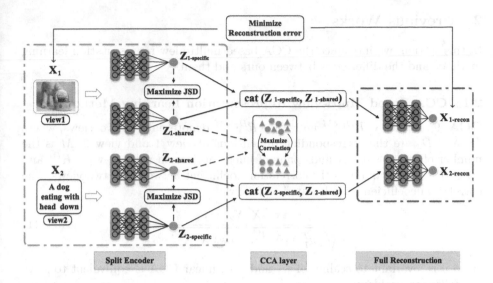

**Fig. 1.** The framework of our proposed method (FR-DCCA): $X_1$ and $X_2$ are the data of two views; $X_{1-recon}$ and $X_{2-recon}$ are the data of reconstruction views; $Z_{i-specific}$ and $Z_{i-shared}$ are outputs of encoders and contain the specific information and shared information from view $i$; $cat\,(\cdot)$ denotes concatenating two parts.

information (specific information) for a single view. Meanwhile, we maximize the JS divergence between them, such that the shared information and specific information of a single view can be semantically disentangled. In Full Reconstruction module, shared information and specific information are concatenated as the input for a decoder to reconstruct the single view. Then we minimize the reconstruction error between original view data and decoder's output. The reconstruction structure guarantees that the information extracted is complete within views. Moreover, the reconstruction advances mutually with correlation maximization. In CCA Layer, only the shared information from two views is fed as inputs, and we align the shared information by maximizing the canonical correlation between them. The CCA Layer maintains consistency between the two views. Finally, we integrate both the specific and shared information from two views to provide complete, compact, more discriminative view representations. Our main contributions are summarized below:

- After systematically analyzing CCA and reconstruction based methods, we catch the contradiction between reconstruction and correlation maximization.
- We propose a novel multi-view representation learning method named FR-DCCA, which not only address this contradiction but also enable the reconstructing and Correlation maximization to benefit from each other.
- Experiments on multiple real-world datasets and diverse downstream tasks demonstrate that our method effectively addresses the contradiction between reconstruction and correlation maximization and outperforms the comparison methods.

## 2   Previous Works

In this section, we introduce the CCA based multi-view representation learning methods and the differences between ours and them.

### 2.1   CCA Based Multi-view Representation Learning Method

**CCA** [9]. Let $X_1 \in R^{D_1 \times M}$ and $X_2 \in R^{D_2 \times M}$ denote data of two views, where $D_1$ and $D_2$ are the corresponding dimensions of view 1 and view 2, $M$ is the number of samples. CCA finds pairs of linear projection vectors, $w_1 \in R^{D_1}$ and $w_2 \in R^{D_2}$, and maximizes the correlation coefficient between the two views. The correlation coefficient is calculated as follows:

$$\rho = \frac{w_1^T X_1 X_2^T w_2}{\sqrt{\left(w_1^T X_1 X_1^T w_1\right)\left(w_2^T X_2 X_2^T w_2\right)}}, \tag{1}$$

since $\rho$ is invariant to scaling of $w_1$ and $w_2$ , linear CCA is equivalent to solve the following problem:

$$\begin{array}{c} \underset{w_1, w_2}{\arg\max} \, w_1^T X_1 X_2^T w_2 \\ \text{s.t.} \quad w_1^T X_1 X_1^T w_1 = 1, w_2^T X_2 X_2^T w_2 = 1 \end{array}. \tag{2}$$

CCA is essentially a data dimensionality reduction method based on linear transformation. However, it is only suited for processing linear data problems.

**KCCA and DCCA.** KCCA [1] and DCCA [2] are two CCA based representative multi-view methods that extract nonlinear features. Inspired by kernel trick [11], KCCA maps the view data to Reproducing Kernel Hilbert Space (RKHS) first and then conducts linear CCA. In RKHS, the inner product is calculated smoothly with a kernel function. DCCA is a deep extension of CCA, which benefits from the DNN's ability of nonlinear representing. As shown in Fig. 2(a), DCCA employs two DNNs, $f$ and $g$, to extract nonlinear features for each view and then projects the outputs of DNNs as in CCA. Finally, the projected features are maximally correlated:

$$\begin{array}{c} \underset{w_f, w_g, U, V}{\arg\max} \, \frac{1}{N} tr \left( U^T f\left(X_1\right) g(X_2)^T V \right) \\ \text{s.t.} \quad U^T \left( \frac{1}{N} f\left(X_1\right) f(X_1)^T + r_{x_1} I \right) U = I \\ V^T \left( \frac{1}{N} g\left(X_2\right) g(X_2)^T + r_{x_2} I \right) V = I \\ u_i^T f\left(X_1\right) g(X_2)^T v_j = 0, when \quad i \neq j \end{array} \tag{3}$$

where $U = [u_1, u_2, ..., u_L]$ and $V = [v_1, v_2, ..., v_L]$ are the projection vectors for view 1 and view 2, $L$ is the size of DNN's output, $(r_{x_1}, r_{x_2}) > 0$ are regularization parameters added to the diagonal of the sample auto-covariance matrices. At last, we utilize the projected DNN's output, $U^T f\left(X_1\right)$ and $g(X_2)^T V$, for downstream tasks.

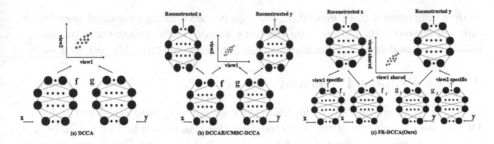

**Fig. 2.** Schematic diagram of CCA based multi-view representation learning methods

**CCA and Reconstruction Based Representation Learning.** The methods based on CCA and reconstruction, which optimize the outputs of DNNs via autoencoder's reconstruction, are further extensions of DCCA. Contrary to aligning views indiscreetly, reconstructing the original view ensures that more information is reserved [10]. DCCAE [21] is a classical method in this style. As shown in Fig. 2(b), it employs two encoders, $f$ and $g$, to extract features from two views and then maximizes the canonical correlation between latent representations. It employs two decoders to reconstruct the original views [10]. DCCAE is formulated to solve the following problem:

$$
\underset{w_f,w_g,w_p,w_q,U,V}{\arg\min} \quad -\tfrac{1}{N}tr\left(U^T f\left(X_1\right) g(X_2)^T V\right) + \tfrac{\lambda}{N}\sum_{i=1}^{N}\|x_i - p\left(f\left(x_i\right)\right)\|^2 \\
+\|y_i - q\left(g\left(y_i\right)\right)\|^2 \\
\text{s.t.} \quad \text{the same as in DCCA}
\tag{4}
$$

where $U$ and $V$ are projection vectors; $\lambda > 0$ is the trade-off parameter between reconstruction and maximizing canonical correlation. We utilize the projected bottleneck features of encoders for downstream tasks.

CMSC-DCCA (Cross-Modal Subspace Clustering via Deep Canonical Correlation Analysis) [8] considers correlations of inter-view data with the correlation matrix and then optimizes reconstruction and CCA objective as in DCCAE.

### 2.2 Differences

Existing CCA based methods, such as DCCA, KCCA, C-DCCA, etc., model the consistency between two views only, but we consider both the consistency and complementarity. As shown in Fig. 2(c), in FR-DCCA, we explicitly disentangle specific information and shared information from a single view via maximizing distance between their probability distributions. Then we apply correlation constraint on shared information to maintain consistency. Meanwhile, one view's specific information is complementary to the other's.

CCA and reconstruction based methods, such as DCCAE, CMSC-DCCA, etc., apply both reconstructing and maximizing canonical correlation on the same representation. In our method, we disentangle specific information and shared information from view data and apply maximizing canonical correlation only on shared information from different views. Then we concatenate shared information and specific information together to reconstruct the original view.

## 3    The Proposed Method

In this section, we introduce the framework of our proposed novel method, FR-DCCA, and the design of the objective function. As shown in Fig. 1, FR-DCCA consists of three parts: Split Encoder module, CCA layer and Full Reconstruction module.

**Split Encoder Module** extracts shared and specific information of each view with different encoders. We assume that $X_1 \in R^{D_1 \times M}$ and $X_2 \in R^{D_2 \times M}$ are data of two views, where $D_1$ and $D_2$ are the corresponding dimensions of view 1 and view 2, $M$ is the number of samples. For view 1, two encoders based on full-connected layers, $E_{1-shared}$ and $E_{1-specific}$ are employed to encode the shared information and specific information, the same for view 2. Then we can obtain the encoded representations, $\left(E_{i-specific}\left(X_i\right) \in R^{k \times M} | w_{E_{i-specifci}}\right)$ and $\left(E_{i-shared}\left(X_i\right) \in R^{k \times M} | w_{E_{i-shared}}\right)$, where $i = 1, 2$ is the view index, and $w_{E_{i-specific}}, w_{E_{i-shared}}$ are the parameters of encoders. To disentangle shared and specific information, JS divergence [7] between the distributions of their encoded representations is maximized:

$$\underset{w_{E_1}, w_{E_2}}{\arg\max} \sum_{i=1,2} JSD\left(E_{i-specific}\left(X_i\right), E_{i-shared}\left(X_i\right)\right), \tag{5}$$

where $JSD\left(\cdot\right)$ denotes the calculation of JS divergence, and $w_{E_i} = \left(w_{E_{i-specific}}, w_{E_{i-shared}}\right)$ are the parameters of pairs of encoders for view $i$.

**CCA Layer** aligns encoded shared information from different views through maximizing the canonical correlation [9] between them. After Split Encoder module, we obtain the encoded representations of shared information and specific information for each view. Then the shared information $E_{1-shared}$ and $E_{2-shared}$ are fed as inputs to the CCA layer. According to the calculation method in DCCAE [21], the CCA layer's optimization goal is:

$$\underset{w_{E_1}, w_{E_2}, U, V}{\arg\max} \frac{1}{M} tr\left(U^T E_{1-shared}\left(X_1\right) E_{2-shared}(X_2)^T V\right)$$

$$\text{s.t.}\quad U^T \left(\frac{1}{M} E_{1-shared}\left(X_1\right) E_{1-shared}(X_1)^T + r_{x_1} I\right) U = I, \tag{6}$$

$$V^T \left(\frac{1}{M} E_{2-shared}\left(X_2\right) E_{2-shared}(X_2)^T + r_{x_2} I\right) V = I$$

$$u_i^T E_{1-shared}\left(X_1\right) E_{2-shared}(X_2)^T v_j = 0, when \quad i \neq j$$

where $U = [u_1, u_2, ..., u_k]$ and $V = [v_1, v_2, ..., v_k]$ are projection vectors for view 1 and view 2, $k$ is the size of the encoded representation, $(r_{x_1}, r_{x_2}) > 0$ are regularization parameters added to the diagonal of the sample auto-covariance matrices, $tr\left(\cdot\right)$ is the trace function of the matrix.

**Full Reconstruction Module.** In this module, we concatenate the encoded shared and specific information from a single view together as the input to reconstruct original view data. For view 1 and view 2, we employ two decoders, $D_1$ and $D_2$, which have the reverse structure with encoders. We obtain representations of shared and specific information after Split Encoder and CCA layer, and then concatenate $E_{1-specific}(X_1)$ and $E_{1-shared}(X_1)$ as the input for decoder $D_1$ to reconstruct the original view 1. Finally, we minimize the mean squared error (MSE) between the output of $D_1$ and original view [10], the same for view 2. MSE [23] is an evaluation of data change. The smaller the value of MSE, the better the accuracy of the predictive model to describe the experimental data. Full Reconstruction module aims to utilize more complete and more complementary information via optimizing the following goal:

$$
\arg\min_{w_{E_1}, w_{E_2}, w_{D_1}, w_{D_2}} \sum_{j=1}^{M} \|x_{1j} - D_1\left(cat\left[E_{1-specific}(x_{1j}), E_{1-shared}(x_{1j})\right]\right)\|^2 \atop + \|x_{2j} - D_2\left(cat\left[E_{2-specific}(x_{2j}), E_{2-shared}(x_{2j})\right]\right)\|^2 \tag{7}
$$

where $w_{D_1}, w_{D_2}$ are the parameters of decoders, $cat[\cdot]$ denotes concatenating the two parts, $j = 1, 2, \cdots, M$ is the sample's index.

**Objective Function.** The method we proposed jointly optimizes three objectives with corresponding regularization parameters. According to equation(5)~(7), the final objective function is summarized as follows:

$$
Loss = \min_{\theta, U, V} - \lambda_1 \sum_{i=1,2} JSD\left(E_{i-specific}(X_i), E_{i-shared}(X_i)\right)
$$
$$
- \frac{\lambda_2}{M} tr\left(U^T E_{1-shared}(X_1) E_{2-shared}(X_2)^T V\right)
$$
$$
- \frac{\lambda_3}{M} \sum_{j=1}^{M} \left\{ \begin{array}{l} \|x_{1j} - D_1\left(cat\left[E_{1-specific}(x_{1j}), E_{1-shared}(x_{1j})\right]\right)\|^2 \\ + \|x_{2j} - D_2\left(cat\left[E_{2-specific}(x_{2j}), E_{2-shared}(x_{2j})\right]\right)\|^2 \end{array} \right\} \tag{8}
$$

where $\lambda_1, \lambda_2, \lambda_3 > 0$ are regularization parameters and $\theta = \{w_{E_1}, w_{E_2}, w_{D_1}, w_{D_2}\}$ is a set of network parameters.

## 4    Experiments

In this section, we compare the performance of FR-DCCA and the most advanced methods on multi-view datasets and diverse downstream tasks.

### 4.1    Comparsion with Related Works

**Baselines**

- **Original:** using original features as inputs to classifiers and clustering.
- **KCCA:** Kernel Canonical Correlation Analysis [1], which is based on CCA kernel trick, applies linear CCA in high-dimensional feature space.

- **DCCA:** Deep Canonical Correlation Analysis [2], which maximizes the canonical correlation between the outputs of two DNNs.
- **C-DCCA:** Category-Based Deep CCA [24], which is based on DCCA and category-based correlation.
- **DCCAE:** Deep Canonical Correlation Analysis Autoencoders [21], which combines DCCA and autoencoders, minimizes reconstruction error to obtain better representations.
- **CMSC-DCCA:** Cross-Modal Subspace Clustering via Canonical Correlation Analysis [8], which considers correlations of inter-view data.

**Datasets**

- **Noisy MNIST digits:** we operate our method on the noisy MNIST dataset used by DCCAE [21]. It is generated from the MNIST dataset [14], which consists of 70K gray digit images scaled by $28 \times 28$. The noisy MNIST dataset is divided into $50K/10K/10K$ for training/validation/testing. We generate the view 1 by rescaling and then randomly rotating the image and generate view 2 by adding random noisy to each pixel.
- **WebKB:** the WebKB is a subset of WWW-pages dataset, which was used for co-training in [4]. The WebKB consists of two views: page text and hyperlinks, and it contains 1051 samples that are divided into $6:2:2$ for training/validation/testing in our experiments.
- **XRMB speech-articulation:** following the setup of DCCAE, we demonstrate FR-DCCA's ability to learn acoustic features for speech recognition on XRMB dataset [22], which simultaneously records speech and articulatory measurements from 47 American English speakers. As in DCCAE, the speakers are divided into $35/8/2/2$ for learning features/training recognizer/validation/testing.

**Settings.** As shown in Fig. 1, the encoders are implemented with three hidden layers and an output layer. Each hidden layer is followed by a ReLu layer. The decoders have the reverse structure with encoders. We use Adam optimizer [13] with learning rate set to 0.001 and set the batch size to 256.

One might expect that a simple linear classifier or clustering method can achieve high accuracy on representations extracted. Thus, we employ the one-versus-one linear SVM [5] and the Spectral Clustering [17] for downstream tasks. We utilize the representation of view 1 for the Noisy MNIST and utilize representations of both page text and hyperlinks for WebKB. Especially, for XRMB, we use all learned features appended to original 39D data and employ a standard hidden Markov model (HMM) based recognizer [21]. For evaluation metrics, we adopt classification error rate (Error) and F1-score in classification and clustering accuracy (ACC) and normalized mutual information (NMI) [16] in clustering. The mean and standard deviations of phone error rate are used to evaluate the recognition ability based on a six-fold experiment for XRMB.

**Table 1.** The clustering accuracy (ACC), the normalized mutual information (NMI), the classification error rate (Error) and the F1 score (F1) on Noisy MNIST and WebKB dataset, the mean and standard deviations of phone error rate on XRMB dataset.

| Method | Noisy MNIST | | | | WebKB | | | | XRMB |
| | ACC | NMI | Error | F1 | ACC | NMI | Error | F1 | Mean (std) PER |
| --- | --- | --- | --- | --- | --- | --- | --- | --- | --- |
| Original | 48.7 | 58.2 | 13.4 | 85.3 | 78.6 | 45.5 | 10.2 | 85.10 | 28.6 (5.3) |
| KCCA | 89.3 | 80.4 | 6.3 | 91.5 | 88.1 | 79.3 | 8.9 | 86.24 | 26.9 (5.7) |
| DCCA | 97.0 | 92.1 | 3.4 | 96.4 | 93.0 | 90.5 | 7.6 | 88.1 | 26.0 (4.9) |
| CSMC | 96.9 | 92.1 | 4.3 | 96.0 | 93.4 | 90.7 | 7.3 | 88.8 | 26.1 (5.1) |
| C-DCCA | 96.5 | 92.2 | 4.5 | 95.8 | 92.7 | 89.4 | 8.1 | 86.8 | 27.0 (5.5) |
| DCCAE | 97.3 | 92.0 | 3.1 | 96.9 | 93.2 | 89.6 | 7.4 | 88.2 | 24.8 (4.1) |
| FR-DCCA | **97.8** | **95.4** | **2.0** | **97.8** | **95.3** | **93.7** | **4.2** | **92.8** | **20.8 (3.0)** |

**Result and Analysis.** The classification and clustering performances of our method and comparison methods on the Noisy MNIST and WebKB and recognition results on XRMB are reported in Table 1. In this table, we can find out following information:

1) Classification and clustering are easier with representations extracted by our method, even a simple linear classifier or clustering method is employed.
2) Our method outperforms all baselines in terms of all metrics considered.
3) Compared to DCCAE, our method boosts the classification accuracy by about 1% and 3.2% on the Noisy MNIST and WebKB; boosts the clustering accuracy by about 0.5% and 2%; improves the recognition rate by about 4%, and gets more stable results on XRMB.

The reason why our method outperforms DCCAE is that we address the contradiction between reconstruction and correlation maximization. We apply correlation maximization only on shared information and use complete information for reconstruction. This contributes to more representative representations.

## 4.2  Ablation Study

**Table 2.** Ablation study on WebKB dataset in terms of cluster accuracy (ACC) and classification error rate (Error).

| Method | ACC | Error |
| --- | --- | --- |
| FR-DCCA - Recon | 92.2 | 7.5 |
| FR-DCCA - Shared | 93.0 | 5.9 |
| FR-DCCA - Specific | 94.3 | 7.4 |
| FR-DCCA | **95.3** | **4.2** |

We conduct an ablation study to analyze the impact of different reconstruction strategies on cluster accuracy and classification error rate: 1) FR-DCCA without reconstruction; 2) without shared for reconstruction; 3) without specific for reconstruction; 4) with both shared and specific for reconstruction (FR-DCCA). We display the ablation results on WebKB in Table 2, we can observe that all reconstruction strategies contribute to classification and clustering. The best strategy is reconstructing with both shared and specific information in FR-DCCA, which preserves the most view information and contributes to more complete and compact representations.

### 4.3 Convergence Comparison

Our method has the same correlation maximization objective with DCCA and DCCAE and has the same reconstruction objective with DCCAE. Thus, we explore the effectiveness by comparing the convergence speed and lowest loss value of our method with DCCA's and DCCAE's.

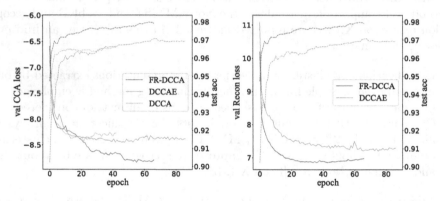

**Fig. 3.** The canonical correlation loss curves of FR-DCCA, DCCA and DCCAE; reconstruction loss curves of FR-DCCA and DCCAE on Noisy MNIST with corresponding classification accuracy (1−error rate) at each epoch.

The canonical correlation loss, reconstruction loss and classification accuracy at each epoch are presented in Fig. 3. We can observe that FR-DCCA converges fastest with the lowest CCA loss and reconstruction loss in validation and achieves the highest classification accuracy on the testing set. It means that our method achieves the highest view consistency and preserves the most view information. The convergence analysis further demonstrates that reconstructing and maximizing the canonical correlation benefits from each other in our method.

## 5    Conclusion

We propose a novel multi-view representation learning method named Full Reconstruction based Deep Canonical Correlation Analysis (FR-DCCA). FR-

DCCA applys reconstruction and correlation maximization on different parts of view information, which not only addresses the contradiction between them but also enables them to benefit from each other. In FR-DCCA, shared and specific information is disentangled by maximizing JS divergence between them, and then we maximize the canonical correlation between shared information from different views to maintain consistency. Meanwhile, we guarantee the complementarity simultaneously via harnessing both the shared and specific information to reconstruct the original view. Finally, we jointly optimize multiple objectives to obtain complete, compact, more discriminative representations. Extensive experiments and analysis demonstrate that FR-DCCA provides significant improvements, and our reconstruction structure is effective. This work is limited to two views and future work includes explorations of more effective estimations of differences between shared and specific information.

**Acknowledgement.** This work was supported by the NSFC Project under Grant No. 62176069 and 61933013, the Innovation Group of Guangdong Education Department under Grant No. 2020KCXTD014 and the 2019 Key Discipline project of Guangdong Province.

# References

1. Akaho, S.: A kernel method for canonical correlation analysis. In: Proceedings of the International Meeting of the Psychometric Society, pp. 2639–2664 (2001)
2. Andrew, G., Arora, R., Bilmes, J., Livescu, K.: Deep canonical correlation analysis. In: Proceedings of the 30th International Conference on Machine Learning, pp. 1247–1255 (2013)
3. Baltrušaitis, T., Ahuja, C., Morency, L.P.: Multimodal machine learning: a survey and taxonomy. IEEE Trans. Pattern Anal. Mach. Intell. **41**(2), 423–443 (2019). https://doi.org/10.1109/TPAMI.2018.2798607
4. Blum, A., Mitchell, T.: Combining labeled and unlabeled data with co-training. In: Proceedings of the Eleventh Annual Conference on Computational Learning Theory, pp. 92–100 (1998). https://doi.org/10.1145/279943.279962
5. Chang, C.C., Lin, C.J.: LIBSVM: a library for support vector machines. ACM Trans. Intell. Syst. Technol. **2**(3), 27 (2011). https://doi.org/10.1145/1961189.1961199
6. Chang, X., Dacheng, T., Chao, X.: A survey on multi-view learning (2013). https://doi.org/10.1109/TKDE.2018.2872063
7. Fuglede, B., Topsoe, F.: Jensen-Shannon divergence and Hilbert space embedding. In: Proceedings of International Symposium on Information Theory, 2004, pp. 31- (2004). https://doi.org/10.1109/ISIT.2004.1365067
8. Gao, Q., Lian, H., Wang, Q., Sun, G.: Cross-modal subspace clustering via deep canonical correlation analysis. In: Proceedings of the AAAI Conference on Artificial Intelligence, vol. 34, pp. 3938–3945 (2020). https://doi.org/10.1609/aaai.v34i04.5808
9. Hardoon, D.R., Szedmak, S., Shawe-Taylor, J.: Canonical correlation analysis: an overview with application to learning methods. Neural Comput. **16**(12), 2639–2664 (2004). https://doi.org/10.1162/0899766042321814

10. Hinton, G., Salakhutdinov, R.: Reducing the dimensionality of data with neural networks. Science **313**, 454–455 (2013). https://doi.org/10.1126/science.1127647
11. Schölkopf, B.: Statistical learning and kernel methods. In: Della Riccia, G., Lenz, H.-J., Kruse, R. (eds.) Data Fusion and Perception. ICMS, vol. 431, pp. 3–24. Springer, Vienna (2001). https://doi.org/10.1007/978-3-7091-2580-9_1
12. Jia, X., et al.: Semi-supervised multi-view deep discriminant representation learning. IEEE Trans. Pattern Anal. Mach. Intell. **43**(7), 2496–2509 (2021). https://doi.org/10.1109/TPAMI.2020.2973634
13. Kingma, D.P., Ba, J.: Adam: a method for stochastic optimization. In: International Conference on Learning Representations (ICLR 2015) (2010)
14. Lecun, Y., Bottou, L., Bengio, Y., Haffner, P.: Gradient-based learning applied to document recognition. Proc. IEEE **86**(11), 2278–2324 (1998). https://doi.org/10.1109/5.726791
15. Li, Y., Yang, M., Zhang, Z.: A survey of multi-view representation learning. IEEE Trans. Knowl. Data Eng. **31**, 1863–1883 (2018). https://doi.org/10.1109/TKDE.2018.2872063
16. Manning, C.D., Raghavan, P., Schütze, H.: Introduction to Information Retrieval. Cambridge University Press, Cambridge (2008)
17. Ng, A.Y., Jordan, M.I., Weiss, Y.: On spectral clustering: analysis and an algorithm. In: Proceedings of the 14th International Conference on Neural Information Processing Systems: Natural and Synthetic, pp. 849–856 (2001)
18. Pei, H., Wei, B., Chang, K.C.C., Lei, Y., Yang, B.: Geom-GCN: Geometric graph convolutional networks. In: International Conference on Learning Representations (2020)
19. Sun, S.: A survey of multi-view machine learning. Neural Comput. Appl. **23**, 2031–2038 (2013). https://doi.org/10.1007/s00521-013-1362-6
20. Wan, Z., Zhang, C., Zhu, P.F., Hu, Q.: Multi-view information-bottleneck representation learning. In: AAAI (2021)
21. Wang, W., Arora, R., Livescu, K., Bilmes, J.: On deep multi-view representation learning. In: Proceedings of the 32nd International Conference on Machine Learning, vol. 37, pp. 1083–1092 (2015)
22. Wang, W., Arora, R., Livescu, K., Bilmes, J.: Unsupervised learning of acoustic features via deep canonical correlation analysis. In: 2015 IEEE International Conference on Acoustics, Speech and Signal Processing (ICASSP). pp. 4590–4594 (2015). https://doi.org/10.1109/ICASSP.2015.7178840
23. Wang, Z., Bovik, A.C.: Mean squared error: love it or leave it? a new look at signal fidelity measures. IEEE Signal Process. Mag. **26**(1), 98–117 (2009). https://doi.org/10.1109/MSP.2008.930649
24. Yu, Y., Tang, S., Aizawa, K., Aizawa, A.: Category-based deep CCA for fine-grained venue discovery from multimodal data. IEEE Trans. Neural Netw. Learn. Syst. **30**(4), 1250–1258 (2019). https://doi.org/10.1109/TNNLS.2018.2856253
25. Zhang, C., Cui, Y., Han, Z., Zhou, J.T., Fu, H., Hu, Q.: Deep partial multi-view learning. IEEE Transactions on Pattern Analysis and Machine Intelligence, p. 1 (2020). https://doi.org/10.1109/TPAMI.2020.3037734
26. Zhou, T., Zhang, C., Peng, X., Bhaskar, H., Yang, J.: Dual shared-specific multi-view subspace clustering. IEEE Trans. Cybern. **50**(8), 3517–3530 (2020). https://doi.org/10.1109/TCYB.2019.2918495
27. Zhu, W., Lu, J., Zhou, J.: Structured general and specific multi-view subspace clustering. Pattern Recogn. **93**, 392–403 (2019). https://doi.org/10.1016/j.patcog.2019.05.005

# Attentional Local Contrastive Learning for Face Forgery Detection

Yunshu Dai[1], Jianwei Fei[1], Huaming Wang[2], and Zhihua Xia[1,2]([⊠])

[1] Nanjing University of Information Science and Technology, Nanjing 210044, China
xia_zhihua@163.com
[2] Jinan University, Guangzhou 510632, China

**Abstract.** In this work, we present a novel representation learning module for face forgery detection called attentional local contrastive learning (ALCL). ALCL is designed to distinguish forged regions from pristine regions using an explicit constraint. Specifically, feature vectors extracted by the backbone are first embedded into a unit hypersphere, and for each local feature vector, ALCL constructs horizontal and vertical triple sets respectively with its adjacent vectors. ALCL minimizes the angle between vectors of the same source while maximizing that between different sources by optimizing their normalized cosine similarity. Moreover, we also propose a multiple scale residual learning (MSRL) module that takes advantage of rich residual information to complement RGB input. We demonstrate the effectiveness of the proposed method through comprehensive experiments. On multiple challenging face forgery benchmarks, our method achieves great performances under both in-domain and cross-domain settings, and also shows good robustness to compression compared to existing works.

**Keywords:** Face forgery detection · Contrastive learning · Local similarity · Image residual learning

## 1 Introduction

Deep learning based face forgery techniques that can manipulate facial expressions or attributes have raised much concern on privacy protection and multimedia security. Thus it is urgent to study face forgery detection as the countermeasures. Prior detection methods focused on obvious visual artifacts left by forgery algorithms, and achieved high detection accuracy with off-the-shelf models [1,2] or artifacts simulation [3]. However, these methods usually overfit traces of specific forgery algorithms, resulting in poor generalization on unseen forgeries. Moreover, the products of face forgery techniques are becoming increasingly realistic with fewer artifacts which challenges detection methods seriously.

Recent works resort to more intrinsic differences between real and forged faces for higher detection accuracy and better generalizability of detectors. A key observation is that the forged faces are more or less inconsistent, whether in temporal domain [4–6] or spatial domain [7,8]. Spatial domain inconsistency refers to the coexistence of different sources in one single face image. Source here represents features like camera pattern noise in real images or Generative Adversarial Networks fingerprints in generated images that can identify image sources [7]. Face forgery algorithms inevitably introduce source that is different from face context by replacing or manipulating facial regions. Thus the coexistence of multiple sources is a primary and intrinsic trace in forged images.

The motivation of our work is in line with this observation. Unlike previous works that directly consider face forgery detection as a binary classification task, we force the model to learn more discriminative local features for different image sources by an additional constraint. Specifically, we propose an Attentional Local Contrastive Learning (ALCL) module to mine the consistency of input face images through maximizing the similarity of local features from the same source, otherwise the opposite. Besides, we also design a Multi Scale Residual Learning (MSRL) module to capture more subtle forgery traces and complement the RGB input. More details are given in Sec. 3.1 and Sec. 3.2. Our contributions are summarized as follows:

- We propose Attentional Local Contrastive Learning to ensure that the model can learn image source inconsistency with local similarity constraints instead of forgery traces left by specific forgery algorithms.
- We propose Multi Scale Residual Learning that is able to adaptively learn rich residual information which is complementary to RGB input, resulting in better performance on compressed data.
- Experiments on large scale benchmarks demonstrate both good generalizability and compression robustness of our method. Ablation studies also show the effectiveness of the proposed modules.

## 2   Related Work

Early works regard face forgery detection as a binary classification problem, and use self-designed deep networks [1,2,9] to identify forged faces. Although these methods have achieved some progress, they lack in-depth study on essential differences between real and forged faces. Thus, researchers are trying to find more intrinsic forgery patterns.

**DeepFake Detection Based on Intrinsic Forgery Patterns.** These works usually leverage the inherent peculiarity of human faces which is difficult to forge, such as heartbeat information [10], behavior habits [4], and the synchronization of lips and sounds [6]. Temporal domain defects of forged videos are also excavated using recurrent neural network [2], long short term memory networks [11], three-dimensional convolution neural networks [5]. Besides, some works have found that the frequency domain provides forgery traces complementary to RGB space, which can be directly used as the input [12] or used for the extraction of high-frequency residuals [8].

**DeepFake Detection Based on Forgery Algorithm Defects.** Forgery algorithms always leave forgery traces at the blending boundary of faces and background [13]. [3] crops out faces from the background and blend the faces back to original images after affine transformation and gaussian blur for simulation of the forgery pipeline. The augmented dataset is dynamically generated to train the detector and prevents from overfitting on specific forgeries. Unlike this method, [14] does not directly train the detector with binary cross entropy, but forces the detector to predict the blending boundary in forged faces.

Different from these works we mentioned above, our method further improves the model by turning its learning goal from forgery boundary to similarity of local features between real and forged regions. Although our method also considers the consistency of face blending boundary, it does not learn the peculiarity of forgery traces, so as to avoid overfitting on specific types of forgery algorithms. Our method does not rely on massive data augmentation but can still achieves good performance under both in-domain and cross-domain settings.

## 3  Methods

The overview of the proposed method is illustrated in Fig. 1. It consists of two key components, one of which is the Multi-Scale Residual Learning (MSRL) module while the other is Attentional Local Contrastive Learning (ALCL) module. The details of MSRL, ALCL and the overall training loss are presented in Sec. 3.1, Sec. 3.2, and Sec. 3.3.

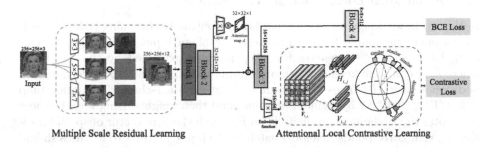

**Fig. 1.** Overview of our method. We use ResNet18 with 4 blocks as the backbone.

### 3.1  Multiple Scale Residual Learning

Recent works on image forensic have found that the forgery traces are more obvious in image residual. For this reason, spatial rich model (SRM) [15] is widely used in face forgery detection methods to extract the high frequency residual with a set of hand-crafted high pass filters (HPF). However, leveraging hand-crafted HPF [16] to obtain the image residual [17] can only cover limited frequency components, which might not able to be generalized well to different types of forgery. Moreover, HPFs are also not scalable to different size. To this end, we introduce a learnable residual extraction module MSRL to replace hand-crafted HPFs with the standard convolutions.

Given an image $I$, classic HPF like SRM firstly predicts the pixel value of position $(i, j)$ according to its neighbour pixels $\mathcal{N}_{i,j}$. Then the residual $R_{i,j}$ can be extracted by $R_{i,j} = P(\mathcal{N}_{i,j}) - I_{i,j}$, where $P(\cdot)$ is the predictor. It is easy to find that $P(\cdot)$ can be replaced using the standard convolutions, let $f$ denotes the convolution, the residual can be modeled as

$$R = f(I) - I = [\sum_{i=1}^{3} I_i * w_i^1, \sum_{i=1}^{3} I_i * w_i^2, \sum_{i=1}^{3} I_i * w_i^3] - I. \tag{1}$$

$w_i$ here denotes the $i$-th kernel of size $k \times k$ for $i$-th channel in the RGB input, and $[\cdot]$ refers to the concatenation of feature maps produced by $w^*$. Unlike traditional HPF, $w$ in Eq. 1 can be updated during the back propagation of model training, which enables $f$ to mine the most discriminative traces adaptively.

However, size of $w$ is fixed and can only cover a fixed receptive field. To capture the forgery traces of different scales, we further construct MSRL module with multiple $f$. Let $f_3$, $f_5$, $f_7$ denote $f$ with kernel size $k$ equals to 3, 5, and 7, and the corresponding residuals are $R_3$, $R_5$, $R_7$, we concatenate all these residuals and the RGB input to form a 12-channel feature maps $[I, R_3, R_5, R_7]$. MSRL provides rich and discriminative residual information which is complementary to RGB input, and supports dynamic update according to different training data.

### 3.2   Attentional Local Contrastive Learning

In this work, we design an Attentional Local Contrastive Learning (ALCL) module to mine the source feature inconsistency of an input face image. Specifically, let $\mathbf{F} \in \mathbb{R}^{h \times w \times c}$ denotes the deep features extracted by the backbone, where $h, w, c$ are the height, width and number of channels respectively, and an additional layer $\pi(\cdot)$ takes $\mathbf{F}$ as input and regresses a 1-channel attention map $A = \pi(\mathbf{F}) \in [0, 1]^{h \times w}$ by sigmoid function, and then weights using $\mathbf{F} \odot A$, where $\odot$ denotes the Hadamard product. Then $\mathbf{F}_{i,j}$ is the feature vector of spatial position $i, j$ that corresponds to a local patch in the input $I$. Any two features should be similar if their corresponding regions in the input are from the same source, i.e., both real or both fake, otherwise, they should be less similar regardless of the size of the forged area.

Then, for each $\mathbf{F}_{i,j}$, ALCL divides its adjacent local features into a vertical set $V_{i,j} = \{\mathbf{F}_{i-1,j}, \mathbf{F}_{i,j}, \mathbf{F}_{i+1,j}\}$ and a horizontal set $H_{i,j} = \{\mathbf{F}_{i,j-1}, \mathbf{F}_{i,j}, \mathbf{F}_{i,j+1}\}$. Both $V_{i,j}$ and $H_{i,j}$ are triple sets that consist of 3 local feature vectors. To impose consistency constraint, all local feature vectors $\mathbf{F}_{i,j}$ are first projected into the same representation space using embedding function which is realized by $1 \times 1$ convolution. Let $\psi$ denotes the upcoming convolution block and the embedding function, then we denotes the new features by

$$\mathbf{F}'_{i,j} = \frac{\psi(\mathbf{F} \odot A)_{i,j})}{||\psi(\mathbf{F} \odot A)_{i,j})||_2}. \tag{2}$$

Equation 2 makes local features fall into a unit hypersphere, and we only have to optimize the angle of any two $\mathbf{F}'_{i,j}$ instead of their euclidean distance. Note that $V_{i,j}$ and $H_{i,j}$ are not strict triple sets since we can not guarantee that they must contain 2 positive samples and 1 negative sample, thus ALCL construct 3 vector pairs for each $V_{i,j}$ or $H_{i,j}$. We take $V_{i,j}$ for example, the triple sets can be divided into 3 pairs: $(F'_{i-1,j}, F'_{i,j}), (F'_{i+1,j}, F'_{i,j}), (F'_{i-1,j}, F'_{i+1,j})$, for each pair, cosine similarity of any two local feature vectors is calculated by:

$$\cos(\mathbf{F}'_a, \mathbf{F}'_b) = \frac{\mathbf{F}'_a \cdot \mathbf{F}'_b}{||\mathbf{F}'_a||\ ||\mathbf{F}'_b||}, \tag{3}$$

where $\mathbf{F}'_a$ and $\mathbf{F}'_b$ denote any two vectors in a triple set. ALCL can not only maximize the similarity of local feature vectors that of the same forgery type but also minimize the similarity of local feature vectors with different types. This ensures that the deep feature maps are more discriminative for downstream layer and classifier.

### 3.3  Loss Functions

Our framework involves two objective to optimize: one is the binary cross entropy loss (BCE) for the main branch that directly outputs real or fake predictions, and the other one is the contrastive loss for ALCL branch. Let $y \in \{0, 1\}$ denotes the ground truth label of input face image, 1 stands for fake and 0 stands for real, the BCE loss is then expressed as

$$L_{BCE} = -\sum_{i=1}^{n} y_i log\hat{y}_i + (1 - y_i)log(1 - \hat{y}_i), \tag{4}$$

where $\hat{y} \in [0, 1]$ is the model prediction. For ALCL branch, we have to utilize the pixel level mask of forged images to obtain the ground truth of pair wise local similarity. Assuming $M \in \{0, 1\}^{H \times W}$ to be the pixel level annotations of a forged face image, we first downsample $M$ to $h \times w$, making its spatial size the same of deep features $\mathbf{F}'$ by average pooling with window size and strides both equal to $(H//h, W//w)$:

$$M' = AveragePooling(M, H//h, W//w) \in [0, 1]^{h \times w \times 1}. \tag{5}$$

Then, $M'_{i,j} \in [0, 1]$ can be the forgery level indicator of the original region with size $(H//h, W//w)$ in the input image, and $M'_{i,j}$ is closer to 1 if more area in its corresponding region is forged. Thus, the ground truth of similarities of local triples can be calculated by:

$$s_{m,n} = \begin{cases} 1 & \text{if } |M'_{i,j} - M'_{m,n}| > 0, \\ 0 & \text{else,} \end{cases} \tag{6}$$

where $(m, n)$ denotes the index of the neigbor in the triples. This indicates that if the corresponding regions of $\mathbf{F}'_{i,j}$ and its neighbor in $V_{i,j}$ or $H_{i,j}$ in the original input image involve different sources, the two feature vectors should be different, otherwise the opposite. The loss of ALCL can be expressed by Eq. 7:

$$L_{ALCL} = s_{m,n} \cos(\mathbf{F}'_{i,j}, \mathbf{F}'_{m,n}) + (1 - s_{m,n}) \min(t - \cos(\mathbf{F}'_{i,j}, \mathbf{F}'_{m,n}), 0). \quad (7)$$

where $t$ is the threshold angle. The total loss is

$$L_{total} = \alpha L_{BCE} + \beta L_{ALCL}, \quad (8)$$

where $\alpha$ and $\beta$ are weights of the two losses.

## 4    Experiment

### 4.1    Experimental Settings

**Datasets.** In this paper, we perform the experiments on multiple large scale face forgery benchmark databases, including FaceForensics++(FF++), Celeb-DF [18], and Faceshifter [19]. FF++ consists of forged faces generated by 4 different forgery algorithms, i.e., Deepfakes (DF),Face2Face (F2F),FaceSwap (FS), NeuralTextures (NT). All of them are applied on 1k pristine videos, so that the entire database contains 5k videos. To evaluate the compression robustness of our method, we use the compressed version of FF++ denoted by C23 and C40 to train and evaluate our method.

**Evaluation Metrics.** We use both Area under the ROC Curve (AUC) and binary classification accuracy (Acc) as the primary evaluation metrics. For the similarity of local feature vector, we adopt normalized cosine similarity.

**Implementation Details.** We construct our framework based on ResNet18 backbone. The model is initiated by ImageNet pretrained weights. The faces are cropped and resized to $256 \times 256 \times 3$. The batch size is 32, iteration number is 200 and model is trained for 50 epochs without early stopping. We adopt Adam as the optimizer with learning rate 0.001, $\beta 1 = 0.9$, and $\beta 2 = 0.999$. The loss weights $\alpha$ and $\beta$ are set to be 10.0 and 1.0 respectively. $t$ is set to be 0.9.

### 4.2    Comparisons with Recent Works

**In-domain Evaluations.** We first evaluate the proposed method on FF++ dataset with different compression levels. As shown in Table 1, compared with existing methods, our method achieves promising results under uncompressed setting and shows more advantages under both light and heavy compression settings. Specifically, F3 Net outperforms our method slightly, but its performances on C23 and C40 data are far behind ours by 0.62% and 0.83%, and the overall performance under all compression settings is 0.4% lower than ours in terms of AUC. Video compression removes the obvious visual artifacts which are always leveraged by existing methods, resulting in significantly performance drop. However, our method is robust to compression and able to preserve high accuracy by making the deep feature maps more discriminative.

**Table 1.** Performances on FF++ with different compression levels (AUC).

| Methods | C0 | C23 | C40 | Average |
|---|---|---|---|---|
| Xception (2019ICCV) [20] | 99.20 | 96.30 | 89.30 | 94.90 |
| Face X-ray (2020CVPR) [14] | 98.80 | 87.40 | 61.60 | 82.60 |
| Two-branch (2020ECCV) [11] | – | 98.70 | 86.59 | – |
| F3 net (2020ECCV) [12] | **99.80** | 98.10 | 93.30 | 97.10 |
| CNN-aug (2020CVPR) [21] | 99.70 | 94.60 | 88.70 | 94.30 |
| Ours | 99.69 | **98.72** | **94.13** | **97.50** |

In Fig. 2, we visualize the $16 \times 16$ local features from different forged faces using t-sne. Orange triangle denotes local feature vectors of forged regions and blue circular denotes that of pristine regions It can be seen that features of real regions gather together and are separated from that of forged regions well.

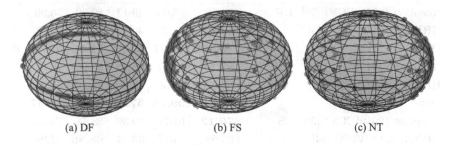

(a) DF                    (b) FS                    (c) NT

**Fig. 2.** Distribution visualization of $\mathbf{F}'_{i,j}$ in block 3 from DF, FS and NT faces.

We further report the detailed performances in terms of binary accuracy in all four forgery types of FF++ (C40) in Table 2. Our method not only outperforms face forgery detection model MesoNet greatly, but also surpasses the state-of-the-art method by 0.84%, 3.95%, 1.99%, 0.78% for each forgery type. And the average accuracy is 1.66% higher.

**Table 2.** Performance on all four forgery types in FF++(C40) (Acc).

| Methods | DF | F2F | FS | NT | Average |
|---|---|---|---|---|---|
| MesoNet (2018WIFS) [1] | 89.52 | 84.44 | 83.56 | 75.74 | 83.31 |
| Face X-ray (2020CVPR) [14] | **94.72** | 87.80 | 92.63 | **78.47** | 88.41 |
| SPSL (2021CVPR) [17] | 93.48 | 86.02 | 92.26 | 76.78 | 87.14 |
| FTTS (2021TCSVT) [17] | 93.88 | 80.76 | 82.99 | 78.03 | 83.91 |
| Ours | **94.32** | **89.07** | **94.25** | 77.56 | **88.80** |

**Cross-domain Evaluations.** The results of FF++ cross-domain evaluations are shown in Table 3. Specifically, ALCL is trained on DF, F2F, FS, NT respectively, and evaluated on all the datasets including those unseen forgery types. We also report the performances of two SOTA detectors Xception and HRNet under the same settings. We can see that our method exceeds others with relatively large improvements under 3 out of 4 cross-domain evaluation settings. While the overall performance of our method is 4.34% and 3.33% lower than that of Xception and HRNet when trained on FS, the results on F2F and FS of ours are still better. Meantime, it can be seen that our results on DF, F2F and NT are higher from about 3% to 14% than other methods. Note that we only use a small ResNet18 network as our backbone while Xception and HRNet are much deeper and wider.

**Table 3.** Cross-domain evaluations on FF++(AUC).

| Model | Train Set | Test Set | | | | Average |
|---|---|---|---|---|---|---|
| | | DF | F2F | FS | NT | |
| Xception (2019ICCV) [20] | DF | 99.38 | 75.05 | 49.13 | 80.39 | 75.99 |
| HRNet (2020CVPR) [14] | | 99.26 | 68.25 | 39.15 | 71.39 | 69.51 |
| Ours | | **100.00** | **88.67** | **52.94** | **92.33** | **83.48** |
| Xception (2019ICCV) [20] | F2F | **87.56** | 99.53 | 65.23 | 65.90 | 79.56 |
| HRNet (2020CVPR) [14] | | 83.64 | 99.50 | 56.60 | 61.26 | 75.25 |
| Ours | | 82.83 | **99.75** | **67.31** | **84.79** | **83.67** |
| Xception (2019ICCV) [20] | FS | **70.12** | 61.70 | 99.36 | 68.71 | **74.97** |
| HRNet(2020CVPR) [14] | | 63.59 | 64.12 | 99.24 | **68.89** | 73.96 |
| Ours | | 54.19 | **66.43** | **99.94** | 61.96 | 70.63 |
| Xception (2019ICCV) [20] | NT | 93.09 | 84.82 | 47.98 | 99.50 | 81.35 |
| HRNet (2020CVPR) [14] | | 94.05 | 87.26 | 64.10 | 98.61 | 86.01 |
| Ours | | **98.86** | **93.44** | **65.60** | 98.72 | **89.16** |

The cross-domain results on Celeb-DF are given in Table 4, under this setting, the model is trained on FF++(C23) and evaluated on both FF++ and Celeb-DF. The proposed method outperforms all other detection approaches on Celeb-DF cross-domain evaluation and the performance on FF++ in-domain is also better. We achieve a significant improvement by 21.21% compared with a similar lightweight model Meso4. We also outperform the recent video-based approach by 2.18%. Note that our result is only frame-level.

## 4.3    Effectiveness of MSRL and ALCL

In this part, we evaluate the effectiveness of proposed MSRL and ALCL respectively, and more quantitative results will be presented in Sec.4.4. Firstly, we visualize the outputs of ALCL for each forgery type in Fig. 3.

**Table 4.** Cross-domain evaluations on Celeb-DF (AUC).

| Method | Training data | FF++ | Celeb-DF |
|---|---|---|---|
| Meso4 (2018WIFS) [1] | FF++ (C40) | 84.70 | 54.80 |
| SMIL (2020ACM MM) [22] | FF++ (C23) | 96.80 | 56.30 |
| Two-branch (2020ECCV) [11] | FF++ (C23) | 93.20 | 73.41 |
| F3 Net (2020ECCV) [12] | FF++ (C23) | 97.97 | 65.17 |
| CNN-aug (2020CVPR) [21] | FF++ (C40) | 88.70 | 68.40 |
| DPNet (2021WACV) [23] | FF++ (C40) | 90.91 | 71.76 |
| MADD (2021CVPR) [24] | FF++ (C0) | 99.80 | 67.44 |
| LRNet (2021CVPR) [25] | FF++ (C0) | **99.90** | 56.90 |
| Nirkin *et al.*(2021TPAMI) [26] | FF++ (C0) | 99.70 | 65.17 |
| Ours | FF++(C23) | 98.72 | **76.59** |

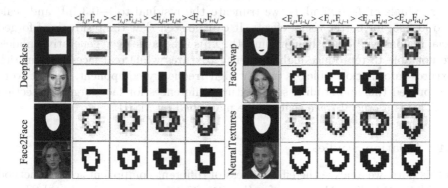

**Fig. 3.** Visualization of pair-wise cosine similarity in different triple sets.

In Fig. 3 the most left column are forgery faces and corresponding pixel level annotations, from left to right are similarity maps of different pairs in triple sets $V_{i,j}$ and $H_{i,j}$ and corresponding ground truth. All the maps are between $[-1, 1]$ and scaled to $[0, 255]$ for visualization. It can be seen, for those adjacent regions that have different sources, the predicted cosine similarities are extremely low. Meantime, we can also find that $< \mathbf{F}_{i,j-1}, \mathbf{F}_{i,j+1} >$ and $< \mathbf{F}_{i-1,j}, \mathbf{F}_{i+1,j} >$ have a greater receptive field, thus are able to mine source inconsistency in a wide range. The dissimilar feature pairs from all different forgery types present low cosine similarity obviously, demonstrating ALCL can be generalizable.

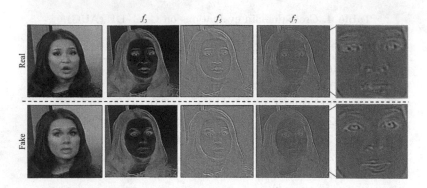

**Fig. 4.** Visualization of outputs of MSRL.

Figure 4 shows the 3 scale residuals extracted by MSRL. From left to right are residuals of $f_3, f_5$, and $f_7$, we truncate the residual to $[-0.3, \inf]$ and scale it to $[0, 255]$ for better visual effects. It can be seen that the residuals of forged facial regions are obviously more smooth. This is because deep generative models are not able to reproduce high frequency textures while real faces contain rich textures information which is usually high frequency component. Recent work also proved this and studied such texture differences for face forgery detection [27].This is a crucial trace that can be magnified by MSRL.

## 4.4  Ablation Studies

In this part, we analyse the effectiveness of different components of our method by ablation studies. Moreover, for the attention map regression in ALCL, we provide both unsupervision and supervision training manners. Note that unsupervision is the default setting above and we use pixel level annotations with pixel level BCE loss in the supervision manner which is denoted by *att-sup*. The results of ablation studies are presented in Table 5.

**Table 5.** Cross-domain evaluations on Celeb-DF and Faceshifter(AUC).

| MSRL | ALCL | *att-sup* | FF++ | Celeb-DF | Faceshifter |
|------|------|-----------|-------|----------|-------------|
|      |      |           | 98.23 | 62.54    | 68.98       |
| ✓    |      |           | 98.34 | 64.71    | 70.90       |
|      | ✓    |           | 98.69 | 75.22    | 74.25       |
| ✓    | ✓    |           | **98.72** | 76.59 | 78.94       |
| ✓    | ✓    | ✓         | 98.36 | **77.51** | **80.31**  |

We can see that the generalizability has a great improvement when the backbone is equipped with ALCL. The MSRL also contributes for both in-domain and cross-domain evaluations slightly. When the attention map in ALCL is trained under supervision, the performance are improved limited on Celeb-DF and Faceshifter while the result on FF++ is lower.

## 5   Conclusion

In this paper, we provided a focused study on intrinsic differences between real and forged faces. We design a novel Attentional Local Contrastive Learning module to ensure the discriminative of features in forged faces and prevent model from overfitting specific forgery traces substantially. We also propose a Multiple Scale Residual Learning module to capture rich residual information. Evaluations on 3 large scale benchmarks have proved the effectiveness and robustness of our method under both in-domain and cross-domain settings.

**Acknowledgements.** This work is supported in part by the National Key Research and Development Plan of China under Grant 2020YFB1005600, in part by the National Natural Science Foundation of China under grant numbers 62122032, and U1936118, in part by Qinglan Project of Jiangsu Province and 333 project of Jiangsu Province, in part by Postgraduate Resarch & Practice Innovation Program of Jiangsu Province under grant number KYCX22-1207.

## References

1. Afchar, D., Nozick, V., Yamagishi, J., Echizen, I.: Mesonet: a compact facial video forgery detection network. In: 2018 IEEE International Workshop on Information Forensics and Security (WIFS), pp. 1–7. IEEE (2018)
2. Sabir, E., Cheng, J., Jaiswal, A., AbdAlmageed, W., Masi, I., Natarajan, P.: Recurrent convolutional strategies for face manipulation detection in videos. Interfaces (GUI) **3**(1), 80–87 (2019)
3. Li, Y., Lyu, S.: Exposing deepfake videos by detecting face warping artifacts. arXiv preprint arXiv:1811.00656 (2018)
4. Agarwal, S., Farid, H., Gu, Y., He, M., Nagano, K., Li, H.: Protecting world leaders against deep fakes. In: CVPR workshops, vol. 1 (2019)
5. Zhang, D., Li, C., Lin, F., Zeng, D., Ge, S.: Detecting deepfake videos with temporal dropout 3dcnn. In: IJCAI (2021)
6. Zhou, Y., Lim, S.N.: Joint audio-visual deepfake detection. In: Proceedings of the IEEE/CVF International Conference on Computer Vision, pp. 14800–14809 (2021)
7. Zhao, T., Xu, X., Xu, M., Ding, H., Xiong, Y., Xia, W.: Learning self-consistency for deepfake detection. In: Proceedings of the IEEE/CVF International Conference on Computer Vision, pp. 15023–15033 (2021)
8. Chen, S., Yao, T., Chen, Y., Ding, S., Li, J., Ji, R.: Local relation learning for face forgery detection. In: Proceedings of the AAAI Conference on Artificial Intelligence, vol. 35, pp. 1081–1088 (2021)
9. Amerini, I., Galteri, L., Caldelli, R., Del Bimbo, A.: Deepfake video detection through optical flow based CNN. In: Proceedings of the IEEE/CVF International Conference on Computer Vision Workshops (2019)

10. Qi, H., et al.: Deeprhythm: exposing deepfakes with attentional visual heartbeat rhythms. In: Proceedings of the 28th ACM International Conference on Multimedia, pp. 4318–4327 (2020)

11. Masi, I., Killekar, A., Mascarenhas, R.M., Gurudatt, S.P., AbdAlmageed, W.: Two-branch recurrent network for isolating deepfakes in videos. In: Vedaldi, A., Bischof, H., Brox, T., Frahm, J.-M. (eds.) ECCV 2020. LNCS, vol. 12352, pp. 667–684. Springer, Cham (2020). https://doi.org/10.1007/978-3-030-58571-6_39

12. Qian, Y., Yin, G., Sheng, L., Chen, Z., Shao, J.: Thinking in frequency: face forgery detection by mining frequency-aware clues. In: Vedaldi, A., Bischof, H., Brox, T., Frahm, J.-M. (eds.) ECCV 2020. LNCS, vol. 12357, pp. 86–103. Springer, Cham (2020). https://doi.org/10.1007/978-3-030-58610-2_6

13. Fei, J., Dai, Y., Yu, P., Shen, T., Xia, Z., Weng, J.: Learning second order local anomaly for general face forgery detection. In: Proceedings of the IEEE/CVF Conference on Computer Vision and Pattern Recognition, pp. 20270–20280 (2022)

14. Li, L., et al.: Face x-ray for more general face forgery detection. In: Proceedings of the IEEE/CVF Conference on Computer Vision and Pattern Recognition, pp. 5001–5010 (2020)

15. Goljan, M., Fridrich, J., Cogranne, R.: Rich model for steganalysis of color images. In: 2014 IEEE International Workshop on Information Forensics and Security (WIFS), pp. 185–190. IEEE (2014)

16. Luo, Y., Zhang, Y., Yan, J., Liu, W.: Generalizing face forgery detection with high-frequency features. In: Proceedings of the IEEE/CVF Conference on Computer Vision and Pattern Recognition, pp. 16317–16326 (2021)

17. Liu, H., et al.: Spatial-phase shallow learning: rethinking face forgery detection in frequency domain. In: Proceedings of the IEEE/CVF Conference on Computer Vision and Pattern Recognition, pp. 772–781 (2021)

18. Li, Y., Yang, X., Sun, P., Qi, H., Lyu, S.: Celeb-df: a large-scale challenging dataset for deepfake forensics. In: Proceedings of the IEEE/CVF Conference on Computer Vision and Pattern Recognition, pp. 3207–3216 (2020)

19. Li, L., Bao, J., Yang, H., Chen, D., Wen, F.: Advancing high fidelity identity swapping for forgery detection. In: Proceedings of the IEEE/CVF Conference on Computer Vision and Pattern Recognition, pp. 5074–5083 (2020)

20. Rossler, A., Cozzolino, D., Verdoliva, L., Riess, C., Thies, J., Nießner., M.: Faceforensics++: learning to detect manipulated facial images. In: Proceedings of the IEEE/CVF International Conference on Computer Vision, pp. 1–11 (2019)

21. Wang, S.Y., Wang, O., Zhang, R., Owens, A., Efros, A.A.: CNN-generated images are surprisingly easy to spot... for now. In: Proceedings of the IEEE/CVF Conference on Computer Vision and Pattern Recognition, pp. 8695–8704 (2020)

22. Li, X., et al.: Sharp multiple instance learning for deepfake video detection. In: Proceedings of the 28th ACM International Conference on Multimedia, pp. 1864–1872 (2020)

23. Trinh, L., Tsang, M., Rambhatla, S., Liu, Y.: Interpretable and trustworthy deepfake detection via dynamic prototypes. In: Proceedings of the IEEE/CVF Winter Conference on Applications of Computer Vision, pp. 1973–1983 (2021)

24. Zhao, H., Zhou, W., Chen, D., Wei, T., Zhang, W., Yu, N.: Multi-attentional deepfake detection. In: Proceedings of the IEEE/CVF Conference on Computer Vision and Pattern Recognition, pp. 2185–2194 (2021)

25. Sun, Z., Han, Y., Hua, Z., Ruan, N., Jia, W.: Improving the efficiency and robustness of deepfakes detection through precise geometric features. In: Proceedings of the IEEE/CVF Conference on Computer Vision and Pattern Recognition, pp. 3609–3618 (2021)

26. Nirkin, Y., Wolf, L., Keller, Y., Hassner, T.: Deepfake detection based on discrepancies between faces and their context. IEEE Trans. Pattern Anal. Mach. Intell. (2021)
27. Yang, J., Li, A., Xiao, S., Wen, L., Gao, X.: Mtd-net: learning to detect deepfakes images by multi-scale texture difference. IEEE Trans. Inf. Forensics Secur. **16**, 4234–4245 (2021)

# Context-Assisted Attention for Image Captioning

Zheng Lian[1,2（✉）] ⓘ, Rui Wang[2], Haichang Li[2], and Xiaohui Hu[2]

[1] University of Chinese Academy of Sciences, Beijing 100049, China
[2] Institute of Software Chinese Academy of Sciences, Beijing 100190, China
lianzheng2017@iscas.ac.cn

**Abstract.** Temporal attention has demonstrated its crucial role with regard to modelling the relationships between semantic queries and image regions in current image captioning task. Nevertheless, most existing attention-based methods ignore the potential effect of the previously attended information on the generation of current attention context. In this paper, we propose a simple but effective Context-Assisted Attention ($CA^2$) for image captioning, which considers the temporal coherence of the attention contexts in the process of sequence prediction. Specifically, $CA^2$ combines the attention contexts from previous time steps with the features of image regions to serve as the input key-value pairs of the attention module for current context generation, which enables the sentence decoder to not only attend to the image regions by tradition but also focus on the historical attention contexts when necessary. Furthermore, we present a regularization method tailored to our $CA^2$, namely Weight Transferring Constraint (WTC), to restrict the total weight assigned to the historical contexts in each decoding step. Experiments on the popular MS COCO dataset demonstrate that our method consistently improves LSTM-based baselines and achieves a competitive performance with 38.7 BLEU-4 and 128.5 CIDEr-D scores.

**Keywords:** Image captioning · Attention mechanism · Temporal coherence

## 1 Introduction

Image captioning [1–3] is a typical sequence prediction task, which aims at automatically generating precise descriptive sentences for images. Current image captioning models generally follow the Encoder-Decoder framework, where the Temporal Attention (TA) plays a vital role in modelling the relationships between the semantic queries and image features. Such an attention mechanism is conducive for the sentence decoder to focus on the most relevant image regions to the current query at each decoding step.

TA-based image captioning methods [1,4,5] have achieved great success in recent years. Motivated by the successful application in neural machine translation, Xu *et al.* [1] first introduced the temporal attention into image captioning

E. Pimenidis et al. (Eds.): ICANN 2022, LNCS 13529, pp. 722–733, 2022.
https://doi.org/10.1007/978-3-031-15919-0_60

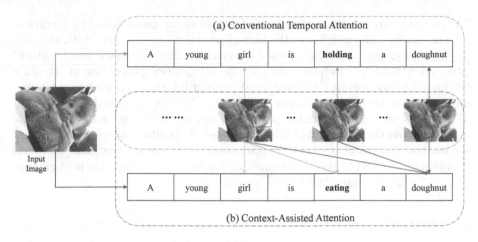

**Fig. 1.** Comparison between (a) Conventional Temporal Attention and (b) our Context-Assisted Attention. At each decoding step, the conventional temporal attention can only attend to the image features, while our method can also focus on the previously attended information to generate the current context.

by proposing a "Show, Attend and Tell" model, where the sentence decoder could capture reliable contextual information from the spatial image features. Afterwards, considering that the generation of non-visual words may require little to no visual information, Lu *et al.* [4] proposed an Adaptive Attention model with a visual sentinel, which provided the decoder with a fallback option to just rely on the language model when necessary. Subsequently, Anderson *et al.* [5] adopted object-level image features detected by a pre-trained Faster R-CNN instead of spatial features as the input key-value pairs of the temporal attention, which further improved the quality of generated captions.

Although temporal attention has recently made remarkable achievements in image captioning, the potential effect of its coherence is still under-explored. So far, only a few researchers [6,7] have conducted preliminary studies on it. Qin *et al.* [6] proposed Look Back method, which introduced the last attention result into the current query to suit visual coherence of human. Lian *et al.* [7] extended the conventional temporal attention with an attention LSTM to capture the weight distribution from previous time steps.

In fact, we humans tend to involuntarily look back upon the previously attended information so as to make a more reasonable attention decision at the current moment. Unfortunately, the Conventional Temporal Attention (CTA) cannot achieve this intention. As illustrated in Fig. 1(a), given an input image, the conventional temporal attention can only attend to the spatial image features and assign high weights to the most relevant regions, which ignores the impact of previously attended contexts on the current prediction. In order to address this problem, in this work, we propose a simple but effective Context-Assisted Attention ($CA^2$) for image captioning, which exploits the temporal coherence of the attention contexts in the sequence prediction. As shown in Fig. 1(b), our

$CA^2$ can not only attend to the spatial features of the given image by tradition, but also assign some weights to the historical attention contexts. With the help of the previous contexts, our method generates a more accurate word "eating" rather than "holding". To further restrict the distribution proportion of attention weights on image features and historical context information, we present a regularization method tailored to our $CA^2$, called Weight Transferring Constraint (WTC), to assist in the training process of the captioning model. We evaluate our method on the popular MS COCO dataset. Experimental results show that our method obtains consistently improvements over the conventional temporal attention on the LSTM-based baselines, and achieves a competitive performance with 38.7 BLEU-4 and 128.5 CIDEr scores.

## 2   Method

### 2.1   Conventional Temporal Attention in Image Captioning

Conventional Temporal Attention (CTA) in image captioning aims at capturing the most relevant context to the current semantic query from image features at each time step of caption generation. Given the current query $q_t$ and the spatial features of $n$ image regions $V = \{v_1, v_2, \ldots, v_n\}$, the temporal attention at time step $t$ can be formulated as:

$$c_t = f_{tatt}(q_t, V), \tag{1}$$

where $c_t$ is the output attention context at current time. $f_{tatt}$ denotes the temporal attention function, which can perform in various manners. In this paper, we adopt the Additive Attention [1] to suit the settings of LSTM-based baselines. At $t$-th time step, the temporal attention in additive manner can be described as follows:

$$u_{t,i} = w_u tanh(w_q q_t + w_v v_i), \tag{2}$$

$$\alpha_{t,i} = \frac{e^{u_{t,i}}}{\sum_{j=1}^{n} e^{u_{t,j}}}, \tag{3}$$

$$c_t = f_{tatt}(q_t, V) = \sum_{i=1}^{n} \alpha_{t,i} v_i, \tag{4}$$

where $w_u$, $w_q$ and $w_v$ are trainable parameters in $f_{tatt}$. $\alpha_{t,i}$ is the attention weight assigned to the $i$-th image region at time $t$.

### 2.2   Captioning Model with Context-Assisted Attention

To achieve a clear explanation of our Context-Assisted Attention ($CA^2$), in this section, we adopt the popular Bottom-Up and Top-Down (BUTD) attention model as the base captioning model and replace the internal temporal attention with our $CA^2$. A complete overview of our proposed $CA^2$ model is depicted

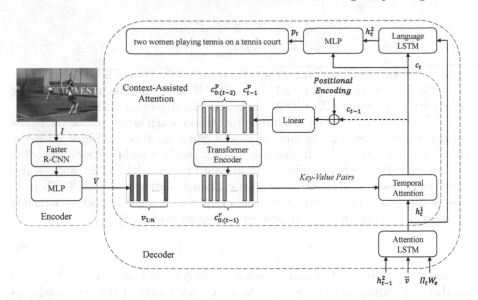

**Fig. 2.** The overview of our $CA^2$ based on the popular bottom-up and top-down attention model with slight modification.

in Fig. 2. It is worth noting that since what we attempt to build is a general extension of the conventional temporal attention in LSTM-based captioning framework, we also consider other state-of-the-art models as baselines and make comparative experiments in Sect. 3.

**Encoder.** Given an input image $I$, we first extract a set of spatial features $A = \{a_1, a_2, \ldots, a_n\}$ using a fixed Faster R-CNN pre-trained on the Visual Genome dataset, where $a_i \in \mathbb{R}^{d_A}$, $n$ is the number of detected regions in $I$, and $d_A$ is the dimension of each feature vector. Instead of directly feeding these features into the sentence decoder, we pass them through a Multi-Layer Perceptron (MLP), which is composed of two linear layers with ReLU activation functions. The encoder function can be summarized as:

$$A' = ReLU(AW_A + b_A), \tag{5}$$
$$V = ReLU(A'W_{A'} + b_{A'}), \tag{6}$$

where $W_A \in \mathbb{R}^{d_A \times d_V}$, $W_{A'} \in \mathbb{R}^{d_V \times d_V}$, and $b_A, b_{A'} \in \mathbb{R}^{d_V}$. Thus, the feature vector $V$ gets the dimension of $n \times d_V$.

**Decoder with $CA^2$.** The decoder is mainly composed of an Attention LSTM, a Context-Assisted Attention module and a Language LSTM. Given the image features $V$, at time step $t$, we feed their mean-pooled features $\bar{v} = \frac{1}{n}\sum_{i=1}^{n} v_i$, the embedding vector of the previously generated word $\Pi_t$ and the last hidden state of the Language LSTM $h_{t-1}^2$ into the Attention LSTM:

$$x_t^1 = [\Pi_t W_e; \overline{v}; h_{t-1}^2]^c, \tag{7}$$

$$h_t^1, m_t^1 = LSTM^1(x_t^1, h_{t-1}^1, m_{t-1}^1), \tag{8}$$

where $[;]^c$ indicates channel-wise concatenation. $\Pi_t$ is the one-hot encoding vector of the current input word, and $W_e \in \mathbb{R}^{|\Sigma| \times d_E}$ is a trainable word embedding matrix for a vocabulary $\Sigma$. $LSTM^1$ indicates the Attention LSTM.

$CA^2$ extends the CTA by combining the previous attention contexts with the image features to serve as the input key-value pairs. As shown in Fig. 2, given the attention context from last time step $c_{t-1} \in \mathbb{R}^{d_C}$, we first add positional encoding to the vector. Here, we use Absolute Positional Encoding [8] (APE), and we also make comparisons with other positional encoding methods in Sect. 3. Then we pass it through a linear layer and combine it with earlier historical attended information to construct a complete set of context vectors $c_{0:(t-1)}^p$.

$$c_{t-1}^p = (c_{t-1} + \Pi_t^p W_e^p) W_p, \tag{9}$$

where $\Pi_t^p$ is the one-hot encoding vector of the current time $t$, $W_e^p \in \mathbb{R}^{L \times d_C}$ is another embedding matrix, and $L$ is the maximum length of the generated captions. $W_p \in \mathbb{R}^{d_C \times d_V}$ is a trainable linear transformation matrix. $c_0$ is initialized to the mean-pooled image features $\overline{v}$.

We further refine these context vectors by using an $N$-layer Transformer Encoder. We describe this refining process as follows for simplicity. More details of the Transformer encoder can be found in [9].

$$c_{0:(t-1)}^r = f_{trans\_enc}(c_{0:(t-1)}^p), \tag{10}$$

where $c_{0:(t-1)}^p, c_{0:(t-1)}^r \in \mathbb{R}^{t \times d_V}$. $f_{trans\_enc}$ indicates the Transformer Encoder layers.

Now, we combine the image features $v_{1:n}$ with the refined context vectors $c_{0:(t-1)}^r$ to serve as the current input key-value pairs for the temporal attention:

$$c_t = f_{tatt}(h_t, [v_{1:n}; c_{0:(t-1)}^r]^s), \tag{11}$$

where $[;]^s$ indicates concatenation along the spatial dimension.

Finally, we feed the current hidden state of the Attention LSTM $h_t^1$ and the attention context $c_t$ output by our $CA^2$ into the Language LSTM.

$$x_t^2 = [h_t^1; c_t]^c, \tag{12}$$

$$h_t^2, m_t^2 = LSTM^2(x_t^2, h_{t-1}^2, m_{t-1}^2), \tag{13}$$

where $LSTM^2$ indicates the function of the Language LSTM. We combine $h_t^2$ with $c_t$ using a residual connection, and feed them into an MLP to produce a probability distribution $p_t$ for prediction of the next word.

$$o_t = ReLU([h_t^2; c_t]^c W_o + b_o), \tag{14}$$

$$p_t = o_t W_r + b_r, \tag{15}$$

where $W_o \in \mathbb{R}^{2d_V \times d_V}$, $b_o \in \mathbb{R}^{d_V}$, $W_r \in \mathbb{R}^{d_V \times |\Sigma|}$, and $b_r \in \mathbb{R}^{|\Sigma|}$.

## 2.3   Training Strategy and Objectives

**Weight Transferring Constraint.** The conventional temporal attention can only attend to the spatial image features, while our $CA^2$ will "transfer" partial weights to the historical attended information. To make the attention distribution more effective, we design a regularization method tailored to our $CA^2$, namely Weight Transferring Constraint (WTC), which restricts the total weights assigned to the previous attention contexts at each decoding step. Given the weight vector of the historical contexts in the whole sequence prediction process $\alpha^c = \{\alpha_1^c, \ldots, \alpha_l^c\}$, where $\alpha_t^c \in \mathbb{R}^t$ and $l$ is the length of the generated caption, WTC can be considered as an auxiliary loss function:

$$L_{wtc}(\theta) = \sum_{t=1}^{l}(\sum_{i=0}^{t-1} \alpha_i^c - \beta + \epsilon)^2, \tag{16}$$

where $\beta$ is a constraint factor. $\epsilon$ is used to prevent gradient explosion in the training stage. We set $\epsilon$ to 1e−8 in this paper.

**Stage 1: Training with Cross Entropy Loss.** We follow the training strategy in the previous studies [5,10]. Given the target ground truth sequence $y_{1:T}^*$, we first train $CA^2$ model by optimizing the cross entropy (XE) loss $L_{xe}$ together with WTC:

$$L_{xe}(\theta) = - \sum_{t=1}^{T} log(p_\theta(y_t^*|y_{1:(t-1)}^*, I)) + \gamma L_{wtc}(\theta), \tag{17}$$

where $\gamma$ is a trade-off coefficient to balance the two losses.

**Stage 2: Reinforcement Learning.** Then we directly optimize the non-differentiable metric by using Self-Critical Sequence Training (SCST):

$$L_{rl}(\theta) = -\mathbb{E}_{w_{1:l} \sim p_\theta}[r(w_{1:l})], \tag{18}$$

where $w_{1:l}$ is the generated caption, and the reward $r(\cdot)$ adopts the CIDEr-D score in this paper.

## 3   Experiments

### 3.1   Dataset and Metrics

We evaluate the performance of our proposed method on the popular MS COCO [11] dataset, which contains a total of 123,287 images. Each image is labeled with at least 5 captions by different AMT workers. To make a fair comparison with other state-of-the-art baselines, we follow the "Karpathy" splits [12] for offline evaluation, where 113,287 images are used for training, 5000 for validation and 5000 for testing. We evaluate our method on different metrics, including BLEU [13], METEOR [14], ROUGE-L [15], CIDEr-D [16] and SPICE [17].

**Table 1.** Performance comparisons of our method with three LSTM-based baselines on MS COCO "Karpathy" test split. Re-implementation results for baselines are reported in the second row for each group. B@N, M, R, C and S are short for BLEU@N, METEOR, ROUGE-L, CIDEr-D and SPICE scores. All values are reported as percentage (%). (–) indicates an unknown metric. The best results are highlighted in bold font.

| Methods | Cross entropy loss | | | | | | Reinforcement learning | | | | | |
|---|---|---|---|---|---|---|---|---|---|---|---|---|
| | B@1 | B@4 | M | R | C | S | B@1 | B@4 | M | R | C | S |
| Att2in [10] | – | 31.3 | 26.0 | 54.3 | 101.3 | – | – | 33.3 | 26.3 | 55.3 | 111.4 | – |
| Att2in (base) | 76.3 | 35.6 | 26.9 | 56.2 | 111.8 | 20.2 | 78.0 | 36.5 | 27.3 | 56.9 | 117.5 | 20.5 |
| Att2in+$CA^2$ | **77.6** | **36.4** | **27.3** | **56.8** | **115.4** | **20.5** | **78.8** | **37.3** | **27.9** | **57.5** | **122.2** | **21.3** |
| BUTD [5] | 77.2 | 36.2 | 27.0 | 56.4 | 113.5 | 20.3 | 79.8 | 36.3 | 27.7 | 56.9 | 120.1 | 21.4 |
| BUTD (base) | 77.2 | 36.8 | 27.6 | 57.0 | 114.8 | 20.7 | 79.9 | 37.2 | 28.0 | 57.7 | 124.7 | 21.6 |
| BUTD+$CA^2$ | **78.2** | **37.9** | **28.0** | **57.6** | **118.2** | **21.2** | **80.8** | **38.5** | **28.5** | **58.6** | **128.2** | **22.3** |
| LB [6] | 77.4 | 36.7 | 27.6 | 57.0 | 114.3 | 20.8 | 79.6 | 37.7 | 28.4 | 58.1 | 124.4 | 21.8 |
| LB (base) | 77.6 | 37.1 | 27.8 | 57.2 | 115.4 | 20.8 | 80.2 | 37.8 | 28.4 | 58.3 | 125.2 | 21.6 |
| LB+$CA^2$ | **78.8** | **38.2** | **28.3** | **57.8** | **118.9** | **21.4** | **80.9** | **38.7** | **28.7** | **58.8** | **128.5** | **22.4** |

## 3.2 Implementation Details

We adopt the Faster R-CNN pre-trained on Visual Genome dataset as the main component of our encoder, which detects 10~100 regions per image and the dimension of each regional feature is 2048. Then we project them into a new dimension of 1024. We verify our $CA^2$ on three LSTM-based models [5,6,10]. For fair comparison with these baselines, we directly use their decoders with the same hyper-parameters. As for the training process, we first train our models with the cross entropy loss and our WTC for 30 epochs. We adopt ADAM optimizer with a learning rate initialized by $4e-4$ and annealed by 0.8 every 3 epochs. Scheduled sampling probability is increased by 0.08 every 3 epochs until a maximum of 0.5. We then optimize the CIDEr-D score with SCST for another 15 epochs. The learning rate in this training stage is initialized by $4e-5$ and annealed by 0.5 when the evaluation metric does not improve in 3 consecutive tests. Batch size is set to 100 for both training stages.

## 3.3 Experimental Results

**Comparing with Conventional Temporal Attention.** To verify the effectiveness and the universality of our $CA^2$ in LSTM-based captioning framework, we conduct comparative experiments on the above mentioned baselines. We replace the conventional temporal attention with our $CA^2$ in these models. The experimental results are reported in Table 1. We observe that our $CA^2$ consistently improves the performances of the baselines across all metrics after both training stages.

**Comparing with State-of-the-Art Methods.** We compare our $CA^2$ models with other LSTM-based state-of-the-art methods in Table 2. The models

**Table 2.** Performance of our $CA^2$ models and other LSTM-based state-of-the-art methods on MS COCO "Karpathy" test split.

| Models | Cross Entropy Loss | | | | | | Reinforcement Learning | | | | | |
|---|---|---|---|---|---|---|---|---|---|---|---|---|
| | B@1 | B@4 | M | R | C | S | B@1 | B@4 | M | R | C | S |
| Att2in [10] | – | 31.3 | 26.0 | 54.3 | 101.3 | – | – | 33.3 | 26.3 | 55.3 | 111.4 | – |
| Att2all [10] | – | 30.0 | 25.9 | 53.4 | 99.4 | – | – | 34.2 | 26.7 | 55.7 | 114.0 | – |
| BUTD [5] | 77.2 | 36.2 | 27.0 | 56.4 | 113.5 | 20.3 | 79.8 | 36.3 | 27.7 | 56.9 | 120.1 | 21.4 |
| GCN-LSTM [18] | 77.3 | 36.8 | 27.9 | 57.0 | 116.3 | 20.9 | 80.5 | 38.2 | 28.5 | 58.3 | 127.6 | 22.0 |
| LBPF [6] | 77.8 | 37.4 | 28.1 | 57.5 | 116.4 | 21.2 | 80.5 | 38.3 | 28.5 | 58.4 | 127.6 | 22.0 |
| SGAE [2] | – | – | – | – | – | – | 80.8 | 38.4 | 28.4 | 58.6 | 127.8 | 22.1 |
| BUTD+RD [19] | – | 36.7 | 27.8 | 56.8 | 114.5 | 20.8 | – | 37.8 | 28.2 | 57.9 | 125.3 | 21.7 |
| BUTD+CATT [3] | – | – | – | – | – | – | – | 38.6 | 28.5 | 58.6 | 128.3 | 21.9 |
| Att2in+$CA^2$ | 77.6 | 36.4 | 27.3 | 56.8 | 115.4 | 20.5 | 78.8 | 37.3 | 27.9 | 57.5 | 122.2 | 21.3 |
| BUTD+$CA^2$ | 78.2 | 37.9 | 28.0 | 57.6 | 118.2 | 21.2 | 80.8 | 38.5 | 28.5 | 58.6 | 128.2 | 22.3 |
| LB+$CA^2$ | **78.8** | **38.2** | **28.3** | **57.8** | **118.9** | **21.4** | **80.9** | **38.7** | **28.7** | **58.8** | **128.5** | **22.4** |

includes (except our baselines): Att2all [10] is the standard "Soft Attention" model optimized with non-differentiable metrics; GCN-LSTM [18] uses Graph Convolutional Networks (GCNs) to explore the semantic and spatial relationships between the objects in images; SGAE [2] uses scene graph to incorporate the language inductive bias for image captioning; RD [19] polishes the raw captions with a ruminant decoder; CATT [3] adopts the front-door adjustment to alleviate the ever-elusive confounding effect. The comparison results show that based on the widely-used BUTD [5] model, our $CA^2$ outperforms most of the previous methods and achieves a competitive CIDEr-D score of 128.2. More than that, our LB+$CA^2$ model obtains a new state-of-the-art CIDEr-D score of 128.5 under the LSTM-based framework.

**Ablation Study.** With respect to the structure of $CA^2$, we verify the effects of various positional encoding methods and the $N$-layer Transformer Encoder, respectively. BUTD model is considered as the baseline in all ablation experiments. For fair comparison with the base model, WTC is not employed to optimize $CA^2$ in this part. We first set $N$ to 1 and compare the effects of different positional encoding methods, including Sinusoidal Positional Encoding [9] (SPE), Absolute Positional Encoding [8] (APE) and Relative Positional Encoding [20] (RPE). Comparative results in Table 3 show that APE achieves the best performance among them and increases 1.0 CIDEr-D score compared with the model without positional encoding.

Based on APE, we then make experiments to find out the influence of the number of Transformer Encoder layers $N$ on the model performance. As reported in Table 4, within limits, the more layers of the Transformer Encoder, the better performance of the model. However, we find that when we change $N$ from 1 to 2, it brings little performance improvement for the model, but higher computation cost. Thus, we determine to set $N$ to 1 in this paper.

We further make ablation study on WTC. By observing the order of magnitude of WTC loss and XE loss, we empirically set the trade-off coefficient $\gamma$ to

**Table 3.** Ablation study on positional encoding methods. The results are reported after cross entropy training stage without WTC.

| Methods | B@4 | M | R | C |
|---|---|---|---|---|
| CTA (base) | 36.8 | 27.6 | 57.0 | 114.8 |
| CA² w/o PE | 37.2 | 27.7 | 57.3 | 116.5 |
| CA² w/SPE | 37.3 | **27.9** | 57.4 | 116.9 |
| CA² w/APE | **37.6** | **27.9** | **57.5** | **117.5** |
| CA² w/RPE | 37.4 | 27.8 | 57.2 | 117.1 |

**Table 4.** Ablation study on the number of Transformer Encoder layers.

| Methods | B@4 | M | R | C |
|---|---|---|---|---|
| CTA (base) | 36.8 | 27.6 | 57.0 | 114.8 |
| CA² (N = 0) | 37.0 | 27.7 | 57.0 | 116.3 |
| CA² (N = 1) | 37.6 | **27.9** | **57.5** | 117.5 |
| CA² (N = 2) | **37.8** | **27.9** | **57.5** | **118.0** |

0.5. From Table 5, we observe that excessively strict constraints will lead to the decline of model performance. When $\beta$ is set to 0.9, the model achieves a much lower CIDEr-D score 116.2 than 117.5 of the baseline without using WTC. Significantly, when $\beta$ is set to 0.5, both the image features and the historical attended information will be assigned half of the attention weight, which helps to enhance the generalization of the model. As a result, CA²+WTC with $\beta = 0.5$ improves the base model from 117.5 CIDEr-D score to 118.2. Experimental results show that optimized with both cross entropy loss and WTC loss, our models are well pre-trained in the first training stage. We then directly optimize our models by using SCST method without WTC regularization.

**Attention Visualization.** We visualize the attention maps for the BUTD models with both CTA and CA² in Fig. 3. When generating the word "santa", not only does our method attend to the image features as the base model does, but also focus on the historical attention contexts, especially those for generating the words "dog" and "wearing". However, the base model only relies on the spatial image features and thus generates a worse caption. It is notable that the attention maps in Fig. 3(b) are not exactly the attention contexts in each time step. Current attention context also contains the summarization of the attended context vectors from previous time steps. We symbolically connect the previous attention maps with the current predicted word to indicate the weight assigned to the historical attention contexts.

**Caption Examples.** We make a qualitative analysis to the capacity for generating captions of our CA² through three examples in Fig. 4. From the examples

**Table 5.** Ablation study on Weight Transferring Constraint. $N$ is set to 1 for $CA^2$.

| Methods | B@4 | M | R | C |
|---|---|---|---|---|
| $CA^2$ (base) | 37.6 | 27.9 | 57.5 | 117.5 |
| $CA^2$+WTC ($\beta = 0.1$) | 37.4 | 27.8 | 57.4 | 117.2 |
| $CA^2$+WTC ($\beta = 0.3$) | 37.7 | 27.9 | 57.5 | 117.8 |
| $CA^2$+WTC ($\beta = 0.5$) | **37.9** | **28.0** | **57.6** | **118.2** |
| $CA^2$+WTC ($\beta = 0.7$) | 37.6 | 27.9 | 57.3 | 117.4 |
| $CA^2$+WTC ($\beta = 0.9$) | 37.0 | 27.6 | 57.1 | 116.2 |

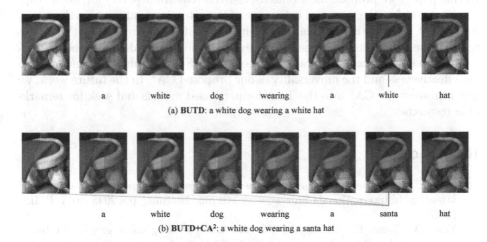

a    white    dog    wearing    a    white    hat

(a) **BUTD**: a white dog wearing a white hat

a    white    dog    wearing    a    santa    hat

(b) **BUTD+CA²**: a white dog wearing a santa hat

**Fig. 3.** Attention visualization. We only depict the attention distribution of one time step for clarity. Darker regions or lines indicate higher attention weights.

| Images | Generated Captions | Ground Truth Captions |
|---|---|---|
| | **BUTD**: a kitchen with a sink and a stove<br><br>**BUTD+CA²**: a kitchen with wooden cabinets and a stove top oven | **GT1**: a kitchen that appears to be missing a cabinet door<br><br>**GT2**: a kitchen with a sink, oven, and wood cabinets and floors<br><br>**GT3**: a kitchen with wood cabinets and white appliances and countertops |
| | **BUTD**: a teddy bear sitting on top of a laptop computer<br><br>**BUTD+CA²**: a teddy bear sitting in front of a computer screen | **GT1**: a stuffed animal is in front of a notebook computer<br><br>**GT2**: a bear is sitting in front of a computer<br><br>**GT3**: a teddy bear sitting in front of an open laptop computer |
| | **BUTD**: a street sign on the side of a pole<br><br>**BUTD+CA²**: a one way sign on the side of a pole | **GT1**: a one way sign pointing to the left; the sky is blue in the background<br><br>**GT2**: a one way sign mounted to the side of a pole<br><br>**GT3**: a close up of a one way sign on a pole |

**Fig. 4.** Examples of the captions generated by our $CA^2$ and its baseline model BUTD as well as their corresponding ground truths. Mistakes are highlighted in red color, and the advantages in describing images are highlighted in blue color. (Color figure online)

we can see, our method is good at discovering the main subjects and grasping the details of the images. As described in the first example, our method focuses on the specific "wooden cabinets" in the image, while the baseline model can only output "sink", which is a general facility to the kitchen. In the third example, our method captures the visual details in the image and generates the "one way sign" instead of the normal "street sign".

## 4    Conclusion

In this paper, we propose the Context-Assisted Attention ($CA^2$) for image captioning to exploit the temporal coherence of the attention contexts. Furthermore, we present a regularization method Weight Transferring Constraint (WTC) to restrict the attention assignment. We evaluate our method under the LSTM-based framework. Experimental results on the MS COCO dataset demonstrate the effectiveness and the universality of our proposed $CA^2$. In the future work, we will introduce the $CA^2$ into the Transformer-based models and seek for remarkable researches.

## References

1. Xu, K., et al.: Show, attend and tell: neural image caption generation with visual attention. In International Conference on Machine Learning, pp. 2048–2057. PMLR (2015)
2. Yang, X., Tang, K., Zhang, H., Cai, J.: Auto-encoding scene graphs for image captioning. In: Proceedings of the IEEE/CVF Conference on Computer Vision and Pattern Recognition, pp. 10685–10694 (2019)
3. Yang, X., Zhang, H., Qi, G., Cai, J.: Causal attention for vision-language tasks. In: Proceedings of the IEEE/CVF Conference on Computer Vision and Pattern Recognition, pp. 9847–9857 (2021)
4. Lu, J., Xiong, C., Parikh, D., Socher, R.: Knowing when to look: adaptive attention via a visual sentinel for image captioning. In: Proceedings of the IEEE Conference on Computer Vision and Pattern Recognition, pp. 375–383 (2017)
5. Anderson, P., et al.: Bottom-up and top-down attention for image captioning and visual question answering. In: Proceedings of the IEEE Conference on Computer Vision and Pattern Recognition, pp. 6077–6086 (2018)
6. Qin, Y., Du, J., Zhang, Y., Lu, H.: Look back and predict forward in image captioning. In: Proceedings of the IEEE/CVF Conference on Computer Vision and Pattern Recognition, pp. 8367–8375 (2019)
7. Lian, Z., Li, H., Wang, R., Hu, X.: Enhanced soft attention mechanism with an inception-like module for image captioning. In: 2020 IEEE 32nd International Conference on Tools with Artificial Intelligence, pp. 748–752 (2020)
8. Devlin, J., Chang, M. W., Lee, K., Toutanova, K.: BERT: pre-training of deep bidirectional transformers for language understanding. In: Proceedings of NAACL-HLT, pp. 4171–4186 (2019)
9. Vaswani, A., et al.: Attention is all you need. Adv. Neural Inf. Process. Syst. **30** (2017)

10. Rennie, S.J., Marcheret, E., Mroueh, Y., Ross, J., Goel, V.: Self-critical sequence training for image captioning. In: Proceedings of the IEEE Conference on Computer Vision and Pattern Recognition, pp. 7008–7024 (2017)
11. Lin, T.-Y., et al.: Microsoft COCO: common objects in context. In: Fleet, D., Pajdla, T., Schiele, B., Tuytelaars, T. (eds.) ECCV 2014. LNCS, vol. 8693, pp. 740–755. Springer, Cham (2014). https://doi.org/10.1007/978-3-319-10602-1_48
12. Karpathy, A., Fei-Fei, L.: Deep visual-semantic alignments for generating image descriptions. In: Proceedings of the IEEE Conference on Computer Vision and Pattern Recognition, pp. 3128–3137 (2015)
13. Papineni, K., Roukos, S., Ward, T., Zhu, W. J.: BLEU: a method for automatic evaluation of machine translation. In: Proceedings of the 40th annual meeting of the Association for Computational Linguistics, pp. 311–318 (2002)
14. Banerjee, S., Lavie, A.: METEOR: an automatic metric for MT evaluation with improved correlation with human judgments. In: Proceedings of the ACL Workshop on Intrinsic and Extrinsic Evaluation Measures for Machine Translation and/or Summarization, pp. 65–72 (2005)
15. Lin, C. Y.: ROUGE: a package for automatic evaluation of summaries. In: Text Summarization Branches Out, pp. 74–81 (2004)
16. Vedantam, R., Lawrence Zitnick, C., Parikh, D.: CIDEr: consensus-based image description evaluation. In: Proceedings of the IEEE Conference on Computer Vision and Pattern Recognition, pp. 4566–4575 (2015)
17. Anderson, P., Fernando, B., Johnson, M., Gould, S.: SPICE: semantic propositional image caption evaluation. In: Leibe, B., Matas, J., Sebe, N., Welling, M. (eds.) ECCV 2016. LNCS, vol. 9909, pp. 382–398. Springer, Cham (2016). https://doi.org/10.1007/978-3-319-46454-1_24
18. Yao, T., Pan, Y., Li, Y., Mei, T.: Exploring visual relationship for image captioning. In: Proceedings of the European Conference on Computer Vision (ECCV), pp. 684–699 (2018)
19. Guo, L., Liu, J., Lu, S., Lu, H.: Show, tell, and polish: ruminant decoding for image captioning. IEEE Trans. Multimed. 22(8), 2149–2162 (2019)
20. Shaw, P., Uszkoreit, J., Vaswani, A.: Self-attention with relative position representations. In: Proceedings of the 2018 Conference of the North American Chapter of the Association for Computational Linguistics: Human Language Technologies, Volume 2 (Short Papers), pp. 464–468 (2018)

# Multi-level Proposal Relations Aggregation for Video Object Detection

Chongkai Yu, Wenjie Chen(✉), and Bing Wu

State Key Laboratory of Intelligent Control and Decision of Complex Systems,
School of Automation, Beijing Institute of Technology, Beijing, China
{3220200825,chenwenjie}@bit.edu.cn

**Abstract.** Video information often deteriorates in certain frames, which is a great challenge for object detection. It is difficult to identify the object in this frame by just utilizing the information of one frame. Recently, plenty of studies have shown that context aggregating information through the self-attention mechanism can enhance the features in key frames. However, these methods only exploit some of inter-video and intra-video global-local information, not all of it. Global semantic and local localization information in the same video can assist object classification and regression. The intra-proposal relation among different videos can provide important cues to distinguish confusing objects. All of this information is able to enhance the performance of video object detection. In this paper, we design a Multi-Level Proposal Relations Aggregation network to mine inter-video and intra-video global-local pro-posal relations. For intra-video, we effectively aggregate global and local information to augments the proposal features of key frames. For inter-video, we aggregate the inter-video key frame features to the target video under the constraint of relation regularization. We flexibly utilize the relation module to aggregate the proposals from different frames. Experiments on ImageNet VID dataset demonstrate the effectiveness of our method.

**Keywords:** Video object detection · Relation aggregation · Global-local information

## 1 Introduction

Recently, the development of deep convolutional neural networks has promoted great progress in object detection of still images [1–4,14]. Most of them adopt the region-based detection paradigm. Applying the single image methods directly on isolated video frames might not produce satisfactory results, due to the fact that objects in videos often contain motion blur, sudden occlusion, rare pose, etc. Videos contain spatio-temporal information that single image object detectors do not exploit, and that can be very valuable to address these issues. Recent studies [5–8] have shown that modeling the object proposal relation of different

The work was supported in part by the National Natural Science Foundation of China under Grants 61773067, 62022015, 62088101, and 61720106011.

frames can effectively aggregate the spatio-temporal context and yield better representation for detection task. However, the previous methods only exploited the global or local information of the same video or the local information between different videos, without fully mining the global and local information within and between videos.

In real life, when people cannot judge what the object of a certain frame in the video is, we naturally hope to find objects in other frames in the video that have high semantic similarity with the current frame and group them into a category. This takes advantage of the global semantic information in the video. When people cannot determine the position of the object, we can infer the position of the object in the frame from adjacent frames, which makes use of the local localization information in the video. Both global and local information is based on intra video. However, when blurry objects with similar appearance or motion characteristics appear in different videos. It is difficult to distinguish them only by intra-video information, because it has little clue about the relations of object changes in different videos. For example, Rabbits and Fox with similar coloration but different motor characteristics could hardly distinguish between blurry frames only by intra-videos information, just as shown in Fig. 3. Therefore, we also need to exploit inter-video information of the relations between object changes to distinguish easily confusing objects.

In this paper, we present Multi-Level Proposal Relations Aggregation to mine inter-video and intra-video global-local proposal relations. Specifically, our framework is mainly divided into inter-video relations aggregation module and intra-video relations aggregation module. For inter-video, inspired by the HVR-Net [23], we select hard training proposals among confused videos and exploit the proposal relations to construct better proposal features. For intra-video, unlike HVRNet, we make significant improvements. We introduce global information from the entire video and utilized a new relational module which can optionally focus on semantic or geometric information. We obtain local information from the frame adjacent to the key frame and global information from the random frame in the whole video. After that, we effectively aggregate global and local information to augments the proposal features of the key frames. The whole framework is shown in Fig. 1.

Our method is tested on the ImageNet VID dataset [10], and we designed some ablation experiments to verify the effectiveness of proposed methods.

## 2   Related Work

### 2.1   Object Detection in Still Images

Thanks to the success of deep neural networks [11–13], object detection in still images [1–4, 14] has recently achieved remarkable successes. The state-of-the-art single image object detectors follow two main approaches: two stage and one stage architectures. The classical two-stage detectors (such as RCNN [15], Fast-RCNN [16], Faster-RCNN [4]) extract regional features from backbone networks based on deep CNNs, and then classifies and refines the corresponding bounding boxes. One-stage object detectors such as SSD [17] and YOLO [14] directly calculate the final detection set taking a dense grid of bounding boxes as input rather than proposals targeting objects of interest. One-stage detectors often maintain computation efficiency but can hardly extend to more complicated tasks. Similarly, it can hardly be extended to proposal-level object semantic features in our work. Thus, we chose the typical two-stage detectors Faster-RCNN as our basic still image detector.

## 2.2    Object Detection in Videos

Since the objects in videos often suffer from problems such as motion blur, sudden occlusion or rare pose, the object detection in still images is not up to the task. The main challenges lie in how to utilize the rich information of videos (e.g. temporal continuity) to improve the accuracy as well as the speed. The main idea of recent methods [5–8,20] towards solving video object detection is to enter multiple frames for feature aggregation to enhance the per frame features. In particular, recent studies have shown that learning proposal relations from different frames can effectively alleviate various difficulty for video object detection [5]. However, most of these methods are limited to part of the information in the video without explore its relations comprehensively.

Local aggregation methods mainly utilize information in local temporal range near the key frame of the video to assist detection. For example, FGFA [20] combines the optical flow field with the feature map of the key frame, and integrates local temporal range information by calculating the approximate feature map of several adjacent frames to the current frame. RDN [5] based on Relation Network [8] enhances the feature of candidate boxes in key frames by directly learning the relation among candidate boxes in local scope. Global aggregation methods seek to find semantic information from the whole video to directly enhance the pixel or box features. Methods like SELSA [6] fuses instance features based on semantic similarity, and adopted completely random sampling frames for feature extraction, ignoring temporal and local semantic information and only using global semantic information. Inter-video aggregation methods mainly use confusable objects between videos to enhance the robustness of detection. HVRNet [23] models hard proposals relations among videos to learn effective feature representations. However, for intra-video, it only makes use of the candidate box features at a local scale.

In contrast to these methods, the proposed Multi-Level Proposal Relations Aggregation can mine inter-video and intra-video global-local proposal relations to enhance the feature representation.

## 3    Method

### 3.1    Overview

In this section, we systematically introduce how we devise Multi-Level Proposal Relations Aggregation to fully utilize the local and global information of intra video and inter video. The whole framework is shown in Fig. 1. It is mainly divided into two parts: intra-video aggregation and inter-video aggregation. For intra-video aggregation, we model the relations between frames through a multi-stage attention module to enhance proposal features in key frames. Local localization information can be obtained by learning the relations between key frames and adjacent frames, and global semantic information can be obtained by learning the relations between key frames and random frames in the whole video. For inter-video aggregation, we select other support videos from the training set for target videos. Just like target video, support video obtains key frames strengthened by the global and local information of their respective videos, and learns the relation between these key frames through the Relation Module to distinguish easily confusing objects.

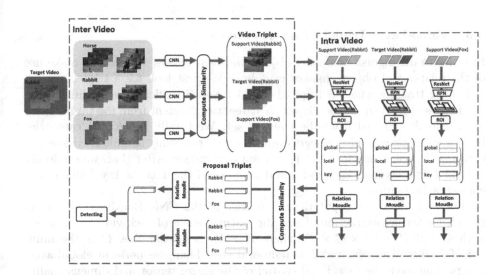

**Fig. 1.** Our multi-level proposal relations aggregation framework. It can mine inter-video and intra-video global-local proposal relations progressively.

## 3.2 Relation Module

The operators we choose to mine the relations between frames are the relation module [5]. Motivated from Multi-Head Attention in [18], given the input of proposals $P = \{p_i\}$, object relation module is devised to enhance each proposal $p_i$ by measuring $M$ relation features as the weighted sum of semantic features from other proposals, where $M$ denotes the number of heads. Then, the mthrelation features of $p_i$ is computed as

$$f_{rela}^m (p_i, P) = \sum_j \omega_{ij}^m \cdot (w_L^m \cdot f_j), m = 1, \cdots, M \qquad (1)$$

where $W_L^m$ is a linear transformation matrix. The relation weight $\omega_{ij}^m$ represents the influence between proposals $p_i$ and $p_j$ which is measured based on their semantic and geometric features. For global frame and Inter-video frame, as geometric features of the proposals in the temporal dimension are redundant and may affect the general performance, we modified Relation Module to remove geometric features and focus only on semantic features. By concatenating all $M$ relation features of each proposal $p_i$ and its original feature, we finally obtain the output augment feature.

$$f_{rm}(p_i, \boldsymbol{P}) = f_i + concat\left[\{f_{rela}^m(p_i, \boldsymbol{P})\}_{m=1}^M\right] \tag{2}$$

After each relation module, we add a fully-connected layer plus ReLU to implement feature transformation.

### 3.3  Video-Level Triplet of Inter Video

In order to distinguish confusing objects between videos, we need to make use of the relations of object changes in videos. We first look for a triplet of hard videos for training which is inspired by HVRNet. Specifically, according to the key frames of the target video input, $K$ categories different from the target video are randomly selected from the training set. We totally get $K + 1$ categories including the target video category, and then we randomly sample $N$ videos per category. Hence, there are $(K + 1) \times N$ support videos. After that, we randomly sample $T$ Frames from each video and take one of them as the key frame of the corresponding video.

For each video, we input their $T$ frames to the CNN Backbone of Faster-RCNN for feature extraction. Thus, the feature tensor of each video is obtained with size of $H \times W \times C \times T$, where $H \times W$ is spatial size, $C$ is the number of feature channels, and $T$ is temporal size. Then, we perform global average pooling along temporal and spatial of the entire tensor and dimensionality reduction to obtain the $1 \times C$ video feature representation. $\boldsymbol{X}_{key}(1) \in \mathbb{R}^{1 \times C}$ and $\boldsymbol{X}_{sup}[(K + 1) \times N] \in \mathbb{R}^{[(K+1) \times N] \times C}$ denote the feature tensor of a target video and all support videos respectively. Both $\boldsymbol{X}_{key}$ and $\boldsymbol{X}_{sup}$ are L2 normalized along with the channel dimension to generate $\hat{\boldsymbol{X}}_{key}$ and $\hat{\boldsymbol{X}}_{sup}$. Cosine similarity map of video $\boldsymbol{S}_v$ is calculated as follows:

$$\boldsymbol{S}_v = S\left(\hat{\boldsymbol{X}}_{key}(1), \hat{\boldsymbol{X}}_{sup}[(K + 1) \times N]\right) \tag{3}$$

$$\boldsymbol{S}_v = \mathbb{R}^{1 \times C} \bigotimes \left[\mathbb{R}^{[(K+1) \times N] \times C}\right]^T \rightarrow \mathbb{R}^{1 \times [(K+1) \times N]} \tag{4}$$

where $\otimes$ denotes matrix multiplication and $[\cdot]^T$ denotes matrix transposition.

Finally, we get similarity scores of each support video and target video from the similarity map $\boldsymbol{S}_v$. From the scores, we get the video triplet consists of the video that is most dissimilar in the class which the target video belongs to and the video that is most similar in the other class.

### 3.4   Global-Local Relation Aggregation of Intra Video

In this part, we mined the global and local proposal relations of intra video. We aggregate global information into local and key frames, and then aggregate local information into key frames to obtain more effective box-level features. As shown in Fig. 1, after finding the video triplet, we input all three videos into the Intra-Video module at the same time. We sample global and local frames from each video and input these sampled frames together with the key frame to RPN and ROI layers of Faster-RCNN. Region Proposal Networks (RPN) is employed to produce object proposals from key frames and all support frames. After that, we apply RoI-Align to extract ROI feature for each proposal. The intra-video aggregation is depicted in Fig. 2.

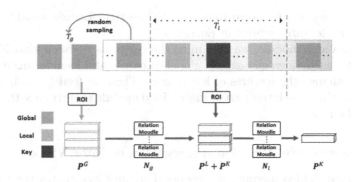

**Fig. 2.** Global-local relation aggregation of intra video. For the same video, the global information comes from the same the global supportive pool $\boldsymbol{P}^G$.

Proposal features of global frames firstly aggregate global information to the proposals of local frames and key frames. Specifically, we randomly select $T_g$ frames from the entire video and use RPN and ROI to generate object proposals. The set of object proposals from global frames are grouped as the global supportive pool, denoted as $\boldsymbol{P}^G = \left\{ p_i^G \right\}$. Then we exploit the Relation Module that only focuses on semantic features to enhance local and key proposals $p_i^{LK}$. In order to fully mine the potential of global Features, we apply $\boldsymbol{N}_g$ Relation Modules to infer relations in a stacked way. For the $n$-th relation module, the $i$-th local proposal $p_i^{LK,n}$ is augmented with the relation features over all in the global supportive pool $\boldsymbol{P}^G$:

$$p_i^{LK,n} = f_{rm}^G \left( p_i^{LK,n-1}, \boldsymbol{P}^G \right), n = 1, \dots, \boldsymbol{N}_g \tag{5}$$

where $f_{rm}^G \left( \cdot \right)$ denotes the global Relation Module that focuses only on semantic features, defined in Eq. (2). Each Relation Module utilizes the transformed features from the previous Relation Module as the inputs of reference proposals.

For local frames, we select $T_l$ adjacent frames around the keyframe. The whole sequence of adjacent frames $\{I_t\}_{t=k-T_l}^{k+T_l}$ is taken as local support frames and $T_l$ represents the temporal span range of local frames. We use RPN and ROI to generate object proposals and aggregate the global information to the local proposal. In order to improve training efficiency and mine more effective local change relations, we select the top-$k$ object proposals with high objectness scores from each local frame as local supportive pool, denoted as $\boldsymbol{P}^L = \{p_i^L\}$. We use Relation Module with geometric features to enhance the proposal features of key frames $p_i^K$ for utilizing the semantic and geometric information of local features. Meanwhile, to take full use of local features, we also apply $N_l$ Relation Module to characterize the relations between local and key frames. The final $i$-th proposal features for key frames $p_i^{K,n}$ is calculated as follows:

$$p_i^{K,n} = f_{rm}^L \left( p_i^{K,n-1}, \boldsymbol{P}^L \right), n = 1,\ldots,N_l \tag{6}$$

where $f_{rm}^L(\cdot)$ denotes the local Relation Module that focuses semantic features and geometric feature, defined in Eq. (2).

By Intra-Video module, we fully mine the relations between global-local and key frame for each video and exploit global semantic and local localization information to enhance the features of key frames. Then we feed the enhanced proposal features into the latter part of Inter Video module to introduce the relations of object changes.

## 3.5   Proposal-Level Relation Aggregation of Inter Video

After the Intra Video module, the proposal feature aggregates the global and local information of their respective videos. To explore the changes of objects between videos, we further search for hard objects from the proposal-level feature. Specifically, like the video-level similarity comparison method in Sect. 3.3, we calculate the cosine similarity map between the proposal features in key frames and those in inter-video frames.

According to the similarity scores of key frames among different videos, we matched each proposal of the target video with the most dissimilar proposal from the same class of the support video, and matched the most similar proposal from other class of the support video. Thus, a set of proposal triplet $p_i^{triplet}$ is obtained for each proposal in the key frame of the target video.

$$p_i^{triplet} = \left\{ p_i^T, p_i^+, p_i^- \right\} \tag{7}$$

where $p_i^T$ represents the proposal from the proposals pool of the target video keyframes $\boldsymbol{P}^T = \{p_i^T\}$. $p_i^+$ is the proposal from the most dissimilar proposal pool in the same category $\boldsymbol{P}^+ = \{p_i^+\}$. $p_i^-$ is the proposal from the most similar proposals pool in the other category $\boldsymbol{P}^- = \{p_i^-\}$.

In order to accurately describe the relations of object changes between videos, we establish the relation model for each proposal triplet, and exploit the proposal features of the support video to enhance the proposal features of the target video. We apply $N_V$ Relation Modules to infer relations in a stacked way to fully study the object relations between videos.

$$p_i^{T,n} = f_{rm}^V \left( p_i^{K,n-1}, p_i^+, p_i^- \right), n = 1, \ldots, N_V \tag{8}$$

$$f_{rm}^V \left( p_i^T, p_i^+, p_i^- \right) = f_i + concat \left[ \{ f_{rela}^m \left( p_i^T, p_i^+ \right) \}_{m=1}^M \right] \\ + concat \left[ \{ f_{rela}^m \left( p_i^T, p_i^- \right) \}_{m=1}^M \right] \tag{9}$$

where $f_{rm}^V (\cdot)$ denotes proposal-level Relation Module, which is similar to the global Relation Module and only focuses on semantic features, excluding geometric features. We calculate relation features for the proposal $p_i^T$ of each target video and other proposals in its corresponding triplet $p_i^{triplet}$. By connecting the two relation features with the original proposal features, we finally obtained the enhanced proposal features that aggregated the hard proposals between videos in Eq. (9).

Inspired by HVRNet, we also add the following relation regularization loss to emphasize the correct constraint on the Inter-Video Relation Module to effectively reduce object confusion between videos.

$$\mathcal{L}_{\text{relation}} = \max \left\{ d \left( p_i^T, p_i^- \right) - d \left( p_i^T, p_i^+ \right) + \lambda, 0 \right\} \tag{10}$$

After the final enhanced features of keyframes are generated, we feed them into the Faster-RCNN head for final detection.

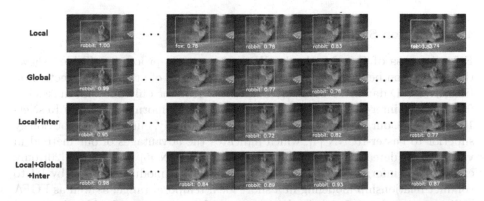

**Fig. 3.** Detection visualization. Obviously, with the addition of different kinds of relation information, the detection performance gradually improves. For confusing objects, only using local information lacks global semantic information of objects and mistakenly recognizes the rabbit as a fox. Using only global information lacks local position information and does not identify object locations. The combination of local and inter information distinguishes confusing objects, but still lacks the location of the object. When introducing all the information, our method successfully detects all objects.

## 4    Experiment

### 4.1    Dataset and Evaluation Experiment

We evaluated our methods primarily on ImageNet VID dataset. ImageNet VID dataset is a large-scale video object detection benchmark with 3862 training videos and 555 validation videos from 30 classes. Following common protocols in [5–7,20,22,23], we utilize ImageNet VID and ImageNet Object Detection (DET) datasets to train our framework. We evaluate our method on validation sets and use mean average accuracy (mAP) as the evaluation metric.

## 4.2   Implementation Details

**Architecture.** We use ResNet-101 [11] as backbone for ablation studies. The whole architecture is shown in Fig. 1. We use Faster-RCNN as our detection module. During training and inference, each frame generates 300 proposals at an NMS threshold of 0.7 IoU. We apply RoI-Align [3] and a 1024-D fully-connected layer after the conv5 stage to obtain the feature vector of each proposal.

**Training Details.** The whole architecture is trained on 4 GPUs of Tesla V100 with SGD. In each training batch, we randomly sample one video as the target video from training set and sample $K = 2$ different categories as support categories. Then, we randomly sample $N = 3$ videos from each of $K + 1 = 3$ categories (including the target category). For each video, we randomly sample $T = 3$ frames. For intra video, we select $T_g = 10$ global frames and $T_l = 21$ local frames.

## 4.3   Ablation Studies

**Effectiveness of Our Methods.** Without any post-processing, Table 1 shows the comparison between our framework and the state-of-art object detection on ImageNet VID dataset. Among all methods, ours is the only one that makes full use of all the inter-video and intra-video global-local information. With ResNet-101 backbone, our method achieves 82.6% mAP. Firstly, our method is obviously superior to Faster-RCNN [4], which indicates the advantages of our method in video object detection. Among all competitors, RDN [5] and FGFA [20] only exploit local information. RDN utilizes the relation module inspired by [8] to conduct relationship modeling in a short local temporal range, as well as FGFA utilizes optical flow information between local frames. Our method has improved 0.8% mAP and 6.3% mAP respectively compared with them. While SELSA [6] only models sparse global connections and TROI [22] adds temporal ROI Align based on SELSA to model with global and local information. Our method exceeds them by 2.3 and 0.6 points. While our method is slightly inferior to HVRNet [23] which aggregates local and inter information and achieves the highest accuracy of 83.2%. However, our method is higher than it when using fewer testing frames as shown in Table 2.

When the number of testing frames is small, our method has higher accuracy than HVRNet. Because in the test phase, for HVRNet, it is only able to use a little temporal span range of local frames. But our method uses the random frames of the entire video to introduce global information. In addition, for the key frames of the same video, the global information comes from the same the

**Table 1.** Comparison with other methods on ImageNet VID.

| Methods | Backbone | Local | Global | Inter | mAP(%) |
|---|---|:---:|:---:|:---:|---|
| Faster-RCNN [4] | ResNet-101 | | | | 73.2 |
| FGFA [20] | ResNet-101 | ✓ | | | 76.3 |
| THP [21] | ResNet-101 | ✓ | | | 78.6 |
| SELSA [6] | ResNet-101 | | ✓ | | 80.3 |
| RDN [5] | ResNet-101 | ✓ | | | 81.8 |
| SLTnet [7] | ResNet-X101+FPN | ✓ | ✓ | | 81.9 |
| TROI [22] | ResNet-101 | ✓ | ✓ | | 82.0 |
| HVRNet [23] | ResNet-101 | ✓ | | ✓ | 83.2 |
| **Ours** | ResNet-101 | ✓ | ✓ | ✓ | 82.6 |

**Table 2.** Number of testing frames.

| Methods | Testing frames | | | | |
|---|---|---|---|---|---|
| | 5 | 11 | 17 | 21 | 31 |
| HVRNet | 80.5 | 81.6 | 82.0 | 82.9 | 83.2 |
| Ours | **81.2** | **82.0** | **82.4** | 82.6 | 82.6 |

global supportive pool $P^G$. Thus there is no need to extract the ROI features of the global frames repeatedly, and the computation is not increased much. As more testing frames are added, the effect of global information on accuracy wears off. Our method gradually saturate after 21 testing frames, slightly lower than HVRNet. This may be that our framework and aggregation method is different from HVRNet, and fall short in the integration method of local and inter information. Just as shown in Table 3, with the local and Inter information, our framework only reaches 82.2%.

**Influence Between the Various Relation Modules.** By using different number of relation modules, we explore the influence of inter-video and intra-video global-local information on our framework when the number of testing frames is 21. We set the corresponding module number to 0 to remove the influence of different information. The results are shown in Table 3. Performance drops to 81.6% mAP and 81.8% mAP with only local or global information. Aggregating both local and global information or both local and inter information, we all achieved 82.2% mAP. The introduction of all the information improves performance again. When the number of Inter Relation Modules $N_V = 3$, the performance reaches the optimal 82.6% mAP. Figure 3 showcases one hard example in video object detection. The introduction of various information improves the accuracy.

Table 3. Number of testing frames.

| Information | Number of relation modules | | | |
|---|---|---|---|---|
| | $N_l$ | $N_g$ | $N_V$ | mAP(%) |
| Local | 4 | 0 | 0 | 81.6 |
| Global | 0 | 4 | 0 | 81.8 |
| Local+Global | 3 | 1 | 0 | 82.2 |
| Local+Inter | 3 | 0 | 3 | 82.2 |
| Local+Global+Inter | 3 | 1 | 1 | 82.5 |
| Local+Global+Inter | **3** | **1** | **3** | **82.6** |

## 5   Conclusion

In this work, we present Multi-Level Proposal Relations Aggregation to mine inter-video and intra-video global-local proposal relations to solve video object detection. Particularly, we flexibly use Relation Module to aggregate the global local information to the key frame, and then aggregate the inter-video key frame features to the target video. Experiments on ImageNet VID datasets demonstrate the effectiveness of our method.

## References

1. Cai, Z., Vasconcelos, N.: Cascade R-CNN: delving into high quality object detection. In: Proceedings of the IEEE Conference on Computer Vision and Pattern Recognition, pp. 6154–6162 (2018)
2. Dai, J., Li, Y., He, K., Sun, J.: R-FCN: object detection via region-based fully convolutional networks. In: Advances in Neural Information Processing Systems, pp. 379–387 (2016)
3. He, K., Gkioxari, G., Dollár, P., Girshick, R.: Mask R-CNN. In: Proceedings of the IEEE International Conference on Computer Vision, pp. 2961–2969 (2017)
4. Ren, S., He, K., Girshick, R., Sun, J.: Faster R-CNN: towards real-time object detection with region proposal networks. In: Advances in Neural Information Processing Systems, vol. 28, pp. 91–99 (2015)
5. Deng, J., Pan, Y., Yao, T., Zhou, W., Li, H., Mei, T.: Relation distillation networks for video object detection. In: Proceedings of the IEEE/CVF International Conference on Computer Vision, pp. 7023–7032 (2019)
6. Wu, H., Chen, Y., Wang, N., Zhang, Z.: Sequence level semantics aggregation for video object detection. In: Proceedings of the IEEE/CVF International Conference on Computer Vision (2019)
7. Cores, D., Brea, V.M., Mucientes, M.: Short-term anchor linking and long-term self-guided attention for video object detection. Image Vis. Comput. **110**, 104179 (2021)
8. Hu, H., Gu, J., Zhang, Z., Dai, J., Wei, Y.: Relation networks for object detection. In: Proceedings of the IEEE Conference on Computer Vision and Pattern Recognition, pp. 3588–3597 (2018)

9. Schroff, F., Kalenichenko, D., Philbin, J.: Facenet: a unified embedding for face recognition and clustering. In: Proceedings of the IEEE Conference on Computer Vision and Pattern Recognition, pp. 815–823 (2015)
10. Russakovsky, O., et al.: ImageNet large scale visual recognition challenge. Int. J. Comput. Vision **115**(3), 211–252 (2015)
11. He, K., Zhang, X., Ren, S., Sun, J.: Deep residual learning for image recognition. In: Proceedings of the IEEE Conference on Computer Vision and Pattern Recognition, pp. 770–778 (2016)
12. Krizhevsky, A., Sutskever, I., Hinton, G.E.: ImageNet classification with deep convolutional neural networks. In: Advances in neural information processing systems, vol. 25, pp. 1097–1105 (2012)
13. Xie, S., Girshick, R., Dollár, P., Tu, Z., He, K.: Aggregated residual transformations for deep neural networks. In: Proceedings of the IEEE Conference on Computer Vision and Pattern Recognition, pp. 1492–1500 (2017)
14. Redmon, J., Divvala, S., Girshick, R., Farhadi, A.: You only look once: unified, real-time object detection. In: Proceedings of the IEEE Conference on Computer Vision and Pattern Recognition, pp. 779–788 (2016)
15. Girshick, R., Donahue, J., Darrell, T., Malik, J.: Rich feature hierarchies for accurate object detection and semantic segmentation. In: Proceedings of the IEEE Conference on Computer Vision and Pattern Recognition, pp. 580–587 (2014)
16. Girshick, R.: Fast R-CNN. In: Proceedings of the IEEE International Conference on Computer Vision, pp. 1440–1448 (2015)
17. Liu, W., et al.: SSD: single shot multibox detector. In: Leibe, B., Matas, J., Sebe, N., Welling, M. (eds.) ECCV 2016. LNCS, vol. 9905, pp. 21–37. Springer, Cham (2016). https://doi.org/10.1007/978-3-319-46448-0_2
18. Vaswani, A., et al.: Attention is all you need. In: Advances in Neural Information Processing Systems, pp. 5998–6008 (2017)
19. Wang, X., Girshick, R., Gupta, A., He, K.: Non-local neural networks. In: Proceedings of the IEEE Conference on Computer Vision and Pattern Recognition, pp. 7794–7803 (2018)
20. Zhu, X., Wang, Y., Dai, J., Yuan, L., Wei, Y.: Flow-guided feature aggregation for video object detection. In: Proceedings of the IEEE International Conference on Computer Vision, pp. 408–417 (2017)
21. Zhu, X., Dai, J., Yuan, L., Wei, Y.: Towards high performance video object detection. In: Proceedings of the IEEE Conference on Computer Vision and Pattern Recognition, pp. 7210–7218 (2018)
22. Gong, T., et al.: Temporal ROI align for video object recognition. In: Proceedings of the AAAI Conference on Artificial Intelligence, vol. 35, no. 2, pp. 1442–1450 (2021)
23. Han, M., Wang, Y., Chang, X., Qiao, Y.: Mining inter-video proposal relations for video object detection. In: Vedaldi, A., Bischof, H., Brox, T., Frahm, J.-M. (eds.) ECCV 2020. LNCS, vol. 12366, pp. 431–446. Springer, Cham (2020). https://doi.org/10.1007/978-3-030-58589-1_26

# Relation-Aware Global-Augmented Transformer for TextCaps

Qiang Li[1,2], Bing Li[1], and Can Ma[1(✉)]

[1] Institute of Information Engineering, Chinese Academy of Sciences, Beijing, China
{liqiang,libing,macan}@iie.ac.cn
[2] School of Cyber Security, University of Chinese Academy of Sciences, Beijing, China

**Abstract.** Text-based image captioning (TextCaps) task aims to describe the given image reasonably based on scene text and visual objects simultaneously. Although previous works have shown great success, they pay too much attention to the text modality while ignoring other important visual information, and the correlations between objects and text are not fully exploited. Moreover, traditional transformer-based architectures ignore global information reflecting the entire image, which may cause object missing and erroneous reasoning problems. In this paper, we propose a Relation-aware Global-augmented Transformer (**RGT**) framework to tackle these problems. Specifically, we utilize a scene graph extracted from the image to explicitly model the relative semantic and spatial relationships of objects via a graph convolutional network, which not only enhances the visual representations but also encodes explicit semantic features of objects. Besides, we add a multi-modal alignment (**MMA**) module as a supplement for the multi-modal transformer to strengthen the association between scene text and objects. Finally, a global-augmented transformer (**GAT**) is designed to get a more comprehensive representation of the image, which could alleviate object missing and erroneous reasoning problems. Our method outperforms state-of-the-art models on the TextCaps dataset, improving from 105.0 to 107.2 in CIDEr.

**Keywords:** Text-based image captioning · Scene graph · Multi-modal alignment · Global-augmented transformer

## 1 Introduction

Image captioning is one of the most extensively researched topics in multi-modal learning and has witnessed great progress. However, traditional image captioning methods do not realize the importance of scene text, so they fail to provide a comprehensive description of the image. To tackle this drawback, the work [16] constructs the TextCaps dataset and proposes the text-based image captioning (TextCaps) task. Given an image, the TextCaps task aims to generate a reasonable description with the consideration of scene text.

E. Pimenidis et al. (Eds.): ICANN 2022, LNCS 13529, pp. 746–758, 2022.
https://doi.org/10.1007/978-3-031-15919-0_62

a

**M4C-Captioner w/o RGT:** a group of cheerleaders with the word *cheerlf* on their *shirts*.

**M4C-Captioner w RGT:** a group of cheerleaders are posing for a photo with the word *cheerlf* on the *back*.

**Human:** Cheerleaders performing an act while wearing Wildcats jerseys.

b

**M4C-Captioner w/o RGT:** a yellow taxi is *driving* down a street with a license plate that says silvertp.

**M4C-Captioner w RGT:** a yellow car with the license plate 131 008 is *parked* in front of a *building*.

**Human:** Several taxis are shown parked in front of a building with taxi 131008 being closest to the camera.

**Fig. 1.** Caption examples from M4C-Captioner without or with RGT.

In order to generate text-related captions, TextCaps models need to understand the text words, capture the visual entities and reason over rich multi-modality information. Although both image captioning and Optical Character Recognition (OCR) techniques are relatively mature, there are still some problems existing in the TextCaps task. Aiming to integrate the text information, current TextCaps methods [16,22,23,25,27] pay too much attention to the text modality while ignoring other important visual information. To be specific, the image visual features are often represented by a set of visual objects extracted from a pre-trained object detector [15], but the correlations between objects and text are not fully exploited. For example, in Fig. 1 (a), existing methods (e.g., M4C-Captioner [16]) describe the image as "a group of cheerleaders with the word cheerlf on their shirts", which incorrectly places the word *"cheerlf"* located on the background to the clothes. Although several practices [22,23] explore the spatial or geometrical relationships, they still cannot solve this problem well.

Besides, most existing methods [16,25,27] leverage multi-modal transformer architecture for modal interaction, which may lead to the object missing and erroneous reasoning problem. As shown in Fig. 1 (b), previous methods miss the crucial object *"building"* so that they predict the car is "driving down a street" instead of "parked in front of a building". This is because they are prone to focus on the local region features while ignoring the global cues.

In this paper, we propose a relation-aware global-augmented Transformer (RGT) framework to address the above problems. Firstly, instead of only localizing and recognizing objects, we model their relationships to enhance the visual representations. The relationships are embodied at both spatial and semantic levels. Specifically, we encode the input image into a scene graph and explicitly model the relative semantic and spatial relationships via a graph convolutional network (GCN). The semantic relationship is then fused with the location features of objects, which enables explicit reasoning about objects and their relationships.

Secondly, we propose a multi-modal alignment (MMA) module as a supplement for the multi-modal transformer, which separates the visual and semantic features of the scene text, and performs attention operations with corresponding object features. In Fig. 1 (a), with the adoption of RGT, our model links the text *"cheerlf"* with the background wall in the image. It shows that the proposed method is conducive to associating the scene text with objects.

Finally, in order to tackle the object missing and erroneous reasoning problems, a global-augmented transformer (GAT) is developed to make full use of global features from the image. In Fig. 1 (b), our model can not only read the plate number on the taxi but also recognize the *building* object and capture the global scene of the *parking* lot.

In summary, our main contributions are as follows:

- We propose a Relation-aware Global-augmented Transformer framework to deal with the TextCaps task. With the introduction of a scene graph and the proposed multi-modal alignment module, the semantic and spatial relationships between scene text and objects can be effectively encoded.
- We design a global-augmented transformer to capture the global information of an image to address objects missing and erroneous reasoning problems.
- Extensive experiments and analyses on the TextCaps dataset are conducted to verify the effectiveness of our method.

## 2   Related Work

**Image Captioning.** Image captioning has made great progress in recent years. Show and Tell [21] creates the Encoder-Decoder model based on CNN and RNN architecture. After that, Show, Attend and Tell [26] introduces the attention mechanism, which can dynamically focus the salient area of the image during the process of generating the caption. Adaptive attention [13] uses a sentinel gate mechanism in visual attention, which can prompt the model to pay attention to visual features or semantic context. BUTD [3] leverages a bottom-up attention mechanism based on top-down attention and uses Faster R-CNN [15] to extract the attention area of the image, instead of traditional grid attention. GCN-LSTM [28] further explores the semantic and spatial information between objects through a graph convolutional network. Recently, due to the tremendous progress made in the transformer architecture in the field of machine translation [19], many works [9,10] have also adopted this self-attention network. Although these works have achieved a lot of success, they have no ability to read and understand text, so they cannot be directly used for text-based image captioning.

**Text-Based Image Captioning and VQA.** Text-based visual question answering (TextVQA) task was first proposed in LoRRA [17]. Its goal is to correctly answer the text-related questions based on the given image. M4C [8] improves the feature representation of OCR tokens and adopts a transformer for multi-modal feature fusion. In addition, it proposes a novel pointer network for iterative decoding. Following a similar motivation, M4C-Captioner [16] proposes the task of text-based image captioning based on M4C. After that, MMA-SR [22] and LSTM-R [23] propose to utilize the inherent spatial relationship between OCR tokens to enhance the connection between them. CNMT [25] improves the performance by improving the OCR capability and removing the repeated words in the caption. Mirroring the success of the visual and language pretraining [12,30], TAP [27] designs text-related pretraining tasks and improves TextVQA and TextCaps performance by noticeable margins. However, these works pay too much attention to the text modality while ignoring other important information. How to effectively represent the relationships between text and objects remains an open question. Additionally, understanding the global image information is indispensable to generate a comprehensive description.

**Scene Graph Generation.** Scene graph is a structured representation of objects, attributes and relationships in an image. Scene graph generation (SGG) [18,29] has received more and more attention due to its superior performance in relational understanding, which also greatly facilitates the visual and language cross-modality tasks. Scene graph-based image captioning methods [7,24] can fully exploit the semantic and spatial relationships between objects in an image. Different from simply using a scene graph to represent relationships between objects, we model the relative semantic and spatial relationships by encoding the scene graph using a graph convolutional network. Our method considers both explicit and implicit relations in an image, which are more interpretable.

## 3 Method

In this paper, we propose a Relation-aware Global-augmented Transformer (RGT) model for Textcaps. Figure 2 shows an overview of our model. It mainly contains three modules: (i) Feature embedding module is used to extract and embed object features and OCR tokens features into a common feature space (Sect. 3.1); (ii) Fusion and reasoning module is used to fuse and reason on the extracted features (Sect. 3.2); and (iii) Caption prediction module iteratively generate caption word which either predicts from a vocabulary word or points to an OCR token (Sect. 3.3).

### 3.1 Feature Embedding Module

For an image $I$, we use Faster R-CNN [15] and Rosetta [6] to obtain a series of object regions $\{x_m^{obj}, m \in (1, M)\}$ and OCR tokens $\{x_n^{ocr}, n \in (1, N)\}$. But these features come from different modalities, we need to embed features extracted from each modality into a $d$-dimensional common feature space. The specific embedding method is shown below.

**Embedding of Objects and Relations.** For the object feature $x_m^{obj}$, we employ Faster R-CNN [15] to obtain the bounding box feature $x_m^{bbox}$ and appearance feature $x_m^{fr}$ of the object. To get the explicit relationships between objects, we encode each image into a scene graph $G = (V, E)$, which treats each object

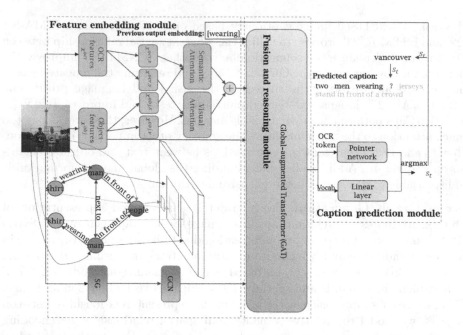

**Fig. 2.** Overview of the proposed RGT architecture.

in the image as a vertex and the relation between objects as an edge. After that, the scene graph is exploited to model the relative semantic and spatial relationships $x_m^{sg} = GCN(G)$ via a graph convolutional network, which computes embedding vectors for all objects in the image. Finally, we project the obtained object features to the $d$-dimensional feature space as follows:

$$x_m^{obj} = LN(W'_{fr}x_m^{fr}) + LN(W'_{bbox}x_m^{bbox}) + LN(W'_{sg}x_m^{sg}) \tag{1}$$

where $W'_{fr}, W'_{bbox}$ and $W'_{sg}$ are learning parameters, and $LN$ means layer normalization.

Instead of handling these object features indiscriminately like previous works, we decouple them to object visual features $x_m^{obj,v}$ and object semantic features $x_m^{obj,s}$ as follows and build the multi-modal alignment module later.

$$\begin{aligned} x_m^{obj,v} &= LN(W'_{fr}x_m^{fr}) + LN(W'_{bbox}x_m^{bbox}) \\ x_m^{obj,s} &= LN(W'_{sg}x_m^{sg}) \end{aligned} \tag{2}$$

**Embedding of OCR Tokens.** Similarly, Faster R-CNN [15] is utilized to obtain OCR tokens' appearance feature $x_n^{fr}$ and bounding box feature $x_n^{bbox}$. Following M4C-Captioner [16], we also use FastText [5] and PHOC (Pyramidal Histogram of Characters [1]) to obtain the semantic features $x_n^{ft}$ and $x_n^{ph}$ of OCR tokens. Finally, we project the obtained OCR token feature to the $d$-dimensional feature space to get the following vector representation:

$$x_n^{ocr} = LN(W_{fr}x_n^{fr} + W_{ft}x_n^{ft} + W_{ph}x_n^{ph}) + LN(W_{bbox}x_n^{bbox}) \tag{3}$$

where $W_{fr}, W_{ft}, W_{ph}$ and $W_{bbox}$ are learning parameters, and $LN$ means layer normalization.

For the multi-modal alignment module later, we subdivide the features of OCR tokens into OCR visual features $x_n^{ocr,v}$ and OCR semantic features $x_n^{ocr,s}$ as follows:

$$\begin{aligned} x_n^{ocr,v} &= LN(W_{fr}x_n^{fr}) + LN(W_{bbox}x_n^{bbox}) \\ x_n^{ocr,s} &= LN(W_{ft}x_n^{ft} + W_{ph}x_n^{ph}) \end{aligned} \tag{4}$$

From the above operations, we can obtain the following six feature vectors: object vector $x^{obj}$, object visual vector $x^{obj,v}$ and object semantic vector $x^{obj,s}$; OCR token vector $x^{ocr}$, OCR token visual vector $x^{ocr,v}$ and OCR token semantic vector $x^{ocr,s}$.

**Multi-Modal Alignment (MMA) module.** We propose a multi-modal alignment module as a supplement for the transformer to fuse multi-modal features as shown in Fig. 3. Specifically, in order to better associate OCR tokens with objects, we perform an attention operation on the visual and semantic features of OCR tokens with corresponding object features separately and then concatenate them as input for GAT. The corresponding formula is shown below:

$$x^{mma} = concat\left(Att\left(x^{ocr,v}, x^{obj,v}\right), Att\left(x^{ocr,s}, x^{obj,s}\right)\right) \tag{5}$$

where $Att$ denotes attention operation, and $concat$ means vector splicing operation.

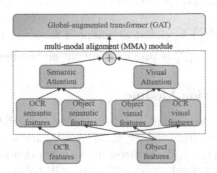

**Fig. 3.** Multi-modal alignment (MMA) module.

### 3.2 Fusion and Reasoning Module

**Global-Augmented Transformer.** Different from previous works, we use a global-augmented transformer to fuse the inter-modal and intra-modal features. For a group of object visual features $x^{fr} = \{v_1, v_2, \cdots, v_M\}$, we can use global feature $x_{obj}^g$ represent the image as follows:

$$x^g_{obj} = \frac{1}{M} \sum_{i=1}^{M} v_i \tag{6}$$

where $M$ is the number of visual features.

As shown in Fig. 4, instead of just considering the region feature, we input both the region feature and global feature into the multi-head self-attention module in each layer of MMT.

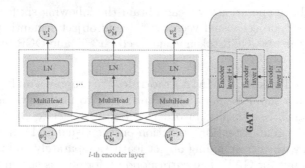

**Fig. 4.** l-th encode layer of the global-augmented transformer (GAT).

The final output $v^{dec}_{t-1}$ at $t$-th time step is as follows:

$$\left[z^{obj}, z^{ocr}, z^{dec}_{t-1}\right] = GAT(\left[x^{obj}_g, x^{ocr}, x^{mma}, x^{dec}_{t-1}\right]) \tag{7}$$

where $x^{obj}_g = \left(x^{obj}; x^g_{obj}\right)$ is global augmented features, $GAT$ denotes global-augmented transformer, $x^{dec}_{t-1}$ is previous output embedding.

### 3.3 Caption Prediction Module

The captions are decoded in an iterative manner. At the $t$-th time step, the caption word is selected from one of fixed vocabulary words $v_k, k \in (1, K)$ or OCR tokens $x^{ocr}_n, n \in (1, N)$. We utilize a linear network and a pointer network to calculate the vocabulary word scores $y^{voc}_t$ and OCR token scores $y^{ocr}_t$ separately. The corresponding formula is as follows:

$$y^{voc}_t = W z^{dec}_{t-1} + b, y^{ocr}_t = PTN(z^{dec}_{t-1}) \tag{8}$$

where $W$ and $b$ are hyperparameters of the linear network, PTN denotes Pointer Network and $z^{dec}_{t-1}$ represents output of GAT. Then we get the concatenation scores $y^{all}_t = [y^{voc}_t; y^{ocr}_t]$ at the $t$-th time step.

Finally, in the prediction process, we take argmax in the concatenation scores and select a word with the highest score from all candidate words as the caption word $S_t$ at the $t$-th time step.

# 4 Experiments

## 4.1 Experimental Setup

**Dataset and Metrics.** We evaluate our model on the TextCaps dataset, which is specifically designed for text-based image captioning task. This dataset contains 28,408 images, and each image corresponds to 5 artificial annotations. For fair comparison, we use the default settings of TextCaps [16], namely 21,953 for training, 3,166 for verification and 3,289 for testing. We use the official code provided by the TextCaps dataset to evaluate our model online. The Metrics include BLEU-4 [14], METEOR [4], ROUGE-L [11], SPICE [2] and CIDEr [20], among which the CIDEr index is the most convincing metric, because it can determine whether the model has captured key information and is more relevant to human evaluation.

**Comparison Methods.** As implementation examples, we employ M4C-Captioner [16] and TAP [27] as baselines to verify the effectiveness of our proposed method. Specifically, TAP is the first attempt to integrate cross-modal pretraining. Then, we compare our models with existing text-based image captioning methods including MMA-SR [22] and CNMT [25].

**Implementation Details.** The dimension $d$ of the common feature space is set to 768. For each image, at most $M = 100$ objects are considered. Following the baseline settings, we set $N = 50$ in the M4C-Captioner based model and $N = 100$ in the TAP based model. Meanwhile, for a fair comparison, we use 4 layers of transformers with 12 attention heads. In addition to the 2048-dimensional visual feature, OCR tokens are also encoded by some semantic features, including a 300-d FastText feature and a 604-d PHOC feature. Each object is equipped with a 128-dimensional scene graph vector as the semantic feature. During training, we use the Adam optimizer and learning rate decay strategy with an initial value of 1e-4.

## 4.2 Main Results

**Evaluation on the TextCaps Validation Set.** To verify the effectiveness of our proposed method RGT, we compare it with other methods on the TextCaps validation set, as shown in Table 1. As we can see, the performance of the M4C-Captioner model without text (lines 1) is far weaker than that using text (lines 2), proving that it is important to consider text information for the TextCap task. Whether using M4C-Captioner and TAP as the baseline, our method is effective and brings noticeable improvement. Our method outperforms M4C-Captioner on all five metrics, especially improving 2.5 in CIDEr. While TAP is a strong pretraining baseline, our method is also effective, bringing a 2.2 improvement in CIDEr.

**Table 1.** Performance of our RGT and other methods on the TextCaps validation set.

| Method | BLEU-4 | METEOR | ROUGE-L | SPICE | CIDEr |
|---|---|---|---|---|---|
| M4C-Captioner w/o OCRs [16] | 15.9 | 18.0 | 39.6 | 12.1 | 35.1 |
| M4C-Captioner [16] | 23.3 | 22.0 | 46.2 | 15.6 | 89.6 |
| M4C-Captioner+RGT | **23.9** | **22.2** | **46.6** | **15.7** | **92.1** |
| MMA-SR [22] | 24.6 | 23.0 | 47.3 | 16.2 | 98.0 |
| CNMT [25] | 24.8 | 23.0 | 47.1 | 16.3 | 101.7 |
| TAP [27] | 25.2 | 23.4 | 47.7 | 16.9 | 105.0 |
| TAP+RGT | **25.9** | **23.5** | **47.9** | **17.0** | **107.2** |

**Table 2.** Performance of our RGT and other methods on the TextCaps test set.

| Method | BLEU-4 | METEOR | ROUGE-L | SPICE | CIDEr |
|---|---|---|---|---|---|
| M4C-Captioner [16] | 18.9 | 19.8 | 43.2 | 12.8 | 81.0 |
| M4C-Captioner+RGT | **19.1** | **20.0** | **43.7** | **12.8** | **82.5** |
| MMA-SR [22] | 19.8 | 20.6 | 44.0 | 13.2 | 88.0 |
| CNMT [25] | 20.0 | 20.8 | 44.4 | 13.4 | 93.0 |
| TAP [27] | 21.5 | 21.7 | 45.4 | **14.5** | 99.5 |
| TAP+RGT | **22.0** | **21.7** | **45.7** | 14.4 | **100.1** |
| *Human* [16] | 24.4 | 26.1 | 47.0 | 18.8 | 125.5 |

**Evaluation on the TextCaps Test Set.** We submit the sentences generated by the proposed RGT method to the website[1] for online testing, and the results are shown in Table 2. The performance of manually labeled captions is provided in the last line, which can be considered as the upper limit of the TextCaps task. It can be seen that our RGT method achieves the best results on most metrics. The improvement further verifies the superior performance and good generalization of our method.

**Ablation Study.** In order to verify the effectiveness of each component in our model, we conduct ablation experiments by removing some modules during training. The results of the experiment are shown in Table 3. It can be seen that all modules we adopted have made positive contributions to the model. Specifically, SG (line1) works best because it can explicitly identify each object in the image and get the relationship between objects so that key information and keywords can be obtained with a larger probability. MMA (line2) has the weakest effect because it is used to assist in grasping the relationship between object and text without generating new entity words, which is less helpful for

[1] https://eval.ai/web/challenges/challenge-page/906/.

**Table 3.** Ablation of each design in RGT on the TextCaps dataset.

| Method | BLEU-4 | METEOR | ROUGE-L | SPICE | CIDEr |
|---|---|---|---|---|---|
| Base (M4C-Captioner+RGT) | **23.9** | **22.2** | **46.6** | **15.7** | **92.1** |
| Base w/o SG | 23.3 | 22.0 | 45.9 | 15.4 | 90.6 |
| Base w/o MMA | 23.8 | 22.1 | 46.3 | 15.7 | 91.3 |
| Base w/o GAT | 23.3 | 22.0 | 46.1 | 15.4 | 90.7 |

obtaining key information. GAT (line3) can obtain the global information of the image and mitigate object missing and erroneous reasoning problems, which is very helpful for the model to obtain comprehensive and accurate information, thus improving the performance of the model.

**Qualitative Analysis.** Aiming to better illustrate the effects brought by our method, in Fig. 5, we show some caption examples generated by M4C-Captioner w/o RGT, M4C-Captioner with RGT, and human on the images of the TextCaps dataset. Our model can recognize objects and identify their relations well by using scene graph information (shown in Fig. 5 a, b, f). In addition, the multi-modal alignment module we adopted can help the model better capture the relationships between scene text and objects (shown in Fig. 5 c, d). The involved global information enables to mitigate object missing and erroneous reasoning drawbacks (shown in Fig. 5 a, b, e) and represent the whole scene of the image (shown in Fig. 5 g, h).

However, it can also be seen that our model still has some shortcomings. For example, our model mistakes the couple for a man (shown in Fig. 5 b) and a card for a book (shown in Fig. 5 d). Besides, our model will be affected by the inaccurate OCR results sometimes (shown in Fig. 5 f, h). These problems are worthy of further study.

**Fig. 5.** Qualitative examples on the TextCaps dataset. Red indicates OCR tokens, yellow represents objects, and blue shows the relations. (Color figure online)

## 5    Conclusions

In this paper, we introduce a Relation-aware Global-augmented Transformer (RGT) model for TextCaps. In the feature embedding module, to explicitly model and reason the relations in an image, we construct a scene graph based on the image content, after which we use the scene graph to explicitly model the relative semantic and spatial relationships via a graph convolutional network. Besides, in order to make the multi-modal fusion more efficient, we propose a multi-modal alignment module as a supplement for the multi-modal transformer, which can strengthen the association between scene text and objects. In the fusion and reasoning module, to get a more comprehensive representation of the image, we propose a global-augmented transformer architecture, which enables us to mitigate object missing and erroneous reasoning problems. Experiments demonstrate the effectiveness and generalization of the method. In the future, we will further explore how to better perform reasoning and learning based on the acquired information.

# References

1. Almazán, J., Gordo, A., Fornés, A., Valveny, E.: Word spotting and recognition with embedded attributes. IEEE Trans. Pattern Anal. Mach. Intell. **36**(12), 2552–2566 (2014)
2. Anderson, P., Fernando, B., Johnson, M., Gould, S.: SPICE: semantic propositional image caption evaluation. In: Leibe, B., Matas, J., Sebe, N., Welling, M. (eds.) ECCV 2016. LNCS, vol. 9909, pp. 382–398. Springer, Cham (2016). https://doi.org/10.1007/978-3-319-46454-1_24
3. Anderson, P., et al.: Bottom-up and top-down attention for image captioning and visual question answering. In: CVPR, pp. 6077–6086 (2018)
4. Banerjee, S., Lavie, A.: METEOR: an automatic metric for MT evaluation with improved correlation with human judgments. In: ACL, pp. 65–72 (2005)
5. Bojanowski, P., Grave, E., Joulin, A., Mikolov, T.: Enriching word vectors with subword information. Trans. Assoc. Comput. Linguist. **5**, 135–146 (2017)
6. Borisyuk, F., Gordo, A., Sivakumar, V.: Rosetta: large scale system for text detection and recognition in images. In: KDD, pp. 71–79 (2018)
7. Gao, L., Wang, B., Wang, W.: Image captioning with scene-graph based semantic concepts. In: ICMLC, pp. 225–229 (2018)
8. Hu, R., Singh, A., Darrell, T., Rohrbach, M.: Iterative answer prediction with pointer-augmented multimodal transformers for TextVQA. In: CVPR, pp. 9989–9999 (2020)
9. Huang, L., Wang, W., Chen, J., Wei, X.: Attention on attention for image captioning. In: ICCV, pp. 4633–4642 (2019)
10. Li, G., Zhu, L., Liu, P., Yang, Y.: Entangled transformer for image captioning. In: ICCV, pp. 8927–8936 (2019)
11. Lin, C.Y.: Rouge: a package for automatic evaluation of summaries. In: Proceedings of the Workshop on Text Summarization Branches Out (WAS 2004) (2004)
12. Lu, J., Batra, D., Parikh, D., Lee, S.: Vilbert: pretraining task-agnostic visiolinguistic representations for vision-and-language tasks. In: NeurIPS (2019)
13. Lu, J., Xiong, C., Parikh, D., Socher, R.: Knowing when to look: adaptive attention via a visual sentinel for image captioning. In: CVPR, pp. 3242–3250 (2017)
14. Papineni, K., Roukos, S., Ward, T., Zhu, W.: Bleu: a method for automatic evaluation of machine translation. In: ACL, pp. 311–318 (2002)
15. Ren, S., He, K., Girshick, R.B., Sun, J.: Faster R-CNN: towards real-time object detection with region proposal networks. In: NIPS, pp. 91–99 (2015)
16. Sidorov, O., Hu, R., Rohrbach, M., Singh, A.: TextCaps: a dataset for image captioning with reading comprehension. In: Vedaldi, A., Bischof, H., Brox, T., Frahm, J.-M. (eds.) ECCV 2020. LNCS, vol. 12347, pp. 742–758. Springer, Cham (2020). https://doi.org/10.1007/978-3-030-58536-5_44
17. Singh, A., et al.: Towards VQA models that can read. In: CVPR, pp. 8317–8326 (2019)
18. Tang, K., Niu, Y., Huang, J., Shi, J., Zhang, H.: Unbiased scene graph generation from biased training. In: CVPR, pp. 3713–3722 (2020)
19. Vaswani, A., et al.: Attention is all you need. In: NIPS, pp. 5998–6008 (2017)
20. Vedantam, R., Zitnick, C.L., Parikh, D.: Cider: consensus-based image description evaluation. In: CVPR, pp. 4566–4575 (2015)
21. Vinyals, O., Toshev, A., Bengio, S., Erhan, D.: Show and tell: a neural image caption generator. In: CVPR, pp. 3156–3164 (2015)

22. Wang, J., Tang, J., Luo, J.: Multimodal attention with image text spatial relationship for OCR-based image captioning. In: MM, pp. 4337–4345 (2020)
23. Wang, J., Tang, J., Yang, M., Bai, X., Luo, J.: Improving OCR-based image captioning by incorporating geometrical relationship. In: CVPR, pp. 1306–1315 (2021)
24. Wang, J., Wang, W., Wang, L., Wang, Z., Feng, D.D., Tan, T.: Learning visual relationship and context-aware attention for image captioning. Pattern Recogn. **98**, 107075 (2020)
25. Wang, Z., Bao, R., Wu, Q., Liu, S.: Confidence-aware non-repetitive multimodal transformers for textcaps. In: AAAI, pp. 2835–2843 (2021)
26. Xu, K., et al.: Show, attend and tell: Neural image caption generation with visual attention. In: ICML, pp. 2048–2057 (2015)
27. Yang, Z., et al.: TAP: text-aware pre-training for text-VQA and text-caption. In: CVPR, pp. 8751–8761 (2021)
28. Yao, T., Pan, Y., Li, Y., Mei, T.: Exploring visual relationship for image captioning. In: ECCV, pp. 711–727 (2018)
29. Zellers, R., Yatskar, M., Thomson, S., Choi, Y.: Neural motifs: scene graph parsing with global context. In: CVPR, pp. 5831–5840 (2018)
30. Zhou, L., Palangi, H., Zhang, L., Hu, H., Corso, J.J., Gao, J.: Unified vision-language pre-training for image captioning and VQA. In: AAAI, pp. 13041–13049 (2020)

# Correction to: Sim-to-Real Neural Learning with Domain Randomisation for Humanoid Robot Grasping

Connor Gäde, Matthias Kerzel, Erik Strahl, and Stefan Wermter

**Correction to:**
**Chapter "Sim-to-Real Neural Learning with Domain Randomisation for Humanoid Robot Grasping" in:**
**E. Pimenidis et al. (Eds.): *Artificial Neural Networks and Machine Learning – ICANN 2022*, LNCS 13529,**
**https://doi.org/10.1007/978-3-031-15919-0_29**

Chapter, "Sim-to-Real Neural Learning with Domain Randomisation for Humanoid Robot Grasping" was previously published non-open access. It has now been changed to open access under a CC BY 4.0 license and the copyright holder updated to 'The Author(s)'. The book has also been updated with this change.

---

The updated original version of this chapter can be found at
https://doi.org/10.1007/978-3-031-15919-0_29

E. Pimenidis et al. (Eds.): ICANN 2022, LNCS 13529, p. C1, 2023.
https://doi.org/10.1007/978-3-031-15919-0_63

# Author Index

Printed in the United States
by Baker & Taylor Publisher Services